Adobe Creative Suite 2 KillerTips Collection

PHOTOSHOP
INDESIGN
ILLUSTRATOR
CS2
KILLER TIPS

ADOBE® CREATIVE SUITE 2 KILLER TIPS COLLECTION

PUBLISHED BY
New Riders
1249 Eighth Street, Berkeley, CA 94710
800-283-9444 • 510-524-2178 • 510-524-2221 (fax)

New Riders is an imprint of Peachpit, a division of Pearson Education.

Copyright © 2006 by Kelby Corporate Management, Inc.

FIRST EDITION: September 2005

All rights reserved. No part of this book may be reproduced or transmitted in any form, by any means, electronic or mechanical, including photocopying, recording, or by any information storage and retrieval system, without written permission from the publisher, except for inclusion of brief quotations in a review.

Composed in Myriad Pro and Helvetica by NAPP Publishing.

Trademarks
All terms mentioned in this book that are known to be trademarks or service marks have been appropriately capitalized. New Riders cannot attest to the accuracy of this information. Use of a term in the book should not be regarded as affecting the validity of any trademark or service mark.

Photoshop is a registered trademark of Adobe Systems, Inc.
InDesign is a registered trademark of Adobe Systems, Inc.
Illustrator is a registered trademark of Adobe Systems, Inc.
Windows is a registered trademark of Microsoft Corporation.

Warning and Disclaimer
This book is designed to provide information about Photoshop, InDesign, and Illustrator tips. Every effort has been made to make this book as complete and as accurate as possible, but no warranty of fitness is implied.

The information is provided on an as-is basis. The authors and New Riders shall have neither liability nor responsibility to any person or entity with respect to any loss or damages arising from the information contained in this book or from the use of the discs or programs that may accompany it.

ISBN 0-321-38545-4

Note: This edition is a collection of these three books:
Photoshop CS2 Killer Tips (ISBN 0-321-33063-3)
InDesign CS/CS2 Killer Tips (ISBN 0-321-33064-1)
Illustrator CS2 Killer Tips (ISBN 0-321-33065-X)

9 8 7 6 5 4 3 2 1

Printed and bound in the United States of America

www.peachpit.com
www.scottkelbybooks.com

Adobe Creative Suite 2 Killer Tips Collection

ABOUT THIS COMBINED BOOK

Thank you for purchasing the *Adobe Creative Suite 2 Killer Tips Collection*. By combining three books into one, you'll get the opportunity to save money and learn the best tips for three exciting applications in the same book.

Photoshop CS2 Killer Tips is the first book in this combined volume, with the index for the book following immediately after the text. This is followed by *InDesign CS/CS2 Killer Tips* and *Illustrator CS2 Killer Tips*, with their respective indexes following immediately after each book, as well.

Hungry for more Killer Books?

Tear into these best-selling titles from
Scott Kelby and feed the creative beast within!

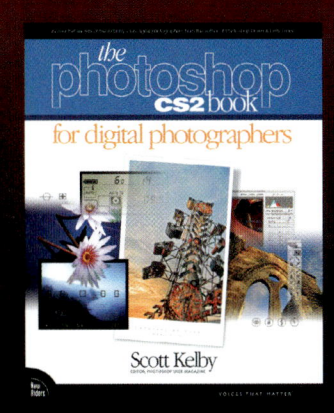

The Photoshop CS2 Book for Digital Photographers *$29.99*

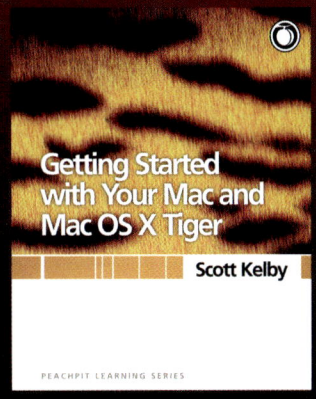

Getting Started with Your Mac and Mac OS X Tiger *$17.99*

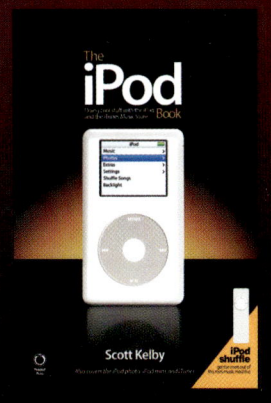

The iPod Book *$18.99*

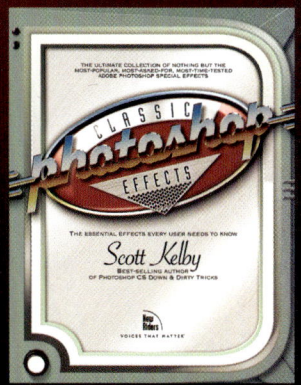

Classic Photoshop Effects *$31.99*

To snag these tasty titles, and track down more information go to
www.scottkelbybooks.com
or call **800-738-8513** today!

Scott Kelby is the #1 Technology Author of 2004

Photoshop CS2 KillerTips

Scott Kelby • Felix Nelson

PHOTOSHOP® CS2 KILLER TIPS

The Photoshop® CS2
Killer Tips Team

TECHNICAL EDITORS
Polly Reincheld
Veronica Martin
Cindy Snyder

PRODUCTION EDITOR
Kim Gabriel

PRODUCTION MANAGER
Dave Damstra

COVER DESIGN AND
CREATIVE CONCEPTS
Felix Nelson

PUBLISHED BY
New Riders

Copyright © 2006 by Scott Kelby

FIRST EDITION: October 2005

All rights reserved. No part of this book may be reproduced or transmitted in any form, by any means, electronic or mechanical, including photocopying, recording, or by any information storage and retrieval system, without written permission from the publisher, except for inclusion of brief quotations in a review.

Composed in Myriad Pro and Helvetica by NAPP Publishing

Trademarks
All terms mentioned in this book that are known to be trademarks or service marks have been appropriately capitalized. New Riders cannot attest to the accuracy of this information. Use of a term in the book should not be regarded as affecting the validity of any trademark or service mark.

Photoshop is a registered trademark of Adobe Systems, Inc.
Windows is a registered trademark of Microsoft Corporation.

Warning and Disclaimer
This book is designed to provide information about Photoshop tips. Every effort has been made to make this book as complete and as accurate as possible, but no warranty of fitness is implied.

The information is provided on an as-is basis. The authors and New Riders shall have neither liability nor responsibility to any person or entity with respect to any loss or damages arising from the information contained in this book or from the use of the discs or programs that may accompany it.

ISBN 0-321-33063-3

9 8 7 6 5 4 3 2 1

Printed in the United States of America

www.newriders.com
www.scottkelbybooks.com

To my sweetheart Kalebra. I can't imagine that the crush I've had on you since the first time we met 20-something years ago will ever fade.
—SCOTT KELBY

To Patty, Alex, Chris, and Earl. They truly are my strength and inspiration.
—FELIX NELSON

ACKNOWLEDGMENTS

The downside of being a co-author is you only get half as much space to thank all of the wonderful people without whom you couldn't do any of this.

First, I want to thank my incredible wife Kalebra. I don't know what she puts in her morning coffee, but it must be working. Every year she gets more amazing, more beautiful, more hilarious, more savvy, and more just plain wonderful. She's my best friend, confidante, advice desk, gourmet chef, favorite artist, and the ultimate business partner. Best of all, she's a world-class mom, and it's an absolute joy seeing her special gifts reflected in our son Jordan. He has no idea how blessed and supremely lucky we both are to have her.

I want to thank my co-author, Felix Nelson, for agreeing to do this book with me. He's an amazing person—a great artist, with seemingly limitless enthusiasm and energy that has him perpetually in a good mood seven days a week.

His combination of talent, business savvy, and humor make him an absolute pleasure to work with, and I continue to learn more from him every day. I want to thank my world class Tech Editor Polly Reincheld for all her hard work and dedication, and thanks to my Production Editor Kim Gabriel for once again bringing the whole project together.

Thanks to Dave Cross and Matt Kloskowski for always sharing their favorite Photoshop tips with me, so I can pass them along to my readers, and thanks to best buddy Dave "Hey You!" Moser for kickin' so much butt out there.

I also want to thank my good friend and business partner Jean A. Kendra for all her support and enthusiasm for my projects. Special thanks to my brother Jeff for everything he does and for being such an important influence in my life. I want to thank everyone at KW Media Group who every day redefine what teamwork and dedication are all about. An extra special thanks to Kathy Siler for the hundreds of things she does that make my life and my work so much easier.

Thanks to Nancy Ruenzel, Scott Cowlin, Rachel Tiley and the entire crew at Peachpit for their commitment to excellence, and for the honor of letting me be one of their "Voices That Matter."

And most importantly, an extra special thanks to God and his son Jesus Christ for always hearing my prayers, for always being there when I need Him, and for blessing me with a life I truly love, and such a warm loving family to share it with.

—SCOTT KELBY

....

First, I'd like to thank my wife Patty, who is the kindest, most understanding and caring person on the face of the planet. Her positive outlook on life, no matter how chaotic the world is around her, is remarkable. A smile from her face can light up an entire room. Then there are my three sons, Earl, Chris, and Alex. Earl is the ultimate in cool. Nothing ever ruffles his feathers. To watch an adorable, curly-headed little boy grow up into such a wonderful young man has been my greatest source of pride. And Chris "the studier" is the hardest-working, nose-to-the-grindstone person you'd ever want to meet. His drive and determination astonishes me. He's just a fantastic kid. Then there's little Alex. It's absolutely amazing how this little person affects my life. No matter how bad or how stressful the day has been, a hug from those tiny little arms and an "I love you Daddy" from those big brown eyes just melt my heart. He makes me realize things are never quite as bad as they appear.

My involvement in this book would not have been possible without the guidance and tutelage of Scott Kelby. He is without a doubt the most energetic, ambitious, and entertaining person I've ever met. His motor just never stops running. I can't begin to tell you how much he's influenced my life. He's a great mentor and a wonderful human being. I also have to thank the partners of KW Media Group (Jim Workman, Jean Kendra, and Kalebra Kelby) for the opportunities they've given me. When it comes to hard work and dedication, they're right up there with Scott. They're an amazing group and I'm a better person for knowing them.

Thanks to Dave Moser and Kim Gabriel who, come hell or high water, make sure the trains run on time. Of course, I can't forget about "Super Dave" Damstra, Dave "#5" Korman, Margie Rosenstien, Taffy Orlowski, and Christine Edwards who do the work of about 20 ordinary designers. They Rock. Thanks to Polly, Veronica, and Cindy, the tech editing "book babes". I'd also like to thank Chris Main and Barbara Thompson, Managing Editors extraordinaire, they could proofread an entire set of encyclopedias in an afternoon, and still have time for beer and a game of darts. And a special thanks to everyone else at KW Media Group, working behind the scenes, from the mailroom to customer service, who make us all look good.

—FELIX NELSON

ABOUT THE AUTHORS

Scott Kelby

Scott is Editor-in-Chief and co-founder of *Photoshop User* magazine, Editor-in-Chief of Nikon's *Capture User* magazine, Editor-in-Chief of *Layers* magazine (The How-To Magazine for Everything Adobe), and is Executive Editor of the *Photoshop Elements Techniques* newsletter.

He is President of the National Association of Photoshop Professionals (NAPP), the trade association for Adobe® Photoshop® users, and he's President of the software training and publishing firm, KW Media Group, Inc.

Scott is an award-winning author of more than 26 books on Photoshop, digital imaging, and technology. In 2004, he was the world's #1 bestselling author of all computer and technology books. His other titles include *Photoshop Down & Dirty Tricks, Photoshop Photo-Retouching Secrets, Photoshop Classic Effects, The Photoshop Elements Book for Digital Photographers,* and he's creator and series Editor for the entire *Killer Tips* series from New Riders.

Scott's latest books include *The iPod Book* and *The Book for Guys Who Don't Want Kids (How to Get Past the Fear of Fatherhood)*. In 2004, Scott was awarded the publishing industry's prestigious Benjamin Franklin Award for the previous edition of this book.

Scott is Training Director for the Adobe Photoshop Seminar Tour, Conference Technical Chair for the Photoshop World Conference & Expo, and he is a speaker at digital imaging trade shows and events around the world. He is also featured in a series of Adobe Photoshop training DVDs and has been training Adobe Photoshop users since 1993.

For more background info on Scott, visit www.scottkelby.com.

Felix Nelson

Felix Nelson is the Creative Director of *Photoshop User* magazine, the Senior Art Director for the National Association of Photoshop Professionals (NAPP), and the Art Director for *Layers* magazine, The How-To Magazine for Everything Adobe. Felix is a contributing author to *Photoshop Effects Magic* from New Riders and served as technical consultant for *Photoshop Down & Dirty Tricks*. Felix is also featured in a Photoshop training video, *Photoshop Photorealistic Techniques*, and is a member of the Photoshop World instructor "Dream Team."

He's a traditional illustrator who took a "digital-u-turn" in 1988 when he was first introduced to a Mac IIcx. His design work and digital illustrations have been featured on NBA-, NFL-, and MLB-licensed sports apparel and have appeared in several national publications.

Felix lives in Spring Hill, Florida, with his wife Patty and sons Alex, Chris, and Earl.

www.scottkelbybooks.com

www.scottkelbybooks.com   TABLE OF CONTENTS

CHAPTER 1   1
Speed Ballin'
Adobe Bridge Tips

Undocumented Bridge Slide Show Tip	2
Scrolling Through the Views	2
Open Any Folder with a Simple Drag-and-Drop	3
Rating Multiple Photos at Once	3
Creating New Folders the Fast Way	4
Separating Your "Best of the Best"	4
Rating Your Images in Full Screen Mode	5
A Sneak Peek at Your Photo's Data	5
Uncluttering Your View	6
Renaming Your Label Colors	6
Keeping Bridge Always on Top	7
Resetting Bridge's Preferences	7
Deleting Folders from Bridge	8
Seeing More Than One Folder of Images at a Time	8
Viewing the Pages of PDFs from within Bridge	9
Seeing Your PDF Pages Bigger	9
How to Get More Than Three Panes	10
How to Know if a Photo Is Open in Photoshop	11
Opening an Image and Hiding Your Bridge Window	11
I Wanna Go Back	12
Faster Color Labeling Shortcut	12
Getting Back to Your Bridge Window After Searching	13
Collections Are Live, Baby!	13
Duplicate Any Photo Fast!	14
Deleting Unwanted Photos Fast	14
Emailing from Bridge	15
Ejecting Discs from within Bridge	15
Rename Any Photo Fast	16
Switching Between Open Bridge Windows	16
Jump to the Largest Thumbnail Size in One Click	17
How to Keep from Losing Your Bridge Changes	17
Batch Renaming Earns a Shortcut	18
Jumping Between Bridge and Photoshop	18
One-Button Refresh for Bridge	19
Changing Metadata Font Sizes	19
Nesting Your Bridge Panes	20
Making the Preview Palette Bigger	20
Saving Bridge Workspaces	21

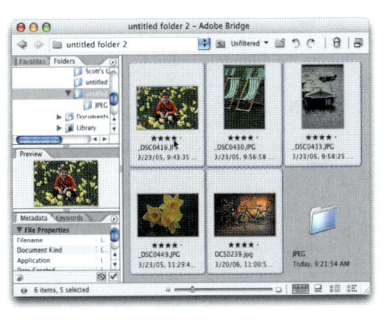

TABLE OF CONTENTS

CHAPTER 2	**23**
Born to Run	
Essential Tips You've Got to Know	
Find All the New CS2 Stuff Fast!	24
The Most Long-Awaited Shortcut Makes Its Debut	24
Cursor Too Small? Make It Bigger	25
Side-by-Side Photo Review	25
Want Some Hints for the Tool You're Currently Using?	26
Don't Use It? Hide It!	26
A Tip for People Who Train New Photoshop Users	27
Lost Your Cursor? Find It Fast!	27
The Hidden Measurement Pop-Up Menu	28
Getting a Fresh Histogram in One Click	28
Using the Lasso Tool? Keep It Straight	29
Can't Remember Selection Shortcuts? Look at the Cursor	29
How to Tame the Select Similar Command	30
Quick Trick to Reapply That Filter	30
Scrubby Slider Shift-Click Trick	31
Escape from the Crop Tool (or Die!)	31
Getting the Startup Window Back	32
Getting Your Warnings Back (Resetting All Dialogs)	32
The Smaller Toolbox Trick	33
Brushes Palette: That's Not a Header, It's a Button	33
Dangerous Intersection?	34
Nudging 10 Pixels at a Time	35
Make That Options Bar Float— Float???	35
Where's the 3D Transform Filter?	36
Supersize It	36
Steal Color from Anywhere	37
Ask Photoshop to Remember More	38
Shrink Those Palettes Down to Size	38
Creating the Über Palette	39
Fix Those Tool Settings Fast	39
Bring Order Back to Your World	40
The Undocumented Fill Shortcut	40
Deselected and Forgot to Save? Don't Sweat It	41
Super-Fast Inches to Pixels	41
Boss Around Your Color Swatches	42
Zoomed In? Don't Use the Scroll Bars	42
Let Photoshop Do the Math When Copying/Pasting	43
Instant Selection from Any Path	43

TABLE OF CONTENTS

www.scottkelbybooks.com

Save Clicks When You Close	44
Been Bingeing on RAM? Maybe It's Time to Purge!	44
Reaching the Free Transform Handles	45
Transforming and Copying at the Same Time	45

CHAPTER 3   47
Life in the Fast Lane
Production Tips

Miss the Old Default Actions?	48
Rearranging Your Brushes	48
Find the Center of Any Document	49
No More Jaggy Lasso Tool Selections	50
Open Up Some Screen Real Estate	51
Let Photoshop Do the Work in Curves	52
Want a Finer Grid? You Got It!	52
You Don't Need the Brushes Palette to Change Brush Size	53
Rotate to Any Angle the Fast Way	53
Get Rid of Unwanted Brushes	54
Brushes Right Where You Want 'Em	54
Navigating the Brush Picker Like a Pro	55
Get More Control Over Your Paint Strokes	55
Speed Tip to Rotate through Open Images	56
Instantly Find the Center of Any Object	56
Making Your Guide Flip	57
Creating Temporary Brushes	58
Reusing Your Last Curve Setting	58
Bringing Back Those Cropped-Away Areas	59
Fix Those Stray Pixels Fast!	60
Getting More Control Over the Magic Wand	60
Making the Color Palette Work Twice as Hard	61
Use Your Last Settings and Save Time	61
Hit Those Channels Fast	62
How to Get an Undo After You've Closed the Document	62
Using the Pen? Stay Away from the Toolbox	63
Put Your Gradient Picker at Your Fingertips	63
Don't Click in That Field!	64
Out of Memory? Try This First	64
How to "Unerase"	65
Let Photoshop Straighten Your Crooked Scans	65
Copy One Layer, or Copy 'Em All	66
Stuck in a Field? Here's How to Escape	66

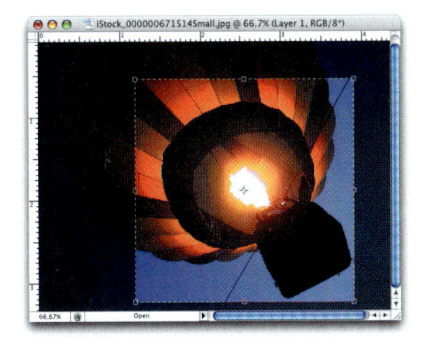

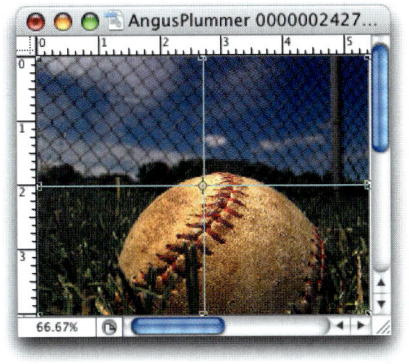

TABLE OF CONTENTS

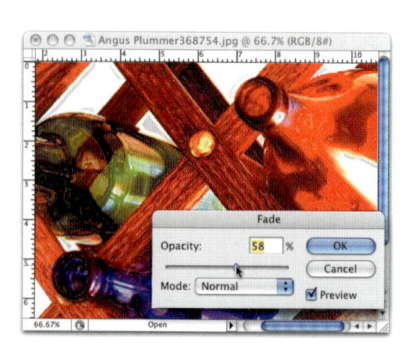

Don't Cancel; Reset and Save Time	67
See Every Tweak with Bigger Filter Gallery Previews	67
Showing One Effect in the Filter Gallery	68
Use the Move Tool Anytime	68
Filter Gallery Zoom Quick Tip	69

CHAPTER 4   71
Greased Lightnin'
Way Cool Tips

Find Things Fast by Color-Coding Them	72
Using Camera Raw Images as Smart Objects	73
Getting More Control Over Vanishing Point	73
Turning Your Vanishing Point Grid	74
Hidden Zoom Feature in Vanishing Point	74
Think You Might Change Sizes? Make It a Smart Object!	75
Making a Smart Object Dumb—Well, Kinda	75
Switching from Warp to Free Transform (and Back Again)	76
Instant Thumbnail Size Control	76
What's Smarter Than Using Guides?	77
Getting Back to the Filter Gallery Defaults	78
Having History Track Your Layer Visibility	78
The Trick to Tricky Extractions	79
Zooming All Your Tiled Images at Once	79
How to Duplicate a Color Stop	80
Removing Edge Fringe When Collaging	80
Cracking the Easter Egg Mystery	81
Undo on a Slider!	81
Resizing Paths the Easy Way	82
The Gaussian Blur Keyboard Shortcut	82
The Advantage of Photo Filter Adjustment Layers	83
Make a Photoshop Client Presentation	83
Moving Your Image in Full Screen Mode	84
Photo-Retouching Safety Tip	84
Lights, Camera, Action: Slide Shows Using Photoshop	85
Photoshop's Hidden Step and Repeat	86
Pausing for a Brush Preview	86
The Undocumented Airbrush Toggle Trick	87
Swapping Crop Fields	87
Let Those Windows Breathe!	88
The Multiple Undo Shortcut	88
Want Arrowheads? Photoshop Can Add Them for You!	89

Dragging-and-Dropping Where You Want	89
Feather a Selection Without the Guessing Game	90
Top-Secret Photoshop Splash Screen	91
Fall in Love with a Temporary Brush, or Not	91
Undo a Save? That's Impossible, Isn't It?	92
Change Brush Softness on the Fly	92
How to Correct One Problem Color	93
Building a Better Background Eraser Tool	94
Custom Brushes: Start with a Clean Slate	95
Timing Is Everything!	95

CHAPTER 5

Fast & Furious

Camera Raw Tips

97

Black-and-White Conversions in Camera Raw	98
Don't Click the White Balance Tool on Something White	99
Updating the Histogram as You Crop	99
Slide Away the Aberrations	100
Seeing Your RAW Image without the Auto Corrections	101
Toggling the Preview On/Off	102
Turning Off Auto Correction for Good	102
How to Undo the White Balance Tool	103
Getting More Readouts Per Eyedropper	103
Shortcuts for Highlight and Shadow Warnings	104
Cancelling a Crop in Camera Raw	104
Removing a Straighten in Camera Raw	105
How to See the Sharpening Now, but Not Apply It	105
Adding Points to Camera Raw's Curve	106
Shortcut for Rotating Images in Camera Raw	106
Cropping Multiple RAW Images at Once	107
Last-Minute Renaming in Raw	107
Bigger Previews in Camera Raw	108
Use Your Favorite Navigation Shortcuts in Camera Raw	108
Make It Always Fit in Camera Raw	109
How About a JPEG with the RAW File? Oh, a TIFF Too?	109
Don't Change Your Camera's Color Space for Raw	110
Making Your Photo Bigger? Do It in Raw!	110
Hiding Your Metadata from Others	111
How to Get Back Where You Started in Camera Raw	112
Bypass Camera Raw's Annoying Save As Dialog	112
Sorting Images in Camera Raw	113

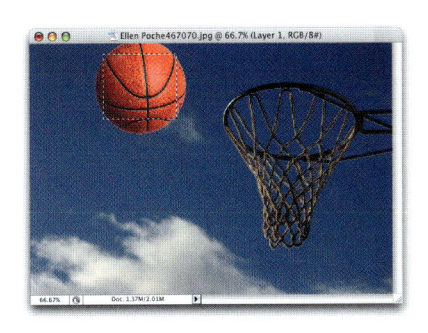

TABLE OF CONTENTS

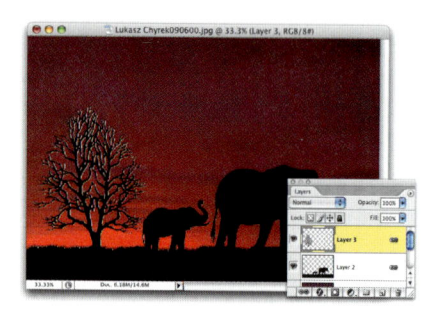

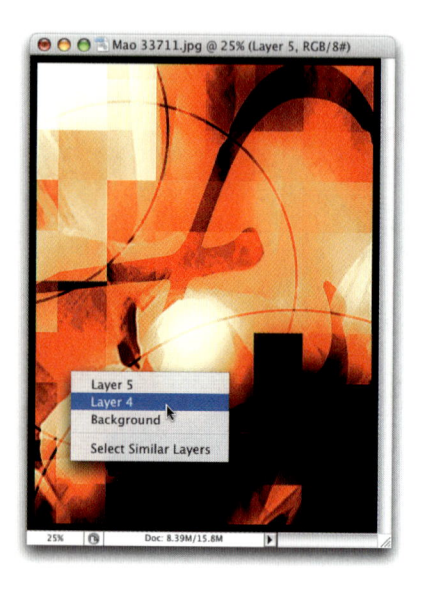

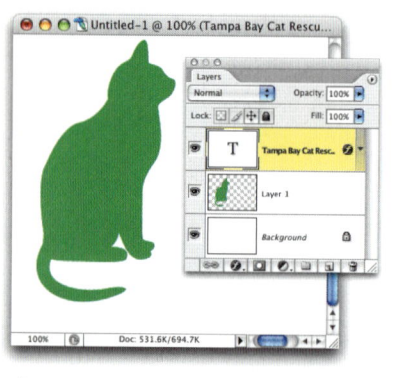

Having Bridge Always Process Your RAW Images	114
How to Tell Camera Raw Which Photo to Use for Edits	114
Like the Edits You Made to One Photo? Apply Them to Others	115
Removing Your Edits to a RAW Image in Bridge	116
Cropping Multiple Images at Once	116

CHAPTER 6 119
Speedy Gonzalez
Layer Tips

Finally, a Shortcut for Creating a Flattened Layer	120
Changing Opacity While You're Transforming	120
Moving Layer Effects from One Layer to Another	121
Faster Flattening	122
Unlinking All Your Linked Layers with a Single Click	122
Temporarily Unlinking a Layer	123
Loading a Layer Selection Has Changed	123
Visual Cues for a Layer's Edge	124
Don't Want a Gap Between Items? Snap to 'Em	125
Moving and Copying Layer Masks	125
Inverting a Mask as You Move It	126
Want to "Drag Select" Layers? You Need to Turn This On	126
Layer Group Super-Speed Tip	127
Almost a Built-In Flattening Shortcut	127
Jump to Any Layer Just by Clicking in Your Image	128
Turning Your Layers into Separate Documents	128
Opening Layered Files without All the Layers	129
Missing Your Background Layer? Here's the Fix	129
Avoiding the Layer Menu	130
Lock All Those Layers in Just One Click	130
Toggle through the Blend Modes	131
Hide Your Other Layers in the Blink of an Eye	131
Why Dragging-and-Dropping Styles Rocks!	132
Applying Layer Styles to Your Background Layer	133
Turn Your Layer Comps into Their Own Docs	133
More Control Over Blends: Advanced Blending	134
Instant Opacity Change	135
Copy a Layer in the Same Location in Another Document	135
Moving Multiple Layers from Document to Document	136
Centering Dragged Layers the Easy Way	137
Easier Drop Shadow Angle Adjustments	137

www.scottkelbybooks.com TABLE OF CONTENTS

Layer Navigation Shortcut	138
Separation Anxiety: Put a Layer Style on a Separate Layer	138
Layer Effects Removal Speed Tip	139
Shapes without the Shape Layer	139
Color-Coding Made Easy	140
Speed Up Photoshop by Merging Layers	140
Can't We All Just Have the Same Style?	141
Layers Palette Navigation Speed Tips	142
View Your Layer Mask as a Rubylith	143
Selecting Just One Object on a Layer	144
Un-Filling for Fun and Profit	144
Secret Opacity See-Through-Part-of-a-Layer Tip	145

CHAPTER 7	**147**
Burn Rubber	
Smokin' Type Tips	

Bigger Font Previews	148
Don't Like the Font Previews? Turn 'Em Off	148
Clicking with the Type Tool Trick	149
Getting Type in a Perfect Circle	149
I Need My Dumb Quotes Again	150
Resetting Your Type	150
One-Click Access to the Copyright Symbol, and More	151
Highlighting Your Text Super Fast!	151
Rendering Text in Just One Click	152
Made to Fit	152
Text-Path-Making Maniac	153
Picture This: Putting a Photo Inside Type	153
Fonts, Fonts, and More Fonts	154
Make Your Text Jump into Action	155
Double Your Pleasure	156
Move Your Type, without Switching Tools	156
Seeing Your Type Change Color	157
Editing Text without Highlighting It	158
Rasterize Times 2, 4, 6...	158
Honey, I Need Some Space: Visually Adjust Kerning	159
Tell Photoshop When You're Done with Type	159
Bring Those Type Layers Together	160
The Long and the Short of Type	161
Made to Fit: Part Two	162
Making the Spell Checker Obey Your Commands	162

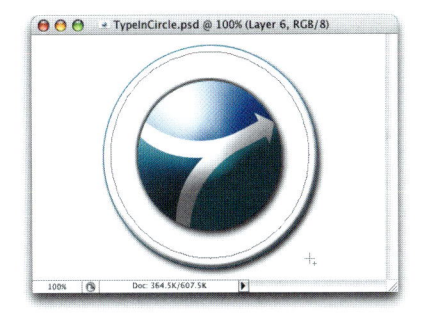

xv

TABLE OF CONTENTS

Editing Type on a Path	163
Exact Sizing for Your Text Columns	163
Removing Those Typographically Incorrect Spaces	164
Don't Have Italic or Bold? Don't Sweat It	164
Tweak All Your Type with One Fell Swoop!	165

CHAPTER 8   167
Speed Two
Image Correction and Prepress Tips

How Accurate Do You Need to Be When Removing Red Eye?	168
Getting Better Shadow/Highlight Results	168
Ditch the Annoying Lens Correction Grid	169
Determining the Motion Angle in Smart Sharpen	170
Getting More Accurate Color Using Replace Color	171
Correcting Highlights? Watch Out for Open Shadows!	171
How to Heal on a Blank Layer	172
Better Healing with a Custom Brush	172
Creating a Custom Shadow/Highlight Default	173
Getting Back Shadow/Highlight's Factory Defaults	173
Healing with Pressure	174
Control the Opacity of Your Healing Process	174
Say Good-Bye to Gradient Banding	175
Sharpening Your Images Like a Pro	175
Five Tips for Getting Rid of Moiré Patterns	176
Scan Line Art at the Resolution You Need	177
Using the High Pass Filter for Sharpening	178
Spot Color Gradient Film Saver	178
Correct in CMYK or RGB?	179
Straightening Scans in 10 Seconds (or Less)	179
Scanners Aren't Just for Flat Objects	180
Are Your Colors Press Ready?	180
Never Swap Colors Again When Cleaning Line Art	181
Let Photoshop Do Your Resolution Math	181
Going to Press? Make Sure Your Monitor Is in the "Right Space"	182
Want Better Gradients on Press? Here's the Tip	183
Getting Before and After Previews	183
Cloning from Image to Image	184
Get More Realistic Drop Shadows on Press	184
Making Sure Your Whites Are Really White	185

TABLE OF CONTENTS

www.scottkelbybooks.com

Try Not to Correct More Than Once	186
More Curve Point Quick Tips	186
Have Photoshop Help Find Your Highlights/Shadows	187
Talkin' 'Bout My Resolution	187
Are You Really Seeing Your Sharpening?	188
Adjusting Curve Points with Precision	188
Apply Unsharp Mask to CMYK Images	189
RGB Flesh Tones: Getting the "Red" Out	189
Once You're in CMYK Mode, Stay There	190
The Simple Tip to Better Color Separations	190
How to Sharpen Flesh Tones in CMYK	191
How to Read Four Areas at Once	191

CHAPTER 9 — 193
Speed Kills
Advanced Tips

Action Insurance Policy	194
Doing Animations? Don't Jump to ImageReady	194
The New Way to Create a Clipping Group	195
Keeping Track of Your Every Move	195
Embed Your Message into Your Photos	196
Managing the Metadata Overload	196
Photoshop's Own Slide Show	197
The Histogram Palette's Visual Cues	197
Seeing Your Full-Color Image While Editing a Channel	198
How to Combine Two Paths into One	198
Power Up Your Layer Styles	199
Freeform/Pen Tool Quick Switch	199
Visual Control Over Your Selections Using Quick Mask	200
Have Photoshop Select the Shadows and Highlights	201
Troubleshooting Actions? Slow Down!	201
Accessing Grayed-Out Filters in CMYK	202
Assigning Metadata to Multiple Files	202
More Control Over Filters	203
Applying Multiple Filters? Not on My Layer!	204
New Snapshot, the Mistake Insurance Policy	204
Saving Your Actions as Printable Text Files	205
3D Print Effects (and Where to Get Those Goofy Glasses)	205
Creating Reusable Diagonal Guides	206
The Secrets of Searching in Bridge	206
Drag-and-Drop Curves for Quick Correction	207

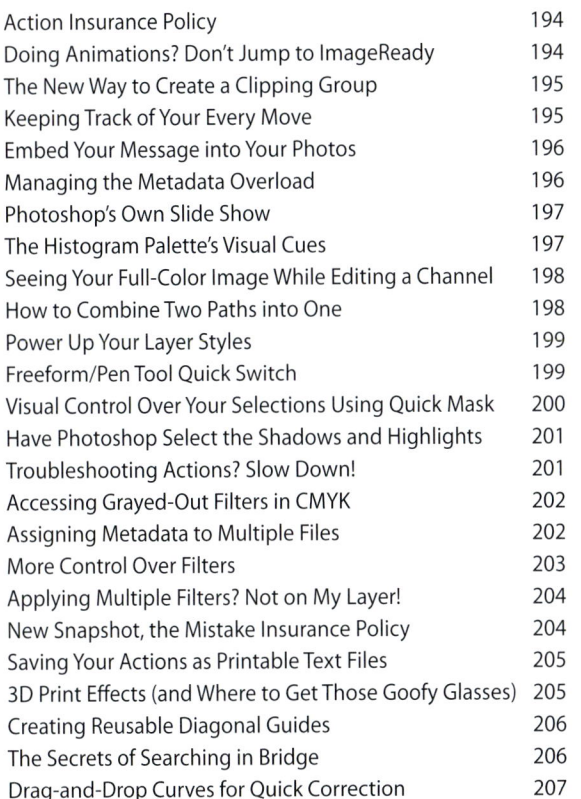

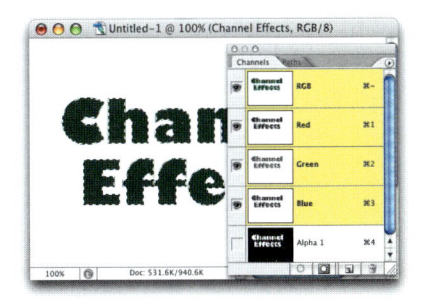

xvii

TABLE OF CONTENTS

Actions Power Tip: Add an Action to Your Action	207
Prepress Cleanups—In a Snap	208
No More Creating Type in Channels	208
Blend Mode Power Tip	209
Let Photoshop Tell You the Highlight and Shadow	209
Using the Lasso—Don't Stop to Navigate	210
Load Any Saved Selection without the Channels Palette	210
Plot Multiple Curve Points in Just One Click	211
Tough Selection Tip	212
Making the Color Picker Show CMYK	213
Moving Multiple Curve Points at Once	213
Add to Your Selections through the Channels Palette	214
Embedding Paths into Actions	214
Measure Twice, Look Once	215
Stroking Half a Path—Half a Path????	215
Locking a PDF Presentation	216
Speeding Up Batch Actions	217
Putting Your Lens Flare on the Spot	217

CHAPTER 10 219
Fast Company
Troubleshooting Tips

The Reappearing/Disappearing Brush Tip	220
Get Print Resolution from Your Digital Camera Images	220
How to Use RGB Filters on Grayscale Images	221
Stop the Crop Snapping	221
Let's Do the Text Warp Again	222
Unlocking the Background Layer	222
Do You Have Enough RAM? Ask Photoshop	223
Getting Better EPS Previews	224
Get Back Your Background Layer	224
Expanding Rectangular Selections	225
Fixing the "Rounded Corners" Selection Problem	226
Making Global Light Work for You	226
Find the Hidden Magnetic Pen Tool Options	227
Let Photoshop Rebuild Your Prefs	227
Stop the "Click-and-Jump-to-That-Layer" Blues	228
Faster Application Switching	228
Will More RAM Make Photoshop Run Faster?	229
Don't Use Crop to Fix Barrel Distortion	229
Getting Smaller Photoshop Files	230

xviii

www.scottkelbybooks.com

TABLE OF CONTENTS

CHAPTER 11	233
Speed Freak	
Killer Web Tips	
Adding Music to Your Flash Web Gallery	234
Lose Those Annoying Numbers in the Upper Left-Hand Corner	234
Need to Shrink the File Size? Use Transparency	235
Crop It Even Closer	235
Let Photoshop Make the File Size Call	236
Zoom Out for Sharper Web Images	236
ImageReady Feature Comes to Photoshop	237
Two Easy Ways to Create Transparency	237
ImageReady Window Speed Tip	238
If It's Web Safe, Don't Use It	238
Change One Preference, Save a Bundle	239
Get the Real 100% View	240
Style Warning for Web Designers	241
Spend More Time Animating, Less Time Clicking	241
Getting to the Hexadecimal Code	242
Get Super-Clean Type for the Web	242
Got a Folder Full of Images for the Web? Batch 'Em!	243
Exercising Your Influence on GIFs	244
Read the Web Color Onscreen	244
ImageReady's Supercharged Eyedropper	245
ImageReady's Auto Tile Maker	246
Make Sure You See It the Same Way They See It	246
Don't Load That Bogus Slice!	247
Use Layer-Based Slices	247
Blur That JPEG and Shrink It Down	248
INDEX	249

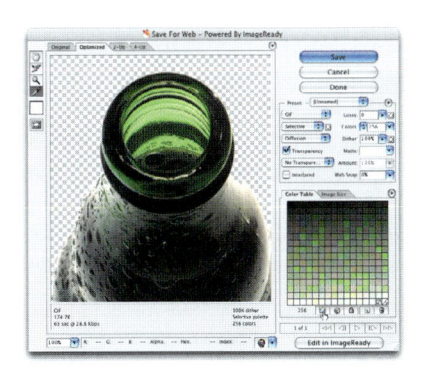

xix

INTRODUCTION

Why we wrote this book

The inspiration for this book came when Felix saw what the car payment would be on a new Porsche Boxster. He came to me and said, "Dude, I gotta write a book." Okay, you know we're kidding, but admit it—don't you secretly wish that for once, when someone was doing something strictly for the money, they'd just come out and say so. Just once, wouldn't you like to hear someone admit it? Well, I hate to disappoint you, but I can tell you unequivocally that Felix and I absolutely did not write this book for the money. We wrote it to get free drugs. All authors get free drugs—it's in every book contract. Always has been.

Actually, the reason we wanted to write this book is because of something that is already in almost every Photoshop book ever written: the tips. You know—those cool little tips littered throughout the sidebars of all great Photoshop books. We found that those little tips were often our favorite parts of the book. In fact, Felix and I agreed that frequently we'd read all those little sidebar tips first—before we'd ever sit down to actually read a chapter. It's those neat little tips that the great authors include that make using Photoshop so much fun (and make their books so great). The only problem is, there's just not enough of 'em.

So we thought, "Wouldn't it be cool if there was a Photoshop book where the whole book, cover-to-cover, was nothing but those little tips on the side!" Then Felix jumped up and yelled, "Let's write that book!" I jumped up and yelled, "Yes, yes! We have to write that book. It's our destiny!" Then Felix yelled, "Then I can get my Porsche!" I mean, he yelled, "This book will help humanity and be written for the common good" (or something like that. I can't remember. Probably because of all the drugs).

> **TIP**
>
> *This is a sidebar tip. Every great Photoshop book has a few of them. But this book is nothing but them. A whole book of cool sidebar tips, without the sidebars.*

Is this book for you?

Is this book for you? Are you kidding? This book is so for you that it secretly freaks you out. Look, we don't know you personally, but we know Photoshop people. You're just like us—you love those little sidebar tips just as much as we do. If you didn't, authors would've stopped adding them to their books years ago, because, frankly, they're a pain in the butt to compile. But we know what you're thinking. Sure, you love those little tips—those inside secrets that make you look smart at parties and gain respect from your peers, homies, peeps, and other esteemed colleagues, but you want something more. You want the one thing that those cool little sidebar tips never seem to have. That's right, graphics. As cool as those sidebar tips are, they're always just a tiny little box with a couple of lines of text (like the sidebar we added above left). So we thought we'd expand the explanations just enough to make them more accessible, and add an accompanying graphic to enhance each tip's innate juiciness. They must remain "juicy." They must be "juicy tips."

Now you're probably wondering, "Guys, Photoshop is one amazing program with an unrivaled power and incredible depth. Couldn't you have come up with at least 1,000 Photoshop tips?" Absolutely. We could have included loads of tips, such as "F7 brings up the Layers palette," and "Press G-Shift-G to get the Paint Bucket tool," but the problem is, those aren't "Killer Tips." Every Photoshop book has those tips. Heck, books about gardening probably even have those Photoshop tips. For a tip to get in this book, it had to be a "Killer Tip." Each tip had to be one that would make the reader smile, nod, and then pick up the phone to call another Photoshop user just to "tune them up" with their newfound power. Remember, these are killer tips, so be careful. Someone could get hurt.

Okay, how do I get started?

In my previous Photoshop books, *Photoshop CS Down & Dirty Tricks* and *The Photoshop CS2 Book for Digital Photographers*, I used a technique that really worked well. I gratuitously mentioned my other books in the introduction, just in case I didn't get to plug them later. No, wait… that's not it. What I did tell the reader was that my books aren't set up like a novel. They're purposely not designed to make you start at Chapter One and read your way through to the back (where hopefully, I'll again have an opportunity to plug, I mean casually mention, my other books). Instead, this book is designed so you can jump in anywhere, in any chapter, and immediately try the tips that interest you the most, regardless of your level of experience in Photoshop. You don't need to load any special images from a CD-ROM or go to a website to download special photos—these are just cool tips. No flaming type, no multilevel glows—just timesaving shortcuts and efficiency tips that will make you faster and better at Photoshop than you'd ever thought you'd be.

Also, like my previous books, we spell out everything. So if you've been using Photoshop for years, don't let it frustrate you because instead of just writing, "Create a new layer," we usually write, "Create a new layer by clicking on the New Layer icon at the bottom of the Layers palette." We do that because we want everyone, at any skill level, to be able to open the book to any page and start applying these cool tips to their work immediately.

This book is built on the premise that "Speed Kills." Because after all, if you get faster at Photoshop, you'll have more time to be creative, and the more time you spend being creative, the more fun you'll have.

Is this book for Macintosh, Windows, or both?

This book is not only for Mac and Windows users, it's for people who don't even have a computer. In fact, it's ideal for anyone with $29.99 (kidding). Because Photoshop is identical on both the Macintosh and Windows operating systems, the book is for both Mac and Windows users. However, the keyboards on a Mac and PC are slightly different, so every time we give a keyboard shortcut, we give both the Mac and Windows shortcuts. (Well, there is one other difference—in Mac OS X you'll find Photoshop's Preferences under the Photoshop menu instead of the Edit menu like it used to be in the Mac OS and still is in Windows.)

How to use this book

This book is designed to be read while moving at a high rate of speed. If you're barreling down the highway going 80 mph, weaving in and out of traffic, that's the ideal time to turn to Chapter Six to read the tip on "How to assist EMS workers with using the Jaws of Life." Okay, admittedly, that's probably not a good idea, so instead, just make sure you open this book in front of your computer so you can dive right into the tips. Remember, the one who dies with the most cool tips wins.

What not to do

You're almost ready to get to the tips, but first a word of caution: "Caution." There. Now you're ready. Actually, we did want to point out that the only two actual sidebar tips in the entire book are on these two pages. So, don't go rippin' through the book looking for all those little sidebar tips, because we intentionally left the sidebars blank. Why? So we could write another book called *The Missing Killer Tips Sidebars*, just in case Felix ever sees what the payment is for a house on the beach.

> **TIP**
>
> You're doing it again! Stop looking at these sidebars. See, they're intoxicating—you're drawn to them even after you know it's not really a tip. Okay, here's a real tip: If you like sidebar tips, buy this book.

Speed Ballin'

ADOBE BRIDGE TIPS

These chapter intros are usually Scott's area of expertise, but when we decided to add Adobe Bridge killer tips to this book, I felt the need to purge myself and release some inner

Speed Ballin'
adobe bridge tips

demons. Now, I don't have a problem with the Bridge software. Not at all, I love Bridge. And it isn't a fear of actual bridges. I dig real bridges, too. It's the word "bridge" itself that has blackened my heart. Even worse, Clint Eastwood, one of my favorite actors of all time, is forever linked to this vile and venomous word.

What created this inner turmoil? What horrific event triggered this kind of repulsive response to a simple word, you ask? The Bridges of Madison County, *that's what. Watching that one movie tainted the word bridge forever. There I was, waiting to hear Dirty Harry utter one of those famous one-liners—"Go ahead, make my day" or "Do you feel lucky punk?" Heck, simply hearing Philo Beddoe say "Right turn, Clyde" just one time could have saved the show. But nope, it wasn't to be. There he was, the outlaw Josey Wales, in a chick flick. Not just a chick flick, but maybe one of the worst films ever documented.*

But hey, that was a long time ago. Maybe I should just let it go and forget about the past. Clint's new movie, Million Dollar Baby, *is getting a lot of good press. I mean, it is Clint Eastwood after all, and it's about boxing. That's got machismo written all over it. Right?*

CHAPTER 1 • Adobe Bridge Tips   **1**

UNDOCUMENTED BRIDGE SLIDE SHOW TIP

Here's one that slipped below the radar—if you're watching a slide show of your images in Bridge (by pressing Command-L [PC: Control-L]), and you come across an image you want to open in Photoshop CS2, just press the letter O.

SCROLLING THROUGH THE VIEWS

Want to quickly scroll through the different thumbnail views in Bridge? Press-and-hold Command (PC: Control) and the Backslash key (\). Hey, don't scoff at this seemingly innocent shortcut—Mac users have been waiting years for any shortcut that makes use of the Backslash key. In the captures shown here, I've scrolled from Thumbnails view to Filmstrip view.

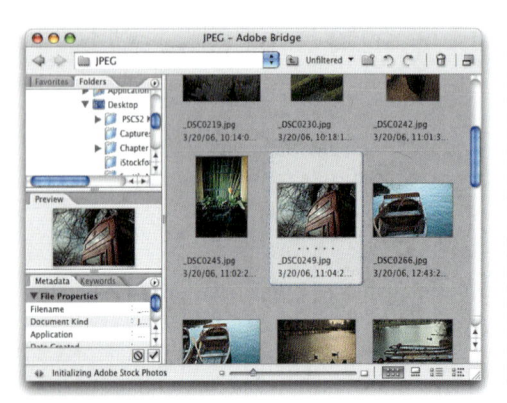

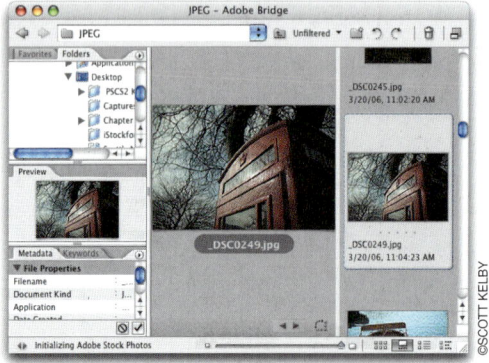

CHAPTER 1 • Adobe Bridge Tips

OPEN ANY FOLDER WITH A SIMPLE DRAG-AND-DROP

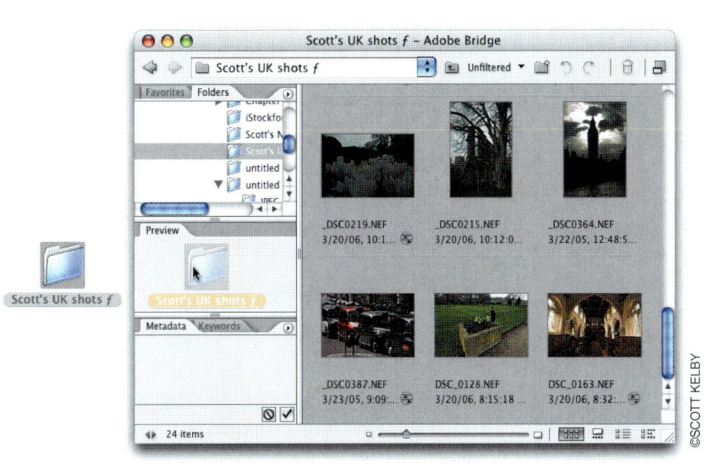

Want to open a folder of images in Bridge? Just drag-and-drop the folder directly onto the Preview panel. That's it. I wish this tip were longer, but it's just not.

RATING MULTIPLE PHOTOS AT ONCE

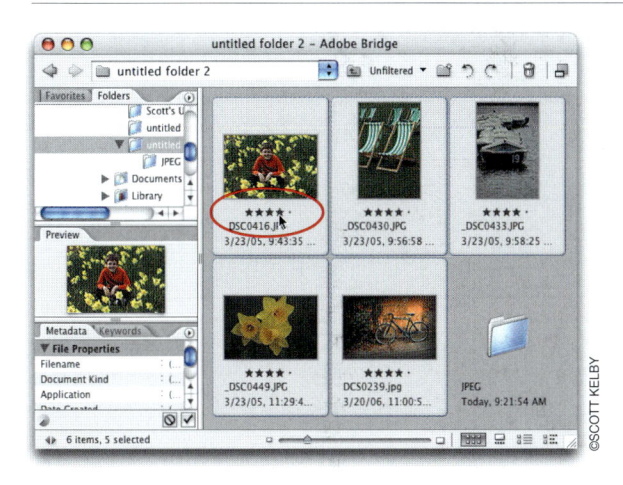

If you see a number of photos in Bridge that you want to have the same rating, first select the images (Shift-click on them or Command-click [PC: Control-click] noncontiguous images), then drag your cursor over the rating area (those five dots that appear below any selected thumbnail). The rating you apply to that one photo will be applied to all your selected photos.

CHAPTER 1 • Adobe Bridge Tips   **3**

CREATING NEW FOLDERS THE FAST WAY

Want to create a folder from right within Bridge? Scroll down to any open space (you'll usually find a blank spot at the bottom of your list of thumbnails, so scroll down there), then Control-click (PC: Right-click) and from the contextual menu that appears, choose New Folder. *Note:* If you don't see any empty space, adjust the size of your images using the Thumbnail Size slider along the bottom of the Bridge window.

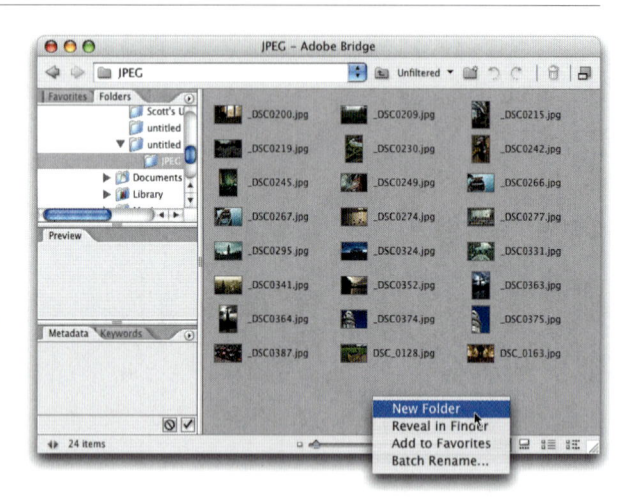

SEPARATING YOUR "BEST OF THE BEST"

If you've rated some of your photos as five-star photos (the best of the bunch), aren't there some five-star photos that are better than the others? You know, the best of your best? Of course there are, and now you can separate just those (so you can really see the cream of the crop). Here's how: First you must view just your five-star photos, so choose Show 5 Stars from the Unfiltered pop-up menu near the top right of the Options Bar. Then Command-click (PC: Control-click) on just your best five-star images to select them. Control-click (PC: Right-click) on any selected image and choose a color from the Label submenu in the contextual menu that appears (I chose Red). That color is now tagging your best five-star images. To see just your red five-star photos, go back to the Filtered pop-up menu (it'll change from Unfiltered to Filtered once you've selected an option), and choose Show Red Label. Now you're seeing your "Best of the Best."

CHAPTER 1 • Adobe Bridge Tips

RATING YOUR IMAGES IN FULL SCREEN MODE

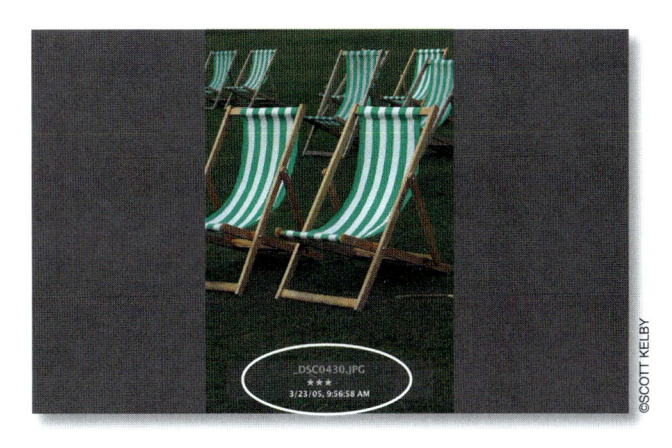

This is one of the most effective ways to sort your photos after you've imported them from your digital camera, because you can only really tell which photos are in sharp focus when they're viewed at nearly full screen. So in Bridge, Shift-click on all the contiguous photos you want to review, press Command-L (PC: Control-L) to launch the slide show, press W to see the images full screen, and then press Spacebar to start the slide show. As a photo appears full screen, just press numbers (1–5) to rate that photo instantly. For example, a photo appears onscreen and it's not that great, type 3 and it gets a three-star rating right on the spot. Try this once, and you'll start doing this all the time. Unless of course, you hate it—then you'll probably never do it again.

A SNEAK PEEK AT YOUR PHOTO'S DATA

You don't have to go digging through your photo's EXIF data to learn more about the image. Just hover your cursor over a photo's thumbnail for a moment, and a little yellow window will pop up with some brief background info, like the file's format, size, pixel dimensions, date created, date modified, resolution, etc. However, this only works if you have Tooltips turned on, so if you don't, press Command-K (PC: Control-K) to open the Bridge Preferences, choose General (from the left side of the dialog), and turn on the checkbox for Show Tooltips; now try the hovering trick again.

CHAPTER 1 • Adobe Bridge Tips

UNCLUTTERING YOUR VIEW

Want to hide all of that distracting info that appears beneath your thumbnails? Just press Command-T (PC: Control-T) and all that stuff (even the file names) is hidden, giving you a clean, unobstructed view of just your images and nothing more. When you want all the distracting junk back, just press the shortcut again.

RENAMING YOUR LABEL COLORS

Although you can't change the color of the color labels themselves, you can change each color's name to something that makes more sense to you when you're sorting your images. For example, if you want change the Green label to read "Keepers," just press Command-K (PC: Control-K) to go to the Bridge Preferences, click on Labels (along the list on the left side of the dialog), and then delete the word "Green" that appears to the right of the green dot and type "Keepers." Click OK to close the Preferences dialog. Now, when you look in the Label menu, it will be updated with your new name.

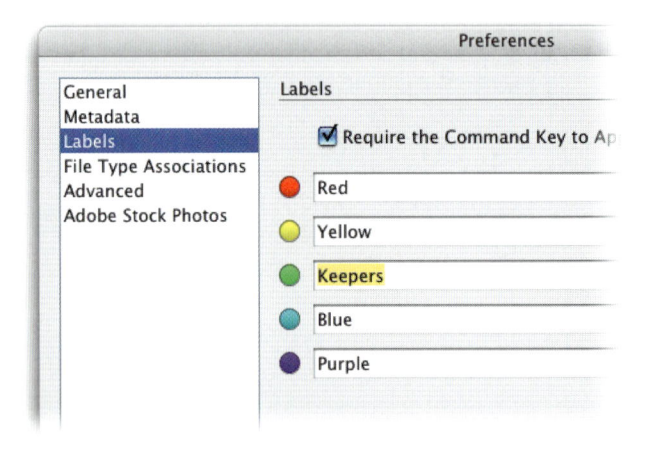

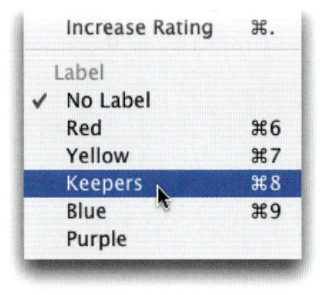

CHAPTER 1 • Adobe Bridge Tips

KEEPING BRIDGE ALWAYS ON TOP

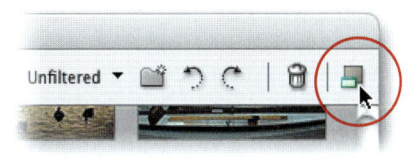

The idea behind Bridge is to use it to manage all your images for all your programs, and if you're doing just that, you'll definitely want to know how to keep Bridge up front and floating above whichever program you currently have open. First, click on the Switch to Compact Mode icon that appears in the upper-right corner of Bridge's Options Bar. Then, once it switches to Compact Mode, a new icon will now appear to the left of that icon—the Switch to Ultra-Compact Mode icon (I kid you not). If you use either Compact Mode, Bridge will remain at the foreground just like a floating palette, no matter which program you're using. To stop the floating, just click on the Switch to Full Mode icon (which had been the Compact Mode icon—it changes its function depending on the mode you're using—I know, it's confusing).

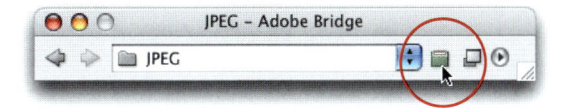

RESETTING BRIDGE'S PREFERENCES

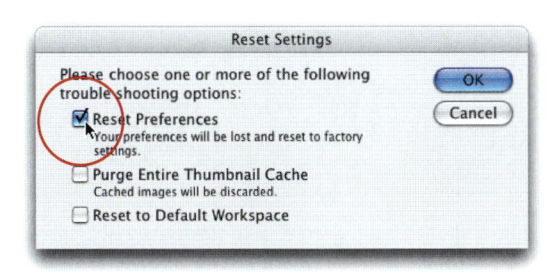

Want all the options in Bridge set back to the factory defaults? Then close Bridge, hold down Command-Option-Shift (PC: Control-Alt-Shift), and then launch Bridge again. A dialog will appear asking what you want to do. Turn on the Reset Preferences checkbox and click OK. Now when Bridge appears, the preferences are factory-fresh.

CHAPTER 1 • Adobe Bridge Tips

DELETING FOLDERS FROM BRIDGE

This is one Adobe snuck into CS2, and they made so little fuss about it, hardly anyone realizes they did it—you can now delete entire folders right within Bridge. Just click on the folder and press Command-Delete (PC: Control-Delete). Now, with great power comes great responsibility, so don't just start deleting stuff all willy-nilly (by the way, I have no idea what willy-nilly means), because those folders have photos in 'em. Even though you'll get a warning dialog before the folder disappears, make sure that before you click OK to delete a folder, that's really what you want to do.

SEEING MORE THAN ONE FOLDER OF IMAGES AT A TIME

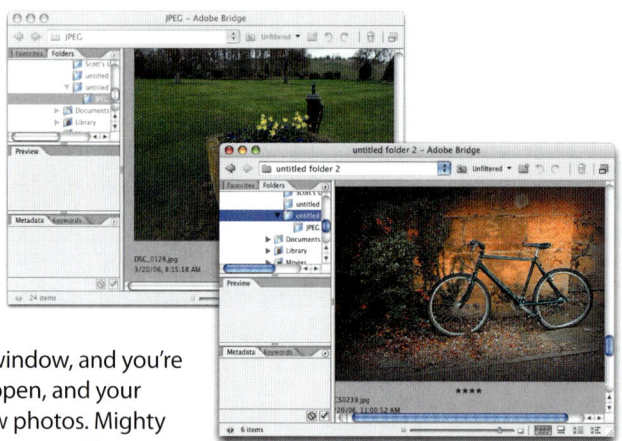

If you'd like to see more than one folder of photos onscreen at the same time, it's no problem, because in CS2 you can have multiple Bridge windows open at the same time. Just press Command-N (PC: Control-N) and a new Bridge window will appear (your previous Bridge window will still be there). Now, navigate to the folder you want to display in this window, and you're set—your original window is still open, and your new window is showing some new photos. Mighty darn handy stuff for a Buckaroo like yourself.

8 CHAPTER 1 • Adobe Bridge Tips

VIEWING THE PAGES OF PDFS FROM WITHIN BRIDGE

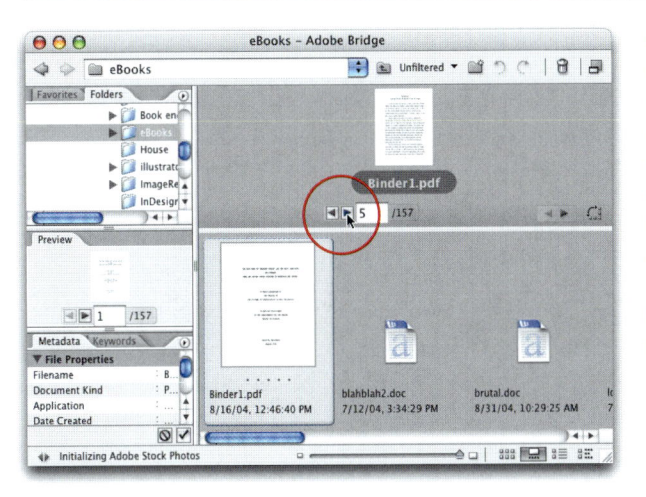

Got a multipage PDF and want to see inside it? No sweat—just switch to Filmstrip view (click the Filmstrip icon near the bottom-right corner of the Bridge window), click on the PDF's thumbnail in Bridge, and little arrow buttons will appear beneath the PDF, which let you move from page to page inside the PDF.

SEEING YOUR PDF PAGES BIGGER

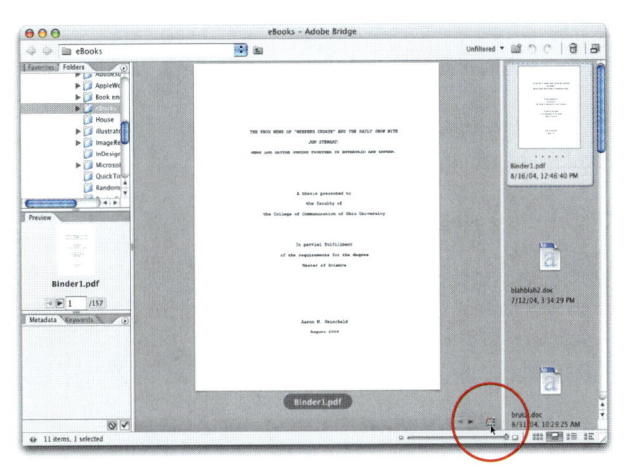

If you're using the previous tip to view PDF documents within Bridge, here's a tip you'll probably want to know to make your PDF's pages appear larger onscreen. If your PDF contains regular letter-sized pages, click the Switch Filmstrip Orientation icon found to the right of the arrow buttons below the PDF. This switches your view so your thumbnails appear along the side, which makes your letter-sized pages larger. Now you can grab the bottom-right corner of the Bridge window and expand it to make your view even bigger, so it's "biggity big" (that's a technical term, not to be used lightly).

CHAPTER 1 • Adobe Bridge Tips

HOW TO GET MORE THAN THREE PANES

That headline is a setup I can hardly resist, but I'm going to totally ignore it and jump right to the tip, although it panes me. (Sorry, I couldn't help it.) By default, Bridge (and the File Browsers that came before it) has three panes visible on the left side of the window (with the Folders and Favorites panels on top, Preview in the middle, and the Metadata and Keywords panels below that). But in CS2 it doesn't have to be just three—you can add more panes (ideal if you're working on a really large monitor). Here's how: Just click-and-drag the tab of the pane you want to have in its own section until it appears right beneath one of the existing panes. When you see a thick, blue horizontal line appear between the two panes, that's your cue—release the mouse button, and your pane has a new home.

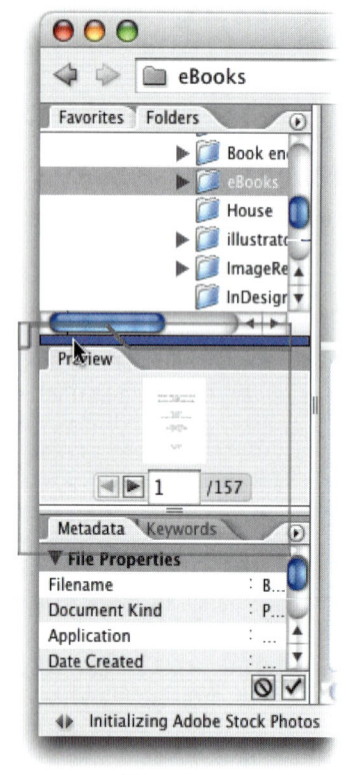

Drag a pane…   *…to get as many sections as you'd like.*

10 CHAPTER 1 • Adobe Bridge Tips

HOW TO KNOW IF A PHOTO IS OPEN IN PHOTOSHOP

If you're in Bridge and notice a little round icon with a bent page has appeared in the bottom-right corner of your thumbnail, that's Bridge's way of telling you that the image is currently open in Photoshop.

OPENING AN IMAGE AND HIDING YOUR BRIDGE WINDOW

One thing that really adds to your desktop clutter is the fact that when you open a photo from Bridge, your Bridge window remains open behind your photo. In most cases, you can still see the top, right-hand side, bottom, or all sides (depending on the size of your image) peeking out from behind your photo. But it doesn't have to be that way. To open a photo and have Bridge automatically close its window, don't just double-click on the thumbnail to open it; instead, Option-double-click (PC: Alt-double-click) on the thumbnail.

CHAPTER 1 • Adobe Bridge Tips   11

I WANNA GO BACK

If you're on a webpage and you want to go back to the previous page, you just hit the Back button, right? Well, luckily Adobe added a Back button to Bridge as well, so to get back to your previous folder of images, just click the Go Back button (it's the left-facing arrow) at the top-left corner of your Bridge window. You can also go to your next folder by clicking the Go Forward button (it's the right-facing arrow), but did I really have to tell you that?

FASTER COLOR LABELING SHORTCUT

By default, the shortcuts for applying a color label require you to hold down the Command key (PC: Control key), so you'd press Command-6 for Red, Command-7 for Yellow, etc. (PC: Control-6, -7, etc.). But if you find yourself using color labels a lot, you can change it so it only takes one key—the number, rather than Command/Control. Just press Command-K (PC: Control-K) to go to the Bridge Preferences, click on Labels (from the list on the left side of the dialog), and then turn off the checkbox for Require the Command Key (PC: Control Key) to Apply Labels and Ratings.

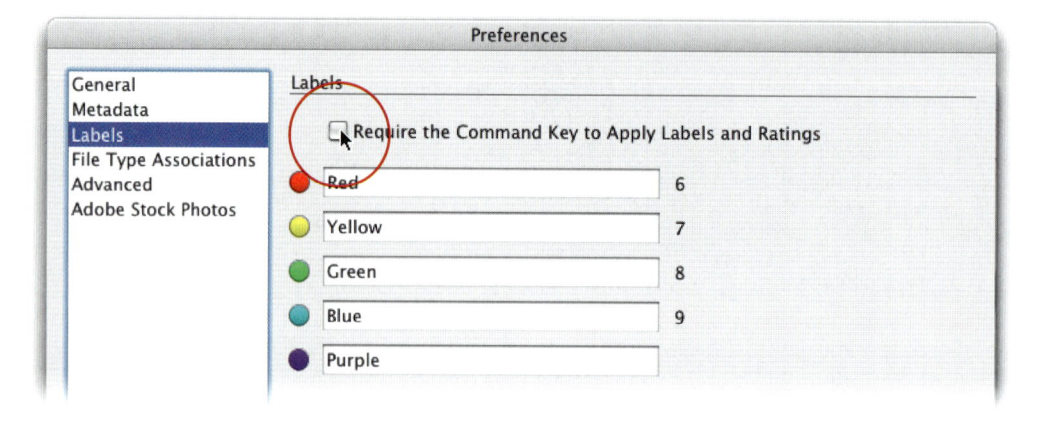

12   CHAPTER 1 • Adobe Bridge Tips

GETTING BACK TO YOUR BRIDGE WINDOW AFTER SEARCHING

When you perform a search (by pressing Command-F [PC: Control-F]), although it at first seems that your results appear within your same Bridge window—they don't. They appear in their own separate window, so if you want to get back to working in Bridge, you have to close the results window.

COLLECTIONS ARE LIVE, BABY!

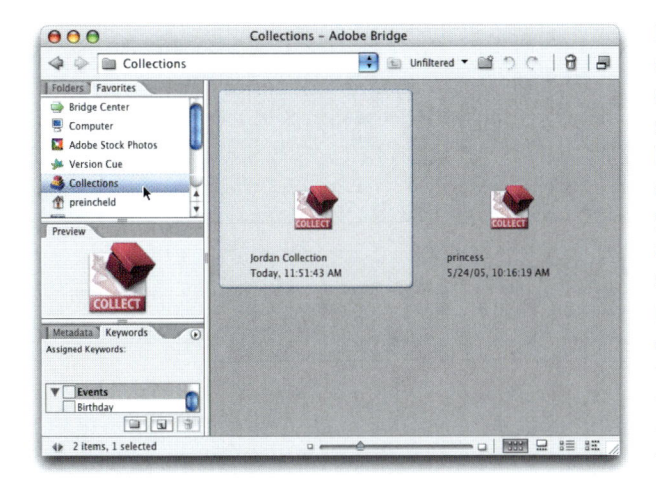

If you create a collection (let's say it's a collection of all photos on your hard disk that have your son's or daughter's name as the keyword), this collection is "live" and by that I mean that anytime you import a new photo and assign that same keyword (your son's or daughter's name), that photo will automatically also appear in that collection (well, technically it updates the next time you click on that collection, but that's technical, right?). To create a collection, just do a search for the keyword you want by pressing Command-F (PC: Control-F), enter your criteria in the Find dialog, and then once the results window appears, click on the Save As Collection button in the top-right corner. To see if your imported image appeared in your collection, click on Collections in the Favorites pane, and double-click on the collection to open it in its own window.

CHAPTER 1 • Adobe Bridge Tips   13

DUPLICATE ANY PHOTO FAST!

Want to duplicate an image in Bridge? Just click on it and press Command-D (PC: Control-D) and it will appear at the bottom of your Bridge window. This used to be the shortcut for Deselect All back in the File Browser of CS, but now it duplicates the image. That's probably got you thinking, "Hey, so if Command-D doesn't deselect all, what shortcut does?" It's Command-Shift-A (PC: Control-Shift-A).

DELETING UNWANTED PHOTOS FAST

Let's say you've opened the photos from your latest shoot (after you've backed them up to CD, of course), and you realize there are only five or six photos that you really want to keep, and you want to delete the rest. Use this tip to make quick work of getting rid of the hundreds you don't want—just Command-click (PC: Control-click) on the five or six you want to keep, then go under the Edit menu and choose Invert Selection. This command selects every photo *but* those five or six you selected. Now you can just press Command-Delete (PC: Control-Delete) to delete all the ones you don't want. Big time saver.

EMAILING FROM BRIDGE

Okay, you can't exactly email from Bridge, but this is the closest thing—you can drag images directly from Bridge right into your email message window. Just open your email program, create a new message, then go to Bridge, find the photo you want, drag-and-drop the thumbnail into your email message window, and it attaches to your message. *Note:* This can vary depending on the email program you use.

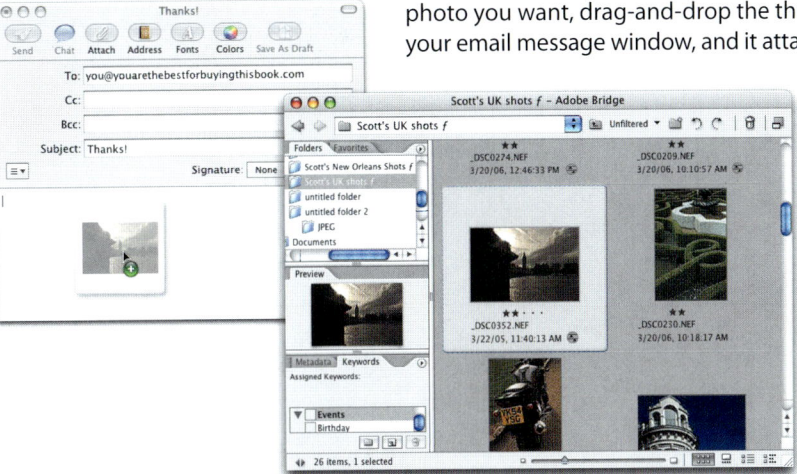

EJECTING DISCS FROM WITHIN BRIDGE

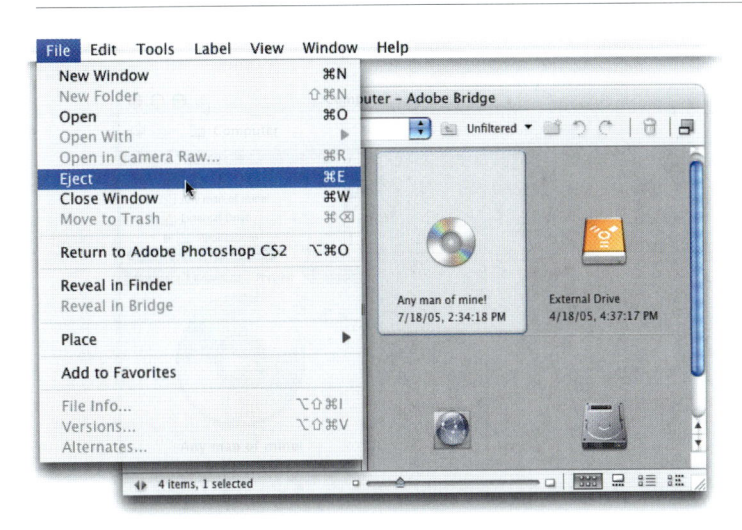

If you've got a CD, jump drive, a camera memory card, etc., hooked up to your computer, you can eject it without leaving Bridge. Just go to the Folders pane, click on the disc you want to eject, then go under Bridge's File menu and choose Eject.

CHAPTER 1 • Adobe Bridge Tips   15

RENAME ANY PHOTO FAST

Want to rename a photo? Just click on its thumbnail then press the Spacebar. Its name will highlight and you can just type in a new one. When you're done, just press the Enter key.

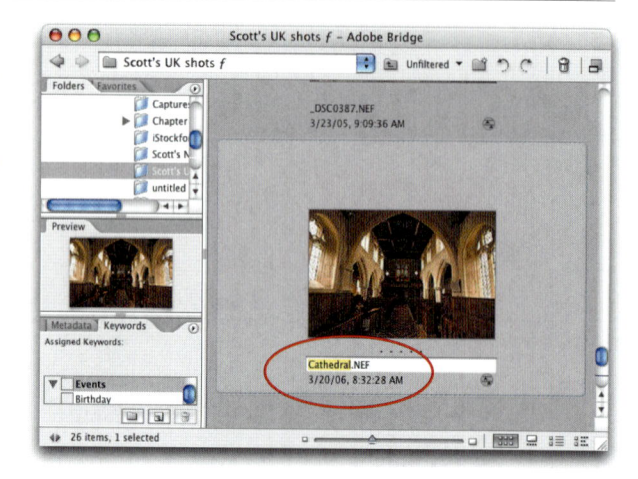

SWITCHING BETWEEN OPEN BRIDGE WINDOWS

As you learned earlier, you can have more than one Bridge window open at a time (which is great for looking at different collections of images at the same time). Well, if you're going to be working with multiple windows, you're going to want to know this shortcut, which toggles you back and forth between open Bridge windows. It's Command-Shift-~ (that's the Tilde key, found right above the Tab key on your keyboard). *Note:* Unfortunately for PC users, this shortcut doesn't work.

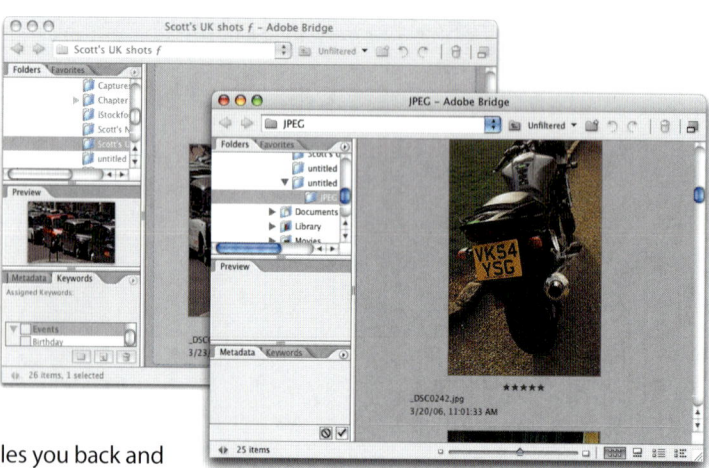

Photoshop CS2 KillerTips

🔴 🟡 🟢 JUMP TO THE LARGEST THUMBNAIL SIZE IN ONE CLICK

If you want to see your thumbnails as large as they can possibly fit within Bridge's main window, just go down to the Thumbnail Size slider (along the bottom of the window) and click on the little rectangle icon that appears at the end of the slider on the right side. This jumps you instantly to the largest possible thumbnail size in just one click.

🔴 🟡 🟢 HOW TO KEEP FROM LOSING YOUR BRIDGE CHANGES

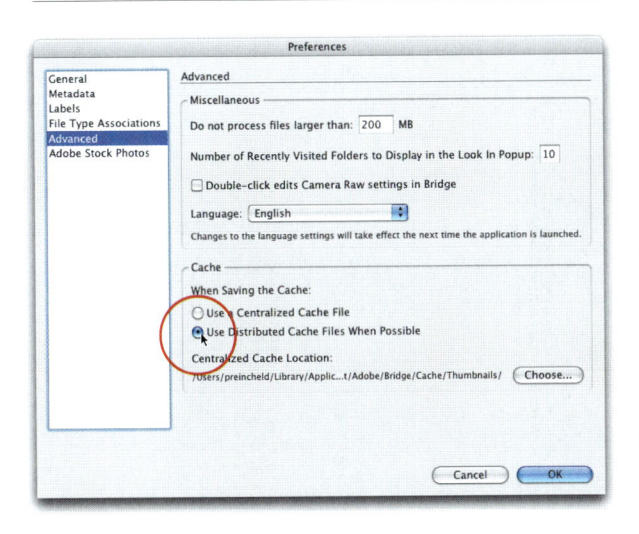

Before there was Bridge, there was the File Browser. One downfall of the File Browser was that if you moved photos from one folder to another, you lost all the changes (and cached thumbnails) you had made while in the Browser because you lost the link to the invisible files that stored that information. But you can change that in Bridge, so your edits (and thumbnail cache) follow wherever you move your folder of images. First, press Command-K (PC: Control-K) to bring up Bridge's Preferences. On the left side of the dialog, click on Advanced, and then click on the Use Distributed Cache Files When Possible option under the Cache section. This makes two normally invisible files now visible, and when you move your folder of images, they move right along with them.

CHAPTER 1 • Adobe Bridge Tips

BATCH RENAMING EARNS A SHORTCUT

Finally, the Batch Rename command (where you rename multiple photos at once) has a keyboard shortcut. It's Command-Shift-R (PC: Control-Shift-R), which brings up the Batch Rename dialog (as shown here).

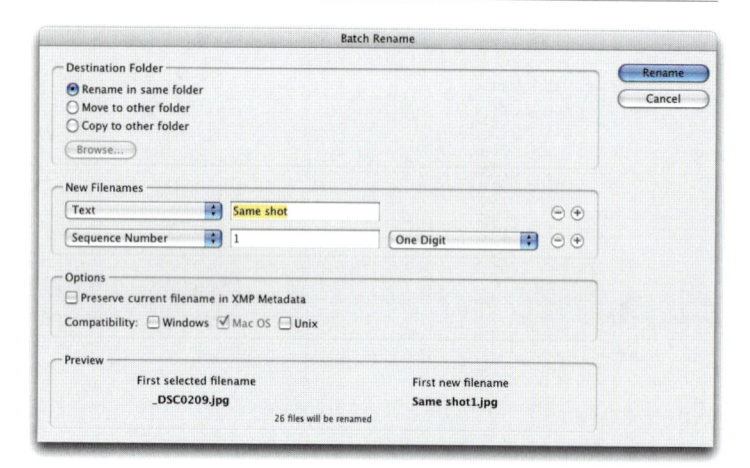

JUMPING BETWEEN BRIDGE AND PHOTOSHOP

Here's a shortcut you'll want to start using to jump you back and forth between Photoshop and Bridge (when they're both already open). It's Command-Option-O (PC: Control-Alt-O).

CHAPTER 1 • Adobe Bridge Tips

ONE-BUTTON REFRESH FOR BRIDGE

When you're working in CS2's Bridge, you've probably noticed that when you plug in a jump drive, memory card, etc., your Folders pane doesn't always update immediately. If that's the case, there's a simple one-button trick—press F5. If you're charging by the hour, you could always choose Refresh from the Folders palette's flyout menu, but that just takes too long. Instead, just press F5 for an instant refresh anytime.

CHANGING METADATA FONT SIZES

If you're older than 17, chances are you'll find the font size Adobe uses for the Metadata palette in Bridge way, way too small. Luckily, Adobe doesn't have many 17-year-olds on the payroll, so they included a way to increase the font size for the metadata. Just click on the flyout menu (it's the little round button with a right-facing triangle in it on the top-right side of the Metadata palette) and choose Increase Font Size from the contextual menu. The cool thing is—you can choose this command more than once, making your font size bigger and bigger each time you choose it.

CHAPTER 1 • Adobe Bridge Tips

NESTING YOUR BRIDGE PANES

Nesting palettes (putting commonly used palettes together in one palette, with just their tabs showing) is very popular in Photoshop, and you're able to do that within Bridge as well. Just drag-and-drop the tab of one palette onto another palette (just like you would outside Bridge). For example, if you'd like all four Bridge pane tabs side-by-side at the top of the Bridge's Panel area, just drag the lower three tabs up to the Folders pane, one by one.

MAKING THE PREVIEW PALETTE BIGGER

Want a taller preview in Bridge for photos taken in a portrait orientation (tall rather than wide)? Just double-click on the Folders (or Favorites) tab, then double-click the Metadata (or Keywords) tab), and they will both "roll up," allowing the Preview pane to expand, giving you a preview that's twice as tall.

CHAPTER 1 • Adobe Bridge Tips

SAVING BRIDGE WORKSPACES

In Bridge, your custom setups can be saved as workspaces. For example, if you shoot a lot of portraits, you could use the previous tip to set up your Bridge window to your liking and then save it by going to the Window menu, under Workspace, and choosing Save Workspace (name it something you'll remember, like "Bridge Portrait"). Then, next time you're looking through some proofs, you can have huge previews in just one click. You can do the same thing for wide horizontal photos—just drag the divider bar along the Panel area to the right until the preview takes up most of the Bridge window. Now switching between huge portrait and landscape previews only takes one click.

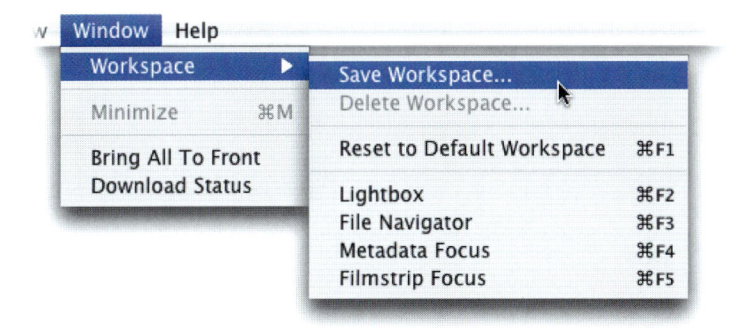

CHAPTER 1 • Adobe Bridge Tips

Born to Run

ESSENTIAL TIPS YOU'VE GOT TO KNOW

Have you ever been to one of those trendy Photoshop parties? You know the ones I mean—where the guests sit around in the study, ensconced in big leather chairs, smoking

Born to Run
essential tips you've got to know

smuggled Cuban cigars, and casually chatting about "calculating this and masking that…," and they keep referring to the time they were out on their yacht with Deke, Ben, and Jack. Don't you hate those parties? Me too. But nonetheless, I don't want to get caught at one of them and be the only goober there who didn't know that Shift-Delete is the undocumented shortcut for bringing up the Fill dialog. Imagine the shame. Then you'd have to pull that old, "Oh, I knew that, I thought you were referring to something in the Curves dialog that I heard at RIT," as they all slowly look away, rolling their eyes, glancing at each other with that "who's the spaz?" look on their faces. Do you want to be that person? Do you want to be that spaz? No? Then read this chapter, dammit. Memorize every word, every line, every keyboard shortcut. Then fire up a fat boy and head for the study. It's time to find a spaz to tease until he's in the fetal position.

FIND ALL THE NEW CS2 STUFF FAST!

Want to instantly find all the areas where Adobe added something new in CS2? Then go under the Window menu, under Workspace, and choose What's New in CS2. This is a custom workspace that puts a color bar over every menu item that has something new in it. For example, now when you look under the Filter menu, you'll see that the filter Vanishing Point is highlighted, as are the submenus Blur, Distort, Noise, and Sharpen. *Note:* When you choose this option, you will likely get a warning dialog telling you that this will change your workspace—just click Yes and enjoy the colorful menus.

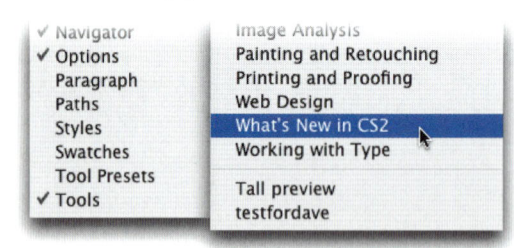

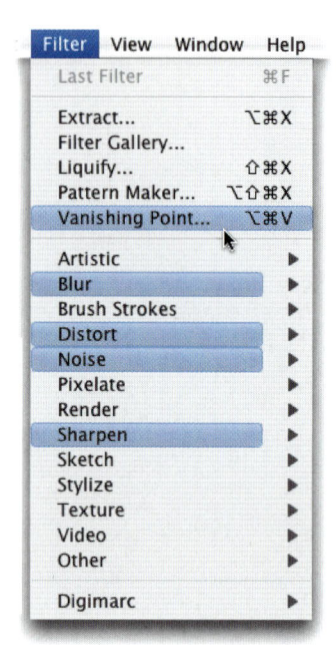

THE MOST LONG-AWAITED SHORTCUT MAKES ITS DEBUT

If there was a keyboard shortcut that we've been waiting for since Photoshop 1.0, it was one for the Image Size dialog. It's one of the most-used dialogs in all of Photoshop, but there's never been a "factory" shortcut for it until now. Press Command-Option-I (PC: Control-Alt-I) and it pops up. Luckily, while Adobe was at it, they went ahead and gave us one for the Canvas Size dialog as well: Command-Option-C (PC: Control-Alt-C).

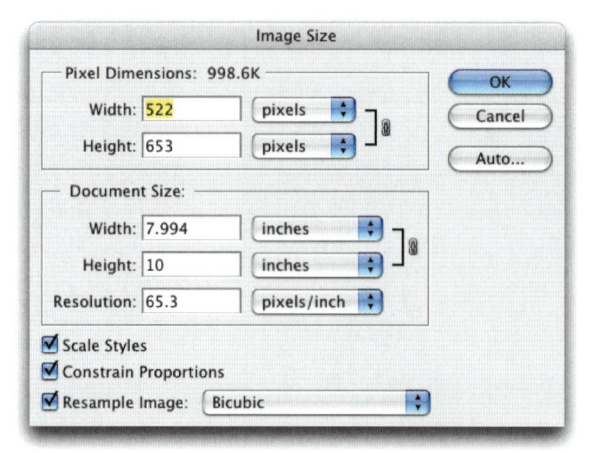

24   CHAPTER 2 • Essential Tips You've Got to Know

CURSOR TOO SMALL? MAKE IT BIGGER

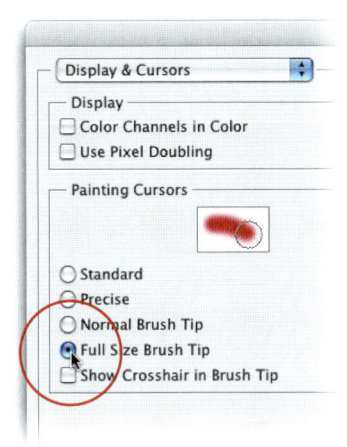

At long last, bigger brush cursors are here. Just go to Preferences under the Photoshop menu (or under the Edit menu in Windows), under Display & Cursors, and choose Full Size Brush Tip. You also have the option of adding a crosshair to the center of your brush cursor by turning on that option (which appears just below Full Size Brush Tip).

SIDE-BY-SIDE PHOTO REVIEW

Want to compare two photos side-by-side? Just open both in Photoshop CS2, then go under the Window menu, under Arrange, and choose Tile Vertically, which places both photos onscreen, side-by-side, at their maximum "fit-in-window" size.

CHAPTER 2 • Essential Tips You've Got to Know   25

WANT SOME HINTS FOR THE TOOL YOU'RE CURRENTLY USING?

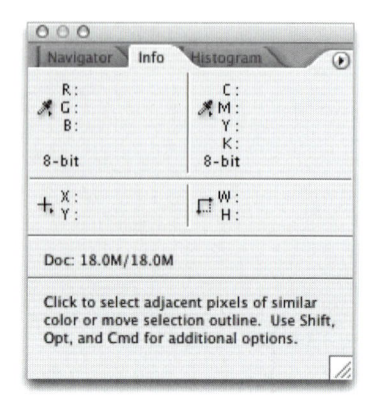

If you want some tips about the tool you currently have selected, just go to the Window menu and choose Info. This brings up the Info palette and at the bottom of the palette you'll find a tip or two for the tool you're using. If you don't see these tips, go to the Info palette's flyout menu and choose Palette Options. When the options appear, at the bottom turn on the checkbox for Show Tool Hints.

DON'T USE IT? HIDE IT!

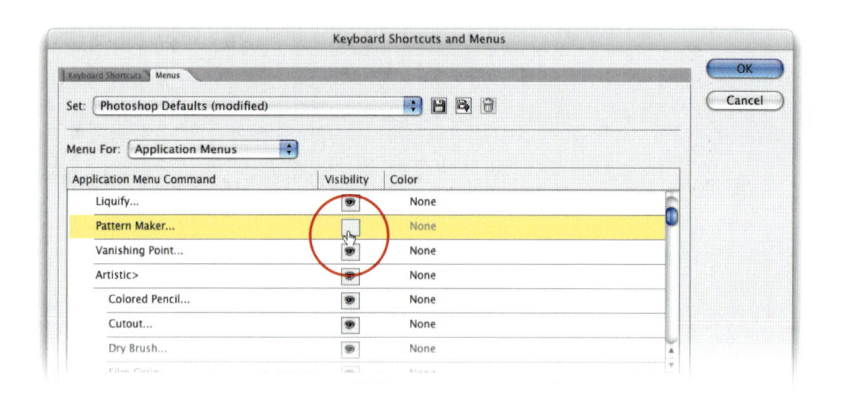

Photoshop has more than a hundred different filters, and most of us probably use just a handful in our daily work. In fact, so far as we've been able to determine (through years of user-testing), only three people in the world today use either the Pattern Maker filter or the Fiber filter, and even they don't like them. So, if there are filters you never use, do they have to hang around clogging up your filter menus? Absolutely not (if you have CS2). Just go under the Edit menu and choose Menus. In the list of Application Menus commands, double-click on Filter to reveal a list of all Photoshop filters. Now, just turn off the Eye icon (a.k.a. the Visibility button) beside the filters you don't want to see. Don't worry, if for some reason you decide you need to temporarily access one of those hidden filters, just go under the Filter menu, to the submenu where it used to appear, and choose Show All Menu Items.

26   CHAPTER 2 • Essential Tips You've Got to Know

A TIP FOR PEOPLE WHO TRAIN NEW PHOTOSHOP USERS

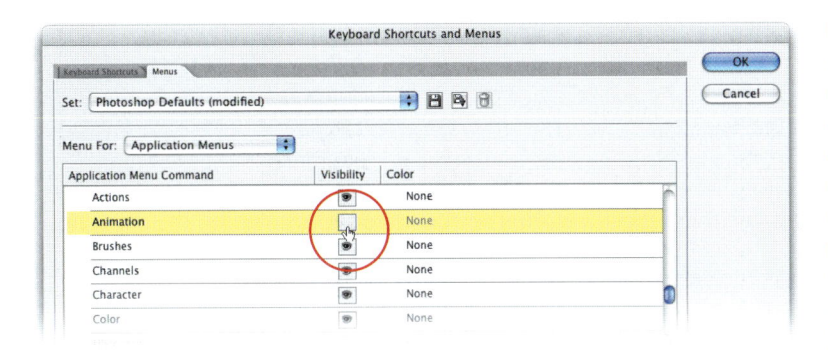

If you're responsible for training beginners, especially in a corporate environment where you're training people to do specific tasks in a specific order (like prepress), you can use this and the previous tip to make your (and their) life easier. First, go to the Menus command (found under the Edit menu) and hide every menu item you don't want them to see or mess with, leaving only the items they'll actually use visible. You can even hide palettes they don't need to see (by double-clicking on the word "Window" in the dialog and turning off the Eye icons to hide palettes). This makes Photoshop appear less cluttered, and therefore less intimidating. As they learn more and get better, you can reveal additional features to them.

LOST YOUR CURSOR? FIND IT FAST!

Where's my cursor?   There it is.

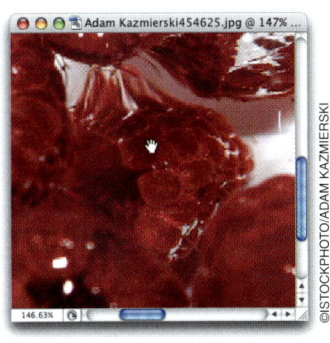

Photoshop's cursors can be easy to lose onscreen, especially if you're working on a big screen or with the crosshair cursor (meaning you have the Caps Lock key active). Well, the next time you're working on an image, and you say to yourself, "Hey, where in the heck is my cursor?" (but you use a different word in place of "heck"), try this—just hold the Spacebar down for a moment. This temporarily changes your cursor into the Hand tool, whose icon is larger, white, and easy to see. Once it appears, you'll see right where your cursor is, and you can release the Spacebar.

CHAPTER 2 • Essential Tips You've Got to Know   27

THE HIDDEN MEASUREMENT POP-UP MENU

You probably already know the trick about entering values in measurement fields in the Options Bar. You can change your unit of measure by typing the appropriate abbreviation after the value (for example, if you want 100 pixels, you'd type in "100 px"). But there's an even easier way (and you don't have to memorize a bunch of abbreviations). Just type your number, Control-click (PC: Right-click) in the field, and a pop-up menu of measurement units will appear. Just choose the one you want and it'll take care of the rest.

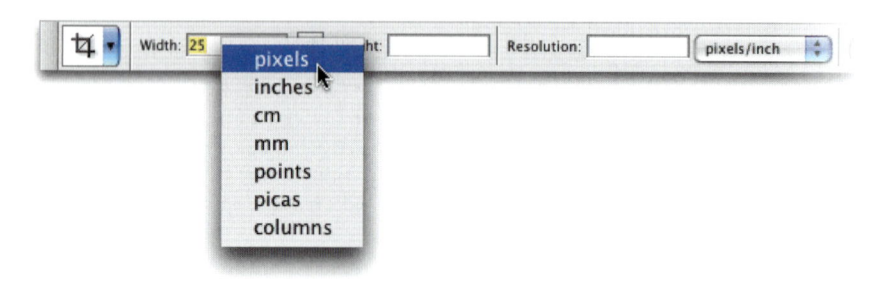

GETTING A FRESH HISTOGRAM IN ONE CLICK

When you have the Histogram palette open to monitor your tonal adjustments to an image, you may see a tiny warning symbol in the top-right corner of your histogram. That's its way of letting you know that you're looking at a histogram reading from the histogram's memory cache—not a fresh reading. If you want to refresh the histogram and get a new reading (and you should), you can click directly on the tiny warning symbol and it will refresh immediately for you.

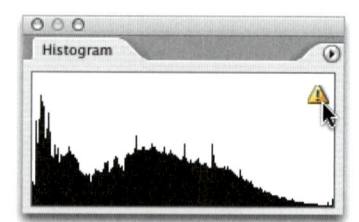

28   CHAPTER 2 • Essential Tips You've Got to Know

USING THE LASSO TOOL? KEEP IT STRAIGHT

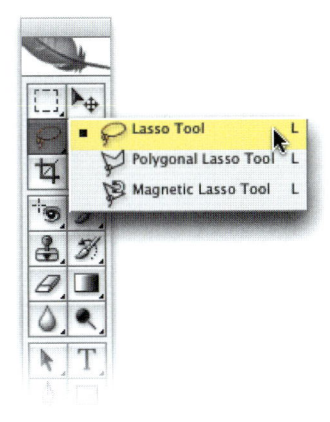

We normally use the Lasso tool (L) for drawing freeform selections, but sometimes you'll find that while drawing your selection you'll need to draw a perfectly straight segment, even for just a few pixels. You can do just that by holding the Option key (PC: Alt key), releasing the mouse button, and continuing to draw your selection. You'll notice that your cursor changes to the Polygonal Lasso tool, and that as you move the mouse, a perfectly straight selection will drag out. When you've dragged the straight selection where you want, click-and-hold the mouse button (to add a point), release the Option/Alt key, and you'll be back to the regular Lasso tool again. Drag the mouse to continue drawing your selection.

CAN'T REMEMBER SELECTION SHORTCUTS? LOOK AT THE CURSOR

If you've made a selection and want to add to that selection, just hold the Shift key and you can add more area to it. Of course, we just told you it was the Shift key, but what if you couldn't remember which key it was? Just press a modifier key (such as Shift, Option/Alt, Command/Control, etc.) then look at your cursor. When you hold the Shift key, a little plus sign appears at the bottom right-hand corner of the cursor to tell you that you can add to the selection. Hold Option (PC: Alt) and a minus sign appears to tell you that you can subtract from the selection. Hold Command (PC: Control) and a pair of scissors appears, telling you that if you click-and-drag the selection, it will cut out the image inside of the selection and move it right along with the cursor.

CHAPTER 2 • Essential Tips You've Got to Know

HOW TO TAME THE SELECT SIMILAR COMMAND

A popular trick for making selections of large areas (such as backgrounds) is to select part of the background that contains most of the colors that appear within that background. Then you can go under the Select menu and choose Similar. Photoshop will then select all the similar colors in your image. This can really speed up the task of selecting an entire background, especially if the background is limited to just a few colors. Here's the tip: Do you know what determines how many pixels out the Similar command selects? Believe it or not, it's controlled by the Magic Wand's Tolerance setting. The higher the setting, the more pixels it selects. Eerie, ain't it? Sooooooo… if you use Similar, and it doesn't select enough colors, go to the Magic Wand tool, increase the Tolerance setting, and then try running Similar again. This all makes perfect sense (at least to an engineer at Adobe).

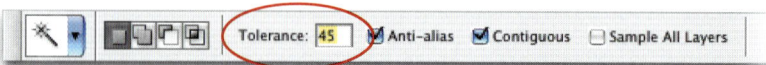

QUICK TRICK TO REAPPLY THAT FILTER

Want a convenient shortcut that lets you run the last filter you applied, without going to the Filter menu? Too bad (just kidding). Simply press Command-F (PC: Control-F). What if you don't want the same settings (ah, I knew you were going to ask that)? Try pressing Command-Option-F (PC: Control-Alt-F), which brings up the dialog for the last filter you applied with the last settings you used.

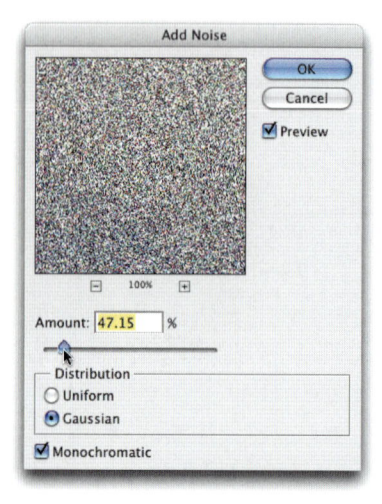

30   CHAPTER 2 • Essential Tips You've Got to Know

SCRUBBY SLIDER SHIFT-CLICK TRICK

Adobe borrowed scrubby sliders, a very cool feature from Adobe After Effects, and put it in Photoshop. You use it by clicking on a field's name, rather than in the field itself, and the value in the field changes as you drag (scrub) over the field's name. However, it scrubs in very small increments. That is, unless you hold the Shift key, which is ideal when you need to make big changes in the field (like from 0 to 256).

ESCAPE FROM THE CROP TOOL (OR DIE!)

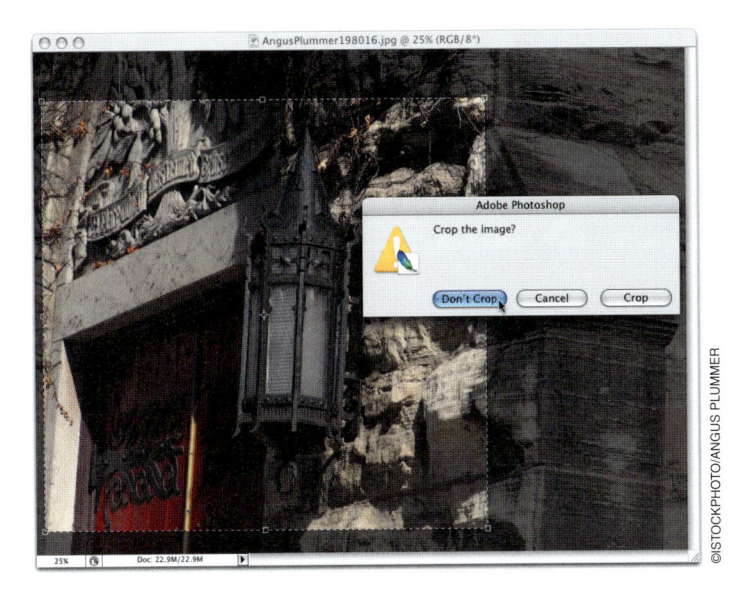

Sometimes when you're using the Crop tool (C), you change your mind and decide not to crop. If this happens to you, do you have to crop and then press the undo shortcut? Nah, press the Escape key to cancel your crop and remove the cropping border. You can also click on the circle with a slash icon (the international symbol for "NO") on the far right of the Options Bar to cancel a crop. Okay, there's one more way: just switch tools—a dialog will appear asking you if you want to complete the crop or not. Just hit Don't Crop.

CHAPTER 2 • Essential Tips You've Got to Know   31

GETTING THE STARTUP WINDOW BACK

When you first launch Photoshop CS2, it brings up a Welcome Screen that has links to tutorials, a list of what's new, etc. There's also a checkbox at the bottom called Show This Dialog at Startup that you'll probably uncheck before too long, because after a short while the Welcome Screen tends to get on your nerves (that's why Adobe put that checkbox there in the first place). However, if you've turned off that checkbox, and then one day you have some extra time and you'd like to explore what the Welcome Screen has to offer, you can temporarily bring it back by going under the Help menu and choosing Welcome Screen.

GETTING YOUR WARNINGS BACK (RESETTING ALL DIALOGS)

One thing I love about Photoshop is that a number of warning dialogs have a magical checkbox that says "Don't show this dialog again" (or something along those lines). However, if you later decide you want these warning dialogs put back into play (this is especially helpful if you're training someone new on your computer), you can have them become active again. Just go under the Photoshop menu (PC: Edit menu), under Preferences, and choose General. In the General section of the Preferences dialog, click on the button at the bottom of the dialog named Reset All Warning Dialogs.

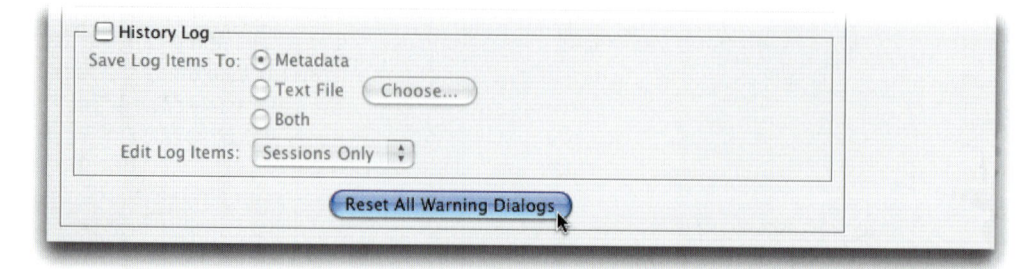

THE SMALLER TOOLBOX TRICK

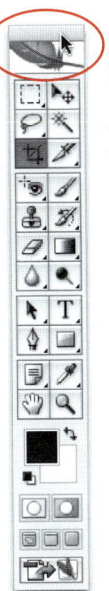

Is that Toolbox taking up too much space, but you don't want to close it, because a few seconds later, sure enough, you'll need a tool? Then just double-click on the very top of your Toolbox and it will tuck up out of the way, leaving just that little tab showing. Need it back fast, just double-click the little tab again and it comes right back.

BRUSHES PALETTE: THAT'S NOT A HEADER, IT'S A BUTTON

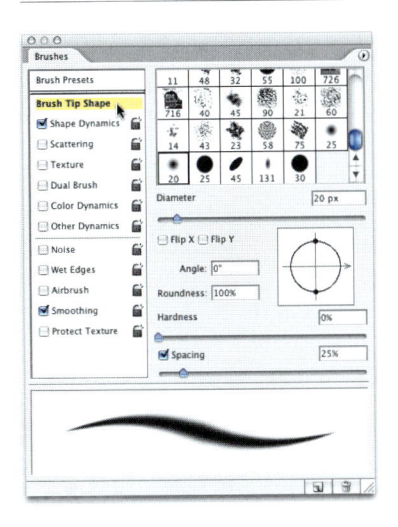

If you look in the expanded Brushes palette (docked in the Palette Well by default), there's a list of controls on the left side of the dialog. At the top it shows Brush Presets, and you might figure that you can click on that and get some options, but the one that catches just about everyone off guard is just below that. It's the header for Brush Tip Shape. It appears to be a header for a list of brush tip options below it, but in reality, it's a button (I know, it doesn't look like a button, but it is). Click right on the words "Brush Tip Shape" and the Brush Tip Shape options are revealed in the main panel on the right.

CHAPTER 2 • Essential Tips You've Got to Know

DANGEROUS INTERSECTION?

You've already learned that if you're using a selection tool (Lasso, Rectangular Marquee, etc.) and you need to add an additional area to your currently selected area, you can hold the Shift key, then any selection you draw with one of those tools will be added. But what if you have a selection and instead you want to create a new selection that will intersect with your existing selection to create an entirely new selection (Whew! That sounds complicated just explaining it)? Here's how: Draw your first selection, then up in the Options Bar you'll find four icons for various selection options. The fourth icon is Intersect with Selection. Click on it, then draw another selection that overlaps your existing selection and all will become clear (grasshopper).

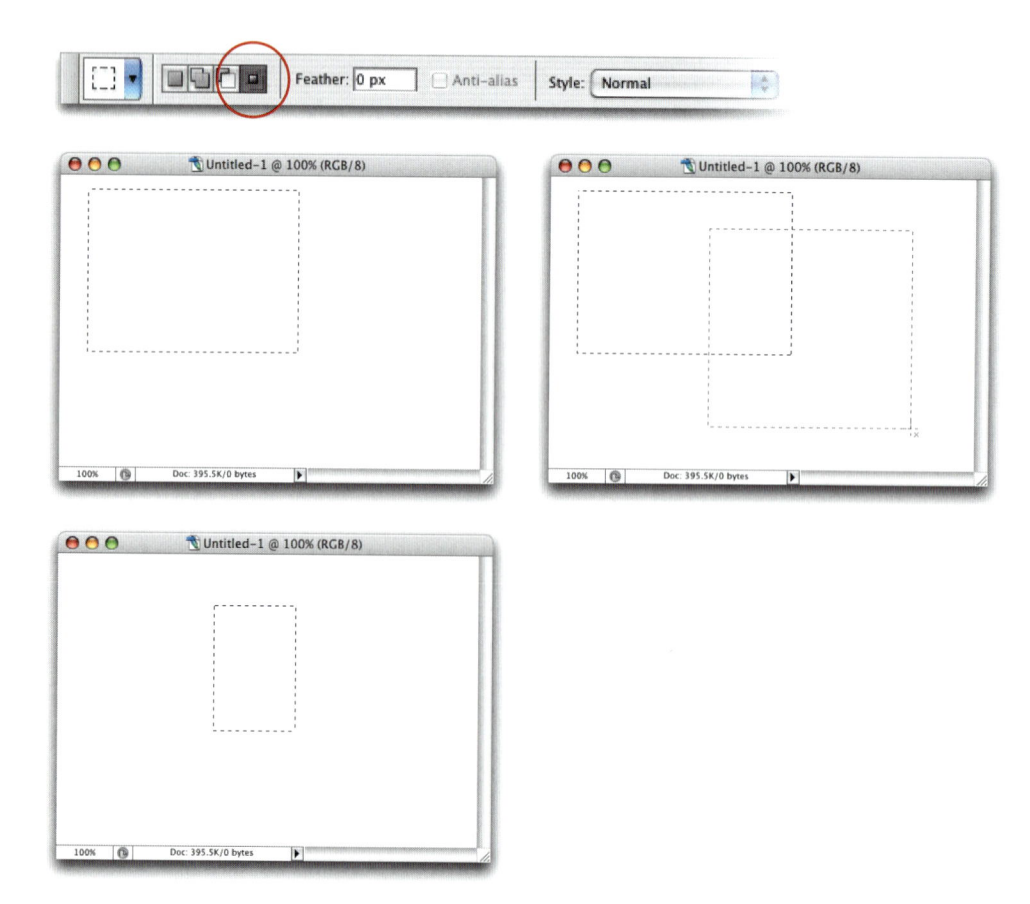

34   CHAPTER 2 • Essential Tips You've Got to Know

NUDGING 10 PIXELS AT A TIME

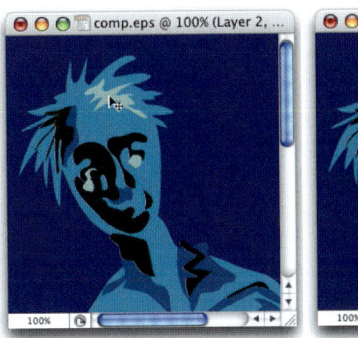

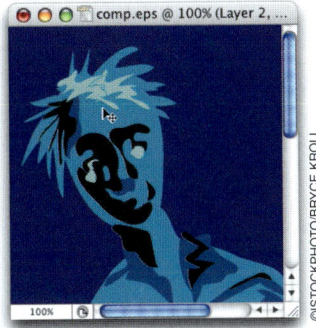

As you know, as long as you have the Move tool (V) selected, you can move (or nudge) your current layer using the Up/Down/Left/Right Arrow keys on your keyboard. For every press of an Arrow, it nudges your layer 1 pixel in that direction. However, if you hold the Shift key and use the Arrow keys, it nudges the object 10 pixels at a time.

MAKE THAT OPTIONS BAR FLOAT— FLOAT???

You may not realize it, but the Options Bar, which seems permanently docked to the top of your work area, can actually be redocked to the bottom of your screen, or you can make it into a floating palette. To make it float, just click on the little tab on the far-left side of the bar, drag it away, and voilà, it floats. To dock it at the bottom of your screen, drag the tab down to the bottom left-hand side of your screen and it snaps into place. You can even hide the Options Bar altogether by choosing Options from the Window menu. You can always get it back by double-clicking on any tool.

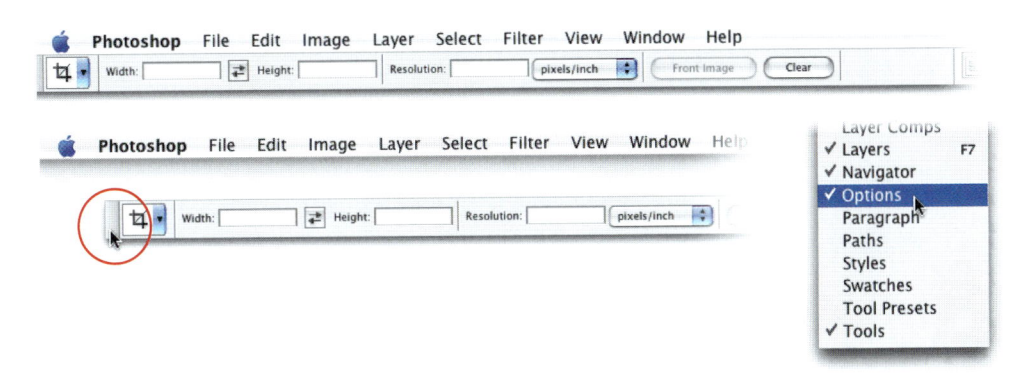

CHAPTER 2 • Essential Tips You've Got to Know   35

WHERE'S THE 3D TRANSFORM FILTER?

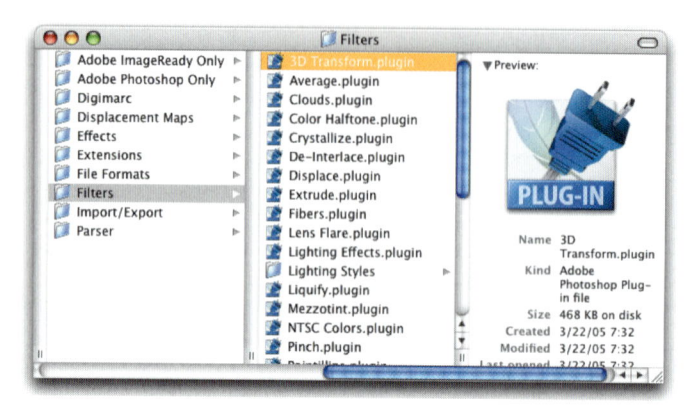

You can kill a lot of otherwise productive time searching for the 3D Transform filter that's been in Photoshop for years. That's because—it ain't there. It no longer installs when you install Photoshop, but Adobe thought that somebody, somewhere, might want to use it for something, so even though it doesn't install, you can find it in the Goodies folder on the Photoshop CS2 Resources and Extras disc. Just drag it into Photoshop's Filters folder (inside the Plug-Ins folder) to get it back in your Filter menu (under Render).

SUPERSIZE IT

This is a super speed trick for getting your image view up (or down) to size. To instantly view your image at 100% size, double-click on the Zoom tool in the Toolbox. To have your image fit as large as possible on your screen (using the Fit On Screen command), double-click the Hand tool.

Double-clicking the Zoom tool

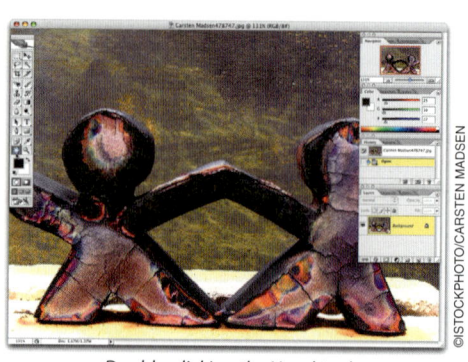

Double-clicking the Hand tool

CHAPTER 2 • Essential Tips You've Got to Know

STEAL COLOR FROM ANYWHERE

In previous versions of Photoshop, you could click the Eyedropper tool (I) on any color within your image, and it would steal that color and make it your new Foreground color. The only drawback was you could only steal colors from within an open document window. Back in Photoshop 7.0, Adobe cut the Eyedropper tool loose from the chains that bound it, and now, as long as you click within an open image first, you can drag right out of your image window and sample a color from, well, anywhere. That includes sampling colors from other applications, Photoshop's own Toolbox and menu bars, and even your computer's desktop pattern. Just remember to click in your image first, and then drag that Eyedropper to a new world of color delights that dare not speak its name.

CHAPTER 2 • Essential Tips You've Got to Know

ASK PHOTOSHOP TO REMEMBER MORE

Photoshop CS2 remembers the last 30 documents that you had open, but by default it only displays the last 10 under the File menu, under Open Recent. However, you're not limited to just 10. Would you rather Photoshop displayed the last 15 instead? Then in Mac OS X, go under the Photoshop menu, under Preferences, and choose File Handling (in Windows, Preferences can be found under the Edit menu). When the dialog appears, under Recent File List Contains, enter the desired number of files (up to 30) that you want to have quick access to under the Open Recent menu.

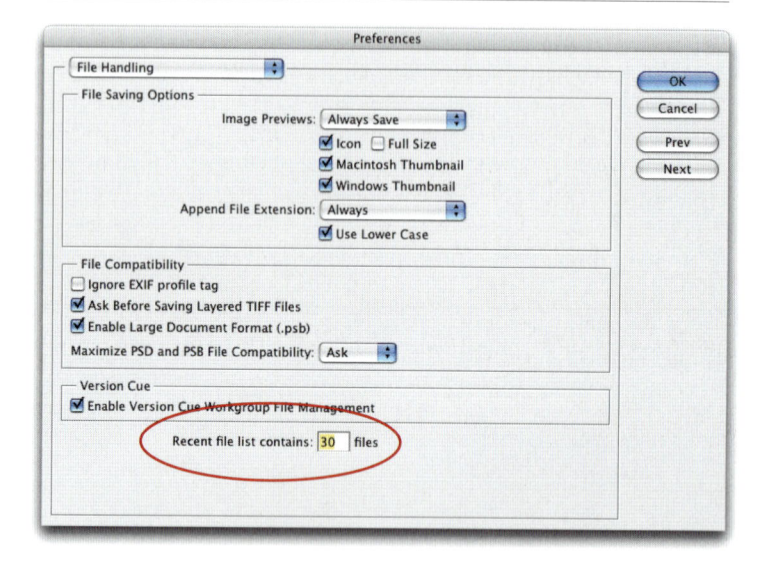

SHRINK THOSE PALETTES DOWN TO SIZE

Are your palettes in the way, but you don't want to hide them all using the Tab key? You can double-click the palette's name tab, and the palette (and any nested palettes) will minimize to just the tab itself, giving you lots of screen real estate. Need the palette back, just double-click on its tab again.

38   CHAPTER 2 • Essential Tips You've Got to Know

CREATING THE ÜBER PALETTE

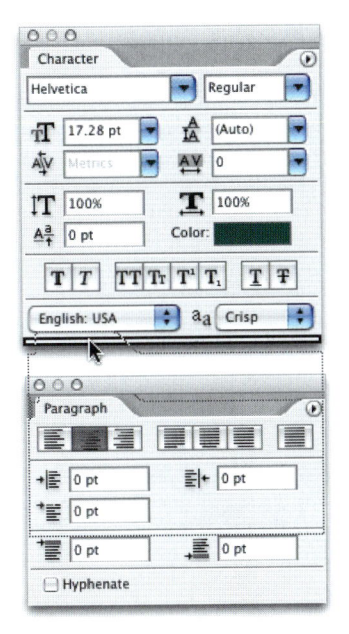

You've been able to nest one or more palettes into another palette since Photoshop 3.0. No big deal, but now you can not only nest but also dock palettes one atop the other, creating a giant über palette. Here's how: Drag the name tab of one palette to the bottom edge of a second palette and slowly drag upward. A thin, black double-line will appear at the bottom of the top palette, letting you know it's "time to dock." Release the mouse button and your palettes will be docked, one on top of the other. Now, when you move the top palette, all docked palettes will move with it as a group.

FIX THOSE TOOL SETTINGS FAST

There's no doubt you'll be "messing" with many, if not all, of the options for the tools you use every day in Photoshop. One day you'll go to use a tool, and you'll have messed with it to the extent that something's just not right. To quickly get back to any tool's default settings, choose the tool from the Toolbox, then Control-click (PC: Right-click) on the tool's icon that appears in the Options Bar on the far left. A contextual menu will appear where you can choose Reset Tool to set it back to its factory-fresh defaults. By the way, while you're there, you can also choose Reset All Tools and they will all revert to their defaults.

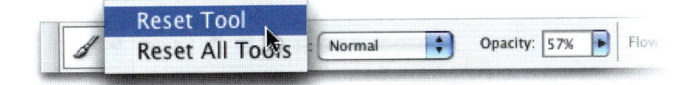

CHAPTER 2 • Essential Tips You've Got to Know   39

BRING ORDER BACK TO YOUR WORLD

In Photoshop, you're constantly moving your palettes around, and before long, you've got one messy set of palettes littering your screen. If your palettes get messy, you're only one simple menu command from having them back at their factory-fresh default locations. Just go under the Window menu, under Workspace, and choose Reset Palette Locations, and all will be right with your world once more (that is, until you mess 'em up again).

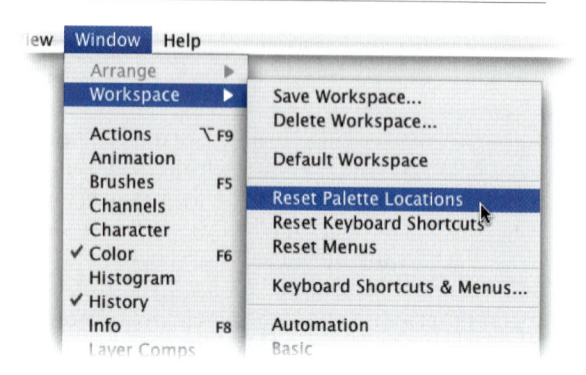

THE UNDOCUMENTED FILL SHORTCUT

There are all sorts of keyboard shortcuts for filling selections, entire layers, and stuff like that, but if you look under the Edit menu, next to the Fill command there's a new little shortcut in CS2 for bringing up the Fill dialog itself (about time!). It's Shift-F5. However, there's an undocumented keyboard shortcut that will do the same trick—it's Shift-Delete (PC: Shift-Backspace). This is a good one to pull on your Photoshop buddies and co-workers as a Photoshop trivia question, because few people know it exists.

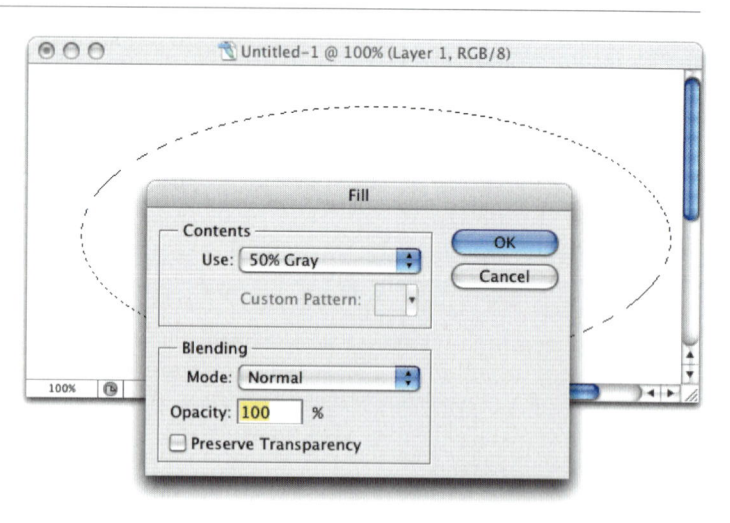

40   CHAPTER 2 • Essential Tips You've Got to Know

DESELECTED AND FORGOT TO SAVE? DON'T SWEAT IT

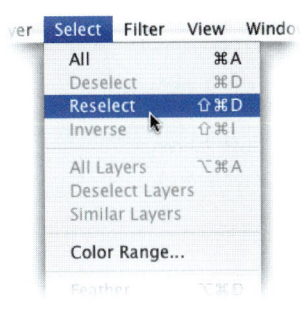

If, after you've created a selection in an image, deselected it, and moved on to other things, you suddenly wish you had that selection back, you're not out of luck. As long as you haven't made another selection (since the one you want to get back), Photoshop remembers your last selection and lets you get it back by going under the Select menu and choosing Reselect. When you choose it, the last selection you created reappears within your image. If you create a selection that, while it's still active, you know you want to keep for later use, then go under the Select menu and choose Save Selection. When the Save Selection dialog appears, click OK, and Photoshop saves it. You can reload it anytime by going under the Select menu and choosing Load Selection. Your selection will be named "Alpha 1" by default, and you can choose to load it (or other subsequent saved selections) from the Channel pop-up menu in the Load Selection dialog.

SUPER-FAST INCHES TO PIXELS

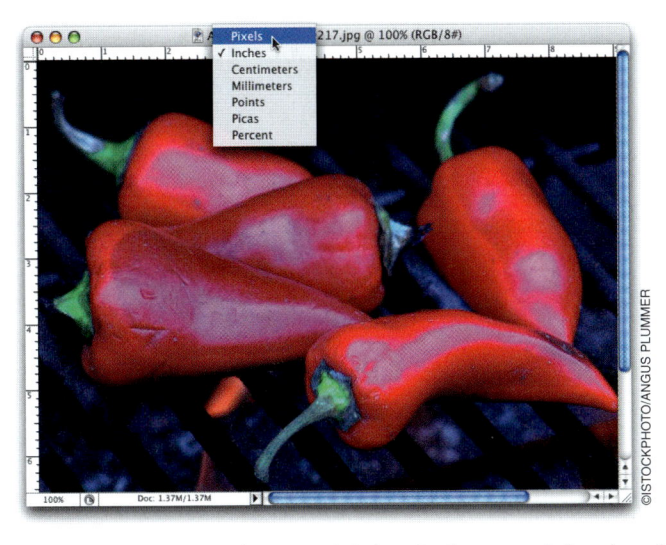

Want to change the unit of measurement for your image? Don't go digging through Photoshop's menus for the Preferences dialog, just Control-click (PC: Right-click) on Photoshop's rulers and a contextual menu will appear with a list of measurement units. (*Note:* If your rulers are not showing, press Command-R [PC: Control-R]). Choose the one you want, and your rulers will instantly reflect the change. If you feel you must access the Units & Rulers Preferences dialog, just double-click anywhere on one of Photoshop's rulers and the dialog will appear.

CHAPTER 2 • Essential Tips You've Got to Know   41

BOSS AROUND YOUR COLOR SWATCHES

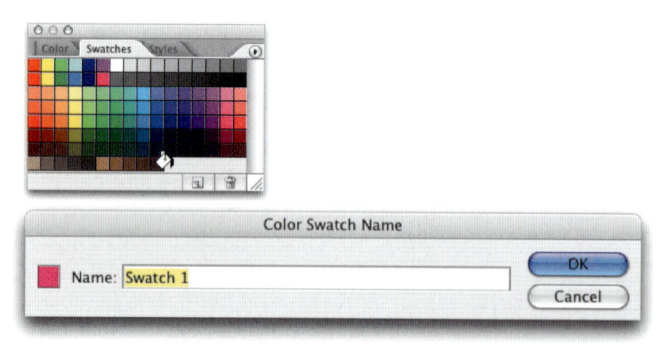

Here are a few tips for using the Swatches palette (found under the Window menu). I'm sure you know that if you click on a color in the Swatches palette, that color becomes your new Foreground color. Here's one you may not have realized—if you Command-click (PC: Control-click) on a swatch, that color now becomes your Background color. Also, you can delete any swatch by holding the Option key (PC: Alt key) and clicking on the swatch you want to remove. You can also add a color to your swatches by setting your Foreground color to the color you want to save and clicking on any open space at the bottom of the Swatches palette.

ZOOMED IN? DON'T USE THE SCROLL BARS

If you've zoomed in on an image, using the scroll bars can be incredibly frustrating, because you move just a tiny bit. Here's how to get around that—don't use the scroll bars. (Okay, there's more to it than that.) Instead, when you're zoomed in, use the Hand tool, but to save time, access it by simply pressing the Spacebar. It temporarily switches you to the Hand, letting you easily navigate through your zoomed image.

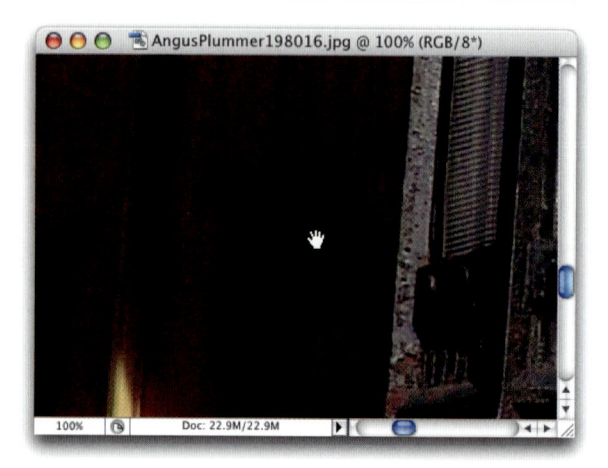

42   CHAPTER 2 • Essential Tips You've Got to Know

LET PHOTOSHOP DO THE MATH WHEN COPYING/PASTING

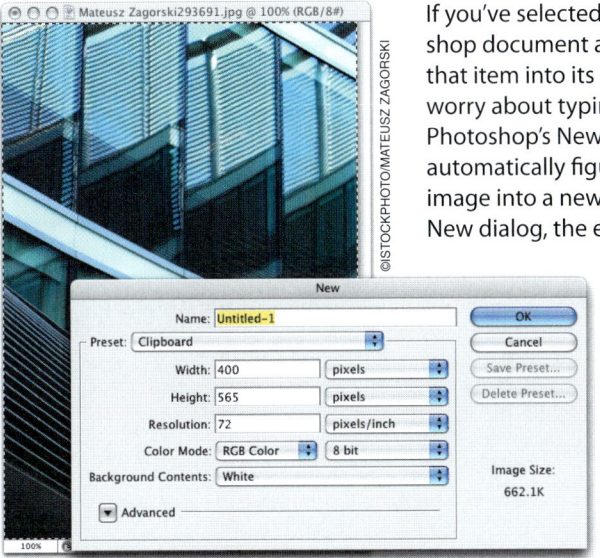

If you've selected something within your Photoshop document and you want to copy-and-paste that item into its own separate document, don't worry about typing the Width and Height into Photoshop's New document dialog. Photoshop automatically figures that you're going to paste that image into a new document, so when you open the New dialog, the exact size of your copied selection has already been entered for you, so just click OK, and then paste your image inside—it'll be a perfect fit.

INSTANT SELECTION FROM ANY PATH

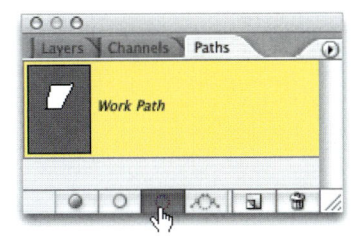

When you're using the Pen tool (P) to create a path, you can go to the Paths palette (under the Window menu) and click on the third icon from the left (at the bottom of the palette) to turn your path into a selection, or you can use the keyboard shortcut Command-Return (PC: Control-Enter). We prefer the keyboard shortcut, because it will do the exact same job faster and saves us from opening the Paths palette, taking up valuable screen real estate. *Note:* If you want to create a selection from an existing path, select that path in the Paths palette and then use the shortcut.

CHAPTER 2 • Essential Tips You've Got to Know

SAVE CLICKS WHEN YOU CLOSE

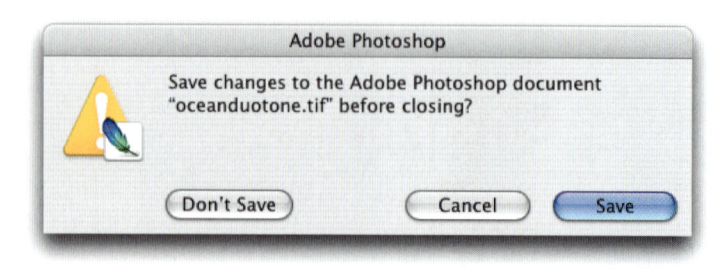

This is such a quick little tip that you might not think that it matters, but it saves a few seconds every time you close a document. If you close a number of documents a day (and my guess is, you do), it really starts to add up fast. When you close a document, Photoshop presents you with a dialog asking, "Save changes to the Adobe Photoshop document before closing?" You have three choices: (1) Don't Save, (2) Cancel, and (3) Save. Here's the shortcut: Press the letter D for Don't Save, press S for Save, and C for Cancel.

BEEN BINGEING ON RAM? MAYBE IT'S TIME TO PURGE!

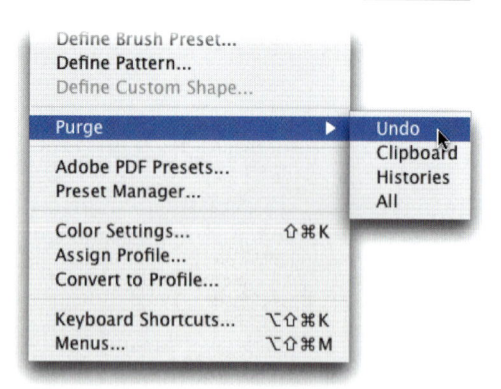

What do you do if the dreaded "Not enough RAM to complete this function" dialog appears? Outside of buying more RAM and installing it on the spot, you might want to purge some of the "junk" hanging around in RAM so you can free up some space to complete the project you're working on. You do this by going under the Edit menu, under Purge, and choosing to empty your Undo, Photoshop's Clipboard, your History States, or everything at once (All). They're in the order you should proceed, so first try purging your Undo and see if that frees up enough memory. If that doesn't do it, try the Clipboard, then Histories. If that doesn't do it, try this super-slick insider tip: Make a tiny (1x1") selection within your document, and then go under the Edit menu and choose Copy three times in a row. Believe it or not, it often works, and has gotten us out of more than one sticky situation.

CHAPTER 2 • Essential Tips You've Got to Know

REACHING THE FREE TRANSFORM HANDLES

If you want to use Free Transform on a layer, but your image extends beyond the edges of your document window (and this happens frequently if you're collaging different photos together), you won't be able to reach the Free Transform handles to scale your image down to size. Here's the keyboard shortcut that lets you reach each and every handle, no matter how far the image extends outside your current canvas area. Just press Command-T (PC: Control-T) to bring up Free Transform, then press Command-0 (zero) (PC: Control-0) and your window will zoom out to exactly the right size to enable you to reach all the handles. Cool!

TRANSFORMING AND COPYING AT THE SAME TIME

Generally, when you apply a transformation to an object (scaling, rotating, distorting, perspective), you apply that transformation to the object itself. However, here's a cool tip if you want to apply a transformation (using Free Transform) on a duplicate of your object, rather than on the original: Press Command-Option-T (PC: Control-Alt-T), then use Free Transform as you usually would. You'll notice that as you begin to transform, the original object remains untouched, and a copy is transformed instead.

CHAPTER 2 • Essential Tips You've Got to Know   45

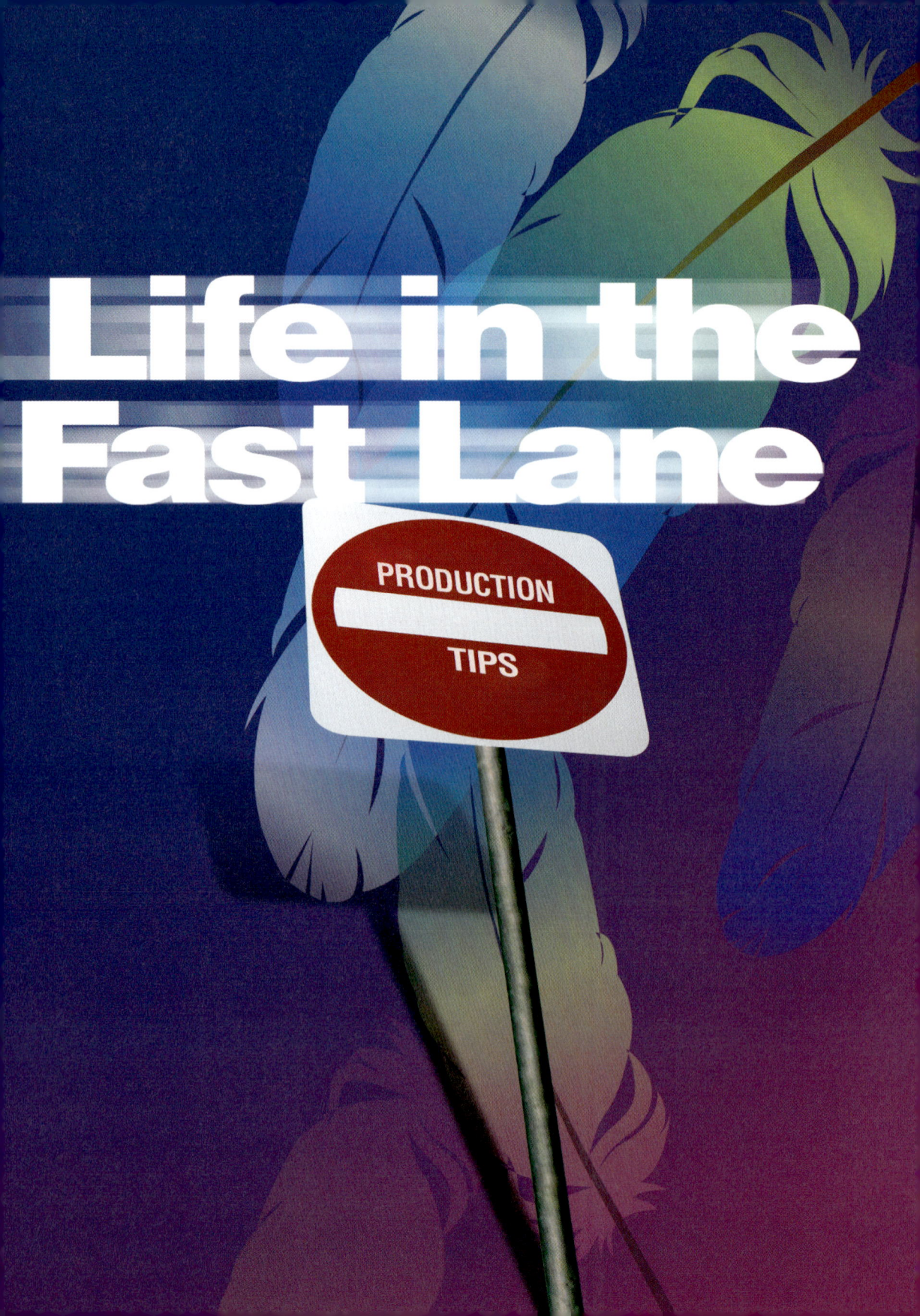

Life in the Fast Lane

PRODUCTION TIPS

Imagine a pig. Wait, not the sloppy grunting kind. Imagine that cute pig from the movie Babe. *Clean, well kempt, with a broad vocabulary and a slightly British accent. Ahh,*

Life in the Fast Lane
production tips

that's better. Now, imagine that he somehow stumbled into a giant vat of grease, jumped out, and began to run at full speed. If you decided to try to catch him with your bare hands (and it's a reasonable assumption that you would), how easy would that be? Now, think of this chapter as "the making of the pig." Now you're the pig, and your competition is trying to catch you. But after learning the tips in this chapter, you're "faster than a greased pig" in Photoshop. Okay, I admit this whole pig thing isn't the greatest metaphor. Let's try this. You're an eagle, a soaring proud bird. And you've somehow fallen into a giant vat of grease. Suddenly, a shot rings out.... I'm not sure I like where this is going. Let's try this: Every day you spend time in Photoshop. Some of it is fun, creative time. Some of it is boring production time, such as making selections, loading brush sets, applying Curves, cropping, transforming—you know, boring stuff. But if you could greatly speed up the boring stuff, that would leave more time for the fun, creative stuff, right? When you strip away all the greased-pig metaphors, that's what this chapter is really about. Run, Babe, run!

CHAPTER 3 • Production Tips   **47**

MISS THE OLD DEFAULT ACTIONS?

If you miss the old default set of actions that has been shipping with Photoshop for years, you can get it back fairly easily. Just go to the Actions palette's flyout menu and choose Sample Actions to reload that old default set.

REARRANGING YOUR BRUSHES

One of the things in Photoshop that just didn't make sense to us was that you couldn't easily rearrange the order of your brushes in the Brushes palette or Brush Picker. Oh sure, you could create a whole new custom set with the brushes you wanted, in the order you wanted them, but it would take a while, and frankly, was such a pain that we only know a handful of people who actually went through the trouble. Well, our wish for easily rearranging brushes is finally here, but the process is a bit hidden beneath the surface. To move a brush from one spot in the palette to another, go under the Edit menu, and choose Preset Manager. In the Preset Manager dialog, under Preset Type, choose Brushes. Then, click-and-drag the brush of your choice to the location of your choice. At last, we are free to move brushes among the herd.

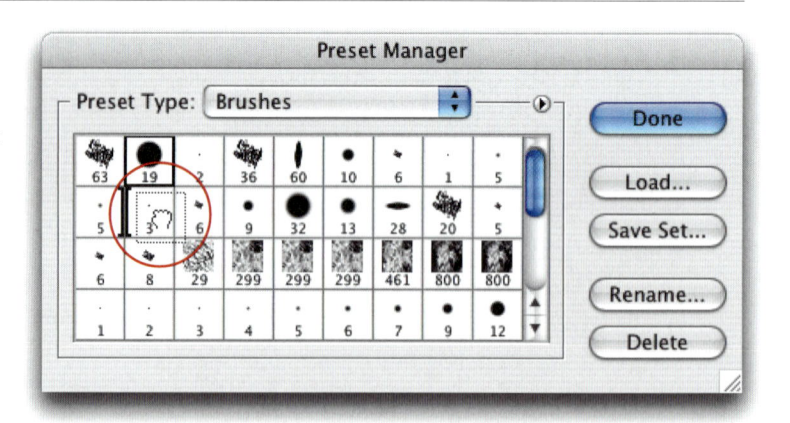

48   CHAPTER 3 • Production Tips

FIND THE CENTER OF ANY DOCUMENT

Need to find the exact center of your image? All you need is a layer filled with your Foreground color, and Photoshop will do the rest (okay, you have to do a little, but Photoshop will certainly help). First, click on the Create a New Layer icon in the Layers palette and press Option-Delete (PC: Alt-Backspace) to fill it with your Foreground color. Make your rulers visible (press Command-R [PC: Control-R]) and drag a guide down from the top ruler. When you get close to the center of the image, the guide will automatically snap to the exact horizontal center. Do the same with the side ruler, and it automatically snaps to the vertical center of your image. (*Note:* If there's not any snapping going on, be sure Snap is turned on under the View menu.)

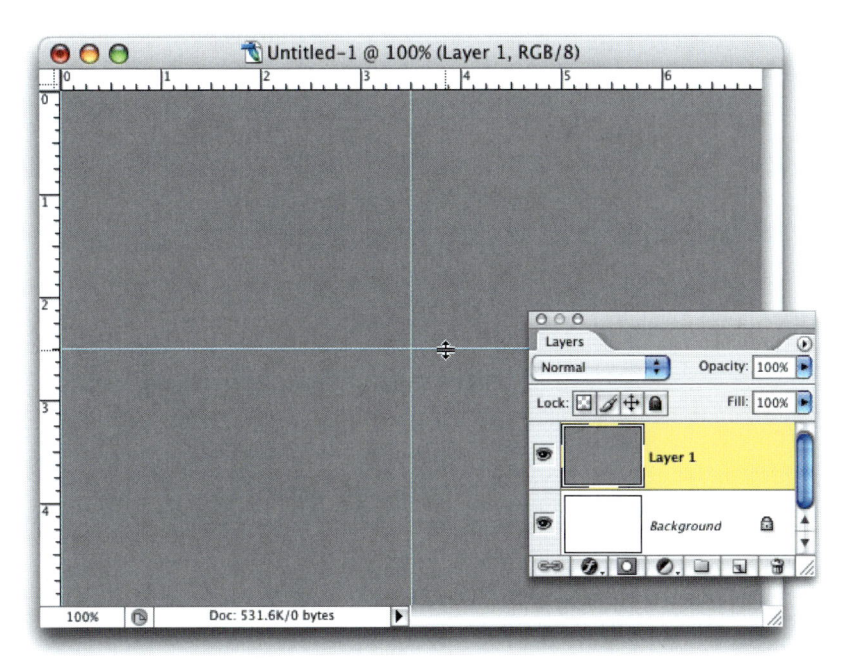

NO MORE JAGGY LASSO TOOL SELECTIONS

Have you ever tried to create a smooth selection using the Lasso tool? It's just about impossible, right? (If it sounds like it isn't, give it a try—open a new document, take the Lasso tool, and draw any random selection, and then look at the selection. It's jaggy—not crazy jaggy, but it's certainly not smooth.) If you were trying to create a selection for an interface design, or a realistic element of some sort, it would just be too jaggy to use. Here's a tip:

(1) Press L to get the Lasso tool and draw around the area you want to use as your selection.

(2) Press the letter Q to enter Quick Mask mode (your selection will now be surrounded with a reddish hue).

(3) Go under the Filter menu, under Noise, and choose Median. As you move the Radius slider to the right, you'll see your edges smooth out.

(4) When it looks nice and smooth, click OK then press the letter Q again to return to Standard mode, and you'll have nothing but a nice rounded selection.

Look at the selection in the first image above. See how those jaggies have been replaced by the smooth edges—courtesy of the Median filter?

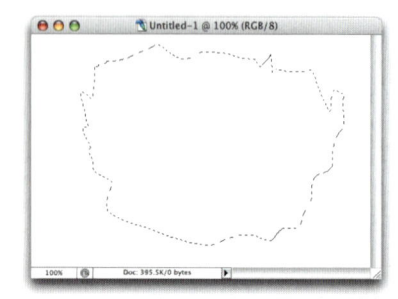

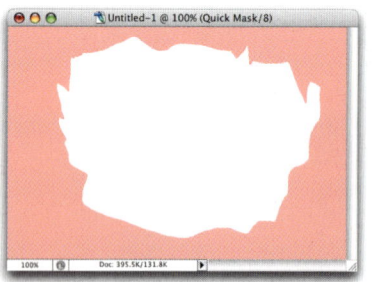

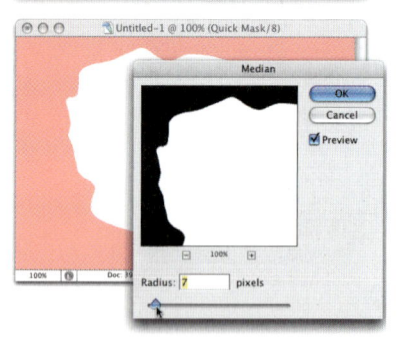

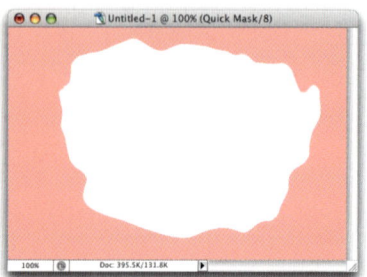

CHAPTER 3 • Production Tips

OPEN UP SOME SCREEN REAL ESTATE

A lot of times when you're working on a project, your screen can get really cluttered with palettes (Photoshop is an especially palette-heavy application). If you want all the palettes out of the way for your convenience while you're working, just press Shift-Tab to hide them, or Shift-Tab to bring them back. The menu bar, the Options Bar, and the Toolbox will still be visible.

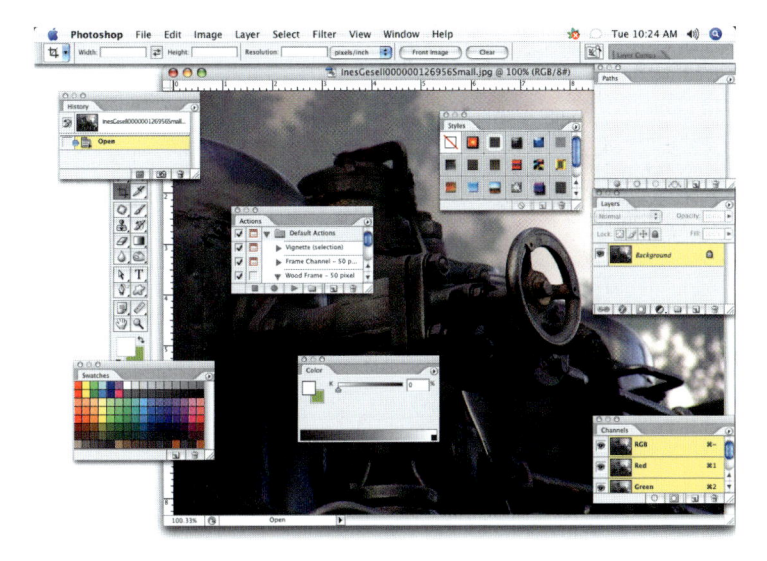

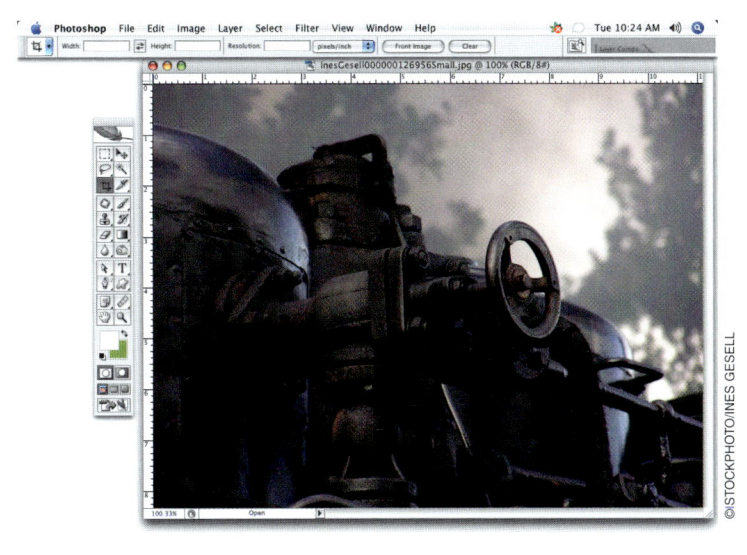

CHAPTER 3 • Production Tips   51

LET PHOTOSHOP DO THE WORK IN CURVES

Let's say you're using the Curves dialog for correcting images and you have an image where you're trying to adjust the color of some green plants. How do you know where that particular green "lives" on the curve so you can dial in and adjust it? Photoshop can tell you—in fact, you can have Photoshop automatically plot that color on the curve for you. With the Curves dialog open, just Command-click (PC: Control-click) on that color within your image. Photoshop will then add a point to the curve that represents the spot you sampled, and now you're ready to tweak it.

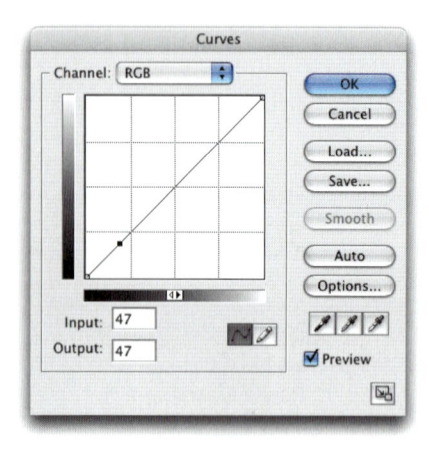

WANT A FINER GRID? YOU GOT IT!

While we're talking Curves, by default the Curves dialog displays a 25% grid. If you'd like a finer grid, you can Option-click (PC: Alt-click) once within the grid, and it will then display a 10% grid.

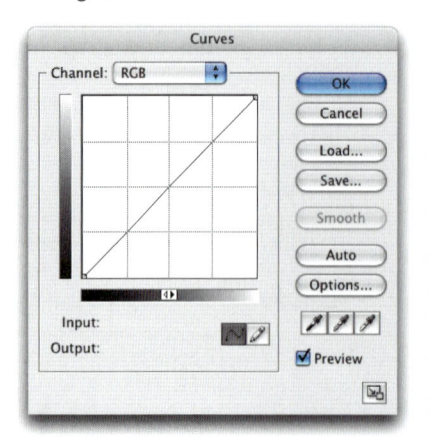

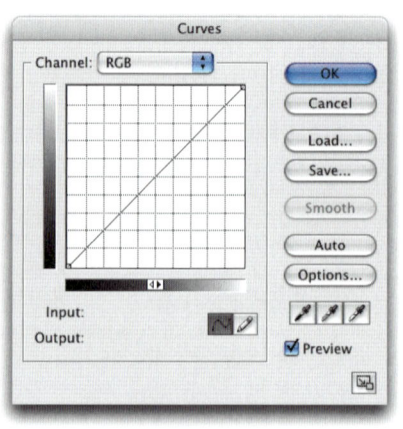

CHAPTER 3 • Production Tips

YOU DON'T NEED THE BRUSHES PALETTE TO CHANGE BRUSH SIZE

In Photoshop CS2 you can increase or decrease the size of your brush by 10 pixels by pressing the Left or Right Bracket keys when the Brush tool (B) is selected. Once your brush is more than 100 pixels in size, it then moves in 25-pixel increments; if you go higher than 200 pixels, it moves in 50-pixel increments until you reach 300 pixels, at which point it moves in 100-pixel increments.

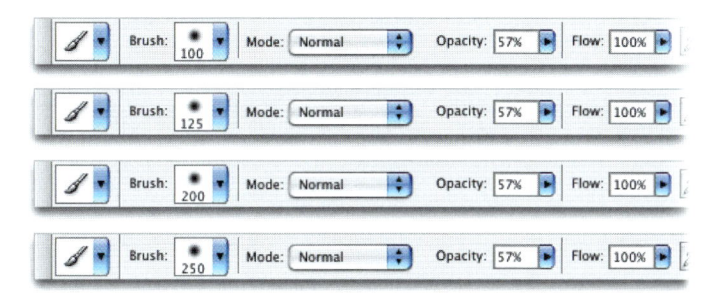

ROTATE TO ANY ANGLE THE FAST WAY

If you have a specific angle that you'd like to rotate a layer to, it's easy. Get the Measure tool (it looks like a ruler and is in the Eyedropper tool's flyout menu in the Toolbox), and click-and-drag out a line at the desired angle. Then go under the Edit menu, under Transform, and choose Rotate. Your layer will instantly rotate to match the angle that you drew with the Measure tool. *Note:* To rotate the Background layer, you must first select it (Command-A [PC: Control-A]).

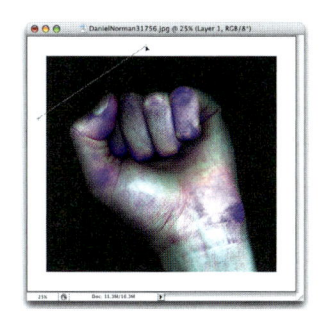

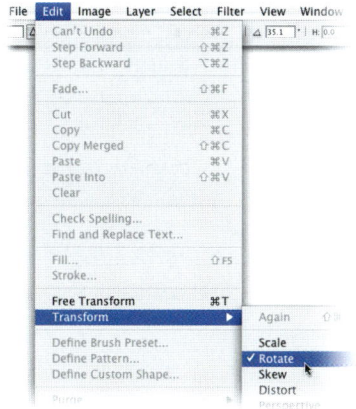

GET RID OF UNWANTED BRUSHES

You probably already know that you can add a brush to the Brushes palette, but did you know that it's even easier to delete them? Just hold the Option key (PC: Alt key) and you'll notice that your cursor changes into a pair of scissors. Click once on the brush you want to delete and that baby's gone—no warning dialog, no chance to change your mind—it's gone.

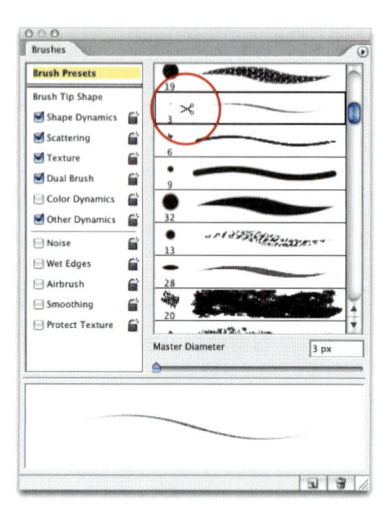

BRUSHES RIGHT WHERE YOU WANT 'EM

Here's a tip that gives you a faster and more convenient way to switch to another preset brush without using the Brushes palette—and you might find that you like it even better. Just press the Control key, then click within your image (PC: Right-click) and the Brush Picker will appear directly under your cursor. Plus, you can even change the Master Diameter of the brush that you choose in the Picker. This is one you'll have to try to appreciate the sheer speed and convenience of putting your brushes at your fingertips anytime.

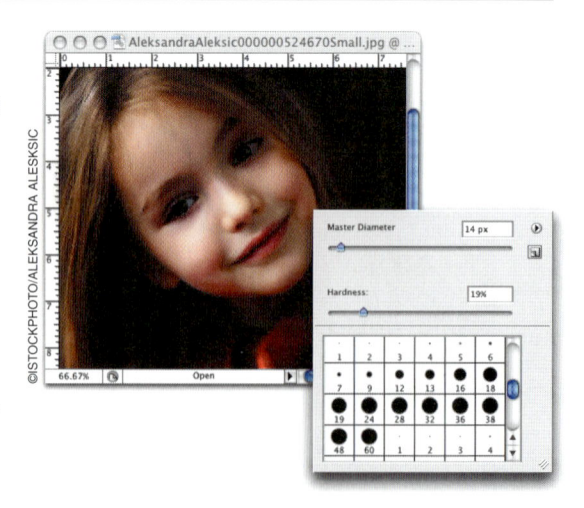

CHAPTER 3 • Production Tips

NAVIGATING THE BRUSH PICKER LIKE A PRO

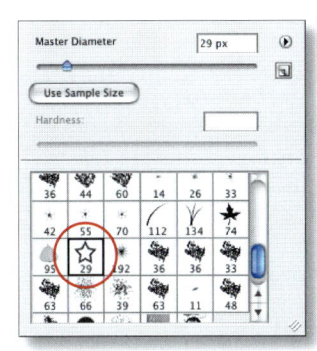

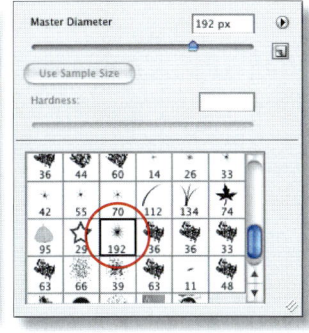

Now that you've learned how to bring up the Brush Picker right where you want it, it wouldn't hurt to learn this quick navigation tip to keep you from spending more time there than necessary. Once you've selected a brush in the Picker, just use the Arrow keys on your keyboard to navigate up, down, left, or right to other brushes in the Picker. Once you choose a brush and you are no longer in the Brush Picker, you can use the Period and Comma keys to move forward and backward through the different brushes. Shift-Comma and Shift-Period will jump you to the first and last brushes in the Brush Picker, respectively.

GET MORE CONTROL OVER YOUR PAINT STROKES

Photoshop lets you affect a brush stroke even after you've painted it by using Photoshop's Fade command (found under the Edit menu). Fade works like "undo on a slider," and dragging the Opacity slider all the way to the left will completely undo your freshly painted brush stroke, but if you stop anywhere before the far-left side, it will instead simply lighten the stroke. You can also use the Mode pop-up menu to alter how your stroke blends with the object below it.

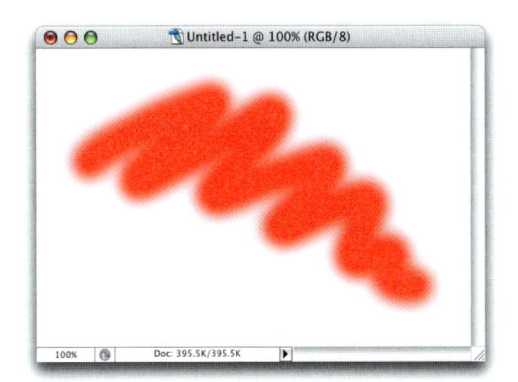

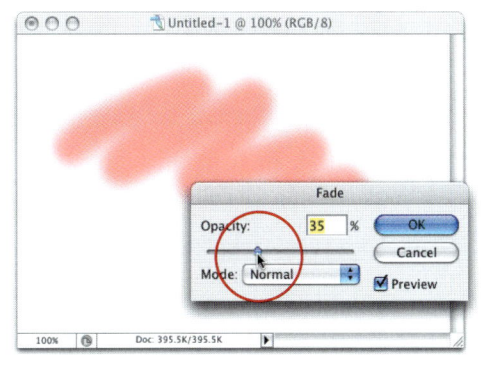

CHAPTER 3 • Production Tips   55

SPEED TIP TO ROTATE THROUGH OPEN IMAGES

Have a bunch of images open on your screen and can't see the one you want? Just press Control-Tab to move from one open image to the next, cycling through all of your open documents.

INSTANTLY FIND THE CENTER OF ANY OBJECT

This is a great tip for quickly finding the exact center of any object on its own layer. You start by pressing Command-T (PC: Control-T) to bring up the Free Transform bounding box. The bounding box has a handle in the center of both sides and center handles at both the top and bottom. Now all you have to do is make Photoshop's rulers visible (Command-R [PC: Control-R]), and then drag out a horizontal and a vertical ruler guide to these handles to mark the center. Better still, if you have the Snap command active in the View menu, the guides will snap to the center of your object as you drag.

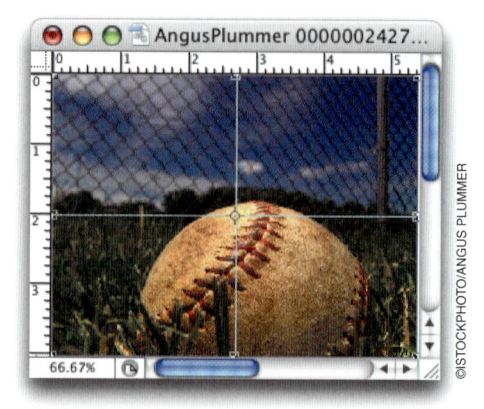

CHAPTER 3 • Production Tips

MAKING YOUR GUIDE FLIP

Just like most page-layout applications, Photoshop has non-printing guides you can pull out anytime you need to align objects or type, but there's also a trick for flipping the guides. To access the guides, make your rulers visible by pressing Command-R (PC: Control-R), then click-and-hold within one of the rulers and drag out a guide. If you pull out a horizontal guide from the top ruler, but really wanted a vertical guide, just press the Option key (PC: Alt key) as you drag and your guide will flip from horizontal to vertical (pretty slick). You can pull out as many guides as you need (there's probably a limit to how many you can use, but we've never reached it). When you're done using a guide, just use the Move tool (V) to drag it back to the ruler where it came from. To remove all of your guides at once, choose Clear Guides from the View menu.

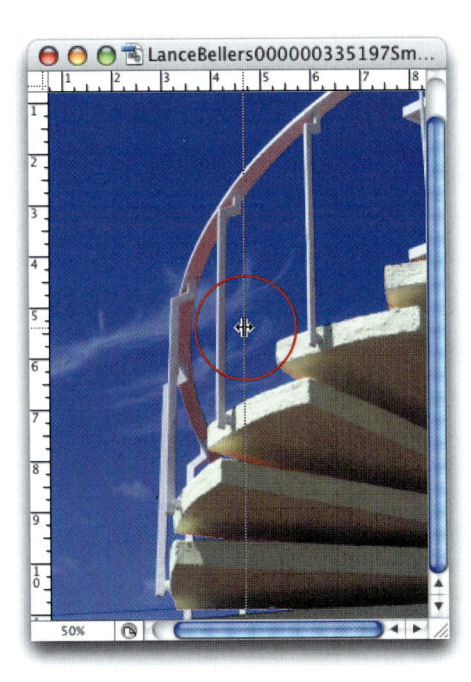

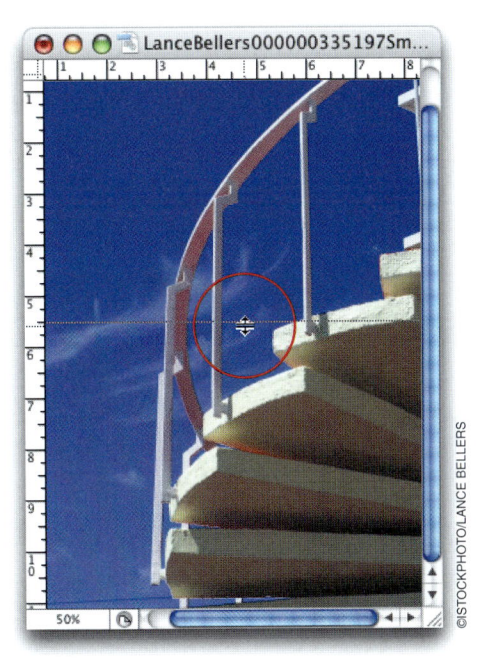

CREATING TEMPORARY BRUSHES

It's easy to create a temporary brush based on your preset brushes in Photoshop. Just click on the Brush thumbnail in the Options Bar to bring up the Brush Picker. Using the Master Diameter slider, you can change your brush size from 1 to 2500 pixels. If you like the size of your new brush and you want to save it, just click the Create a New Brush Preset icon at the top right of the dialog. The Brush Name dialog will appear so you can name your new brush. When you click OK, the new brush will immediately be added to your Brush Picker (and Brushes palette).

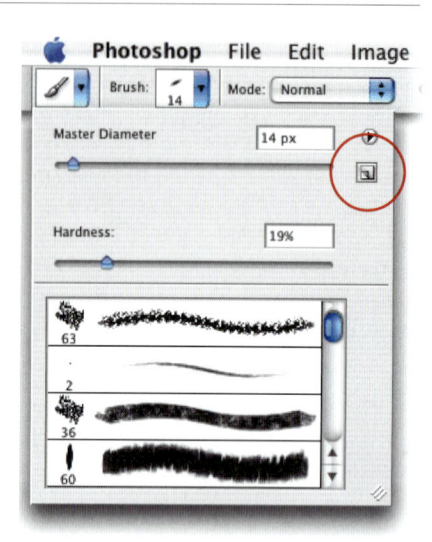

REUSING YOUR LAST CURVE SETTING

Once you've applied a curve setting to an image, it's very possible that you'd like to use that exact same setting again, or maybe you'd just like to tweak that setting a bit. Well, you can. To bring up the Curves dialog with the last curve you used still in place, press Command-Option-M (PC: Control-Alt-M).

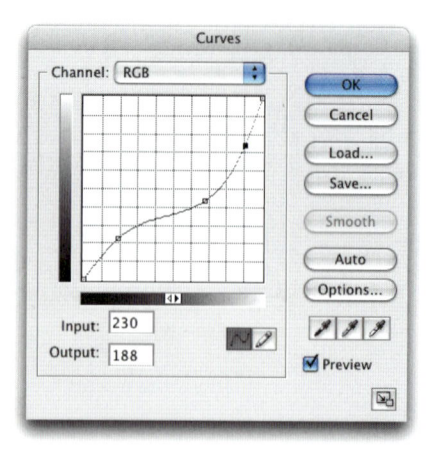

58   CHAPTER 3 • Production Tips

BRINGING BACK THOSE CROPPED-AWAY AREAS

When you're using the Crop tool (C) to crop images, you'll find that you actually have some options on how the area you're cropping away is handled after the crop. For example, in the Options Bar (as long as you're not on the Background layer) you'll see an option that lets you either Delete the cropped areas or simply Hide them from view (in other words, the areas are still there, they just expand out into the canvas area). If you choose the Hide option, it crops the image window down to the size of the crop, but since the cropped-away areas are still really there, you can use the Move tool (V) to drag these cropped areas back into view.

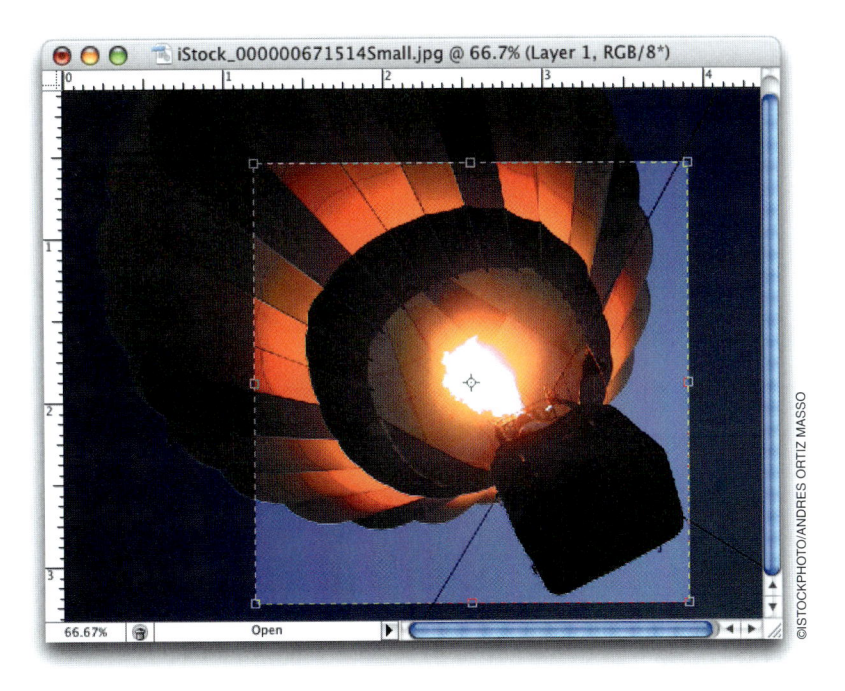

CHAPTER 3 • Production Tips

FIX THOSE STRAY PIXELS FAST!

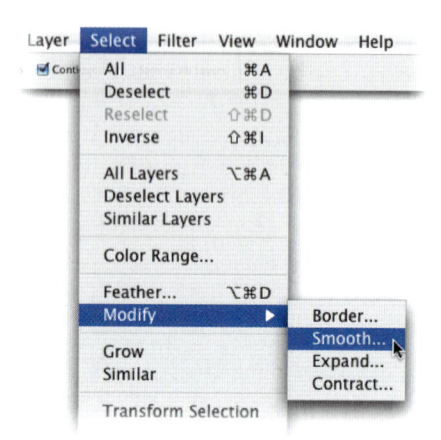

Sometimes when making a selection with the Magic Wand tool (W) or Color Range command (under the Select menu), Photoshop will leave little stray pixels unselected. You can tell where they are because they appear to twinkle on and off, kind of teasing…nay, taunting you, because your selection is not complete. Luckily, there's a quick way to rein in those renegade stray pixels. Go under the Select menu, under Modify, and choose Smooth. Enter a Sample Radius of 1 pixel and click OK. That will usually do the trick—those stray pixels are now selected.

GETTING MORE CONTROL OVER THE MAGIC WAND

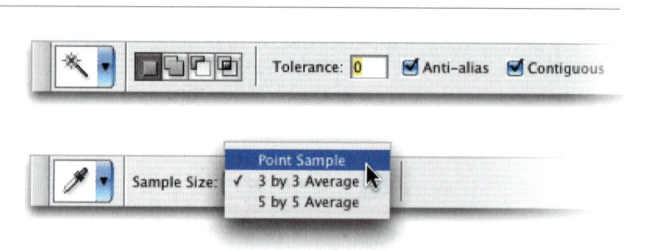

By default, the Eyedropper tool's Sample Size feature (in the Options Bar) is set to Point Sample, which comes into play if you're using it to read values for color correction. But for now, it's important to know that the Sample Size option chosen for the Eyedropper tool (I) actually affects how the Magic Wand tool (W) makes its selection (the two have an undocumented relationship). If you increase the Eyedropper's Sample Size to 3 by 3 or 5 by 5 Average, the Magic Wand will select an average of a much larger range of pixels in the sample area. This is important to know, because if you don't have Point Sample chosen and you set the Magic Wand Tolerance to 0, it won't just select the individual pixel you click on—it will select all of the pixels that match any of the pixels in a 3 by 3 or 5 by 5 area. The next time your Magic Wand isn't behaving the way it used to, check to see if you have changed the Eyedropper tool's Sample Size.

MAKING THE COLOR PALETTE WORK TWICE AS HARD

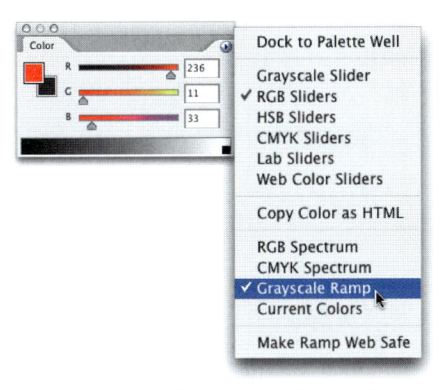

If you use the Color palette (under the Window menu) to select colors, you're probably already using the color ramp at the bottom of the palette for making quick color selections, but here are two tips that make using the ramp faster and easier. First, the color ramp doesn't have to use the same color mode as the color sliders above it; for example, you can have RGB for your sliders and grayscale as your ramp. This is great because it gives you two different models to choose from without digging through menus. You can choose the color modes for both the sliders and the ramp from the Color palette's flyout menu. The second tip is that if you quickly want to change color ramps, Shift-click on the ramp. Every time you Shift-click, it will rotate to the next color mode.

USE YOUR LAST SETTINGS AND SAVE TIME

This is a tip that will save you time when you're making tonal adjustments using Levels, Curves, Color Balance, etc. (most anything that appears under the Adjustments submenu under the Image menu). When you bring up one of the tonal adjustment dialogs, it always displays its default settings, but if you hold the Option key (PC: Alt key) when choosing it from the Adjustments menu, instead of coming up with the default settings, it will display the last settings you used in that particular dialog. You can also add the Option (PC: Alt) key to the keyboard shortcuts. For example, the shortcut to bring up the Levels dialog is Command-L (PC: Control-L), but if you add Option (PC: Alt) to those keys, the Levels dialog will open with your last-used settings.

CHAPTER 3 • Production Tips   61

HIT THOSE CHANNELS FAST

When you're in the Curves dialog (Command-M [PC: Control-M]), if you're charging by the hour, you can certainly travel up to the Channel pop-up menu and choose each individual channel you want to work on, but if you want to do it the fast way, just press Command-1 for Red, Command-2 for Green, and Command-3 for Blue (PC: Control-1, Control-2, etc.). If you need to return to the composite RGB channel, press Command-Tilde (PC: Control-Tilde). By the way, the Tilde key looks like ~, and it lives right above the Tab key on your keyboard. Don't feel bad. Nobody knows what the Tilde key is. We're not sure it's a real symbol at all. We think it was made up so there wouldn't be an empty space there on your keyboard. Hey, it's somewhat plausible.

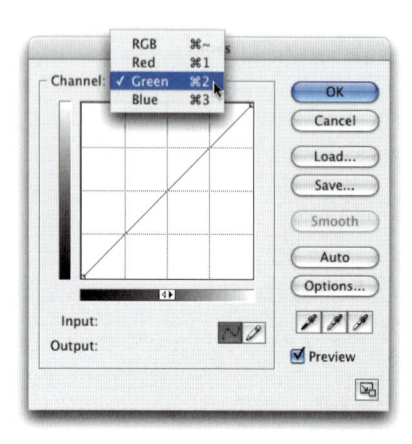

HOW TO GET AN UNDO AFTER YOU'VE CLOSED THE DOCUMENT

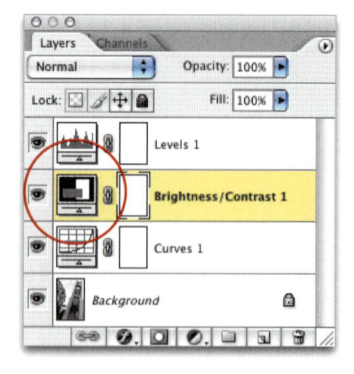

As you probably already know, the History palette keeps track of the last 20 changes to your document, and you can use it for multiple undos when working on a project. The only bad part is that when you close your document, your undos (in History) are automatically deleted. However, there is a way to save an undo, as long as it's a tonal adjustment (such as Curves, Levels, Color Balance, etc.), by creating adjustment layers. Just click on the half-white/half-black circle icon at the bottom of the Layers palette and choose your tonal adjustment from the pop-up menu to create an adjustment layer. These adjustment layers are saved along with your file. That way, the next time you open the file, you can go back and edit your Curves, Levels, etc., adjustment by double-clicking on the adjustment layer's thumbnail. The last-applied adjustment will appear, and you can edit it live. If you decide you don't want the original adjustment applied at all, you can drag the adjustment layer into the Trash icon at the bottom of the Layers palette. You can also add a Gradient fill, a Pattern fill, and even a Solid Color fill as an adjustment layer, giving you an undo at a later date, because again, they're saved as layers with the file.

CHAPTER 3 • Production Tips

USING THE PEN? STAY AWAY FROM THE TOOLBOX

Want to save trips to the Toolbox when using the Pen tool (P)? You're in luck. Better yet, you don't even have to hold down any modifier keys (such as Option/Alt, etc.), because Photoshop will do the work for you. Here's why: When you draw a path, move your cursor over a line segment and your Pen cursor automatically changes to the Add Anchor Point tool, so you can click anywhere along that path to add a point. Move your cursor over an existing point, and it changes into the Delete Anchor Point tool (click on the point, and it's deleted). This is called Auto Add/Delete, and it's on by default (you can turn it off, should you want to, using the checkbox in the Options Bar).

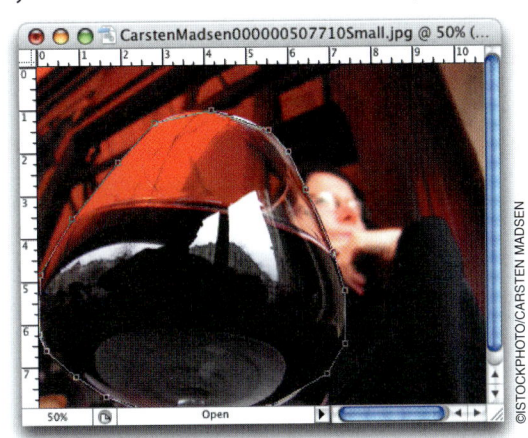

PUT YOUR GRADIENT PICKER AT YOUR FINGERTIPS

Want to make the Gradient Picker appear where your cursor is in your image window? You can do this when you have the Gradient tool (G) active, allowing access to your gradient library, by Control-clicking (PC: Right-clicking) within your image area. It also works with the Custom Shape Picker. Here's an even slicker trick: You can use the Return or Enter key instead to bring up the Gradient or Custom Shape Pickers.

CHAPTER 3 • Production Tips   63

DON'T CLICK IN THAT FIELD!

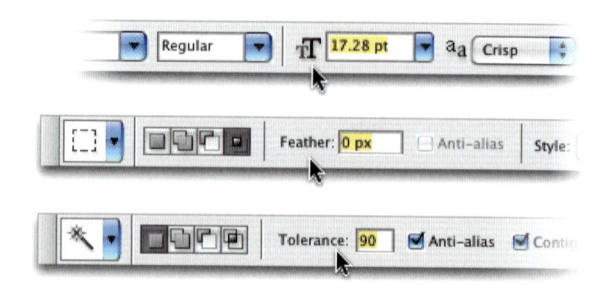

Those tiny little fields up in the Options Bar can really be a pain sometimes, especially if you're trying to highlight a field, delete the current value, and type in a new one. Instead of doing all that, just click on the field's name and Photoshop will automatically highlight the entire field for you. That way, you can just type in new values and it will automatically replace the old values. Great thing is, this doesn't just work in the Options Bar; it works in many of Photoshop's palettes, including the Character and Paragraph palettes.

OUT OF MEMORY? TRY THIS FIRST

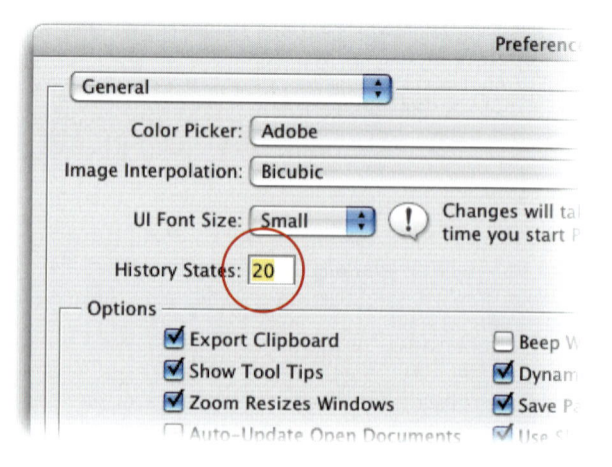

Here's a tip for avoiding those nasty out-of-memory warning dialogs. One of the reasons Photoshop needs so much memory is that by default it keeps a snapshot of the last 20 things you did to your document, thus allowing you to undo your previous 20 steps. (You can see the running list of your last 20 steps in the History palette.) As you might expect, storing 20 steps takes a mighty chunk of memory, and if you're running a little low (or getting those evil out-of-memory warnings), one thing you might try is lowering the amount of steps Photoshop stores. In Mac OS X, go under the Photoshop menu, under Preferences, under General, and you'll find a field for History States. (In Windows you'll find Preferences under the Edit menu.) You can lower this number (try 8 States for starters), and you may avoid the dreaded memory warnings. Just remember, by lowering the States, you don't have 20 undos anymore.

64 CHAPTER 3 • Production Tips

HOW TO "UNERASE"

You probably already know that you can use the History Brush (Y) as an "undo" on a brush, and that by default, the History Brush paints back to how your image looked when you first opened it. But did you know that the Eraser tool has a similar function? That's right; the next time you've got the Eraser tool (E) active, look up in the Options Bar and you'll see a checkbox for Erase to History. Normally, the Eraser tool erases to your Background color, but when you turn on this checkbox, it erases back to what the image looked like when you opened it.

LET PHOTOSHOP STRAIGHTEN YOUR CROOKED SCANS

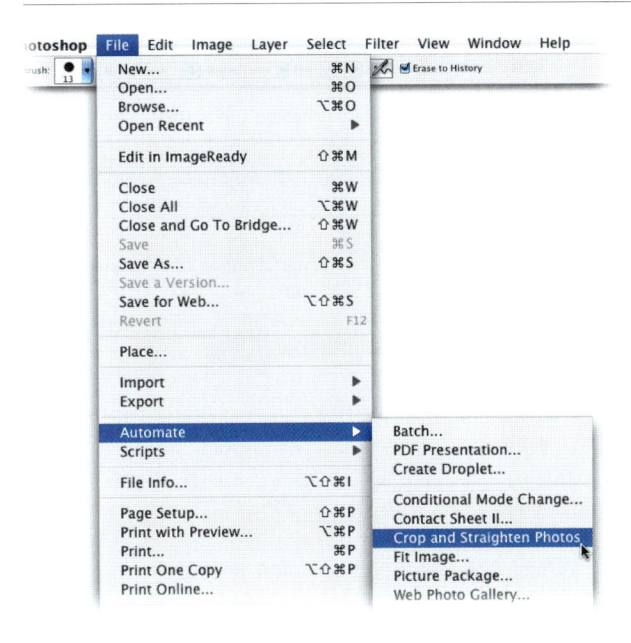

That's right—straightening is totally automated in Photoshop CS2. In fact, try out this ideal situation: Toss two or three photos casually onto your scanner bed, without taking the time to carefully align them, and scan them all with just one pass of your scanner. Then, open the single scan of the three photos in Photoshop, go under the File menu, under Automate, and choose Crop and Straighten Photos. Photoshop will then crop, straighten, and even put each photo into its own separate document. Nice.

CHAPTER 3 • Production Tips   65

COPY ONE LAYER, OR COPY 'EM ALL

If you're working on a layered document, and you make a selection and copy that selection, by default Photoshop only copies the information on your currently active layer (and that's a good thing). However, there may be times when you want to copy your selection as if the image was flattened (in other words, you want to copy everything on all visible layers). If that's the case, press Command-Shift-C (PC: Control-Shift-C), and you'll copy as if the image was flattened, not just on the active layer.

STUCK IN A FIELD? HERE'S HOW TO ESCAPE

This is one of those tips that keeps you from pulling your hair out. Sometimes when you're editing values in a field (for example, you're typing numbers in the Opacity field for a layer) and you've entered the number you want, Photoshop doesn't automatically take you out of that field (meaning your cursor is still flashing in the Opacity field). It gets worse if you've switched to another layer (besides the Background layer) and you want to use a keyboard shortcut to switch tools. For example, you press the letter T to switch to the Type tool, but instead of getting the Type tool, you get an error sound because your cursor is still in the Opacity field (you can't type letters in a number field). Here's how to get around it: Just press the Return (PC: Enter) key on your keyboard to lock in the change in your field and release your keyboard for other tasks.

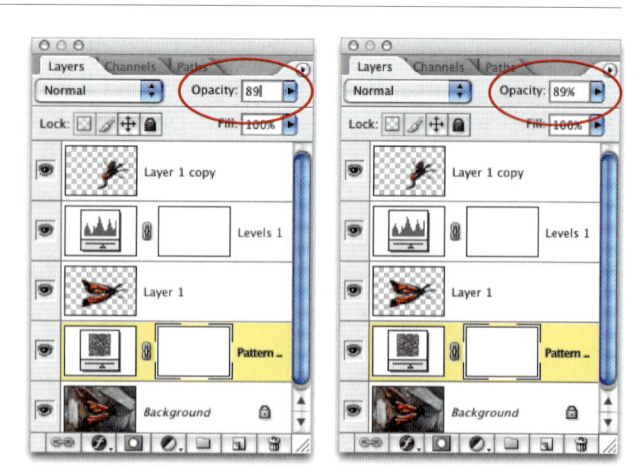

CHAPTER 3 • Production Tips

DON'T CANCEL; RESET AND SAVE TIME

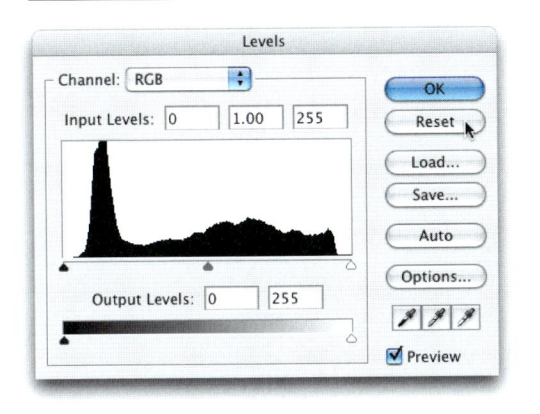

Most of Photoshop's dialogs (but not all) will let you use this little tip, which can save you loads of time. When you're making changes in a dialog (let's use the Levels dialog as an example) and decide that you don't like the changes you've made, one option is to click the Cancel button to close the dialog, leaving your image unchanged. Then you can reopen the dialog and try again. This is an incredible waste of valuable time, so instead, Photoshop lets you "reset" the dialog—putting the settings back to what they were when you first opened it. Just hold the Option key (PC: Alt key) and look at the Cancel button—it changes into the Reset button. Click it, and it resets the dialog automatically, as if you hadn't made any changes at all. Big, big time saver.

SEE EVERY TWEAK WITH BIGGER FILTER GALLERY PREVIEWS

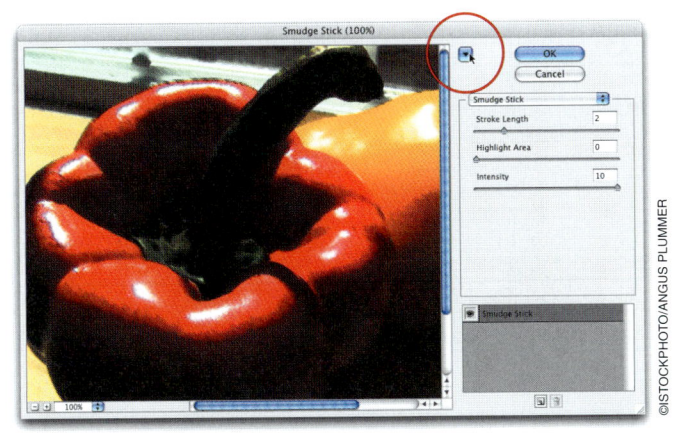

Once you've chosen a filter from the Filter Gallery (under the Filter menu), you'll probably want to spend some time tweaking the settings. If that's the case, you'll also need to see a larger preview of your work so you can really see the effects of each little tweak. You can do that by clicking on the triangle button, to the left of the OK button. This hides the center column (the list of filters) and expands the Preview pane into its space, giving you the full preview experience.

SHOWING ONE EFFECT IN THE FILTER GALLERY

The idea behind the Filter Gallery (under the Filter menu) is the stacking up of one filter on top of the next, but if you want to see any one of the filters by itself, just Option-click (PC: Alt-click) on the Eye icon beside that filter in the filter stack, and all the other filters will be hidden from view. Option-click (PC: Alt-click) on the same Eye icon to bring them all back into view.

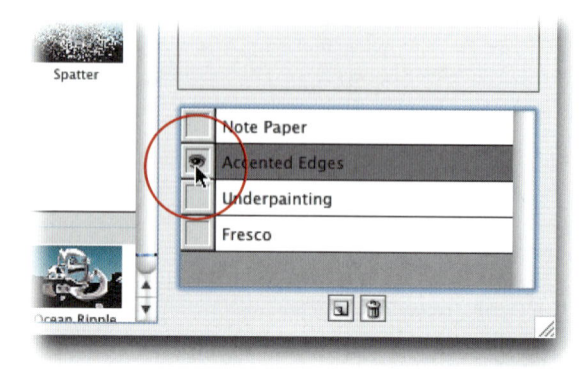

USE THE MOVE TOOL ANYTIME

When you're using just about any of Photoshop's tools, you can temporarily switch to the Move tool at any time by simply holding the Command key (PC: Control key). It's temporary, and as soon as you release it, you're back to the tool you started with.

68 CHAPTER 3 • Production Tips

FILTER GALLERY ZOOM QUICK TIP

If you're in the Filter Gallery (under the Filter menu) and want to zoom quickly to a particular level of magnification, just Control-click (PC: Right-click) anywhere within the preview window and a contextual menu of zoom views will appear.

CHAPTER 3 • Production Tips

Greased Lightnin'

WAY COOL TIPS

Why is this chapter named "Way Cool Tips"? It's because "Boring Regular Tips" was already taken (psych!). Actually, it's because this is where a lot of the really cool tips wound

Greased Lightnin'
way cool tips

up that didn't fit into any of the other categories. I don't really have anything else to say about this chapter, so instead, let's fill this space by singing a verse of "Greased Lightnin'" from the motion picture Grease. *"We'll get some overhead lifters, and four-barrel quads, oh yeah (keep talkin', whoa, keep talkin'). Fuel-injection cutoff and chrome-plated rods, oh yeah (I'll get the money, I'll see you get the money), with the four-speed on the floor, they'll be waitin' at the door, you know that ain't no…." Hey, wait a minute—that next word is a cuss word. Okay, no problem, we'll skip over that word and continue, "…we'll be getting lots of…." Gees, another nasty word. I've been singing that song for years and never really noticed how nasty it was. Just to be safe, let's just jump to the end of the chorus, "…you know that I ain't braggin', she's a real…." Oh, that's just wrong! I'm stopping right here.*

FIND THINGS FAST BY COLOR-CODING THEM

If there are particular areas of Photoshop you use a lot, you can make finding them in the menus even faster by color-coding your favorite menu items. Here's how: Go under the Edit menu and choose Menus. When the dialog appears, scroll down to the menu you want and double-click on it. Now scroll down until you find the command you want to color-code, and then click on the word "None" to the far right of that item (under the Color column) and a menu of colors will appear. Choose the color you want for that item, and from now on it will appear highlighted in that color. This is ideal if you're training new Photoshop users. For example, you could color-code certain items for when they're doing prepress (maybe make those items appear in red) and choose another color for when they're designing Web graphics.

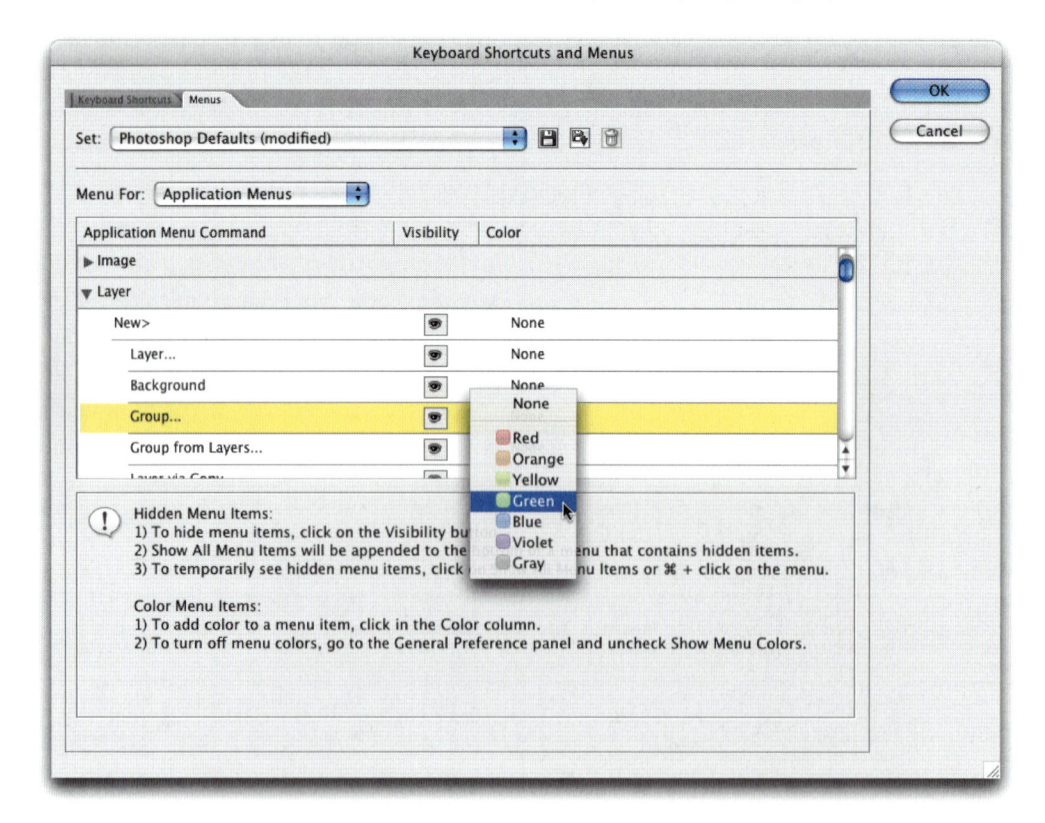

CHAPTER 4 • Way Cool Tips

USING CAMERA RAW IMAGES AS SMART OBJECTS

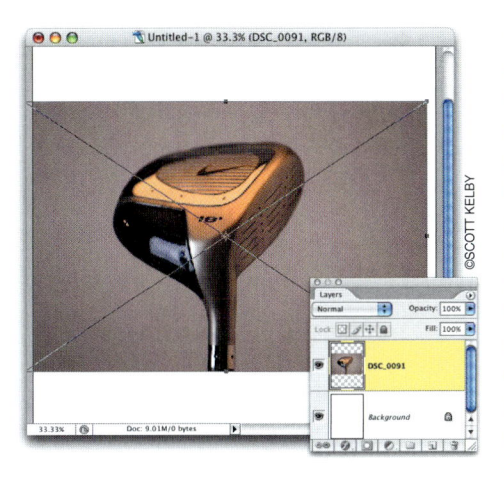

You can add any RAW image to your existing document as a Smart Object. Just use the Place command (under the File menu) and navigate your way to the RAW image. When you choose the RAW image, Photoshop will first open Camera Raw so you can process it. When you click Open in the Camera Raw dialog, it will place itself into your document as a Smart Object (and it will have a bounding box around it so you can determine the size you want it to appear within your document). Once you've sized the placed image, press Return (PC: Enter) to lock it into position. If you need to make any edits to the RAW photo after it's placed into your document as a Smart Object, just double-click on the Smart Object's thumbnail in the Layers palette and your RAW image will reopen in Camera Raw. Make your changes, click OK, and it will automatically update in your main document. Sweeeeeettttt!

GETTING MORE CONTROL OVER VANISHING POINT

When you apply the Vanishing Point filter, by default it applies the effect to your Background layer, which means once Vanishing Point "does its thing," you don't have any control over the results. If it's too light, too dark, you want to change the color, blend mode, etc., you're out of luck. That's why, before you run the Vanishing Point filter, you should create a new blank layer by clicking on the Create a New Layer icon at the bottom of the Layers palette. That way, the object (text, whatever) to which you apply Vanishing Point winds up on its own separate layer, where you can control everything from color to opacity and more.

CHAPTER 4 • Way Cool Tips   73

TURNING YOUR VANISHING POINT GRID

Need to wrap your Vanishing Point filter grid around a corner? No sweat—just hold the Command key (PC: Control key), drag a center point, and the grid will bend around the corner.

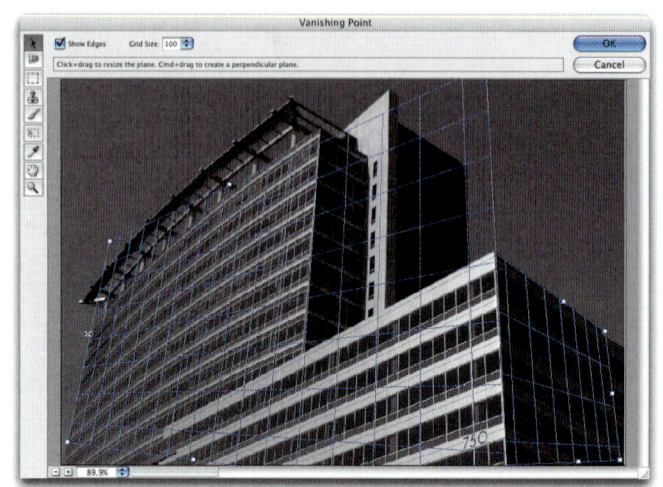

HIDDEN ZOOM FEATURE IN VANISHING POINT

If you're using Vanishing Point and need to quickly zoom in on an area, just move your cursor over that area, then press-and-hold the letter X on your keyboard to zoom in on the area where your cursor is. To zoom back out, release the X key.

Before

After

THINK YOU MIGHT CHANGE SIZES? MAKE IT A SMART OBJECT!

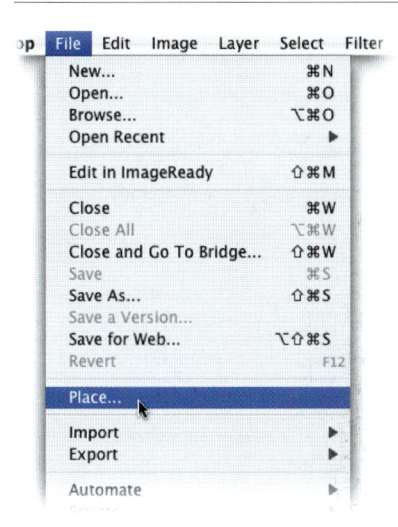

If you're building a collage, or some other document that has images on different layers, and you think you might wind up resizing some of the images, rather than just dragging-and-dropping opened photos into your main document, make them Smart Objects. That way, when you resize them (especially helpful if you increase their size), it calls upon the original image to make a clean resize (instead of a blurry, pixelated version). To create a Smart Object, you only have to change one thing—instead of opening the photo, go under the File menu and choose Place instead.

MAKING A SMART OBJECT DUMB—WELL, KINDA

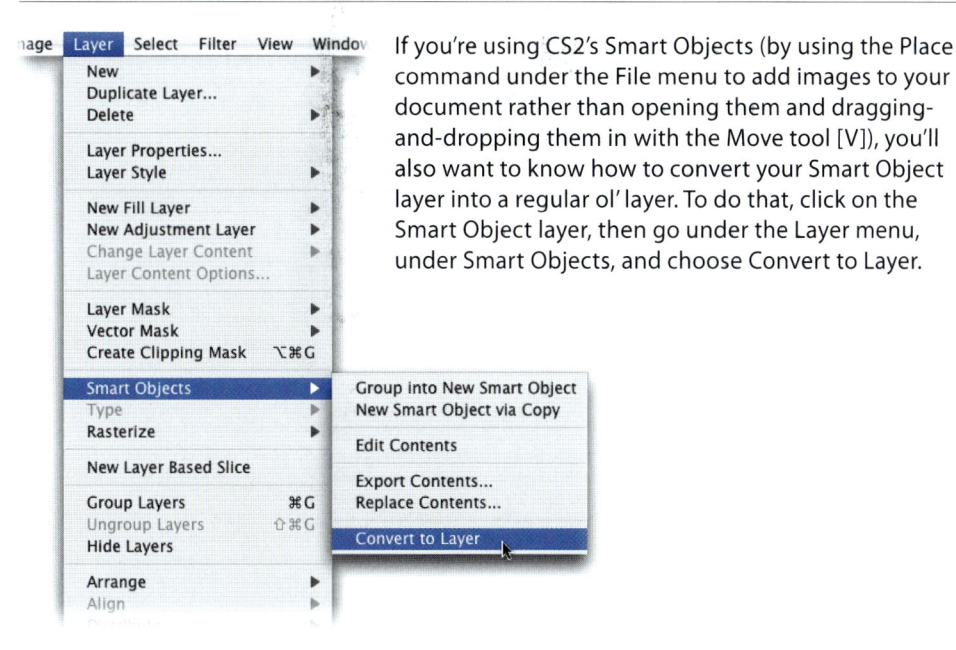

If you're using CS2's Smart Objects (by using the Place command under the File menu to add images to your document rather than opening them and dragging-and-dropping them in with the Move tool [V]), you'll also want to know how to convert your Smart Object layer into a regular ol' layer. To do that, click on the Smart Object layer, then go under the Layer menu, under Smart Objects, and choose Convert to Layer.

CHAPTER 4 • Way Cool Tips

SWITCHING FROM WARP TO FREE TRANSFORM (AND BACK AGAIN)

If you're using CS2's Warp Image feature (which is accessed by pressing Command-T [PC: Control-T] to bring up Free Transform, then Control-clicking [PC: Right-clicking] inside the Free Transform bounding box and choosing Warp from the contextual menu), there's a good chance you'll need to resize the image once you start warping it. If that happens, there's a button you can click that will switch back to Free Transform. It's near the top-right corner of the Options Bar, and clicking the button will toggle you between Warp and Free Transform.

INSTANT THUMBNAIL SIZE CONTROL

Want to change the size of your thumbnail preview in your Layers, Channels, or Paths palette? Just hold the Control key (PC: Right-click) and click in an open area of the palette (such as the space under your Background layer, or beneath the bottom channel in the Channels palette), and a pop-up menu of thumbnail sizes will appear. For instance, in the Layers palette you can choose from No, Small, Medium, or Large Thumbnails, instantly changing your thumbnail view.

CHAPTER 4 • Way Cool Tips

WHAT'S SMARTER THAN USING GUIDES?

Oh wait. I know this one. It's…it's…Smart Guides! (That's right, for 500 points.) These little below-the-radar additions to CS2 are there to help you align objects on layers, but they don't show up just on the edges of your object. As you drag your layer, they look for angles and corners within your layer, and the guides then extend out from there. That's why they're called "Smart." To turn them on within your multilayered file, all you have to do is go under the View menu, under Show, and choose Smart Guides. Once they're enabled, they appear automatically as you drag. They're handier—and smarter—than you'd think.

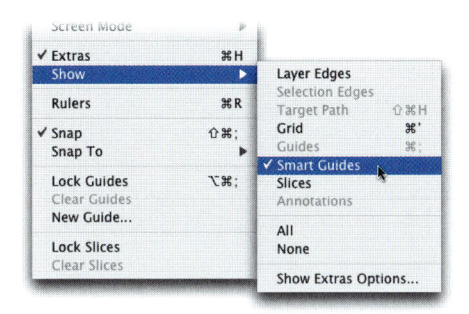

CHAPTER 4 • Way Cool Tips   77

GETTING BACK TO THE FILTER GALLERY DEFAULTS

Let's say you've tried all the filters in the Filter Gallery, and changed each setting so much that you can't remember what the default, out-of-the-box settings were. Well, you're out of luck (kidding). Here's a trick for getting back to those default settings for any filter the Filter Gallery supports (like any of the Artistic filters, the Sketch filters, etc.): Open one of these filters (by choosing it from the Filter menu) and when it opens in the Filter Gallery, press-and-hold the Command key (PC: Control key) and you'll see that the Cancel button changes into the Default button. Click it (while still holding down Command/Control) and the default settings will magically reappear.

HAVING HISTORY TRACK YOUR LAYER VISIBILITY

By default, the History palette tracks the last 20 things you did in Photoshop, but (weird as this may sound) it doesn't track when you hide or show a layer. For some reason, it just doesn't record that. Well, that is unless you know this tip: Go to the History palette's flyout menu and choose History Options. When the History Options dialog appears, turn on the checkbox for Make Layer Visibility Changes Undoable. Now, you can undo your showing and hiding of layers from the History palette.

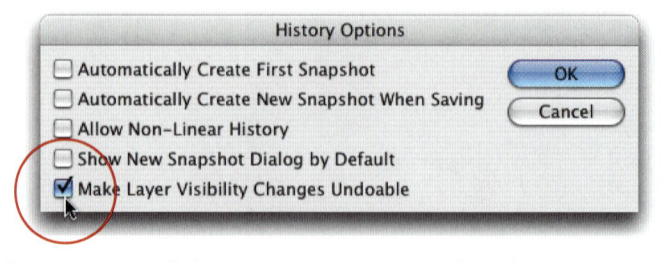

78   CHAPTER 4 • Way Cool Tips

THE TRICK TO TRICKY EXTRACTIONS

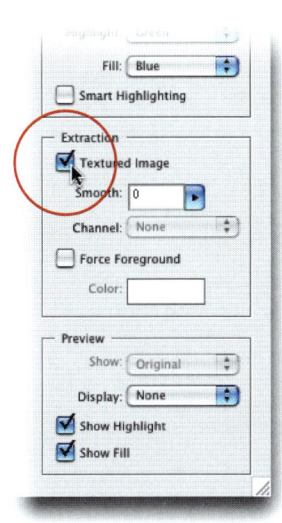

Adobe's own Julieanne Kost (Photoshop guru and instructor supreme) showed this at the Photoshop World Conference & Expo, and it had everybody's jaw dropping, but little has been said of it since, even though it's built into Photoshop CS2's Extract function (found under the Filter menu). It's called Textured Image and you use it when you're dealing with a tough extraction—a person with a dark shirt posing on a dark background, for example—and Extract can't really tell where the shirt ends and the background begins. Turning this on helps detect the edges by examining the texture, and if it detects a texture (like you might find in a shirt), it can often help pull you out of a tight situation.

ZOOMING ALL YOUR TILED IMAGES AT ONCE

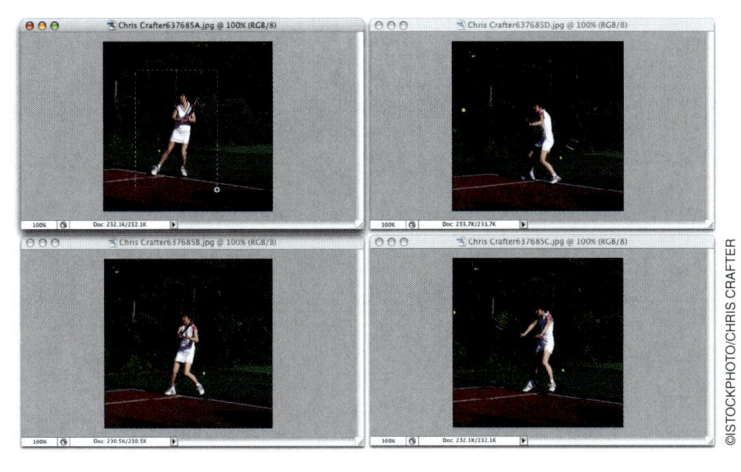

If you've chosen to tile your open windows (in the Window menu, under Arrange, choose Tile Horizontally [or Vertically]), in Photoshop CS2 you get some hidden functionality. If you want all the tiled images to be displayed at the same level of magnification, just hold the Shift key, grab the Zoom tool (Z), zoom in on one of the images, and all the other tiled images will jump to that same magnification. This is great when you're trying to compare a number of similar images for detail.

CHAPTER 4 • Way Cool Tips

HOW TO DUPLICATE A COLOR STOP

Here's the scenario: You're making a custom gradient using the Gradient tool (G) (by double-clicking the gradient thumbnail in the Options Bar to get to the Gradient Editor) and you need to duplicate one or more of the color stops. No problem. Once you've created one gradient color stop, you can make copies by Option-dragging (PC: Alt-dragging) it. Also, as long as you keep the Option key (PC: Alt key) down while you drag, you can jump right over other existing stops. It's a color stop love fest, can you feel it?

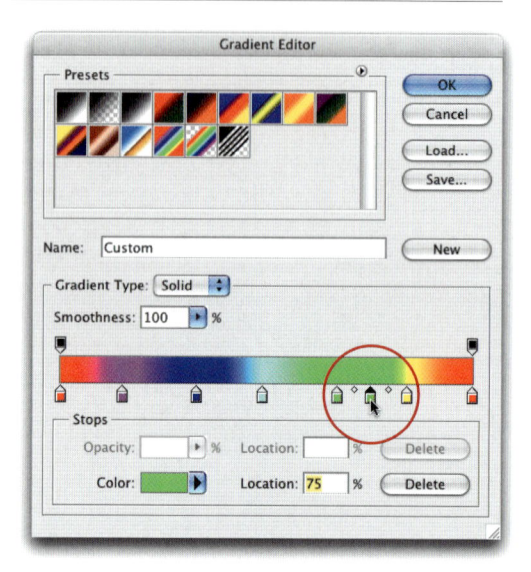

REMOVING EDGE FRINGE WHEN COLLAGING

Any time you're creating a collage, you'll eventually add an image that has little white pixels around the edges of your object. Here's a tip for getting rid of that "fringe." Go under the Layer menu, under Matting, and choose Defringe. Try the default setting of 1 pixel and click OK. What this does (here's the techno speak) is replace the edge pixels with a combination of the pixel colors in your object and the colors in the background (whew, that hurt). That usually does the trick. If it doesn't, undo it, then try a 2- or 3-pixel Defringe.

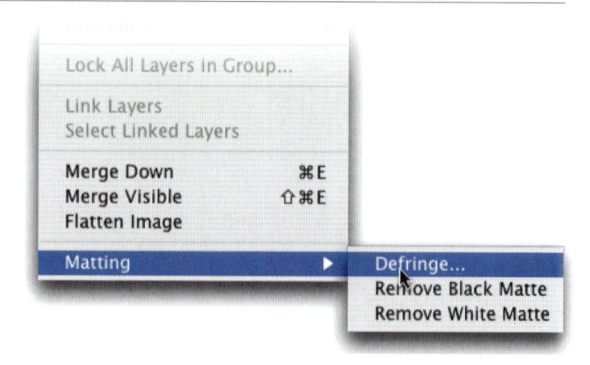

CRACKING THE EASTER EGG MYSTERY

Easter Eggs are usually funny little messages hidden within an application (engineer humor just cracks us up). Photoshop has a few of its own, but one of the lesser-known Easter Eggs is Merlin Lives. To see this Easter Egg, go to the Paths palette (under the Window menu), hold the Option key (PC: Alt key), and in the palette's flyout menu, choose Palette Options. When you do, a tiny floating palette will appear with a picture of Merlin and just one button named "Begone," which closes the dialog. I have to party with those engineer guys.

UNDO ON A SLIDER!

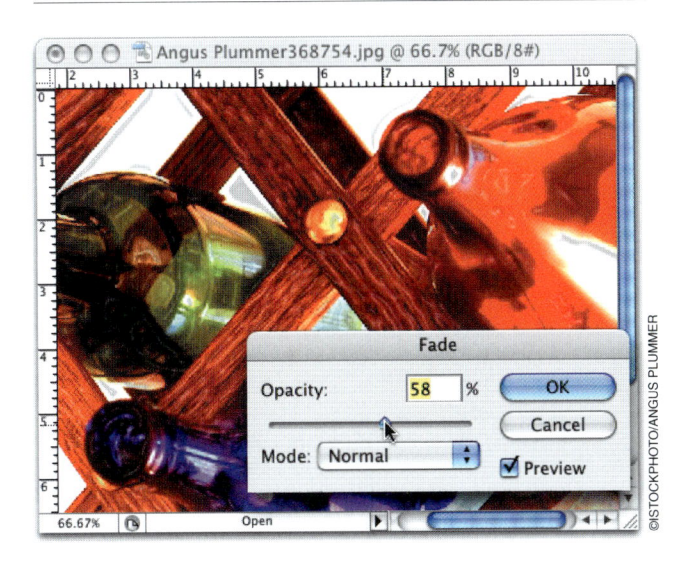

If you apply a technique (such as a filter or a paint stroke) and the effect is too intense, you can always undo the effect by pressing Command-Z (PC: Control-Z). But if you just want to decrease the intensity, instead of completely undoing it, go under the Edit menu and choose Fade. Want a less intense effect? Just move the Opacity slider to the left. The farther you drag, the less intense the effect. Drag all the way to the left, and the effect is undone.

CHAPTER 4 • Way Cool Tips

RESIZING PATHS THE EASY WAY

When you're working with paths, you can visually resize your path by using the Path Selection tool. To do this, press A to get the tool, then go up in the Options Bar and turn on the checkbox for Show Bounding Box. This puts a Free Transform-like bounding box around your path, and you can use this bounding box to resize your path by dragging the handles (remember to hold the Shift key to resize it proportionately).

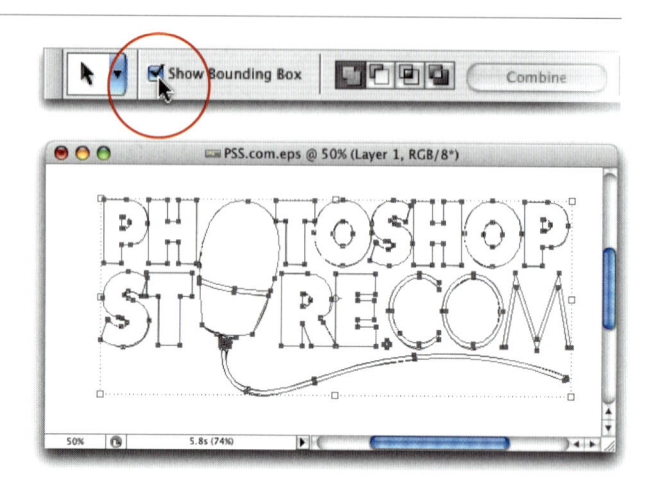

THE GAUSSIAN BLUR KEYBOARD SHORTCUT

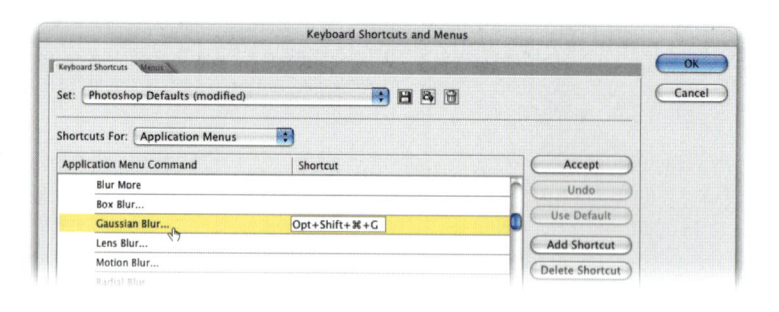

I thought that would get your attention. That's because you know there's no keyboard shortcut for applying a Gaussian Blur. But there is in my copy of Photoshop CS2. How is that possible? Because I created one, and you can too. Just go under the Edit menu and choose Keyboard Shortcuts to bring up the Keyboard Shortcuts dialog. Then, from the Shortcuts For pop-up menu, choose Application Menus. In the list of menus in the window beneath it, double-click on Filter to reveal all the choices under the Filter menu. Scroll down to Gaussian Blur, then click on its name. This brings up a field where you can enter the shortcut by pressing the keys you want to use. I recommend using Option-Shift-Command-G (PC: Alt-Shift-Control-G) because there are so few shortcuts not already being used by Photoshop. Click OK, and not only is the shortcut activated but your custom shortcut now appears in the Filter menu to the right of Gaussian Blur.

THE ADVANTAGE OF PHOTO FILTER ADJUSTMENT LAYERS

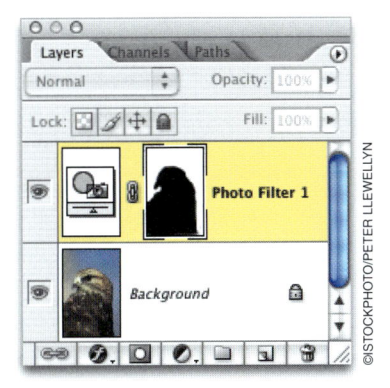

One of the most brilliant things Adobe did when they added Photo Filters to Photoshop (these filters replicate the old traditional screw-on lens filters) was to make them adjustment layers. You can create one by clicking on the Create New Adjustment Layer pop-up menu in the Layers palette and choosing Photo Filter. After you apply a Photo Filter from the resulting dialog (let's say, for example, you used Warming Filter 81 to warm a cool photo), you can get the Brush tool (B), set your Foreground color to black, and paint over any areas of the photo you don't want to be warmed. This gives you a level of flexibility you wouldn't get any other way.

MAKE A PHOTOSHOP CLIENT PRESENTATION

To hide all your palettes and all your menus, and to display your current image centered on your monitor with a cool black frame around your image, just press the letter F twice, then press the Tab key (F, F, Tab). To return to your regular Photoshop work area, press F, then Tab. You'll be the envy of all your friends, and eventually they'll write folk songs about you. It's almost embarrassing.

CHAPTER 4 • Way Cool Tips

MOVING YOUR IMAGE IN FULL SCREEN MODE

In Photoshop CS2 you can pull off something users have been wanting for years—the ability to change the placement of your entire image once you're in Full Screen mode (where your image is centered onscreen, surrounded by a black border with no menus, palettes, or tools visible). Just enter Full Screen mode (press F, F, then Tab), hold the Spacebar, and your cursor will change into the Hand tool. Click-and-drag your entire image anywhere on the screen you'd like. To return to regular mode, press F, then Tab.

PHOTO-RETOUCHING SAFETY TIP

Here's a tip that many photo retouchers use—do all your retouching on a layer above your image. That way, you don't damage the underlying image, and you have control over opacity and blend modes you normally wouldn't have. It's also easy to erase areas you wish you hadn't retouched. The key to making this work is to get the Clone Stamp tool (S) and in the Options Bar, turn on the Sample All Layers option. That way you can sample from the underlying image and then paint on the layer above it (believe it or not, by default Photoshop doesn't let you do that—it only lets you clone from the active layer to that same layer).

84   **CHAPTER 4** • Way Cool Tips

LIGHTS, CAMERA, ACTION: SLIDE SHOWS USING PHOTOSHOP

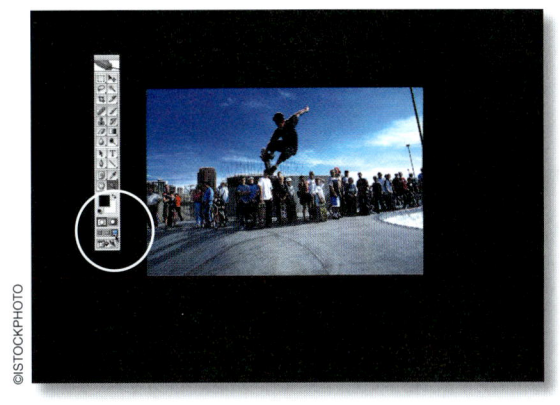

Shift-click to see multiple photos in Full Screen mode.

You can create a mock slide show presentation by opening multiple images in Photoshop and then pressing Control-Tab to rotate through the images. Plus, you can hold the Shift key and click on the Full Screen Mode icon near the bottom of your Toolbox to allow your images to fill the full screen (holding Shift will switch all of your open images to the Full Screen mode at once). Press Tab to hide your palettes and you're all set to give a slick presentation. To exit your mini-slide show, press Tab to see the Toolbox, and then Shift-click on the Standard Mode icon.

Shift-click to exit your slide show in Full Screen mode.

CHAPTER 4 • Way Cool Tips   85

PHOTOSHOP'S HIDDEN STEP AND REPEAT

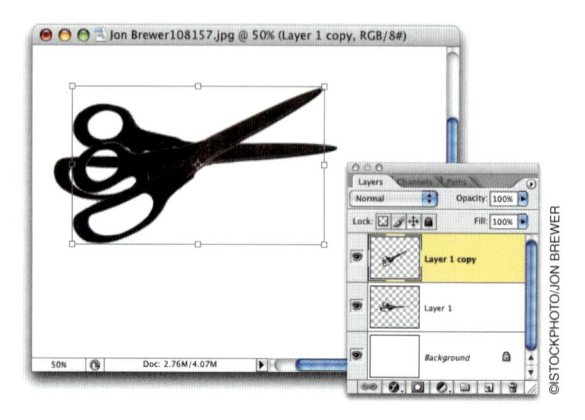

Although Photoshop doesn't have a visible Step and Repeat function (like many vector or page-layout programs do), it still has the feature—it's just a bit hidden. For example, let's say you have an object on a layer, and you want to duplicate and move or rotate that object a number of times in succession (a typical step-and-repeat), here's how you can do it in Photoshop CS2: Start by going to the original layer with the object, then press Command-Option-T (PC: Control-Alt-T) to bring up a special version of Free Transform. Now you can transform your object (move it, rotate it, skew it, etc.), then press Return (PC: Enter) to lock in your transformation. You'll notice that your original object remains untouched on its layer and you now have a new layer with the transformed object. Now press Command-Option-Shift-T (PC: Control-Alt-Shift-T) and this will create a duplicate of your last move, and at the same time it creates a new layer, thereby giving you a step-and-repeat (you have to try this once, and you'll immediately "get it").

PAUSING FOR A BRUSH PREVIEW

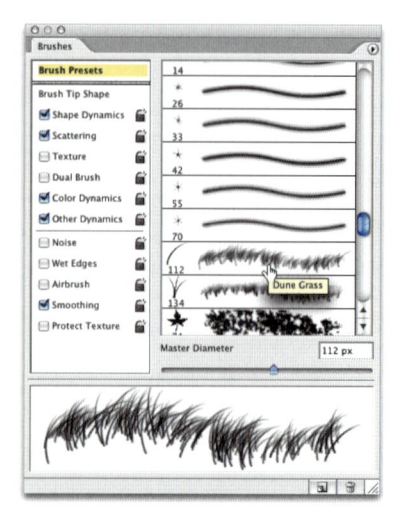

If you're choosing your brush tips from the expanded Brushes palette, you don't have to actually click on a brush to see the large preview of it at the bottom of the Brushes palette (which is nested in the Palette Well by default). Instead, pause your cursor right over the brush you want to preview, and in just a second the preview will appear, even though you didn't actually click on the brush tip. The catch is: The Show Tool Tips checkbox must be turned on in the General Preferences for this "pause preview" to work.

THE UNDOCUMENTED AIRBRUSH TOGGLE TRICK

This cool, undocumented shortcut comes from our good friend, Web wizard, and all-powerful overlord of every Photoshop keyboard shortcut known to man, Michael Ninness (author of the book *Photoshop 7 Power Shortcuts*, from New Riders, ISBN 0735713316). Here's the tip: As you probably know by now, the Airbrush tool has been gone from the Toolbox since 7.0, but you can add Airbrush control to some painting tools by clicking on the Airbrush icon found in the Options Bar of most Brush tools. However, that takes a lot of trips up to the Options Bar. Ah, if only there were a keyboard shortcut that would let you toggle this Airbrush feature on and off at will. Well, there is, and thanks to Michael, we can share it here—it's Option-Shift-P (PC: Alt-Shift-P). Makes you want to buy Michael's book, doesn't it?

SWAPPING CROP FIELDS

Adobe snuck a little button into the Options Bar that's hardly noticeable. It works with tools such as the Crop tool (C), and it's a big time saver. For example, for the Crop tool it swaps the measurements in the Width and Height fields, so if you have the Crop tool set to crop to exactly a 5x7", if you click this Swaps button, it will now crop to 7x5". See? I told you it was handy.

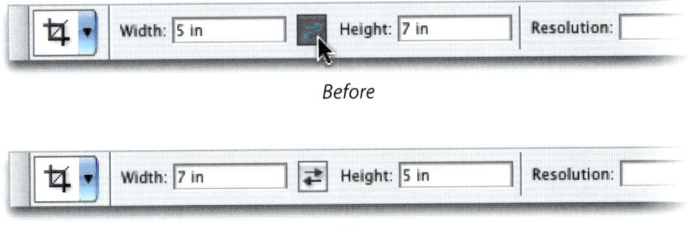

Before

After

CHAPTER 4 • Way Cool Tips

LET THOSE WINDOWS BREATHE!

Since version 3.0, Photoshop has done something called "protecting the palettes" (I don't know if that's its official name, but we've always heard it called that). What it means is that as you increase the size of your image using the Zoom tool (Z), Photoshop stops increasing the size of the image window when it reaches the left edge of your open palettes (if you have turned on the Resize Windows To Fit checkbox in the Options Bar). When it reaches this safety zone, the window stops growing, and only the image within the window continues to zoom. The only way to get around this (in previous versions of Photoshop) was to close your palettes. Then you could zoom the window as large as you'd like. However, Adobe addressed this problem back in Photoshop 6.0, and now if you want to keep the window growing, choose Ignore Palettes in the Options Bar when using the Zoom tool.

THE MULTIPLE UNDO SHORTCUT

Need to back up a few steps to readjust a setting? Piece of cake. Here's a shortcut to do just that. You can step back through your History palette (found under the Window menu) by pressing Command-Option-Z (PC: Control-Alt-Z) a few times. This doesn't delete the items, but takes you back a step in the History palette each time you apply the shortcut.

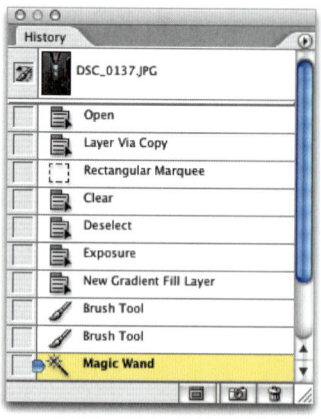

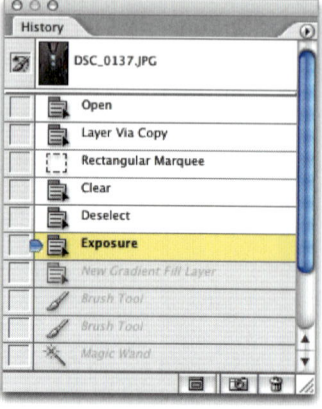

Before *After*

88 **CHAPTER 4** • Way Cool Tips

WANT ARROWHEADS? PHOTOSHOP CAN ADD THEM FOR YOU!

This one is pretty slick because it's been a feature in Photoshop for a while, but eight out of 10 Photoshop users will tell you Photoshop can't create arrowheads on the ends of lines (if it makes you feel any better, nine out of 10 dentists didn't think Photoshop could do it either). Here's how: First, go under the Shape tools (in the Toolbox) and choose the Line tool. Then, up in the Options Bar, you'll see icons for the Shape tools. Directly to the right of these eight icons is a down-facing triangle. Click on that triangle and out pops a dialog where you can click a checkbox to add arrowheads to either the beginning or end of your line, and you can choose the Width, Length, and even the Concavity (there's that dentist thing again).

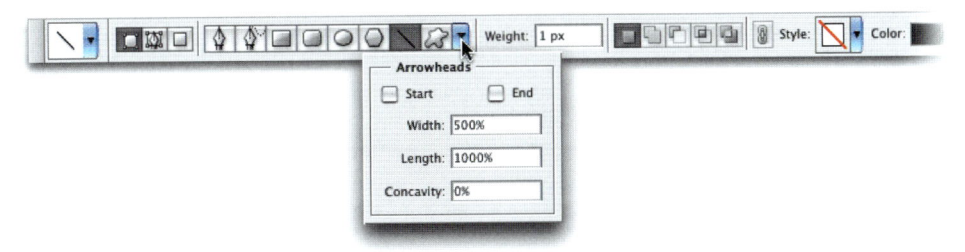

DRAGGING-AND-DROPPING WHERE YOU WANT

If you drag an image from one document to another, the dragged image appears right at the spot where you let go of the mouse button. You may know that if you hold the Shift key when you drag-and-drop the image, the dragged image will automatically be centered within the receiving image. But you can go one better—make a selection in the receiving document, then hold the Shift key before you drag. Your image will be centered within the selection, instead of within the entire document. Scary, isn't it? You can also copy-and-paste the selection and Photoshop will center the pasted image in the selection.

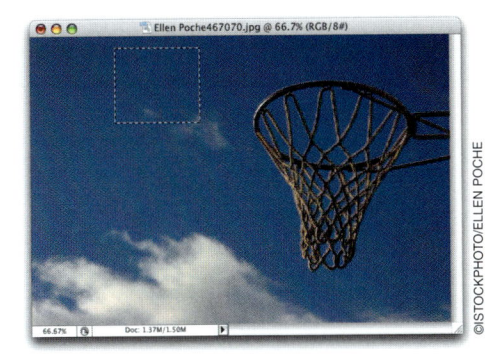

CHAPTER 4 • Way Cool Tips

FEATHER A SELECTION WITHOUT THE GUESSING GAME

Most of us try to guess how many pixels will give us the nice, soft selection we're looking for when we use the Feather Selection dialog (under the Select menu). Sometimes we guess right, and other times we press Command-Z (PC: Control-Z) to undo the damage before trying again. Try this instead: Make your selection first, and then press Q to turn on the Quick Mask mode. Now make the edge fade out by going under Filter, under Blur, and choosing Gaussian Blur. You can see how much of a blur you'll need to soften the edges as you adjust the Radius amount. When you're done, press Q to get back to Standard mode with the selection already made with the exact amount of feathering that you want.

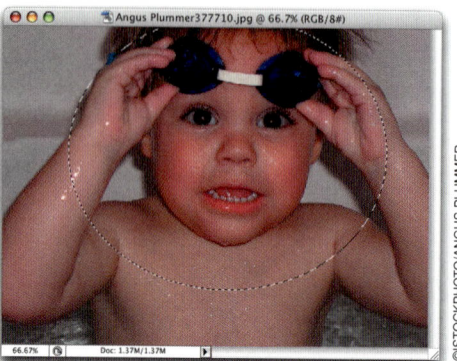

CHAPTER 4 • Way Cool Tips

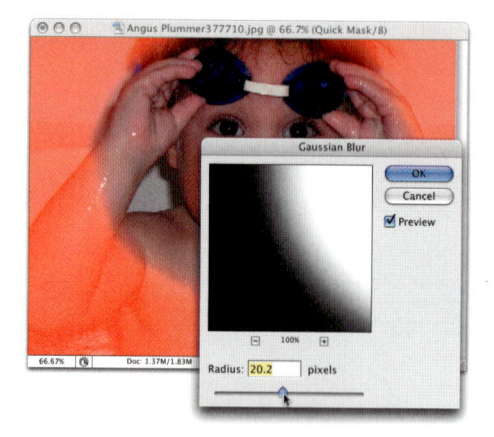

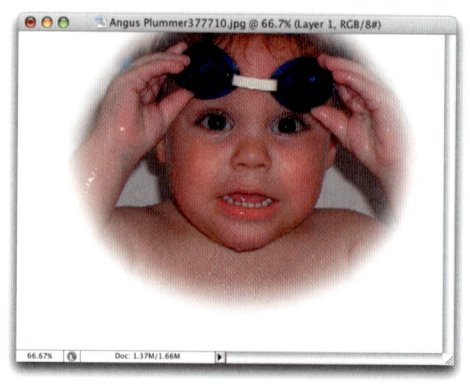

TOP-SECRET PHOTOSHOP SPLASH SCREEN

If you want to see the secret Photoshop beta startup screen (the pre-release version of Photoshop CS2), just hold the Command key (PC: Control key) and choose About Photoshop from the Photoshop menu (or Help menu on a PC). It will show you the splash screen, displaying CS2's secret pre-release code name. I'm telling you, those engineers know how to party.

FALL IN LOVE WITH A TEMPORARY BRUSH, OR NOT

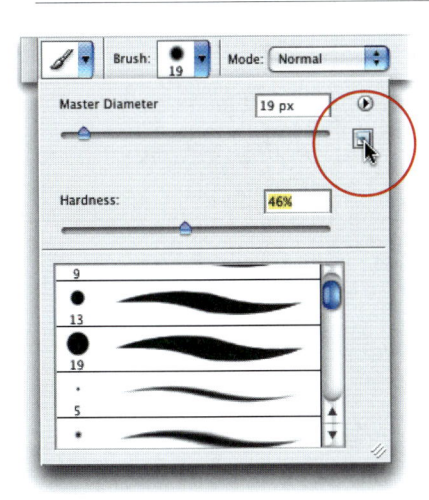

You can create a temporary brush anytime in Photoshop by playing with the options in the Brushes palette (which is nested in the Palette Well by default). After you make your choices, start painting. When you switch to another brush, the temporary brush you just created is gone. If you fall in love with your temporary brush (which is considered illegal in 48 states) and want to save it, before you change brush sizes, click on the Brush thumbnail in the Options Bar, and when the Brush Picker appears, click on the New Preset Brush icon in the upper right-hand corner, you sick pup.

CHAPTER 4 • Way Cool Tips 91

UNDO A SAVE? THAT'S IMPOSSIBLE, ISN'T IT?

This is a great trick we learned from our buddy Mike Ninness, and the first time we saw it, we said, "Hey, wait a minute, that can't be." Oh, but it be. It's how to undo a Save. This is especially helpful after you've flattened an image, saved the file, then realized that you needed to change something on a layer. This only happens to us about every other day, and here's the keyboard shortcut to fix it: Command-Option-Z (PC: Control-Alt-Z). Press it a few times after you've flattened and saved, and look in your Layers palette to see all the layers come a-rumbling right back. Pretty slick stuff.

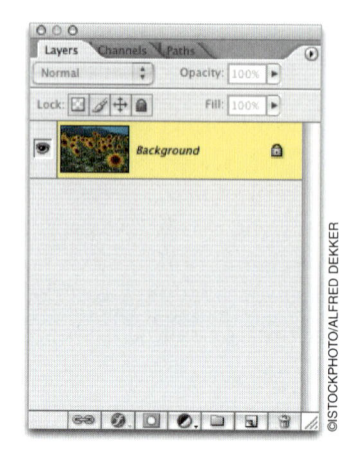

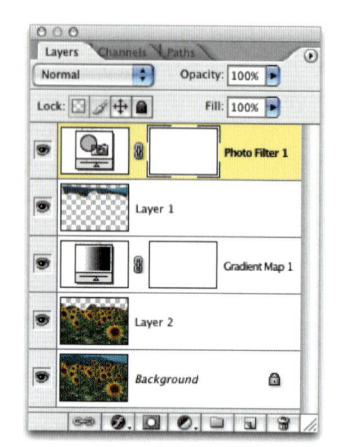

CHANGE BRUSH SOFTNESS ON THE FLY

You can increase or decrease the softness of a round brush in Photoshop without changing the size of the brush by pressing Shift-Left Bracket or Shift-Right Bracket. That's almost too easy.

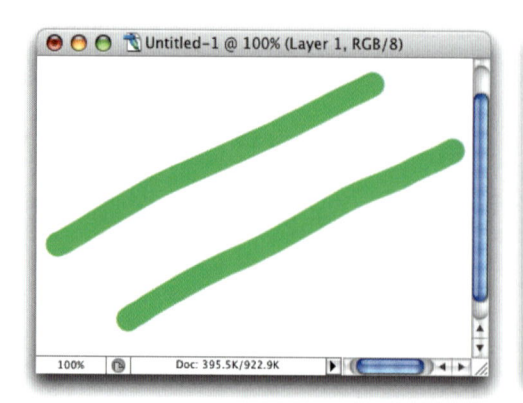

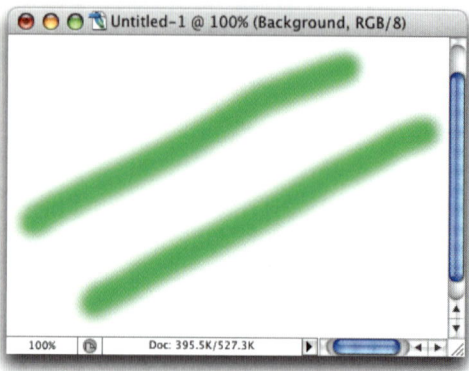

92   CHAPTER 4 • Way Cool Tips

HOW TO CORRECT ONE PROBLEM COLOR

Let's say you have an image, but the sky doesn't look as vibrant as you'd like, and you want to increase the amount of blue without affecting the rest of the image. Try this on for size: Open an image that contains a daylight sky. Click on the Create New Adjustment Layer pop-up menu at the bottom of the Layers palette and choose Color Balance. In the Color Balance dialog, drag the Blue slider all the way to the right (it looks bad now, but trust me) and click OK. Now, press B to switch to the Brush tool. Press the letter X until your Foreground color is black, and with a large, soft brush, start painting over the areas you don't want blue. As you paint, the blue Color Balance you added is painted away. The sky is much bluer, but you can paint away the added blue from the other areas. To really see the before/after difference, click the Eye icon next to the adjustment layer.

Before

After

CHAPTER 4 • Way Cool Tips

BUILDING A BETTER BACKGROUND ERASER TOOL

Here's a tip for making Photoshop's Background Eraser tool much more effective. Choose the Background Eraser tool (it's in the Eraser tool's flyout menu in the Toolbox), and in the Options Bar, lower the Tolerance setting to 20%. Click on the Brush thumbnail to open the Brush Picker and choose a large, hard-edged brush. Then, press P to switch to the Pen tool, making sure that the Paths icon (middle one at left in the Options Bar) is selected. Draw a path just outside the edge of the object you want to isolate (you don't have to be precise; in fact, stay just outside the edges of the object and draw straight lines all the way around the image). Go to the Paths palette (under the Window menu), and in the palette's flyout menu, choose Stroke Path. When the dialog appears, under Tool, choose Background Eraser, and click OK. The Background Eraser will instantly trace around your image, following the path you created. Now that the edges have been erased, you can use the regular Eraser tool to erase the rest of the background area.

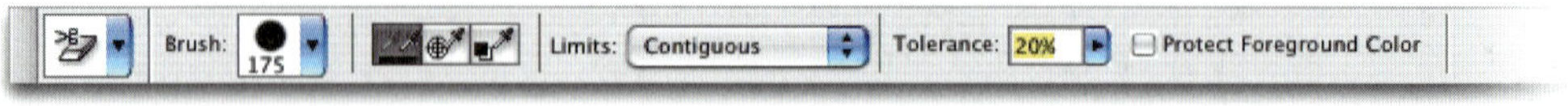

94 CHAPTER 4 • Way Cool Tips

CUSTOM BRUSHES: START WITH A CLEAN SLATE

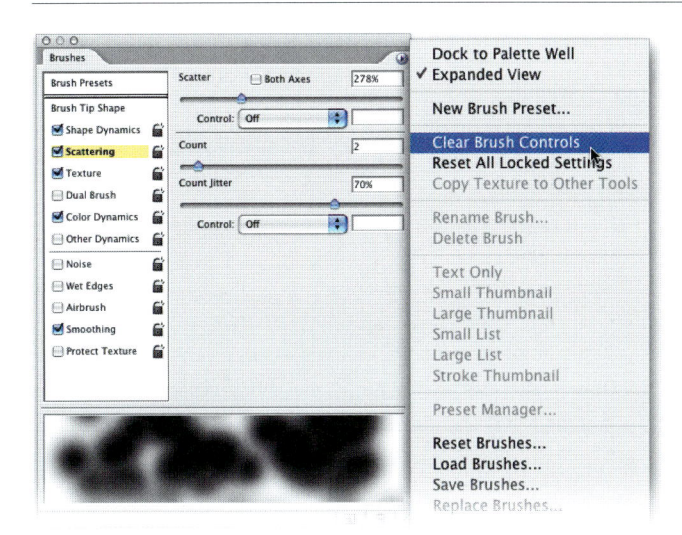

If you're going to build your own custom brush in Photoshop, sometimes it's easier to start with an existing brush and edit it. The problem is that you may have all sorts of settings already in place (Texture, Scattering, Shape Dynamics, etc., along with all their individual options). To set everything back to their defaults could take a while. At least it would if you didn't know this cool little trick: Click on the brush you want to use as your starting point for your custom brush, and in the Brushes palette, click on the options you want to edit (like Texture, Scattering, etc.). Then, from the palette's flyout menu, choose Clear Brush Controls, and all the selected options will be instantly reset to their default settings.

TIMING IS EVERYTHING!

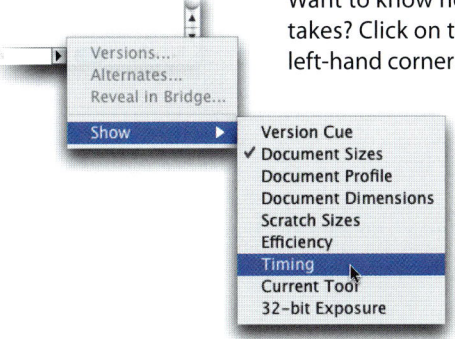

Want to know how long a particular Photoshop command takes? Click on the right-facing triangle toward the bottom left-hand corner of your image window. From the pop-up menu that appears, under Show, choose Timing. This starts the equivalent of a stopwatch that times your Photoshop commands in seconds. This is great for speed tests, pitting one machine against another. Which one runs the fastest Smart Sharpen? Time it and find out.

CHAPTER 4 • Way Cool Tips

Fast & Furious

CAMERA RAW TIPS →

Hey there, it's me again (Felix). So here we are halfway through this book and Scott is having entirely too much fun writing these chapter intros. In fact, I just walked past his office

Fast & Furious
camera raw tips

and he was grinning from ear to ear. I asked what was so funny. He mumbled something about an old What's Happening!! *episode and how Raj, Dwayne and Rerun just crack him up. But I saw the chapter intro template on his PowerBook. I knew what he was up to.*

So, how can I best describe this chapter (before Scott discovers I snuck another one in while he's pretending to watch back-to-back episodes of Good Times, *and* Mama's Family*)? Well, it's like this. Imagine that Camera Raw is like* The Facts of Life. *You know, Tootie was the backbone of that show and Blair was simply riding her coattails after the second season. Sorry, I got sidetracked. The tips in this chapter are more like* Different Strokes. *You remember when Arnold would say, "What you talkin' 'bout Willis?" Now that was sitcom writing at its finest. Dang, I'm doing it again. Let me get back on track. OK, Camera Raw is really more like* Mork and Mindy. *Nanu-nanu is just another way to describe the histogram and how it... No, that's no good. I got it. Imagine you're Weezy, George Jefferson is the Metadata and Florence is like your digital camera's color space, and...*

CHAPTER 5 • Camera Raw Tips **97**

BLACK-AND-WHITE CONVERSIONS IN CAMERA RAW

Believe it or not, Camera Raw is great for creating black-and-white conversions. Start by opening a RAW image, then lowering the Saturation to –100. Adjust the Exposure and Shadows sliders to create a nice contrasty image, then drag the Contrast slider to the right to give the image even more contrast. Now try all the different White Balance presets until you find the one that looks best for your particular conversion. You can even add sharpening if you like by clicking on the Detail tab and adjusting the Sharpness slider. And best of all, you can create a surprisingly good black-and-white image before it actually enters Photoshop CS2.

DON'T CLICK THE WHITE BALANCE TOOL ON SOMETHING WHITE

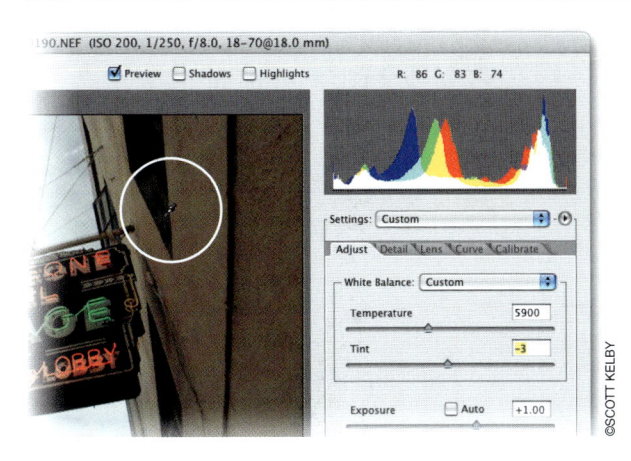

The White Balance tool (I) actually works best by clicking on something in your photo that is light gray, rather than clicking on something that is supposed to be white. Once you've clicked on a light gray area, use the Tint and Temperature sliders if you want to tweak the white balance a little bit, but use the White Balance tool to do most of the work.

UPDATING THE HISTOGRAM AS YOU CROP

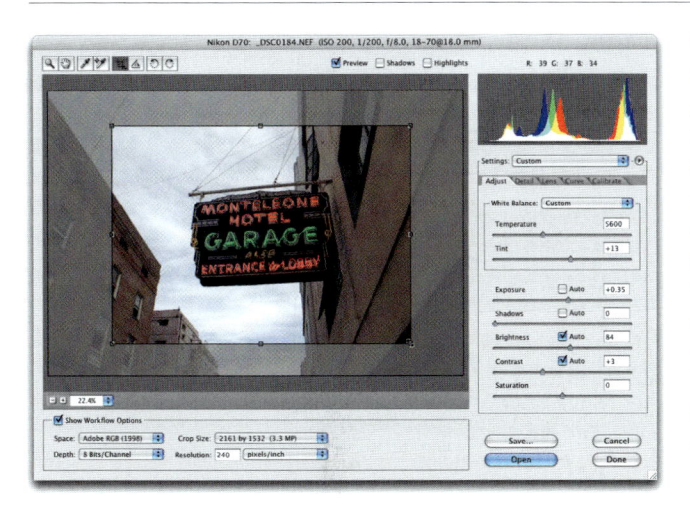

The fact that Camera Raw has cropping built in should be cool enough, but its Crop tool (C) is smarter than Photoshop's. For example, when you drag out a cropping border in Camera Raw, take a look at the histogram in the top-right corner—it instantly updates to show you the histogram for *just* the areas that appear inside your cropping border. Sweet!

CHAPTER 5 • Camera Raw Tips   99

SLIDE AWAY THE ABERRATIONS

If you see areas of bright-colored fringe appearing around objects in your RAW photos, you're suffering from Chromatic Aberrations (well, you're not, but your camera's lens is). Under the Lens tab in Camera Raw, there are two sliders (Fix Red/Cyan Fringe and Fix Blue/Yellow Fringe) that let you slide those problems away, but seeing the problem clearly enough to eliminate the fringe is your first challenge. That's why you'll want to know this tip: If you hold the Option key (PC: Alt key) while you're dragging either Chromatic Aberration slider, it will only show the two channels you're adjusting in the preview area, making it easier to see—and repair—the problem.

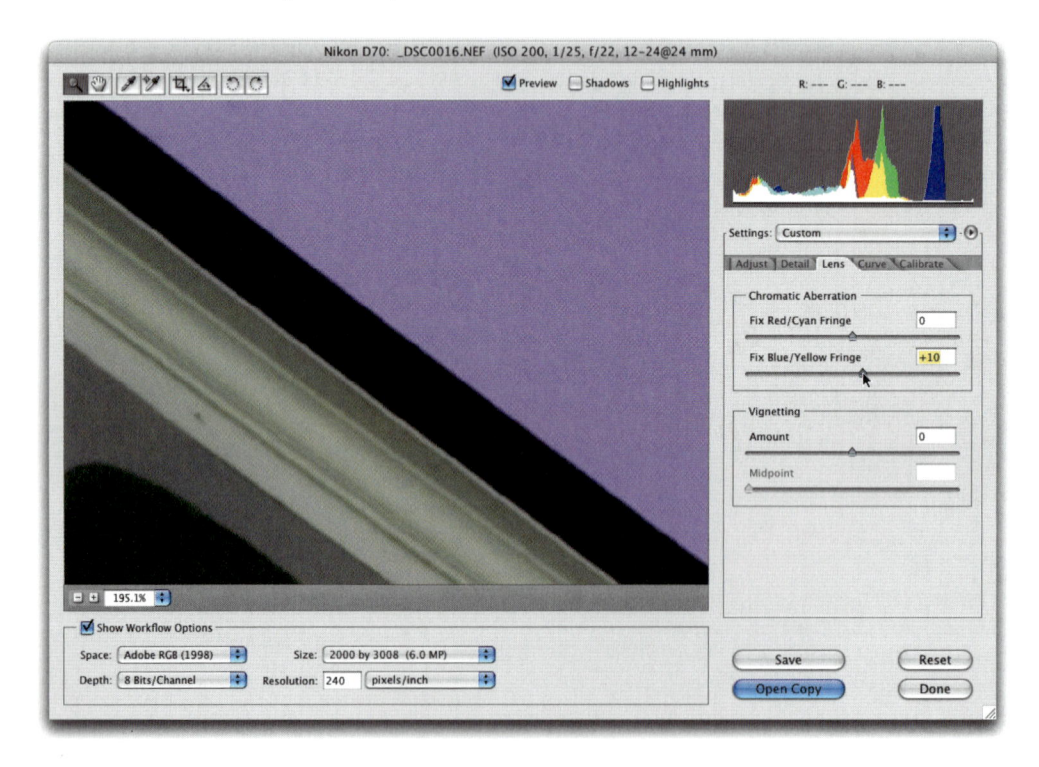

CHAPTER 5 • Camera Raw Tips

SEEING YOUR RAW IMAGE WITHOUT THE AUTO CORRECTIONS

By default, when you open a RAW image in Photoshop CS2, Camera Raw looks at the EXIF data embedded into your photo by your digital camera to find out which type of camera it was taken with, and once it knows, it applies a set of Auto corrections to the photo's exposure, shadows, brightness, and contrast. If you'd like to see what your RAW image looked like before Camera Raw applied these Auto corrections, just press Command-U (PC: Control-U), and it turns off all the Auto corrections to give you a clear, uncorrected view. Pretty bad, eh? So press Command-U (PC: Control-U) to turn those bad boys right back on.

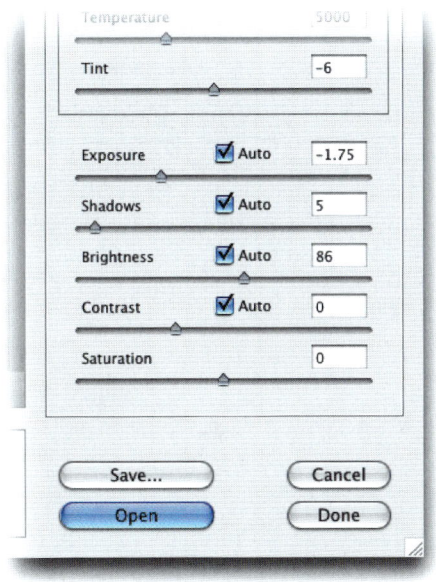

Default Auto corrections 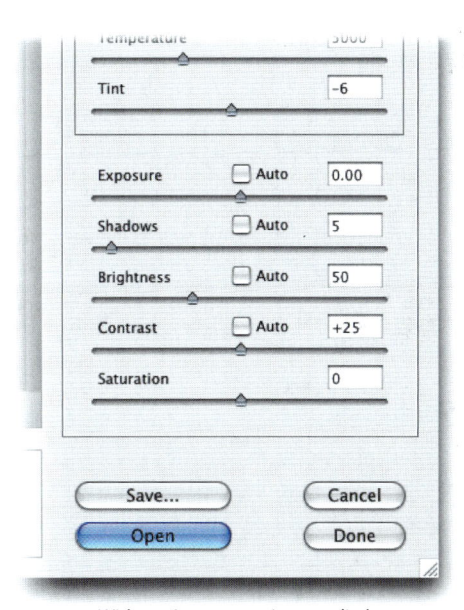 *Without Auto corrections applied*

CHAPTER 5 • Camera Raw Tips   101

TOGGLING THE PREVIEW ON/OFF

So, have the adjustments you've made in Camera Raw helped or hurt your photo? Just press the letter P and you'll quickly find out. This turns the preview of your changes off, and shows how the original file looked before you started tweaking it. To turn the preview back on, just press P again.

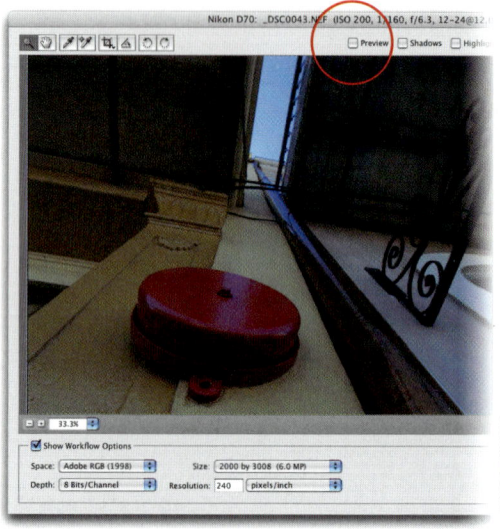

TURNING OFF AUTO CORRECTION FOR GOOD

If you don't like the Auto corrections that are applied to your RAW images by default, you can change things so that when you open photos from your camera, it will no longer perform any Auto corrections. Here's how: Open a RAW image and press Command-U (PC: Control-U) to turn off all the Auto corrections in Camera Raw. Then go under the flyout menu (to the right of the Settings pop-up menu) and choose Save New Camera Raw Defaults. Now, when you open a photo taken with the same camera make and model, it will no longer apply any of the Auto settings.

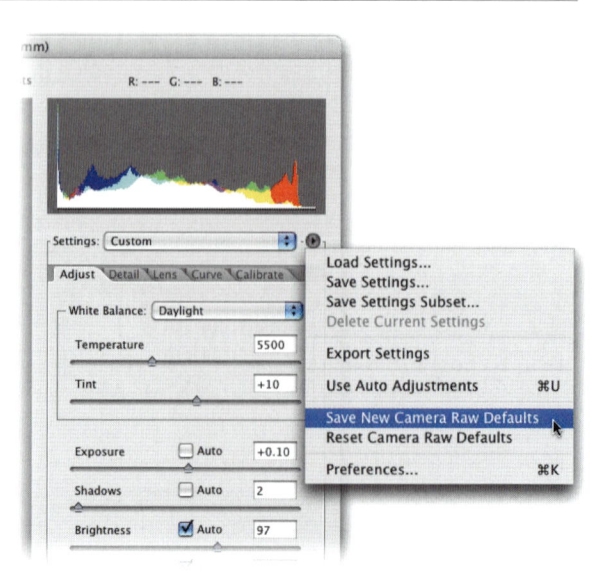

102   CHAPTER 5 • Camera Raw Tips

HOW TO UNDO THE WHITE BALANCE TOOL

If you used the White Balance tool (I) to set the white balance in your image, and you don't like the results, you can undo your white balance setting by double-clicking on the White Balance tool in Camera Raw's Toolbox.

GETTING MORE READOUTS PER EYEDROPPER

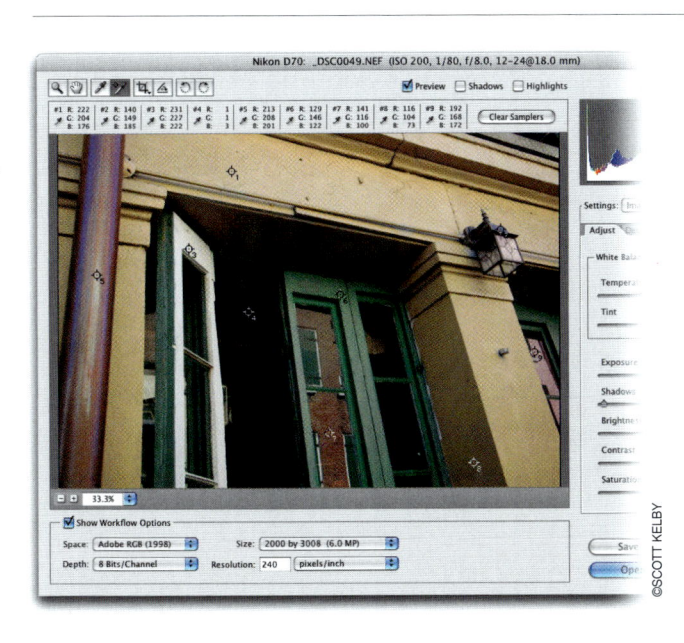

In Photoshop CS2, the Color Sampler tool can give you readings from up to four different places, but the Color Sampler in Camera Raw is more powerful and monitors even more areas for you. Each time you click the tool, another set of readings appears at the top of the Camera Raw dialog, and although it looks like six is the maximum number of color samplers you can add to your image (because the top of the Camera Raw dialog looks full), you can actually add three more (for a total of nine color samplers). Try it, and you'll see the six samplers squeeze to accommodate three more samplers. Now, I have to say, if you need to monitor the color in nine different areas of your image, perhaps working with RAW images shouldn't be your biggest concern.

CHAPTER 5 • Camera Raw Tips

SHORTCUTS FOR HIGHLIGHT AND SHADOW WARNINGS

If you're going to be using CS2's new Highlight and Shadow clipping warnings, here are two shortcuts you'll need to know: Press the letter O to turn on the Highlight clipping warning (everything that appears highlighted in red is clipping), and press U to toggle on/off the Shadow clipping warning (everything that appears in blue is clipped to solid black with no detail).

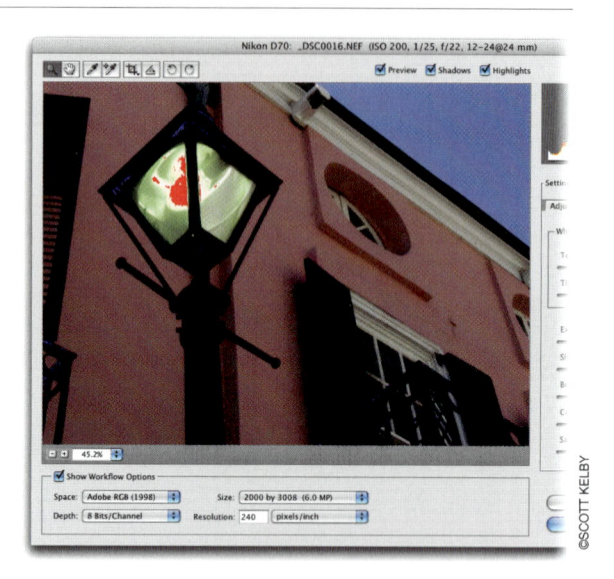

CANCELLING A CROP IN CAMERA RAW

If you're using the Crop tool (C) in Camera Raw, and decide you want to cancel your Crop, just click on the Crop tool, then press the Escape key on your keyboard.

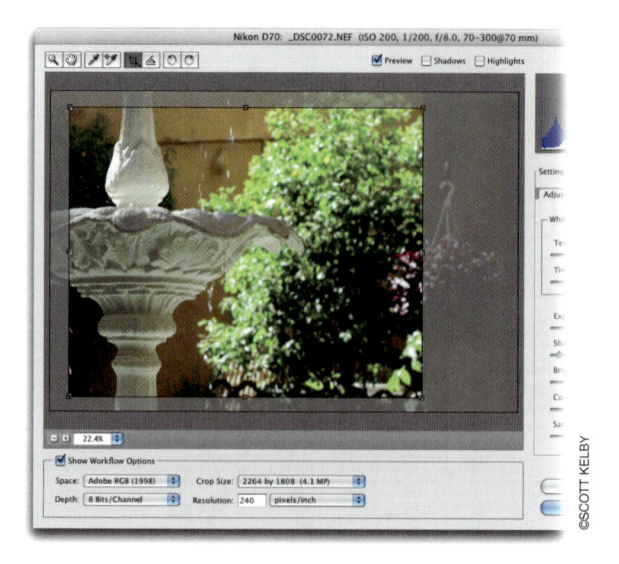

104   CHAPTER 5 • Camera Raw Tips

REMOVING A STRAIGHTEN IN CAMERA RAW

The Straighten tool (A) and the Crop tool (C) in Camera Raw are pretty much tied together. So much so, in fact, that if you want to cancel your straightening, you have to first click on the Crop tool (if it's not active by default after dragging with the Straighten tool), then press the Escape key on your keyboard.

HOW TO SEE THE SHARPENING NOW, BUT NOT APPLY IT

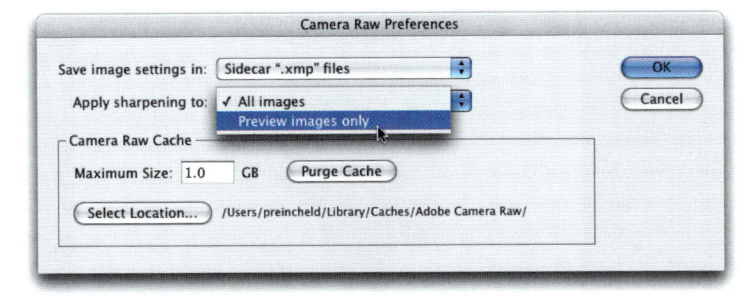

Many pros prefer to apply their sharpening in Photoshop itself, using Unsharp Mask or the Smart Sharpen filter, rather than in Camera Raw. If that sounds like you, wouldn't it be nice to just see what the sharpening would look like, even if you don't apply it? Of course, you could simply adjust the Sharpening slider (under the Detail tab) for a moment, look at the image, then slide it back—but there's a better way. While you have an image open in Camera Raw, press Command-K (PC: Control-K) to open the Camera Raw Preferences. When the dialog appears, change the Apply Sharpening To pop-up menu so it shows Preview Images Only. That way, any sharpening you apply in Camera Raw will only be applied to the preview you see onscreen in Camera Raw, and not the photo itself, so you can apply it later in Photoshop.

CHAPTER 5 • Camera Raw Tips   105

ADDING POINTS TO CAMERA RAW'S CURVE

Camera Raw in CS2 has its own curves adjustments (under the Curve tab), but adding a point to the curve is different in Camera Raw than it is in Photoshop. To plot a point on your curve in Photoshop, you just click the Eyedropper on the spot in your image you want plotted. But in Camera Raw, you have to Command-click (PC: Control-click) the Eyedropper instead.

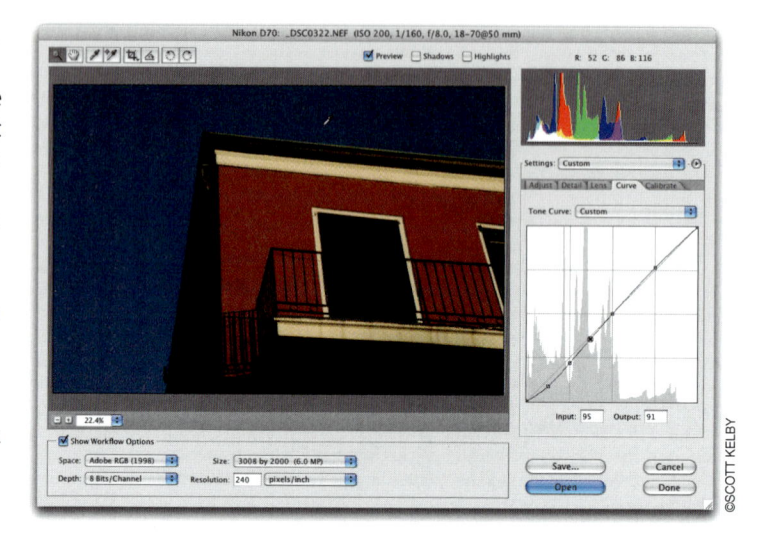

SHORTCUT FOR ROTATING IMAGES IN CAMERA RAW

Save yourself a trip up to Camera Raw's Toolbox the next time you need to rotate an image. Just press L on your keyboard to rotate to the left or press R to rotate to the right. To rotate completely around, just keep pressing either letter.

CROPPING MULTIPLE RAW IMAGES AT ONCE

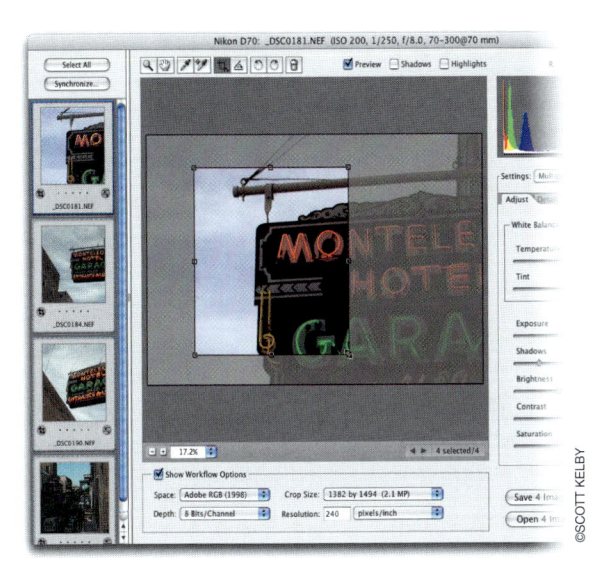

Want to crop just one RAW image and have that exact same crop applied to a number of similar RAW images at once? In Adobe Bridge, just Command-click (PC: Control-click) on all the RAW images you want to crop, then press Command-R (PC: Control-R) to open them in Camera Raw. Next, click the Select All button in the top-left corner of the Camera Raw dialog. Now press C to get the Crop tool, drag out your cropping border within the image in the preview area, and as you drag it out for the current photo, all the other selected photos will get the same cropping treatment, which will be reflected immediately in the list of images on the left side of Camera Raw.

LAST-MINUTE RENAMING IN RAW

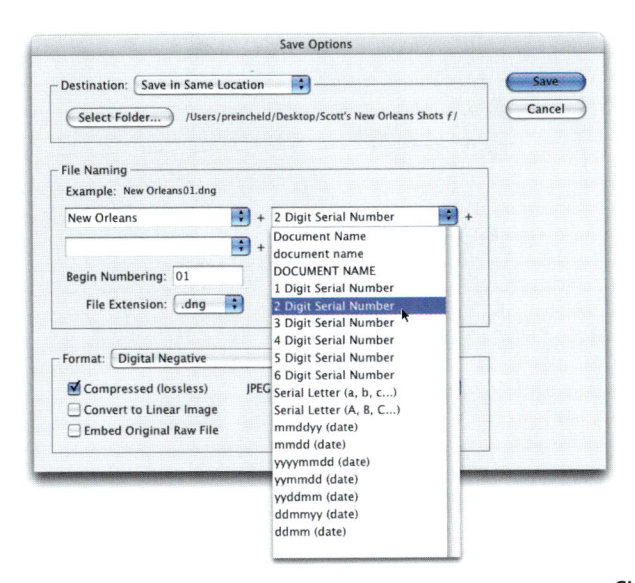

If you haven't renamed your photos, and you're busy processing them in Camera Raw, don't sweat it—you'll have an opportunity to rename them when you save them. In fact, when you choose Save in the Camera Raw dialog, the Save As screen that appears lets you batch rename the photos as they're saved. Just type the name you want in the first field, then the numbering scheme you want to use (after all, they can't all have the exact same name, right?).

CHAPTER 5 • Camera Raw Tips   107

BIGGER PREVIEWS IN CAMERA RAW

If you want a larger preview window in Camera Raw, you're only one click away. Just turn off the Show Workflow Options checkbox in the bottom-left corner of Camera Raw, and those options will be tucked out of sight, and your preview area will be expanded.

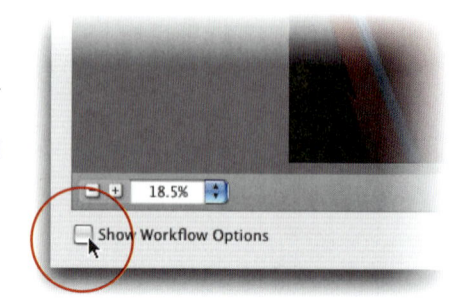

USE YOUR FAVORITE NAVIGATION SHORTCUTS IN CAMERA RAW

If you want to change the size of your preview window in Camera Raw, you can use most of the same keyboard shortcuts you already use in Photoshop. For example, to zoom in press Command–+ (Plus Sign) (PC: Control–+), and to zoom out press Command–– (Minus Sign) (PC: Control––). To jump to Fit on Screen view, double-click on the Hand tool. To jump to 100% size, double-click on the Zoom tool. To temporarily get the Hand tool, press-and-hold the Spacebar, then click-and-drag within the preview area.

108 CHAPTER 5 • Camera Raw Tips

MAKE IT ALWAYS FIT IN CAMERA RAW

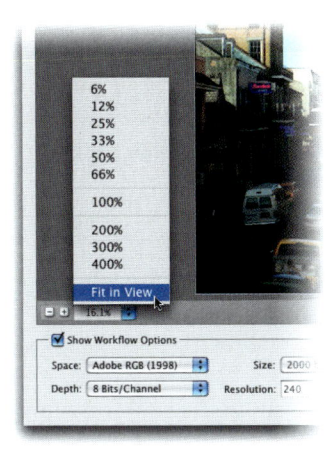

Here's a new viewing option—it's called Fit in View. It's found in the Zoom pop-up menu in the bottom-left corner of Camera Raw's preview window, and when you select it, it displays your entire photo as large as it can in the preview area.

HOW ABOUT A JPEG WITH THE RAW FILE? OH, A TIFF TOO?

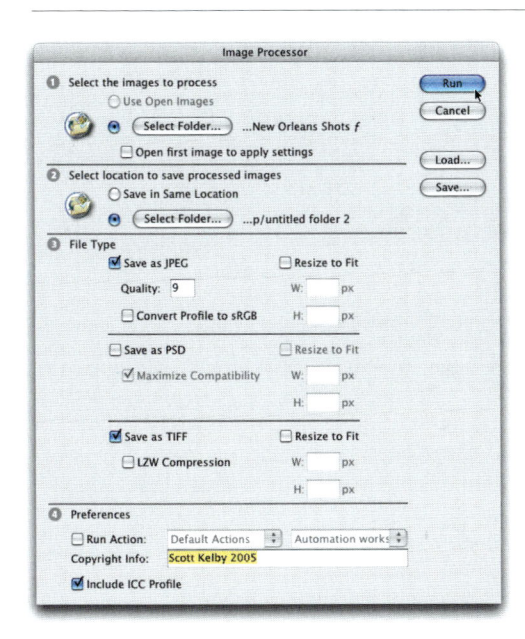

If you decide that you want to create JPEGs from all your RAW images, the entire process is automated in CS2, but you don't do it from Camera Raw—you do it within Photoshop. You start by going under Photoshop's File menu, under Scripts, and choosing Image Processor. When the dialog appears, choose your folder of RAW photos, then choose the folder where you want the new JPEGs saved. In the third section, you choose the file type and the size you want your images to be. Do you want just JPEGs, or also TIFFs and PSDs as well? It's up to you. If you like, you can apply an action to your images and a copyright while you're at it. Once you've entered your preferences and clicked Run, Image Processor automatically creates separate folders (inside the folder you indicated in section two) for each type of file (JPEG, TIFF, or PSD).

CHAPTER 5 • Camera Raw Tips   109

DON'T CHANGE YOUR CAMERA'S COLOR SPACE FOR RAW

If you're shooting only in RAW (and not RAW+JPEG), then you don't have to worry about changing the color space in your digital camera to match the edit space in Photoshop. That's because you'll actually choose the color profile that will be assigned to the photo right before you process the RAW file—it comes in "untagged." It's RAW after all, right? So choose your color profile from the Space pop-up menu in the bottom-left corner of the Camera Raw dialog before you open the image in Photoshop. (*Note:* If you don't see the Space menu, turn on the Show Workflow Options checkbox.)

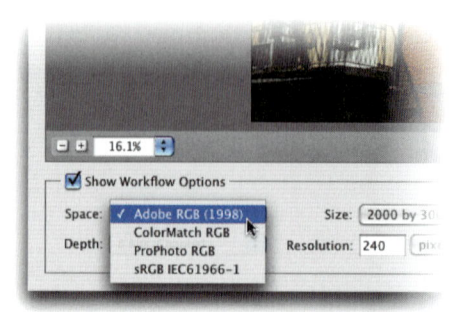

MAKING YOUR PHOTO BIGGER? DO IT IN RAW!

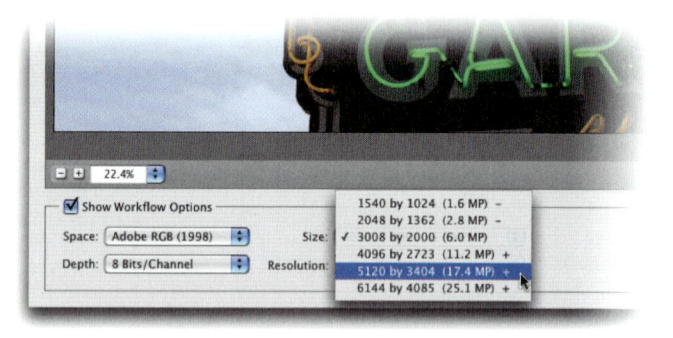

Another advantage of working with RAW images comes when you need to make your image larger than the original. Of course, this is generally thought of as a big no-no because making a photo bigger than its original usually means a major loss of sharpness and quality, but if you're shooting RAW, well…not so much. Well, not nearly as much. So, all you have to do is go to Camera Raw's Workflow Options (in the bottom-left corner of the dialog), and from the Size pop-up menu choose a larger size (make sure you also choose 8 Bits/Channel for your depth), and you'll get much better results from your forbidden upsizing than you would have if you tried to do the same thing in Photoshop using the Image Size dialog (under the Image menu).

110 CHAPTER 5 • Camera Raw Tips

HIDING YOUR METADATA FROM OTHERS

If you're providing photos to magazines, websites, or really just about anybody, you might want to strip out your metadata, or anybody with Photoshop will be able to learn a lot about you. For example, they'll know what kind of camera and lens you have (including make and model), what day you took the photo, edited the photo, and so on. Luckily, stripping the data out is easy, because you don't really strip it out. Just do this: Open the photo in Photoshop. Press Command-A (PC: Control-A) to select all, then press Command-C (PC: Control-C) to copy the photo into memory. Press Command-N (PC: Control-N) to create a new blank document in the same size, color mode, and resolution of your copied photo. Don't change anything; just click OK. When the new document appears, press Command-V (PC: Control-V) to paste your copied photo into your new document. Press Command-E (PC: Control-E) to merge this image layer with your Background layer, and save the file. The embedded EXIF data is left behind, giving you a clean image with no personal data attached.

CHAPTER 5 • Camera Raw Tips   111

HOW TO GET BACK WHERE YOU STARTED IN CAMERA RAW

If you've made a number of adjustments in Camera Raw, and you're not happy with them and just want to get back to where you started, go to the Camera Raw Settings pop-up menu (it's just above the White Balance pop-up menu) and choose Camera Raw Defaults. That'll put the photo back to how it looked when you opened it.

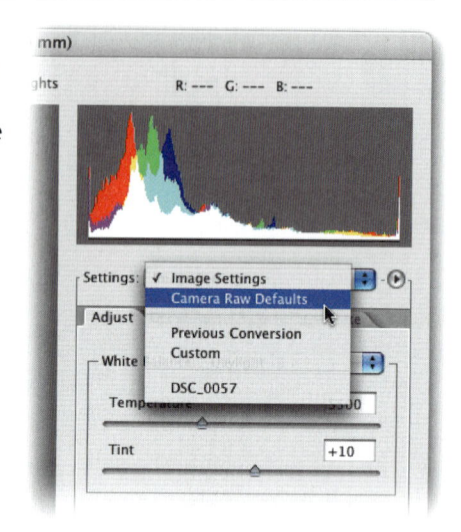

BYPASS CAMERA RAW'S ANNOYING SAVE AS DIALOG

If you've been processing images and you want to quickly save a file with the settings you've just applied, you don't have to have the whole Save As dialog appear, which just takes up time and space. Instead, hold the Option key (PC: Alt key), and then click the Save button. It will simply save your image and apply the settings you selected without closing the Camera Raw dialog. It's faster, it's funner, and it's all gooder as well.

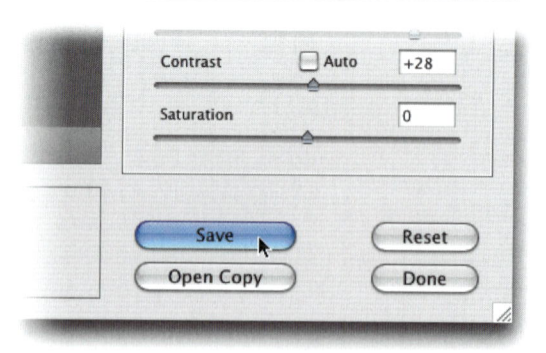

SORTING IMAGES IN CAMERA RAW

When most of us think about sorting or rating images, we think about Bridge, but believe it or not, you can pretty much do the same thing right within Camera Raw. For example, let's say you open 60 images in Camera Raw. You can toggle through the different images by clicking on the left/right arrows in the bottom-right side of the preview window. To delete any image you don't like, click on the Trash icon in the Toolbox (it only appears when you have multiple images open). To add a star rating to a file, just click on it in the list of images on the left side of the dialog and drag out your rating below the image's thumbnail.

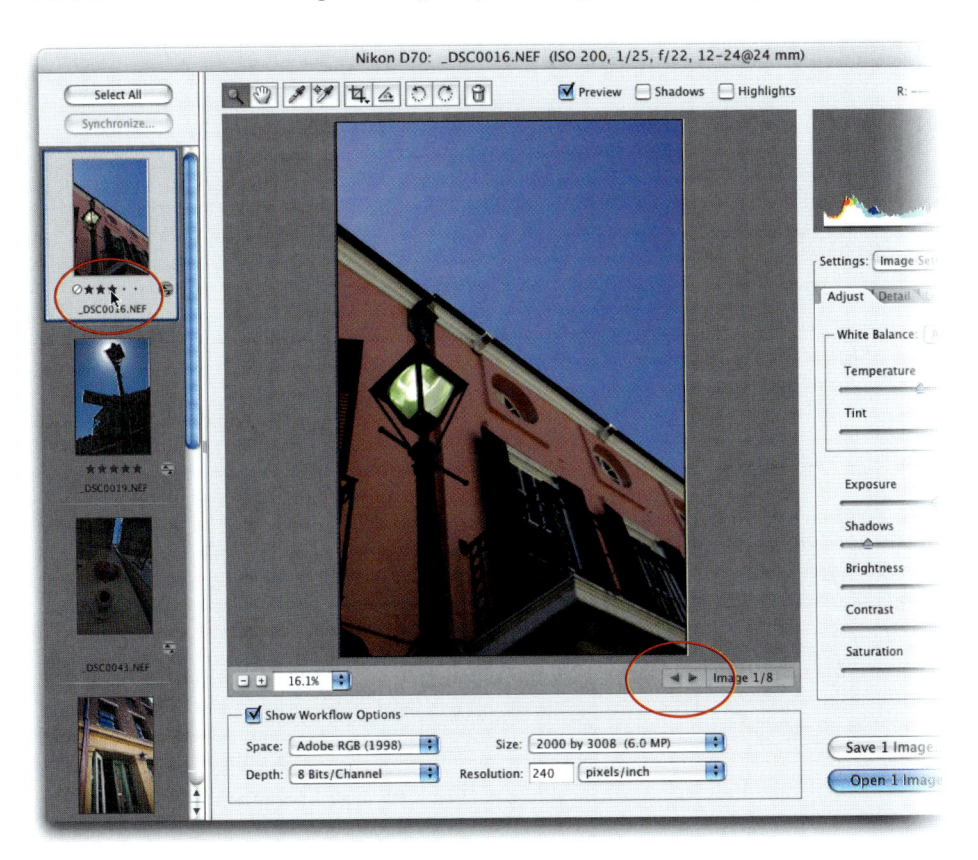

CHAPTER 5 • Camera Raw Tips   113

HAVING BRIDGE ALWAYS PROCESS YOUR RAW IMAGES

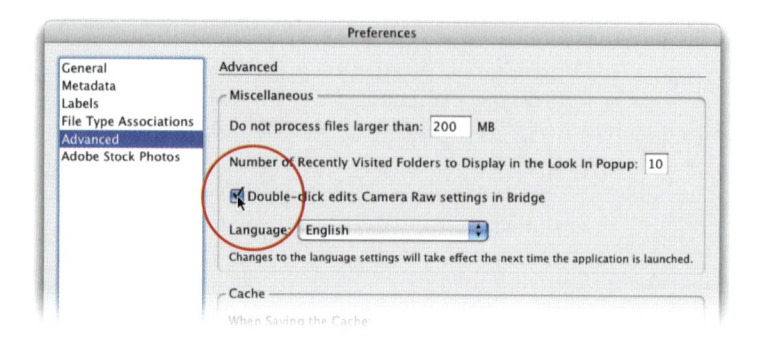

Double-clicking on a RAW image in Bridge opens that image in Photoshop's Camera Raw, but if you'd prefer to always have RAW images processed by Bridge's Camera Raw instead, just press Command-K (PC: Control-K) to open Bridge's Preferences, and in the list on the left side of the dialog, click on Advanced. When the Advanced options appear, turn on the checkbox named Double-Click Edits Camera Raw Settings in Bridge.

HOW TO TELL CAMERA RAW WHICH PHOTO TO USE FOR EDITS

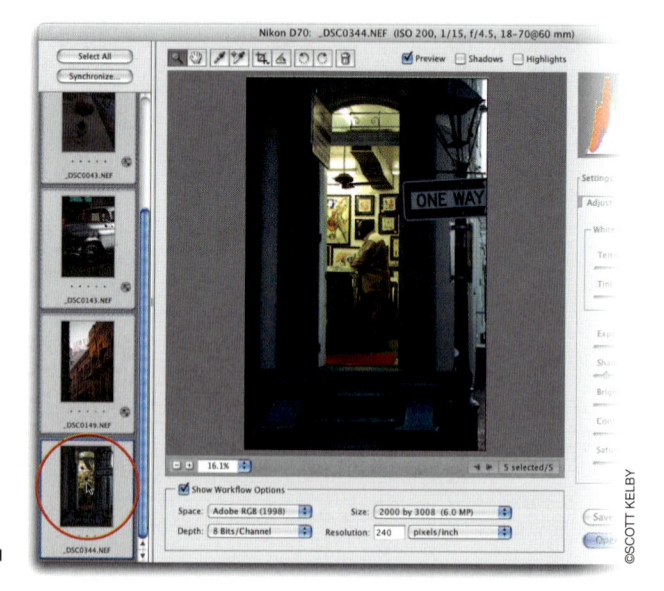

When you open multiple RAW images in Camera Raw, if you press Command-A (PC: Control-A) to select them all, any change you make to the top image in the list will be made to all the other selected images. But what if you'd prefer to edit the fourth or fifth image down, and have all the rest adjusted the same way (rather than having to adjust the first photo in the list)? It's easy—once all the photos are selected, Option-click (PC: Alt-click) on the photo along the left side that you want to base all your edits on. That photo will now appear in the preview window, and changes you make to it will also be applied to all other selected RAW photos.

114   CHAPTER 5 • Camera Raw Tips

LIKE THE EDITS YOU MADE TO ONE PHOTO? APPLY THEM TO OTHERS

If you've got a number of photos open in Camera Raw, and you make some edits to one of those photos, and you think to yourself, "Hey, that doesn't look bad," you can quickly apply those same edits to other images. Here's how: Once you've made your edits to an image, Command-click (PC: Control-click) on the photos along the left side of the dialog to which you want to apply the same edits. Then click on the Synchronize button in the top-left side of Camera Raw. This brings up a dialog with a checkbox list of all the edits you can do in Camera Raw. If you want all the changes you applied to the first image to be applied to your selected images, choose Everything from the Synchronize pop-up menu at the top of the dialog. If you only want a few edits applied, uncheck the checkboxes beside the options you don't want.

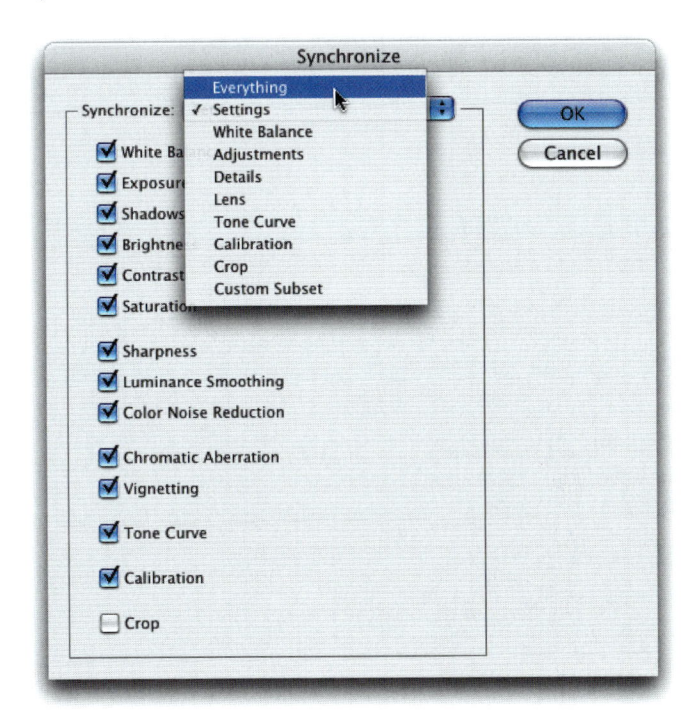

REMOVING YOUR EDITS TO A RAW IMAGE IN BRIDGE

If you've edited a RAW photo in Camera Raw, you'll see a little round two-slider icon below the RAW photo's thumbnail in Bridge. If you want to remove those edits, and return the image to the original unedited version (like it just came out of your camera), Control-click (PC: Right-click) on the thumbnail and choose Clear Camera Raw Settings.

CROPPING MULTIPLE IMAGES AT ONCE

If you've opened multiple images in Camera Raw, you can apply cropping to one of those images and then have that exact same cropping applied to as many other open images as you'd like, in just two clicks. First crop your selected image in the preview window using the Crop tool (C). Now select the other photos you want to crop by Command-clicking (PC: Control-click) on them in the list of open photos on the left side of the Camera Raw dialog. Then click on the Synchronize button. When the dialog appears, from the Synchronize pop-up menu at the top, choose Crop and click OK. All your selected photos will be cropped the same way you cropped the first photo.

116 CHAPTER 5 • Camera Raw Tips

CHAPTER 5 • Camera Raw Tips

Speedy Gonzalez

LAYER TIPS →

I know I'm supposed to write something compelling to make you want to read this chapter, but honestly, they're layer tips. Not that they're unimportant—they totally are. But

Speedy Gonzalez
layer tips

when you say it—"layer tips"—it just doesn't have enough oomph! This chapter name needs more oomph! By the way, as an aside, if you look up the word "oomph" in the 2003 Webster's Abridged Dictionary, Oxford Version, for the actual definition, it's "a bulkiness or powerful quality that is brought on by most chapter heads, with the notable exception of 'Layer Tips.'" Hey, I'm not making this stuff up. Those Webster guys are serious (especially the one who had his own show and was friends with Michael Jackson).

FINALLY, A SHORTCUT FOR CREATING A FLATTENED LAYER

I'm not talking about flattening your image. I'm talking about a new layer that contains a flattened version of your whole layered document, without flattening your layers. That's right—one layer that looks like your flattened document. You could do this in previous versions, but it took a little doin'. Now, it's just one simple keyboard shortcut, and it even creates the layer for you—it's Command-Option-Shift-E (PC: Control-Alt-Shift-E).

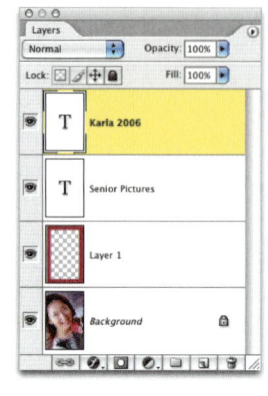

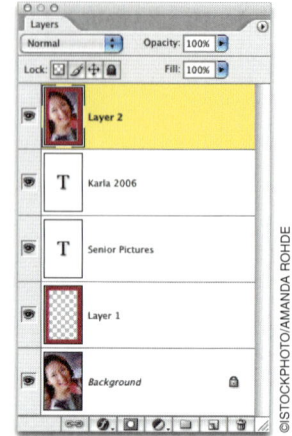

CHANGING OPACITY WHILE YOU'RE TRANSFORMING

Until CS2, this was impossible, but now when you have Free Transform active on a layer and you need to change the opacity of the layer you're transforming, you can do it by just going to the Layers palette and lowering the Opacity setting. But it's not just Opacity—you can change the blend mode as well. If you do photo restoration, or wind up having to take a head shot from one photo and composite it on another (the groom's eyes were closed, etc.), you know what a time saver this will be.

MOVING LAYER EFFECTS FROM ONE LAYER TO ANOTHER

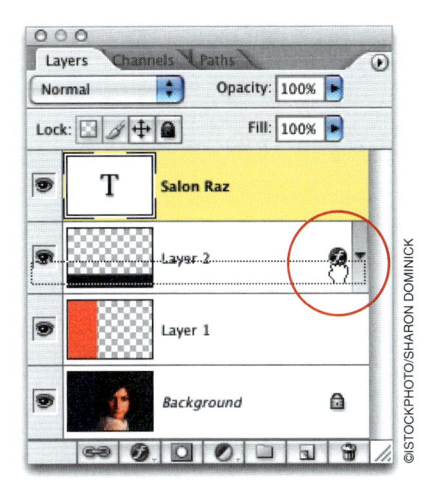

In previous versions of Photoshop, when you wanted to move an applied effect (like a drop shadow or bevel and emboss) from one layer and have it appear on another layer, you'd copy the effect from your original layer, then paste it onto your preferred layer, then go back to the original layer and drag the effect into the Trash. Four steps are just too much. How about only one—just drag the little round "*f*" icon from the active layer to the layer you want it on, and it relocates to that layer. If you want to duplicate the effect (rather than move it), just Option-drag (PC: Alt-drag) the icon.

CHAPTER 6 • Layer Tips   121

FASTER FLATTENING

In the past, if you wanted to flatten an image, there was only one way to do it—go to the Layers palette's flyout menu and choose Flatten Image. But in CS2, it's finally right at your fingertips. Just Control-click (PC: Right-click) on any image layer's name in the Layers palette and choose Flatten Image from the contextual menu that appears. It's not perfect, but it's faster than digging through the flyout menu. *Note:* The options in the contextual menu depend upon the type of layer on which you Command/Control-click.

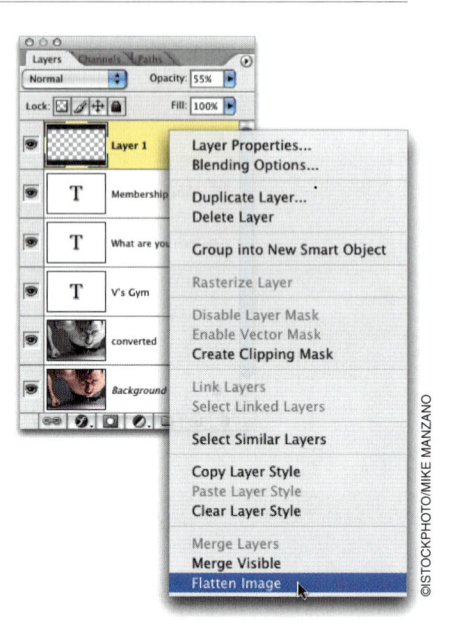

UNLINKING ALL YOUR LINKED LAYERS WITH A SINGLE CLICK

Here's another one we've been waiting (patiently, I might add) for a long time—the ability to unlink all your linked layers with a single click. Just click once on the Link icon at the bottom of the Layers palette and all layers linked to your current linked layer will be unlinked. See, if you just wait long enough….

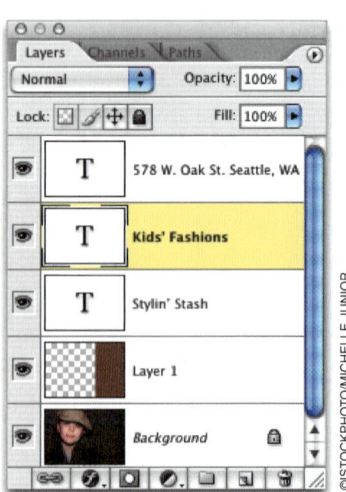

122   CHAPTER 6 • Layer Tips

TEMPORARILY UNLINKING A LAYER

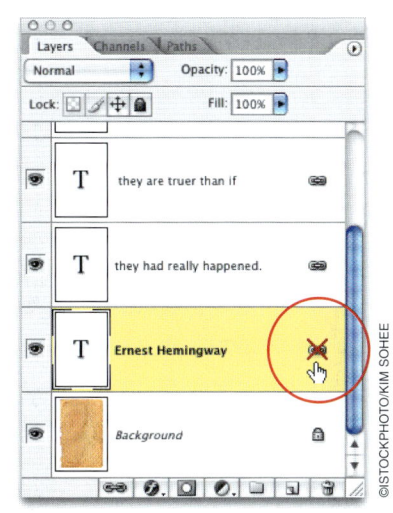

If you have a layer linked to another layer in CS2, you'll see a Link icon appear to the right of the layer's name (it appears there now, because the old Link column that used to appear to the left of layers is gone). If you hold the Shift key and click directly on that Link icon, that layer will be temporarily unlinked (you'll see a red X appear through that layer's Link icon). To relink it, just Shift-click on that icon again.

LOADING A LAYER SELECTION HAS CHANGED

For years now, when you wanted to put a selection around everything on a particular layer, you would Command-click (PC: Control-click) on that layer in the Layers palette, and it pretty much didn't matter where you clicked, as long as you clicked. Well, in CS2, it matters. You now have to click directly on the layer's thumbnail to get the selection to load. So what happens if you Command-click (PC: Control-click) on the other part of a layer (the layer's name for example)? It highlights that layer, so you can select multiple layers at a time.

CHAPTER 6 • Layer Tips   123

VISUAL CUES FOR A LAYER'S EDGE

Want to see where the edges of your current layer appear (especially handy if you're working with layers with soft edges)? Just go under the View menu, under Show, and choose Layer Edges. Now a thin blue border will appear around the edges of the currently selected layer to give you a visual cue of your layer's boundaries.

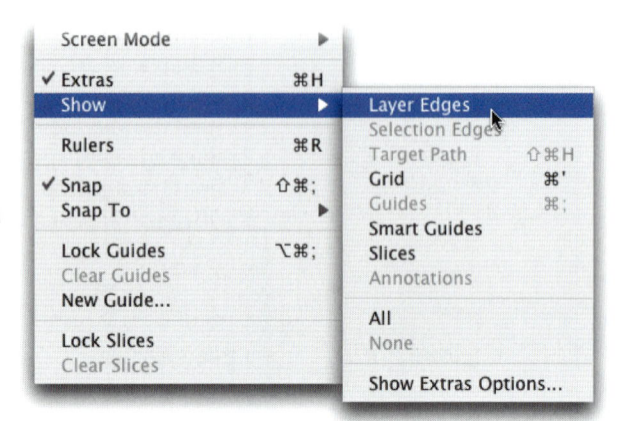

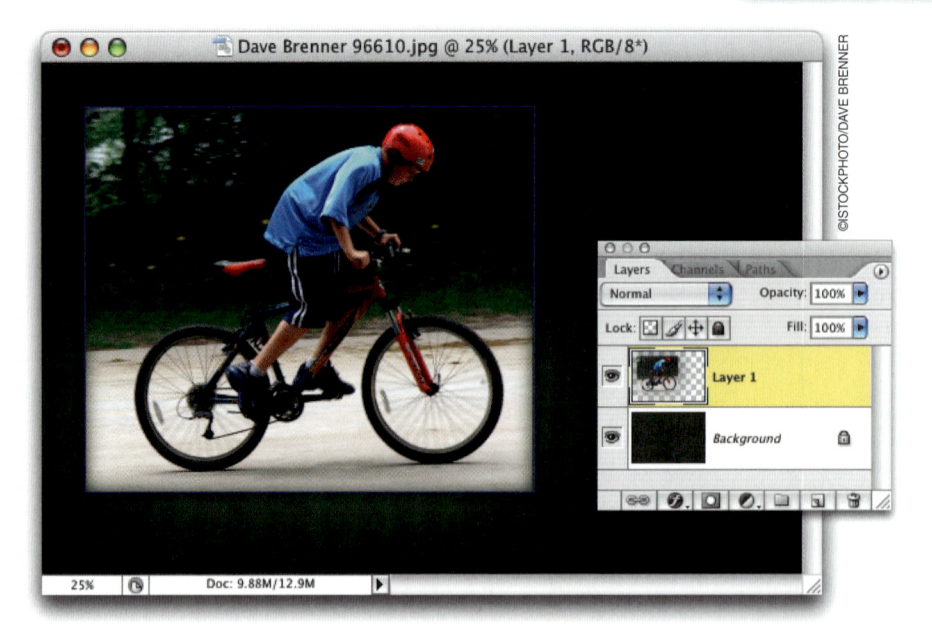

CHAPTER 6 • Layer Tips

DON'T WANT A GAP BETWEEN ITEMS? SNAP TO 'EM

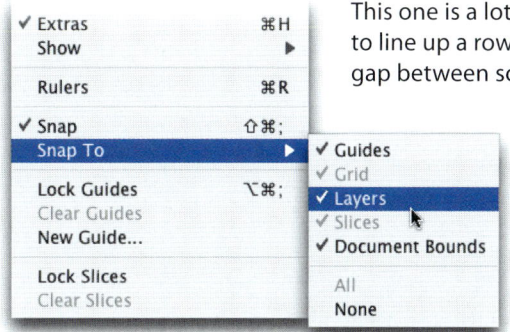

This one is a lot handier than it sounds. If you've ever tried to line up a row of objects, the last thing you want is a little gap between some of them (I just ran across this problem when I was trying to line up a row of television monitors for a video wall I was creating). Well, you don't have to have that gap anymore, because in CS2 you can actually have the layer you're moving snap right to the layer you're trying to align it to. Just go under the View menu, under Snap To, and choose Layers.

MOVING AND COPYING LAYER MASKS

If you wanted to move a layer mask from one layer to another, you used to have to jump through a few hoops, but in CS2 it's much easier. Just click directly on the layer mask's thumbnail and drag it to the layer where you want it. If you want a duplicate of a layer mask (rather than just moving it from one layer to another), press-and-hold the Option key (PC: Alt key) before you drag.

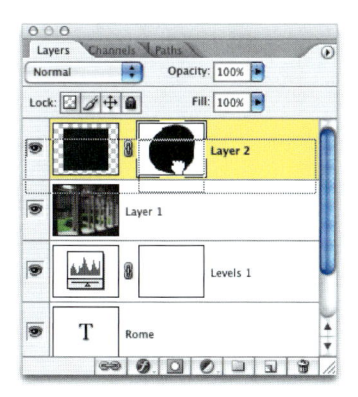

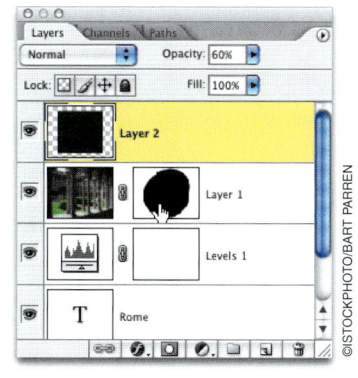

CHAPTER 6 • Layer Tips   125

INVERTING A MASK AS YOU MOVE IT

This isn't a hard tip, but it's the kind of thing that only advanced users would want to do. It's the hidden shortcut for inverting a layer mask as you duplicate it (see what I mean?) Well, anyway, here's the tip: First hold the Shift key, then click-and-drag the layer mask thumbnail to the layer you want it to appear on. If you want to invert and duplicate the mask (rather than move it), hold the Option key (PC: Alt key) as well—so the shortcut is Option-Shift (PC: Alt-Shift) to duplicate and invert.

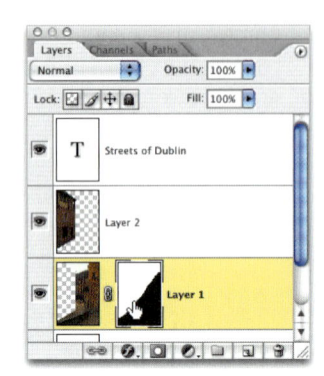

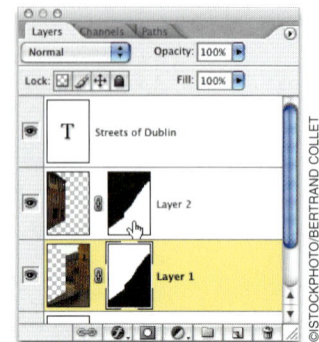

Here we duplicated and inverted the mask.

WANT TO "DRAG SELECT" LAYERS? YOU NEED TO TURN THIS ON

Although CS2 lets you "drag select" layers (and by that I mean you can drag out a selection around objects on layers in your document, and any layers your selection touches will become active in the Layers palette as if you linked them together), you have to know where to turn this feature on. First, press V to get the Move tool, then in the Options Bar turn on the checkbox for Auto Select Layer. Now, click-and-drag within your image and any layer that falls within your selection becomes active. Now you can move them as one unit.

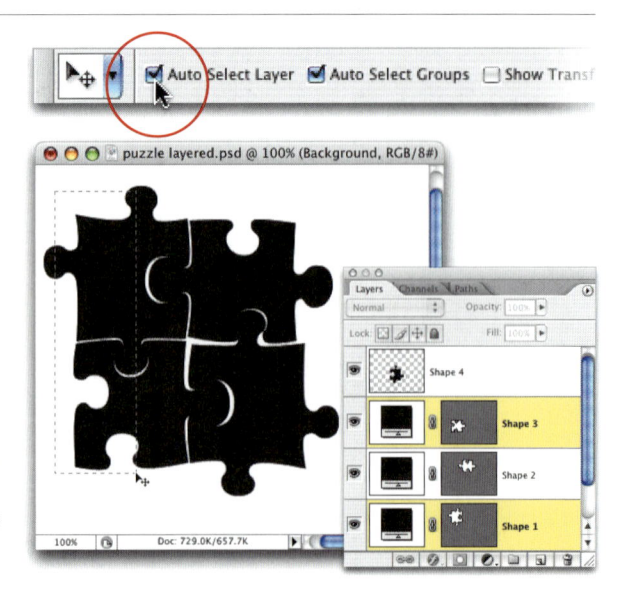

126   **CHAPTER 6** • Layer Tips

LAYER GROUP SUPER-SPEED TIP

Want a quicker way to create a Layer Group? Command-click (PC: Control-click) on all the layers you want to include in this new Group. Then press-and-hold the Shift key and click on the Create a New Group icon at the bottom of the Layers palette. This will create a brand new Group consisting of all of your linked layers.

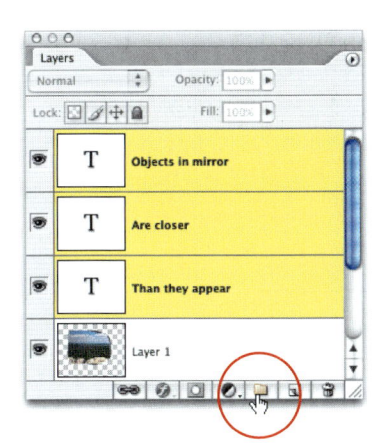

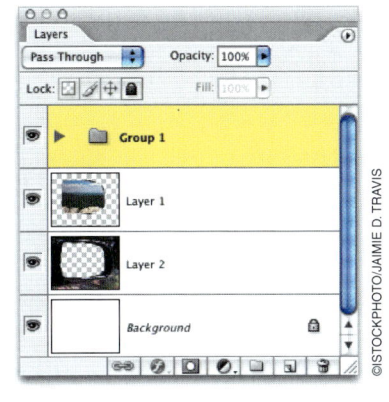

ALMOST A BUILT-IN FLATTENING SHORTCUT

I say "almost" because it works "almost" all the time. If you have a multilayered file and want to quickly flatten it, you can usually press Shift-Command-E (PC: Shift-Control-E). The only time it doesn't work is when you have a hidden layer, because what you're pressing is the new keyboard shortcut for Merge Visible. If all your layers are visible, it flattens them, but if even one layer is hidden, it won't merge all the layers, only the visible ones. So you can use this "almost" all of the time.

CHAPTER 6 • Layer Tips   127

JUMP TO ANY LAYER JUST BY CLICKING IN YOUR IMAGE

You can jump to any layer in your document without going to the Layers palette. Press V to switch to the Move tool. Now, press-and-hold the Command key (PC: Control key), and click on an object in your image that you want, and you'll instantly jump to that object's layer.

TURNING YOUR LAYERS INTO SEPARATE DOCUMENTS

If you have a multilayered document and want to turn each layer into its own separate document, just go under the File menu, under Scripts, and choose Export Layers To Files.

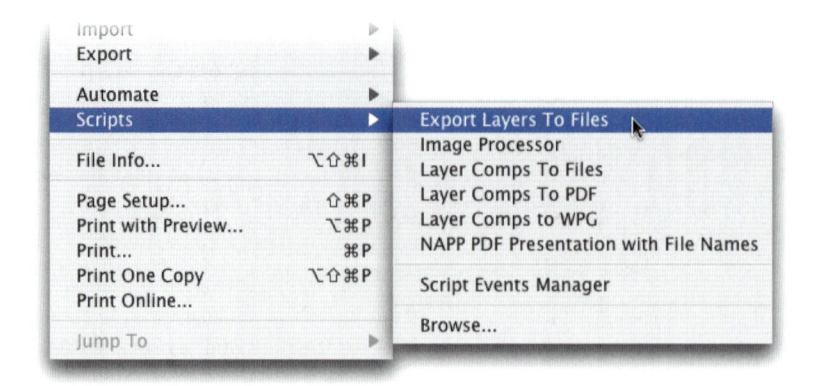

CHAPTER 6 • Layer Tips

OPENING LAYERED FILES WITHOUT ALL THE LAYERS

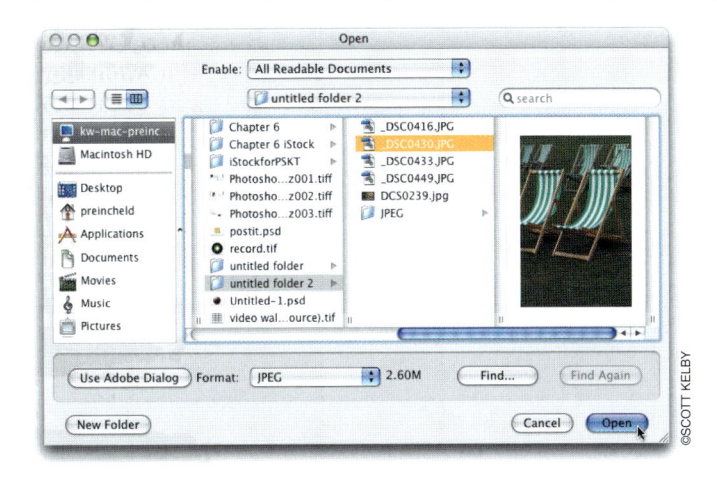

If you have a large multi-layered file, you know it can take a while to open, and that's fine—it's part of working with large files. But sometimes you're not going to actually work on the file, and you just want to open it, take a quick look at it, and then close it (maybe you just want to see if it's the version of the file you're looking for). So why waste time opening a huge multilayered file if you just want to take a quick look? Well, you don't have to—just go under the File menu, choose Open, and navigate to the layered file, but before you click the Open button, hold Option-Shift (PC: Alt-Shift). By holding those two keys down before you choose Open, it opens a flattened version of your layered file. Pretty darn slick.

MISSING YOUR BACKGROUND LAYER? HERE'S THE FIX

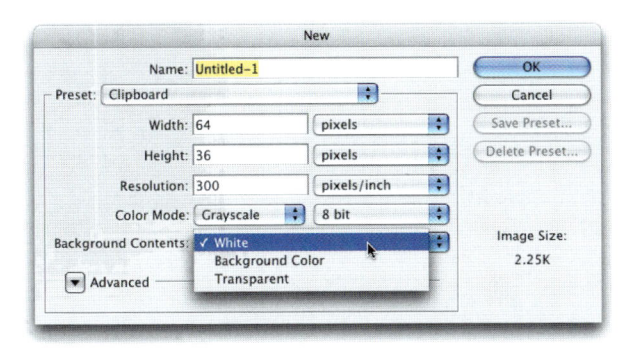

If you're opening new documents and they don't have a Background layer, there's a reason (of course there's a reason, everything has a reason; we just happen to know what it is). The reason is that you've selected the Transparent option in the New document dialog. That seems like a reasonable thing to do; everybody wants transparency, right? However, what it tells Photoshop is "Don't worry about creating a Background layer." To get Background layers again, the next time you're in the New dialog, under Background Contents, make sure you choose White, and from then on, you'll have Background layers in your documents.

CHAPTER 6 • Layer Tips   129

AVOIDING THE LAYER MENU

Once you've applied a layer style to a layer, if you need to access some related commands that are in the Layer menu, you don't need to go up to the menu bar and go digging through the submenus. Instead, Control-click (PC: Right-click) on the little "ƒ" icon that appears to the right of your layer's name in the Layers palette. A contextual menu will appear with most of the Layer Style menu commands right at your fingertips—without the searching and digging through menus.

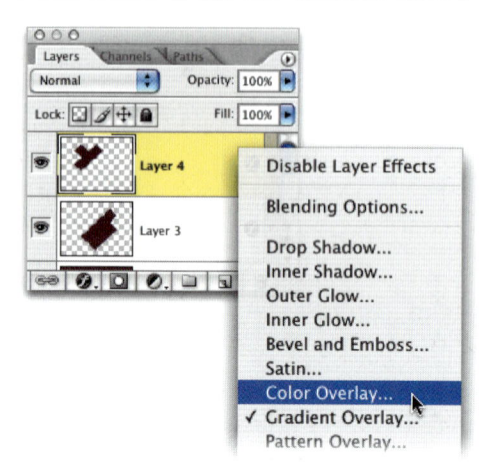

LOCK ALL THOSE LAYERS IN JUST ONE CLICK

You can lock all of your linked layers at once by choosing Select Linked Layers from the Layers palette's flyout menu, then choosing Lock Layers from the same menu. They'll kick and scratch for a while, but they'll eventually calm right down.

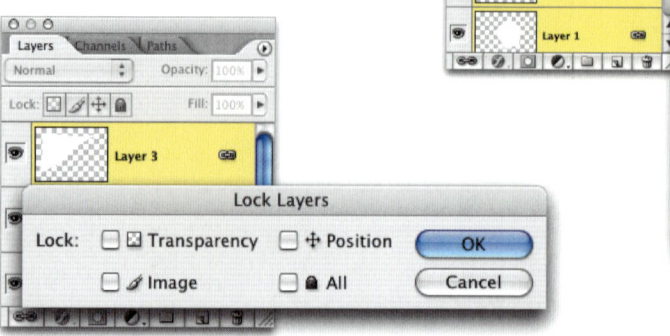

130 CHAPTER 6 • Layer Tips

TOGGLE THROUGH THE BLEND MODES

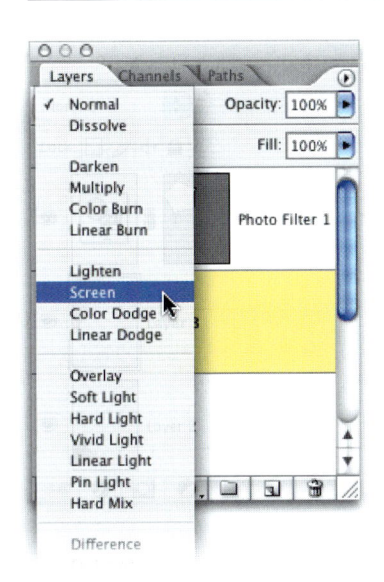

When I'm struggling to get just the right effect by changing the layer blend modes, it's great to be able to rotate through each mode without having to go back to the layer blend mode pop-up menu every time. To do this, simply switch to the Move tool (V), then press Shift–+ (Plus Sign). Every time you press it, it goes to the next blend mode.

HIDE YOUR OTHER LAYERS IN THE BLINK OF AN EYE

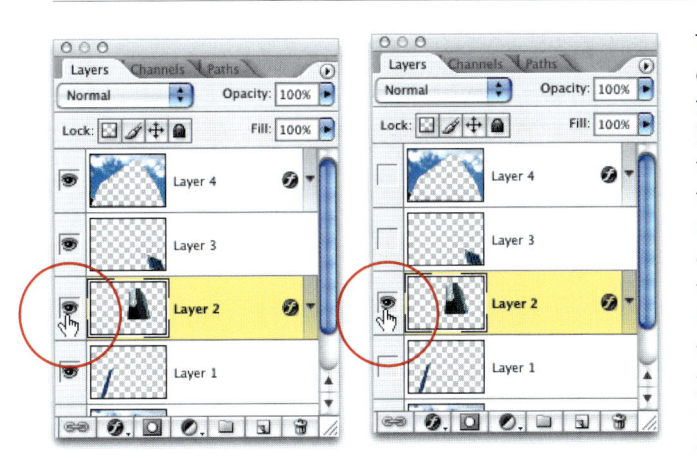

To hide an individual layer, click on the Eye icon in the first column next to that layer in the Layers palette. To make the layer visible again, click on the spot where the Eye icon used to be. If you want to keep one layer visible and hide all the others, hold the Option key (PC: Alt key) and click on the Eye icon beside the layer you want to keep visible. To make the other layers visible again, repeat the process.

CHAPTER 6 • Layer Tips   131

WHY DRAGGING-AND-DROPPING STYLES ROCKS!

You probably already know that you can apply styles to an image from the Styles palette, and you may even know that rather than just clicking on them, you can drag-and-drop these styles right from the palette straight onto your current layer. But what's the advantage of dragging-and-dropping? Isn't it actually harder to drag-and-drop, rather than just clicking once? The advantage is that you can drag-and-drop styles to any layer, not just your currently active layer. You can also drag-and-drop effects between different open documents (like we did here).

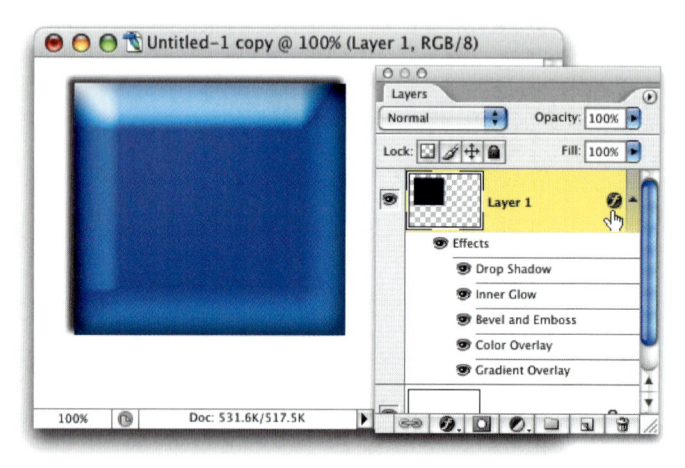

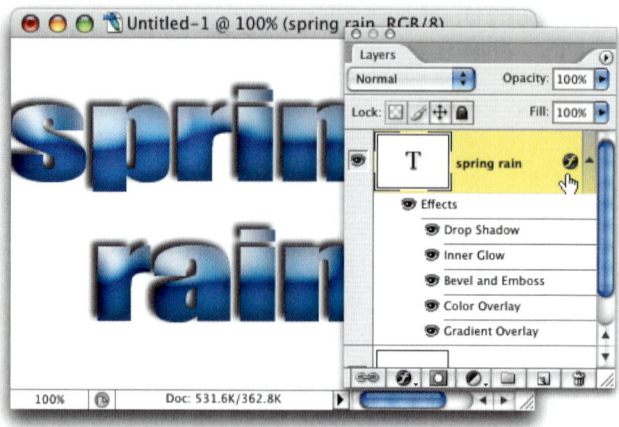

APPLYING LAYER STYLES TO YOUR BACKGROUND LAYER

How do you apply a layer style to your Background layer? You can't. That is, unless you double-click on your Background layer. This brings up the New Layer dialog where you can rename your Background layer, and when you do, it turns into a regular layer. Now you can apply layer styles to your heart's content. Want an even faster way? Just hold the Option key (PC: Alt key) and double-click, then you won't get the dialog at all—it will just convert it into a new layer named Layer 0.

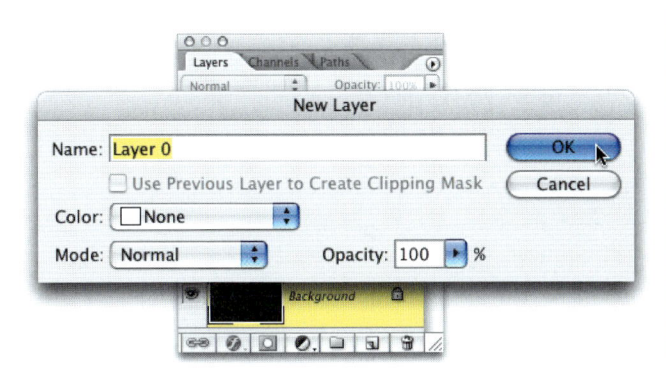

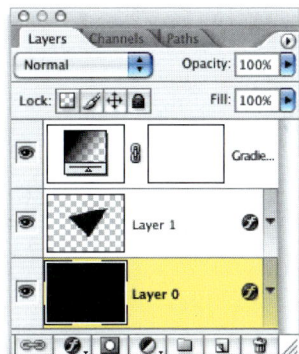

TURN YOUR LAYER COMPS INTO THEIR OWN DOCS

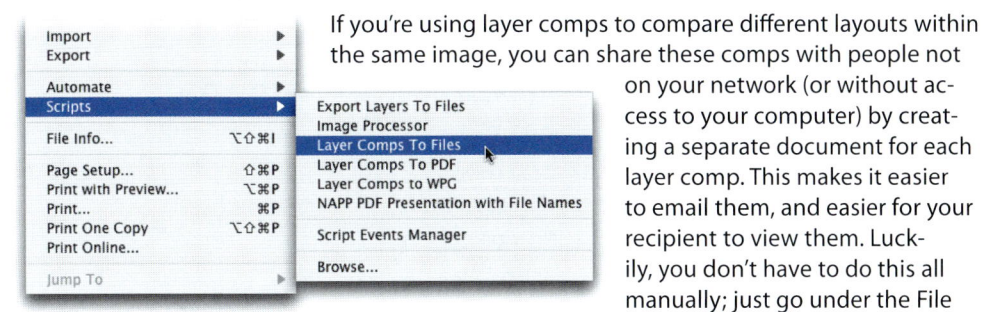

If you're using layer comps to compare different layouts within the same image, you can share these comps with people not on your network (or without access to your computer) by creating a separate document for each layer comp. This makes it easier to email them, and easier for your recipient to view them. Luckily, you don't have to do this all manually; just go under the File menu, under Scripts, and choose Layer Comps To Files.

CHAPTER 6 • Layer Tips   133

MORE CONTROL OVER BLENDS: ADVANCED BLENDING

Using blend modes is a great way to get the layer you're on to interact with the layers beneath it. The only problem is you don't have much control over these blend modes—they either look the way you want them to, or not. They're pretty much an "on" or "off" tool. If you're looking for that next level of control over how layers interact with each other, you need the advanced Blending Options. These are found by double-clicking in the empty space just to the right of the layer's name in the Layers palette. What appears onscreen looks like the Layer Style dialog (and in fact, it is), but if you look closely, you'll see two bars with sliders at the bottom of the dialog giving you control over how your layered images interact. Here's another quick tip: If you hold the Option key (PC: Alt key) before you drag one of the sliders, it will split the slider in two, which gives you smoother transitions and more usable blend effects.

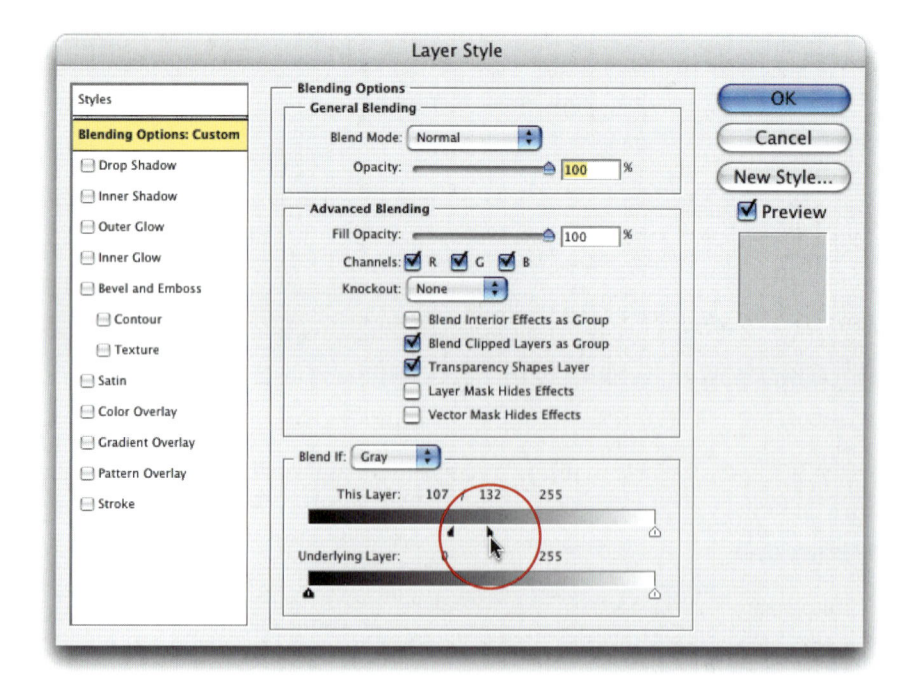

INSTANT OPACITY CHANGE

Anytime you want to change the Opacity of the layer you're currently working on, just switch to the Move tool (V) and press a number key on your keyboard: 4 = 40% Opacity, 5 = 50% Opacity, etc. If you want an exact percentage, such as 52%, then type 52. (*Note:* You have to type quickly, or you'll get 50%, then 20%.)

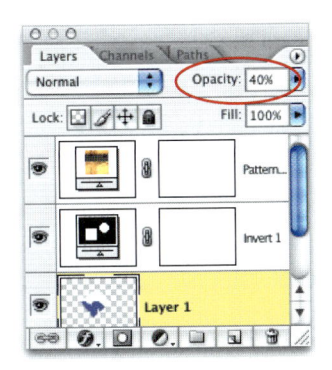

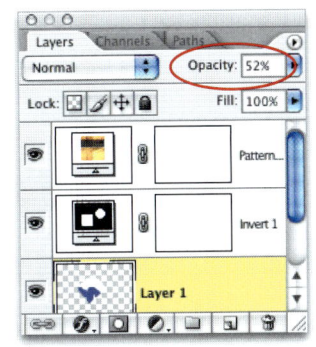

COPY A LAYER IN THE SAME LOCATION IN ANOTHER DOCUMENT

To make a copy of your current layer and have it appear in the exact location in a different Photoshop document, Control-click (PC: Right-click) on the layer in the Layers palette that you want to copy, and choose Duplicate Layer. When the Duplicate Layer dialog appears, choose the Destination from the Document pop-up menu, and click OK.

CHAPTER 6 • Layer Tips   135

MOVING MULTIPLE LAYERS FROM DOCUMENT TO DOCUMENT

Want to move more than one layer at a time from one document to another? It's easy, as long as you know where to drag from. First, Command-click (PC: Control-click) to select your layers and then click the Link icon at the bottom of the Layers palette to link your layers together. Then, make sure that you drag your layer from within your document itself, rather than trying to drag the layer from the Layers palette. Dragging a layer from the Layers palette to another document is fine, as long as you only want to drag one layer at a time.

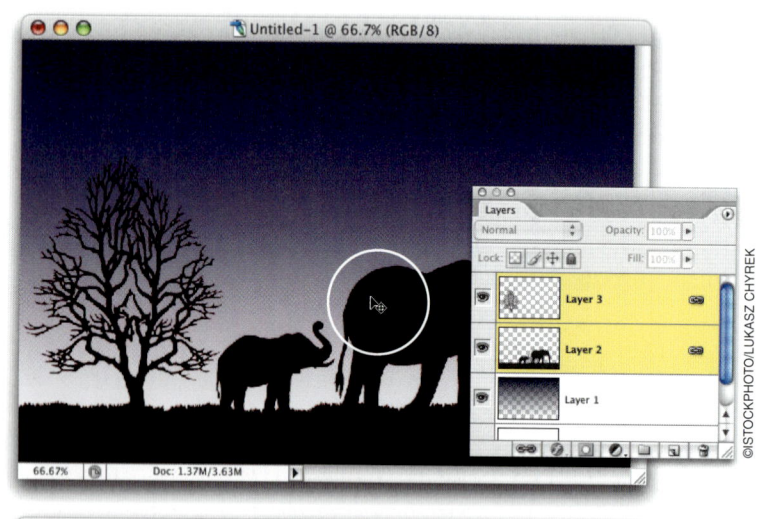

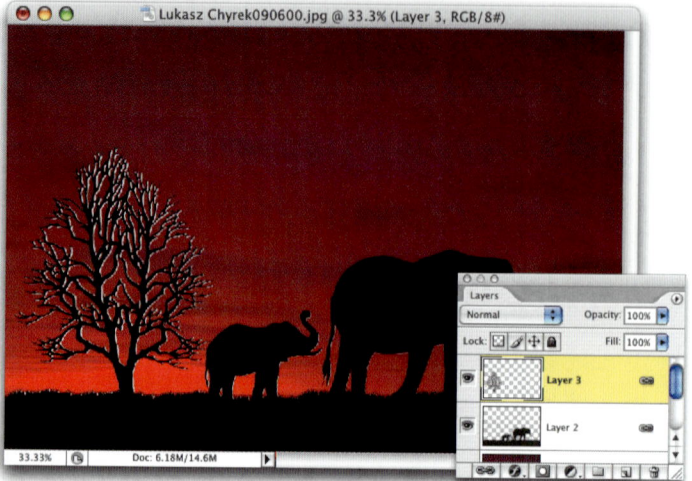

136   CHAPTER 6 • Layer Tips

CENTERING DRAGGED LAYERS THE EASY WAY

When dragging a layer from one document to another, the object will appear in the new document at the point where your cursor was when you released the mouse button. If you'd prefer that the layer appear perfectly centered within the other document, just hold the Shift key as you drag, and when you release the mouse button, the object will be perfectly centered.

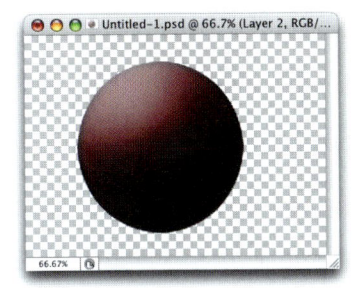

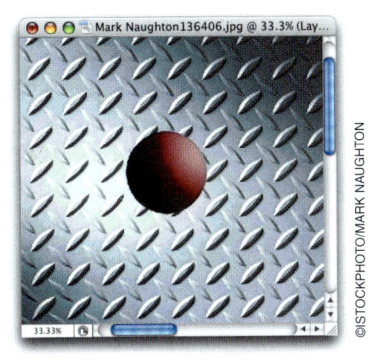

EASIER DROP SHADOW ANGLE ADJUSTMENTS

If you're creating a drop shadow using Photoshop's built-in layer styles (from the Add a Layer Style pop-up menu in the Layers palette), rather than setting the Distance and Angle numerically, you can adjust it visually. Just move your cursor outside the dialog right into your image, click on the shadow itself, and drag it where you'd like it.

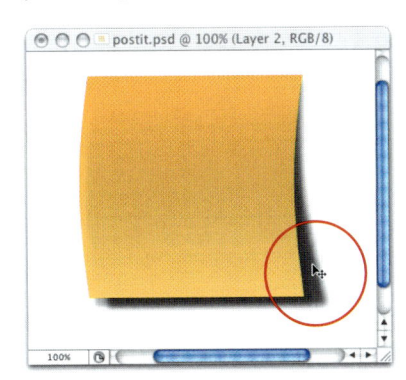

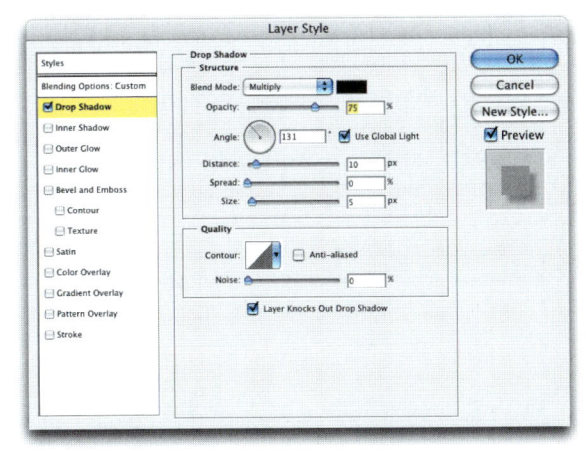

CHAPTER 6 • Layer Tips

LAYER NAVIGATION SHORTCUT

If you're working on a large, multilayered document and you have the Move tool (V) active, you can jump to the layer you want by Control-clicking (PC: Right-clicking) on a portion of the image. A contextual menu will appear with a list of the layers beneath the point where you clicked your cursor. To make one of those layers the active layer, just choose it from the menu. It's important to note that if there aren't any layers beneath where you're clicking (or the layers are transparent where you're clicking), the only layer that will appear in the menu is the Background layer.

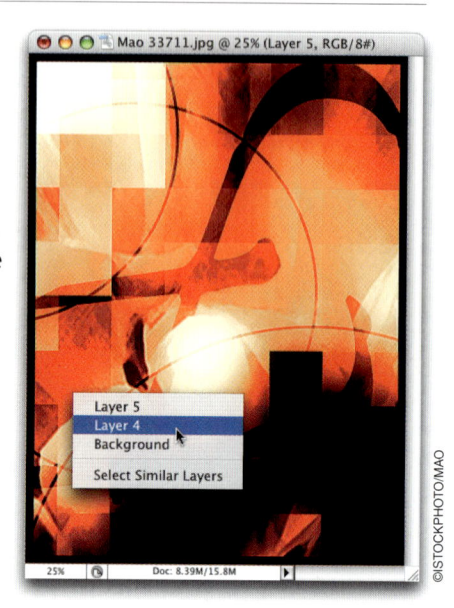

SEPARATION ANXIETY: PUT A LAYER STYLE ON A SEPARATE LAYER

When you apply a layer style to a layer using the Add a Layer Style pop-up menu in the Layers palette, you've done just that—applied a style to a layer, and that style is married to that layer. However, if you'd like to edit your effect separately from the layer, you can ask Photoshop to put the layer style on its own separate layer (or layers if necessary). To do this, click on your layer, then go under the Layer menu, under Layer Style, and choose Create Layer. Your effect will now appear on its own layer beneath your current layer. *Note:* If you apply a bevel effect, it will create multiple separate layers.

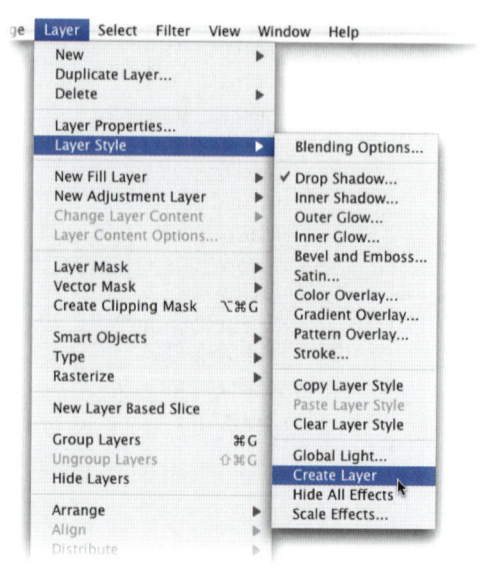

138   CHAPTER 6 • Layer Tips

LAYER EFFECTS REMOVAL SPEED TIP

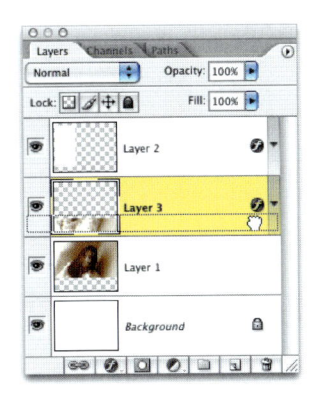

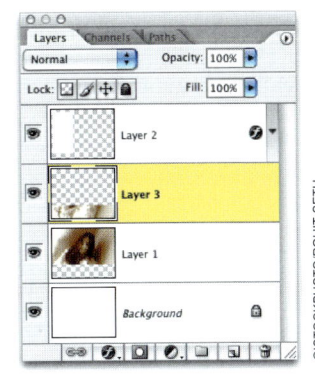

If you want to remove all the layer effects applied to a particular layer, don't drag them all into the Trash one by one. The fastest way is to simply drag the Layer Effects icon (it looks like a little "*f*") directly into the Trash icon at the bottom of the Layers palette, and all the effects go right along with it.

SHAPES WITHOUT THE SHAPE LAYER

If you use Photoshop's Shape tools, by default they create a Shape layer (which is basically a layer filled with your Foreground color with a clipping path in the shape of your shape, if that makes any sense). We've had loads of email from users asking us, "Do I have to have that funky Shape layer? Can't I just have the shape without the layer and clipping path?" Absolutely! When you choose one of the Shape tools, look in the Options Bar and on the far left you'll see three icons. Click on the third icon from the left and you'll get just the shape—no Shape layer, no paths, no kidding.

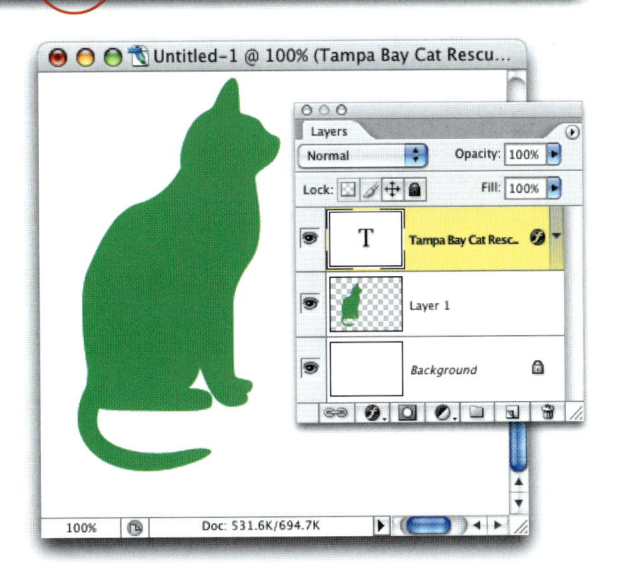

CHAPTER 6 • Layer Tips   139

COLOR-CODING MADE EASY

In Photoshop you can color-code layers and layer sets for quick visual identification. One way to do this is to bring up the Layer Properties dialog (from the Layers palette's flyout menu) and choose your colors from a pop-up menu. But there's a much faster way—at least if you know this shortcut: Control-click (PC: Right-click) on the Eye icon next to the layer you want to color-code and a contextual menu of colors will appear where you can choose the shade you'd like.

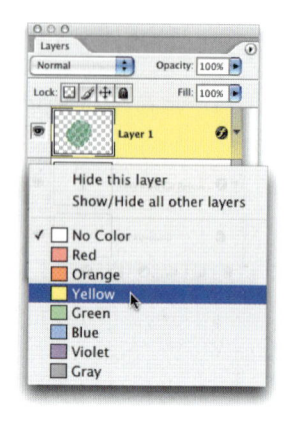

SPEED UP PHOTOSHOP BY MERGING LAYERS

Every time you add a layer to Photoshop, it adds quite a bit of file size to your image. The larger your file size, the slower Photoshop goes. If you're creating a document that has lots of layers, before long, your file size is going to get pretty huge. One way to keep things lean and mean is to merge any layers that don't need to be separate. You do this by clicking on the topmost image layer in the

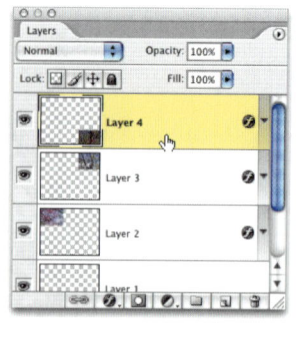

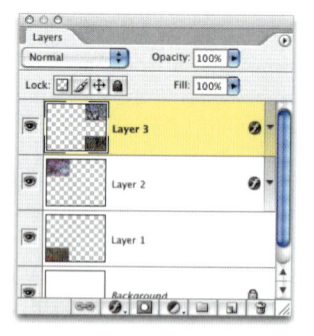

©ISTOCKPHOTO/RANDALL CHET

Layers palette, and then pressing Command-E (PC: Control-E). This merges the current layer with the layer directly beneath it. Think of it this way—every time you merge two layers, your file size drops and Photoshop gets faster. It's like a keyboard shortcut that adds more horsepower. *Note:* If one merge doesn't drop your file size, try merging again.

140   CHAPTER 6 • Layer Tips

CAN'T WE ALL JUST HAVE THE SAME STYLE?

Want to apply a style that's on one layer to a bunch of other layers? It's easy (if you know the trick). Just link all the layers that you want to have that same style by Command-clicking (PC: Control-clicking) on them and clicking the Link icon at the bottom of the Layers palette. Then Control-click (PC: Right-click) on the layer's name with the style you want to copy and choose Select Linked Layers from the contextual menu that appears. Control-click (PC: Right-click) again and choose Paste Layer Style, and your style(s) will instantly paste to every linked layer.

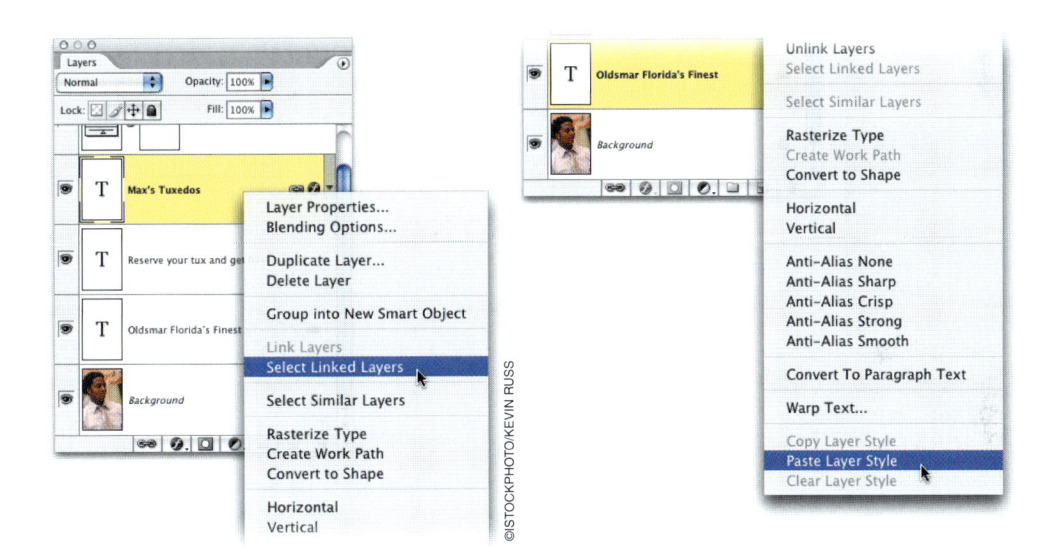

CHAPTER 6 • Layer Tips   141

LAYERS PALETTE NAVIGATION SPEED TIPS

The less you need to be in the Layers palette, the better (at least when it comes to speed), so here are some shortcuts you'll want to know: When you want to select multiple layers, press Option-Shift-Left Bracket ([) (PC: Alt-Shift-Left Bracket) to select layers beneath your current layer. To select layers above your current layer, press Option-Shift-Right Bracket (]) (PC: Alt-Shift-Right Bracket). To move your current layer down one layer at a time, press Command-Left Bracket (PC: Control-Left Bracket). To move it up one layer at a time, press Command-Right Bracket (PC: Control-Right Bracket). To switch to the layer beneath your current layer, press Option-Left Bracket (PC: Alt-Left Bracket). To switch to the Layer above your current layer, press Option-Right Bracket (PC: Alt-Right Bracket). To move your layer to the top of the layer stack, press Command-Shift-Right Bracket (PC: Control-Shift-Right Bracket). To move your layer to the bottom of the layer stack (above your Background layer), press Command-Shift-Left Bracket (PC: Control-Shift-Left Bracket). Trust us, it's worth memorizing this stuff.

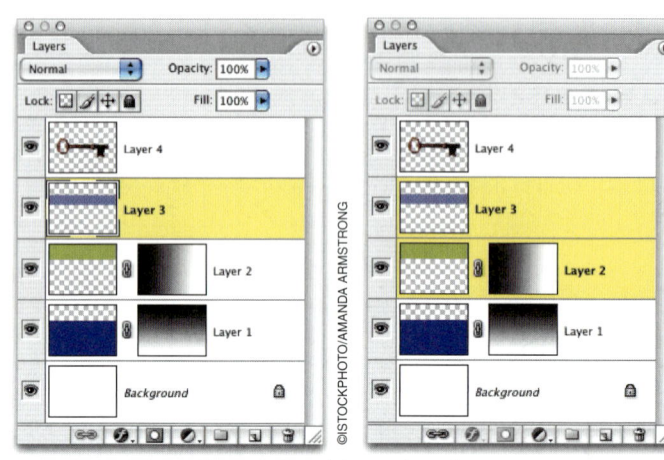

Here we selected the next layer down.

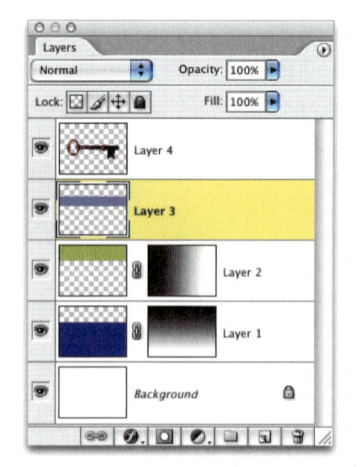

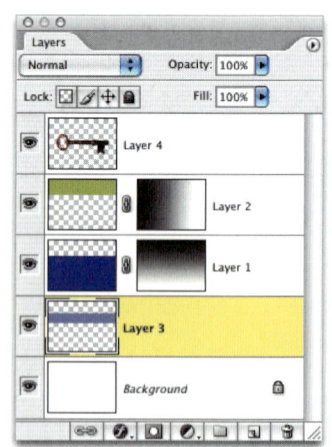

Here we moved our layer to the bottom of the layer stack.

VIEW YOUR LAYER MASK AS A RUBYLITH

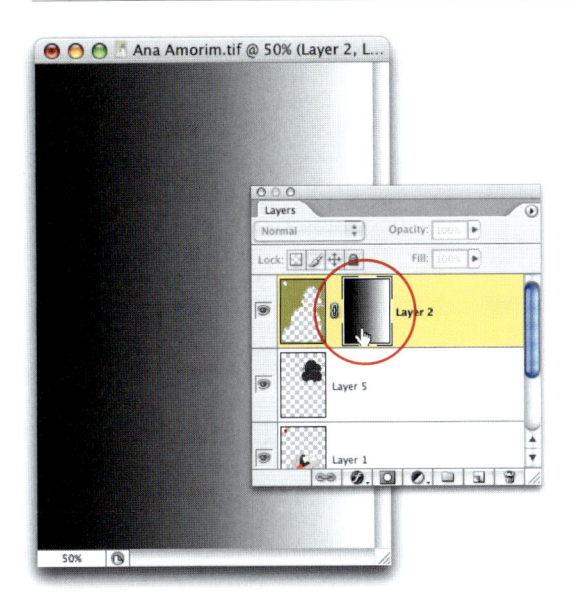

If you want to view your layer mask by itself (rather than how the layer mask affects your overall image), hold the Option key (PC: Alt key) and click directly on the layer mask thumbnail in the Layers palette. This will display just the mask itself. You can also view the layer mask like a Rubylith (a red overlay used in traditional masking) that appears over your image by pressing the Backslash key (\) on your keyboard.

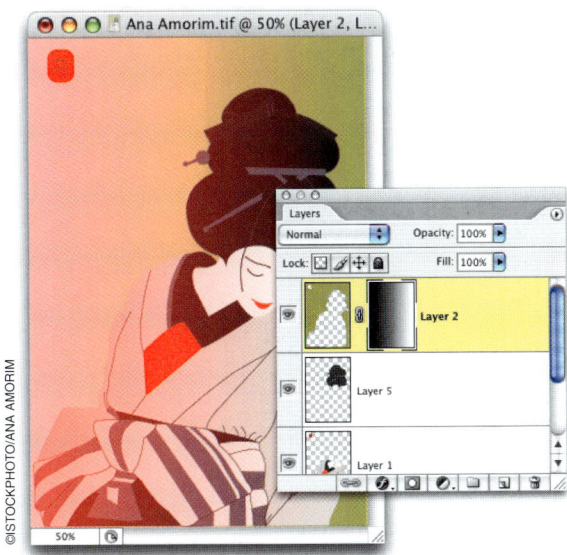

CHAPTER 6 • Layer Tips   143

SELECTING JUST ONE OBJECT ON A LAYER

If you have multiple objects on the same layer (like a few words of type that have already been rasterized) and you want to select just one item on that layer (for example, you want to put a selection around one letter so you can move it independently of the rest of the letters), here's how: Use any selection tool to create a loose selection around the object. Hold the Command key (PC: Control key), and then press the Up Arrow key once and the Down Arrow key once. The entire object will become perfectly selected without disturbing anything else on the layer. Now you can move it, edit it, or tweak it separately because it is a "floating selection."

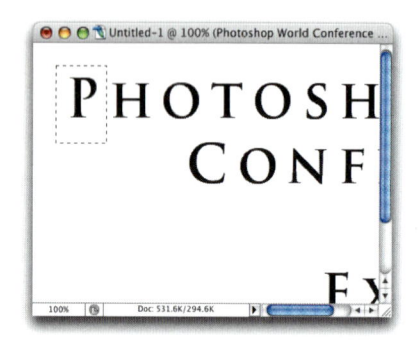

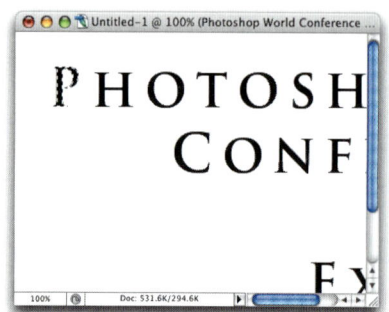

UN-FILLING FOR FUN AND PROFIT

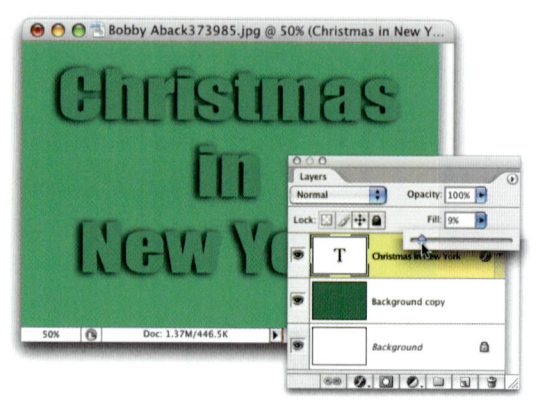

Back in Photoshop 7.0, Adobe brought a once-buried command front and center when they added the Fill option to the Layers palette. This isn't your average everyday fill. No sir, this is a special freaky fill that only works when you've applied a layer style to a layer. To see it in action (and immediately understand its power), create some text, and then apply a drop shadow. Lower the regular Opacity of this layer, and you'll notice that both your type and the shadow fade at the same time. Now raise it back up to 100%. Then lower the Fill amount (in the Layers palette) and you'll notice that the type fades away, but the drop shadow stays at 100%. Ahhhhhh. Makes you stop and think, doesn't it?

144 CHAPTER 6 • Layer Tips

SECRET OPACITY SEE-THROUGH-PART-OF-A-LAYER TIP

This is a pretty wild tip—how to make just one part of a layer have a lower opacity. We know it sounds impossible, but this is totally cool. Start by making a selection on any area of the layer that you want to become transparent, while the rest of the layer remains at 100%. Then go under the Edit menu and choose Fill. When the Fill dialog appears, from the Mode pop-up menu choose Clear. Then lower the Opacity of the fill to whatever percentage you'd like, then click OK and voilà—part of your layer has opacity, while the rest remains at 100%. Majorly cool! (*Note:* You have to think in reverse here. Clear set to 100% Opacity will make the selected area completely transparent.) Wait, what if you decide later that you want to fill it back in? Here's how: Just start making copies of your layer by pressing Command-J (PC: Control-J), and as you do, you'll see the transparency disappear. You may have to make five or more copies, but son of a gun if it doesn't work. When it looks right, hide all but those copied layers, and from the Layers palette's flyout menu, choose Merge Visible.

CHAPTER 6 • Layer Tips   145

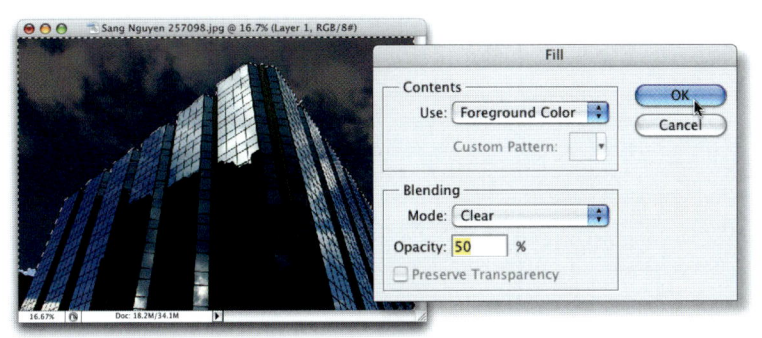

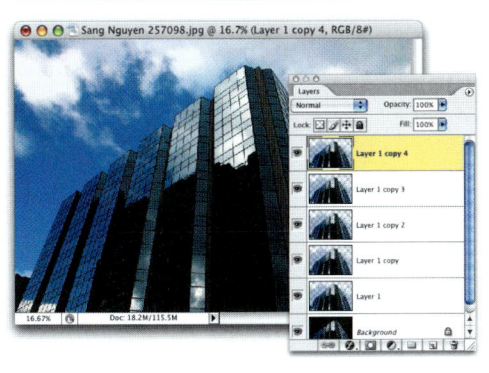

Burn Rubber

TYPE TIPS

Do you remember the song "Burn Rubber" by the Gap Band from back in the early '80s? Remember it goes: "Burn rubber on me, Charlene... whoa, no...." Not ringing any bells?

Burn Rubber
smokin' type tips

It doesn't matter. This chapter has nothing to do with burning rubber—I was just curious to see if you're as old as I am (which is young. Very young. I heard that song accidentally on an oldies station in my dad's car). This chapter is dedicated to making the time you spend using type in Photoshop more productive. Here's the weird thing about Photoshop type—back in version 6.0, Adobe added most of the high-end typography features found in Adobe's high-end page-layout program, InDesign. Which made me think, "Why?" I can't imagine setting a book or magazine article in Photoshop, because when Photoshop type gets below 12 points, it starts to get fuzzy, so laying out columns of text and tweaking the balance, spacing, and paragraph specs for columns of type just doesn't make sense. Then I figured out what's going on. Somebody at Adobe must be hittin' the crack pipe. Could that be it? Or is it so not, that it freaks you out.

BIGGER FONT PREVIEWS

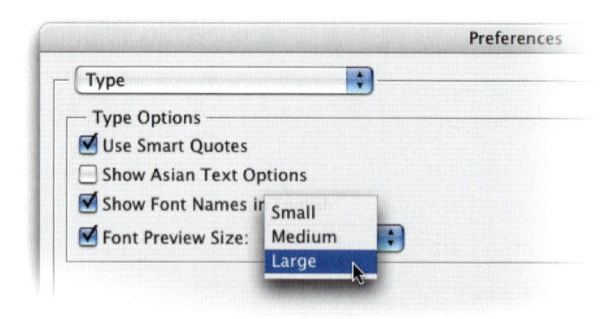

In Photoshop CS2, Adobe added font previews (where you can see a preview of how each font looks, right in the Font menu itself), but the previews are so small, it's still hard to tell the difference among fonts. Luckily, there is a way to make those previews large enough so they actually are usable—just press Command-K (PC: Control-K) to bring up Photoshop's Preferences, then press Command-9 (PC: Control-9) to jump to the Type preferences. In the Font Preview Size pop-up menu, choose Large, and now your font previews will be significantly larger.

DON'T LIKE THE FONT PREVIEWS? TURN 'EM OFF

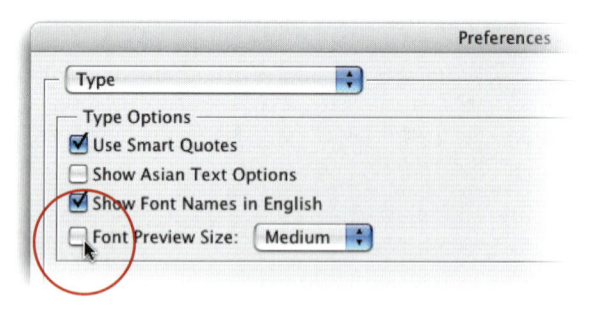

I know everybody and their uncle has been waiting patiently for years to get font previews in the Font menu, but personally, they drive me nuts. Maybe it's the type freak in me that has led me to memorize what my favorite installed fonts are, but whatever it is, I hate seeing those previews (plus, it does slow the Font menu down a bit), so I turn it off. If you have the same level of disdain that I do for font previews, here's how to turn them off: Press Command-K (PC: Control-K) to bring up Photoshop's Preferences, then press Command-9 (PC: Control-9) to jump to the Type preferences. Now turn off the checkbox next to the Font Preview Size pop-up menu, and they're wiped from your Font menu.

CLICKING WITH THE TYPE TOOL TRICK

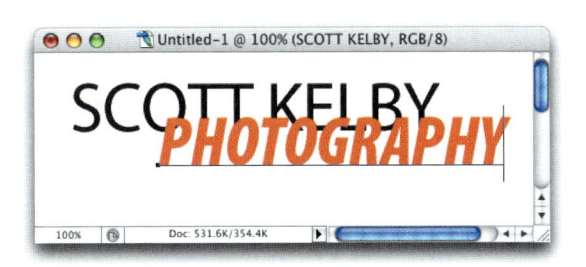

Here's one I learned from my buddy Matt Kloskowski, and it's something that has been driving me crazy for years, and I had no idea there was a way around it. It happens when you've already got some Type layers in your document, and you want to create some new type. When you click the Type tool (T) within your document, if you're anywhere in the vicinity of any other type, Photoshop thinks you want to add to that type (rather than creating some new type), so it puts your cursor in with your existing Type layer. Arrrrrggghh! Here's how to get around it—just hold the Shift key before you click the Type tool, and it ignores any nearby Type layers, letting you create a brand new string of type. Thanks to Matt for keeping me (us) from standing out on a ledge somewhere.

GETTING TYPE IN A PERFECT CIRCLE

Now that Photoshop can really give you type in a circle, getting a perfect circle that you can add type to is not as obvious as you'd think. To get this perfect circle, click on the Shape tools in the Toolbox and choose the Ellipse tool from the flyout menu (or press Shift-U). Then go up to the Options Bar, and in the group of three icons from the left, click on the middle icon, which creates a regular path, rather than a Shape layer or a pixel-based shape. Then, press-and-hold the Shift key, and drag out your circle (the Shift key constrains the shape to a perfect circle). Now you can press T to switch to the Type tool and move your cursor over the circle. When it changes into a Type on a Path cursor, click on the circle and get to typin'.

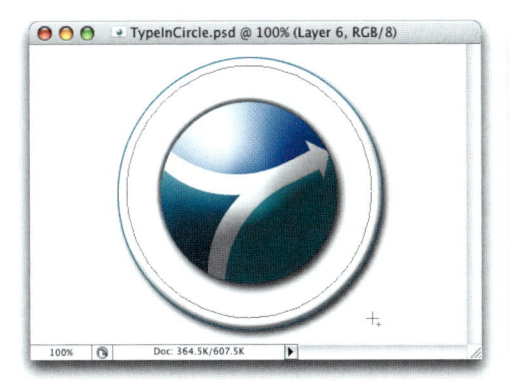

CHAPTER 7 • Smokin' Type Tips

I NEED MY DUMB QUOTES AGAIN

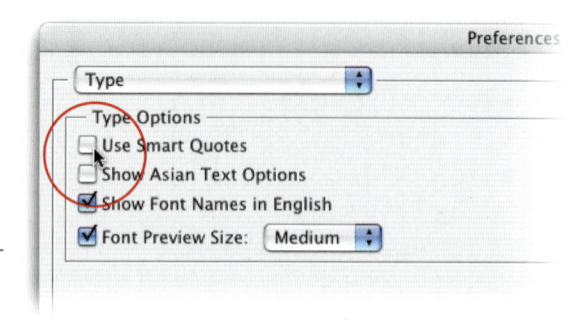

In all previous versions of Photoshop, when you typed in a quote mark (") or apostrophe ('), what Photoshop gave you was the typographically incorrect inch mark (") or foot mark (') instead. They're called "dumb quotes." Luckily, back in Photoshop 7.0, Adobe brought these typographically challenged dummies into line, and now they're properly applied as "curly quotes" by default, which is great. That is unless you have to actually type an inch mark or a foot mark. Here's the workaround—when it comes time to type an inch or foot mark, go under the Photoshop menu, under Preferences, and choose Type (in Windows, Preferences can be found under the Edit menu). In the resulting dialog, turn off Use Smart Quotes, and then type your characters. When you're done, return to the Type Preferences and turn them back on to bring typographic order to your world.

RESETTING YOUR TYPE

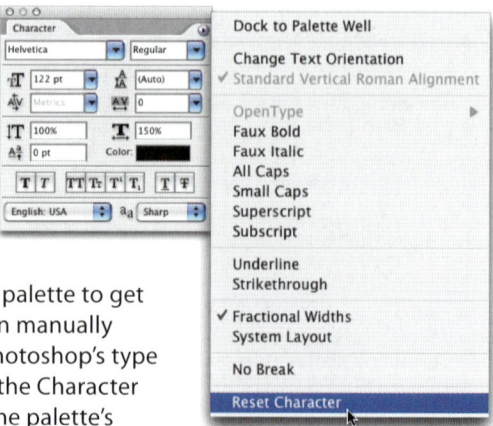

If you're into typography, Photoshop gives you loads of typographical control. You can adjust everything from tracking, kerning, and dozens of other characteristics. The downside is—the Character palette (where we make most of these tweaks) keeps your last-used settings as a default. If you did some major type tweaking to your last line of type, it might need some major "undoing" in the Character palette to get you back to normal type settings. Rather than manually resetting every field, you can quickly reset Photoshop's type to its "default" standard settings by going to the Character palette and choosing Reset Character from the palette's flyout menu.

150   CHAPTER 7 • Smokin' Type Tips

ONE-CLICK ACCESS TO THE COPYRIGHT SYMBOL, AND MORE

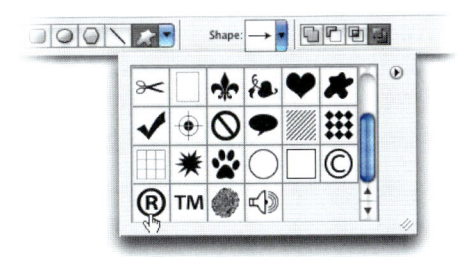

Looking for some special type characters, like ©, ™, or ®? If you're not fussy about these characters not actually being a font, you can find them in the default set of Custom Shapes. Just get the Custom Shape tool (press Shift-U until you have it), click on the Shape thumbnail in the Options Bar, which opens the Custom Shape Picker, and you'll find all three special characters there, in the default set of shapes.

HIGHLIGHTING YOUR TEXT SUPER FAST!

When you want to automatically highlight the type in a Type layer *and* switch to the Type tool at the same time to make some copy changes, just double-click directly on the "T" thumbnail on the Type layer you want to edit in the Layers palette, and blam! You're ready to go.

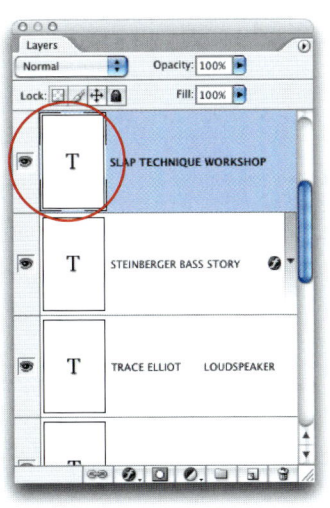

CHAPTER 7 • Smokin' Type Tips

RENDERING TEXT IN JUST ONE CLICK

If you need to convert your Type layer into an image layer, you can save some time by simply Control-clicking (PC: Right-clicking) directly on the Type layer name that appears in the Layers palette. A contextual menu will appear where you can choose Rasterize Type to instantly render your type.

MADE TO FIT

To create a text box for your type to fit within, press T to select the Type tool, then click-and-drag out the area you want for your text box. Your type will now fit within that box. When you're finished entering your text, just press Enter on your numeric keypad (or Command-Return [PC: Control-Enter] on your laptop) to get out of the text bounding box.

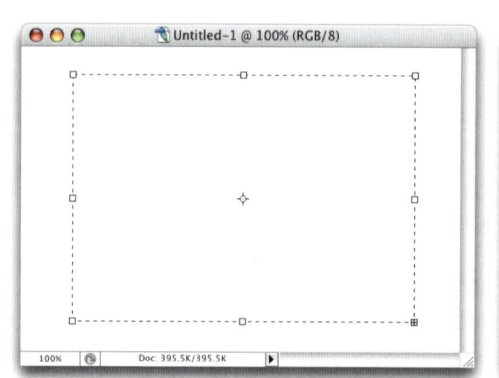

152   CHAPTER 7 • Smokin' Type Tips

TEXT-PATH-MAKING MANIAC

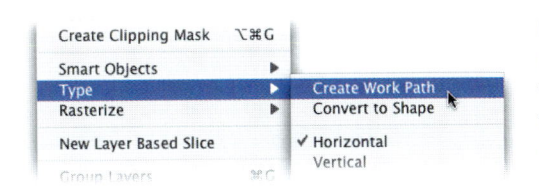

If you want to convert your Type layer into paths (as if you meticulously drew the type with the Pen tool—your clients won't have to know), simply go under the Layer menu, under Type, and choose Create Work Path.

PICTURE THIS: PUTTING A PHOTO INSIDE TYPE

First, set your Foreground color to black by pressing D. Press T to choose the Type tool and create your text (you don't have to rasterize the type). Then, open the image you want to appear inside your type and use the Move tool (V) to drag-and-drop it into your type document (it should appear on the layer above your Type layer. If it doesn't, just go to the Layers palette and move it on top of your Type layer). To put your image inside the type, press Command-Option-G (PC: Control-Alt-G) to create a clipping mask and whammo—your image is masked into your type. You can reposition the image by using the Move tool. And since you didn't rasterize your Type layer, your text remains totally editable—just click on the Type layer and start editing. You can add layer styles to your Type layer to further enhance the effect. If you're not crazy about the image you picked, click on the image layer and press the keyboard shortcut again to release the mask. Now remove the image.

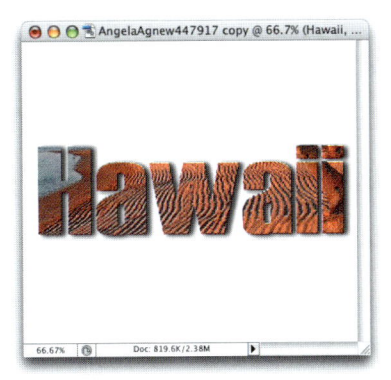

CHAPTER 7 • Smokin' Type Tips   153

FONTS, FONTS, AND MORE FONTS

Here's a tip to quickly change typefaces and see the change while you make it. First, highlight the type you want to change, and then press Command-H (PC: Control-H) to hide the highlighting (the type is still highlighted; the highlight is just hidden from view). Then, up in the Options Bar, click once in the Font field, then use the Up/Down Arrow keys on your keyboard to scroll through your installed typefaces. Man, do I love this one.

154   CHAPTER 7 • Smokin' Type Tips

MAKE YOUR TEXT JUMP INTO ACTION

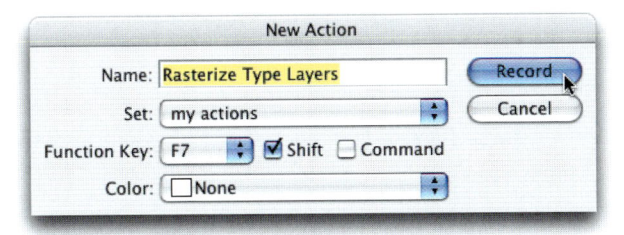

Earlier, I gave you the quick tip for rasterizing your type by Control-clicking (PC: Right-clicking) on your Type layer in the Layers palette, then choosing Rasterize Type from the contextual menu that appears. Believe it or not, there's an even faster way, if you don't mind spending a minute or two setting it up. You can create an action that rasterizes the type for you with just one key. Here's how: Use the Type tool (T) to create a Type layer, then make the Actions palette visible (from the Window menu). Choose New Action from the Actions palette's flyout menu. Name your new action "Rasterize Type Layers," assign it an action set from the Set pop-up menu, then from the Function Key pop-up menu, assign an F-key to this action. Click the Record button, then go under the Layer menu, under Rasterize, and choose Type. Now go back to the Actions palette and click on the Stop icon at the bottom of the palette (it's the first icon from the left). That's it—your action is written. Test it by creating a Type layer, then pressing the F-key you assigned to your action. It should instantly rasterize (you'll know if it worked, because the "T" icon on the Type layer will no longer be visible).

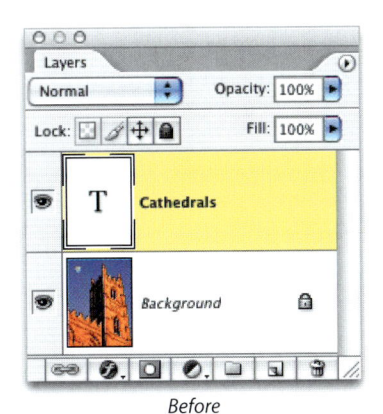

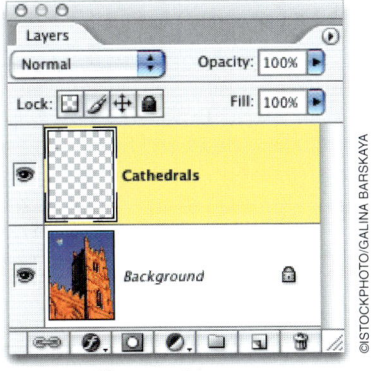

Before

After rasterizing type

CHAPTER 7 • Smokin' Type Tips   155

DOUBLE YOUR PLEASURE

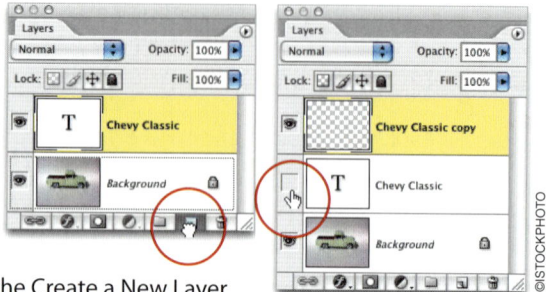

We've already talked about rasterizing text, but once you've rasterized your Type layer into a regular image layer, your type is no longer editable (meaning you can't go back and change typefaces, type in a different word, adjust leading or kerning, etc.). Here's a quick way around that limitation. Before rasterizing (rendering) your type, duplicate the Type layer by dragging it to the Create a New Layer icon at the bottom of the Layers palette. Then, hide the original Type layer from view (by clicking on the Eye icon next to the original Type layer) and rasterize the duplicate Type layer (see previous tip). That way, if you ever need to go back and change the word (or font, leading, etc.), you have the original editable Type layer still available. Just simply make it visible by clicking in the empty box where the Eye icon used to be.

MOVE YOUR TYPE, WITHOUT SWITCHING TOOLS

Here's a tip that can save you a lot of tool switching when formatting your type. Once you create your type with the Type tool (T), and while your cursor is still blinking somewhere in the text, if you need to move the type, you don't have to switch to the Move tool—just move your Type cursor away from your type (either above, below, or an inch or so to the right or left), and your cursor will temporarily change to the Move tool. You can now simply click-and-drag your type. If you want to edit your type some more, just move your cursor back to the type and click where you need to make edits.

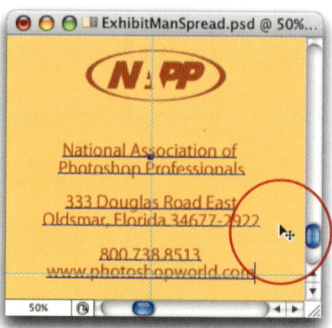

SEEING YOUR TYPE CHANGE COLOR

In Photoshop, you can change the color of your type without even selecting it first. "Why is that important?" you may ask. If you highlight your type to change its color using the Foreground color swatch in the Toolbox, the highlighting hides the color of your type so you can't see any of your color changes while you're in the Color Picker. So instead, after you commit your type by pressing the Enter key, click on the Color swatch in the Options Bar (without highlighting your type first) when you have the Type tool (T) active. As you change colors in the resulting Color Picker, you'll see your type update on the fly.

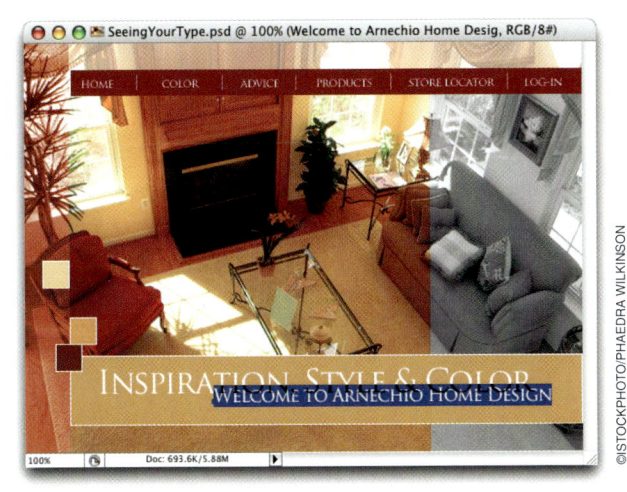

CHAPTER 7 • Smokin' Type Tips

EDITING TEXT WITHOUT HIGHLIGHTING IT

Here's a cool little tip for changing your text without having the Type tool active. Just click on your Type layer (in the Layers palette), then go under the Window menu and choose Character. When the Character palette appears, you can make changes to your type size, color, font, tracking, etc. It freaks you out, doesn't it?

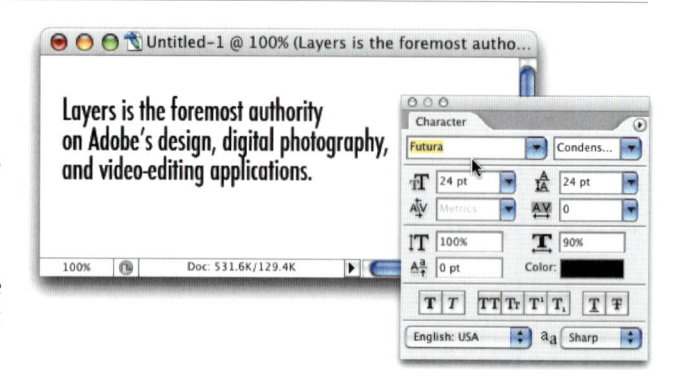

RASTERIZE TIMES 2, 4, 6...

If you have multiple Type layers and you want to convert them all to image layers, there's a way to do it without individually rasterizing each. Simply go under the Layer menu, under Rasterize, and choose All Layers. This will rasterize all the Type layers at once.

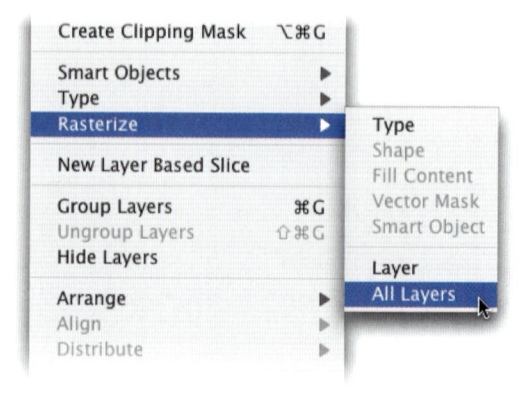

HONEY, I NEED SOME SPACE: VISUALLY ADJUST KERNING

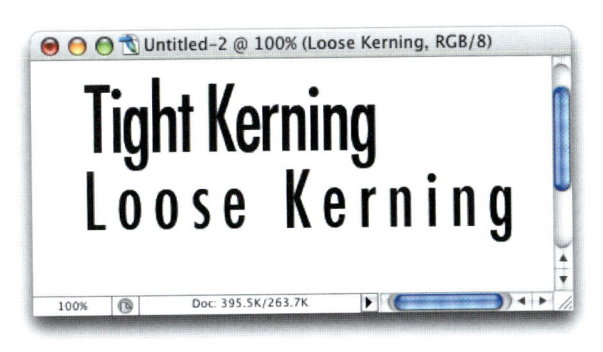

You can visually control the spacing between your type (which is much better than numerically trying to figure it out) by using the same keyboard shortcuts for adjusting type that Adobe Illustrator uses. Here's how: To set the tracking tighter (tightening the space between each letter or word in a group), highlight the type with the Type tool (T), then press Option-Left Arrow (PC: Alt-Left Arrow) to tighten. Press Option-Right Arrow (PC: Alt-Right Arrow) to add more space between a selected group of letters or words. To adjust the space between two individual letters (called kerning), click your cursor between the two letters and use the same keyboard shortcuts mentioned above.

TELL PHOTOSHOP WHEN YOU'RE DONE WITH TYPE

As you probably know, you can jump to most any tool in the Toolbox by pressing a single-key keyboard shortcut. (If you didn't know that, sell your copy of Photoshop. Kidding. Just turn to Chapter 2 for some essential tips.) Here's the problem: While creating type with the Type tool (T), if you press one of those one-key shortcuts (let's say the letter P for the Pen tool), instead of jumping to the Pen tool, Photoshop types the letter "p". It'll drive you nuts. Okay, you won't go nuts, but at the very least you'll have a lot of typos. The reason is this: You have to tell Photoshop that you're done editing your type. You do this in one of three ways: (1) Click on the checkmark icon at the far right of the Options Bar, (2) press the Enter key on your numeric keypad (or Command-Return [PC: Control-Enter] on your laptop), or (3) switch to another tool manually by clicking on it in the Toolbox. Any of these three tells Photoshop that you're done and lets you use the single-key shortcuts to switch tools.

CHAPTER 7 • Smokin' Type Tips

BRING THOSE TYPE LAYERS TOGETHER

How do you merge two Type layers together? Unfortunately, while they're still editable Type layers, you can't—you have to rasterize the layers first. Technically, you rasterize just one (the bottom of the two Type layers), and then make the top Type layer active and press Command-E (PC: Control-E) to merge these two layers together. However, when you do that, the top Type layer will automatically rasterize as the two layers are combined into one, so there's really no way around it—with the exception of this little tip: Highlight the editable type on the top layer and choose Cut from the Edit menu. Switch to the lower Type layer, click your Type cursor once at the end of the type, press Return (PC: Enter) to start a new line, then choose Paste from the Edit menu to paste the contents of the top Type layer into the bottom Type layer. Then drag the old top Type layer into the Trash icon at the bottom of the Layers palette. Although it takes a little effort, now you have both layers combined into one layer (your goal), but the type remains totally editable (the bonus).

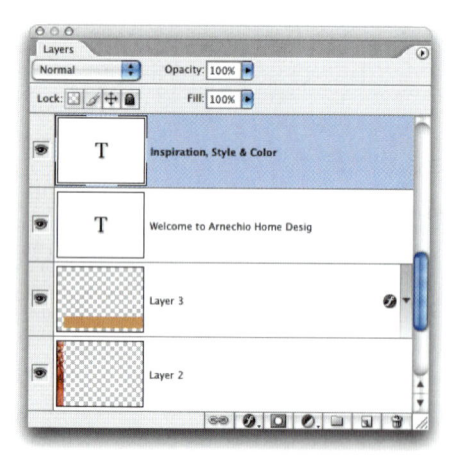

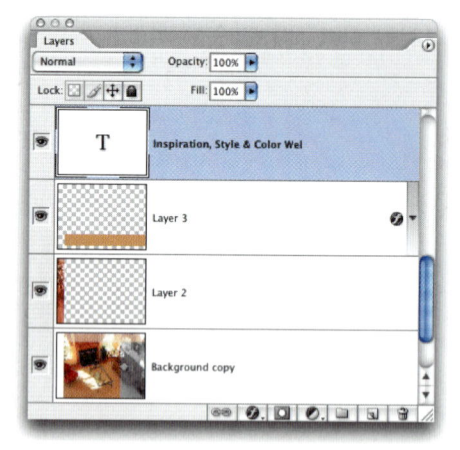

160   CHAPTER 7 • Smokin' Type Tips

THE LONG AND THE SHORT OF TYPE

Although the Character palette has numeric controls for making your type fatter (horizontal scaling) or taller (vertical scaling), it's usually easier to do these two functions visually (rather than numerically). Here's how: First set your type, then with the Type cursor still blinking somewhere in the text, press-and-hold the Command key (PC: Control key) to bring up the Free Transform bounding box. To make your type fatter, click on the center (or corner) handle on either side, release the Command/Control key and drag outward. To make your type taller, grab the center (or corner) handle on the top or bottom, release the Command/Control key, and drag upward or downward.

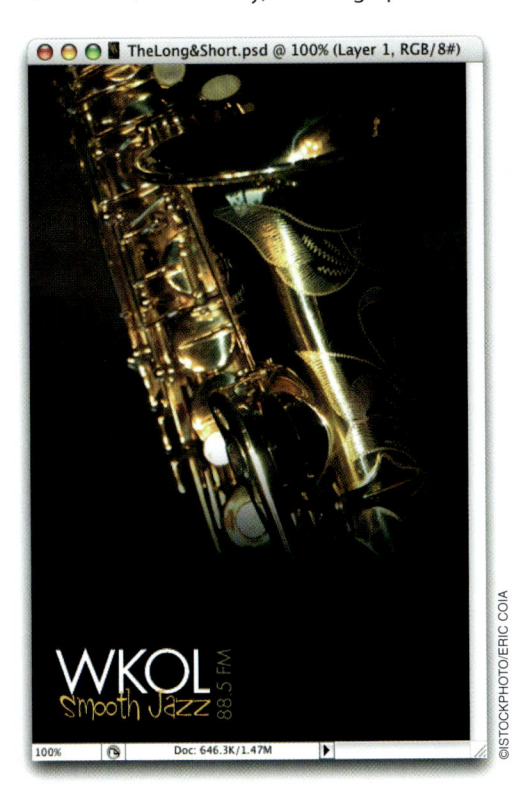

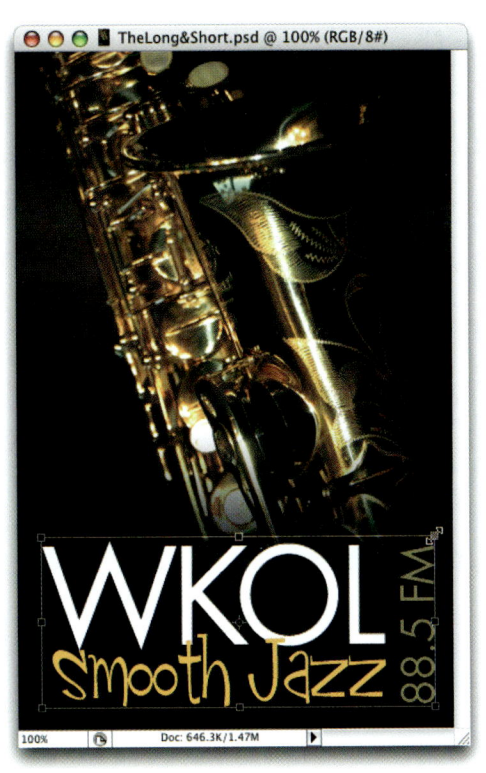

MADE TO FIT: PART TWO

This tip relates to a previous tip, where you created what's called a "text box" so that your type wraps within a text block, rather than running in one straight line. The tip is this: If you've created some standard type by just clicking and typing rather than creating a paragraph text box, you're not out of luck. While the Type layer is active, just go under the Layer menu, under Type, and choose Convert to Paragraph Text. Now your type will wrap within the text box boundaries, and you can edit the boundaries by adjusting the corner and center points.

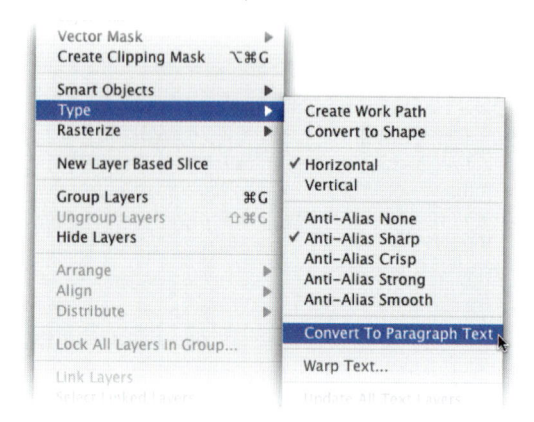

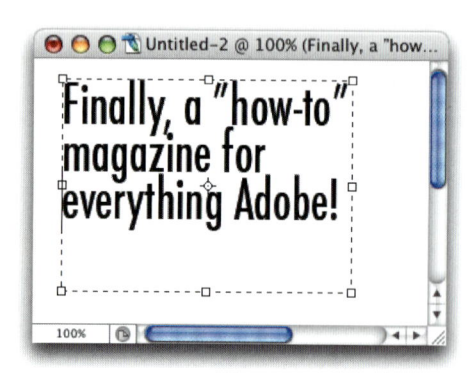

MAKING THE SPELL CHECKER OBEY YOUR COMMANDS

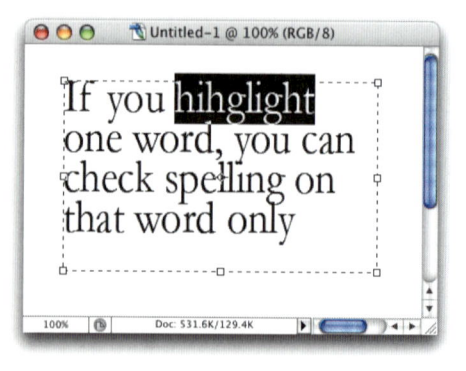

Photoshop's spell checker isn't just window dressing; it has a very robust spell-checking function, akin to Adobe InDesign's own spell checker, but if you understand how it works, you can save yourself some time and frustration. Basically, if you highlight some text on a layer, it checks just the highlighted text, so if you highlight one word, it just checks that one word (even if there are dozens of words in your paragraph). If you choose to spell check but don't have anything highlighted, it checks your entire document, regardless of how many Type layers you have. It's also helpful to know that it only checks real Type layers (layers that have a capital "T" as their thumbnail image in the Layers palette), and it cannot spell-check any layers with text that have been rasterized (converted from a Type layer into a regular image layer).

162   CHAPTER 7 • Smokin' Type Tips

EDITING TYPE ON A PATH

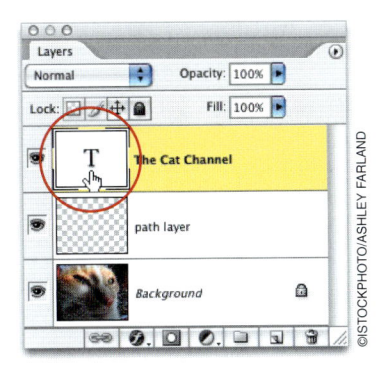

If you've created some type on a path, highlighting that type to edit it (to change the font, color, spelling, etc.) can be kind of tricky. That's why it's quicker to go to the Layers palette and double-click directly on the "T" thumbnail icon. This will highlight all the type on this layer, making it easy to type in some new text, or change some of the attributes.

EXACT SIZING FOR YOUR TEXT COLUMNS

We already showed you how to create a column of type by clicking-and-dragging the Type tool to create your text box so your text will wrap within that column. But here's a quick little tip that lets you tell Photoshop exactly the width and height you'd like your type column to be (rather than just clicking-and-dragging it out visually). With the Type tool, just hold the Option key (PC: Alt key) and click in your document and the Paragraph Text Size dialog will appear where you can enter the exact size you'd like for your column.

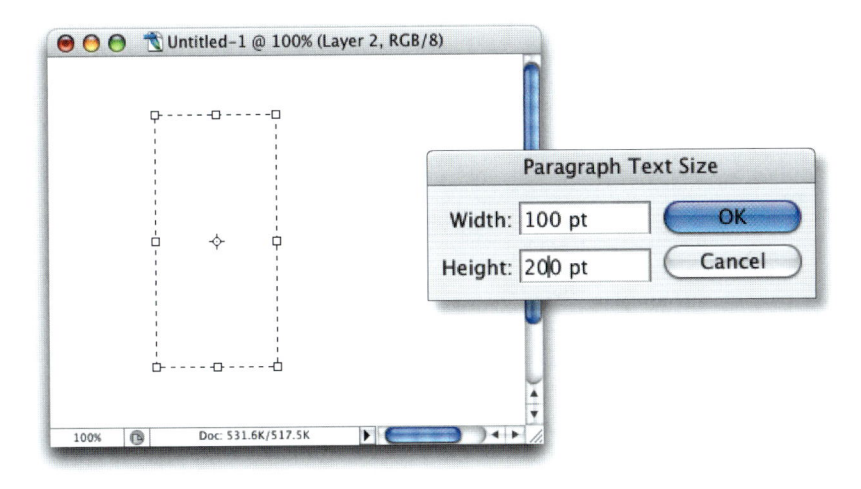

CHAPTER 7 • Smokin' Type Tips   163

REMOVING THOSE TYPOGRAPHICALLY INCORRECT SPACES

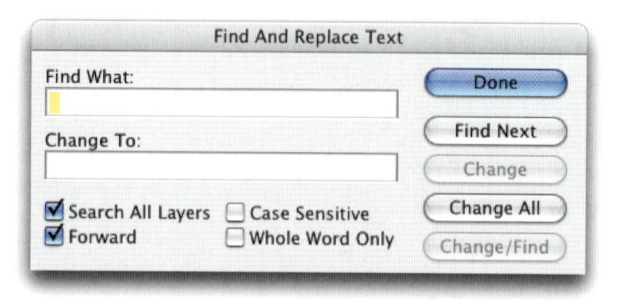

If you're trying to set type that looks typographically correct in Photoshop, there's an old habit you'll have to break, and that's the curse of putting two spaces at the end of every sentence. This is a holdover from people who at one time used traditional typewriters, where adding two spaces was necessary, but in typesetting that's a huge no-no. About 70% of the text I copy-and-paste from text files that people give me has two spaces, but I use this Photoshop tip to fix the problem in just seconds. First, go under the Edit menu and choose Find and Replace Text. In the Find field, press the Spacebar twice (entering two spaces), then in Change To, press the Spacebar just once. Click Change All, and every time Photoshop finds two spaces at the end of a sentence, it will replace it with just one, making you typographically correct.

DON'T HAVE ITALIC OR BOLD? DON'T SWEAT IT

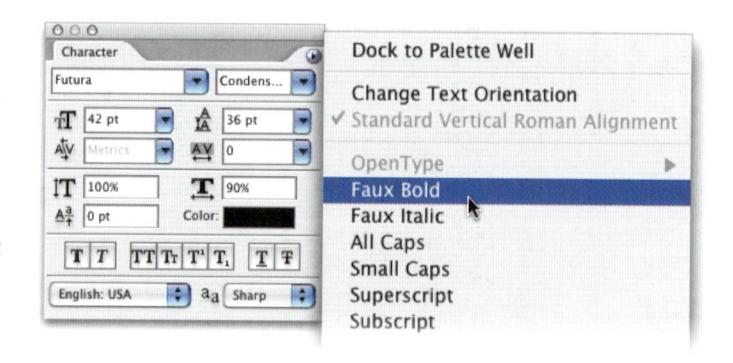

If you have a typeface that doesn't have a bold or italic version available, don't sweat it—Photoshop can make a fake bold or italic version for you. They're called faux bold and faux italic (don't pronounce them "fox bold" or the French will get really cranky about it. It's pronounced "fo," as in "Fe, Fi, Fo, Fum"). To apply a faux style to the type, highlight your type and choose Faux Bold or Faux Italic from the Character palette's flyout menu. Here's another tip: Don't forget to turn off these faux styles when you're done, because they don't automatically turn themselves off. Vive le Français!

TWEAK ALL YOUR TYPE WITH ONE FELL SWOOP!

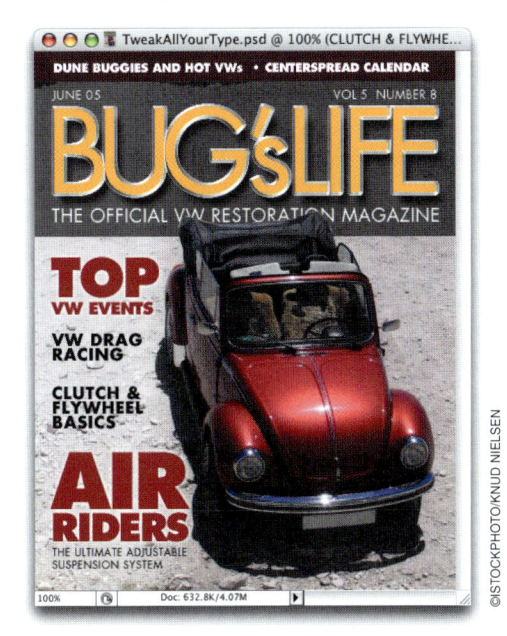

This is a pretty darn slick tip for changing the font, size, or color of a number of different Type layers all at once. Here's how it's done: First, link all the layers that you want to adjust by Command-clicking (PC: Control-clicking) on each Type layer, then clicking on the Link icon in the bottom left corner of the palette. Linking the layers helps you keep track of your text. Now, just choose the Type tool (T) and go straight to the Options Bar or the Character palette. The change you make to one Type layer will also affect all the selected Type layers. The key is *not* to highlight your type. Schweeeet!

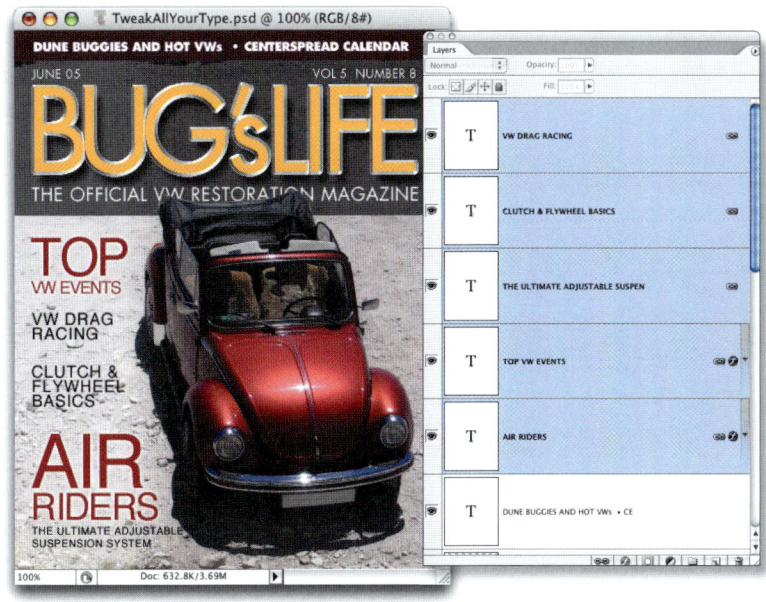

CHAPTER 7 • Smokin' Type Tips

Speed Two

IMAGE CORRECTION AND PREPRESS TIPS

We're getting near the end of the book, and I'm growing tired. Dark figures dance across the windows like so many shadows gathering dust for the fall harvest (see, this is

Speed Two
image correction and prepress tips

why they don't let me write chapter intros at 2:30 a.m. anymore). Originally, this chapter was going to be a catchall chapter—a place for all those tips that couldn't find a home, but as luck would have it, we had so many image correction and prepress tips, they actually took over the catchall chapter by force. Now, because we stuck these tips toward the back of the book, does it mean that these tips aren't as good, aren't as important, or aren't as cool as the tips in all the other chapters? Yes, that's exactly what it means. These are the tips that just aren't worth a darn, so don't even waste your time reading them, because frankly, I'm not sure how many of them really work. Oh, I'm sure one or two do, but at this point, I'm just making stuff up. I know there are many new users of Photoshop that will be reading this book, so I think a description of the term "prepress" is in order. "Pre," as you know, means before, and "press" is derived from the Latin word meaning "to unwrinkle one's pants with an iron." So, basically, read this chapter before you wrinkle your pants.

HOW ACCURATE DO YOU NEED TO BE WHEN REMOVING RED EYE?

Not very. That's right, when you're using the Red Eye tool (Shift-J until you have it), you can click directly on the red that appears in the pupil, but if you're afraid that you won't be able to click directly

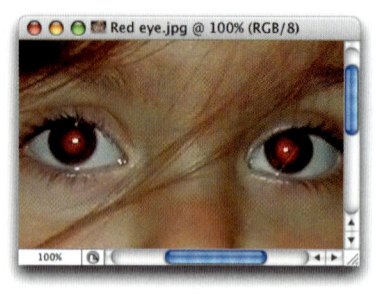

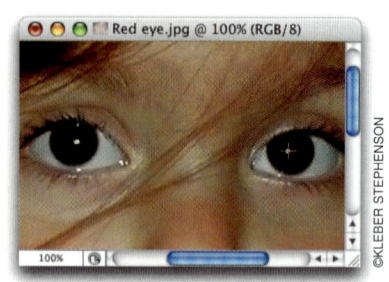

Before

After

on the red area (which can happen due to squinting, eye lashes, etc.), don't sweat it. Just click somewhere near where the red eye appears, and it will still remove the red eye. The tool is sensitive enough to search out any red that's even near where you clicked, so that's why the answer to the question "how accurate do you need to be when clicking?" is "not very."

GETTING BETTER SHADOW/HIGHLIGHT RESULTS

The Shadow/Highlight feature in Photoshop is pretty amazing, but as amazing as it is, sometimes opening up the shadows can give your photo a "milky" look to it, making it obvious that you made adjustments using Shadow/Highlight. Well, here's a tip for getting around that. First open Shadow/Highlight by going under the Image menu, under Adjustments, then choosing Shadow/Highlight. When the dialog opens, click on the Show More Options checkbox. Then, in the Shadows area up top, lower the Amount from the default setting of 50% to something more like 20%. Then increase the Tonal Width a bit and the Radius setting quite a bit, until the shadows are opened, but it doesn't look "milky" or over-processed. Once you've done this, you can slowly increase the Amount slider, but stop if it starts to look milky.

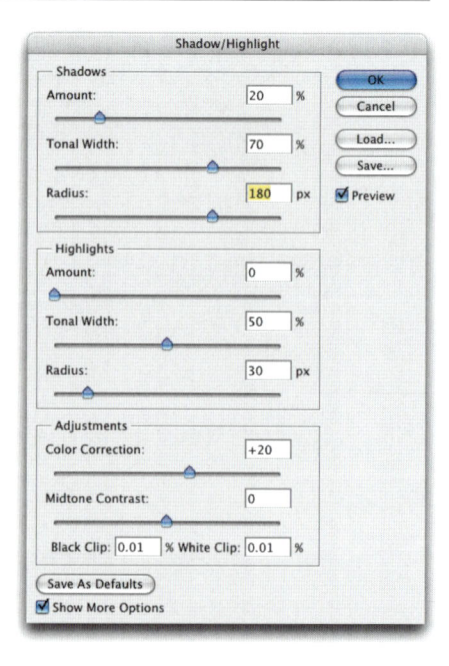

168 CHAPTER 8 • Image Correction and Prepress Tips

DITCH THE ANNOYING LENS CORRECTION GRID

I love the Lens Correction filter in CS2, but I dearly hate the grid that appears over every image every time I open one, and it's on by default, so you have to manually turn it off. However, if you're like me (and you know you are), and you want that grid off fast, there is a workaround—you can save your own custom setting with the grid turned off. But to do that, you have to change something (or the Save Settings will be grayed out). I found a workaround that has virtually no effect on your image. Open the Lens Correction filter (found under the Filter menu, under Distort), and then increase the Vignette Midpoint to 51% (a 1% increase). Then, at the bottom of the dialog, turn off the checkbox for Show Grid. Now, in the Settings flyout menu, you'll be able to choose Save Settings.

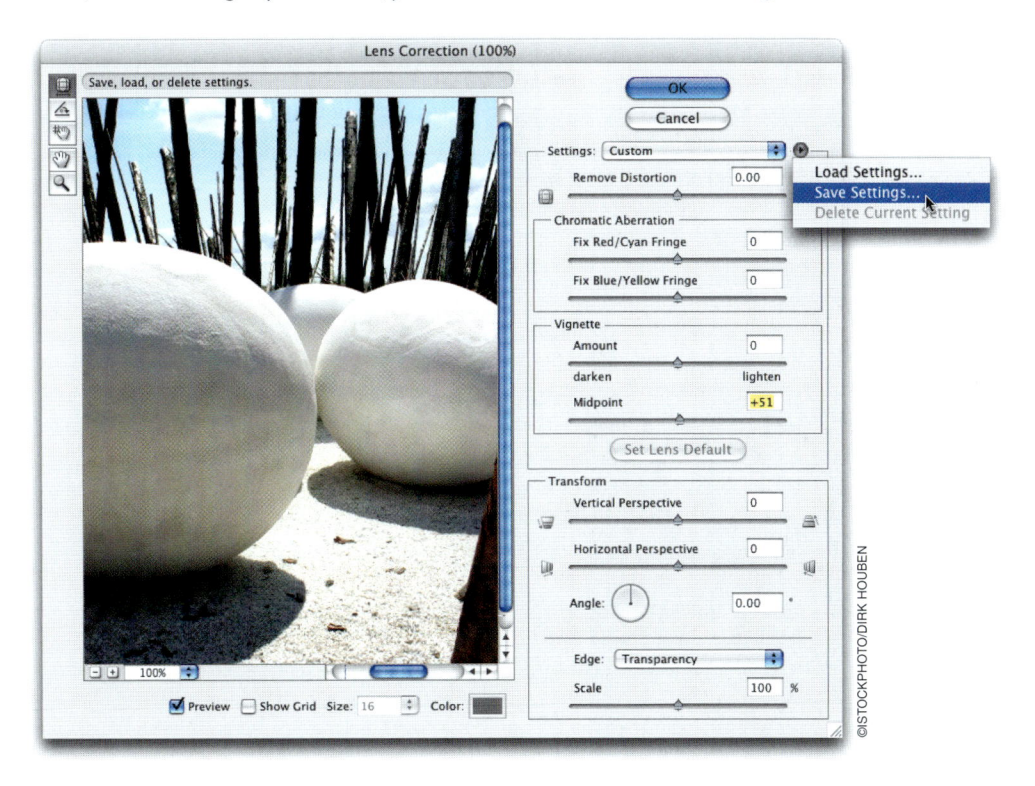

DETERMINING THE MOTION ANGLE IN SMART SHARPEN

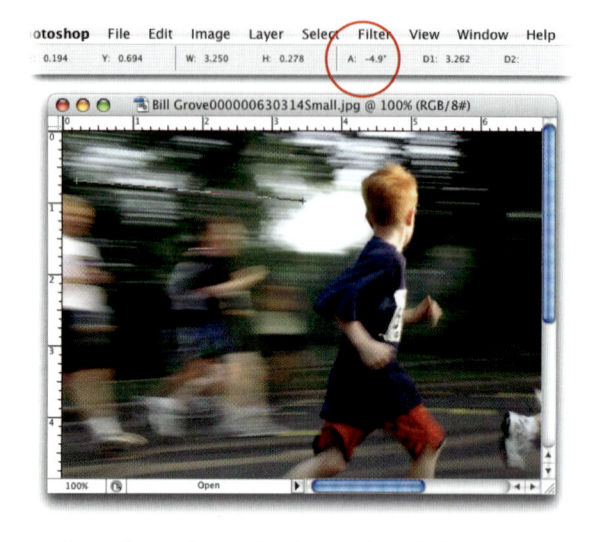

Here's a tip I picked up from our buddy and NAPP Help Desk Director Peter Bauer. In Smart Sharpen (under Filter, choose Sharpen), there's a special form of sharpening that removes visible motion blur. This sharpening is called (are you ready for this?) Motion Blur sharpening, and you choose it from the Remove pop-up menu in the Smart Sharpen dialog. But here's the catch—you have to be able to determine the angle of the blur for Smart Sharpen to remove it. So, that's where Pete's tip comes in. You grab the Measure tool (nested under the Eyedropper tool in the Toolbox), and drag it along the angle of the blur. Then, look in the Options Bar and you'll see the angle degree listed after the letter A. That's the number you enter in the Motion Blur Angle field within Smart Sharpen. Very clever, Mr. Bauer.

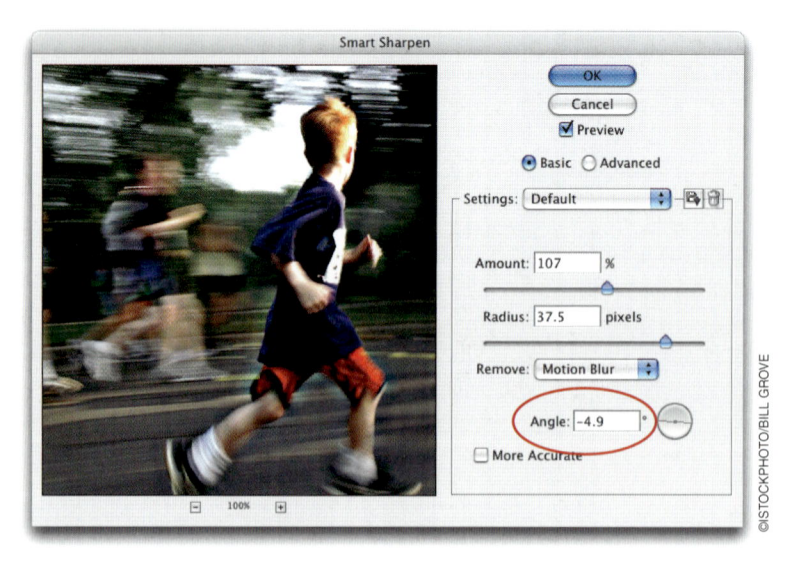

170   CHAPTER 8 • Image Correction and Prepress Tips

GETTING MORE ACCURATE COLOR USING REPLACE COLOR

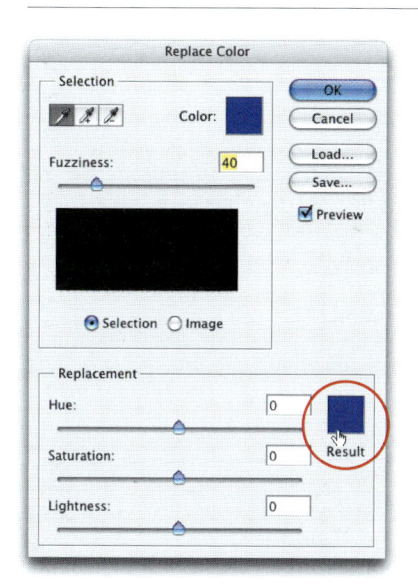

If you're using Replace Color (under the Image menu, under Adjustments) to select an area within your photo and replace it with a different color, the new color is pretty much an approximation, because you're dragging sliders, rather than inputting the exact RGB or CMYK build you're looking for. In Photoshop CS2, there's a way around this. Once you've selected the area of color you want to replace, click on the color swatch to the right of the sliders in the Replacement section (it wasn't there in previous versions). This brings up the Color Picker, where you can enter the exact RGB or CMYK values for your new color.

CORRECTING HIGHLIGHTS? WATCH OUT FOR OPEN SHADOWS!

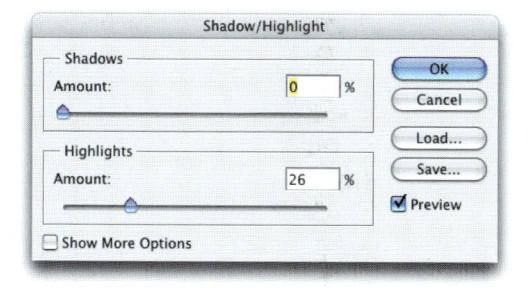

If you open the Shadow/Highlight command (found in the Image menu, under Adjustments) to open up the shadows in your photo, you're in good shape from the get-go because it automatically increases the shadow area by 50%. That's great, if that's what you're after. But what if you're trying to pull back the highlights in a photo? Shadow/Highlight doesn't know that and by default still opens up your shadows by 50%. The way to combat this is to immediately drag the Shadows slider all the way to the left when the dialog appears, so now you can adjust (pull back) the highlights by dragging the Highlights slider to the right, which affects just the highlights and not the shadows.

CHAPTER 8 • Image Correction and Prepress Tips   171

HOW TO HEAL ON A BLANK LAYER

One of the cornerstones of professional retouching is to always perform your retouches on their own separate layer. That way you never "bruise" (damage) the pixels of the original image. However, when using the Healing Brush in Photoshop 7.0, you really had no choice—you had to use it on the same layer. In Photoshop CS2, you can heal to another layer. But first, there's a little setting you have to change. Get the Healing Brush from the Toolbox, then up in the Options Bar, turn on the checkbox for Sample All Layers. Next, click on the Create a New Layer icon at the bottom of the Layers palette to create a new blank layer above your Background layer and do your "healing" there.

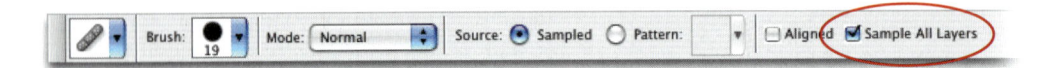

BETTER HEALING WITH A CUSTOM BRUSH

I have to give credit for this incredible tip to NAPP member Stephanie Cole, who showed it to me after the Midnight Madness session at the Photoshop World Conference & Expo in LA. She pointed out how you can get a real mottled-looking result sometimes when using the Healing Brush. However, she found that when you change the brush shape (by clicking on the Brush thumbnail in the Options Bar) to a tall thin brush, it heals using a star-shaped stroke. This greatly reduces the mottling often associated with the Healing Brush, creating a smoother-looking, more natural retouch. My thanks to Stephanie for allowing me to share her very slick trick.

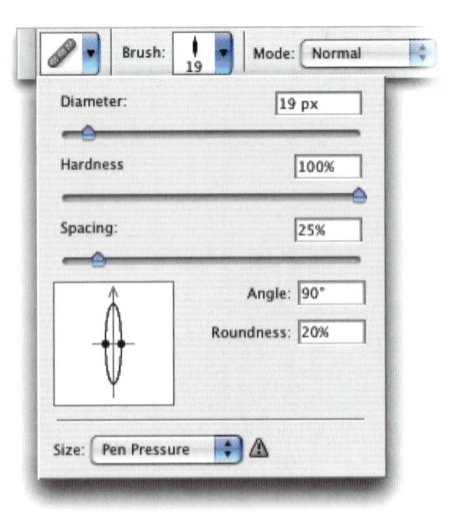

172   CHAPTER 8 • Image Correction and Prepress Tips

CREATING A CUSTOM SHADOW/HIGHLIGHT DEFAULT

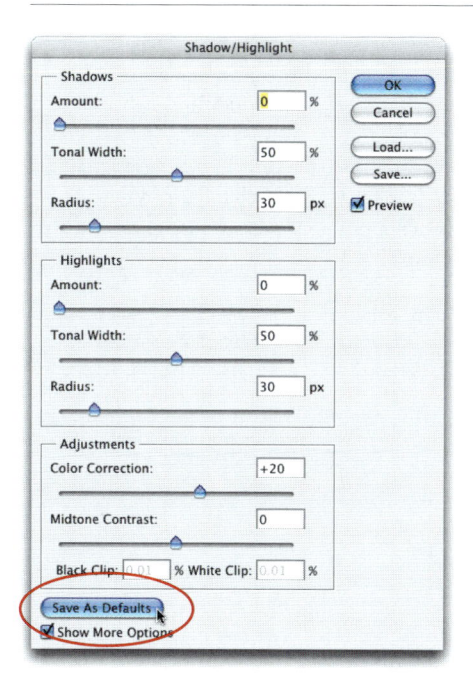

By default, the Shadow/Highlight adjustment command decreases the shadows by 50%, but if you'd prefer to have Shadow/Highlight open flat (with no automatic shadow adjustment), you can set your own defaults. That way, you decide how much, and when, the shadows get opened. You do this by going under the Image menu, under Adjustments, choosing Shadow/Highlight, and then dragging the Shadows Amount slider to 0%. Click on the Show More Options checkbox, and at the bottom of the expanded dialog click on the Save As Defaults button. That's it: Now you get to decide if the shadows get opened up, and how much, because everything's set flat.

GETTING BACK SHADOW/HIGHLIGHT'S FACTORY DEFAULTS

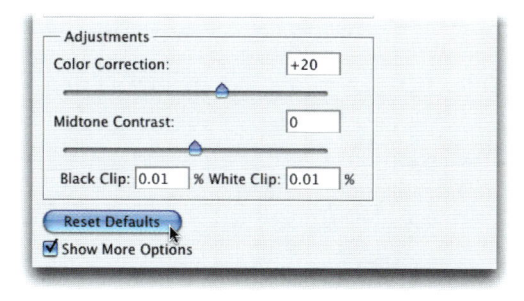

Don't ever be concerned about experimenting in Photoshop CS2's amazing Shadow/Highlight feature—mess with the sliders all you want, because you can always get back to the factory-default settings, even if you've overridden them by saving your own defaults. You do this within the Shadow/Highlight dialog (under Image, under Adjustments) by clicking on the Show More Options checkbox. Then, hold the Shift button, and you'll see the Save As Defaults button at the bottom of the expanded dialog change to the Reset Defaults button. Click it, and the factory defaults are back, baby!

CHAPTER 8 • Image Correction and Prepress Tips

HEALING WITH PRESSURE

If you're using a Wacom tablet and wireless pen with Photoshop, you've probably already uncovered the secret hiding place where Adobe tucked the pressure sensitivity controls. (*Hint:* They're in the Brushes palette.) But if you want to use pressure sensitivity with the Healing Brush, it's in a totally different spot. To turn it on, press Shift-J until you have the Healing Brush tool, then in the Options Bar, click directly on the Brush thumbnail, and a menu will pop up (it's not the standard Brush Picker). At the bottom of the menu, you'll see a Size pop-up menu, where you can choose Pen Pressure.

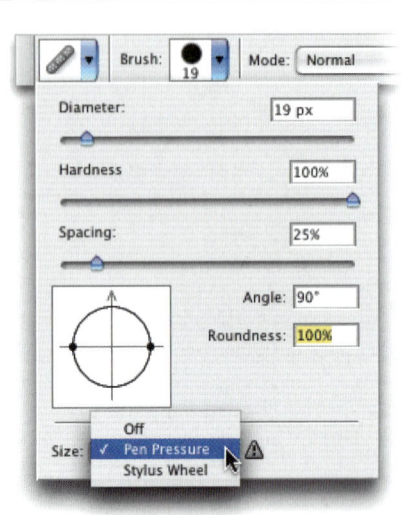

CONTROL THE OPACITY OF YOUR HEALING PROCESS

I don't know if you've noticed, but Photoshop's Healing Brush (Shift-J) doesn't have an option for controlling its opacity (the way the Clone Stamp, Brush, Eraser, and other tools have). But there is a workaround if you want to use the brush and have some control over its opacity. Just go ahead and use the brush first; then to lower the opacity of your stroke, go under the Edit menu and choose Fade Healing Brush. When the Fade dialog appears, lower the Opacity slider to the desired amount. It's a bit clunky, but it works.

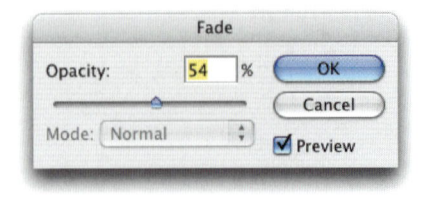

SAY GOOD-BYE TO GRADIENT BANDING

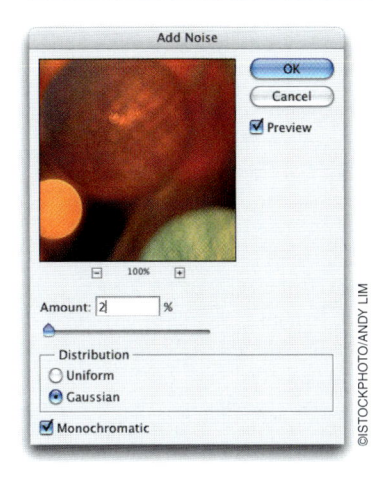

If you've printed an image with a gradient in it, you're probably familiar with banding (a visible line where one color ends and the next starts, like bands of color, instead of a smooth transition from one color to the next). There's a very popular tip for getting rid of banding that's very effective for high-resolution imaging. Open the image in Photoshop and go under the Filter menu, under Noise, and choose Add Noise. When the Add Noise dialog appears, for Amount enter 2, for Distribution choose Gaussian, turn on the Monochromatic checkbox, and then click OK. You'll see a little bit of this noise when viewing the image onscreen, but when printed at high resolution, the noise disappears and hides the banding. We add noise to every gradient we create for just that reason.

SHARPENING YOUR IMAGES LIKE A PRO

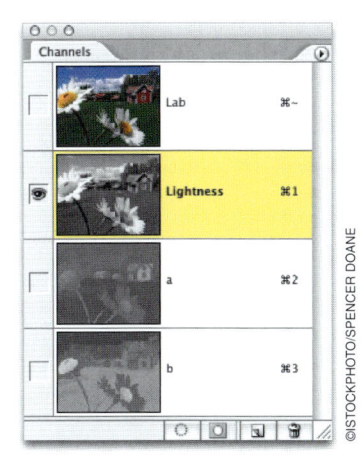

Just about every image that is brought into Photoshop, whether from a scanner, digital camera, CD-ROM, etc., needs to be sharpened. The undisputed tool for this task is Photoshop's Unsharp Mask filter. The only downside of using this filter is that getting the level of sharpening you'd like can sometimes cause color shifts and halos, and it can also accentuate dust or specs within the image. There are two ways around this, and what's great about these methods is they let you apply a higher level of sharpening without causing color shifts or other problems: (1) Convert your file from RGB mode to Lab Color. Then go to the Channels palette and click on the Lightness channel. Now apply the Unsharp Mask filter (twice if you need it), then switch back to RGB mode (don't worry, there's no harm in this RGB-to-Lab-to-RGB mode conversion). (2) If you're working on a CMYK image, apply the Unsharp Mask filter, then go under the Edit menu and choose Fade Unsharp Mask. When the Fade dialog appears, change the Mode pop-up menu to Luminosity and click OK (which pretty much does the same thing as method 1; it applies the sharpening to the luminance of the image, not the color).

CHAPTER 8 • Image Correction and Prepress Tips   175

FIVE TIPS FOR GETTING RID OF MOIRÉ PATTERNS

If you scanned an image that already has been printed in one form or another, you're bound to get a moiré pattern over your image (moiré patterns are a series of dots or spots that appear on your image). These spots are your scanner picking up the halftone screen that was applied when the image was printed.

Here are five quick tips for removing moiré patterns:

1. Go under the Filter menu, under Noise, and choose Despeckle. There are no numbers to input or sliders to adjust—it either works or it doesn't, but luckily, it works about 75% of the time. However, if you run Despeckle and it doesn't work, undo it. That's because Despeckle adds a slight blur to your entire image, and if it doesn't work, there's no sense in leaving that blur applied, eh?
2. Apply a 1-pixel or less Gaussian Blur. This will usually work if method 1 doesn't. Again, if this technique doesn't remove the moiré pattern, undo it to reduce unnecessary blurring.
3. Go under the Filter menu, under Noise, and choose Median. Enter 1 pixel and click OK. I know I'm sounding like a broken record, but if it doesn't work, undo it. You know why.
4. Reduce the resolution of your scan to twice the line screen it will be printed at. For example, if you scanned it at 300 dpi and you're going to print it at 100-line screen, lower the resolution of the file to 200 ppi and that'll probably do the trick. If this image is going to be used on the Web, when you lower the resolution to 72 ppi, that'll probably do it.
5. Lastly, try rescanning the image with the image rotated slightly on the scanner bed. This is a last resort, but if all else fails, this will probably do the trick. Once the image is in Photoshop, you'll have to straighten the scan, but at least the moiré pattern will be gone.

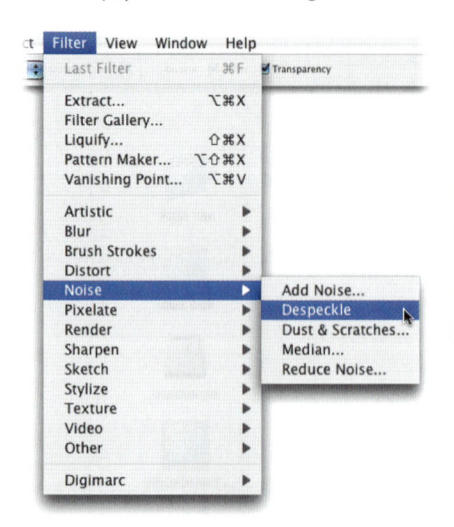

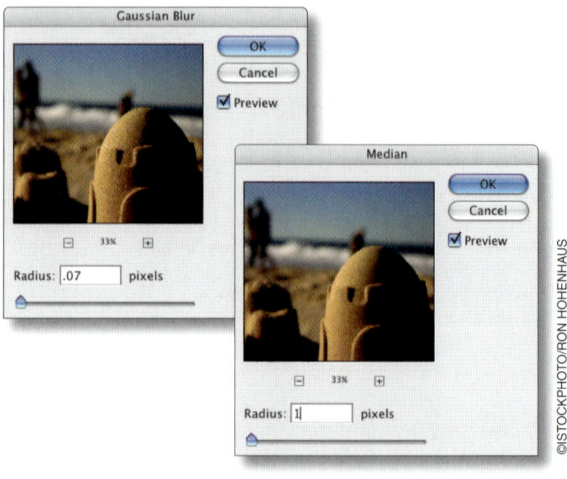

CHAPTER 8 • Image Correction and Prepress Tips

SCAN LINE ART AT THE RESOLUTION YOU NEED

If you're scanning black-and-white line art for reproduction in print, here are two quick tips that'll help you get better results:

1. Scan the line art image at the dpi you'll be printing it. This is the one time we break our long-standing "don't-scan-at-too-high-a-resolution" rule—but only when it comes to line art. If you're going to output your line art on a 600-dpi laser printer, scan it at 600 dpi. If you're going to output it to high-resolution film negs, scan it at 1,200 dpi (that's about as high as you'll need to go).
2. Scan your line art images in Grayscale mode. If you do, then you can apply filters such as the Unsharp Mask to help clean and define the lines, and you can use Levels to brighten the white areas.

Note: If you scan in Bitmap mode, you won't be able to use these two important line art cleanup tips, because they're not supported in Bitmap mode.

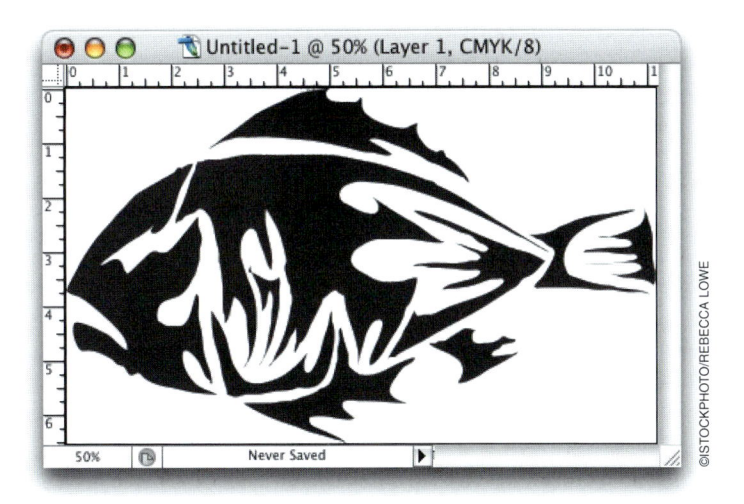

CHAPTER 8 • Image Correction and Prepress Tips

USING THE HIGH PASS FILTER FOR SHARPENING

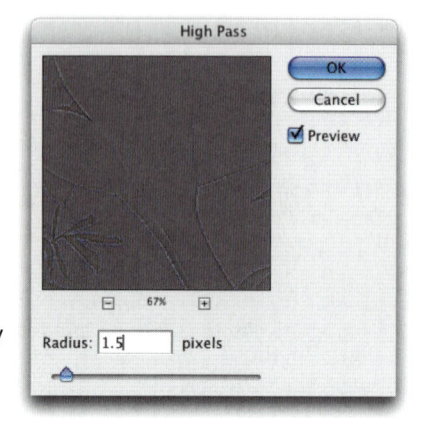

There's a sharpening technique that's really gaining popularity that works especially well on images with lots of well-defined edges (such as buildings, cars, furniture, etc.). It's actually a layer technique combined with a filter, but it's very easy (and often very effective) to apply. Start by duplicating the Background layer of the image you want to sharpen by pressing Command-J (PC: Control-J). Then, go under the Filter menu, under Other, and choose High Pass. When the High Pass dialog appears, enter a Radius of 1.5 pixels (a good starting point) and click OK to apply the filter. It will change your image into a gray mess, but don't sweat it (yet). To bring the sharpening into your image, change the blend mode of this layer to Soft Light. The gray will disappear, and the edges of your image will appear sharper. You can also try the Hard Light mode to increase the sharpening effect. Still not enough? Make a copy of the layer for a multiplying effect. Is one copy not enough sharpening, but two are too much? You can control the sharpening amount in two ways: (1) Switch between Soft Light and Hard Light, or (2) lower the Opacity setting of the layer to dial in just the right amount of sharpening.

SPOT COLOR GRADIENT FILM SAVER

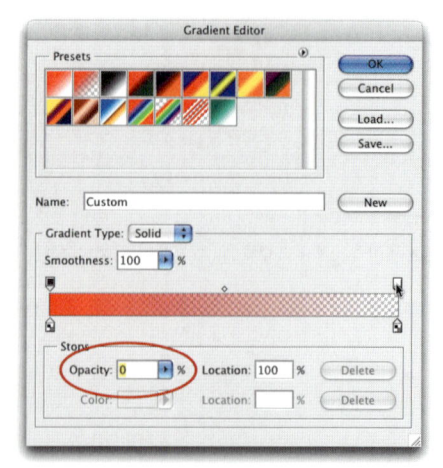

If you're creating a gradient using a spot color that fades to white, to make sure your gradient appears just on the spot separation plate, create the gradient to go from the spot color to a 0% tint of the same spot color (for example, go from 100% red to 0% red). Just click on the color's opacity stop (that appears above the stop in the color ramp) and then lower the Opacity in the bottom-left corner of the Gradient Editor. That way, when you do your seps, the entire gradient will appear on the red separation.

CORRECT IN CMYK OR RGB?

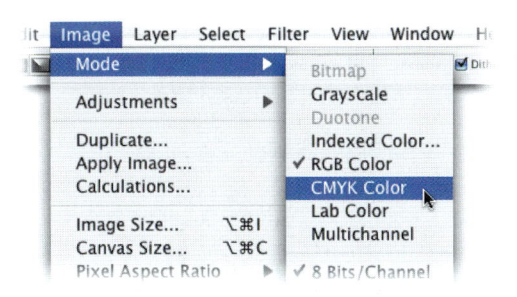

We've been asked the question of whether to correct in CMYK or RGB a hundred times. As a general rule, we try to do as much color correction as possible in RGB mode, and if we're going to use the image on press, we only convert to CMYK at the end of the correction process. The main reason is that CMYK mode throws away data—a lot of data—and why would you want to correct an image with significantly less data than your scanner can capture? We want as much data as possible while correcting images, and when we're done, then we'll convert to CMYK (under Image, choose Mode) and toss the data that won't be used on press.

STRAIGHTENING SCANS IN 10 SECONDS (OR LESS)

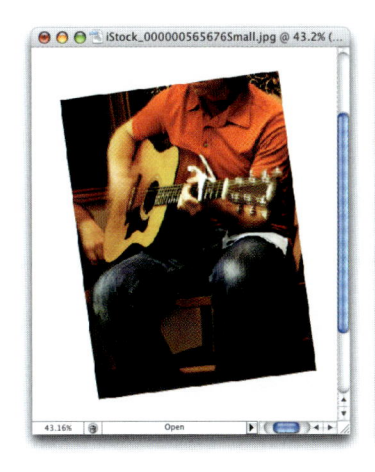

If you've scanned an image and it's crooked when you bring it into Photoshop, you can fix it in about 10 seconds flat. Just switch to the Measure tool (it lives behind the Eyedropper tool in the Toolbox) and drag it along the top edge of the image you want to straighten. That's the hard part (and that should give you an idea of how easy this technique is). Next, go under the Image menu, under Rotate Canvas, and choose Arbitrary. Photoshop automatically enters the amount of rotation (courtesy of your earlier measurement), so all you have to do is click OK and bam!—the image is perfectly straightened.

CHAPTER 8 • Image Correction and Prepress Tips

SCANNERS AREN'T JUST FOR FLAT OBJECTS

Even though your flatbed scanner is normally used for scanning (you guessed it) flat images, it doesn't mean you can't scan images that have more dimension (such as a watch, a ring, a yo-yo, you name it). The only problem is, scanning an image that lifts the lid adds lots of ambient light into your scan, introducing so many outside colors and reflections that it makes the scan all but unusable. The tip for getting around this is deceivingly simple: Just put a black sweater (or black felt cloth) around the object you're going to scan, and you'll get great-looking scans, even with the lid open. The black sweater soaks up that ambient light and you'll be amazed at how natural and balanced your scanned objects will look.

ARE YOUR COLORS PRESS READY?

If you're working on an image that will be printed on a printing press and you select a color that's outside the range of what a CMYK press can reproduce, you'll get what's called a Gamut Warning right within Photoshop's Color Picker. This is just to let you know that the color you've chosen is outside the CMYK gamut. Just below the warning is a tiny color swatch showing you what the color you picked will really look like when printed in CMYK mode. To find out where that color resides within the Color Picker, click once directly on that tiny swatch and Photoshop will pick that color for you.

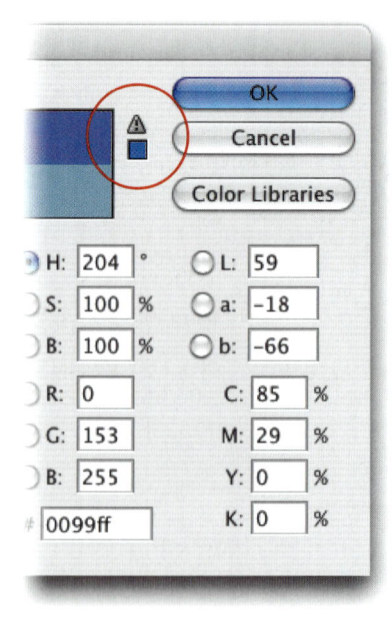

CHAPTER 8 • Image Correction and Prepress Tips

NEVER SWAP COLORS AGAIN WHEN CLEANING LINE ART

When cleaning up line art images with the Pencil tool, you can spend a lot of time going back and forth to the Toolbox to switch your Foreground color to black (to fill in missing pixels) and then to white (to erase pixels that shouldn't be there in the first place). It does help if you use the keyboard shortcut D to set your Foreground to black, and then X to make white your Foreground color, but there's actually a faster way. Once you select the Pencil tool, go in the Options Bar and turn on Auto Erase. What the Auto Erase option does is pretty neat—when you click the Pencil in a black area of pixels, it paints white; when you click it on a white pixel, it automatically paints black. It happens automatically—so you never have to switch colors again—saving you a ton of time, travel, and keystrokes.

LET PHOTOSHOP DO YOUR RESOLUTION MATH

You don't need a calculator to determine how much resolution you need for printing to a particular line screen—Photoshop will do all the math for you, right inside the Image Size dialog. Here's how: Open the image you want to print. Go under the Image menu and choose Image Size. When the dialog appears, click on the Auto button (it's right under the Cancel button). When the Auto Resolution dialog appears, all you have to do is type in the line screen of the device you're printing to and then choose a Quality setting. Here's how Photoshop does its resolution math:

Draft: This just lowers your resolution to 72 ppi (ideal for onscreen use, the Web, etc.).
Good: This takes the line screen and multiplies it by 1.5.
Best: This doubles the line screen (multiplies it by 2).

When you click OK, Photoshop enters the math it just did into the Resolution field of the Image Size dialog.

CHAPTER 8 • Image Correction and Prepress Tips

GOING TO PRESS? MAKE SURE YOUR MONITOR IS IN THE "RIGHT SPACE"

By default, the RGB space for your monitor is set to sRGB, which is an okay mode for designing Web graphics. However, if you're producing graphics for print, the sRGB mode is just about the worst RGB space your monitor could possibly be set at. It clips off lots of colors that are actually printable in CMYK mode, and therefore is pretty unsuitable for prepress work. We recommend changing your RGB workspace to an RGB space that's more appropriate for doing print work. We like Adobe RGB (1998), which is a very popular RGB space for prepress work. You choose this RGB space under the Photoshop menu, under Color Settings (in Windows, Color Settings can be found under the Edit menu). When the Color Settings dialog appears, under the Working Spaces area, choose Adobe RGB (1998) from the RGB pop-up menu.

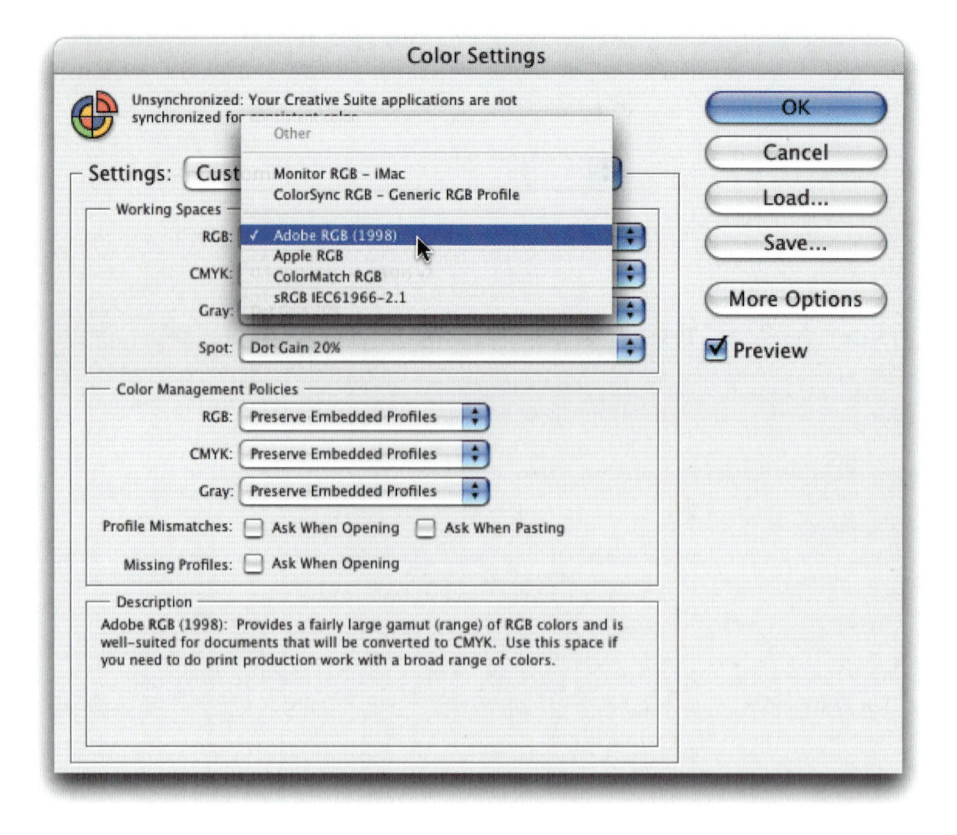

WANT BETTER GRADIENTS ON PRESS? HERE'S THE TIP

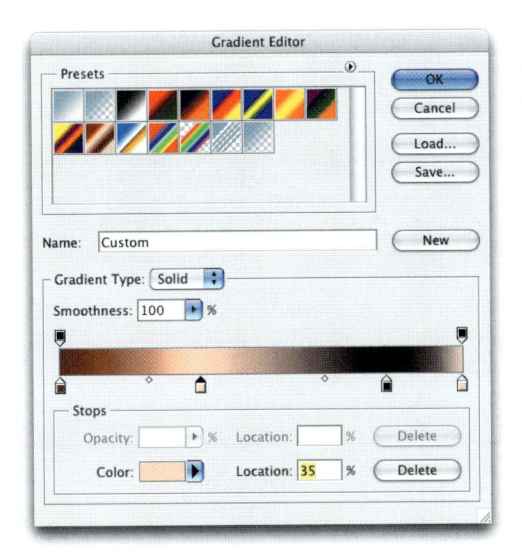

If you're designing a job that will ultimately go to a printing press in CMYK mode and it's going to contain one or more gradients, you'll get better printed results (less color shifts) if you create those gradients after you convert to CMYK mode.

GETTING BEFORE AND AFTER PREVIEWS

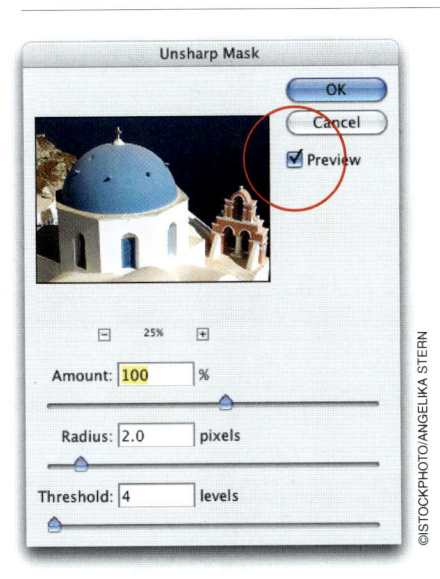

If you're applying a correction filter, such as the Unsharp Mask filter, you can get a before and after view of your image even before you click the OK button (and then press Command-Z [PC: Control-Z] to undo/redo the filter). Instead, click-and-hold on the preview box inside the Unsharp Mask filter. When you click-and-hold, you get the before preview in the window; when you release the mouse button, it shows you how the image will look with the filter applied. Pretty handy. If you need to see the full preview onscreen, you can toggle the Preview checkbox on or off. Another tip is to hold the Command or Option (PC: Control or Alt) button while in a filter dialog, and then your cursor changes into the Zoom tool. You can then zoom in or out in your preview window by clicking within it.

CHAPTER 8 • Image Correction and Prepress Tips

CLONING FROM IMAGE TO IMAGE

If you're retouching an image using the Clone Stamp tool (S), not only can you clone from the image you're in but you can also clone from any other image that you have open. All you have to do is make sure both images are open at the same time. Go to the other image, Option-click (PC: Alt-click) on the area you want to clone from, switch back to the image you're working on, and then start painting. When you do, you'll be cloning image data from the other image.

GET MORE REALISTIC DROP SHADOWS ON PRESS

Here's a quick tip for getting more realistic drop shadows in print: Add some noise. When you choose Drop Shadow from the Add a Layer Style pop-up menu in the Layers palette, there's a slider for adding noise to your shadows in the Layer Style dialog. When you add just a small percentage, it makes your shadows appear more realistic when they show up in print.

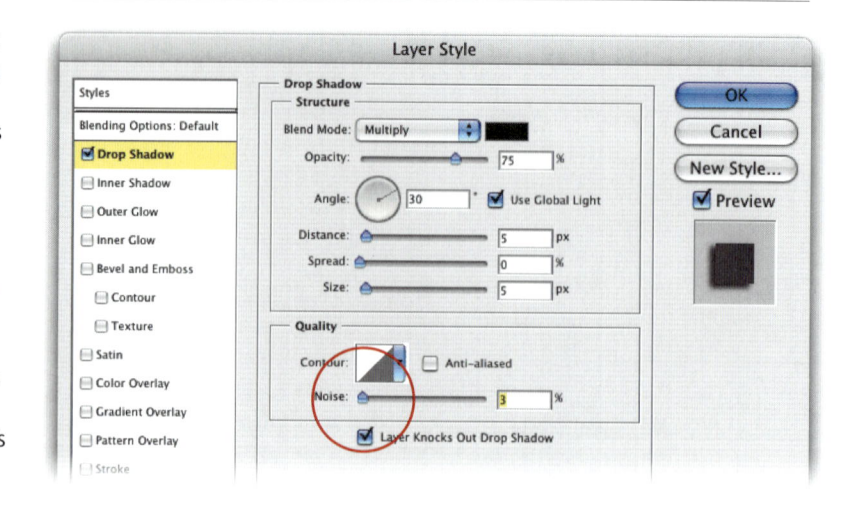

184 CHAPTER 8 • Image Correction and Prepress Tips

MAKING SURE YOUR WHITES ARE REALLY WHITE

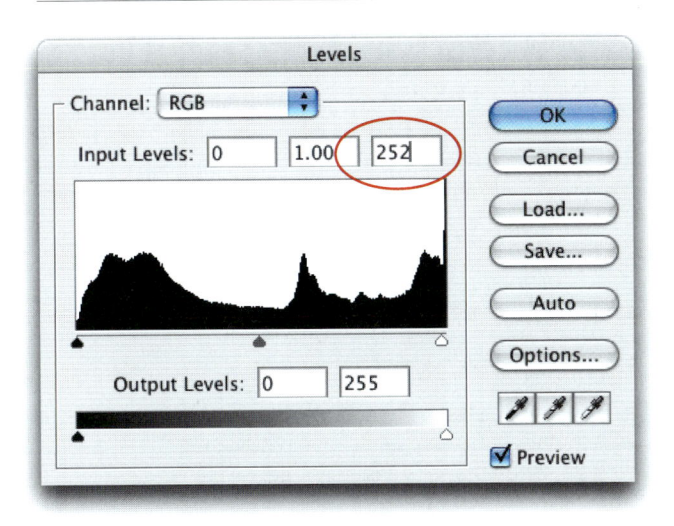

If you have an image that appears to have solid white areas (maybe the background surrounding a logo), but when you put the Eyedropper on that area, it gives you a 1% or 2% reading in one of the CMYK values in your Info palette, you can use Levels to gets those areas back down to 0% so they don't print with a dot. Here's how: Go under the Image menu, under Adjustments, and choose Levels. The third field from the left (at the top of the dialog) shows your current highlight value (your white point setting). The default value will be 255. Enter 252 or 250, then move your cursor over the white area in question and look in the Info palette to see if the readings are now all 0% (that change should be enough to remove the stray colors). When it's right, click OK, and you'll have solid white in your white areas.

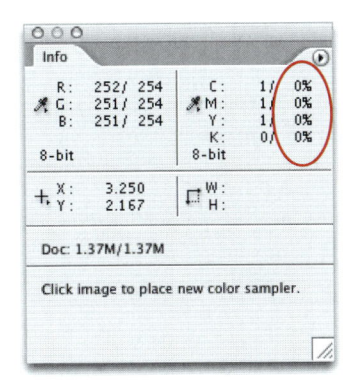

CHAPTER 8 • Image Correction and Prepress Tips   185

TRY NOT TO CORRECT MORE THAN ONCE

When correcting images in Curves, Levels, etc., it's best to try to do all your corrections at one time rather than changing each setting individually (by that I mean, don't set a highlight in Curves, then close and reopen it to set a shadow). The reason is, each time you apply a tonal correction, it puts some strain on the quality of the image. So to keep your image from having unnecessary data loss, when you open Curves or Levels, make your shadow, highlight, and midtone adjustments, and then click OK to apply all three adjustments at once.

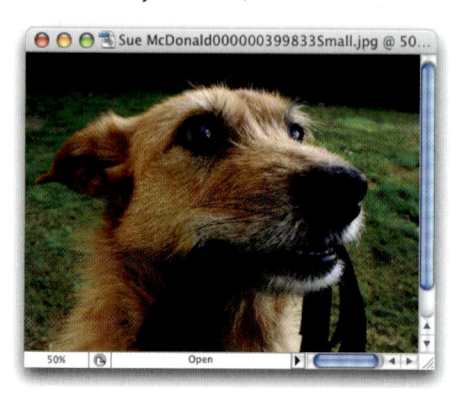

MORE CURVE POINT QUICK TIPS

When you're working in Curves (Command-M [PC: Control-M]), once you've plotted a curve point, you can rotate over to the next point in your curve by pressing Control-Tab (PC: Right-click-Tab). To rotate back to the previous point, add the Shift key to make it Shift-Control-Tab (PC: Shift-Right-click-Tab). If you've got one or more points selected and want to deselect all your points, just press Command-D (PC: Control-D) to release all your points.

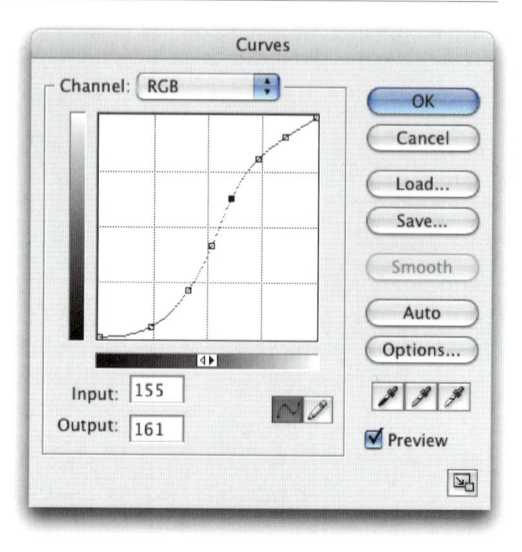

186 CHAPTER 8 • Image Correction and Prepress Tips

HAVE PHOTOSHOP HELP FIND YOUR HIGHLIGHTS/SHADOWS

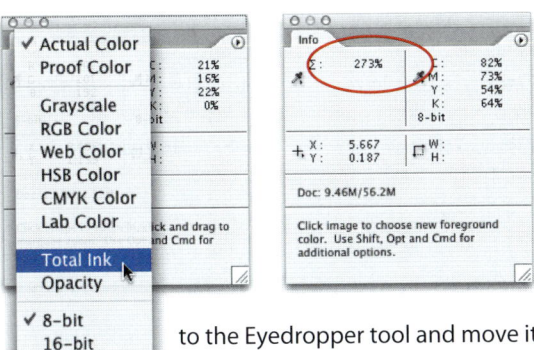

Not sure where the highlight or shadow points in your image are located? Let Photoshop help. Go under the Window menu and choose Info. In the RGB readout, click on the tiny Eyedropper icon to the left of the readout. A pop-up menu will appear with a list of values you can measure. Choose Total Ink from this pop-up menu. Next, press I to switch to the Eyedropper tool and move it over your image in the areas you think might be the darkest. Now, in the Info palette, look for the highest number. When you find the area in your image with the highest number (the highest amount of total ink), you've found the shadow point. Do the same to find the highlight—just look for the lowest number. When you locate that number, you've found the highlight.

TALKIN' 'BOUT MY RESOLUTION

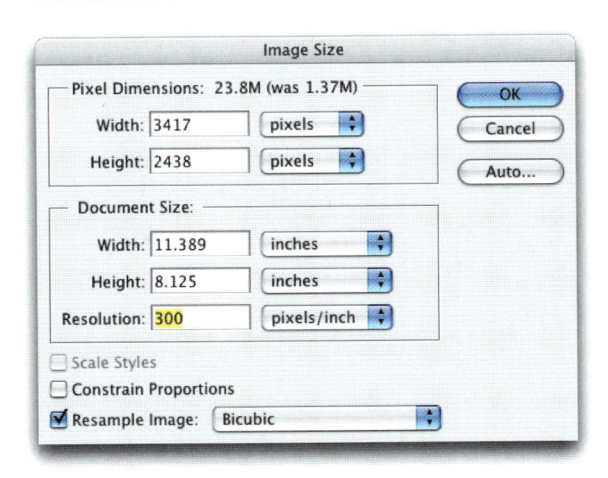

Here's a lingo tip about resolution. Although images can have a resolution from 1 to more than 2,000 ppi, when it comes to talking resolution, there are three basic resolutions that are pretty common. Low-res (short for resolution) is normally 72 ppi, and low-res images are primarily used for onscreen viewing (such as the Web, slide presentations, digital video, etc.). Medium-res is generally 150 ppi and is commonly used for printing to inkjet and laser printers. When people use the term high-res, it's almost always referring to 300 ppi, which is more than sufficient resolution for printing to a printing press. Anything above 300 ppi is still considered high-res, but you'd say it like this: "I made a 600-ppi high-res scan." Which resolution is right for you? Nice try. That's a whole book unto itself.

CHAPTER 8 • Image Correction and Prepress Tips

ARE YOU REALLY SEEING YOUR SHARPENING?

When you apply sharpening to your image using the Unsharp Mask or Smart Sharpen filter (under Filter, choose Sharpen), make certain that when you apply it, you're viewing the image at 100% size. Most other views won't give you an accurate view of how the sharpening is really affecting the image. To make sure you're viewing at 100%, just double-click the Zoom tool in the Toolbox.

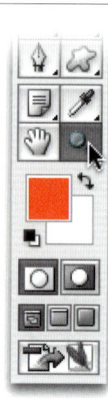

ADJUSTING CURVE POINTS WITH PRECISION

Once you've plotted a point on a curve in the Curves dialog (Command-M [PC: Control-M]), you can adjust these points by clicking-and-dragging them, but many people find it easier to plot the point by using the Up/Down Arrow keys on their keyboard. This adjusts the Output of the point in increments of 2. To adjust the Input, use the Left/Right Arrow keys. To make larger moves, hold the Shift key while using the Arrow keys and your points will move in increments of 15.

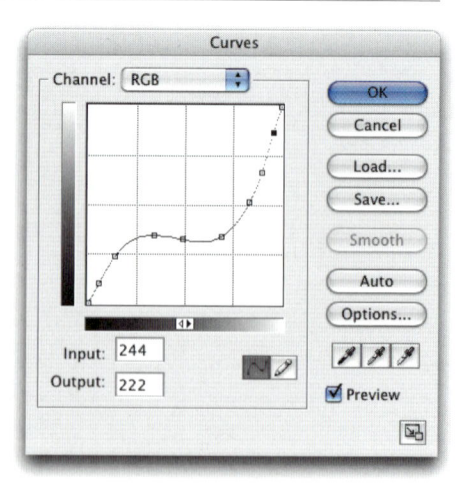

CHAPTER 8 • Image Correction and Prepress Tips

APPLY UNSHARP MASK TO CMYK IMAGES

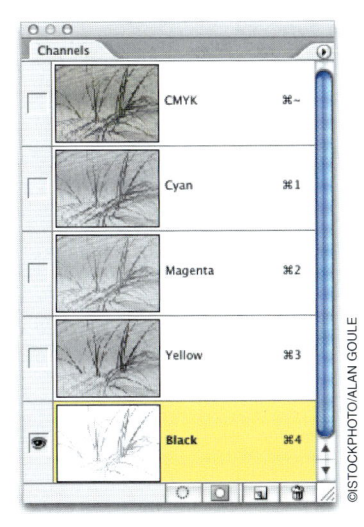

If you've already converted your image to CMYK mode and you want to quickly sharpen your image without introducing color shifts or halos, go to the Channels palette (under the Window menu), click on the Black channel, and apply your Unsharp Mask there. Applying the filter just to the Black channel will enable you to apply a higher level of sharpening without damaging the image.

©ISTOCKPHOTO/ALAN GOULE

RGB FLESH TONES: GETTING THE "RED" OUT

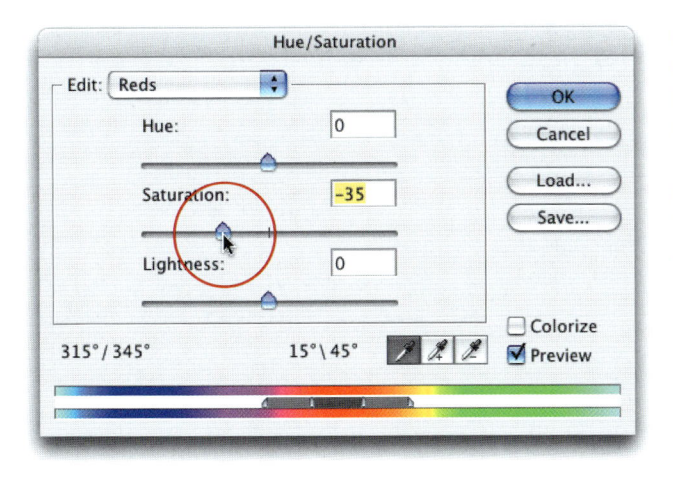

If you're working on an RGB image and you've done your basic color correction but the flesh tone in your image still seems too red (a common problem), here's a tip to fix it fast. First, select the flesh tone areas in your image (using the Lasso tool, etc.). Add a slight feather by going under the Select menu and choosing Feather. Enter a 1-pixel feather for low-res images; 3–5 pixels for high-res images. Go under the Image menu, under Adjustments, and choose Hue/Saturation. From the Edit pop-up menu, choose Reds. Now lower the Saturation slider until your skin tones look more natural and click OK.

CHAPTER 8 • Image Correction and Prepress Tips   189

ONCE YOU'RE IN CMYK MODE, STAY THERE

You've read some techniques in this chapter that require you to be in either RGB mode or Lab Color mode; however, if for any reason your image is already in CMYK mode, do not (I repeat, do not) convert to RGB or Lab mode for any reason. Once you've converted to CMYK mode, the data loss from the conversion has already occurred, and switching back to RGB mode won't bring back those lost colors. What's worse is, if you switch from CMYK to RGB (or Lab), when you convert back to CMYK mode, you'll go through another CMYK conversion and damage your image even more. The moral of this story is—once you're in CMYK mode, stay there.

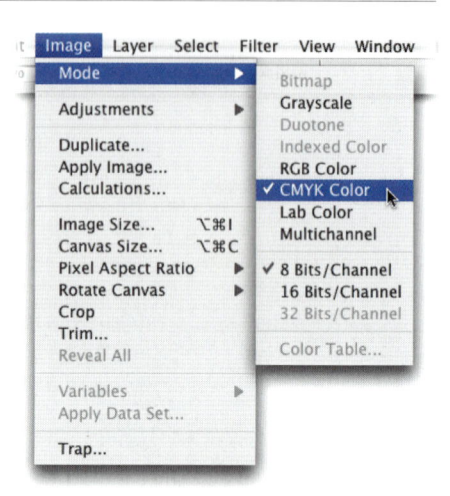

THE SIMPLE TIP TO BETTER COLOR SEPARATIONS

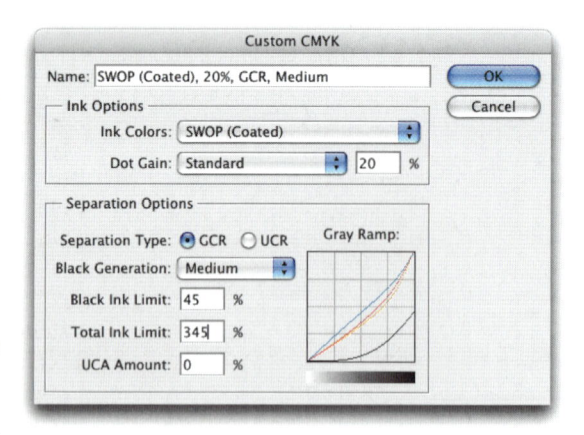

Converting from RGB mode to CMYK mode for printing is easy, just choose CMYK from the Mode menu under the Image menu. However, getting great-looking separations on press takes more than just choosing the CMYK menu command. Before you convert to CMYK mode, call the print shop that's printing your job and ask them for their Photoshop CMYK separation setup. They'll provide you with custom settings to input in the Custom CMYK dialog that will give you a separation that's tuned to their particular printing press. Once they provide you with those settings, you input them by going under the Edit menu and choosing Color Settings. When the Color Settings dialog appears, click on the CMYK pop-up menu, and at the top of the menu choose Custom CMYK. The Custom CMYK setup dialog will appear, where you can enter the settings given to you by the print shop. Once entered, then you can make your CMYK conversion, and you'll get a better separation that's specially tuned to the press your job will be printed on.

190 CHAPTER 8 • Image Correction and Prepress Tips

HOW TO SHARPEN FLESH TONES IN CMYK

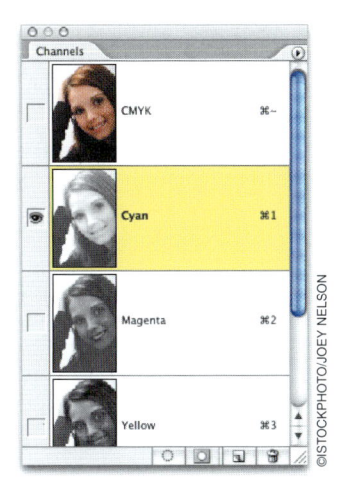

When you're sharpening CMYK images, the toughest areas to sharpen are often the flesh tones. Usually, because of the soft nature of skin, you'll need a lot of sharpening, which can introduce noise and color shifts, particularly in flesh tone areas. One tip that's often used to combat this is to apply your sharpening to just the Cyan channel in the Channels palette in images where flesh tone is the focal point (such as in portraits).

HOW TO READ FOUR AREAS AT ONCE

Photoshop's Color Sampler tool lets you sample up to four different color readings from within your image at the same time. The cool thing is, anytime you have one of Photoshop's paint tools (Brush, Pencil, etc.), you can instantly access the Color Sampler by holding Option-Shift (PC: Alt-Shift). Click to add a color sampler and the Info palette immediately pops up to show you the reading. Each time you add a sampler, the Info palette expands to show that reading (leaving your earlier readings still visible). To delete any sampler, press Option-Shift (PC: Alt-Shift) again and just move the cursor back over the sampler and it will change into a pair of scissors. Click right on the sampler in your image to delete it. (*Hint:* You have to click directly on the sampler or it won't work, and this doesn't work for all painting tools.)

CHAPTER 8 • Image Correction and Prepress Tips 191

Speed Kills

ADVANCED TIPS

Before you attempt any of the tips in this chapter, I have to tell you, you'll need a fairly thorough knowledge of calculus, and it wouldn't hurt if you kept a scientific calculator

Speed Kills
advanced tips

handy either. In fact, ideally, you'd put together a team with varied backgrounds and skill sets to really get anything out of this chapter. Believe it or not, that's what some people expect from an "Advanced Tips" chapter—tips that are very complicated and involved. But just because you're a more advanced user, doesn't mean the tips should be harder; it just means the tips apply to more advanced areas of Photoshop use, such as masking, curves, paths, and fun stuff like that. The tips should be easy to do, just covering more advanced topics. But if you really feel you need a complicated and involved tip to get your money's worth, here goes: Open a blank RGB document at 72 ppi. Then take a photograph of your family and tape it to the outside of your monitor. Using the Brush tool, choose a large soft-edged brush, and draw what you see. When complete, it should look exactly like the photograph. Happy now?

ACTION INSURANCE POLICY

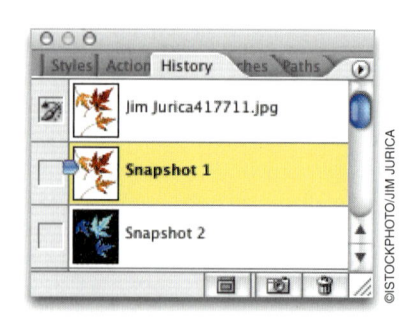

Have you ever written an action, and after it's done, you wish you hadn't run it in the first place? Maybe the effect just doesn't look right on the image, or there's a mistake or missing step in your action? Well, here's a tip that will help you, not just when you're testing your action, but even after you've perfected it. Bring up the Actions palette (found under the Window menu), click on the Create New Action icon, and once you're recording, make the first step of your action creating a snapshot. To do this, just open the History palette (under the Window menu) and click on the Create New Snapshot icon at the bottom of the palette. That way, if after the action runs, you don't like the results, you can just click on the saved snapshot in the History palette, and the image will instantly return to how it looked when you opened it.

DOING ANIMATIONS? DON'T JUMP TO IMAGEREADY

In previous versions of Photoshop, if you wanted to create an animation, you'd have to jump to Image-Ready (Photoshop's Web graphics sibling that comes preinstalled with Photoshop). Although ImageReady still comes with Photoshop CS2, you don't need to jump over there to do your animations; now you can do them right within Photoshop. Just go to the Window menu and choose Animation, and ImageReady's familiar-looking Animation palette will appear across the bottom of your Photoshop screen, and a row of buttons for animation options will appear near the top of your Layers palette.

194 CHAPTER 9 • Advanced Tips

THE NEW WAY TO CREATE A CLIPPING GROUP

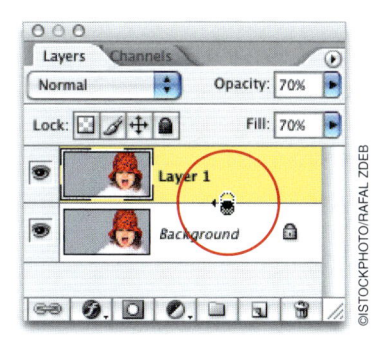

If you're used to the old Command-G (PC: Control-G) shortcut to clip the layer you're on into the layer beneath, then you're going to have some frustrating times in CS2. That's because Command-G (PC: Control-G) now creates a Layer Group, not a clipping group (or clipping mask as Adobe renamed it in CS). To create a clipping mask, you have to use the old shortcut from pre-CS versions of Photoshop, which is to hold the Option key (PC: Alt key) and in the Layers palette click once right between the two layers (your cursor will change to two overlapping circles—that's your cue to click). You unclip them the same way.

KEEPING TRACK OF YOUR EVERY MOVE

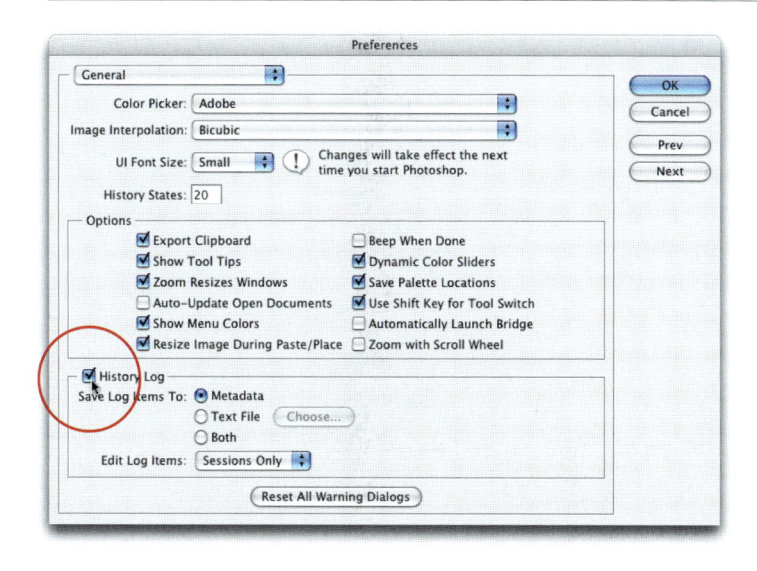

If you'd like to keep a running record of every step, every tweak, every movement—virtually every little thing you've done to your image in Photoshop CS2—you can do just that. It's called History Logging. Basically, it keeps a running log (in the background) of all your History States, and it can save it to a text file that you can open and view later. To turn on this History Log, go under the Photoshop menu (PC: Edit menu), under Preferences, and choose General. At the bottom of the Preferences dialog, turn on the checkbox for History Log, then choose if you want the log items embedded into the file (metadata), written to a text file, or both.

CHAPTER 9 • Advanced Tips   195

EMBED YOUR MESSAGE INTO YOUR PHOTOS

As you know, your digital camera embeds background info into your photos (called EXIF data), and Photoshop embeds its own info when you edit the image (called File Properties). However, in Photoshop CS2 you can add your own info (called IPTC data) in the IPTC Core area within the Metadata palette in Adobe Bridge. This is where you might embed your copyright info, website, or other comments that people viewing your file might find important. To add your info, just click next to any IPTC item that has a Pencil icon to the right of it, and a field will appear where you can enter your own custom info.

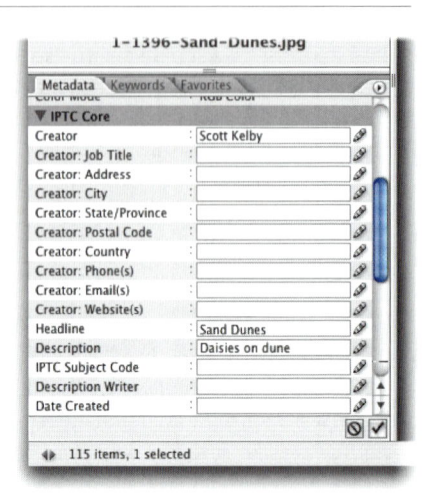

MANAGING THE METADATA OVERLOAD

The Metadata palette in Bridge provides much more information than the average person will ever need. If you don't need all this "metadata overload," you can set it up so it only displays the data you care about, giving you a more orderly, easier-to-read Metadata palette. To do this, go to Bridge's Metadata palette, click on the flyout menu, and choose Preferences. In the dialog that appears, uncheck any fields you don't need displayed, turn on the checkbox at the bottom for Hide Empty Fields, and click OK.

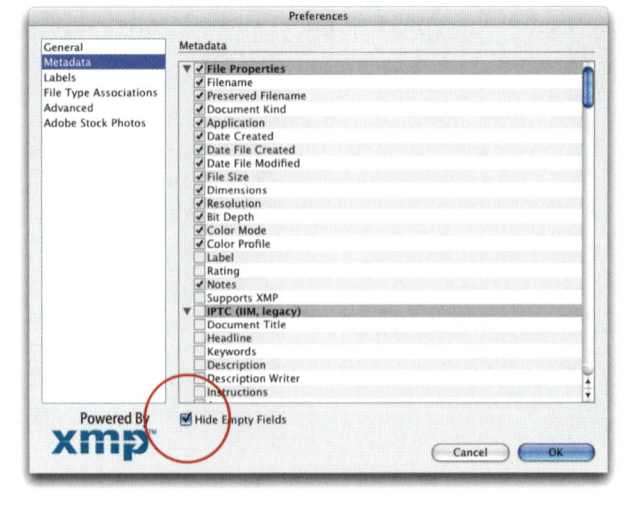

196   CHAPTER 9 • Advanced Tips

PHOTOSHOP'S OWN SLIDE SHOW

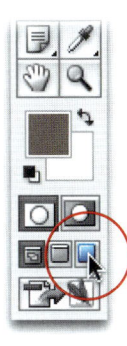

If you don't want to create a full PDF Presentation, you can create a mini slide show right within Photoshop. Just open all the images you want in your slide show, then Shift-click on the Full Screen Mode icon near the bottom of the Toolbox (it's the third icon from the left), and press the Tab key on your keyboard. To step through your slide show, press Control-Tab.

THE HISTOGRAM PALETTE'S VISUAL CUES

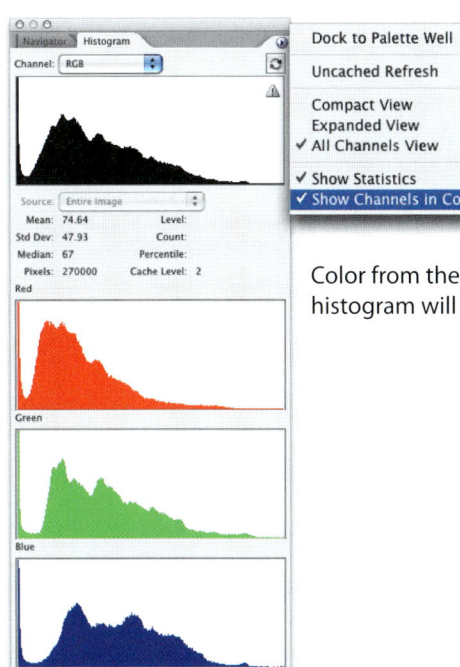

When you're using Photoshop's Histogram palette (under the Window menu), not only can you see a histogram of each individual channel (select the All Channels View option from the Histogram palette's flyout menu), but you can use color as your visual cue to quickly see which channel is which. Just choose Show Channels in Color from the palette's flyout menu, and then the Red channel histogram will appear in red, the Green in green, etc.

CHAPTER 9 • Advanced Tips   197

SEEING YOUR FULL-COLOR IMAGE WHILE EDITING A CHANNEL

When you're working on an individual channel in the Channels palette (under the Window menu), by default Photoshop displays your current channel on-screen in grayscale. If you make changes to that channel, you only see how the change affects that channel. However, there is a little-known trick that lets you see the full-color image, while editing the currently selected channel. While you're editing the channel, just press the Tilde key (~), which is right above the Tab key on your keyboard, and you'll see the full RGB preview as you edit.

HOW TO COMBINE TWO PATHS INTO ONE

If you're using the Pen tool (P), and you've created multiple paths within your document, these paths are totally separate, and are moved independently of one another. However, if you want these paths to move as one unit—combine them. Just switch to the Path Selection tool (Shift-A until it comes up), then go up to the Options Bar and click on the Combine button. Now when you move one path, all the combined paths move right along with it.

198   CHAPTER 9 • Advanced Tips

POWER UP YOUR LAYER STYLES

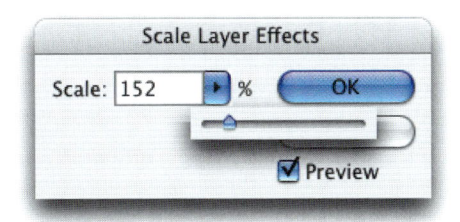

Here's a little-known tip for controlling the intensity of your layer styles. This is particularly helpful if you've applied a number of different layer styles to a layer, and want to affect them all at the same time, rather than tweaking each one individually. It's called Scale Effects, and it's buried in the Layer menu, at the bottom of the Layer Style submenu. Choose it, and a dialog appears with a slider set to 100% by default. As you increase the amount (up to 1000% maximum), it increases the "scale" of all your effects. For example, if you increased the scale of a Drop Shadow layer style, the shadow would become blurrier and its distance from the object would become greater. If you adjusted a Stroke layer style, the stroke would become thicker, etc. Pretty powerful stuff.

FREEFORM/PEN TOOL QUICK SWITCH

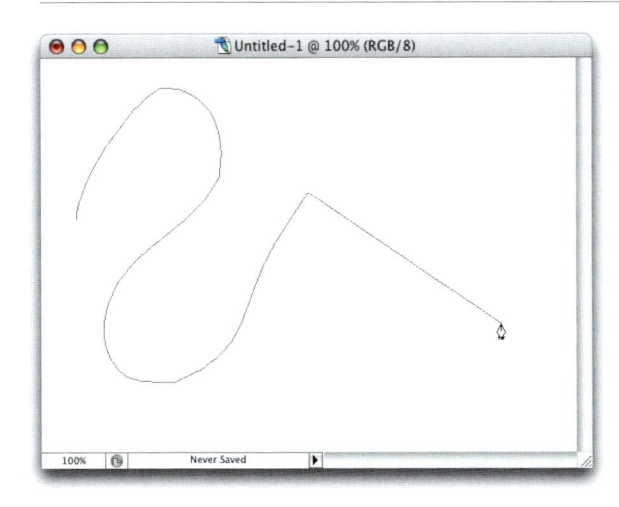

If you're using the Freeform Pen tool (Shift-P until it comes up), there are times when you may want to temporarily switch to the regular Pen tool so you can draw a straight-line segment. You can actually do this by holding the Option key (PC: Alt key) and then releasing the mouse button. This temporarily switches you to the regular Pen tool so you can draw your straight-line segment by moving the mouse. When you're done, click-and-hold, release Option/Alt, and you're back to the Freeform Pen tool.

CHAPTER 9 • Advanced Tips   199

VISUAL CONTROL OVER YOUR SELECTIONS USING QUICK MASK

Did you know that you can use Quick Mask mode to expand or contract your selections visually? Here's how: Create a selection (using any of Photoshop's selection tools), and then switch to Quick Mask mode (press the letter Q). Now you can go to the Levels dialog (under the Image menu, under Adjustments) and tweak the size of your selection. Moving the midtones Input Levels slider to the far left makes the selected area smaller (contracting the selection). Moving the midtones Input Levels slider to the far right makes the selected area larger (expanding the selection). The changes here usually aren't drastic, so you'd use this technique when a small adjustment to your selection is necessary, but seeing it like this beats the heck out of guessing.

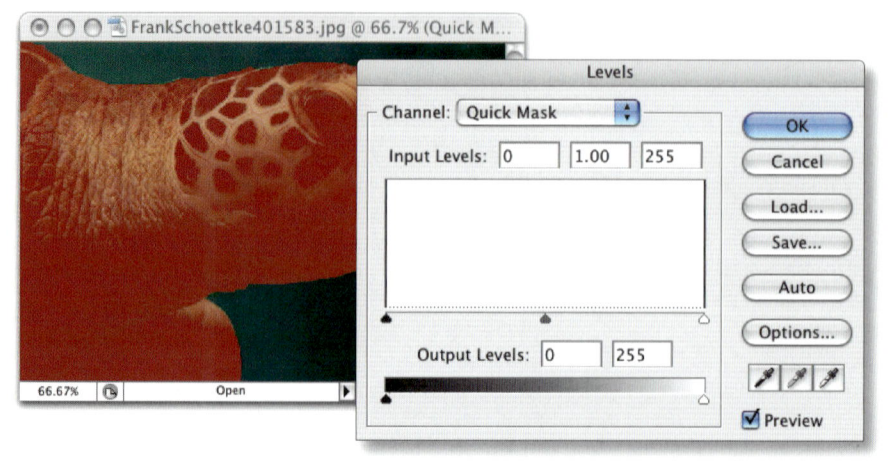

CHAPTER 9 • Advanced Tips

HAVE PHOTOSHOP SELECT THE SHADOWS AND HIGHLIGHTS

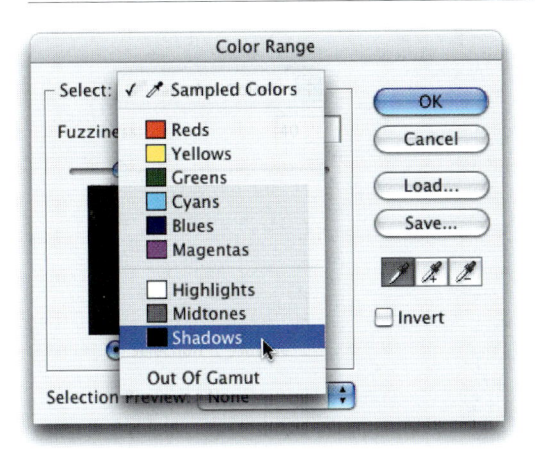

This is a trick we use for prepress and for photo retouching because it instantly lets you select all the shadow areas (or highlight areas if you wish) for a particular image, and it's so easy because Photoshop does all the work. To have Photoshop select just the shadow areas in your image, go under the Select menu and choose Color Range. When the dialog appears, in the Select pop-up menu, choose Shadows (or Highlights), and click OK. The shadow areas are instantly selected. This is ideal for situations where your scanner has plugged up the detail in the shadow areas (pretty common in most sub-$1,000 desktop scanners). Once the shadows are selected, you can "open them up" by going to the Levels dialog (under the Image menu, under Adjustments) and moving the midtones Input Levels slider to the left to bring back some of the shadow detail lost in the scan.

TROUBLESHOOTING ACTIONS? SLOW DOWN!

If you're an advanced user, chances are you're no stranger to using actions, and in fact, you probably create your own (rather than using the default actions that ship with Photoshop, many of which redefine the term "useless"). If you do create your own actions, you've already found that you spend more time troubleshooting your actions than you do creating them in the first place. Well, this little tip makes the troubleshooting process a lot easier, and saves you both time and frustration. The problem is (and this won't sound like a problem) Photoshop runs actions so quickly that you don't see each step, or each dialog, so tracking down a missing or wrong step is just about impossible. Luckily, you can actually slow down your action, or even put a pause between each step, by using Photoshop's Playback Options dialog found in the Actions palette's flyout menu. When it appears, you can choose to play your action Step by Step, seeing everything as it happens, or you can choose to enter the number of seconds you'd like it to pause. Then, when you replay the action, you can see everything step by step and track down the culprit.

CHAPTER 9 • Advanced Tips   201

🔴 🟡 🟢 ACCESSING GRAYED-OUT FILTERS IN CMYK

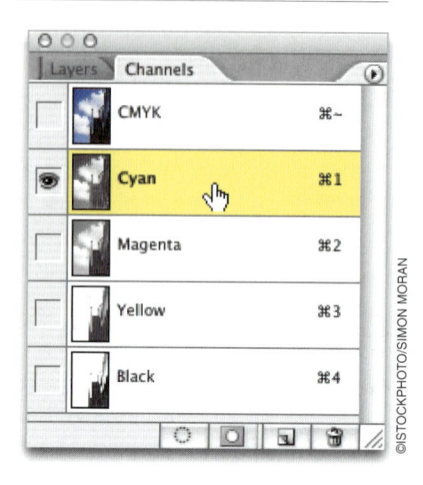

One of the bad things about converting from RGB mode to CMYK mode (under the Image menu) is that many of Photoshop's coolest filters can only be applied in RGB mode, and once you're in CMYK mode, many of them are grayed out in the Filter menu, so they can't be accessed. So what do you do if you really want to use one of those filters? (Whatever you do, don't convert back to RGB mode, then back to CMYK. That's image suicide.) Instead, try this tip: In the Channels palette, click on the Cyan channel. Go to the Filters menu and you'll notice that all those grayed-out filters are now suddenly available. All you have to do now is apply the filter you want to each channel individually (once each on Cyan, Magenta, Yellow, and finally the Black channel), and the filter will appear as though you applied it to the entire image (in reality, you did—you just did it the more laborious way). One way to speed up this process is to create an action that will do it all for you with one click of the mouse.

🔴 🟡 🟢 ASSIGNING METADATA TO MULTIPLE FILES

Want to assign metadata to more than one photo at a time in Bridge? (Perhaps you want to embed your copyright info into 30 or more photos at once.) Just Command-click (PC: Control-click) on all the photos you want to affect, then enter the custom info you want (in one of the IPTC fields in the Metadata palette) and that info will be added to every selected photo at once.

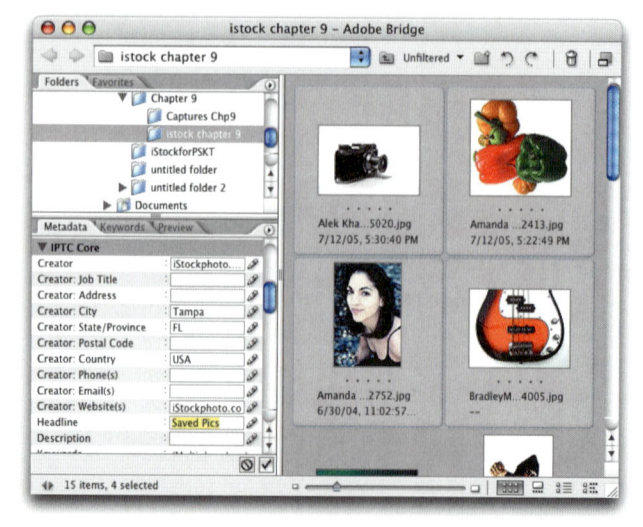

202   CHAPTER 9 • Advanced Tips

MORE CONTROL OVER FILTERS

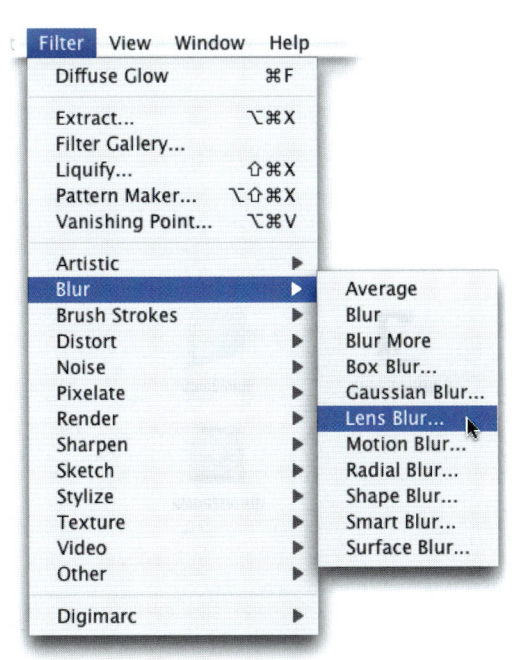

We love Photoshop's Fade command (which acts like an "undo on a slider"), and when it comes to applying filters, we use it all the time to gain more control (including blending mode control) over filters we apply. The only downside to the Fade command (which is found under the Edit menu) is you can only use it one time—you get one opportunity to Fade, or choose a Blend Mode, then you're stuck. Here's a tip to keep the control of your filters for as long as you'd like: When you're about to apply a filter, make a duplicate of the layer before you apply the filter by pressing Command-J (PC: Control-J) and then apply the filter. This keeps the application of your filter fully editable—you can change blend modes as often as you like, change opacity, add a layer mask to determine where the filter shows and where it doesn't, or even toss the layer in the Trash and start over.

CHAPTER 9 • Advanced Tips   203

APPLYING MULTIPLE FILTERS? NOT ON MY LAYER!

Thinking of applying a number of different filters to a particular layer? Don't do it. Instead, make a copy of your layer by pressing Command-J (PC: Control-J), then apply the first filter. Make another copy of the layer and apply the second filter; make another copy, apply the third filter, and so on. You can use Photoshop's layer blend modes in the Layers palette to get the effect that one filter is applied on top of the others, and now you've got full control over each individual filter applied. If you don't like one of the filters, just drag that layer into the Trash. Better yet, you've got blend and opacity control you wouldn't have by simply applying filter over filter.

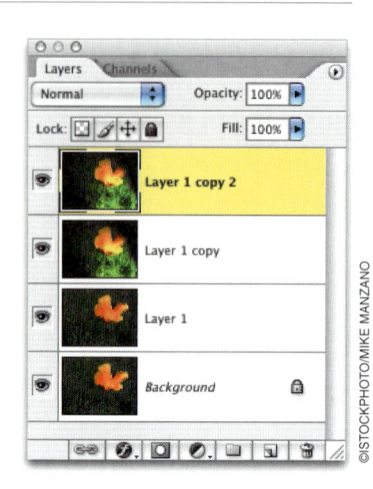

NEW SNAPSHOT, THE MISTAKE INSURANCE POLICY

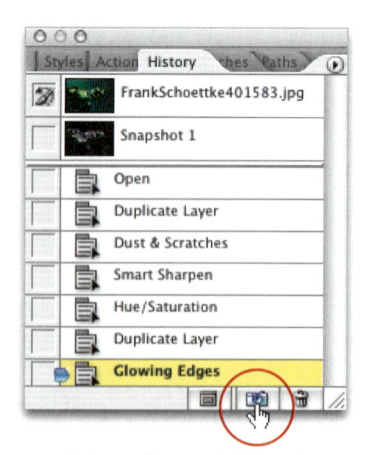

The great thing about Photoshop's History feature is that you can (by default) undo your last 20 steps. Perhaps even more important is that you can always return to how the image looked when you opened it, so you never really do any permanent damage (as long as the file is open). However, what if you opened an image, worked on it for a while, and it was really looking great, but about 10 minutes later, it took a turn for the worse (this happens to us more often than we'd care to admit). If you undo the last 20 steps, it may not take you back far enough to the point that you want to return to, and the only other choice is to go all the way back to where you started. Here's a tip to keep you from pulling your hair out: Any time your image is at a stage where you think it looks pretty good, go to the History palette, and at the bottom of the palette, click on the Create New Snapshot icon. Think of it as an insurance policy, so that if things go bad, you can at least return to that spot and try again. It's not a bad idea to create a new snapshot about every five minutes when you're working on a big project. To keep from loading up on snapshots, when you create a new one, delete one or two snapshots before it.

204   CHAPTER 9 • Advanced Tips

SAVING YOUR ACTIONS AS PRINTABLE TEXT FILES

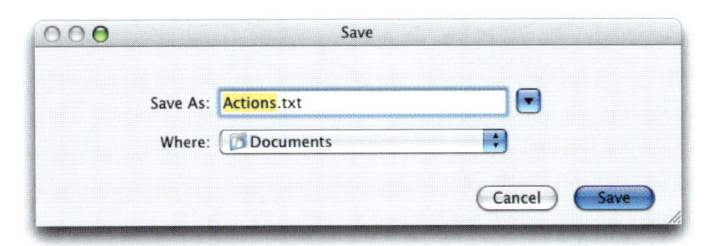

This is a totally undocumented actions tip, and if you need it, it's a real lifesaver. Once you've created an action, you can actually save a text document with all the action steps so you can have a printed hard copy of your action. Here's how: In the Actions palette, click on the action set containing the action that you want to save as a text document. Hold Command-Option (PC: Control-Alt) and from the Actions palette's flyout menu, choose Save Actions. When the Save dialog appears, you'll notice that the three-letter file extension is TXT (indicating it's a text file) rather than ATN (which is the Photoshop action format). Click OK and you've got a text file you can open in any word processor to print out your steps.

3D PRINT EFFECTS (AND WHERE TO GET THOSE GOOFY GLASSES)

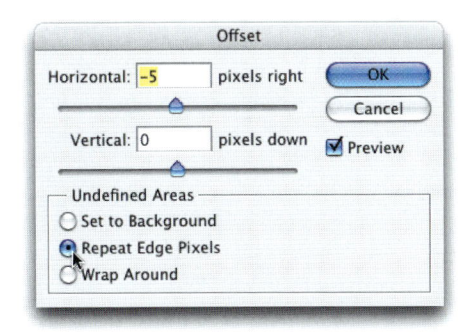

For a brief time back in the 1950s, 3D movies were all the rage, but it was short-lived, probably because you had to wear those cheesy-looking 3D glasses to experience the effect. Although 3D has come a long way since then, unfortunately you still have to wear the cheesy glasses. Be that as it may, the 3D effect is starting to appear again in print ads in trendy magazines, which generally include the paper 3D glasses in the magazine. This effect can be created in Photoshop, no problem. The hardest part is finding a supplier for 3D glasses (okay, we'll help on that part too. Try 3D Glasses Direct at www.3dglasses.net). Here's a tip on how to create the 3D effect in Photoshop: Open an RGB image, then go to the Channels palette and click on the Red channel. Go under the Filter menu, under Other, and choose Offset. For Horizontal enter –5 and set Vertical to zero. For Undefined Areas, choose Repeat Edge Pixels, then click OK. In the Channels palette, click on the RGB channel to reveal the effect. Then, lastly, you have to determine which part you want to appear as "coming out of the image" toward the person viewing it. Switch to the History Brush (Y), and using a soft-edged brush, paint over the area you want to "jump out" from the image. As you paint with the History Brush, you'll see your original untouched image paint back in (don't sweat it, that's what it's supposed to do). Now all you have to do is order the glasses.

CREATING REUSABLE DIAGONAL GUIDES

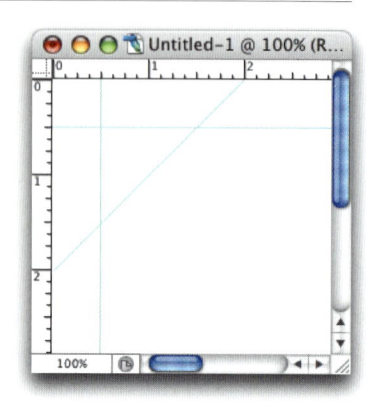

If you've used Photoshop's rulers at all, you know that you have your choice of either a vertical or horizontal guide. That's not a bad thing, but there's one thing missing—a diagonal guide. Since Photoshop doesn't have one, here's a tip for making your own: Start by clicking the Create a New Layer icon in the Layers palette, then double-click on your Foreground color swatch and in the resulting Color Picker, set it to R: 161, G: 253, B: 253 (the color Photoshop uses for its built-in guides). Switch to the Line tool found in the Shapes tools (Shift-U until it comes up), and on this new layer draw a diagonal line where you want your guide to appear (make sure you have the Fill Pixels icon selected in the Options Bar). It's not a bad idea to copy that layer into a separate document and save it on your drive—so anytime you need a diagonal line, you can just open that document and drag it right in.

THE SECRETS OF SEARCHING IN BRIDGE

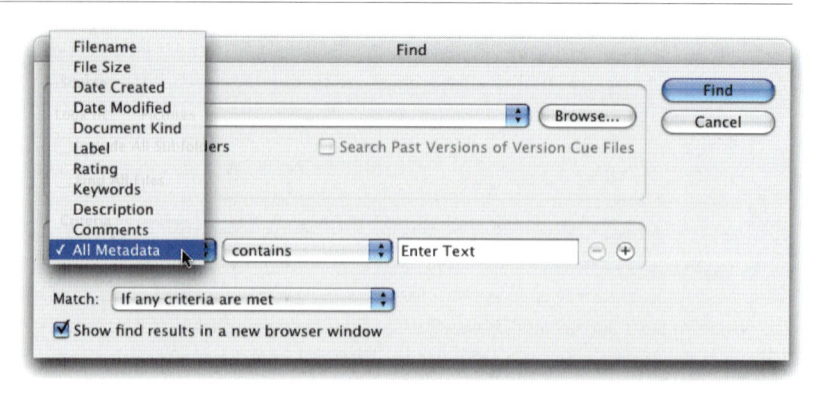

Don't get caught in the trap of thinking that you have to assign keywords to your photos before you can start using Bridge's Find function (although keywords certainly make it easier). But to find out just how much power the Find function really has, just press Command-F (PC: Control-F), then choose your options from the pop-up menus in the Criteria section. If you remember you shot the photo you're looking for with a certain camera, you can search All Metadata for that make and model. You can also search by Rating, Date Created, and a host of other criteria.

206   CHAPTER 9 • Advanced Tips

DRAG-AND-DROP CURVES FOR QUICK CORRECTION

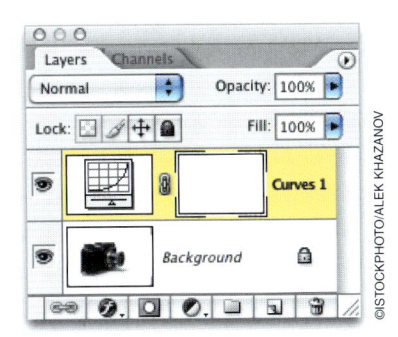

If you're color-correcting a number of images that are basically the same (for example, catalog shots or high school yearbook shots, where the lighting and composition are pretty much the same), you may want to apply the same Curve setting to a number of images. Rather than saving the Curve setting and loading it each time, try this tip: Use the Create New Adjustment Layer pop-up menu at the bottom of the Layers palette to create a Curves adjustment layer, and then just drag-and-drop that adjustment layer from your current image to your target image.

ACTIONS POWER TIP: ADD AN ACTION TO YOUR ACTION

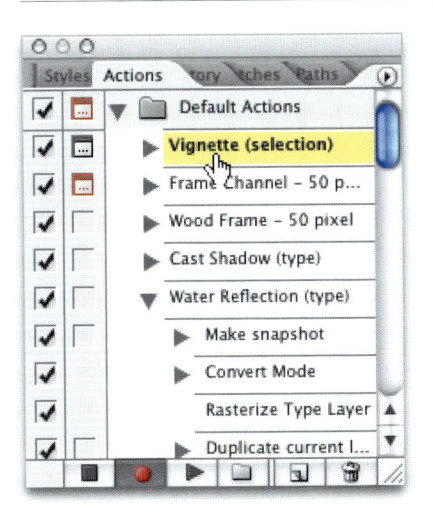

Here's an actions power tip: Did you know that you can build an action that will include an existing action? Here's how it's done: As you're recording your action, just go to the Actions palette, click on the existing action you want to include in your current action, and click the Play button at the bottom of the Actions palette. The existing action will now be added as a step in your current action (pretty scary stuff).

CHAPTER 9 • Advanced Tips   207

PREPRESS CLEANUPS—IN A SNAP

This is a great tip if you're zoomed in close to an image for retouching, or checking it in prepress for spots or specs, because it lets you check the entire image in a very methodical way—using your keyboard to navigate zone by zone. Here's how:

Press the Home key to jump to the upper-left corner of your image window.
Press the End key to jump to the lower-right corner of your image window.
Press the Page Up key to scroll upward one full screen.
Press the Page Down key to scroll downward one full screen.
Press Command-Page Up (PC: Control-Page Up) to scroll one full screen to the left.
Press Command-Page Down (PC: Control-Page Down) to scroll one full screen to the right.

Once you've learned these shortcuts, you can start by pressing the Home key (jumping you to the upper left-hand corner of your image). Clean that area then press the Page Down key to move methodically down the left side of your image until you reach the bottom of your window. Then press Command-Page Up (PC: Control-Page Down) to move one screen to the right, clean that area, then press the Page Up key to move methodically up the image until you reach the top. Repeat these steps until you're finished. The advantage of doing it this way, besides the sheer speed of using keyboard shortcuts, is that you'll see every area of the image without missing a spot.

NO MORE CREATING TYPE IN CHANNELS

If you've ever tried to create and format type in a channel, you know what a pain it can be. Especially because, when you're working in a channel, it doesn't create an editable Type layer, so you're really limited to how you can format and, of course, edit your type. So instead of creating type in a channel (which many special channel-type effects call for), just create your type on a layer as usual. In fact, don't go to the Channels palette at all—just pretend you're not using channels. Once you've got your type formatted and adjusted just the way you want it on your regular Type layer, Command-click (PC: Control-click) on your Type layer's thumbnail in the Layers palette. This puts a selection around your type. Now you can go under the Select menu and choose Save Selection. When the dialog appears, click OK, and it saves your perfectly formatted type as (you guessed it) a channel. Now you can delete your Type layer, and you're left with an Alpha channel with perfectly formatted type.

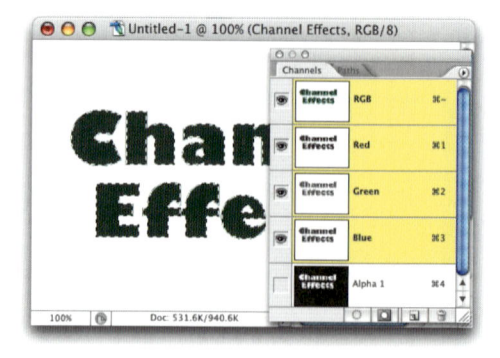

208 CHAPTER 9 • Advanced Tips

BLEND MODE POWER TIP

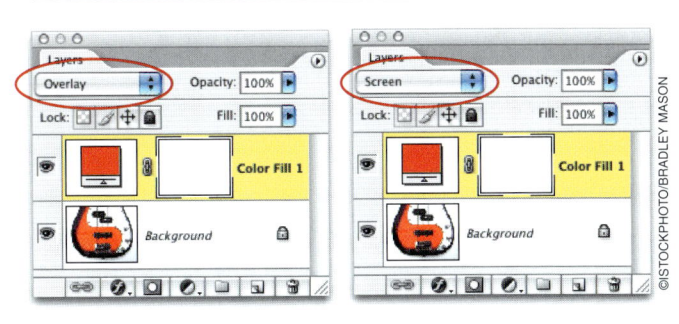

Once you understand layer blend modes, you wind up using them all the time. Chances are by now you know which individual modes you want to use (such as Overlay, Multiply, Soft Light, Hard Light, Screen) and which ones you'll probably never use (such as Dissolve). If you know which ones you want to apply, you can use a keyboard shortcut to jump right to the blend mode you want. For example, to jump to the Overlay mode for a layer, press Option-Shift (PC: Alt-Shift) and the first letter of the mode you want, in this case, the letter O (making the shortcut Option-Shift-O [PC: Alt-Shift-O]). For Screen mode, you'd press Option-Shift-S (PC: Alt-Shift-S), and so on. (*Note:* If you have a tool selected that has a blend mode in its Options Bar, such as the Brush tool [B], the keyboard shortcut will change that tool's blend mode instead of the layer blend mode.)

LET PHOTOSHOP TELL YOU THE HIGHLIGHT AND SHADOW

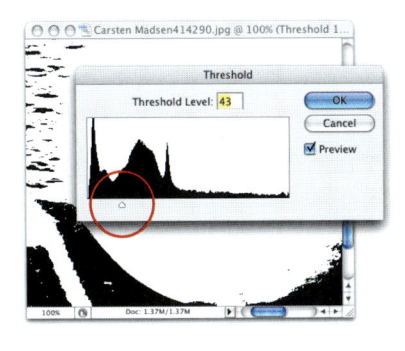

We use this tip to have Photoshop help us determine which are the darkest (shadow) points and which are the lightest (highlight) points in an image when we're color-correcting. We start by choosing a Threshold adjustment layer from the Create New Adjustment Layer pop-up menu at the bottom of the Layers palette. When the Threshold dialog appears, we drag the slider all the way to the left and the image turns completely white. We then slowly drag the slider back to the right, and the first black pixels that appear onscreen are the shadow areas. We make a mental note of that area as our shadow point. Then we drag the slider all the way to the far right (the image turns black). As we drag slowly back toward the left, the first white pixels that appear are the highlight points in the image. We note them as well. We now know where the shadow and highlight points are in the image, and we can use them, along with the Eyedropper tools in the Curves dialog (Command-M [PC: Control M]), to set the proper shadow and highlight areas to remove any color casts. *Note:* When you've determined where the shadow and highlight areas are, you can then delete the Threshold adjustment layer by dragging it into the Trash icon at the bottom of the Layers palette.

CHAPTER 9 • Advanced Tips   209

USING THE LASSO—DON'T STOP TO NAVIGATE

If you're using the Lasso tool (L), you have a surprising amount of navigation control, even while you're dragging out your selection. For example, if you're drawing a selection and you need to scroll over a bit, just press-and-hold the Spacebar, and right where your cursor is, the Hand tool will appear. Then you can move the image while you're still selecting (try it once and you'll see what we mean). When you let go of the Spacebar, you're right where you left off, and you can continue your selection. Here's another Lasso tip: If you're drawing a selection and reach the edge of your document window and need to scroll over, hold the Option key (PC: Alt key), let go of the mouse button, move your mouse to the edge of your image window, and you can nudge the screen over (again, this is one you have to try once to understand it). It's like you're using the Lasso tool to slide the image over. When you're done sliding, press the mouse button and release Option/Alt to continue selecting. Incidentally, while selecting, you can also use the zoom in/out tricks: Command–+ (Plus Sign) (PC: Control–+) and Command–– (Minus Sign) (PC: Control––).

LOAD ANY SAVED SELECTION WITHOUT THE CHANNELS PALETTE

If you're working on an RGB image and you've saved a selection (by drawing a selection and choosing Save Selection from the Select menu), you can instantly reload that selection at any time, without going to the Channels palette. If you have only one saved selection, just press Command-Option-4 (PC: Control-Alt-4), and the selection will instantly appear onscreen. If you have a second saved selection, press Command-Option-5 (PC: Control-Alt-5), and so on. The key to remember is that the RGB channels take up the 1, 2, and 3 spots, so always start with 4 to load your first Alpha channel. *Note:* If you're working with CMYK images, remember to always start with 5, because the CMYK channels take up the first four spots.

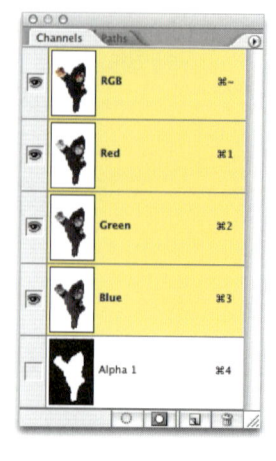

PLOT MULTIPLE CURVE POINTS IN JUST ONE CLICK

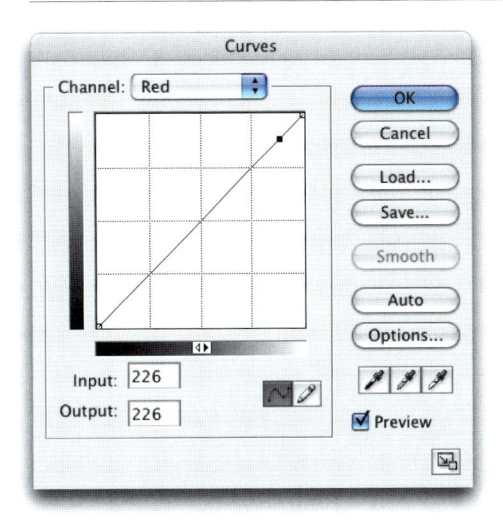

Earlier in the book, we showed you how Photoshop will plot a point on the curve for you if you Command-click (PC: Control-click) on a color in your image that you want plotted. However, there's a power tip that we waited until now to share—if you add the Shift key, making it Command-Shift-click (PC: Control-Shift-click), Photoshop will add a point for that spot on all the color channels for you. This works in both RGB and CMYK modes.

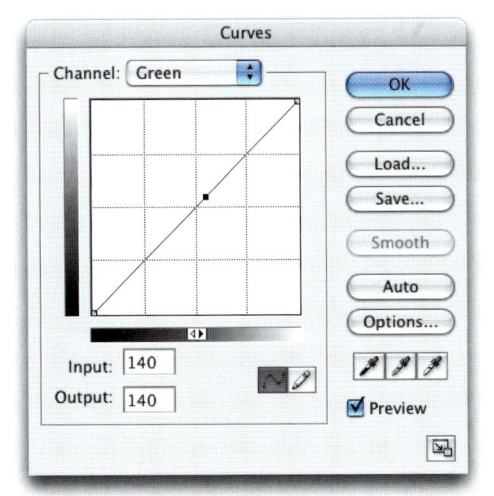

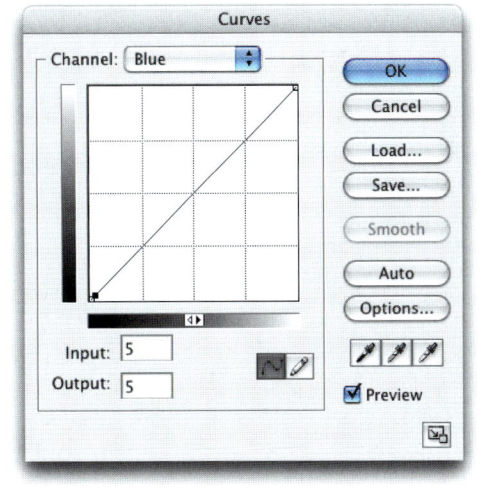

CHAPTER 9 • Advanced Tips   211

TOUGH SELECTION TIP

If you're struggling to make a selection of an image that's against either a background of a similar color or a very busy background, here's a masking tip to make the process easier: Add a Levels or Curves adjustment layer above your image layer using the Create New Adjustment Layer pop-up menu, and use it to dramatically increase the contrast in the image to help make the edges stand out. This will often help make the difference between the object's edge and the background more obvious. The great part is, you can totally damage the look of the image because you're using an adjustment layer. When your selection is in place, just drag the adjustment layer onto the Trash to delete it, and your image is back to normal, but you've got that "impossible" selection still in place.

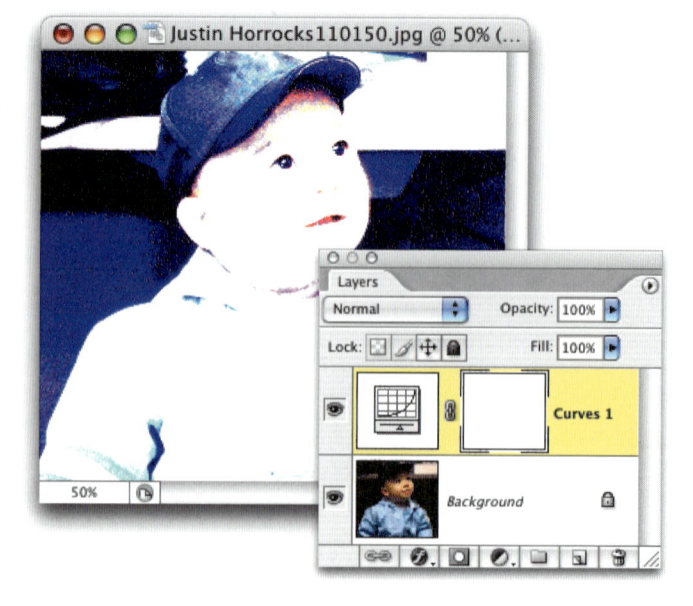

212   CHAPTER 9 • Advanced Tips

MAKING THE COLOR PICKER SHOW CMYK

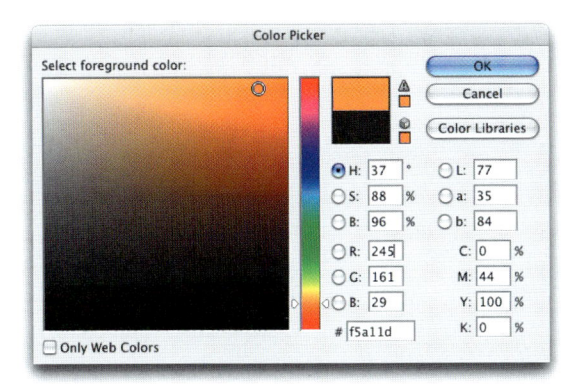

If you're working in CMYK mode and you go to the Color Picker, it still displays RGB colors. This is a bit of a problem, because you think you're picking one color, but when you start to paint or fill with that color, you get the CMYK desaturated version. Here's a tip to get around that. When you're in CMYK mode and you go to the Color Picker, press Command-Y (PC: Control-Y), which is the shortcut for Proof Colors (found under the View menu). When you do this with the Color Picker open, it changes all the colors in the Color Picker to CMYK colors. That way, when you pick a color in the Color Picker, it looks the same when you paint or fill with it in your CMYK image.

MOVING MULTIPLE CURVE POINTS AT ONCE

If you're working in the Curves dialog (Command-M [PC: Control-M]) and you want to make more than one point active at the same time, click on one point (to make it active) then hold the Shift key and click on another. As long as the Shift key is held down, you can click on as many points as you'd like to make them active at the same time.

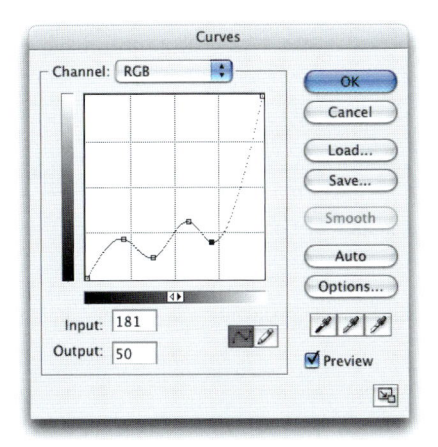

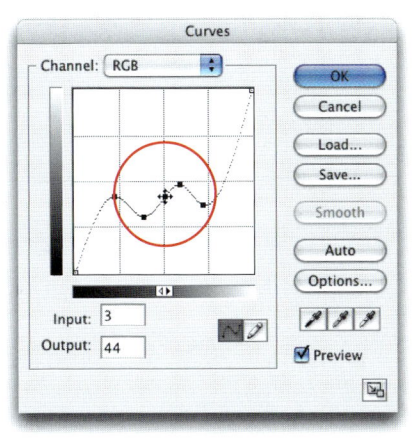

CHAPTER 9 • Advanced Tips   213

ADD TO YOUR SELECTIONS THROUGH THE CHANNELS PALETTE

If you've got the Channels palette open and you have multiple saved Alpha channels, you can load any Alpha channel as a selection by holding the Command key (PC: Control key) and clicking directly on the channel's name. This instantly loads the selection. An even better tip: If you hold the Command key (PC: Control key) then add the Shift key (making it Command-Shift/Control-Shift) and click on another Alpha channel, it adds that to your current selection. You can keep adding more selections to your original selection until, well… until you run out of Alpha channels.

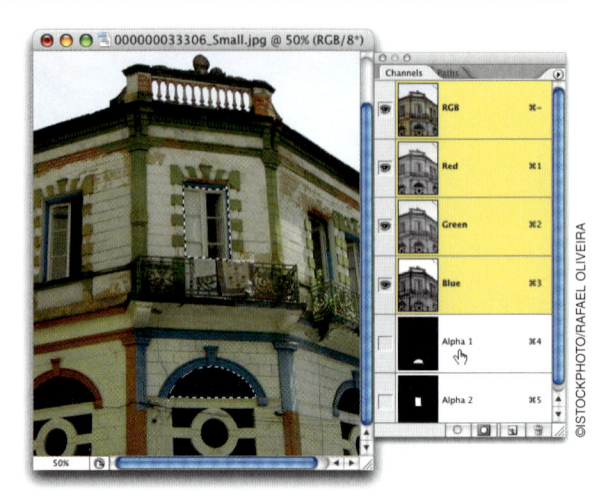

EMBEDDING PATHS INTO ACTIONS

If you're creating actions and you want your action to include a path that you've created, you can do that, but you have to draw your path first, before you record your action. Once you've drawn your path, and it comes to the part of your action that requires the path, go to the Action palette's flyout menu, choose Insert Path, and that path will be stored along with the action.

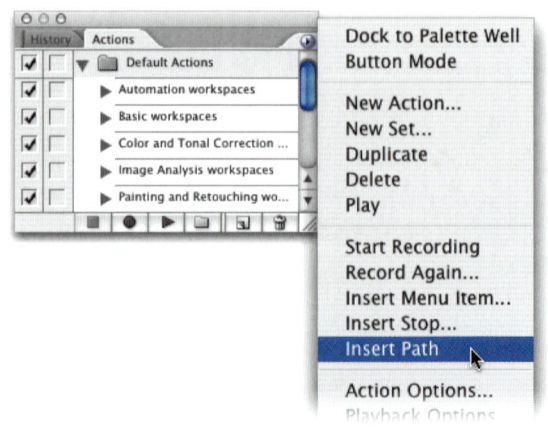

MEASURE TWICE, LOOK ONCE

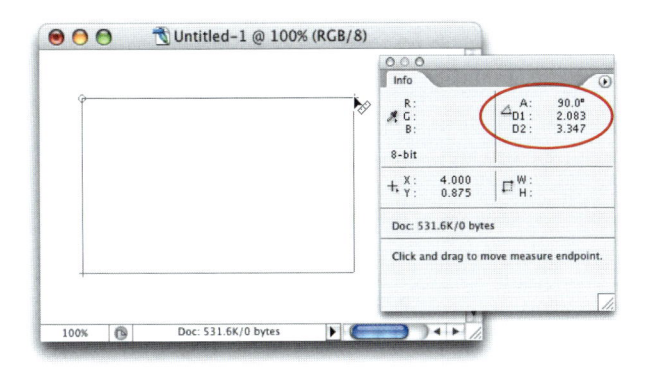

If you need to measure more than one side of an object (for example, if you're measuring a box, and you need the height and width), you can measure both at the same time. First, open the Info palette under the Window menu (so you can see the measurements that the Measure tool generates), then get the Measure tool (Shift-I until it comes up) and click-and-drag it along the first edge. Release the mouse when you reach the end of the edge. Then hold the Option key (PC: Alt key), click on the end of the first line, and continue on in a different direction. You'll notice that another measurement line appears. Now, look in the Info palette and you'll see your two measurements listed under D1 and D2.

STROKING HALF A PATH—HALF A PATH????

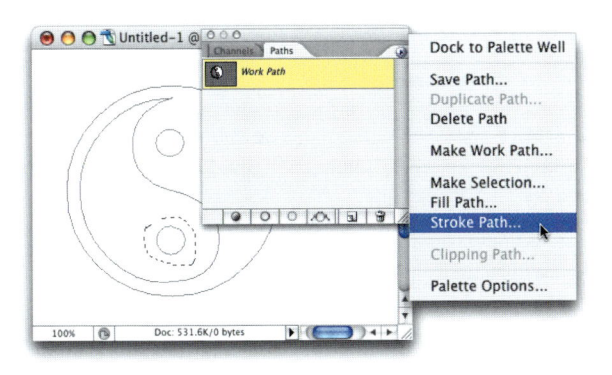

This is a mind-blowing advanced tip (not because it's hard—it's simple—but if you use the Pen tool [P], warning—your mind is about to spontaneously combust). Here's the scoop: If you're an advanced user, you already know that you can draw a path and then apply a stroke along that path (using the paint tool of your choice) by choosing Stroke Path from the Paths palette's flyout menu. But dig this: If you draw your path, but only want to stroke a portion of that path, all you have to do is make a selection (using any selection tool) of the part of the path you want stroked. Then when you choose Stroke Path, it will only stroke the area of your path that is contained within your selection. Boom! That was the sound of our heads exploding.

CHAPTER 9 • Advanced Tips   215

LOCKING A PDF PRESENTATION

If you're using Photoshop to create a PDF Presentation slide show (under the Automate submenu in the File menu) so you can email it to your clients for proofing, one of your concerns may be that your client will just print your photos out to a photo-quality printer, leaving you out in the cold (so to speak). But you can pull the plug on their printing aspirations. When saving your PDF Presentation, under Output Options, choose Presentation, then hit Save. It'll ask you to name your PDF presentation (you're not done yet), so name it and click Save. Then, a PDF options dialog will appear. Under Security (in the options along the left side), turn on the checkbox for Use a Password to Restrict Printing, Editing and Other Tasks under Permissions. Enter (and memorize) a password. Then, make sure Printing Allowed and Changes Allowed are set to None. Click Save PDF and it'll ask for your password one more time. Now, when you email the PDF Presentation, printing will be grayed out, and even if they have the full version of Acrobat, they won't be able to copy-and-paste your photos into something else for printing.

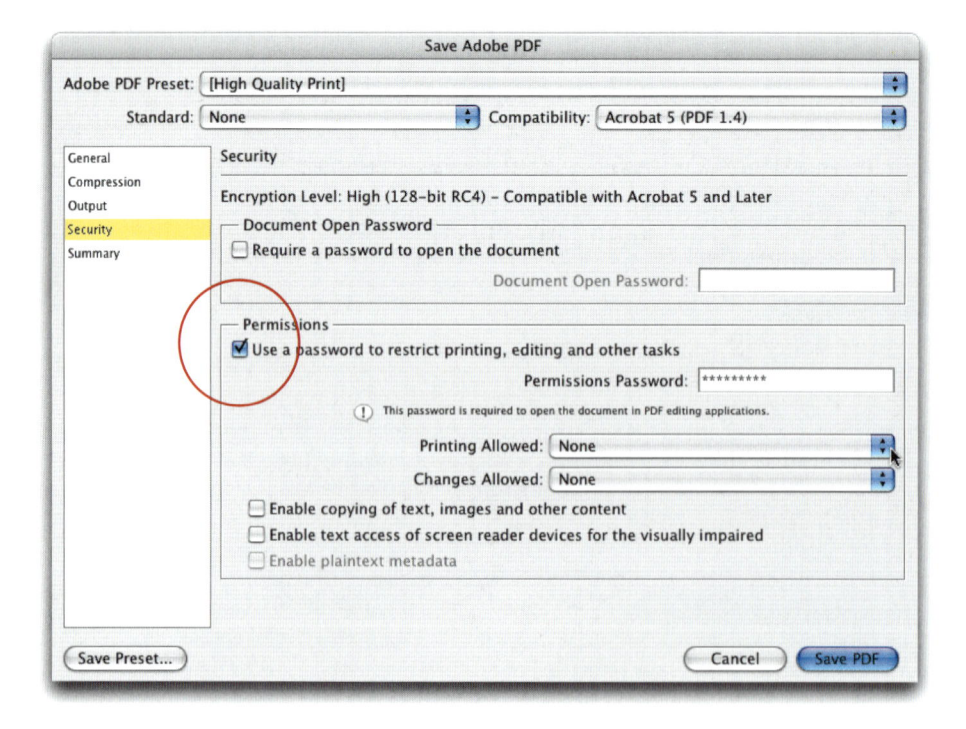

216 CHAPTER 9 • Advanced Tips

SPEEDING UP BATCH ACTIONS

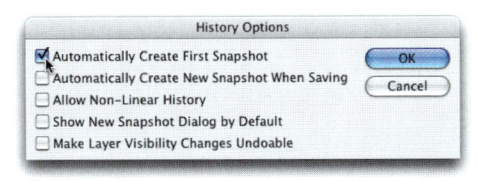

If you're running a Batch action on a folder full of images, one of the things that can really slow the process down is the fact that the History palette keeps creating History States (undos) for each image. To keep your Batch actions running at full speed, there are two things you can do: In the History palette's flyout menu, under History Options, turn off the checkbox for Automatically Create First Snapshot. Secondly, go under the Photoshop menu, under Preferences, and choose General (in Windows, Preferences can be found under the Edit menu). In the History States field, lower the number from 20 (the default) to 2 and click OK, then your Batch will run like a greased pig. Don't forget to increase your History States or change your History Options back after you're done batching or you'll be down to two undos.

PUTTING YOUR LENS FLARE ON THE SPOT

This tip lets you precisely position the center of the Lens Flare filter by using the Info palette and a little-known feature of the Lens Flare dialog. First, open the Info palette (found under the Window menu), then put your cursor over the precise spot in your image where you'd like the center of your lens flare to appear. Look in the Info palette, under the X and Y coordinates, and write down those two coordinates (I knew one day I'd find a use for the X and Y coordinate readings). Then go under the Filter menu, under Render, and choose Lens Flare. There's a fairly large preview window in the center of the dialog. Hold the Option key (PC: Alt key), click once on the preview window, and it brings up the Precise Flare Center dialog. Enter those X and Y coordinates you wrote down earlier (you did write them down, right?), click OK, and your lens flare is precisely positioned.

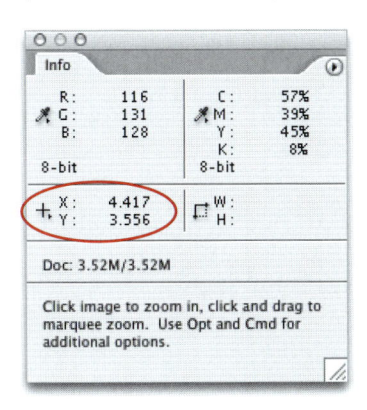

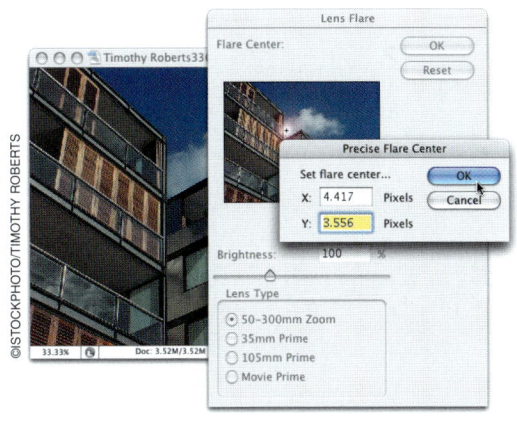

CHAPTER 9 • Advanced Tips   217

Fast Company

TROUBLESHOOTING TIPS

I've got to be honest with you, I'm not sure you really need this chapter, so let's do a little quiz to start things off, and if for some reason you fail this impromptu quiz, then you'll have to

Fast Company
troubleshooting tips

read the chapter. Pass, and you jump straight to Chapter 11. Ready? Begin (you have 12 minutes for the first segment). Question One: If Photoshop crashes while copying a 50-MB file into Clipboard memory, do you (a) pack up your computer, call Billie Joe MacAllister, and ask him to meet you at the Tallahatchie bridge; (b) completely disrobe, sit cross-legged on the floor while burning candles around the Photoshop product box; (c) press Shift-Alt-Control-Delete-Tilde-Tab-Escape-Enter-Option-F15-Backslash, proving you have 11 fingers; or (d) all of the above? Answer: It was a trick question. Obviously, the real answer would have been "b," except you never, never dare to have an open flame anywhere near your Photoshop product box. Sorry, grasshopper—turn the page and start reading.

THE REAPPEARING/DISAPPEARING BRUSH TIP

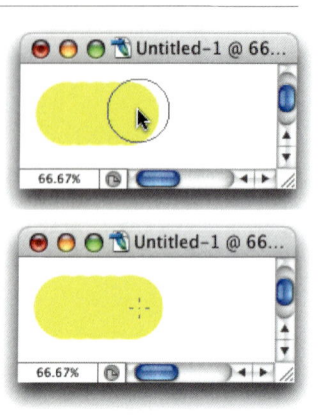

This one gets more people because it's a feature that acts like a bug. Has this ever happened to you? You're working in Photoshop, you're using the Brush tool (B), and everything seems fine. But a little later in your session, you get the Brush tool again, and it no longer displays the size of the currently selected brush tip. Instead, it displays a little crosshair cursor. So you go to the Preferences dialog and choose Display & Cursors, and sure enough, you've got Normal Brush Tip chosen as your preference, but for some strange reason, it's not showing your brush size; it's showing that stupid crosshair. Here's the problem: Check your Caps Lock key. It's turned on, and turning it on changes your Brush cursor from displaying brush size to displaying the crosshair. This is actually a feature to be used when you need to see the precise center of your brush. The problem is it's assigned to the Caps Lock key, so every time you turn on Caps Lock when you're working with type, you just temporarily switched your Brush cursor (or any cursor for that matter). Does Adobe need to find a better key for this feature/bug? You betcha! Will it happen? Not as far as I know.

GET PRINT RESOLUTION FROM YOUR DIGITAL CAMERA IMAGES

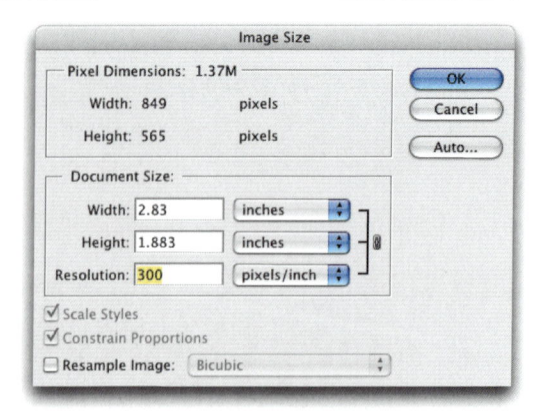

Problem: You imported an image from your digital camera and although the physical dimensions of the image are rather large, the resolution shows up as only 72 ppi. How can you get enough resolution to print this image? Solution: Go under the Image menu and choose Image Size. Turn off Resample Image, then in the Resolution field, type the resolution you need for the specific device you'll be printing to. When you do this, Photoshop will automatically input the Height and Width that would result from using that resolution (the image size will definitely be smaller—the higher the resolution needed, the smaller the physical dimensions of your image). All you have to do is click OK and Photoshop will do the math, creating an image in the new smaller size, with the new higher resolution. The good news is that by doing it this way, there's absolutely no loss of quality to the file whatsoever.

220   CHAPTER 10 • Troubleshooting Tips

HOW TO USE RGB FILTERS ON GRAYSCALE IMAGES

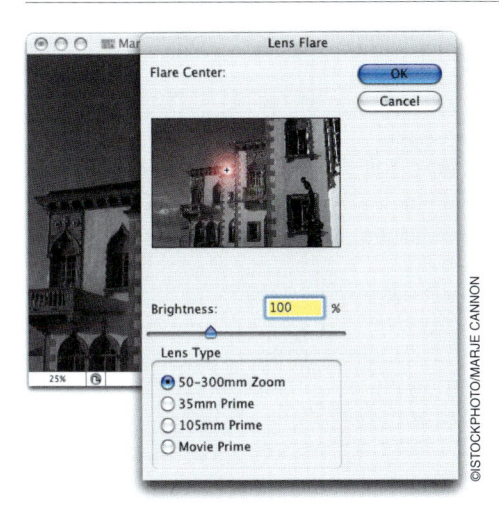

If you're working on grayscale images, you'll find there are some Photoshop filters that won't work (they're grayed out, so you can't access them). Of course, it's always the really cool filters, such as Lens Flare and Lighting Effects, that are grayed out. But don't be dismayed (in fact, be "mayed") because you can still use those filters—just switch to RGB mode (it's found under the Image menu, under Mode), apply the filters, then switch back to Grayscale mode. It won't affect the color of your image because, well, there is no color—you're working on a grayscale image. Switching to RGB doesn't suddenly pour color onto your image; your grayscale image will still look grayscale in RGB. When you switch back to Grayscale mode (after applying the filters), you'll get a warning asking, "Discard color information?" You can safely click OK, because after all, there was no color to begin with.

STOP THE CROP SNAPPING

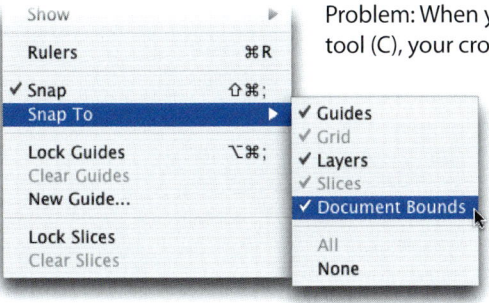

Problem: When you're trying to crop an image using the Crop tool (C), your cropping border tries to snap to the edges of your document window. This might be happening when drawing large Marquee selections as well. Solution: Press Command-Shift-; (PC: Control-Shift-;), which is the shortcut for turning off this snapping. The only downside is it turns off all snapping (like Snap To Guides, Snap To Grid, etc.). If you just want the Crop snapping (or Marquee snapping) off, go under the View menu, under Snap To, and choose Document Bounds, and your tools will no longer try to snap to your, well, document bounds.

CHAPTER 10 • Troubleshooting Tips   221

LET'S DO THE TEXT WARP AGAIN

I get more people than you can "stick a shake at" asking me about this problem. If you go to use Photoshop's Warped Text function, you might get a warning that states, "Could not complete your request because the type layer uses a faux bold style." A faux bold style? What in the wide world of sports is that? Actually, it's a feature of Photoshop (that was introduced back in version 5.0) that lets you create a fake (faux) bold or italic type style for fonts that don't really have a bold or italic type style. It's toggled on/off in the Character palette's flyout menu. In Photoshop 7.0, Adobe added the option in the warning dialog to "Remove attribute and continue." All you have to do is click OK to remove the faux bold and now you can warp your text. Life is good.

UNLOCKING THE BACKGROUND LAYER

Can't move the Background layer? That's because back in Photoshop 6.0, Adobe locked the Background layer from movement. That wouldn't be so bad, except that if you look at the top of the Layers palette, you can see that "Yup, the checkbox to lock movement is turned on," but the frustrating part is that it's also grayed out, so you can't simply uncheck it to unlock it. The only way around this is to double-click on the Background, which brings up the New Layer dialog. Click OK, and your Background layer becomes Layer 0 and is unlocked. Now you can move it.

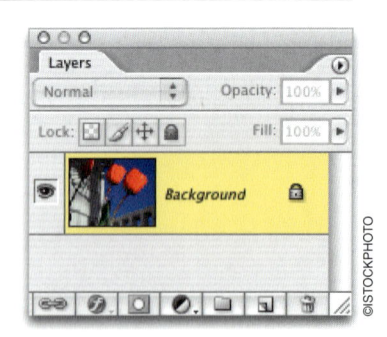

222   CHAPTER 10 • Troubleshooting Tips

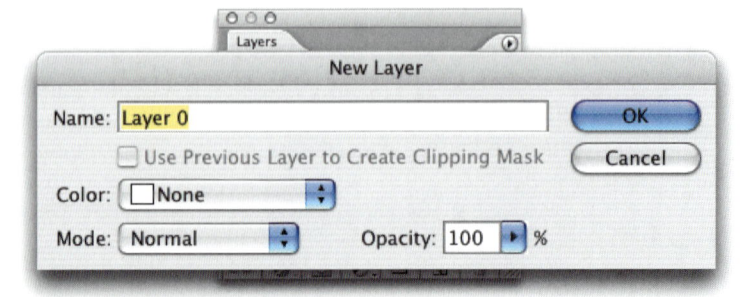

DO YOU HAVE ENOUGH RAM? ASK PHOTOSHOP

Not sure if you have enough RAM? Just ask Photoshop. Believe it or not, it can tell you. Here's how: Open a document that's indicative of the type of image you normally work on. Work on the image, doing typical stuff, for about 10 minutes. Along the bottom left-hand corner of your document window, just to the right of the current document magnification readout, is the status bar. By default, it's set to display your document's file size, but if you click-and-hold on the right-facing triangle to the right of it, a pop-up menu of options will appear. Choose Show, then Efficiency. If the percentage shown is 100%, you're gold, baby! That means that Photoshop is running at peak efficiency, because 100% of the time your image manipulations are being handled in RAM. If the efficiency number shown is, say, 75%, this means that 25% of the time, Photoshop ran out of RAM and had to use free hard drive space to make up for it, which means Photoshop ran much slower 25% of the time. An efficiency of 75% is pretty much as low as you want it to go. If it shows anything less than 75%, it's time to buy more RAM. Pronto!

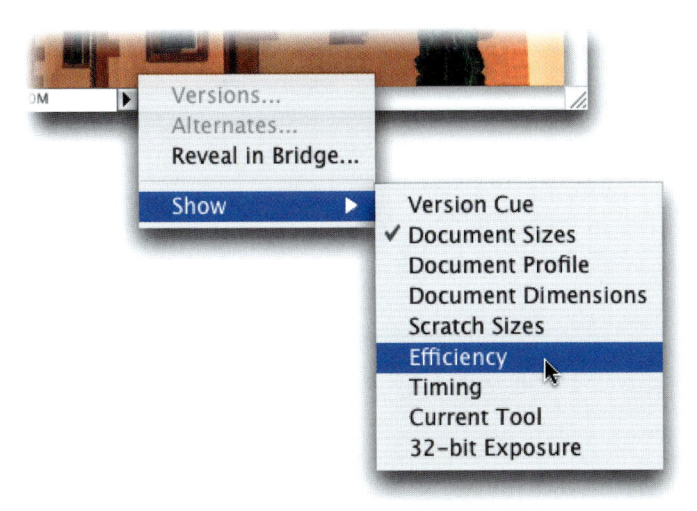

GETTING BETTER EPS PREVIEWS

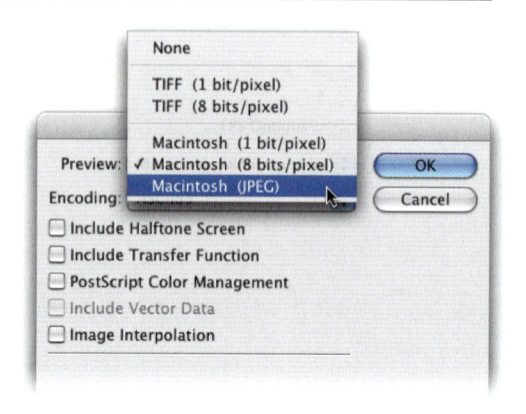

Problem: The image looked great in Photoshop, but now that you've converted it to CMYK, saved the file as a TIFF, and placed it into QuarkXPress, InDesign, PageMaker, etc., the image looks awful—way oversaturated and totally whacked. Reason: The preview of CMYK TIFFs just looks like that, so don't freak out—if it looked right in Photoshop, it should print fine. Okay, what if you saved the file as an EPS, and when you place the image into your page-layout app, the color of the image looks okay, but it's not crisp and clear, but pixelated. Reason: By default, the preview embedded within EPS images is a lame 256-color preview. Solution: When you choose Save As (from the File menu), choose Photoshop EPS in the Format pop-up menu, click Save, and the EPS Options dialog will appear. In the Preview pop-up menu, choose JPEG. That way, it sends a 24-bit, full-color preview, rather than the lame 256-color preview.

GET BACK YOUR BACKGROUND LAYER

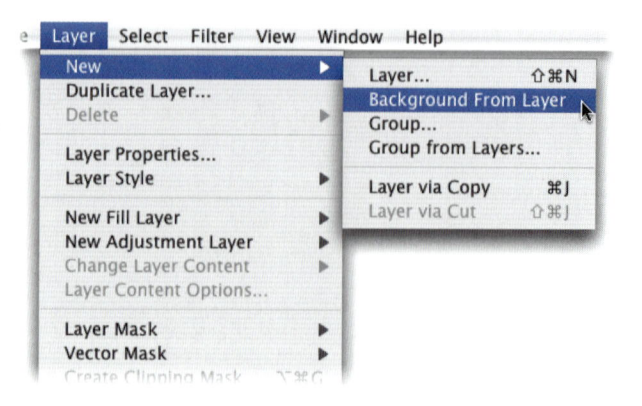

Lost your Background layer? It happens. It's heartbreaking, but it happens. If you suddenly find yourself staring at a Layers palette and there's no Background layer (chances are you accidentally converted your Background layer into a regular layer), here's how to get a Background layer again: Click on the Create a New Layer icon, then go under the Layer menu, under New, and choose Background From Layer, and Photoshop will take your new blank layer and create a solid white Background layer at the bottom of your layer stack.

224   CHAPTER 10 • Troubleshooting Tips

EXPANDING RECTANGULAR SELECTIONS

If you've ever tried to expand a rectangular selection by more than five or six pixels, you know what happens. The crisp, sharp-edged corners that you start off with become rounded. Here's the fix: Don't use the Expand command (found under the Select menu, under Modify). First, make your selection and press Command-T (PC: Control-T) to bring up the Free Transform bounding box. Go to the Options Bar and Control-click (PC: Right-click) in the Width and Height fields to change the measurements from Percent to Pixels. Now, simply add the amount of pixels you want to expand to the existing number. For example: If the field reads 110 pixels, and you want to expand it by 10 pixels, enter 120 pixels in the field and press Enter to apply the transformation. Don't forget to change both the Width and Height fields. That's it—perfectly expanded corners.

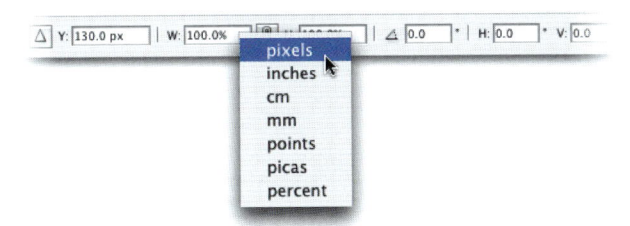

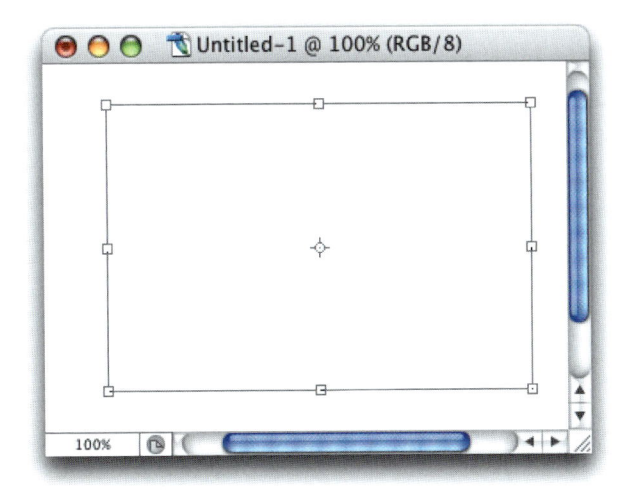

CHAPTER 10 • Troubleshooting Tips   225

FIXING THE "ROUNDED CORNERS" SELECTION PROBLEM

Ever have this happen? You draw a selection with the Rectangular Marquee tool (M) and the corners of your selection are rounded, rather than nice and straight? This happens to a lot of people, especially if they've been drinking. If you haven't been drinking but you're suffering from rounded-corner selections, look up in the Options Bar, and you'll see a field for Feather. Chances are there's some number other than zero in this field, and what's happening is every time you draw a selection with that tool, it's automatically feathering (softening) the edge. What probably happened is you intentionally (or accidentally) added a feather amount at some time, then later forgot to set it back to its default of zero. So to fix it, just highlight the field and type 0 (zero). Incidentally, this is a great Photoshop prank to play on co-workers, friends, soon-to-be-enemies, etc., because the Feather field is usually the last place they'll look.

MAKING GLOBAL LIGHT WORK FOR YOU

Problem: You applied a drop shadow to an object on one layer, then later you applied a bevel on another layer, but in the Bevel and Emboss options in the Layer Style dialog, you notice that the position of your drop shadow just moved when you changed the angle of your bevel. Reason: Adobe uses a feature (that acts like a bug) called Global Light. The idea behind it makes sense, yet we've never run into the scenario it was created for. The idea is this: You've created an image with lots of drop shadows, all casting in a particular direction. If the client saw your work and said, "Hey, instead of having the shadows go down and to the right, can we make all the shadows go up and to the left?" If that unlikely event ever occurred, you'd be set, because all you'd have to do is move one shadow and all the other shadows on other layers would move to the exact same angle. It's a great idea; it just never happens (okay, it's probably happened somewhere, once). Solution: In the Layer Style dialog, deselect the Use Global Light checkbox. Now you can move the angle of your current layer style separately from the rest of your image. Life is good once more.

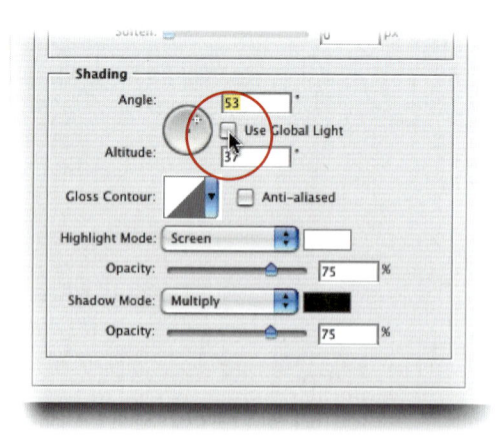

226   CHAPTER 10 • Troubleshooting Tips

FIND THE HIDDEN MAGNETIC PEN TOOL OPTIONS

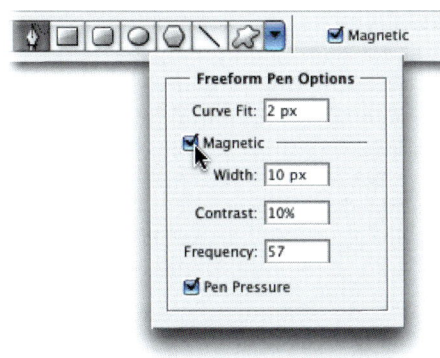

I know what you're thinking—finding the Magnetic Pen tool options? I didn't even know there was a Magnetic Pen tool in the first place. Adobe has done a great job of hiding it. For some reason they must hate this tool. Anyway, to get to the Magnetic Pen tool (the magnetic part means it snaps to well-defined edges to help you draw accurate paths around objects), you have to start by choosing the Freeform Pen tool from the Toolbox (it's nested with the Pen tool). Only then will the subterranean Magnetic checkbox surface in the Options Bar. However, to access the all-important Magnetic options so you have a chance in hell of actually controlling this tool, you have to dig deeper into the underground world of CS2 to make these options bubble to the top. Click on the down-facing black triangle to the right of the Custom Shape tool icon in the Options Bar to reveal a pop-down menu few will ever see—the Freeform Pen Options. In this rarely viewed menu, you'll find a checkbox for Magnetic, and clicking on it will bring the grayed-out Magnetic options to life, and open a treasure chest of newfound riches (also known as more boring options).

LET PHOTOSHOP REBUILD YOUR PREFS

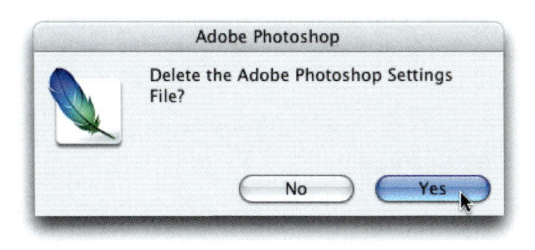

If you need to delete Photoshop's current preferences file (which is a common "first-line-of-defense" troubleshooting move), you don't have to go digging around your drive. All you have to do is hold the Command, Option, and Shift keys (PC: Control-Alt-Shift) when you first launch Photoshop, and you'll be greeted with a dialog asking you if you want to delete the Photoshop Settings File. If you do, click Yes, and Photoshop will build a new, factory-fresh set of preferences for you.

CHAPTER 10 • Troubleshooting Tips   227

STOP THE "CLICK-AND-JUMP-TO-THAT-LAYER" BLUES

Problem: All of a sudden, every time you click on a layer with the Move tool, it jumps to that layer. Solution: Somehow you turned on a feature called Auto Select Layer, which lets you make a layer active by just clicking on it with the Move tool. To turn this feature off, press V to get the Move tool, and up in the Options Bar, turn off the checkbox for Auto Select Layer. Besides, you never really need to turn this feature on, because you can just hold the Command key (PC: Control key) and click on any layer in your image window.

FASTER APPLICATION SWITCHING

Do you often copy-and-paste images from Photoshop into other applications (such as FileMaker Pro, Word, etc.)? I'm not talking about importing a TIFF or EPS, I'm talking about copying the object, switching to another application, and pasting your copied image from the Clipboard. You don't? Great, then we have a tip for you that will speed up your application-switching pretty dramatically. Go under the Photoshop menu, under Preferences, under General, and turn off the checkbox for Export Clipboard (in Windows, Preferences can be found under the Edit menu). Here's what's happening when it's turned on: Whatever you last copied in Photoshop gets transferred to your system's Clipboard memory when you switch to another application, just in case you want to paste it. If you have a large image in Clipboard, it'll take some time to export the image to the other application (or it'll be so large it won't export at all—you'll get a warning dialog instead). So, turn off that preference, and wait no more.

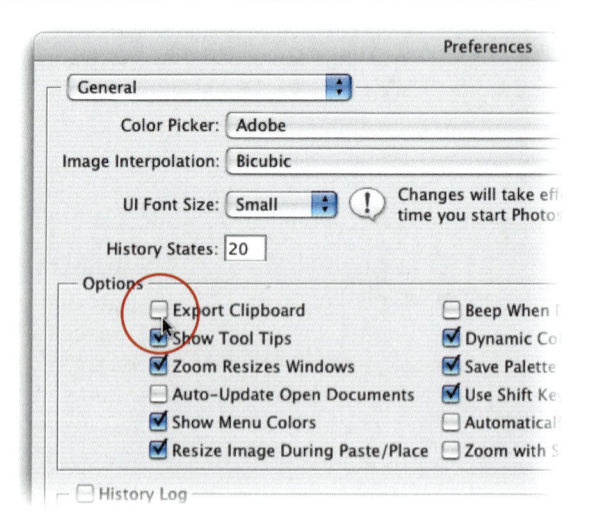

WILL MORE RAM MAKE PHOTOSHOP RUN FASTER?

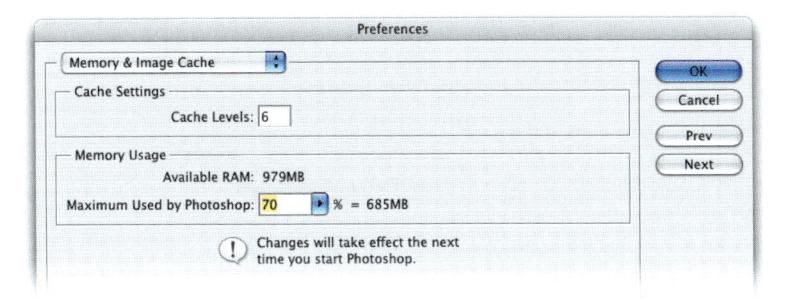

Problem: You added more RAM to your system and assigned more RAM to Photoshop, but it doesn't seem to run any faster. Reason: Adding RAM doesn't always make Photoshop run faster. It only works if you didn't have enough RAM to begin with. Adding RAM will only help to make your computer run as fast as it can, but it won't make your 800-MHz computer run at 801 MHz. For example, if you work on Web images and the average image you work on is 3 MB, you only need about 15 or 20 MB assigned to Photoshop to have it run at full speed. If you've got that, and add another 256 MB of RAM, Photoshop won't run any faster, because Photoshop only needs that 15 or 20 MB that you already had. Freaky. To check your RAM usage, go under the Photoshop menu, under Preferences, and choose Memory & Image Cache (on a Windows PC, Preferences are under the Edit menu).

DON'T USE CROP TO FIX BARREL DISTORTION

Problem: You're trying to fix barrel distortion that appears on a photo you're editing, but using the Crop tool's Perspective feature is a guessing game. You try the crop and it doesn't look right; you have to undo it, and guess again. Solution: Don't use the Crop tool's Perspective feature (found in the Options Bar), even though it was specifically designed to address barrel distortion. Use the standard Free Transform command instead by pressing Command-T (PC: Control-T) and then pressing-and-holding the Command (PC: Control) key while you drag the corner handles to create your perspective. Doing this gives you a live onscreen preview as you work, so fixing the distortion takes just a few seconds—unlike Crop's Perspective.

CHAPTER 10 • Troubleshooting Tips

GETTING SMALLER PHOTOSHOP FILES

Do your Photoshop PSD file sizes seem a little large? It may be because of a Preferences setting that makes Photoshop save a flattened version of your Photoshop image, along with your layered Photoshop file. Why does Photoshop do this? Because there's a slight possibility you might share this file with someone using Photoshop 2.5 (just like there's a slight possibility that Congress will vote to cut their own salaries), and Photoshop 2.5 didn't support layers, so it can't read your layered document. But because, by default, that flattened version is included in your layered file, guess what—2.5 can open the flattened image. What luck! Who cares? I'd rather have smaller file sizes all year long, and if you would too, go under the Photoshop menu (the Edit menu in Windows), under Preferences, under File Handling, then in the File Compatibility section, for Maximize PSD and PSB File Compatibility, change Ask to Never. Think about this one for a minute and you'll wonder why this is turned on by default. Think about it for two minutes and you'll wonder why it's in Photoshop at all. Don't spend too much time on it, or you'll start to wonder who's the poor soul that's stuck on version 2.5.

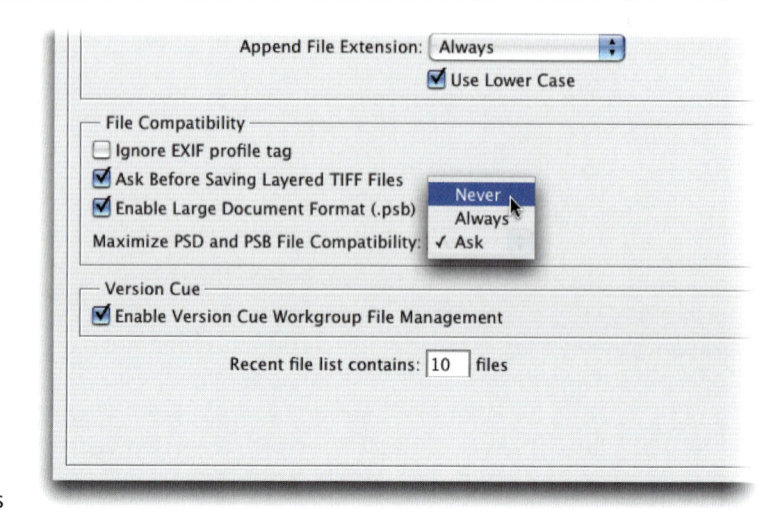

Speed Freak

KILLER WEB TIPS →

The reason I call this chapter "Killer Web Tips" is that most of the tips in this chapter came from a buddy of mine who's now serving time in Raiford State Penitentiary for

Speed Freak
killer web tips

manslaughter. Technically, he's not really a killer, and technically this chapter should have been called "Web Tips from a Killer" rather than "Killer Web Tips," but really, would you have bought this book if that was the name of this chapter? You would have? Wow! You're my kind of person (or trusty, as my friend likes to call them). Seriously though, in this chapter we're going to look at some tips to make optimizing your graphics easier and faster, while making your file sizes as small as possible. If you incorporate these tips into your Web work, before you know it, you'll be earning more money, and then when you have enough money, you can buy cartons of cigarettes to bribe the guards. See, it all works out in the end.

ADDING MUSIC TO YOUR FLASH WEB GALLERY

In CS2 Adobe added two Flash-based templates you can use for your online Web Photo Gallery. Even cooler is the fact that you can now add a background music track to one of these Flash galleries. Just follow these steps: First find the MP3 audio track you want to use as your background music and rename the file as "useraudio.mp3". Then open your Photoshop CS2 application folder, navigate to Presets, and choose Web Photo Gallery. Inside that folder look for either Flash Gallery 1 or Flash Gallery 2. Depending on which gallery you chose within Photoshop, drag-and-drop your audio file into the corresponding folder. That's it! You've got background music.

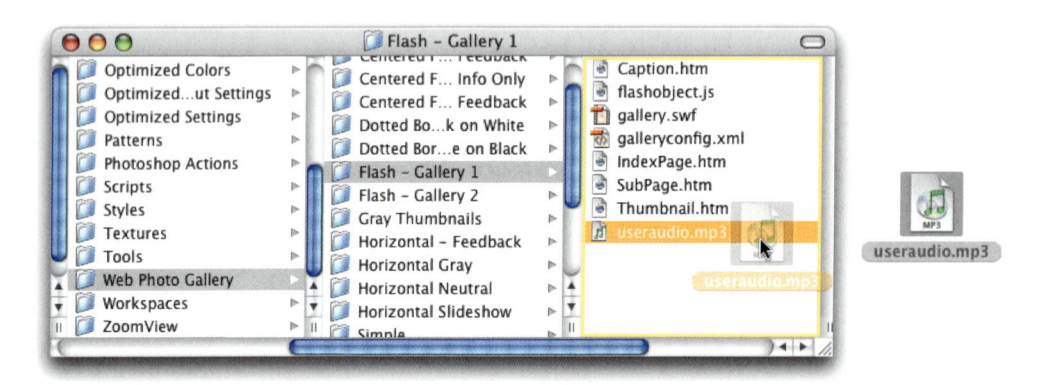

LOSE THOSE ANNOYING NUMBERS IN THE UPPER LEFT-HAND CORNER

We get more letters from people who ask us, "How do I get rid of that number in the top left-hand corner of my image?" This little puppy appears if you accidentally click on the Slice tool in the Toolbox. Even if you notice your error and immediately switch to another tool, it's too late. The "slice number" is already in place. To make it go away, go under the View menu, under Show, and choose Slices. Then try not to accidentally click on the Slice tool again. (Sorry, I felt like scolding somebody. You know, just for fun.)

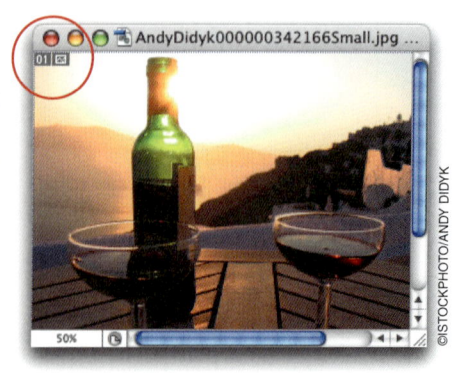

NEED TO SHRINK THE FILE SIZE? USE TRANSPARENCY

Want a killer tip for squeezing even more size out of your GIF Web images? Make something transparent. That's right, if you can pick an area of your image to make transparent, your file size will drop like a rock. For example, if you're putting a logo over a white background and you can make the white area around the logo transparent, your file size will be significantly smaller, because the transparent areas are virtually ignored when determining file size, because, after all, there's nothing there.

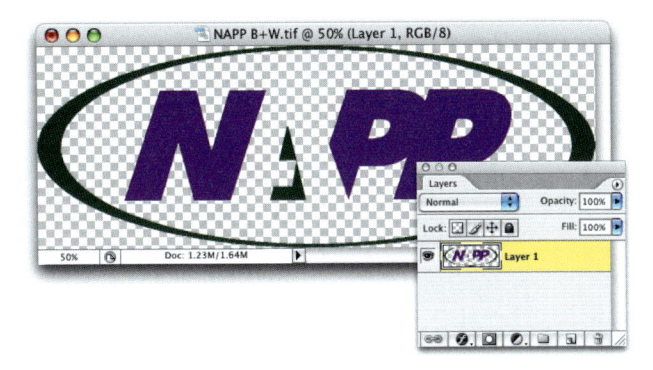

CROP IT EVEN CLOSER

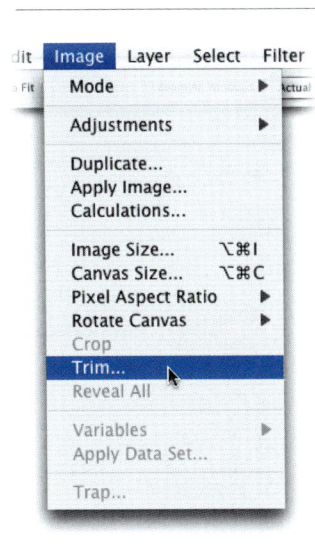

When you're designing graphics for the Web, you don't want even one extra pixel of unused space, because it adds to the overall file size of the image. Because of that, you want to crop your Web graphics as tightly as possible. Luckily for us (you, them, etc.), Photoshop CS2 can do it for you automatically. Just choose Trim from the Image menu, click OK in the dialog, and it will crop your Web graphic as tightly as possible for the smallest possible file size. It does this by looking at the pixel color in the upper left-hand corner of your image and cropping down until it hits another color. (*Note:* The Trim dialog also gives you the option to base the crop on the bottom right-hand corner pixel color or transparent areas.) This works especially well when creating type for the Web, because you'll often create it on a white background.

CHAPTER 11 • Killer Web Tips   235

LET PHOTOSHOP MAKE THE FILE SIZE CALL

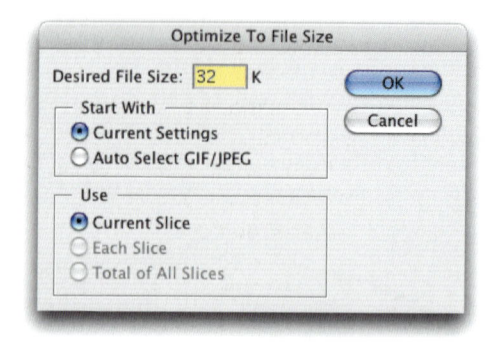

Oftentimes you have a target size you're trying to hit when creating Web graphics; for example, you're creating a Web banner and your file size limit is 32 K. If that's the case, and you know the target size, why not let Photoshop do all the work? Here's how: Under the File menu, go to Save for Web. In the Save for Web dialog, just to the right of the Settings pop-up menu, is a right-facing triangle. Click-and-hold it and when the pop-up menu appears, choose Optimize to File Size. In the dialog, enter the target file size you need your graphic to be and click OK to have Photoshop optimize the graphic to fit your target file size. If it doesn't matter to you whether it's a GIF or JPEG, choose Auto Select GIF/JPEG and Photoshop will "make the call."

ZOOM OUT FOR SHARPER WEB IMAGES

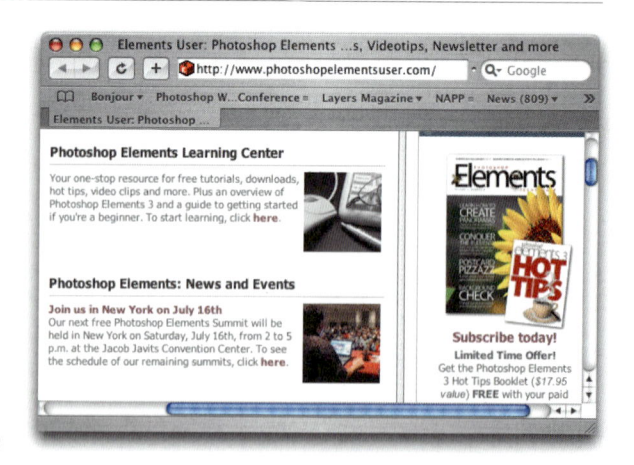

This is a tip we use almost daily when we have to greatly reduce the size and/or resolution of an image. Sometimes when you make a drastic size/resolution change, it can really make the resulting image blurry, so what we do is simply zoom out on the image so that the window and image are at either 50% or 25% view. Then, we take a screen capture of our image window at the new smaller size. That way, the image still looks sharp, but it's much smaller when we open the screen capture in Photoshop. The trick to making this work is using either a 50%, 25%, or 12.5% view size for making the capture. If you view the image at 66.7%, 33.3%, or 16.7%, the image won't be as crisp (because of the way Photoshop draws the image at those views).

236 CHAPTER 11 • Killer Web Tips

IMAGEREADY FEATURE COMES TO PHOTOSHOP

One of our favorite little features from Adobe ImageReady has made its way into Photoshop—it's called Slices From Guides. What it does is slice your image (for the Web) where your guides are positioned. To make use of this handy little number, just make your rulers visible by pressing Command-R (PC: Control-R), drag out guides where you'd like your slices applied, and then press the letter K to use the Slice tool. With the Slice tool selected, look up in the Options Bar and you'll find a button called Slices From Guides. Click the button and Photoshop will do the rest.

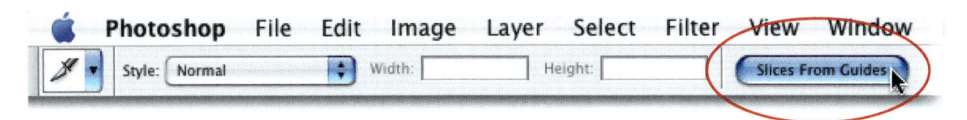

TWO EASY WAYS TO CREATE TRANSPARENCY

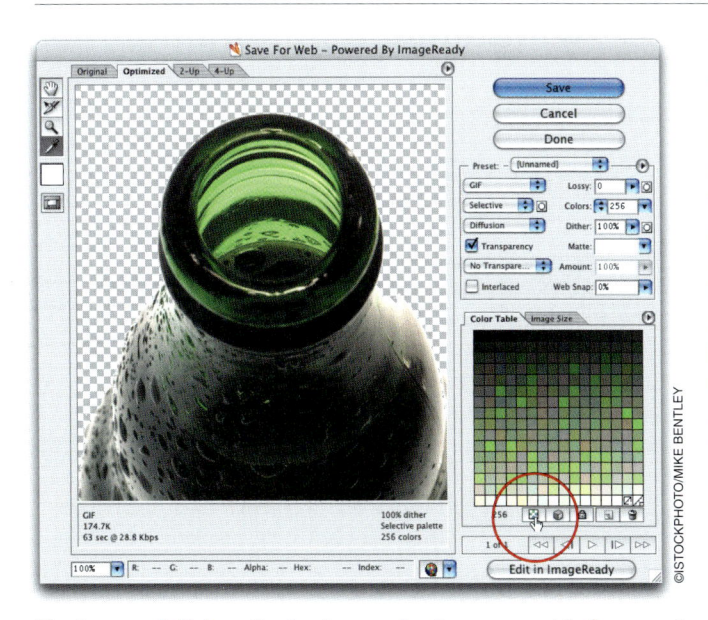

The most common method for making a background transparent back in Photoshop 6.0 is still available to you in Photoshop CS2, and that's to go to the Layers palette and simply delete the Background layer. That's it. This leaves only the layers that were above the Background layer (which already have background transparency). Now, there's another easy way, and that's to go to Photoshop's Save for Web command, switch to the Eyedropper tool in the Save for Web's Toolbox, and click on the background color you want to become transparent. Then, just below the Color Table on the bottom right of the dialog, click on the first icon, which creates transparency from your selected color.

CHAPTER 11 • Killer Web Tips   237

Photoshop CS2 KillerTips

IMAGEREADY WINDOW SPEED TIP

If you're using Adobe ImageReady (which comes installed with Photoshop as part of the package), by default the image window displays the original (un-optimized version) of your image. However, if you want to quickly view the optimized version, a 2-Up version (original and optimized side-by-side), or the 4-Up version (your original and three other optimized options), you can use the quick tip Command-Y (PC: Control-Y) to rotate through your four view choices. A big time saver.

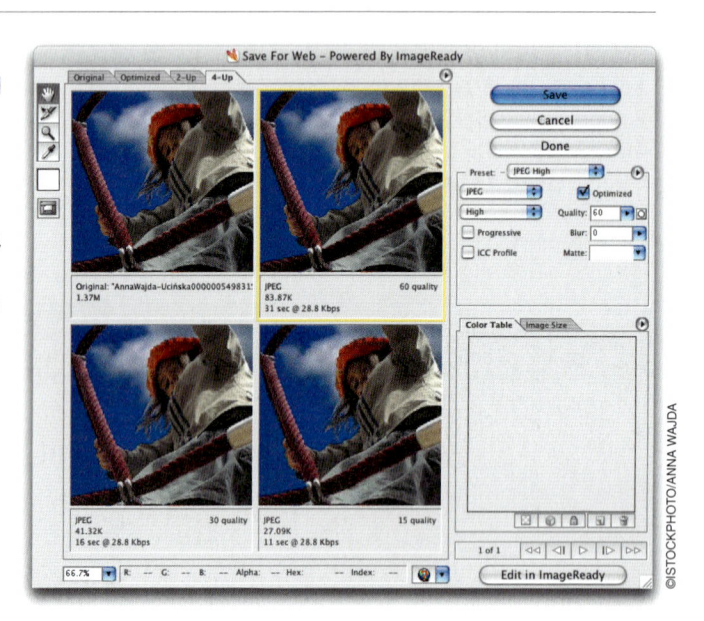

IF IT'S WEB SAFE, DON'T USE IT

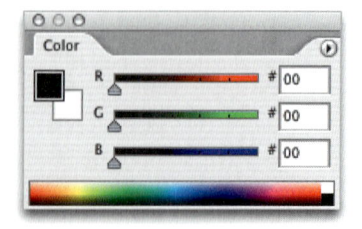

The one palette that we absolutely don't use at all anymore is the Web-safe Color palette (choose Web Color Sliders from the Color palette's flyout menu). Why? You don't need it—and it can make your file sizes significantly larger than necessary. The Web-safe colors were created back when most computer users had computers that could only display a maximum of 256 colors. Out of those 256, the "Web-safe" colors were the 216 colors that were the same on both Macintosh and Windows browsers. Even back then you could still use a non-Web-safe color, but it might dither to the next closest Web-safe color so the color might be off a bit. However, if you've ever looked at a row of monitors at the computer store, you'll notice the color is slightly different on every one, but that's another story. Luckily these days, you'd be hard-pressed to find anyone using such a lame computer that it only displays 256 colors. They haven't sold a computer like that for literally years.

238 CHAPTER 11 • Killer Web Tips

CHANGE ONE PREFERENCE, SAVE A BUNDLE

If you're creating Web graphics with Photoshop and you're not using the Save for Web feature (which is perfectly fine not to do), make sure you go under the Photoshop menu (in Mac OS X), under Preferences, and choose File Handling (in Windows, Preferences can be found under the Edit menu). In the Image Previews pop-up, change the setting from Always Save to Never Save. Image Previews are those tiny thumbnail icons that are visible on your system. They look cute, but they take up big space—often accounting for 70% of your file size. Turn them off, and you'll save file size big time. (Save for Web does this automatically, so if you're using that feature, don't sweat it.)

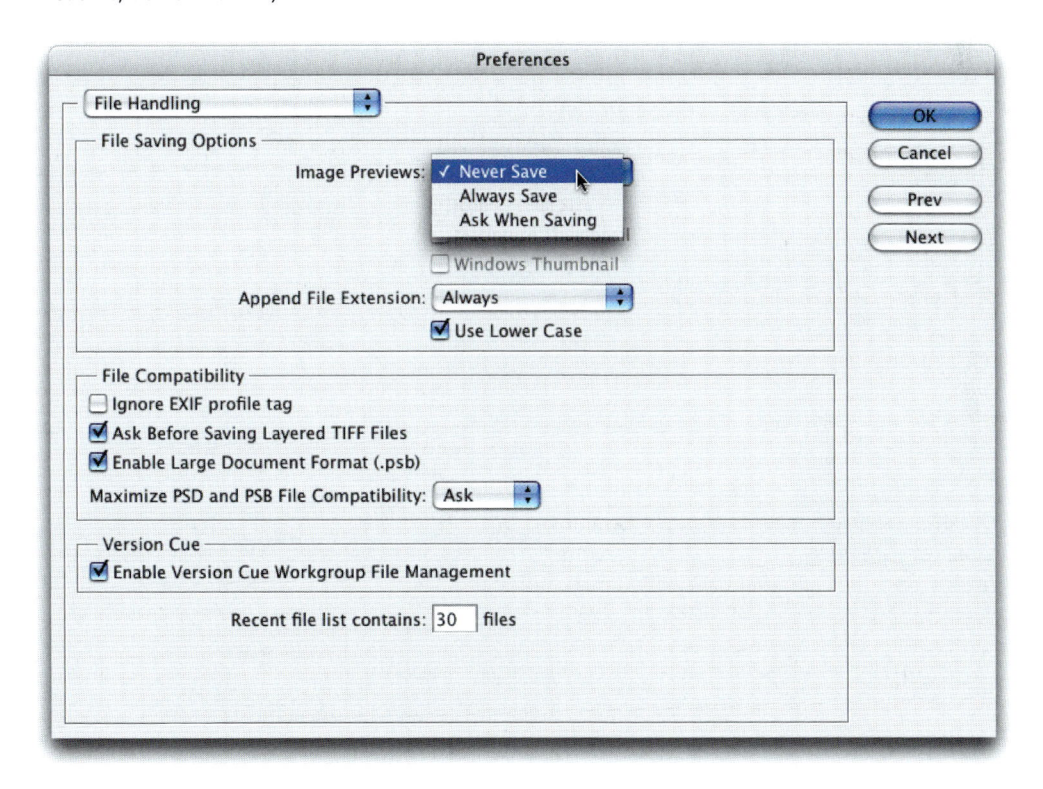

CHAPTER 11 • Killer Web Tips   239

GET THE REAL 100% VIEW

When creating Web graphics, it's often important to view your graphic at the same size your audience will view it. To view your image at 100%, just double-click on the Zoom tool. If your image is too big when viewed at 100%, just zoom out until the view of your image is the size you'd like it to appear on the webpage (use the zoom-out shortcuts—click with the Zoom tool while holding the Option/Alt keys, etc.), then look in the lower-left corner of the image window and you'll see the percentage of zoom. Write that down, then go under the Image menu and choose Image Size. When the Image Size dialog appears, in the Height pop-up menu in the Pixel Dimensions section, choose Percent. Then enter the percentage amount you wrote down earlier. By default, Photoshop will enter the Width when you enter the Height setting to keep your image proportional (if not, make sure the Constrain Proportions checkbox is turned on at the bottom). Click OK and it resizes your image to the exact size you want it to appear on the webpage.

240   CHAPTER 11 • Killer Web Tips

STYLE WARNING FOR WEB DESIGNERS

If you're designing Web graphics using Photoshop and ImageReady, you're probably spending a decent amount of time swapping back and forth between the two apps. The two programs share many of the same features and commands. However, they don't share custom styles that you've saved in Photoshop's Styles palette. So just be forewarned: If you create a custom style in Photoshop, don't expect to find that same style in ImageReady.

SPEND MORE TIME ANIMATING, LESS TIME CLICKING

If you're building Web animations in ImageReady, you don't have to keep clicking the tiny controls at the bottom of the Animations palette. Instead, navigate using these quick shortcuts: To play your animation, press Shift-Spacebar. To stop it, press Shift-Spacebar again. Press Option-Left Arrow (PC: Alt-Left Arrow) to go to the previous frame. Press Option-Right Arrow (PC: Alt-Right Arrow) to go to the next frame. To quickly jump back to the beginning of your animation, press Option-Shift-Left Arrow (PC: Alt-Shift-Left Arrow).

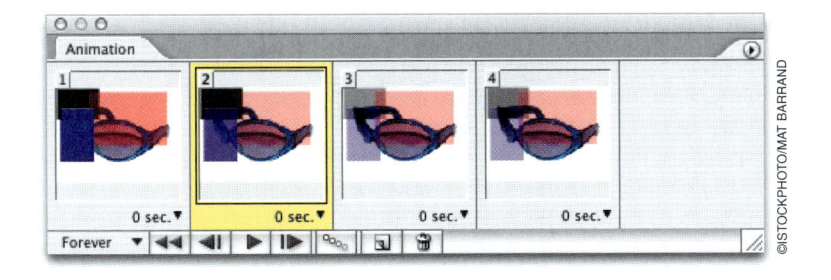

CHAPTER 11 • Killer Web Tips

GETTING TO THE HEXADECIMAL CODE

As you may know, there are hexadecimal codes for the colors used in webpages. Not only does Photoshop know these hexadecimal codes, it can extract them from an image and let you paste them into your HTML code editor. First, press the letter I to switch to the Eyedropper tool, and then hold the Control key (PC: Right-click) and click on a color within your image. A contextual menu will appear where you can choose Copy Color as HTML. Now you can switch to your HTML editor and choose Paste to copy the HTML code into your app.

GET SUPER-CLEAN TYPE FOR THE WEB

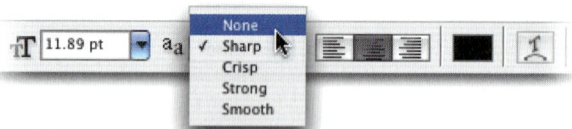

If you've been faced with having to create small type on the Web (usually 12 points or fewer), you know the smaller you go, the blurrier your type gets. That's because of the anti-aliasing that's automatically applied to the type, which works fine at larger sizes but tends to run together at smaller sizes, making your type look fuzzy. You can adjust the amount of aliasing (from the Options Bar), but here's a tip that many Web designers feel works even better: Once you get below 12 points, start adding positive tracking to your type (anywhere between 20 to 50 points) in the Character palette. This increases the amount of space between letters, and therefore, decreases the amount of blurriness. Increasing the space between your letters this way minimizes the effects of anti-aliasing and makes your type cleaner and more readable at smaller sizes. As a general rule—the smaller the type, the larger the tracking amount.

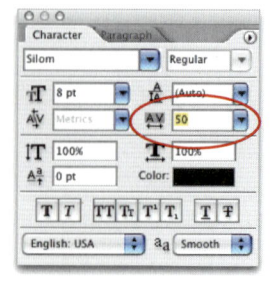

242   CHAPTER 11 • Killer Web Tips

GOT A FOLDER FULL OF IMAGES FOR THE WEB? BATCH 'EM!

Do you have a whole folder of images that you're going to convert to Web graphics? If the images are somewhat similar, don't do them one at a time—automate the process using actions. Start by opening one image from the folder. Go to the Actions palette (under the Window menu) and click on the Create New Action icon. Give this action a name (something like Optimize as JPEGs) then go about the business of optimizing this one graphic into a JPEG for the Web. When you're done optimizing it, click the Stop button at the bottom of the Actions palette. Then go under the File menu, under Automate, and choose Batch. In this dialog, under Play, choose the name of the new action you just created. Under Source, choose the folder of images you want converted using that action, and under Destination, choose what you want to happen to those images after they're converted. Click OK, and Photoshop will convert that folder with absolutely blinding speed. This one tip can really change the way you work, especially if you create for print first, then repurpose for the Web afterward.

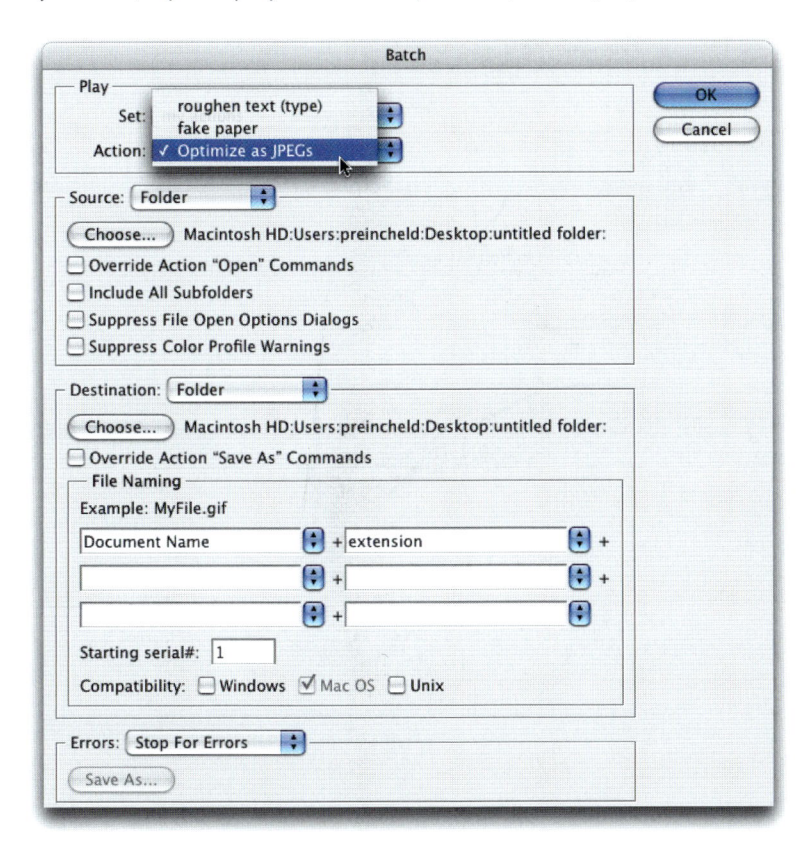

CHAPTER 11 • Killer Web Tips   243

EXERCISING YOUR INFLUENCE ON GIFS

This is an old trick we use to influence how Photoshop builds its color table when creating GIF images. We put a selection around the area of the image that's most important to us (for example, if we had a product shot, we'd put a selection around it), then we'd convert to Indexed Color (by choosing it from the Mode submenu under the Image menu). Photoshop will look at the colors contained in your selection and build the Indexed Color Table giving preference to those colors. It's another slick way to use less colors, creating a smaller file, but with a better-looking image.

READ THE WEB COLOR ONSCREEN

Want to know the hexadecimal Web color values of any color in your image? The Info palette can tell you instantly. Go under the Window menu and choose Info. In the Info palette, click on the little Eyedropper icon next to the CMYK readout and a pop-up menu appears. Choose Web Color, and you'll get the hexadecimal readouts right in the palette.

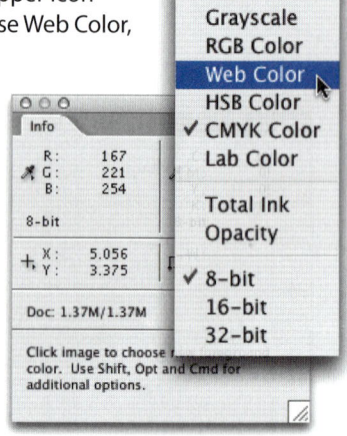

IMAGEREADY'S SUPERCHARGED EYEDROPPER

In previous versions of Photoshop, you could only use the Eyedropper tool to sample a color from other open images in Photoshop, but for some reason, ImageReady had a supercharged Eyedropper. If you clicked the mouse button within your image and held it down, you could leave your image window and sample colors from, well… just about anything—including your computer desktop or any other open application. Freaky! Fortunately, Adobe finally added this same power to Photoshop's Eyedropper tool.

CHAPTER 11 • Killer Web Tips   245

IMAGEREADY'S AUTO TILE MAKER

ImageReady has a built-in tool for creating seamless backgrounds. It's called Tile Maker and it's found under the Filter menu, under Other. It brings up a dialog where you can choose how much you want to blend the edges of your images (the default setting of 10 percent works fairly well for most images), but you can increase it if it doesn't look smooth enough to you.

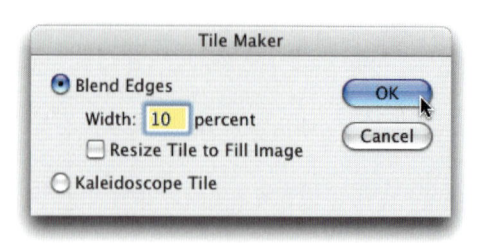

MAKE SURE YOU SEE IT THE SAME WAY THEY SEE IT

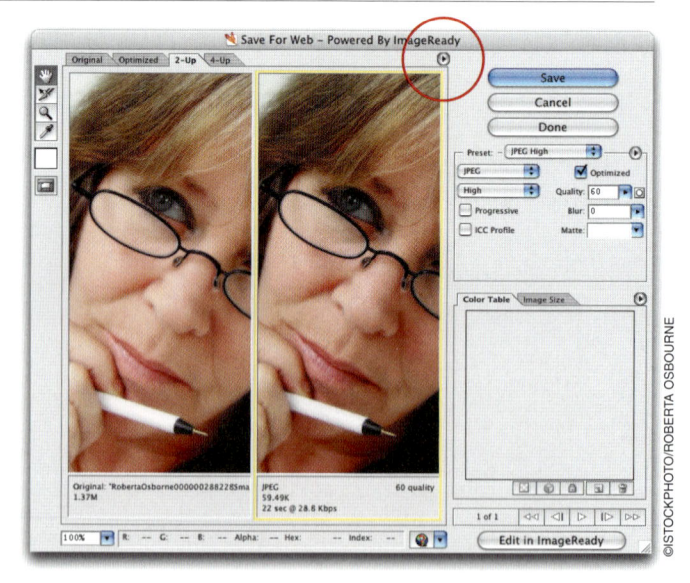

If you're designing Web graphics on a Macintosh, you can be sure they're going to be viewed by lots of people using a PC, and vice versa. A design problem arises because the monitors on Macs and on PCs display with different levels of brightness. For example, if you design Web graphics on a Macintosh, they'll look more than 10% darker when viewed on a PC using Windows. Photoshop will let you see an approximation of how those graphics will look when viewed on a PC. Here's how: Choose Save for Web from the File menu. Then, at the top right of the preview window you'll see a pop-up menu called the Preview Menu. From that menu, choose Standard Windows Color to get a preview of how your currently opened graphic will look when viewed on a standard Windows monitor. Windows designers can do the same thing and view how their Web graphics will look when viewed on a Mac (they'll look lighter). Knowing how your graphics will look on each platform will help you find a happy middle ground that looks good on both.

DON'T LOAD THAT BOGUS SLICE!

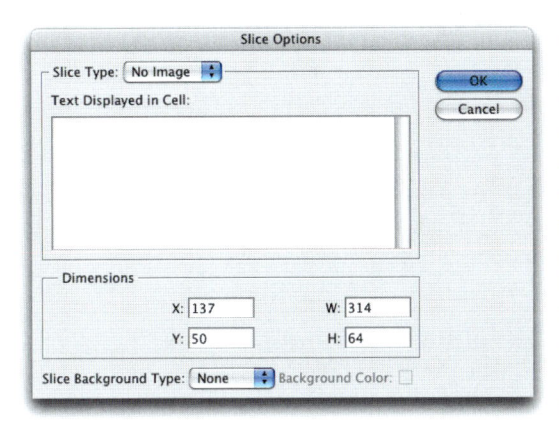

If you're slicing images for the Web in Photoshop (using the Slice tool), here's a tip to save even more space. If you have a slice in your image that's going to be the same color as your background (for example, you've got a solid white slice going on a solid white background), you can save file size by having that slice load no image at all. Sound like a plan? (I thought you'd like that.) Here's how to do it: Once your slice is in place, make it active (using the Slice Select tool), and then double-click within the selection to get the Slice Options dialog. In the Slice Type pop-up menu, choose No Image and click OK. That way, when Photoshop generates its HTML for the page, there will be no image in that spot, just the white background showing through, giving you a faster loading webpage. Pretty sweet!

USE LAYER-BASED SLICES

If you're getting ready to slice an image for the Web and you still have your layers intact, don't flatten that image before you slice. Instead, let Photoshop create the (layer-based) slices for you. There are two main advantages: (1) it's easier. You don't have to drag out slices—Photoshop does it automatically, perfectly slicing at the size of your layer. But even better is (2), when you create a layer-based slice, you can move the layer and (get this) Photoshop will automatically adjust all the slices to accommodate your move, and it will create a new slice for your layer as well. If you slice manually and move your layer—you're out of luck—the old slice stays right where it was. Plus, creating a layer-based slice couldn't be easier. Click on the layer you want to slice, then go under the Layer menu and choose New Layer Based Slice—Photoshop does the rest.

CHAPTER 11 • Killer Web Tips

BLUR THAT JPEG AND SHRINK IT DOWN

Here's a cool tip for when you're creating JPEG images. This tip doesn't work for all images, but can really come in handy for others. The tip is this: Because of the way JPEG compression works, if you can slightly blur your image, the file size will be smaller. You could just add a Gaussian Blur, or you could blur the image directly from the Save for Web dialog by entering a number in the Blur field. However, you're usually better off putting a selection around the important areas of your image, then inverting the selection (by choosing Inverse from the Select menu) and blurring just the background. That way, the important parts stay sharp, and the noncritical areas become more compressed.

Index

3D print effects, 205
3D Transform filter, 36
24-bit preview, 224

A

aberrations, chromatic, 100
About Photoshop command, 91
actions
    adding to existing actions, 207
    batch, 217
    default, 48
    embedding paths into, 214
    playback of, 201
    recording, 207
    saving as text files, 205
    slowing down, 201
    snapshots of, 194
    testing, 194
    text, 155
    troubleshooting, 201
Actions palette, 48, 207, 214, 243
Add Anchor Point tool, 63
Add Noise command, 175
adjustment layers, 62, 83, 212
Adobe Bridge, 1–21
    adding panes, 10
    Back button, 12
    creating folders from, 4
    deleting folders from, 8
    duplicating images in, 14
    ejecting discs from, 15
    emailing from, 15
    Full Screen Mode, 5, 84
    hiding Bridge window, 11
    image info in, 5–6
    jumping to/from Photoshop, 18
    keeping in foreground, 7
    nesting palettes/panes, 20
    opening folder of images in, 3
    opening multiple windows, 8
    preferences, 6–7, 17
    previewing images in, 20
    processing RAW images, 114
    rating photos in, 3–5
    refreshing, 19
    renaming images from, 16
    resetting defaults, 7
    scrolling through views, 2
    searching in, 13, 206
    slide shows in, 2, 5
    switching between open windows in, 16
    viewing PDFs in, 9
Adobe Photoshop CS2. *See* Photoshop CS2
Airbrush tool, 87
alignment
    layers, 125, 138
    objects, 57, 77, 125
All Channels View option, 197
All Layers option, 158
Alpha channels, 208, 214
ambient light, 180
Amount slider, 168
animations, 194, 241
Animations palette, 241
application switching, 228
arrowheads, 89
ATN files, 205
Auto correction, 101–102
Auto Erase option, 181
Auto Resolution dialog, 181
Auto Select Layer feature, 126, 228

B

Back button, 12
background color, 42, 65, 237
Background Eraser tool, 94
Background layers
    deleting, 237
    locking/unlocking, 222
    missing, 129, 224
    renaming, 133
    sharpening images, 178
    styles, 133
background music, 234
backgrounds
    blurring, 248
    seamless, 246
    tiled, 246
    transparent, 237
banding, 175
barrel distortion, 229
batch actions, 217
batch conversions, 243
Batch Rename command, 18
batch renaming, 18, 107
Bauer, Peg, 170
Bitmap mode, 178
black-and-white conversions, 98
black-and-white images, 98, 177
black frame, 83
blend modes, 131, 134, 209
Blur filters, 82, 90, 176
blurring
    backgrounds, 248
    Despeckle command, 176
    Gaussian Blur filter, 82, 90, 176
    JPEG images, 248
    motion blur, 170
bold text, 164, 222
borders, 84, 124
bounding boxes, 82, 152
Bridge. *See* Adobe Bridge
brightness, 246
browsers, 238
Brush Picker, 48, 55, 58, 91, 94
Brush Sample, 91, 174
brush strokes, 55, 172, 174
Brush tool, 220
brushes
    accessing, 54
    airbrush control, 87
    creating, 58
    custom, 95, 172
    default settings, 95
    disappearing tips, 220
    Healing Brush, 172, 174
    History Brush, 205
    presets, 33, 48, 54, 58
    previewing, 86
    rearranging, 48
    removing, 54
    resizing, 53
    samples, 91, 174

brushes *(continued)*
  shape of, 33, 63, 172
  softness, 92
  switching between, 54
  temporary, 58, 91
  troubleshooting, 220
  undo feature, 65
Brushes palette, 34, 86

C

cache files, 17
camera memory cards, 15, 19
Camera Raw, 97–116. *See also* RAW images
  Auto corrections and, 101–102
  black-and-white conversions, 98
  bypassing Save As dialog, 112
  Chromatic Aberrations, 100
  color space, 110
  cropping and, 99, 104, 107
  curves adjustment, 106
  editing RAW images, 114–116
  navigation shortcuts, 108
  previews in, 102, 108–109
  rating/sorting images in, 113
  renaming images in, 107
  resetting defaults, 112
  rotating images, 106
  sharpening and, 105
  updating histogram, 99
  viewing options, 102, 108–109
  White Balance tool, 99
  Workflow Options, 110
Camera Raw dialog, 103
cameras. *See* **digital cameras**
Cancel button, 67
canvas area, 24, 45, 59, 179
Canvas Size dialog, 24
CDs, ejecting, 15
Channel pop-up menu, 62
channels
  Alpha, 208, 214
  CMYK, 210
  color, 197–198, 211
  editing content on, 198
  Lightness, 175
  RGB, 210
  selecting, 62

  type/text in, 208
  viewing, 197
Channels palette
  accessing filters, 202
  adding to selections with, 214
  channel display, 198
  sharpening images, 175, 191
  type/text in channels, 208
  Unsharp Mask, 189
Character palette, 150, 158
characters, special, 151
Chromatic Aberration slider, 100
Clear Brush Controls command, 95
Clear Guides command, 57
clipboard, 228
clipping groups, 195
clipping masks, 195
clipping paths, 139
clipping warnings, 104
Clone Stamp tool, 184
cloned images, 184
CMYK channels, 210
CMYK images, 191
CMYK mode
  accessing filters in, 202
  caution about switching from, 190
  color corrections, 179
  Color Picker, 213
  conversions, 190, 202
  gradients and, 183
  printing and, 180, 183
  sharpening images, 189
  vs. RGB mode, 179, 190
collage, 75, 80
collections, 13
color
  accuracy of, 171
  background, 42, 65, 237
  banding, 175
  channels, 197–198, 211
  CMYK. *See* CMYK mode
  copying, 37
  correcting. *See* color correction
  fills, 49, 213
  foreground, 157
  fringe, 100
  GIF images, 244

  hexidecimal codes, 242, 244
  hue, 189
  indexed, 244
  Lab, 175, 190
  labels, 4, 6, 12
  layers, 140
  menu items, 72
  organizing items by, 72
  press-ready, 180
  previewing, 224
  replacing, 171
  RGB. *See* RGB mode
  sampled, 37, 103, 191, 245
  saturation, 189
  separations, 178, 190
  Similar command, 30
  spot, 178
  sRGB, 182
  swapping, 181
  type, 157
  Web and, 238, 244
  Web-safe, 238
Color Balance, 93
color-coding items, 72
color correction. *See also* **image correction**
  accuracy of color, 171
  CMYK vs. RGB mode, 179
  correcting single color, 93
  Curves adjustment layer for, 207
  default settings, 173
  drag-and-drop feature, 207
  flesh tones, 189
  highlights, 171
  multiple corrections, 186
  multiple images, 207
color modes
  CMYK. *See* CMYK mode
  grayscale images and, 177, 221
  Lab Color, 175, 190
  RGB. *See* RGB mode
Color palette, 61
Color Picker
  CMYK mode, 213
  Gamut Warning, 180
  replacing color, 171
  RGB mode, 213
color profile, 110

250

color ramp, 61
Color Range command, 60
Color Range dialog, 201
Color Sampler tool, 103, 191
color space, 110, 182
color stops, 80
color swatches, 42, 157, 180
columns, 163
commands
    About Photoshop, 91
    Add Noise, 175
    Batch Rename, 18
    Clear Brush Controls, 95
    Clear Guides, 57
    Color Range, 60
    Convert to Layer, 75
    Convert to Paragraph Text, 162
    Create Layers, 138
    Create Work Path, 153
    Despeckle, 176
    Eject, 15
    Expand, 225
    Export Layers To Files, 128
    Fade, 203
    Flatten Image, 122
    Free Transform, 45, 229
    Image Size, 240
    Insert Path, 214
    Invert Selection, 14
    Layer Edges, 124
    Load Selection, 41
    Merge Visible, 127, 145
    Paste Layer Style, 141
    Place, 73, 75
    Purge All, 44
    Rasterize Type, 152, 155
    Refresh, 19
    Replace Color, 171
    Rotate, 53
    Sample Actions, 48
    Save, 91
    Save Actions, 205
    Save for Web, 236–237, 246
    Save Selection, 41
    Select Linked Layers, 130
    Shadow/Highlight, 171, 173
    Show All Menu Items, 26
    Similar, 30
    Tile Vertically, 25
    Timing, 95
    Web Color, 244
Compact Mode, 7
contextual menus, 122
Contrast slider, 98
Convert to Layer command, 75
Convert to Paragraph Text command, 162
copying items
    color, 37
    images, 14, 43
    layer masks, 125
    layers, 66, 135
copyright symbol, 109, 151
Create Layers command, 138
Create Work Path command, 153
Crop snapping, 221
Crop tool, 31, 59, 87, 104–107, 221
cropping. *See also* trimming
    Camera Raw and, 99, 104, 107, 116
    cancelling a crop, 104
    images, 31, 59, 107, 116
    multiple images, 107, 116
    RAW files, 99, 104, 107, 116
    snapping and, 221
    Web graphics, 235
cursors
    finding fast, 27
    lost, 27
    resizing, 25
    selection shortcuts and, 29
    Type cursor, 156
curve points, 106, 186, 188, 211, 213
curves
    adjusting, 106, 186, 188
    Camera Raw and, 106
    drag-and-drop, 207
    reusing settings, 58
Curves adjustment layer, 207
Curves dialog, 52, 186, 213
Custom CMYK dialog, 190
Custom Shape tool, 151
custom shapes, 63, 151, 173
customizing
    brushes, 95, 172
    highlights, 173
    shadows, 173
    shapes, 151
    styles, 241

D

data. *See also* metadata
    EXIF, 101, 111, 196
    IPTC, 196, 202
Delete Anchor Point tool, 63
deleting items
    folders, 8
    images/photos, 14, 113
    layers, 237
    preferences, 227
deselecting items, 14
Despeckle command, 176
diagonal guides, 206
digital cameras
    color space in, 110
    EXIF data, 196
    image resolution, 220
    importing images, 220
    make/model, 102
discs, ejecting from Bridge, 15
Display & Cursors preferences, 25, 220
distortion, 229
docked palettes, 35, 39
Document Bounds option, 221
documents. *See* files
drag-and-drop
    color correction, 207
    Curves adjustment layer, 207
    to email program, 15
    images/photos, 15, 89
    layers, 126, 132, 136–137
    opening folders with, 3
    styles, 132
    thumbnails, 15
drawing lines, 206
Drop Shadow layer style, 184
drop shadows
    adding noise to, 184
    angle adjustments, 137
    Global Light feature and, 226
    layers and, 137
    problems with, 226
dumb quotes, 150
Duplicate Layer dialog, 135

E

Easter Eggs, 81
edge fringe, 80, 100
edges
   detecting, 79
   smoothing, 50
   softening, 90, 124
   viewing, 124, 212, 227
editing
   applying edits, 115
   channel content, 198
   on paths, 163
   RAW images, 114–116
   removing edits, 116
   text, 157–158, 163
effects
   3D, 205
   Filter Gallery, 67–69, 78
   layers, 139, 199
   modifying intensity, 81
   moving between layers, 121
   print, 205
   scaling, 199
   undoing, 81
Eject command, 15
ejecting discs, 15
emailing images, 15
EPS files, 224
EPS Options dialog, 224
erasing items, 94
Escape key, 31, 104–105
EXIF data, 101, 111, 196. *See also* info, image
Expand command, 225
Export Clipboard option, 228
Export Layers To Files script, 128
Exposure slider, 98
extensions
   ATN, 205
   PSD, 230
   TXT, 205
Extract function, 79
Eye icon, 131, 140
Eyedropper icon, 244
Eyedropper tool, 37, 187, 237, 242, 245

F

Fade command, 203
Fade dialog, 174–175
Favorites pane, 10
Feather field, 226
Feather Selection dialog, 90
feathered selections, 90
feathering, 90, 226
fields, escaping, 66
File Browser, 14, 17. *See also* Adobe Bridge
File Handling preferences, 239
files. *See also* images
   assigning metadata to, 202
   closing, 44
   converting layers to, 128
   determining exact center of, 49
   EPS, 224
   finding, 206
   GIF, 235, 244
   JPEG, 243
   layered, 128–129
   PDF, 9
   PSB, 230
   PSD, 109, 230
   recalling previous settings, 61
   recent, 38
   saving changes, 44
   size of, 140, 230, 235–236, 248
   text, 205
   transparency and, 235
Fill dialog, 40
Fill option, 144
fills
   color, 49, 213
   gradient, 62
   pattern, 62
   shortcuts, 40
   "un-filling" layers, 144
Filmstrip view, 9
Filter Gallery, 67–69, 78
Filter menu, 24, 26, 67–68
filters
   3D Transform, 36
   accessing in CMYK mode, 202
   applying, 30, 203
   Blur, 82, 90, 176
   controlling, 203

   Gaussian Blur, 82, 90, 176
   grayscale images and, 221
   hiding/showing, 26
   layers and, 204
   Lens Correction, 169
   Lens Flare, 217
   multiple, 204
   Photo Filters, 83
   reapplying previous, 30
   RGB, 221
   Smart Sharpen, 95, 170, 188
   Unsharp Mask, 175, 188–189
   Vanishing Point, 73–74
Find and Replace Text dialog, 164
Find function, 206
finding items
   cursors, 27
   files, 13, 206
   highlights, 187, 209
   images/photos, 13, 206
   items in Bridge, 13, 206
   layers, 224
   metadata, 206
   shadows, 187, 209
   text, 164
Fit in View option, 109
Fit on Screen view, 36, 108
Flash-based templates, 234
Flash galleries, 234
Flatten Image command, 122
flattened images, 127, 230
flattened layers, 120, 122, 127, 230
flesh tones, 189, 191
floating selections, 144
Folder pane, 19–20
folders
   creating, 4, 109
   deleting, 8
   Image Processor, 109
   moving, 17
   opening, 3
   viewing multiple, 8
   Web images, 243
fonts. *See also* text; type
   changing, 154
   metadata, 19, 28
   previewing, 148
   resizing, 158

foreground color, 157
Foreground Color Swatch, 157
formats
    GIF, 235–236
    JPEG, 109, 224, 236
    PDF, 9, 197, 216
    PSD, 109, 230
Free Transform bounding box, 56, 76, 225, 229
Free Transform command, 45, 120, 229
Free Transform handles, 45
Freeform Pen options, 227
Freeform Pen tool, 199
fringe, edge, 80, 100
Full Mode, 7
Full Screen Mode, 5, 84
Full Size Brush Tip option, 25

G

gamut problems, 180
Gamut Warning, 180
gaps, 125
Gaussian Blur filter, 82, 90, 176
GIF files/images, 235–236, 244
GIF format, 235–236
Global Light feature, 226
Go Back button, 12
Go Forward button, 12
gradient banding, 175
Gradient Picker, 63
Gradient tool, 63, 80
gradients
    CMYK mode and, 183
    color separations, 178
    color stops, 80
    prepress work and, 183
    spot color, 178
graphic elements. *See also* **images**
    cropping, 235
    for Web, 235, 240, 246
graphics tablet, 174
grayscale images, 221
Grayscale mode, 177, 221
grids, 52, 74, 169
groups
    clipping, 195
    Layer Groups, 127, 195
guides
    diagonal, 206

flipping, 57
slicing images at, 237
Smart Guides, 77
snapping to center, 56

H

Hand tool, 36, 42, 84, 108, 210
handles, Free Transform, 45
hard light, 178, 209
Healing Brush tool, 172, 174
hexidecimal codes, 242, 244
hiding
    filters, 26
    image info, 6
    layers, 78, 131
    menus, 27, 83
    metadata, 111
    palettes, 83
High Pass dialog, 178
High Pass filter, 178
Highlight clipping warnings, 104
highlighting text, 151
highlights. *See also* **light**
    adjusting, 168, 171
    customizing, 173
    default settings, 173
    finding, 187, 209
    selecting, 201
histogram, updating, 99
Histogram palette, 197
History Brush, 65, 205
History feature, 204
History Logging, 195
History Options, 78, 217
History palette
    batch actions, 217
    snapshots, 204
    tracking layer visibility, 78
    undo feature, 62, 88
History States, 217
horizontal guides, 206
HTML code, 242
HTML editor, 242
hue, 189
Hue/Saturation dialog, 189

I

Ignore Palettes option, 88
image correction, 167–181. *See also* **color correction**

Auto, 101–102
CMYK vs. RGB mode, 179
Curves adjustment layer for, 207
default settings, 173
drag-and-drop feature, 207
flesh tones, 189
gradient banding, 175
healing process, 172, 174
highlights, 168, 171, 173
Lens Correction filter, 169
moiré patterns, 176
multiple corrections, 186
multiple images, 207
red eye removal, 168
shadows, 168, 173
sharpening. *See* sharpening images
Image Previews feature, 239
Image Processor script, 109
Image Size command, 240
Image Size dialog, 24, 181, 240
ImageReady
    animations, 194
    Slices From Guides, 237
    styles and, 241
    Tile Maker, 246
    Web animations, 241
    window speed tip, 238
images. *See also* **files; graphic elements; photographs**
    before and after views, 183
    assigning metadata to, 196, 202
    barrel distortion, 229
    batch converting for Web, 243
    black-and-white, 98, 177
    black frame around, 83
    changing placement of, 84
    cloning, 184
    CMYK, 191
    collage, 75, 80
    collections of, 13
    copying, 14, 43
    correcting. *See* image correction
    cropping. *See* cropping
    deleting, 14, 113
    deselecting, 14
    determining if open in Photoshop, 11
    dragging, 89

images *(continued)*
   editing. *See* editing
   emailing, 15
   finding, 206
   fit-in-window size, 25
   fitting to screen, 36
   five-star, 4
   flattened, 127, 230
   flesh tones, 189, 191
   grayscale, 221
   importing, 220
   info about, 5–6
   JPEG, 248
   line art, 177, 181
   moving with Hand tool, 84
   navigating between, 56
   numbers, 107, 234
   opening, 11
   optimized, 238
   pasting, 43
   placing inside type, 153
   previewing, 239
   rating, 3–5, 113
   RAW. *See* RAW images
   renaming, 16, 18, 107
   resizing, 75, 110
   resolution. *See* resolution
   retouching, 84
   RGB, 189
   rotating, 106
   scaling, 45
   scanned, 65, 176–177
   sharpening, 175, 178, 188, 191
   side-by-side review of, 25
   size of, 36, 75, 110, 240
   sliced, 237, 247
   tiled, 79
   viewing at 100% size, 36, 240
   Web. *See* Web images
importing images, 220
indexed color, 244
info, image, 5–6. *See also* **EXIF data**
Info palette, 215, 217
Insert Path command, 214
Internet. *See* **Web**
Intersect with Selection icon, 34
Invert Selection command, 14
IPTC data, 196, 202
italic text, 164, 222

J
jaggies, 50
JPEG files, 109, 243
JPEG format, 109, 224, 236
JPEG images, 248
jump drives, 15, 19

K
kerning, 159
keyboard
   navigation, 208
   text spacing, 159
keyboard shortcuts
   Animations palette, 241
   blend modes, 209
   in Camera Raw, 108
   Canvas Size dialog, 24
   color labeling, 12
   creating flattened layers, 120
   cursor and, 29
   Fill dialog, 40
   flattening images, 122, 127
   Gaussian Blur filter, 82
   hiding thumbnail info, 6
   highlight/shadow warnings, 104
   Image Size dialog, 24
   inverting masks, 126
   jumping between Bridge/Photoshop, 18
   Layers palette, 142
   loading selections, 123
   Mac OS–based systems, xxi
   modifier keys, 29
   moving effects between layers, 121
   multiple undos, 88
   navigation, 108, 208
   reapplying filters, 30
   rotating images, 106
   scrolling through views, 2
   selection, 29
   switching between windows, 16
   unlinking layers, 122–123
   Windows-based systems, xxi
   for zooming, 74
Keyboard Shortcuts editor, 82
Keywords pane, 10
Kloskowski, Matt, 149
Kost, Julieanne, 79

L
Lab Color mode, 175, 190
labels, 4, 6, 12
Lasso tool
   drawing straight segments, 29
   jaggies and, 50
   navigation control with, 210
   tips for, 50, 210
layer blend modes, 204
Layer Comps To Files script, 133
Layer Edges command, 124
layer effects, 121, 139
Layer Effects icon, 139
Layer Groups, 127, 195
layer masks
   copying, 125
   inverting, 126
   moving, 125–126
   thumbnails, 125
   viewing as Rubyliths, 143
   viewing separately, 143
Layer menu, 130
Layer Properties dialog, 140
Layer Style dialog, 130, 134, 137, 184, 226
layered files, 128–129
layers
   activating, 138
   adjustment, 62, 83, 212
   aligning, 125
   aligning objects on, 77, 125
   background. *See* Background layers
   blank, 172
   blend modes, 131, 134
   centered, 137
   color-coding, 140
   comparing layouts, 133
   converting Smart Object layers to, 75
   converting to separate documents, 128
   converting type layers to image layers, 152
   copying, 65–66, 135
   creating, 120
   Curves Adjustment, 207
   deleting, 237

dragging between documents, 126, 132, 136–137
drop shadow angles, 137
edges. *See* edges
effects, 139, 199
file size and, 140
filters and, 204
finding, 224
flattened, 120, 122, 127, 230
grouping, 127
healing on, 172
hidden, 78, 127, 131
jumping to, 128, 138, 142, 228
layer-based slices, 247
linked, 122–123, 127, 130, 141
locking/unlocking, 130, 222
merging, 127, 140, 160
moving, 142
navigating, 128, 138, 142, 228
nudging pixels in, 35
opacity, 135, 144–145
problems with, 222, 224, 228
retouching and, 84
rotating, 53
selecting, 123
selecting objects on, 144
Shape, 139
showing, 78
slices, 247
snapping to, 125
styles, 132–133, 137–138, 141, 199
switching between, 142
tips for, 119–145
tracking visibility, 78
transparency, 138, 144
Type, 149, 151–152, 160
"un-filling," 144
unlinking, 122–123
Layers palette, 130, 142
Lens Correction filter, 169
Lens Flare filter, 217
Levels dialog, 185
light. *See also* **highlights**
ambient, 180
Global Light feature, 226
hard, 178, 209
soft, 178, 209
Lightness channel, 175

line art, 177, 181
Line tool, 206
lines
arrowheads, 89
drawing, 206
measurement, 215
Link icon, 122–123, 136, 141, 165
linked layers, 122–123, 127, 130, 141
Load Selection command, 41
loading selections, 41, 123, 210, 214
locked layers, 130, 222
Luminosity mode, 175

M
Mac OS–based systems, xxi, 38, 238, 246
Magic Wand tool, 60
Magnetic Pen tool, 227
Marquee snapping, 221
masks
clipping, 195
inverting, 126
layer. *See* layer masks
Quick Mask mode, 200
selections and, 200, 212
Unsharp Mask filter, 175, 188–189
Measure tool, 170, 179, 215
measurement units, 28, 41, 87, 215
memory
checking usage, 229
clipboard, 228
out-of-memory warnings, 64
performance and, 229
problems with, 64, 223, 229
purging, 44
requirements for, 223
undo feature and, 64
memory cards, 15, 19
menus
color-coding, 72
contextual, 122
filter, 24, 26, 67–68
hiding, 27, 83
Layer, 130
new features, 24
Merge Visible command, 127, 145
merging layers, 127, 140, 160
"Merlin Lives" Easter Egg, 81
messages. *See also* **warnings**
Easter Eggs, 81

Gamut Warning, 180
out-of-memory warnings, 64
resetting warning dialogs, 32
metadata
assigning to multiple files, 202
assigning to photographs, 196, 202
display options, 196
font sizes, 19, 28
hiding, 111
searching, 206
Metadata palette, 19, 28, 196, 204
Metadata pane, 10
midtones Input Levels slider, 200–201
moiré patterns, 176
monitor
brightness, 246
CMYK mode and, 182
cross-platform issues, 246
prepress work and, 182
motion blur, 170
Motion Blur sharpening, 170
Move tool, 35, 68, 138, 156, 228
music, 234

N
navigation
in Camera Raw, 108
between images, 56
jumping to layers, 128, 138, 142, 228
jumping to tools, 159
keyboard, 208
Lasso tool, 210
layers, 128, 138, 142, 228
nesting palettes/panes, 20
New dialog, 129
New Layer dialog, 222
New Snapshot button, 204
Ninness, Michael, 87, 92
noise, 175, 184, 191

O
objects
3D, 180
aligning, 77, 125
finding center of, 56
gaps between, 125
on layers, 77, 125, 144

255

objects *(continued)*
   measuring, 215
   scanning, 180
   selecting, 144
   Smart Objects. *See* Smart Objects
   snapping to layers, 125
   Step and Repeat function, 86
   transforming, 45
opacity
   changing, 120
   healing process, 174
   layers, 135, 144–145
   sharpening and, 178
   transforming and, 120
Opacity slider, 81, 174
Open button, 129
Open Recent menu, 38
optimization
   comparing image versions, 238
   graphics for Web, 236, 243
   window speed and, 238
Optimize to File Size option, 236
Options Bar, 35, 64

P

paint strokes, 55
painting, 93, 181, 191, 205, 215
palettes
   Actions, 48, 207, 214, 243
   Animations, 241
   Brushes, 33, 86
   Channels. *See* Channels palette
   Character, 150, 158
   Color, 61
   default locations, 40
   docked, 35, 39
   hiding, 83
   hiding/showing, 38, 51
   Histogram, 197
   History. *See* History palette
   Info, 215, 217
   Layers, 130, 142
   Metadata, 19, 28, 196, 204
   minimizing, 38
   nesting, 20
   Paths, 43, 215
   Preview, 20
   protecting, 88

   saving, 92
   Swatches, 42
   Web-safe Color, 238
   zooming, 88
panes, 10, 20
Paragraph Text Size dialog, 163
Paste Layer Style command, 141
pasting items
   images, 43
   layer styles, 141
Path Selection tool, 82
paths
   combining, 198
   editing type on, 163
   embedding into actions, 214
   resizing, 82
   selections and, 43
   Stroke Path tool, 94, 215
   stroking portion of, 215
   text, 152
Paths palette, 43, 215
patterns, 62, 176
PDF files, 9
PDF format, 9, 197, 216
PDF Presentations, 197, 216
PDF Security dialog, 216
Pen tool
   Auto Add/Delete option, 63
   combining paths with, 198
   Magnetic options, 227
   path selection, 43
   switching to Freeform tool, 199
   tips for, 63
Pencil tool, 181
performance, 229
perspective, 73–74, 229
Perspective feature, 229
Photo Filters, 83
Photo Gallery. *See* **Web Photo Gallery**
photographs. *See also* **files; images**
   before and after views, 183
   assigning metadata to, 196, 202
   barrel distortion, 229
   batch converting for Web, 243
   black-and-white, 98, 177
   black frame around, 83
   changing placement of, 84
   cloning, 184

CMYK, 191
collage, 75, 80
collections of, 13
copying, 14, 43
correcting. *See* image correction
cropping. *See* cropping
deleting, 14, 113
deselecting, 14
determining if open in Photoshop, 11
dragging, 89
editing. *See* editing
emailing, 15
finding, 206
fit-in-window size, 25
fitting to screen, 36
five-star, 4
flattened, 127, 230
flesh tones, 189, 191
grayscale, 221
importing, 220
info about, 5–6
JPEG, 248
line art, 177, 181
moving with Hand tool, 84
navigating between, 56
numbers, 107, 234
opening, 11
optimized, 238
pasting, 43
placing inside type, 153
previewing, 239
rating, 3–5, 113
RAW. *See* RAW images
renaming, 16, 18, 107
resizing, 75, 110
resolution. *See* resolution
retouching, 84
RGB, 189
rotating, 106
scaling, 45
scanned, 65, 176–177
sharpening, 175, 178, 188, 191
side-by-side review of, 25
size of, 36, 75, 110, 240
sliced, 237, 247
tiled, 79
viewing at 100% size, 36, 240
Web Photo Gallery, 234

Photoshop 7 Power Shortcuts, 87
The Photoshop CS2 Book for Digital Photographers, xxi
Photoshop CS Down & Dirty Tricks, xxi
Photoshop CS2
   color-coding menu items, 72
   Easter Eggs, 81
   History Logging, 195
   IPTC data, 196
   jumping to/from Bridge, 18
   new features, 24
   performance, 229
pixels
   expanding selections by, 225
   feathered, 90
   fixing stray, 60
   nudging, 35
   painting, 181
   removing edge fringe, 80
   selection smoothing and, 60
Place command, 73, 75
Playback Options dialog, 202
points
   center, 162
   corner, 162
   curve, 106, 186, 188, 211, 213
   white, 185
preferences
   Adobe Bridge, 6–7, 17
   brush size, 220
   deleting, 227
   Display & Cursors, 25, 220
   Export Clipboard, 228
   File Handling, 239
   flattening files, 230
   Mac OS–based systems, xxi
   rebuilding, 227
   Windows-based systems, xxi
Preferences dialog, 32, 195, 220
prepress cleanups, 208
prepress tips, 167, 182–186
presentations, 83, 85, 197, 216
presets
   brushes, 33, 48, 54, 58
   White Balance, 98
press-ready colors, 180
pressure sensitivity controls, 174
Preview palette, 20

Preview pane, 10, 67
Preview panel, 3
previews
   before and after views, 183
   brushes, 86
   in Camera Raw, 102, 108–109
   color, 224
   EPS files and, 224
   fonts, 148
   landscape, 21
   portrait, 21
   RGB, 198
   sharpening, 105
   switching between, 21
   thumbnails. *See* thumbnails
   toggling on/off, 102
printing
   3D print effects, 205
   CMYK mode, 180, 182–183
   color space and, 182
   resolution, 181, 220
   text files, 205
production tips, 46–69
Proof Colors option, 213
PSB files, 230
PSD files, 109, 230
PSD format, 109, 230
Purge All command, 44

Q
Quick Mask mode, 200
quotation marks, 150

R
Radius slider, 50
RAM
   checking usage, 229
   clipboard, 228
   out-of-memory warnings, 64
   performance and, 229
   problems with, 64, 223, 229
   purging, 44
   requirements for, 223
   undo feature and, 64
Rasterize Type command, 152, 155
rasterizing type, 155–156, 158
rating images, 3–5, 113
RAW images. *See also* **Camera Raw**
   Auto corrections, 101–102

   color space, 110
   creating JPEGs from, 109
   cropping, 99, 104, 107, 116
   editing, 114–116
   previewing, 102, 108–109
   processing in Adobe Bridge, 114
   resizing, 110
   as Smart Objects, 73
Rectangular Marquee tool, 226
rectangular selections, 225–226
red eye, 168
Refresh command, 19
rendering text, 152
Replace Color command, 171
Resample Image option, 220
Reset button, 67
Reset Preferences option, 7
resolution
   digital camera images, 220
   high, 187
   images, 220
   low, 187
   medium, 187
   printing images, 181, 220
   printing presses and, 187
   scanned images, 176–177
   Web and, 187
retouching process, 84, 172
RGB channels, 210
RGB filters, 221
RGB images, 189
RGB mode
   color corrections, 179
   Color Picker, 213
   conversions, 190, 202
   grayscale images, 221
   sharpening images, 175
   vs. CMYK mode, 179, 190
RGB preview, 198
RGB space, 182
Rotate command, 53
rotating
   images, 106
   layers, 53
   scans, 179
Rubylith, 143
rulers, 41

S

Sample Actions command, 48
Sample All Layers option, 84
Sample Size option, 60
sampled color, 37, 103, 191, 245
samples, brush, 91
saturation, 98, 189
Saturation slider, 189
Save Actions command, 205
Save As dialog, 112
Save button, 112
Save command, 92, 107
Save for Web command, 236–237, 246
Save Selection command, 41
saves, undoing, 92
saving
    actions as text files, 205
    Bridge workspaces, 21
    in Camera Raw, 107, 112
    changes to files, 44
    palettes, 92
    selections, 41
    for Web, 236–237, 246
Scale Layer Effects dialog, 199
scaling images, 45
scans
    3D objects, 180
    highlights and, 201
    resolution, 176–177
    shadows and, 201
    straightening, 65, 179
screen cleanup, 51
scripts
    Export Layers To Files, 128
    Image Processor, 109
    Layer Comps To Files, 133
scroll bars, 42
scrubbing, 31
scrubby sliders, 31
search feature
    files, 13, 206
    highlights, 187, 209
    items in Bridge, 13, 206
    layers, 224
    metadata, 206
    photos, 13, 206
    shadows, 187, 209
    text, 164

Select Linked Layers command, 130
selections
    adding to with Channels palette, 214
    Auto Select Layer feature, 126
    contracting, 200
    "drag selecting" layers, 126
    expanding, 200, 225
    feathered, 90
    floating, 144
    intersecting, 34
    Lasso tool, 210
    layers, 123
    loading, 41, 123, 210, 214
    masking and, 200, 212
    multiple layers, 123
    objects, 144
    paths as, 43
    Quick Mask mode and, 200
    rectangular, 225–226
    rounded corners, 225–226
    saving, 41
    shortcuts, 29
    tips for, 212
    transforming, 45
separation, color, 178, 190
Shadow clipping warnings, 104
Shadow/Highlight command, 168, 171, 173
shadows
    adding noise to, 184
    adjusting, 168, 173
    custom, 173
    decreasing, 173
    default settings, 173
    drop. *See* drop shadows
    finding, 187, 209
    open, 171, 173
    problems with, 226
    selecting, 201
Shadows Amount slider, 173
Shadows slider, 98, 171
Shape layer, 139
Shape Picker, 151
Shape tools, 139, 151
shapes
    arrowheads, 89
    brush, 33, 63, 172
    circles, 149

    custom, 63, 151, 173
sharpening images
    Camera Raw and, 105
    CMYK images, 171
    flesh tones, 171
    High Pass filter, 178
    Motion Blur sharpening, 170
    previews, 105
    Smart Sharpen feature, 95, 170
    Unsharp Mask filter, 175, 188–189
Sharpening slider, 105
Sharpness slider, 98
shortcuts
    Animations palette, 241
    blend modes, 209
    in Camera Raw, 108
    Canvas Size dialog, 24
    color labeling, 12
    creating flattened layers, 120
    cursor and, 29
    Fill dialog, 40
    flattening images, 122, 127
    Gaussian Blur filter, 82
    hiding thumbnail info, 6
    highlight/shadow warnings, 104
    Image Size dialog, 24
    inverting masks, 126
    jumping between Bridge/Photoshop, 18
    Layers palette, 142
    loading selections, 123
    Mac OS–based systems, xxi
    modifier keys, 29
    moving effects between layers, 121
    multiple undos, 88
    navigation, 108, 208
    reapplying filters, 30
    rotating images, 106
    scrolling through views, 2
    selection, 29
    switching between windows, 16
    unlinking layers, 122–123
    Windows-based systems, xxi
    for zooming, 74
Show All Menu Items command, 26
Show Channels in Color option, 197
Show Tool Hints option, 26
Similar command, 30

Slice Options dialog, 247
Slice Select tool, 247
Slice tool, 234
sliced images, 237, 247
Slices From Guides feature, 237
slide shows, 2, 5, 85, 197, 216
sliders, 31, 81
Smart Guides, 77
Smart Object layers, 75
Smart Objects
    camera RAW images as, 73
    creating, 75
    resizing images and, 75
smart quotes, 150
Smart Sharpen filter, 95, 170, 188
Snap command, 56
Snap To feature, 125, 221
snapping
    to center of image, 49, 56
    cropped images and, 221
    to layers, 125
    objects, 125
snapshots, 194, 204
soft light, 178, 209
Space menu, 110
Spacebar, 42
spacing, text, 159, 164
special characters, 151
spell checking, 162
spot color, 178
sRGB color space, 182
star ratings, 4–5, 113
startup window, 32, 91
Step and Repeat function, 86
stops, color, 80
straight quotes, 150
straight segments, drawing, 29
Straighten tool, 105
Stroke Path tool, 94, 215
strokes
    brush, 55, 172, 174
    paint, 55
    paths, 94, 215
styles
    Background layers, 133
    custom, 241
    dragging and dropping, 132
    ImageReady and, 241
    layers, 132–133, 137–138, 141, 199

text, 164, 222
Swatches palette, 42
Switch Filmstrip Orientation icon, 9
symbols, 151
Synchronize button, 115–116

T
Temperature slider, 99
templates, Flash-based, 234
text. *See also* fonts; type
    actions, 155
    bold, 164, 222
    columns, 163
    editing, 157–158, 163
    faux styles for, 164, 222
    finding, 164
    highlighting, 151
    horizontal scaling, 161
    italic, 164, 222
    kerning, 159
    multiple adjustments to, 164
    rendering, 152
    replacing, 164
    spacing, 159, 164
    spell checking, 162
    styles, 164, 222
    vertical scaling, 161
    warped, 222
    wrapping, 162
text boxes, 152, 162
text files, 205
text paths, 153
Textured Image extraction, 79
Threshold adjustment layer, 209
thumbnail cache, 17
Thumbnail Size slider, 17
thumbnails. *See also* previews
    in Bridge, 2, 4
    file size and, 239
    image info, 5–6
    layer masks, 125
    loading selections, 123
    renaming, 16
    scrolling through, 2
    size of, 17, 76
    turning off, 239
TIFF files, 109
Tilde key (~), 16, 62
Tile Horizontally command, 79

Tile Maker, 246
Tile Vertically command, 25, 79
tiled backgrounds, 246
tiled images, 79
Timing command, 95
Tint slider, 99
tonal adjustments, 61–62
Toolbox
    hiding/showing, 33
    jumping to tools in, 159
tools
    Add Anchor Point, 63
    Airbrush, 87
    Background Eraser, 94
    Brush, 220
    Clone Stamp, 184
    Color Sampler, 103, 191
    Crop, 31, 59, 87, 104–107, 221
    Custom Shape, 151
    default settings, 39
    Delete Anchor Point, 63
    Eyedropper, 37, 187, 237, 242, 245
    Free Transform, 229
    Freeform Pen, 199
    Gradient, 63, 80
    Hand, 42, 84, 210
    Healing Brush, 172, 174
    jumping to, 159
    Lasso. *See* Lasso tool
    Line, 206
    Magic Wand, 60
    Magnetic Pen, 227
    Measure, 179, 215
    Move, 35, 68, 156, 228
    Path Selection, 82
    Pen, 43, 63, 82, 198–199, 227
    Pencil, 181
    Rectangular Marquee, 226
    Shape, 139, 151
    Show Tool Hints option, 26
    Slice, 234
    Slice Select, 247
    Straighten, 105
    Stroke Path, 94, 215
    Type, 149, 151, 156, 159
    Zoom, 36, 88, 240
Tooltips, 5, 86
training tips, 26–27

transformations
    3D Transform filter, 36
    Free Transform bounding box, 225
    Free Transform command, 45
    Free Transform handles, 45
    Free Transform tool, 229
    objects, 45
    opacity and, 120
    selections, 45
transparency
    backgrounds, 237
    creating, 237
    file size and, 235
    layers, 138, 144
Transparent option, 129
Trash icon, 113
Trim dialog, 235
trimming, 235. *See also* **cropping**
troubleshooting, 219–230
    actions, 201
    banding, 175
    barrel distortion, 229
    brushes, 220
    chromatic aberrations, 100
    Crop snapping, 221
    deleting preferences, 227
    eliminating fringe, 100
    EPS previews, 224
    faux styles, 222
    gamut problems, 180
    grayscale images, 221
    layer navigation, 228
    memory problems, 64, 223, 229
    moiré patterns, 176
    performance, 229
    print resolution, 220
    rebuilding preferences, 227
    resetting warning dialogs, 32
    selection problems, 225–226
    shadows, 226
    Warped Text function, 222
TXT files, 205
type. *See also* **fonts; text**
    in channels, 208
    in circular format, 149
    color, 157
    editing, 157, 163
    moving, 156

    on paths, 163
    placing photos inside, 153
    rasterizing, 155–156, 158
    resetting, 150
    sharpness of, 242
    styles, 164, 222
    for Web, 242
Type cursor, 156
Type layers, 149, 151–152, 160
Type tool, 149, 151, 156, 159
typeface tips, 147–165

U

undo feature
    brushes, 65
    History Brush, 65
    History palette, 62, 204
    modifying effects, 81
    multiple undo shortcut, 88
    out-of-memory warnings and, 64
    undoing saves, 92
Units & Rulers Preferences dialog, 41
Unsharp Mask filter, 175, 188–189

V

vanishing point, 73–74
Vanishing Point filter, 73–74
vertical guides, 206

W

Wacom tablet, 174
warning dialogs, 32
warnings. *See also* **messages**
    clipping, 104
    Gamut Warning, 180
    highlight, 104
    out-of-memory warnings, 64
    resetting warning dialogs, 32
Warp Image feature, 76
Warp option, 76
warped text, 222
Web
    color and, 238, 244
    image resolution and, 187
    sliced images, 247
    tips for, 233–248
    type size and, 242
Web animations, 241
Web browsers, 238

Web Color command, 244
Web images. *See also* **images**
    batch converting images to, 243
    cropping, 235
    cross-platform issues, 246
    sharpness of, 236
    viewing at 100% size, 240
    zooming and, 236
Web Photo Gallery, 234
Web-safe Color palette, 238
webpages, 246–247
Welcome Screen, 32
white, 99
white balance, 98–99, 103
White Balance presets, 98
White Balance tool, 99, 103
white point setting, 185
windows
    opening multiple, 8
    rotating through, 238
    speed of, 238
    startup, 32, 91
    switching between, 16
    Welcome Screen, 33
    zooming, 88
Windows-based systems, xxi, 217, 229, 238, 246
wireless pens, 174
Workflow Options, 110
workspace, 21, 24, 40, 182

X

X coordinates, 217

Y

Y coordinates, 217

Z

Zoom tool, 36, 88, 240
zooming
    in Camera Raw, 108
    entering zoom percentages, 240
    Filter Gallery, 69
    keyboard shortcuts for, 74
    palettes, 88
    for sharper web images, 236
    tiled images, 79
    vanishing point, 74
    windows, 88

COLOPHON

The book was produced by the author and design team using all Macintosh computers, including a Power Mac G5 1.8-GHz, a Power Mac G5 Dual Processor 1.8-GHz, a Power Mac G5 Dual Processor 2-GHz, a Power Mac G4 Dual Processor 1.25-MHz. We use LaCie, Sony, and Apple Studio Display monitors.

Page layout was done using Adobe InDesign CS. We use a Mac OS X server, and burn our CDs to our CPU's internal Sony DVD RW DW-U10A.

The headers for each technique are set in Adobe Myriad Pro Semibold at 11 points on 12.5 leading, with the Horizontal Scaling set to 100%. Body copy is set using Adobe Myriad Pro Regular at 9.5 points on 11.5 leading, with the Horizontal Scaling set to 100%.

Screen captures were made with Snapz Pro X and were placed and sized within Adobe InDesign CS. The book was output at 150 line screen, and all in-house printing was done using a Tektronix Phaser 7700 by Xerox.

ADDITIONAL RESOURCES

ScottKelbyBooks.com
For information on Scott's other Macintosh and graphics-related books, visit his book site. For background info on Scott, visit www.scottkelby.com.

http://www.scottkelbybooks.com

Layers Magazine
Layers—The How-To Magazine for Everything Adobe—is the foremost authority on Adobe's design, digital video, digital photography, and education applications. Each issue features timely product news, plus the quick tips, hidden shortcuts, and step-by-step tutorials for working in today's digital market. America's top-selling computer book author for 2004, Scott Kelby is editor-in-chief of *Layers*.

www.layersmagazine.com

National Association of Photoshop Professionals (NAPP)
The industry trade association for Adobe® Photoshop® users and the world's leading resource for Photoshop training, education, and news.

http://www.photoshopuser.com

KW Computer Training Videos
Scott Kelby is featured in a series of Photoshop training DVDs, each on a particular Photoshop topic, available from KW Computer Training. Visit the website or call 813-433-5000 for orders or more information.

http://www.photoshopvideos.com

Photoshop Down & Dirty Tricks
Scott is also author of the best-selling book *Photoshop CS Down & Dirty Tricks*, and the book's companion website has all the info on the book, which is available at bookstores around the country.

http://www.scottkelbybooks.com

Adobe Photoshop Seminar Tour
See Scott live at the Adobe Photoshop Seminar Tour, the nation's most popular Photoshop seminars. For upcoming tour dates and class schedules, visit the tour website.

http://www.photoshopseminars.com

Photoshop World
The convention for Adobe Photoshop users has now become the largest Photoshop-only event in the world. Scott Kelby is technical chair and education director for the event, as well as one of the instructors.

http://www.photoshopworld.com

The Photoshop CS2 Book for Digital Photographers
This book cuts through the bull and shows you step by step the exact techniques used by today's cutting-edge digital photographers, and it shows you which settings to use, when to use them, and why.

http://www.scottkelbybooks.com

Photoshop Hall of Fame
Created to honor and recognize those individuals whose contributions to the art and business of Adobe Photoshop have had a major impact on the application or the Photoshop community itself.

http://www.photoshophalloffame.com

Before NAPP   *After NAPP*

How'd they do that?

You'll learn how and more from the
National Association of Photoshop Professionals (NAPP)

You're invited to join NAPP, the most complete resource for Adobe® Photoshop® training, education, and news.

Member Benefits:

- Annual subscription to *Photoshop User* magazine
- Killer tips, video tutorials, action downloads plus more
- Free online tech support

- Discounts on educational books, training DVDs, and seminars
- Exclusive discounts on hardware, software and everything in between
- Individual online portfolios

NAPP

The National Association of Photoshop Professionals
A one-year membership is only $99
(includes a one-year subscription to *Photoshop User* magazine)

Join today! Call 800-738-8513
www.photoshopuser.com

Corporate, educational and international memberships available.
Adobe and Photoshop are registered trademarks of Adobe Systems, Inc.

NAPP's Official Publication

Join today and get "Best of Photoshop User: The Seventh Year" DVD free ($69.99 value).
(Special new member discount code NAPM-1UM).

iStockphoto™

High-res, royalty-free images for $3 or less

Over 370,000 high-quality images
6,000 new files each week
No subscription fees – ever
Absolutely free to join

istockphoto.com

I love my image.

#575850 "Stroll" Aleksandra Aleksic, Serbia (exclusive to iStock) istockphoto.com/aldra

TWO GREAT NEW PHOTOSHOP PLUG-INS FROM MEDIA LAB

medialab.com

.01 | Build a professional website... *without ever leaving Photoshop!*

Power to the people! Pixel-perfect CSS design has never been easier.
—Fabrice Grover | Freelance designer

SiteGrinder has truly freed my creativity. I was thrilled and impressed!
—Paul Milazzo | Racer's Edge Photography

PRODUCT DESCRIPTION:

SiteGrinder is a Photoshop plug-in that intelligently generates an entire multi-page website from a Photoshop design using simple layer naming. With a click of the mouse, **SiteGrinder** creates styled text, graphics, buttons, hyperlinks, menus, and page navigation.

SiteGrinder instantly turns your Photoshop skills into professional web authoring skills. If you're already a web expert **SiteGrinder** can convert complex interactive designs into working pages amazingly quickly.

FEATURES:
- Instant styled web text from type layers
- Graphical buttons and rollovers
- Text buttons and rollovers
- Multiple text and graphic popups
- Multilevel graphic and text menus
- Automatic page navigation
- Uses modern, professional web standards
- Create links to any web resource
- Integrates well with other tools

SYSTEM REQUIREMENTS:
Photoshop 6 or later for Mac OS X & Windows
Photoshop Elements 3 or later for Mac OS X & Windows

site grinder — Only **$129.00** — Download the free demo from *medialab.com*

.02 | Photoshop to FLASH... *in a flash!*

"There simply is no better way to transfer work from Photoshop to Flash."
— Jayse Hansen | Creative Art Director | cytekstudios.com

PRODUCT DESCRIPTION:

PSD2FLA is a plug-in for Adobe Photoshop that lets you save your layered Photoshop design as a Flash 5 .fla file.

Yes, you read that correctly, **PSD2FLA** saves as an editable Flash .fla file, as opposed to a .swf file. This means you can immediately open your Photoshop design directly in Flash and begin to edit, adding animation, interactivity, etc.

FEATURES:
- Create a multi-layered Flash .fla file from a multi-layered Photoshop File!
- Flash files are fully editable and ready to go.
- Supports Flash 5 and later.
- Layers positioned in Flash exactly as they are in Photoshop.
- Flash layers are produced with their Photoshop names intact.
- Optionally ignore hidden layers.

SYSTEM REQUIREMENTS:
Photoshop 4 or later for Mac OS X & Windows

Only **$89.00** → Download the free demo from *medialab.com*

InDesign CS/CS2 Killer Tips

InDesign® CS/CS2 KillerTips

INDESIGN® CS/CS2 KILLER TIPS

The InDesign® CS
Killer Tips Team

TECHNICAL EDITORS
Chris Main
Polly Reincheld

EDITOR
Richard Theriault

PRODUCTION EDITOR
Kim Gabriel

PRODUCTION
Dave Damstra
Dave Korman

**COVER DESIGN AND
CREATIVE CONCEPTS**
Felix Nelson

SITE DESIGN
Stacy Behan

Update for InDesign® CS2

EDITOR
Ted Waitt

PRODUCTION EDITOR
Connie Jeung-Mills

TECHNICAL REVIEW
Lynn Grillo

IMAGES
Kelly McCathran

COMPOSITOR
Owen Wolfson

PUBLISHED BY
New Riders

Copyright © 2006 by Scott Kelby

FIRST EDITION: September 2005

All rights reserved. No part of this book may be reproduced or transmitted in any form, by any means, electronic or mechanical, including photocopying, recording, or by any information storage and retrieval system, without written permission from the publisher, except for inclusion of brief quotations in a review.

Composed in Myriad, Helvetica Black, and Cronos by NAPP Publishing

Trademarks
All terms mentioned in this book that are known to be trademarks or service marks have been appropriately capitalized. New Riders cannot attest to the accuracy of this information. Use of a term in the book should not be regarded as affecting the validity of any trademark or service mark.

InDesign is a registered trademark of Adobe Systems, Inc.
Windows is a registered trademark of Microsoft Corporation.

Warning and Disclaimer
This book is designed to provide information about InDesign tips. Every effort has been made to make this book as complete and as accurate as possible, but no warranty of fitness is implied.

The information is provided on an as-is basis. The authors and New Riders shall have neither liability nor responsibility to any person or entity with respect to any loss or damages arising from the information contained in this book or from the use of the discs or programs that may accompany it.

ISBN 0-321-33064-1

9 8 7 6 5 4 3 2 1

Printed and bound in the United States of America

www.peachpit.com
www.scottkelbybooks.com

For my wonderful wife Kalebra, for enabling me to marry the girl of my dreams.
—SCOTT KELBY

For all designers out there who push the creative envelope and continue to design great things.
—TERRY WHITE

A NOTE ABOUT THIS BOOK

This book has been updated for InDesign CS2. With the exception of the final chapter, "What's New in InDesign CS2," the majority of the tips in this book are applicable in both CS and CS2.

ACKNOWLEDGMENTS

I learned a while back the real downside of being a co-author: You only get half as much space to thank all of the talented people who make a book like this possible.

First, I want to thank the most amazing woman I've ever known—my wife, Kalebra. You meet very few people in your life who are truly inspiring, truly giving, compassionate to a fault, and literally a joy to be around—and she is every one of those and more. She's my best friend, confidante, a world-class mom, gourmet chef, advice desk, and one heck of a savvy business woman. It's an absolute joy seeing her special gifts reflected in our son Jordan (who has no idea how blessed we both are to have her in our life).

I want to thank my co-author, Terry White, for agreeing to do this book with me. Besides being one of my very best friends, Terry knows more about InDesign than anyone I've ever known, so he was my first, and only, choice as this book's co-author. But Terry's much more than just an InDesign expert: He's a uniquely talented individual whose passion and dedication touch everything he does, and everyone he meets; and I'm truly honored to be able to work with him.

I want to thank my home team at KW Media Group, who constantly redefine what "kickin' butt" really means. In particular, I want to thank my Creative Director Felix Nelson; my Editor Richard Theriault; my Tech Editors Chris Main and Polly Reincheld; and Production Editor Kim Gabriel. Also thanks to Barbara Thompson, Dave Korman, Daphne Durkee, and Dave "The Michigan Layout Machine" Damstra. I'd put them up against any production team in the business—they're that good.

I also want to thank wonderful, crazy, loving Dad Jerry for being so "him," and thanks to my brother Jeff for having so much "him" in him. Thanks to my friends and business partners, Jim Workman and Jean A. Kendra, and thanks to coach Joe Gibbs for coming back to the Redskins, which is better than anything I could say or do for my absolutely wonderful Executive Assistant Kathy Siler.

Thanks to Nancy Ruenzel, Scott Cowlin, Kim Lombardi, Gary Paul Prince, and everyone at Peachpit for their commitment to excellence, and for the honor of letting me be one of their "Voices That Matter."

And most importantly, an extra special thanks to God and his son Jesus Christ for always hearing my prayers, for always being there when I need Him, and for blessing me with a life I truly love, and a warm loving family to share it with.

—SCOTT KELBY

Co-authoring this book would not have been possible if not for the continued inspiration and support of my friends, family, and colleagues. While there aren't enough pages to thank and acknowledge everyone, I would like to acknowledge my wife Carla, who has constantly supported my efforts; my two daughters Ayoola and Sala, both visions of beauty and motivation; my sister Pam, who is always there for me to bounce ideas and problems off of; and of course, my mom and dad.

I would like to thank all my friends, team members, managers, and colleagues at Adobe, including Sue Scheen, Lynn Grillo, Adam Pratt, Mike Richman, Colin Smith, Steve Whatley, Noha Edell, Ashwini Jambotkar, Gary Cosimini, Lisa Forrester, Tim Cole, Julieanne Kost, Rye Livingston, Diane Olson, Peggy Snyder, Russell Preston Brown, Dave Helmly, Jim Ringham, Rick Borstein, Donna Zontos, Lisa Avalos, the entire Americas Sales Team, and the InDesign Product Team.

I would also like to thank all my friends in the Mac community for their continued support and help over the years, especially Steve Wozniak, Sandy Kaye, Calvin Carson, Mia Sasser, Mike Arlow, Mary and Joseph Grey, Carmela Z. Robertson, Shirley Kussner, Chita Hunter, Lori Autrey, Lesa Snider, Phyllis Evans, David Syme, Leonard Mazerov, Kwesi Ohene Aquil, and Piankhi Blount.

Last but certainly not least, I would like to especially thank Scott Kelby and the folks at KW Media Group for the opportunity to collaborate on this project. I would also like to thank all InDesign users worldwide.

—TERRY WHITE

ABOUT THE AUTHORS

Scott Kelby

Scott is Editor-in-Chief and co-founder of *Photoshop User* magazine, Editor-in-Chief of Nikon's *Capture User* magazine, and Editor-in-Chief of *Layers* magazine. He is President of the National Association of Photoshop Professionals (NAPP), the trade association for Adobe® Photoshop® users, and he's President of KW Media Group, Inc., a Florida-based software education and publishing firm.

Scott is author of the best-selling books *Photoshop CS Down & Dirty Tricks, The Photoshop CS2 Book for Digital Photographers,* and *Photoshop CS2 Killer Tips* and he's creator and Series Editor for the Killer Tips series of books from New Riders.

Scott is Training Director for the Adobe Photoshop Seminar Tour, Conference Technical Chair for the PhotoshopWorld Conference & Expo, and he is a speaker at graphics trade shows and events around the world. He is also featured in a series of Adobe Photoshop training DVDs and has been training creative professionals since 1993.

For more background info on Scott, visit www.scottkelby.com.

Terry White

Terry White, Technical Resources Manager–Adobe Systems Inc., is a technologist at heart. He loves computers and all things tech. Terry has been with Adobe for seven years, and has extensive knowledge of Adobe's Creative Professional product line. In his current position as Technical Resources Manager for North America, he leads a team of Applications Engineers who focus on professional publishing, Web authoring, and digital video. Terry has been active in the industry for over 18 years and is the founder and president of MacGroup-Detroit—Michigan's largest Macintosh Users group—and a columnist for *Layers* magazine.

TABLE OF CONTENTS

CHAPTER 1 — 1
Who's Zoomin' Who
Navigating and Other Essentials

Undo a Zoom? You Can with This Hidden Shortcut	2
Set Your Own Defaults	2
The "Jump to Any Page" Shortcut	3
Get to the First Page Fast!	3
Open or Close All Your Side Tab Palettes with One Click	4
Speed Tip: Highlighting Fields	4
New Docs without the New Document Dialog	5
Reset the New Document Dialog	5
Save Time when Creating New Documents	6
See Your Whole Spread Onscreen	6
Fit Spread in Window Even Faster!	7
Not Just the Page or Spread—See the Whole Pasteboard	7
Speed Zooming	8
The Speedway to a 100% View	9
Jump to a 200% Enlargement of Where You're Working	9
The Secret Zoom Field Shortcut	10
Better Navigation While Zoomed In	10
Switch to the Zoom Tool Temporarily	11
Choose When Your Baseline Grid is Visible	11
Those Pesky Ruler Guides	12
Your Toolbox, Your Way	12
Float the Control Palette	13
Shrink the Control Palette	13
Manage Palette Clutter	14
Fit More in Your Layers Palette	15
Make an Über-Palette	15
Set Your Workspace Once, and It's Yours Forever!	16
Hide All Palettes and Toolbox with One Click	16
One Click Hides Palettes, But Leaves Toolbox Visible	17
Hide Just Palettes	17
Side-Tab a Group of Palettes	18
How to Preview Your Document	18
Save Every Open Document with One Keystroke	19
A Bigger View in the Navigator Palette	19
I Want to See It All	20
The Five Most Important One-Key Tool Shortcuts	20
No Keyboard Shortcut? Make One!	21
Coming Over from QuarkXPress? Use Quark Shortcuts	21
Print Your Custom Keyboard Shortcuts	22
Bring Back Those Hidden Warning Dialogs	22

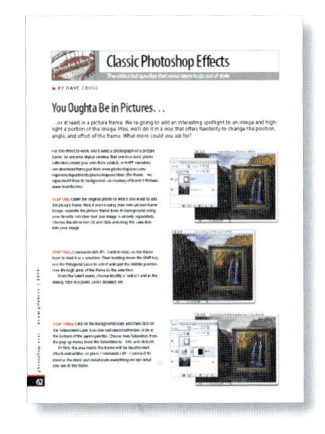

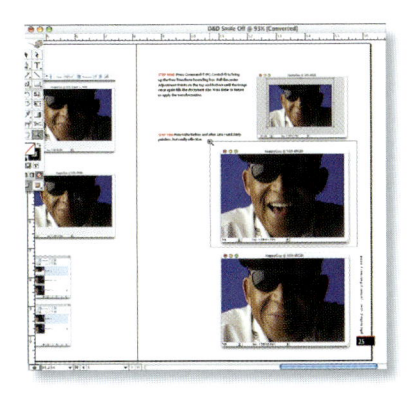

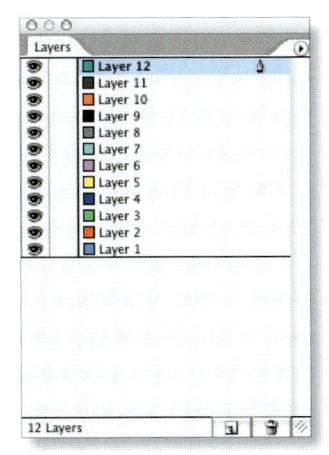

ix

TABLE OF CONTENTS

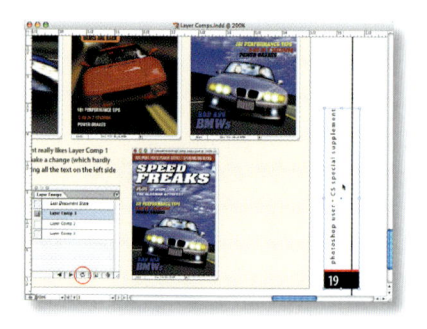

CHAPTER 2	**25**
Stereo Type	
Tweakin' Your Text	
The Type Tool Super Shortcut	26
The Hidden Options for Type on a Path	26
Set Your Type Defaults	27
Set Default Character and Paragraph Styles	27
Fast Font Size Changes from the Keyboard	28
Jumping Up 2 Points at a Time Not Enough for You?	28
Waiting on the Real Text? Fake It	29
Tip for Magazine and Newspaper Editors	29
Make Your Own Custom Placeholder Text	30
Control Palette Stunts (Swapping Type and Paragraph Fields)	30
Type Preferences Shortcut	31
The Secret to Kerning Visually	31
Why are Parentheses in My Kerning Field?	32
Tighten the Space Between Words Visually	32
Adjust Leading Visually	33
Adjust Horizontal Scaling Visually	33
The Speed Lane to 100% Horizontal Scaling	34
Don't Know the Right Point Size? Just Drag Your Text	34
Changing Multiple Text Blocks at Once	35
Apply Character Formatting to Multiple Text Blocks	35
Shortcut to the New Character Style Dialog	36
Shift Baseline without the Character Palette	36
Get Rid of Those Nasty Double-Spaces	37
Get Rid of Weird Characters	37
Faster Fixes for Bad Characters	38
Make That Sentence All Caps the Fast Way	38
Highlight Character Palette Fields Fast	39
Quick Type Tweaking in the Character Palette	39
Find the Right Font Fast—Scroll Through Them	40
Jump to the Right Font	40
Change Fonts Automatically, without Style Sheets	41
Paste Text into InDesign	41
Paste Text while Retaining Your Type Formatting	42
Drag-and-Drop Text into InDesign	42
Get Control Over Your Imported Text	43
How to Deselect Everything	43
One Column to Multi-Columns the Fast Way	44
Need a ™? How About a ©?	44
How to Use Glyphs	45
Glyph Characters Too Small? Head for the Mountains	45
Five Key Shortcuts for Selecting Text	46
Edit While You Check Spelling	46
Save Time When Checking Spelling	47

TABLE OF CONTENTS

Voilà! The Trick to Spell-Checking Foreign Languages	47
How to Stop a Word from Being Hyphenated	48
It's Okay to Use the Bold Shortcut	48
When Fonts Collide (How to Add Ligatures)	49
Set Type Justification the Fast Way	49
Indent Paragraphs (How and How Much)	50
Doing a Pull Quote? Better Hang Those Quote Marks, Bunky	50
Add Drop Shadows to Text	51
Make Your Text Frame Fit the Text	52
How to Move Objects While Your Text is Selected	53
Get Live Text Wrap Previews While You Move	53
Apply Gradients to Editable Type	54
Faster Text Frame Moving	54
Get the Grabber When You've Got the Type Tool	55
Choose Custom Fonts and Sizes in Story Editor	55
Access Master Page Text Frames on a Regular Page	56
Use the Right Dash	56
Not Just a Space. A "Special" Space	57

CHAPTER 3
Color Blind
Working with Color

Drag from Palette to Palette	60
Create Your Gradients with Drag-and-Drop	60
Create a Default Set of Colors	61
Steal Colors from Another Document	61
Not Just for Text Style Sheets—But Color Style Sheets Too	62
Eyedropper Trick #2	62
Save Time by Dragging and Dropping Color	63
Delete Multiple Swatches	63
If You Didn't Use It, Lose It	64
Merge Swatches	64
Change the Order of Your Swatches	65
Save Tints as Swatches	65
Avoid Tint Weirdness	66
Tint Weirdness #2	66
Name Color Swatches After Their Values	67
How to Name Swatches (And Why You Should)	67
Load the Pantone Colors	68
Import Just a Few, Or All, of the Pantone Colors	68
Speed Through the Swatches Palette	69
The Smart Way to Edit Swatches	69
Speed Through the Color Ramp	70
Get Solid Black, Or Solid White, in One Click	70
Get Your Colors in Gamut with One Click	71

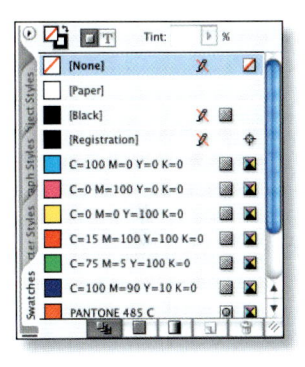

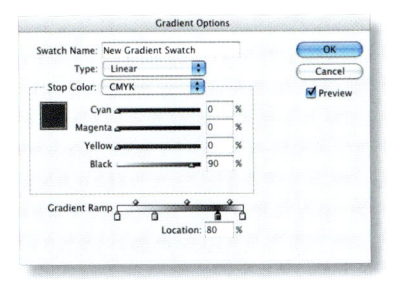

TABLE OF CONTENTS

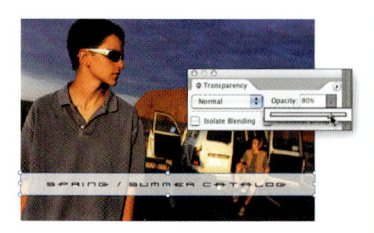

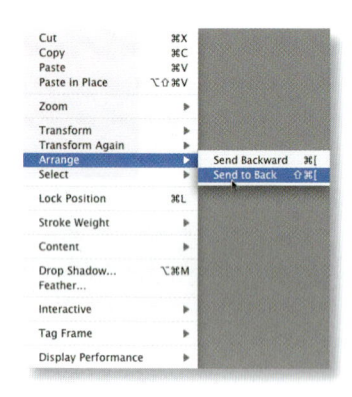

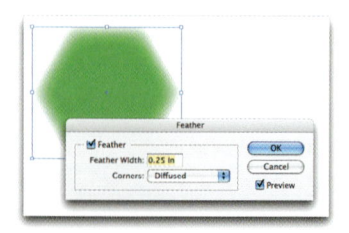

Create Perfect Shades	71
Get the Color Palette into Tint Mode	72
Help with Creating Colors	72
One Click to No Fill or Stroke	73
Swap the Fill and Stroke	73
Return to the Default Black Stroke, No Fill	74
Drag-and-Drop Colors from the Toolbox	74
Get Live Gradient Previews	75
Reapply the Last-Used Gradient	75
Color Management when Importing Photos	76
Gradient Palette Shortcut	76
Make Sure All the Colors in Your Book Match	77
Blue and Yellow Make Green	78
Stop Playing Hit-or-Miss	78

CHAPTER 4 — 81
Drawing Fire
Drawing with InDesign

Edit One Object in a Group	82
Turn Your Font into a Graphic	82
Smooth Out Those Jaggy Paths	83
Add Soft Edges to Objects	83
Backscreening Effects	84
How Many Sides with That Polygon?	84
Adjust Polygon Sides and Points on the Fly	85
Experiment with Size	85
The Subtle Art of Frame Scaling	86
Don't Copy and Paste It—Dupe It	86
Select an Object Behind Another Object	87
Select an Object Behind Another (Version 2)	87
Send Objects Forward or Backward	88
Keep on Sending Objects Forward and Backward	88
Set Your Default Fill and Stroke Colors	89
Auto Add/Delete Path Points	89
Move Just One Side of Your Curve	90
How to Stop One Path and Start Another	90
How to Remove One Direction Point from a Curve	91
Cutting the Cheese (Or Making a Perfect Half Circle)	91
Point It Out	92

CHAPTER 5 — 95
Turn the Page
Working with Pages

Drag Pages from One Doc to Another	96
When One Master Page Just Doesn't Cut It	96

TABLE OF CONTENTS

www.scottkelbybooks.com

Be Flexible with the Size of Your Layout	97
Spread Beyond Two Pages	97
Make It a Template	98
Underestimating the Page Count	98
Add Pages the Fast Way	99
Larger Page Icons	99
Have It Your Way	100
Make Your Guide Stretch Across Spreads	100
Get Rid of Unwanted Guides Fast	101
Delete All Your Guides at Once	101
Add a Guide Exactly Where You Want It	102
Get Both a Horizontal and Vertical Guide	102
Copy Those Guides	103
Shortcut for Locking Guides	103
Toggle Guides On/Off	104
Create Your Own Custom Guides Layout	104
Assign Guides to a Layer	105
Get Organized with Layers	105
Select Everything on One Layer	106
Stack It Up in the Right Order	106
Delete Any Layers You're Not Using	107
See the Real Page Numbers	107
Create New Sections (with Their Own Page Numbers)	108
One Is the Loneliest Number	108
Jump to the Page You Need	109
Make All Master Page Items Editable	109
Make Just One Master Page Item Editable	110
Assign Master Page Attributes to a Page	110
You Will Be Assimilated	111
From Text Frame to Graphics Frame Fast	111
Make a TOC Style	112
TOC: More Options	112
Style vs. Entry Style	113
Give Me Dots	113
Link Docs Together In a Book	114
Create a PDF from Your Book	114
Synchronize a Book	115
Book Pagination	115
Create Index Entries	116
Index Cross-Referencing	116
Hey, There's No PDF Button on the Book Palette	117
Add Documents to a Book from the Desktop	117
I Want Just One Document	118
Take It to the Web	118

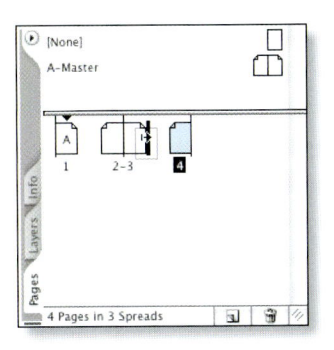

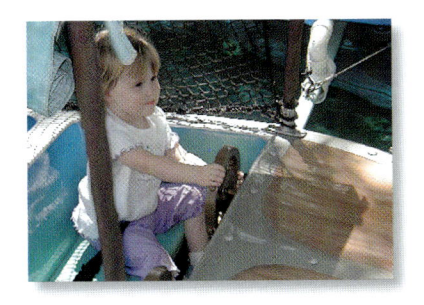

TABLE OF CONTENTS

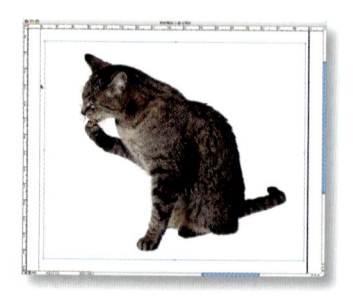

CHAPTER 6	**121**
Contains Graphic Images	
Working with Graphics	
Create a Vignette without Leaving InDesign	122
Don't Be a Square	122
Try Out Blending Modes	123
Use the Paste Into Command	123
Government-Mandated Drop Shadows	124
Create Fake Glows	124
Drag-and-Drop from the OS	125
Show Import Options for More Control	125
Place PDF Files Too	126
Text Wrap: Take It Or Leave It	126
Wrap It, Wrap It Good	127
Who's the Master Now?	127
From One Vector Lover to Another	128
I Don't Want to Draw No Stinkin' Boxes	128
I Have to Draw Boxes First. It's My Life	129
Make the Graphic Fit	129
Size Does Matter	130
The Resize-Multiple-Objects Trick	130
Move the Graphic without Moving the Frame	131
Three-in-One	131
Look at Me When I'm Talking to You	132
Don't Use the Force to Align Objects	132
Give Your Objects a Restraining Order	133
Copy and Paste Is So 1980s	133
Step and Repeat Instead of Copy and Paste	134
Don't Move It to the Same Place—Copy It	134
Paste Remembers Layers	135
Where's the Library Palette?	135
Add Objects to the Library	136
Drag from the Library onto the Page	136
Double-click Library Items to Name Them	137
Save Time Searching in Your Library	137
Add Keywords to Items Already in the Library	138
Search the Library	138
Narrow Your Library Search	139
How to Recover from a Library Search	139
Thumbnails in the Library are Cool, But...	140
Don't Print This!	140
Go Stand in the Corner and Think About What You've Done	141
Relink to a New Graphic	141
Replace Graphics	142
Make a Picture	142
Who Took That Placed Digital Photo? InDesign Knows	143

xiv

TABLE OF CONTENTS

www.scottkelbybooks.com

Fade That Image Back	143
Stacking Order is Everything	144
Identify Pages with Transparent Objects	144
Transparency Flattener Styles	145
Use Transparency from Photoshop	146
Use Photoshop Alpha Channels	146
Generate Clipping Paths Automatically	147
Use the Transparency Flattener Preview	148
Override Flattener Settings Spread by Spread	149

CHAPTER 7	151
Cool Hand Luke	
Way-Cool Tips	
The Trick to Shrinking Your InDesign File Size	152
Copy Drop Shadows with the Eyedropper	152
Use Multiple Views of the Same Document	153
Want to Speed Up InDesign? Turn Off Plug-ins	153
Image-by-Image High-Quality Display	154
Set Your Own Display Performance	154
Create Bleeds and Slugs without Oversized Pages	155
View Bleeds and Slugs Using Preview	155
Use Pathfinder to Join Shapes	156
Enter Measurements in Your Unit of Choice	156
Use the Story Editor to Edit Blocks of Text	157
Open QuarkXPress Documents in InDesign	158
Open PageMaker Documents in InDesign	158
Use the Info Palette to Get Image Details	159
Use the Measure Tool Instead of Rulers	159
Unembed Embedded Graphics to Make Your Printer Happy	160
You're the One (Layer)	160
Drag to Make Visible or Lock Layers	161

CHAPTER 8	163
Hidden Treasure	
Little-Known Features	
View Menus in Alphabetical Order	164
Want to Use Inches? Type (˝)	164
Reshape Frames with the Pencil Tool	165
Create Gradients the Easy Way	165
Get Rounded Rectangles with Corner Effects	166
Reset Your Zero Point	166
Change Attributes Using Percentages	167
Getting PageMaker Features in InDesign	167
See Your Pages Before You Open Them	168
The Deleting Stunt	168
Drag-and-Drop from iPhoto	169

xv

TABLE OF CONTENTS

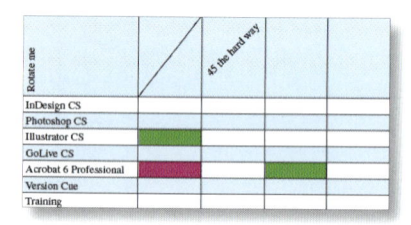

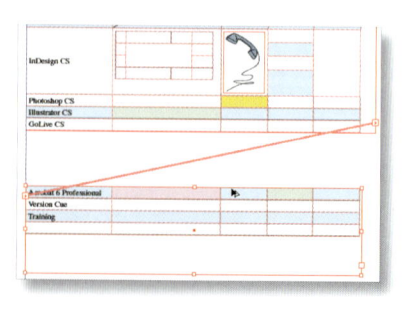

Drag-and-Drop from Adobe Bridge	169
Create a Specific-Sized Frame in One Click	170
Create a Duotone Effect Right within InDesign	170
Add Hyperlinks or Bookmarks to Any Object	171
Let the Good Times Scroll	171
Scale Selected Objects without Grouping	172
Stroke Your Styles, Baby	173
Four-Color Process On a Spot Color Budget	174
Could You Please Change That Spot Color?	175
Back to the Future	175
Something Wrong in Neverland? Delete the Preferences	176
Kick the Keyboard Habit	176
Get to the Units/Increments Preferences Fast	177
Speed Lane to the Move Dialog	177
Speedy Scaler	178

CHAPTER 9 — 181
Portable People
Making PDFs

Place a Movie in Your Document	182
Pick a Different Poster Frame	182
Import a Sound When You Don't Have Video	183
Flash in the Pants	183
Embed Multimedia Files	184
Make Interactive Buttons	185
When a Static Button is Not Enough	186
Define a PDF Export Style	188
Use a PDF Export Style	188
Add a Hotlink to Your Website	189
Create a Dynamic Link to Another Page	189
Recognize Hyperlinks from Word Automatically	190
Get Rid of the Black Boxes Around Your Links	190
Use Layers to Give Your Client a Choice of Content	191
Create Bookmarks to Walk Them Through Your Document	191
Create Bookmark Groups	192
Trust No One—Password Protect It	192
Don't Give Away the Farm—Disallow Printing	193
Disallow Editing	194
Compatibility with Older Versions of Acrobat	194
Use Spreads	195
What's All the Buzz About PDF/X?	195
Make It Small but Keep It Lookin' Good	196
Create PDFs with Transparency	196
Place InDesign Pages into Other InDesign Documents Via PDF	197

TABLE OF CONTENTS

CHAPTER 10 — 199
Waiting Tables
Working with Tables

Place Graphics in a Table	200
Go Plaid, Baby	200
Fill Individual Cells with Color	201
Rotate Text in Tables	201
Select Rows and Columns	202
Select the Entire Table	202
Resize Rows and Columns	203
Running Headers and Footers	203
Place Word and Excel Tables	204
Convert Text to Table	204
Nested Tables	205
Make Big Ones Out of Little Ones	205
Time to Split Cells	206
Remove the Table Stroke	206
Insert a Row at the End with a Tab	207
Insert Rows and Columns	207
Bring Order to Table Chaos!	208
Line Up and Fly Right	208
Create Diagonal Lines	209
Angled Text? Make It So	209
It Just Won't Fit	210

CHAPTER 11 — 213
Blue Prints
Printing and the Creative Suite

Print to Different Printers with Ease	214
Avoid Separation Surprises on Press	215
How Many Plates Do You Really Have?	215
Use the Ink Manager to Eliminate Rogue Plates	216
Preflight for the Most Common Problems	216
Preflight: Show Problems Only	217
Package It Up	217
Non-Printing Objects—Print Them Anyway	218
Cycle Through Your Print Settings	218
Switch Printers On the Fly	219
Speed Up Printing	219
Print Panel Navigation Shortcut	220
Change Your Line Screen When Going Monochrome	220
Print Separations Like a Pro	221
Print the Slug	221
Access Printer-Specific Features	222
Download PPD Fonts Anyway!	222
Scale Pages to Fit Your Media Size	223
When Your Service Provider Won't Take an InDesign File	223

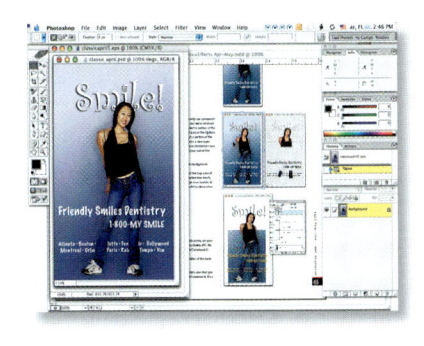

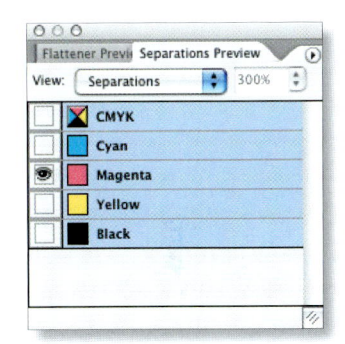

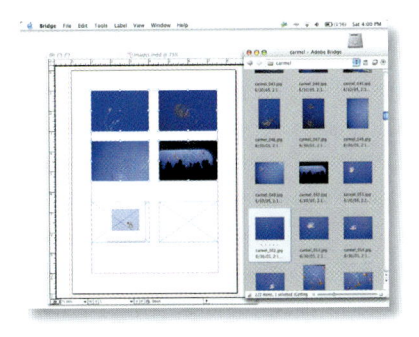

TABLE OF CONTENTS

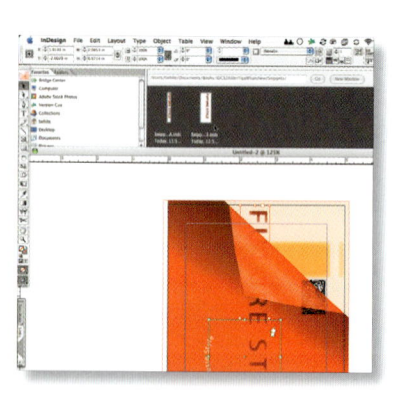

Pull the Plug on Auto-Updating	224
Place Native Photoshop Files	224
Place Native Illustrator Files	225
Share Color Settings with Photoshop and Illustrator	226
Edit Your Graphics and Have Them Auto-Update	227
Going from Print to the Web?	228

CHAPTER 12
New Attitude

What's New in InDesign CS2	231
Drag-and-Drop from the Bridge	232
Open the Bridge from InDesign	233
Place a Stock Photo Comp Image	233
Purchase a Stock Photo Image from InDesign	234
Snippets	235
WYSIWYG Font Menus	236
Drag-and-Drop Text	236
Dynamic Spelling	237
Autocorrect	237
Multiple User Dictionaries	238
Import Text Files to the Dictionary	238
Footnotes	239
Paste without Formatting	239
Overset Text in the Story Editor	240
Frame-Based Baseline Grids	240
Photoshop Layer Controls	241
Object Styles	242
Selectively Load Styles	243
Quick Apply	243
Apply Next Style	244
Reset to Base Style	244
Clear Overrides	245
Align Away/Towards Spine	245
Word Import	246
Fill Frame Proportionally	247
Anchored Objects	248
Transform Again	248
Shape Conversions	249
Drop Shadow Noise & Spread Options	249
Import Multi-Page PDFs	250
Save Back to InDesign CS	251
Move Pages Dialog Box	252
Lock Column Guides	252
Data Merge	253
Create Printer Spreads	254
Multi-Page Export to JPEG	254

Index 255

IF YOU'RE THINKING THIS IS THE INTRODUCTION, YOU'RE WAY OFF BASE

That's because this book has no introduction.
We're not saying "it needs no introduction." This book desperately needs an introduction. It's crying out for an introduction—begging for one (if you will), but we sat down and intentionally decided not to write one. Why? Because we have mental problems. Deep-rooted psychological problems that will probably one day become the syllabus for college-level study. Why? Why would two men of otherwise unremarkable lives decide to go against time-honored traditions, which all book publishers hold sacred, and not write an introduction? Well, we'll tell you—it's because nobody reads introductions. Nobody. Not you. Not us. Nobody. See, you're not reading one now.

So why do authors even write introductions?
Their publishers force them to. It's true. They're forced to write an introduction, even though the publishing company knows full well that no one will read it, not even editors from the publishing company itself. Here's an example: "We were going to right an entroduction; but know one kares enuff to chech it." See—an editor would never let that slip by, but they don't even run introductions by part-time interns. Yet there it is—in print—in a book from a major computer book publishing company (at least they were until this book hit the shelves). Are we concerned? Nah. They'll never learn that a severely messed-up sentence wound up in the published version of the book, because that would require having a least one person read it; and you know darn well that person doesn't exist.

Why do books need an introduction, anyway?
We have no idea. Okay, it's probably so the authors can tell the reader how to use the book (we assume it's stuff like "Once you reach the bottom of a right-facing page, turn the page to continue," but since we don't read introductions, that's purely a guess). On the other hand, if we *were* to write an introduction (and don't worry, we're not) we'd probably tell you what makes this book different from other books.

What makes this book different from other books?
Well, it has a road sign on the cover, and most books don't. Besides that, the one thing that makes this book different is that the whole book, cover-to-cover, is just tips. Tips to make you more efficient, faster, and have more fun while you're using InDesign. There are no detailed descriptions of how to check out managed documents over a workgroup server, or how to adjust the Hyphenation Zone (we know you're disappointed, because those two sound like a lot of fun)—instead, we cut through the bull and give you nothing but the inside shortcuts, cool workarounds, and proven tricks that help you get twice the work done in half the time. The stuff that makes you faster, better, and worth more to your clients and your company.

Do we really need to work faster?
Yes. Next question.

> **TIP**
>
> *This is a sidebar tip. Every great computer book has a few of them. But this book is nothing **but** them. A whole book of cool sidebar tips, without the sidebars.*

Come on. Is working faster that important?
It's *that* important. Nobody wants to do things "the hard way." The slow way. The frustrating way. Your time is important, and if you're working more efficiently in InDesign, you'll have time for other important things like trying different layouts, exploring creative possibilities, and maybe even a dinner break. That's what this book is all about. Other books sprinkle a few sidebar tips throughout their pages, but this book is nothing but those sidebar tips.

What's a sidebar?
It's one of those gray boxes on the left and right of this spread, with the word "TIP" at the top. That's how most books handle tips—in a box, in the sidebar of the book. As cool as those sidebar tips are, there are two problems: (1) There are never enough of them, and (2) those tips are usually in just a tiny little box with a couple of lines of text (like the sidebar shown at right). So in this book, we include literally hundreds of tips, and we thought we'd expand the explanations enough to make them more accessible, and then add a screen capture if (a) it helps make the tip easier to understand, or (b) if the page just looks really boring without one.

So what exactly is a "Killer Tip"?
"Use the Type tool to create type." Technically, that is a tip. It's a lame tip. It's a boringly obvious tip, and it's definitely not a Killer Tip. To be a "Killer Tip" it's supposed to make you nod and smile when you read it. A Killer Tip is one that you can't wait to show off to your page-layout buddies, because you'll look like the big pro and they'll look like the big schmo. (Schmo is one of those words that doesn't make it into enough computer books. Why? Because editors remove words like "schmo" from all non-introduction areas. It's what they do for fun.)

Is this book for you?
If you've come this far, knowing all the while that you were indeed reading what some might call "The book's introduction" (not Terry and I mind you, some other people—bad people), then this book is absolutely for you. However, if you had no idea—you were completely unaware, either consciously or subconsciously, that you were in fact reading the book's introduction—then we're afraid you may be somewhat gullible and therefore in danger of being taken advantage of and we want to protect you from that by having you buy this book, and paying the bookstore twice the published price (hey, it's worth a shot).

Okay, how do I get started?
This book isn't set up like a novel—you can jump in anywhere, start on any page and immediately try the tips that interest you most. Also, don't forget to read each chapter's intro page—it's critical to your understanding of what's in that particular chapter (that's totally not true, but it took a long time to write those intros, so we use little lies like this to get you to read them. Sad, isn't it?).

Wait! One last thing!
Actually, there's nothing else. Gotcha! Okay, now turn the page and get to "tippin'!"

TIP

You're doing it again! Stop looking at these sidebars. See, they're intoxicating—you're drawn to them even after you know it's not really a tip. Okay, here's a real tip: If you like sidebar tips, buy this book.

Who's Zoomin' Who

NAVIGATING AND OTHER ESSENTIALS

Since we (and by "we" I mean "me") spend so much of our lives (which is to say "mine") navigating through documents, it would save us loads of time each day if we

Who's Zoomin' Who
navigating and other essentials

were to get incredibly efficient at navigating. Now, what would we do with all that extra time? Would we go home early? Spend more time with our family? Nope. We'd do what designers love doing best—zooming. When no one's around, we zoom in and out of our documents repeatedly. We zoom in to a 400% view, then back out to 50%; in to a 1200% view, and back out to 12.5%. Why? Nobody knows. Scientists have studied this for years, and still—nothin'. I think it's a power thing. Maybe that's why there are about a gazillion ways to zoom, magnify, nudge, and otherwise move through our InDesign pages. We (and by "we" I mean "you") secretly love the power of knowing that at any given time, for no apparent reason, we can zoom in to a 4000% enlargement of one character of text. It's weird. It's annoying. But we love it (by "we" I mean "you," and by "it" I mean "it").

UNDO A ZOOM? YOU CAN WITH THIS HIDDEN SHORTCUT

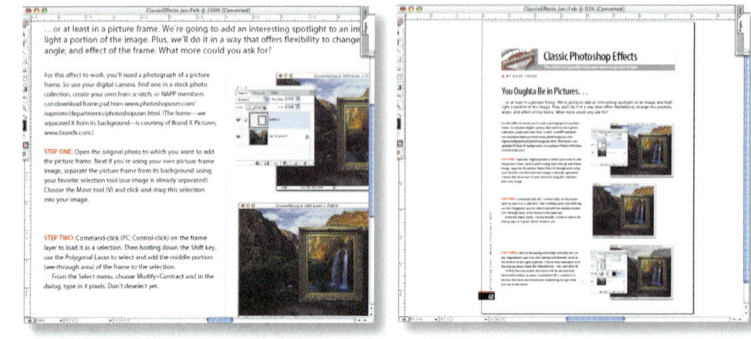

Here's one of those hidden shortcuts that are incredibly handy, but we've met so few people who know them that hardly anyone uses them (of course, you'll start using this one now, and that's a good thing). Once you've zoomed in on something, you know there's no "undo" for zooming. Or is there? You can toggle between your current view and your zoomed-in view by pressing Option-Command-2 (PC: Alt-Control-2). This is another one of those tips that you'll try once, and then use it again and again.

SET YOUR OWN DEFAULTS

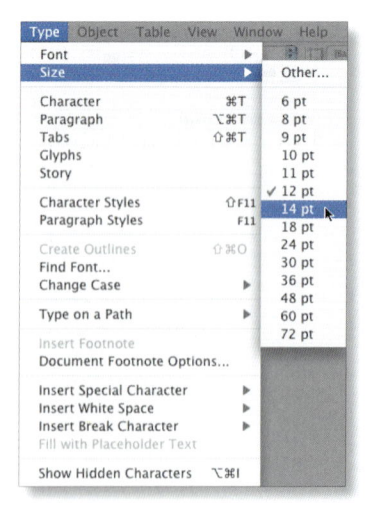

Want your default font to be different? Want the default stroke to be .5 instead of 1 point? Want the default Text Wrap to be Wrap Around Bounding Box? It's easy to set the overall defaults—you just have to know this one thing—set them all while there is no document open. That's right, close all your open documents, make all your changes, then these new changes become your defaults. Freaky, I know.

CHAPTER 1 • Navigating and Other Essentials

THE "JUMP TO ANY PAGE" SHORTCUT

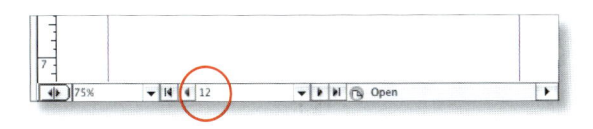

If you're working on a multipage document and you know which page you want to jump to, we've got a very fast way to get there. Just press Command-J (PC: Control-J) and the Page Number field highlights. Enter the page number, then press Enter and BAM—you're there. If you're trying to get to a master page (and you know the name of the master page you want), use the same shortcut but instead of entering a number, just type in the first few letters of the master page and it will jump to that page.

GET TO THE FIRST PAGE FAST!

Want to jump directly to the first page in your document? We're not talking about the page you have auto-numbered as page 1, because if you're working on a book or a magazine, that could well be page 354. Nope, we're talking about jumping to the actual first page in your document. To jump right there, press Command-J (PC: Control-J) to highlight the Page Number field, then type "+1" and press Enter to jump to the very first page.

CHAPTER 1 • Navigating and Other Essentials

OPEN OR CLOSE ALL YOUR SIDE TAB PALETTES WITH ONE CLICK

Want to open (or close) all of the side tab palettes at once, with just one click? Just hold the Option key (PC: Alt key), then click on any open side palette's tab and they'll all open (or close) at once. Pretty darn handy.

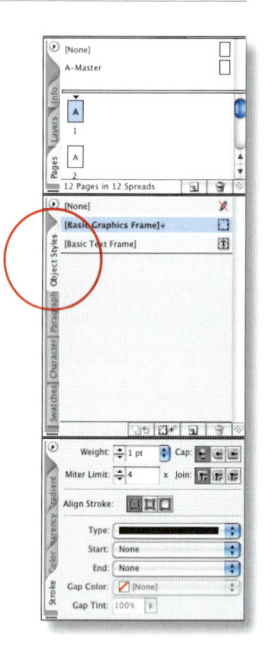

SPEED TIP: HIGHLIGHTING FIELDS

Want to highlight a field fast? Just click once on the icon for that field and it will automatically highlight the value that's currently there. This saves a bunch of time because once you click, you can immediately type in a new value to replace the old one. Plus, not only is this a faster way to select a field, it's easier than trying to get your cursor in those tiny fields, and then highlight the numbers. Try this once—you'll use it again and again.

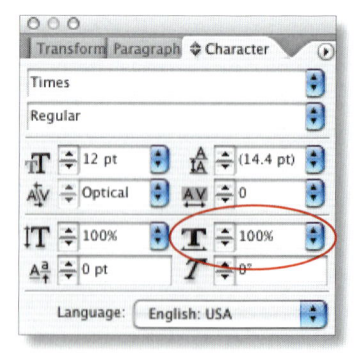

4   CHAPTER 1 • Navigating and Other Essentials

NEW DOCS WITHOUT THE NEW DOCUMENT DIALOG

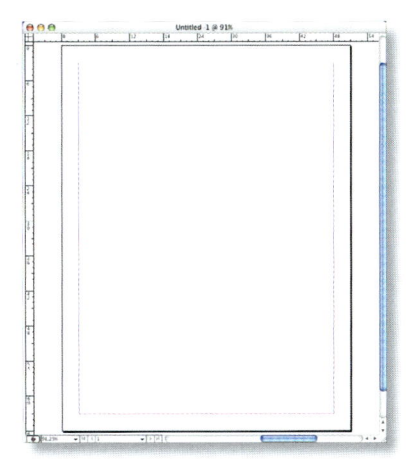

Want another new document that's the same size and specs as the last document you created? Just press Option-Command-N (PC: Alt-Control-N) and the new doc will instantly appear, based on the settings you last used—no New Document dialog, no muss, no fuss.

RESET THE NEW DOCUMENT DIALOG

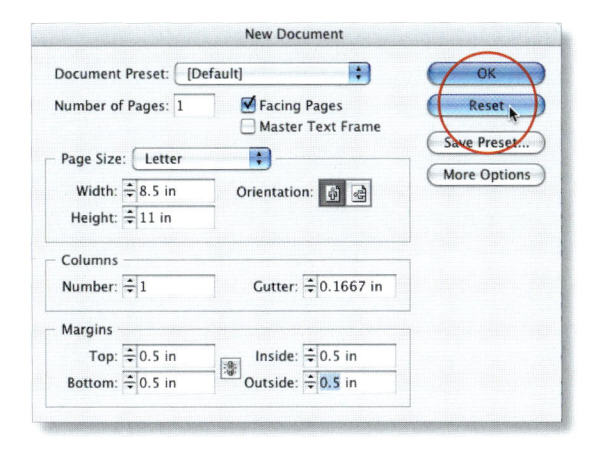

If you're entering values in the New Document dialog, and you change your mind or make a mistake, you don't have to hit the Cancel button and start all over. Instead, just hold the Option key (PC: Alt key) and you'll see the Cancel button change into the Reset button. Click it, and it will return all the settings to what they were when you opened it.

CHAPTER 1 • Navigating and Other Essentials

SAVE TIME WHEN CREATING NEW DOCUMENTS

If you find yourself creating new documents in a non-standard size (for example, rather than letter-size documents, perhaps you create 6x4˝ postcards fairly often), you can create and save your own custom preset size and have it appear in the Document Preset pop-up menu in the New Document dialog. Here's how: Go under the File menu, under New, and choose Document. In the New Document dialog, enter your own custom width, height, margins, etc., and then click the Save Preset button (as shown) and a dialog will appear where you can name your new document preset. When you click OK, this new preset will appear in the Document Preset pop-up menu.

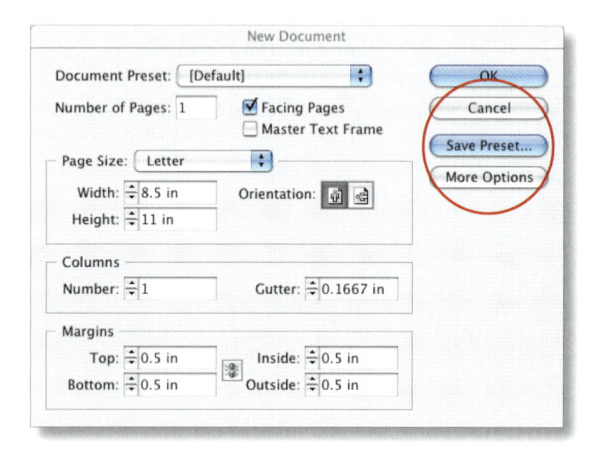

SEE YOUR WHOLE SPREAD ONSCREEN

If you're working on a spread and press the shortcut for Fit Page in Window (Command-Zero [PC: Control-Zero]) it will fit the entire height of your page in the window, but you'll probably have to scroll to the right or left to see your entire spread. That is, unless you press Option-Command-Zero (PC: Alt-Control-Zero) instead, which gives you Fit Spread in Window rather than just Fit Page in Window.

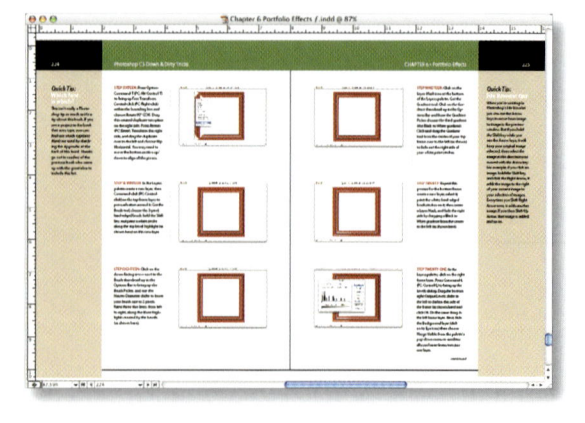

CHAPTER 1 • Navigating and Other Essentials

FIT SPREAD IN WINDOW EVEN FASTER!

If you want an even faster way to see your full page or spread as large as possible on your monitor (see previous tip), save yourself a trip all the way up to the View menu in the menu bar or using the Command-Option-Zero (PC: Control-Alt-Zero) shortcut, and instead just double-click directly on the Hand tool in the Toolbox and it'll jump right to the Fit Spread in Window view.

NOT JUST THE PAGE OR SPREAD—SEE THE WHOLE PASTEBOARD

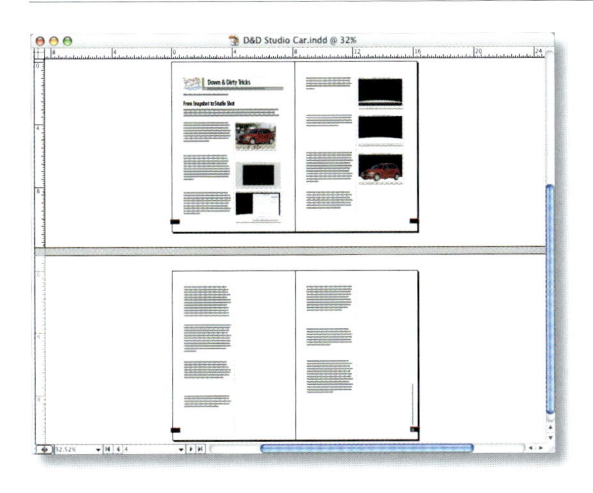

If you're anything like us (and we feel you are), you use the pasteboard area outside your page to store things you think you might need later (like extra blocks of text, photos, logos, etc.). But if you're like us, then you probably lose track of which page you were on when you placed those things just beyond your page borders. If that's the case, just press Shift-Option-Command-Zero (PC: Shift-Alt-Control-Zero) to see the entire pasteboard fitted to your screen.

CHAPTER 1 • Navigating and Other Essentials   7

SPEED ZOOMING

Our favorite way to zoom in to and out of our document doesn't use the Zoom tool at all. Instead, we feel the fastest way is to press Command–+ (PC: Control–+) to quickly zoom in, and then Command-minus sign (PC: Control-minus sign) to zoom out. With each press, your view zooms in (or out, depending on which shortcut you use), and it's so fast, it'll probably wind up being your favorite way too!

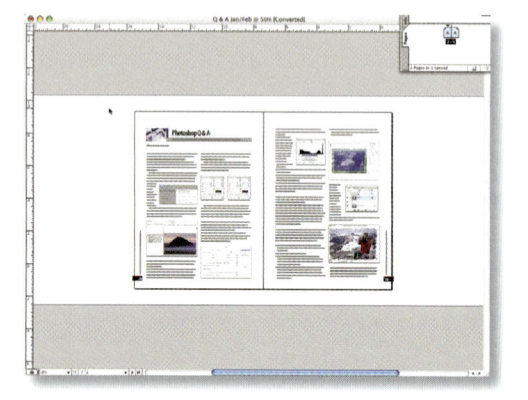

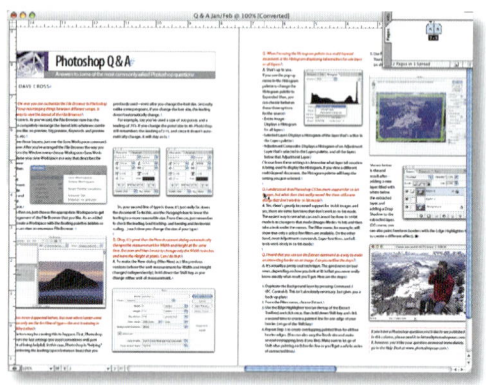

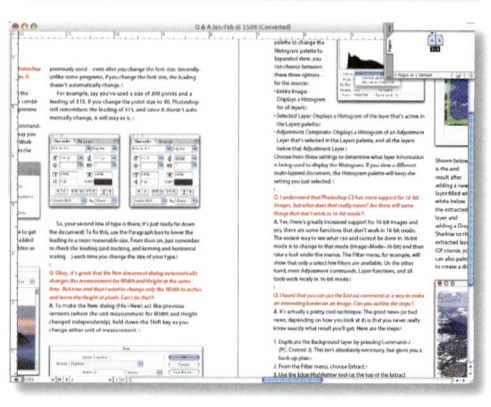

THE SPEEDWAY TO A 100% VIEW

Want to see your document at its full 100% size? Just double-click directly on the Zoom tool (magnifying glass) in the Toolbox. Don't get the tool, just double-click on it.

JUMP TO A 200% ENLARGEMENT OF WHERE YOU'RE WORKING

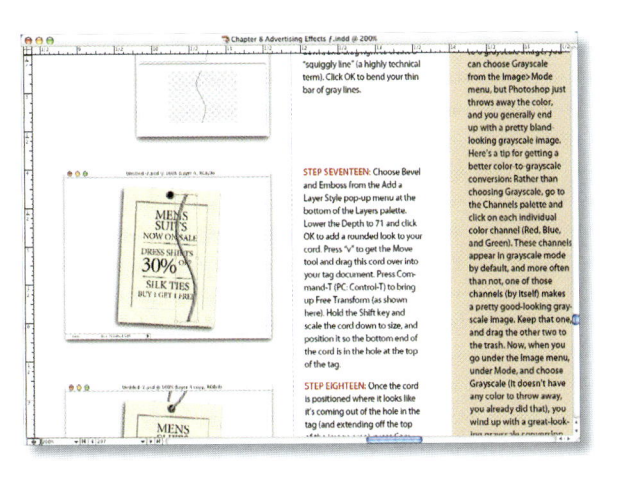

If you want to jump quickly to a 200% view of the area right where you're working in your document, you're just one keystroke away. As long as you've clicked on anything in that area (an object, some type, anything), you can press Command-2 (PC: Control-2) and you'll be zoomed into that exact area at a 200% magnification.

CHAPTER 1 • Navigating and Other Essentials   9

THE SECRET ZOOM FIELD SHORTCUT

If you know exactly the percentage amount you want to zoom in (or out), you can highlight the Zoom field (in the bottom left corner of your document window) and type in the amount. However, if it seems like a lot of trouble to head down there, highlight the field manually, and then type in the percentage, you'll love this tip: Just press Option-Command-5 (PC: Alt-Control-5) and the field will highlight automatically. All you do is type in your desired percentage, then press Enter. You don't even have to type the percentage symbol, just type in the number, hit the Enter key, and it zooms!

BETTER NAVIGATION WHILE ZOOMED IN

If you've zoomed in close on your document, there's a much easier way to navigate around your document than trying to use the scroll bars. Instead, once you're zoomed in, just hold Option-Spacebar (PC: Alt-Spacebar) and your current tool temporarily changes to the Hand tool, so you can click within your document area and move the document right where you want it. When you're done navigating, just release the keys and you're right back to the tool you were last using.

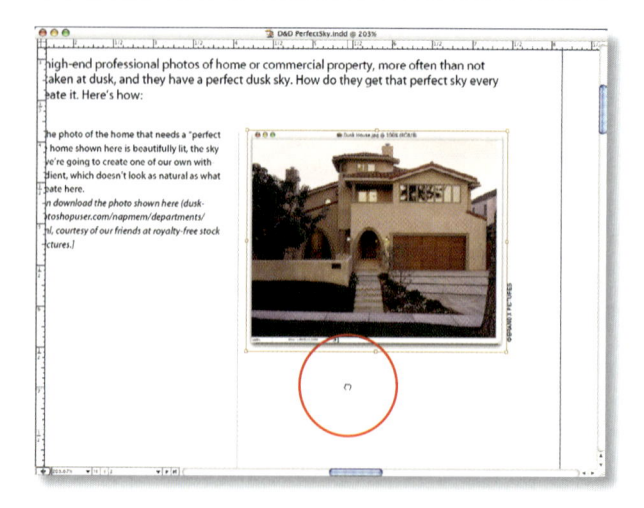

CHAPTER 1 • Navigating and Other Essentials

SWITCH TO THE ZOOM TOOL TEMPORARILY

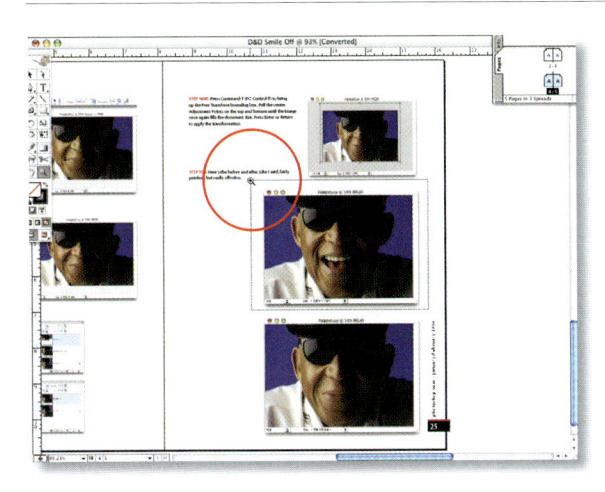

Anytime you want to zoom in on a precise area, you can temporarily switch from the tool you're using to the Zoom tool by holding Command-Spacebar (PC: Control-Spacebar). When you release the keys, you're back to the tool you were originally using. To zoom out, add the Option key (PC: Alt key) to the shortcut.

CHOOSE WHEN YOUR BASELINE GRID IS VISIBLE

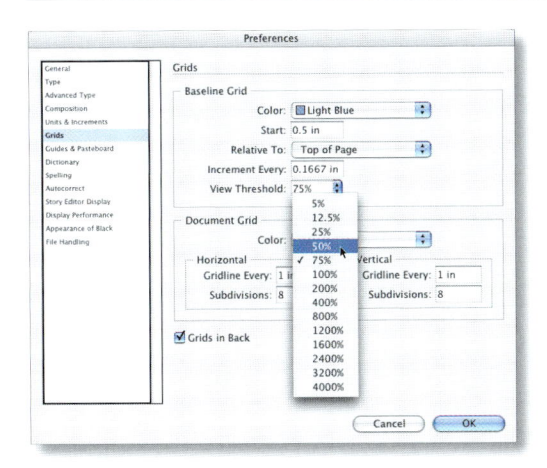

If you use the Baseline Grid feature (under the View menu, choose Show Baseline Grid), you can decide at which page magnifications this grid remains visible. For example, by default if you zoom out to less than a 75% view, the once-visible grid is hidden. However, if you want to still see the grid at smaller magnifications, you can control the "threshold" at which it's visible by going under InDesign (PC: Edit), under Preferences, under Grids, and lowering the View Threshold amount. I have to say—that's pretty slick.

CHAPTER 1 • Navigating and Other Essentials   11

THOSE PESKY RULER GUIDES

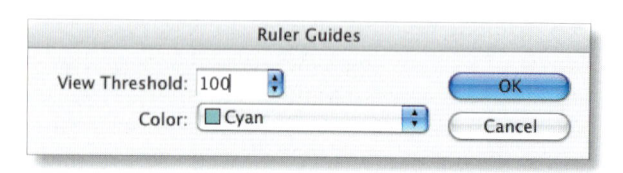

Ruler guides can be a blessing and they can be a pain. That's why there's an option to hide them. However, manually hiding ruler guides and then showing them can be frustrating too. In most cases you want to see the guides when you're zoomed in and not when you're zoomed out. You can control that "threshold" just like you can for the Baseline Grid (see previous tip). Before you drag out your guides, choose Ruler Guides from the Layout menu and change the View Threshold to 100%. Now when you drag new guides onto the page, they will be visible only when you're zoomed in to 100% or greater. When you're zoomed out to 99% or less they will disappear.

YOUR TOOLBOX, YOUR WAY

Don't like the default tall, two-column Toolbox? No sweat. Just double-click the little tab at the very top of the Toolbox (circled in red here), and the bar will switch to a single-row vertical Toolbox (shown at far right). Double-click it again, and it will switch to a horizontal single-row bar (shown below). How do you get back to the default, two-column vertical Toolbox? Just double-click that little tab one more time.

Single-row horizontal

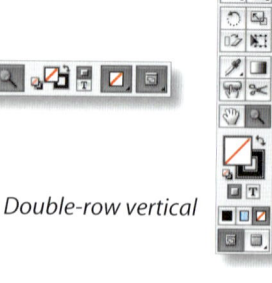

Double-row vertical

Single-row vertical

12   CHAPTER 1 • Navigating and Other Essentials

FLOAT THE CONTROL PALETTE

Although the Control palette is docked at the top of your screen by default, it doesn't have to be that way. You can make it a floating palette by clicking directly on the little vertical tab on the far left of it and just dragging it off. If you want to dock it at the bottom of your screen, click on that little tab again (not the end of the palette, the little tab just to the right of it, shown here circled in red) and drag it to the bottom left-hand corner of your screen.

SHRINK THE CONTROL PALETTE

If you decide that you like floating the Control palette, rather than having it docked at the top of the screen, so it stays out of the way (see previous tip), you're really going to love this tip: Once it's floating, if you double-click on the far left tab, the entire bar will tuck away, leaving only a small floating tab. To see the Control palette again, double-click on the tab again.

CHAPTER 1 • Navigating and Other Essentials   13

MANAGE PALETTE CLUTTER

Although the side tab palette concept of InDesign goes a long way to help keep your screen free of palettes, there are some other things you can do to minimize your palette clutter. First, if you see small, double-headed black arrows in the palette's tab, right before the palette's name, you can click on those arrows to expand or collapse the palette's extra options (as shown in the middle capture here). If you really want to save some space, double-click directly on a palette's tab and it "tucks up" so that just the tab remains visible. Even if you have nested palettes (more than one palette grouped together), double-clicking on any of their tabs tucks them all up. To reveal the full palette(s), just double-click on the tab again.

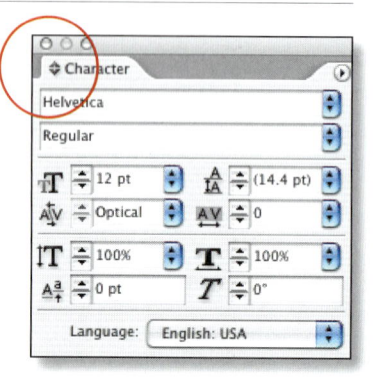

Full-sized palette

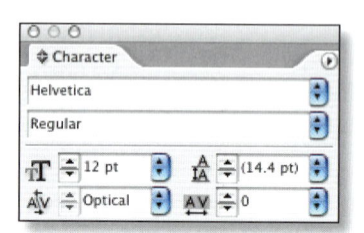

Options hidden

Just the tabs

14   CHAPTER 1 • Navigating and Other Essentials

FIT MORE IN YOUR LAYERS PALETTE

If you're working with a lot of layers, your Layers palette can get pretty full pretty quick. But there's a trick you can use to help see more layers without making the Layers palette larger (and believe me, making the palette take up more space is not our goal). To fit more layers in your Layers palette, choose Small Palette Rows from the palette's flyout menu. In the example shown here, the regular palette (shown left) lets you access all of your layers; but by choosing Small Palette Rows, you are able to add—and see—many more layers at once.

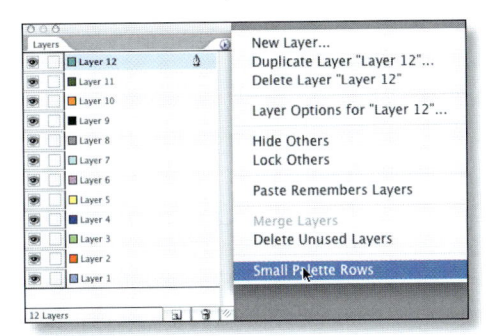

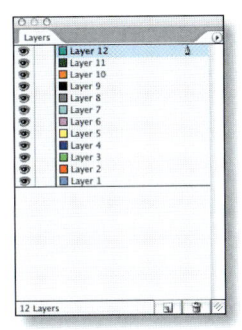

MAKE AN ÜBER-PALETTE

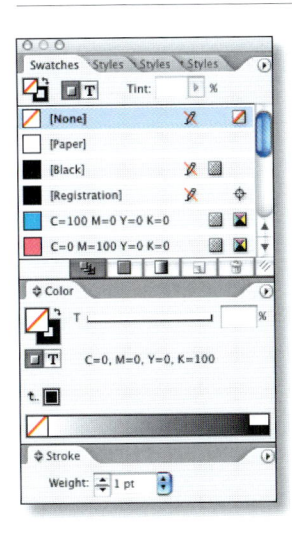

Adobe has devised a number of different ways to reduce palette clutter, but some people (you know who you are) want the opposite—all their favorite palettes visible all the time in one big palette (we call this an "über-palette"). Here's how to make your own: Once you've nested three or four of your favorite palettes together, open another palette, grab its name, and drag it to the bottom of your main palette. Move it around until a black highlight bar appears along the bottom of the top palette (you have to line up the tip of your mouse with the bottom of the palette). Release your mouse button, and this palette will "dock" vertically to the bottom of your top palette, which is the beginning of your own über-palette. Keep docking more palettes to the bottom or nesting more palettes until all your favorites are visible in one long palette (like the one shown here).

CHAPTER 1 • Navigating and Other Essentials   15

InDesign CS/CS2
KillerTips

SET YOUR WORKSPACE ONCE, AND IT'S YOURS FOREVER!

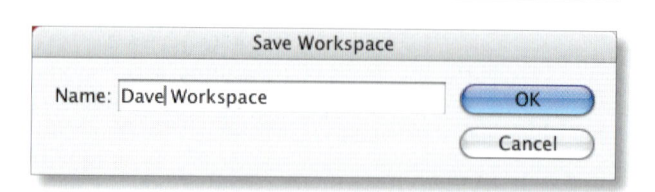

When you first launch InDesign, all the palettes, Toolbox, etc. are in their default positions (basically, they're where Adobe decided they'd be), but you can just as easily set up your own custom workspace so that every time you work, all the palettes, Toolbox, etc. are right where you want them, with only the palettes you want visible. To do this, first, put everything where you want it (in other words, set up your workspace your way). Then go under the Window menu, under Workspace, and choose Save Workspace. A dialog will appear where you can name your workspace. Click OK, then to get to your custom workspace anytime, just go under the Window menu, under Workspace, and choose your named workspace. Saving your own custom workspace is ideal for anyone who shares a computer with other users, or for anyone who likes different setups for different tasks.

HIDE ALL PALETTES AND TOOLBOX WITH ONE CLICK

When the palette clutter really gets to you (and believe me, it will), and you want a clean, completely uncluttered view of your document, just press the Tab key on your keyboard; and every palette, even your Toolbox, will be hidden from view. Once the blood returns to your head, you can press Tab again to bring them all back.

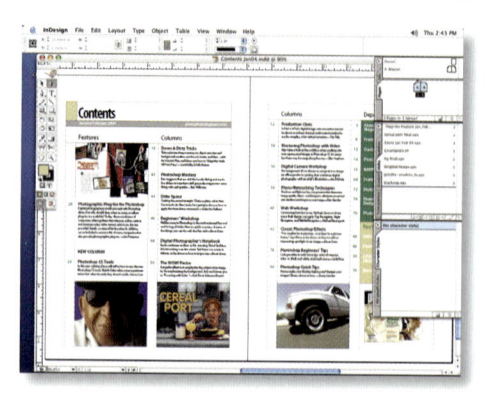

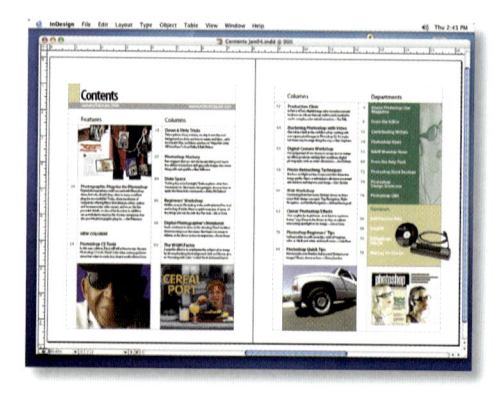

16 CHAPTER 1 • Navigating and Other Essentials

ONE CLICK HIDES PALETTES, BUT LEAVES TOOLBOX VISIBLE

Want to hide all your palettes, but keep the Toolbox visible? With no items selected in your document, click the little palette icon in the Control palette (circled here in red) and you're there! If you do have any items selected, this will cycle the appropriate palettes for that object.

HIDE JUST PALETTES

Even though the side tabs of InDesign only take up a tiny bit of space, sometimes even that is too much and you just want them out of the way. If you want to hide your palettes, but leave your Control palette and Toolbox still visible, just press Shift-Tab and they'll hide until you press Shift-Tab again. When will you use this little shortcut most? Probably to reach the vertical scroll bar on the right side of your document window (at least, that's when we use it).

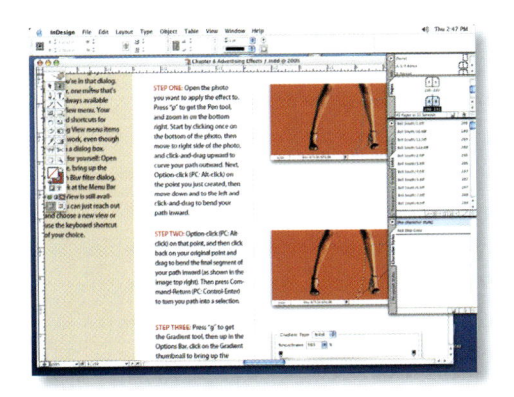

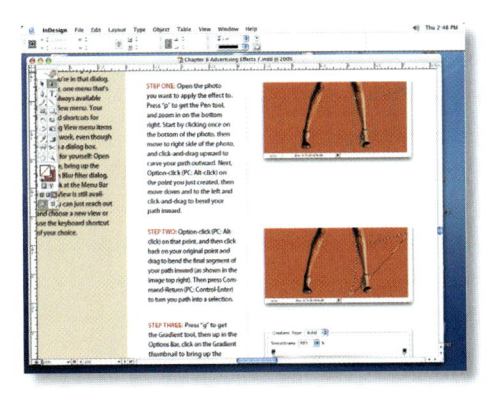

SIDE-TAB A GROUP OF PALETTES

What happens if you have three palettes nested together, and you drag one of those tabs over to the right side of your screen to make it a side tab? Well, sadly only that particular palette becomes a side tab—the others that were nested with it just remain onscreen. Don't you wish there was a way you could nest all three palettes at once, instead of one at a time? There is: Hold Option (PC: Alt) before you drag the tab, then all the palettes will become side tabs as a group.

HOW TO PREVIEW YOUR DOCUMENT

If at any time you want a preview of how your document will look, without all the guides, non-printing elements, etc., you can click on the Preview Mode button at the bottom of the Toolbox (or press the letter "w" on your keyboard when you're not in the Type tool), and you'll get the clean unfettered view. If you've added slugs or bleeds, there are special previews that will show them as well, just choose those views from the Preview Mode flyout menu (as shown here).

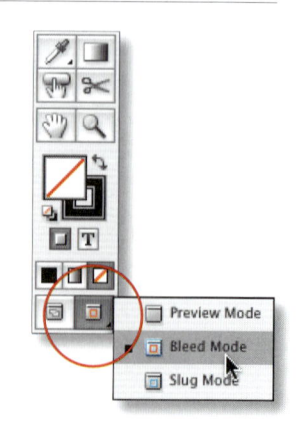

18 CHAPTER 1 • Navigating and Other Essentials

SAVE EVERY OPEN DOCUMENT WITH ONE KEYSTROKE

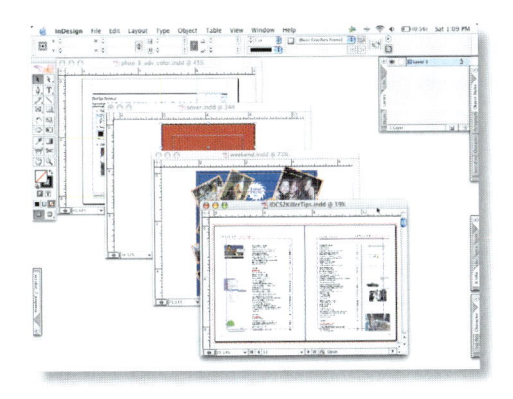

If you have a number of different documents open and you have a sneaking suspicion that your system's getting ready to take a dive (i.e., crash), here's a keyboard shortcut that can save your life (okay, it's a lifesaver, but it won't actually save your life). Just press Shift-Option-Command-S (PC: Shift-Alt-Control-S) and every open document will be saved. Nothing like a one-keystroke insurance policy, eh?

A BIGGER VIEW IN THE NAVIGATOR PALETTE

This one surprises a lot of people who always use the tiny Navigator palette at its default size (left picture). If you want a larger preview in the Navigator palette, it resizes like a window—just grab the bottom right-hand corner and drag it out. As the palette's window gets bigger, so does the thumbnail of your page (right picture).

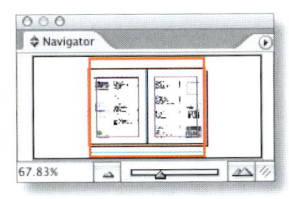

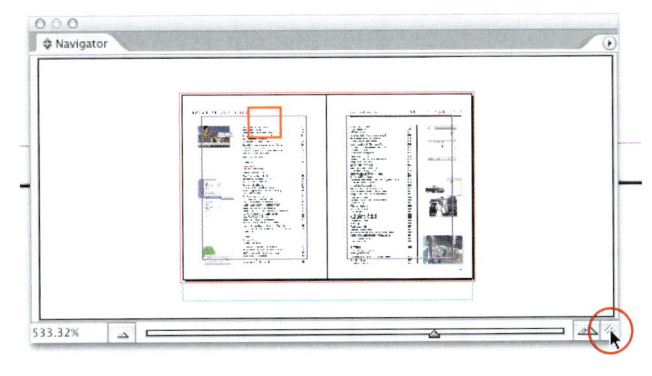

CHAPTER 1 • Navigating and Other Essentials

InDesign CS/CS2
KillerTips

I WANT TO SEE IT ALL

The Navigator palette is sweet for being able to see your entire spread at one time and to zoom in on specific areas; but with today's monitors you can pretty much accomplish that anyway. Don't give up on the Navigator, though. Choose View All Spreads from the Navigator palette's flyout menu. Now you can see all the spreads in one view and navigate to any spot in your document with a click-and-drag.

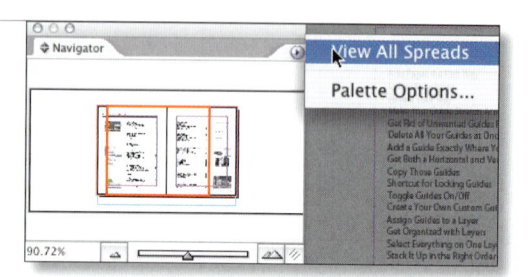

THE FIVE MOST IMPORTANT ONE-KEY TOOL SHORTCUTS

Want to start saving loads of time every single day? Then learn these five easy-to-remember one-key shortcuts, so you can switch to the most popular tools quickly.

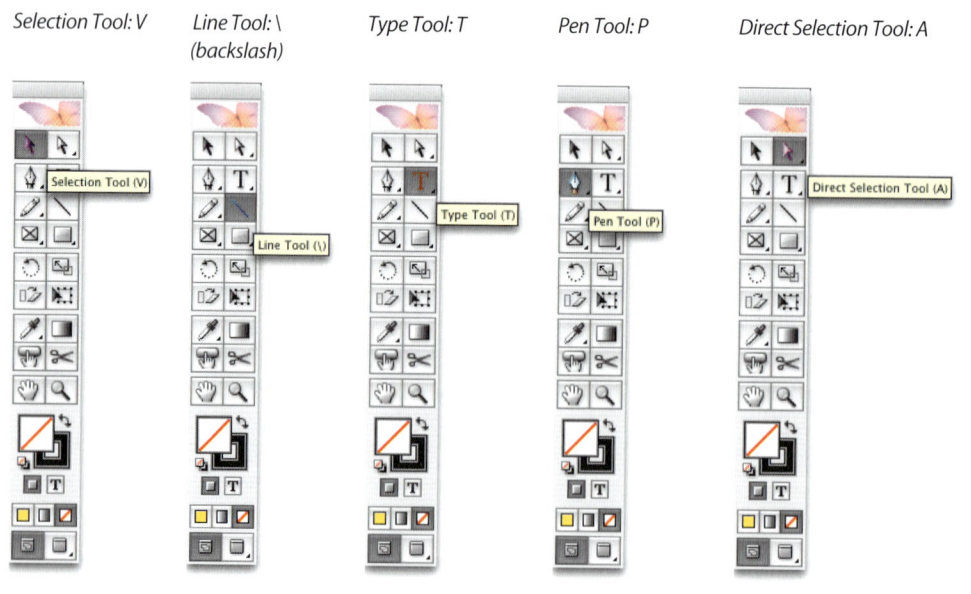

Selection Tool: V

Line Tool: \ (backslash)

Type Tool: T

Pen Tool: P

Direct Selection Tool: A

Learn just those five, and you'll be amazed at how much your efficiency improves.

20   CHAPTER 1 • Navigating and Other Essentials

NO KEYBOARD SHORTCUT? MAKE ONE!

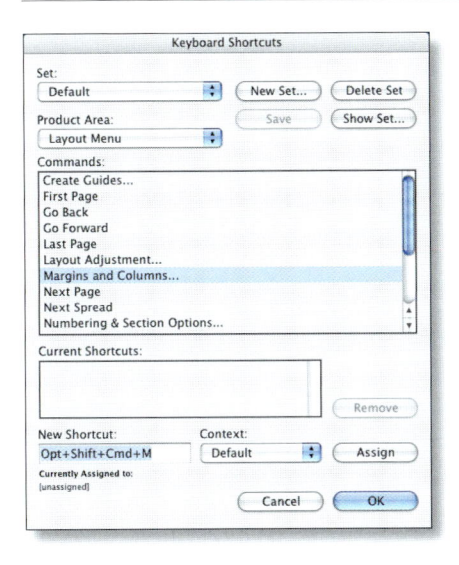

If you find yourself using a command that doesn't have a keyboard shortcut (like the Margins and Columns dialog, for example), then just make one. Go under the Edit menu and choose Keyboard Shortcuts. When the dialog appears, from the Product Area pop-up choose whichever menu the command appears under (in the example shown here, Margins and Columns appears under the Layout Menu). Then in the list of commands that appears, click on the command that you want to assign a keyboard shortcut (as shown here). If there's already a shortcut, it will appear in the Current Shortcuts window. If not, add your own: Click once in the New Shortcut field, then type in the keystrokes of the shortcut you want to use, click Assign, then click OK. Cool!

COMING OVER FROM QUARKXPRESS? USE QUARK SHORTCUTS

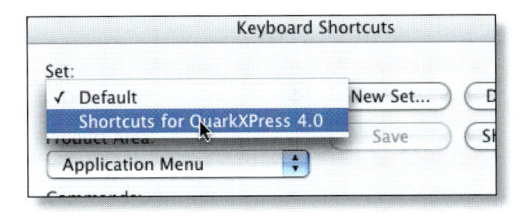

If you're coming to InDesign after leaving QuarkXPress (in fact, I'd guess most people using InDesign did just that), you can make the transition easier by having InDesign load all of QuarkXPress's same keyboard shortcuts. That way, you don't have to relearn how to do, well…everything. Here's how to load 'em: Go under the Edit menu and choose Keyboard Shortcuts. When the dialog appears, choose Shortcuts for QuarkXPress 4.0 from the Set pop-up menu at the top of the dialog (as shown here) and then click OK. That's all there is to it. (Note: Changing this makes an excellent prank to pull on co-workers. Not that you'd ever do it, but wouldn't it be hilarious to watch them as they learn that none of their keyboard shortcuts seem to work? Hmmmmm.)

CHAPTER 1 • Navigating and Other Essentials   21

PRINT YOUR CUSTOM KEYBOARD SHORTCUTS

If you've decided to add your own custom set of keyboard shortcuts to InDesign, how are you going to remember them all? You don't have to—just print out your custom set by going under the Edit menu and choosing Keyboard Shortcuts. Then in the dialog, click on the Show Set button (as shown) and it will launch your text editor and display a list of all the keyboard shortcuts in your set (as shown here), which you can then print as a reference. How sweet is that?

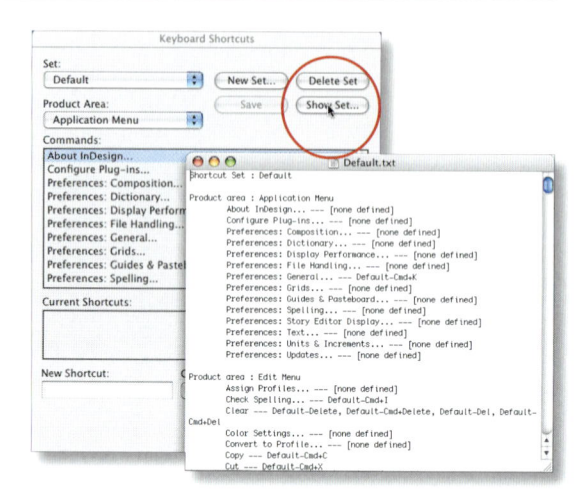

BRING BACK THOSE HIDDEN WARNING DIALOGS

Chances are you've had a warning dialog pop up more than once. And if you have, chances are you've clicked on the checkbox that says something along the lines of "Don't show again." However, sure enough, at some point you'll want to remember what that warning said (or perhaps now you're sharing your computer with someone else, and you want him to see the warning). To get those scary warning dialogs back, go under the InDesign menu (PC: Edit menu), under Preferences, to General, and at the bottom of the dialog click the Reset All Warning Dialogs button (as shown). Then click OK.

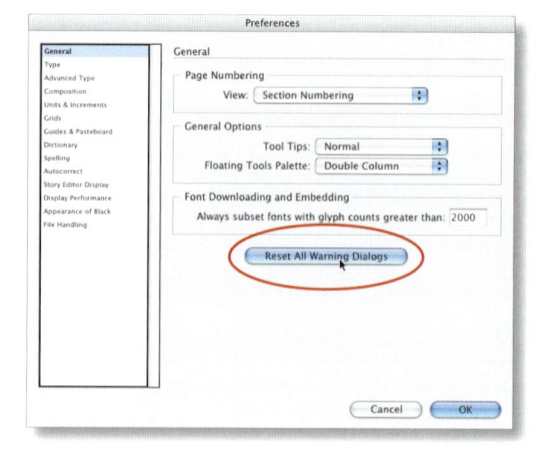

CHAPTER 1 • Navigating and Other Essentials

CHAPTER 1 • Navigating and Other Essentials

Stereo Type

TWEAKIN' YOUR TEXT

If there's one area where InDesign undeniably reigns supreme, it's type tweaking. You can flat-out set some seriously righteous type in this program; and

Stereo Type
tweakin' your text

it's packed with so many high-end typographic features that I'm not sure that even Adobe knows what half of them do. But here's the thing: If you take the time to learn some of these type tips, not only will you work faster and smarter, but you'll also be well on your way to becoming a total type snob. Once you reach that lofty plane, ah my friend, life will be sweet. You'll look down on people who set type for coupons, newspaper ads, flyers, and other such nonsense. You'll laugh at their lack of ligatures. You'll scoff at their un-hung punctuation. You'll cackle at their non-curly quotes while you hiss and glare at them with the utter disdain, contempt, and loathing they deserve. They're beneath you. They're "double-spacers" and they should be dealt with accordingly. But even though you openly mock them, somewhere deep inside your soul, in a place you seldom dare venture, you know that before this chapter you, too, were one of them. An "under-liner." A "no-superscripter." A (dare I say it?) "non-kerner."

THE TYPE TOOL SUPER SHORTCUT

If you've got a layout with text frames in place on your page, when you decide to enter some text in a particular frame you don't have to go to the Toolbox to switch to the Type tool. Instead, when you have either of the Selection tools, just double-click inside any visible text frame. You'll immediately switch to the Type tool, and your cursor will be in place, ready for you to type.

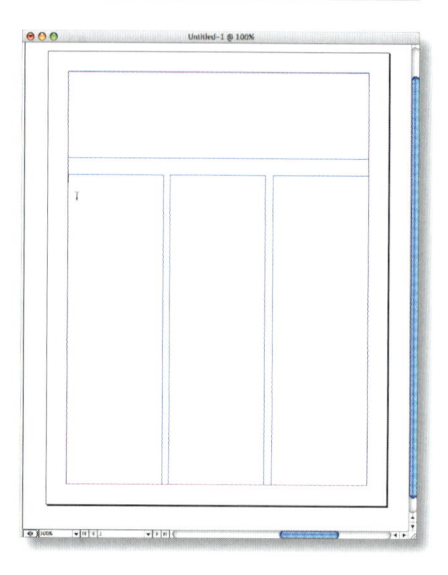

THE HIDDEN OPTIONS FOR TYPE ON A PATH

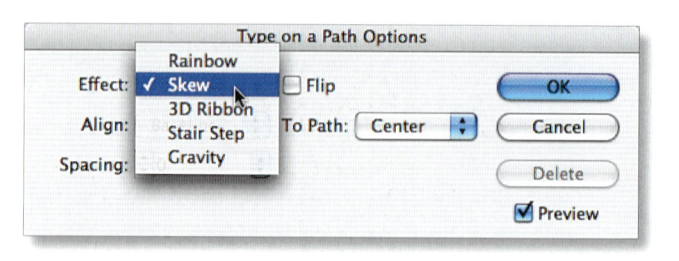

Want more control over how your type on a path works? Then go to the Toolbox and just double-click directly on the Type on a Path tool to bring up its options. (Note: To get to the Type on a Path tool, click-and-hold on the Type tool in the Toolbox, then choose the Type on a Path tool from the flyout menu.) Perhaps one of the coolest options is the Effect pop-up menu, where you can apply different type-on-a-path effects, even after the type is already on the path.

26   CHAPTER 2 • Tweakin' Your Text

SET YOUR TYPE DEFAULTS

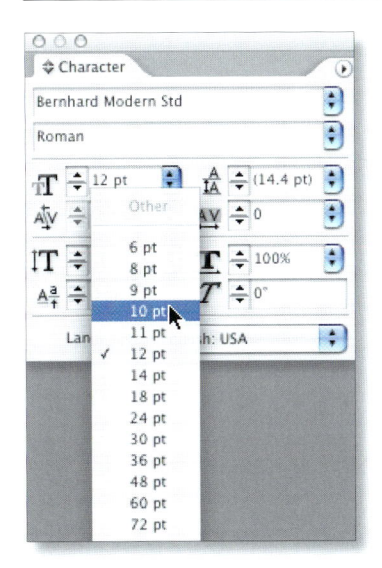

You can set the type defaults (default font, size, etc.) for your document very easily. Just make sure nothing is selected (to make sure, go under the Edit menu and choose Deselect All). Then get the Type tool, go to the Character palette and set everything the way you want it, and those now become your defaults. See, we told you it was easy.

SET DEFAULT CHARACTER AND PARAGRAPH STYLES

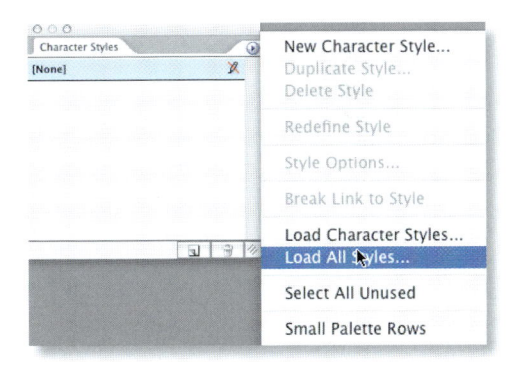

You can set default styles, and the easiest way is to import styles from an existing document that already has the styles you want. Here's how: First make sure no documents are open. Then go under the Type menu and choose Character Styles or Paragraph Styles—doesn't matter which. Then from the palette's flyout menu choose Load All Styles. This brings up a standard Open A File dialog. Navigate your way to your existing document that has the styles you want to use as your defaults, then click Open. That's it—the styles from that document are now imported, and those styles are now your default paragraph and character styles.

CHAPTER 2 • Tweakin' Your Text   27

FAST FONT SIZE CHANGES FROM THE KEYBOARD

When it comes to resizing your fonts, save yourself trips to the Control palette or the Character palette and use these shortcuts instead. To jump up 2 point sizes at a time, highlight your text and press Shift-Command-> (PC: Shift-Control->). Perfect for making quick little adjustments. To make your highlighted type shrink by 2 points at a pop, press Shift-Command-< (PC: Shift-Control-<).

JUMPING UP 2 POINTS AT A TIME NOT ENOUGH FOR YOU?

When using the shortcut in the previous tip, you may find that jumping up only 2 points at a time (the default) just isn't enough for you. You may want to jump to 6 points, 8, or even 10 points every time you press that shortcut. If that's the case, go under the InDesign menu (PC: Edit menu), under Preferences, and choose Units & Increments. In the Keyboard Increments section, under the Size/Leading field you'll see 2 entered as the current amount. You know what to do from here, right? Right!

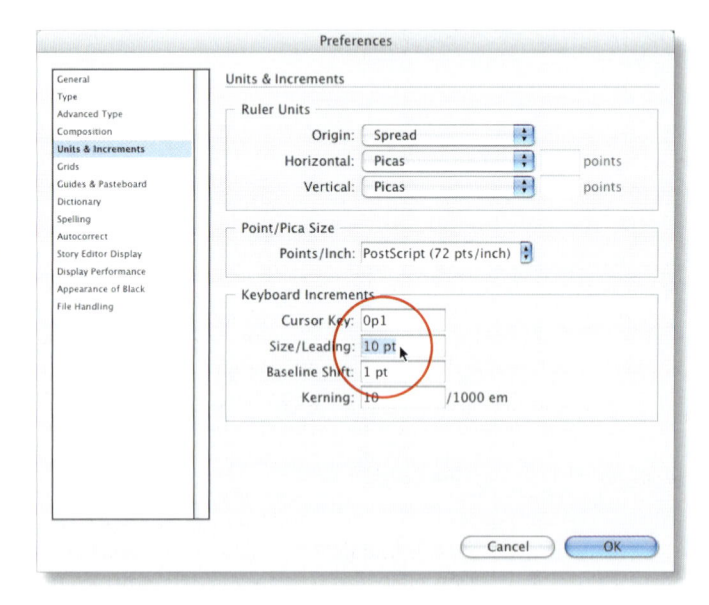

WAITING ON THE REAL TEXT? FAKE IT

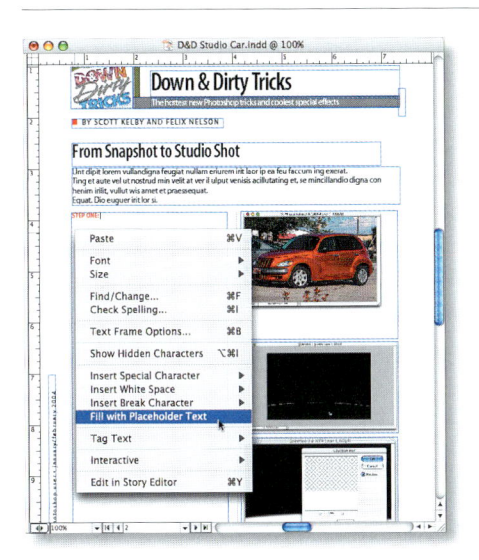

Many times when you're creating a layout for a publication, book, or print ad, you don't have the final copy (or any copy, for that matter) to use in your layout. But that doesn't have to stop you, because you can have InDesign add "dummy" text to flow into your text columns. Here's how: Create your columns, then Control-click (PC: Right-click) in your text frame and choose Fill With Placeholder Text from the pop-up menu that appears. The frame will be filled with sample text that you can use for layout purposes until the final text is delivered from the writers (and writers are always late—just ask any editor).

TIP FOR MAGAZINE AND NEWSPAPER EDITORS

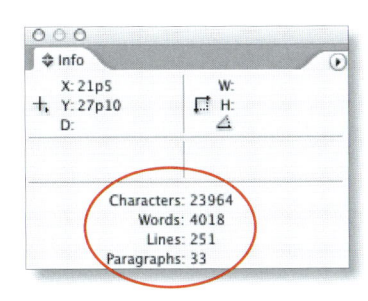

If you're working on a magazine or newspaper, you're working with writers; and chances are you're in charge of giving them (or at the very least, your editors) the word counts for their articles. If that's the case, InDesign can help. Put your text frames in place on the page where the article will appear, then go under the Type menu and choose Fill With Placeholder Text to fill the text frames with sample text. Now all you have to do is look at InDesign's built-in word count, which is found by going under the Window menu and choosing Info. At the bottom of the Info palette, you'll find the "counts," and the second one down is the word count for your selected text. (Note: If you don't see this information, it's just hidden. Go to the Info palette's flyout menu and choose Show Options.)

CHAPTER 2 • Tweakin' Your Text   29

MAKE YOUR OWN CUSTOM PLACEHOLDER TEXT

If you don't like what InDesign's built-in placeholder text says, you can create your own custom placeholder text and use it instead. Just open the text file you want to use in your word processing application, then save that file and name it Placeholder.txt. Lastly, just drop that file in the InDesign folder. That's it—now it will use your custom text as the placeholder text.

CONTROL PALETTE STUNTS (SWAPPING TYPE AND PARAGRAPH FIELDS)

When you have the Type tool, you can pull a pretty handy Control palette stunt that lets you decide whether the Control palette displays type attributes or paragraph attributes. Just press Option-Command-7 (PC: Alt-Control-7) and it swaps between the two Control palette layouts. How helpful is this? Massively!

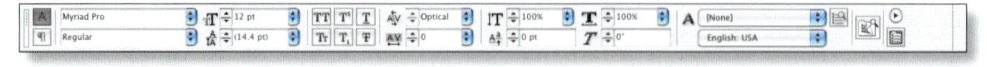

Type options

Paragraph options

TYPE PREFERENCES SHORTCUT

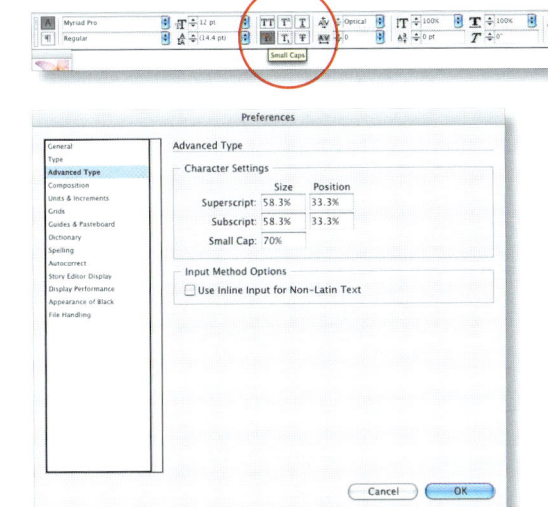

If you're using the Type tool and you want to get to the Type preferences fast, just Option-click (PC: Alt-click) on either the Superscript, Subscript, or Small Caps button up in the Control palette. This shortcut makes great sense, because in the Advanced Type Preferences dialog you can adjust the default Superscript, Subscript, and Small Cap settings.

THE SECRET TO KERNING VISUALLY

Adjusting the space between two letters can certainly be done by going to the Character palette and manually entering numbers in the Kerning field, but that's so un-design-like. Good kerning is such a visual thing (and designers are such visual people) that entering numbers should be a last resort—we want to kern visually. Here's how it's done: Click your cursor between the two letters you want to kern, then press Option-Left Arrow (PC: Alt-Left Arrow) to kern (move) the letters closer together. Press Option-Right Arrow (PC: Alt-Right Arrow) to move them farther apart. Then, when it's time to kern another set of letters, use just the Left/Right Arrow keys to move your cursor to the letters, then add the Option key (PC: Alt key) to visually kern this set of letters.

CHAPTER 2 • Tweakin' Your Text   31

WHY ARE PARENTHESES IN MY KERNING FIELD?

That's InDesign's way of letting you know that the number you see in the field was generated by InDesign's Auto Kerning feature, which uses kerning pairs to adjust the space automatically between a pair of letters that are known to cause a spacing problem. You're welcome to change the kerning if it doesn't look right to you, but at least the parens let you know how (and why) that kerning value got there in the first place.

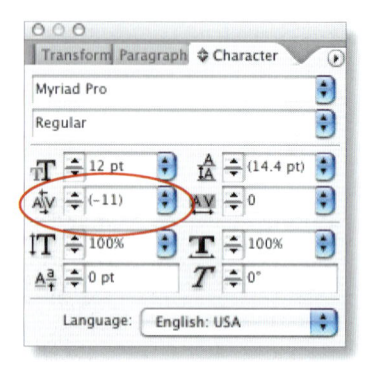

TIGHTEN THE SPACE BETWEEN WORDS VISUALLY

When tracking words (adjusting the space between a number of selected letters or words), what exactly is the right amount? Nobody knows. That's because you have to do it visually, rather than numerically, to get it to look right. That's why it's so important to know this keyboard shortcut: Highlight the letters, or words, whose tracking you want to adjust, then press Option-Left Arrow (PC: Alt-Left Arrow) to tighten the spacing by moving the letters closer together or Option-Right Arrow (PC: Alt-Right Arrow) to move the letters farther apart.

ADJUST LEADING VISUALLY

Adjusting the vertical spacing between lines (known as leading) is another one of those adjustments that it's best to do visually rather than by the numbers. Just highlight the lines you want to adjust, then press Option-Up Arrow (PC: Alt-Up Arrow) to move the lines closer together, or Option-Down Arrow (PC: Alt-Down Arrow) to add more space between the lines.

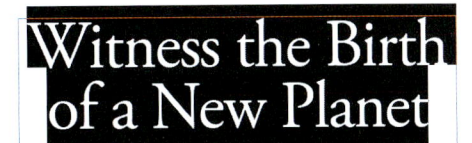

ADJUST HORIZONTAL SCALING VISUALLY

Want to make your type thinner or thicker without having to type values in the Horizontal Scale field in the Character palette? Try this: Switch to the Selection tool, select your text frame, hold the Command key (PC: Control key), grab one of the center points on the sides of your text frame, and drag inward to make the type thinner, or outward to make the letters wider (as shown below).

CHAPTER 2 • Tweakin' Your Text

THE SPEED LANE TO 100% HORIZONTAL SCALING

As you know, we use horizontal scaling to make our letters thicker (like 120% or 130%) or thinner (I like to set all my body copy at 95%), and since we're always tweaking our horizontal scaling, wouldn't it be great if there was a shortcut for a quick return to the standard 100%? Well there is (you knew we were setting you up, right?). Just press Shift-Command-X (PC: Shift-Control-X) and your highlighted text will return to its good ol' default of 100% horizontal scaling.

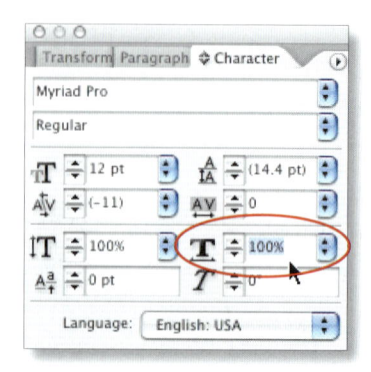

DON'T KNOW THE RIGHT POINT SIZE? JUST DRAG YOUR TEXT

If you want to make your text much larger, but you're not sure which point size is right—do it visually. Instead of highlighting the type and entering a number in the Font Size field, get the Selection tool and click on the text block, hold Shift-Command (PC: Shift-Control), grab a corner point of the text block and drag diagonally upward to enlarge it, or diagonally inward to shrink it.

PROVEN STRENGTH

PROVEN STRENGTH

CHAPTER 2 • Tweakin' Your Text

CHANGING MULTIPLE TEXT BLOCKS AT ONCE

If you want to change an attribute (like font, size, leading, etc.) in a number of text blocks at once, just get the Selection tool (the solid arrow), Shift-click on each text frame you want to adjust, switch to the Type tool, then go up to the Control palette and make your changes. Any changes you make will now be applied to all of the selected blocks of text.

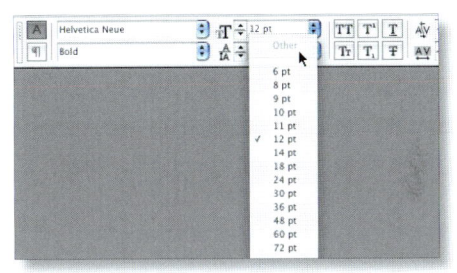

APPLY CHARACTER FORMATTING TO MULTIPLE TEXT BLOCKS

This is one of our favorite InDesign tips, because it makes your type-tweaking life so much easier. If you have character formatting styles set up, you don't have to apply them one at a time. As in the previous tip, just get the Selection tool, Shift-click on every text block that you want to have a particular character formatting style, but this time go to the Character Styles palette or Paragraph Styles palette, click on the style, and BAM—they all change at once. Life is good.

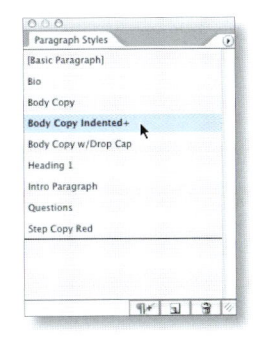

CHAPTER 2 • Tweakin' Your Text

SHORTCUT TO THE NEW CHARACTER STYLE DIALOG

Want a one-click way to get to the New Character Style dialog? Just go up in the Control palette and double-click the capital "A" that appears on the far right (just before the Character Styles pop-up menu) and the New Character Style dialog will pop right up.

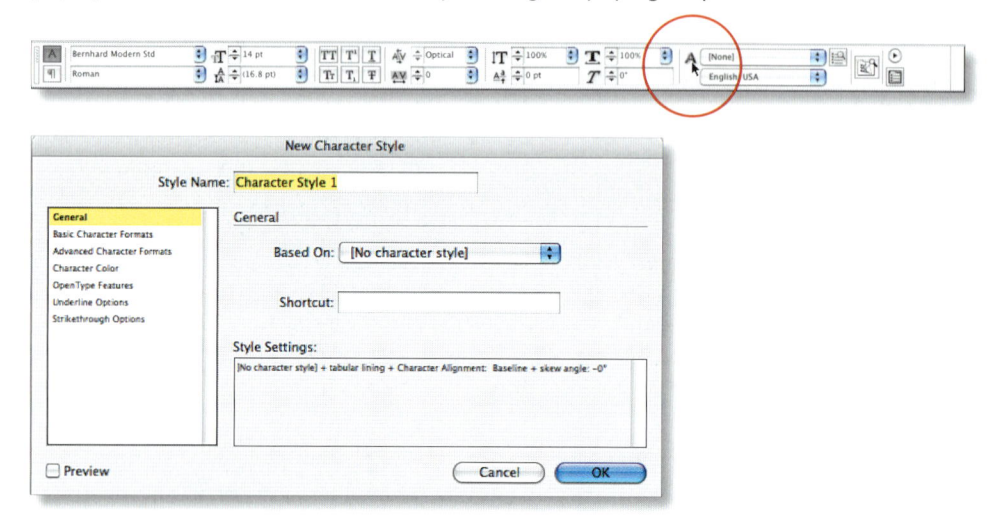

SHIFT BASELINE WITHOUT THE CHARACTER PALETTE

Need to shift something up off the baseline (like the ® symbol) or move something down (like the 2 in H$_2$0)? You can do it using a keyboard shortcut: Highlight the character you want to shift, then press Shift-Option-Up Arrow (PC: Shift-Alt-Up Arrow) to move the character up, or Shift-Option-Down Arrow (PC: Shift-Alt-Down Arrow) to move the character down.

36 CHAPTER 2 • Tweakin' Your Text

GET RID OF THOSE NASTY DOUBLE-SPACES

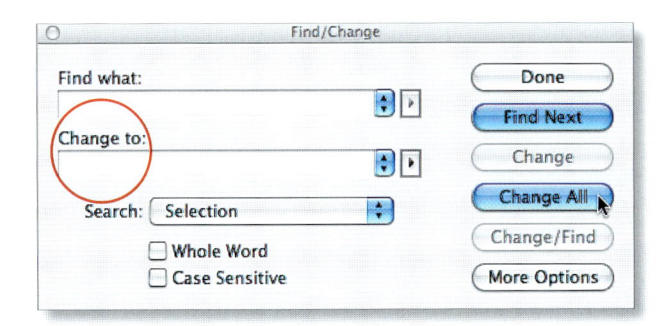

If you're importing text from a word processing document, there's a pretty good chance that the person who entered the text used the time-honored tradition of putting two spaces between sentences (a holdover from the days of using a typewriter). That's fine on a typewriter, with its monospace letters, but it looks terrible in today's typography and those double-spaces have to be removed. Here's how: Go under the Edit menu and choose Find/Change. Click in the Find What field, then press the Spacebar twice (you're telling it to find all double-spaces). Then tab to the Change To field and press the Spacebar once. Click the Change All button, and every double-space will instantly be changed to a single space. Pretty slick little trick, eh?

GET RID OF WEIRD CHARACTERS

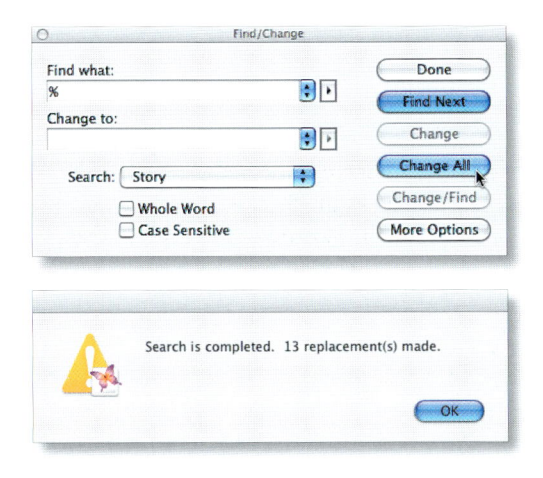

If you convert a QuarkXPress document into an InDesign document, you'll sometimes wind up with weird extra characters (like the % symbol appearing right in the middle of a word) throughout the document (at least, that usually happens to us). If so, you can have InDesign get rid of all of 'em, fast. Here's how: First select the weird character, then press Command-C (PC: Control-C) to copy it into memory. Then go under the Edit menu and choose Find/Change. When the dialog appears, click in the Find What field and then press Command-V (PC: Control-V) to paste the weird character into that field. Leave the Change To field blank, then click the Change All button. This then removes all the weird characters and replaces them with nothing. How sweet is that?

CHAPTER 2 • Tweakin' Your Text

FASTER FIXES FOR BAD CHARACTERS

In the previous tip, we showed you how to replace bad characters that appear when importing type or converting a QuarkXPress document to InDesign by using Find/Change under the Edit menu. Well, if you've had to replace those characters once, it's even faster the second time. Why? It's because InDesign remembers the last 15 finds and changes. So if you convert a second document, you don't have to copy the offending bad character into the Find What field—instead just choose it from the field's pop-up menu, because it's already there. This can absolutely save loads of time when cleaning up a messy document.

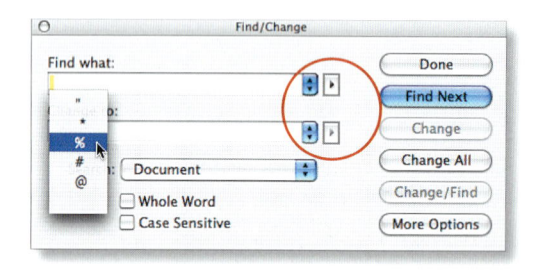

MAKE THAT SENTENCE ALL CAPS THE FAST WAY

If you've typed something, and then wish you'd entered it in all caps, you're only about three seconds away from having just that. Highlight the text you want in caps, and then press Shift-Command-K (PC: Shift-Control-K) and it's changed to all caps lickety-split.

The Standard of Luxury for New Car Owners

THE STANDARD OF LUXURY FOR NEW CAR OWNERS

HIGHLIGHT CHARACTER PALETTE FIELDS FAST

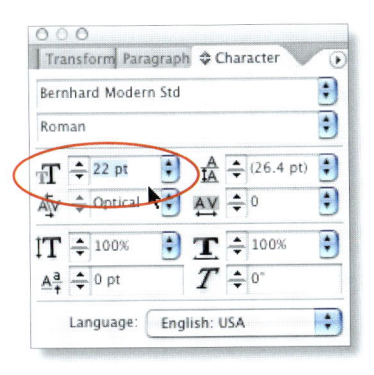

The next time you need to make a change in the Character palette, don't click your cursor in the tiny little field and then type in a new number—instead just click on the field's icon and the field will highlight, so all you have to do is type in the new amount. Sweet.

QUICK TYPE TWEAKING IN THE CHARACTER PALETTE

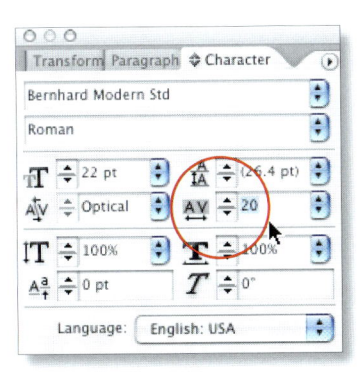

To keep working at maximum speed, we usually try to avoid using the Character palette as much as possible (having to type in values just takes too long), but if you have to work in the Character palette, here's a tip that speeds things up—as in the previous tip, when you want to adjust a value, just click on the icon for that field (to highlight the value already in that field), but instead of typing in a value, use the Up/Down Arrow keys on your keyboard to quickly increase or decrease the current amount. When you've got the number you want, press Enter.

CHAPTER 2 • Tweakin' Your Text

FIND THE RIGHT FONT FAST—SCROLL THROUGH THEM

If you're not sure which font to use for a project, try this: Highlight the text in question, then just click your cursor once in the Font field (up in the Control palette, as shown here, or in the Character palette) and then use the Up/Down Arrow keys on your keyboard to move up and down the list of fonts. Each time you press an arrow key, the font will change to the next one in the list, which makes finding the right font a breeze.

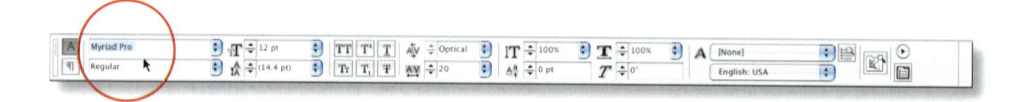

JUMP TO THE RIGHT FONT

If you know the name of the font you want, you don't have to scroll all the way through the font list to get to it. Just highlight the current font's name in the Font field (either in the Control palette or the Character palette) with your cursor, then type in the first letter of the font you want, and it will jump to that font. (Okay, technically it'll jump to the first font in the list that starts with that letter. So, if you have a lot of fonts, you might want to type in the first two or three letters, so it homes in on the exact font you want.)

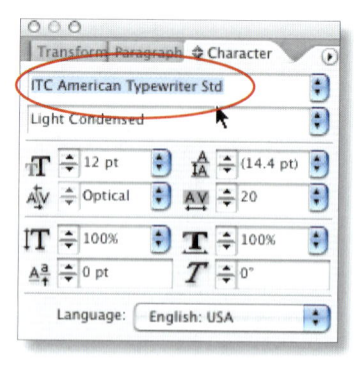

CHAPTER 2 • Tweakin' Your Text

CHANGE FONTS AUTOMATICALLY, WITHOUT STYLE SHEETS

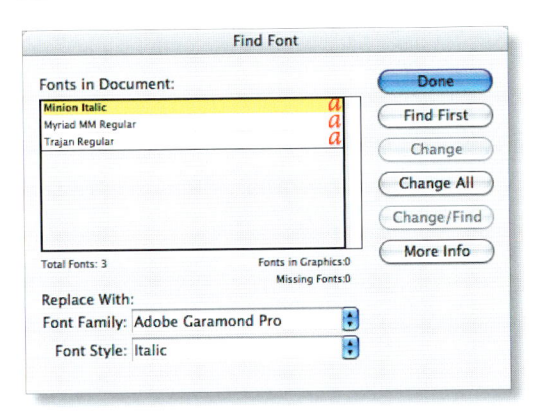

Let's say you have a multipage document, and all of the captions are in the font Minion Italic. If you used style sheets, you could change all the captions to a different face, say Adobe Garamond Pro Italic, very easily, but what if you didn't build style sheets (hey, it happens all the time)? Here's what to do: Go under the Type menu and choose Find Fonts. A list of the fonts used in your current document will appear in the window. Click on the font you want to replace (in this case, Minion Italic), then choose the Font Family and Font Style you want it replaced with from the pop-up menus at the bottom left of the dialog (in this case, Adobe Garamond Pro Italic). Click the Change All button, and all instances of Minion Italic in your document will be replaced with Adobe Garamond Pro Italic.

PASTE TEXT INTO INDESIGN

If you're copying a small amount of text into your InDesign document, perhaps from a word processing program (such as Microsoft Word), probably the quickest way to do so is simply to highlight the text in your word processing program, press Command-C (PC: Control-C) to copy it, then switch to InDesign and press Command-V (PC: Control-V) to paste it in. If you can see your InDesign document onscreen, an even quicker way may be to click on the highlighted text in the word processing program and drag-and-drop it on the InDesign document.

CHAPTER 2 • Tweakin' Your Text   41

PASTE TEXT WHILE RETAINING YOUR TYPE FORMATTING

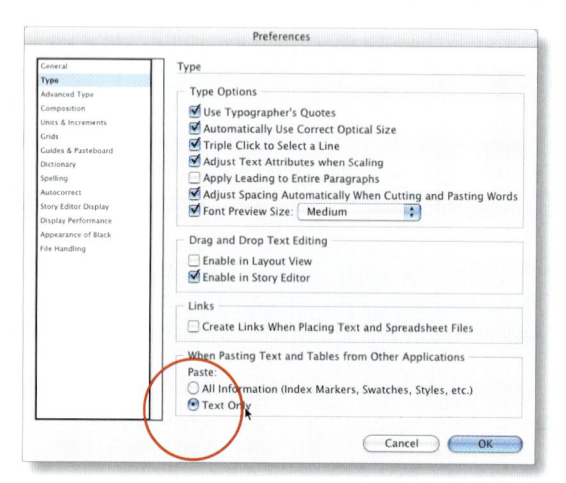

In previous versions of InDesign, if you pasted in text from another application, it kept the formatting of the original application. Personally, this drove me absolutely insane. In fact, it was the only thing about InDesign that I could say I really hated. But now, I can tell my therapist to cancel my standing Tuesday appointment because InDesign gives you the option to retain the formatting done in other applications, or to have your pasted text use the text formatting (font, size, leading, etc.) you're already using in InDesign. Just go to the InDesign menu (PC: Edit menu), under Preferences, choose Type, and in the When Pasting Text and Tables from Other Applications section, select Text Only. (Also, see "Paste Without Formatting" on page 239.)

DRAG-AND-DROP TEXT INTO INDESIGN

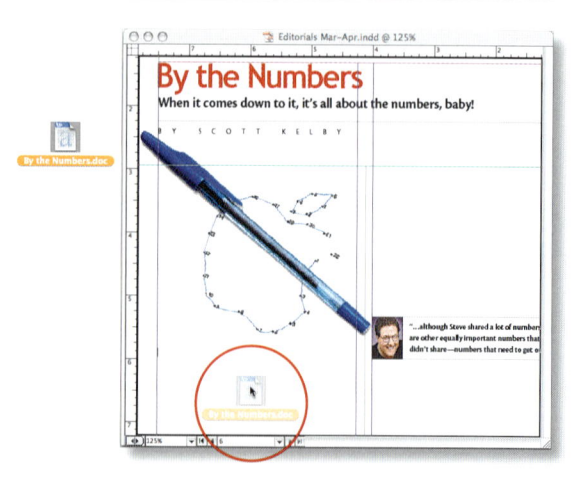

If you can see a text document on your desktop, you can actually drag-and-drop that text file from the desktop right into an open InDesign document, and the text will appear in its own text box. Weirder yet—it doesn't just work on text—try it on a graphic. That's right, it'll just drag-and-drop right on in.

42   CHAPTER 2 • Tweakin' Your Text

GET CONTROL OVER YOUR IMPORTED TEXT

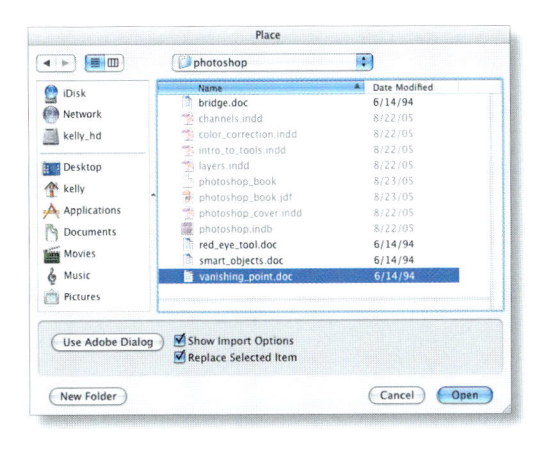

If you're importing text into InDesign, you can have a lot of control over how the text is imported by holding just one key. First, go under the File menu and choose Place. In the Place dialog, before you double-click on a text file to import it, just hold the Shift key, then double-click on it (or you can simply check Show Import Options). The Import Options dialog will appear, where you can control how your type will be imported and how certain aspects will be handled (like whether you want the quotes converted to typographer's quotes).

HOW TO DESELECT EVERYTHING

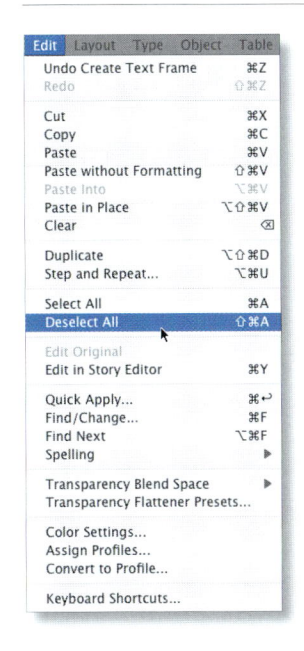

If you have multiple items selected in InDesign, you may want to deselect—well—everything. If you're charging by the hour, go under the Edit menu and choose Deselect All. If you're charging by the job, just press Shift-Command-A (PC: Shift-Control-A).

CHAPTER 2 • Tweakin' Your Text   43

ONE COLUMN TO MULTI-COLUMNS THE FAST WAY

If you've imported some text, you can instantly create multiple columns in that text by switching to the Selection tool (the black arrow on the left in the Toolbox), holding the Option key (PC: Alt key), and double-clicking on the text frame. This brings up the Text Frame Options dialog, and there you can choose how many columns you'd like your text split into. Turn on the Preview checkbox for a live preview of how your columns will look.

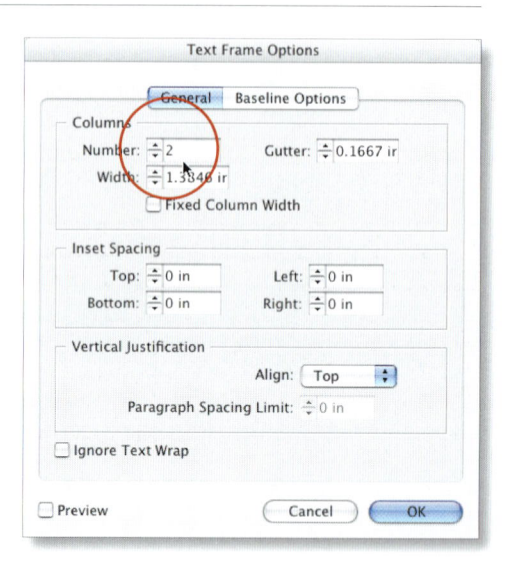

NEED A ™? HOW ABOUT A ©?

Characters like ©, ™, and ® are called "special characters" and you can have InDesign insert these directly into your document. When you come to a situation that calls for a special character, just Control-click (PC: Right-click) right where your type cursor is and a pop-up menu will appear. Choose Insert Special Character from the pop-up menu and then choose which special character you want inserted from the submenu that appears (as shown here).

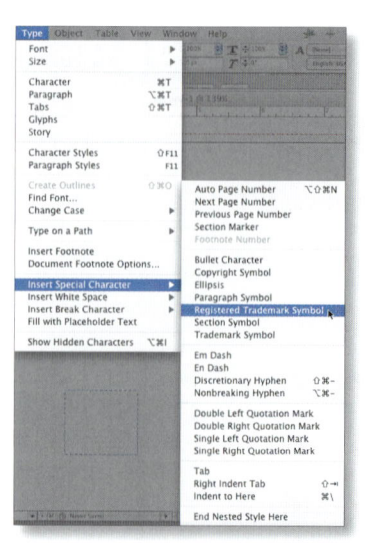

HOW TO USE GLYPHS

If you're reading this tip, and you're into typography, you already know that many fonts have glyphs (extra characters used in professional typesetting, like real fractions, alternate letters, swash letters, etc.). Well, you can find a font's glyphs and insert them directly by going under the Type menu and choosing Glyphs to bring up the Glyphs palette. From there, you can see all the alternate letters for the currently selected typeface, and if you want to insert one of those characters into your document, just double-click directly on the box that contains that character.

GLYPH CHARACTERS TOO SMALL? HEAD FOR THE MOUNTAINS

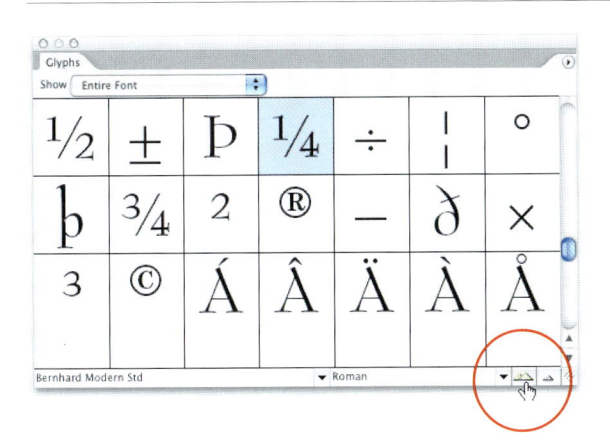

If the default size of the alternate characters in the Glyphs palette appears too small (and it is), just click on the left mountain button at the bottom of the palette and the characters will jump up to the next size. Click it again, they get even larger. To make the glyphs smaller, just click on the right mountain button. So give these mountains a couple of good clicks and this palette will be much easier to use.

CHAPTER 2 • Tweakin' Your Text   **45**

FIVE KEY SHORTCUTS FOR SELECTING TEXT

If you find yourself working a lot with type (especially if you're editing text), you can save loads of time by learning a few simple shortcuts for selecting type. For example:

1. To select an entire word, just double-click on it.
2. To select characters to the left of where your text cursor is located, just press Shift-Left Arrow. To select characters to the right, press (duh) Shift-Right Arrow. Each time you press the Shift-Arrow keys, it adds more characters to the selection.
3. To select a whole line of text, triple-click on it.
4. To select an entire paragraph, quadruple-click (it's easier than it sounds).
5. And last, Shift-Command-\ (PC: Shift-Control-\) selects the line where your text cursor is.

Use these five simple shortcuts, and you'll save more time every day than you'd ever imagine.

EDIT WHILE YOU CHECK SPELLING

The spelling checker may look like a dialog, but if you give it a closer look you'll find it's actually a floating palette. How is that different? Well, since it's a floating palette, you can be in the middle of a spell-check, leave the palette, make an adjustment to your document, and then go back to the Check Spelling palette and pick right up where you left off. We usually wind up doing this when we accidentally click the Ignore button—and right when we do, we realize we missed a misspelled word; so we leave the palette, manually type the correct spelling right into the document, then we return to the Check Spelling palette and finish the job.

SAVE TIME WHEN CHECKING SPELLING

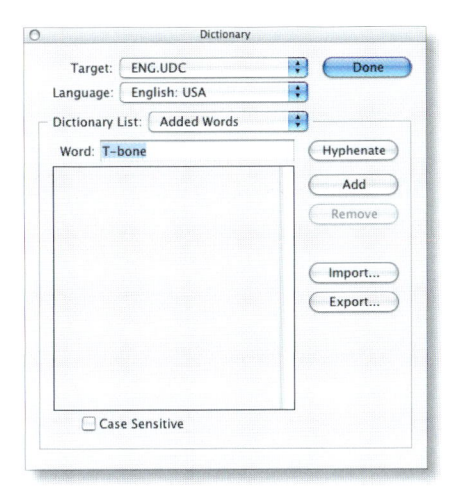

Like most spelling checkers, InDesign's checker lets you add words it doesn't recognize during the spell-checking process (words like your name or your company's name), but you'll save time if rather than waiting until these names come up during a spell-check, you enter them now, in the InDesign Dictionary. Go under the Edit menu, under Spelling, and choose Dictionary. This brings up a dialog where you can enter your name, your company's name, and other words that the built-in dictionary just won't recognize.

VOILÀ! THE TRICK TO SPELL-CHECKING FOREIGN LANGUAGES

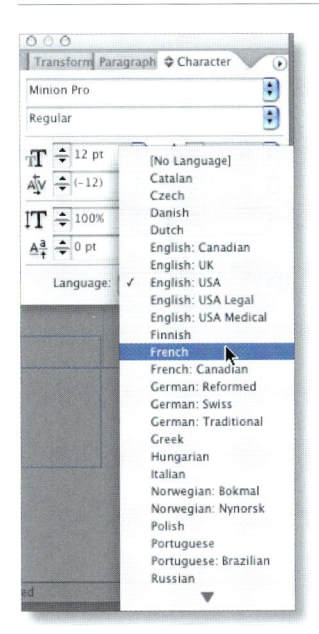

InDesign comes with a number of international dictionaries built right in, so if you're like Frasier and like to work as many French words and phrases as possible into everyday language, at least now you can make sure they're spelled right. Just highlight the French (German, Italian, Spanish, etc.) word you want to check, then go to the Character palette and at the bottom you'll see a pop-up list of languages (if you don't see this pop-up list, it means your Character palette's options are hidden, so just go to the palette's flyout menu and choose Show Options). The language is set to English: USA by default (at least ours is) so change it to French, which loads the French dictionary. Now you can use the Check Spelling palette (under the Edit menu, choose Spelling, and then Check Spelling) just like always, but now it'll check your French words. C'est magnifique!

CHAPTER 2 • Tweakin' Your Text

HOW TO STOP A WORD FROM BEING HYPHENATED

If you have a word that you never want to be hyphenated (some words like "inappropriate" or "invisible" generally shouldn't be hyphenated, because in these usages the prefix "in" stands for "not"), you can let InDesign know that's what you want by entering the word into the Dictionary (found under the Edit menu, under the Spelling menu) with a ~ (tilde) before the word and clicking the Add button. Once it sees that, it won't hyphenate that word.

IT'S OKAY TO USE THE BOLD SHORTCUT

Back in the olden days of digital layout programs, if you highlighted some text, then used the keyboard shortcut for bold, it looked for a bold version of your current font. If it didn't find a bold version, it would fake it. This usually looked horrible, but most people were working on pretty awful non-PostScript printers, so really—who cared? Worse than that, sometimes it looked bold onscreen, but that bolding went away when you printed the document. But InDesign is smarter than that. If you highlight some text and press the international standard for bold text: Shift-Command-B (PC: Shift-Control-B), InDesign will apply the next heaviest weight of your typeface. If there is no bold version of your current font, it will (get this) just ignore it. So basically, you're safe to use the shortcut—it won't burn you like it did in the old days. Same thing for italics: Press Shift-Command-I (PC: Shift-Control-I); if there's not an italic version, it'll just ignore it, but best of all, it won't show a fake italic onscreen.

48   CHAPTER 2 • Tweakin' Your Text

WHEN FONTS COLLIDE (HOW TO ADD LIGATURES)

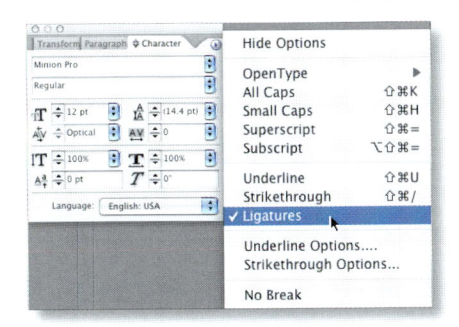

Certain lowercase letters, because of their design, collide (touch) when you use them side by side, such as the lowercase "f" and "i" in the word "finally." Typographers feel that collision looks really bad. It looks "inelegant" (if that's actually a word), so the type designers invented ligatures. Ligatures are custom-made combinations of two normally colliding characters that have been engineered into one beautiful character. They're designed to touch, but in an elegant way. Today, most professional quality typefaces include a set of ligatures; you just have to activate them by going to the Character palette's flyout menu and choosing Ligatures. It then looks for instances of lowercase letter combinations (like fi or fl) and converts them on the fly. If you want your type to look its best, you'll definitely want to start using ligatures.

SET TYPE JUSTIFICATION THE FAST WAY

You don't have to head to the Paragraph palette or Control palette to set your type as left justified, right justified, or centered because the keyboard shortcuts all use the first letter of the justification style. For example, for left justification use Shift-Command-L (PC: Shift-Control-L) and the "L" is for left. We're not going to embarrass you by telling you the other two—they're pretty obvious.

CHAPTER 2 • Tweakin' Your Text   49

INDENT PARAGRAPHS (HOW AND HOW MUCH)

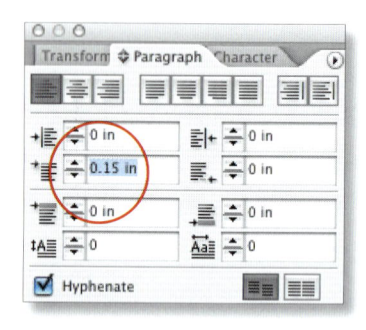

We use indents to tell the reader "Here's a new paragraph," and creating these indents is easy—just open the Paragraph palette (opening the Character palette will usually get you one click from the Paragraph palette, because they're nested together by default), then in the second field from the top, enter the amount you want for your indent. So, how much should you indent? It's up to you, but many professionals agree that the exact proper amount is the width of a capital "M" in the typeface you're using. (For example, the typeface we're using here is Myriad, and in that face an indent of .10 is approximately equal to one capital letter M. Now, personally, we think .10 isn't enough indent so we generally use a .15-inch indent for most of our standard body copy regardless of the typeface; but hey, that's just us.)

DOING A PULL QUOTE?
BETTER HANG THOSE QUOTE MARKS, BUNKY

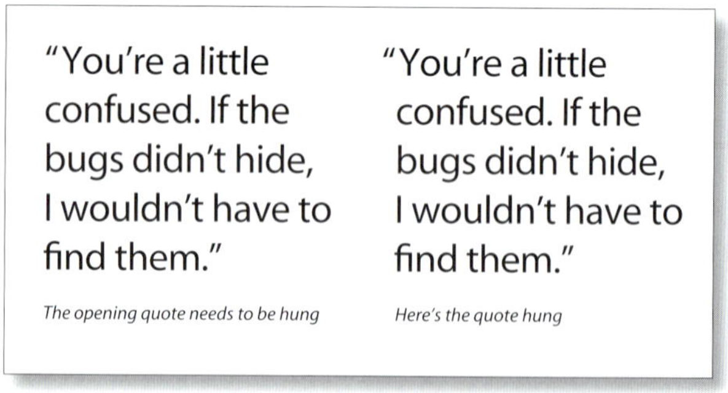

If you're pulling a quote out of some text (this is hugely popular in magazines), then you're going to have quotes around the text, right? Well, if you do this, the pros always (always) "hang" their punctuation. By hanging, we mean the opening quote literally hangs outside the text block to the left, as if it started one character before the actual text begins (you can see an example here). How important is hanging your quotes? Adobe made a separate palette just for it—the Story palette, which is found under the Type menu. When the palette appears (shown here), turn on the checkbox for Optical Margin Alignment, then enter the point size of your type, so it properly aligns your quotes. That's it, bunky.

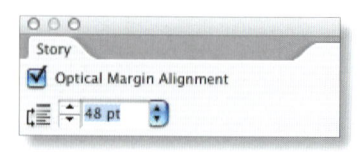

"You're a little confused. If the bugs didn't hide, I wouldn't have to find them."

The opening quote needs to be hung

"You're a little confused. If the bugs didn't hide, I wouldn't have to find them."

Here's the quote hung

CHAPTER 2 • Tweakin' Your Text

ADD DROP SHADOWS TO TEXT

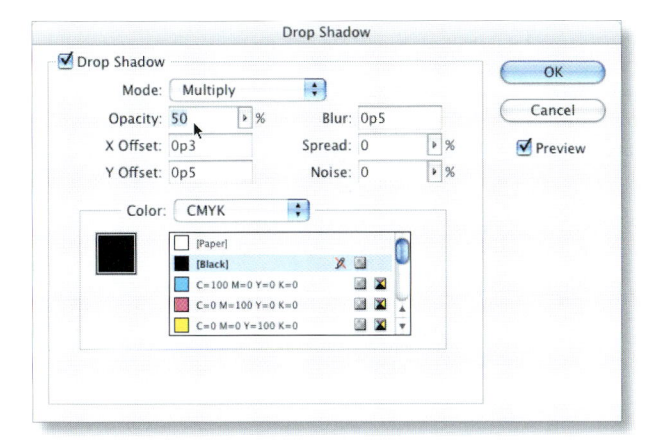

Want to add a drop shadow to your text? (If you do, make sure it's large display-sized text—something like 36 points or larger.) Select your text block with the Selection tool, then go under the Object menu and choose Drop Shadow. When the Drop Shadow dialog appears (by default it's turned off— I know, that doesn't make sense), you have to turn it on by clicking on the Drop Shadow checkbox at the top left corner of the dialog. Then you'll also want to turn on the Preview checkbox (it's off by default—don't get me started) so you can actually see what the shadow looks like before you click OK.

CHAPTER 2 • Tweakin' Your Text   51

MAKE YOUR TEXT FRAME FIT THE TEXT

If you've been using InDesign for a while (before the CS version), you are going to lose your mind with this little improvement. You know how you drag out a text frame, then you start typing in your text, but the text frame is always WAY bigger than the text, so if you want it to fit snugly, you have to resize the frame manually? Not anymore. Thankfully, Adobe felt your pain and now to fit your text frame snugly around your text, just switch to the Selection tool, go up to the Control palette, and click on the Fit Frame to Content button and suddenly your whole world makes sense.

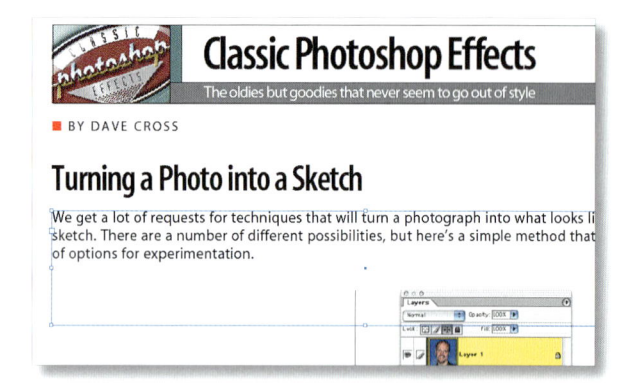

52   CHAPTER 2 • Tweakin' Your Text

HOW TO MOVE OBJECTS WHILE YOUR TEXT IS SELECTED

Okay, this may sound a bit esoteric, but it's more useful than you'd think. Here's a typical scenario: You highlight some text to adjust it, you start increasing the size of the text, and it starts to overlap another object on the page (a photo, a box, a graphic—whatever). So you have to switch to the Selection tool, move the object out of the way, and then switch back to the Type tool and re-highlight your text. A pain, right? Right. But instead, even while your text is highlighted, you can hold the Command key (PC: Control key) to switch temporarily to a mini-Selection tool so you can reposition the object while your text remains highlighted. Release the Command key (PC: Control key) and you're back to your Type tool, saving loads of time and aggravation. This is only one scenario where you'll use this—believe me, you'll find a dozen more.

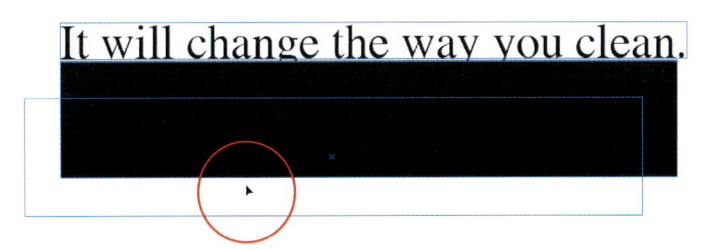

GET LIVE TEXT WRAP PREVIEWS WHILE YOU MOVE

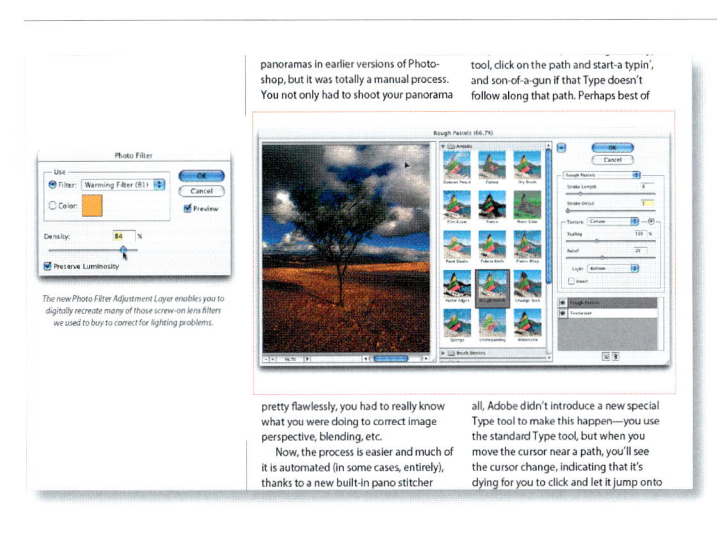

If you've applied text wrap to a graphic, and you move the graphic, it waits until you release the mouse button to "re-wrap." But if you'd like to see a live text wrap while you move your graphic, just click on the graphic and hold a moment before you drag; then when you drag, the text will re-wrap in real time as you move.

CHAPTER 2 • Tweakin' Your Text   53

APPLY GRADIENTS TO EDITABLE TYPE

InDesign is one of the few programs out there that will let you apply a gradient to type and have that type still editable (most require that you convert your type into a graphic before you apply a gradient; and once it's converted you can no longer change the font, leading, spacing, etc.). To do this "live type gradient," you just set your type, click on the text frame with the Selection tool to select it, then in the Toolbox click the Formatting Affects Text icon (the "T" just below the Fill/Stroke swatches). Now open the Gradient palette (it's found under the Window menu), create the gradient you want, and your type will be filled with that gradient.

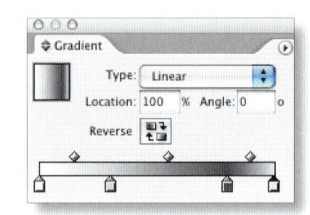

FASTER TEXT FRAME MOVING

If you're adjusting your layout, when it comes to moving your text frames around, it's good to know this little tip: If you click, hold, and drag a text frame, you'll see the text displayed as you drag; and because InDesign is rendering this text live as you drag, it moves slower. However, if you want to reposition text frames as fast as possible, don't click, hold, and drag—just click and immediately drag. Then InDesign only displays a "ghost" of the frame (the outline with no contents, shown here with a blue outline) and it moves at full speed.

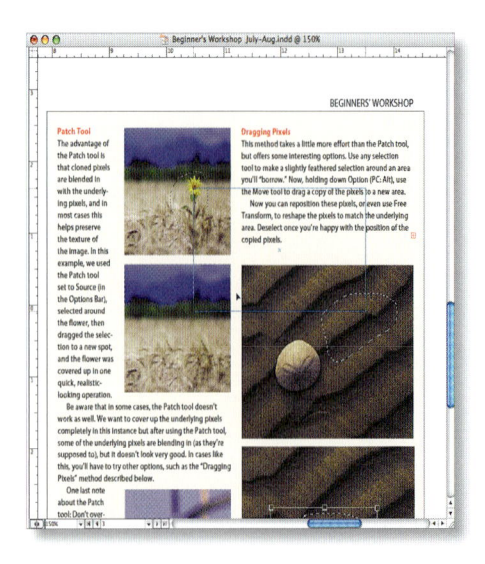

CHAPTER 2 • Tweakin' Your Text

GET THE GRABBER WHEN YOU'VE GOT THE TYPE TOOL

When you're working with any tool except the Type tool, you press the Spacebar to get the Hand tool (which you click-and-drag to move around your document), but when you have the Type tool there's a different shortcut—instead hold the Option key (PC: Alt key) when you have a text insertion point, and your Type tool will temporarily change into the Hand tool.

CHOOSE CUSTOM FONTS AND SIZES IN STORY EDITOR

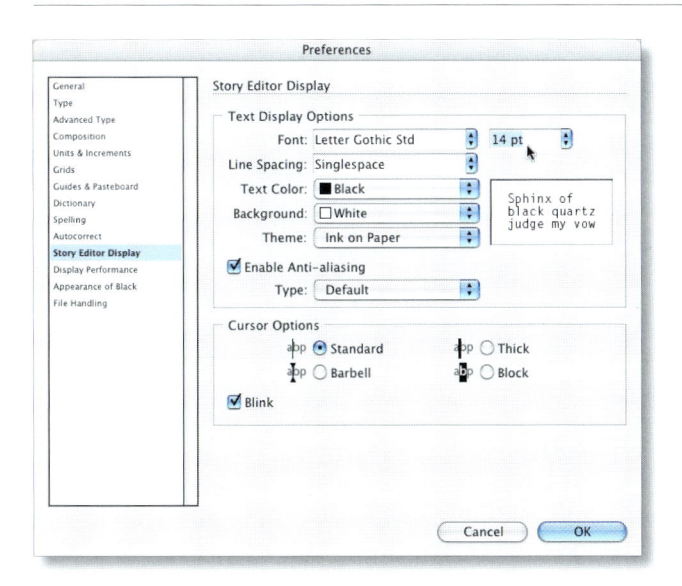

If you're using the Story Editor feature in InDesign (which means you're secretly an old PageMaker freak), then you'll be happy to know you have some control over the font and size of the Story Editor text display. Just go under the InDesign menu (PC: Edit menu), under Preferences, under Story Editor Display, and you'll find a host of controls, including font, font size, and even what your cursor looks like while you're in the Story Editor.

CHAPTER 2 • Tweakin' Your Text   55

ACCESS MASTER PAGE TEXT FRAMES ON A REGULAR PAGE

If you set up text frames on a master page in your document, those frames aren't accessible within a regular page. That is, unless you know this trick—just Shift-Command-click (PC: Shift-Control-click) on the text frame. This overrides the master page, so that frame is made active (as shown here), and a text frame placed on the master page becomes editable on a regular page.

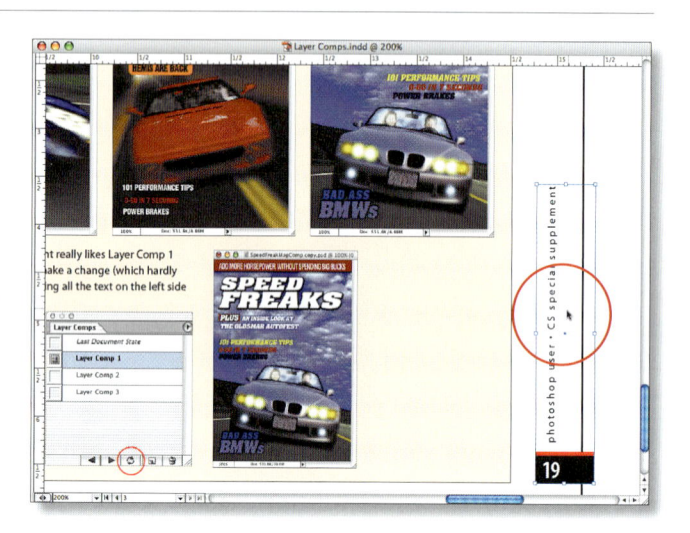

USE THE RIGHT DASH

Okay, if you're using InDesign, you're no longer typing on your computer. Now you're "setting type." Since you don't want it to be a dead giveaway that you're not a professional typographer, you'll need to use the right dashes—typographer's dashes (in other words, you'll only use hyphens to hyphenate words and that's it). For example, to express time (like "the party is from 8:00 p.m.–10:00 p.m.") you use an "en" dash, which is longer than a regular dash (or hyphen). You get an en dash by pressing Option-Hyphen (PC: Alt-Hyphen). When you've got an abrupt change in thought, but you don't want to end the sentence or use a comma, use an "em" dash, which is a really long dash—like that one there (usually used without a space—right up against the next letter). To get an em dash press Shift-Option-Hyphen (PC: Shift-Alt-Hyphen).

> Using a Hyphen
> The party is from 8:00 p.m.-10:00 p.m.
>
> Using an En Dash
> The party is from 8:00 p.m.–10:00 p.m.

56 CHAPTER 2 • Tweakin' Your Text

NOT JUST A SPACE. A "SPECIAL" SPACE

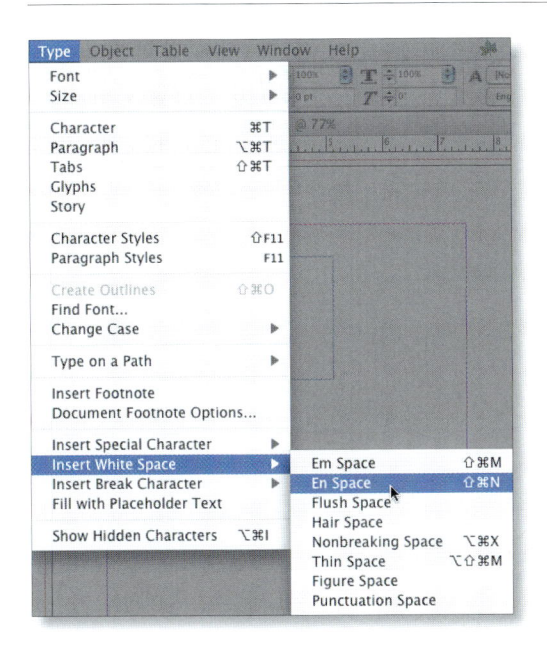

When you're working with type, sometimes a regular old Spacebar space is too big. Sometimes you need something less. A mini-space, if you will. Well, InDesign is chock-full of freaky, I mean "professional," spaces. You find them by going under the Type menu, under Insert White Space, and you'll find a whole submenu of spaces, including popular typographer's spaces like en and em spaces. My favorite is Hair Space. I have no earthly idea what it is, but I just like the name. (Okay, I do know—a hair space is just what it sounds like it would be: a really, really thin space that is $1/24$ the width of an em space. Ants use these fairly often.)

CHAPTER 2 • Tweakin' Your Text   57

Color Blind

WORKING WITH COLOR

Now why would anyone title a chapter about working with color "Color Blind"? Well, here's the thing. It's always been our credo (by the way, I have no idea what a

Color Blind
working with color

credo is) to title our chapters with the name of a song or a movie, and then below the title, the real description of the chapter appears as a subhead. Is this a good plan? No. But it's what we do (it's that credo thing again). So, is there a song named "Color Blind"? Yup (it's by Michael W. Smith). I originally wanted to use Color Me Badd, which was the name of a group that had some hits back in the 80s (remember "I want to sex you up"?), but I didn't think Color Me Badd sounded positive enough. Color Me Good has a better feeling, but I couldn't find a band named Color Me Good; so Color Blind, while not a stellar chapter name, won the nod. By the way, there's also a song named "Color Blind Dog" by Dishpan, and I briefly considered that as well, but I hate chapter names that make you feel sad (e.g., "That poor little dog," etc.).

DRAG FROM PALETTE TO PALETTE

Here's a nice time saver—if you've created a color in the Color palette, the quickest way to save that color to your Swatches palette is to just drag-and-drop it. Just click directly on the preview swatch in the Color palette, and drag that over to the Swatches palette. Again, you'll see the cursor change to a hand with a plus (+) sign, and a black horizontal line will appear in the Swatches palette right where your swatch will appear—all you have to do is let go of the mouse button and that custom color will now be saved as a color swatch in your Swatches palette.

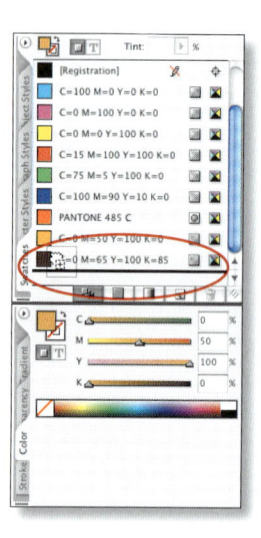

CREATE YOUR GRADIENTS WITH DRAG-AND-DROP

InDesign has a way to create your gradients—drag-and-drop. That's right, just grab a color swatch from the Swatches palette and drag it right onto a Color Stop in the Gradients palette and the stop takes on that color. Freaky!

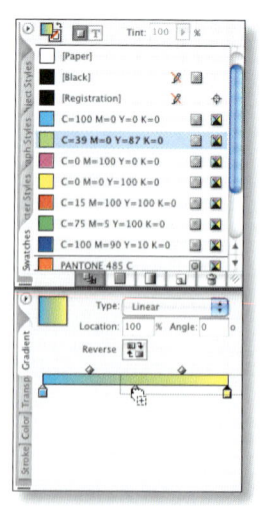

CHAPTER 3 • Working with Color

CREATE A DEFAULT SET OF COLORS

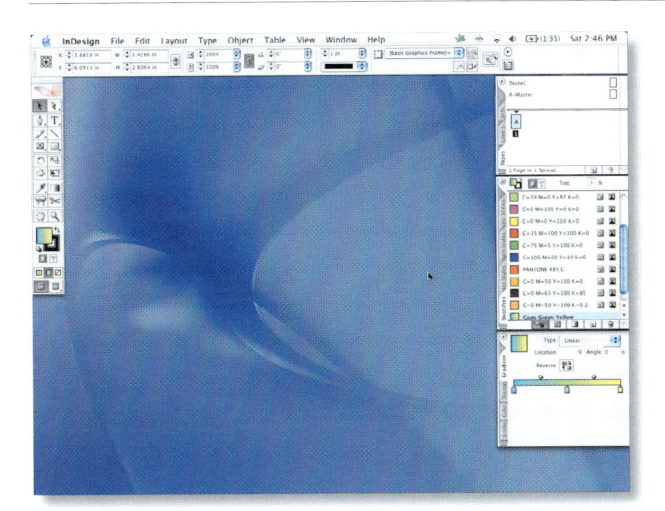

If you'd like a special set of custom colors to appear as your default colors (so every time you open a new document, those colors are already in place), it's fairly simple. Just close any open documents, then go to the Color palette, create your new colors, drag-and-drop them to the Swatches palette and you're done! The next time you open a new document (and for all future documents), these new custom colors are set as the default swatches.

STEAL COLORS FROM ANOTHER DOCUMENT

If you've taken the time to create some custom colors in one document, you can steal those colors, all at once, and move them into your new document. Here's how: Just go to the Swatches palette and from its flyout menu choose Load Swatches. When the Open A File dialog appears, navigate to the document you want to steal colors from, then click Open, and the swatches from that document will load into your currently open Swatches palette.

CHAPTER 3 • Working with Color   61

NOT JUST FOR TEXT STYLE SHEETS—BUT COLOR STYLE SHEETS TOO

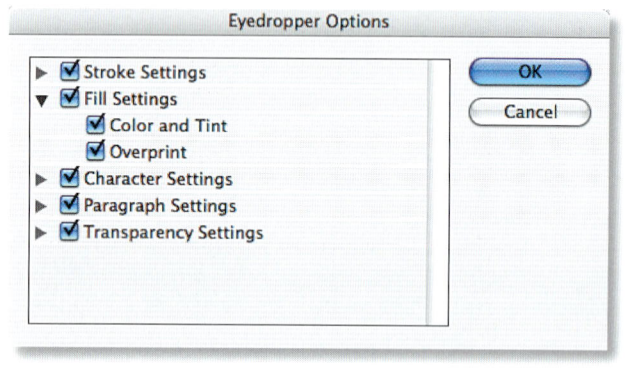

If you've painstakingly created a custom fill and stroke pattern for an object, and later on you want to apply those exact same specs to another object, you don't have to rebuild it all from scratch. Start by clicking on the new object, then get the Eyedropper tool and click on the object whose attributes (fill, stroke width, color, etc.) you want to steal. When you click, all those attributes will be applied to your new object. How do you control how many attributes the Eyedropper picks up? Just go to the Toolbox, double-click on the Eyedropper, and an Eyedropper Options dialog will appear (shown here) where you can choose which attributes it copies and which it ignores.

EYEDROPPER TRICK #2

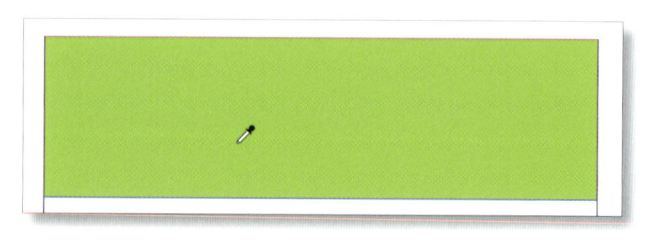

Okay, so you've applied the attributes of one object to another—now how do you sample a different object? If you click on it with the Eyedropper tool, it'll change to the attributes of the first object that you sampled from. Do you have to first switch to the Selection tool? Nope. While you have the Eyedropper tool, just hold the Option key (PC: Alt key) and then click on the new object, and rather than filling, it will sample those attributes of the second object.

62 CHAPTER 3 • Working with Color

SAVE TIME BY DRAGGING AND DROPPING COLOR

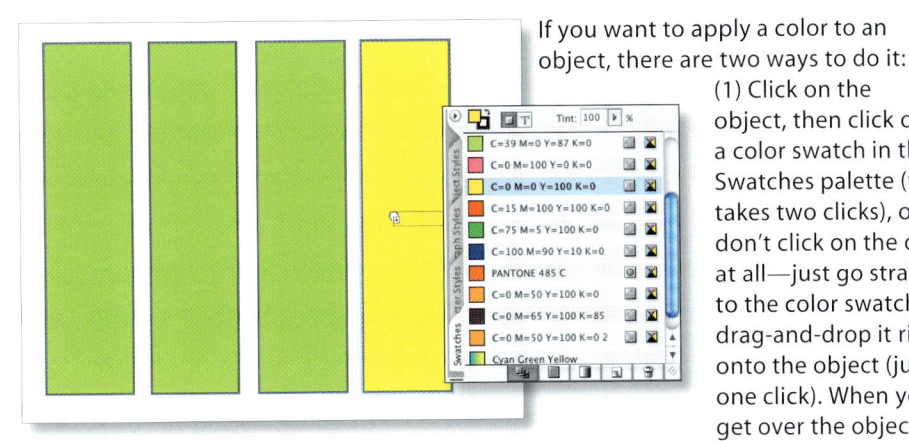

If you want to apply a color to an object, there are two ways to do it: (1) Click on the object, then click on a color swatch in the Swatches palette (which takes two clicks), or (2) don't click on the object at all—just go straight to the color swatch and drag-and-drop it right onto the object (just one click). When you get over the object you want to drop a color onto, the cursor will change to a hand with a plus (+) sign, so you know it has recognized that you're dragging and dropping color. This is a big time saver and as many times as we apply color, it can save you hundreds of clicks in no time.

DELETE MULTIPLE SWATCHES

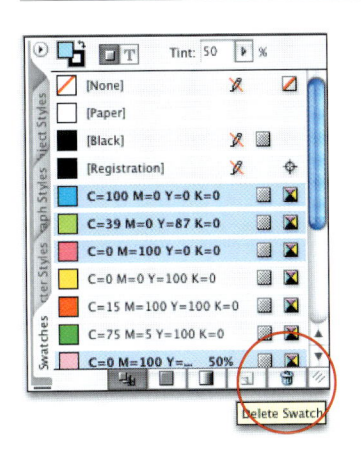

To delete multiple swatches from the Swatches palette, just hold the Command key (PC: Control key), click on all the swatches you want to delete (which selects them), then just click once on the Trash icon at the bottom of the Swatches palette.

CHAPTER 3 • Working with Color   63

IF YOU DIDN'T USE IT, LOSE IT

When you want to send your document to a printer or service provider, you should make the document as simple as possible to alleviate any potential doubt or confusion as to what you did. Therefore, you should delete any unused color swatches from the Swatches palette so that your printer will know exactly which colors are used in the document. InDesign has no single command to do this, but you can do it in two steps. Choose Select All Unused from the Swatches palette's flyout menu. This will highlight all your unused swatches, then just click the Trash icon at the bottom of the Swatches palette to delete them all in one click.

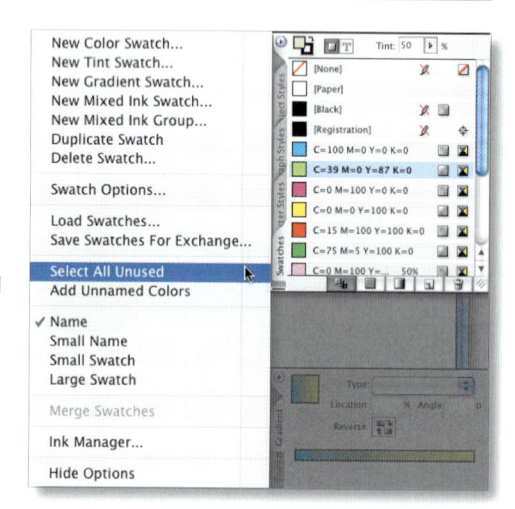

MERGE SWATCHES

An alternative way to delete swatches is to simply merge the swatches you don't want into one swatch you do want. Here's how: Start by clicking on the swatch you want to keep, then Command-click (PC: Control-click) on the swatches you want to delete. Now, to merge them go to the palette's flyout menu and choose Merge Swatches. All that will be left is the first swatch you clicked on (the one you wanted to keep) and the others are long gone!

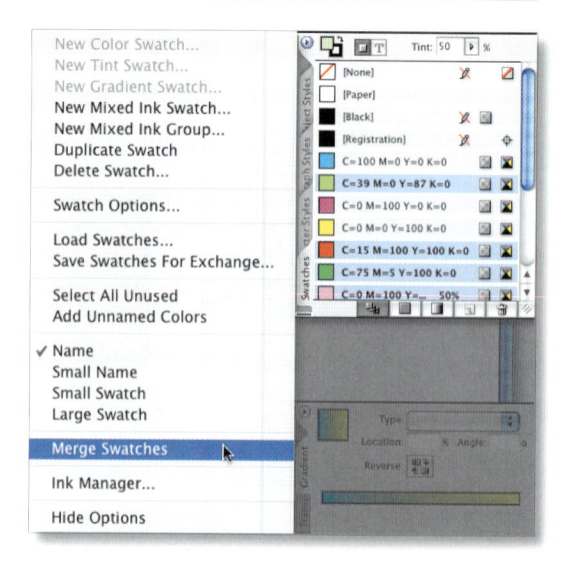

CHANGE THE ORDER OF YOUR SWATCHES

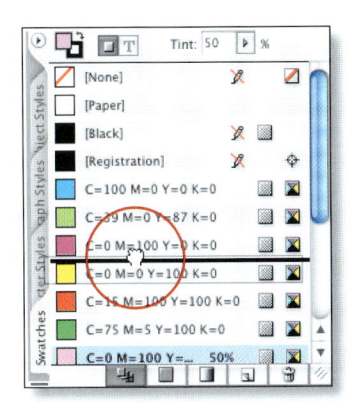

If you're familiar with Photoshop's Layers palette, you'll have no problem rearranging InDesign's color swatches because they work in a very similar manner. Just click on the swatch you want to move, and drag it up (or down) the Swatches palette to the location where you want it.

SAVE TINTS AS SWATCHES

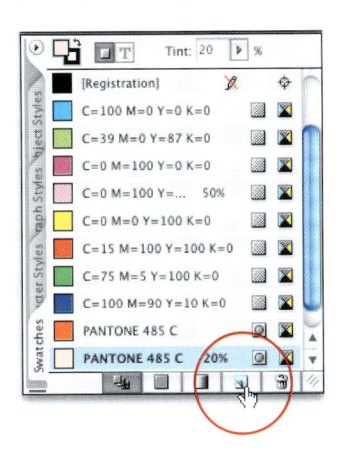

Creating a tint of the color currently selected in the Swatches palette is easy; just move the Tint slider at the top of the palette from 100% to a lower number. However, once you raise that Tint slider back up to 100% (perhaps you're now working on a different swatch), your tint is now long gone. To avoid that, you have to save your custom tint as a swatch—first click on the color you want to use as the tint base. Then use the Tint slider to create the tint you want. Once the tint looks right, click the New Swatch icon at the bottom of the Swatches palette and that tint is now saved as a totally separate color. Changes you make in the Color palette will no longer affect your tint because now it is saved as its own separate swatch.

CHAPTER 3 • Working with Color   65

InDesign CS/CS2
KillerTips

AVOID TINT WEIRDNESS

InDesign handles tints differently than you might think, and that's why we included this tip to keep you from experiencing tint "weirdness." The Tint control in the Swatches palette is really a "master" Tint slider because it applies the tint percentage to every swatch you click on. So if you click on one swatch, and lower the tint of that swatch to 62%, then you click on another swatch, that swatch also becomes a 62% tint. If you raise it back to 100%, you also just raised the previous swatch (the one you originally set to 62%) back to 100%. In fact, if you save a 52% tint as a swatch, and if you even as much as click on that swatch, it moves the master Tint slider to 52% for all your swatches. Yes, it's weird, but we thought you should know.

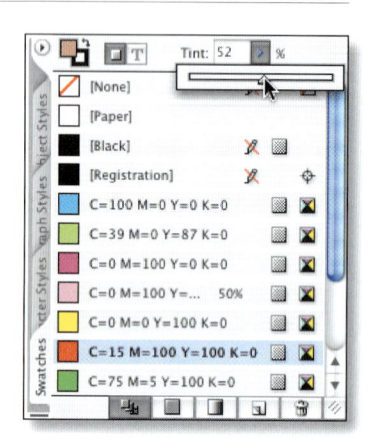

TINT WEIRDNESS #2

Just when you thought it couldn't get any weirder, there's this: Let's say you clicked on a purple swatch, lowered the tint to 40%, then saved it as its own separate swatch (so the Tint slider would no longer affect it). Then you did the same thing again for tints that are 20% and 30%. If you were to edit your purple swatch (let's say you added more red) it would automatically affect (or update, if you will) all your other tints. They're somehow tied to the "mother swatch." This can either be a cool feature or an annoying bug—it just depends on how you look at it.

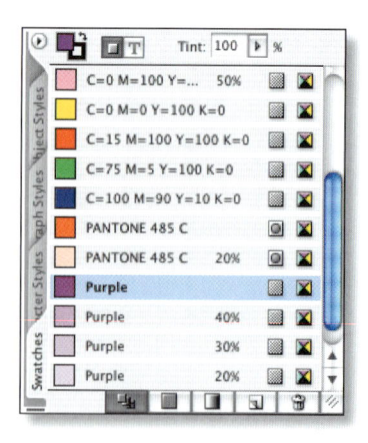

CHAPTER 3 • Working with Color

NAME COLOR SWATCHES AFTER THEIR VALUES

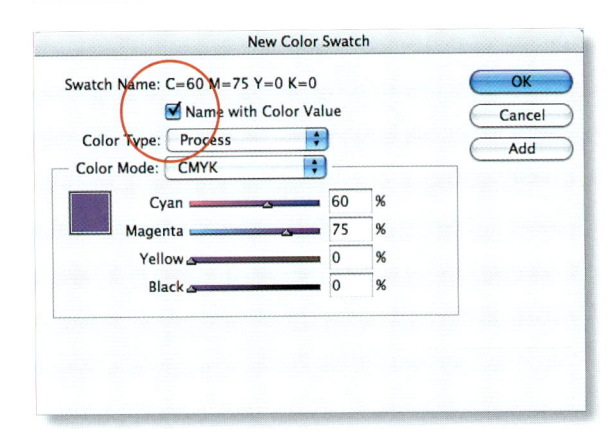

Do you ever get tired of trying to figure out or remember what colors you used in a previous layout? Are you trying to re-create that same shade of blue that worked so well for you last year? When you create a new process swatch in the New Color Swatch dialog, the box labeled Name with Color Value is turned on by default. This automatically names your swatch with the values of cyan, magenta, yellow, and black that you've used. It will also update if you go back later and change your mind.

HOW TO NAME SWATCHES (AND WHY YOU SHOULD)

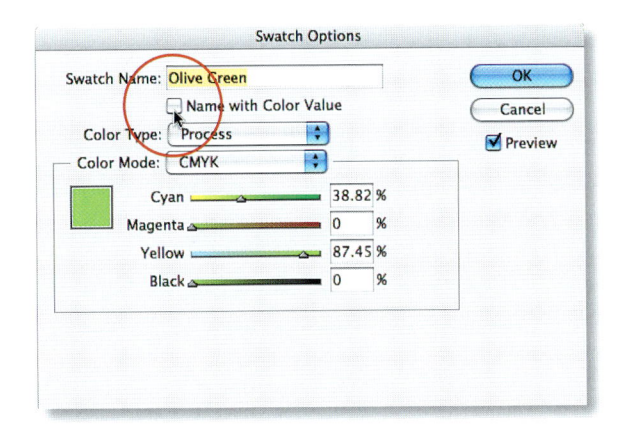

As mentioned in the previous tip, when you create a new color swatch, by default it's named using the build of the color (i.e., C=39, M=0, Y=87, K=0). Unless you're a prepress operator, it's not the most descriptive name. To rename it with a "human" name (like "Olive Green" or "Frank"), go to the Swatches palette and double-click directly on the swatch. That'll bring up the Swatch Options dialog. The Swatch Name field is not accessible until you turn off the Name with Color Value checkbox. Then a field appears where you can name the swatch. Besides sheer ease of use, if you're using spot color on a printing press, there's another reason to rename your swatches—so the pressman can figure out which colors to put on press, because spot colors aren't color builds like process colors.

CHAPTER 3 • Working with Color

LOAD THE PANTONE COLORS

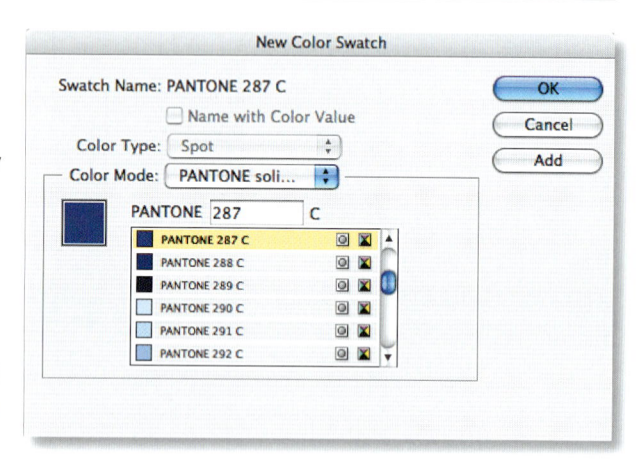

If you've been wondering where the Pantone colors are hiding, we can help. Go to the Swatches palette and from its flyout menu choose New Color Swatch. A New Color Swatch dialog will appear (shown here) and if you click on the Color Mode pop-up menu, you'll see a list of all the color libraries, which are installed with InDesign. Choose the one you want (in this case, PANTONE solid coated) and that set immediately loads. To choose a particular color, type the number in the PANTONE field.

IMPORT JUST A FEW, OR ALL, OF THE PANTONE COLORS

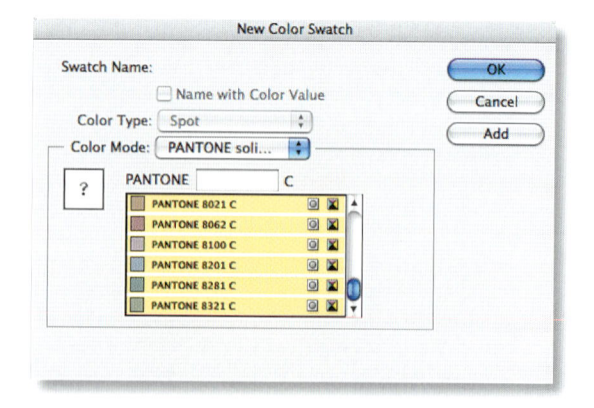

In the previous tip we showed you how to choose an individual Pantone color as your color swatch, but what if you want to import seven or eight Pantone swatches? What if you want to import them all? Here's how: To import multiple Pantone colors, go to the Swatches palette and choose New Color Swatch from the palette's flyout menu. Then from the Color Mode pop-up menu choose which Pantone color set you want. That set will load, and they will be displayed as a list in the dialog. Command-click (PC: Control-click) on the individual Pantone swatches you want to import, then click the Add button. If you want to import the entire Pantone set into your Swatches palette, click on the first visible Pantone swatch, then scroll to the bottom of the list, hold the Shift key and click on the last swatch, then click OK, and all the Pantone swatches in that set will load into your Swatches palette, where you'll spend the rest of your natural life scrolling through the hundreds of swatches.

CHAPTER 3 • Working with Color

InDesign CS/CS2
KillerTips

SPEED THROUGH THE SWATCHES PALETTE

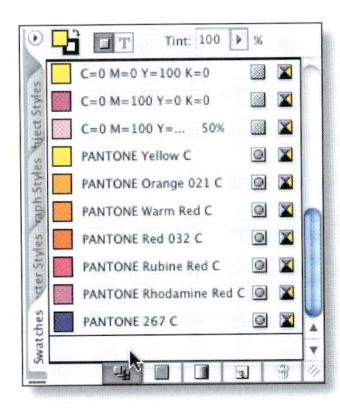

Want to get to a particular color in your Swatches palette in a hurry? Hold Option-Command (PC: Alt-Control) and click within your Swatches palette (you'll see a thin black highlight line appear around the list area of your Swatches palette). Now you can simply type in the first letter (or first few letters) of the name of the color swatch you want and it'll jump right to that swatch (this is yet another reason why you want to name your color swatches). This is particularly helpful if you've loaded an entire Pantone set.

THE SMART WAY TO EDIT SWATCHES

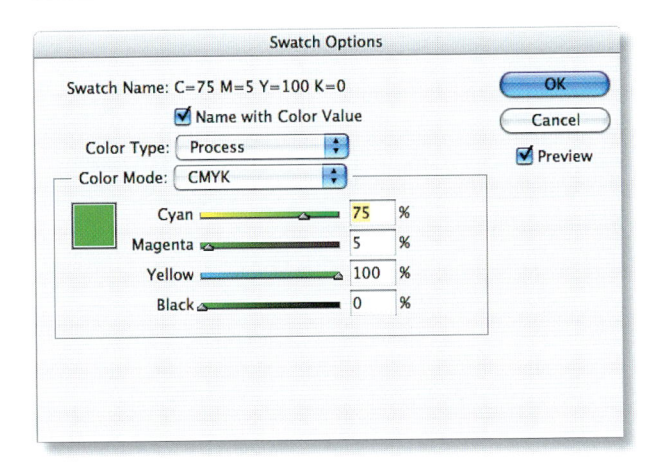

If you have objects selected in your document, you have to be careful about editing color swatches. If you simply head over to the Swatches palette and double-click on a swatch to edit it, in the split second before the Swatch Options dialog appears, all your selected objects will change to that color. But you can get around that with this important tip—before you double-click on a swatch, hold Shift-Option-Command (PC: Shift-Alt-Control). Then you can double-click on any swatch, edit the color, and not worry about affecting any selected object. (Of course, if you edit the color swatch for the selected objects, those objects will change color when you click OK, but you knew that, right?)

CHAPTER 3 • Working with Color   69

SPEED THROUGH THE COLOR RAMP

When you're using the Color palette, there's a ramp (spectrum) at the bottom of the palette where you can click directly on any color within the currently selected color model (RGB, LAB, or CMYK). You change which color model is selected by choosing it from the palette's flyout menu, but there's an even faster way—just Shift-click anywhere in the ramp, and the next color model will appear in the ramp.

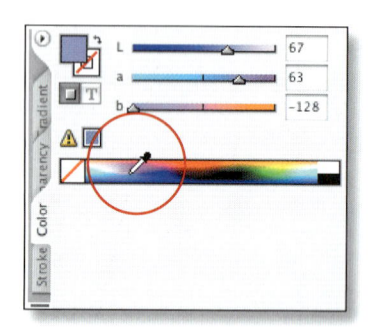

GET SOLID BLACK, OR SOLID WHITE, IN ONE CLICK

I know a lot of longtime users who didn't realize that if you're looking for solid white or solid black, there's a shortcut that will keep you moving at full speed. At the bottom of the Color palette is a color spectrum, and at the end of this spectrum are two swatches: one white, one black. If you need either color, go right there and you're one click away.

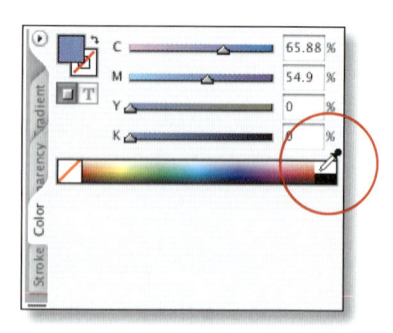

GET YOUR COLORS IN GAMUT WITH ONE CLICK

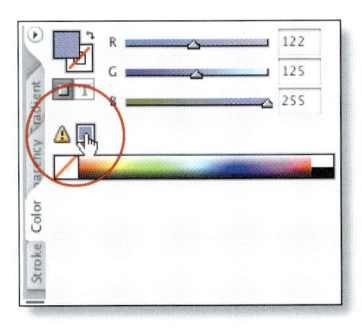

If you create a color that is out of the CMYK printing gamut (out of range of what a CMYK printing press can print), you'll see a little yellow warning symbol (shown here) appear just above the color spectrum in the Color palette. So the warning tells you it's out of gamut, but how do you get that color in gamut? Just click directly on the warning symbol, and it will give you the closest in-gamut color available.

CREATE PERFECT SHADES

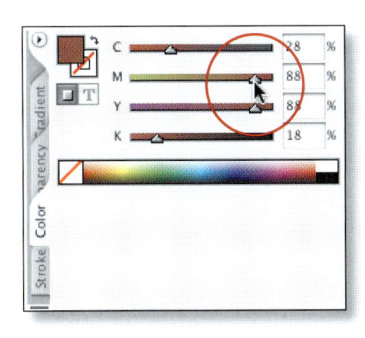

If you've created a color (using the Color palette, of course) and then you decide you want to see a lighter shade of that same color, here's a trick you'll love—just hold the Shift key, grab one of the color sliders (as shown here) and all the other sliders will move right along with it, giving you either a lighter shade (if you drag left with CMYK; right with RGB) or a more saturated version of the color (if you drag right with CMYK; left with RGB).

GET THE COLOR PALETTE INTO TINT MODE

Want to get the Color palette into tint mode fast (where it gives you the 100% to 0% Tint slider)? Just click on any swatch in the Swatches palette and the Color palette then switches immediately to tint mode (as shown here).

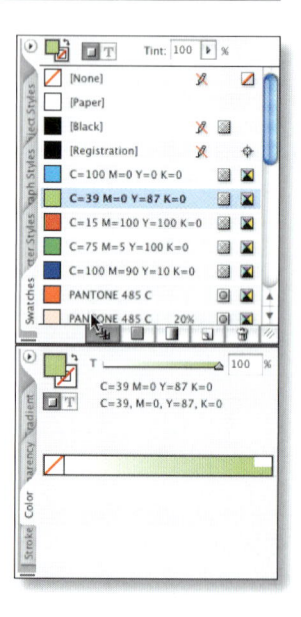

HELP WITH CREATING COLORS

Not sure which colors to mix to create an olive color? Look to the sliders, Luke. If you look in the Color palette, the sliders appear in color. That's not just for looks—those sliders show you exactly where to drag to get the color you want. If you're in CMYK and the sliders look black, lower the black amount until you can start to see some color. If you don't see olive there, drag the top slider to the left and look at the color sliders—is it closer or farther away from olive? In just a few seconds of experimenting, you'll probably see just which sliders you need to drag where. (Here's a hint—to get to olive, start with just the green slider, then add a little red.)

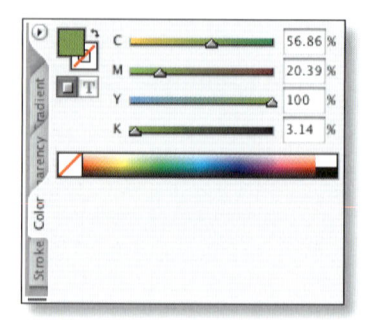

72   CHAPTER 3 • Working with Color

ONE CLICK TO NO FILL OR STROKE

Want to quickly set your current fill (or stroke) to None? Save yourself a trip to the Toolbox and just press the "/" (slash) key.

SWAP THE FILL AND STROKE

If you've been adjusting the stroke color and decide now you want to swap the fill color and the stroke color, you could of course head over to the Toolbox and click the Swap Fill and Stroke icon, or you could use this handy shortcut—Shift-X and it'll do it for you.

CHAPTER 3 • Working with Color

RETURN TO THE DEFAULT BLACK STROKE, NO FILL

The default settings for InDesign's stroke and fill are black for the stroke, and no fill (so if you were to draw a box, it would be empty in the middle, with a thin black stroke around it). To get back to these default settings anytime, press the same key as Photoshop uses to reset its default Foreground/Background colors—the letter "d." Of course, you could click the little Default Fill and Stroke icon (circled here) to return to the default colors, but who has time for that, eh?

DRAG-AND-DROP COLORS FROM THE TOOLBOX

Earlier we talked about how you can drag-and-drop color from the Swatches palette onto an object within your document; but you can do the exact same thing from the Toolbox—if you want to apply the current selected fill or stroke color, just click on the Fill or Stroke thumbnail and drag-and-drop it right where you want it.

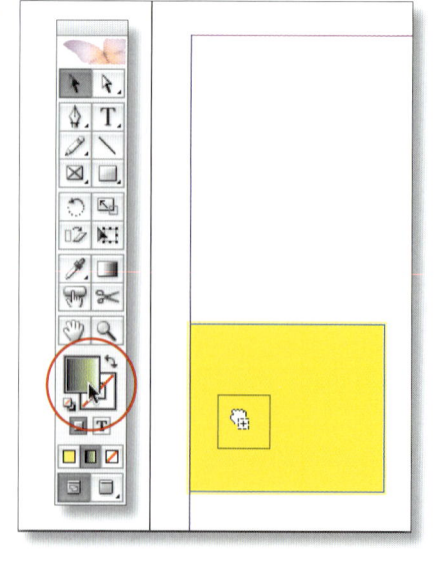

74   CHAPTER 3 • Working with Color

GET LIVE GRADIENT PREVIEWS

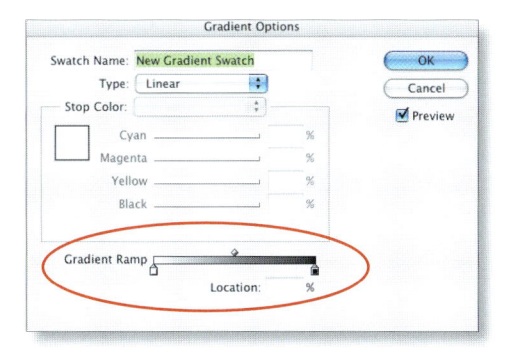

If you're creating a gradient to apply to an object (or text), once you've applied the gradient, you can adjust the gradient ramp and see how the adjustments will affect the selected object live, in real time. Here's how: Just click on the object that has the gradient applied, then go to the Swatches palette where you'll see your gradient selected. Double-click on it, and the Gradient Options dialog will appear (as shown here). At the bottom of the dialog is a Gradient Ramp with all your color stops. If you click the Preview button (it's off by default) the changes you make in this Gradient Ramp are updated live onscreen, saving you from having to guess how your changes will affect your object.

REAPPLY THE LAST-USED GRADIENT

If you recently applied a gradient, you can reapply that same gradient by selecting an object and just pressing the period (.) key. (That's a shortcut that keeps you from going to the bottom of the Toolbox and hitting the Apply Gradient icon shown here, which also applies the last gradient used.)

CHAPTER 3 • Working with Color   75

COLOR MANAGEMENT WHEN IMPORTING PHOTOS

If you've set up a color management system within Adobe Photoshop, InDesign can take advantage of it, including reading embedded color profiles of imported images and assigning color profiles. In InDesign CS2, color management is on by default. Go to Edit>Color Settings. From there, you can control how your images are color managed. What does that mean? That's a whole book unto itself. Check out Bruce Fraser, Fred Bunting, and Chris Murphy's *Real World Color Management* from Peachpit Press.

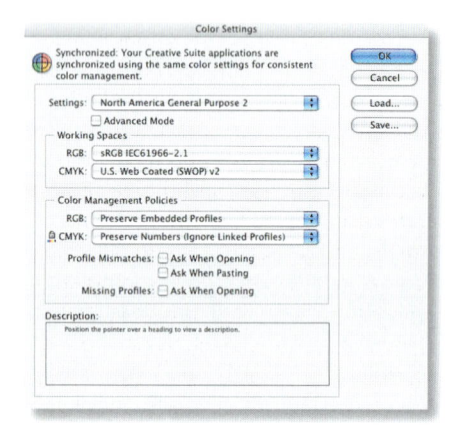

GRADIENT PALETTE SHORTCUT

Here's a quick way to get the Gradient palette open—just double-click on the Gradient tool in the Toolbox and it will pop right up.

MAKE SURE ALL THE COLORS IN YOUR BOOK MATCH

If you're creating a book, magazine, or other project that uses multiple documents, it's important that all your color swatches match exactly (in other words, you don't want one version of red in one section, and then a slightly different shade in another). Well, InDesign lets you make sure all your colors match exactly by syncing all the swatches in your separate documents together, so they're all using the exact same "red." Here's how: Go under the File menu, under New, and choose Book. Save your book (which brings up the Book palette), then press the + sign at the bottom of the palette to add the chapters you want sync'd together. Once you have all the chapters in your Book palette, choose Synchronize Book from the palette's flyout menu. By default, it not only syncs your color swatches, but it syncs your Character Styles and Paragraph Styles as well. (If you want to sync only your color swatches, choose Synchronize Options from the flyout menu and turn off the checkboxes for Character Styles and Paragraph Styles.)

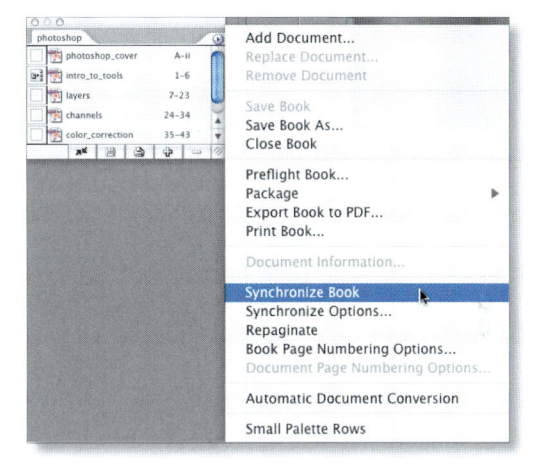

BLUE AND YELLOW MAKE GREEN

Takes you back to your elementary school days, doesn't it? Rather than getting out the finger paints, overlap two objects of different colors. Bring up the Attributes palette from the Window menu. Select just the top object and check the Overprint Fill box. When your document prints, the color on top will be mixed with the color below.

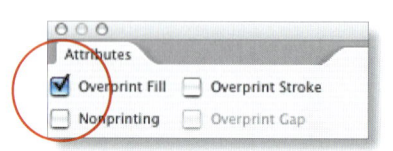

STOP PLAYING HIT-OR-MISS

Overprinting doesn't have to be a guessing game. Nor do you have to keep wasting color ink and paper. If you have objects set to overprint, simply choose Overprint Preview from the View menu to see exactly how those inks will be mixed together.

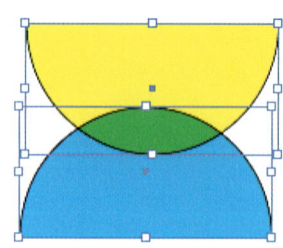

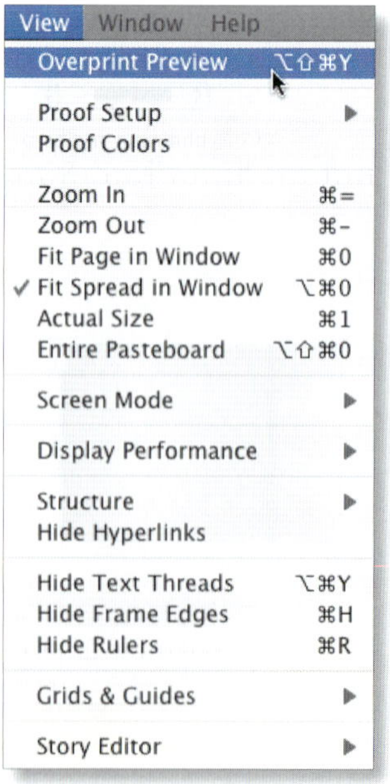

78   **CHAPTER 3** • Working with Color

CHAPTER 3 • Working with Color

Drawing Fire

DRAWING WITH INDESIGN

I know what you're thinking: "I didn't know you could draw with InDesign." Nobody does. Well, somebody does, but he's not talkin'. Actually, InDesign has a number

Drawing Fire
drawing with InDesign

of shape tools and a Pen tool, so you can draw quite a few things. Of course—it really helps if you know how to draw. If not, you'll wind up with a bunch of polygons, rectangles, circles, and the occasional oval. So, if you can't draw, should you still read this chapter? No. Don't read it.

Skip immediately to the next chapter and pretend this one doesn't exist. It's not for you. It's not intended for your viewing, so please do us all a favor and just move on before you create a scene. Now, why would we tell you not to read this chapter? To hook you. Now that we've told you not to read this chapter, you're definitely going to read it. You're dying to read it. It's killing you that there might be things in here, naughty things, that you're not supposed to read, so even though you can't draw as much as a stick-man, you're going to read every single line, every page, and drink it all up because you know there's more to this chapter than we're letting on. See, you're smarter than we thought.

CHAPTER 4 • Drawing with InDesign   **81**

EDIT ONE OBJECT IN A GROUP

If you've grouped some objects together and you need to scale (or edit) only one of them, just get the Direct Selection tool (the hollow arrow) and click on the object you want to edit; that one object will be selected, rather than the entire group. In the example shown here, we selected one circle within the grouped image, changed the color, and increased its size.

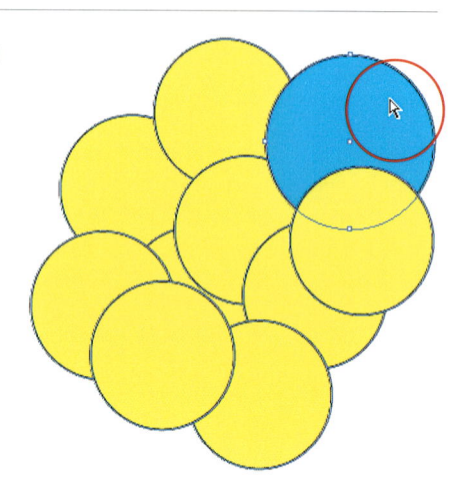

TURN YOUR FONT INTO A GRAPHIC

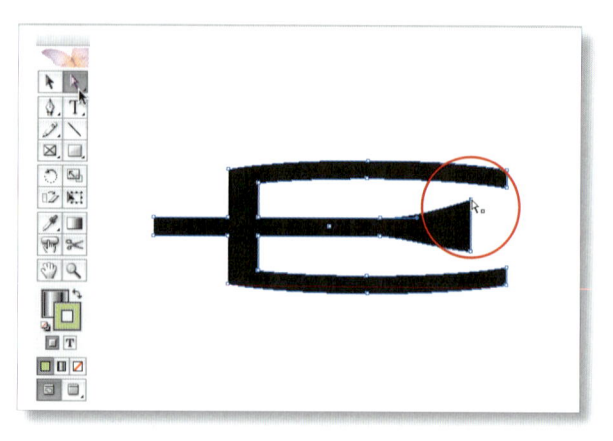

Want to do some freaky things to your type? Then you'll have to convert it from type into a graphic—and at that point, the rules of typography go out the window. You can stretch, squeeze, distort, and torment your type just as you would any other graphic object. To do this, select your text, then go under the Type menu and choose Create Outlines. This changes your type into paths (as if you had drawn each letter manually with the Pen tool); because it now has paths, you can use the Direct Selection tool (as shown here) to grab points and extend them (for creating custom type logos) or use the Pen tool to add, subtract, and otherwise edit its anchor points.

82 CHAPTER 4 • Drawing with InDesign

SMOOTH OUT THOSE JAGGY PATHS

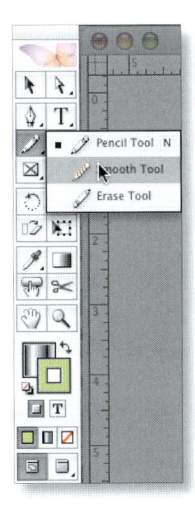

Got a jaggy path? (It happens all the time, especially if you're drawing your paths with a mouse instead of a Wacom graphics tablet.) The problem is usually caused by having too many points (which makes things look jaggy, rather than nice and smooth). Well, you can fix those jaggy paths with the seldom-used (but very powerful) Smooth tool. Get the Smooth tool from the Toolbox (it's under the Pencil tool—which is probably why nobody's found it) and just trace over areas of your path that have too many points. It removes any extraneous anchor points while trying to keep your original shape as intact as possible. Try it once and you'll see what we mean. It's smooooooth!

ADD SOFT EDGES TO OBJECTS

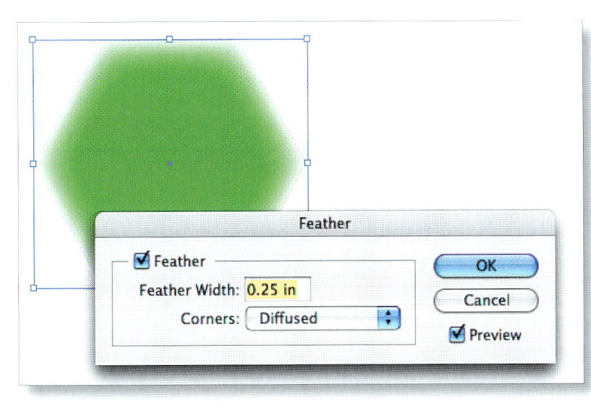

If you want to add a soft edge effect to an object, just Control-click (PC: Right-click) on the object and choose Feather from the pop-up menu that appears. This brings up the Feather dialog (shown here), where you can enter the amount of feathering you'd like (the higher the number, the softer the edges of your selected object will appear). Also, the Preview checkbox is off by default (don't get me started), so to actually see what's happening as you apply the feathering, click this Preview checkbox.

CHAPTER 4 • Drawing with InDesign   83

BACKSCREENING EFFECTS

If you want to put text that is easily seen over a photo in InDesign, then you'll want to know this backscreening trick. Just use the Rectangle tool to draw a rectangle over the area of the photo where you want text to appear. Fill this rectangle with white (or paper) from the Swatches palette, then go under the Window menu and choose Transparency to bring up that palette. Lower the opacity (as shown here) so you can see the photo behind the box. Now you can add your text and it will be easily seen over the photo.

HOW MANY SIDES WITH THAT POLYGON?

If you want to specify how many sides your polygon will have before you draw it, just double-click the Polygon tool, which is found under the Rectangle tool in the Toolbox, to bring up the Polygon Settings dialog (shown here). You can enter how many sides you'd like your polygon to have, and how "pointy" you want each side to be (using the Star Inset field).

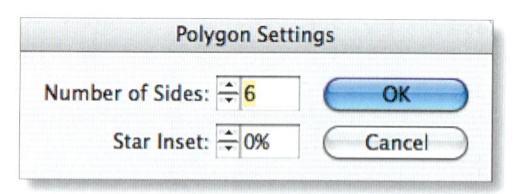

CHAPTER 4 • Drawing with InDesign

ADJUST POLYGON SIDES AND POINTS ON THE FLY

There's a little-known polygon shortcut that lets you adjust the number of sides to your polygon while you're creating it. While you're dragging (and you must be dragging—it doesn't work if you're stopped), just press the Up Arrow key on your keyboard to increase the number of sides, and the Down Arrow key to decrease them. You can also adjust how "pointy" your polygon is by pressing the Left and Right Arrow keys as you drag.

EXPERIMENT WITH SIZE

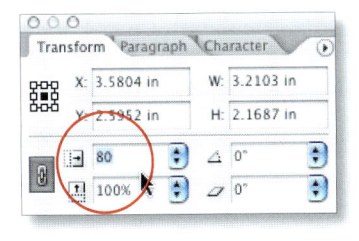

If you're resizing an object and you're not sure of the exact percentage you want to scale up (or down, for that matter), here's a tip that can save you some time. Once you've entered your percentage in either the Control or Transform palette, don't just press Enter. Instead, press Shift-Enter. That way, it applies the scaling, but if it's not the right amount (and if you're guessing, your first guess probably isn't) the scaling field remains highlighted; so you can simply type in another guess without having to re-highlight the field manually. Yeah, it's a small thing, but things like this add up fast.

CHAPTER 4 • Drawing with InDesign   85

THE SUBTLE ART OF FRAME SCALING

Here's a really helpful tidbit that can save you lots of time and aggravation. If you've created a frame and imported a graphic into it, and then you want to scale the frame, the tool you use makes all the difference. What I mean by this is if you click on a frame with the Selection tool (the black arrow), when you scale the frame (by pressing Shift-Command [PC: Shift-Control] and dragging), it scales both the frame and the object inside it at the same time. However, if you switch to the Direct Selection tool (the hollow arrow) and click in the frame, it scales only the graphic inside the frame and not the frame itself. (Although it looks as if the frame is scaling along with it, when you switch back to the Selection tool and click on the frame, you'll see that the frame is still the same size, but the graphic inside has been scaled up.) See, it's the little things.

DON'T COPY AND PASTE IT—DUPE IT

If you want a duplicate of an object or text block, don't waste time copying and pasting (it's way too slow). Instead, just Option-click (PC: Alt-click) on the object with either the Selection or Direct Selection tool and drag yourself off a duplicate (it's called "drag copying"). When you hold the Option (Alt) key and click, your cursor changes into a double-arrow (as shown here) to let you know you're about to "drag copy." When you do this, you just see a copy of the duplicated frame (as shown) until you release the mouse button, and then you'll see the frame's contents.

86   CHAPTER 4 • Drawing with InDesign

SELECT AN OBJECT BEHIND ANOTHER OBJECT

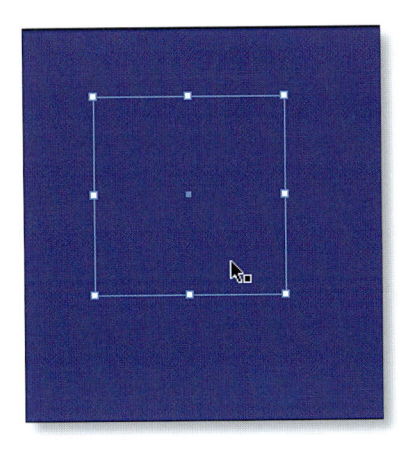

If you want to move an object (some text, a graphic, whatever) but that object is covered by another object, just Command-click (PC: Control-click) on the covering object and the object directly behind it will become selected (as shown in the example). If the top object is covering more than one object (in other words, there are objects layers-deep behind it), keep Command-clicking (each click selects the next object back) until the object you want becomes selected. (Here we've selected a square behind a dark blue object.)

SELECT AN OBJECT BEHIND ANOTHER (VERSION 2)

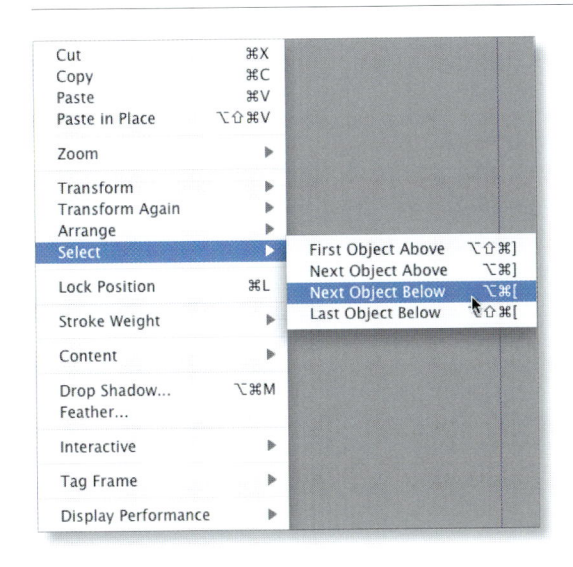

Another quick way to select an object that is behind another object is to Control-click (PC: Right-click) on the top object and from the pop-up menu that appears, go under Select and choose Next Object Below (as shown here).

CHAPTER 4 • Drawing with InDesign   87

SEND OBJECTS FORWARD OR BACKWARD

If one object is covering another object, you can send the top one behind the covered one by clicking on the top object and pressing Command-[(PC: Control-[). This sends the top object backward. In the example shown here, the star was covered by a large blue square, but we clicked on the square and used the shortcut to send that object back behind the star, making it visible (as shown). If at this point you want the blue box to cover the star again, just click on the box, then press Command-] (PC: Control-]) to bring it forward.

KEEP ON SENDING OBJECTS FORWARD AND BACKWARD

Another way to move objects in front of or behind other objects is to select the top object, then Control-click (PC: Right-click) and in the pop-up menu that appears, go under Arrange and choose Send Backward to move the current object back one level, or choose Send to Back to move the object as far back as it can go on that layer (meaning no other objects are behind it).

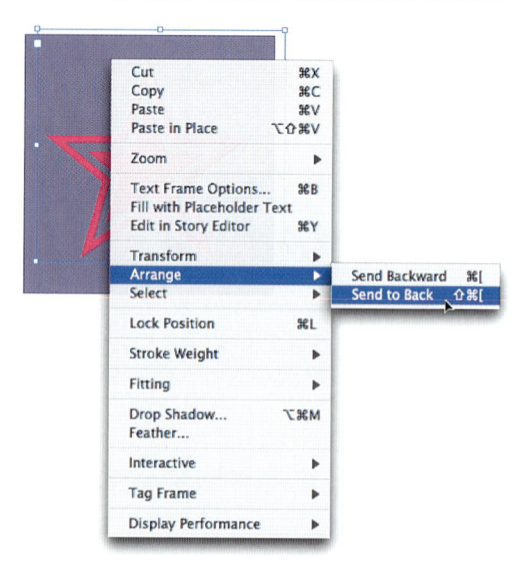

88   CHAPTER 4 • Drawing with InDesign

SET YOUR DEFAULT FILL AND STROKE COLORS

InDesign's default fill and stroke settings are no fill with a black stroke, but you can change that to anything you'd like. Just launch InDesign but don't open any documents. While no documents are open, go to the Swatches palette, click on the Fill icon and choose your new default fill color, then do the same for the stroke. These are now your default settings.

AUTO ADD/DELETE PATH POINTS

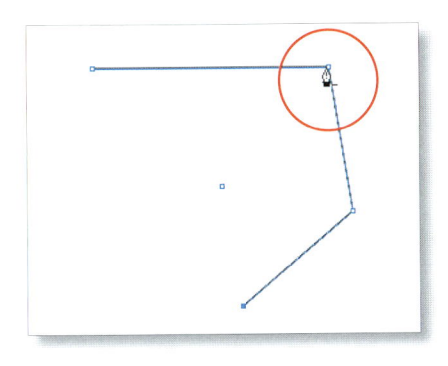

If you're drawing a path with the Pen tool and you decide you want to delete a point you've created, you go back to the Toolbox and choose the Delete Anchor Point tool, right? You don't have to. You can add and delete points using the regular Pen tool; and best of all, you don't even have to memorize a shortcut—just move your Pen tool over an existing point and it immediately changes to the Delete Anchor Point tool (as shown here)—so you can just click on that point and it's gone. Want to add a point? Just move your Pen tool directly over an existing path and it immediately turns into the Add Anchor Point tool, so you can just click to add a point. Move away from the path, and you're back to the regular ol' Pen tool.

CHAPTER 4 • Drawing with InDesign   89

MOVE JUST ONE SIDE OF YOUR CURVE

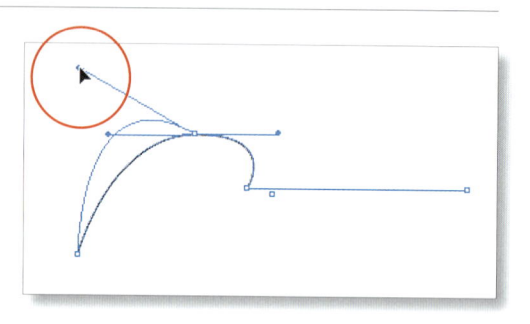

If you've created a curve using the Pen tool, when you go to adjust that curve you'll see two direction lines. They kind of work like a teeter-totter in that when you adjust the direction point on one side of the line, the other side of the line moves in reaction (one side goes up, the other side goes down). But there's a little-known trick that lets you adjust just one side of the direction lines, leaving the other side undisturbed. Just press Shift-C to switch to the Convert Direction Point tool, then use it to click on one direction point on one of the direction lines (as shown here). Now when you make your adjustment, it affects only that one side. This, my friends, will change your life (well, at least your life as it relates to editing paths).

HOW TO STOP ONE PATH AND START ANOTHER

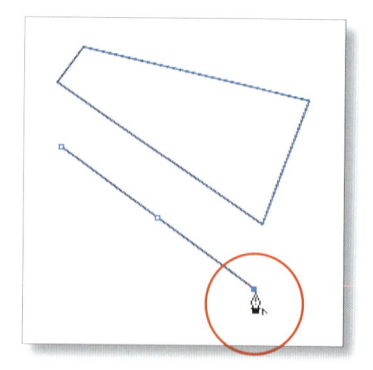

If you're drawing an open path, and want to stop drawing that path and move on to another (without actually closing the old path), try this: Move your cursor to an area away from your original path and Command-click (PC: Control-click). This deselects the first path, and now you're ready to move on to your next path.

90   CHAPTER 4 • Drawing with InDesign

HOW TO REMOVE ONE DIRECTION POINT FROM A CURVE

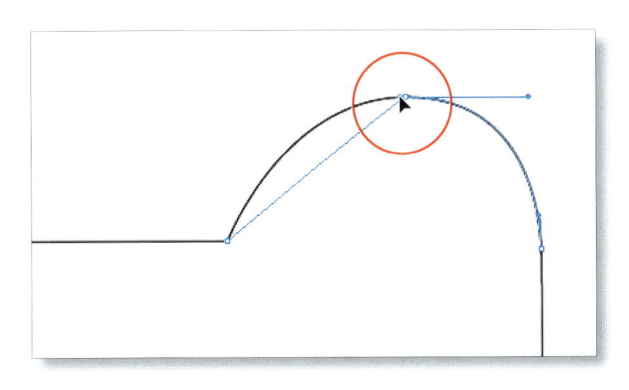

Ya know how curve anchor points have two direction lines and two direction points? Well, they don't have to—if you prefer that just one side of the curve is curved and the other side is straight, you can delete the other side of the curve. Here's the trick: Use the Direct Selection tool to select the anchor point of the curve that has the direction line you want to delete, then drag the direction point back in toward the center until it actually touches the curve's anchor point. You're basically just tucking it back in. When it hits that anchor point—it's gone—that side of the curve now becomes a straight segment (as shown here).

CUTTING THE CHEESE (OR MAKING A PERFECT HALF CIRCLE)

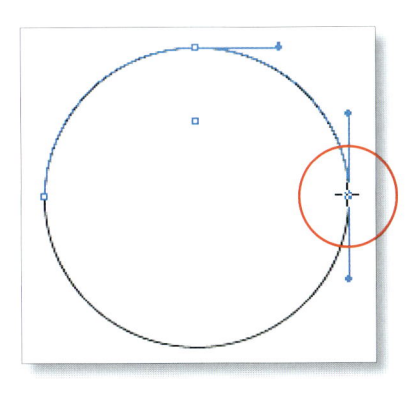

If you've ever tried to draw a half circle, you know how frustrating it can be. This tip will make you look like an expert with the Pen tool (even though you won't be using the Pen tool at all). Use the Ellipse tool to draw a perfect circle (hold down the Shift key to constrain it as you're drawing it). Then use the Scissors tool to click (cut) the two side points. You can simply delete the half that you don't need, and you will end up with a perfect half circle.

CHAPTER 4 • Drawing with InDesign

POINT IT OUT

When simple lines aren't enough to make your point, draw an arrow instead. Well, you can't actually draw an arrow; okay, you *could*, but who wants to? Draw a line and then go to the Stroke palette and make sure that you have chosen Show Options in the Stroke palette's flyout menu. Using either the Start or End pop-up menu, choose the arrowhead or tail that you like best. Make sure that your stroke Weight is high enough to show the stroke and arrowhead that you desire.

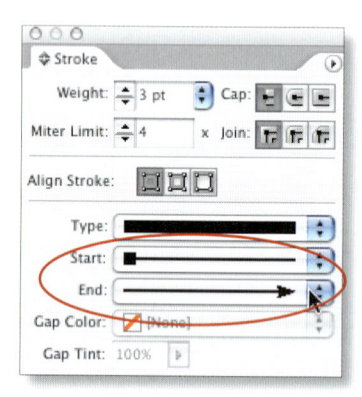

InDesign CS/CS2
KillerTips

CHAPTER 4 • Drawing with InDesign

Turn The Page

WORKING WITH PAGES →

This is a big chapter. And by big I mean large. Do you see where I'm going with this? Because honestly, I have no idea whatsoever. Well, I have some idea, but I'm still

Turn the Page
working with pages

forming it as I go. In the meantime, this chapter is all about working with page layout, adding pages, changing pages, numbering pages, mastering pages, and even mastering master pages (and I'm not even sure that's a real thing). Now, what if you only work with single-page documents and therefore you never really "Turn the Page"? You still have to read this chapter. Why? Because at the end of this chapter we have a drawing for some fabulous prizes (selected especially for you), so make sure you put your business card in the box at the door when you're finished so you're entered in the drawing. (By the way, if you asked yourself anything along the lines of "Where's the door?" or "Did I remember to bring my business cards?" perhaps working with pages isn't your biggest concern.)

DRAG PAGES FROM ONE DOC TO ANOTHER

This feature of InDesign is very, very slick. If you want to copy a page from one document to another, you can literally drag-and-drop it. Here's how: Start by making sure both documents are open onscreen, then go to the Pages palette, click on the page you want to copy, and then drag-and-drop it right into the new page area (you know—the area within the margins) and the page will be copied into that document. That is mighty cool!

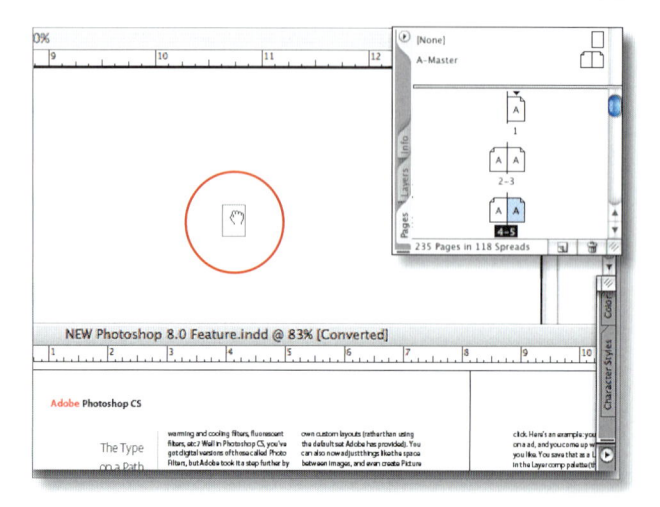

WHEN ONE MASTER PAGE JUST DOESN'T CUT IT

Yeah, I know what you're thinking, you could just create two master pages, but hierarchical master pages kick multiple master pages' butt! Let's say that you're doing pages for a catalog and all of the pages will have your logo, website URL, and a color bar. However, the catalog will also be divided into sections and each section will have the section name on the color bar as well as other things that pertain to only that section. This tip will make that chore child's play. Create your first master page using the default A-Master Page that will be used throughout the document. Then, create your master page for the first section by choosing New Master from the Pages palette's flyout menu. Now drag the first master page you created on top of the section master page, and your section master page will have all the elements on it from both master pages. When you make changes to the main master page, those changes will ripple through all your sections, too.

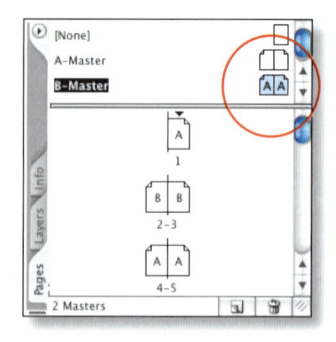

96 CHAPTER 5 • Working with Pages

BE FLEXIBLE WITH THE SIZE OF YOUR LAYOUT

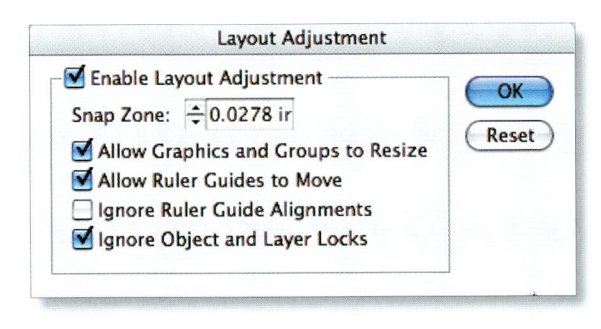

Change is inevitable and nothing is more frustrating than having to change your layout's dimensions. Say that suddenly the layout needs to change from tall to wide. Yikes! Rather than struggling to reposition all your elements manually, try this tip next time you need to make severe page size or orientation changes: Choose Layout Adjustment from the Layout menu and check the box labeled Enable Layout Adjustment. Now when you change your page orientation or dimensions, InDesign will do its best to keep everything positioned the way it was, but moving and resizing things to fit on the new layout.

SPREAD BEYOND TWO PAGES

The next time you need to create a gate fold, try this tip: Open the Pages palette and turn off Allow Pages to Shuffle in the palette's flyout menu. Now when you drag pages next to each other in the Pages palette (you have to drag a page almost on top of the existing page until you see a black vertical bar, as shown in center), they will stay next to each other. Gate folds are typically three side-by-side panels. This tip lets you achieve that look.

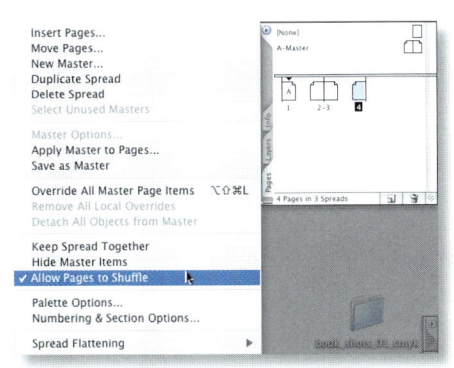

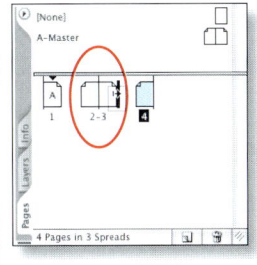

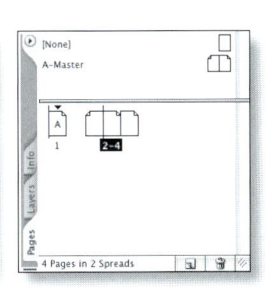

CHAPTER 5 • Working with Pages   97

MAKE IT A TEMPLATE

If you're creating a document that is published repeatedly, you might want to consider making templates of your documents rather than opening them and performing a Save As each time. Templates are more efficient and less likely to corrupt on you as time goes by. As you open and save the same document again and again, you could have a problem that continues to build every time the document is used. With a template, you start fresh each time. Make all the frames and elements in your document that will be used each time it's published. Then choose Save As from the File menu. Change the Format pop-up menu to InDesign CS2 Template and click Save. The next time you need to work on the publication, just open the file through the File menu and it will open "untitled" and fresh.

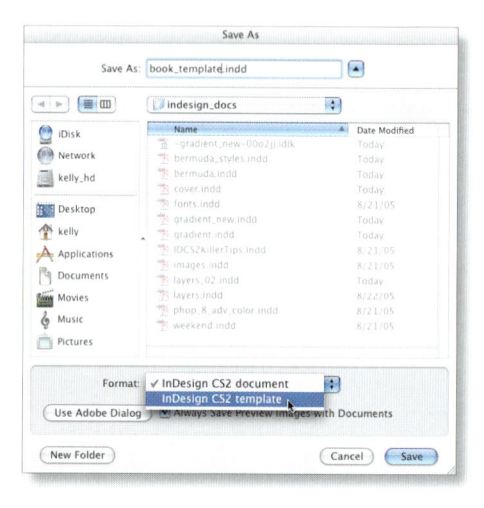

UNDERESTIMATING THE PAGE COUNT

Okay, you need to add more pages. You've searched frantically under the menus and don't see a way to do it. For some reason, Adobe doesn't think that adding pages should be a menu command. Go to the Pages palette and either click the Create New Page icon at the bottom of the palette or use the Pages palette's flyout menu and choose Insert Pages to add more than one at a time.

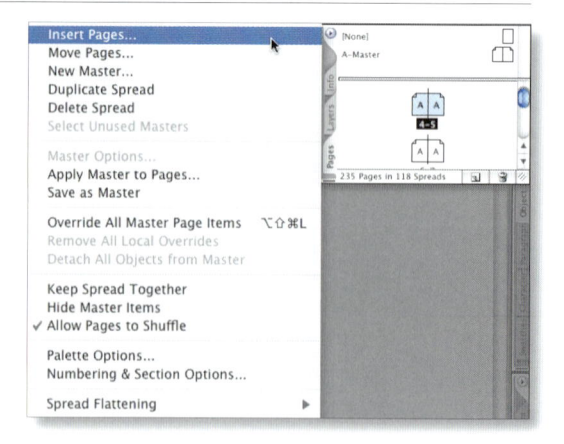

98 CHAPTER 5 • Working with Pages

ADD PAGES THE FAST WAY

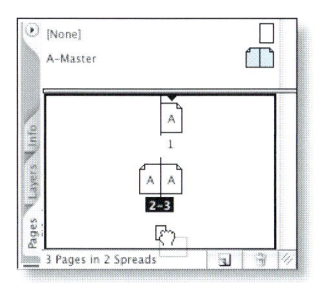

Do you want an even faster way to add pages to your document without choosing Insert Pages from the Pages palette's flyout menu and then adding pages manually in the dialog as mentioned in the previous tip? Instead, just click-and-drag the page icon from the top section of the Pages palette to the main section. Each time you do, it adds a page.

LARGER PAGE ICONS

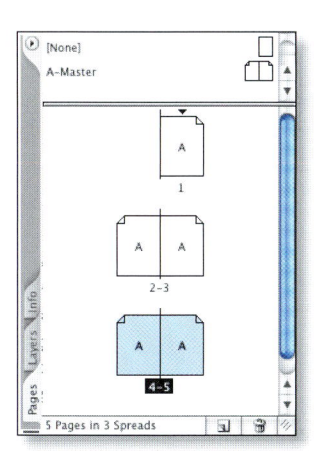

Admittedly, those page icons in the Pages palette are pretty small, but they don't have to be. If you'd prefer larger page icons, just choose Palette Options from the Pages palette's flyout menu, and a dialog will appear where you can choose your page icon size from a pop-up menu. (In the example shown here, we chose Extra Large.)

CHAPTER 5 • Working with Pages   99

HAVE IT YOUR WAY

I guess people get really passionate about the way the Pages palette looks. I for one couldn't care less as long as the features are there. However, if it bugs you that the pages are listed vertically instead of horizontally, choose the Palette Options from the Pages palette's flyout menu and go nuts. You can even decide who's on top, Masters or Pages. Go figure!

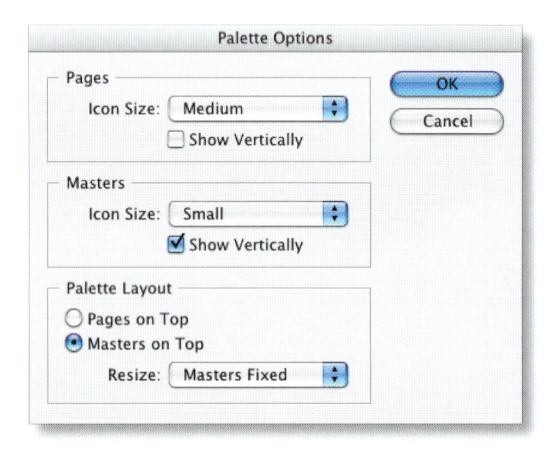

MAKE YOUR GUIDE STRETCH ACROSS SPREADS

When you're working with two-page spreads, if you pull down a horizontal guide from the top ruler, the guide only appears on the current page, not across the spread. If you'd like to have your guide appear across the whole spread (great for lining up blocks of text on facing pages), just hold the Command key (PC: Control key) before you click on your ruler, then drag it down.

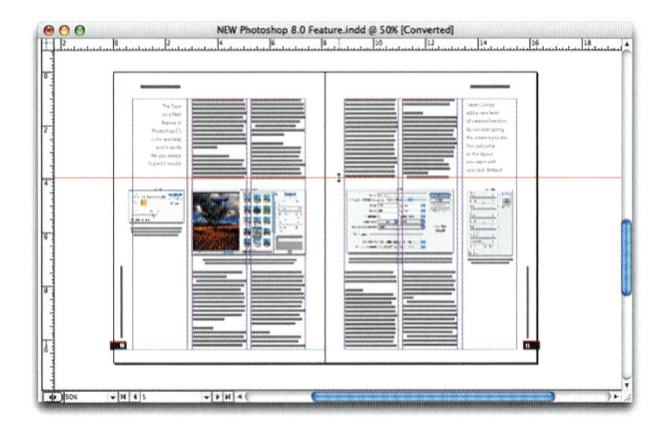

100 CHAPTER 5 • Working with Pages

GET RID OF UNWANTED GUIDES FAST

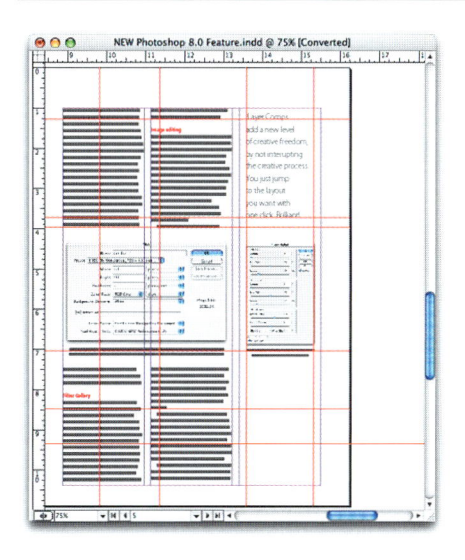

Want to get rid of some ruler guides fast? Just take the Selection tool, click-and-drag a selection over the ones you want to delete to select them (by default, when they're selected they turn the same color as the layer they are on in the Layers palette), then press Delete (PC: Backspace) to delete them. Tip: It's easier if you select guides either right above the page or to the right of the page in the pasteboard area, so you don't accidentally select other objects on the page.

DELETE ALL YOUR GUIDES AT ONCE

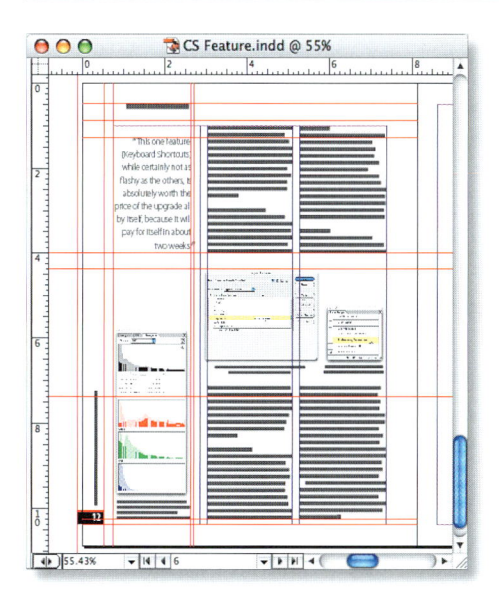

Want all your guides on a page or spread to disappear for good with extreme prejudice? Just press Option-Command-G (PC: Alt-Control-G), which selects all your guides, then press Delete (PC: Backspace) to erase them all.

ADD A GUIDE EXACTLY WHERE YOU WANT IT

Know exactly where you want your guide? Then instead of dragging it out from the rulers, just double-click in either the top or side ruler where you want the guide to appear, and it will appear right there. Sweet!

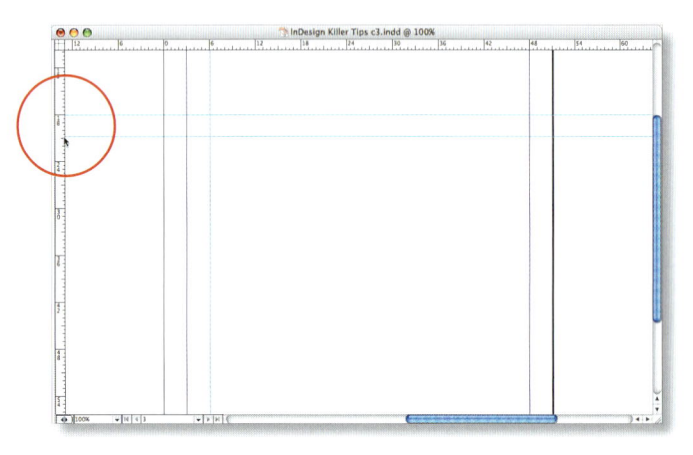

GET BOTH A HORIZONTAL AND VERTICAL GUIDE

If you drag from the top ruler down, you get a horizontal guide. If you drag the left-side ruler, you get a vertical guide. But did you know that if you hold the Command key (PC: Control key) and click in the top left corner (where the two rulers meet) you can drag out both a horizontal and vertical guide at the same time?

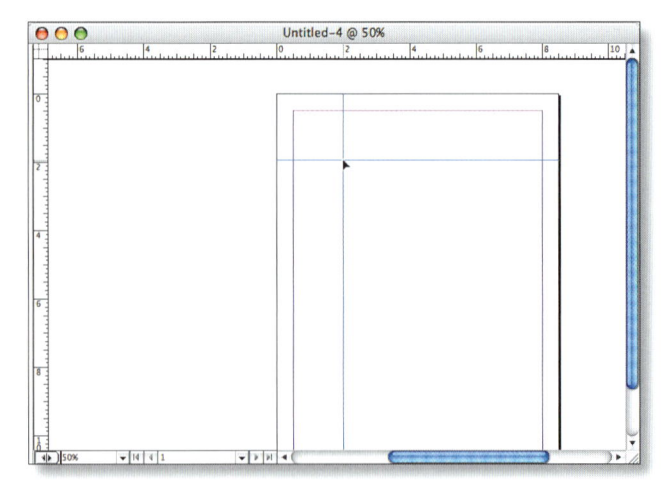

COPY THOSE GUIDES

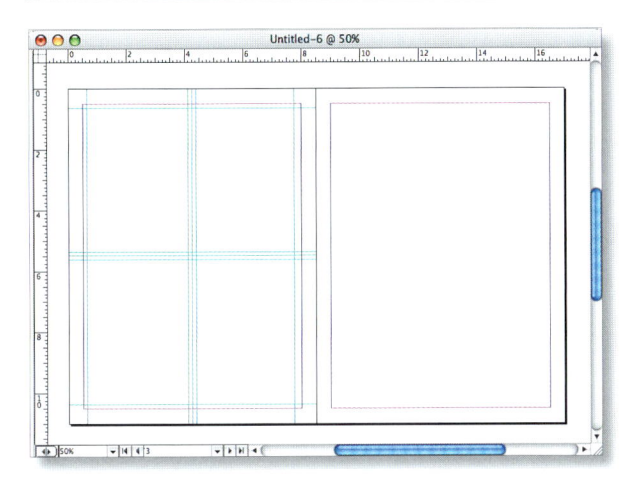

If you want to move the guides you have set up on one page to another page in your document (or in another document, for that matter), you can copy and paste them just like anything else. First get the Selection tool, then Shift-click on each guide you want to copy (to select them), then press Command-C (PC: Control-C) to copy them. Switch to the page where you want the guides and press Command-V (PC: Control-V). Couldn't be easier. If you're pasting these guides into a different document, make sure the document you're pasting into has the same physical dimensions or the guides will be out of place when pasted.

SHORTCUT FOR LOCKING GUIDES

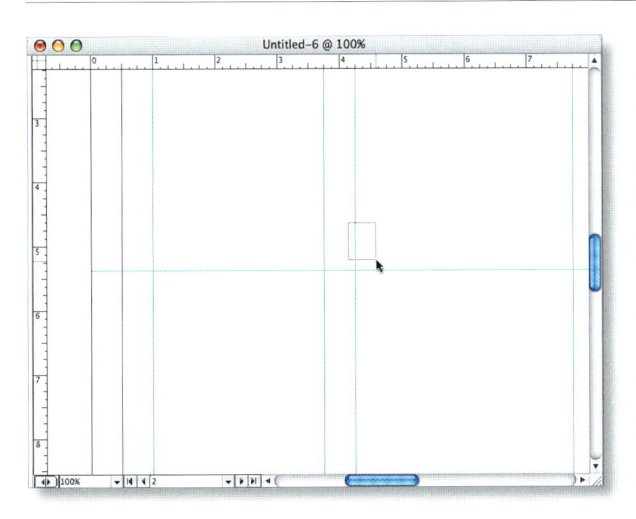

If you're using guides to set up your page layout, you usually don't want to move a guide accidentally, or it'll mess up your layout. That's why you'll want to know this shortcut: Option-Command-; (PC: Alt-Control-;) which locks all your guides down so they can't be moved. If you then try to select a guide (as we're trying to do in the capture shown here), it ignores your attempts. If you decide later that you want to unlock them, just press the same shortcut.

CHAPTER 5 • Working with Pages   103

InDesign CS/CS2
KillerTips

TOGGLE GUIDES ON/OFF

Here's one of the most useful shortcuts in all of InDesign. When you want a clean, no-guides look on your page (and by clean I mean no ruler guides, no margin guides, no column guides—nothing but page, baby), press Command-; (PC: Control-;).

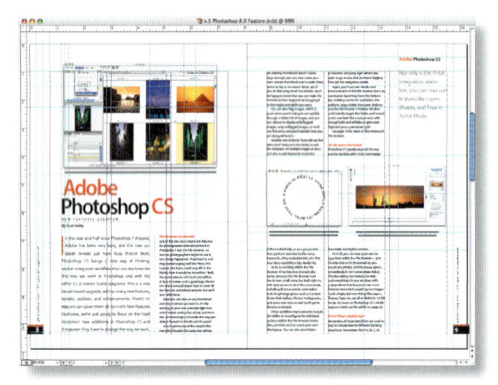

Guides visible

Guides hidden

CREATE YOUR OWN CUSTOM GUIDES LAYOUT

Dragging guides from the rulers is so 1980s. The next time you need to get guides on the page and have them perfectly spaced apart, try this: Choose Create Guides from the Layout menu. Now you have a dialog with a Preview option to specify how many rows and columns you want and how far they will be spaced apart from each other, known as the gutter.

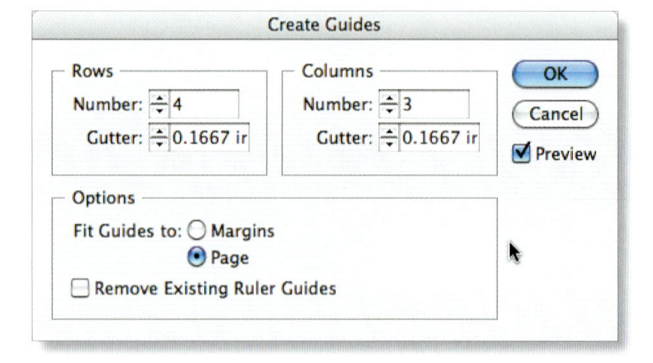

104 CHAPTER 5 • Working with Pages

ASSIGN GUIDES TO A LAYER

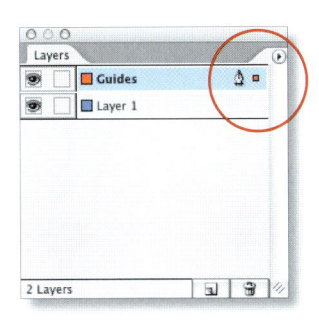

Hiding guides (View>Hide Guides) is an all-or-nothing deal. Sometimes you only need to hide some of the guides but not all of them. This tip will make your life easier. In the Layers palette Option-click (PC: Alt-click) on the Create a New Layer icon and name the new layer "guides". Now use the Selection tool to select the guides you want on that layer. A little box will appear in the Layers palette at the right side of the layer that contains the selected guides. Drag-and-drop this little box to the new guides layer to assign them to their own layer. Now you can click on the Eye icon for this layer to turn it off or on whenever you want to hide or show the guides.

GET ORGANIZED WITH LAYERS

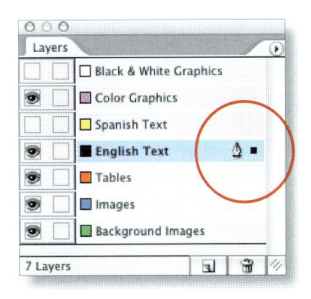

Stop creating different documents to show different versions of the same brochure. Use layers instead. If most of your layout is going to contain the same elements but some of the elements and text will need to change, try putting the "changeable" items on different layers. You can create more layers than you'll probably need and it doesn't add any significant weight to the document, so go nuts. Bring up the Layers palette from the Window menu and click on the Create a New Layer icon to add layers (Option-click [PC: Alt-click] if you want to name it at the same time). Then select objects on the page. In the Layers palette you'll notice a tiny little square appears on the right-hand side of the layer that contains the selected object. Drag the little square to move those objects to their respective layers.

CHAPTER 5 • Working with Pages   105

SELECT EVERYTHING ON ONE LAYER

Select All does just what you would expect—it selects everything (except, of course, items on locked layers and master items). However, there are those times when you just want to select everything on a single layer. Here's a quick way to do it. Hold down the Option (PC: Alt) key and click on the name of a layer in the Layers palette. Now everything on that layer is selected, but everything else is left alone.

STACK IT UP IN THE RIGHT ORDER

Stacking order is vitally important when it comes to printing with transparency. You should have your background images on the bottom, your photos next, then your vector graphics, and then your text on top. An easy way to accomplish this is to simply make layers for the aforementioned objects in the Layers palette. You can also reorder several groups of objects at any time by dragging a layer up or down in the Layers palette.

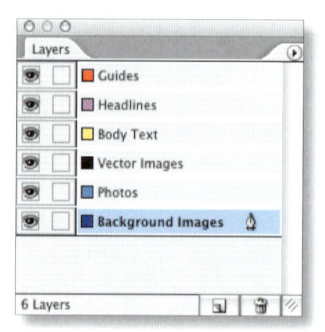

DELETE ANY LAYERS YOU'RE NOT USING

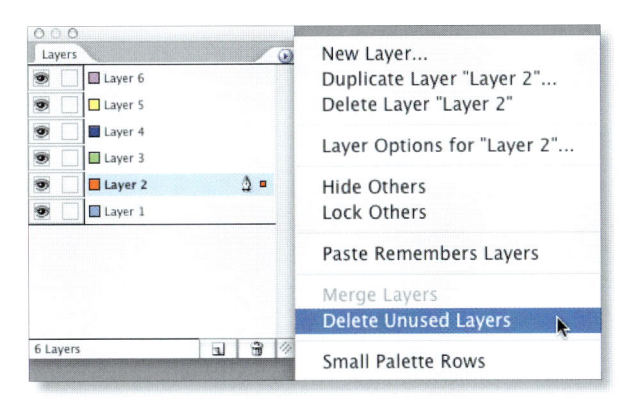

Got some layers you didn't wind up using (it happens pretty frequently)? Then choose Delete Unused Layers from the Layers palette's flyout menu and they're gone in a hurry!

SEE THE REAL PAGE NUMBERS

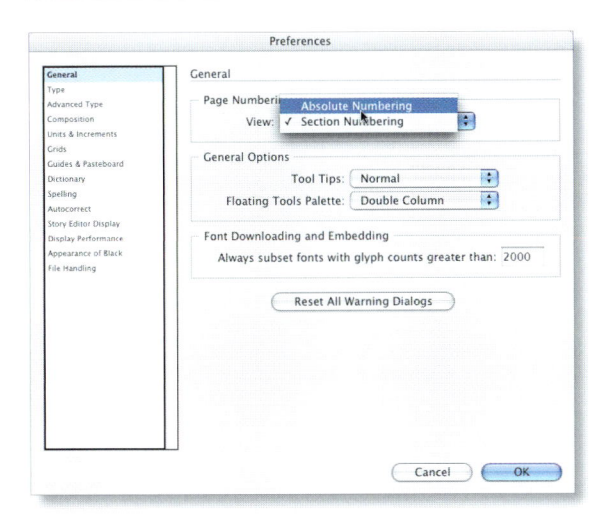

By default, the page numbers you see in the page number field in the bottom left-hand corner of your document window are based on the auto-page numbering setting for your document. For example, if you created your document starting with page 326, the second page in your document will be page 327. However, if you want to see the real number of pages in your document, rather than the auto-numbering version, go to InDesign's Preferences (Command-K [PC: Control-K]), select General, and change the Page Numbering View pop-up menu from its default setting of Section Numbering to Absolute Numbering (as shown).

CHAPTER 5 • Working with Pages   107

CREATE NEW SECTIONS (WITH THEIR OWN PAGE NUMBERS)

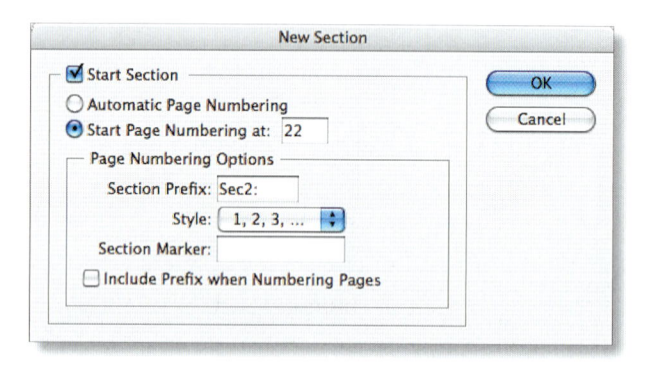

You can create a new section in your document, with its own separate page numbering scheme, by going to the Pages palette's flyout menu and choosing Numbering & Section Options. When the dialog appears, click the Start Section checkbox, then click the Start Page Numbering At radio button and enter the starting page number you want for your new section. Click OK and the page you're currently on will start your new section. So within your document, you could have pages 1, 2, 3, 4, 5, 6, 7, then 22, 23, 24, etc.

ONE IS THE LONELIEST NUMBER

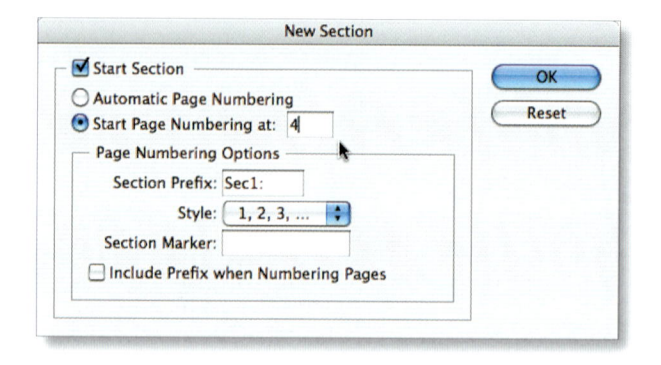

Numbering pages automatically is child's play. But what about when you want page numbering to start on a specific page or to start over again on a specific chapter? Try this tip: In your multiple-page document go to page 3 and choose Numbering & Section Options from the Layout menu. With this dialog you can start the page numbering at a specific number, as well as change the style of numbering that will be used until the next section break or the end of the document.

108   CHAPTER 5 • Working with Pages

InDesign CS/CS2
KillerTips

JUMP TO THE PAGE YOU NEED

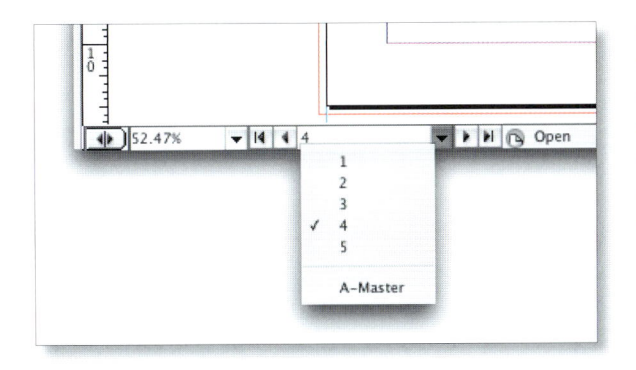

If you know which page you want to go to, there's a quick way to get right where you want to be—click on the down-facing arrow to the right of the current page number (down in the bottom left-hand corner of your image window).

MAKE ALL MASTER PAGE ITEMS EDITABLE

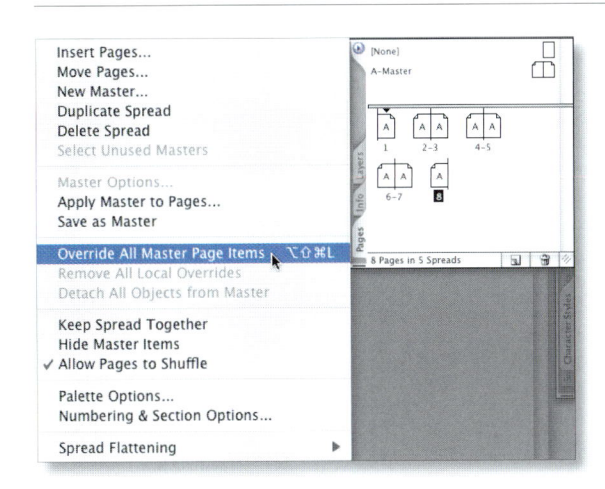

If you want to access all the items on your master page while you're working on a regular page, you're just one quick click away. Go to the Pages palette's flyout menu and choose Override All Master Page Items (as shown here). Now those master page items that were once "off limits" are live on your page (not just your current page—every page).

CHAPTER 5 • Working with Pages   109

MAKE JUST ONE MASTER PAGE ITEM EDITABLE

If you want to edit just one master page item, just Shift-Command-click (PC: Shift-Control-click) on the item and it becomes live on your page so you can reposition it, move it, or even delete it. However, it only becomes live on your current page—it remains on the master page as far as any other pages in your document are concerned. If you truly want that item demoted from master page item to just a regular item on your page, once it's selected you can go to the Pages palette's flyout menu and choose Detach Selection From Master (as shown here).

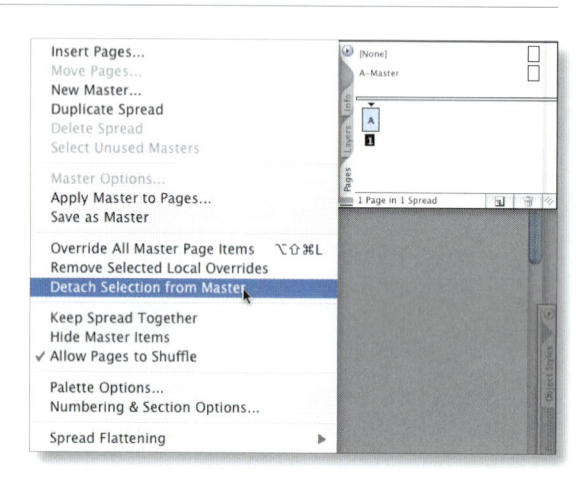

ASSIGN MASTER PAGE ATTRIBUTES TO A PAGE

If you're working on a page in your document and decide you want the objects on a master page to appear on that page, just go to the Pages palette, click on the thumbnail for the master page you want to apply, and drag-and-drop it right onto the page thumbnail icon for the page you're on. This applies the master page attributes to that page.

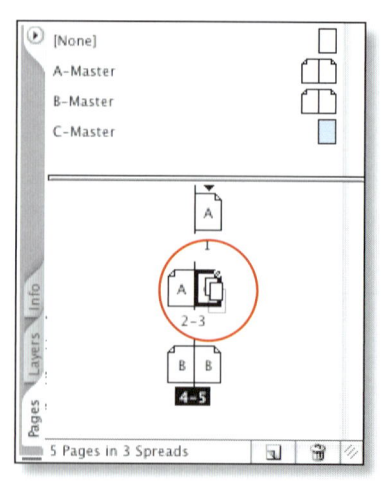

CHAPTER 5 • Working with Pages

YOU WILL BE ASSIMILATED

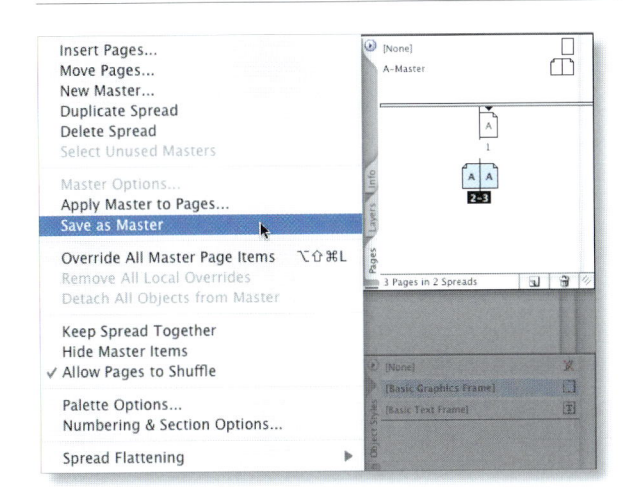

You've created such a wonderful page that you want all other pages in your document to look like it. However, you didn't create it on a master page. No problem, simply choose Save As Master from the Pages palette's flyout menu.

FROM TEXT FRAME TO GRAPHICS FRAME FAST

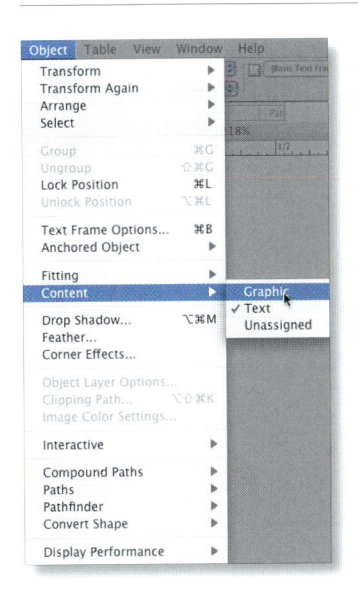

If you like to set up your pages with all the text and graphics frames before any actual content is added to the page, then you'll really find this helpful. If you have a text frame in place and decide you want to use it to hold a graphic instead, you don't have to delete the text frame and create a new graphics frame—just change its frame type by clicking on the frame, going under the Object menu, under Content, and choosing Graphic. The same works vice versa to change graphics frames into text frames.

CHAPTER 5 • Working with Pages 111

MAKE A TOC STYLE

A table of contents sounds like a simple thing until you try to do one with InDesign. It doesn't have to be hard (it just is). A TOC Style is a set of options to build your table of contents. You can build a new one simply by choosing Table of Contents Styles from the Layout menu and clicking the New button in the dialog. Give your style a catchy name like "TOC Style 1." At this point all you really need to do is tell it which of your paragraph styles will be included as TOC entries and click OK. More tips follow.

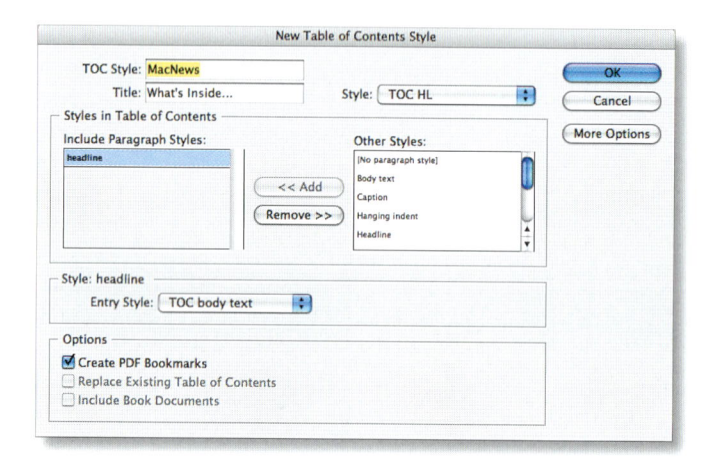

TOC: MORE OPTIONS

In the New Table of Contents Style dialog there is a More Options button. As usual this means, er, umm, more options are available. With more options showing you get the choice of where you want your page numbers, what kind of character (such as a Tab) is between the text entry and the number, and the ability to sort the entries in alphabetical order. See—I told you it meant more options.

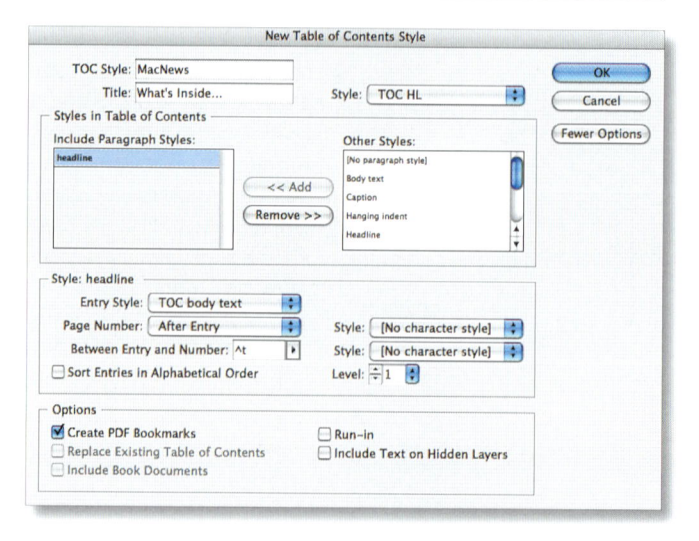

112   CHAPTER 5 • Working with Pages

STYLE VS. ENTRY STYLE

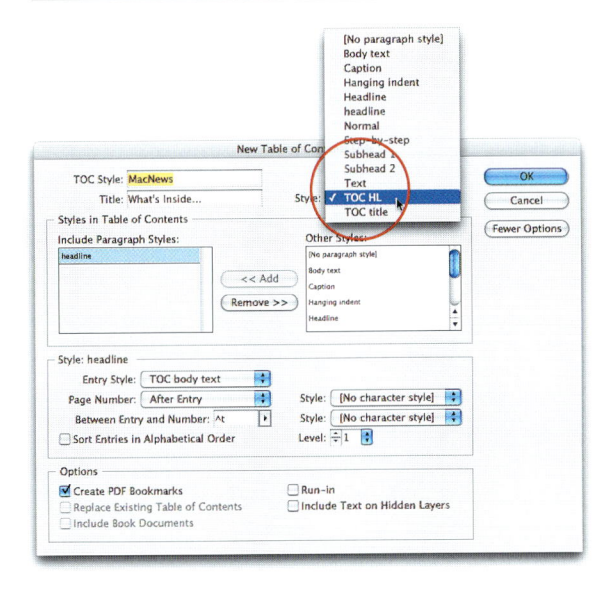

The New Table of Contents Style dialog makes too much use of the word "style." I mean it's all over the place. Let's face it, this dialog needs an overhaul. The easiest way to make sense of it is to remember that when you see just the word "style" by itself, it refers to stylizing the item to the left of it in the dialog. For example, if you wanted to pick a paragraph style for your title, you would choose it from the Style pop-up menu to the right of the Title field. Ahhhh, now it makes sense! Keep in mind that you should create all your paragraph styles first before trying to create a TOC Style.

GIVE ME DOTS

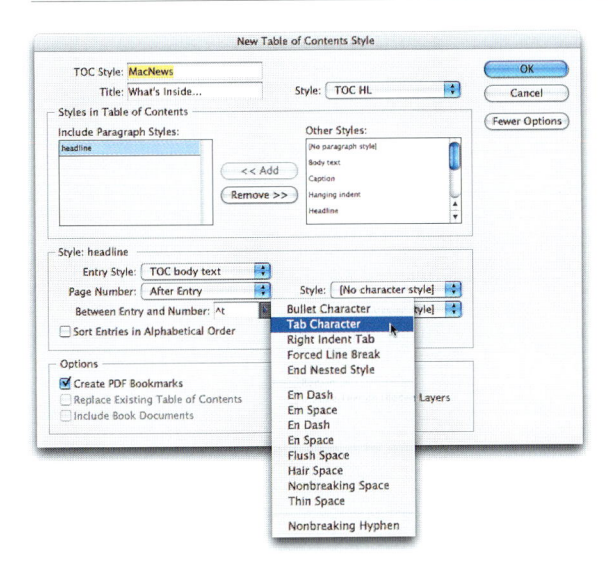

It's very common to have a series of leader dots between each table of contents entry and its page number. Click the More Options button in the New Table of Contents Style dialog and for the Between Entry and Number option choose Tab Character from the pop-up menu. Now to get the dots to appear you will have to create a Leader Tab in your Entry Style paragraph style sheet.

CHAPTER 5 • Working with Pages   113

LINK DOCS TOGETHER IN A BOOK

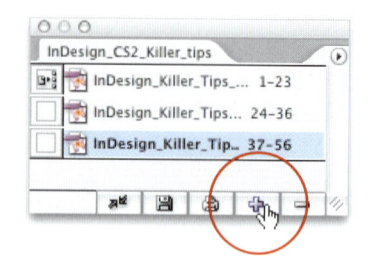

Just because InDesign can create a single document that's 9,999 pages long, that doesn't mean it's a good idea. If you're working on a document that's going to be more than a couple hundred pages long, it's probably a good idea to think about breaking it up into smaller sections/documents. You can still have the benefits of a single document by using the Book feature. Create two or more InDesign documents and then choose File>New>Book. You will be prompted to save your Book document and then you'll get a Book palette. From here you can use the Plus sign at the bottom of the palette to add individual documents to the book.

CREATE A PDF FROM YOUR BOOK

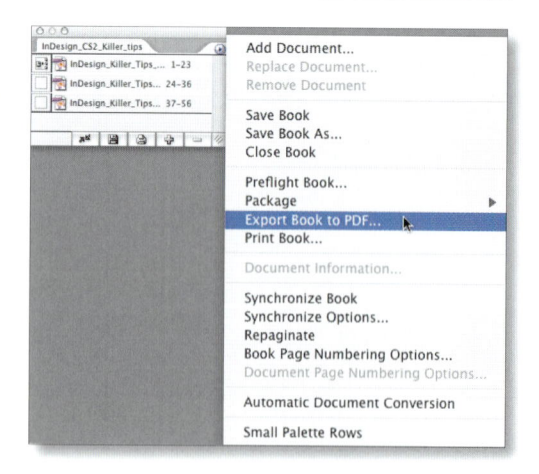

Once you have an InDesign Book document, you can create a single PDF from all the documents it includes. Simply choose Export Book to PDF from the Book palette's flyout menu. While you're in that menu, check out the variety of cool things you can do there. You know, like printing the entire book. Hey, that could come in handy.

SYNCHRONIZE A BOOK

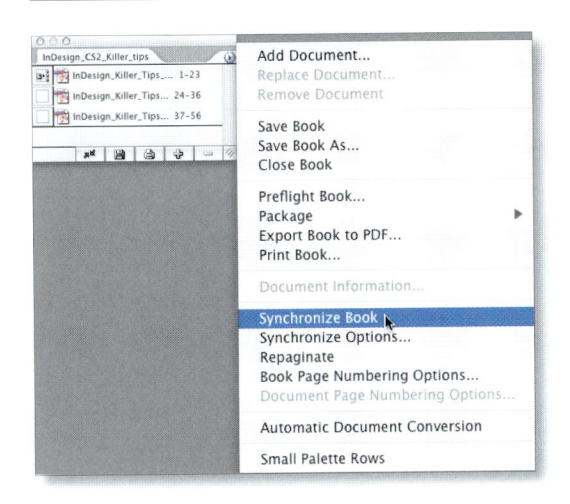

People are so helpful. They often want to take on some of your workload and ask nothing in return. Yeah, right! However, if you do have someone helping you create your book by supplying InDesign documents, you may want to make sure everyone's on the same page. Choose Synchronize Book from the Book palette's flyout menu to make sure that all the documents in the book have the same TOC, character and paragraph styles, as well as trap presets and swatches.

BOOK PAGINATION

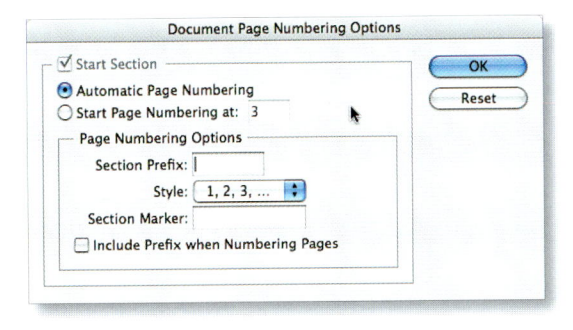

Page numbering is important, so use this tip to make sure that your book's page numbers come out the way you want. You can verify the page numbering options for each individual document in your book to make sure that they are all set to automatic numbering (or whatever you like) by choosing Document Page Numbering Options from the Book palette's flyout menu. Then all you have to do is enter page numbering options within the same menu to set your favorite way of numbering for the entire book.

CHAPTER 5 • Working with Pages   115

CREATE INDEX ENTRIES

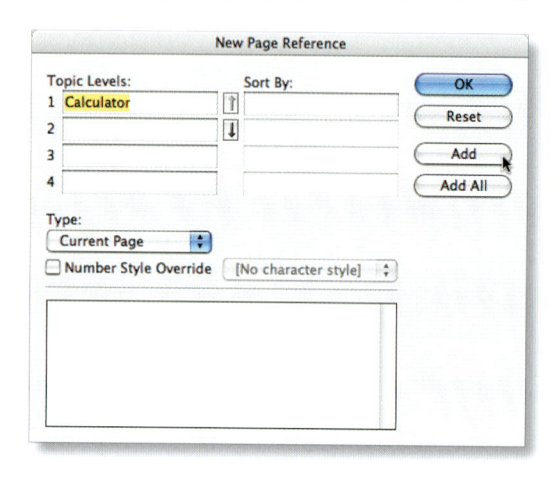

Before you can build an index, you have to specify some words that you want to appear in it. Unfortunately InDesign has no mind-reading feature so the program has no idea of what should be in the index and what shouldn't. Bring up the Index palette from the Type & Tables flyout menu under Window or hit Shift-F8 on the keyboard. Now simply highlight a word that you want included in the index and click the Create a New Index Entry button at the bottom of the Index palette. In the New Page Reference dialog you can choose the topic level and how the word is sorted. Once you hit OK, your word is added to the Index palette in alphabetical order.

INDEX CROSS-REFERENCING

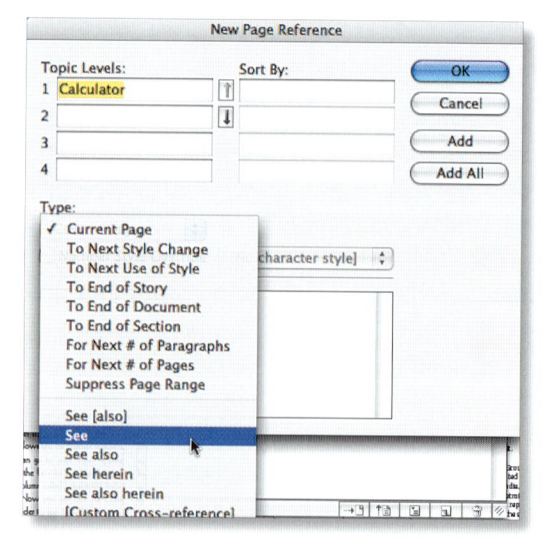

Doesn't it drive you crazy when you take time to look up a word in the index of a book you're reading only to find "See blah blah blah"? Then you have to go look up another word. Well now you, too, can drive your readers crazy. When you create an index entry in the New Page Reference dialog, simply change the Type pop-up menu from Current Page to See, See Also, etc. Then in the Referenced field that appears under the Type pop-up, either type in the index entry that they really should go to or drag-and-drop the entry from the list of index items in the box below it.

116   CHAPTER 5 • Working with Pages

HEY, THERE'S NO PDF BUTTON ON THE BOOK PALETTE

True, but there is a Print button that you can use to create a PDF. Hold down the Option key (PC: Alt key) and click the Print button. Now you will be prompted to export to PDF instead of printing.

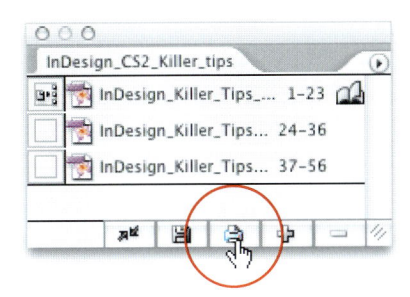

ADD DOCUMENTS TO A BOOK FROM THE DESKTOP

Hey, we all enjoy navigating Open dialogs, but sometimes just to break up the monotony you can actually drag stuff from the desktop. Here's a tip for all you book lovers: With the Book palette open, simply drag an InDesign document into the palette from the desktop (or any other folder in your computer) to add it to the book.

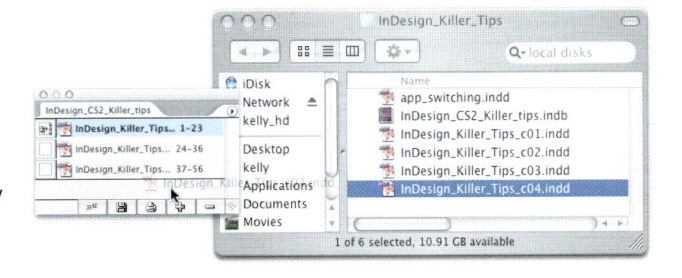

I WANT JUST ONE DOCUMENT

Although the Book palette lets you treat multiple documents like a single big document, sometimes you just want to do something to an individual document. Maybe you only want to print one document in the book. Once you highlight a single document or multiple documents in the Book palette (Command-click [PC: Control-click] on all the documents you want to select), you can use the Book palette's flyout menu to choose your option. You'll notice that it now says it will apply commands to the selected documents; for example, Print Book becomes Print Selected Documents.

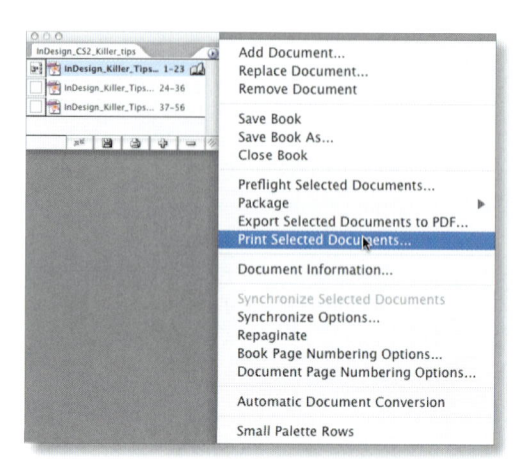

TAKE IT TO THE WEB

With a book of multiple InDesign documents, going to the Web can be a challenge. I mean c'mon, who wants to open up and export individual documents? If you're doing that, stop it! Try this tip: Open your book document and from the Book palette's flyout menu go to Package and choose Book For GoLive. To take full advantage of this, you will need Adobe GoLive CS or higher. If you have GoLive CS or higher, you can then move the package folder into the InDesign Packages area of your site and start to repurpose your content for the Web.

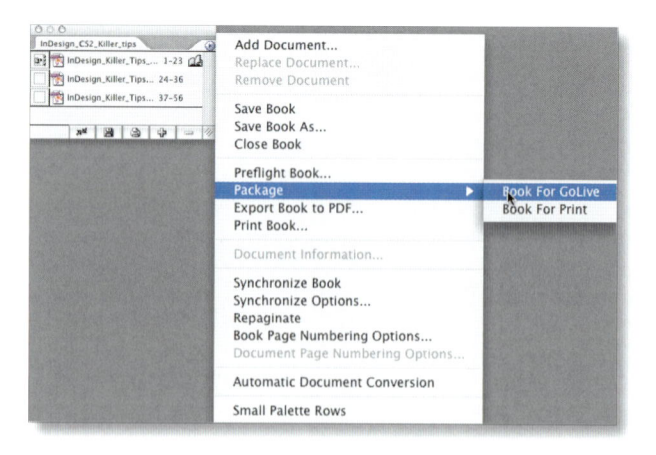

CHAPTER 5 • Working with Pages

Contains Graphic Images

WORKING WITH GRAPHICS

Although there's a lot you can do right within InDesign, sometimes you have to reach outside InDesign and import a graphic. Yes, it's unseemly, but people (even fine

Contains Graphic Images
working with graphics

people like yourself) do it every day right out in broad daylight. If you're one of those (a graphic importer/exporter), at some point you're going to want some help, mostly some tips to make you faster, better, and all-around more gooder (gooder? I meant "bester"). Oh yes, that day's a-comin' and when it does, we'll be there. We'll be there to greet you with open arms and share with you a level of graphic tips so rich, so graphic, so graphically rich that one dare not speak its name. You'll be able to do things to imported graphics that would make a lesser man blush, a steady woman swoon, and small children pass out cold. You're about to become a "Graphic Master," and you'll command an army of tips so vast, and so powerful, that no QuarkXPress-using adversary would dare stand in your shadow. This is powerful stuff. Use it with great care.

CREATE A VIGNETTE WITHOUT LEAVING INDESIGN

Hard-edged photos went out in the 90s. The new craze is to have images with ragged or vignetted borders. If you want ragged borders, you'll still need Photoshop for that. However, you can create a nice soft-edge border with this tip: Select your photo with the Selection tool. Then choose Feather from the Object menu. Click the Feather and the Preview checkboxes and enter your desired feather amount or simply click into the Feather Width field and use the Up and Down Arrow keys to increase or decrease the amount of feathering visually.

DON'T BE A SQUARE

Sure, we will all use the Rectangle Frame tool to lay out most things in our documents. However, with this tip you can add a little flair to your text and graphic frames. After you draw a frame, choose the Pen tool and click-and-drag it on the edge of your frame. You just added a curve point, which you can use to create a nice curve in your frame.

122   CHAPTER 6 • Working with Graphics

TRY OUT BLENDING MODES

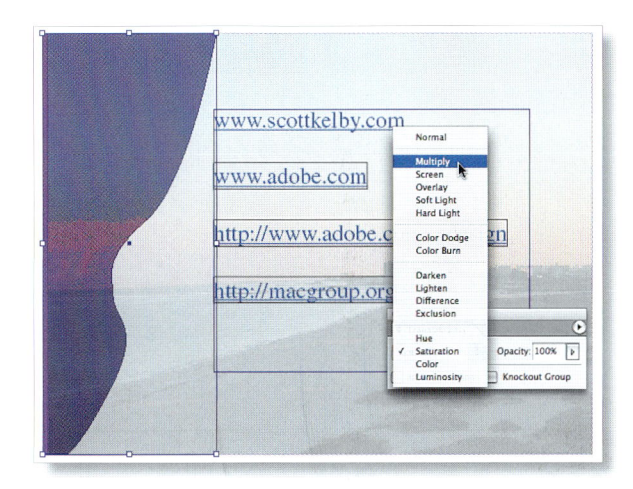

InDesign brings you the same blending modes you've grown to know and love in Photoshop. To create a nice effect without having to do it in another app, try selecting a vector shape filled with your favorite color (well, maybe one of the colors you're using in the job would be a better choice) that is stacked on top of another object and choose Multiply from the pop-up menu at the top of the Transparency palette. The beauty of this tip is that when you swap out the image underneath the vector shape, you'll get a different effect. Try the other blending modes and amaze your friends.

USE THE PASTE INTO COMMAND

Putting a graphic inside of text always goes over well visually. The next time you have the text and graphic already on the page, try this tip to make use of what you already have: Highlight the text with the Type tool and choose Create Outlines from the Type menu. Switch to the Direct Selection tool, select your graphic, and hit Copy from the Edit menu. Then select your outlined text and choose Paste Into from the Edit menu. While you have the Direct Selection tool selected, you can still drag your image around inside the text to position it to your liking.

CHAPTER 6 • Working with Graphics

GOVERNMENT-MANDATED DROP SHADOWS

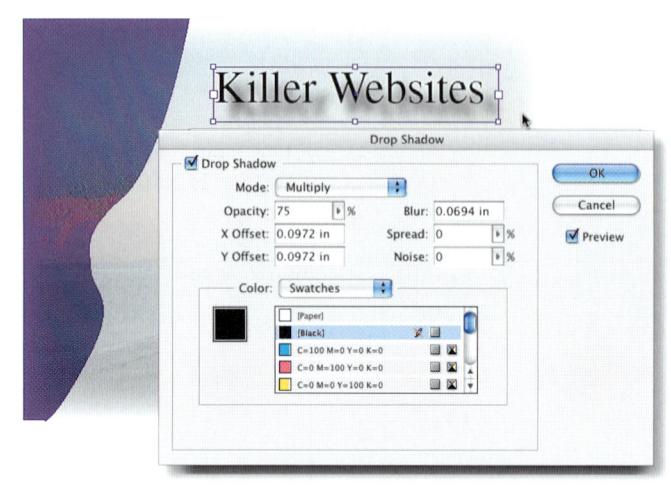

It's hard to pick up any publication that doesn't have at least one manually created drop shadow. Therefore, it's perfectly okay for you to have at least one if not several in your publication. You can create drop shadows on both text and images. Drop shadows and feathers are frame-based, so that means that even for text you select the frame with the Selection tool, not the Type tool. Once you have your frame selected, choose Drop Shadow from the Object menu. Click the Preview and the Drop Shadow checkboxes. Now you can choose the amount of offset, opacity, and blurriness.

CREATE FAKE GLOWS

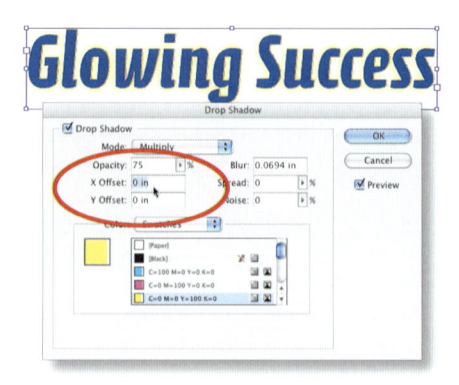

InDesign really has no glow feature, but you can fake one using the drop shadow feature. Select your frame with the Selection tool (it works really nicely on large text) and choose Drop Shadow from the Object menu. Click on the Preview and Drop Shadow checkboxes, create a drop shadow with a nice glow color such as green or yellow, and choose zero for both offsets. Your text will appear to have a glow around it.

DRAG-AND-DROP FROM THE OS

File>Place, File>Place, File>Place—that's what we do all day long to bring stuff into InDesign. There's a better way! It's called drag-and-drop. This tip will make your production go much faster. Chances are the graphics you want to place in your document are in a folder. Go to that folder in the Finder (Windows Explorer) and simply drag those images onto the page. You can even do more than one at a time. Just Command-click (PC: Control-click) on the graphics you want, then drag-and-drop them.

SHOW IMPORT OPTIONS FOR MORE CONTROL

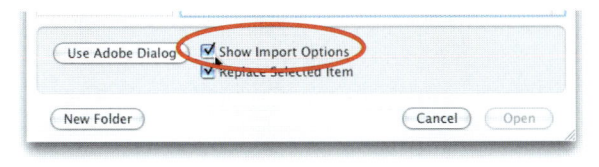

Get more choices when placing files by turning on the checkbox for Show Import Options in the Place dialog. With this option turned on, whether you're placing text, graphics, or PDF files there will be more choices of how those items are placed. For example, if you want to bypass the manual page breaks in a Word document, choose No Breaks in the Manual Page Breaks pop-up menu.

CHAPTER 6 • Working with Graphics   125

PLACE PDF FILES TOO

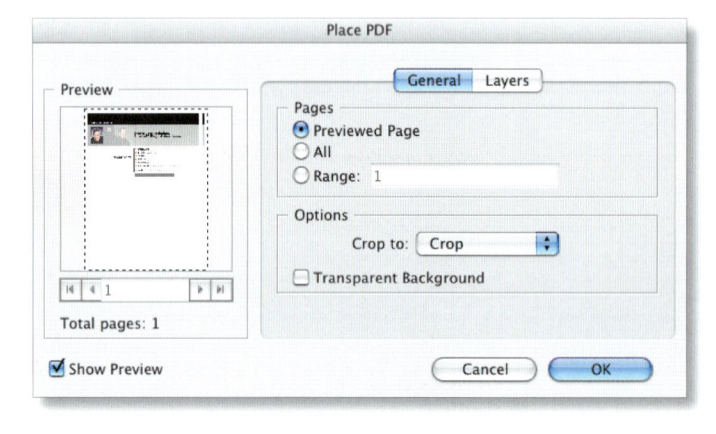

InDesign can place PDF files on your pages. Big surprise, right? Of course, you'd expect that Adobe would allow you to place its own graphics standards, but the way you do it can determine how InDesign will import them. After choosing Place under the File menu, select a PDF. Then, from the Place PDF dialog, you can choose from a number of options for placing your PDF. (Also, see "Import Multi-Page PDF" on page 250.)

TEXT WRAP: TAKE IT OR LEAVE IT

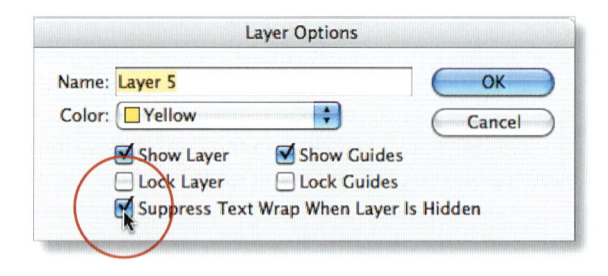

Text wrap is a wonderful thing, but sometimes you want your text to wrap based on using different objects. Say you want to show your customer two different versions of a page and each version has a different main graphic but uses the same text. Here's a tip that will make your day. Put each graphic on its own layer and then put the text on its own layer too. Then go to the Layers palette and double-click the name of one of the layers containing a graphic. In the Layer Options dialog, check the box labeled Suppress Text Wrap When Layer Is Hidden. Repeat this for each layer with a graphic. Now for each graphic, hide the other graphic layers and then in the Text Wrap palette (Window>Type & Tables>Text Wrap) set a text wrap to your liking. Now because you chose to suppress the text wrap in the Layer Options dialog, whenever you hide a layer it will also remove the text wrap for the graphic on that layer; when you make a layer visible, the text wrap will be there again.

126   CHAPTER 6 • Working with Graphics

WRAP IT, WRAP IT GOOD

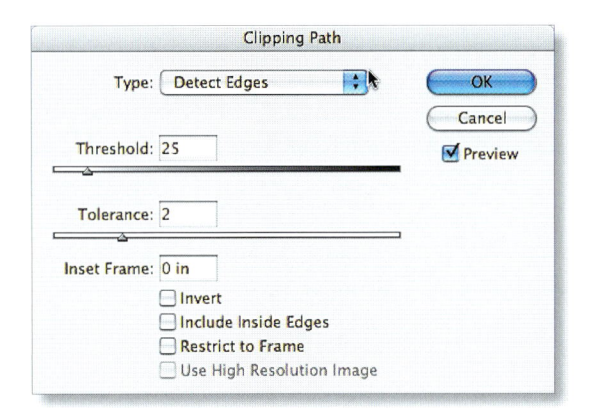

InDesign's text wrap makes text stay away from an object. However, with EPS and Illustrator files you can perform an extra step to get the text to wrap around the actual shape of the graphic and not just the frame. Select the graphic and choose Clipping Path from the Object menu. Then choose Detect Edges from the Type pop-up menu. Click OK. Now when you choose to Wrap Around Object Shape (the third icon from the left in the Text Wrap palette), your text will wrap around the shape of the actual graphic, not the frame.

WHO'S THE MASTER NOW?

This one comes up a lot. Master pages are great in that they allow you to put something on a single page and have it appear on several pages in your document. However, there are those times when you need to do something to a graphic on a particular page but you can't because it's on a master page. But there's a way around that: Simply press Shift-Command (PC: Shift-Control) and click on the master page item you want to change on your page. Now you can do whatever you want to it because it's no longer tied to the master page.

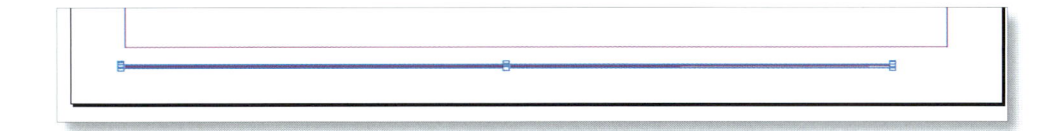

CHAPTER 6 • Working with Graphics   127

FROM ONE VECTOR LOVER TO ANOTHER

Although Adobe InDesign and Illustrator are both vector-based, Illustrator's drawing tools kick InDesign's drawing tools' butt. This tip will give you the best of both worlds. Draw your cool illustration in Illustrator. Make sure you've set Illustrator's preferences (Illustrator>Preferences [PC: Edit>Preferences]) for File Handling & Clipboard to AICB (Adobe Illustrator Clipboard). Now copy your masterpiece, go to InDesign, and paste it. If you use the Direct Selection tool, you'll be able to edit the points in InDesign that originated in Illustrator.

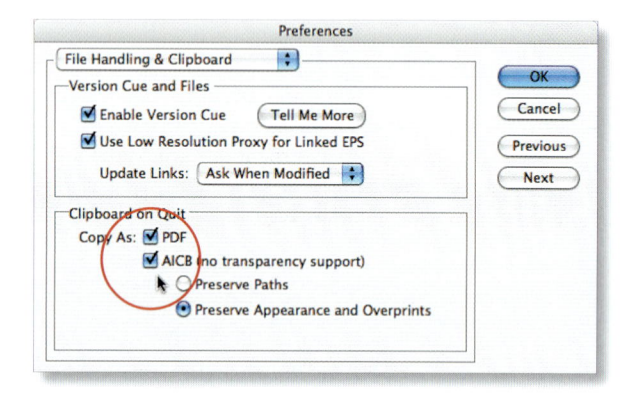

I DON'T WANT TO DRAW NO STINKIN' BOXES

Designers just want to design. Working with grids and drawing boxes just seems so unnatural. If what you just read pushed your buttons, then you'll love this tip. You can place text or graphics into InDesign without drawing frames first. When you place a graphic or drag it in, InDesign will build a frame for it on the fly.

128   CHAPTER 6 • Working with Graphics

I HAVE TO DRAW BOXES FIRST. IT'S MY LIFE

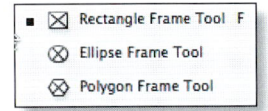

If you're the kind of person who has to have structure in your world and the thought of placing a graphic with no predefined area for it to go into makes you nauseated, then by all means draw frames first. InDesign has about 11 million frame tools for drawing them. There are two main types: the ones with an "x" in them and the ones without an "x." InDesign actually doesn't care which ones you use. The "x"s are to make Quark"X"Press users feel better.

MAKE THE GRAPHIC FIT

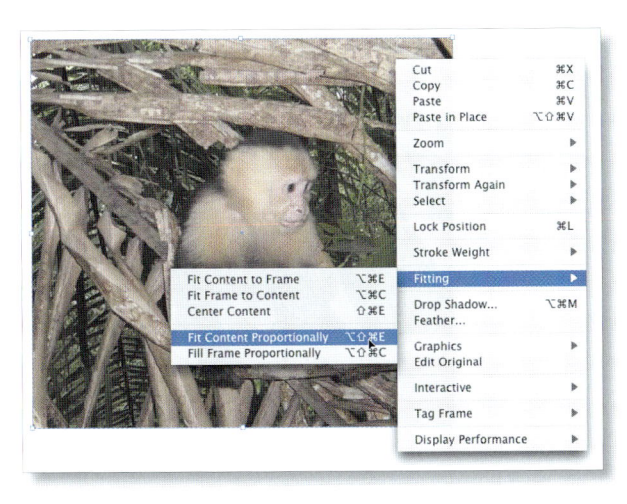

When a graphic needs to fit in a certain spot on your page, try this tip to make it easier. Draw a frame in the space you've allotted for the graphic. Now place the graphic in that frame. In most cases you will want the graphic to fit in the frame proportionally. With that in mind, choose Object>Fitting>Fit Content Proportionally.

CHAPTER 6 • Working with Graphics   129

SIZE DOES MATTER

Quickly, you need to resize a graphic. Whoa—when you grab the frame handle and pull, it just resizes the frame! This is the default behavior of InDesign. If you want to size the graphic and the frame at the same time, use the Selection tool and hold down the Command (PC: Control) and Shift keys as you drag one of the corner handles. This will resize the graphic proportionally.

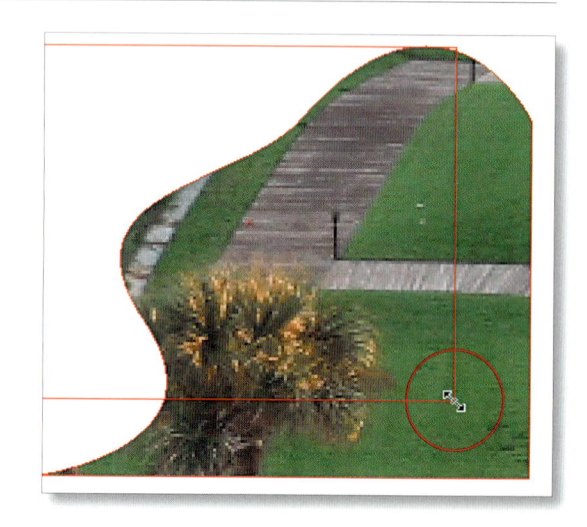

THE RESIZE-MULTIPLE-OBJECTS TRICK

Want to resize several objects at once? No sweat—just Shift-click on everything you want to scale (as shown here), then press Command-G (PC: Control-G) to group them together. Now when you grab a corner and drag outward, they all resize together. Note: This "group-it-then-resize-it" trick works on objects, but not on type.

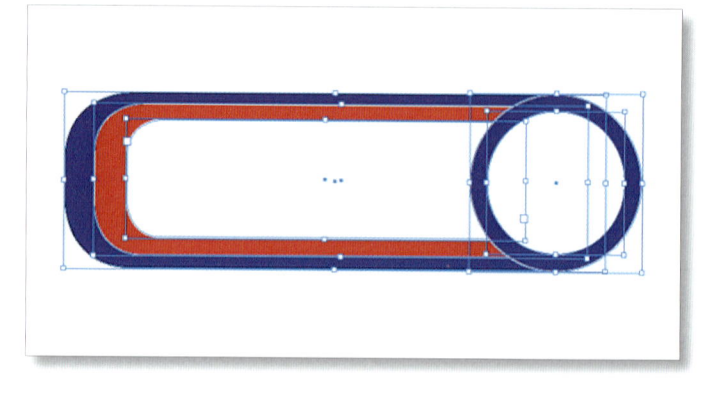

130   CHAPTER 6 • Working with Graphics

MOVE THE GRAPHIC WITHOUT MOVING THE FRAME

The frame is exactly where it needs to be. However, the graphic in the frame is not in the right position to show the part of it that you want. People often use frames to crop large photos, and you can "crop" a graphic by repositioning it in a frame so that only the part you want is visible. Use the Direct Selection tool to drag the graphic around in the frame without moving the frame. If you click-and-hold for a second, you'll get a live preview of the image as you reposition it in the frame.

THREE-IN-ONE

I want to move it, size it, and rotate it. Use this tip to do all three with one tool. It's called the Free Transform tool. That funky-looking tool in the Toolbox with the dotted box and the arrow icon can do three things. With the Free Transform tool you can move your graphics as well as size them (without holding down any keys) and rotate them. If you drag in the middle of the frame, you'll move it. If you grab a corner handle, you'll size it; and if you move just outside the corner handles, you'll be able to rotate it (shown here).

CHAPTER 6 • Working with Graphics   131

LOOK AT ME WHEN I'M TALKING TO YOU

Nothing is more distracting than to have the subject of your article facing away from the article or off the page. Don't go back to Photoshop; let InDesign flip your image. Use the flyout menu on the far right corner of the Control palette to Flip Horizontal.

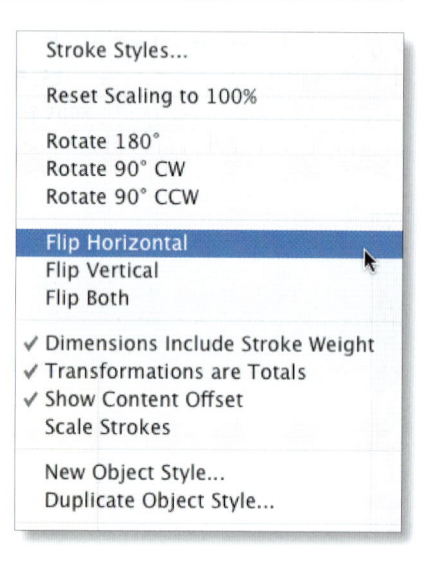

DON'T USE THE FORCE TO ALIGN OBJECTS

Using the Force or your naked eye is probably not the best way to line things up on a page. The next time you need objects to line up, simply choose Align from the Window menu. Now select the objects that you wish to line up and then click one of the horizontal or vertical alignment icons on the Align palette.

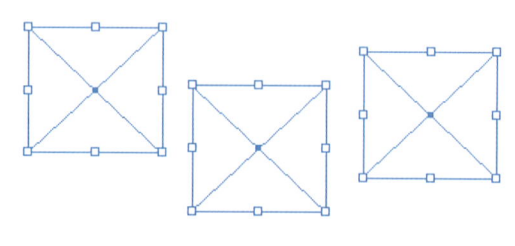

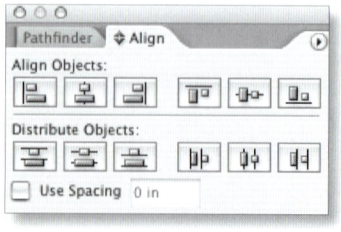

132   CHAPTER 6 • Working with Graphics

GIVE YOUR OBJECTS A RESTRAINING ORDER

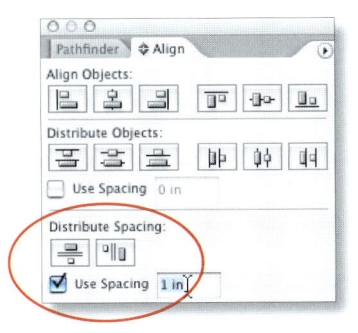

If you want the objects on your page to be a certain distance from each other, try this tip: Using the Align palette, make sure that Show Options in the palette's flyout menu is on. Turn on the checkbox for Use Spacing, and type the exact spacing you want in the Use Spacing field. Select your objects and click either the Distribute Vertical or Distribute Horizontal Space icon in the Align palette.

Before using Distribute Spacing

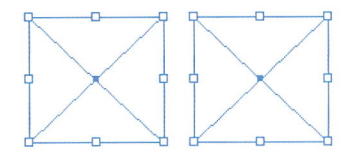

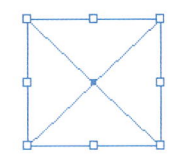

After using Distribute Spacing of 1˝

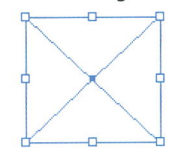

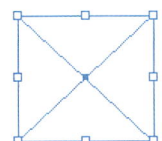

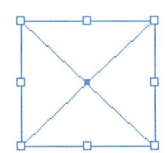

COPY AND PASTE IS SO 1980S

The next time you need to make a copy of something on the page, simply hold down the Option key (PC: Alt key) and drag the object with the Selection tool. This will make a copy of the object wherever you drag it.

CHAPTER 6 • Working with Graphics

STEP AND REPEAT INSTEAD OF COPY AND PASTE

Okay, I know there is some value to copy and paste. However, hitting paste 50 million times to get copies of the same object on the page is a drag. Try this tip: Select your object and choose Step and Repeat from the Edit menu. Now you can specify how many you want and how far apart they should be with the Horizontal and Vertical Offset options.

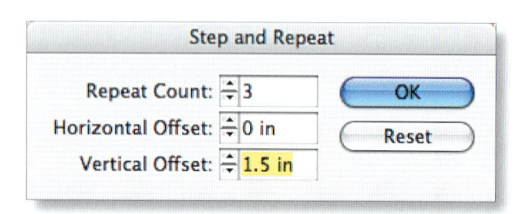

DON'T MOVE IT TO THE SAME PLACE—COPY IT

Have you ever wanted to create a copy of something in the same exact place as the original? This is especially useful and necessary when you're trying to get things to be in the same place on different pages. Next time you need that, try this tip. Copy the object (Command-C [PC: Control-C]) that you want to appear in the same spot on a different page, navigate to that page, and choose Paste in Place from the Edit menu.

PASTE REMEMBERS LAYERS

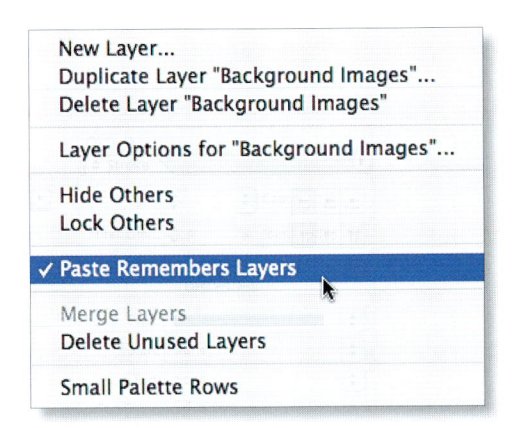

To keep things on the layers where they belong, you can use the Paste Remembers Layers option in the Layers palette's flyout menu. For example, if you have a photos layer and you want to copy a photo on page 1 and paste it on page 16, but you also want it to still be on the photos layer when you paste it, this tip makes it possible.

WHERE'S THE LIBRARY PALETTE?

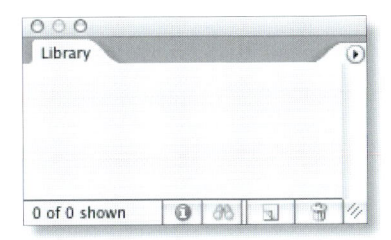

If you've looked for the Library palette under the Window menu (where all the other palettes are) you already know—it's not there. So where is this hidden palette? Believe it or not, you have to create it. That's right—you have to go under the File menu, under New, and choose Library. Then a Save dialog appears and you have to save your new library (and you can give it a custom name too). When you click OK, only then does the palette appear. Then, if you close the Library palette, to get back to it you have to go through the Open command in the File menu. If you think this is a weird way to access a palette, you're probably right.

CHAPTER 6 • Working with Graphics

ADD OBJECTS TO THE LIBRARY

Now that you have your library created, rather than sit there and stare at an empty palette, you can either drag items from your pages into the Library palette or you can simply select an object and click the New Library Item icon at the bottom of the Library palette.

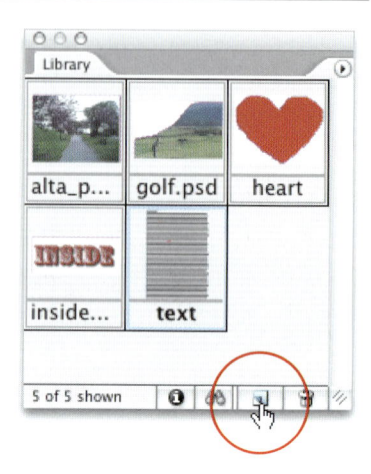

DRAG FROM THE LIBRARY ONTO THE PAGE

Okay, you've got items into your library. How do you use them? Just drag them onto the page from the Library palette. You could also use the Place Item(s) command from the Library palette's flyout menu, but how much fun is that?

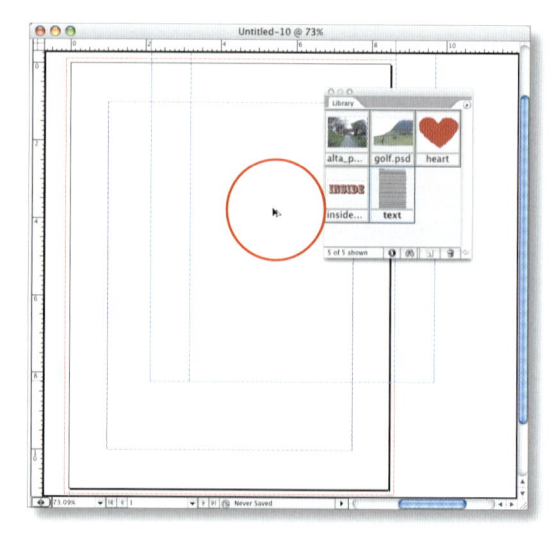

DOUBLE-CLICK LIBRARY ITEMS TO NAME THEM

If you created an object or frame and dragged it into a library, most likely it went into your library as "Untitled." That's going to make it hard to search for later. Use this tip to name your library items: Open your library and double-click each item you wish to name in the Library palette. When the Item Information dialog appears, simply key in a better name and click OK.

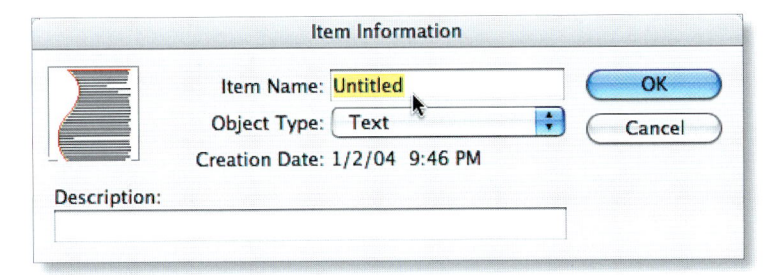

SAVE TIME SEARCHING IN YOUR LIBRARY

If you're adding items to your InDesign Library palette, you can save yourself some time and assign keywords (for searching purposes) right when you add each object to your library. Just hold the Option key (PC: Alt key) before you drag the item into the Library palette, and the Item Information dialog will appear so you can assign your keywords in the Description field at the same time. Big time saver.

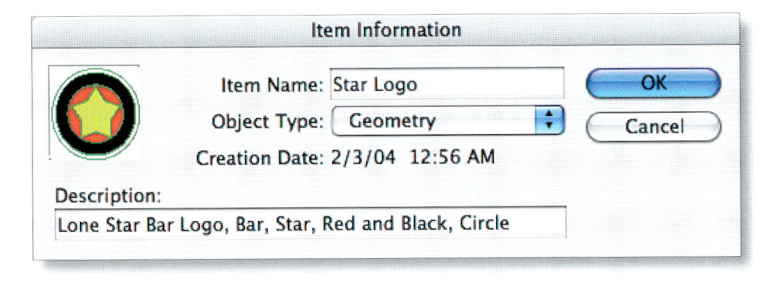

ADD KEYWORDS TO ITEMS ALREADY IN THE LIBRARY

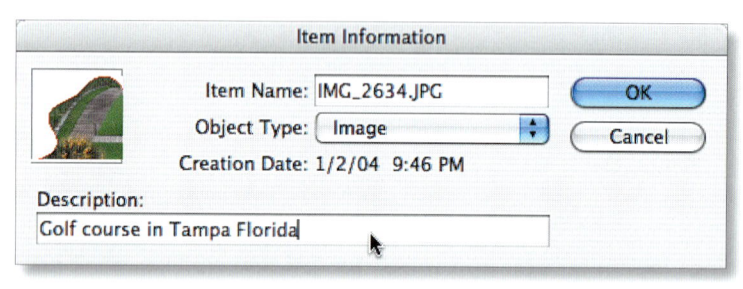

If you want to add keywords to items that are already in the library, simply double-click on a library item and enter keywords into the Description field. Then you can use these keywords to search for these library items later by clicking on the Show Library Subset button at the bottom of the Library palette.

SEARCH THE LIBRARY

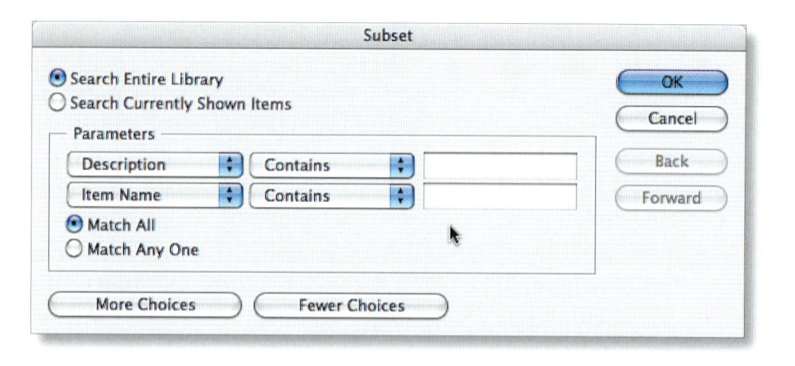

If you have dozens or even hundreds of items in an InDesign library, scrolling up and down the list looking for what you want will get old pretty quick. The next time you're looking for something in particular, click the little set of binoculars on the bottom of the palette. This will bring up a Subset dialog that allows you to search the item name as well as other attributes. Each time you click the More Choices button you will be given the ability to add more choices to narrow down your search.

138   CHAPTER 6 • Working with Graphics

NARROW YOUR LIBRARY SEARCH

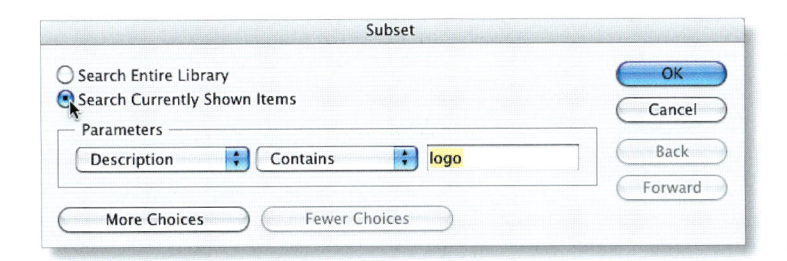

Okay, picture this: You've done a library search using the word "logo" and about 60 logos show up in your search results. Not good. Here's how to narrow that search—once your search results have appeared, click the Show Library Subset button (it looks like a pair of binoculars) at the bottom of the Library palette. When the Subset dialog appears, click on Search Currently Shown Items, change the first Parameters pop-up menu to Description, then add another keyword. When you click OK, it will only search within the results of your previous search, helping you narrow things down to find the item you're looking for.

HOW TO RECOVER FROM A LIBRARY SEARCH

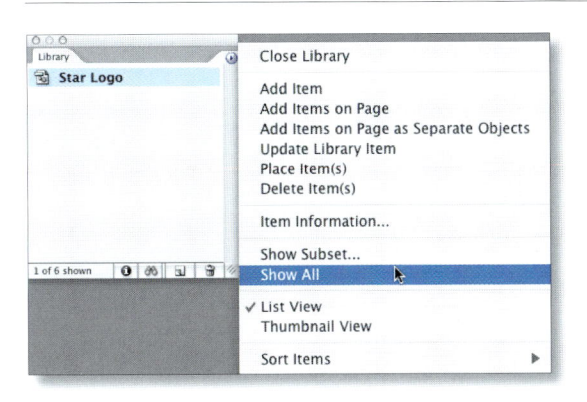

If you've done a successful search for a particular item, the library now displays only the item you searched for. Once you've used the item, how do you get to see the whole library again, and not just your search item? Go to the Library palette's flyout menu, choose Show All (as shown here) and all the items in your library will be visible once again.

CHAPTER 6 • Working with Graphics 139

THUMBNAILS IN THE LIBRARY ARE COOL, BUT…

For a visual person, having thumbnails is cool, but they take up a lot of space. If you want to maximize your Library palette, try this: Choose List View from the Library palette's flyout menu. Now your Library palette will list all the names of the objects it contains and you'll see a lot more items in the same space than you did with Thumbnail View.

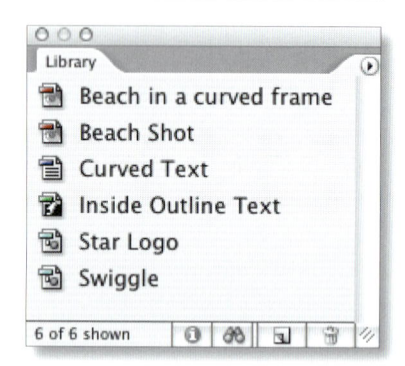

DON'T PRINT THIS!

Hey, sometimes you just want something on the page for show. Maybe it's a note to your production department or some other logo or stamp of approval. With this tip you can make it non-printing. Select an object and bring up the Attributes palette from the Window menu. Now simply click the Nonprinting checkbox.

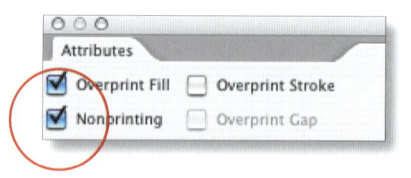

140   CHAPTER 6 • Working with Graphics

GO STAND IN THE CORNER AND THINK ABOUT WHAT YOU'VE DONE

By default all operations in the Control palette affect selected objects from the center of the object. You can change that behavior with this tip: The icon on the left side of the Control palette has nine handles. You can click on any one of those handles to dictate where your measurements and operations will happen. We like the upper-left corner best, don't ask why.

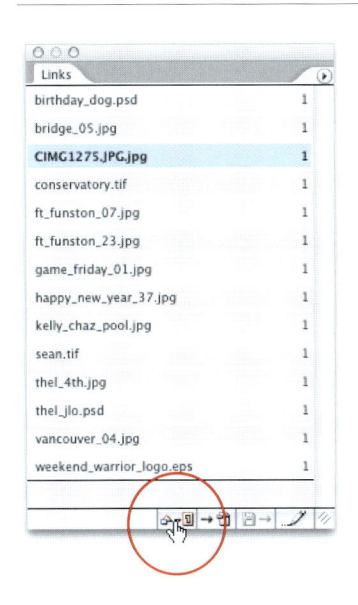

RELINK TO A NEW GRAPHIC

Your client gave you a picture and you placed it. But since then you've rotated it, you've scaled it, you've done all kinds of things to it to get it just the way you wanted it on the page. Now the phone rings and your client says, "Use the other picture"! Skip all those four-letter words, and try this: Bring up the Links palette from the Window menu and hit the Relink button at the bottom. Now select the other picture and click Open. Your picture will be replaced and all your transformations will be intact.

CHAPTER 6 • Working with Graphics   141

REPLACE GRAPHICS

It happens. You've changed your mind and you want to use a different graphic. No problem. Select the graphic that you want to replace on the page and choose Place from the File menu. Find your new graphic and make sure that at the bottom of the Place dialog you have Replace Selected Item checked. When you bring in the new graphic, it will automatically replace the selected one in the same frame.

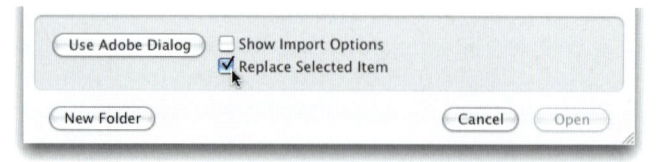

MAKE A PICTURE

Sometimes a PDF just won't do. You may need a graphic from your layout for your website or an image to send to a client. The next time you need a JPEG of an image on your page, try this tip: Select the objects you want to be in the JPEG file. Choose Export from the File menu, then select JPEG as the Format, and click Save. When the Export JPEG dialog appears choose Selection instead of Page. You can set the quality and then click the Export button.

InDesign CS/CS2
KillerTips

🔴 🟡 🟢 WHO TOOK THAT PLACED DIGITAL PHOTO? INDESIGN KNOWS

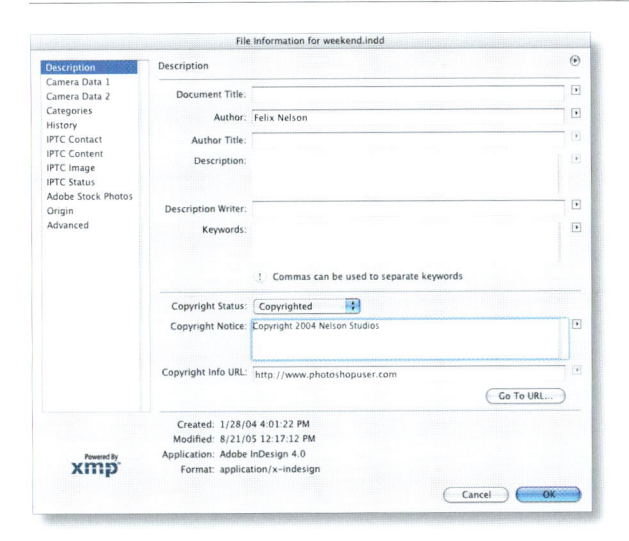

If you place a digital photo into InDesign and you want to credit the photographer who took the shot, InDesign might be able to tell you. Click on the photo, then go under the File menu and choose File Info. This brings up a dialog that displays information embedded into the digital photo itself. In the left column, click on Description (as shown) and if the photographer who took the shot entered his copyright info, you'll see the author's name (as shown here). In the File Information dialog highlight the author/photographer's name and hit Command-C (PC: Control-C) on the keyboard. Hit Cancel to close the File Info window. All you have to do now is create a text frame under or at the side of your photo and paste in the photographer's name.

🔴 🟡 🟢 FADE THAT IMAGE BACK

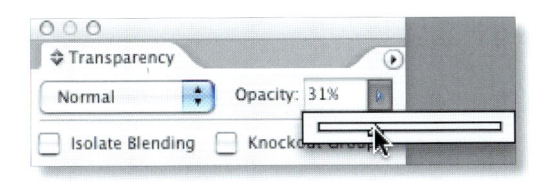

Sometimes you just want to fade or backscreen an image into the background. The next time you want that look, select your image with the Selection tool and drag the Opacity slider to the left in the Transparency palette.

CHAPTER 6 • Working with Graphics   **143**

STACKING ORDER IS EVERYTHING

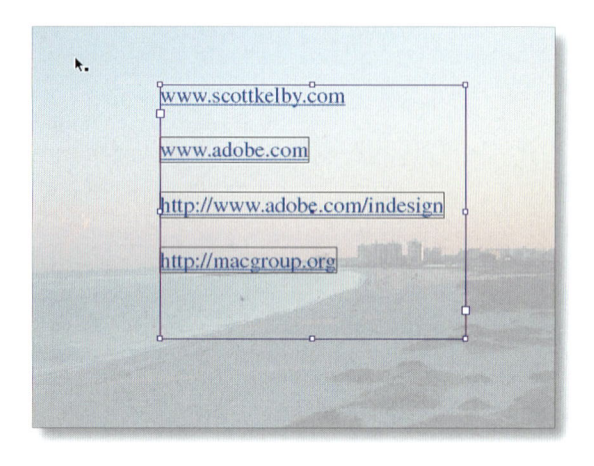

Some people freak out at the mere mention of transparency in a page layout program; but transparency used properly does work! Simply follow the stacking order rules to eliminate the most common transparency issues. You can use layers to make it easier or you can simply remember to always put on top the items you don't want affected by transparency. A good thing to have unaffected by transparency is type. If you have a transparent object on top of type, the type will most likely rasterize. So to prevent that from happening, put your background images on the bottom of the stacking order (or bottom layer), then your photos, then your vector graphics, then your body text and headlines.

IDENTIFY PAGES WITH TRANSPARENT OBJECTS

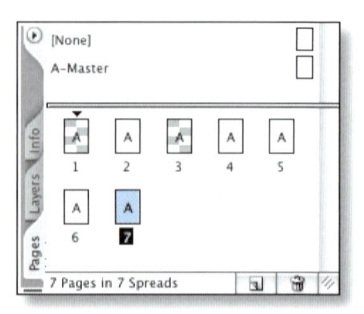

Sometimes you don't want transparency, or maybe you want to make sure you're not using transparency on certain pages. This tip will show you which pages use transparency and which ones don't. Go to the Pages palette and you'll see that the pages with a checkerboard icon use transparency and the plain white ones do not.

144 CHAPTER 6 • Working with Graphics

TRANSPARENCY FLATTENER STYLES

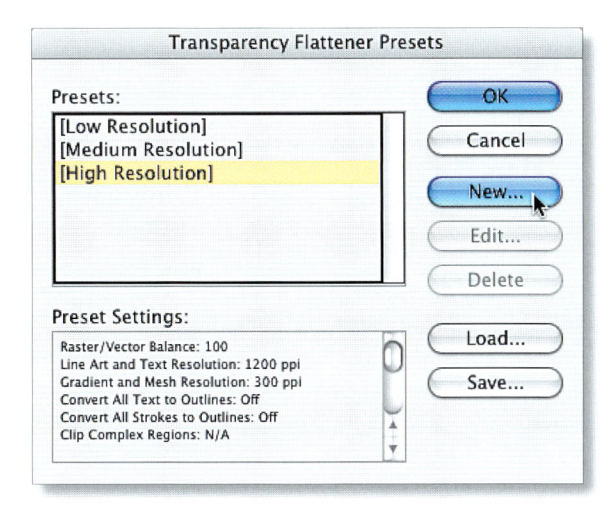

The key to successfully outputting documents that contain transparency lies in the Transparency Flattener styles. Unless you're the printer or service provider, there is no way for you to know how to create a transparency flattener style that will work best. However, if you are printing your own InDesign documents with transparency, try this to improve your results: Choose Transparency Flattener Presets from the Edit menu. Three presets appear there by default. You can experiment with your own settings by highlighting one of the existing ones and clicking the New button. Adjust the sliders and options, name it, and click OK. You will be able to choose your transparency flattener style in the Print dialog's Advanced options. Experiment until you achieve your desired results on your output device.

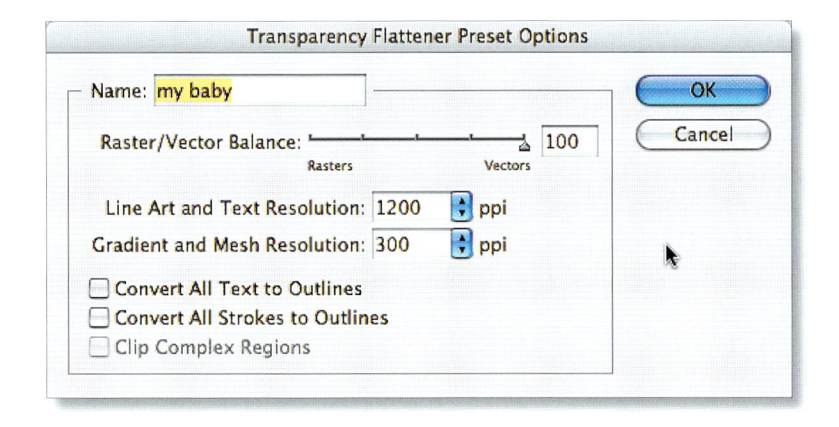

CHAPTER 6 • Working with Graphics   145

USE TRANSPARENCY FROM PHOTOSHOP

Say goodbye to clipping paths. Photoshop has great tools for eliminating the background from an image. Well, now you can take advantage of that work in your page layout. Simply make an image transparent in Photoshop by putting it on its own layer and eliminating the Background layer. Save it as a native Photoshop file (.PSD) and then place (File>Place) that native file in InDesign. Once it is placed, you can layer it on top of other elements and see through it.

USE PHOTOSHOP ALPHA CHANNELS

Photo retouchers will often use alpha channels as masks or saved selections. The next time you want to eliminate the background of a placed Photoshop image, check to see if it has an alpha channel. Select the placed Photoshop image on your page and choose Clipping Path from the Object menu. Choose Alpha Channel from the Type menu. If there are alpha channels in the image, you will be able to choose them in the Alpha pop-up menu.

GENERATE CLIPPING PATHS AUTOMATICALLY

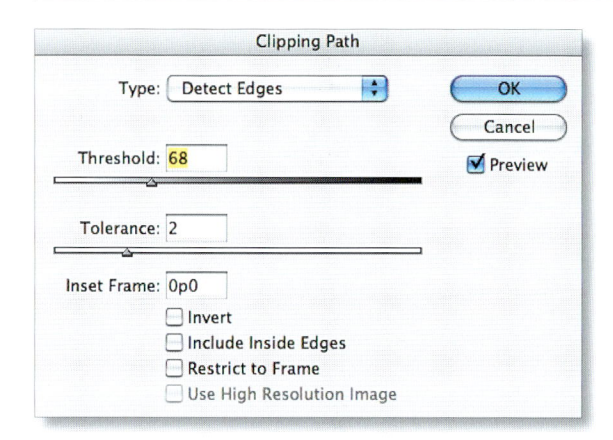

Although InDesign can bring in native Photoshop files with transparent layers, there are times that you will still have clipping paths. For example, older images that already have clipping paths in them or vector images that you wish to run text around. If you have an image with a fairly simple background that has not been erased in Photoshop, try this to eliminate it in InDesign: Place (File>Place) your image and then choose Clipping Path from the Object menu. Then choose Detect Edges from the Type pop-up menu. While Preview is checked, you can use the Threshold and Tolerance sliders to eliminate the background. Use the Invert option to eliminate darker tones. Click OK when you're done.

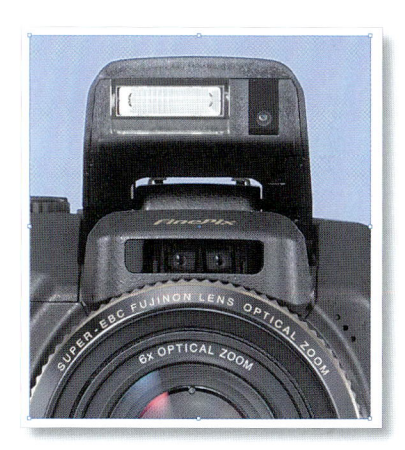

CHAPTER 6 • Working with Graphics   147

USE THE TRANSPARENCY FLATTENER PREVIEW

Printing transparency doesn't have to be hit-or-miss. The next time you're going to send your printer an InDesign document that contains transparency, you can use the Flattener Preview palette to see how your document will most likely look printed. Choose Window>Output> Flattener Preview. This feature is fairly processor-intensive, so it defaults to an off state. Choose from the various previews under the Highlight pop-up menu in the Flattener Preview palette to see which objects in your document contain transparency and more importantly which objects on your pages will be affected by transparency. You can also see what effect your transparency flattener styles will have on your document. Remember to set the Highlight pop-up back to None when you're done.

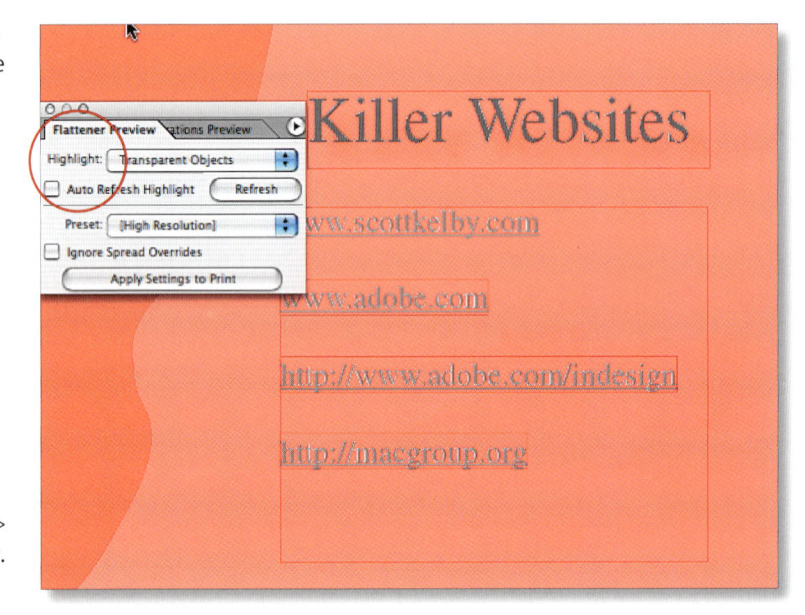

148   CHAPTER 6 • Working with Graphics

OVERRIDE FLATTENER SETTINGS SPREAD BY SPREAD

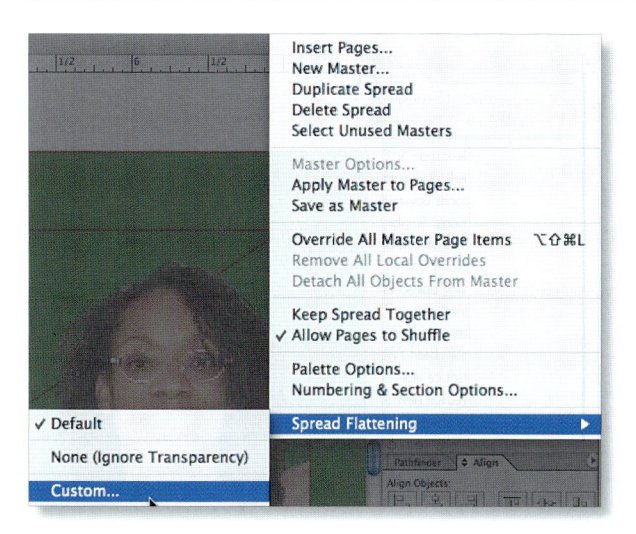

If you have a document that mixes both high-res and low-res graphics, then one transparency flattener style is probably not going to be enough. If your document contains mostly high-res images, then go to the spread that contains the low-res images and choose Custom from the Spread Flattening submenu from the Pages palette's flyout menu. This will bring up the same kind of flattener settings that you used in setting up your flattener style, but these settings will apply only to this spread.

CHAPTER 6 • Working with Graphics 149

Cool Hand Luke

WAY-COOL TIPS

As you might guess, there are a bunch of tips that are so cool they defy categorization. They don't belong in page layout or navigation. They'd be out of

Cool Hand Luke
a bunch of way-cool tips

place with those "nerdy" tips. These are the tips that you'll find hanging out with the cool kids. Sipping champagne with P. Diddy and rollin' in a Bentley bling-blingin' it with some 20-inch rims. These tips are so cool they can't be confined by convention. These are tips untrammelled. They need to bust out on their own, free to roam and spread their innate coolness wherever the pages take them. These are the tips you take out for a spin. The ones you use to impress your friends and humiliate your enemies. The ones you casually pull out at InDesign parties out in L.A. (Do they really have InDesign parties out in L.A.? Not without these tips they don't.) So use these sparingly. Pull them out when you need 'em—when you need to stake your claim, mark your territory, and generally establish who's the "king" of InDesign. Because remember, when you strip away all the typography, all the design, and all the CMYK separations, it all comes down to this—"Whoever dies with the most tips wins."

CHAPTER 7 • Way-Cool Tips   151

THE TRICK TO SHRINKING YOUR INDESIGN FILE SIZE

If you've ever taken a look at the file size of your InDesign documents, you've probably noticed that they get pretty big pretty quick, and that normally doesn't create a problem—unless you're emailing your pages (which we do quite often). Well, here's a neat trick for greatly shrinking the file size of a bloated InDesign document. Reopen the file in InDesign, then change something. Anything. Move a guide, type a space, etc., and then don't just choose Save: Instead go under the File menu, choose Save As, and save over the old file using the exact same name. For some reason, when you Save As (using the same name) it creates a much smaller file size for the exact same document. Sounds crazy, but it works like a charm.

COPY DROP SHADOWS WITH THE EYEDROPPER

Putting a drop shadow on an image or text is easy (just select it with the Selection tool and go to Object>Drop Shadow). However, after you've tweaked that shadow to get it just right, you may need to apply the same shadow to another object or objects in the document. Drop shadows are a frame attribute and therefore you can use the Eyedropper tool to add the same shadow to other elements. Simply select the other objects by Shift-clicking on them with the Selection tool, switch to the Eyedropper tool, and then click on the edge of the frame containing the shadow. All your selected frames will have the same shadow settings with just a single click. It's tricky at times and works best if you click just to the right of the frame's edge.

152   CHAPTER 7 • Way-Cool Tips

USE MULTIPLE VIEWS OF THE SAME DOCUMENT

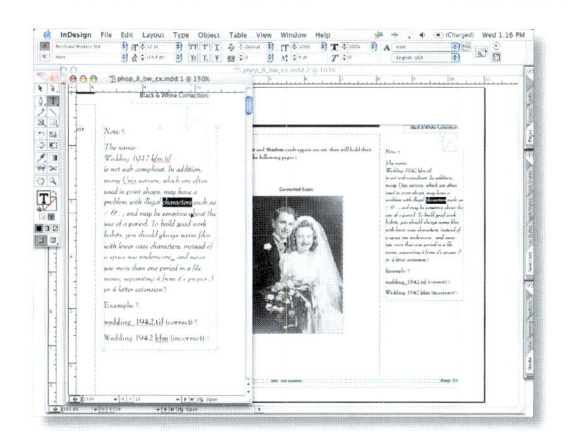

Sometimes you need to be zoomed in and out at the same time. Without causing a rift in the space-time continuum, you can simply choose Window>Arrange>New Window. This will give you another view of the same document that you can zoom in or out on. You can even tile the windows to see both views at the same time.

WANT TO SPEED UP INDESIGN? TURN OFF PLUG-INS

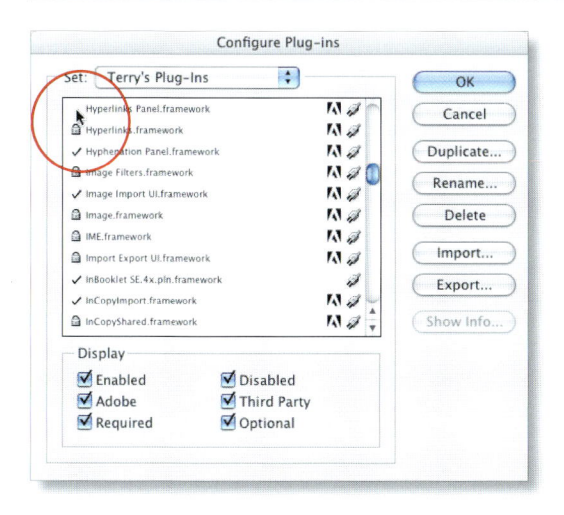

For the most part, InDesign is an application made up of plug-ins. This allows Adobe and third parties to change and add to InDesign without the delays we often see in other products. InDesign also includes lots of functionality that you may not need. Therefore, you can speed things up by turning off plug-ins that you don't use. Choose Configure Plug-ins from the InDesign menu (PC: Edit menu), and then click Duplicate because you're not able to modify the default set. Then, turn off plug-ins that you don't use by clicking on the checkmark in the left-hand column next to each of them, such as the Hyperlinks Panel (as shown here), then click OK. You have to quit and relaunch InDesign for your changes to take effect.

CHAPTER 7 • Way-Cool Tips   153

InDesign CS/CS2 KillerTips

IMAGE-BY-IMAGE HIGH-QUALITY DISPLAY

If you're wondering why your images sometimes look as if you're seeing them through a burlap sack, it's because InDesign defaults to a Typical Display view—typical of 1986 page-layout apps, that is. Well, you don't have to live with this anymore. Simply Control-click (PC: Right-click) on your image with the Selection tool. This will bring up the contextual menu and from there you can choose Display Performance>High Quality Display. This works on any kind of image in an InDesign document, but works extremely well on native Illustrator, EPS, and PDF files placed in your

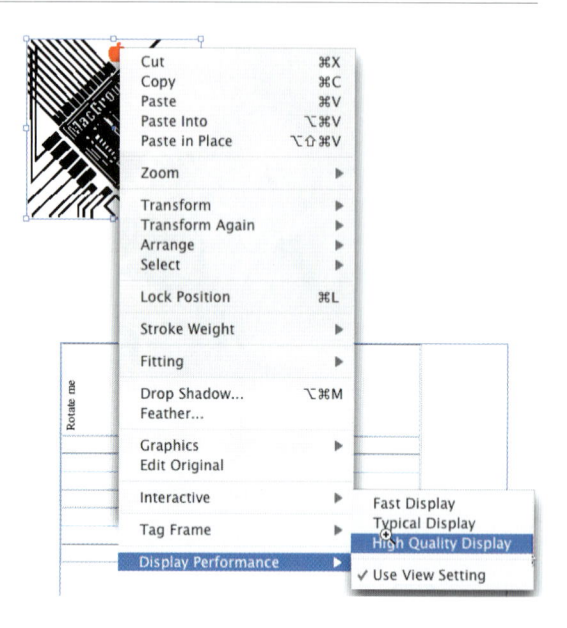

SET YOUR OWN DISPLAY PERFORMANCE

As mentioned in the previous tip, you can control the display of your graphics on a frame-by-frame basis. But what's even cooler than that is that you can really fine-tune the difference between Optimized, Typical, and High Quality Display. Just go to the InDesign menu (PC: Edit menu), under Preferences, and choose Display Performance. Then, in the Adjust View Settings section, you can decide on the image quality for each setting.

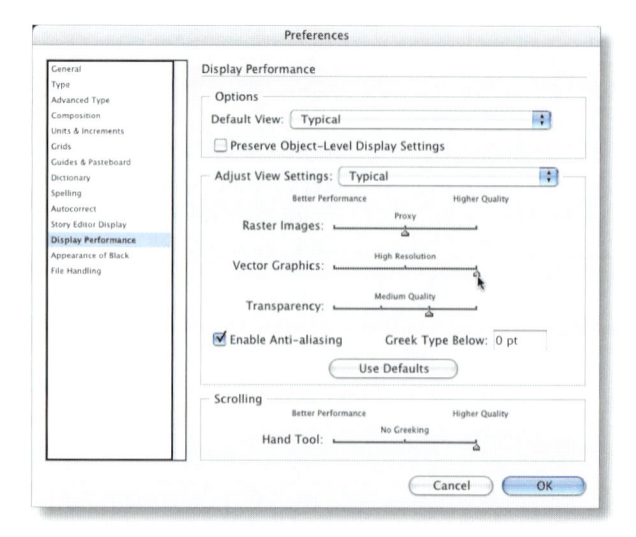

154   CHAPTER 7 • Way-Cool Tips

CREATE BLEEDS AND SLUGS WITHOUT OVERSIZED PAGES

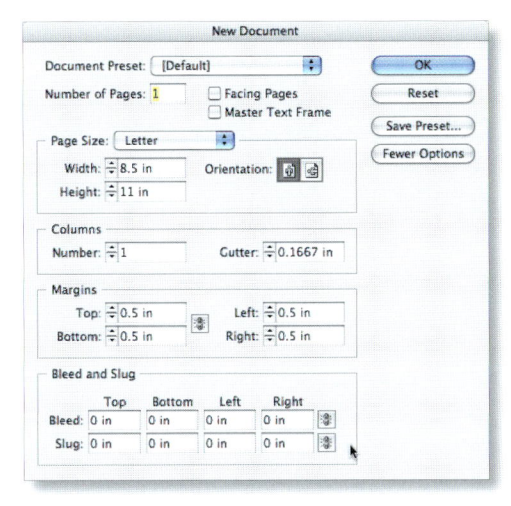

Hey, are you still creating oversized pages just to represent your bleed and slug information? Now you don't have to anymore. The New Document dialog allows you to create extra space around your document page for either bleed or slug information. Just click on the More Options button in the New Document dialog and you'll be presented with two extra sets of measurements at the bottom. You can enter measurements for either the bleed or the slug. This way, you can create your document at the actual finished size, yet still account for all the extra stuff that you have to put outside the document area. You can even control whether or not the bleed or the slug will print in the Marks and Bleed section of the Print dialog.

VIEW BLEEDS AND SLUGS USING PREVIEW

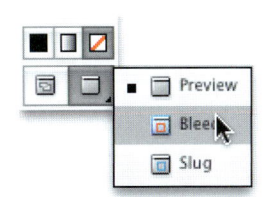

Creating extra space around your document to represent the bleed or the slug is one thing, but what about viewing this information? Or better yet, turning this extra space off when you don't want to see it. In addition to the Normal View and Preview Modes, InDesign offers you Bleed Mode and Slug Mode. You can get to these extra views at the bottom of the Toolbox by simply holding down your mouse button on the Preview Mode icon and you'll get a choice among Preview, Bleed, and Slug.

CHAPTER 7 • Way-Cool Tips   155

USE PATHFINDER TO JOIN SHAPES

Drawing irregular-shaped frames with the Pen or Polygon tool is okay, but sometimes it's a lot easier to just take two shapes and join them together. Simply draw two or more overlapping shapes with InDesign's various shape tools. Then, using the Selection tool, hold down the Shift key and select each shape. Now, choose Pathfinder from the Window menu. Once the Pathfinder palette appears, click the first icon to join them together as one frame for text or graphics.

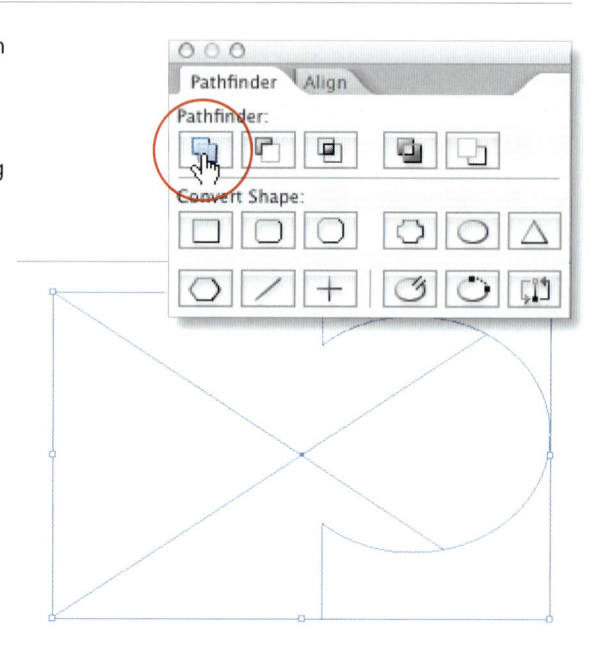

ENTER MEASUREMENTS IN YOUR UNIT OF CHOICE

Everyone has his or her favorite unit of measurement. For many, it's inches. However, there are those times when you need to enter points, picas, etc. into a dialog. Well, without changing your Preferences, you can simply enter the measurement in your system of choice as long as you put the abbreviation for it after the numbers. For example, if you wanted to enter 400 points into a dialog that's expecting inches, you would simply type "400pt".

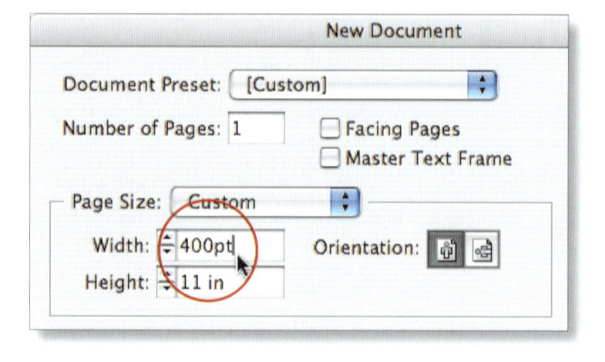

156   CHAPTER 7 • Way-Cool Tips

USE THE STORY EDITOR TO EDIT BLOCKS OF TEXT

Okay, there is one thing we miss from our old PageMaker days. Yup, you guessed it, the Story Editor. It's back, and the Story Editor is way-cool because it allows you to enter text and make changes or corrections to your InDesign documents in a nice, easy-to-read word processing-type view. Simply place your cursor anywhere in your text frame and choose Edit in Story Editor from the Edit menu. Now you can make all the changes you want, no matter how many pages your text spans or frames you have linked.

OPEN QUARKXPRESS DOCUMENTS IN INDESIGN

Impress your friends! Open their QuarkXPress documents right in front of them inside of InDesign. InDesign supports opening XPress 3.3 through 4.1 documents natively. Simply go up to the File menu and choose Open. Point to your XPress document and click Open. Within moments the XPress document will be converted and opened as an untitled InDesign document complete with all its master pages, style sheets, and content.

OPEN PAGEMAKER DOCUMENTS IN INDESIGN

Well, it wouldn't be fair if InDesign could open only QuarkXPress documents, now would it? InDesign can also open PageMaker 6.0–7.0 documents—with no additional plug-ins.

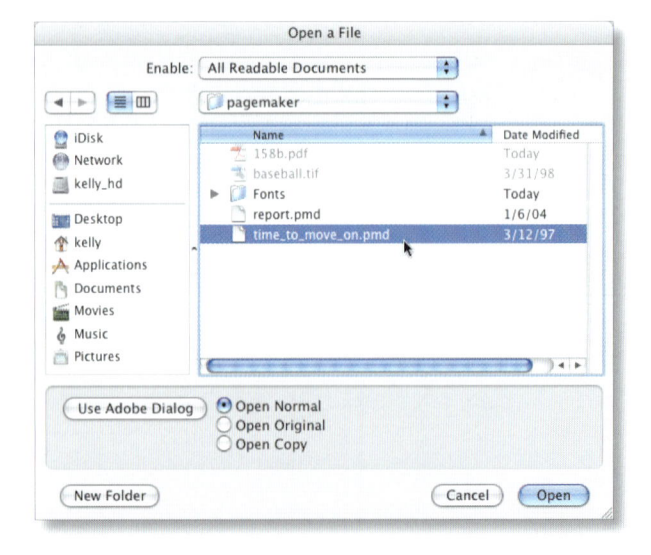

CHAPTER 7 • Way-Cool Tips

USE THE INFO PALETTE TO GET IMAGE DETAILS

It's 4:45 p.m. and the document you're working on needs to be in the printer's hands by 5:00 when you think, "Did I convert that image to CMYK or not?" With the Info palette, you can simply click on an image to find out not only what color space it uses but also what type of image it is and its resolution. If you don't see that information in the Info palette, just choose Show Options from its flyout menu.

USE THE MEASURE TOOL INSTEAD OF RULERS

So—on your page is an image containing a person. You want to make sure your surrounding images are the same exact size as the person. One question remains. How big is the person? With the new Measure tool (found in the Eyedropper tool's flyout menu in the Toolbox) you can click on one side of the person and drag to the other side and the Info palette will show you exactly how big the person within the image is.

CHAPTER 7 • Way-Cool Tips   159

UNEMBED EMBEDDED GRAPHICS TO MAKE YOUR PRINTER HAPPY

Embedded graphics are taboo with most printers and service providers. If you don't believe that, call one and ask if you can embed all your graphics in your next InDesign job and they'll pass out right there on the spot. Luckily, if you or someone else has embedded graphics in a document you can select the graphic, go to the Links palette (under the Window menu) and choose Unembed File from the flyout menu. InDesign even gives you the choice of relinking to the original image or to a new folder that it will create containing the unembedded graphic(s).

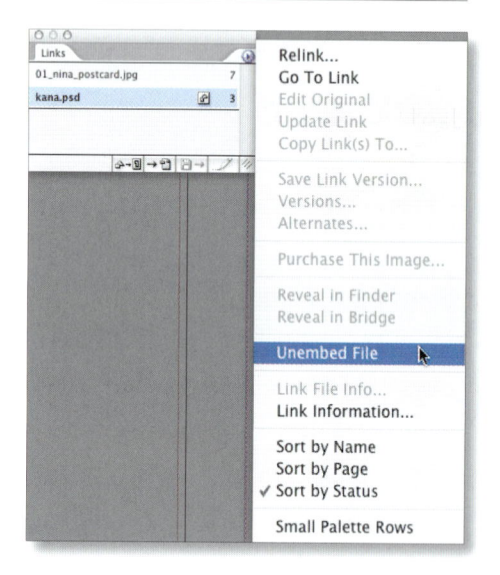

YOU'RE THE ONE (LAYER)

Don't just click your way through your layers to turn them off one by one in the Layers palette. By holding down the Option key (PC: Alt key), you can click the Eye icon of the one layer that you want to be visible and turn off all other layers at the same time. This is sometimes referred to as soloing.

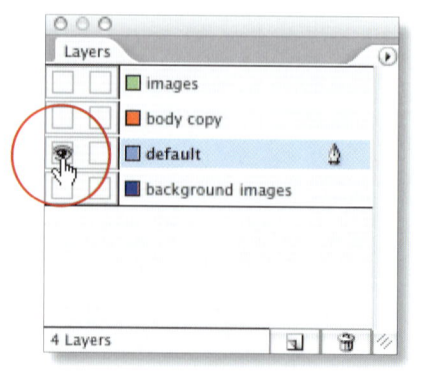

160   CHAPTER 7 • Way-Cool Tips

DRAG TO MAKE VISIBLE OR LOCK LAYERS

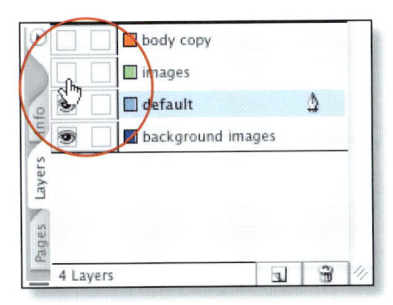

Although InDesign doesn't have any levers like the ones found in the Enterprise's transporter room, it has something just as cool: You can drag the visibility or locking/unlocking of layers. That's right, just click-and-drag through the column of Eye or Pencil icons in the Layers palette to make several layers visible/invisible or locked/unlocked all at once. You can even make the transporter sound effects while you do it. We won't tell.

Hidden Treasure

LITTLE-KNOWN FEATURES

Are there really InDesign features you don't know about? Of course there are. If there weren't, how could we put together an entire chapter on hidden features? Here's the

Hidden Treasure
little-known features

thing: Every time a new version of InDesign is announced, Adobe boasts about the top 10 or so megafeatures that are sure to get lots of press. But each new version contains way more than just the 10 or 12 features you read about in the news. There are often nearly a hundred overall enhancements, improvements, and new features; but these are often overlooked due to space constraints or sheer lack of intestinal fortitude. So what happens to these "other" features? They remain hidden. Buried, if you will, in a cacophony of echoing nothingness until someone rises up to lift the veil of secrecy and expose these hidden gems to the light of day. It's not us, but surely someday someone will write a chapter on it. We can only hope.

VIEW MENUS IN ALPHABETICAL ORDER

How much time do we all spend looking through the menus for that one command that we know is there somewhere? You just saw it yesterday, but you're frantically dropping down through the menus trying to find it. You know what it's called, but you just don't see it. You begin to reach for the manual but then you say to yourself, "Nah, that would take even longer. I'll find it eventually. Anything is better than looking in the manual." Try this: Hold down the Shift-Option-Command keys (PC: Shift-Alt-Control) and click on any menu. BAM, it's now displayed in alphabetical order.

WANT TO USE INCHES? TYPE (″)

A number of applications let you enter values in fields and then decide the unit of measure after you type in the value. (For example, if you want 72 points, you'd enter 72 pt, or for three inches you'd type 3 in.) InDesign also lets you type in the inch symbol (″) after the value. (For example, to enter 7.3 inches in a field, you'd just type 7.3″.)

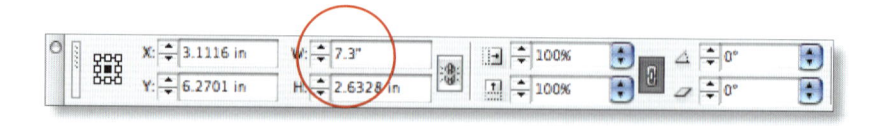

164   CHAPTER 8 • Little-Known Features

RESHAPE FRAMES WITH THE PENCIL TOOL

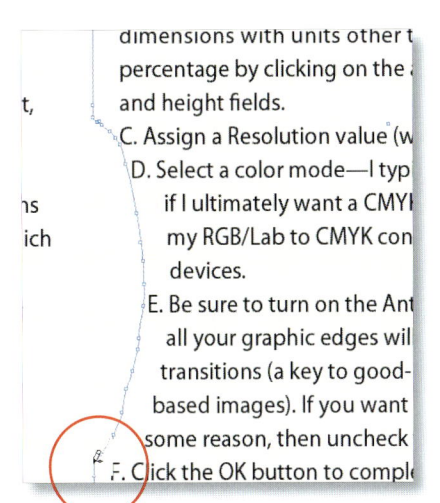

We get a kick out of this one every time we show it. The world is not just rectangles (unless you live in a Tetris game). You can modify the shape of your text and image frames by drawing on the edge of the frame with the Pencil tool. Just select the frame with the Selection tool, switch to the Pencil tool (N), and start drawing (make sure you start and finish right on the edge).

CREATE GRADIENTS THE EASY WAY

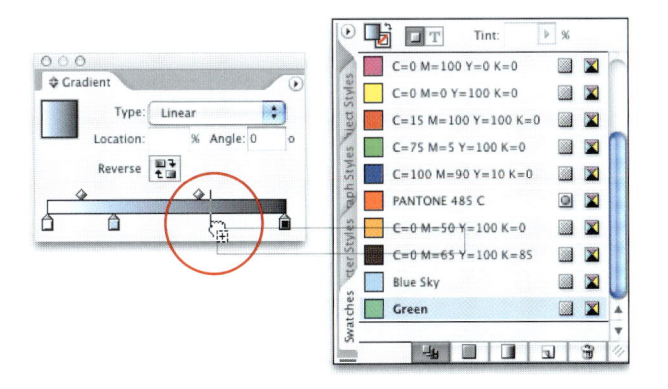

Creating gradients in InDesign used to be a lesson in patience. Now InDesign makes it much easier. Simply click-and-drag existing swatches from the Swatches palette to the gradient bar in the Gradient palette. Once you're done, you can even click on the gradient swatch in the Gradient palette and drag it back to the Swatches palette to keep your newly created gradient.

CHAPTER 8 • Little-Known Features   165

GET ROUNDED RECTANGLES WITH CORNER EFFECTS

Stop looking for the Rectangle with Rounded Corners tool. It doesn't exist. Create your rectangle frame with the regular Rectangle tool and then choose Corner Effects from the Object menu. From this dialog you can choose Rounded from the pop-up menu and then the amount of roundness you want in the Size field. Be sure to click the Preview checkbox so that you can see your changes as you make them. You can also use the Up and Down Arrow keys on your keyboard to adjust the Size up/down. Add the Shift key to change it by larger increments.

RESET YOUR ZERO POINT

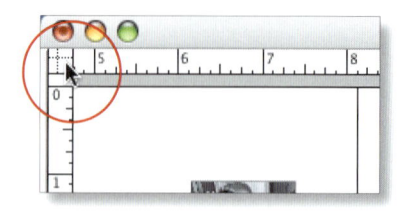

You probably already know that if you click-and-drag at the point where your rulers meet (in the very upper left-hand corner of your document window), you can pull out the zero point (the point where your ruler starts at zero). Many designers find this handy for measuring objects on their page; however, trying to drag the point back up into the corner is a little tricky. Luckily, you don't have to. Just double-click right up in that spot where the zero point used to be, and the zero point will snap right back into place.

166   CHAPTER 8 • Little-Known Features

CHANGE ATTRIBUTES USING PERCENTAGES

Some people think in percentages. You know the ones. The folks who were in business school while you were in design school. They'll yell out things like "Make that 33% larger." When they do, don't reach for the calculator. This tip will make you glad that you slept through that math class. Simply highlight the text you want to change, and then in the Control palette highlight the field for the attribute that you want to change and key in the percentage. For example, enter 150% in the Font Size field to make your type grow by 50%. Now Tab out of it to apply it.

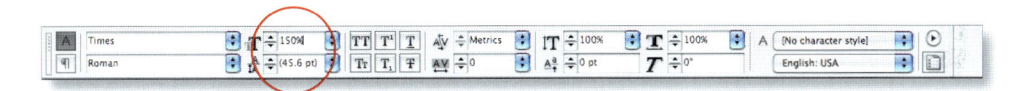

Before scaling 150%   After scaling 150%

GETTING PAGEMAKER FEATURES IN INDESIGN

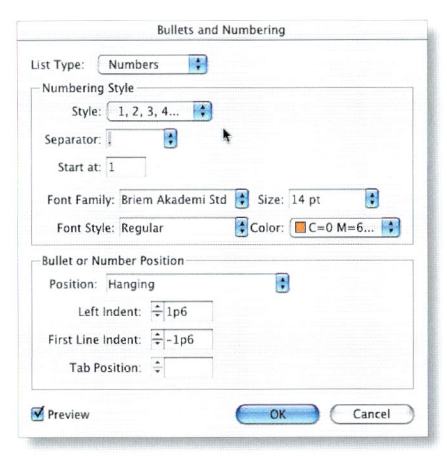

Since Adobe officially stopped developing or supporting PageMaker in early 2004, a lot of PageMaker users are making the jump to InDesign. If you're one of those, InDesign eases the transition a bit by making some of PageMaker's features and functionality available in InDesign (it kind of makes you feel a bit more at home). You can access PageMaker favorites like the PageMaker Toolbar, bullets and numbers, and PageMaker templates, plus training on how to make the jump to InDesign. For more details, visit Adobe.com.

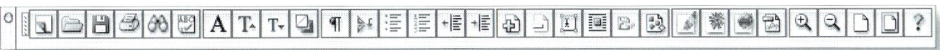

CHAPTER 8 • Little-Known Features   167

SEE YOUR PAGES BEFORE YOU OPEN THEM

Wouldn't it be great if you could get a preview of your InDesign document before you actually open it? It can't be done, but wouldn't it be great? (Just kidding.) You can do it, if you make one little change in InDesign's Preferences. Go into Preferences and choose File Handling. When the dialog appears, go to the Saving InDesign Files section and turn on the checkbox for Always Save Preview Images with Documents (as shown). From this point on, as you save or update documents in InDesign, you'll see a preview of those documents when you use the Open A File dialog.

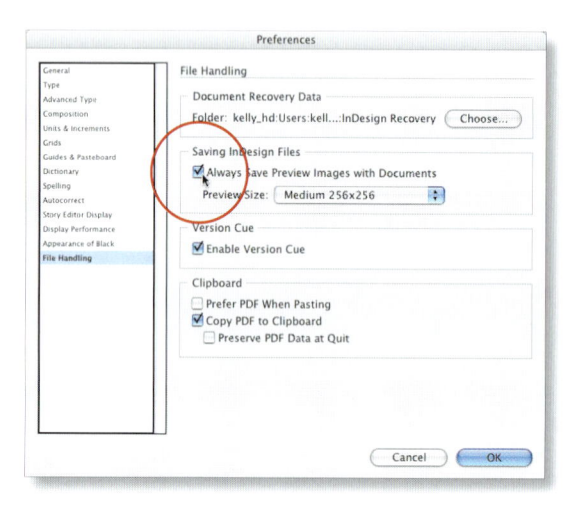

THE DELETING STUNT

This is one of those tricks you'll only use when somebody else is looking (in particular, when a QuarkXPress user is watching you use InDesign). Just click on an object you want to delete within InDesign, and drag it right out of InDesign and straight into the Trash on your desktop (Mac OS) or the Recycle Bin (Windows) and the object will be deleted from the document. It's not a particularly practical tip, but it's great for showing off at Quark parties.

168   CHAPTER 8 • Little-Known Features

DRAG-AND-DROP FROM IPHOTO

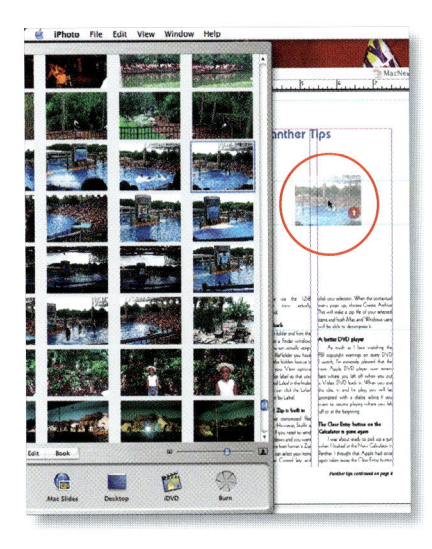

If you're on the Mac, chances are you have a few photos in iPhoto. Wanna use those pictures in InDesign? Don't export, just drag-and-drop. That's right, simply create or open an InDesign document and launch iPhoto. Now simply select the image you want, and drag it right into your open document.

DRAG-AND-DROP FROM ADOBE BRIDGE

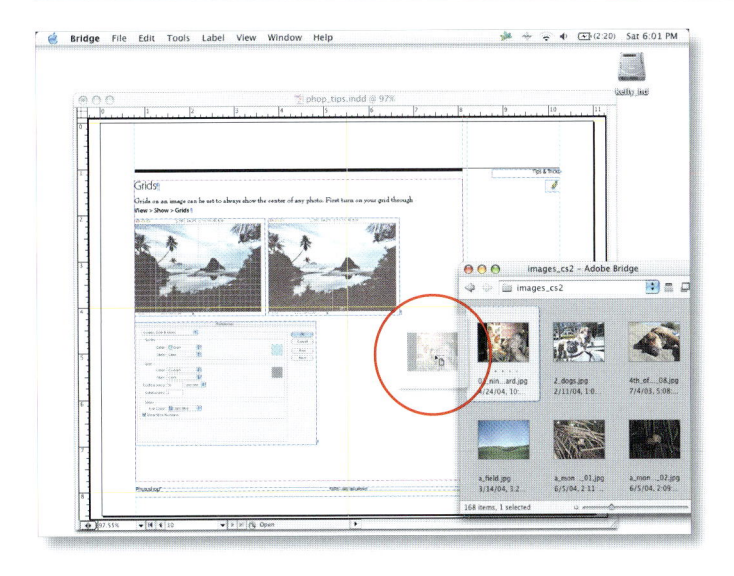

Adobe Bridge is awesome. It allows you to view hundreds of photos at once in any given folder. Wouldn't it be cool if you found that perfect photo and then wanted to use it in InDesign? Okay, do it! Open Adobe Bridge and find your image. Create or open an InDesign document and drag the image right into it from Adobe Bridge.

CHAPTER 8 • Little-Known Features   169

CREATE A SPECIFIC-SIZED FRAME IN ONE CLICK

So you need a frame that's exactly 2.3x4.7″ and you've given up trying to draw it by hand? Stop pulling out guides. Simply choose one of the frame tools and click once on the page. Now you can specify whatever size you need in the resulting dialog and click OK.

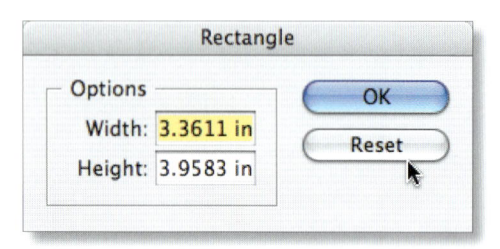

CREATE A DUOTONE EFFECT RIGHT WITHIN INDESIGN

Okay, so you're on a budget and you can only print a two-color job. Well, there's no problem creating the text in any color, but what about your photos? Who wants to live with just grayscale? Colorizing TIFFs is not a new thing, but this tip will take it to a whole new level. When you select your grayscale TIFF or Photoshop placed image with the Selection tool and click-and-drag a swatch in the Swatches palette to the image, it will colorize the shadows. You've just faked a duotone without ever touching Photoshop. That's cool, but wait! Now simply click on a different swatch (don't click-and-drag, just click) and it will colorize the highlights.

170 CHAPTER 8 • Little-Known Features

ADD HYPERLINKS OR BOOKMARKS TO ANY OBJECT

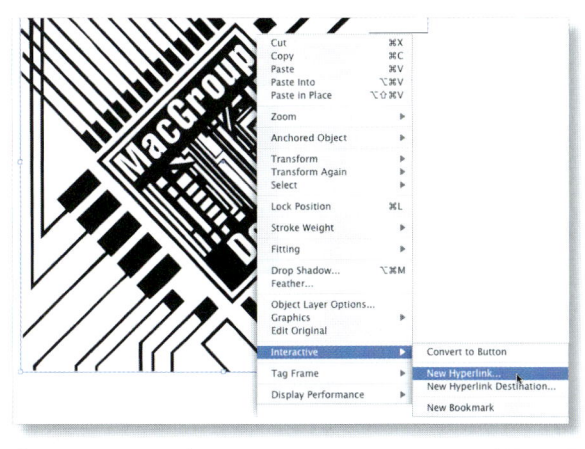

We sometimes wish that either print or the Web would go away; but guess what, they're both here to stay (at least for a while). This means that you'll sometimes create documents that need to get repurposed. We make PDFs all the time from InDesign documents, but here's a tip to make your PDFs just that much cooler. Select any image on the page with the Selection tool, bring up the contextual menu on it (Mac: Control-click [PC: Right-click]), and choose New Hyperlink from the Interactive submenu. You can now create a URL or Page link so that when the user clicks this image in the PDF, it will go to the webpage or document page of your choice.

LET THE GOOD TIMES SCROLL

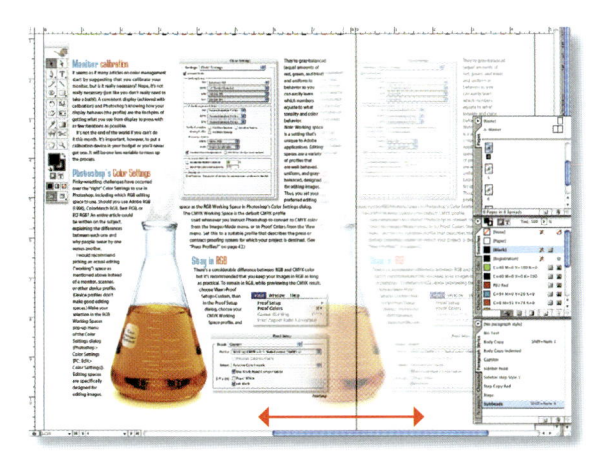

So you're one of those people who thinks a single-button mouse pretty much blows, and you've invested in a multi-button, optical mouse with a scroll wheel. You even took it up a notch and got a wireless one. Check this out—instead of just scrolling up and down your pages with the scroll wheel, hold down the Shift key and scroll left and right.

CHAPTER 8 • Little-Known Features

SCALE SELECTED OBJECTS WITHOUT GROUPING

You've got 10 minutes before it's time to leave for the day. You just finished your layout, and your customer (art director, spouse… the list goes on and on) changes his mind and wants the layout to be printed on postcards instead of the original spec, which was a poster. Instead of reaching for the closest weapon, select all the objects (Mac: Command-A [PC: Control-A]) in the layout (yes, including the text), and go to the Control palette at the top of your screen. Make sure that your scale percentage fields are linked, enter a new percentage in either field, and everything gets scaled uniformly.

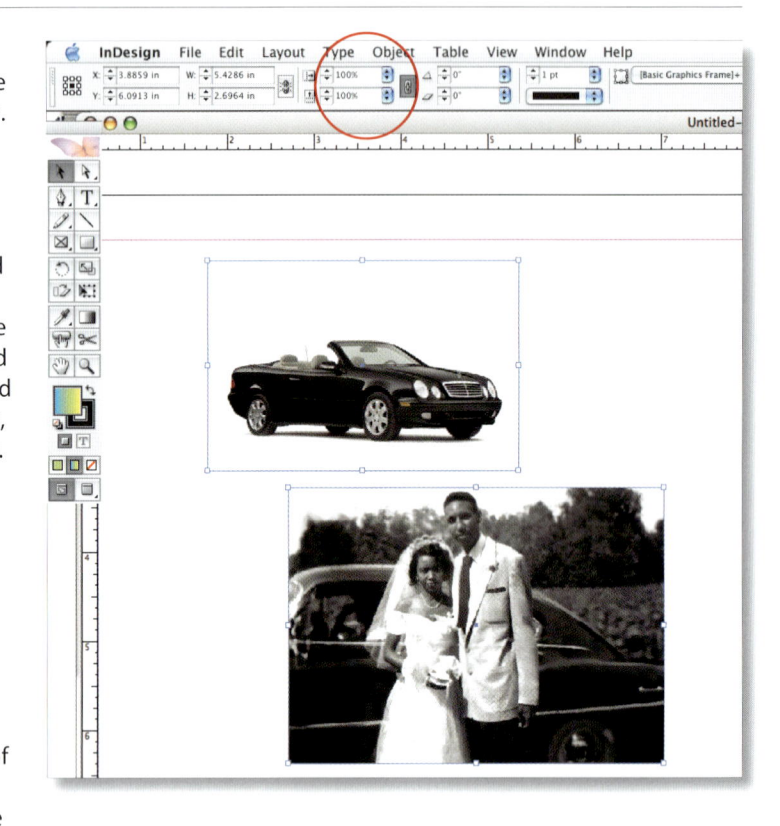

172   CHAPTER 8 • Little-Known Features

STROKE YOUR STYLES, BABY

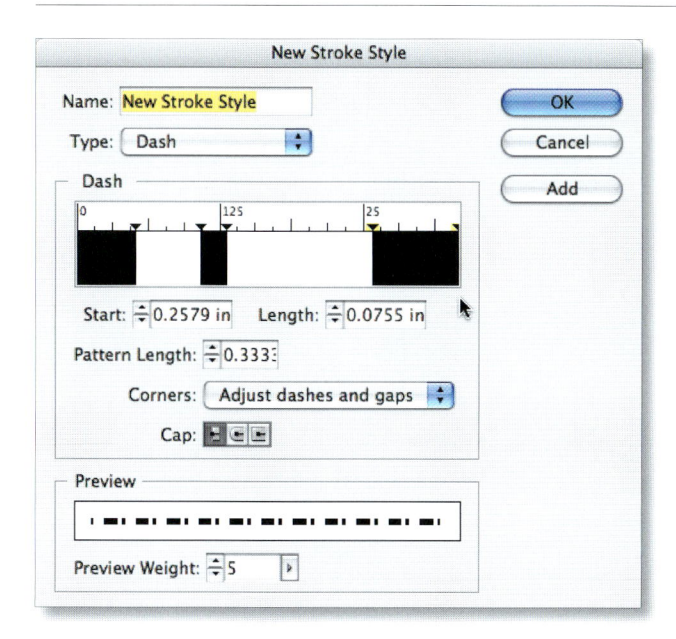

We all get very tired of the same old line styles: solid, thick-thick, thick-thin, etc. These line styles have been around for years, and using them shows the age of your design concepts. So let's break with tradition. You need a funky new line style for your funky new design (funky is a good word—or at least it was a few years ago). From the Window menu, get the Stroke palette and choose Stroke Styles in the flyout menu, and as quickly as you can, hit the New button so that you're not mesmerized by the existing styles. Now pick the kind of stroke you want in the Type pop-up menu and then design it by clicking in the area right below the ruler. You can drag the little triangles on the ruler to make the dashes thicker or thinner, or click on an empty white space to add another element to the line. To delete a dash, click-and-drag it down, and it will disappear. Once you've created a cool design, click OK.

FOUR-COLOR PROCESS ON A SPOT COLOR BUDGET

You want to create a kick-butt layout, but your customer can only afford two-color printing. Use this tip and save the day. Mix those inks! Create the two swatches representing your spot colors by going to the Swatches palette's flyout menu and choosing New Color Swatch. In the Color Type field select Spot, move the sliders to select your color, then click OK. You'll do this again for your second color. Now from the Swatches palette's flyout menu, choose New Mixed Ink Group. In this dialog you will see cyan, magenta, yellow, and black plus the two spot colors you created (shown circled in red). Click the little empty box in front of your spot swatches. At this point you have to do a little math. You have to give each ink an initial value (it can be zero), a repeat value for the number of steps you want, and then an incremental percentage for each step. Your goal is not to exceed 100% total. So whether you start out at zero and do five repeats at 20% each or 10 repeats at 10% each, you don't want to go over 100%. If you do, don't worry; InDesign will warn you and then cap it off at 100% anyway. After doing this for each swatch, just click the Preview Swatches button. This will show you dozens of swatches that you can use throughout your job, and no matter how many you use, you will only be using two inks at the end of the day.

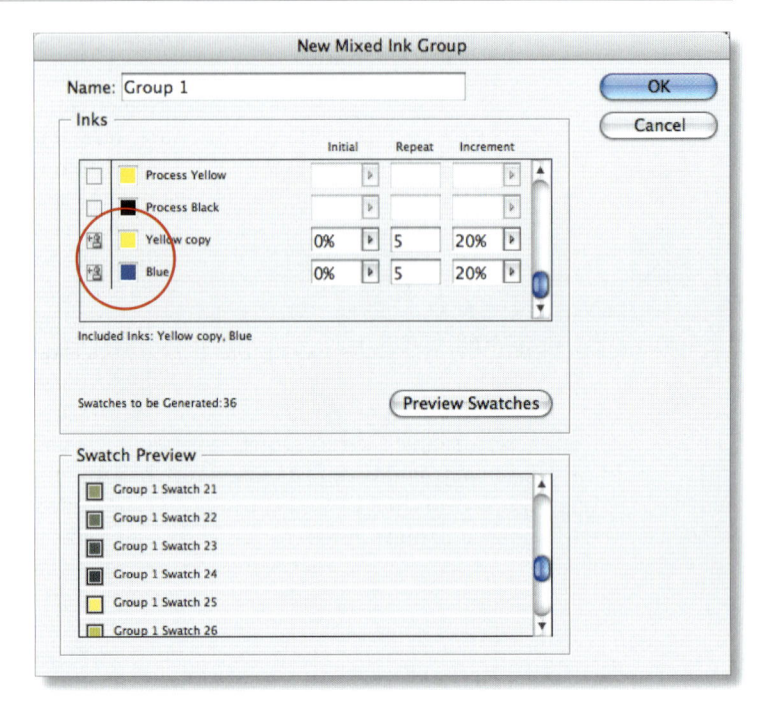

InDesign CS/CS2 KillerTips

COULD YOU PLEASE CHANGE THAT SPOT COLOR?

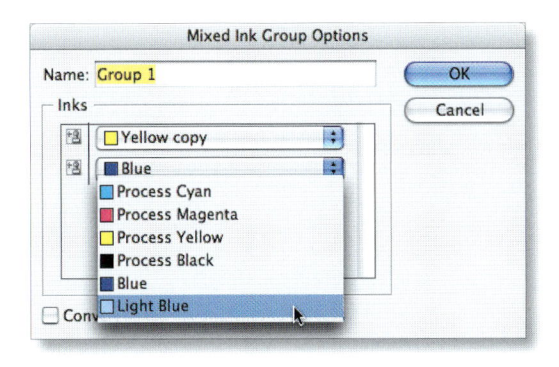

The phone rings. You check your caller ID and it's your customer with yet another last-minute change. This time, however, he wants to do the unthinkable. He wants you to change one of the spot colors you're using in your mixed ink group. I know, I know, it's bad enough that he wouldn't even spring for full color and here he is asking you to make a significant change like this. No need to think those thoughts. Go to the Swatches palette and double-click on the mixed ink group you created in the previous tip. Then in the Mixed Ink Group Options dialog, simply click on the pop-up menu with the swatch representing the color you want to change and choose the new swatch. BAM, all of your color swatches and the corresponding objects that you used them on will be updated! Don't forget, you still charge for the hours of work this would have normally caused you.

BACK TO THE FUTURE

Why is there screaming in the cubicle next to you? Did they lose power? Did their computer crash? No, actually they just hit Save when they meant to hit Save As. Now they've just wiped out a previous version of their document. You walk over and say, in your most sympathetic voice, "Let me see what I can do." Hit the Undo command (Mac: Command-Z [PC: Control-Z]) a few times to take the document back to the original and then choose Save As from the File menu. Yes, you just "saved" the day again.

CHAPTER 8 • Little-Known Features   175

SOMETHING WRONG IN NEVERLAND? DELETE THE PREFERENCES

If for some reason InDesign is misbehaving and you want to start out with a fresh set of preferences, rather than hunting for them in your system, you can have InDesign automatically delete them for you. First, quit InDesign, hold down Shift-Control-Option-Command (PC: Shift-Control-Alt), and relaunch InDesign. A dialog will ask if you want to delete the InDesign preference files. Click Yes and it will automatically delete the prefs and create a fresh default set at the same time. (Note: If you're launching InDesign from the Dock in Mac OS X, make sure to click on the InDesign icon first to start launching it, and then hold down the keys immediately afterwards.)

KICK THE KEYBOARD HABIT

There must be a 12-step program out there somewhere for reducing your dependency on keyboard shortcuts. Actually, keyboard shortcuts are pretty cool, but I must admit that I know only a few. Therefore, I've become totally hooked on contextual menus. Try this tip the next time you're looking for a command to run on a particular object. Rather than wandering through the menus aimlessly, simply hold down the Control key (PC: Right-click) and click on the object to bring up a menu of the most commonly used commands for such an object.

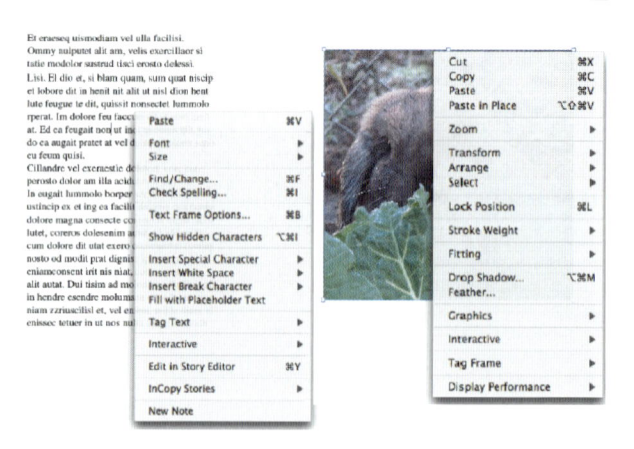

176 CHAPTER 8 • Little-Known Features

GET TO THE UNITS/INCREMENTS PREFERENCES FAST

When you're working with type, some people prefer to work in points (usually typographers), some prefer pixels (Web designers), and others prefer centimeters (freaks). If you've got the Type tool and want to quickly get to the Units & Increments Preferences dialog to make a quick change or two, just Option-click (PC: Alt-click) on the Kerning icon in the Control palette and it will bring up the dialog for you—no more digging around in the InDesign (PC: Edit) menu.

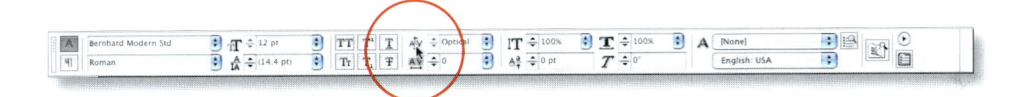

SPEED LANE TO THE MOVE DIALOG

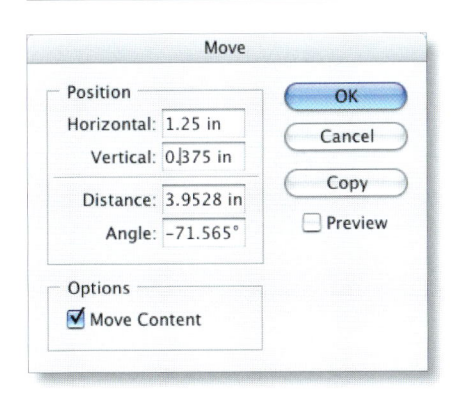

If you want to move an object precisely using the Move dialog, here's a quick way to get at it. Click on the object you want to move, then go up to the Control palette and Option-click (PC: Alt-click) on either the X or Y coordinate icon and the Move dialog (shown here) will appear. How's that for fast?

CHAPTER 8 • Little-Known Features   177

SPEEDY SCALER

Okay, now that you know how to bring up the Move dialog, surely you'll want a quick way to bring up the Scale dialog, for resizing objects with extreme precision. Just click on the object you want to scale, then Option-click (PC: Alt-click) on either of the Horizontal or Vertical Scale icons up in the Control palette (shown here circled in red) and the Scale dialog will appear.

InDesign CS/CS2
KillerTips

CHAPTER 8 • Little-Known Features

Portable People

MAKING PDFs

I don't get it. Why is this chapter named "Portable People"? See, this is what happens when people start using acronyms for everyday items—they lose touch

Portable People
making PDFs

with the meanings behind the acronyms. The "portable" part is the first word in PDF (which stands for Portable Document Format) and the song "Portable People" is from the band Ten Years After. (Sadly, I couldn't find a song or movie with PDF in the title, except for "Strawberry PDF 23" from the Brothers Johnson.) But do people care about that—about preserving the meaning behind the acronym? No. People are just too busy to pronounce full words anymore, so everything has to be an acronym. So basically, this chapter is about using IDCS2 to create PDFs so you can FTP them to a URL using DSL to UPS for NMR (that last one is the real acronym for Nuclear Magnetic Resonance. I threw it in just for effect).

PLACE A MOVIE IN YOUR DOCUMENT

Print and QuickTime usually have nothing to do with each other. After all, print is usually CMYK and static; and QuickTime is usually RGB and moving. So why would you ever want to place a QuickTime movie in an InDesign document? To go out to PDF and the Web. Choose Place from the File menu and then point to a QuickTime movie. You will be able to bring it in, and on your print document it will be a static image; but when you Export to PDF or Package for GoLive it will go out as a fully functional QuickTime movie.

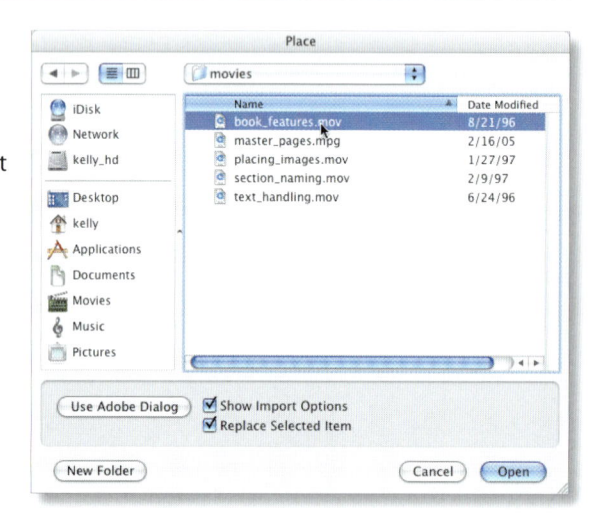

PICK A DIFFERENT POSTER FRAME

Most QuickTime movies fade in from black. A black rectangle in your print document is probably not what you're looking for. So to avoid having a dull-looking print document, PDF, or website, simply choose an image as the Poster Frame (the frame that displays when the movie isn't playing). Double-click your placed QuickTime movie and in the Movie Options dialog change the Poster pop-up menu to Choose Image as Poster. Click the Browse button and go find a nice CMYK Photoshop image or TIFF to be used as your poster. You probably want to create the image ahead of time in Photoshop to be the same size as your movie so it fits seamlessly.

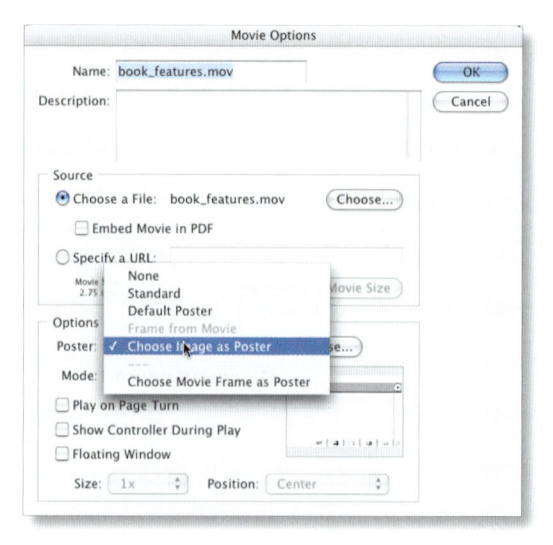

182   CHAPTER 9 • Making PDFs

IMPORT A SOUND WHEN YOU DON'T HAVE VIDEO

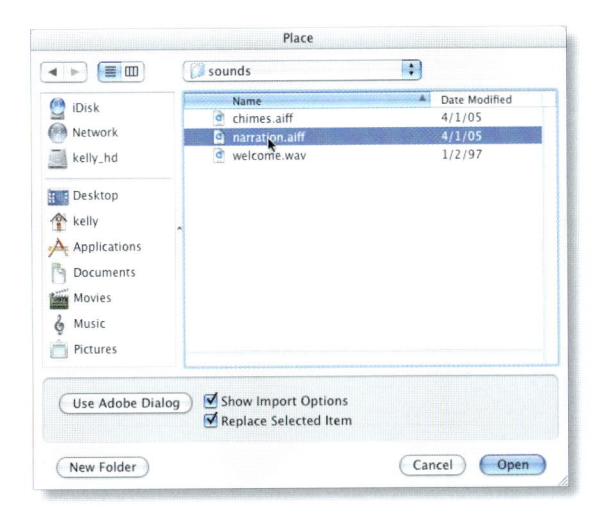

Placing movies is cool, but you can also place sounds. Why? Let's say you actually wanted to narrate your document to your client. You can record the narration in your favorite sound recording app, save it as a QuickTime movie and then place it in your InDesign document. Now when you export it to PDF the sound will go with it. You might want to check out other tips in this chapter to create multimedia buttons that will play your sound.

FLASH IN THE PANTS

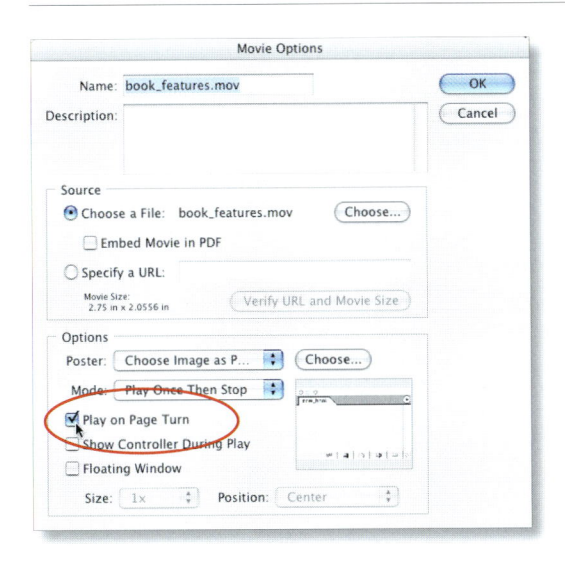

Another tip to spruce up your InDesign-generated PDFs would be to add Flash (.SWF) animation. You can place .SWF files just like you do movies. However, once you place your .SWF animation you will need to double-click on it, and in the Movie Options dialog enable the Play on Page Turn option to get it to start playing/animating when the PDF is opened.

CHAPTER 9 • Making PDFs   183

EMBED MULTIMEDIA FILES

PDFs have supported multimedia files such as QuickTime movies for some time now, but it has always been a pain because the multimedia files were never really in the PDF. They were linked and you always had to remember to send them separately to your client. The next time you want to make a PDF truly portable, click on the General category on the left-hand side of the Export Adobe PDF dialog; choose Acrobat 6 in the Compatibility pop-up menu in the Options section; and in the Multimedia pop-up menu, select Embed All. The advantage to this is that you'll have one PDF that contains everything. The downside is that the person receiving this PDF will need Adobe Reader 6 or higher (or the full version of Acrobat 6 or higher) to view it.

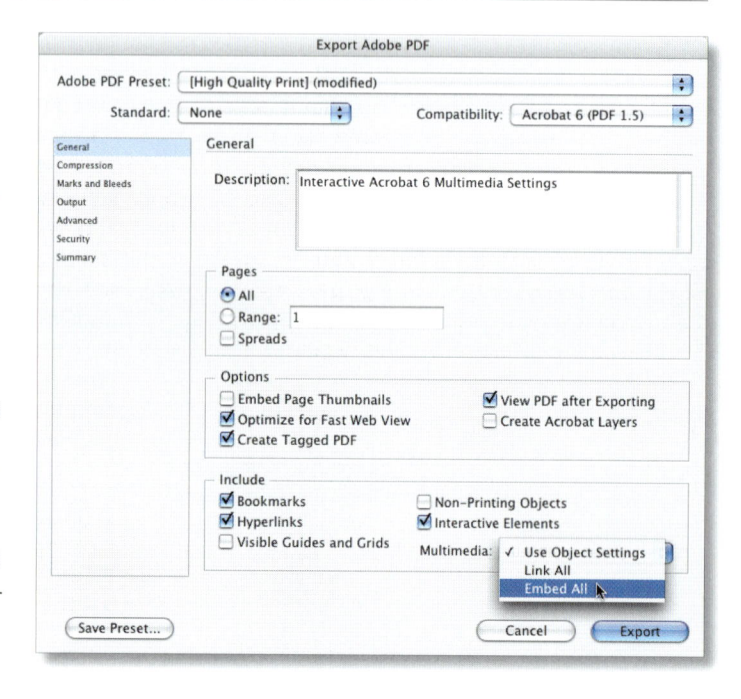

184   CHAPTER 9 • Making PDFs

MAKE INTERACTIVE BUTTONS

PDFs can be interactive and you can use this tip to make buttons that will do things in exported PDFs. For example, if you place a QuickTime movie, you can make a button to alert the recipient of your PDF file that it is a movie that can be played. I would suggest that you create a graphic that looks like a "Play Movie" button and place it near your movie. Use the Button tool to drag a new button around your graphic. Then double-click it with the Selection tool to get to the Button Options dialog. Next, click on the Behaviors button at the top of the dialog and create a behavior that plays the movie upon mouse up. In the Event pop-up menu choose Mouse Up. In the Behavior pop-up menu choose Movie, and you'll see two more pop-up menus appear: one for choosing which movie the button interacts with and another for the Play Options. Once you've set your options, click the Add button and then click OK.

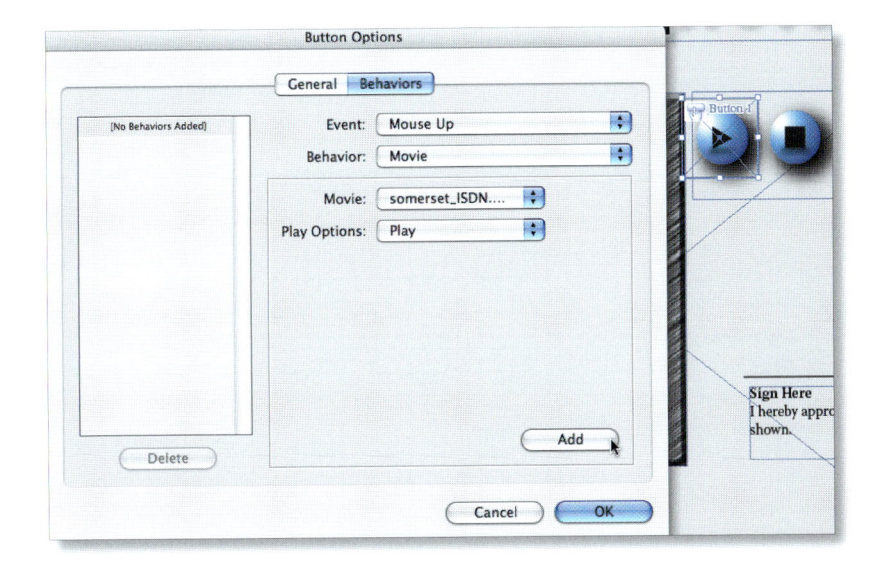

CHAPTER 9 • Making PDFs   185

WHEN A STATIC BUTTON IS NOT ENOUGH

Let's take the interactive button tip to a whole new level. Making a button is one thing (see previous tip); making a button rollover is even cooler. If you have an image that you want to be displayed when someone mouses over a button, it can be done. You will need two buttons: the image that you want to appear when someone mouses over the button and the actual button that becomes visible when they mouse over it.

1. Select the image that you want to appear and convert it to a button by choosing Convert to Button from the Object menu's Interactive submenu.

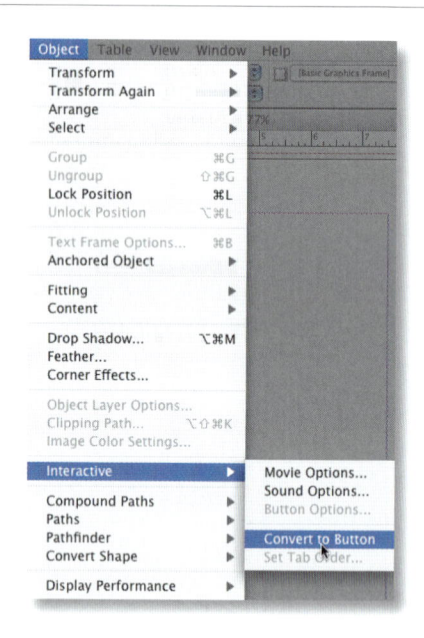

2. Double-click on your newly created graphic button with the Selection tool and name it "over image" in the Button Options dialog. Change the Visibility in PDF pop-up menu to Hidden and click OK.

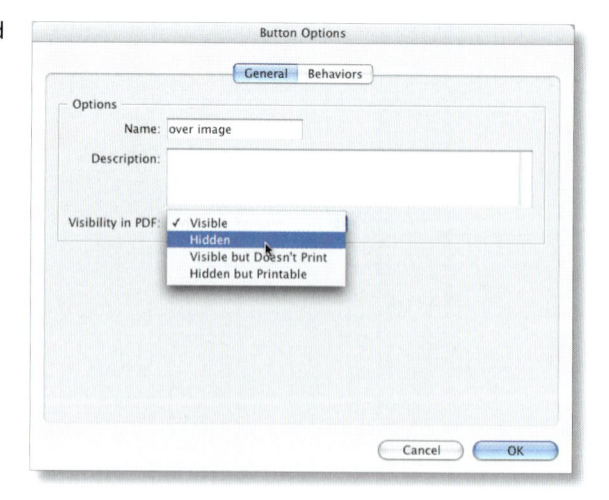

186 CHAPTER 9 • Making PDFs

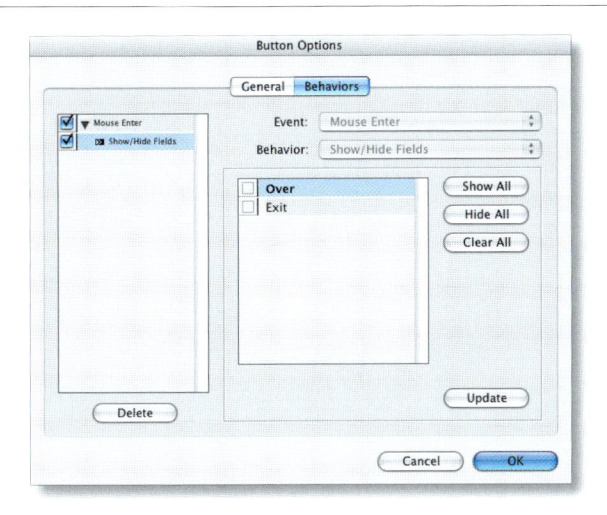

3. Use your Selection tool to double-click on your original button, then click the Behaviors button and add two Behaviors. The first one will be on Mouse Enter and it will show the over image. So change the Event pop-up menu to Mouse Enter and the Behavior pop-up to Show/Hide Fields. Click on the checkbox next to "over image" and then click the Update button.

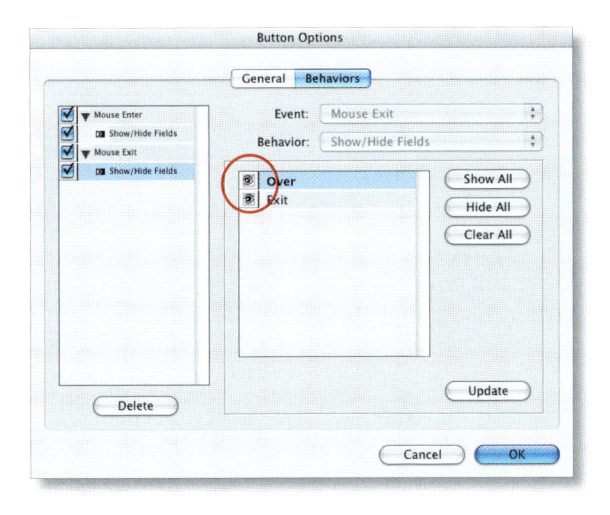

4. The second one should be a Mouse Exit Behavior that will hide the over image. So change the Event pop-up to Mouse Exit and click the checkbox next to "over image" until you have an Eye icon with a red slash through it. Click the Update button, then the OK button. Now when you export to PDF you will have a rollover button.

CHAPTER 9 • Making PDFs   187

DEFINE A PDF EXPORT STYLE

Once you have a good set of settings for exporting PDF files, you can use this tip so that you don't have to constantly remember what the settings were and enter them each time: Choose Export from the File menu and Save. When the Export Adobe PDF dialog appears, key in all of your favorite settings for each category. Once you're done, click the Save Preset button, name your preset, and click OK. Your new preset will appear in the Preset pop-up at the top of the Export Adobe PDF dialog.

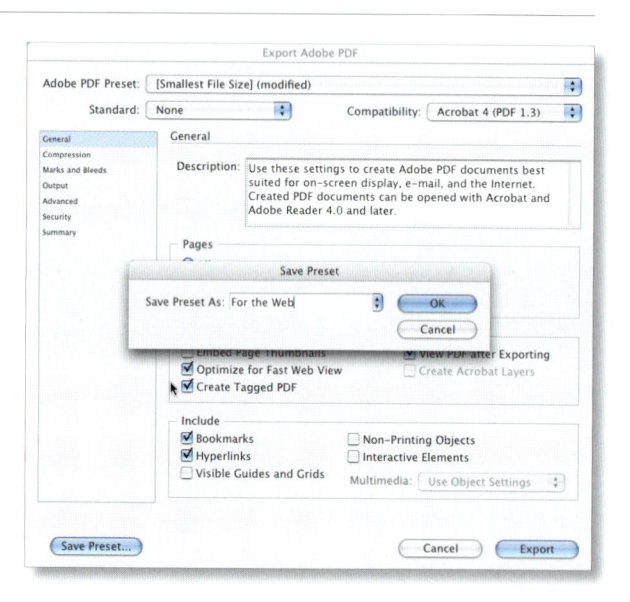

USE A PDF EXPORT STYLE

Once you've defined a PDF export style like the one in the previous tip, you can export to a PDF file with those same settings by choosing your saved preset from the Adobe PDF Presets menu under the File menu. The Export Adobe PDF dialog will appear and it will already have all of your settings in it.

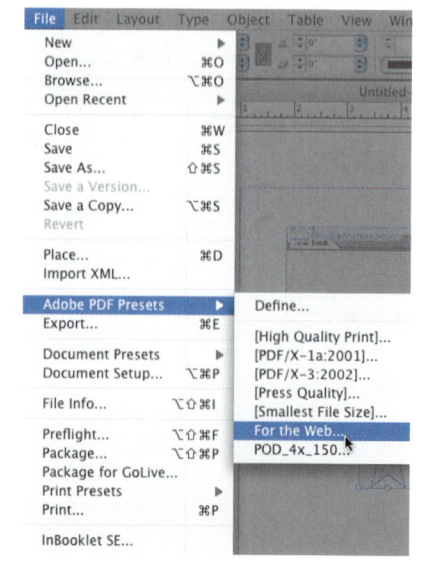

ADD A HOTLINK TO YOUR WEBSITE

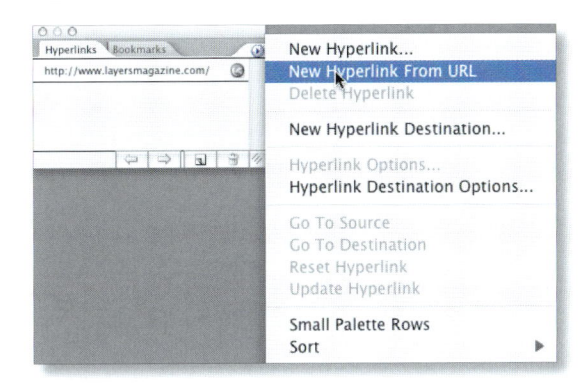

If you're going to export your document to PDF, InDesign can add interactive hyperlinks that will be live in the PDF. If you've already keyed in a valid URL in your document, such as www.macgroup.org, highlight that URL with the Type tool and open the Hyperlinks palette from the Interactive submenu in the Window menu. Then, from the Hyperlinks palette's flyout menu choose New Hyperlink From URL. The hyperlink will be added to the Hyperlinks palette and will automatically be active upon exporting to PDF.

CREATE A DYNAMIC LINK TO ANOTHER PAGE

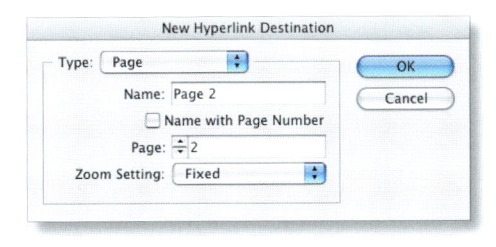

Creating hyperlinks to the Web is one thing, but your needs may be as simple as creating a link that merely goes to another page in your PDF. Luckily, InDesign does this automatically when you use the Table of Contents feature. But what about the ones you want to create yourself? Here's a tip that you can use when you want to make your own page links: Go to the page that you want to be able to jump to. Choose New Hyperlink Destination from the Hyperlinks palette's flyout menu. It should default to Page in the Type pop-up menu and give you the page number that you are setting as the destination. Click OK, then go to the page that you want to be able to jump from and select an object or text that people will be able to click on to jump to your destination page. Choose New Hyperlink from the Hyperlinks palette's flyout menu. In the New Hyperlink dialog, name your link if you desire and choose the destination you created from the Name pop-up menu. When you export your PDF, your link will be active. In the General category of the Export Adobe PDF dialog, be sure to check the Hyperlinks checkbox in the Include section.

CHAPTER 9 • Making PDFs   189

RECOGNIZE HYPERLINKS FROM WORD AUTOMATICALLY

You can cut down on some of your work if you're using Microsoft Word as your writing tool for import into InDesign. If you know you want to end up with hyperlinks in your final PDF, you can author them right inside Word. The valid formats are http://www.yoursite.whatever, http://yoursite.whatever, www.yoursite.whatever, and somebody@somedomain.whatever. If you use any of these formats in Word and place the Word document in InDesign, they will automatically be converted into active links.

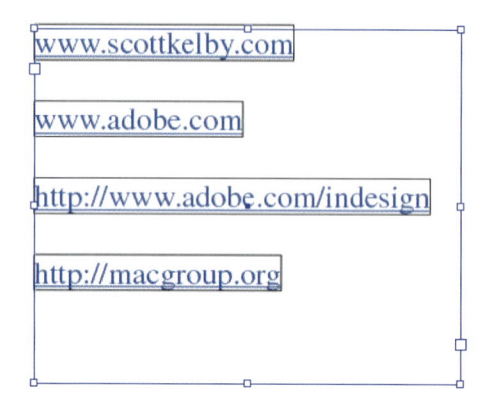

GET RID OF THE BLACK BOXES AROUND YOUR LINKS

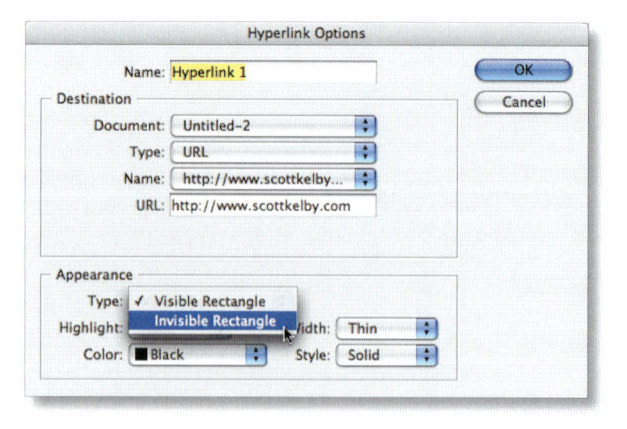

One side effect of bringing in Word files that contain URLs is that they will appear to have a black box around them onscreen and on the printed page. This is because InDesign defaults to a visible rectangle around links. To avoid this, bring up the Hyperlinks palette (Window>Interactive>Hyperlinks) and double-click one of the imported links in the palette. They are usually called "Hyperlink 1," "Hyperlink 2," etc. In the Hyperlink Options dialog, under Appearance, change the Type pop-up menu to Invisible Rectangle. You can do this for each imported hyperlink or, if you have several links, Shift-click to select them all and then perform this operation once to remove the visible rectangle from all of them at once.

USE LAYERS TO GIVE YOUR CLIENT A CHOICE OF CONTENT

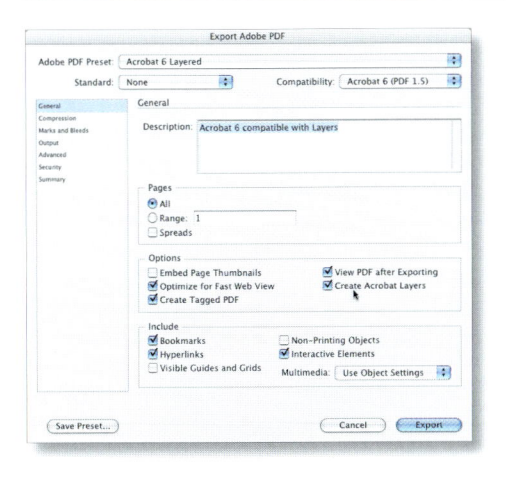

If you want to really impress your clients, give them a couple of choices for design or content. Use this tip to create one PDF with multiple choices. It's all about layers! Create three layers and call them "Design 1," "Design 2" and "Design 3." Now assign content to each of the layers. If necessary, you can build other layers on top of these three that will have the same content no matter which design is below. Then turn off the Design 2 and Design 3 layers by clicking on their Eye icons in the Layers palette. From File>Adobe PDF Presets, choose Define and click New. Name your preset and in the Compatibility pop-up menu choose Acrobat 6 (PDF 1.5). Turn on the option to Create Acrobat Layers in the Options section. Click OK, and then select that preset from the Presets menu in the Adobe PDF Presets dialog. Click Done. When you save your file using this preset, this will make a layered Acrobat 6 (PDF 1.5) compatible file. Anyone with Adobe Reader 6 or higher (or the full version of Acrobat 6 or higher) will be able to turn your layers on or off.

CREATE BOOKMARKS TO WALK THEM THROUGH YOUR DOCUMENT

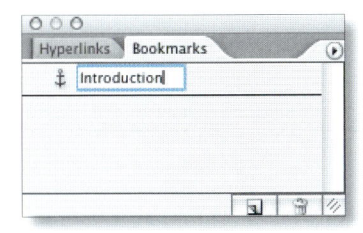

PDF bookmarks have been around almost since day one. However, it's usually a manual task to create them in the full version of Acrobat. Here's a tip on how you can create them right inside of InDesign. Open the Bookmarks palette from the Window menu's Interactive submenu. Go to the page you want to create a bookmark for (we suggest going in order from the beginning of the document to the end) and click the Create New Bookmark icon at the bottom of the Bookmarks palette. This will create a bookmark called "Bookmark." While it's still selected you can rename it right then and there. Do this for each page that you want to bookmark.

CHAPTER 9 • Making PDFs   191

CREATE BOOKMARK GROUPS

If you have bookmarks that could be grouped together under one heading, for example, pages in a particular chapter, you can group them together before exporting your PDF. To create a bookmark group, simply drag one bookmark directly on top of another. When it highlights, you can release and it will then indent to the right to indicate that it is now a part of a group.

TRUST NO ONE—PASSWORD PROTECT IT

You don't have to be James Bond to need good document security. If you're sending sensitive information over the Internet, having a secured PDF may help you sleep a little better. Click the Security category in the list down the left-hand side of the Export Adobe PDF dialog. From that window you can check the option Require a Password to Open the Document. Then, in the Document Open Password field enter a password that you will share with the recipient in another communication such as a phone call. When you export your PDF, InDesign will ask you to confirm that you know the password and then you'll be all set.

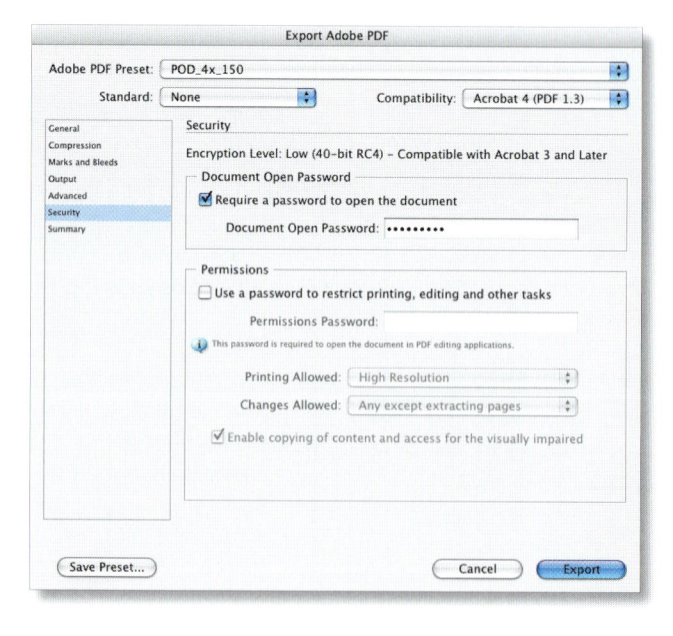

DON'T GIVE AWAY THE FARM—DISALLOW PRINTING

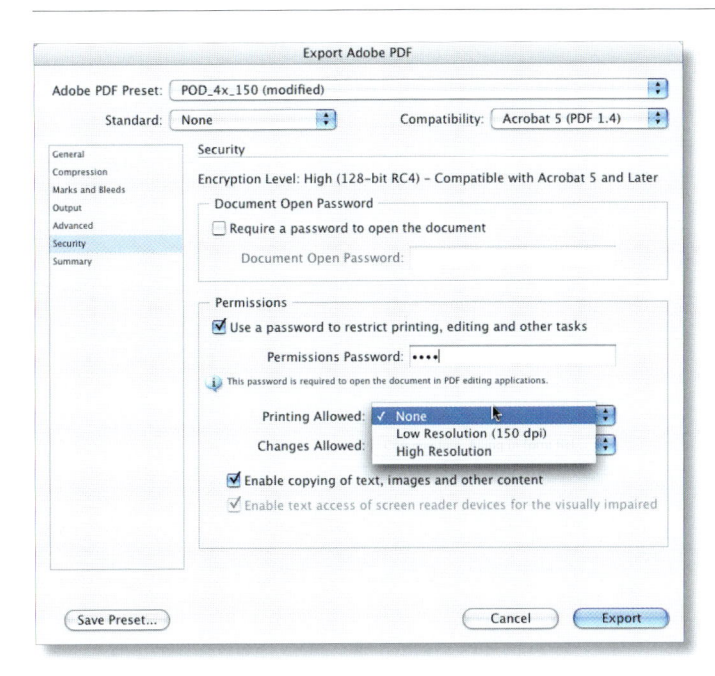

Just because you want to show your customers a proof electronically, that doesn't mean that you want to be taken advantage of. Send them a PDF, but send them one that won't allow them to print. Or send them one that only prints low res. In the Security section of the Export Adobe PDF dialog, there is an option for Use a Password to Restrict Printing, Editing and Other Tasks. Check this box to make the Printing Allowed pop-up menu active. In the Printing Allowed pop-up you can choose among None, Low Resolution (150 dpi), and High Resolution. (Note: The Low Resolution option is not available if you have the PDF compatibility set to Acrobat 4.) Before you export your PDF, choose None and enter a password in the Permissions Password field. The recipient will be able to open and navigate your PDF, but all printing options will be grayed out.

CHAPTER 9 • Making PDFs   193

DISALLOW EDITING

Another way of securing a PDF, especially one that you will be posting to your website, is to disallow editing it. This is especially useful for contracts, press releases, and annual reports. Click the Security category in the Export Adobe PDF dialog, check the box for Use a Password to Restrict Printing . . . , and choose None in the Changes Allowed pop-up menu. You will need to give it a Permissions Password and then export your PDF.

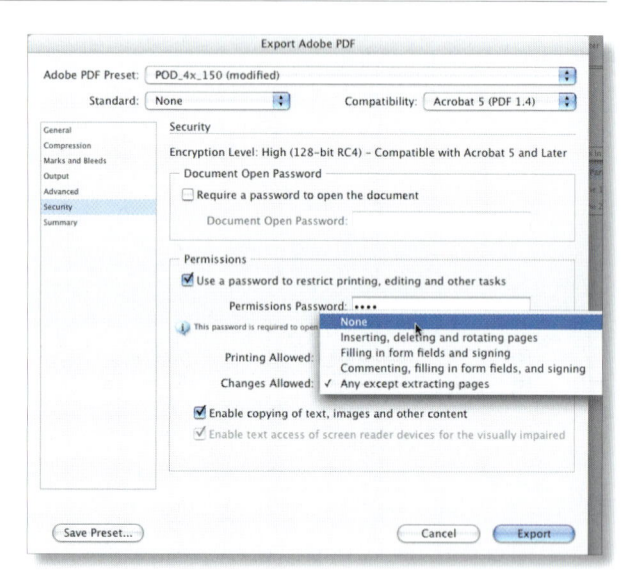

COMPATIBILITY WITH OLDER VERSIONS OF ACROBAT

It's a fact that not everyone you work with will be upgrading his or her software at the same time that you do. When you need to send someone a PDF and you're not sure which version of Acrobat he has, use the lowest common denominator, Acrobat 4 (PDF 1.3), in the Compatibility pop-up menu of the Options section in the General category of the Export Adobe PDF dialog.

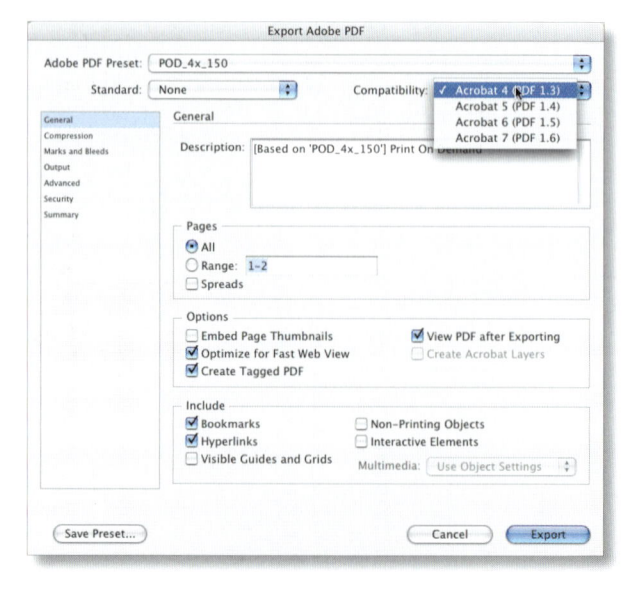

194 CHAPTER 9 • Making PDFs

USE SPREADS

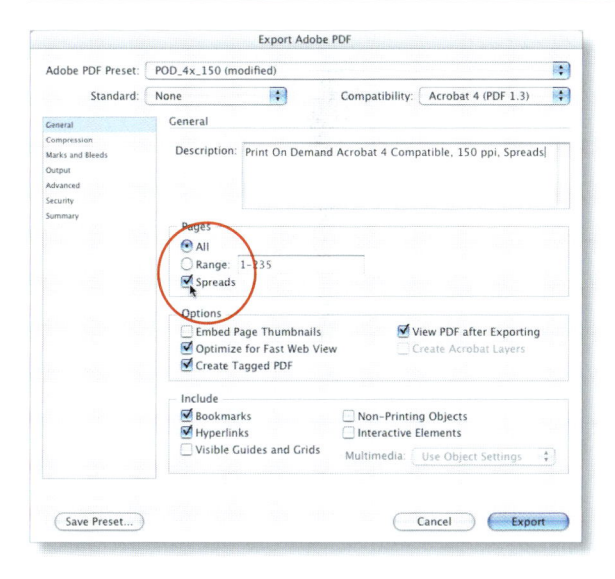

If you've used spreads in your document, chances are that you'll want spreads when you go to PDF. Therefore, all you have to do is check the Spreads checkbox in the Export Adobe PDF dialog. Now your PDF will mimic your InDesign document's side-by-side pages.

WHAT'S ALL THE BUZZ ABOUT PDF/X?

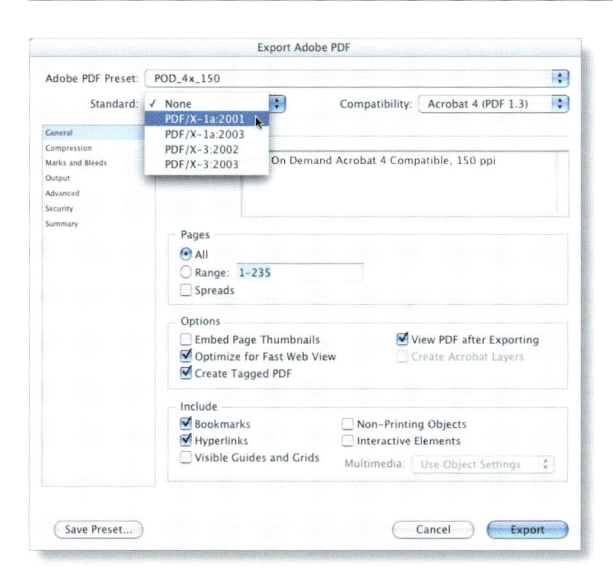

PDF/X is a subset of PDF designed specifically for printing. It strips out all the whizzbang multimedia, hyperlinks, and other non-print-related baggage in your PDF files. There are two main PDF/X formats: PDF/X-1a and PDF/X-3. PDF/X-1a is for a CMYK (and spot color) only workflow; and PDF/X-3 supports a color-managed workflow, which could include RGB. To create the most print-reliable/print-ready PDF that you can out of InDesign, choose PDF/X-1a: 2001 from the Standard pop-up menu in the Export Adobe PDF dialog.

CHAPTER 9 • Making PDFs   195

MAKE IT SMALL BUT KEEP IT LOOKIN' GOOD

We all want the smallest PDF we can get, especially for posting on the Web or for sending via email. However, InDesign's default settings for Screen resolution PDFs can leave a little to be desired for PDFs containing color images, especially if users will be zooming in on them. Our tip for keeping PDFs small, but still looking good, is to start with the Screen preset in the Export Adobe PDF dialog, and then in the Compression category on the left side of the dialog, change the resolution for color images from 72 ppi to 150 ppi. This will make your PDF a little larger, but it will make your photos look a lot better.

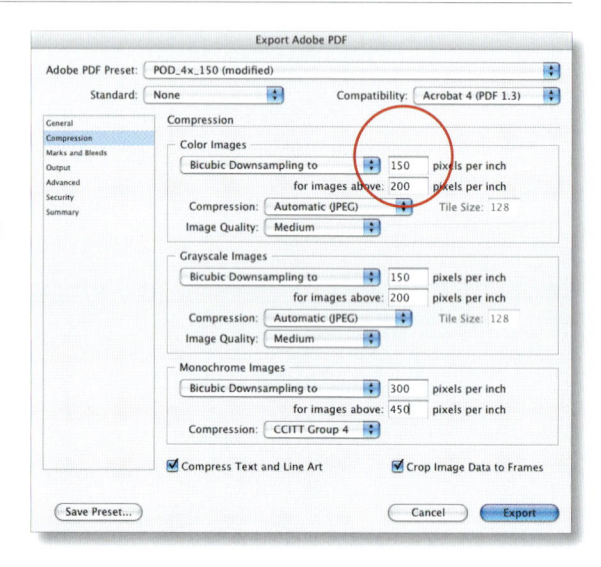

CREATE PDFS WITH TRANSPARENCY

If you have used any of InDesign's transparency effects or placed native Photoshop files with transparency, you have to make a choice when going out to PDF. You have to decide whether to create a flattened PDF or a PDF that supports transparency. By making an Acrobat 4 (PDF 1.3)-compatible PDF, you're taking the transparency flattening into your own hands. However, if you want to maintain the transparency in the PDF, you should create an Acrobat 5 or higher PDF—Acrobat 5 and higher support transparency natively. Flattening will then only take place upon printing.

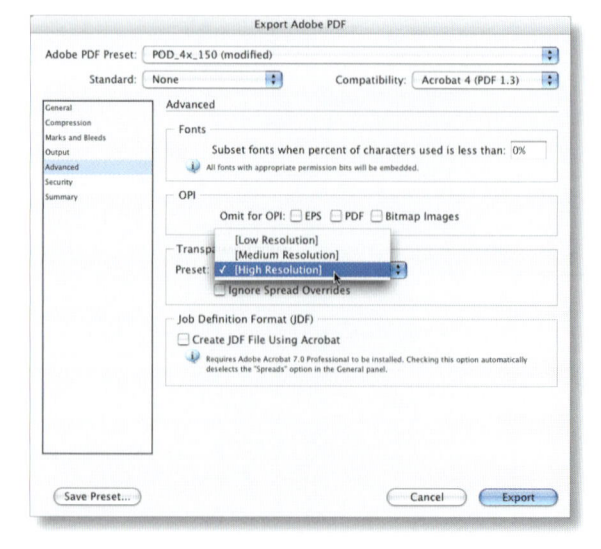

196   CHAPTER 9 • Making PDFs

PLACE INDESIGN PAGES INTO OTHER INDESIGN DOCUMENTS VIA PDF

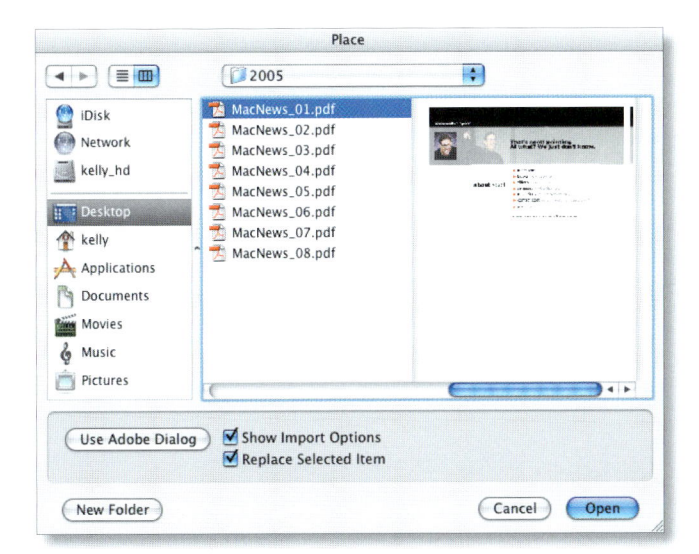

If you need to bring an InDesign page that you've already created into a new InDesign document, such as an ad or form, a quick way to do so is to export (File>Export) the ad or form as a PDF and then place (File>Place) the PDF in your new document.

Waiting Tables

WORKING WITH TABLES

If you're ready for some tear-the-roof-off, go insane, break-all-the-rules, frat-party-gone-wild, uncontrollable good times, then start working in tables. It's off the hook.

Waiting Tables
working with tables

I remember this one night I was at a bachelor party in Vegas. We had a limo and we were hittin' all the clubs up and down the strip, and we wound up at Rain at The Palms. The drinks were flowin', the music was pumpin', lights were flashing, and things were getting a bit crazy out on the dance floor, when all of a sudden, one of my buddies yelled out, "Hey, let's go set some complex tables in InDesign." The next thing you know, we piled back in the limo, headed for the Bellagio's business center, and were setting tables, editing individual cells, and reformatting nested tables until like two in the morning. Suddenly, the cops burst in and one of the SWAT guys pointed a Ruger Mini-14 rifle right at me and screamed, "Any of you boys been filling individual cells with color?" I didn't blink. I just stared at him with that "I just placed an Excel spreadsheet" stare until he decided to stand down, and they finally left. Just another wild night of setting tables in InDesign.

PLACE GRAPHICS IN A TABLE

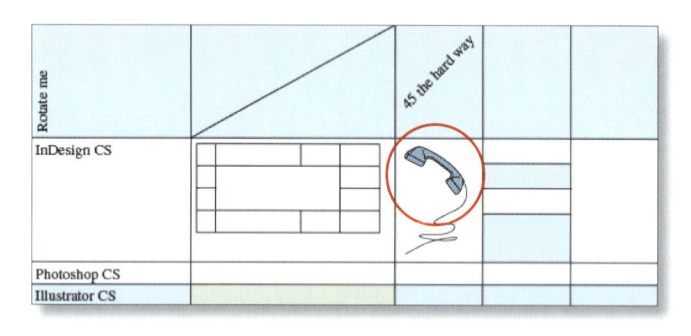

So you've exhausted all the clever ways of using text in tables and now you want to spice up your tables with graphics. Perhaps you want to do a comparison chart or maybe a catalog page with a graphic next to each description. Although InDesign doesn't have an actual graphics cell, you can still place graphics into table cells as inline graphics. Simply place your cursor in a table cell with the Type tool and then choose Place from the File menu to find your graphic for placement. Once you place it, InDesign will automatically create a frame for your graphic. You can also copy/cut frames from existing pages and paste them into table cells by selecting your frames with the Type tool, going to Edit>Cut (or Copy), then clicking within your table cell and choosing Edit>Paste.

GO PLAID, BABY

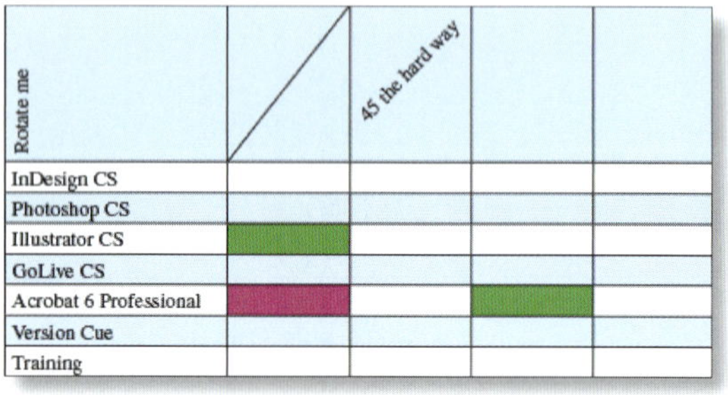

Liven up your tables with a little color. But rather than simply filling all the cells with the same color, try alternating fills. First, highlight all the cells in your table using the Type tool. Now, either Control-click (PC: Right-click) or choose Table>Table Options>Alternating Fills from the menu bar. In the Table Options dialog you can specify a pattern in the Alternating Patterns pop-up menu, as well as what colors will be used (here we selected Every Other Row filled with blue and white).

200   CHAPTER 10 • Working with Tables

FILL INDIVIDUAL CELLS WITH COLOR

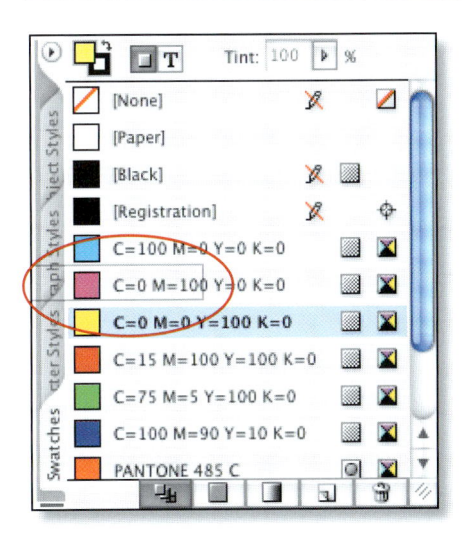

Sometimes you just want to fill a cell with a single color and call it a day. Alternating fills is sweet, but not always necessary. Simply drag a color from your Swatches palette, drop it on any table cell, and the cell will fill with that color. Now you can go home.

ROTATE TEXT IN TABLES

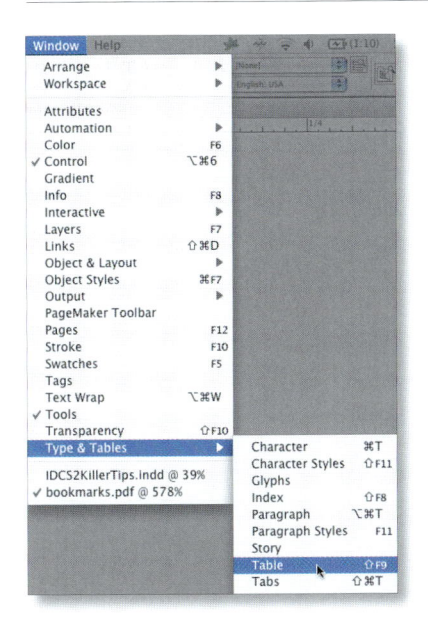

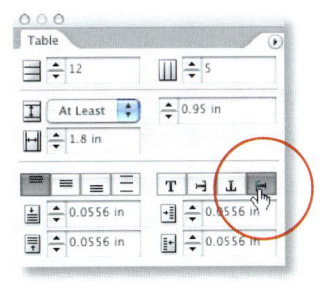

One of the cool ways to make your table stand out is to rotate some of the text. This is especially effective in the headers above the columns. Simply put the cursor in the table cell that you want to rotate and bring up the Table palette from the Window menu in the Type & Tables submenu. Now click the letter "T" icon that represents how you want your text rotated. You may have to increase your row height to accommodate your new choice.

CHAPTER 10 • Working with Tables   **201**

InDesign CS/CS2
KillerTips

◉ ◉ ◉ SELECT ROWS AND COLUMNS

One of InDesign's least obvious functions is how you go about selecting rows and columns in a table. Here's how you do it: Choose the Type tool and hover it near the left edge of the table, or near the top of the table if you want to highlight a column. Once you see an arrow pointing to the right or down, click to select the row or column the arrow points to. You can also click-and-drag to select multiple rows or columns at once.

◉ ◉ ◉ SELECT THE ENTIRE TABLE

The day has come when you need to select an entire table and modify it all at once. This tip lets you do it in one click. Simply go to the upper-left corner of the first instance of the table and hover the Type tool above the corner until the cursor changes to a diagonal arrow. Now, just click and the entire table will be selected, no matter how many pages it spans.

202   CHAPTER 10 • Working with Tables

RESIZE ROWS AND COLUMNS

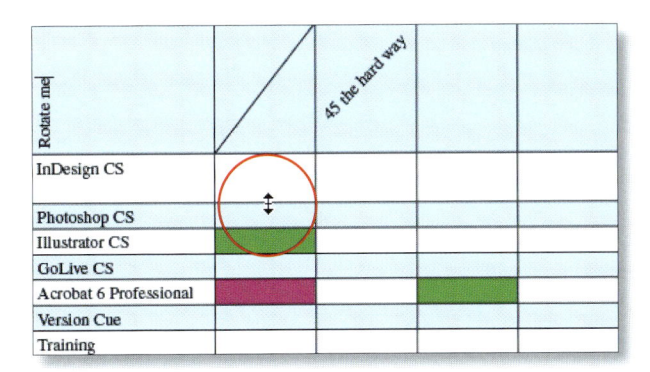

One quick way to resize a single row or column is to simply switch to the Type tool and hover over the line separating two rows or two columns. The cursor should change into a double-arrow pointer. This is the indicator that you can now drag left or right to resize columns, up or down to resize rows.

RUNNING HEADERS AND FOOTERS

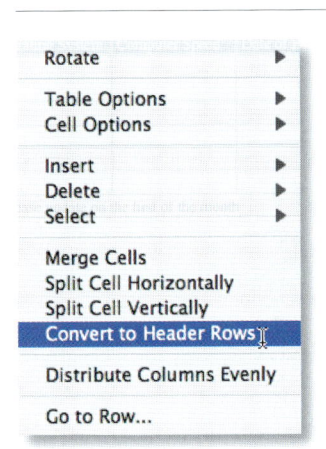

We often like to have headings above each column in a table to identify the contents to the reader. However, if you split up (link) a table from one page to another or even multiple places on the same page, headings don't carry over. This tip is a lifesaver. With the Type tool, highlight the first row or however many rows it takes to contain your header. Now Control-click (PC: Right-click) on the table and choose Convert to Header Rows from the contextual menu. This will place the same header on top of each instance of the table. The same tip works for selecting the last line(s) of the table and choosing Convert to Footer Rows.

CHAPTER 10 • Working with Tables   203

PLACE WORD AND EXCEL TABLES

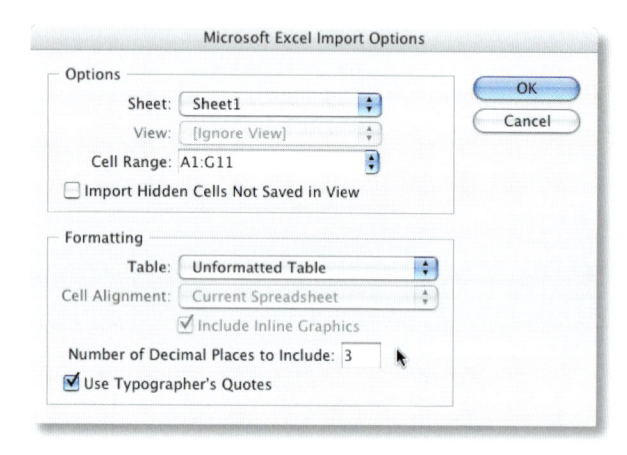

Graphic designers just love getting files from their colleagues who use Microsoft Office products. We especially crave Microsoft Excel documents that need to be laid out in a page-layout program. Well actually, life is about to get a lot better. The next time they ask, "Can I send it to you in Excel?" you can still hem and haw, but say, "Yes!" Choose Place from the File menu and then in the Place dialog point to either an Excel or Word document that contains a table and click Open. In the Import Options dialog you can choose options such as importing the table as formatted or unformatted. Once you click OK, all you have to do is place it. InDesign will automatically convert it to an InDesign table. You can still grumble if it makes you feel better.

CONVERT TEXT TO TABLE

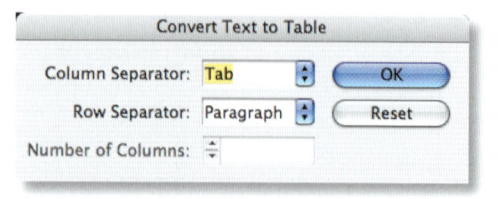

We often get information that needs to be laid out from a database. And while databases have come a long way, they still don't spit out the friendliest types of documents. Ooooohhhh, tab-delimited text, how cool is that? Not! That's okay, go ahead and place it. Now highlight the tab-delimited text with the Type tool and choose Convert Text to Table from the Table menu. Now you've got a table that's a lot more flexible to deal with than just the raw text.

204   CHAPTER 10 • Working with Tables

NESTED TABLES

Sometimes creating a table and merging cells together still doesn't give you enough flexibility. So try this tip the next time you need to create a complex table. It's called nested tables. Simply use the Type tool to click your cursor in an existing table cell and choose Insert Table from the Table menu. Now in the Insert Table dialog you can specify the number of rows and columns that you need for the table within a table.

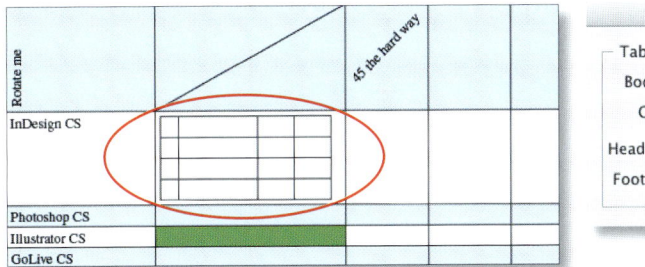

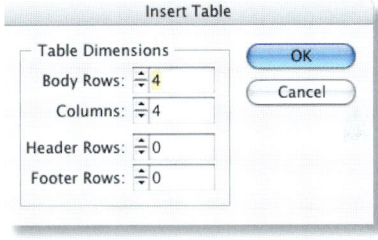

MAKE BIG ONES OUT OF LITTLE ONES

Instead of trying to cram that large graphic or tons of text into a tiny little table cell, try this tip: Highlight multiple cells with the Type tool and choose Merge Cells from the Table menu.

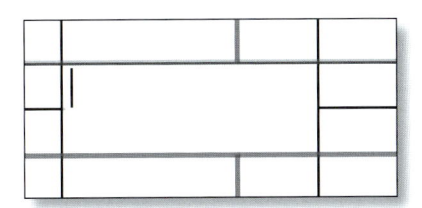

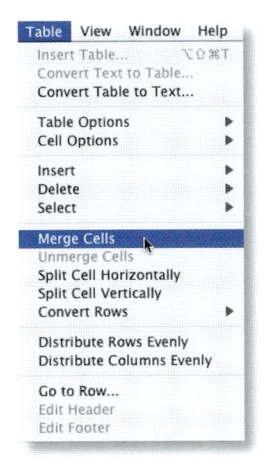

CHAPTER 10 • Working with Tables   205

TIME TO SPLIT CELLS

Okay, now it's time to make more cells instead of fewer. Just as you can merge cells together, you can also split them to make more cells. Highlight one or more cells and choose Split Cell Horizontally or Split Cell Vertically from the Table menu.

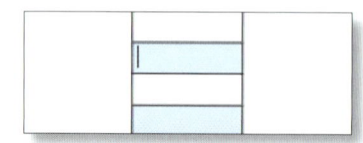

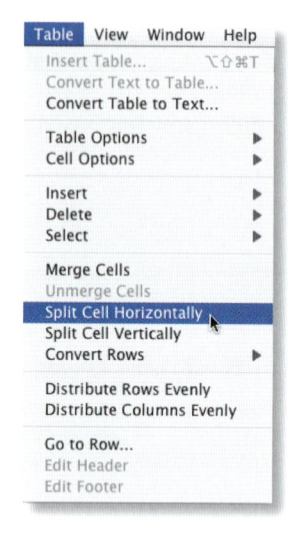

REMOVE THE TABLE STROKE

One of the first things that people want to do after setting up their table is to get rid of the lines between the rows and columns. Actually it's easier than you think. InDesign uses the same stroke metaphor for tables that it uses for everything else. To get rid of a stroke, highlight the rows and columns and from the Color or the Stroke palette choose None for color or zero for the stroke weight.

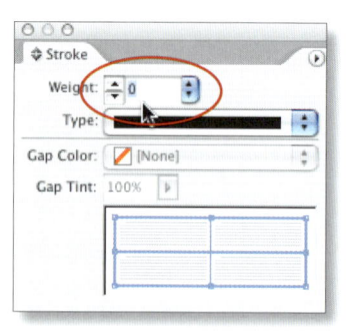

INSERT A ROW AT THE END WITH A TAB

You need to add one more row at the end of the table because someone (usually the customer) decided to add "one more thing." No problem, simply use the Type tool to put your cursor in the last cell of the table and (here it comes) press the Tab key on the keyboard. That will automatically add a row onto the end of your table.

INSERT ROWS AND COLUMNS

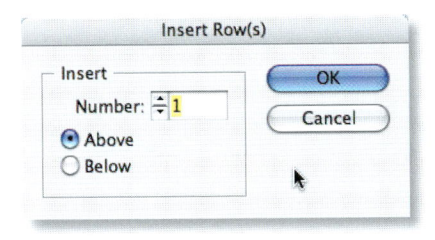

Creating a table with eight rows and four columns sounded like a great idea at the time, but now you need to add another row in the middle of the table to key in some information that you forgot. Use this tip to add as many rows or columns as you want. With the Type tool, put your cursor in a row either above or below where you want to insert more rows. Now choose Insert>Row from the Table menu. You will get a dialog asking how many rows you want and whether you want to insert them above or below the row you have selected. This tip works the same way if you put your cursor in a column and choose Insert>Column from the Table menu.

CHAPTER 10 • Working with Tables

BRING ORDER TO TABLE CHAOS!

So you've become a junkie for dragging the width and height of your columns and rows all willy-nilly? Now you've decided you want nice evenly spaced rows and columns. So use this tip next time to bring everything back to order. Use the Type tool to highlight the rows or columns in which you want to distribute the space evenly. Now choose either Distribute Rows Evenly or Distribute Columns Evenly from the Table menu. Like magic, the space in your rows and columns will be evenly spaced.

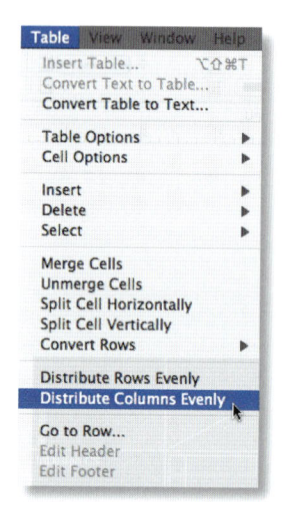

LINE UP AND FLY RIGHT

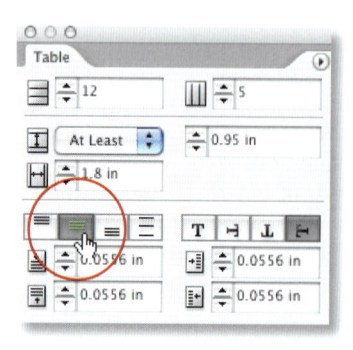

At this point you're probably a pro at putting text in cells. Now how about aligning it? The cool part is that you do it the same way you align text that's not in a cell. Simply select the cells with the Type tool and choose your options from the Control palette or from the Paragraph palette. If you want text aligned in the center of the cell, you can do that from the Control or Table palette (Window>Type & Tables>Table).

208   CHAPTER 10 • Working with Tables

CREATE DIAGONAL LINES

I don't quite understand why, but you might want to have diagonal lines in your table cells. Rather than painstakingly drawing them one by one, you can have InDesign draw them for you. Highlight the cells where you need them and choose Diagonal Lines from the Cell Options submenu under the Table menu. You can choose a diagonal line that leans to the left, right, or both. How exciting! If only Adobe had seen fit to allow your text to be rotated to match the angle, you would really be in good shape.

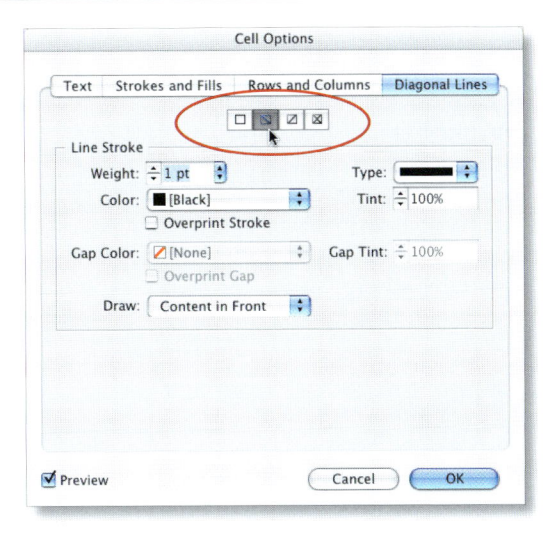

ANGLED TEXT? MAKE IT SO

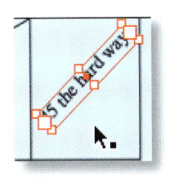

That last tip may have left you obsessed with having text on an angle in a table cell. Give it up; the feature just isn't there. However, you can fake it by rotating the text first and then pasting the rotated text into the cell. Create a small text frame with the Type tool, type your text, and then use the Rotate tool to rotate it to whatever degree you like. Then select the frame with the Selection tool and cut it (Mac: Command-X [PC: Control-X]). Now simply click with the Type tool into the cell where you want it and paste it in (Mac: Command-V [PC: Control-V]). It's not perfect, but it works!

CHAPTER 10 • Working with Tables   209

IT JUST WON'T FIT

Hey, guess what? It won't fit and nobody likes reading 4-point type—so stop trying to cram that big table at the bottom of your page. Place your table where you want it to be and then collapse the bottom of the frame by clicking on the frame's bottom center handle and dragging up with the Selection tool until it fits on the page. Now you should have a red plus sign on the bottom right. Click the plus sign and continue placing your table on the next page. You'll make your readers a lot happier.

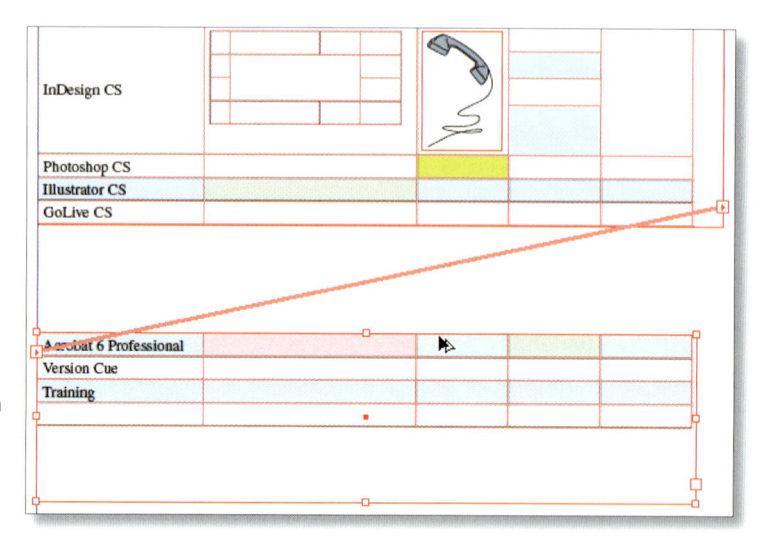

InDesign CS/CS2
KillerTips

Blue Prints

PRINTING AND THE CREATIVE SUITE

So how do tips on printing and on working with other Creative Suite applications belong in the same chapter? Do you want some fluffy-sounding run-around answer

Blue Prints
printing and the Creative Suite

or do you want the truth? Believe me, I can make it sound pretty compelling if you're up for the fluff answer. No? You want the truth? Okay, I'm going to give it to you straight, but if I tell the absolute truth, it's understood that you won't hold it against us in any way. Deal? Deal. Here's the thing: We had enough printing tips to easily fill a chapter, but we were short on the "Suite" tips. Although we originally planned on having an entire "Working with the Creative Suite" chapter, we just couldn't come up with enough tips, so we had to bury our Creative Suite tips within some other chapter. The type and layout chapters were so long we couldn't add them there, and although the tips were pretty good, they weren't really cool enough for the way-cool tips chapter; so basically they ended up here. Hey, you said you wanted the truth, but now that you've heard it, admit it—you wish you had asked for the fluffy compelling-sounding reason. See, this is what they mean by "The truth hurts."

PRINT TO DIFFERENT PRINTERS WITH EASE

It's not uncommon for people to have two or more printers these days. Each printer, of course, has its own way of working and its own driver and its own settings. Rather than having to remember which settings you used the last time, use saved Print Presets. Choose File>Print Presets>Define and click New in the Print Presets dialog. Now you can choose a printer and all the settings you want for that printer. Name your settings and click OK. The next time you want to print with those settings, simply choose your setting from the File menu's Print Presets submenu (as shown below, left). The Print dialog will appear and your settings will already be in place. All you have to do is hit Print.

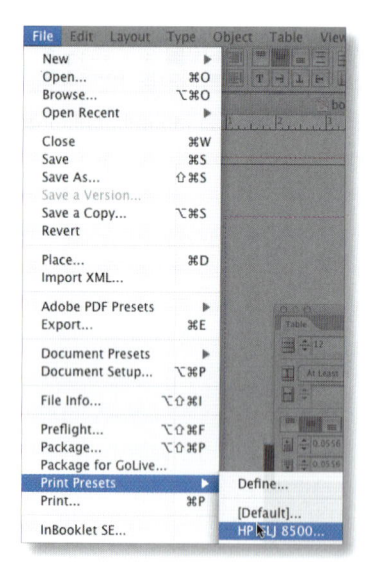

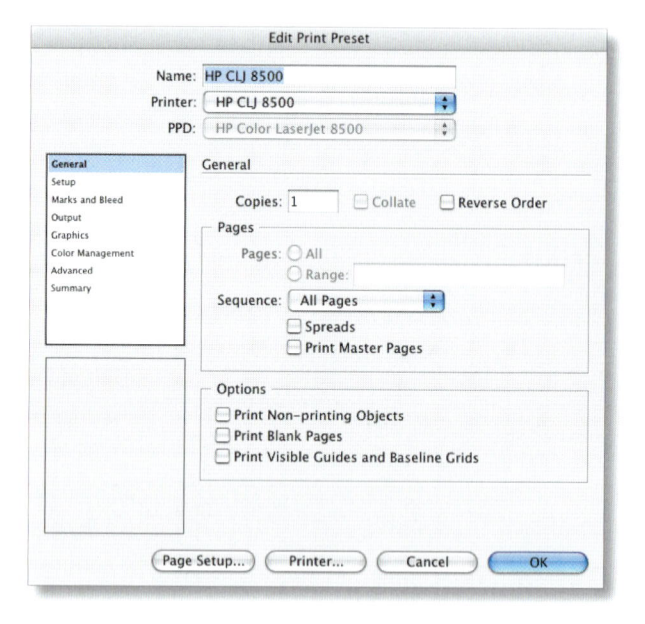

AVOID SEPARATION SURPRISES ON PRESS

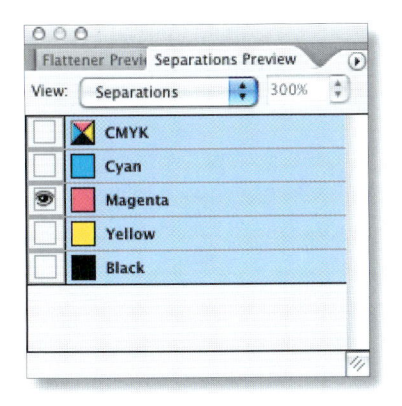

If you'll be color-separating your InDesign file, there's a way to get a preview of your results before the actual separation to film (or plates) occurs—which is helpful in avoiding costly surprises on press. Just go under the Window menu, under Preview, and choose Separations Preview to bring up the Separations Preview palette (as shown here). From the palette's View pop-up menu, choose Separations and then you can view individual plates by turning their visibility on/off using the Eye icons (just as you would in the Layers palette).

HOW MANY PLATES DO YOU REALLY HAVE?

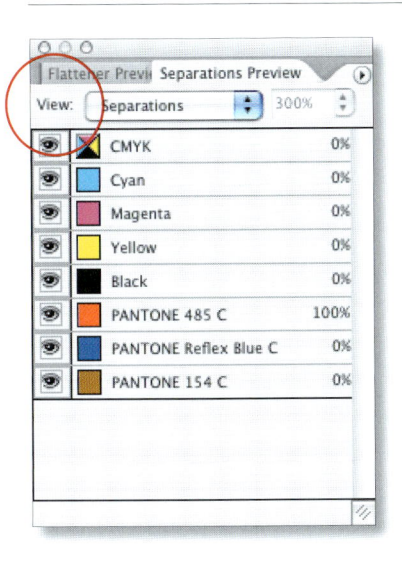

More often than we'd like to admit we may create a job with more colors than we anticipated. This is usually done by accident and can be a real pain in the butt to track down. Here's a tip that will make your day: Choose Window>Output>Separations Preview. Then just as in the previous tip, choose Separations from the View pop-up menu at the top of the Separations Preview palette. This will show you how many plates your job uses. You can find that rogue plate by simply hiding all the other plates by clicking on the Eye icons.

CHAPTER 11 • Printing and the Creative Suite   215

InDesign CS/CS2 KillerTips

USE THE INK MANAGER TO ELIMINATE ROGUE PLATES

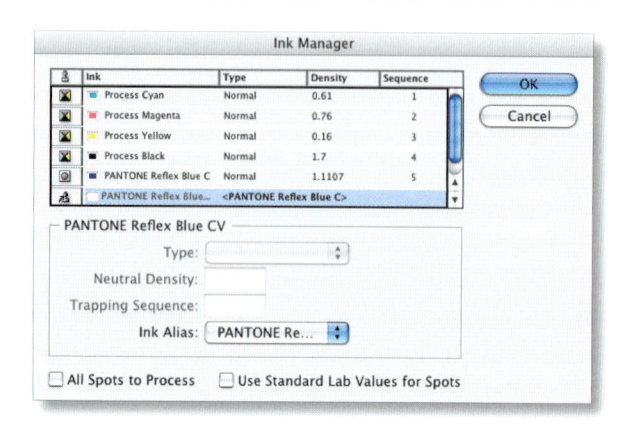

Sometimes you end up with extra plates in your job due to colors that come in from placed graphics. The color is the same as one that you have already defined, but it has a different name. You can fix this using the Ink Manager. You can access the Ink Manager either from the Separations Preview palette's flyout menu or in the Output panel of the Print dialog. Click the color that you want to alias to another existing color in the Ink Manager dialog. Then choose the second color in the Ink Alias pop-up menu. Any objects using this extra color will now be on the plate of the ink that you choose to alias.

PREFLIGHT FOR THE MOST COMMON PROBLEMS

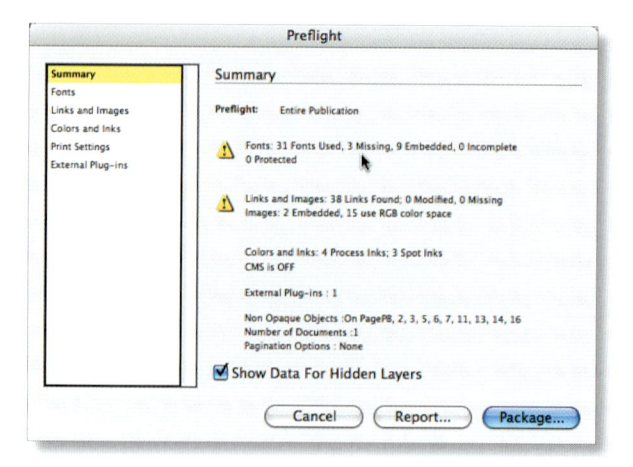

After you send a job out to be printed, the only time you want to hear from the printer is to know that the job is done. So check for the most common mistakes before you burn your CD or FTP your files. Choose Preflight from the File menu and InDesign will automatically run through your entire document looking for missing fonts, broken links, missing fonts placed in vector graphics, extra color plates, and graphics using the RGB color space.

216   CHAPTER 11 • Printing and the Creative Suite

PREFLIGHT: SHOW PROBLEMS ONLY

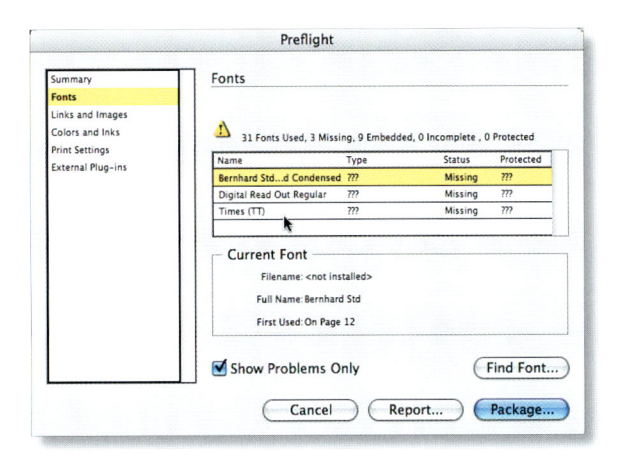

When I'm looking at my Preflight results I really don't care about what's right. I care about what's wrong! In each of the Preflight panels, there is an option to Show Problems Only. If you check that box Preflight will list only the problems in any of the respective panels.

PACKAGE IT UP

Although many people have moved to a PDF workflow, there are still many printers out there that want to work with the native files. You've placed graphics from all over your hard drive, you've used various fonts, and you don't want to have to go gathering up all that stuff manually. Well there is a solution for this: Choose Package from the File menu. The great thing about this is that it will automatically run Preflight too, so if you know you're going to package the document, you don't have to run Preflight manually. The Package feature copies all of the InDesign document, the links, and even the fonts to a location/folder of your choice. Then all you have to do is Stuff it, Zip it, FTP it, or burn it to a CD and transport it to your printer.

CHAPTER 11 • Printing and the Creative Suite

NON-PRINTING OBJECTS—PRINT THEM ANYWAY

Okay, so you've defined objects in your document as non-printing, but now you want to print them anyway. Rather than going back through the document and one by one making them printable again, just click the Print Non-Printing Objects box in the Options section of the Print dialog. This way, you won't miss any, and you won't have to worry about making them non-printing again.

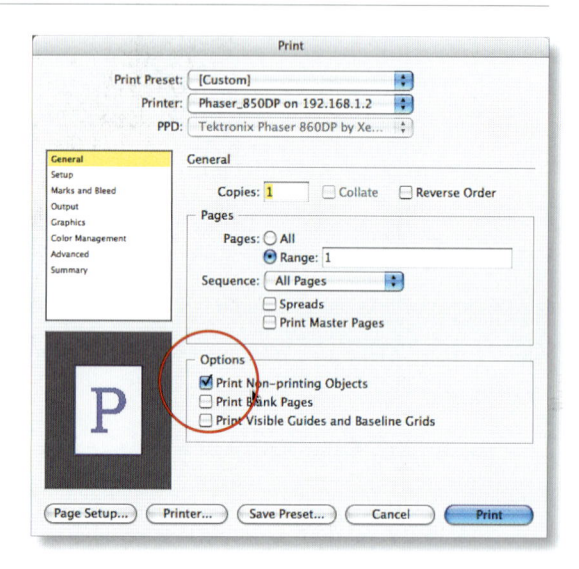

CYCLE THROUGH YOUR PRINT SETTINGS

It's not a print preview, but it's the next best thing. When you want to see the current settings for printing your document, simply click the box where you see the big "P" in the lower left of the Print dialog. Each time you click inside the box it will cycle to your next print setting, as shown here.

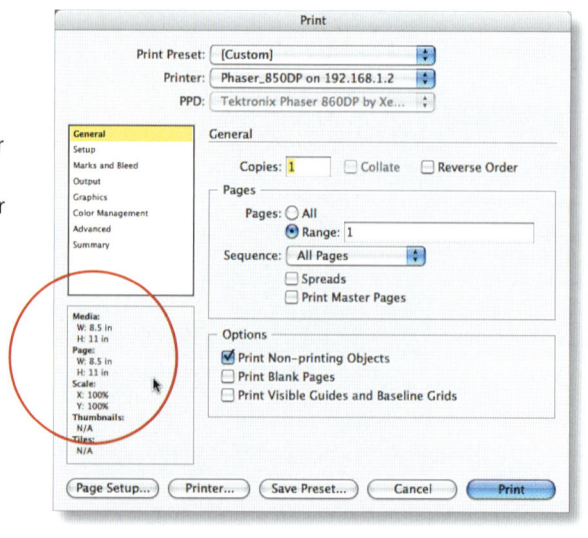

218   CHAPTER 11 • Printing and the Creative Suite

SWITCH PRINTERS ON THE FLY

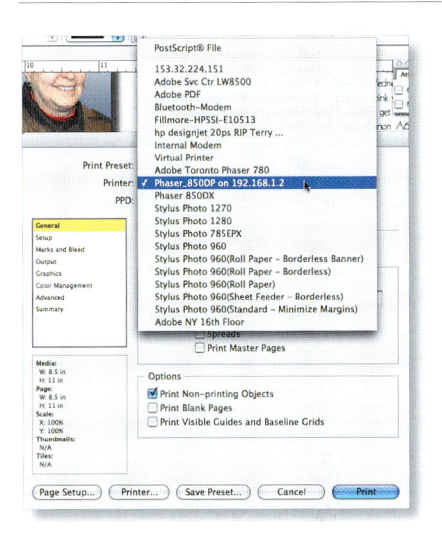

Mac users, the Chooser is gone. This is a good thing because you can now switch printers in any Mac OS X-native application's Print dialog. InDesign's Print dialog also has one extra choice that you may not have noticed. It's the Print Preset pop-up menu. So if you've created a print preset that you wanted to choose from the File menu, but you chose Print by mistake, don't cancel; just choose it from the Print Preset pop-up and you're ready to go.

SPEED UP PRINTING

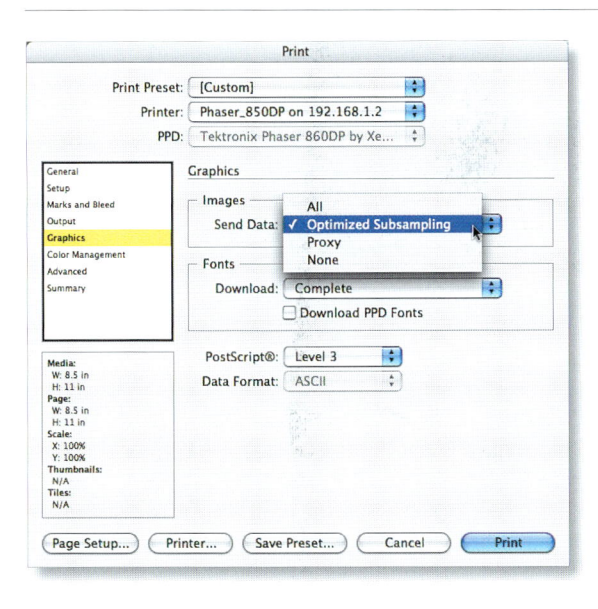

When you print from InDesign you probably want the fastest, most accurate printing you can get, right? To speed things up, switch to the Graphics category of the Print dialog and make sure that the Send Data pop-up menu in the Images section is set to Optimized Subsampling. This option will send down only as much data as your printer can handle. For example, if you had a 1,200-dpi image and you had only a 600-dpi printer, sending down 1,200 dpi would be a waste of time. Optimized Subsampling sends only the right amount of image data.

CHAPTER 11 • Printing and the Creative Suite   219

PRINT PANEL NAVIGATION SHORTCUT

The Print dialog has several panels for choosing your print options. Here's a tip to let you cycle through them quickly. Simply use your Up and Down Arrow keys on your keyboard to take you through the various panels.

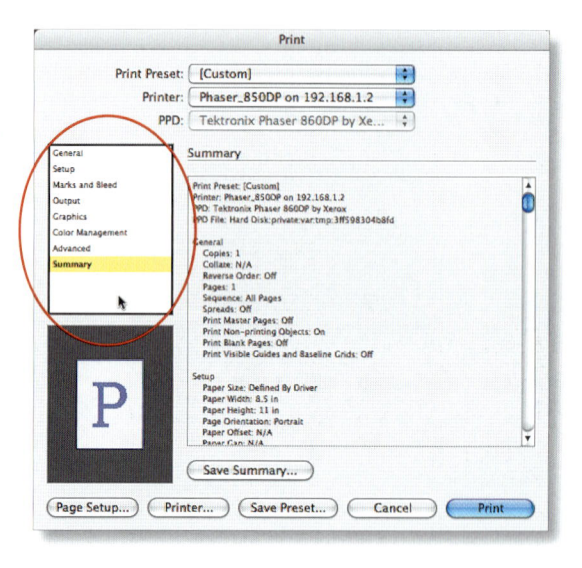

CHANGE YOUR LINE SCREEN WHEN GOING MONOCHROME

Not everyone can afford four-color printing. There are folks out there still using monochrome printers and making plates from laser prints or even running copies on a copier. You can vary the line screen that will be used on your monochrome printer. Choose the Output panel on the left of the Print dialog and change the Color pop-up menu to Composite Gray and then change the Screening pop-up menu to Custom. You'll notice that now you can enter your own Frequency (lines per inch) as well as an Angle (although 45° will work for most folks).

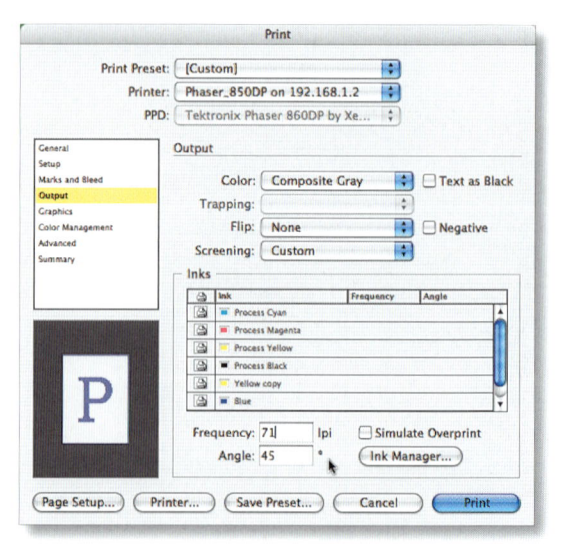

PRINT SEPARATIONS LIKE A PRO

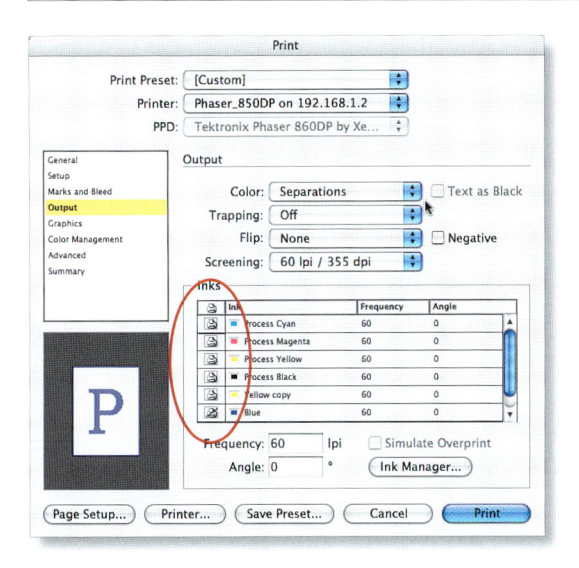

By default InDesign prints color in Composite mode. If you're printing to your color printer, that's what you want. However, if you're printing to an image setter or plate maker, chances are you want a separate plate or piece of film for each color. Switch to the Output panel in the Print dialog and choose Separations from the Color pop-up menu. In the Inks section you will be able to manually turn on and off which plates you want to print by clicking on the tiny printer icons on the left.

PRINT THE SLUG

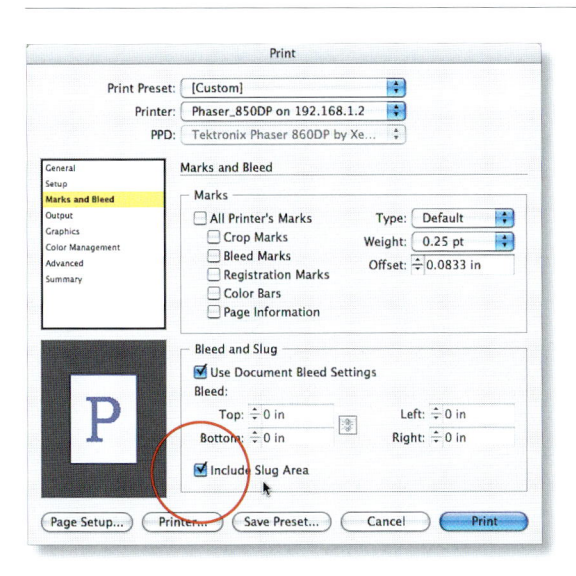

When you create an InDesign document you have the option of creating a slug area. This area is typically used by ad agencies and designers to place information about the job and its print settings. In the Marks and Bleed category in the Print dialog, go to the Bleed and Slug section, where you have the option whether to Include Slug Area when you print the document. It's off by default.

CHAPTER 11 • Printing and the Creative Suite   221

InDesign CS/CS2
KillerTips

ACCESS PRINTER-SPECIFIC FEATURES

Unfortunately InDesign's Print dialog may not include every single option that is available in your printer driver. For example, our Tektronix Phaser 850DP can do duplexing, but those controls aren't in the InDesign Print dialog. When you want to access all of the options available to your printer, click the Printer button at the bottom of the Print dialog. This will allow you to access the normal OS-level printer driver to enable the options that InDesign is missing.

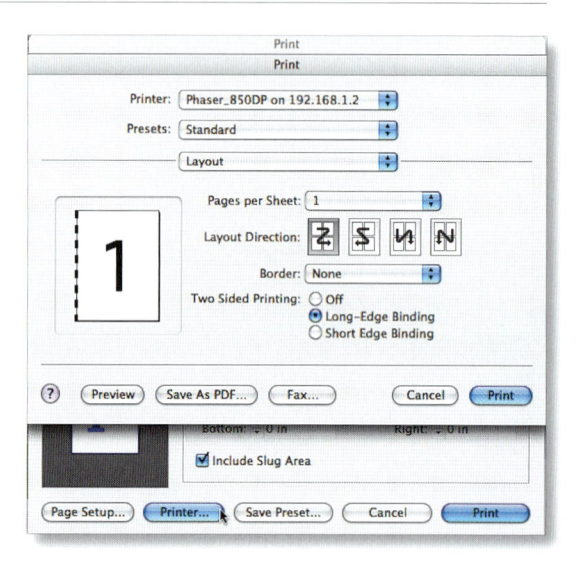

DOWNLOAD PPD FONTS ANYWAY!

You used Times Roman and it's coming out Courier. How can this be? Times Roman is built into the printer. If you have fonts that are built into the printer but they're not printing right, switch to the Graphics panel of the Print dialog (yeah, I know that's the first place you'd look, right?); and for the Fonts option enable the checkbox for Download PPD Fonts. This will force InDesign to download the fonts that should be in the printer anyway.

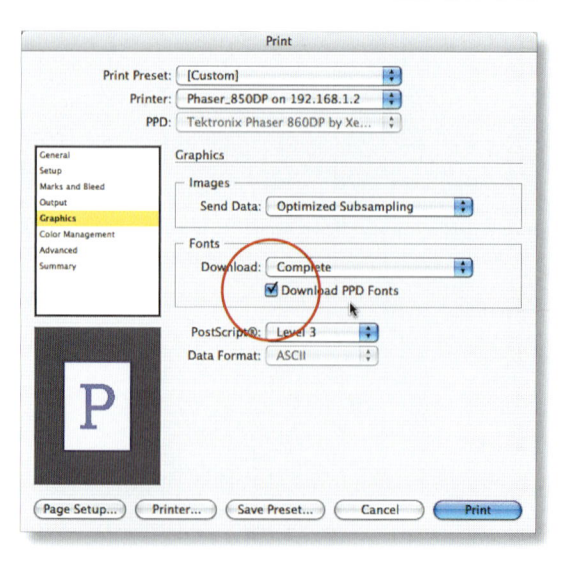

222 CHAPTER 11 • Printing and the Creative Suite

SCALE PAGES TO FIT YOUR MEDIA SIZE

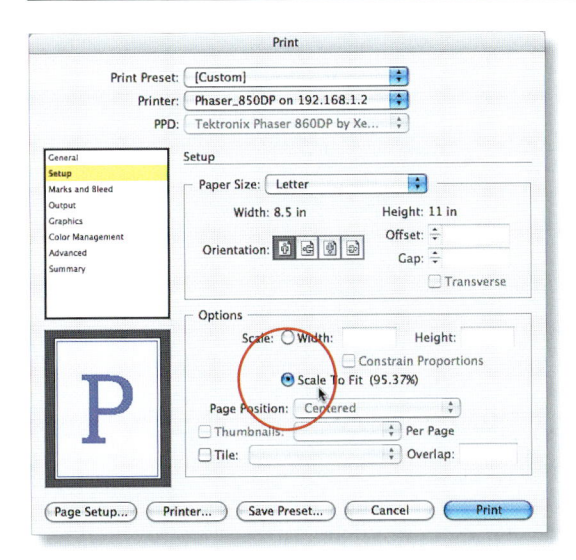

If you have something that was designed for a large page and need to shrink it down to fit the media that you're currently printing to, this tip will save you time. Rather than scale the objects in the document, simply choose Scale To Fit in the Setup panel of the Print dialog and print your job.

WHEN YOUR SERVICE PROVIDER WON'T TAKE AN INDESIGN FILE

If your printer or service provider flat-out refuses to accept InDesign files, smack 'em. Okay, maybe that's not a good idea. Work around the problem. In most cases, they would probably accept a PDF. If not, you can export the pages as EPS files or even print PostScript. If your printer/service provider isn't open to any of these options, it may be time to move to another printer/service provider. At http://partners.adobe.com you can find print houses that are eagerly accepting InDesign files.

CHAPTER 11 • Printing and the Creative Suite   223

InDesign CS/CS2
KillerTips

🔴 🟡 🟢 PULL THE PLUG ON AUTO-UPDATING

If Adobe comes out with a free maintenance update for InDesign, they really want you to have it (read as: really, really, really!). That's why they've included a feature that goes to Adobe's website and checks for updates automatically. This auto-check feature is actually pretty helpful and these updates are designed to make your work easier by fixing bugs or other potential problems; but some people just hate the fact that it goes out and searches without their specifically asking it to. If you're one of those people (you know who you are), then go under the InDesign menu (PC: Edit menu), under Preferences, and choose Updates. When the Preferences dialog appears, uncheck Automatically Check for Updates Every Month. From that point on, it's up to you to check for updates from Adobe, and if you know that in reality you're likely to forget (like us), you may not want to turn this feature off after all.

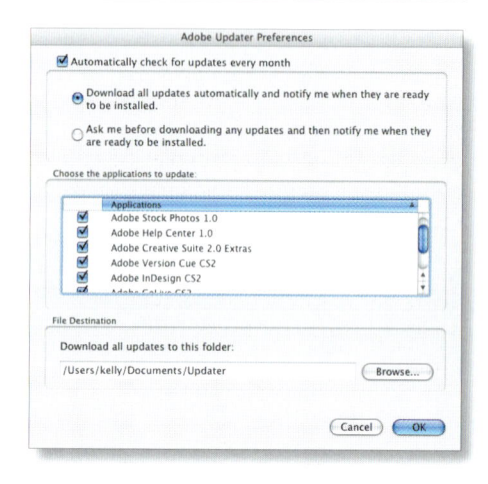

🔴 🟡 🟢 PLACE NATIVE PHOTOSHOP FILES

Although TIFF files are still the norm, they're not the most convenient to work with. Chances are that you have used layers in creating your Photoshop artwork. In making a TIFF you would probably do a Save As to create a flattened TIFF and now you have two files to deal with. Instead of making TIFFs just place (File>Place) the native Photoshop document. InDesign will automatically flatten it in the print stream.

224   CHAPTER 11 • Printing and the Creative Suite

PLACE NATIVE ILLUSTRATOR FILES

InDesign works with Illustrator in two ways. You can either copy and paste vector paths from Illustrator into InDesign or you can place (File>Place) native Illustrator files. The advantage of copying and pasting vector paths is that they are converted to InDesign vectors and can be modified in InDesign. The disadvantage is that there is no link back to the original Illustrator drawing. The advantage of placing native Illustrator files is that you maintain all the effects and transparency and a link back to the original .AI file. However, placed Illustrator files cannot be modified in InDesign.

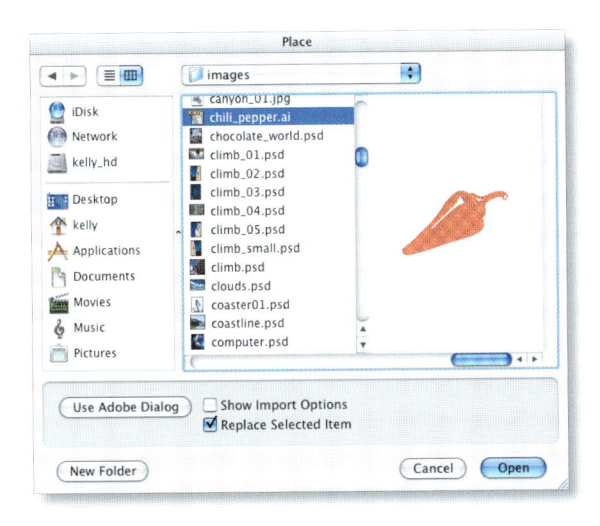

CHAPTER 11 • Printing and the Creative Suite   225

SHARE COLOR SETTINGS WITH PHOTOSHOP AND ILLUSTRATOR

InDesign, Photoshop, and Illustrator all share the same color management settings. Therefore, when you've spent time getting color right in Photoshop, InDesign can use those same settings. Choose Color Settings from the Edit menu. Click Load, and choose the custom color settings you created and named in Photoshop. If you didn't create custom settings, then simply match the settings that you used in the other apps for consistent color in all three programs.

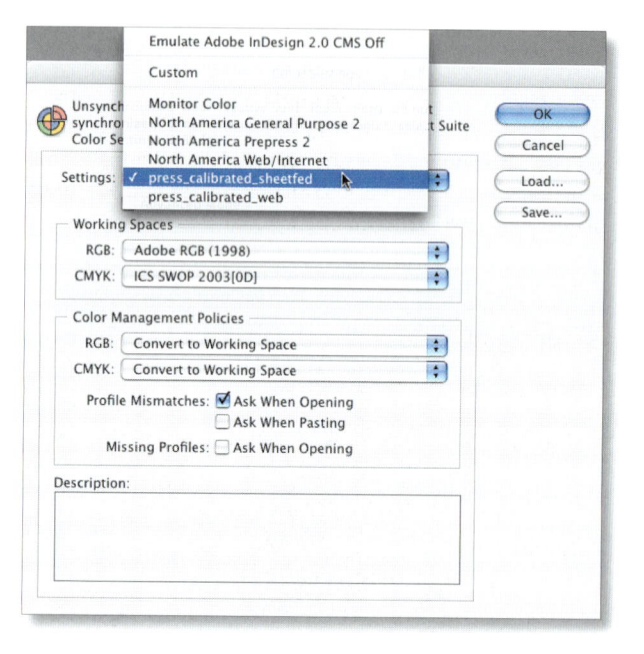

EDIT YOUR GRAPHICS AND HAVE THEM AUTO-UPDATE

If you're working with placed graphics created in either Adobe Photoshop or Adobe Illustrator (and our guess is you are) you can edit a placed image directly by holding the Option key (PC: Alt key) and double-clicking on the image. This opens the image in the application that created it (Photoshop or Illustrator) so you can edit the image as you'd like. (You can also Control-click [PC: Alt-click] your image and choose Edit Original, as shown here.) When you resave the images after your edits and return to InDesign, these edited images will automatically be updated in your InDesign document. Mighty cool.

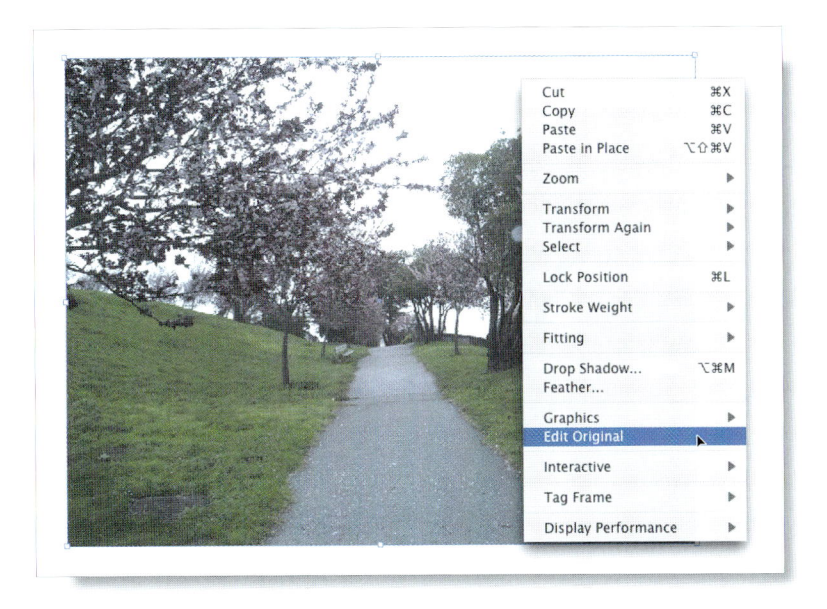

CHAPTER 11 • Printing and the Creative Suite

GOING FROM PRINT TO THE WEB?

If the boss comes by and says something like, "That new brochure design looks great! Can we get a version up on the Web?" your first reaction might be to create a PDF (which in many cases is the right reaction), but what if you want a standard HTML webpage instead? If you're using Adobe GoLive as your Web authoring application, InDesign can make your conversion much easier. Just go under the File menu and choose Package For GoLive. Though InDesign will let you save the package anywhere you like, it makes it a whole lot easier if you save it to the InDesignPackages folder located in your GoLive site's web-data folder. After you choose a location to save your "package," you'll be greeted with a dialog (shown here) that offers options such as the ability to package all—or just a portion—of your document. Click the Package button, and you're ready to open your file (and images) in GoLive for further editing.

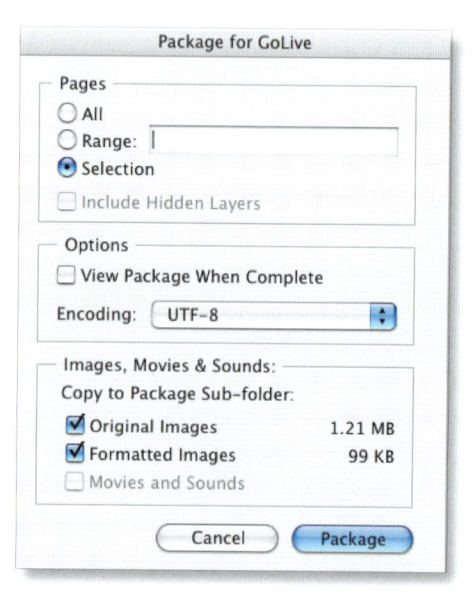

CHAPTER 11 • Printing and the Creative Suite

New Attitude

WHAT'S NEW IN INDESIGN CS2

There's nothing like cracking open a new piece of software, going through the arduous installation process, waiting with bated breath, only to see what appears at first

New Attitude
what's new in InDesign CS2

glance to be the same old interface. Believe it or not, that's a good thing. Imagine the panic in the streets and rioting in San Jose if every time someone installed an upgrade everything was totally different and moved around just for the sake of making things different and moving things around. Although InDesign CS2 looks a lot like InDesign CS, there's a lot of new stuff in there. In this chapter we'll take you through the new features that matter most. You'll be up and running in no time, thumbing your nose at those poor misfortunate souls who are still working the way they always did since InDesign 2 and not taking advantage of the things you're about to learn. You could read this chapter and then hold a class for everyone, but that's so not like you.

DRAG-AND-DROP FROM THE BRIDGE

Whether you bought InDesign CS2 as a stand-alone application or as part of the Adobe Creative Suite 2, you also received an additional application called Adobe Bridge. The Bridge is neat because it allows you to see a folder full of images without having to open them up one by one. Here's a tip for laying out your next job faster. Use the Bridge to navigate to the folder containing all the assets you need to place in your layout. Then simply drag the images from the Bridge directly onto your InDesign page. You can either drag images into existing frames or let InDesign create the frames for you on the fly. You can even drag multiple images at once and then sort them out once they are on the page.

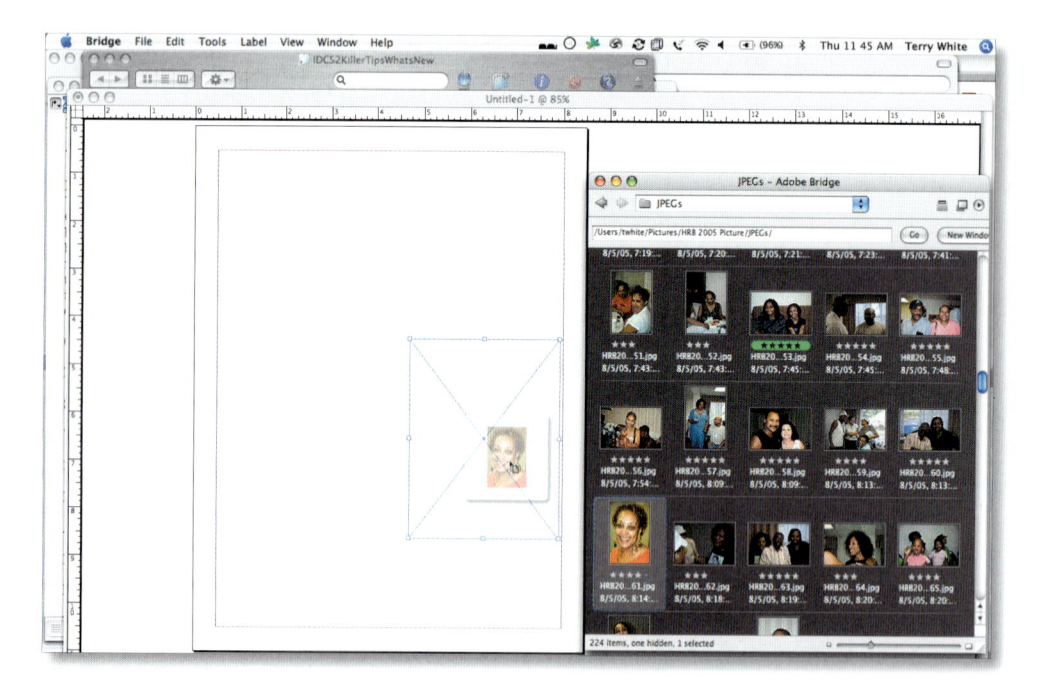

OPEN THE BRIDGE FROM INDESIGN

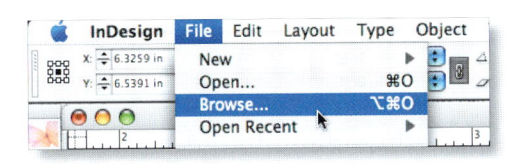

Using Adobe Bridge is like having your own image palette accessible anytime you need it. However, finding and launching the Bridge can be a pain. But there are a couple of easy ways to access the Bridge directly from InDesign CS2. The first way is to choose Browse from the File menu, or use the keyboard shortcut: Command-Option-O (PC: Control-Alt-O). The second way is to simply click the Go To Bridge button right on the Control bar.

PLACE A STOCK PHOTO COMP IMAGE

With the Bridge you can search the world's leading stock photography houses. When you find a stock image you like and you want to test it in your layout, the Bridge allows you to download a low-res comp image. Rather than trying to find that image later via the Place command, simply drag it in from the downloaded comps area of the Bridge. Just drag the thumbnail from the Bridge to your existing frame or directly to your page in InDesign.

CHAPTER 12 • What's New in InDesign CS2   233

PURCHASE A STOCK PHOTO IMAGE FROM INDESIGN

Which images are yours and which are stock photo comps? That may be a question that comes to mind after you've started placing lots of stock photo comps mixed in with your own images. This tip will not only make it easy for you to tell which images are which, but it will also allow you to go ahead and purchase the images you need. If you do decide to purchase an image, it will automatically download and replace the comp image. Simply bring up your InDesign Links palette. You'll see all the links in your document. The stock photo comps will have a small film negative icon on them to the right of the name of the link. That's a dead giveaway that will tell you which links are stock photo comps and which ones aren't. In order to purchase an image, simply select Purchase This Image from the Links palette flyout menu.

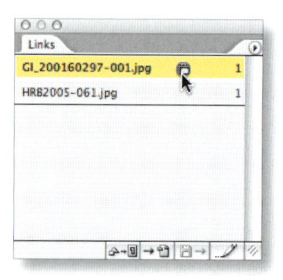

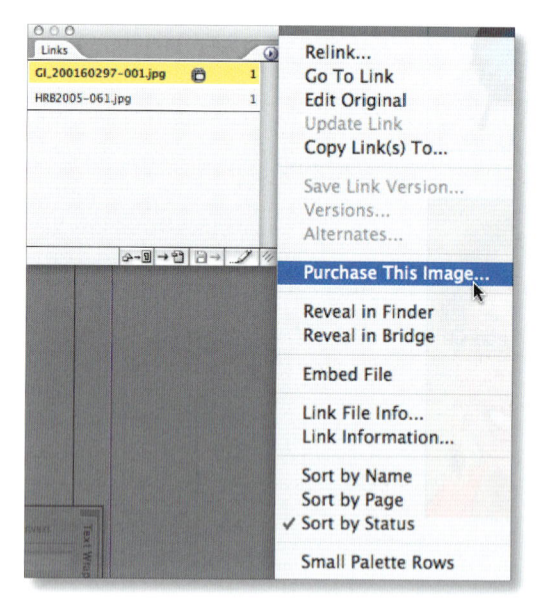

SNIPPETS

Almost everyone is familiar with InDesign Libraries, right? You know, those palettes that you can create by choosing New > Library from the File menu. Once one is open, you can drag-and-drop page elements into it. As long as you keep that library open (or even if you open it later), you can drag elements from it onto other InDesign pages in the same document or other documents. Now imagine if these elements weren't tied to an InDesign Library? That's where Snippets come in. The next time you want to use elements from one InDesign document in another InDesign document, simply drag the elements to the desktop or a Bridge window and it will create an XML-based Snippet that can be used in any other InDesign page or document. You can even email Snippets. It's like having Library elements without the Library file.

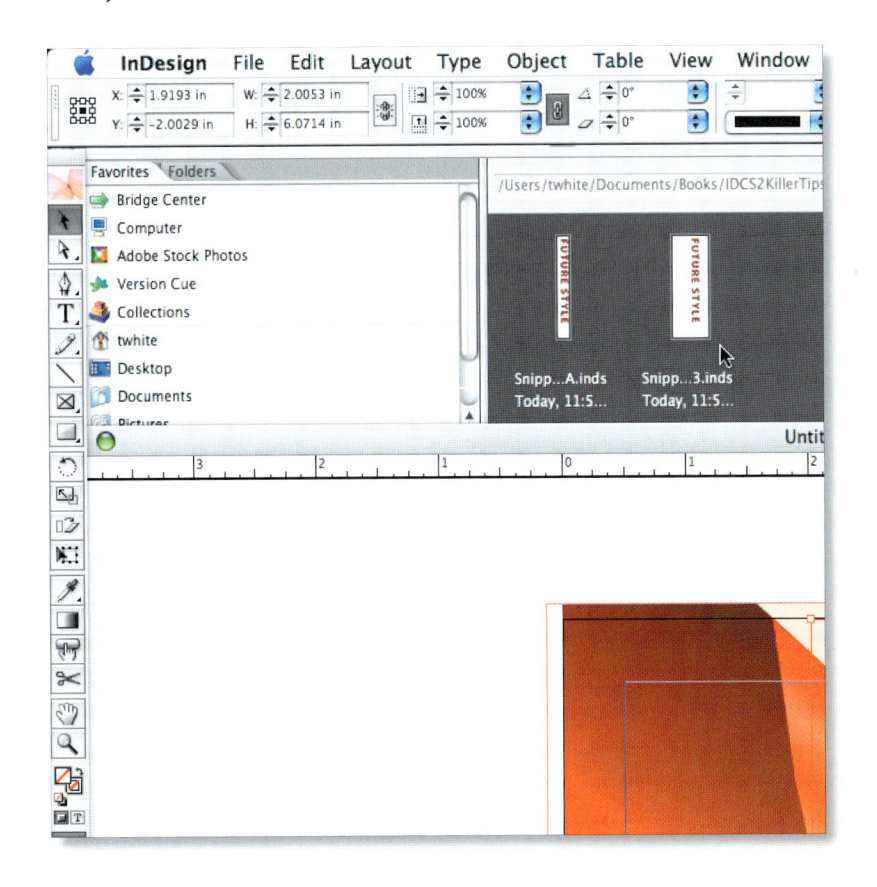

WYSIWYG FONT MENUS

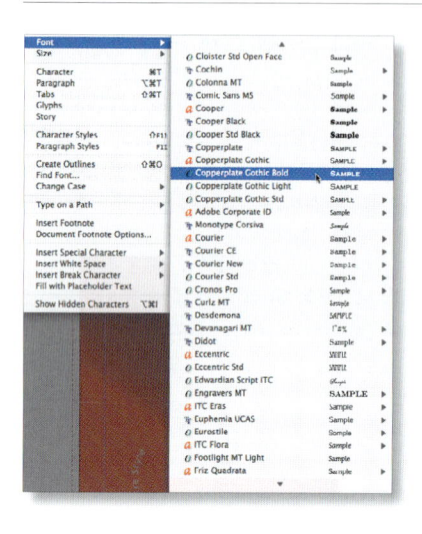

Choosing between different fonts is a daily exercise in the page layout world. It's pretty cool that you can just start typing the name of the font that you want to get to in the Control palette. But what if you're not sure which font you want to use until you see it? Now you can simply choose the Font menu (under the Type menu) and not only will it show you the names of the fonts, but it will also show you what type of font it is and provide a sample of what the font looks like. If it's an OpenType font it will have an "O" to the left of the font's name. An "a" denotes a PostScript Type 1 font, and a "TT" means it's a TrueType font. So if your service provider wants you to avoid TrueType fonts, you can easily do that by scanning the list and avoiding those font types.

DRAG-AND-DROP TEXT

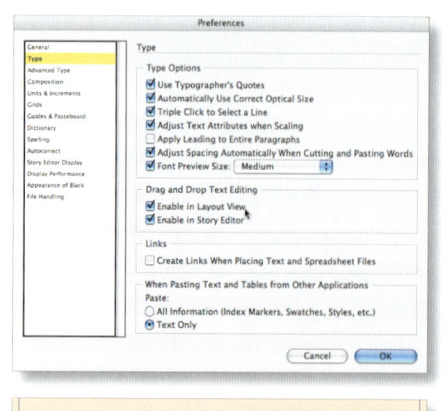

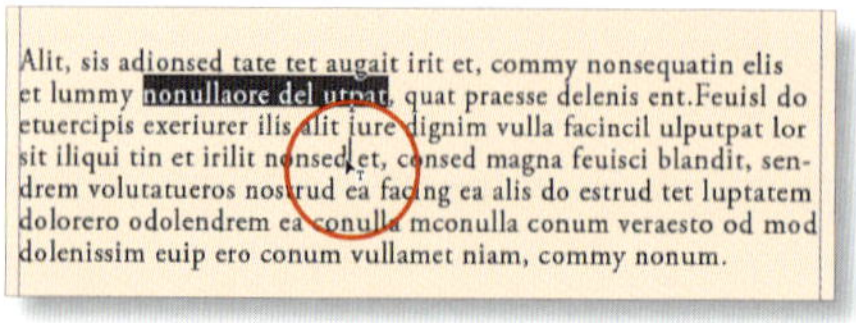

When you highlight text in an InDesign document and start dragging the Type tool across it again, by default it will simply make a new selection. If you want the behavior to change so that you can drag-and-drop your highlighted text, try this tip: Choose Type from the Preferences menu and check Enable in Layout View from the Drag and Drop Text Editing section. Now, if you use the Type tool and hover over highlighted text on the page, you'll notice that there is a little pointer with a "T". You can now drag that highlighted text to another location either in the same frame or a different frame.

236 CHAPTER 12 • What's New in InDesign CS2

InDesign CS/CS2
KillerTips

DYNAMIC SPELLING

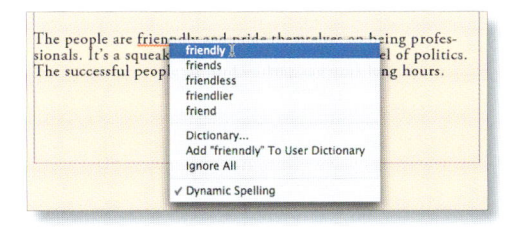

I've used Microsoft Word for years and years, mainly because it has one thing that I really like: Dynamic Spelling. I like having my spelling checked as I type. In InDesign CS2, this is now a built-in capability. However, it's off by default. You can enable it by choosing Dynamic Spelling from the Spelling menu (under the Edit menu). Any words in your document that are not in the dictionary will be underlined in red. You can then Control-click (PC: Right-click) on them to bring up a list of suggested words that InDesign thinks you're trying to spell.

AUTOCORRECT

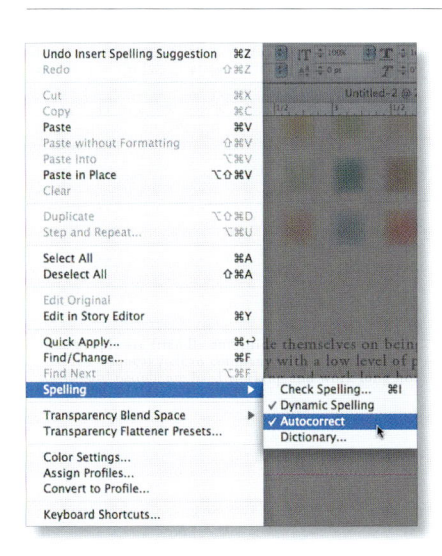

If you're not the world's most accurate typist, you'll love Autocorrect. Autocorrect is off by default in InDesign. However, if you enable it (choose Autocorrect from the Spelling menu under the Edit menu) and type a commonly misspelled word —such as "teh"— InDesign will correct it as "the". You can even add your own Autocorrect words by going to the Autocorrect preferences (in the Preferences dialog) and adding them.

CHAPTER 12 • What's New in InDesign CS2   237

MULTIPLE USER DICTIONARIES

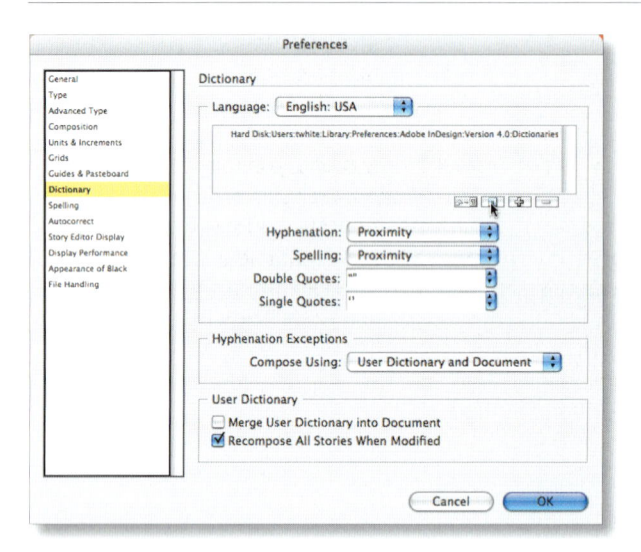

InDesign CS2 documents can now be spell checked against multiple dictionaries simultaneously. So you can spell check using the user dictionary that you normally add words to, and you can also choose additional dictionaries, such as a dictionary of corporate terms, from the Dictionary preferences. Or, if you want to create a new dictionary altogether, you can do that by adding it in the Dictionary preferences.

IMPORT TEXT FILES TO THE DICTIONARY

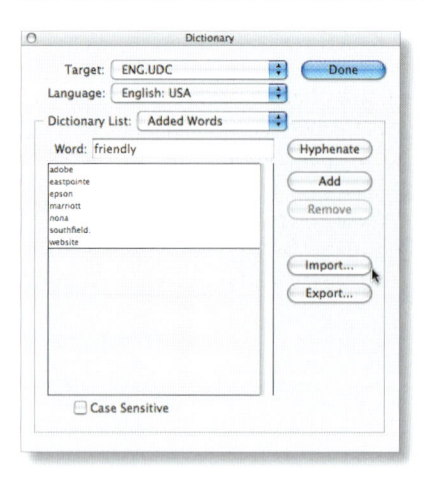

If you work in a workgroup where everyone uses InDesign, here's a tip to increase the speed and consistency of your spell checking. Type a list of words that are specific to your kind of work, such as technical terms, acronyms, etc. Then export or save that list as a text file (.txt). Choose Dictionary from the Spelling menu (under the Edit menu) and click the Import button to select the text file you created. After each user does this, you will all have the same words in your user dictionaries—plus the words you've already added.

238   CHAPTER 12 • What's New in InDesign CS2

FOOTNOTES

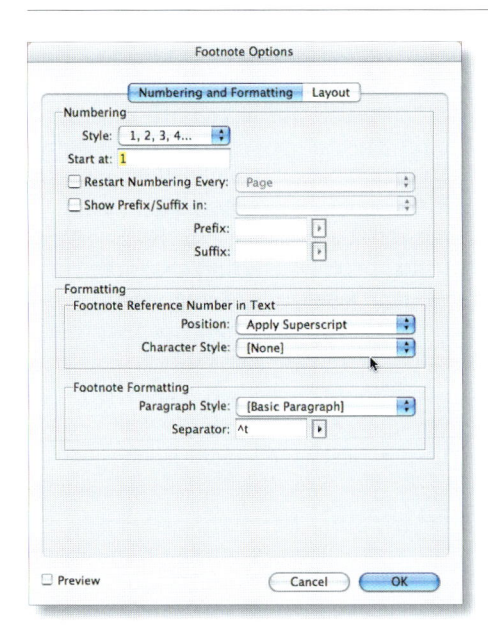

Stop building your footnotes manually! InDesign CS2 has an automatic footnote capability. That's not really the tip, though. The tip is that not only can you choose Insert Footnote from the Type menu, you can also control how that footnote looks using style sheets: Choose Document Footnote Options from the Type menu and assign a Character Style to your Footnote Reference Number and a Paragraph Style to your Footnote Formatting.

PASTE WITHOUT FORMATTING

InDesign tries to do the right thing by pasting text exactly as it was formatted in the source document. However, this can be frustrating when you're just trying to paste raw text that you want to format yourself. This tip will end the frustration. Copy your text from any application (such as Microsoft Word) and then choose Paste Without Formatting from the Edit menu in InDesign CS2. Your text will be pasted as raw text that you can then stylize however you'd like.

CHAPTER 12 • What's New in InDesign CS2   239

OVERSET TEXT IN THE STORY EDITOR

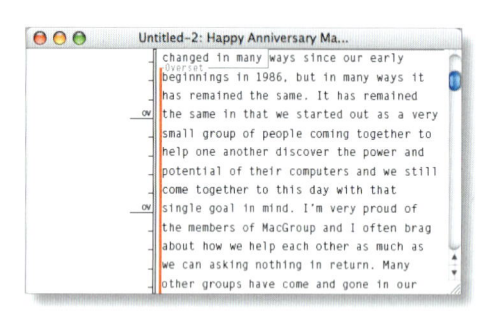

A question that has plagued desktop publishers since day one is this: "How much text is left to place?" The next time you place text in a frame and you get the red plus sign indicating that there is more text, try this tip to know exactly where you stand. Put your cursor on the last line of text that's showing in the frame. Then bring up that text in the Story Editor by choosing Edit in Story Editor from the Edit menu. Now you'll see your overset text, indicated by a red vertical line.

FRAME-BASED BASELINE GRIDS

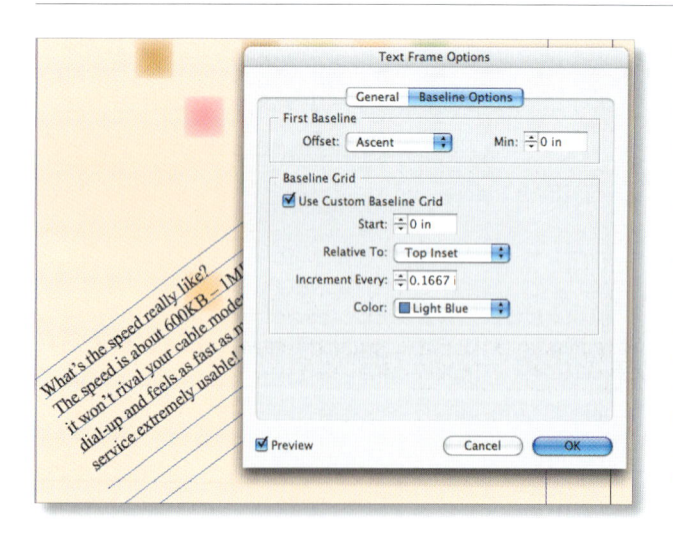

Baseline grids have been around for years, working behind the scenes on your pages to keep your columns of text even across the page. However, the functionality of a baseline grid completely falls apart if you have text in a frame and the frame needs to be rotated. The text can't line up to the page's baseline grid if the frame is on an angle. If you find yourself in this situation, try this tip. First, you have to create your text and align it to the grid by clicking the Align to Baseline Grid button in the Paragraph options of the Control palette. You'll probably also want to Show the Baseline Grid in the View menu (under Grids & Guides). Once your text is aligned in the frame, that's when you can go ahead and rotate the frame.

CHAPTER 12 • What's New in InDesign CS2

PHOTOSHOP LAYER CONTROLS

InDesign has always been able to place native Photoshop files. However, you were only able to get the current state of the Photoshop layers. (In other words, if a Photoshop file had three layers but only two were turned on, you'd only get those two layers when you placed the file.) Now you can actually turn the layers on and off of a placed Photoshop file directly in InDesign. If the Photoshop file contains Layer Comps (groups of layers turned on and off) you can control those, too. Place a native Photoshop file that contains at least two layers. With the image selected on the page choose Object Layer Options (from the Object menu). You'll then be able to turn layers on and off for that one instance of the placed Photoshop file. Be sure to enable the Preview checkbox so that you can see the updates live. This tip also works for placed PDF files that contain layers.

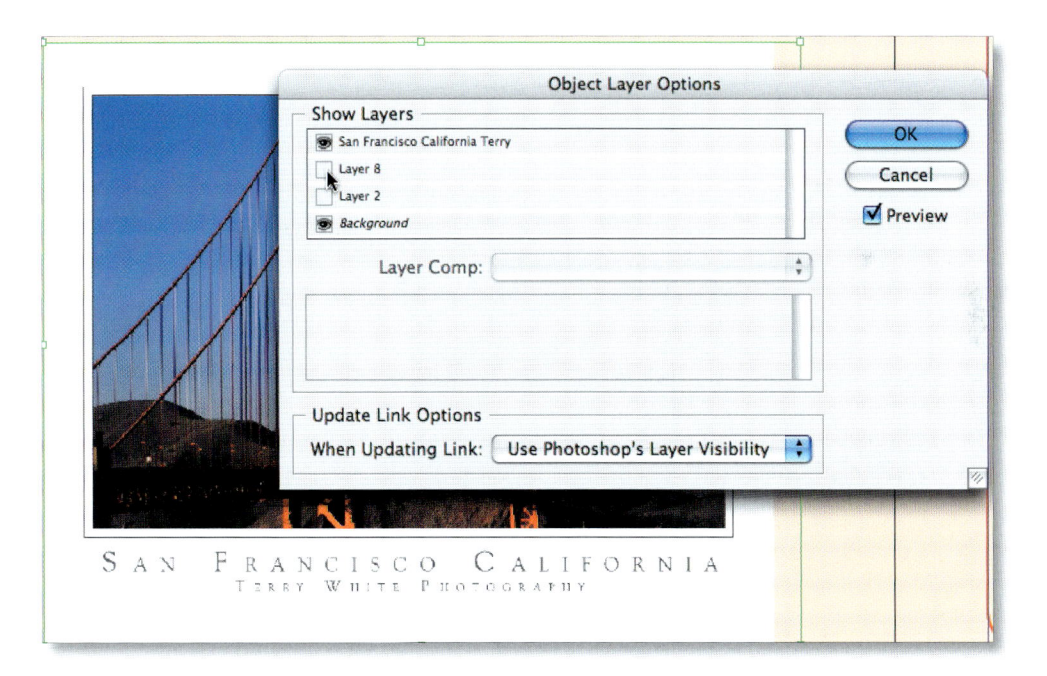

CHAPTER 12 • What's New in InDesign CS2   241

OBJECT STYLES

Paragraph and character style sheets have been around almost as long as desktop publishing itself. They allow you to quickly format paragraphs and individual character selections. Up until now, style sheets only applied to text. But what about your objects? The frames that you place your text and images into can contain attributes such as transparency settings, strokes, number of columns, etc. We've always had to set these attributes one-by-one in the past. With this tip, you can streamline your workflow. Create or select a frame already on the page. Give it whatever attributes you want, such as a stroke and a drop shadow. Then bring up the Object Styles palette and click the Create New Style button at the bottom. This will create a new Object Style that contains those attributes. You can then select other frames in your document and simply click on your new Object Style to assign it to the frames you selected.

SELECTIVELY LOAD STYLES

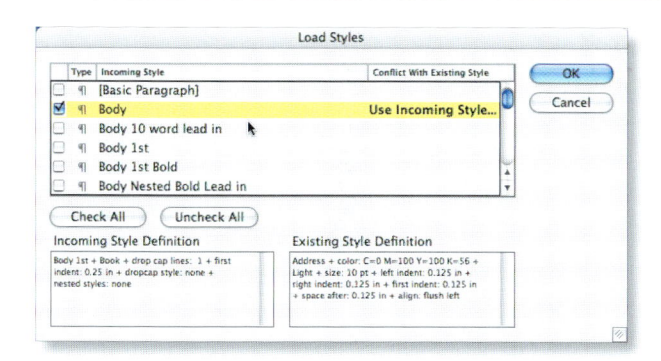

You spent time creating this really cool style sheet in the document you worked on last week and now you need to use it in your new document. The problem is that the document you already created has about a million other style sheets that you don't need in the new document. There is a solution! You can selectively load styles from one InDesign document into another. Open or create the new document and then bring up the style palette for the styles that you want to import. For example, bring up the Paragraph Styles palette and then choose Load Paragraph Styles from the flyout menu. You'll get a dialog box asking you to choose the document from which you want to import styles. Now you have the option to choose just the styles you want to import.

QUICK APPLY

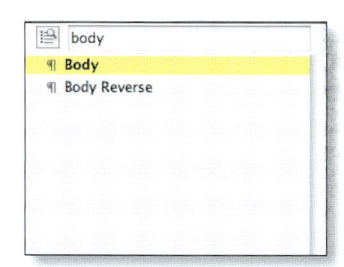

Have you ever caught yourself digging for the right style palette? You can see the Paragraph Styles palette, but the Character Styles and Object Styles palettes don't jump out at you. What if you could apply styles without having the palettes open at all? Use this tip to quickly apply paragraph, character, or object styles depending on what you have selected on the page: Press Command-Return (PC: Control-Return) to bring up the Quick Apply palette. Type in the name of the style you want to apply. Once it's highlighted you can simply press Return to apply the style and the palette goes away.

CHAPTER 12 • What's New in InDesign CS2   243

APPLY NEXT STYLE

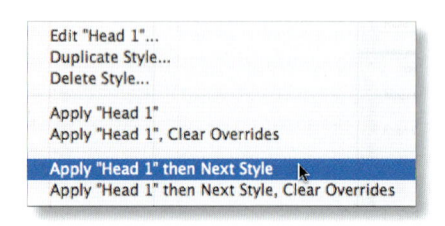

When you create a Paragraph Style you have the option to choose a Next Style. That means that, when you hit Return, InDesign automatically switches to another style that you've assigned as the Next Style. For example, if after typing a headline you always type the author's name, you could set up a Next Style where the Author style immediately follows the Headline style. Catchy, huh? This works great as long as you're typing directly into InDesign. If you're placing text, use this tip to apply all of your Paragraph Styles at once: Highlight all the text that you want to apply the styles to, then Control-click (PC: Right-click) on the first style you want to apply. You'll get a contextual menu that allows you to apply the style you clicked on, as well as the Next Style that you've defined. This effect will ripple through the rest of the highlighted text, applying all your Next Styles.

RESET TO BASE STYLE

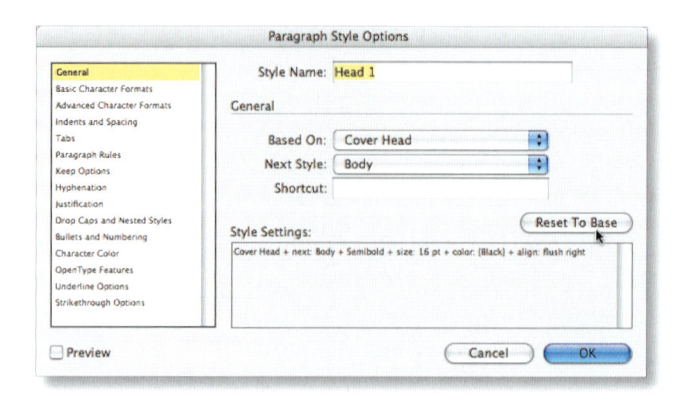

If the style sheet you're creating is getting out of hand and you want to reset it back to the base settings, bring up the style definition and press the Reset To Base button to quickly restore the original attributes in a new style you're specifying or editing.

244 CHAPTER 12 • What's New in InDesign CS2

InDesign CS/CS2
KillerTips

CLEAR OVERRIDES

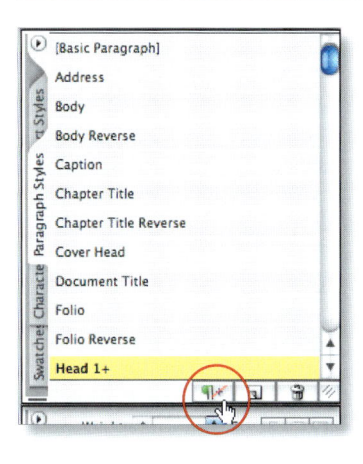

When applying paragraph styles, sometimes the paragraph you're applying it to may have some local overrides, with certain words being bold, italicized, or maybe even a different font. In previous versions of InDesign, the tip would be to hold down the Option key and click the style to override this individual formatting. You can still do it that way in InDesign CS2, but now there is also a new button at the bottom of the Paragraph Styles and Object Styles palettes that will do the trick: Place your cursor in the paragraph with the overrides that you want to clear and press the Clear Overrides button.

ALIGN AWAY/TOWARDS SPINE

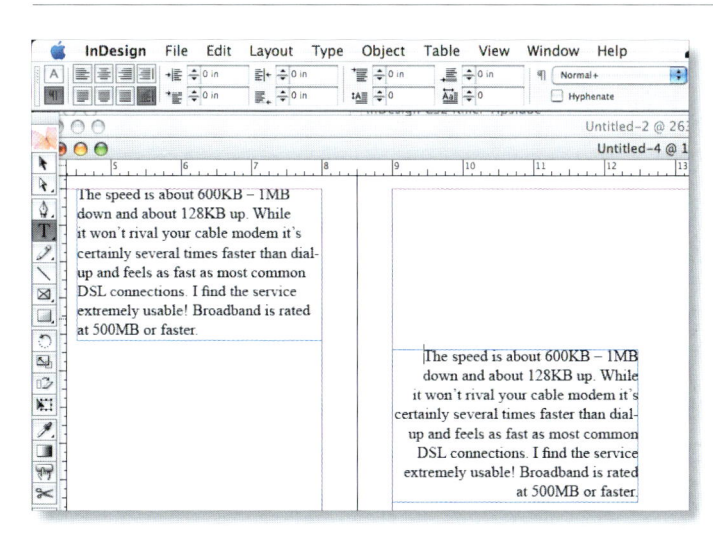

You can align text using a variety of different options, such as Align Left, Align Center, Align Right, Justified, etc. The next time you want to align text based on its location in relation to the spine, try this tip: Put your cursor in the paragraph that you want to align toward or away from the spine and go to the Paragraph options in the Control palette. There you will find one button to align your text toward the spine and one to align your text away from the spine. In the image here, you can see that the text is set to align away from the spine, and it automatically shifts to align left or right depending on what side of the spine it's on.

CHAPTER 12 • What's New in InDesign CS2   245

WORD IMPORT

If you're in the page layout world, receiving Word files from people is a fact of life. InDesign can place Word files pretty easily. By default, they come in as they were formatted in Word. However, if you want to control exactly how the text comes in, choose Place from the File menu and make sure you check the Show Import Options checkbox. Now choose a Word file to place and you'll get a dialog box that lets you control just about every aspect of how the file is formatted as it is imported. You can choose to accept or discard the formatting already in place. Also, don't forget to check out the Customize Style Import option at the bottom of the dialog, which allows you to map the incoming Word styles to your InDesign styles.

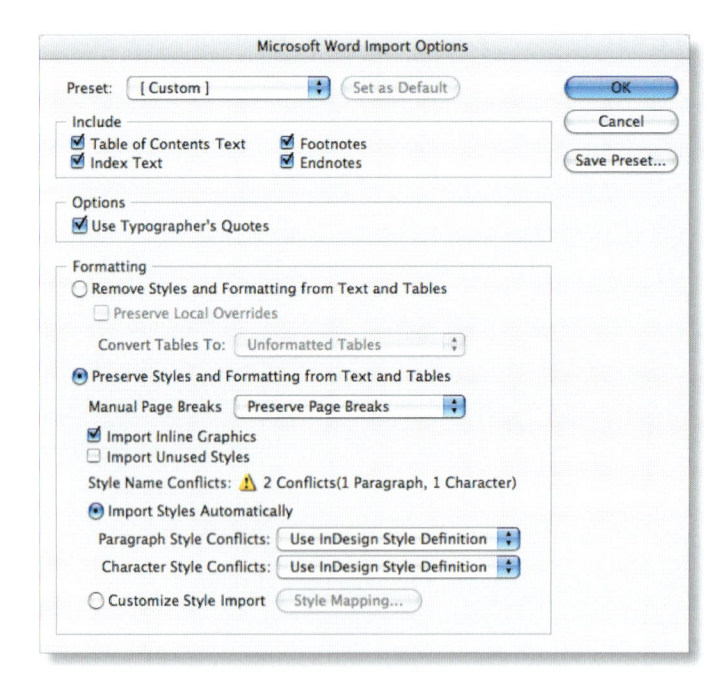

FILL FRAME PROPORTIONALLY

I gotta say that the new Fill Frame Proportionally command is probably my favorite new "little thing I love about InDesign." As you know, when you create a frame in InDesign and then place an image into it, there's a strong chance that the proportions are not going to match. When you use the Fit Content Proportionally command, there will inevitably be some space left over on either the right side or the bottom. This is fine if you need to see 100% of the image. However, if it's a photo where the edges can be cropped, then you will probably scale it manually to fit the frame perfectly. (It's the true perfectionist in you showing through.) Next time, use this tip: Place your photo and instead of using Fit Content Proportionally, use Fill Frame Proportionally. This will fill the frame completely without distorting or stretching the image. InDesign may have to do some cropping to achieve this, but you can always use the Direct Selection tool to reposition the image if necessary.

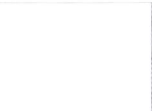

ANCHORED OBJECTS

Go beyond simple inline graphics with Anchored Objects. Yeah, it may sound like a marketing pitch, but this is a really useful tip. If you need your graphics to move along with your text—whether it be inside or, better yet, outside the text frame—try the following: Insert your cursor in the text that the graphic is related to. Then choose Insert from the Anchored Object menu (under the Object menu). This will present you with a dialog box with numerous options for the placement of the object frame in relation to the anchor inside the text. One option I would recommend is Relative to Spine, which automatically aligns your object to the left or right of the text frame depending on which side of the spine it's on. This is key in book and magazine publishing.

TRANSFORM AGAIN

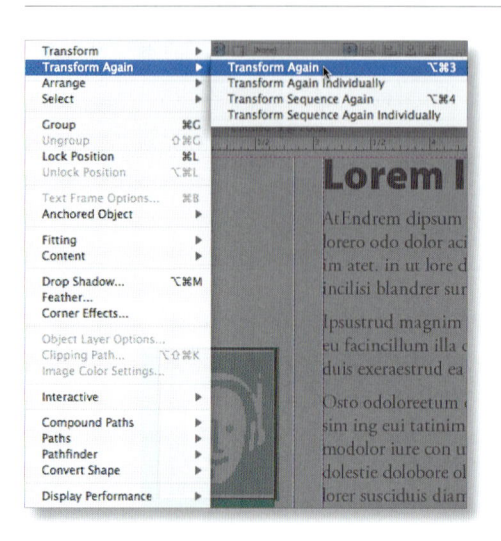

Sometimes you get something just right on the first try. Don't you wish you could just tell InDesign to "do it again?" That's what Transform Again lets you do. If you move or rotate an object, you can select other objects that you want moved or rotated in the same fashion. Go to Transform Again (under the Object menu) and choose Transform Again Individually. The objects that you selected will be transformed just like the last object. If you want the selected objects to be transformed as a group, you can do that, too, by choosing Transform Again.

CHAPTER 12 • What's New in InDesign CS2

SHAPE CONVERSIONS

Drawing that circle sounded like a great idea—at first. Now you wish that it were a rectangle instead. Don't delete it and start over. Convert it instead. You can convert the shape of a frame to a different shape by choosing Convert Shape from the Object menu and choosing the shape you need.

DROP SHADOW NOISE & SPREAD OPTIONS

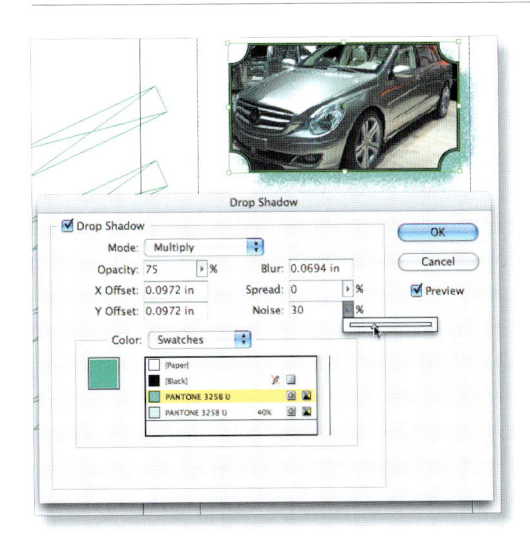

You can have a lot of fun in InDesign creating drop shadows and feathering objects, including text frames. However, until now the drop shadow options were pretty basic. There is a design effect that I refer to as "grunge"; you see it everywhere in design today. Now you can create those grungy, noisy kinds of drop shadows directly in InDesign. Select an object on the page and choose Drop Shadow from the Object menu. You'll notice that you now have options for Spread and Noise. Spread controls the amount of softness from the object to the edge of the shadow, and Noise does just what it sounds like it would do: it adds noise to the shadow itself.

CHAPTER 12 • What's New in InDesign CS2   249

IMPORT MULTI-PAGE PDFS

Placing PDF files into InDesign gives you the added flexibility of repurposing content to use in a different layout. However, it would be a pain to place a multi-page PDF one page at a time. The next time you want to place a PDF that contains two or more pages into InDesign, first make sure that you don't have any frames selected in InDesign. Then choose Place from the File menu and make sure your Show Import Options checkbox is checked. Choose a PDF with two or more pages; when you click Open you'll get the Place PDF dialog box. You can then choose to place all of the pages or select a page range. Once you click OK you can place each page into existing frames or you can have InDesign create the frames for you on the fly.

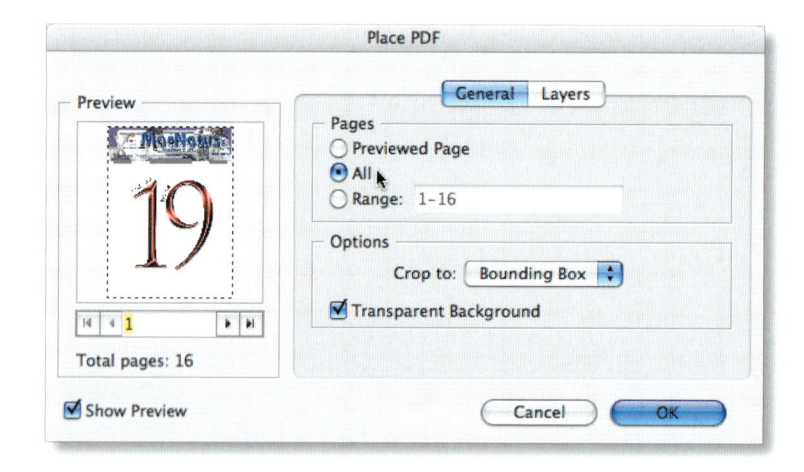

SAVE BACK TO INDESIGN CS

Not everyone moves to the new version of an application at once. You may be on InDesign CS2 and still have colleagues on InDesign CS. At first glance it may appear that there is no way to save an InDesign CS2 document back to CS. However, there is a way. What you need to do is choose Export from the File menu in InDesign CS2. When the Export dialog box appears, choose InDesign Interchange from the Format pop-up menu. Give the file a name, pick a location, and click Save. This creates an .inx file that InDesign CS can open (with the latest updates). Another use of the .inx format is for troubleshooting a problematic document. If you're having problems with an InDesign CS2 document, try exporting it to InDesign Interchange format. Then open it back up again in InDesign CS2 and save it with a different name. In effect, this will rebuild the document and that may solve your problem.

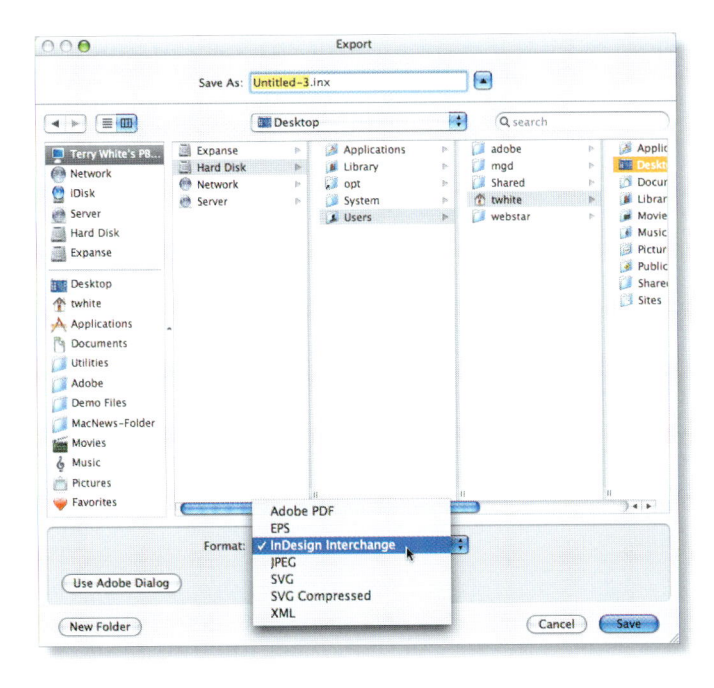

CHAPTER 12 • What's New in InDesign CS2

MOVE PAGES DIALOG BOX

You can move pages around in the Pages palette easily enough by simply dragging them around. As long as you have a document with only a few pages, this works fine. However, if you have more pages than will fit in one window of the Pages palette, moving pages and having to scroll up and down can be a pain. The next time you find yourself in this situation, use the Move Pages dialog box instead. Bring up the Pages palette and choose Move Pages from the Pages palette menu. You can then specify a page range, and place them either before or after the page that you designate. This is way faster than drag-and-drop and it's much more efficient.

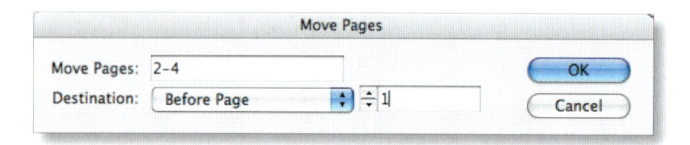

LOCK COLUMN GUIDES

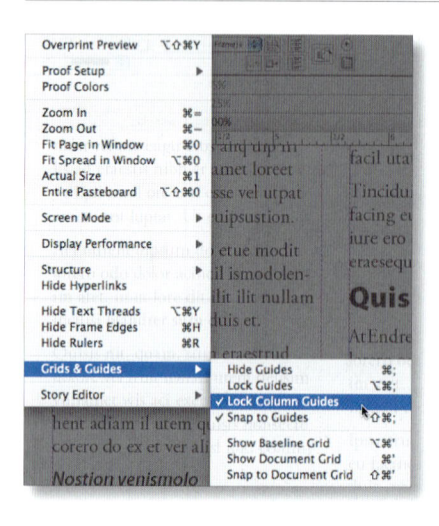

Locking and unlocking guides is probably second nature to you, and up until now it's been all or nothing. But let's say that you want to lock your column guides in place but still have the flexibility of moving your ruler guides around. The next time you find yourself in this situation, go to the Grids and Guides menu (under the View menu) and choose Lock Column Guides. This will lock only the column guides and leave you free to move your regular ruler guides around.

DATA MERGE

Data Merge is not technically new to InDesign; however, it is now included in InDesign CS2. Remember Mail Merge in your word processor? Mail Merge allows you to use a tab or comma delimited list and put fields in your form letter that automatically populate from the data in your list. Data Merge in InDesign CS2 takes this to a whole new level, allowing you to merge not only text, but images as well. First, define the list with the text that you want to populate your InDesign document. Then, in that list you need to include the path to each image on your hard drive for each record. Using the Data Merge palette (which is found under the Window menu, under Automation), you can drag the fields into your InDesign layout.

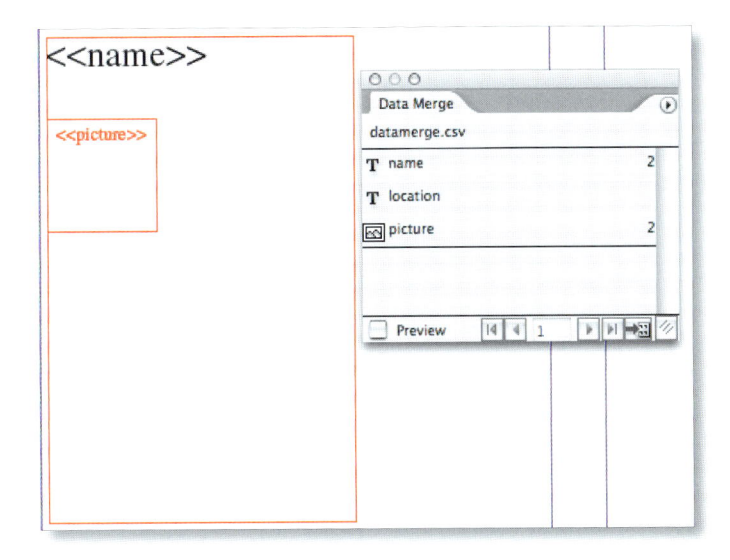

CREATE PRINTER SPREADS

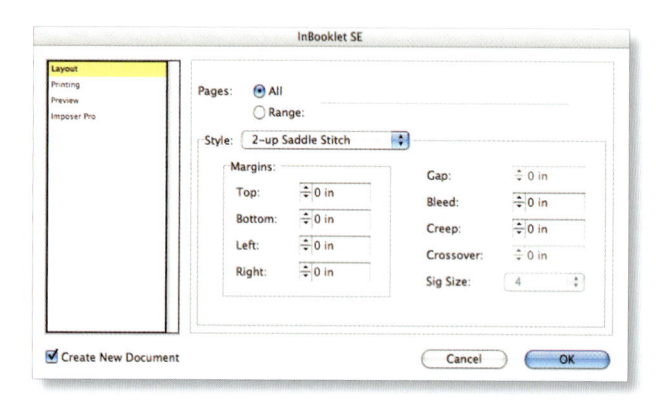

Another subtle change in InDesign CS2 is the inclusion of the InBooklet SE plug-in. Along with Data Merge, this plug-in was originally only available with the InDesign CS PageMaker Plug-in Pack. Now it's included in InDesign CS2. When you design your documents, you're likely in Reader Spreads (pages 1, 2, 3, 4, etc.). However, when you print your document for assembly in a book, it often needs to be in Printer Spreads (pages 8 & 1, 7 & 2, 6 & 3, etc.). Once your publication is designed, you can choose InBooklet SE from the File menu and set up your book. To verify your settings before actually generating the new document, click the Preview option on the left. Once you're satisfied, click OK and InDesign will build a new document for you.

MULTI-PAGE EXPORT TO JPEG

Sometimes you just need a JPEG. With the Export JPEG feature in InDesign, you can now—with one command—export all your pages as individual JPEG files. Choose Export from the File menu and choose JPEG as the format from the pop-up menu at the bottom. Make sure you give it a file name and location and click the Save button. The next dialog box to appear will allow you to choose a page range and quality settings. When you click the Export button, InDesign CS2 will export each page as a separate JPEG in the location you chose.

254   CHAPTER 12 • What's New in InDesign CS2

Index

A

Acrobat, 194. *See also* **PDF files**
Add Anchor Point tool, 89
Adobe Bridge
    drag-and-drop from, 232
    opening, 233
    stock photos and, 233, 234
alignment
    objects, 132–133
    table text, 208
    with spine, 245
alpha channels, 146
animation, 183
arrowheads, 92
arrows, 92
attributes
    changing with percentages, 167
    master page, 110
    paragraph, 30
    type, 30
Autocorrect, 237
auto-check feature, 224

B

backgrounds, 146, 147
backscreening effects, 84
Baseline Grid feature, 11, 240
baseline shift, 36
black
    poster frames, 182
    swatches, 70
Bleed Mode, 155
bleeds, 155
blending modes, 123
bold text, 48
Book feature, 114
Book palette, 114–115, 117–118
bookmarks, 171, 191–192
books
    adding documents to, 117
    creating PDFs from, 114
    linking documents together in, 114
    pagination, 115
    single document in, 118
    synchronizing, 115
Bridge. *See* **Adobe Bridge**
button rollovers, 186–187
buttons, interactive, 185–187

C

cells, 200–201, 205–209
channels, alpha, 146
Character palette, 39
Character Style dialog, 36
characters
    glyph, 45
    replacing bad, 37–38
    selecting, 46
    special, 44
    styles, 27, 36
Check Spelling palette, 46–47
circles, 91
Clear Overrides, 245
clipping paths, 127, 147
color
    blending modes, 123
    duotone effects, 170
    fill, 89
    glow, 124
    highlights, 170
    Illustrator and, 226
    Photoshop and, 226
    plates, 215–216
    settings for, 226
    spot, 174–175
    stroke, 89
    swatches. *See* swatches
    in tables, 200–201
color separations, 215, 216
colorizing photos, 170
columns
    locking guides for, 252
    table, 201–208
    text, 44
contents, 112–113
contextual menus, 175
Control palette, 13, 30, 141
Convert Direction Point tool, 90
copying items, 103, 133–135
Create Outlines command, 82
cross-references, 116
curve points, 122
curves, 90, 91, 122

D

dashes, 56, 173
Data Merge, 253
defaults, 2
deleting
    dashes, 173
    guides, 101
    layers, 107
    objects, 168
    preferences, 175
    swatches, 63, 64
Deselect All command, 43
dictionaries, 47–48, 238
    importing text files into, 238
    spell checking with multiple, 238
digital photos, 143
Direct Selection tool, 82, 86
direction lines, 91
direction points, 91
Display Performance settings, 154
documents. *See also* **files; pages**
    adding Flash animations to, 183
    adding to books, 114, 117
    bookmarks, 191–192
    changing defaults, 2
    creating, 5, 6
    dragging pages between, 96
    embedding multimedia files in, 184
    multiple views of, 153
    new, 5, 6
    packaging, 217
    PageMaker, 158

documents *(continued)*
　passwords, 192–194
　PDF. *See* PDF files
　placing movies in, 182
　placing sound in, 183
　preflighting, 216, 217
　presets, 6
　previewing, 18, 168
　publishing on Web, 118, 228
　QuarkXPress, 37, 158
　saving, 19, 175
　spreads, 6–7
　templates, 98
　versions, 194
　zooming in/out. *See* **zooming**
drag-and-drop feature
　from Adobe Bridge, 169, 232
　graphics, 125
　from iPhoto, 169
　library items, 136
　pages between documents, 96
　swatches, 60
　text, 42, 236
drawing, 81–92
drop shadows, 51, 124, 152, 249
"dummy" text, 29, 30
duotone effects, 170
Dynamic Spelling, 237

E

editing
　disallowing, 194
　graphics, 227
　Story Editor, 157
　swatches, 69
　text blocks, 157
effects
　backscreening, 84
　duotone, 170
　glow, 124
Ellipse tool, 91
em dashes, 56
em spaces, 57
en dashes, 56
en spaces, 57
EPS files, 223

Excel tables, 204
exporting
　books to PDF, 114, 117
　as JPEG files, 142, 254
　multimedia files, 184
　PDF files, 188, 192–193
Eyedropper tool, 152

F

fading images, 143
feathering, 83, 124
fields
　highlighting, 4
　Size/Leading, 28
　Zoom, 10
File Handling option, 168
files. *See also* **documents**
　EPS, 223
　Illustrator, 225
　JPEG, 142
　multimedia, 184
　PDF. *See* PDF files
　Photoshop, 224
　reducing size of, 152
　TIFF, 170, 224
　Word, 190
Fill Frame Proportionally command, 247
fills, 89
Find/Change command, 37
Find Fonts command, 41
finding library items, 138–139
Fit Frame to Content button, 52
Flash animation, 183
flattened PDF files, 145, 148, 149, 196
Flattener Preview palette, 148
fonts
　changing automatically, 41
　finding, 40, 41
　glyphs, 45
　jumping to, 40
　ligatures, 49
　PPD, 222
　previewing, 236
　resizing, 28

　in Story Editor, 55
　turning into graphics, 82
font types, 236
footers, table, 203
footnotes, automatic, 239
formatting. *See* **styles**
frames
　filling proportionally, 247
　fitting to content, 52
　for graphics, 111, 128–131
　poster, 182
　reshaping, 165
　scaling, 86
　size of, 170
　text. *See* text frames
Free Transform tool, 131

G

gate folds, 97
glow effect, 124
glyphs, 45
GoLive, 118, 228
Gradient palette, 165
gradients, 54, 165
graphics, 121–149. *See also* **images; objects**
　auto-updating, 227
　buttons, 185–187
　copying, 133
　dragging/dropping, 125
　editing, 227
　embedded, 160
　frames for, 111, 128–131
　inline, 200
　on master pages, 127
　moving, 131
　pasting, 133
　pasting inside text, 123
　placing in tables, 200
　relinking, 141
　replacing, 142
　resizing, 129–130
　rotating, 131
　text wrap and, 126–127
　turning fonts into, 82
　unembedded, 160
　vector, 128

grids, 11
grouped objects, 82
guides, 100–105. *See also* **rulers**
   adding, 102
   assigning to layers, 105
   column, 252
   controlling, 12
   copying, 103
   custom layouts, 104
   hiding/showing, 12, 105
   horizontal, 102
   locking/unlocking, 103, 252
   removing, 101
   toggling on/off, 104
   two-page spreads and, 100
   vertical, 102
gutter, 104

H

half circles, 91
Hand tool, 10, 55
headers, table, 203
highlighting fields, 4
highlights, 170
HTML pages, 228
hyperlinks, 141, 171, 189–190
hyphenation, 48
hyphens, 48, 56

I

Illustrator, 128, 225, 226
Illustrator files, 225
images. *See also* **graphics; photographs**
   fading, 143
   flipping, 132
   getting details about, 159
   high-quality display, 154
   merging, 253
   removing background from, 146, 147
importing
   links, 190
   options for, 125
   placing PDF files, 126

   sound, 183
   text, 43, 239
InBooklet SE plug-in, 254
indenting paragraphs, 50
InDesign
   changing defaults, 2
   dictionary, 47, 48
   little-known features, 163–178
   opening QuarkXPress files in, 158
   performance, 153
   printers/service providers and, 223
   saving InDesign CS2 files for InDesign CS, 251
   updates to, 224
InDesign CS2, new features of, 231–254
   Autocorrect, 237
   Data Merge, 253
   dictionaries
     importing text files into, 238
     spell checking with multiple, 238
   drag-and-drop from Adobe Bridge, 232-233
   drop shadow options, 249
   Dynamic Spelling, 237
   Fill Frame Proportionally, 247
   font types, previewing, 236
   fonts, previewing, 236
   footnotes, automatic, 239
   guides, locking column, 252
   images, merging, 253
   InDesign CS, saving CS2 files for, 251
   JPEG files, exporting pages as, 254
   layers, controlling Photoshop files and, 241
   Next Style, 244
   Object Styles, 242
   objects
     anchored, 248
     transforming, 248
   overrides, clearing, 245

   pages, moving, 252
   PDF, importing multi-page, 250
   printer spreads, creating, 254
   Quick Apply, 243
   shapes, converting, 249
   Snippets, 235
   style sheets, resetting, 244
   styles, loading selectively, 243
   text
     aligning in relation to spine, 245
     drag-and-drop, 236
     merging, 253
     pasting without formatting, 239
     rotating frames, 240
     viewing overset, 240
   Word files, importing, 246
InDesign Interchange Format, 251
index creation, 116
Info palette, 159
Ink Manager, 216
inks, 216
interactive buttons, 185–187
iPhoto, 169
italic text, 48
items. *See also* **objects**
   copying, 103, 133–135
   deselecting all, 43
   dragging from library, 136
   locked, 161
   pasting, 133–135

J

jaggy paths, 83
JPEG files, 142, 254
jumping
   to fonts, 40
   to pages, 3, 109
justification, 49

257

K

kerning text, 31–32
keyboard shortcuts. *See also* **shortcuts**
    creating, 21
    custom, 21, 22
    one-key tool shortcuts, 20
    printing as reference, 22
    QuarkXPress, 21
    saving all open documents, 19
    text selection, 46
keywords, 137–139

L

languages, foreign, 47
layers
    controlling Photoshop files and, 241
    deleting unused, 107
    locking/unlocking, 161
    organizing documents, 105
    pasting and, 135
    PDF files, 191
    selecting everything on, 106
    soloing, 160
    stacking order, 106
    transparency and, 144
    visibility of, 161
Layers palette, 15
layouts, 97, 104
leader dots, 113
leading, 33
library, 135–140
Library palette, 135–140
ligatures, 49
line screen, 220
lines
    adding arrowheads to, 92
    diagonal, 209
    direction, 91
    selecting, 46
    spacing between, 33
    styles, 173
    in tables, 206
links, 141, 171, 189–190
Links palette, 141

locked items
    guides, 103
    layers, 161

M

master pages
    attributes, 110
    changing master items on, 127
    graphics on, 127
    hierarchical, 96
    making master items editable, 109–110
    saving as, 111
    text frames on, 56
Measure tool, 159
measurement units, 141, 156, 164, 177
menus, 164, 175
Microsoft Excel, 204
Microsoft Word, 190, 204, 239
Mixed Ink Group option, 174, 175
monochrome printers, 220
Move dialog, 177
movies, 182, 185
multimedia files, 184

N

navigation, 1–22, 220
Navigator palette, 19–20
nested tables, 205
New Document dialog, 5
New Mixed Ink Group option, 174, 175
Next Object Below command, 87
Next Style command, 244
numbers, page, 107–108, 115

O

Object Styles, 242
objects. *See also* **graphics; items**
    adding soft edges to, 83
    adding to library, 136
    aligning, 132–133
    anchored, 248
    bookmarks, 171
    deleting, 168
    Distribute Spacing option, 133
    dragging to page, 136
    duplicating, 86
    grouped, 82
    links to, 171
    moving, 53, 177
    non-printing, 140, 218
    resizing, 85–86, 130, 178
    scaling, 85–86, 172, 178
    selecting behind other objects, 87
    sending forward/backward, 88
    transforming, 248
    transparent, 144
Optimized Subsampling option, 219
overrides, clearing, 245

P

Package feature, 217
page breaks, 125
page counts, 98
page icons, 99
PageMaker documents, 158
pages, 95–118. *See also* **documents**
    dragging between documents, 96
    dynamic links to, 189–190
    gate folds, 97
    inserting, 98–99
    jumping to, 3, 109
    master. *See* master pages
    moving, 252
    numbering, 107–108, 115
    placing via PDF, 197
    saving as master, 111
    scaling to fit media, 223
    two-page spreads, 100
Pages palette, 99, 100
pagination, 107–108, 115
palettes. *See also specific palettes*
    changing to side tabs, 18
    closing, 4
    favorites, 13
    floating, 13
    hiding, 14, 17

Navigator, 19–20
nesting, 18
opening, 4
organizing, 14
resizing, 15, 19
showing, 13, 14, 16
paragraphs
   attributes, 30
   indenting, 50
   selecting, 46
   styles, 27
passwords, 192–194
Paste Into command, 123
pasteboard, 7
pasting
   items, 133–135
   text, 41–42, 239
path points, 89
Pathfinder, 156
paths
   clipping, 127, 147
   hidden options for type on, 26
   jaggy, 83
   starting/stopping, 90
   type on, 26
PDF files, 181–197
   bookmarks, 191–192
   disallowing editing, 194
   disallowing printing, 193
   dynamic links to pages, 189–190
   embedding multimedia files in, 184
   export styles, 188
   exporting books to, 114
   exporting documents to, 114, 117
   file size, 196
   flattened, 145, 148, 149, 196
   hyperlinks, 189–190
   importing multi-page, 250
   interactive buttons in, 185–187
   layers in, 191
   older versions, 194
   passwords, 192–194
   placing InDesign pages via, 197
   placing movies in, 182
   placing on InDesign pages, 126
   placing sound in, 183
   printers/service providers and, 223
   resolution, 196
   spreads, 195
   transparency, 196
PDF format, 117
PDF/X formats, 195
Pen tool, 89
Pencil tool, 165
performance, 153, 154, 219
photographs. *See also* **images**
   author name, 143
   colorizing, 170
   digital, 143
   dragging/dropping from Adobe Bridge, 232
   dragging/dropping from iPhoto, 169
   duotone effects, 170
   iPhoto, 169
   vignettes, 122
Photoshop, 224, 226
Photoshop files, 224
pixels, 177
placeholder text, 29, 30
plates, 215–216, 220, 221
plug-ins
   InBooklet SE, 254
   turning off, 153
point size, 34
points, 177
Polygon tool, 84
polygons, 84–85
poster frames, 182
PPD fonts, 222
preferences
   deleting, 175
   type, 31, 236
   units of measurement, 177
Preflight option, 216, 217
presets
   documents, 6
   PDF export style, 188
   print, 214
   screen, 196
previewing
   documents, 18, 148, 168
   slugs, 155
   swatches, 174
   transparency flattener, 148
Print panels, 220
Print Presets dialog, 214
printer spreads, creating, 254
printers
   monochrome, 220
   multiple, 214
   options available to, 222
   presets, 214
   switching, 219
printing
   disallowing, 193
   non-printing objects, 140, 218
   to PDF, 117
   separations, 221
   settings for, 218
   slugs, 221
   speeding up, 219
   transparent items, 148
pull quotes, 50

Q

QuarkXPress, 21, 37, 158
QuarkXPress documents, 37, 158
Quick Apply command, 243
QuickTime movies, 182, 185
quote marks, 50

R

Rectangle tool, 166
rectangles, rounded, 166
resolution, 196
rollover buttons, 186–187
rotating
   frames, 240
   graphics, 131
   text, 201, 240
rows, 201–208
rulers, 159, 166. *See also* **guides**

S

Save As command, 175
Save command, 175
Scale dialog, 178

259

scaling
    frames, 86
    objects, 85–86, 172, 178
    pages to fit media, 223
    text, 33–34
Scissors tool, 91
Screen preset, 196
scroll wheel, 171
scrolling, 171
searches
    Find/Change command, 37
    Find Fonts command, 41
    library, 138–139
sections, 108
Select All command, 106
selections
    characters, 46
    columns, 202
    Deselect All command, 43
    Direct Selection tool, 82, 86
    on layers, 106
    lines, 46
    objects behind other objects, 87
    paragraphs, 46
    rows, 202
    Select All command, 106
    shortcuts for, 46
    tables, 202
    text, 46, 53
    words, 46
separations, color, 215, 216
separations, printing, 221
shadows, drop, 51, 124, 152
shapes
    converting, 249
    frames, 165
    half circles, 91
    joining with Pathfinder, 156
shortcuts. *See also* **keyboard shortcuts**
    Character Style dialog, 36
    text selection, 46
    Type Tool, 26
Size/Leading field, 28
Slug Mode, 155
slugs, 155, 221
Small Palette Rows option, 15
Smooth tool, 83

Snippets, 235
soloing layers, 160
sound, 183
spaces, professional, 57
spacing
    Distribute Spacing option, 133
    between letters, 31–32
    between lines, 33
    removing double-spaces, 37
special characters, 44
spelling checker, 46–47, 237
spot colors, 174–175
spreads
    PDF files, 195
    viewing, 6–7
Step and Repeat function, 134
stock photos, 233, 234
Story Editor, 55, 157, 240
Stroke palette, 173
strokes, 89, 173
style sheets, resetting, 244
styles
    character, 27, 36
    default, 27
    line, 173
    loading selectively, 243
    paragraph, 27
    PDF export, 188
    retaining when pasting text, 42
    strokes, 173
    text blocks, 35
    TOC, 112–113
    transparency flattener, 145, 149
Swatch Options dialog, 67
swatches
    black, 70
    changing order of, 65
    custom, 61
    default, 61
    deleting, 63, 64
    dragging between palettes, 60
    editing, 69
    gradients, 60, 165
    merging, 64
    naming, 67
    Pantone, 68
    previewing, 174
    spot colors, 174–175
    tints, 65–66
    white, 70
Swatches palette, 60–61, 69, 165
.SWF animation, 183

T

table of contents, 112–113
tables, 199–210
    cells, 200–201, 205–209
    cleaning up, 208
    color in, 200–201
    columns, 201–208
    converting text to, 204
    Excel, 204
    fitting on page, 210
    headers/footers in, 203
    nested, 205
    placing graphics in, 200
    removing lines between, 206
    rotating text in, 201
    rows, 201–208
    selections, 202
    Word, 204
templates, 98
text, 25–57. *See also* **fonts; type; words**
    aligning, 208, 245
    angled, 209
    attributes, 30
    backscreening, 84
    bolded, 48
    converting to tables, 204
    dragging/dropping, 42, 236
    drop shadows, 51
    glow effect, 124
    hyphenation, 48
    imported, 43
    italicized, 48
    justification, 49
    kerning, 31–32
    leading, 33
    making all caps, 38
    merging, 253
    pasting, 41–42, 239
    pasting graphics into, 123
    placeholder, 29, 30
    point size, 34

resizing, 28
rotating in frames, 240
rotating in tables, 201
scaling, 33–34
selecting, 46, 53
spacing. *See* spacing
special characters, 44
spell checking, 46–47
tracking, 32
transparent, 84
viewing overset, 240
word counts, 29
wrapping, 53, 126–127

text blocks
duplicating, 86
editing, 157
formatting, 35

text frames. *See also* **frames**
changing to graphics frames, 111
fitting text in, 52
master page, 56
rotating, 240
speeding up, 54

thumbnails, 140
TIFF files, 170, 224
Toolbox, 12, 16
tools, 20. *See also specific tools*
tracking words, 32

transparency
identifying pages with, 144
layers and, 144
PDF files, 196
stacking order and, 144
text, 84

transparency flattener preview, 148
transparency flattener styles, 145, 149
transparent items, printing, 148
type, 25–57. *See also* **fonts; text**
applying gradients to, 54
attributes, 30
defaults, 27
justification, 49
on paths, 26
preferences, 31
Type tool, 25, 55

U

Undo command, 175
unit of measurement, 141, 156, 164, 177
Units & Increments Preferences dialog, 177
URLs, 190

V

vector graphics, 128
View All Spreads option, 20
vignettes, 122

W

warning dialogs, 22
Web, publishing on, 118, 228
Web authoring, 228
Websites, 189–190
word count feature, 29

Word files, 190, 239, 246
Word tables, 204
words. *See also* **text**
checking spelling of, 46–47
hyphenating, 48
keywords, 137–139
library searches, 138–139
selecting, 46
space between, 32
tracking, 32
workspace, custom, 16
wrapping text, 53, 126–127

Z

zero point, 166
Zoom field shortcut, 10
Zoom tool, 11
zooming
with Hand tool, 10
in/out, 153
specifying percentage amount for, 9, 10
speed zooming, 8
undoing zooms, 2

creative **solutions**

It all starts here...
at **bhphotovideo.com** you'll find the latest products, award winning live support and worldwide shipping all at your finger tips. Or you can drop by our DreamStore at **420 9th Ave, New York City**

B&H
PHOTO · VIDEO · PRO AUDIO

800-336-7097

Hungry for more Killer Books?

Tear into these best-selling titles from Scott Kelby and feed the creative beast within!

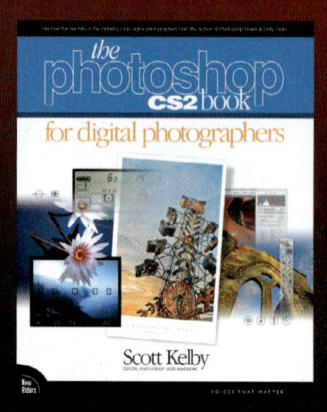

The Photoshop CS2 Book for Digital Photographers *$29.99*

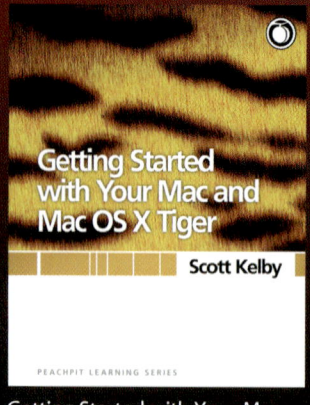

Getting Started with Your Mac and Mac OS X Tiger *$17.99*

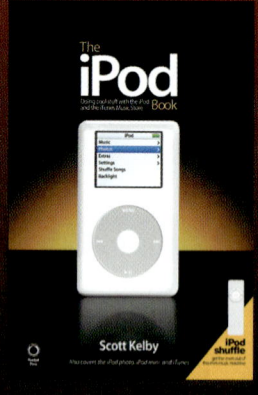

The iPod Book *$18.99*

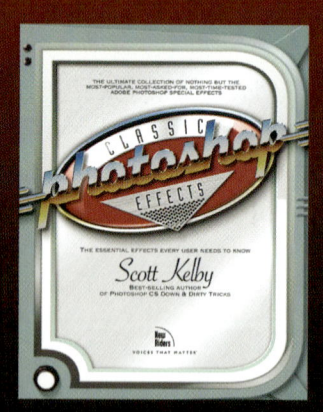

Classic Photoshop Effects *$31.99*

To snag these tasty titles, and track down more information go to
www.scottkelbybooks.com
or call 800-738-8513 today!

Scott Kelby is the #1 Technology Author of 2004

Illustrator CS2 Killer Tips

Illustrator CS2 KillerTips

ILLUSTRATOR® CS2 KILLER TIPS

The Illustrator® CS2
Killer Tips Team

TECHNICAL EDITORS
Cindy Snyder
Kim Doty

PRODUCTION EDITOR
Kim Gabriel

PRODUCTION MANAGER
Dave Damstra

**COVER DESIGN AND
CREATIVE CONCEPTS**
Felix Nelson

PUBLISHED BY
New Riders

Copyright © 2006 by Kelby Corporate Management, Inc.

FIRST EDITION: October 2005

All rights reserved. No part of this book may be reproduced or transmitted in any form, by any means, electronic or mechanical, including photocopying, recording, or by any information storage and retrieval system, without written permission from the publisher, except for inclusion of brief quotations in a review.

Composed in Myriad Pro and Helvetica by NAPP Publishing.

Trademarks
All terms mentioned in this book that are known to be trademarks or service marks have been appropriately capitalized. New Riders cannot attest to the accuracy of this information. Use of a term in the book should not be regarded as affecting the validity of any trademark or service mark.

Illustrator is a registered trademark of Adobe Systems, Inc.
Windows is a registered trademark of Microsoft Corporation.

Warning and Disclaimer
This book is designed to provide information about Illustrator tips. Every effort has been made to make this book as complete and as accurate as possible, but no warranty of fitness is implied.

The information is provided on an as-is basis. The authors and New Riders shall have neither liability nor responsibility to any person or entity with respect to any loss or damages arising from the information contained in this book or from the use of the discs or programs that may accompany it.

ISBN 0-321-33065-X

9 8 7 6 5 4 3 2 1

Printed and bound in the United States of America

www.peachpit.com
www.scottkelbybooks.com

To the most important people in my life: my Mom and Dad, my sisters Julie and Deb, and my family: Marlene, Stephanie, and Michael.
—Dave Cross

To those that I have trained over the years—thank you for making this all worth it and allowing me to do what I love to do.
—Matt Kloskowski

ACKNOWLEDGMENTS

There are many, many advantages to having a co-author on a book like this one, and one pretty big drawback. I think the advantages are pretty obvious: the whole two-heads-are-better-than-one thing. It has been a great pleasure to work with Matt on this book—and on the many other things we work on together on a day-to-day basis. So, what's the downside? I only have half a page for my acknowledgments, whereas last time I had a full page. Oh well…

If you've read any books that are produced at KW Media, you've probably read the author going on and on about how great the team is at KW, but it really is true! I can't imagine being able to produce high-quality books like this one without our great team (I know I certainly wouldn't want to try). You people are all CRAZY—and I love you for it. Thanks to Kim Gabriel for her unbelievable scheduling/balancing act routine, to Felix Nelson for always tweaking our designs to make them better, to our newest Technical Editors Cindy Snyder and Kim Doty for jumping right into the fire and making sure everything worked, and to Dave Damstra for once again making things fit and look pretty. My continuing gratitude to Scott Kelby, Kalebra Kelby, and Jean Kendra for convincing me to move to Florida, and for making this such a cool place to work. Mr. Moser, what can I say but thank you sir, again (as you were).

Thanks to the artists who very generously provided artwork for us to use in the book. It is much better as a result of their stunning Illustrator work.

Finally, I need to acknowledge my family for their love and support. As I write this, it's my 21st wedding anniversary and my 18-year-old daughter is about to head off to college. It's hard to believe that it's been that long, since every day is like a honeymoon (a honeymoon with two grown kids, I guess). Marlene, you are the love of my life and I look forward to every minute we spend together. Stephanie and Michael, there may be fathers who are prouder of their kids than I am, but I find that hard to believe. You make me smile just thinkin' about ya. (Yes Cassy, you too). All-in-all, I consider myself one darn lucky guy.

—*DAVE CROSS*

First, I'd like to thank my co-author and boss, Dave Cross, for involving me with this book. Not only is he an all-around great guy but he's a constant reminder to me of a 100% "class act" in this business. It's an honor to work with him. I'd also like to thank my co-workers and friends at KW Media Group who, in a short time, have shown me how they continually push the boundaries of quality and excellence in every aspect of this business.

I'd also like to thank the illustrators who have allowed us to use their work in this book and the folks at Adobe, namely Julieanne Kost and Terry White, for quickly getting us up to speed on the latest version of Illustrator. Special thanks go out to the folks at Peachpit Press, as well, for helping me do what I love, which is to train and educate people.

Next, I'd like to thank my family. My mom, dad, brother, and sister have always been a great source of inspiration and support to me. Without you, I'd never have gotten such a great start to such a wonderful life.

Speaking of wonderful lives, my greatest thanks goes to my wife, Diana, and two sons, Ryan and Justin, for making my life the best I could have ever dreamed of. The three of you are the reason I wake up every day, and I can never express my gratitude to you for making me feel like the luckiest husband/dad ever.

—*MATT KLOSKOWSKI*

ABOUT THE AUTHORS

Dave Cross

Dave Cross is Senior Developer, Education and Curriculum, for the National Association of Photoshop Professionals and is involved in all aspects of the training that is provided to NAPP members, including the content of seminars, conferences and workbooks. He also creates the very popular weekly QuickTime-based tutorials that appear on the members' website. Dave is an Adobe Certified Instructor in Photoshop CS2 and Illustrator CS2, and is a Certified Technical Trainer.

Prior to joining NAPP, Dave lived in Canada and trained thousands of users across North America. He has been using and teaching Illustrator and Photoshop since their original versions, starting in 1987. Dave co-authored the *Photoshop World Dream Team Book, Volume One*, and is the author of *The Photoshop CS2 Help Desk Book*. Dave writes the "Classic Photoshop Effects" and "Beginners' Workshop" columns for *Photoshop User* magazine, teaches at the Photoshop World Conference & Expo, and is the Lead Instructor for the Photoshop Seminar Tour. He also is featured on a series of DVDs, such as *Best of Photoshop User, Photoshop CS2 for Beginners*, and *Photoshop CS2 Layer Techniques*.

In his spare time, Dave is the Graphics Editor for *Layers* magazine, and enjoys freaking out his Florida co-workers by wearing shorts to work every day, simply "because he can." Dave lives in Odessa, Florida, with his wife, Marlene, and children, Stephanie and Michael.

Matt Kloskowski

Matt Kloskowski is the Education and Curriculum Developer for the National Association of Photoshop Professionals, where he eats, sleeps, and breathes Photoshop and Adobe training to NAPP members. Matt has written four books on Photoshop and Illustrator, including *Photoshop CS2 Savvy, Extreme Photoshop CS*, and *Illustrator CS Most Wanted*. He's featured on various training DVDs available from www.photoshopvideos.com, and is a regular contributing writer to *Photoshop User* magazine, *Layers* magazine, and the *Photoshop Elements Techniques* newsletter. Matt is an instructor at Photoshop World and the Mac Design Conference, and is an Adobe Certified Expert in Photoshop, as well as a Macromedia Flash Certified Developer. He teaches basic and advanced Photoshop classes for Sessions Online School of Design (www.sessions.edu).

www.scottkelbybooks.com

TABLE OF CONTENTS

CHAPTER 1   1
Basic Training!
Basic Tips You Can't Live Without

Make Yourself Famous	2
Additional Content	3
More Additional Content	4
Wacom Pen Tablets Work in Illustrator Too	5
Ongoing Feedback	6
Timing Is Everything	6
The Ever-Changing Palette	7
Quick Delete from Palettes	7
Locking and Unlocking Guides	8
Choose the Best Selection Tool for the Job	8
Direct Selection Secret	9
Quick Selection Tool	9
Hide Bounding Box	10
Quick Move Dialog	10
Selecting the Next Object Below	11
Create by Measure	11
Position Shapes as You Draw	12
Drawing Curves More Easily	12
Simplifying a Path	13
Select None	13
Everything Else But	14
What Happens When You Can't See an Object?	14
Even It Out	15
Reflect vs. Flip	15
Tool Preferences	16
Name a Swatch	16
Reset the Default Fill and Stroke Colors	17
Color Picker	17
Hide or Show Multiple Layers Easily	18
Filters vs. Effects?	18
Edit Existing Patterns and Symbols	19
Use Text Import Options	19
Scale Text Frame But Not Text	20
Multiple Glyph Choices	20
Effecting a Stroke or a Fill	21
Transform Again	21
Create Your Own Crop Marks	22
Open a Template	22
Make Your Own Template	23
Save for Microsoft Office	24
View Actions in Button Mode	24
"Hidden" Keyboard Commands	25

TABLE OF CONTENTS

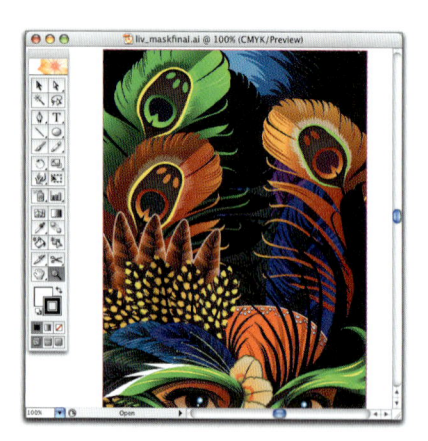

CHAPTER 2	27
The View	
Viewing, Doing, Undoing, and More	
How Many Undos?	28
Actual Size, Fit in Window	28
Really Fit in Window	29
Switching Between Multiple Open Windows	29
Default Workspace to the Rescue!	30
Your Own Personal Workspace	31
Give Your Custom Workspace a Shortcut	31
Control Bar Getting in Your Way?	32
Palette Shortcuts and Control Palette All in One	32
Center That Guide	33
Center Guides Automatically	33
Change Guide Direction	34
Make Guides from Objects	34
Lock a Guide to an Object	35
Change Locked Guide into a Path	35
Lock Everything Else	36
Get a New Perspective on Guides	36
Auto Add Rulers to Every New Document	37
Measure from Where You Want	38
Reset the Rulers	38
Change Ruler Measurement	39
Measure the Way You Want	39
Multiple Tools?	40
Your Logo Ready Anytime	41
Simulate Paper Color	42
Show/Hide Center Point	43
Angled Grid	43
Everything You Wanted to Know About…	44
Get Object Info	44
Actions Within Actions	45
Save That View	45
Two Views, One Document	46
Pinpoint in the Navigator	46
Hide and Show Palettes	47
Change Your Mind in Mid-Zoom	48
The One-Slide Slide Show	48
Remember One Palette Shortcut	49
Zoom Tool Shortcut	49
Hand Tool Shortcut	50
Keep Only Selected Objects	50
Be Precise	51
Front and Center	51
Seeing Red	52
Add the Unrecordable	52
Hide Your Guides in One Click	53

TABLE OF CONTENTS

www.scottkelbybooks.com

Free Resources	53
Back To Basics	54
Don't Squint, Click	54
New Document the Same as Last Time	54
Reset the Page	55
Change Tools Quickly	55
Multiple Pages?	56

CHAPTER 3 — 59
Tool Time
Creating in Illustrator CS2

Photo Inside of Type	60
Start with a Font	60
Mapping Made Easy	61
Find Your Favorite Logo?	61
Change Star Shape, Part One	62
Change Star Shape, Part Two	62
Send Up a Flare	63
Permanent Pathfinder	63
Spray On, Spray Off	64
Years in Graph Data	64
That's Out of One Hundred	65
Edit Graph Designs	66
Sliding Graph Designs	67
Drag-and-Drop Instead of Copy-and-Paste	68
Change Tool Settings on the Fly	68
Make Your Own Spirograph	69
Convert to Shape	69
Let the Blend Tool Do the Math	70
More Blending	71
Yet More Blending	71
Bend the Blend	72
Shapes Around a Circle	72
Change the Blend	73
Outline Stroke	73
Live Trace Not Working How You'd Like? Try This	74
Is Live Trace Still Not Working How You'd Like?	
Take It a Step Further	75
Viewing Reference Photos When Using the Mesh Tool	76
Gradient Brushes	77
Divide Objects Below	78
Change Grids on the Fly	78
Live Interlocking Objects	79
Live Interlocking Objects, Part 2	80
Creating Wireframes	80
Add to a Shape to Create a Shape	81
Move Points as You Draw	81
Auto Add/Delete Getting in Your Way	82

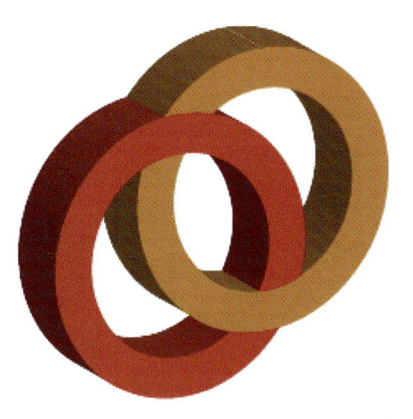

TABLE OF CONTENTS

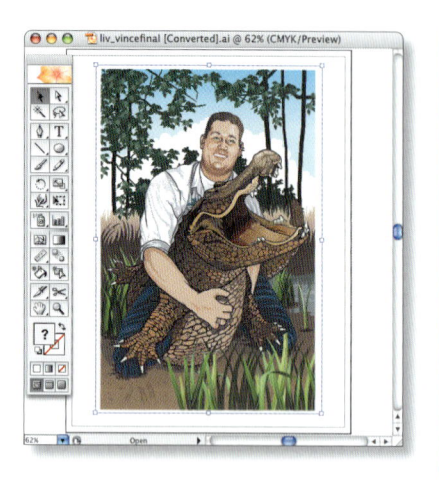

Multiple Objects as a Mask	82
Round Those Corners	83
Same Width and Height	83
Changing Arcs	84
Close a Path Automatically	84
Preserve Brush Stroke Options	85
Disable Auto Add/Delete	86
Split into Grid	86
The Perfect Star	87
Target Practice	87
Opacity Masks	88
Vintage Texture Effect	89

CHAPTER 4 — 91
Nip/Tuck
Selecting, Editing, and Transforming

Save a Selection	92
Reshape Paths by Drawing	92
Reshape Paths by Painting?	93
Editing a Type Path	93
Cut or Add a Point	94
Join vs. Average & Join	94
Average and Join in One Step	95
The True Center	95
Bigger or Smaller a Bit at a Time	96
Scale Tool Cloning	97
Keep Proportions	97
Quick Flip	98
Liquify Brush Size	98
Select Same, Again	99
Select Color from Swatches	99
Selecting Groups	100
Selecting Mesh Points Easily	100
Selecting Multiple Mesh Points Easily	101
Let Illustrator Calculate It for You	101
Editable Transformations	102
Rotate with Care	102
Rotation by the Numbers	103
Repeat Last Pathfinder	103
Transform by Number	104
Free Transform	104
Pick The Best Transformation	105
Select Behind	105
New Stroke Options in Illustrator CS2	106
Scale Strokes & Effects	106
Odd Numbers	107
Move and Copy	107

TABLE OF CONTENTS

Straight Cuts	108
Move It by Measure	108
Draw and Smooth	109
Simplify Path	109
Magic Wand Not Working?	110
Copy While Transforming	110
Transform Again and Send to Back	111
Transform Again, Again	111
Aligning the Fast Way	112
Align to a Specific Object	113
Convert Dashed Stroke to Outline	114
Make a Mesh with Text	114
Drag-and-Drop	115
The Missing Twist Tool	115
CHAPTER 5	**117**
Different Strokes	
Colors, Swatches, Fills, and Strokes	
Your Colors, Every Time	118
Slightly Lighter, Somewhat Darker	118
Grab Only the Color	119
Make Your Own Patterns	119
Transform Just the Pattern	120
Color the Opposite	120
Use Global Color	121
Borrow Some Color	122
Persistent Swatches	122
Color from Anywhere	123
Gradient Palette Shortcut	123
One-Color Gradient	124
Color Stop	124
Duplicate a Color Stop	125
Swap Stops	125
Use a Swatch as a Stop	126
Quick Stroke Change	126
Change Color Modes in the Color Palette	127
Use Multiple Strokes in Appearance	127
Round Joins	128
Apply Sampled Colors	128
Change Live Paint Behavior	129
Same Color Again	129
Fill and Stroke from the Keyboard	130
None in a Hurry	130
Want the Opposite?	131
Make a Spot Color	131
Complementary Colors	132
Invert the Color	132

xiii

TABLE OF CONTENTS

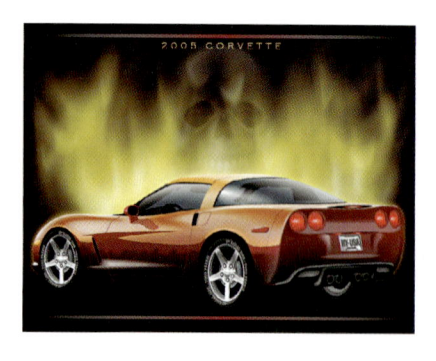

Replace One Swatch with Another	133
Grayscale or Color Gray	133
Find a Color	134
Grayscale Print from a Color File	134
Save Swatch Libraries	135
Expand a Gradient	136
Test Page	136
Fade to Nothing	137
Use Preview Bounds	138
One-Time Preview Bounds	138

CHAPTER 6 — 141
Sultans of Swing
A Killer Collection of Illustrator Artists

Scott Hinton	142
David Pounds	143
Philip J. Neal	144
Mike Sellers	145
Todd Ferris	146
Scott Weichert	147
John Schwegel	148
Jib Hunt	149
Brooke Nuñez	150
Erwin Haya	151
Mark Anderson	152
Christian Musselman	153

CHAPTER 7 — 155
Get Smart
Layers and Transparency

Dim Images	156
Name the New Layer	156
White Really Isn't White	157
Hide Other Layers	158
Change One Layer to Outline View	158
Change Other Layers to Outline View	159
Release the Layers!	160
Copy an Object to a Layer	160
Duplicate the Entire Layer	161
Select Everything on a Layer	162
Select Everything on Multiple Layers	162
Lock All Other Layers	163
Use Layers to Unlock Individual Objects	163
Locate Layer	164
Jump to a Layer	164
Custom Layer Row Size	165
Expand All Sublayers	165

New Layer on Top	166
New Layer Below	166
Target a Layer	167
Moving Targets	167
Moving Targets, Part Two	168
Paste Remembers Layers	168
Mirror Reflections	169
Layer Comps?	170
Selecting Multiple Layers	171
Move Objects to a Different Layer	172
Vector Templates?	173
Don't Print	174
No Sublayers	174
Hide Template	175
When Select All Doesn't Work	175
Merge Selected	176
Collect in a New Layer	177

CHAPTER 8 — 179
Extreme Makeover
Symbols, Brushes, Appearance, Filters, and Effects

What Is New Art Has Basic Appearance?	180
Effect Gallery	180
Scrubby Sliders	181
Creating Arrowhead Designs	181
Symbolism Chooser	182
Using the Eyedropper to Sample Appearance	182
Drag an Appearance	183
Merge Styles	183
Instant Lichtenstein or Pop Art Dot Effect	184
Apply the Same Effect Again	185
Filters vs. Effects? What's the Difference?	185
Reset Effect and Filter Settings	186
Add a Second Stroke	186
Drop Shadows	187
Check Document Raster Effects Settings	188
Breaking a Link to a Style	189
Disappearing Effects When Switching Between RGB and CMYK	189
Add Stroke to Placed Image or Photo	190
Redefine Symbols	191
Viewing the Intensity of the Symbol Tools	191
More Intensity, Different Size	192
Change Multiple Symbols	192
New Symbol and Instance	193
Select All Instances (and Replace Them Too)	193
Replacing Symbols	194
Reverse Engineering a Graphic Style	194

TABLE OF CONTENTS

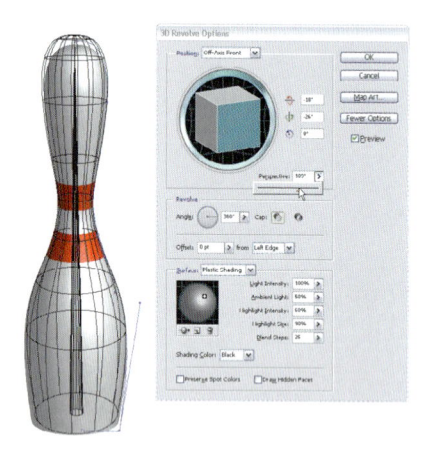

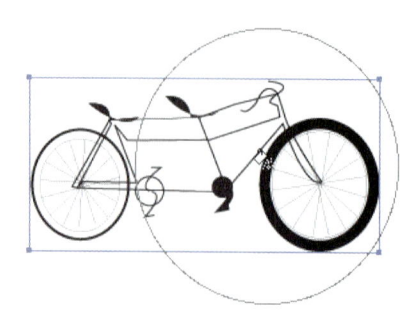

Why Are Some Filters and Effects Grayed Out?	195
See 3D Effects While You're Applying Them	195
Rotate 3D Objects the Right Way	196
Creating a 3D Banner	197
Adding Text to the Banner	198
Get Your Artwork in 3D	199
3D as a Style	200
Stain Removal	201
Scatter Brush Options	201
Scatter Enhancers	202
Symbol Stacking Order	202
Make Your Own Bevels for 3D	203
Stain Repellant	204
Getting More Symbols in Illustrator	204
Free! 1,000+ Scientific Symbols for Illustrator	205
Brush Options vs. Options of Selected Object	206
Birthday Brush	206

CHAPTER 9 — 209
Trading Spaces
Text, Text, Text

Selecting Text	210
Picking the Next Word	210
Select by Paragraphs	211
Change the Default Font in Illustrator	212
Pick a Font by Name	213
Move All Tabs at Once	213
Change Tab Style	214
Delete All Tabs	215
Evenly Spaced Tabs	215
Tab Leaders	216
Line Up the Tab Ruler	216
Align On	217
Angled Tabs	218
Scroll the View with Text	219
Quick Edit	219
Hanging Indents	220
Reset All Settings	220
Colored Text, Colored Box	221
Horizontal to Vertical Type	221
Kern from the Keyboard	222
Tracking with the Keyboard	222
Control Number of Recent Fonts	223
Font Preview—Or Not	223
Reset Kerning and Tracking	224
Open and Start Editing	224
Edit Imported Text	225

xvi

TABLE OF CONTENTS

www.scottkelbybooks.com

Reset Horizontal Scaling	225
Set Leading to the Font Size	226
Increase or Decrease Leading	226
Convert Paragraph Text	227
Cleaning Up Your Text	228
Make Your Own Typeface	229

CHAPTER 10 — 231

Whose Line Is It Anyway?
…And More Text

Transforming Type	232
Drag-and-Drop Text from Desktop	232
Before and After Legacy Text	233
Type Size by Math	234
Gradient-Filled Text	234
Hide the Highlight	235
Clear the Override	235
Override the Override	236
Load Styles from Other Documents	236
Angled Margins	237
Character Rotation	237
Convert Warped Text to Outlines	238
Edit Warped Text	238
Type on a Circle	239
Stop Flipping	240
Baseline Shift Amount	240
Type Not on a Path	241
Copy from Text	241
Thread Text into a New Box	242
Hide Text Threads	243
Threaded Text Blocks of Any Shape	244
Stop the Threading	244
Thread Text on Two Paths	245
Text Wrap Around a Photo	245
Make a Fraction	246
Don't Have an Open Type Font?	246
Automatic Ordinals	247
Global Change Case	248
Blend Two Text Objects	249
Your Styles in Every Document	249
Columns and Rows Galore	250
Columns and Rows in Any Shape	250
Turn Off Typographer's Quotes	251
Pull It Together	251

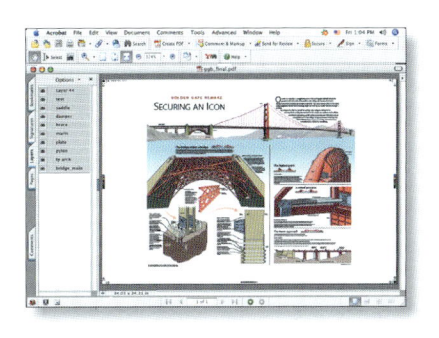

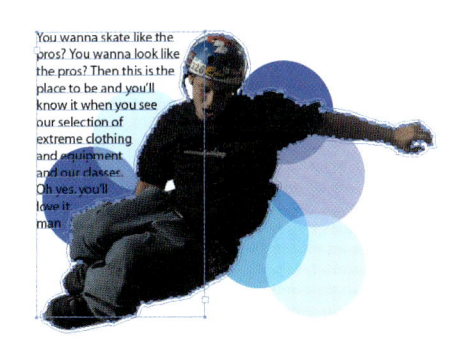

xvii

TABLE OF CONTENTS

CHAPTER 11	253
Friends	
Illustrator with Other CS2 Applications	
Export in Photoshop Format	254
Open an Illustrator File In Photoshop	254
Place an .ai File into Photoshop	255
Drag-and-Drop into Photoshop	255
Drag-and-Drop from Desktop	256
Open a PSD File in Illustrator	257
Place a PSD File into Illustrator	258
Place in Illustrator from Adobe Bridge	259
Change Between Embedded and Linked Graphics	260
Editing Linked Images	260
Vector Shapes in Photoshop	261
Without Warning	262
No Visible Image	263
Copying-and-Pasting Between Illustrator and Photoshop	263
Drag from Illustrator to Make a Path in Photoshop	264
Your Illustrator Logo Built Into Photoshop	265
Export Paths from Photoshop	266
Borrow Shapes from Photoshop to Use in Illustrator	266
Common Color Settings	267
Take Your Swatches Anywhere	268
Info for Photoshop	269
Metadata Templates to Save You Time	270
Show Images or Photos in Outline Mode	271
Dashed Lines in Photoshop (Thanks to Illustrator)	272
Stop Clipping When Saving as an EPS	273
Illustrator Layers in Acrobat	274
Open a PDF in Illustrator	275
Place a PDF with Spot Color	275
Sending a File to a Service Bureau	276
Reduce File Size	276
Cleaning Up Your Illustrations	277
Save for Older Versions of Illustrator	277
Trial Separation	278
Printing Even Larger Than Illustrator Will Let You	279
Save Preset for Printing	280
Saving Print Settings	281
Save for Web Right Within Illustrator	281
Start Over in Save for Web	282
Remember Your Save for Web Settings	282
Optimize by File Size	283
Flattener Preview	283
Get Your Gradients to Print	284
Miss the Old Gal?	285

INTRODUCTION

> **TIP**
>
> *This is a sidebar tip. Every great computer book has a few of them. But this book is nothing but them. A whole book of cool sidebar tips, without the sidebars.*

The idea behind this book

The very first *Killer Tips* book was created based on the premise that the first thing everyone reads in any book is the sidebars. You know, the quick little tips that are typically accompanied by some icon to emphasize their importance. We're no different: We get a new book and flip through it, looking for the tips and then (maybe) will get around to reading the actual text in the chapter. This book is a blatant attempt to capitalize on the popularity of the *Photoshop Killer Tips* book by making up a bunch of stuff and slapping a cover onto it that implies it might actually be useful. Of course we're kidding here—only a handful of the tips were made up; the majority of the others work fine (the ones we tested anyway).

This *Killer Tips* book is a little different from the others in the series, as we revisited the question, "What makes a tip a killer tip?" and realized that it really depends on your experience with the software. To a beginner, a "killer" tip could be a simple shortcut that the more experienced Illustrator user has known for years. So, we created a "Basic Training" chapter with a whole series of what amount to "Killer Tips for Beginners." But throughout the pages, the underlying theme is the same as all the *Killer Tips* books—speed. Get it done fast and do it accurately (and enjoy the new speed at which you can create your works of art).

Is this book for you?

Yes. There, that was simple wasn't it? Yes, you should buy this book. Read it if you must, but definitely buy it. No, really, this book is aimed at the two main types of Illustrator users out there. There's the everyday Illustrator users who have been creating all kinds of cool designs but just want to be faster. They crave speed and quicker ways to get their artwork done. These users will find all kinds of productivity tips and important reminders of speedier methods and helpful techniques. Then there's the other kind of Illustrator user: the ones who own the software and use it occasionally or are just getting started. They will enjoy the fact that some of the tips cover the important principles of the program, particularly the ones that aren't self-evident.

Of course, one of the biggest challenges in a book like this is to decide which tips are "too" basic, which tips "everyone knows," and which tips are way beyond comprehension except for rocket scientists. Our simple solution was to throw darts at a dartboard filled with tip-laden sticky notes, and hope that all the best tips didn't get left out. We believe the odds were in our favor. Seriously, our goal was to provide a wide range of tips, so if the first couple cause you to say, "Jeez, I knew that!" that's great! That means you've done a good job of teaching yourself about Illustrator. Keep on truckin', though, and we know you'll find tips that will change your life (or at least make things go a lot faster).

Is this book for Mac or Windows, or both?

This book is for anyone that owns Illustrator: any platform, any version. Yes, if you run Illustrator 88 on your Mac SE, you can benefit from the seven tips that relate to your version. Of course, if you are using Illustrator CS2 on OS X or Windows, then all of these tips will be of interest to you. For each tip that includes a keyboard command, we give you both the Macintosh and Windows version of the shortcut. Sorry, but due to space constraints we had to cut the Amiga keyboard shortcuts from each tip. Maybe next time.

How to use this book

The beauty of a book like this lies in its simplicity: Start reading anywhere, stop reading when you're finished. Remember, the first chapter is really aimed more at inexperienced users (but it's okay for you to read that one too, even if you feel pretty comfortable with Illustrator—you never know what you might have missed).

If you really want to take best advantage of this book, we would recommend using it with at least three of the following: candlelight, hot tub, wine, favorite companion, barbershop quartet music. Can you imagine anything more romantic? Reading aloud some Illustrator tips by candlelight to your loved one, to the *a capella* strains of "Heart of My Heart"…

ANOTHER TIP

You're doing it again! Stop looking at these sidebars. See, they're intoxicating—you're drawn to them even after you know it's not really a tip. Okay, here's a real tip: If you like sidebar tips, buy this book.

Basic Training

BASIC TIPS YOU CAN'T LIVE WITHOUT

Let's start at the very beginning, that's a good place to start. Do re mi, do re mi… Who'd-a thunk that Maria was an Illustrator user?

Basic Training!
basic tips you can't live without

Okay, so this chapter has little or nothing to do with The Sound of Music, *although it could be argued that these tips will be music to your ears when you realize how productive they'll make you. (Ha! They said it couldn't be done, but we were sure it would somehow be possible to work a classic movie musical into a chapter intro.) Before you have any second thoughts about returning the book to its place of purchase, let us reassure you that these introductions are in no way a reflection of the practical and useful tips that follow them. Go ahead, breathe that big sigh of relief.*

CHAPTER 1 • Basic Tips You Can't Live Without

MAKE YOURSELF FAMOUS

OK, so it's a stretch to include this tip anywhere, but I thought it was cool. Make yourself famous by appearing in the Credits that display on a PC when you choose Help>About Illustrator and click on the Credits button. Just modify the file located in Adobe Illustrator CS2\Support Files\Contents\Windows. The file name is CreditsText.utxt and it opens in any basic text editor. Add your name into it, save it, and show the credits. You can impress all of your friends by saying you were on the product team. (Okay, maybe that's exaggerating a bit. They probably won't believe you, but it's still fun.)

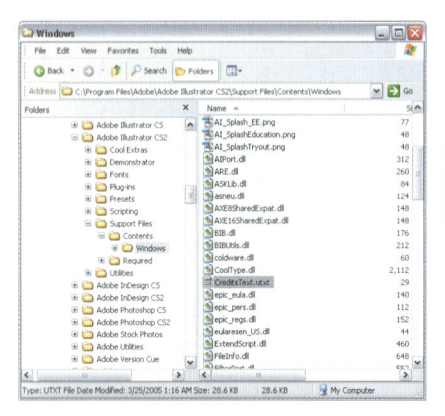

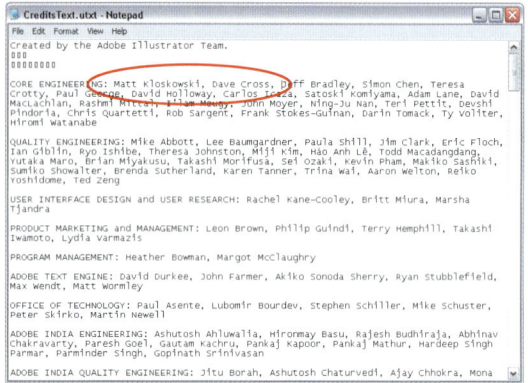

ADDITIONAL CONTENT

If you haven't realized this yet, Illustrator CS2 comes with a ton of extra content. This includes fonts, symbols, swatches, gradients, styles, and custom brushes. I can't stress this one enough. If you need some creative inspiration, then check out this content. It's located right inside the Presets folder (in the Adobe Illustrator Applications or Program File on your hard drive) and is categorized based on what type of preset it works with (i.e., brushes, patterns, gradients, symbols, etc.).

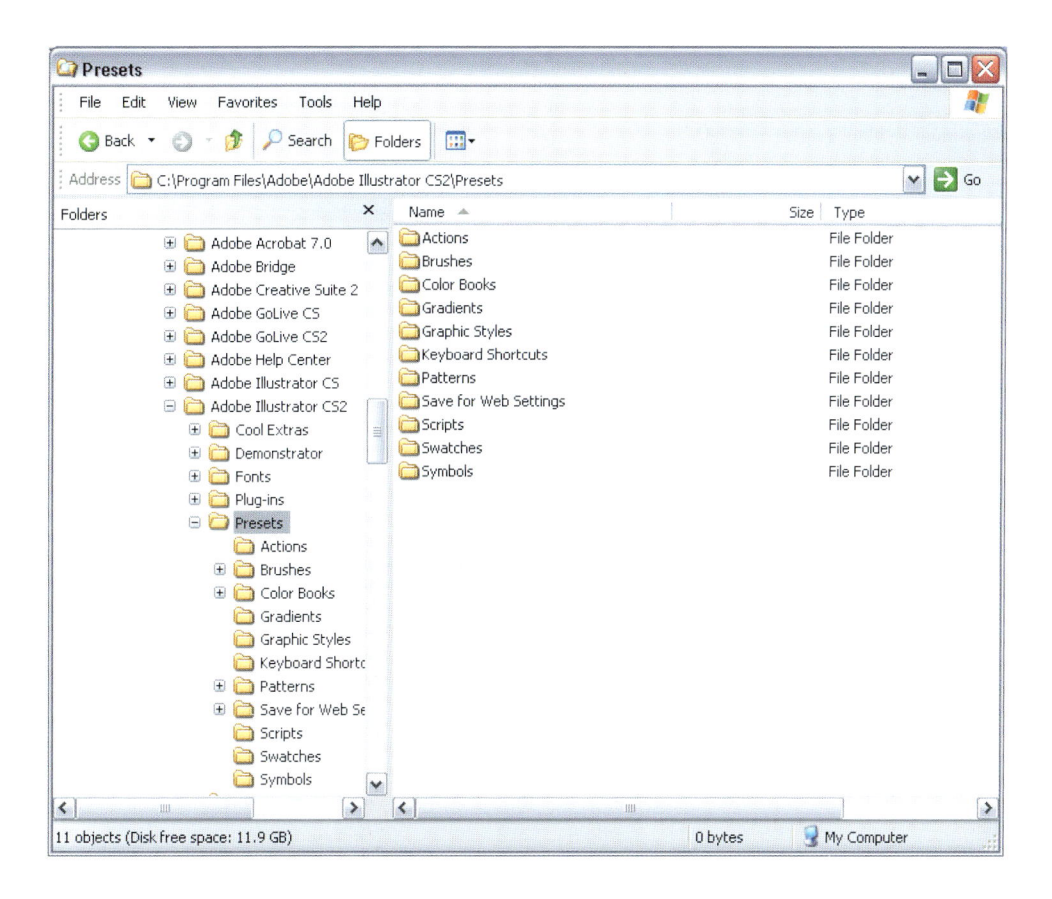

CHAPTER 1 • Basic Tips You Can't Live Without

MORE ADDITIONAL CONTENT

If you liked the previous tip, but thought to yourself, "How am I supposed to ever see all of this content so I can choose what I like?" then I've got some good news and some bad news for you. Which do you want first? I always take the good news first, so that's where we'll start. Illustrator CS included a PDF file called Additional Content.pdf that showed a high resolution preview of all the presets. The bad news is that Illustrator CS2 doesn't, so it's basically a guessing game. Don't let that stop you, though. If you have Illustrator CS, then the PDF file is located in Illustrator CS\Additional Content.pdf. If you don't have CS and only have CS2, we've made the file available for download at http://www.peachpit.com/title/032133065X.

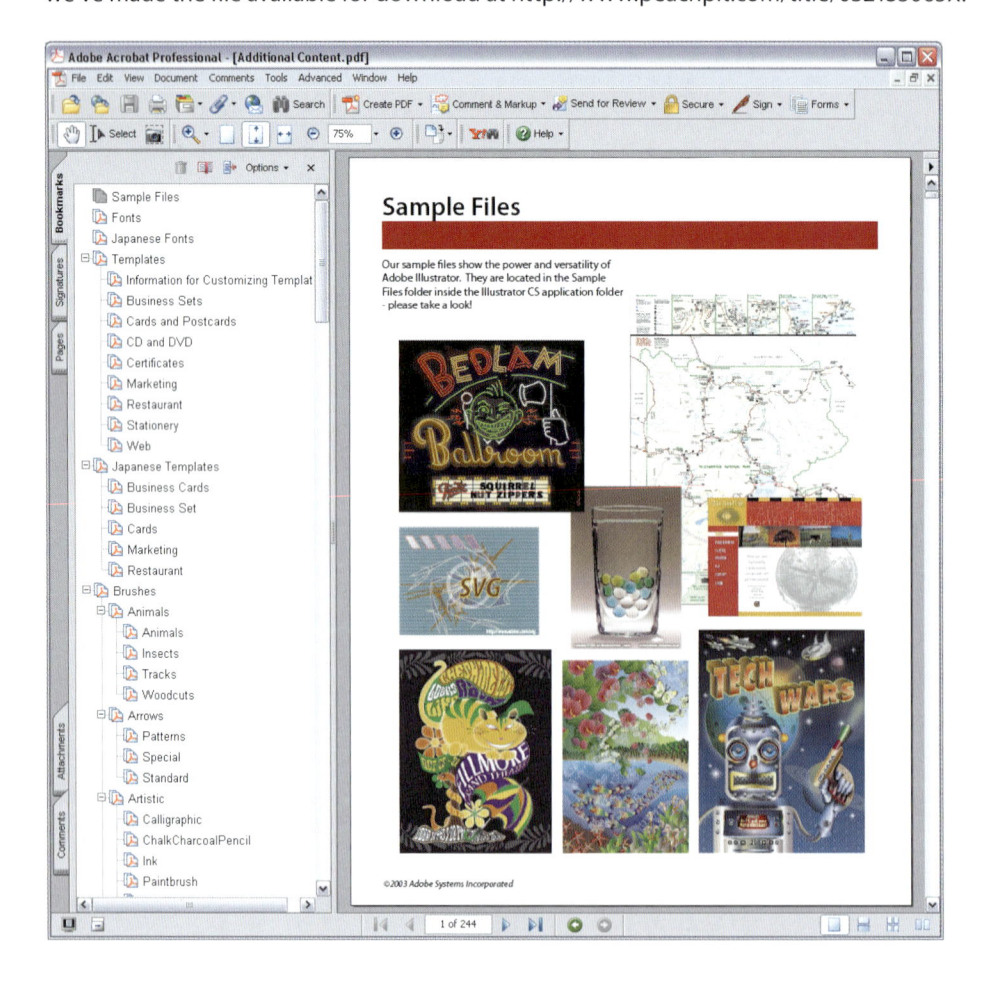

WACOM PEN TABLETS WORK IN ILLUSTRATOR TOO

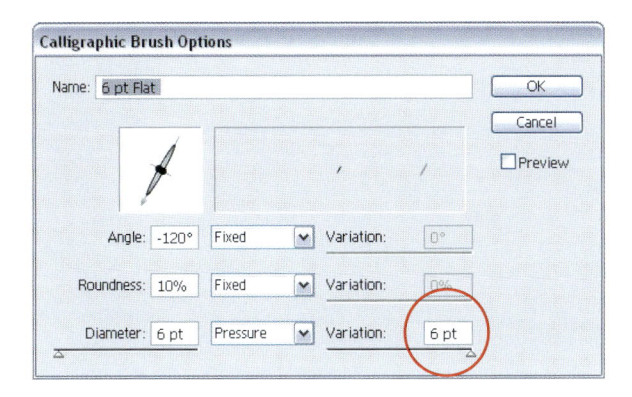

Many people don't know that Wacom pen tablets work great in Illustrator. It mimics traditional drawing techniques because you actually hold a Wacom pen just like you would a drawing pen or pencil. Also, the pressure-sensitive nature of the Wacom pen allows you to control the width of brush strokes in Illustrator. Try it out. Grab the pen and tablet and double-click on any Calligraphic Brush in the Brushes palette (under the Window menu) to bring up the Calligraphic Brush Options dialog. Under one of the settings, such as Diameter, select Pressure, make the variation setting higher, and click OK. Then try drawing on the artboard. Press down softer and harder with the pen and you'll see that the strokes do indeed reflect how hard you are pressing.

Pressing lightly with the Wacom pen

Pressing harder with the Wacom pen

Pressing very hard with the Wacom pen

CHAPTER 1 • Basic Tips You Can't Live Without

ONGOING FEEDBACK

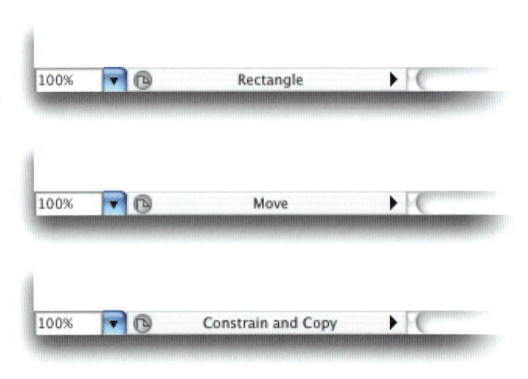

If you're ever unsure that you're holding down the correct modifier key, check out the Status Bar in the lower left hand corner: It constantly changes based on what you're doing. For example, if you have the Rectangle tool (M) active it will display "Rectangle." Press-and-hold the Command key (PC: Control key) and start to drag the object and it will display "Move." Throw in Option-Shift (PC: Alt-Shift) while dragging, and the display will change to "Constrain and Copy." It's a simple but effective way to reassure yourself that you're using the correct keys. *Note:* If you do not see the tool name, click on the Status Bar and under Show, choose Current Tool.

TIMING IS EVERYTHING

One of the more important principles of using keyboard modifiers is that the same key will have different effects, depending on when you use it. For example, with the Direct Selection tool (A) active, holding down the Option key (PC: Alt key) will select the entire path. If you don't let go of the Option key when you drag, you'll get a copy. So in this case, to move a path without copying it, press-and-hold the Option key and click on the path, then let go of the Option key before dragging the path.

CHAPTER 1 • Basic Tips You Can't Live Without

THE EVER-CHANGING PALETTE

Many Illustrator palettes have more than one display size—in some cases, multiple sizes. You can use a palette's flyout menu to choose Show Options or Hide Options, but it can be faster to double-click on the tab at the top of the palette. To see if a palette has multiple sizes, just keep double-clicking on the tab to switch among the collapsed, basic, and expanded views. (Why collapse palettes? To save space without closing palettes or to move them out of the way.)

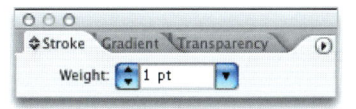

Collapsed palette

Basic size

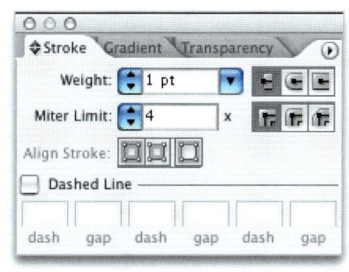

Expanded palette

QUICK DELETE FROM PALETTES

To delete anything from a palette, without getting a dialog like this example asking you to confirm your choice, hold down the Option key (PC: Alt key) as you click on the palette's Trash icon. This applies to brushes, swatches, layers, etc.

CHAPTER 1 • Basic Tips You Can't Live Without

LOCKING AND UNLOCKING GUIDES

By default, all guides that you add to a document are locked. To unlock all the guides in one quick step, press Command-Option-; (PC: Control-Alt-;). This also works the other way around: Once you've unlocked all the guides, use the same shortcut to lock all guides.

CHOOSE THE BEST SELECTION TOOL FOR THE JOB

Trying to determine when to use the Selection tool (V) versus the Direct Selection tool (A)? Here's a simple suggestion: Think of the Selection tool as the "move" tool and the Direct Selection tool as the "reshaping" tool. Actually, I suppose that the Selection tool should be thought of as the move/resize tool, since those are the two functions it performs. So, anytime you need to decide between tools, ask yourself, "Do I need to move/resize the object or reshape it?" That will help you pick the correct selection tool.

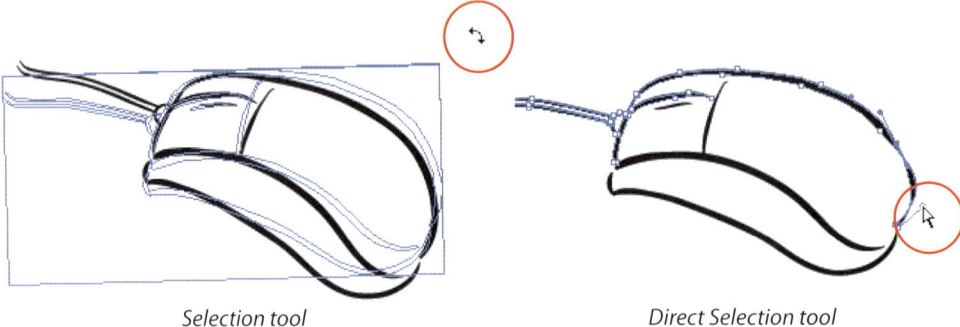

Selection tool

Direct Selection tool

CHAPTER 1 • Basic Tips You Can't Live Without

DIRECT SELECTION SECRET

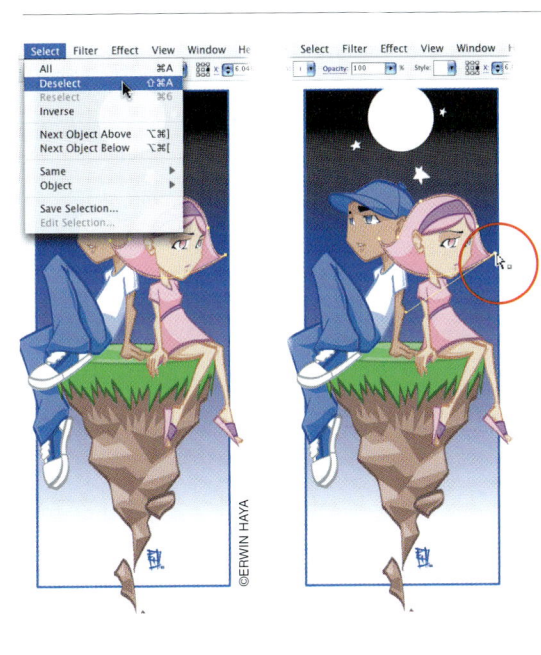

If you're having trouble getting the Direct Selection tool (A) to select only one individual point, here are two "secrets" to success. (1) Make sure nothing is selected by either clicking away from any object or by pressing Command-Shift-A (PC: Control-Shift-A). (2) If you click on the fill of an object, the Direct Selection tool will act just like the Selection tool. So, make sure no anchor points are selected, and then position your mouse over one anchor point and click.

QUICK SELECTION TOOL

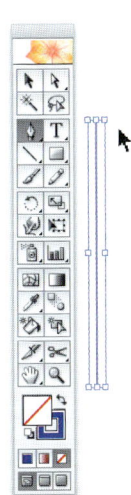

If you need to use the Selection tool (V) and then return to the tool you were using, here's how to do it. With any tool selected, press-and-hold the Command key (PC: Control key) to temporarily activate the Selection tool. (Actually, it will activate the last selection tool you used, so you may get the Direct Selection tool.) Once you've used the Selection tool, let go of the key to return to whatever tool you had been using.

CHAPTER 1 • Basic Tips You Can't Live Without   9

HIDE BOUNDING BOX

Here's a shortcut that you'll want to memorize—the ability to show and hide the bounding box. The bounding box is a great way to resize objects without switching to the Scale tool (S). On the other hand, sometimes the bounding box is very distracting, so the option to show or hide it is very useful. Just press Command-Shift-B (PC: Control-Shift-B) each time you want to toggle the bounding box on and off.

QUICK MOVE DIALOG

A quick way to access the Move dialog is to double-click on the Selection tool. That saves you from having to dig down in the Object menu to get to the command.

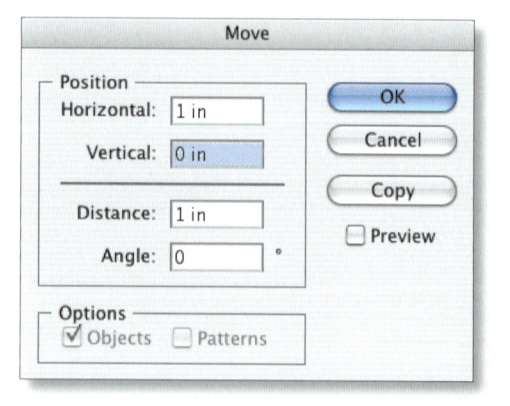

CHAPTER 1 • Basic Tips You Can't Live Without

SELECTING THE NEXT OBJECT BELOW

If you know there's an object hidden under another object and you need to select it, use the contextual menu. With the Selection tool (V), click on the top object, then Control-click (PC: Right-click) and from the contextual menu choose Select>Next Object Below (as we did here to select the airplane). You'll notice there are similar commands for objects above.

CREATE BY MEASURE

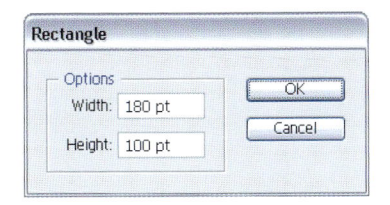

You can create an object at a specific size by choosing the appropriate shape tool (Rectangle, Star, etc.) and then clicking on the artboard. In the subsequent dialog, enter the exact measurements you'd like to use and click OK. To create a shape that's centered on the position of your click, hold down the Option key (PC: Alt key) when you click on the artboard. *Bonus:* Want to know the size of the shape you just created by dragging? Click once using that shape's tool and check out the numbers in the dialog (then click Cancel).

CHAPTER 1 • Basic Tips You Can't Live Without

POSITION SHAPES AS YOU DRAW

With any of the shape tools, you can change the position of the shape while you create it on the artboard. Simply hold down the Spacebar to "interrupt" the tool you're using, allowing you to move the shape. Let go of the Spacebar to continue drawing the shape.

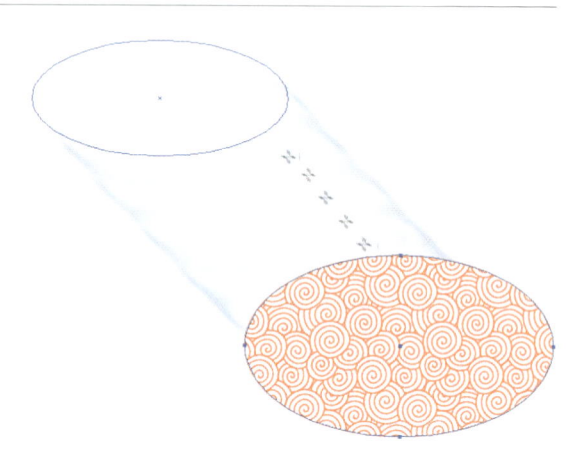

DRAWING CURVES MORE EASILY

If you're new to drawing curves with the Pen tool (P), here's a quick method to create a simple curve. Use the Pen tool to draw two straight lines that create a triangle that points in the direction you want your curve. Then hold down the Option key (PC: Alt key) to activate the Convert Anchor Point tool. Click on the anchor point where the two lines meet and drag outwards to create a curve.

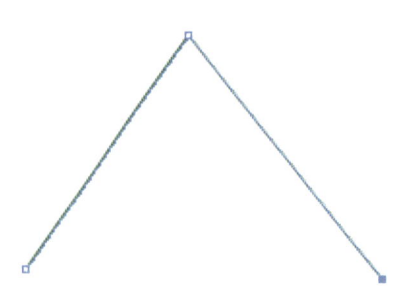

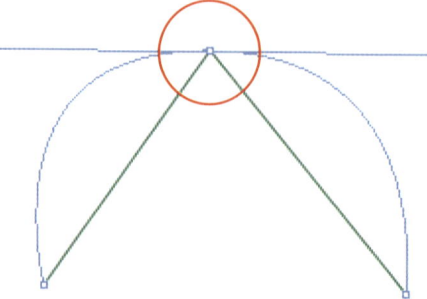

SIMPLIFYING A PATH

One of the basic rules of Illustrator should be to use the minimum number of anchor points that you can get away with on a path. This will keep your objects as simple as possible, which will help streamline the printing process. An easy way to reduce the number of anchor points on a path is to select the path and use the Simplify command (Object>Path>Simplify).

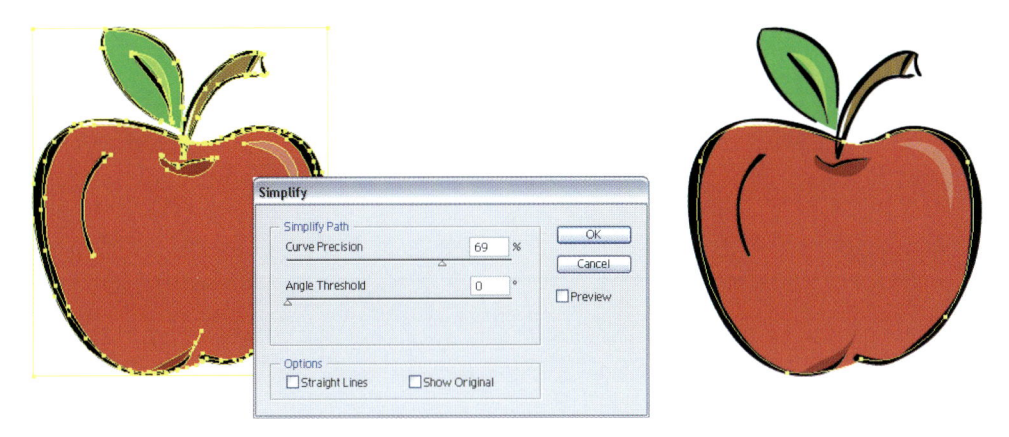

SELECT NONE

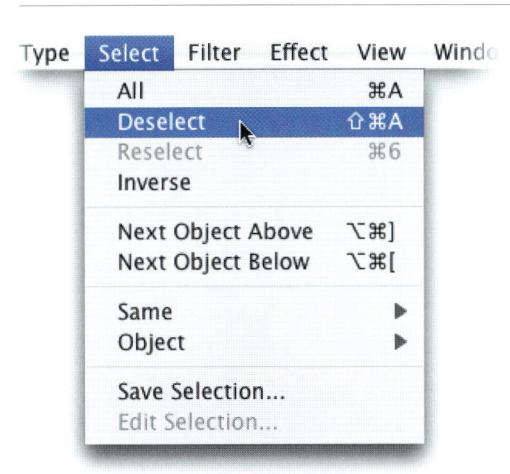

Hopefully, you know that the command to select everything (Select All) is Command-A (PC: Control-A). That's pretty standard in most programs. In Illustrator, it's just as easy to ensure that nothing is selected. To do this, press Command-Shift-A (PC: Control-Shift-A). Or, if you want to do it the "old-fashioned way," go to the Select menu and choose Deselect (as shown here).

CHAPTER 1 • Basic Tips You Can't Live Without   13

EVERYTHING ELSE BUT

To select everything except one object, select the object, then from the Select menu choose Inverse.

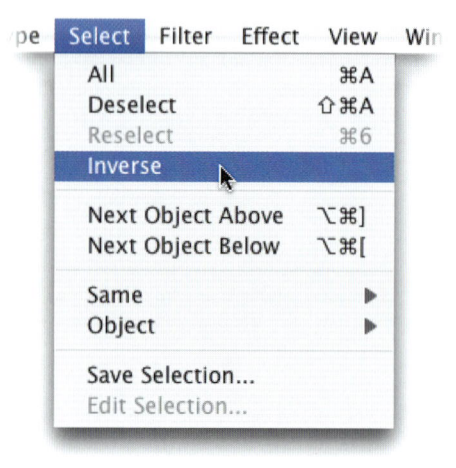

WHAT HAPPENS WHEN YOU CAN'T SEE AN OBJECT?

If you have objects that have no stroke or fill, they are—in effect—hidden. To select one of these paths, look for a small square to appear beside the Selection tool (V). This tells you that you are directly over a path. You can also click-and-drag in the general area of the object using one of the selection tools to select the path.

EVEN IT OUT

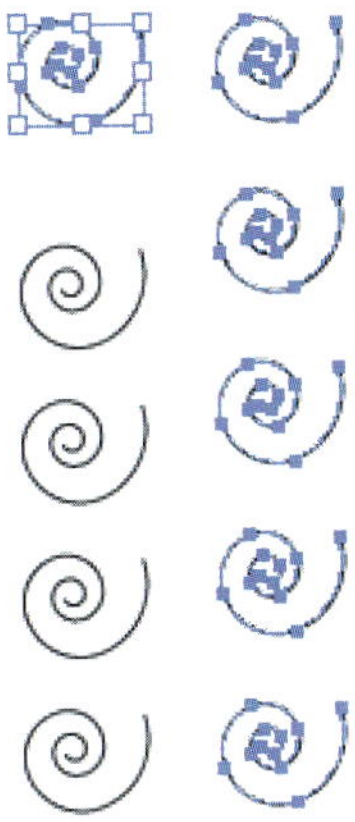

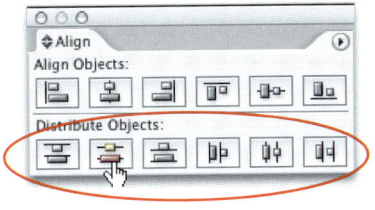

You've created a bunch of objects, with nice even spaces between them, then you decide that the top object needs to be up higher. You move the top object and, of course, the other objects are no longer evenly spaced. The solution? Select all the objects and in the Align palette (Window>Align), click the Horizontal or Vertical Distribute icons.

REFLECT VS. FLIP

In almost every application, there are commands called Flip Vertical and Flip Horizontal—in Illustrator they're not so obvious. There's the Reflect tool (O), but that's more like a mirror reflection than a flip. In other words, Reflect Horizontal is the equivalent of Flip Vertical. That's because "horizontal" indicates the angle of your mirror, which—in effect—flips your object vertically. In case you find that too confusing, commands for Flip Horizontal and Flip Vertical are found in the flyout menu in the Transform palette (Window>Transform).

Original  *Reflect Horizontal*  *Flip Horizontal*

CHAPTER 1 • Basic Tips You Can't Live Without   15

TOOL PREFERENCES

A number of tools have individual preferences or options that you can change to affect the way the tool performs. To open a tool's preferences or options, double-click any of these tools in the Toolbox: Line, Arc, Rectangular Grid, Polar Grid, Flare, Paintbrush, Pencil, Smooth, Eyedropper, Blend, Paint Bucket, Paint Selection, Measure, and any Liquify, Symbolism, or Graph tools.

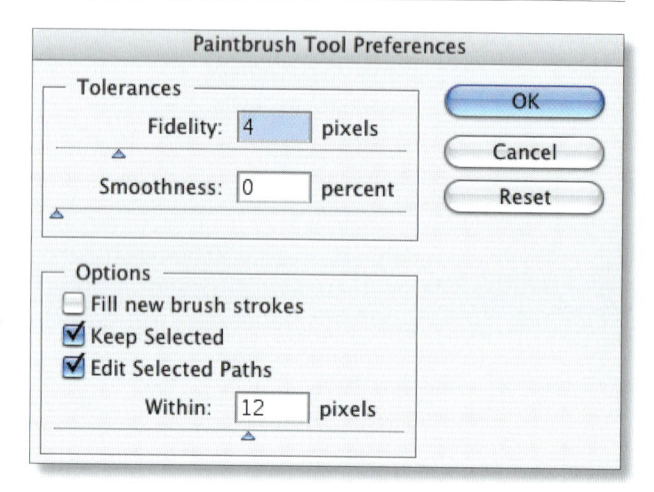

NAME A SWATCH

After creating a new swatch, you can always name it after the fact by double-clicking on it. Or you can name a new swatch as you create it by pressing the Option key (PC: Alt key) as you click on the New Swatch icon at the bottom of the Swatches palette (Window>Swatches).

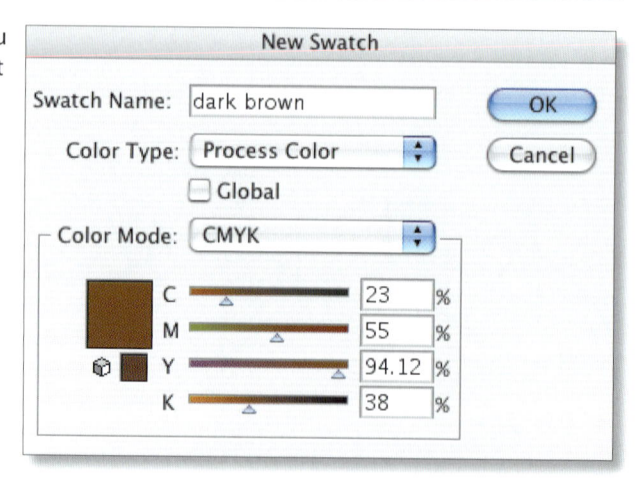

CHAPTER 1 • Basic Tips You Can't Live Without

RESET THE DEFAULT FILL AND STROKE COLORS

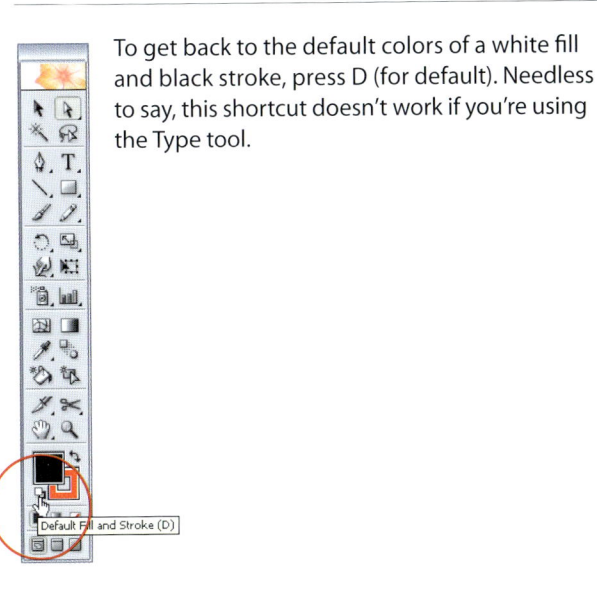

To get back to the default colors of a white fill and black stroke, press D (for default). Needless to say, this shortcut doesn't work if you're using the Type tool.

COLOR PICKER

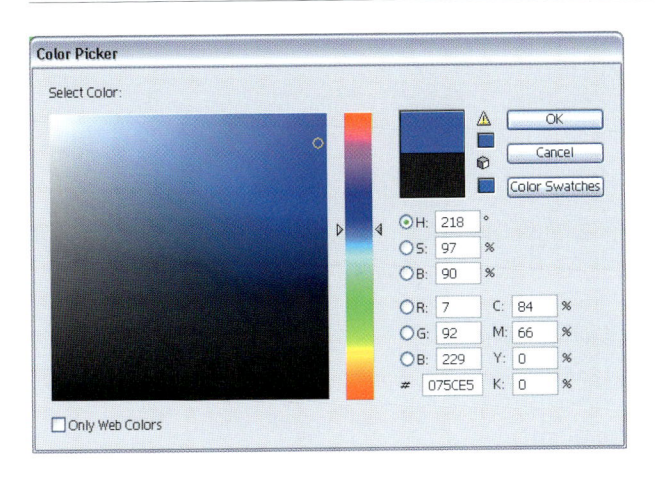

To access a Photoshop-style Color Picker, double-click on either the Fill or Stroke icon near the bottom of the Toolbox or in the top-left of the Color palette. Choose a color visually or numerically, click OK, and you're done.

CHAPTER 1 • Basic Tips You Can't Live Without   17

HIDE OR SHOW MULTIPLE LAYERS EASILY

If you have a long list of layers or sublayers and need to hide a bunch of them—but not all of them—click-and-drag through the Eye icons in the Layers palette to hide or show the layers. Of course, this only works with contiguous layers, but it sure works well, and fast.

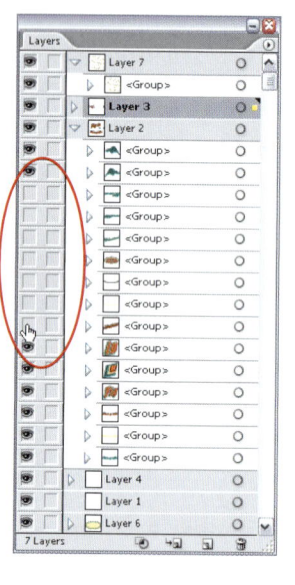

FILTERS VS. EFFECTS?

What's the main difference between the two? Effects are more flexible, allowing you to edit the effect through the Appearance palette (Window>Appearance), but they require more memory and processor power. Filters are "permanent" (although you can choose Undo from the Edit menu), but typically they don't take as long to process. In our example, we first applied the Roughen filter (Filter>Distort>Roughen), and then we applied the Roughen effect (Effect>Distort & Transform>Roughen), which is editable in the Appearance palette.

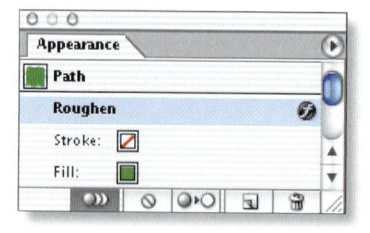

Filter

Effect

18   CHAPTER 1 • Basic Tips You Can't Live Without

EDIT EXISTING PATTERNS AND SYMBOLS

If you see a pattern in the Swatches palette (Window>Swatches) or symbol in the Symbols palette (Window>Symbols) that you'd like to adapt by changing colors or by adding or deleting objects, drag the swatch or symbol onto the artboard. Patterns are editable, but with symbols you'll have to choose Object>Expand to be able to edit the original artwork. Once you've made your changes (using the Direct Selection tool, most likely), select the objects and drag them back into their appropriate palettes, which creates a new pattern or symbol.

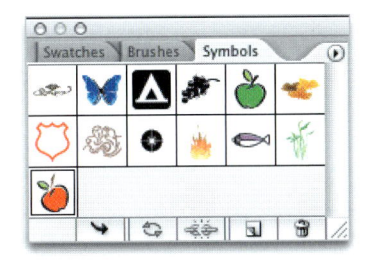

USE TEXT IMPORT OPTIONS

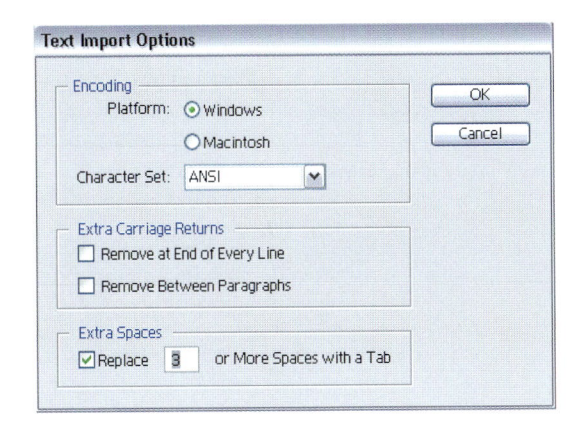

You can make your life a little easier when you place text by setting the options in the importing options dialog that appears before the text is placed. Depending on the type of text file, you'll get a different dialog upon placing (File>Place). Word documents, for example, offer a few choices, such as including a table of contents or removing text formatting. Text files (TXT) will cause the Text Import Options dialog to open, with more options such as removing extra carriage returns or replacing extra spaces with a tab.

CHAPTER 1 • Basic Tips You Can't Live Without   19

SCALE TEXT FRAME BUT NOT TEXT

To make a text frame bigger, so the text reflows, click with the Selection tool (V) to make the bounding box visible. Then click-and-drag on a handle to resize the text frame without affecting the size of the type. In contrast, if you select a text frame with the Selection tool, and then use the Scale tool (S) or Free Transform tool (E), any adjustments to the text frame will scale the size of the text inside the frame.

Scaling text frame with Selection tool

Scaling text frame and text with Free Transform tool

MULTIPLE GLYPH CHOICES

Take a look in the Glyphs palette (Window>Type>Glyphs), and if an OpenType font is selected in the pop-up menu at the bottom of the palette, you will see a small black triangle at the bottom right of some of the characters. The triangle indicates that there is more than one choice for that character. Click-and-hold on one of these characters to see the choices, move your cursor over the character that you want, and release the mouse button to add that character to the artboard. This palette also serves as a great preview of a font—just choose a different typeface from the pop-up menu for an instant preview of the characters in that font.

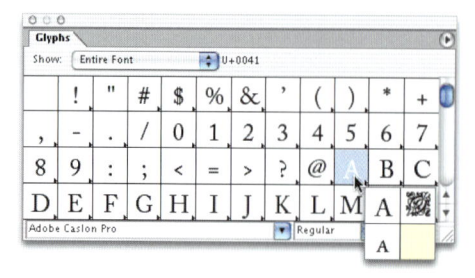

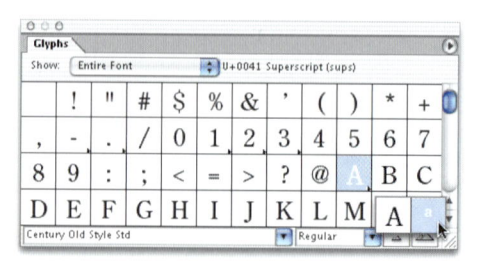

Adobe Caslon Pro offers multiple choices as compared to Century Old Style

20   CHAPTER 1 • Basic Tips You Can't Live Without

EFFECTING A STROKE OR A FILL

One of the advantages of the Appearance palette (Windows>Appearance) is the option to affect only the stroke or only the fill of a selected object. A great example of that is to apply an effect (not a filter) to only the stroke, or only to the fill. In the Appearance palette, click on the word Stroke and then apply an effect from the Effect menu. (In our example, we used the Roughen effect under Distort & Transform in the Effect menu—first applied just to the stroke, and then applied only to the fill.)

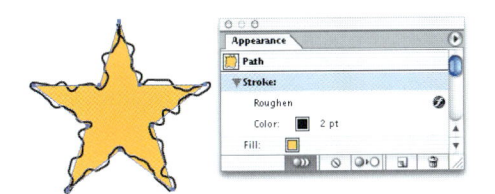

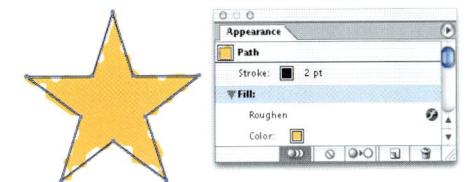

TRANSFORM AGAIN

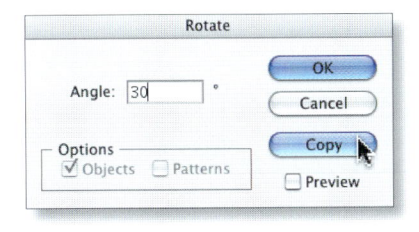

Don't be fooled by the shortcut for this command: Command-D (PC: Control-D). In many applications that's the shortcut for Duplicate, but not in Illustrator. In this program the command is called Transform Again, and it's quite different from duplicating (in a very good way). Transform Again is a shorter way of saying, "Whatever you just did, do it again." So if you just rotated an object 30º, pressing Command-D (PC: Control-D) will rotate the object another 30º. The object will not be duplicated unless that's part of the original transformation. For example, if you drag an object with the Option key (PC: Alt key) held down to move a copy, Transform Again will move another copy the exact same distance and angle. This is an extremely powerful command that has many uses! (Just remember not to do any additional operation, or you will alter your Transform Again command.)

CHAPTER 1 • Basic Tips You Can't Live Without   21

Illustrator CS2
KillerTips

CREATE YOUR OWN CROP MARKS

You can easily create crop marks around a graphic (to indicate where a graphic should be trimmed, for example). Just draw a rectangle that represents the crop area (don't worry about fill or stroke, they'll automatically change). With the rectangle selected, go to Object>Crop Area>Make. If you ever need to change the crop marks, use Object>Crop Area>Release and then edit the rectangle. (*Note:* The cropping object must be a non-rotated rectangle that is not being used as a clipping mask.)

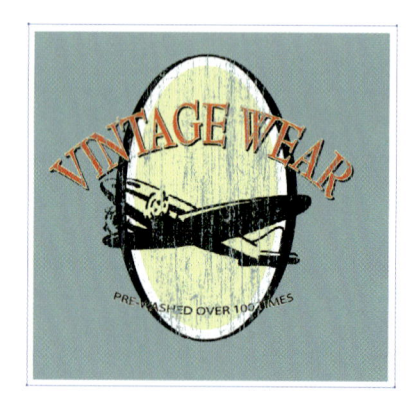

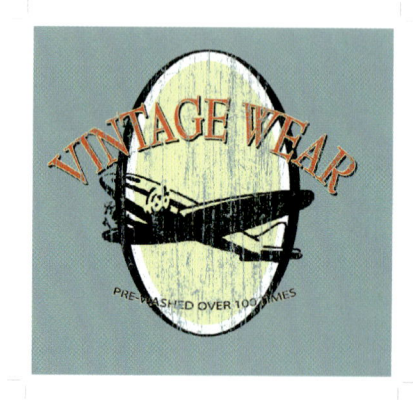

OPEN A TEMPLATE

Adobe was kind enough to provide many useful templates and a simple way to make use of them, so why not take advantage of it? If you need to design artwork for a CD, for example, choose File>New From Template. You should be directed to the templates folder (Illustrator CS2\Cool Extras\Templates), where you select from the various folders. In this example, we opened the template in the Extreme Sports folder called DVD Label.ait. A new, untitled document is created that contains all the artwork, ready to edit, and the original template artwork is untouched, ready for next time.

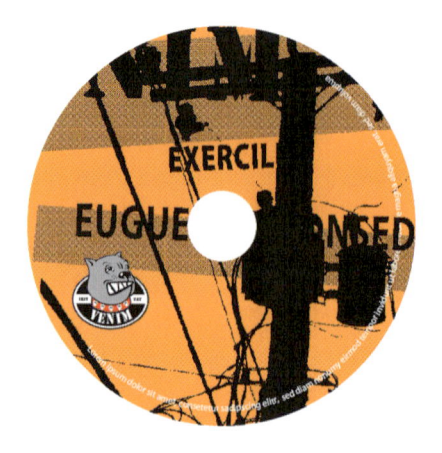

22   CHAPTER 1 • Basic Tips You Can't Live Without

MAKE YOUR OWN TEMPLATE

You can easily make your own template and save it in a format that will automatically be opened as an untitled copy of your artwork. Create your artwork complete with sample text, guides, and the colors you want, and then use File>Save As Template. Name the file and save it in the Templates folder for easy retrieval (it should default to AIT format, but check just to be sure). From then on, use the File>New From Template command to open your template—ready to edit—then save it as a regular Illustrator document.

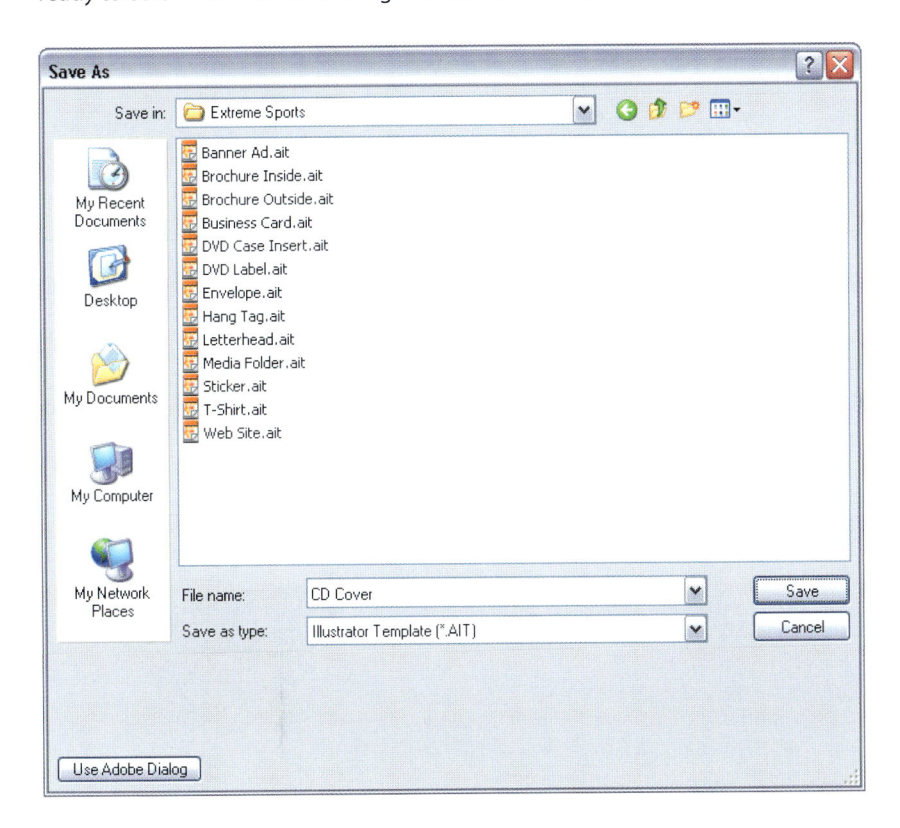

SAVE FOR MICROSOFT OFFICE

Imagine that this command under the File menu is really called "Save As a PNG File, But Without Seeing Any Options." Sure, PNG is a great format for use in MS Office, but personally, I'd like a little more control over how it's saved, such as the resolution and whether the background is transparent. To be able to see—and change—the save options, use the File>Export command instead of Save for Microsoft Office. Choose PNG in the Format (PC: Save As Type) pop-up menu, name the file, and click Export (PC: Save) to see the PNG Options dialog, where you can make changes. (Or you could select the Save for Web command in the File menu, choosing PNG in the pop-up menu under Preset.)

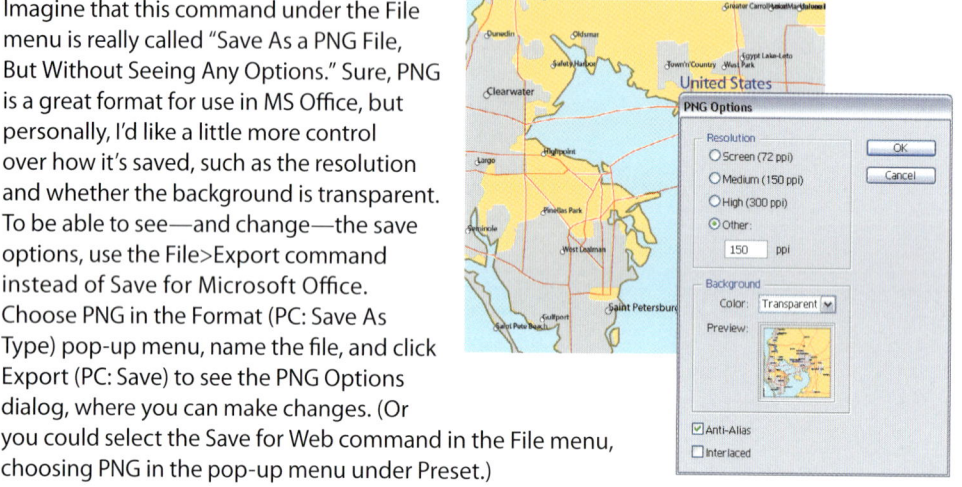

VIEW ACTIONS IN BUTTON MODE

In the Actions palette (found under the Window menu), you can record, edit, and play automated functions to speed up your work. In the Actions palette's standard view, every step of an action is visible and can be turned on and off. The other possible view is Button Mode (chosen from the palette's flyout menu). In Button Mode, you only see the name of the action and its keyboard shortcut, if one has been assigned. So you can use this display mode to either click on an action to play it, or to remind yourself of the F-key shortcut.

Standard view   *Button Mode view*

To return to standard view, go back to the palette's flyout menu and deselect Button Mode. (*Note:* If you've assigned a modifier key to your shortcut, such as the Shift key, this will not be reflected in the Button Mode—for some reason. You'll only see the Function key listed.)

24   CHAPTER 1 • Basic Tips You Can't Live Without

"HIDDEN" KEYBOARD COMMANDS

In Chapter 2, we show you how to customize your own keyboard shortcuts. Here's one little extra tip that you may discover on your own, but we thought we'd make sure that you did by adding it in here. There are a few unusual commands that are kinda "hidden" in the Keyboard Shortcuts dialog (Edit>Keyboard Shortcuts). With Menu Commands selected in the top-left pop-up menu, scroll down to the very bottom of the dialog and click on the triangle beside any of the Other options (e.g., Other Select, Other Text, etc.). Look in those lists and you'll find useful keyboard commands, such as Switch Selection Tools or New Swatch.

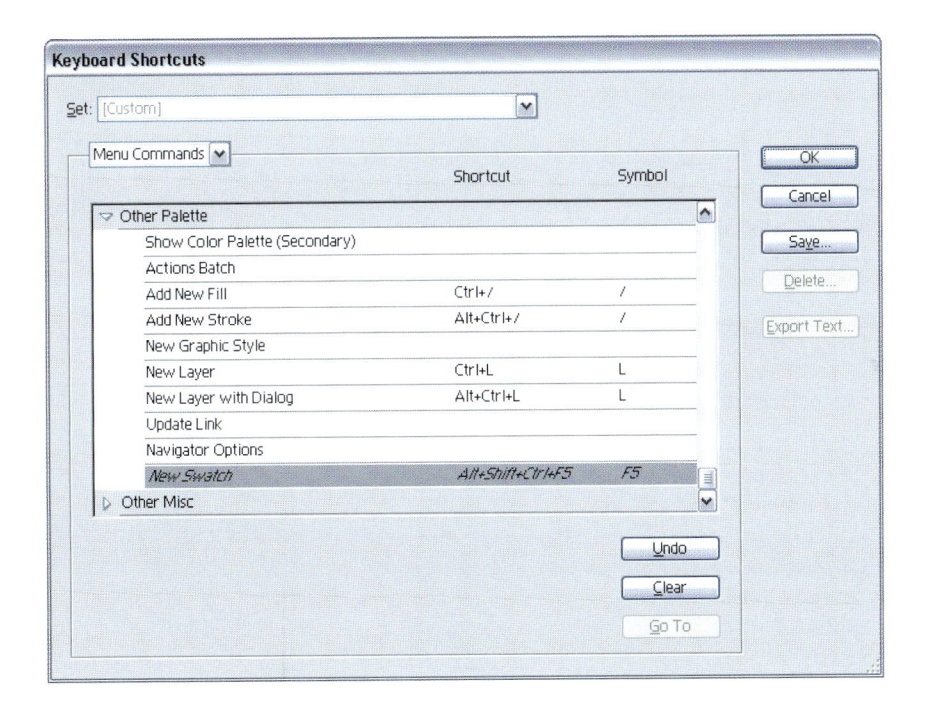

The View

VIEWING, DOING, UNDOING, AND MORE

Most people remember it vividly: The first time you zoom in on a vector image and still see sharp, clean edges. Brings a tear to

The View
viewing, doing, undoing, and more

the eye doesn't it? When you've lived in a world dominated by Photoshop and pixels—you know, that slightly superior, "look what I did to this photo" attitude—it is such a rush to zoom in to 20,000% without even a hint of jaggedness! You know what we're talking about right? Right? Hmmm, maybe it's just vector junkies like us that experience that thrill? But you have to admit, custom views and workspaces rock, right? Right???

HOW MANY UNDOS?

Illustrator has (virtually) unlimited undos. Of course, you could keep pressing Command-Z (PC: Control-Z) over and over again until you run out of undos, but there is an easier way to know how many undos you actually have available. Click on the Status Bar at the bottom-left of the document window (next to your document size). From the pop-up menu that appears, under Show, choose Number of Undos. Now, you can see how many you've got and undo away.

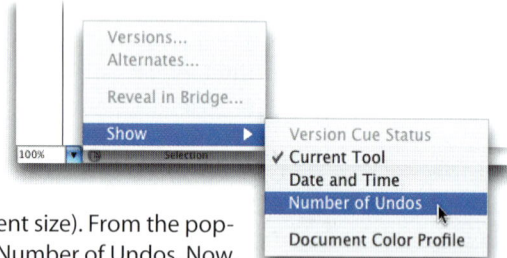

ACTUAL SIZE, FIT IN WINDOW

In Illustrator, there is often more than one way to do things, and zooming in and out is no different. You can use keyboard shortcuts to change the view to Actual Size (Command-1 [PC: Control-1]) and Fit in Window (Command-Zero [PC: Control-Zero]), and you can also change to these views using the Toolbox. Double-click on the Zoom tool to change to Actual Size view, double-click on the Hand tool to change to Fit in Window.

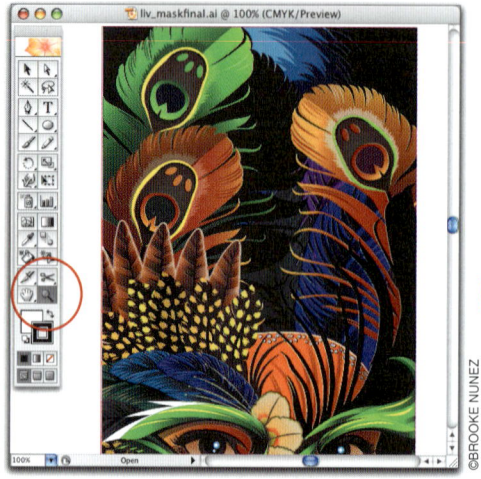

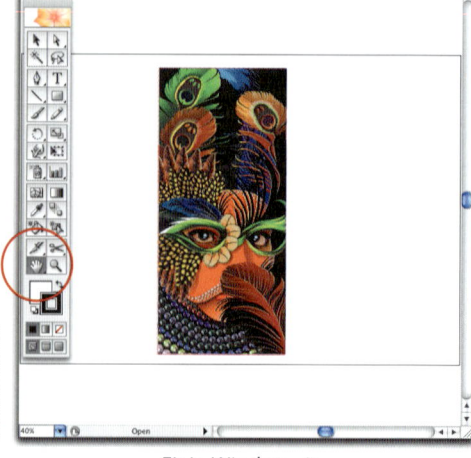

Actual Size view

Fit in Window view

28   CHAPTER 2 • Viewing, Doing, Undoing, and More

REALLY FIT IN WINDOW

Press Command-Zero (PC: Control-Zero) to change the view to Fit in Window. If that's not zoomed out far enough, try this: Hold down the Command key (PC: Control key) and double-click on the Zoom tool in the Toolbox. The view will change to 3.13%, the smallest zoom view possible, which is ideal for those poster-size images.

SWITCHING BETWEEN MULTIPLE OPEN WINDOWS

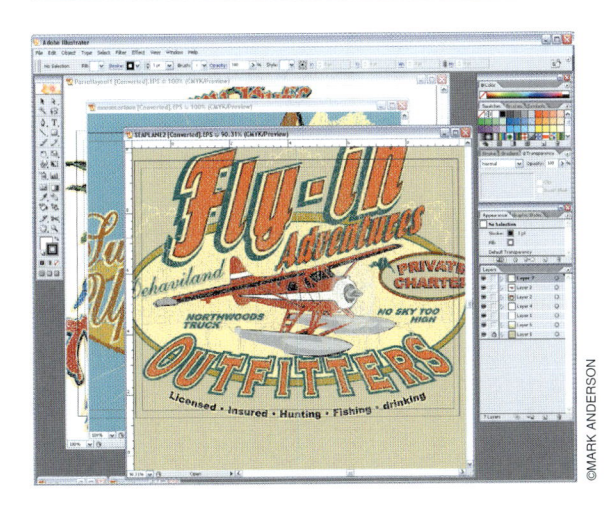

Before Illustrator CS2, the only way you could switch between open windows was to go through the Window menu and choose the file you'd like to work on. Or, if you were adventurous, you could always do (our personal favorite) the window/palette shuffle and just try to maneuver your open windows around the screen. You'll be happy to know that Illustrator CS2 for the PC now has a keyboard shortcut to switch between open windows. Just press Control-Shift-F6 to cycle through each open window.

CHAPTER 2 • Viewing, Doing, Undoing, and More   29

DEFAULT WORKSPACE TO THE RESCUE!

With Illustrator CS2, we now have the ability to use workspaces. Basically, a workspace is the way that, well, the workspace is set up (i.e., palette and Toolbox locations). This is huge if you're like us and your palettes become a jumbled mess halfway through working on your images, or if you're an instructor in a classroom and find it tedious to manually reset palette locations of 20 or 30 computers after a class. To help out, just choose Window>Workspace>[Default]. This will reset the Toolbox and the palettes to their default locations.

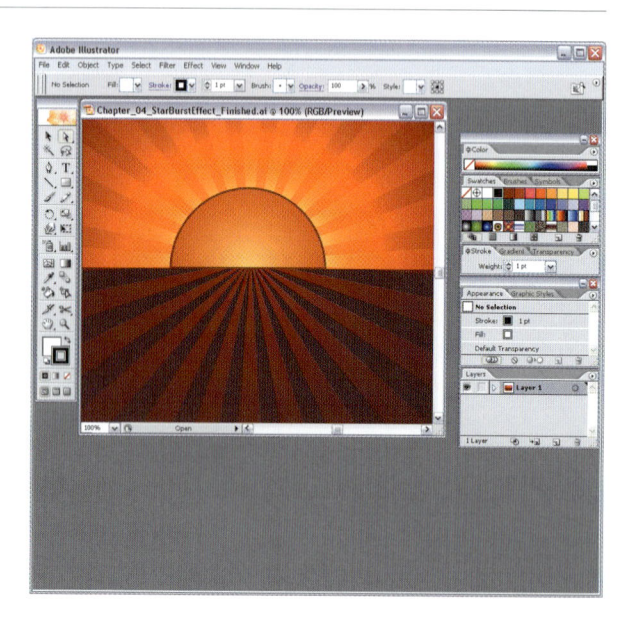

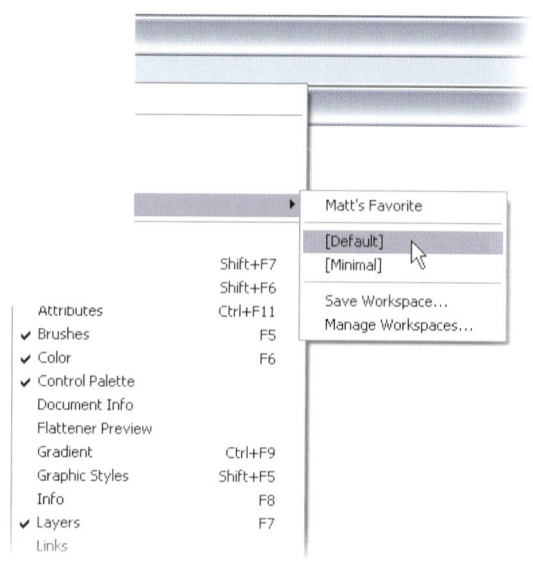

CHAPTER 2 • Viewing, Doing, Undoing, and More

YOUR OWN PERSONAL WORKSPACE

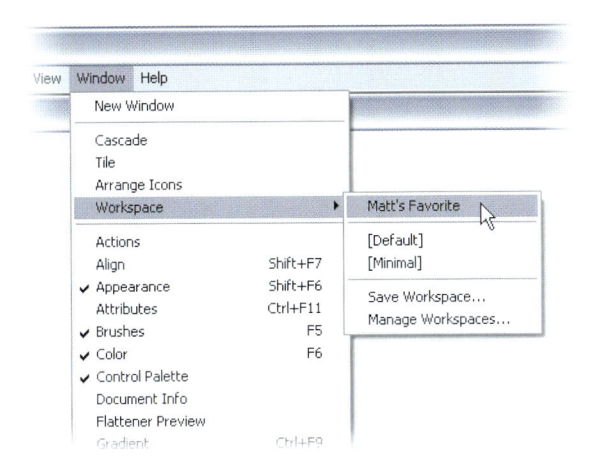

One of the most useful areas of the new Workspace feature in CS2 is the ability to create your own personal workspaces. To do this, set up the palettes you want where you want them. Then choose Window>Workspace>Save Workspace. Give it a meaningful name and you're in business. Now, if your palettes ever get to the point where everything is a mess (come on, you know it happens to you), then just go under Window>Workspace and pick your own personal workspace. It'll be right near the top of the menu.

GIVE YOUR CUSTOM WORKSPACE A SHORTCUT

Although you can save your own workspace (Window>Workspace>Save Workspace) in CS2, you cannot assign it a keyboard shortcut. Instead, record an Action: Click the Create New Action button at the bottom of the Actions palette (Window>Actions), give it a function-key shortcut and press Begin Recording. Then use the flyout menu in the Actions palette to choose Insert Menu Item and go to Window>Workspace to select your custom workspace. Press the Stop Playing/Recording button at the bottom of the Actions palette, and from now on you can press that F-key to change to your workspace.

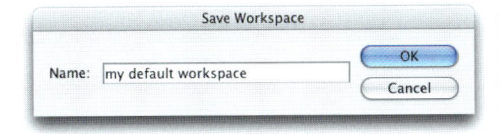

CHAPTER 2 • Viewing, Doing, Undoing, and More   31

CONTROL BAR GETTING IN YOUR WAY?

The new context-sensitive Control palette in Illustrator CS2 is a great way to discover new features and find existing features faster. The ability to access selection-based tools from a single location eliminates the need for multiple palettes. However, sometimes it can be cluttered, especially if you find you don't use many of its features. If this is the case, then turn some of them off. Just click the small right-facing arrow all the way at the far right of the palette to get the flyout menu. Then click on any items you don't want it to display anymore.

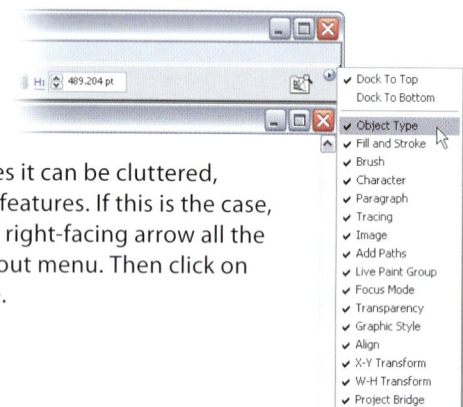

PALETTE SHORTCUTS AND CONTROL PALETTE ALL IN ONE

If you use the new Control Palette often, but still have the need to use some of the extended settings that normally appear in a specific palette, then just click on any of the setting names that are underlined and highlighted in blue. For example, the Control Palette displays Opacity, but no Blend Mode settings that you'd normally find in the Transparency palette. Instead of moving to the Transparency palette, just click on the word Opacity and a small palette will pop up below it allowing you to change more than just Opacity.

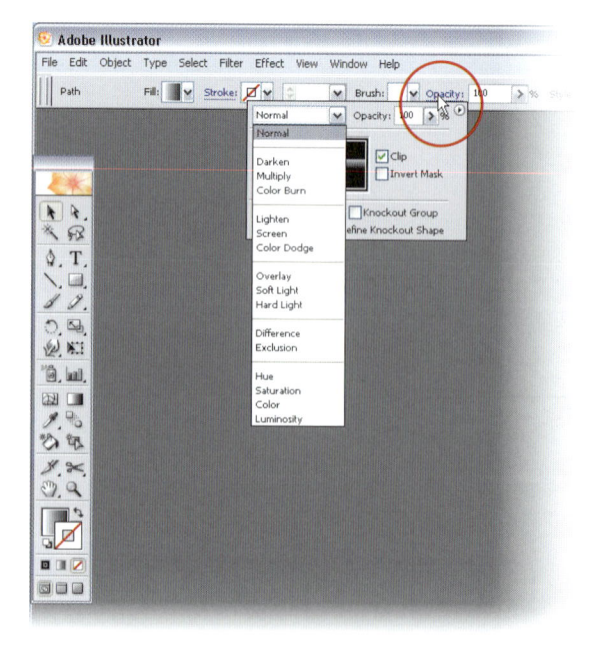

CHAPTER 2 • Viewing, Doing, Undoing, and More

CENTER THAT GUIDE

If you drag a guide from the ruler onto the page and you want to make sure it is centered horizontally or vertically, try this: Press Command-Option-; (PC: Control-Alt-;) to unlock the guides. If necessary, make sure that only the one guide is selected by deselecting every guide and then clicking on the guide you want centered. Then in the Align palette (Window>Align), use the flyout menu to select Align to Artboard. Click on the Vertical Align Center icon (or Horizontal Align Center icon, depending on the direction of the guide).

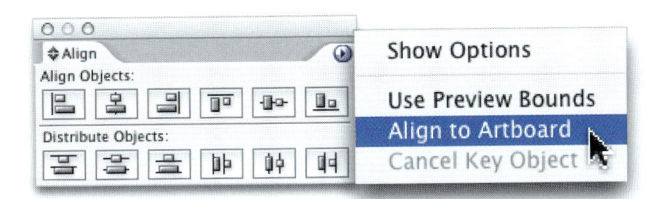

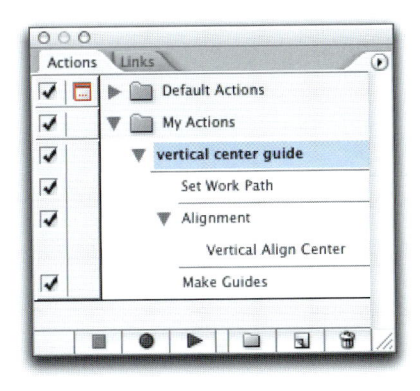

CENTER GUIDES AUTOMATICALLY

You may be thinking, why not record an action to add centered guides automatically? (I know I was.) You can, but with a bit of a trick. Problem is, you cannot record adding a guide to the page, so you have to use another method. Use the Pen tool (P) (with the Shift key held down) to draw a horizontal line that is wider than the current page, and keep the line selected. In the Actions palette under the Window menu, click the Create New Action icon, give your action a name, and press Begin Recording. Then use the Action palette's flyout menu and choose Insert Select Path. Next, click on the Vertical Align Center icon in the Align palette (be sure the Align to Artboard option is selected in the palette's flyout menu), followed by View>Guides>Make Guides. Click the Stop Playing/Recording icon in the Actions palette. Of course, you could also record an action for a vertically centered guide and/or both horizontally and vertically centered guides.

CHAPTER 2 • Viewing, Doing, Undoing, and More

CHANGE GUIDE DIRECTION

As in many applications, you can add non-printing guides to a document by clicking on one of the rulers and dragging onto the document. As you click on a ruler and drag a guide onto the document, the guide will be based on the ruler you've used (top ruler creates horizontal guides, side ruler creates vertical guides). To override this, press the Option key (PC: Alt key) as you drag from the ruler and you'll get the opposite guide. (Press and release Option/Alt to switch back and forth.)

Horizontal guide pulled from top ruler

Guide changed to vertical using this tip

MAKE GUIDES FROM OBJECTS

Not satisfied with only horizontal or vertical guides (and why should you be)? Then make your own. Create any object you want to use as a guide, make sure it is selected, and then from the View menu choose Guides>Make Guides (or press Command-5 [PC: Control-5]). To turn your guide back to a regular object, first unlock the guide using Command-Option-; (PC: Control-Alt-;), then use View>Guides>Release Guides (Command-Option-5 [PC: Control-Option-5]).

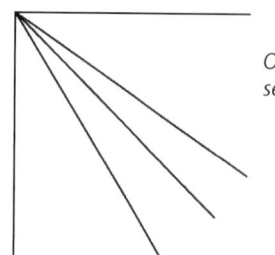

Object selected

Object converted to guides

34 CHAPTER 2 • Viewing, Doing, Undoing, and More

LOCK A GUIDE TO AN OBJECT

If you want to have a guide that is locked to an object so that the guide moves with that object, here's the secret. Create and position a path that you'll use as the guide with either the Pen tool (P) or Line tool (\). Select the path and the other object(s) and press Command-G (PC: Control-G) to group all the objects together. Deselect everything (Command-Shift-A [PC: Control-Shift-A]), and then use the Direct Selection tool (A) to select only the path that you want as a guide. Press Command-5 (PC: Control-5) to convert the path to a guide. From then on, the guide will move with the group.

Path and object grouped

Path as guide locked to object

CHANGE LOCKED GUIDE INTO A PATH

To quickly change a locked guide into an editable path, hold down Command-Shift (PC: Control-Shift) and double-click on the guide. One very practical way to make use of this shortcut is when you want to adjust a guide. Use this shortcut, move the guide, then press Command-5 (PC: Control-5) to turn it back into a guide.

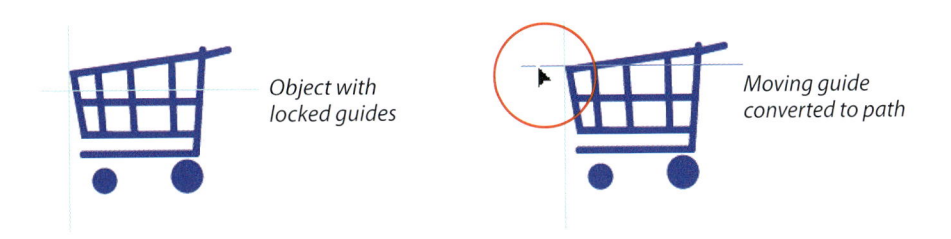

Object with locked guides

Moving guide converted to path

CHAPTER 2 • Viewing, Doing, Undoing, and More

LOCK EVERYTHING ELSE

If you have one or more objects selected and you want to lock everything else, you can do that in one easy step. After selecting the object(s) you want to keep unlocked, press Command-Option-Shift-2 (PC: Control-Alt-Shift-2). To unlock everything, press Command-Option-2 (PC: Control-Alt-2).

GET A NEW PERSPECTIVE ON GUIDES

In a previous tip, you saw how you can turn any object into a guide. Take this a step further and start using guides as a perspective grid. Just draw straight lines that match the perspective of the objects you'll be drawing. Once you're happy with your perspective grid, turn the lines into guides by choosing View>Guides>Make Guides. Then you can ensure that you'll be drawing to proper perspective throughout your illustration. You can even turn on Smart Guides (Command-U [PC: Control-U]) to help you align your paths to this new perspective grid.

36   CHAPTER 2 • Viewing, Doing, Undoing, and More

AUTO ADD RULERS TO EVERY NEW DOCUMENT

If you use rulers often in Illustrator and get frustrated by having to add them into each new document, then this tip is for you. You can automatically add rulers to each new document by modifying the Illustrator startup file located in your Applications or Program Files, in Adobe Illustrator CS2, in the Plug-ins folder. There are two files, so be sure to change both the CMYK and RGB files.

1. Quit Illustrator.
2. This step is optional. In the Adobe Illustrator CS2 Plug-ins folder, duplicate the current default startup file—Adobe Illustrator Startup_CMYK or Adobe Illustrator Startup_RGB—and give it a different name. (This creates a copy of the original startup file in case you need it again. You only need to do this once to back up the original if you want.)
3. Open one of the default startup files—Adobe Illustrator Startup_CMYK or Adobe Illustrator Startup_RGB—depending on which type of document you intend to use.
4. Choose View>Show Rulers.
5. Now, here's the trick. You can't just save this file because you haven't really made any changes that Illustrator will register yet. So, create a rectangle on the artboard using the Rectangle tool (M). Then just delete it.
6. Save the new file as Adobe Illustrator Startup _CMYK or Adobe Illustrator Startup_RGB (depending on which you opened) in the Plug-ins folder.
7. Restart Illustrator.

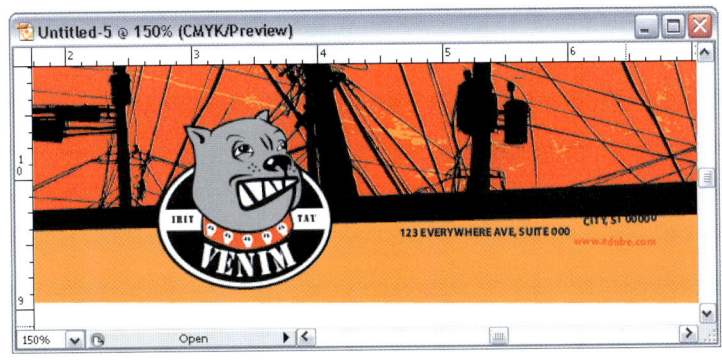

CHAPTER 2 • Viewing, Doing, Undoing, and More

MEASURE FROM WHERE YOU WANT

By default, the rulers display with the top left of the page set to zero for the horizontal ruler, while the vertical ruler displays zero at the bottom left of the page. To change the ruler origin, click on the top left corner of the rulers and drag to wherever you want to set zero.

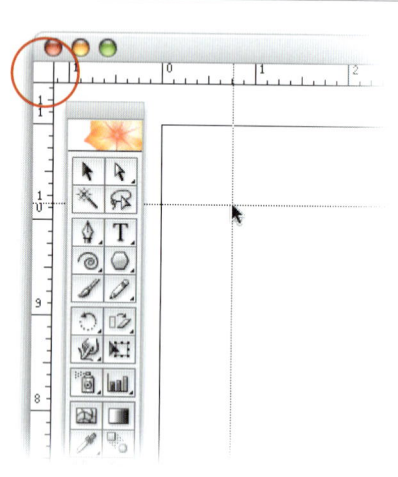

RESET THE RULERS

If you have changed the ruler origins and want to put them back to the default setting, double-click on the top left corner between the two rulers.

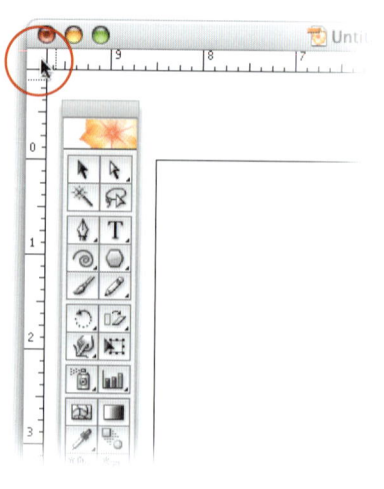

CHANGE RULER MEASUREMENT

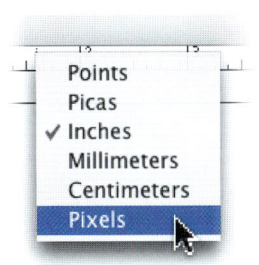

The unit of measurement in Illustrator is determined in the Preferences (Illustrator>Preferences>Units & Display Performance [PC: Edit>Preferences>Units & Display Performance]). This will affect all aspects of the program that use measurements, including the rulers. However, if you need to quickly override the current measurements, just Control-click (PC: Right-click) anywhere on the ruler and choose your new unit of measurement.

MEASURE THE WAY YOU WANT

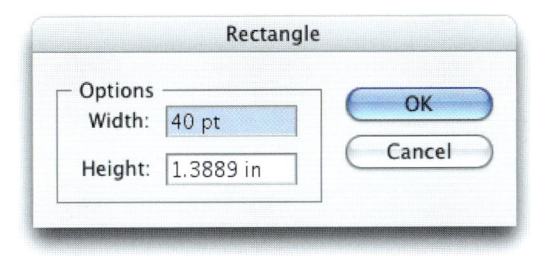

You set the default general unit of measurement in your Preferences (under the Units & Display Performance category) and that becomes the unit used by every dialog and palette (except Stroke and Type). It is possible, however, to override that default simply by typing in the unit you want to use. For example, if your default is set to inches, you can create a rectangle that's 40 points wide by clicking once with the Rectangle tool (M) on the artboard and then typing "40 pt" in the dialog. Use these shortcuts: in for inches, cm for centimeters, pt for points, px for pixels, or mm for millimeters.

CHAPTER 2 • Viewing, Doing, Undoing, and More   39

MULTIPLE TOOLS?

Any tool in the Toolbox that displays a small triangle in the bottom right-hand corner has a set of "hidden" tools that can be popped up by clicking-and-holding on the current tool. Instead of popping up hidden tool menus all the time, make your life easier by tearing off commonly used tool menus. Just click-and-hold on the tool to pop up the other tool choices, and then drag over to the bar at the end of the tool menu. When you release the mouse, the tool menu becomes a floating palette that you can position anywhere you want. If you're really efficient (lazy?) you can add multiple tool menus all over the place. Tear off tool menus and position them all over the screen. This way, if you have a large monitor, you can always have a Type tool nearby without moving too far.

YOUR LOGO READY ANYTIME

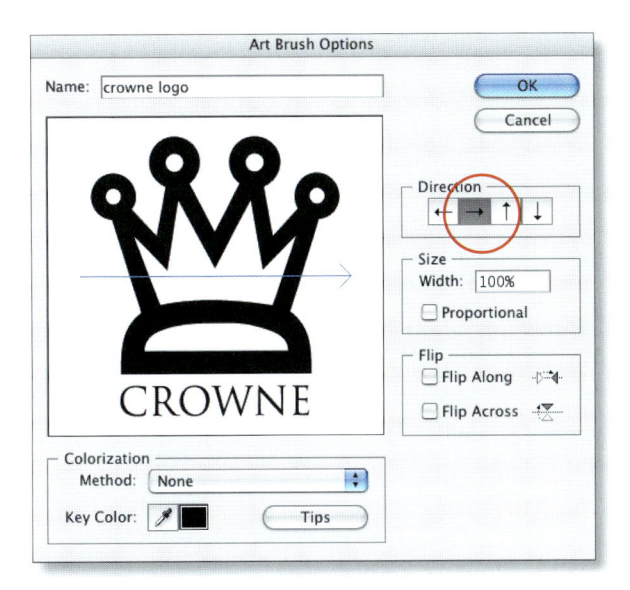

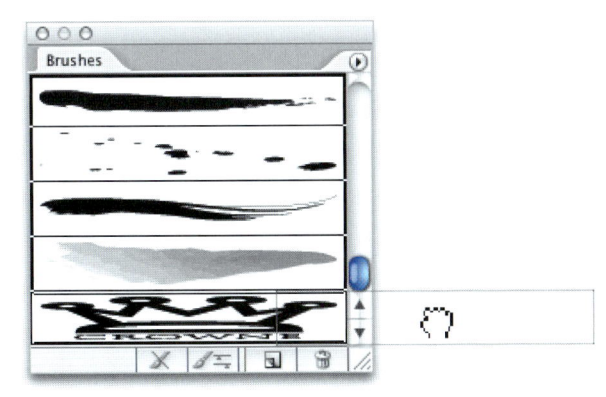

Here's a simple way to have your logo (or any other art you need) readily available in every new document you create. Open either the CMYK or RGB Adobe Illustrator Startup file (found in Illustrator CS2>Plug-ins) and paste your logo into that document. Select your logo (if it has text, you'll have to create an outline by going to Type>Create Outlines) and from the Brushes palette (under the Window menu) click on the New Brush icon. Choose New Art Brush as the type of brush and in the Art Brush Options dialog, click on the second Direction symbol so the arrow displays from left to right. Name your brush and click OK. Delete the artwork and save the document. From then on, you'll be able to click-and-drag the logo from the Brushes palette onto any new document.

CHAPTER 2 • Viewing, Doing, Undoing, and More

SIMULATE PAPER COLOR

To help simulate what your artwork would look like printed on colored paper, you can change the color of the artboard. From the File menu, choose Document Setup and navigate to the Transparency category. In the View section, click on the top swatch to choose your paper color, then check Simulate Colored Paper. Click OK and the entire artboard will display in your chosen color. This eliminates the need to draw a separate box filled with the paper color. *Note:* The simulated paper will not display properly if you choose Show Transparency Grid from the View menu.

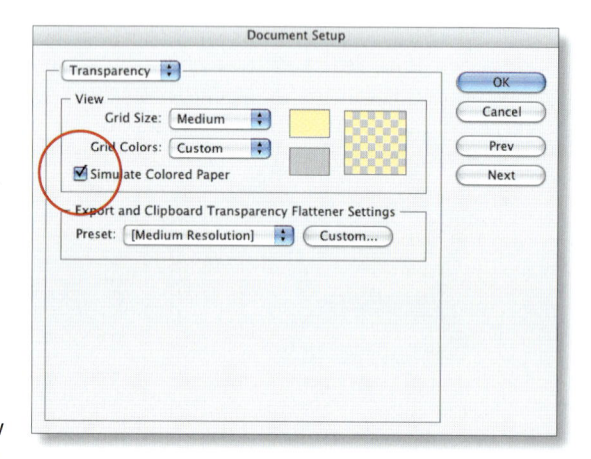

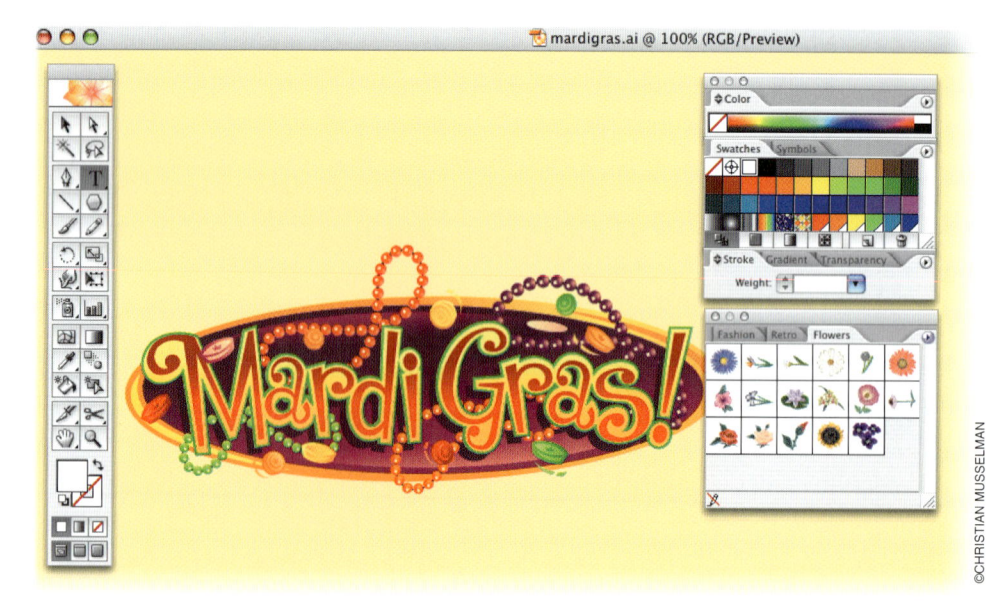

CHAPTER 2 • Viewing, Doing, Undoing, and More

SHOW/HIDE CENTER POINT

Some objects, such as rectangles and ellipses, always show the center point, while others, such as polygons, do not. You can choose whether or not to show the center point using the Attributes palette in the Window menu. With the object selected, look in the Attributes palette and click on the small Show Center or Don't Show Center icon. This does not change the default setting for that tool. Instead, you'll have to do this for each object.

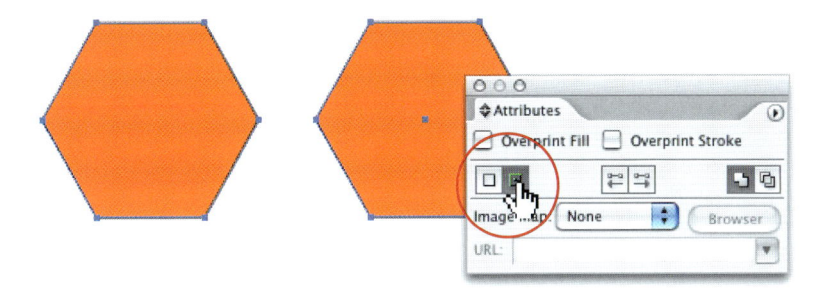

ANGLED GRID

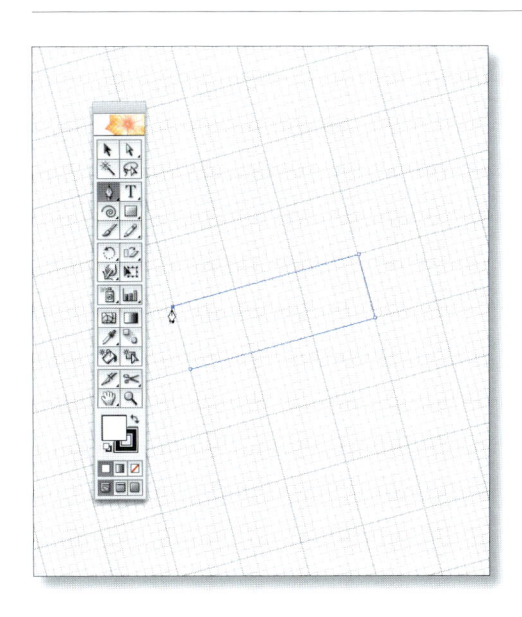

You can show a non-printing grid by using View>Show Grid, or by pressing Command-" (PC: Control-"). Once the grid is showing, there's no rule that says it must be perfectly horizontal—why not angle the grid to help you create angled objects? Just go to the Preferences dialog by pressing Command-K (PC: Control-K) and change the Constrain Angle field from zero degrees to whatever angle you want your grid to follow. Hold down the Shift key to force tools to precisely follow the angled grid. Once you're done, put it back to zero.

CHAPTER 2 • Viewing, Doing, Undoing, and More   43

EVERYTHING YOU WANTED TO KNOW ABOUT…

Your document. Want to know what fonts you used, how many objects there are, or if images are linked or embedded? Try the Document Info palette, found under the Window menu. Then use the flyout menu to access all kinds of information about your document. You can even save the information as a text file by choosing Save, in the flyout menu.

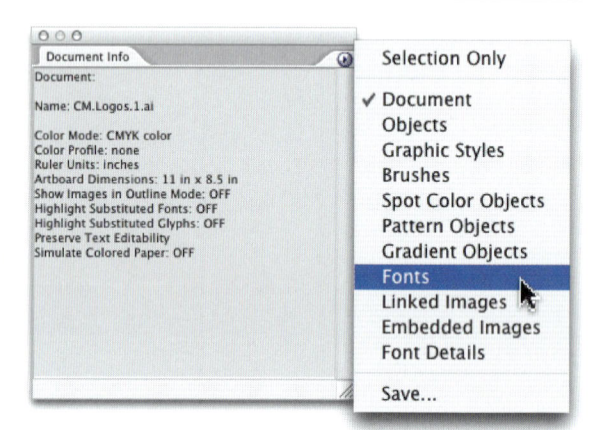

GET OBJECT INFO

To see a quick summary of everything you need to know about a selected object, use the Document Info palette (Window>Document Info), and choose Selection Only from the flyout menu. Go back to the flyout menu to view other options such as Spot Color Objects, Fonts, Linked Objects, or to save a text file containing all the information.

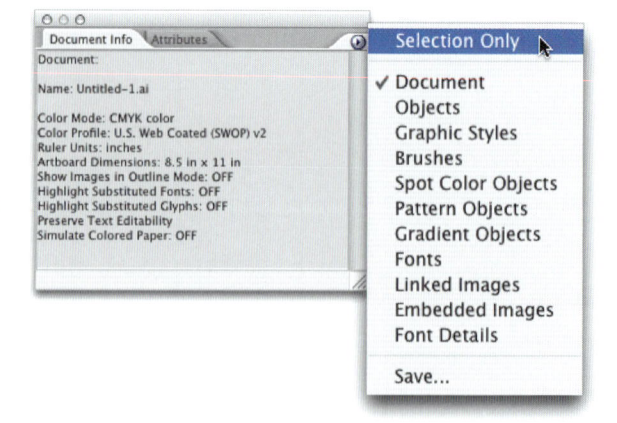

ACTIONS WITHIN ACTIONS

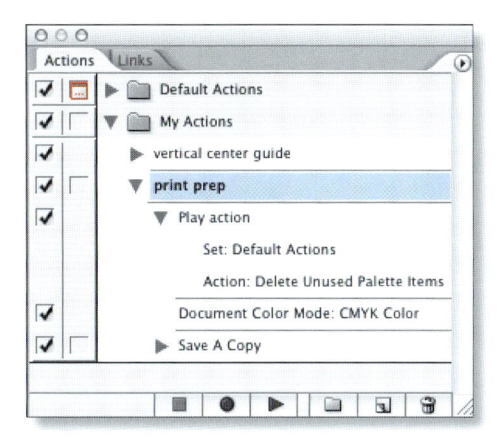

If you've recorded some actions for key operations, you can make use of these actions in another action. Confused? Here's an example: You have previously recorded an action that scales, rotates, and copies a selected object. Now you want to build on those steps and add to them. Rather than re-creating these steps, the first thing you record in the new action is to play the existing action. (Click the Create New Action icon, play the actions you want, then stop recording.) Simply put, you create an action that plays one or more actions. (It's easier than it sounds—try it, you'll like it!)

SAVE THAT VIEW

If you find yourself zooming in and out and scrolling a lot in a document, try saving specific views. To do this, simply change to the view you wish to save by zooming in or out and positioning your view. Then from the View menu choose New View, name the view, and from then on that view will be available at the bottom of the View menu. You can even create views that are in Outline mode rather than the Preview mode. The views you create are saved with the document itself (they are specific to that document as opposed to being global views).

CHAPTER 2 • Viewing, Doing, Undoing, and More   45

Illustrator CS2
KillerTips

TWO VIEWS, ONE DOCUMENT

It's often tempting to zoom way in to look at fine details in your document—remember, Illustrator lets you zoom in to 6,400%. At the same time, it's easy to get carried away and zoom in more than you need, or at least more than the naked eye can see. Here's one way to have the best of both worlds. Create a second view of your document and keep it at Actual Size while you zoom in on the other window. From the Window menu, choose New Window, then manually adjust the window sizes so you can see both windows and pick a zoom level for each window.

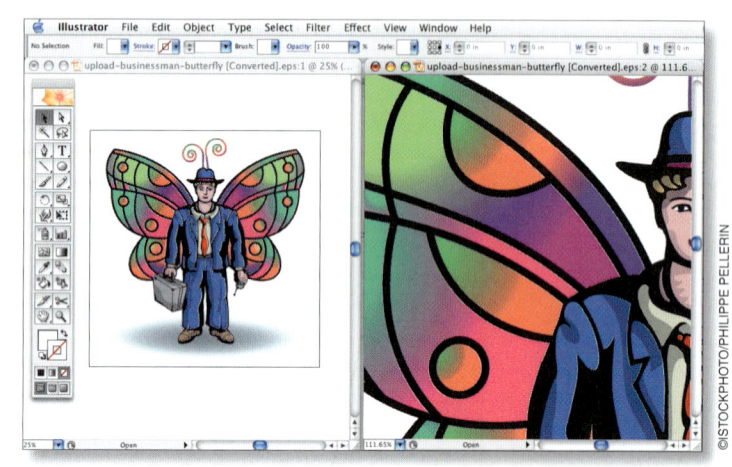

PINPOINT IN THE NAVIGATOR

One of the advantages of using the Navigator palette (found under the Window menu) is that no matter how big your document is, you'll always see a thumbnail view in the Navigator. The red box indicates the portion of the document you are currently viewing in your window. To take full advantage of this thumbnail view and zoom in to a specific location in the document, hold down the Command key (PC: Control key) and click-and-drag in the Navigator thumbnail view. To return to a smaller view, Command-click (PC: Control-click) on the thumbnail again.

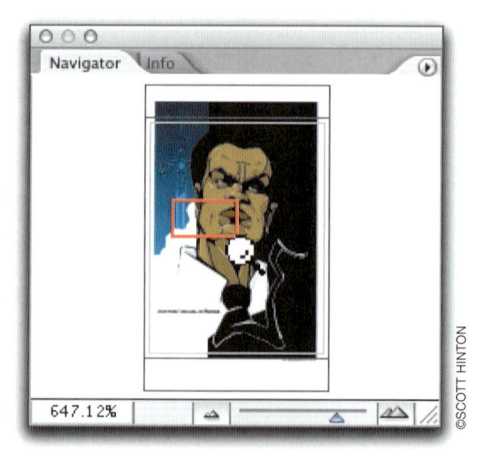

46   CHAPTER 2 • Viewing, Doing, Undoing, and More

HIDE AND SHOW PALETTES

To make more room to work, temporarily hide the floating palettes by pressing the Tab key (with any tool active other than a Type tool). The Tab key acts like a toggle switch, so to show the palettes again, press Tab again. The only problem is that the Toolbox disappears too, so if you want to keep the Toolbox and hide the rest of the palettes, press Shift-Tab. As before, press the same shortcut to show the palettes again. (This is a better method than the alternative, which is spending all your time dragging palettes around to get them out of the way.)

©DAVID POUNDS

CHAPTER 2 • Viewing, Doing, Undoing, and More   47

CHANGE YOUR MIND IN MID-ZOOM

If you start to click-and-drag with the Zoom tool (Z) to zoom in on a specific area and then realize you've positioned your mouse in the wrong place, don't let go of the mouse button. Press-and-hold the Spacebar, reposition your cursor, then let go of the Spacebar to continue selecting the zoom area. Once you try this one, you'll find yourself using it more often than you think.

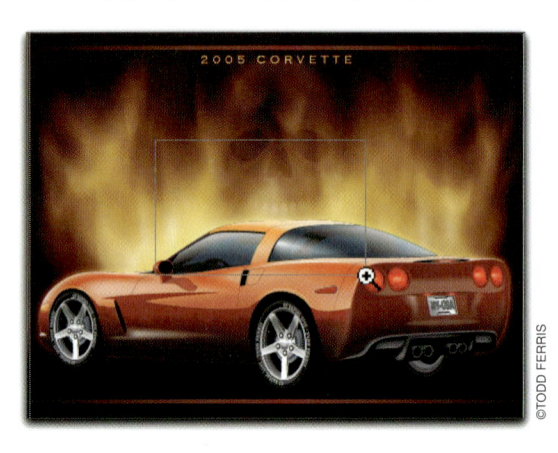

THE ONE-SLIDE SLIDE SHOW

To present your artwork without the distraction of floating palettes and menus, follow these steps: From the View menu, choose Hide Artboard, then go back to the View menu and choose Hide Page Tiling. Now press the Tab key followed by F and F again. Tab hides all the palettes and pressing F cycles through full-screen views, one of which is Full Screen mode with no menus. If the rulers are showing, press Command-R (PC: Control-R) to hide them. (You can still use the Hand tool [H] to position your graphics, or use your zoom shortcuts to change your magnification.) To return to Standard Screen mode, press Tab and F, and then from the View menu show whatever else you want (rulers, artboard, page tiling, etc.).

Before   *After*

REMEMBER ONE PALETTE SHORTCUT

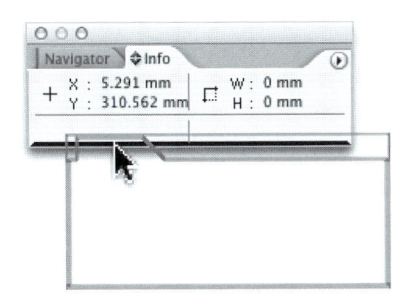

If you are having a hard time remembering keyboard shortcuts to show and hide all the floating palettes, focus on one shortcut. Pick a palette shortcut that you do remember (such as F8 for Info), and then dock other palettes into that one. To do this, click on the palette tab and drag onto the bottom of the chosen palette until a solid line appears. This will dock the palettes together, and now the one shortcut will hide and show multiple palettes at once.

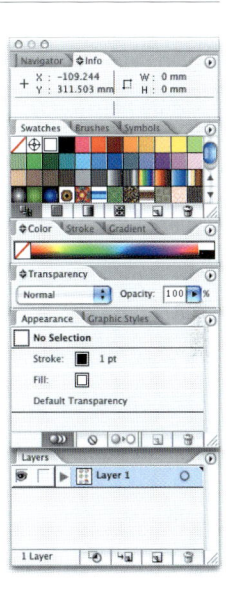

ZOOM TOOL SHORTCUT

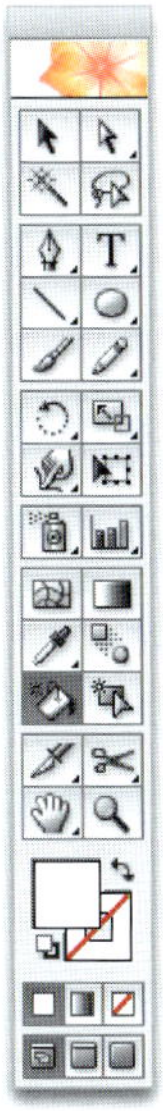

Rather than moving all the way over to the Toolbox to click on the Zoom tool, press Command-Spacebar (PC: Control-Spacebar). This will interrupt whatever tool you are using and activate the Zoom tool. Click to zoom in, and then release the keys to return to whatever tool you were using. To zoom out, add the Option key (PC: Alt key), making the shortcut Command-Option-Spacebar (PC: Control-Alt-Spacebar).

CHAPTER 2 • Viewing, Doing, Undoing, and More   49

HAND TOOL SHORTCUT

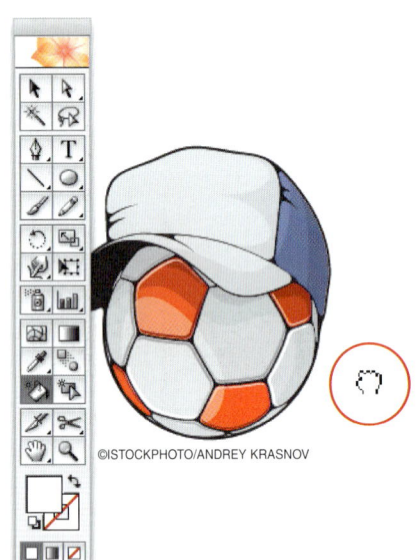

Don't bother clicking on the Hand tool in the Toolbox to scroll your view, either. Just hold down the Spacebar. This will activate the Hand tool so you can scroll, then let go of the Spacebar to continue with your current tool. This works with all tools except the Type tools. (There is a trick, but you'll have to peek at the text chapter.)

KEEP ONLY SELECTED OBJECTS

As a quick way to hide all the objects you're not currently working on, try this: Select the object or objects you want to work on, then press Command-Option-Shift-3 (PC: Control-Alt-Shift-3). All the unselected objects will be hidden. To show all objects again, press Command-Option-3 (PC: Control-Alt-3).

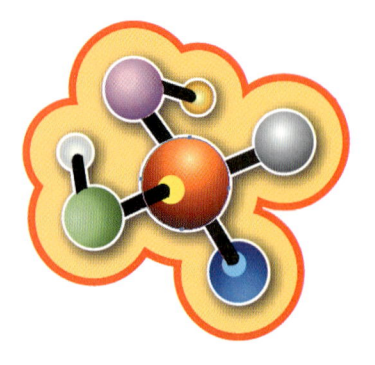

50   CHAPTER 2 • Viewing, Doing, Undoing, and More

BE PRECISE

If you want a more precise cursor, press the Caps Lock key. For many (but not all) tools, the tool cursor will change to a crosshair. To switch back to the regular tool cursors, release the Caps Lock key. Here's another way to look at this: If you use a tool and suddenly it isn't looking like the normal tool icon anymore, chances are the Caps Lock key is on. Turn off Caps Lock and there's your tool icon again.

FRONT AND CENTER

To ensure that an object is exactly centered on your page, use the Align palette (Window> Align or Shift-F7) with one minor change. From the palette's flyout menu, choose Align to Artboard. Then click on the Horizontal and Vertical Align Center icons to align your selected object to the page.

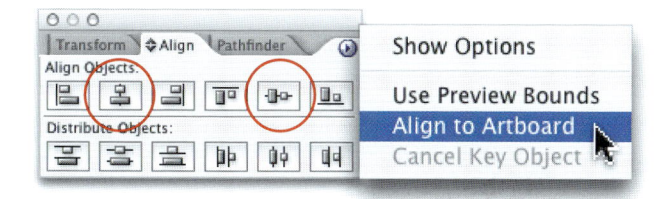

CHAPTER 2 • Viewing, Doing, Undoing, and More   51

SEEING RED

If you're working on artwork that contains lots of red, the red View Box in the Navigator palette (Window>Navigator) might be a little difficult to see. In this situation (or if you just don't like the color red), you can change the color of the View Box by using the flyout menu in the Navigator palette and choosing Palette Options. In the resulting dialog, choose the color you'd like to use for the View Box.

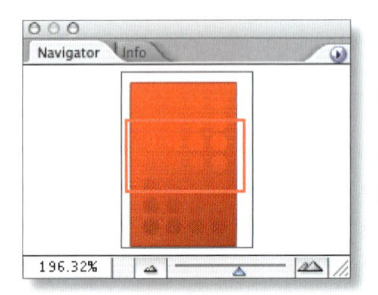

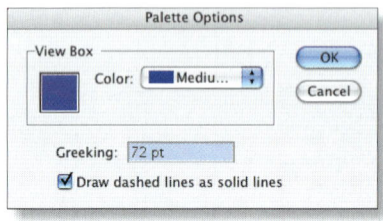

ADD THE UNRECORDABLE

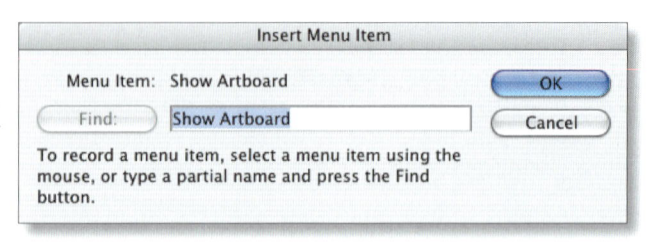

There are some functions that cannot be recorded in an action—such as painting tools, tool options, effects, view commands, and preferences. (In action-speak these are called unactionable.) To add these functions into an action, click the Create New Action icon in the Actions palette (Window>Actions), and choose Insert Menu Item from the palette's flyout menu to record non-recordable operations. With the Insert Menu Item dialog open, go to the menu command you'd like to use and it will be added automatically in the dialog.

52 CHAPTER 2 • Viewing, Doing, Undoing, and More

Illustrator CS2 KillerTips

HIDE YOUR GUIDES IN ONE CLICK

Although it is possible to hide/show guides with the shortcut Command-; (PC: Control-;), you can give yourself even more control by putting guides on their own layer. Click the Create New Layer icon in the Layers palette (under the Window menu), name the layer "guides," and then add guides to that layer. Then you can hide the guides by clicking on the Eye icon beside the layer name. To take this a step further, you could create several guide layers to give yourself even more options over which guides you'd like to be visible.

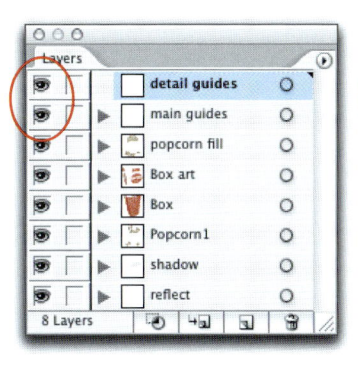

FREE RESOURCES

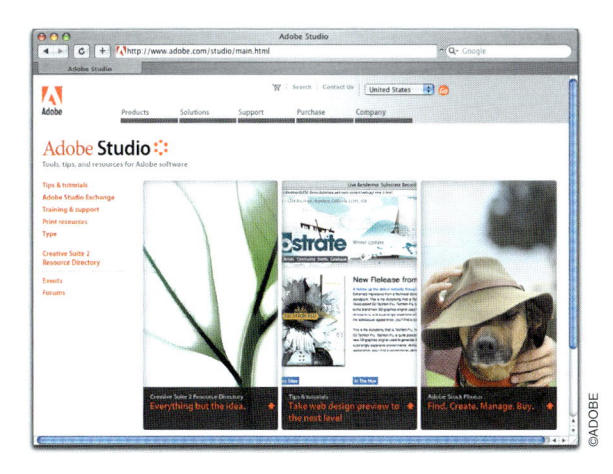

If you need some tips or tutorials, or you would like to download brushes, symbols, styles, actions, etc., check out the downloads through the Adobe Studio Exchange website: www.adobe.com/studio/main.html. Click on Adobe Studio Exchange on the left side of the screen and choose the downloads you're interested in from the pop-up menu.

CHAPTER 2 • Viewing, Doing, Undoing, and More   53

BACK TO BASICS

You may encounter situations when Illustrator starts behaving strangely. For example, tools aren't working the way they should or colors or patterns aren't displaying properly. In cases like this, you probably need to reset the Illustrator Preferences. Although it is possible to find the file and delete it, there is an easier way, especially since you need to launch Illustrator to create new preferences anyway. To reset the preference settings as you launch Illustrator CS2, hold down Command-Option-Shift (PC: Control-Alt-Shift). *Note:* Unlike previous versions, no dialog will appear, but the settings will be reset.

DON'T SQUINT, CLICK

Having trouble focusing in on those tiny little fields in a palette? Instead, just click on the name of the field and it will highlight. Then type away and you're all set!

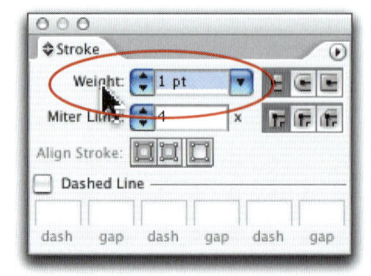

NEW DOCUMENT THE SAME AS LAST TIME

To create a new document with the same settings (width, height, orientation, color mode) as the last document you created, press Command-Option-N (PC: Control-Alt-N).

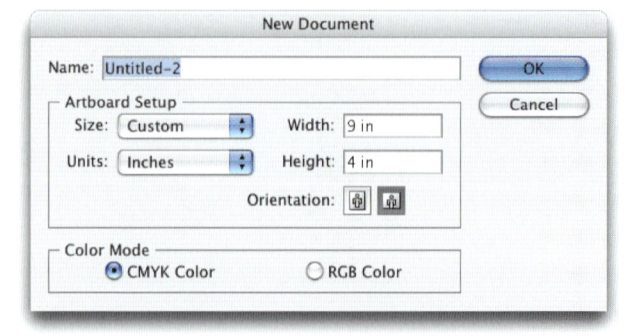

54   **CHAPTER 2** • Viewing, Doing, Undoing, and More

RESET THE PAGE

You can use the Page tool (nested under the Hand tool in the Toolbox) to set the page tiling in a document—wherever you position the mouse will be the bottom left corner of the page tiling (this also represents the printable area on your printer). If you've experimented with the Page tool and you want to get the page tiling back to "normal" (i.e., centered relative to the page), double-click on the Page tool in the Toolbox.

CHANGE TOOLS QUICKLY

There are many sets of tools that you access in the Toolbox by pressing-and-holding on the visible tool, which pops up a menu of additional tools. Another method to switch quickly between tools in a set is to hold down the Option key (PC: Alt key) and click on the visible tool. Each time you click, you'll switch to the next tool in the set.

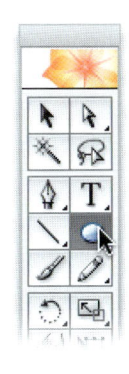

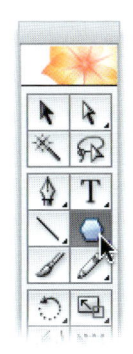

CHAPTER 2 • Viewing, Doing, Undoing, and More

MULTIPLE PAGES?

Some people wish that they could create multipage documents in Illustrator. Well, with quite a bit of effort, you can (if you have Acrobat Distiller). First, go to File>New to create a document that is the size of all your pages side by side. For example, a four-page letter-size document would be set up as a landscape page with a width of 34 inches (8.5 x 4) and a height of 11 inches. Either choose View>Show Page Tiling or create guides to help you show the separation of the pages. Once you've finished designing your "superpage" and are ready to turn it into a multipage document, go to File>Print and in the Media section choose your orientation (we use Letter for Size, and in the Orientation section check the Portrait Up icon). Go to the Setup category (in the list on the left side of the dialog) and set the Tiling to Tile Full Pages. Then create a Postscript file by changing the Printer pop-up menu to Adobe PostScript File. (*Note:* You may need to change your PPD pop-up menu to select the correct print driver, depending on your system's setup.) Click the Save button and give the file a name followed by ".ps" as the file extension. Now launch Acrobat Distiller, open your saved PS document, and the Distiller will save the PDF file as a multipage document.

CHAPTER 2 • Viewing, Doing, Undoing, and More

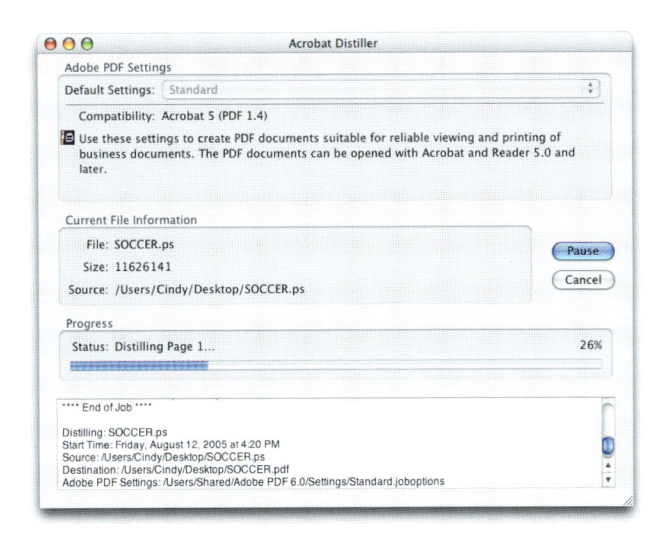

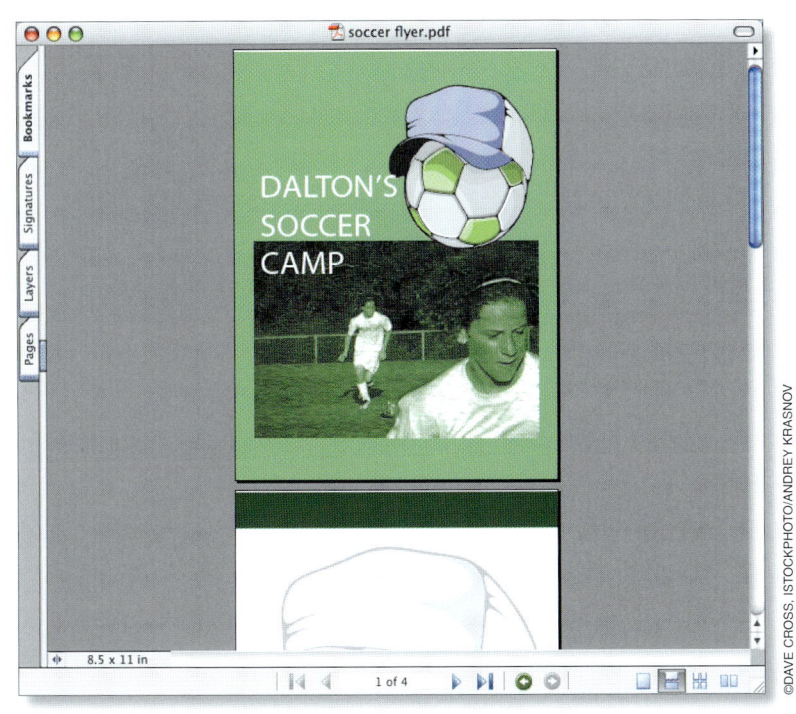

Illustrator CS2
KillerTips

CHAPTER 2 • Viewing, Doing, Undoing, and More

Tool Time

CREATING IN ILLUSTRATOR CS2

You can never have enough tools. The more tools you have at your disposal, the more options you have for constructing your

Tool Time
creating in illustrator CS2

job. Just the other day, Matt was at The Home Depot considering what tools were missing from his collection—tools that would make his life easier. You're probably expecting me to cleverly relate this to using Illustrator's tools, but I really wasn't planning to. I just wanted to talk about our fascination with power tools and the tools we hope to get someday. In fact, just in case you're feeling generous, I can happily provide our wish list of dream tools. Meanwhile, I guess we'll have to make do with this collection of tips on using Illustrator's tools to create stuff (as I imagine, I can hear the sweet sound of a radial saw and smell the aroma of freshly cut pine).

Illustrator CS2 KillerTips

PHOTO INSIDE OF TYPE

To fill text with a photo and keep the text editable, place an image into Illustrator (File>Place), then create some text with the Type tool (T) and position it on top of the photo. With the Selection tool, select both the photo and the type, and from the Object menu, select Clipping Mask>Make, or press Command-7 (PC: Control-7). (In our example, we added a stroke by selecting the text with the Selection tool and changing the Stroke color in the Toolbox to black to make the type easier to see.) Use the Type tool to edit the text or the Direct Selection tool (A) to move the photo. To cancel the effect completely, select the photo and text, then go back to the Object menu and choose Clipping Mask>Release. Let's review the most important aspect of this technique: The masking object (in this case, the text) needs to be on top.

©DAVE CROSS

START WITH A FONT

Stuck for a design idea, or searching for some clip art? Why not check out your built-in symbol fonts such as Webdings, Dingbats, etc.? Get the Type tool (T) and click-and-drag out a text box. Choose a font type and pick a large size. Open the Glyphs palette (Window>Type>Glyphs) and use this palette to pick the shape (letter) you want to use. Once you've found a design you like, double-click on it to add it to the text box. Then, select the symbol in the text box with the Selection tool and from the Type menu, choose Create Outlines (or press Command-Shift-O [PC: Control-Shift-O]). Use the Direct Selection tool (A) to edit and work with the object(s).

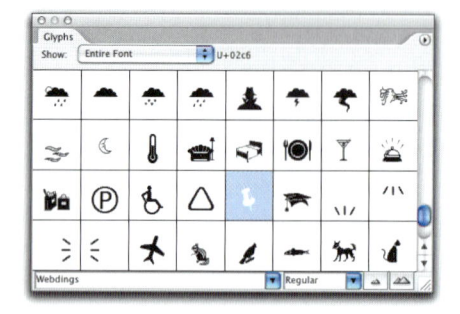

60   CHAPTER 3 • Creating in Illustrator CS2

Illustrator CS2 KillerTips

MAPPING MADE EASY

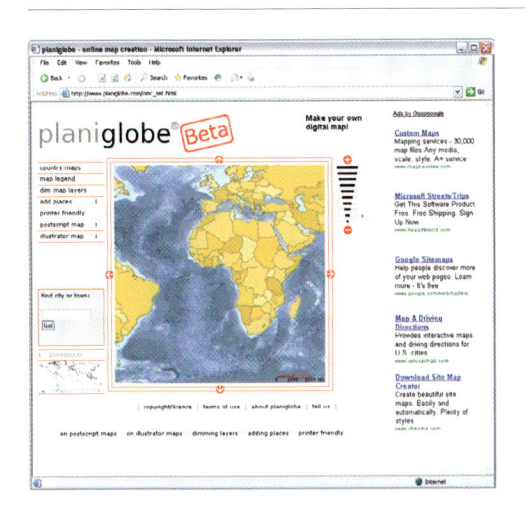

Looking for high-resolution maps and don't want to create your own? Planiglobe.com is a website that can generate them for you. You can generate maps interactively, zoom in and out, search for places, and add your own locations to a map. The PS and .ai versions (which you can download) are compatible to the PostScript® Level 1 language and the Illustrator® 7.0 format, respectively.

FIND YOUR FAVORITE LOGO?

This site is actually on our Most Valuable list. It's called Brandsoftheworld.com and can be found at, you guessed it, www.brandsoftheworld.com. The site is intended for browsing and exchange of the world's famous brand logos. The main goal behind the website is to enable designers to access vector forms of well-known brand logos that they can use in their presentations, given the permission of the copyright owner. The website also enables designers to upload their own works and professional details. Check it out—you'll love it!

CHAPTER 3 • Creating in Illustrator CS2   61

CHANGE STAR SHAPE, PART ONE

When you click-and-drag with the Star tool (nested under the Rectangle tool in the Toolbox) to create a star (duh), the distance between the outer radius (Radius 1) and inner radius (Radius 2) remains constant (Star 1). To experiment with the star shape, start to drag with the Star tool, then press-and-hold the Command key (PC: Control key). The inner radius will remain constant, so as you drag outward, you'll create longer points on the star (Star 2). Keep in mind that from then on, every subsequent star will have the same relationship between the two radii. To change this, you'll have to click once, enter a new value for Radius 2 and click OK (you can delete the star if you like).

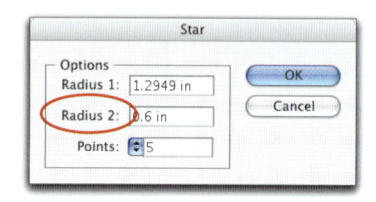

Star 1   *Star 2*

CHANGE STAR SHAPE, PART TWO

Try this one at your own risk—it's very cool, but it can also make the Star tool act strangely from then on, so make sure you read the "how to get back to normal" part of this tip. Ready? Click-and-drag with the Star tool and don't let go throughout this whole procedure. Press the Down Arrow key to make a three-pointed star. Tap the Command and Option keys (PC: Control and Alt keys), then press the Up Arrow key to get multiple-point multi-stars (the star will continue to change each time you hit the Up Arrow key). To experiment even further, press-and-hold the Command key (PC: Control key) to play with the radius (as in the previous tip). The Star tool will create unusual stars like this from now on, so here's how to get it back to normal. Start to drag and tap the Command and Option keys (PC: Control and Alt keys) to get back to one star. You may also need to hit the Down Arrow key to return to a five-pointed star and drag while pressing-and-holding the Command key (PC: Control key) to get back to a more typical radius.

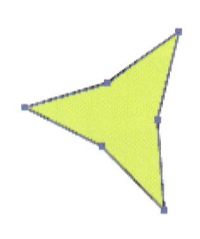

CHAPTER 3 • Creating in Illustrator CS2

SEND UP A FLARE

The Flare tool (nested under the Rectangle tool in the Toolbox) creates its design in a couple of steps. First, click-and-drag to create the flare and its rays from the center outward. If you like, continue to hold down the mouse and press the Up or Down Arrow keys to change the number of rays. Once you release the mouse, the flares are done and you can move on to the rings. Position the mouse where you want the large ring to be positioned and click. If you're not satisfied, use the undo command (Command-Z [PC: Control-Z]) to undo just the rings. Position the mouse again and, for a bit of variety, click-and-hold the mouse as you press the tilde key (~) to randomize the rings. (Oh, and if you haven't figured this out already, flares look better when they appear on top of a darker shape.)

PERMANENT PATHFINDER

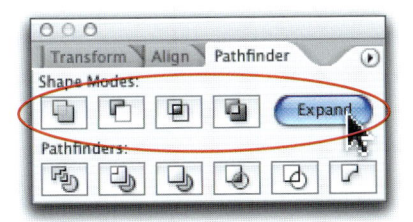

By default, clicking on the top row of icons in the Pathfinder palette creates a "live" effect that can be edited. Clicking on the Expand button makes the effect "permanent." If you want to create a permanent effect right away, press-and-hold the Option key (PC: Alt key) as you click on the Pathfinder icons of your choice.

CHAPTER 3 • Creating in Illustrator CS2   63

SPRAY ON, SPRAY OFF

To add symbols to a document, choose a symbol from the Symbols palette (under the Window menu), then use the Symbol Sprayer tool (Shift-S) to add symbols where you want them. With the Symbol Sprayer tool active, you can remove the active symbol by pressing-and-holding the Option key (PC: Alt key), which effectively turns the Symbol Sprayer tool into a symbol eraser.

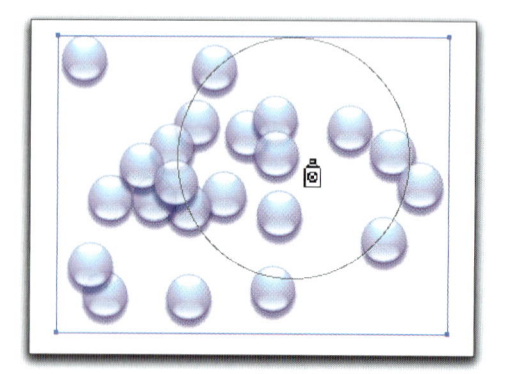

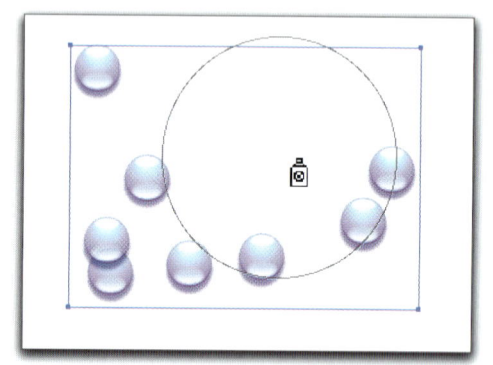

YEARS IN GRAPH DATA

Here's a challenge: You've entered data to create a graph, and you've labeled the information with the year for each column of data. Problem is, Illustrator sees the year as part of the data and will include it in the graph. Solution? Surround the year with quotation marks in the Graph Data palette (Object>Graph>Data), and Illustrator will use it as a label rather than as part of the chart data.

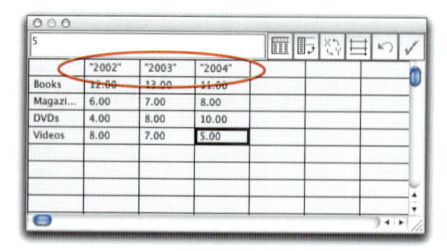

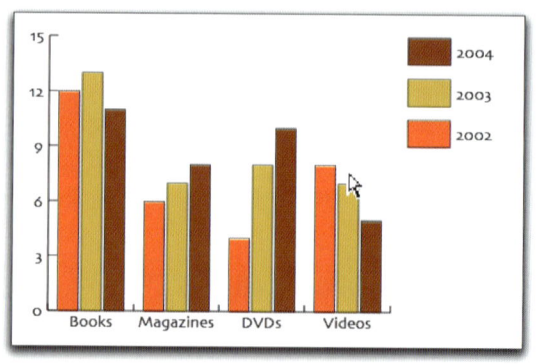

64   **CHAPTER 3** • Creating in Illustrator CS2

THAT'S OUT OF ONE HUNDRED

By default, the value axis on a graph will be slightly more than the largest value in your data. To set a specific maximum value (such as 100), select the graph, and go to Object>Graph> Type. In the dialog, choose Value Axis from the pop-up menu at the top. Check the Override Calculated Values box and enter the maximum value (100 in our example). *Note:* The maximum value you choose will become the default, so be prepared to change it back the next time you create a graph.

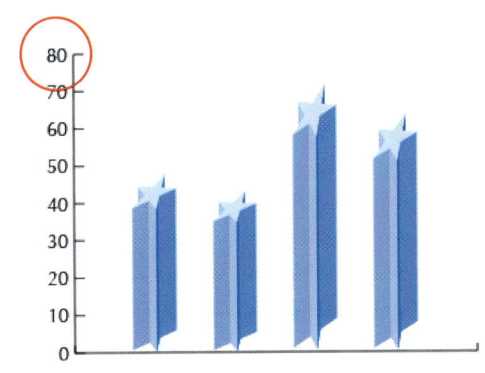

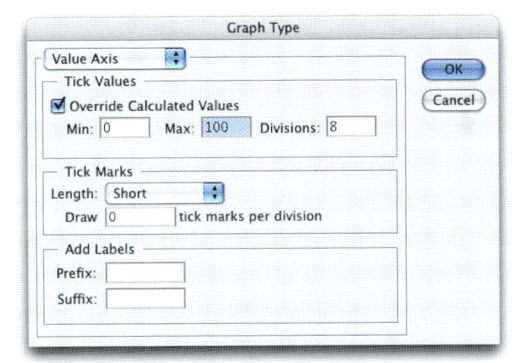

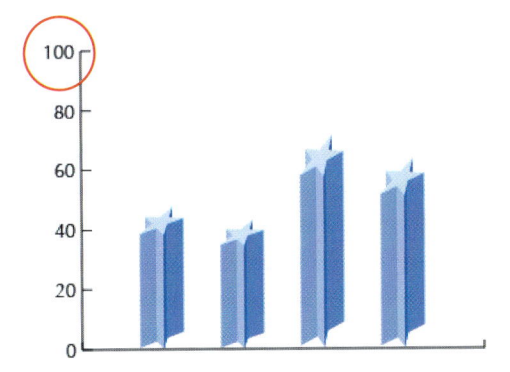

EDIT GRAPH DESIGNS

Illustrator comes with some pretty good graphic designs that you can use to replace the plain old columns created by the graph tools. In your computer's Applications folder (PC: Program Files folder), in Adobe Illustrator CS2>Cool Extras>Sample Files folder, choose the Graph Designs folder, and open one of the documents called Column & Marker Designs. To edit an existing design, go to the Object menu and choose Graph>Design. In the dialog, select the design from the list, click the Paste Design button, and then click OK. Edit the design, select it, and then use the same command, but this time click the New Design button to create a new column design. Name your design and click OK. (*Hint:* The column designs that contain a plus sign beside their names are sliding column designs [see next tip]). Save and close the design document. To apply a column design to a selected graph, use this command: Object>Graph>Column. Now pick your new design!

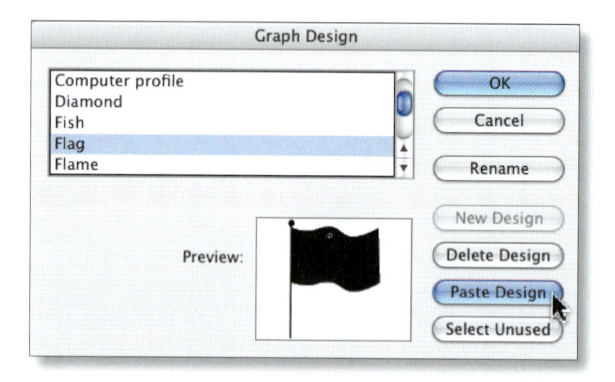

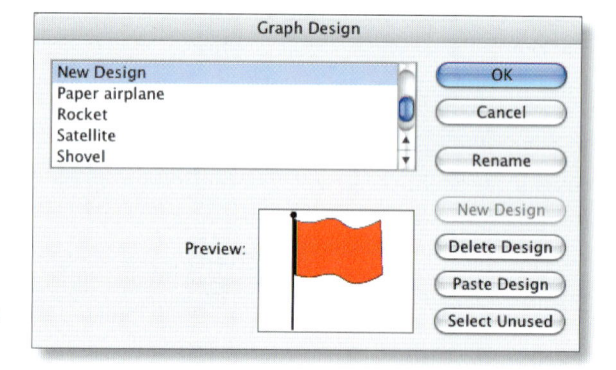

66 CHAPTER 3 • Creating in Illustrator CS2

SLIDING GRAPH DESIGNS

One of the most effective graph elements is a sliding column design. For example, use a martini glass as a column design where the top and bottom of the glass remain the same but the middle portion slides to grow taller. To do this, create your glass design and use the Pen tool (P) to create a horizontal line to indicate where the sliding should take place. Select the artwork and the line, then group them (Command-G [PC: Control-G]). Use the Direct Selection tool (A) to select the sliding line and from the View menu choose Guides>Make Guides. Then select the entire design and from the Object menu select Graph>Design. In the dialog, click the New Design button and use the Rename button if you want to call it something other than "New Design." To replace your graphic with this sliding design, select the graph and use Object>Graph>Column. In the dialog, choose your new design and from the Column Type pop-up menu choose Sliding. Here's a comparison of the difference between sliding and scaling column designs.

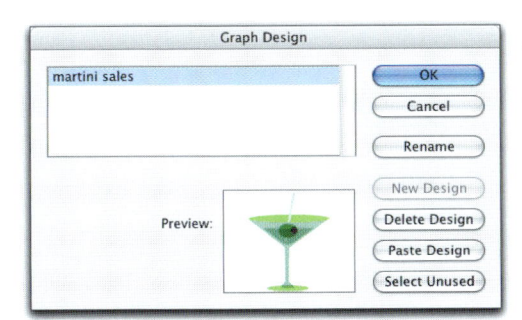

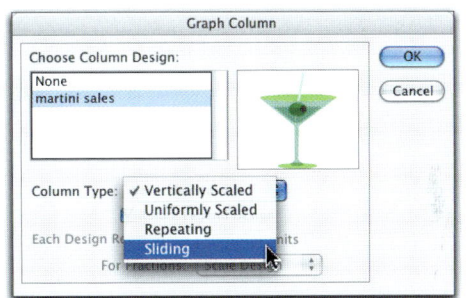

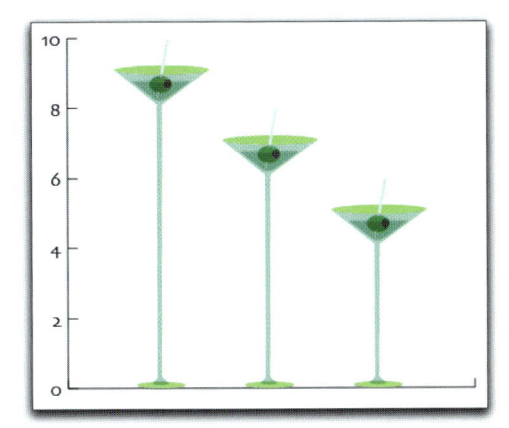

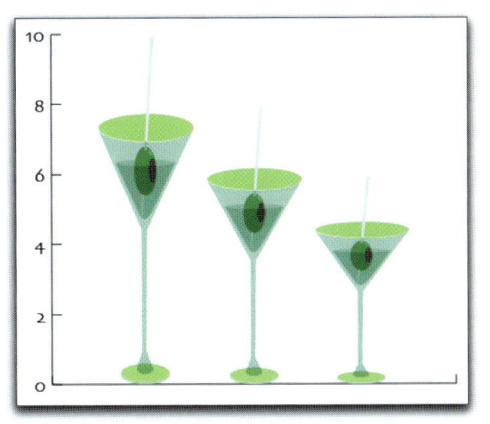

Sliding Column Design

Scaling Column Design

CHAPTER 3 • Creating in Illustrator CS2

DRAG-AND-DROP INSTEAD OF COPY-AND-PASTE

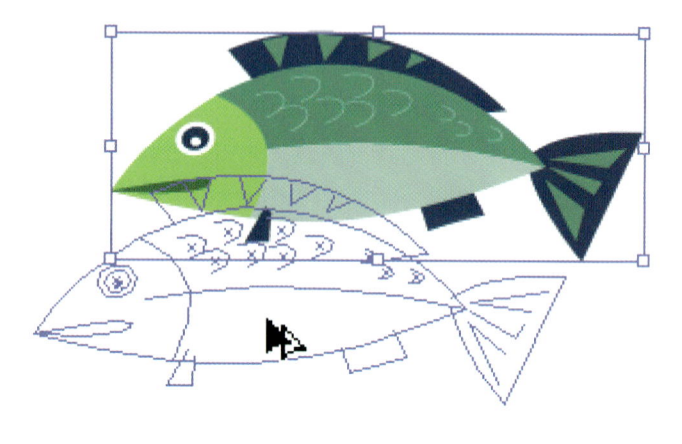

If you need to make a copy of an object, don't copy-and-paste (you could, but that's the slow way because you then have to move the pasted object where you want it). Instead, just press-and-hold the Option key (PC: Alt key) as you drag the object with the Selection tool (V) and you'll make a copy and position it in one step. If you want to make a copy perfectly aligned with the original, after you've started dragging, press-and-hold the Shift key, in addition to the Option key (PC: Alt key).

CHANGE TOOL SETTINGS ON THE FLY

As you drag the mouse to create shapes with tools such as the Star, Polygon, and Spiral tools (nested under the Rectangle tool on the Toolbox), use the Up and Down Arrow keys to increase or decrease the number of points, sides, or segments as you draw the shape. Here we used the Down Arrow key as we dragged out a shape with the Polygon tool.

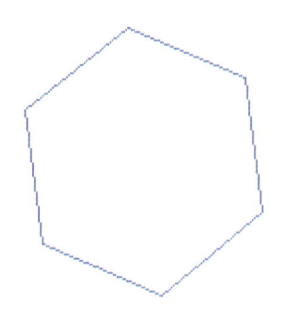

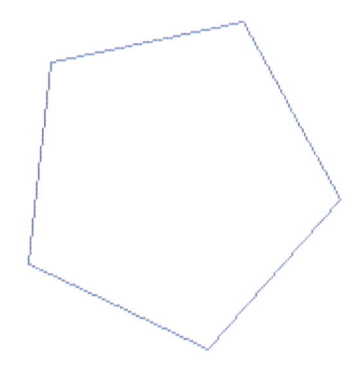

68   CHAPTER 3 • Creating in Illustrator CS2

MAKE YOUR OWN SPIROGRAPH

With many of the drawing tools, you can create multiple shapes by holding down the tilde key (~) as you drag. It's an interesting way to create wire frame shapes—or a computerized spirograph. (*Note:* Make sure you let go of the tool before you let go of the tilde key, or all of your wire framework will disappear and you'll be left with one object.)

CONVERT TO SHAPE

Here's a cool way to add a box to text without having to make a separate shape. Select a text object with the Selection tool (V) and in the Appearance palette (Window>Appearance), choose Add New Fill from the flyout menu. Then go to the Effect menu and choose Convert to Shape>Rectangle. In the dialog, in the Relative section, enter how much larger than the text you want the rectangle. Change the text and the rectangle grows with the text. (*Hint:* If you can't see the text because of the box's color, double check the Appearance palette to make sure the Characters tab is above the Fill tab. Then highlight your text with the Type tool (T) to change its color. Here we use black text on a yellow-filled box.)

CHAPTER 3 • Creating in Illustrator CS2

LET THE BLEND TOOL DO THE MATH

Like a built-in calculator, the Blend tool (W) can do a form of calculation for you. For example, you draw two lines some distance apart, and now you want five more lines evenly spaced between the two original lines. Rather than doing any math to figure out how far apart to space the lines, just create a blend between the two objects. With the Blend tool, click on one line, avoiding anchor points. Then, Option-click (PC: Alt-click) on the other line. In the dialog, enter the number of new lines you want for the specified steps. Illustrator does the math and evenly spaces the new lines between the two originals. (And, since the effect is live, the spacing will automatically update if you move either of the two original objects, or change the angle of one of the lines.)

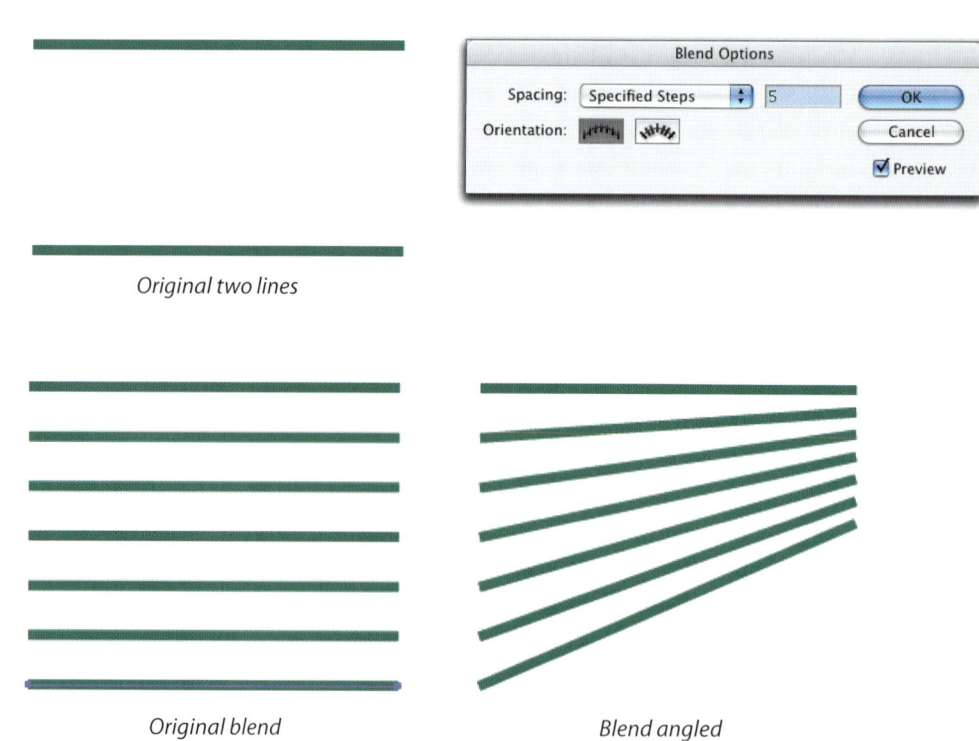

Original two lines

Original blend

Blend angled

MORE BLENDING

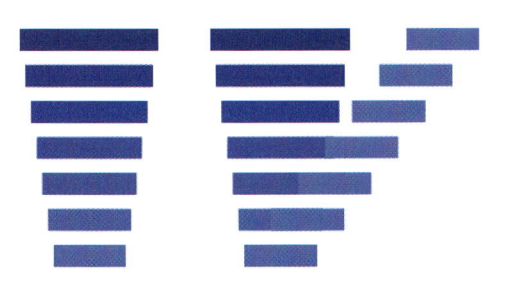

If you've created a blend between two objects and want to add to the blend, one way is to make a copy of the start or end object. Use the Direct Selection tool (A) with the Option key (PC: Alt key) held down, and drag a copy of the object. As you let go, the blend will be updated to include the newly copied object (using the same number of blend objects that are in the original blend).

YET MORE BLENDING

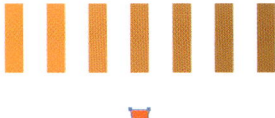

Here's another way to add to an existing blend using any shape you want. Create the shape you want to add to the blend and then go to the Layers palette. Find the Blend and click on the triangle to show its sublayers. Click on the new object and drag it to the Layers palette into the blend's sublayers. The blend will be determined by the position of the new object, so find the object in the palette and drag it to the top of the blend layers. This will make a new blend between it and the last object in the original blend. A middle position redraws the blend with the new object in the middle of the original blend. Positioning it at the bottom of the blend layers means the new blend will form between the new object and the first object in the original blend.

CHAPTER 3 • Creating in Illustrator CS2   71

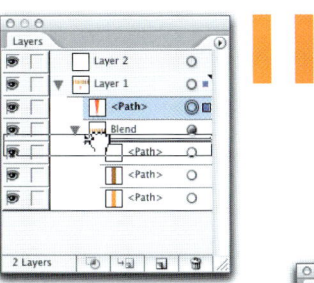

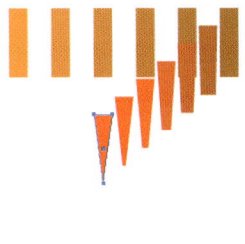

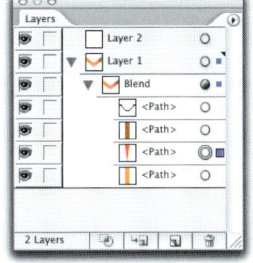

BEND THE BLEND

Here's how to take a blend and turn it up a notch. After creating a blend, draw a path for the blend to follow. Shift-click with the Selection tool (V) to select the path and the entire blend (all the objects in the blend), and from the Object menu choose Blend>Replace Spine. The straight line between the first and last objects in the blend will be replaced with your path. If the objects are not evenly spaced out along the path, see the next tip.

SHAPES AROUND A CIRCLE

If you use a circular path for the Replace Spine command, chances are the objects in your blend will not be evenly distributed around the circle. There's a simple trick to make sure the objects in your blend are evenly spaced around the circle: Select the path, and with the Scissors tool (C) click somewhere on the path of the circle to create an open path (don't move anything, just click once to cut the path). The blended objects will automatically be distributed along the path. (*Note:* Try this for any path, not just circles.)

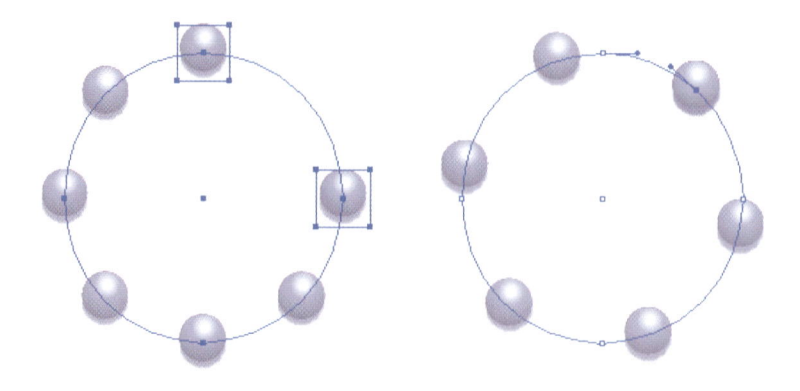

72   CHAPTER 3 • Creating in Illustrator CS2

CHANGE THE BLEND

After you've created a blend (and it's still live), you can change the number of steps in the blend by going to the Object menu and choosing Blend>Blend Options (or double-clicking the Blend tool in the Toolbox). In the dialog, change the number of Specified Steps and the blend will update. An even quicker way is to check the Preview box at the bottom of the dialog, and use the Up and Down Arrow keys for an instant update.

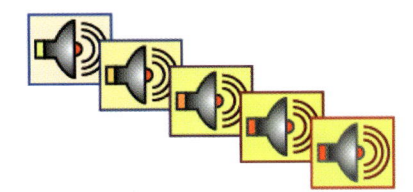

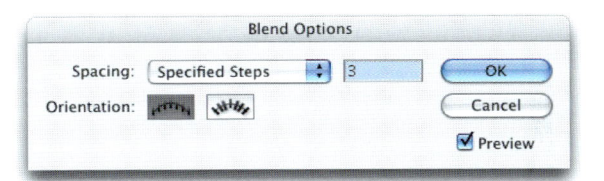

OUTLINE STROKE

One simple way to make a shape that you can use as a building block to create your design, is to convert a path with a thick stroke into an object. Draw a path, add a thick stroke (Window>Stroke), and then from the Object menu choose Path>Outline Stroke. In our example, we then straightened the ends and made multiple copies.

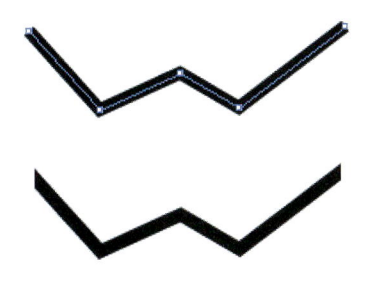

CHAPTER 3 • Creating in Illustrator CS2

LIVE TRACE NOT WORKING HOW YOU'D LIKE? TRY THIS

If you've imported a number of sketches into Illustrator and have tried to run Live Trace (under the Object menu) on them, you may have realized it doesn't always work as good as you'd like. You can try to change the Tracing Options to better fit the sketch that you're tracing, but that still doesn't always do the trick. If that's the case, then try this: Duplicate the sketch layer (go to Window>Layer, and choose Duplicate from the Layer palette's flyout menu) and, on the Transparency palette, change the Blend Mode of the duplicate to Multiply. Then duplicate the layer copy a couple more times. Each time, you'll see the sketch get darker and darker. However, since we can't run Live Trace on several layers at once, we have to flatten the artwork. First, press Command-A (PC: Control-A) to select all the layers. Then, choose Object>Rasterize. Don't worry about the resolution setting since you're just going to run Live Trace on this sketch anyway, just click OK. Now you'll be able to run Live Trace on this image and the results should look much better.

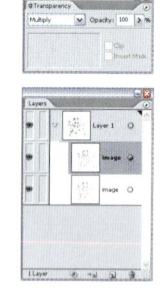

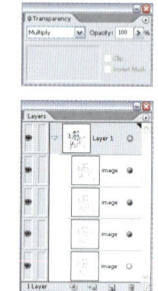

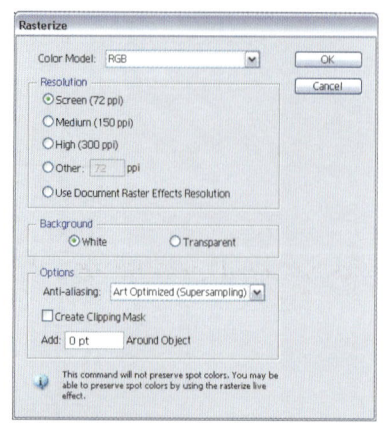

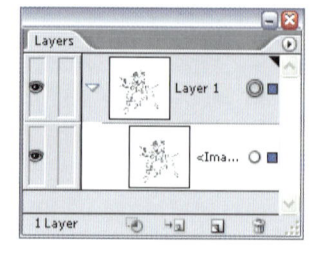

CHAPTER 3 • Creating in Illustrator CS2

IS LIVE TRACE STILL NOT WORKING HOW YOU'D LIKE? TAKE IT A STEP FURTHER

If the previous tip doesn't do the trick when working with Live Trace, then you may have to resort to some more extreme measures. Try opening the sketch in Photoshop. Choose Image>Adjustments>Levels to display the Levels dialog box. Try moving the black slider under Input Levels toward the right to darken the lines. When you're done, click OK, save the image, and import this sketch into Illustrator again. Using Levels in Photoshop will help give Illustrator more definition with which to trace the image and you should come out with a much better result.

Original Sketch

Live Trace applied without Levels adjustment

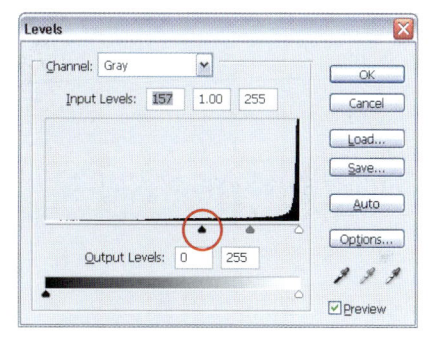

Levels adjustment in Photoshop

Levels-adjusted sketch in Illustrator before Live Trace

Live Trace applied to Levels-adjusted sketch

CHAPTER 3 • Creating in Illustrator CS2

Illustrator CS2 KillerTips

VIEWING REFERENCE PHOTOS WHEN USING THE MESH TOOL

Here's a great tip for working with the Mesh tool (U). Often, illustrators will use a reference photo as a starting place to create their work. Well, if you're using the Mesh tool, it can often be useful to switch between Outline and Preview modes because the colors you're adding may cover up the reference photo. Here's the tip: Be sure that when you bring your reference photo into Illustrator, that you place it as a template layer. This will ensure that you're able to view it in Outline mode. If not, when you switch to Outline mode, all you'll see are the outlines and no photo.

©MATT KLOSKOWSKI

CHAPTER 3 • Creating in Illustrator CS2

GRADIENT BRUSHES

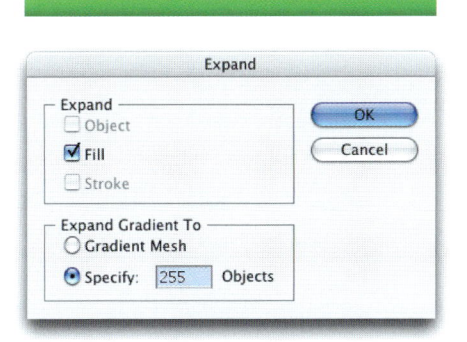

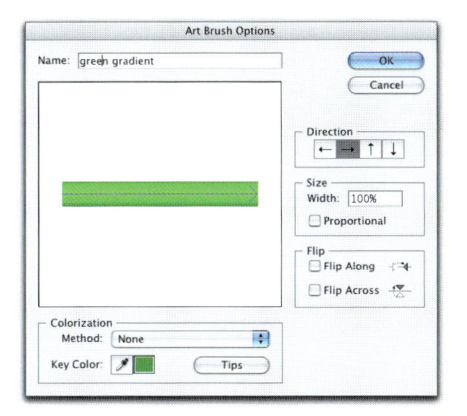

You can make gradients follow a path by making an art brush. Start by making a rectangle with the Rectangle tool (M) and change the fill to Gradient (the center thumbnail near the bottom of the Toolbox under the Fill and Stroke thumbnails). Use the Gradient and Color palettes (under the Window menu) to change the color and style of the gradient. (To add additional color stops, Option-click on a stop and drag it sideways.) From the Object menu, choose Expand. In the dialog, change the number of objects—the number you use will depend on the final use of the artwork, screen versus print. Make sure that no banding is visible once you've expanded the gradient, meaning there are no lines visible in the gradient. If there is banding, you'll have to undo (Command-Z [PC: Control-Z]) and try a higher number. Then in the Layers palette (found under the Window menu), scroll down the layer information until you see the object's clipping path and drag it to the palette's Trash icon. With the expanded gradient still selected, from the Brushes palette's flyout menu choose New Brush and select New Art Brush. Give your brush a name and select other options, such as direction and size. Now you have a gradient brush that you can apply to any path.

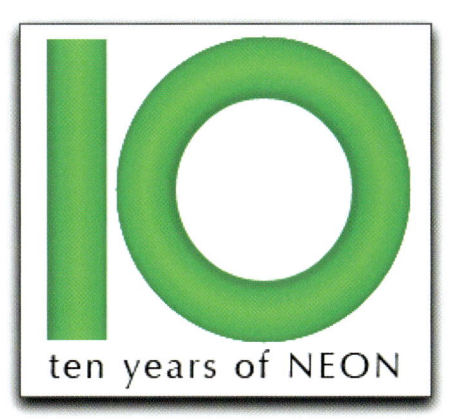

CHAPTER 3 • Creating in Illustrator CS2   77

DIVIDE OBJECTS BELOW

This one's a little odd since it breaks a fundamental rule of Illustrator: Make sure you have selected all the objects you want to work with. In the case of the command called Divide Objects Below, it won't work if more than one object is selected. Simply create the object that will do the dividing and position it over the other (filled) object(s) to be divided. Then choose Object>Path>Divide Objects Below. (If you have too many objects selected, it won't work and you'll get a warning dialog.)

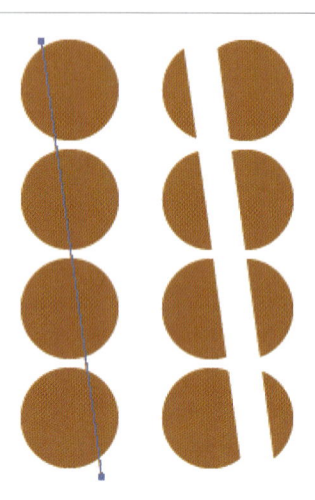

CHANGE GRIDS ON THE FLY

By default, the Rectangular Grid tool (nested under the Line tool in the Toolbox) creates equal spacing between the horizontal and vertical dividers. To change the spacing as you drag a grid, press X or C to move horizontal dividers left or right, and press V or F to move vertical dividers up or down. (Here we pressed C as we dragged out the grid.)

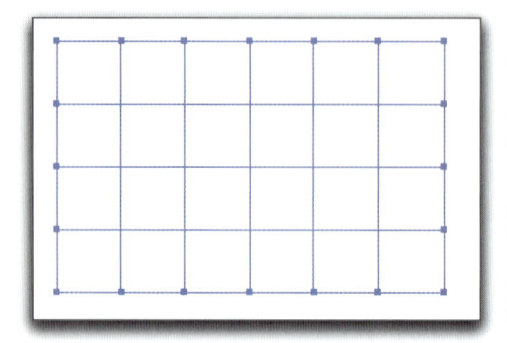

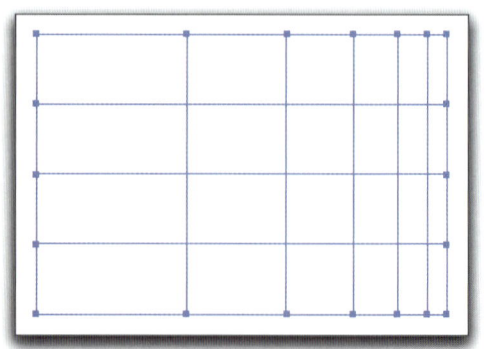

CHAPTER 3 • Creating in Illustrator CS2

LIVE INTERLOCKING OBJECTS

Using the Live Paint Bucket (K), you can easily create interlocking objects that remain live. Create two overlapping objects that have outlined paths (Object>Path>Outline Stroke), select them both, and click on the selected objects with the Live Paint Bucket to turn them into a Live Paint Object. Pick the color of one of the objects and click again with the Live Paint Bucket tool where the objects overlap. Now you can use the Direct Selection tool (A) to reposition either object while keeping the interlocking look.

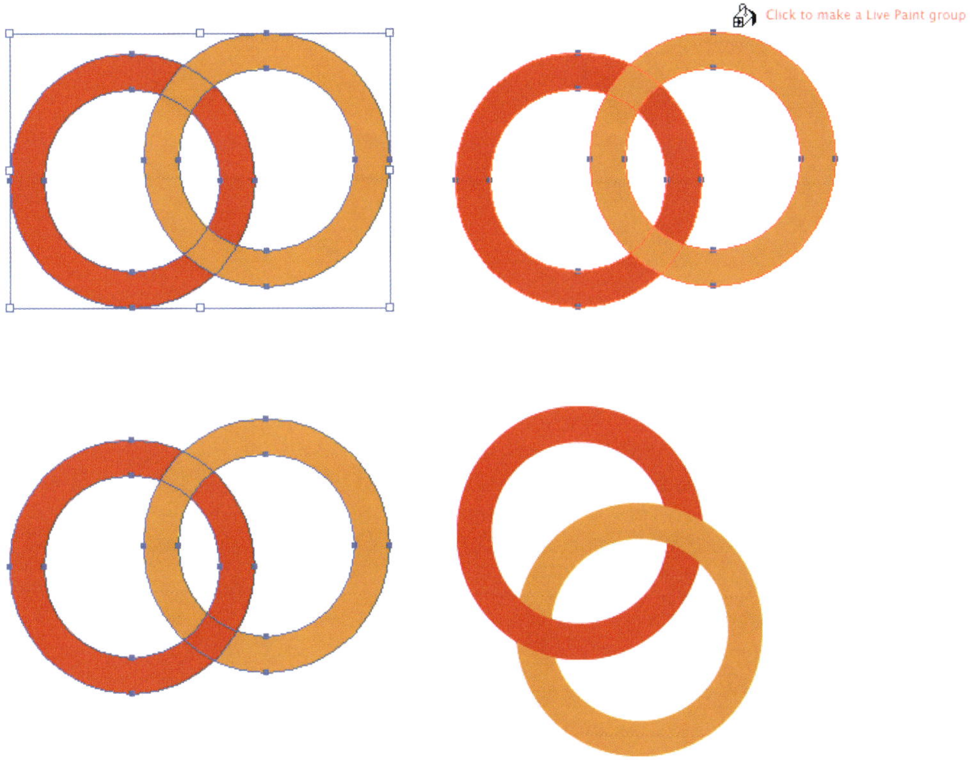

CHAPTER 3 • Creating in Illustrator CS2   79

LIVE INTERLOCKING OBJECTS, PART 2

Okay, so it is a bit of a stretch to make this a separate tip, but frankly, it's just easier to separate this. Once you've created a Live Paint interlocking object like in our last tip, you can take it up a notch by applying the Effect>3D>Extrude & Bevel to the objects. They'll still be interlocked, you can reposition them, and they're in 3D!

CREATING WIREFRAMES

Ever see that cool black and white line view of your 3D objects when you're editing the lighting cube in the 3D effects dialog box? It's called a wireframe, and creating that effect in Illustrator CS2 is easier than ever. Just create an object and apply some 3D effect to it (Effect>3D>Extrude and Bevel or Revolve). At the bottom of the resulting 3D effect options dialog, change the Surface setting pop-up menu from Plastic to Wireframe, and you'll always have that effect instead of the default shaded view.

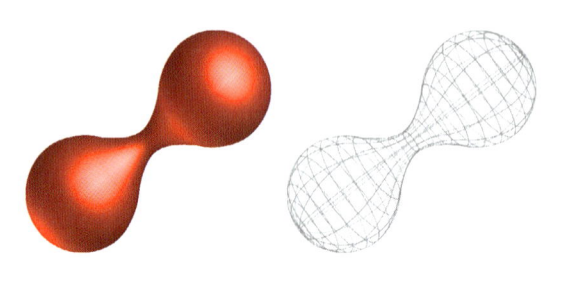

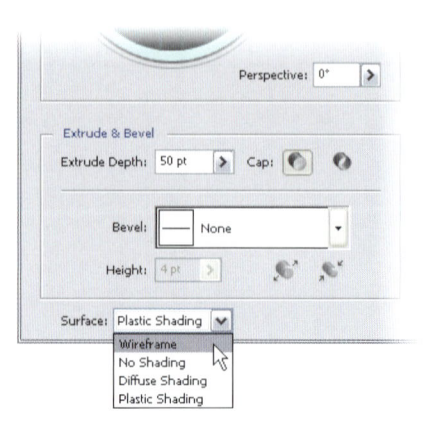

CHAPTER 3 • Creating in Illustrator CS2

ADD TO A SHAPE TO CREATE A SHAPE

Sometimes it's easier to create a simple shape and then add to it with more anchor points. For example, to create a map pointer, draw a rectangle with the Rectangle tool (M) and then use the Add Anchor Point tool (+) to add three anchor points along the bottom. Press A to get the Direct Selection tool, then click-and-drag out the middle of the three anchor points you added. There you have it!

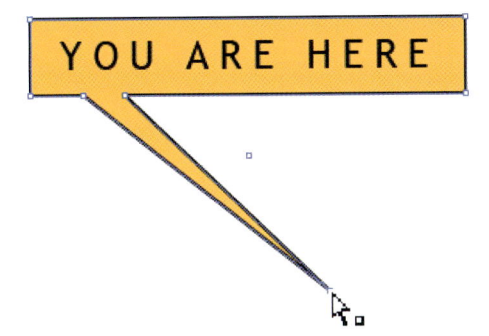

MOVE POINTS AS YOU DRAW

With the Pen tool (P), you can change your mind about the positioning of the anchor points as you draw. Without letting go of the Pen tool, press the Spacebar and drag to move the active anchor point. Let go of the Spacebar to continue drawing with the Pen tool.

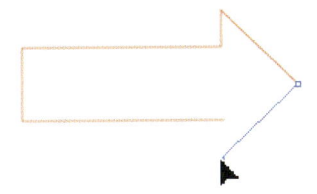

CHAPTER 3 • Creating in Illustrator CS2

AUTO ADD/DELETE GETTING IN YOUR WAY

By default, Illustrator automatically adds or deletes a point on an existing path when you move the Pen tool (P) near it. However, this doesn't help much when you don't want to add or delete from the path, but instead want to create an entirely new path altogether. There is a preference setting to disable this, but there is also a quick way to disable it using the keyboard. Just hold down the Shift key when you're near the path and you see the cursor with the little plus sign next to it. Instead, you'll see the cursor with the small x next to it meaning you're going to start a new path altogether.

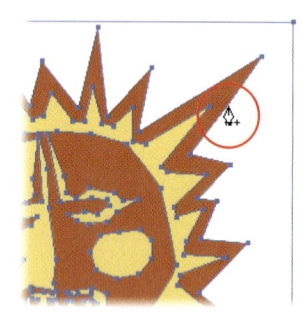

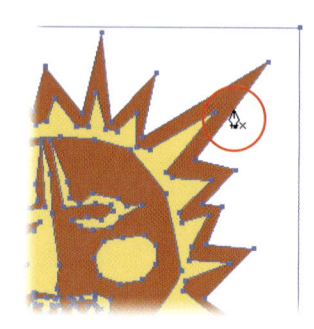

MULTIPLE OBJECTS AS A MASK

If you try to use more than one object as a clipping mask, only the last object you created will act as a mask—the others will be ignored. To use those multiple objects as a mask, you'll first have to select all the objects and from the Object menu, choose Compound Path>Make, or press Command-8 (PC: Control-8). Then position the compounded objects on top of the object you're masking, and use the Object>Clipping Mask>Make command, or press Command-7 (PC: Control-7).

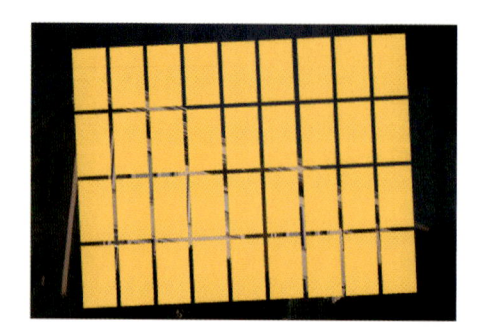

ROUND THOSE CORNERS

As you are dragging the Rounded Rectangle tool (nested under the Rectangle tool in the Toolbox) to create a rounded-corner rectangle (duh), you can change the radius (size) of the rounded corners. Just press the Up or Down Arrow key to increase or decrease the corner radius, or press the Left Arrow key to jump to the minimum radius or the Right Arrow key to change to the maximum radius. (The minimum radius is zero, while the maximum radius depends on the size of the rectangle you are creating. The "maximum" maximum radius is 8,192 points—ideal for those building-sized rectangles.)

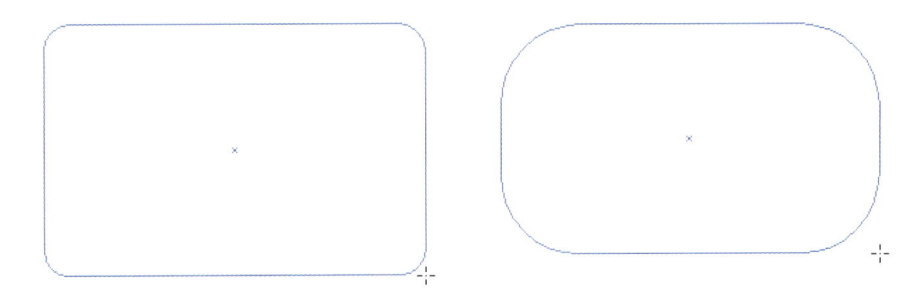

SAME WIDTH AND HEIGHT

Click on the artboard with a tool to get the dialog where you can enter the width and height. To make the width and height both the same amount, enter your number in the width field, and then click on the word Height to use the same measurement.

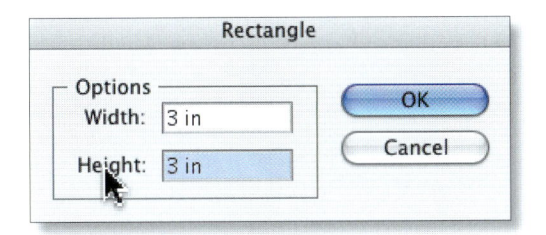

CHAPTER 3 • Creating in Illustrator CS2

CHANGING ARCS

You can change the performance of the Arc tool by holding down a couple of keys. As you drag with the Arc tool (nested under the Line tool in the Toolbox), press C to switch between an open and closed arc (like we did here). Press F to flip the axis of the arc.

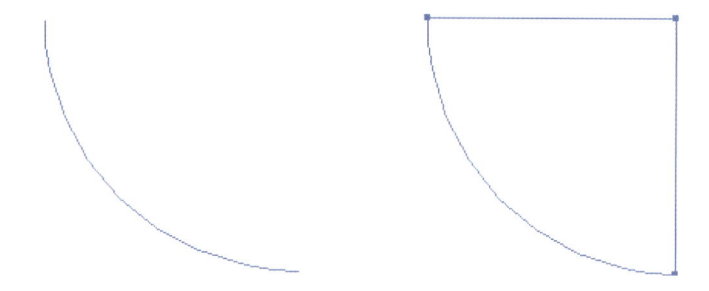

CLOSE A PATH AUTOMATICALLY

To create a closed path with the Paintbrush tool (B) or the Pencil tool (N), start drawing, then click-and-hold the Option key (PC: Alt key). Continue drawing, and when you're ready to have the path closed for you, let go of the tool. Once the path has closed, then release the Option key (PC: Alt key).

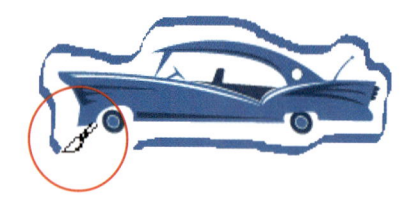

CHAPTER 3 • Creating in Illustrator CS2

PRESERVE BRUSH STROKE OPTIONS

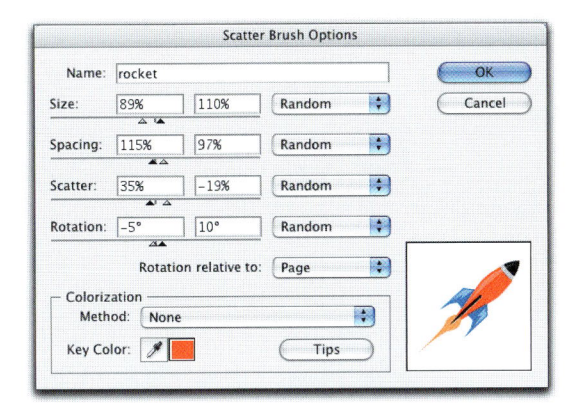

When you create a Scatter brush (go to Window>Brushes, and on the Brushes palette's flyout menu, choose New Brush, then Scatter Brush), you can set various options such as size, scatter amount, rotation, and more. If you apply a different Scatter brush to a stroke created with your new Scatter brush, you'll lose those brush options—unless you hold down the Option key (PC: Alt key) when you click on the new brush that you want to assign a brush stroke to.

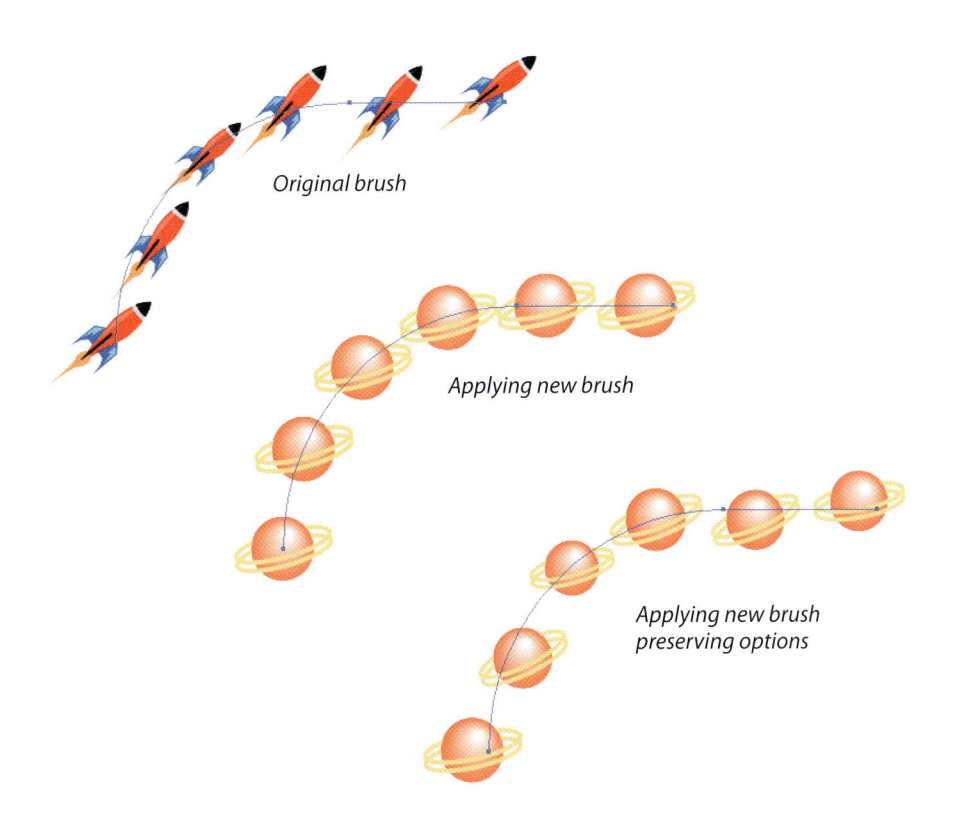

Original brush

Applying new brush

Applying new brush preserving options

CHAPTER 3 • Creating in Illustrator CS2   85

DISABLE AUTO ADD/DELETE

By default, the Pen tool (P) automatically adds anchor points to an existing path, and deletes existing anchor points. In some situations, that option may actually be a hindrance, especially if you're trying to create a new path very close to an existing path. To temporarily make the Pen tool act as simply a *Pen* tool, go to the Preferences (Command-K [PC: Control-K]) and check the Disable Auto Add/Delete box in the General Preferences. As always, remember to return the Pen to "normal" after you're done.

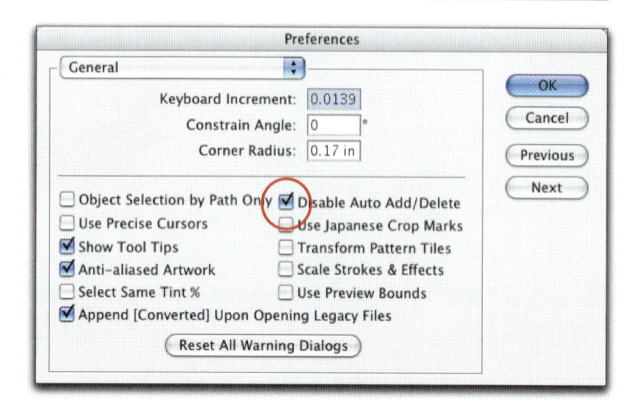

SPLIT INTO GRID

If you need to make a series of rectangles that are evenly spaced apart, draw a rectangle in the overall width you need. Then from the Object menu, choose Path>Split Into Grid. Click the Preview checkbox and then enter the number of rows to indicate the number of objects you want. You can also enter specific widths, gutters (space between columns), or the total width or height you need. There is also the option of creating guides for your grid.

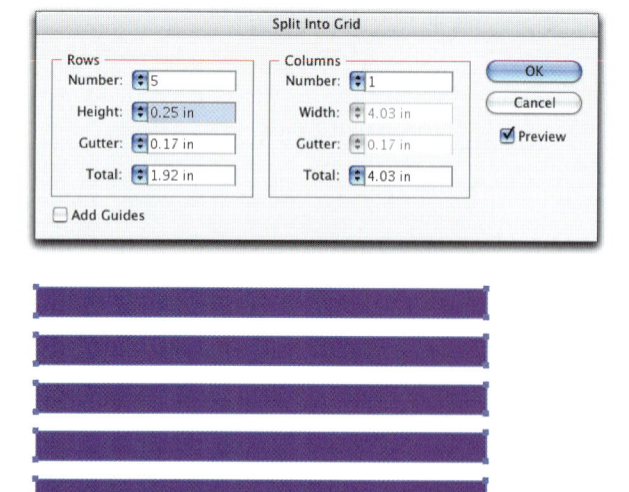

86   CHAPTER 3 • Creating in Illustrator CS2

THE PERFECT STAR

If you start to draw a star (needless to say, with the Star tool that is nested under the Rectangle tool in the Toolbox), and the settings are not what you want, it's because the tool is remembering the last settings you used for the radius. To create the "perfect" star without having to change the settings, press-and-hold Option-Shift (PC: Alt-Shift) while clicking-and-dragging the star. Option/Alt changes the radius to the "ideal" setting for a perfect star and shift will ensure the sides of the star are straight.

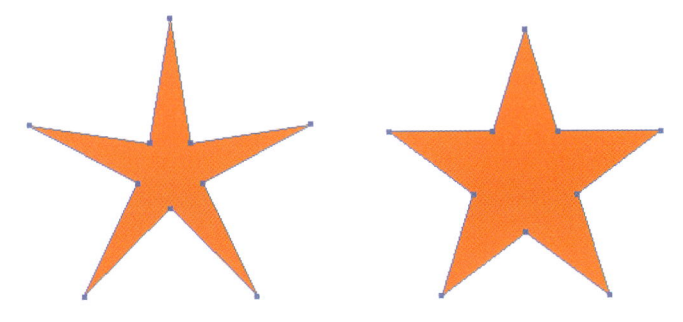

TARGET PRACTICE

Need a series of circles, each slightly larger than the last? Here's a very simple method: Use the Polar Grid tool (found under the Line tool in the Toolbox). As you drag with the tool, use the Up or Down Arrow key to increase or decrease the number of circles. Use the Left or Right Arrow key to increase or decrease the number of dividers. You can always use the Direct Selection tool (A) to edit the results.

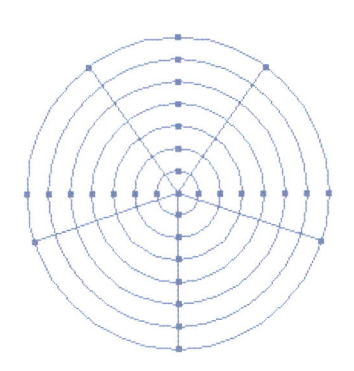

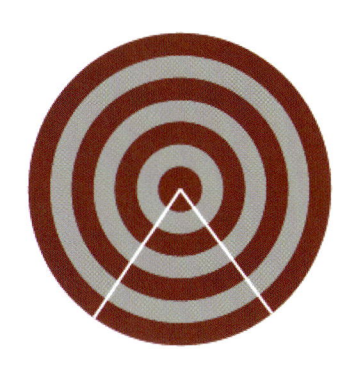

OPACITY MASKS

An opacity mask adds the ability to make portions of an object transparent. To create an opacity mask, draw an object filled with black or shades of gray and position it over the object to which you want to apply the mask (black completely hides objects, gray creates partial transparency). Select both objects and from the Transparency palette's flyout menu, choose Make Opacity Mask. Deselect the Clip checkbox. To temporarily disable the opacity mask, press-and-hold the Shift key and click on the mask thumbnail in the Transparency palette. To see the mask and edit it, press-and-hold the Option key (PC: Alt key) and click on the mask thumbnail. To return to the normal view, click on the object thumbnail (on the left in the palette).

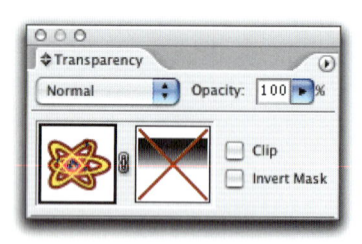

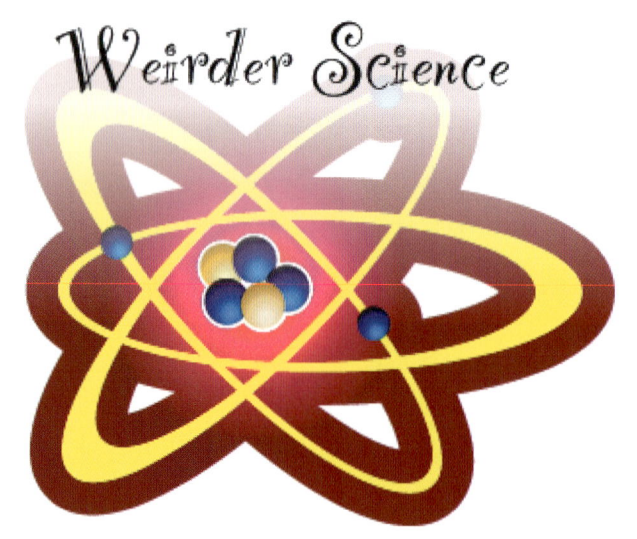

88 CHAPTER 3 • Creating in Illustrator CS2

VINTAGE TEXTURE EFFECT

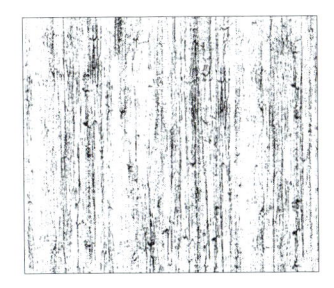

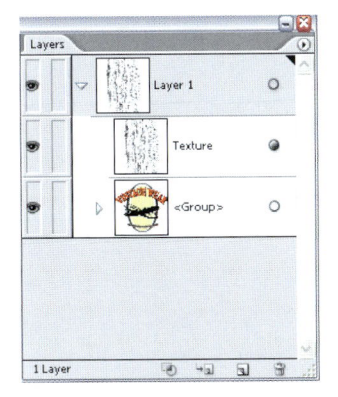

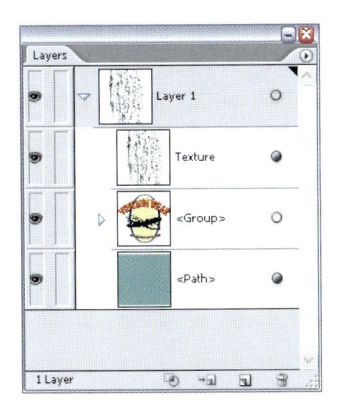

Have you ever seen that old vintage/weathered style t-shirt? It looks like it's been washed a thousand times but in reality it hasn't. How do you know? Because you can buy this style of a t-shirt today brand new and I'm betting that the manufacturer hasn't washed it that many times already. Anyway, it's a nice effect and can easily be added to any of your artwork using Illustrator. First, open any graphics that you'd like to apply this vintage effect to. Then group them together, so you just have one object to work with. Next, import a grayscale texture image from anywhere—it could have been created in Photoshop or scanned in on a flatbed scanner. Place the texture on a layer above the artwork that you want to add the vintage effect to. Then select both the texture layer and the group containing the artwork and choose Make Opacity Mask from the Transparency palette's flyout menu. All the areas that were black will now be the color of whatever is behind the grouped graphics (in this case the white artboard). If you want, you can add a rectangle in a layer below the group to change the color.

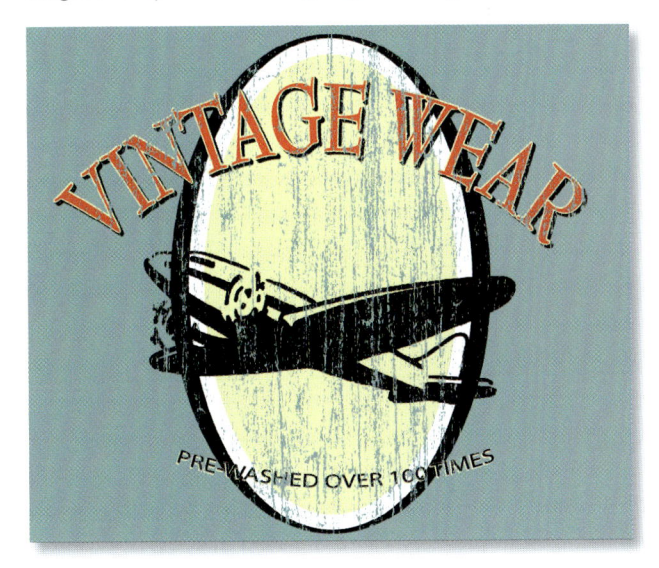

CHAPTER 3 • Creating in Illustrator CS2   89

Nip/Tuck

SELECTING, EDITING, AND TRANSFORMING

Back in the first version of Illustrator, the Status Bar changed on the fly to give you continuous feedback about the tools you were

Nip/Tuck
selecting, editing, and transforming

using. Why are we telling you this? A couple of reasons: First, it establishes fake credibility since no one can go back and check to see if this is true or if we just completely made it up. Second, we wanted to demonstrate the power of any statement that starts, "Back in the first version of Illustrator…" Got your attention, didn't it? As a special bonus available only to you, the reader, we're giving you the go-ahead to make claims about the original Illustrator. You just never know when it could come in handy. Hey, you may even want to go for it and use something like this: "Back when I used to copy artwork from Illustrator 88 into the original Photoshop…" You'll thank us later.

SAVE A SELECTION

If you've made a challenging selection of a number of objects, you don't want to have to do that again, so save yourself the effort. With the objects selected, go to the Select menu and choose Save Selection. Give your selection an appropriate name and click OK. From then on, if you need to make that difficult selection, just choose it from the bottom of the Select menu. (If you have deleted one or more objects from the page, whatever objects remain in that saved selection will be selected.)

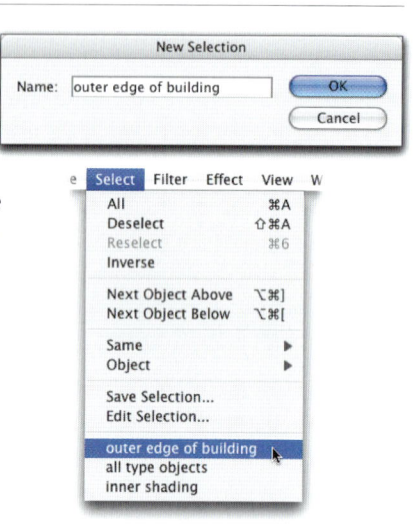

RESHAPE PATHS BY DRAWING

Use the Pencil tool (N) to reshape any existing path by drawing. Make sure the path is selected, then click-and-drag with the Pencil tool to redraw the path. You must start fairly close to the path for Illustrator to recognize that you are redrawing versus creating a new path. How close? That depends on the preference for the Pencil tool. Double-click on the Pencil tool in the Toolbox to set the distance from the path in the Options section of the dialog—just click Edit Selected Paths and choose your pixel amount.

92 CHAPTER 4 • Selecting, Editing, and Transforming

RESHAPE PATHS BY PAINTING?

So, does this concept also work with the Paintbrush tool (B)? Well, kinda. The Paintbrush tool can only be used to reshape paths that were created with the Paintbrush tool (whereas the Pencil tool will reshape any path, including those created with the Paintbrush tool). Double-click the tool in the Toolbox to change its preferences, just like the Pencil tool (see previous tip).

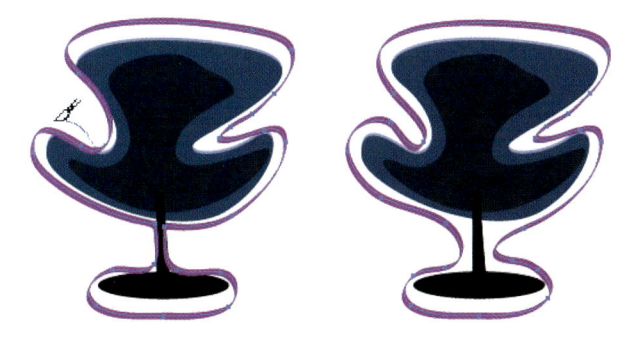

EDITING A TYPE PATH

It's easy enough to create type on a path in Illustrator. Just create a path, grab the Type tool (T), and click on the path to start aligning your type to it. However, once you do this, it appears as if your path is gone. Don't worry, it's not. Just switch to the Direct Selection tool (A), and click on the actual path. Don't click on the type, because that will just select the entire object. You want to make sure you click on the path to display any anchor points or directional handles. Then, you're free to manipulate the path just as you would any other path in Illustrator.

CHAPTER 4 • Selecting, Editing, and Transforming

Illustrator CS2
KillerTips

CUT OR ADD A POINT

When you are using the Scissors tool (C) to cut a path, you may want to add an anchor point or two to help edit the path. Rather than switching to the Pen tool (P) or the Add Anchor Point tool (+), just press-and-hold the Option key (PC: Alt key) and the Scissors tool will switch (temporarily) to the Add Anchor Point tool. Click on the path to add a point, then let go of the Option key to return to the Scissors tool.

JOIN VS. AVERAGE & JOIN

It's important to recognize the difference between Join and Average & Join. If you select the end-points of two paths with the Direct Selection tool (A) and choose Object>Path>Join (Command-J [PC: Control-J]), a straight path will be created to join the two paths. If you want the paths to be joined together using a common point, first choose Average (Command-Option-J [PC: Control-Alt-J]), then use Join.

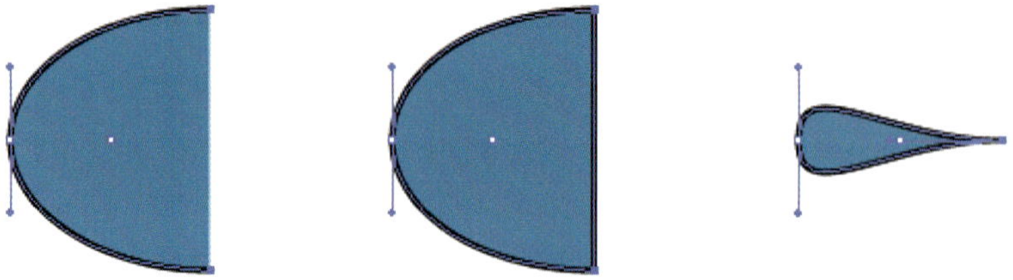

Join *Average and Join*

94 CHAPTER 4 • Selecting, Editing, and Transforming

AVERAGE AND JOIN IN ONE STEP

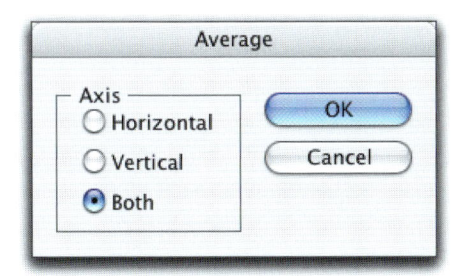

As shown in the previous tip, to join two open paths using a common point, you select the end-points of both paths with the Direct Selection tool (A). Choose Average from the Object menu (Object>Path>Average), click Both for Axis in the resulting dialog, and then click OK to make the two anchor points share one location. Then it's back to the Object menu to choose Path>Join. To trim the process down to one step, just select the two end-points, press Command-Option-Shift-J (PC: Control-Alt-Shift-J) to Average and Join in one step.

THE TRUE CENTER

When you use the Attributes palette (Window>Attributes) to show the center of a star, you'll note that the center point isn't exactly centered. Rather than try to explain why this happens (which isn't really important since we can't change it), let's see how to find the true center of a star. Select the object, then choose Edit>Copy (Command-C [PC: Control-C]), and then Edit>Paste in Front (Command-F [PC: Control-F]). From the Object menu choose Path>Average (Command-Option-J [PC: Control-Alt-J]). In the dialog, click Both for Axis. The point that appears is the true center of the object.

CHAPTER 4 • Selecting, Editing, and Transforming

BIGGER OR SMALLER A BIT AT A TIME

Perhaps you are trying to scale one object to fit within a second object, or you need to make an object smaller, but you're not sure by how much. Try this method: With the object selected, double-click on the Scale tool and enter 98% if you're scaling down, or 102% if you're making it larger. That will scale the object 2% smaller or larger. (You can choose Copy from the dialog to make a smaller or larger copy of your object, like we did in our example here.) Then press Command-D (PC: Control-D) to repeat the transformation. Each time you press this shortcut, the object will scale by 2% (smaller or larger, depending on the value you entered), allowing you to scale a bit at a time.

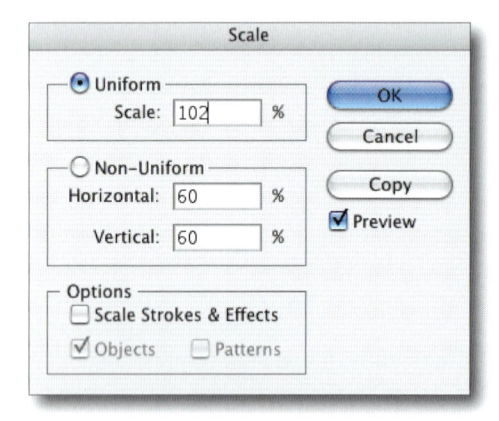

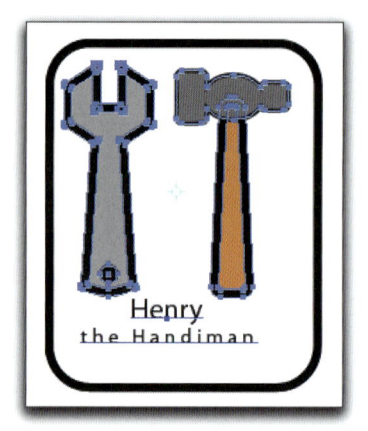

96 CHAPTER 4 • Selecting, Editing, and Transforming

SCALE TOOL CLONING

Here's a neat trick when using the Scale tool (S). While you're scaling an object, try pressing-and-holding the Option key (PC: Alt key), and that will make a duplicate copy of the object for scaling instead of modifying the original. This just saves you the step of creating the duplicate first and lets you do it all in one step.

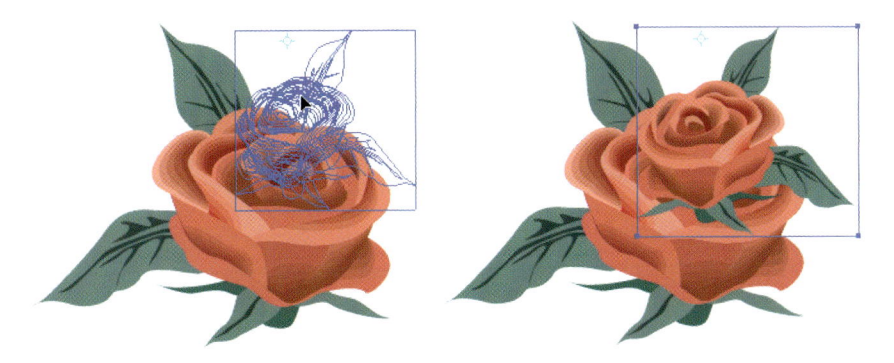

KEEP PROPORTIONS

When you use the Transform palette (Window>Transform) to change the size of an object, you can enter the width and the height for a selected object and press Return (PC: Enter). Another option is to enter either width or height and keep the other measurement proportionate by pressing Command-Return (PC: Control-Enter). For example, if your object is 1.5 inches high by 3 inches wide, change the width from 3 to 6 inches and press Command-Return (PC: Control-Enter), and the height will automatically change to 3 inches.

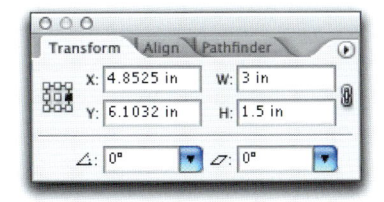

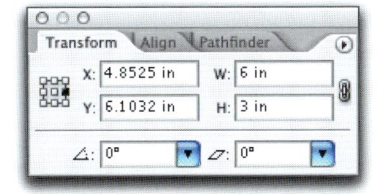

CHAPTER 4 • Selecting, Editing, and Transforming

QUICK FLIP

When you need to flip an object horizontally or vertically, ignore the Reflect tool and jump right to the Transform palette (Window>Transform). Select the object and from the palette's flyout menu, choose either Flip Horizontal or Flip Vertical.

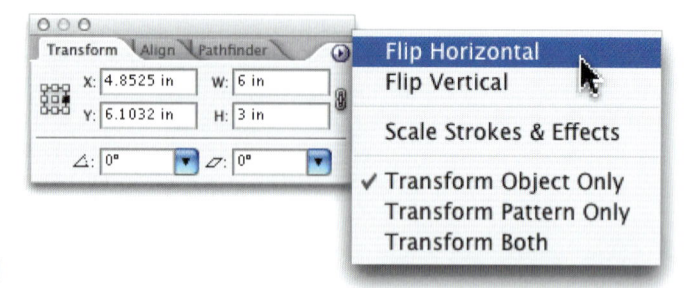

LIQUIFY BRUSH SIZE

When you are using any of the liquify tools (Warp, Twirl, etc.) and your brush is the wrong size, press-and-hold the Option key (PC: Alt key), and drag to change the size. Drag outwards to make the size larger, drag inwards to make it smaller. (*Note:* Using Option/Alt alone will alter the brush size non-proportionally. If you want to keep the brush as a perfect circle but change its size, use Option-Shift [PC: Alt-Shift].)

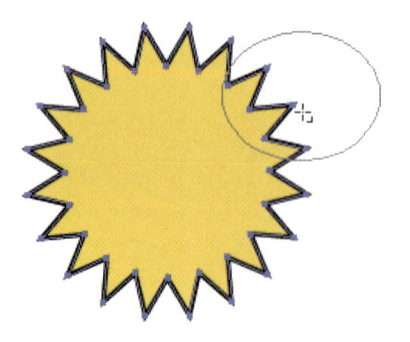

SELECT SAME, AGAIN

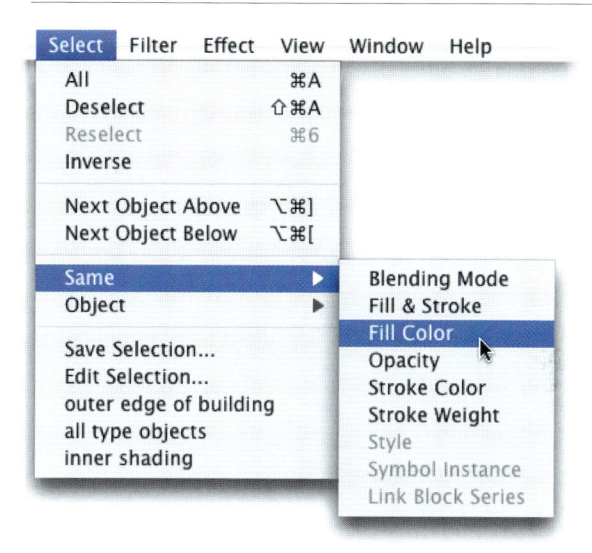

Use the Select>Same options to select objects that have the same Fill Color, Fill & Stroke, Blending Mode, etc. Then, the next time you need to make a selection using the same "select same" criteria, press Command-6 (PC: Control-6). (*Note:* If your selection requires a fill and/or stroke color(s), make sure you have those colors selected in the Toolbox.)

SELECT COLOR FROM SWATCHES

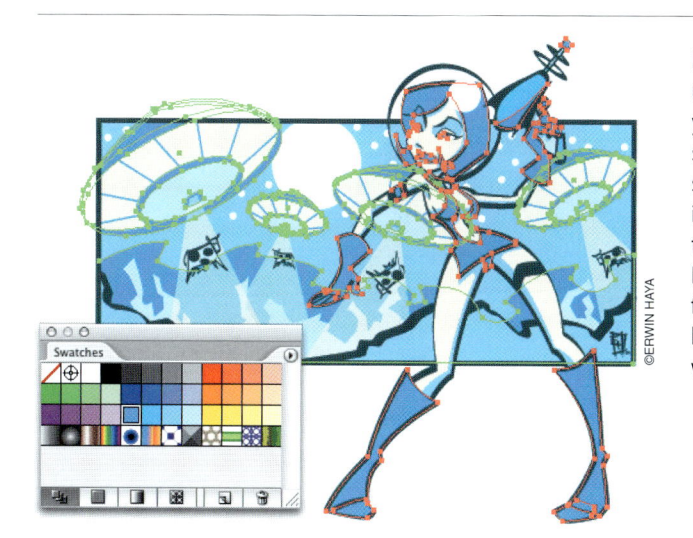

If you want to see if you've used a specific color in your document—and if so, where—with nothing selected, click on the swatch in the Swatches palette and then use Select>Same> Fill Color and every object filled with that color will be selected (regardless of which layer they're on).

CHAPTER 4 • Selecting, Editing, and Transforming

SELECTING GROUPS

Use the Direct Selection tool (A) to select individual paths and anchor points, even when they're part of a group. To select the entire path, press-and-hold the Option key (PC: Alt key) as you click on the path. To take this a step further, each time you click on the same path—with the Option key (PC: Alt key) held down—you will select the group that contains the path, and then the group that contains the group, and so on. You'll really have to try this one to see how useful it is!

SELECTING MESH POINTS EASILY

Here's a great tip when working with the Mesh tool (U). Many times, you'll need to select an existing mesh point to change its color or placement. Well, if you use the Mesh Tool to select points, you'll find that you wind up inadvertently adding a mesh point here or there because you didn't click on the exact point. Instead of using the Mesh tool for this, try pressing-and-holding the Command key (PC: Control key) and that'll switch to the Direct Selection tool (A). Now you won't have to worry about adding mesh points that you didn't want all over the place.

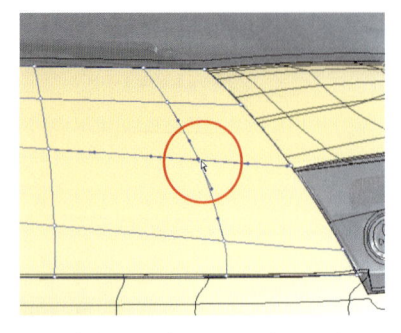

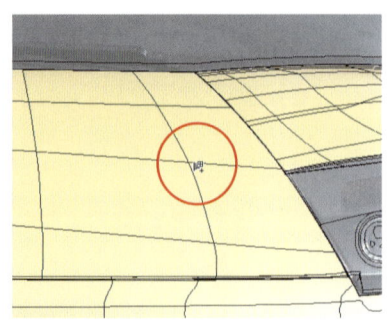

Clicking in the wrong place will inadvertently add a new mesh point

CHAPTER 4 • Selecting, Editing, and Transforming

SELECTING MULTIPLE MESH POINTS EASILY

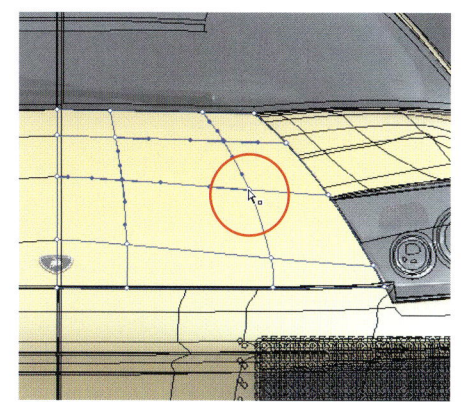

Take the previous tip a step further by adding the Shift key into the mix. While holding down the Command key (PC: Control key) to select certain points, hold down the Shift key to select multiple points. This comes in handy when you want to change the color of several mesh points at once.

Several points selected at once

LET ILLUSTRATOR CALCULATE IT FOR YOU

You can perform simple math in the Transform palette or the Control palette, both found under the Window menu. For example, if you need to make an object one-third of its width, just click after the current size in the Width field and type /3. Use / for divided by, * for multiplied by and + or - for, well, you know. Then press Return (PC: Enter) and Illustrator will do the calculation and transform accordingly.

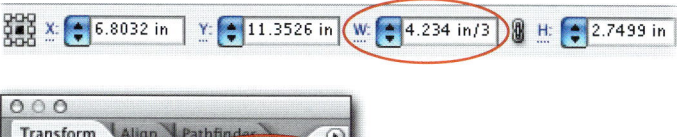

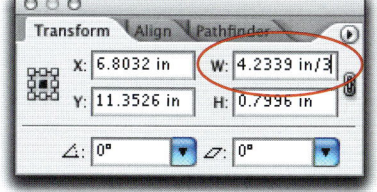

CHAPTER 4 • Selecting, Editing, and Transforming   101

EDITABLE TRANSFORMATIONS

When you use any of the transformation tools such as Scale (S) or Rotate (R), the effect is permanent once you save and close the document. For example, rotate an object, save the document, and close it. Next time you reopen the document, there is no easy way to undo this change. Instead, consider using the Transform command under the Effect menu. You'll find it here: Effect>Distort & Transform>Transform. In the dialog, check the Preview option and then apply whatever transformation you like. Once you've clicked OK, you'll always be able to access and edit these transformations (even after closing the document) by selecting the object, looking in the Appearance palette, and double-clicking on Transform.

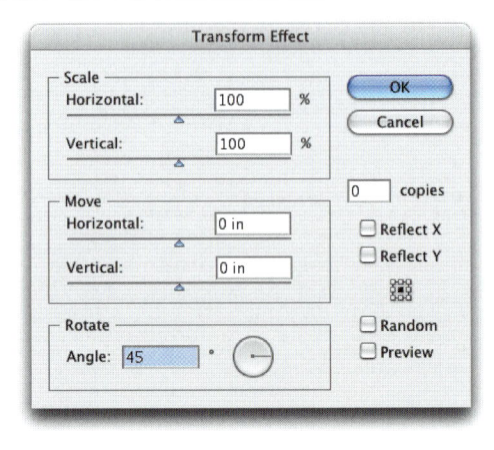

ROTATE WITH CARE

When you're using the Rotate tool (R), keep this in mind. If you leave the cursor too close to the original rotate bounding box, the results can be somewhat erratic. For more precise control, move the cursor farther away from the object you're rotating. That will give you more control over positioning it.

102   CHAPTER 4 • Selecting, Editing, and Transforming

ROTATION BY THE NUMBERS

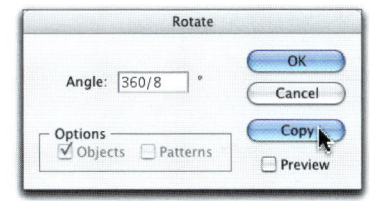

To rotate and copy an object a specific number of times so you end up with even angles between objects, let Illustrator figure it out for you. Select your object, then with the Rotate tool (R), press-and-hold the Option key (PC: Alt key), and click on the bottom of the object. In the Rotate dialog, enter 360/x, with x being the number of objects you want. Then click Copy. The object will be copied and rotated the correct number of degrees. Then press Command-D (PC: Control-D) x-2 times (with x being the number you used before) to complete the effect. For example, for eight objects you'd enter 360/8 in the Rotate dialog, click Copy, and then press Command-D six times (since you already have the original and the first copy).

REPEAT LAST PATHFINDER

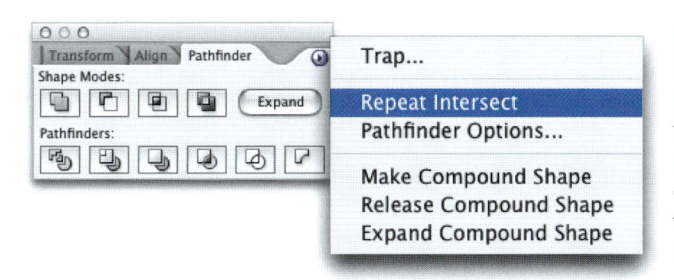

Need to repeat the last Pathfinder effect you just used? Use the flyout menu in the Pathfinder palette (found under the Window menu) and choose Repeat (name of Pathfinder), or press Command-4 (PC: Control-4).

CHAPTER 4 • Selecting, Editing, and Transforming   103

TRANSFORM BY NUMBER

With all transformation tools, such as Scale, Rotate, and Shear, you can transform manually by dragging the mouse or numerically. Double-click on any transformation tool to get a dialog for a numeric transformation. By default, the reference point for the transformation is the center of the object. But to open the dialog and set a different reference point, press-and-hold the Option key (PC: Alt key) and click in the spot you'd like to use as a reference point.

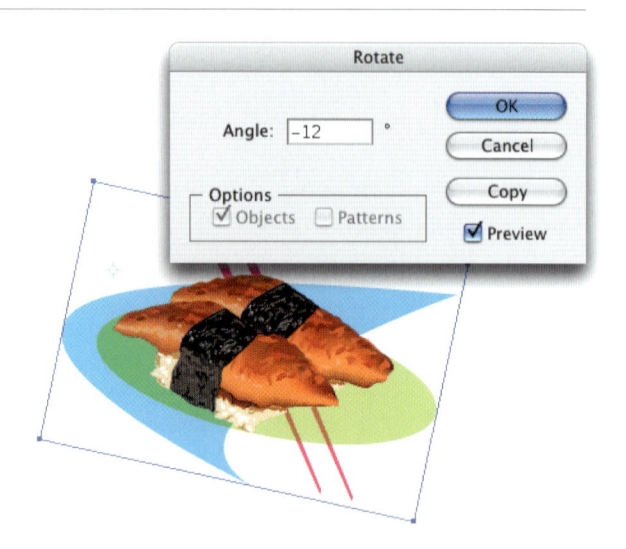

FREE TRANSFORM

Add all kinds of extra functions to the Free Transform tool (E) by using a number of different keys, after you click on a corner handle. For example, press-and-hold the Command key (PC: Control key) as you click-and-drag to distort; press Command-Option-Shift (PC: Control-Alt-Shift) to distort perspective; press Command-Option (PC: Control-Alt) to shear an object; press-and-hold Shift to scale; etc.

104 CHAPTER 4 • Selecting, Editing, and Transforming

PICK THE BEST TRANSFORMATION

When you want to transform multiple objects, you have a couple of choices. One option is to select the objects and use transformation commands (Object>Transform), such as Scale or Rotate. This will transform the objects as if they were one object. The other choice is the Transform Each command (Object>Transform>Transform Each). Use this dialog to transform the separate objects, and take advantage of a preview.

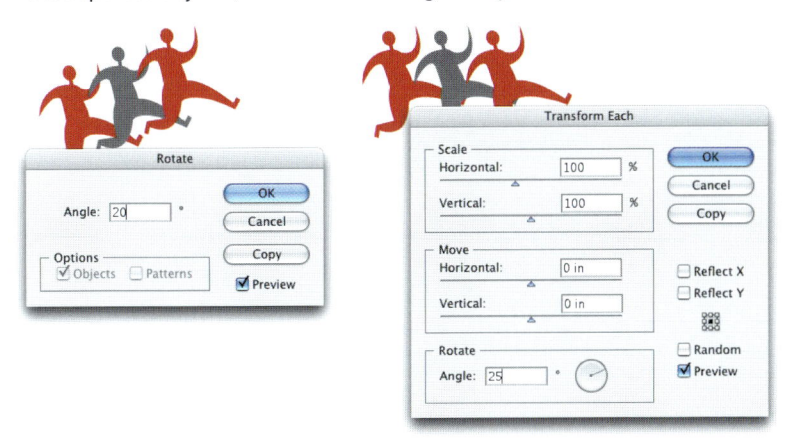

SELECT BEHIND

To select an object hidden behind another object, select the top object, and then press Command-Option-left bracket ([) (PC: Control-Alt-left bracket). That will select the next object, below the selected object. Keep pressing the same shortcut to select the next object down. To select back the other way (Select>Next Object Above), press Command-Option-right bracket (]) (PC: Control-Alt-right bracket). In our example, we selected the top object (part of the face), and used the shortcut to select the next object below.

CHAPTER 4 • Selecting, Editing, and Transforming   105

NEW STROKE OPTIONS IN ILLUSTRATOR CS2

This one is new and it may slip under your radar if you aren't looking closely at CS2's new feature list. In the Stroke palette, you'll see options for aligning a stroke. The default used to be center, which means that half of the stroke width would flow along the inside of the path and half would flow along the outside of the path. However, there was no way to change it. But now you can change this to outside or inside as well.

Center *Inside* *Outside*

SCALE STROKES & EFFECTS

When you scale an object to make it larger or smaller, you'll have to decide whether you want the stroke and effects to scale also (in general, this is usually the best choice). Although this option is controlled by the General Preferences (under the Illustrator menu in OS X or the Edit menu in Windows), there is a quicker way to change this setting. Double-click on the Scale tool to open its dialog. Either check or uncheck the Scale Strokes & Effects box, and that will not only change the setting for the selected object, but will also change the preference from then on.

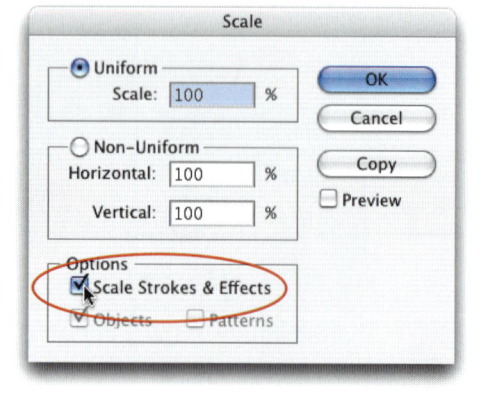

106 **CHAPTER 4** • Selecting, Editing, and Transforming

ODD NUMBERS

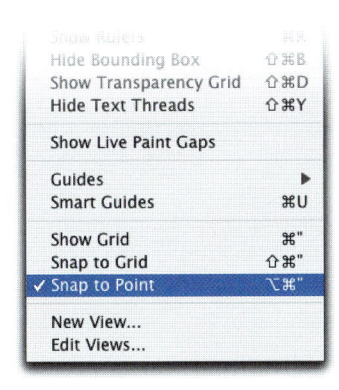

You may find that you enter a value in the Transform palette and, after pressing Return (PC: Enter), you get an odd value. For example, you type in 3 for the width, but after pressing Return (PC: Enter), it says 3.01. One factor that can cause this is a function called Snap to Point. Turn this off from the View menu or press Command-Option-" (PC: Control-Alt-"), and you should now get the exact value you enter.

MOVE AND COPY

To move an object to a specific area and copy it, use the Transform palette. Enter the amount you'd like to move the object in the X or Y field and press-and-hold the Option key (PC: Alt key) as you press Return (PC: Enter). Keep in mind the reference point in the proxy.

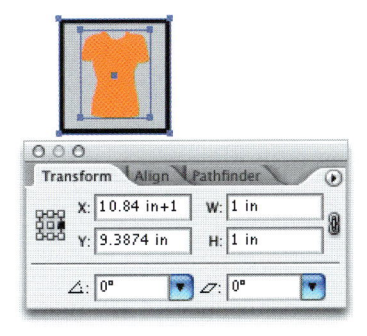

CHAPTER 4 • Selecting, Editing, and Transforming   107

STRAIGHT CUTS

Here's a weird one: The Knife tool (Shift-K) doesn't use the Shift key to cut in a straight line. Although every other tool uses Shift as a constraint for straight lines, with the Knife tool you hold down the Option key (PC: Alt key) to cut in a straight line. Use Option-Shift (PC: Alt-Shift) to cut in a straight horizontal or vertical line.

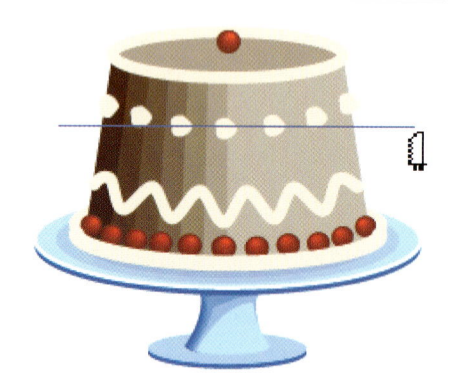

MOVE IT BY MEASURE

The Move command (Object>Transform>Move) and the Measure tool (nested under the Eyedropper tool in the Toolbox) work very nicely together. Start by selecting your object, then click-and-drag with the Measure tool to "measure" the distance and angle you want to move the object. The numbers will appear in the Info palette (Window>Info), but more importantly, the Move command will use these measurements. Use the Move command (Command-Shift-M [PC: Control-Shift-M]) and click OK to move the object the specific distance and angle you just measured.

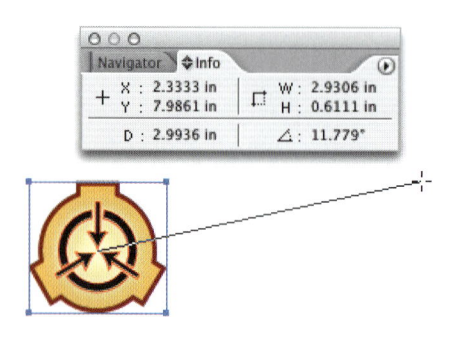

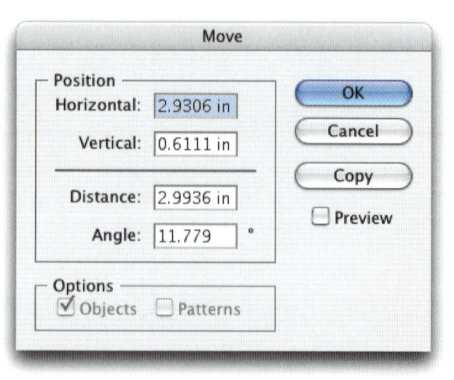

108 CHAPTER 4 • Selecting, Editing, and Transforming

DRAW AND SMOOTH

When you're using the Pencil tool (N) and need to smooth out your path, just hold down the Option key (PC: Alt key) before clicking-and-dragging to temporarily activate and use the Smooth tool. Then let go of the key to return to the Pencil tool.

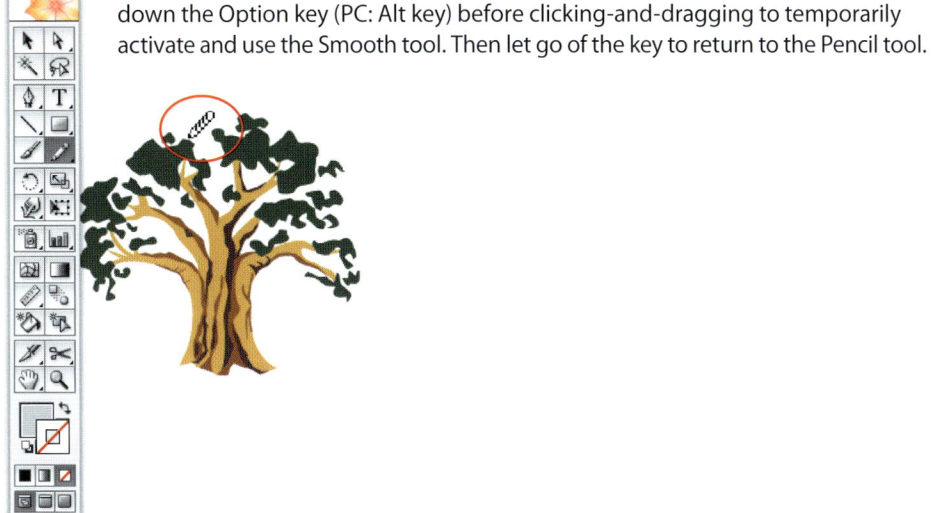

SIMPLIFY PATH

When you use the Simplify command (Object>Path>Simplify) to adjust a path, take advantage of the Show Original option to compare the effects of the Simplify command with the original path. The original path will be shown in red, while the simplified path will display in blue.

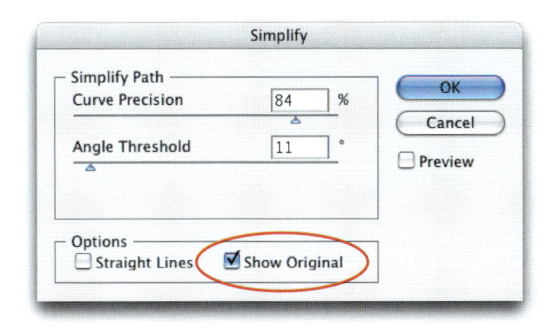

CHAPTER 4 • Selecting, Editing, and Transforming   **109**

MAGIC WAND NOT WORKING

If the Magic Wand tool (Y) isn't doing its job the way you think it should (i.e., it's not selecting objects that it should be selecting), make sure the blending modes are not causing a problem. Double-click on the Magic Wand tool in the Toolbox to open its palette and uncheck Blending Mode. Why? When it is checked, the wand will only select objects with the same fill *and* the same blending mode. (*Note:* If this option isn't showing, go to the palette's flyout menu and select Show Transparency Options).

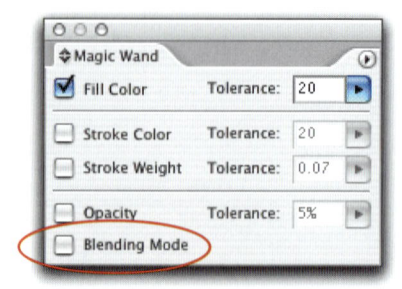

COPY WHILE TRANSFORMING

Selecting an object's bounding box while using the Selection tool (V) is a great way to make quick transformations, such as scaling and rotating without switching to the transformation tools. However, one thing it cannot do is to make a copy when rotating or scaling. To do this, you must use a transformation tool and hold down the Option key (PC: Alt key) as you rotate or scale.

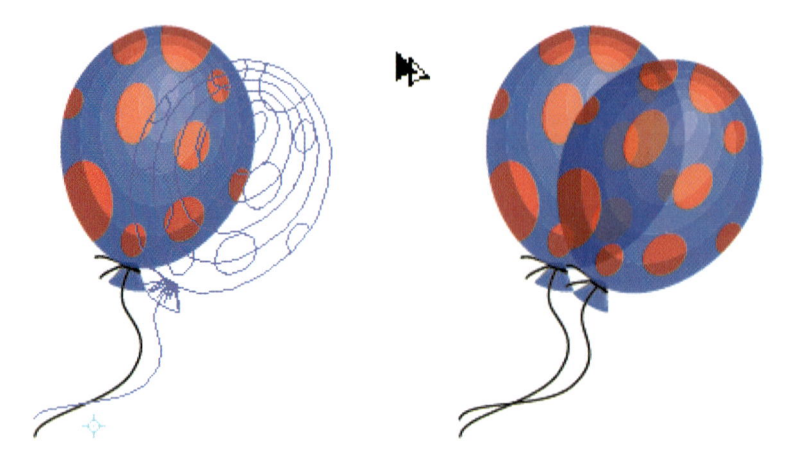

110 CHAPTER 4 • Selecting, Editing, and Transforming

TRANSFORM AGAIN AND SEND TO BACK

An earlier tip told you not to do any additional operation after transforming an object or the Transform Again command wouldn't work. Well, here's one important exception to that rule. You can use the Arrange commands (such as Object>Arrange>Send to Back and Bring to Front) and still retain Transform Again. For example, you scale a circle by Option-clicking (PC: Alt-clicking) on the object with the Scale tool (S) and pressing Copy to make a larger circle. By default, the larger circle will be in front, so use Object>Arrange>Send to Back to reposition the new circle. Then press Command-D (PC: Control-D) to Transform Again (copy and scale the larger circle), and then once again use the Object>Arrange>Send to Back command.

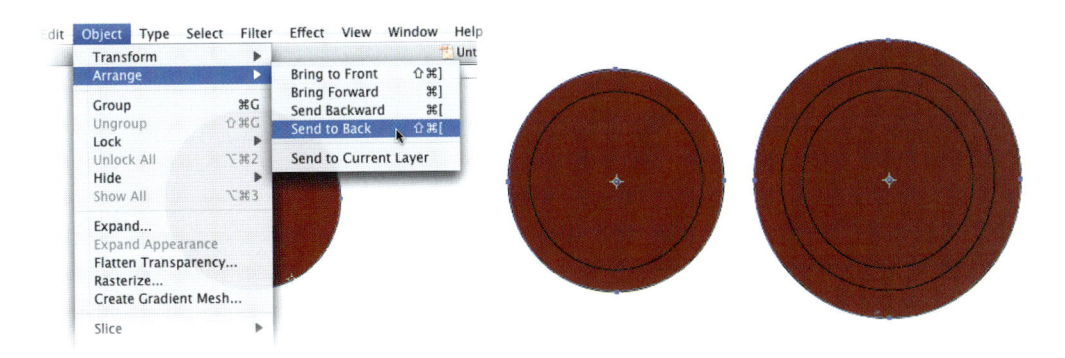

TRANSFORM AGAIN, AGAIN

You know that pressing Command-D (PC: Control-D) after transforming an object will apply the transformation again. However, did you know that you can do the same thing to an anchor point? Just select the Direct Selection tool (A) and move a single anchor point on the object. Here's the tip, though: You won't be able to press Command-D (PC: Control-D) to redo that transformation/move. You'll need to manually go through the Object menu under Transform>Transform Again to do this because pressing the Command key (PC: Control key) reverts the tool back to the Selection tool (V).

CHAPTER 4 • Selecting, Editing, and Transforming

ALIGNING THE FAST WAY

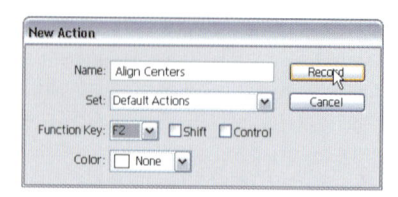

A very common task in Illustrator is aligning objects horizontally and/or vertically. However, there's no keyboard shortcut for this task, and if you find yourself doing it a lot, then it can indeed become a nuisance. Well, don't let that stop you. Just record an action that does it for you. First, draw two objects on the artboard and select both of them. Then choose Window>Actions to display the Actions palette. Click the Create New Action button at the bottom of the palette, and be sure to assign a function key shortcut to it on the resulting dialog. Press Begin Recording, then align the Horizontal and Vertical centers of the two selected objects. Press the Stop Playing/Recording button at the bottom of the palette and you're done. Now just press the F-key shortcut you assigned to the action whenever you want to align selected objects.

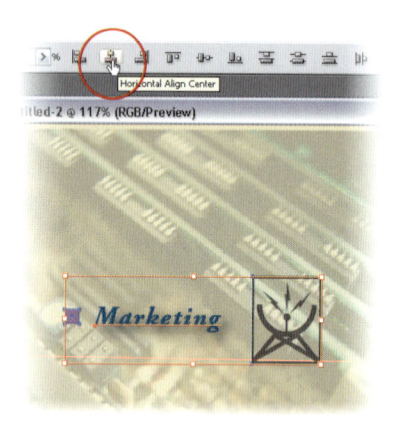

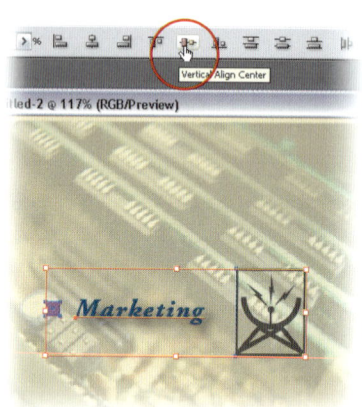

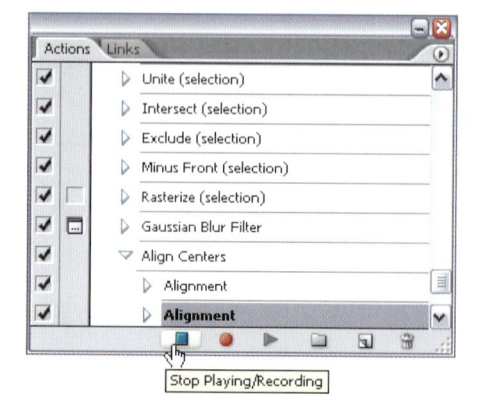

112   CHAPTER 4 • Selecting, Editing, and Transforming

ALIGN TO A SPECIFIC OBJECT

The Align palette (Window>Align) is a simple way to take a number of selected objects and line them up vertically or horizontally by their edges or centers. You can control this alignment by lining up all objects with one specific object. To do this, select all the objects and then click on one object (all the objects will stay selected). Then click on the appropriate icon in the Align palette (or Control Palette) and all the objects will align relative to the object you clicked on. For example, we aligned all of the objects by selecting them and then clicking on the eye graphic. Then we clicked on the Horizontal Align Center icon in the Align palette.

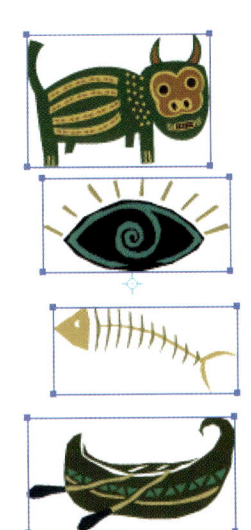

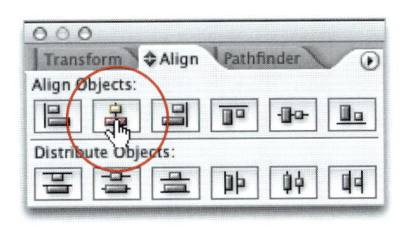

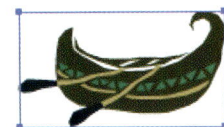

CHAPTER 4 • Selecting, Editing, and Transforming   113

CONVERT DASHED STROKE TO OUTLINE

At first glance, it doesn't appear that it's possible to convert a dashed line to an outline. If you use either the Object>Expand or Object>Path>Outline Stroke command, you get a solid line. The solution? Select the path and from the Object menu choose Flatten Transparency. In the dialog, move the Raster/Vector Balance slider to 100, make sure Convert All Strokes to Outlines is checked, and click OK. You'll end up with an outlined dashed line (where each dash is a separate object).

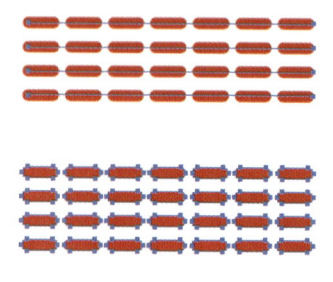

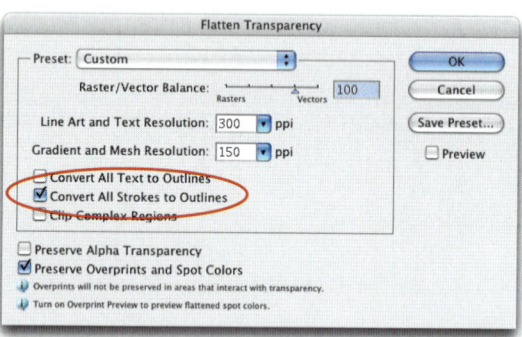

MAKE A MESH WITH TEXT

Here's a cool tip that comes courtesy of David Creamer in *Mac Design Magazine*. As an interesting way of transforming text without creating outlines, select the type with the Selection tool (V), and use the Object>Envelope Distort>Make with Mesh command (Command-Option-M [PC: Control-Alt-M]). The trick is to make the mesh have only one row and one column. Then use the Mesh tool (U) to distort the corner handles. To edit the text, select it again with the Selection tool, and go back to Object>Envelope Distort and choose Edit Contents (Command-Shift-V [PC: Control-Shift-V]).

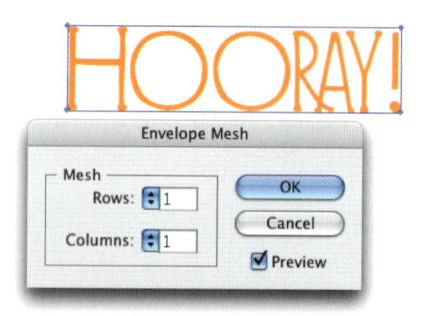

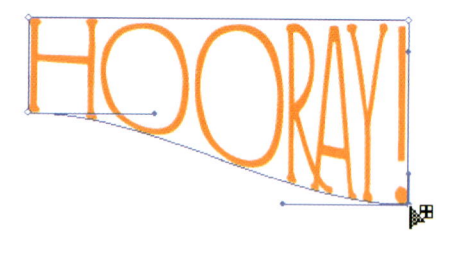

114   CHAPTER 4 • Selecting, Editing, and Transforming

DRAG-AND-DROP

Instead of copying-and-pasting from one document to another, just drag-and-drop. Select an object and use either selection tool to drag the object to a second open document. There's only one catch: If you drag from a document with objects on multiple layers, in the other document all objects will end up on one layer. To avoid this, use the Layers palette flyout menu, and choose Paste Remembers Layers—then the layers will be preserved when you select your object and drag-and-drop.

©BROOKE NUNEZ

THE MISSING TWIST TOOL

In Illustrator 10, there was a Twist tool (which was also named the Twirl tool in previous versions) nested under the Rotate tool, but it is not in CS2. Why? You'll have to ask Adobe that one, although we understand that it has to do with the inability of the Twist tool to twist things back to the way they were. Now if you want to twist an object, you'll have to use Effect>Distort & Transform>Twist. Although you have to distort numerically, the advantage of using the effect is that you can easily change the settings (by double-clicking on Twist in the object's Appearance palette [found under the Window menu]).

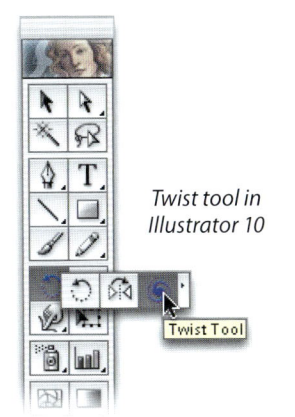

Twist tool in Illustrator 10

Twist tool gone from Illustrator CS2

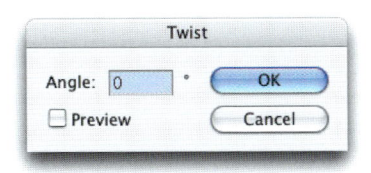

Effect>Distort & Transform>Twist

CHAPTER 4 • Selecting, Editing, and Transforming   115

Different Strokes

COLORS, SWATCHES, FILLS, AND STROKES

These are smokin' tips. Literally, they're hoodlum tips, standing on the street corner, smoking. Tips from the wrong side of

Different Strokes
colors, swatches, fills, and strokes

town, that could easily lead astray all the other tips that are working so hard to stay on the straight and narrow. Ever heard Illustrator users talking about their preferences being corrupted and having to delete them? Do you think that just happens by accident? Oh no, my friend. Be very, very careful. Don't get too close to these tricks or your life may never be the same. We understand the temptation—getting more work done in less time, it's heady stuff. It may not seem like much of anything at first. You record an action to save yourself some time, but before you know it, you're doing batch actions…and using keyboard shortcuts like there's no tomorrow…and it all starts from associating with those bandana-wearing, rough-talking, good-for-nothing tips. Hey, don't say we didn't warn you.

YOUR COLORS, EVERY TIME

You can customize the Swatches palette (Window>Swatches) to have your choice of colors, patterns, and gradients appear in every document. To do this, you need to open a document called Adobe Illustrator Startup, found in the Illustrator CS2 Applications (PC: Program Files) folder under Plug-ins. There are actually two documents, one for RGB and one for CMYK. Open the document that corresponds with whatever color schematic you use most often. Once the document is open, add or delete swatches for colors, gradients, and patterns. Save the document, restart Illustrator, and from then on, the Swatches palette will contain your swatches.

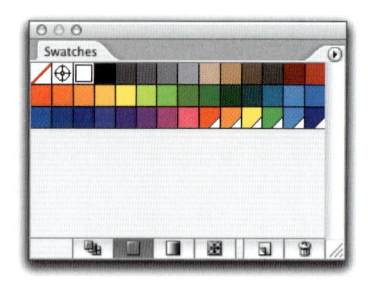

SLIGHTLY LIGHTER, SOMEWHAT DARKER

If you have created a color using CMYK or RGB sliders in the Color palette (Window>Color) and now you want a slightly lighter or darker version of that color, you can adjust all the sliders at the same time. Hold down the Shift key as you drag one slider and the other three sliders will move together, creating a lighter or darker shade of the color.

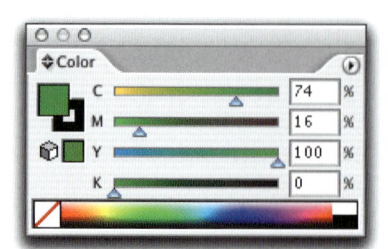

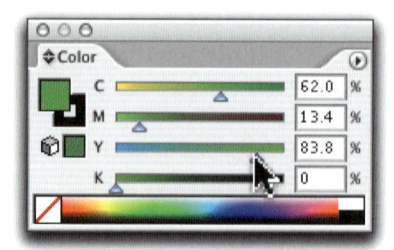

118 CHAPTER 5 • Colors, Swatches, Fills, and Strokes

Illustrator CS2
KillerTips

GRAB ONLY THE COLOR

By default, the Eyedropper picks up everything—fill and stroke color, stroke attributes, transparency, etc. (These options are set by double-clicking on the Eyedropper tool in the Toolbox.) To pick up only the color (without changing the default settings) press-and-hold the Shift key and click with the Eyedropper on an object that has the color you need.

©ISTOCKPHOTO/MARK STAY

MAKE YOUR OWN PATTERNS

Anything you drag into the Swatches palette (Window>Swatches) will become a pattern, but it takes a bit of planning to create a seamless repeating pattern. Start by creating a square with no stroke—pick a fill color if you want your pattern to have a background. Draw the shape you want in your pattern, center it, and then copy it four times, lining up each one's center on each corner of the square. Select the square, Copy it (Command-C [PC: Control-C]) and Paste in Back (Command-B [PC: Control-B]), and then change the fill to none. Select all the pieces (Command-A [PC: Control-A]) and drag them into the Swatches palette. Now you can use the pattern swatch to fill any object.

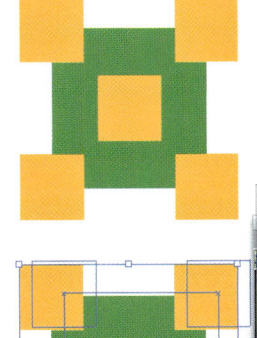

CHAPTER 5 • Colors, Swatches, Fills, and Strokes   119

TRANSFORM JUST THE PATTERN

It's possible to transform only the pattern within an object, without moving the object itself. You can do this with any of the transformation tools (Rotate, Scale, Shear, etc.) while holding down the tilde (~) key. Keep the key held down as you transform—don't let go or the object will be transformed instead.

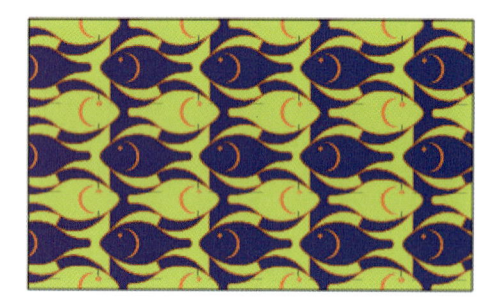

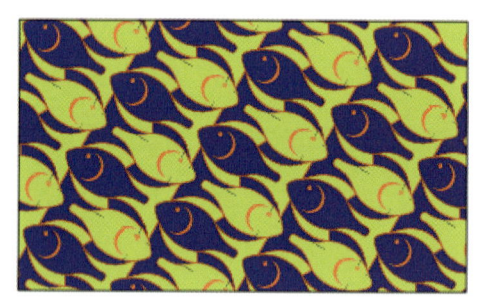

COLOR THE OPPOSITE

If you need to change the fill of an object and the stroke is active (or vice versa), the Color palette offers a simple solution. With the object selected, press-and-hold the Option key (PC: Alt key) as you click on the color ramp at the bottom of the Color palette, and the color will be applied to the opposite of what is active. That is, if the stroke is active, Option-click (PC: Alt-click) to apply the color to the fill. This only works when you click on the color ramp or the black or white squares to the right of the color ramp—it does not work in the Swatches palette.

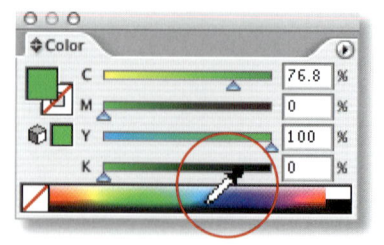

USE GLOBAL COLOR

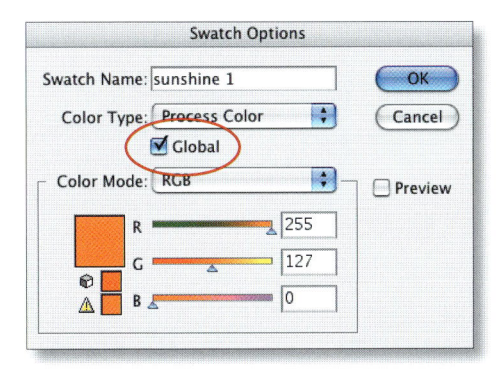

Global color lets you create a document in which you can easily change colors at once, throughout all objects. Start by creating a new swatch in the Swatches palette (Window>Swatches) by using the palette's flyout menu and choosing (strangely enough) New Swatch. Click on the Global checkbox. Use this color to fill and/or stroke images, using different percentages of the color (just make sure you have the color selected and then adjust the Tint percentage slider in the Color palette). You can also create a gradient using different percentages of the global color by dragging the swatch to the gradient ramp in the Gradient palette. Later, if you need to change all objects to a different color, you can either edit the global color by double-clicking it in the Swatches palette, or create a new global color swatch and press-and-hold the Option key (PC: Alt key) as you drag it over the original global color swatch. (Before replacing the global color, make a duplicate of the swatch by dragging it onto the New Swatch icon in the Swatches palette.)

CHAPTER 5 • Colors, Swatches, Fills, and Strokes

BORROW SOME COLOR

You can grab colors (and more) from an existing Illustrator document without opening the file. From the Swatches palette (Window>Swatches), use the flyout menu and choose Open Swatch Library, then select Other Library. Then browse and find the document you want and click Open. A second Swatches palette will open with all the swatches from the other document. (One way to use this is to create for each client or project a document that contains only the swatches you use for that purpose, then load them as you need them.)

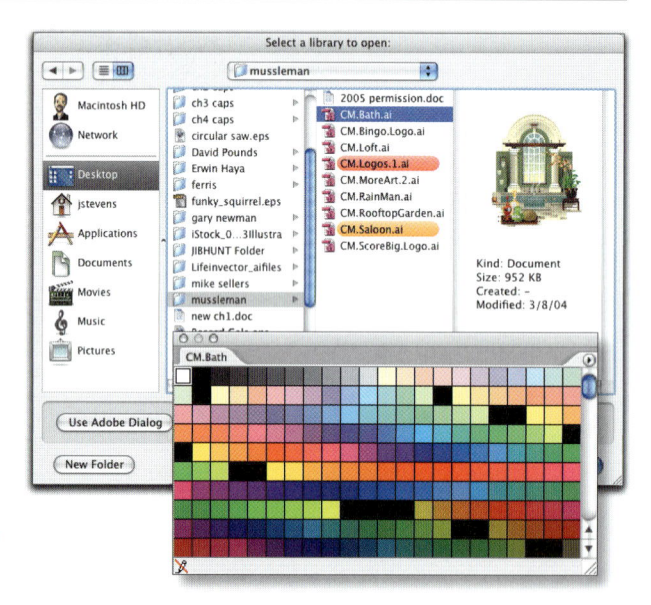

PERSISTENT SWATCHES

After you've loaded swatches from a preset library, you can make sure that library loads each time you launch Illustrator. To do that, first load the library from the Swatches palette's flyout menu. Once it's open, position the palette where you want it to appear, then use the flyout menu from that library's palette, and choose Persistent. (This also works for Symbols and Brushes libraries, but doesn't work on libraries that you've opened from another Illustrator document.)

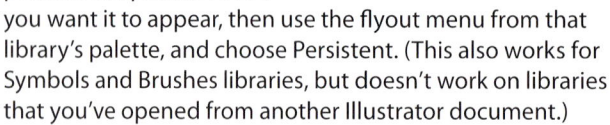

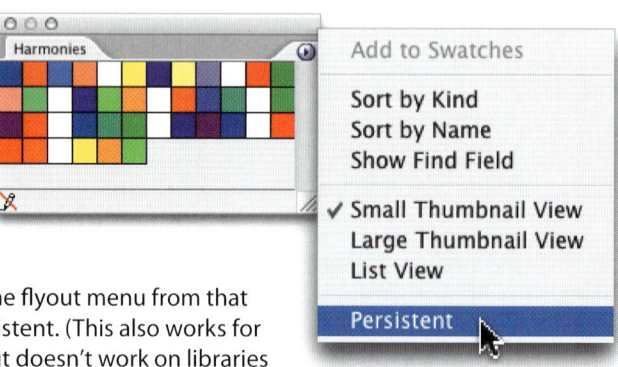

122   CHAPTER 5 • Colors, Swatches, Fills, and Strokes

COLOR FROM ANYWHERE

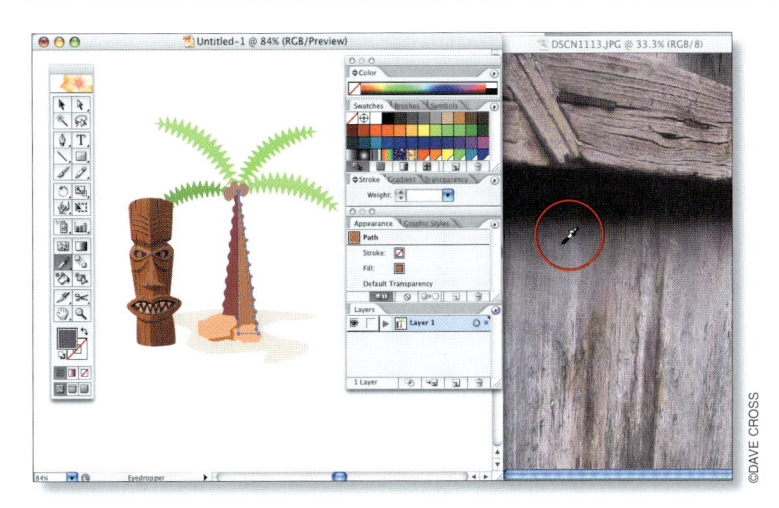

You can sample color from anywhere on your computer—or anything you can see, that is. Just take the Eyedropper tool (I) and click-and-hold anywhere on the artboard. Then, while still holding, drag the Eyedropper tool over any color you can see, including in other applications, other files, or on your desktop. In this example, we're sampling a color from a photo that's open in Photoshop.

GRADIENT PALETTE SHORTCUT

Here's a quick way to open the Gradient palette: Just double-click on the Gradient tool in the Toolbox and the palette will open (or move to the front if it's hidden behind other palettes).

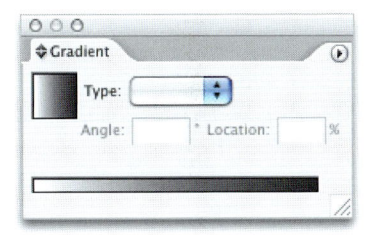

CHAPTER 5 • Colors, Swatches, Fills, and Strokes 123

Illustrator CS2 KillerTips

ONE-COLOR GRADIENT

To create a gradient using only one spot color, you'll get better printing results if you create a gradient that goes from 100% to 0% of the same color (rather than using white as the second color). Just drag your spot color twice to the Gradient Slider in the Gradient palette (found under the Window menu), then select the second color stop, go to the Color palette, and change its percentage to zero in the Tint Percentage field.

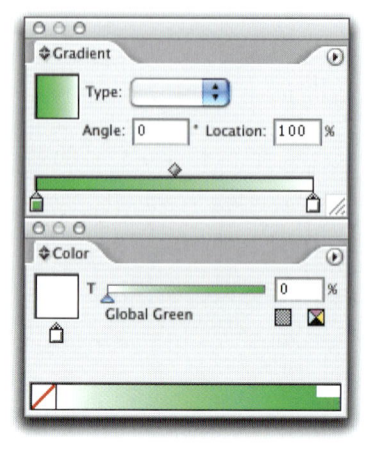

COLOR STOP

You can pick a color from an object in a document and use it to color a gradient stop. In the Gradient Slider, click on the stop you want to change and then pick the Eyedropper tool. Hold down the Shift key and click on an object to use its fill color for the gradient stop.

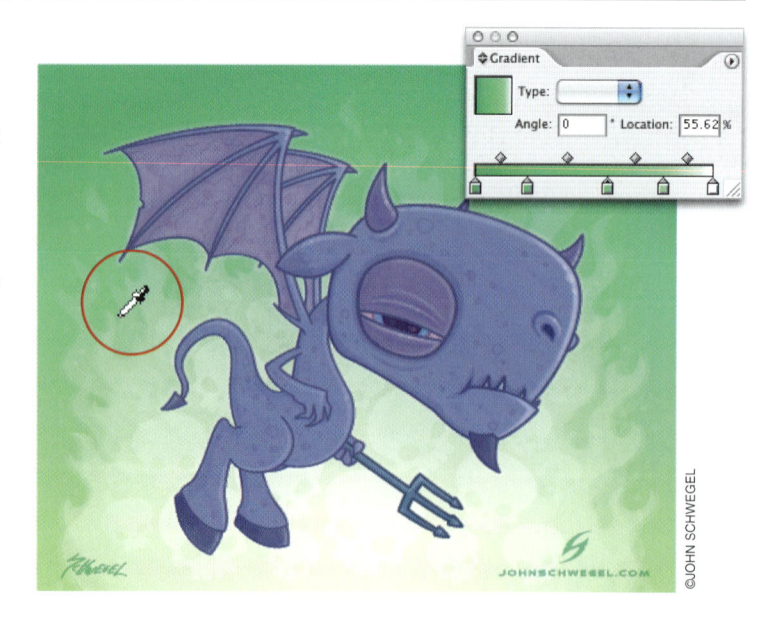

124 CHAPTER 5 • Colors, Swatches, Fills, and Strokes

DUPLICATE A COLOR STOP

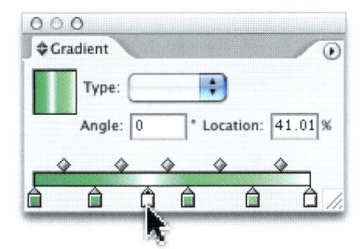

If you need to use the same color elsewhere in a gradient, you can easily copy a stop. In the Gradient Slider on the Gradient palette (Window>Gradient), press-and-hold the Option key (PC: Alt key), and then click on a stop and drag a copy to create a new color stop on the gradient.

SWAP STOPS

In the Gradient Slider on the Gradient palette (Window>Gradient), you can swap colors by holding down the Option key (PC: Alt key), and dragging an existing stop (the color you want) on top of another stop (the color you want to replace).

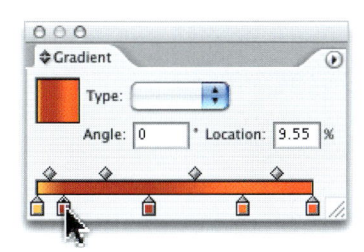

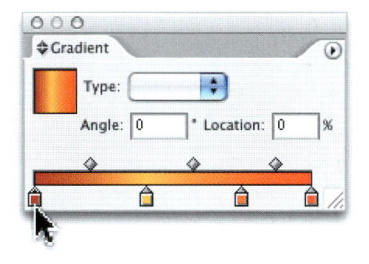

CHAPTER 5 • Colors, Swatches, Fills, and Strokes   125

USE A SWATCH AS A STOP

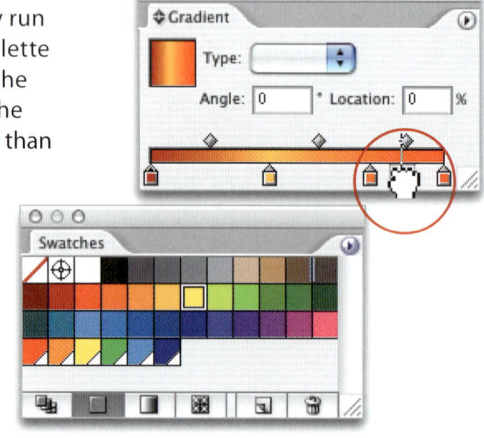

If you have selected an object filled with a gradient and you try to edit the gradient, you may run into a challenge. If you go to the Gradient palette (Window>Gradient), click on a color stop in the Gradient Slider, and then click on a swatch, the object's color will change to the swatch rather than editing the gradient. To apply a swatch to a color stop, click on the stop, hold down the Option key (PC: Alt key), and click on a swatch in the Swatches palette (Window>Swatches). You can also click-and-drag a swatch from the Swatches palette and drop it onto the Gradient Slider to create a new stop in that color (just don't let go of the swatch—click-and-drag in one step). If your stop changes color, but your gradient doesn't reflect the change, simply click on the stop and slide it a little. The gradient will then change.

QUICK STROKE CHANGE

Here's a great, quick way to change the stroke of a path, even if it's not selected. Just drag a swatch from the Swatches palette or Color palette (both found under the Window menu) onto an unselected path. If the stroke is not active in the Toolbox, press-and-hold the Shift key once you start to drag the swatch onto the path.

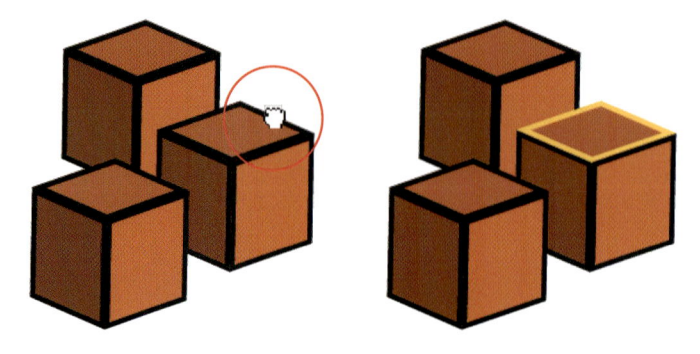

126   CHAPTER 5 • Colors, Swatches, Fills, and Strokes

CHANGE COLOR MODES IN THE COLOR PALETTE

If you need to change the color mode being used by the Color palette (from RGB to CMYK, for example), just press-and-hold the Shift key, and click on the color ramp at the bottom of the palette. With each click, you'll cycle through the various color modes.

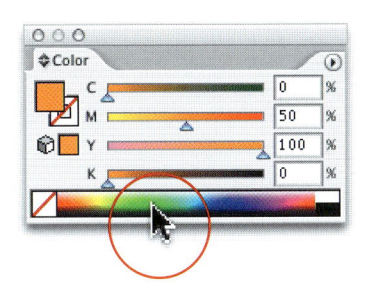

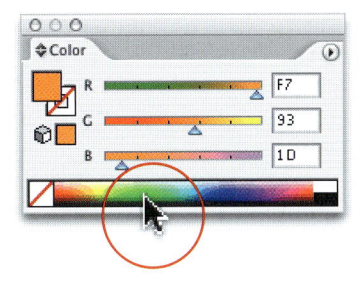

USE MULTIPLE STROKES IN APPEARANCE

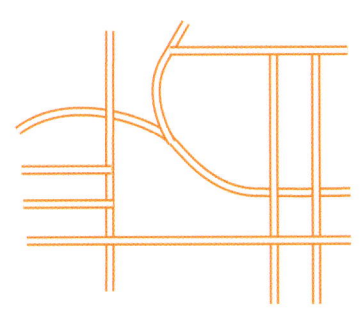

Here's a great way to use multiple strokes without creating multiple objects. Draw your path and in the Appearance palette (Window>Appearance), use the flyout menu to Add New Stroke. Double-click on each stroke in the Appearance palette and adjust the stroke width, color, and stacking order (using the Stroke palette, Color palette, etc.) to get the effect you want. (In our example, we chose a white, 5-point stroke and placed it above our wider 10-point stroke.) If you are working with multiple objects and need to get the "intersecting streets" look, select all the paths and press Command-8 (PC: Control-8) to create a compound path.

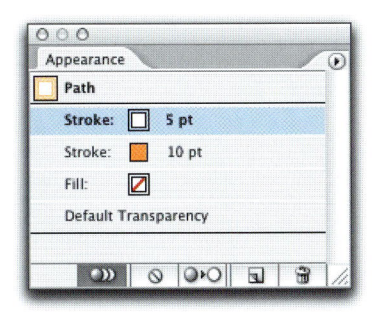

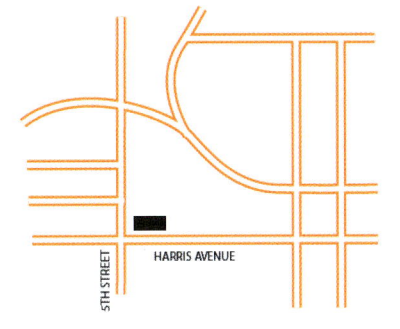

CHAPTER 5 • Colors, Swatches, Fills, and Strokes   127

ROUND JOINS

When you create a path that has a sharp corner, you have a couple of options for making it "less pointy" (how's that for technical terminology?). In the Stroke palette (found under the Window menu), you can either adjust the Miter Limit field by entering a lower number or, in many cases, it is simpler to change the join from Miter Join to Round Join or Bevel Join by clicking on one of the Join icons. (The same concept applies to the corners of a rectangle.) Remember to expand the Stroke palette (using the palette's flyout menu) if you can't see the Miter Limit or Join icons.

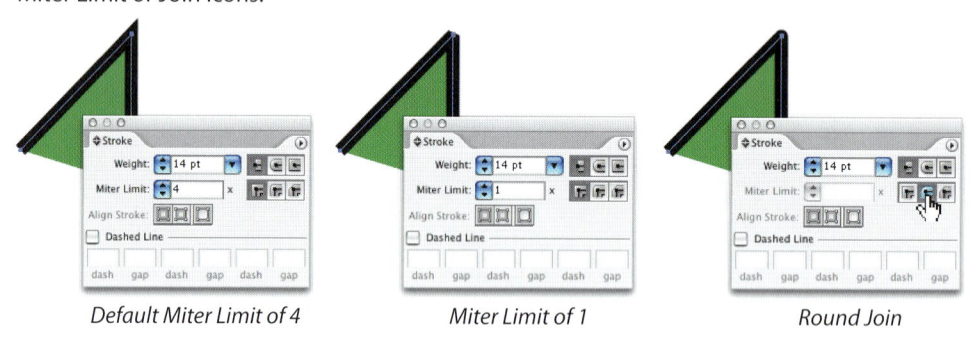

Default Miter Limit of 4   *Miter Limit of 1*   *Round Join*

APPLY SAMPLED COLORS

After you've sampled a color from an object with the Eyedropper tool (I), you can apply the color to an unselected object by pressing-and-holding the Option key (PC: Alt key). This turns the Eyedropper tool into the Black-tipped Apply-it Eyedropper tool (okay, we made up that name)—click and the color is applied.

128   CHAPTER 5 • Colors, Swatches, Fills, and Strokes

CHANGE LIVE PAINT BEHAVIOR

By default, the Live Paint Bucket (K) will paint only the fill of the area you've hovered over. (It paints with the Fill and Stroke colors showing in your Toolbox. To use the colors of another object, such as the small star in our image, click on that object and then Command-click [PC: Control-click] on the object you want to paint.) If you want to change the stroke color of an object using the Live Paint Bucket, press-and-hold the Shift key while hovering over the stroke and the cursor will change to a paintbrush, indicating you're now painting the stroke. (The other option is to double-click on the Live Paint Bucket and change the tool options to Paint Fills and Paint Strokes. Then the tool will affect either fill or stroke, depending on where it is positioned. You will see a paint bucket when you are hovering over the fill and a paintbrush when you are hovering over the stroke.)

SAME COLOR AGAIN

The Toolbox displays the last solid color and gradient fills you've used. After you have selected an object, check to see if your last-used color or gradient appears in the icons (shown here) just below the Fill and Stroke colors near the bottom of the Toolbox. If so, you can apply the last solid fill color you used by pressing the comma (,) key. To fill an object with the last gradient you used, press the period (.) key. Of course, this won't work if you're using the Type tool (T). (*Note:* Although Illustrator implies you should use the Shift key by showing < and > in the Toolbox, you don't need to do this. Instead, consider the keys as the comma and period keys.)

CHAPTER 5 • Colors, Swatches, Fills, and Strokes   129

FILL AND STROKE FROM THE KEYBOARD

Before you choose a color, you need to indicate whether you are working on the fill or stroke for the selected object. At the bottom of the Toolbox, look at the two icons that represent the Fill (left) and Stroke (right). The icon in front indicates which is active, fill or stroke. If the stroke is active and you want to work on the fill (or vice versa), press X. Each time you press X, you will toggle between an active fill or stroke (unless you are using the Type tool).

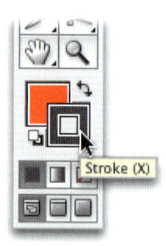

Fill selected after pressing X

Stroke selected after pressing X

NONE IN A HURRY

Need to change the fill or stroke of an object to None? After indicating whether you want to affect the fill or the stroke (see previous tip), press the forward slash key (/). (If you need a reminder as to which slash key to use, look at the "None" symbol, as shown here. And if you're using the Type tool [T], stop it. It won't work for this tip.)

130   CHAPTER 5 • Colors, Swatches, Fills, and Strokes

Illustrator CS2 KillerTips

WANT THE OPPOSITE?

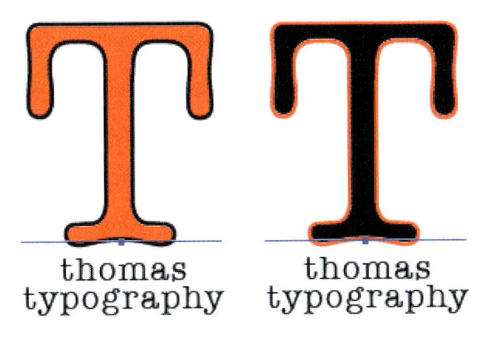

Okay, so you have an object that has a red fill and a black stroke and now you want to see it the other way around. Press Shift-X and the fill and stroke will be swapped (in this case resulting in a black fill and red stroke).

MAKE A SPOT COLOR

When you click on the New Swatch icon in the Swatches palette (Window>Swatches), you'll get, yes, a new swatch. However, the swatch will be a process color. If you want a spot color swatch, hold down the Command key (PC: Control key) as you click on the New Swatch icon. To edit your spot color, head to the Color palette (Window>Color).

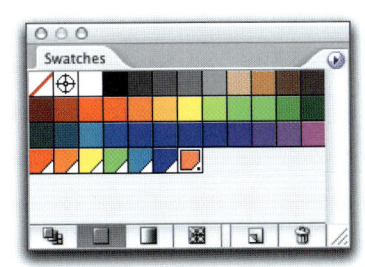

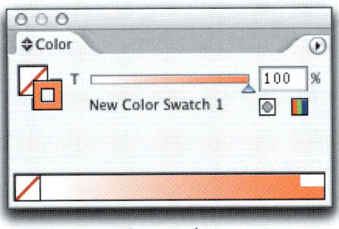

Spot color

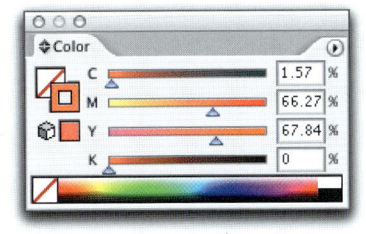

Process color

CHAPTER 5 • Colors, Swatches, Fills, and Strokes   131

COMPLEMENTARY COLORS

To choose the complementary color of the current fill or stroke (depending on which one is active in the Toolbox) of a selected object, hold down the Command and Control keys (PC: Control only), and click in the color ramp at the bottom of the Color palette. (Or, use the flyout menu in the Color palette and choose Complement.)

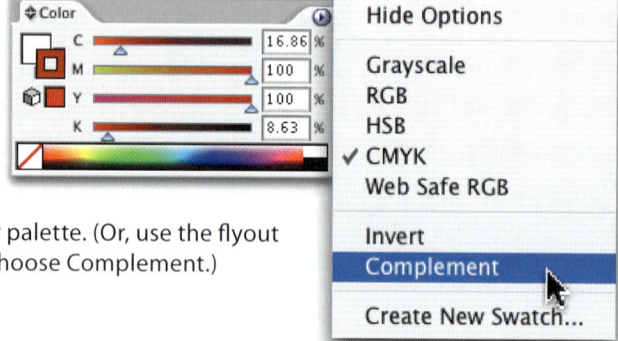

INVERT THE COLOR

To pick the inverse of the current fill or stroke (depending on which one is active in the Toolbox) of a selected object, press-and-hold Command-Shift (PC: Control-Shift), and click on the color ramp on the bottom of the Color palette. (Or, use the flyout menu in the Color palette and choose Invert.)

REPLACE ONE SWATCH WITH ANOTHER

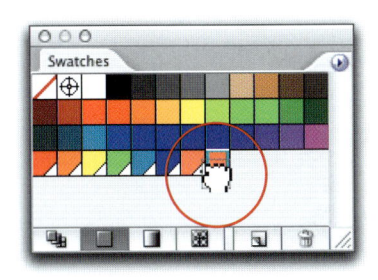

If you've used a color or gradient for various objects and you want to replace that color with another one, press-and-hold the Option key (PC: Alt key), and drag the new replacement swatch over the original swatch. If you're using global color, meaning you've checked Global in the New Swatch dialog when you created the color, all objects using the original global color will change to the new color. (*Note:* Doing this will remove the original swatch from the palette. So, if you want to keep the original color, drag the swatch onto the New Swatch icon to duplicate it before using this replacement method.)

GRAYSCALE OR COLOR GRAY

Huh? Okay, so you want to fill an object with 60% gray. You could change the Color palette (Window>Color) to Grayscale from the flyout menu and enter 60 in the Tint Percentage field. However, that means that your object will always be gray, so you won't be able to change it to color in the Color palette, unless you first change the mode of that object to CMYK. Instead, stick with CMYK and just enter 60 in the K field—that way you can always change to a color from the Color palette whenever you want.

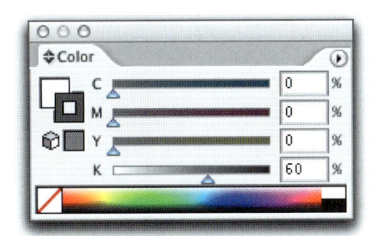

CHAPTER 5 • Colors, Swatches, Fills, and Strokes   133

FIND A COLOR

If you need to pick a specific Pantone color, go to the Window menu and choose the appropriate Pantone library from the Swatch Libraries. Use the flyout menu in the Pantone palette and choose Show Find Field. Then enter the Pantone number you need in the Find field (type in only the number, there's no need for "Pantone").

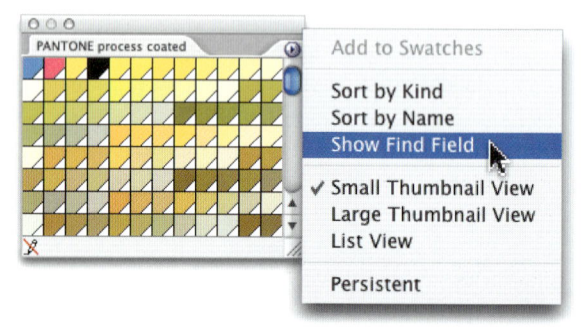

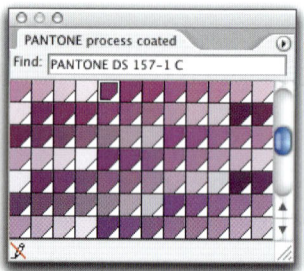

GRAYSCALE PRINT FROM A COLOR FILE

Although it is possible to print a grayscale version of a document using the Print command, on some color inkjet printers the results may be less than satisfactory. Instead, make a quick grayscale version of your document by selecting all the artwork and from the Filter menu, choosing Colors>Convert to Grayscale (gradients and patterns will not be converted). If you like, save as a different name, or just print and then undo the filter.

SAVE SWATCH LIBRARIES

You can edit Illustrator's startup documents to customize your palettes, but this doesn't really help if you are constantly changing sets of swatches. Instead, consider saving and using libraries. Add and delete swatches until the Swatches palette contains your choice of swatches and then use the palette's flyout menu to choose Save Swatch Library. Name it and save it in the Swatches folder in the Illustrator CS2 Applications (PC: Program Files) folder under Presets. Restart Illustrator, and from then on you can access your library from the Window>Swatch Libraries>(yourlibrary).

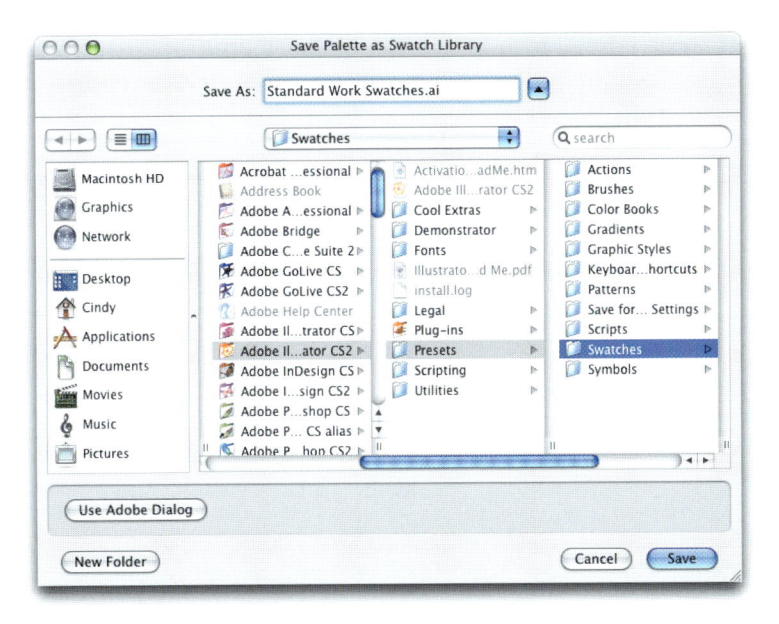

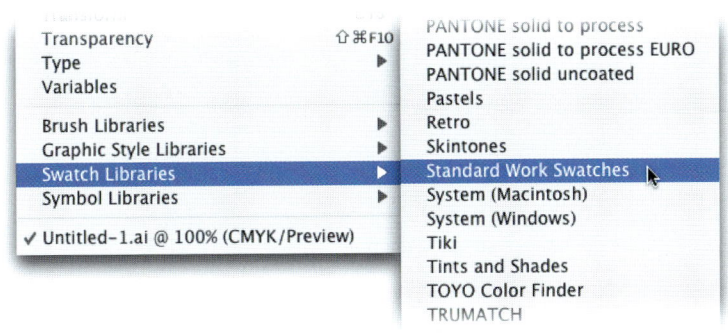

CHAPTER 5 • Colors, Swatches, Fills, and Strokes   135

EXPAND A GRADIENT

There are times when you may have to expand a gradient to convert it to a series of objects (for example, if you are having trouble getting a gradient to print and/or look the way you want). With the object selected, go to the Object menu and choose Expand. In the dialog, choose between Gradient Mesh and Specify Objects. To expand a gradient-filled object with the last-used settings, press-and-hold the Option key (PC: Alt key) as you choose Object>Expand.

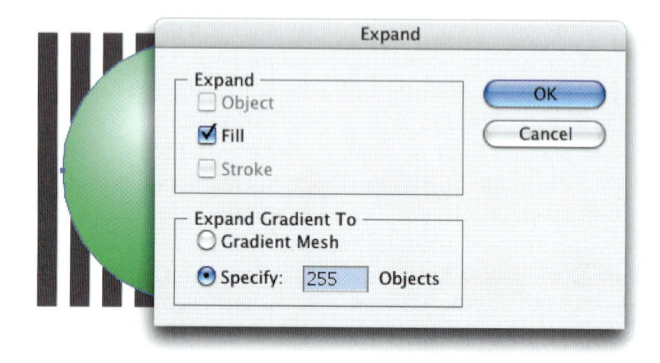

TEST PAGE

Considering how different shades of colors, grays, and stroke widths can look on different printers, you may want to create a printer test page that contains boxes filled with a variety of shades of gray, standard colors, paths with different stroke widths, and type in various small font sizes. Anytime you want to decide on the best color, shade, or stroke width to use, print your test page, and use that as your guide. (If your final output is always the same printer, create a test page that contains every swatch and gradient and use it to choose swatches based on the printed version rather than the screen.)

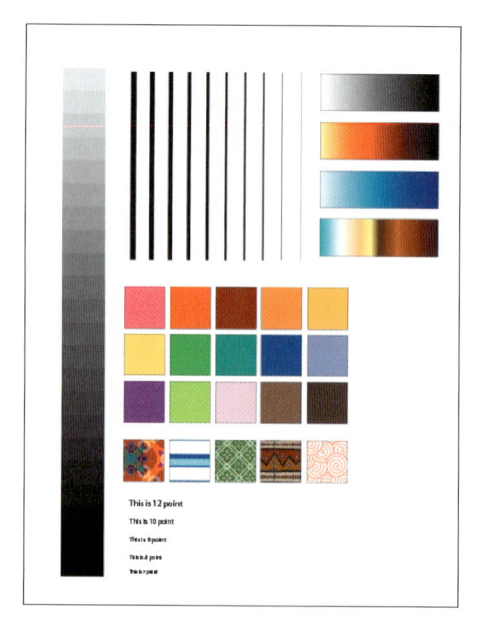

136   CHAPTER 5 • Colors, Swatches, Fills, and Strokes

FADE TO NOTHING

Unfortunately, in Illustrator you cannot create a gradient that goes from a color to transparent as you can in Photoshop. To work around this, create a gradient using the color you need plus white. Fill the object with the gradient and then create an opacity mask to gradually change the object to transparent. To do this, create a rectangle slightly bigger than your object and position the rectangle over the object. Fill the rectangle with a black-to-white gradient, positioning the black over the area of the original object where you want the gradient to be see-through. Select both objects and from the Transparency palette (Window>Transparency), use the flyout menu to choose Make Opacity Mask. If you need to adjust the effect, click on the mask thumbnail (that's to the right of your object) in the Transparency palette and then adjust the position of the rectangle and/or the gradient. To return to regular editing, make sure you click on the object's thumbnail (that's to the left of the mask) in the Transparency palette.

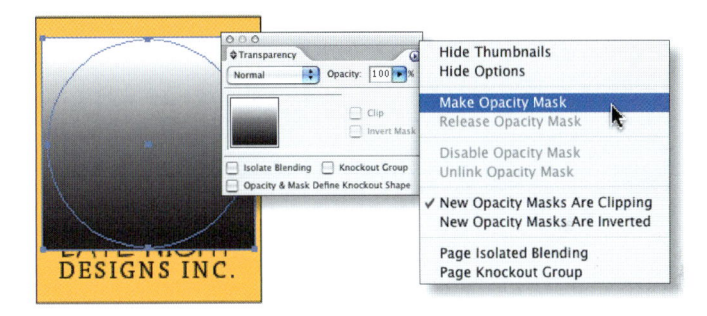

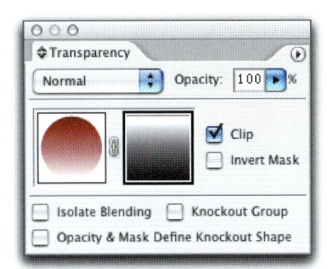

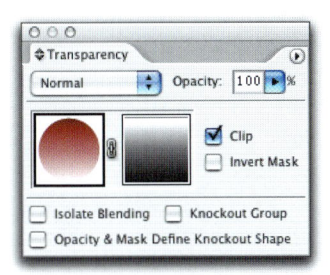

Edit the mask

Edit the object

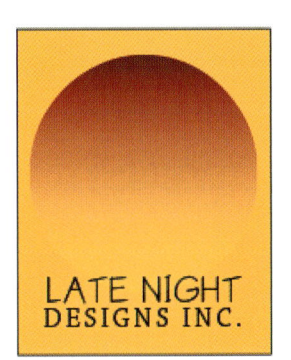

CHAPTER 5 • Colors, Swatches, Fills, and Strokes 137

Illustrator CS2 KillerTips

USE PREVIEW BOUNDS

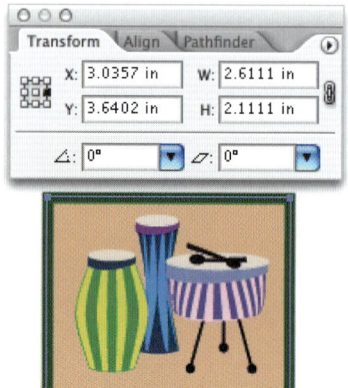

By default, Illustrator uses the path of an object for measurements, alignments, etc., ignoring the stroke width. No matter how thick the stroke, the size of the object will be measured based on the position of the path. If you want to use the stroke width (and position) as the reference rather than the path, press Command-K (PC: Control-K) to go to the Preferences dialog and check Use Preview Bounds. From then on, all operations will be measured based on the thickness and position of the stroke, as shown here in the Transform palette (Window>Transform).

ONE-TIME PREVIEW BOUNDS

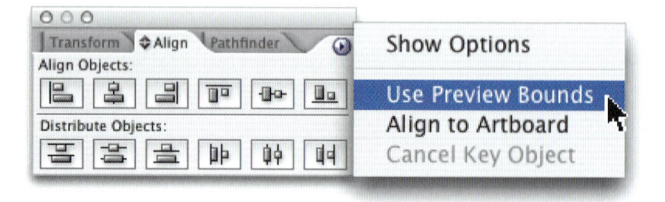

The only downside to the previous tip is that you change the setting for all operations to use the stroke width. If you're using the Align palette (Window>Align), there is a quicker way for one-time uses. Use the flyout menu in the Align palette and click on Use Preview Bounds to turn it on when you want to use it and turn it off when you're done. In other words, the Align palette temporarily overrides the Preferences setting.

138   CHAPTER 5 • Colors, Swatches, Fills, and Strokes

CHAPTER 5 • Colors, Swatches, Fills, and Strokes

Sultans of Swing

A KILLER COLLECTION OF ILLUSTRATOR ARTISTS

Okay, so this isn't really a chapter but more of a bonus section to the book. We thought it would be cool to show you what some

Sultans of Swing
a killer collection of illustrator artists

of the hottest artists out there are doing with Adobe Illustrator. These folks continually imagine new ways to combine the tools in Illustrator to create some stunning results. Plus, it's our way of thanking these folks who have allowed us to use their artwork in this book. We're continually amazed by the work that we see in this industry and we hope you enjoy the creative inspiration that we've added here.

Illustrator CS2 KillerTips

Scott Hinton
scotthinton@bitwisesystems.com

142   CHAPTER 6 • A Killer Collection of Illustrator Artists

Illustrator CS2 KillerTips

David Pounds
davidpounds@hisnet.org

CHAPTER 6 • A Killer Collection of Illustrator Artists   143

Illustrator CS2
KillerTips

Philip J. Neal
www.pneal.com • Philip@3pixels.net

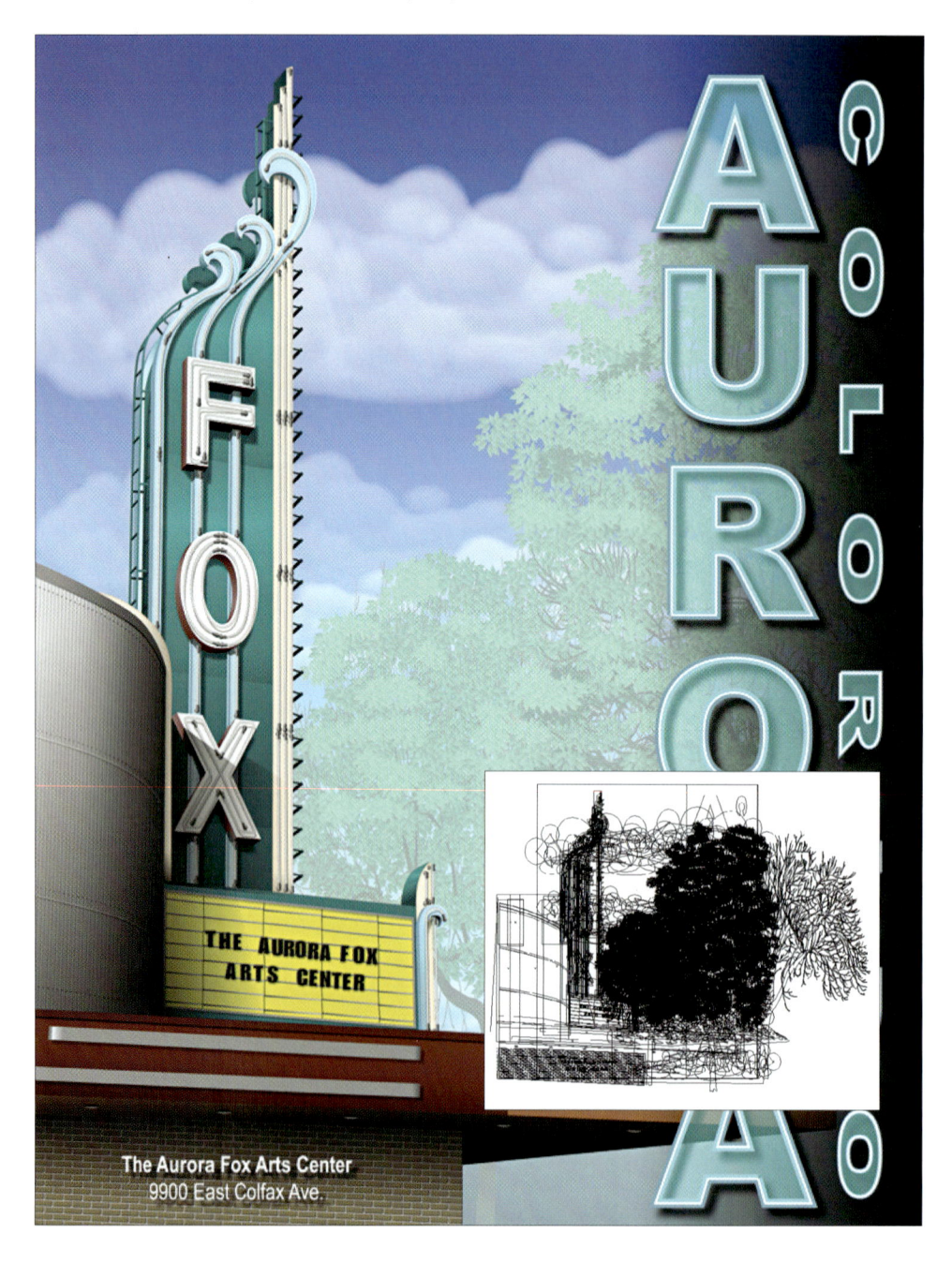

144 CHAPTER 6 • A Killer Collection of Illustrator Artists

Illustrator CS2
KillerTips

Mike Sellers
www.circlenlinestudios.com • mike@circlenlinestudios.com

CHAPTER 6 • A Killer Collection of Illustrator Artists   145

Illustrator CS2
KillerTips

Todd Ferris
www.warking.com • twf9999@optonline.net

146 CHAPTER 6 • A Killer Collection of Illustrator Artists

Scott Weichert

www.weichertcreative.com • scott@weichertcreative.com

CHAPTER 6 • A Killer Collection of Illustrator Artists   147

Illustrator CS2 KillerTips

John Schwegel
www.johnschwegel.com • john@johnschwegel.com

148   CHAPTER 6 • A Killer Collection of Illustrator Artists

Illustrator CS2
KillerTips

Jib Hunt
www.jibhunt.com • jib@jibhunt.com

CHAPTER 6 • A Killer Collection of Illustrator Artists

Brooke Nuñez
www.lifeinvector.com • brooke@lifeinvector.com

150 CHAPTER 6 • A Killer Collection of Illustrator Artists

Erwin Haya
www.onesickindividual.com • erwinhaya@hotmail.com

CHAPTER 6 • A Killer Collection of Illustrator Artists

Illustrator CS2
KillerTips

Mark Anderson
www.bigwhiskeyart.com

152   CHAPTER 6 • A Killer Collection of Illustrator Artists

Illustrator CS2 KillerTips

Christian Musselman
www.christianmusselman.com • chris@christianmusselman.com

CHAPTER 6 • A Killer Collection of Illustrator Artists   153

Get Smart

LAYERS AND TRANSPARENCY

Imagine you have a stack of clear plastic sheets—you know, acetate. Each sheet has a colored graphic printed on it. Now imagine

Get Smart
layers and transparency

that you carefully overlay one sheet on top of another to create an informational graphic that shows a step-by-step procedure. With us so far? Okay, now imagine that you're standing beside an overhead projector (remember those?) with your stack of acetates, with your palms sweating, heart pounding, anxiously waiting for your presentation to start. Phew, we don't know about you, but that brings back nerve-wracking memories of the days before PowerPoint and data projectors. Makes working with Illustrator layers so easy that it's laughable. Ha ha ha… Ha!

DIM IMAGES

A common approach to creating artwork in Illustrator is to import a photograph or a scanned image (File>Place) and to trace over it. You can make this procedure a little easier by putting the placed image on its own layer and then making it a template. Use the Layers palette's flyout menu to choose Template. The placed image will automatically be dimmed. To change the setting for the template, double-click on the layer in the Layers palette to open the Layer Options dialog. In the Dim Images To field, enter a percentage. Then click on the Create New Layer icon at the bottom of the Layers palette and use your favorite creation tools to trace over the dimmed image.

NAME THE NEW LAYER

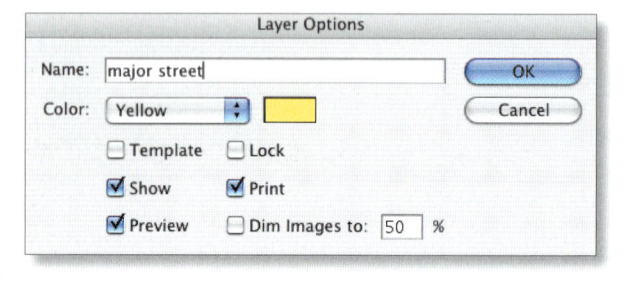

When you add a new layer by clicking on the Create New Layer icon in the Layers palette (Window>Layers), the layer is automatically named "Layer x" (with x representing the next number). To create a new layer and name it, Option-click (PC: Alt-click) on the Create New Layer icon to open the Layer Options dialog where you can enter a name for the layer.

WHITE REALLY ISN'T WHITE

OK, maybe the title is exaggerated a bit. White is still white. But, the artboard in Illustrator isn't really white and will not reflect any transparency settings that white would normally influence. A little confused on what this means? Try this. Create an illustration or graphic in Illustrator—any small object should do—but just be sure it has no fill and a colored stroke, and you don't have anything in the layers below it. Select it, then in the Transparency palette (Window>Transparency), change the blend of that object to Soft Light. Nothing should happen. Now, add a rectangle with a white fill and no stroke to a layer below your object and you should see that top object disappear wherever it intersects with the white rectangle below it. This means that even though the artboard is white, it's not REALLY white.

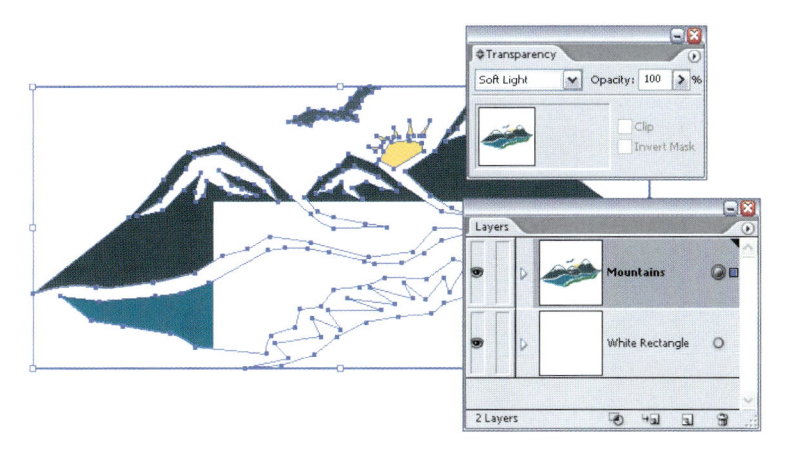

CHAPTER 7 • Layers and Transparency 157

HIDE OTHER LAYERS

A quick way to view just one layer and hide all the rest of the layers is to press-and-hold the Option key (PC: Alt key) and click on the Eye icon beside the layer you want to view in the Layers palette. All the other layers will be hidden. Repeat to show all the layers again.

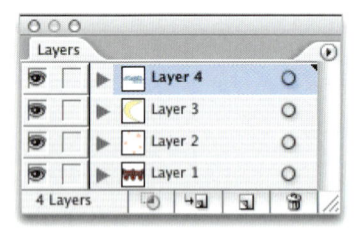

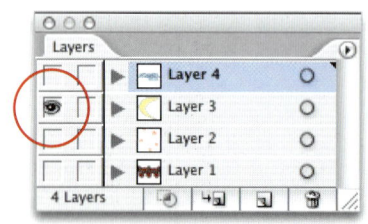

CHANGE ONE LAYER TO OUTLINE VIEW

Changing to Outline view (Command-Y [PC: Control-Y]) is a great way see all the paths and anchor points. If you want to change only one layer to Outline view (rather than the entire document), press-and-hold the Command key (PC: Control key) and click on its Eye icon.

158   CHAPTER 7 • Layers and Transparency

CHANGE OTHER LAYERS TO OUTLINE VIEW

When your artwork is in Outline view (Command-Y [PC: Control-Y]), things move faster since you're not waiting for the screen to redraw. Here's one way to take advantage of almost everything being in Outline view. Press-and-hold Command-Option (PC: Control-Alt) and click on the Eye icon beside the layer you need to change every other layer into Outline view, while your current layer remains in Preview view.

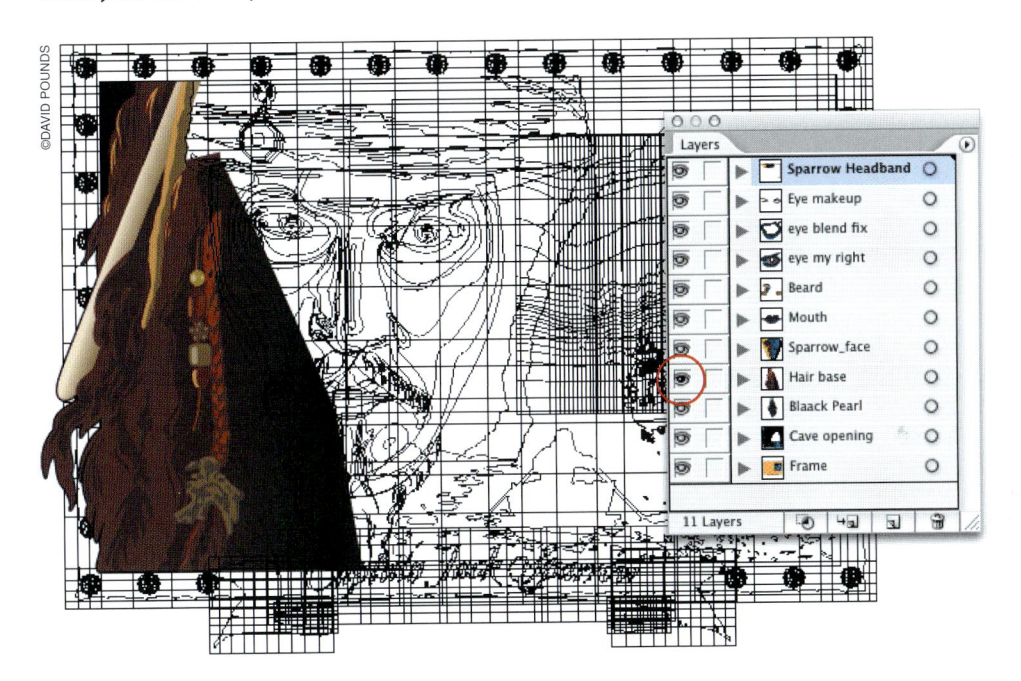

CHAPTER 7 • Layers and Transparency   159

RELEASE THE LAYERS!

If you find yourself creating Web animations, then Illustrator and its Blend Tool (W) can be your best friend. However, when you expand a Blend in Illustrator (Object>Blend>Expand) it leaves you with a Group. This makes it difficult to export to Photoshop or ImageReady for animation since exporting to PSD will flatten the Group layer. To get around this, immediately after Expanding the Blend, choose Release to Layers (Sequence) from the Layers palette's flyout menu. This will convert all of the paths in the group to layers, thus preserving each object when you export to a PSD file.

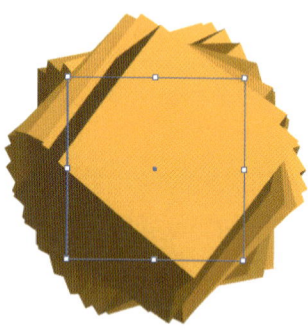

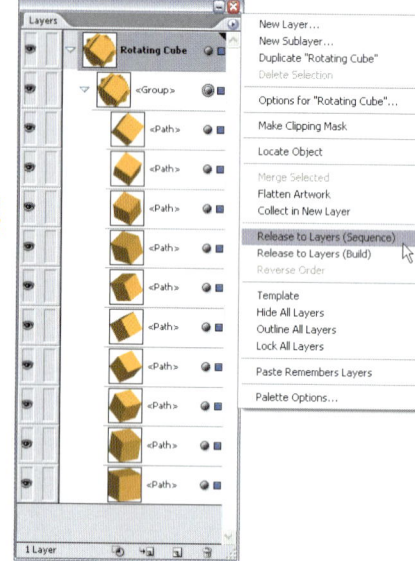

COPY AN OBJECT TO A LAYER

To move a selected object onto a different layer, look for the tiny square to the far right of the current layer's name in the Layers palette. Drag that square to a different layer and the object will move to that layer. However, if you want to copy the object so that it stays on its current layer and a copy appears on a different layer, hold down the Option key (PC: Alt key) as you drag the small square.

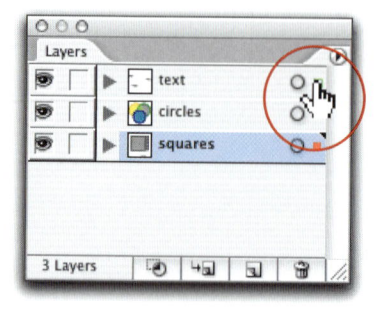

160   CHAPTER 7 • Layers and Transparency

DUPLICATE THE ENTIRE LAYER

To quickly make an exact duplicate of a layer—and therefore, of all the objects on that layer—click on the layer name, then press-and-hold the Option key (PC: Alt key) as you drag that layer onto the Create New Layer icon at the bottom of the Layers palette.

CHAPTER 7 • Layers and Transparency   161

SELECT EVERYTHING ON A LAYER

How many times have you wanted to select every single object on a layer? Of course, the Select>All command won't help since every object on every layer would be selected. Here's the solution: In the Layers palette, locate the layer whose objects you want to select and either click on the small box (or empty space) to the right of the round button to the far right of the layer name, or Option-click (PC: Alt-click) on the name of the layer. All the objects on that layer will be selected.

SELECT EVERYTHING ON MULTIPLE LAYERS

To take the previous tip a step further, if you need to select all of the objects on multiple layers, Option-Shift-click (PC: Alt-Shift-click) on the names of the contiguous layers whose objects you need to select, or Command-Option-click (PC: Control-Alt-click) to select non-contiguous layers.

162   CHAPTER 7 • Layers and Transparency

LOCK ALL OTHER LAYERS

Locking objects is a very effective way to work—you can still see the objects but you cannot select or alter them by mistake. To lock every layer except the one you're working on, Option-click (PC: Alt-click) on the empty box next to the Eye icon on your current layer. All the layers, except the one you're working on, will be locked. Repeat the same operation to unlock all the layers.

©TODD FERRIS/POSE BY STEVE FERRIS

USE LAYERS TO UNLOCK INDIVIDUAL OBJECTS

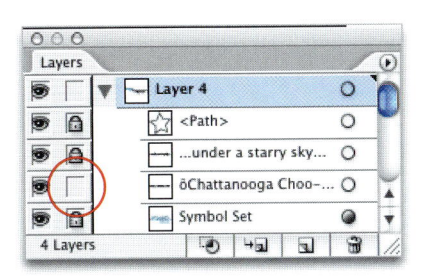

For many people, the first shortcuts they memorize are used to lock and unlock objects. Unfortunately, Command-2 (PC: Control-2) will lock one object, while Command-Option-2 (PC: Control-Alt-2) will unlock all objects. Sadly, there is no keyboard command to unlock just the last object that you locked a moment ago. The Layers palette offers a great alternative: Expand the layer by clicking on the triangle beside the layer's name, and then click the Lock icon to the left of the individual sublayer (object) you need to work with. (This only works if sublayers are locked, rather than the entire layer being locked.)

CHAPTER 7 • Layers and Transparency

LOCATE LAYER

If you need to figure out what layer or sublayer an object is on, try this method. Click on the object to select it and then from the Layers palette's flyout menu, choose Locate Object. The sublayers will be expanded to reveal the location of the selected object.

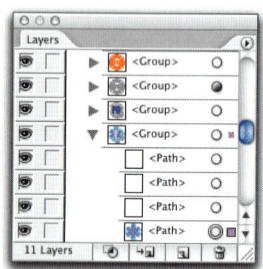

JUMP TO A LAYER

Here's a Windows-only tip that lets you jump to a specific layer in a long list in your Layers palette. Press-and-hold Control-Alt and click in the Layers palette. A solid black line will appear around the interior of the palette. Start typing the layer name to jump to that layer. (If you have a bunch of layers called "Layer 1," "Layer 2," and so on, just type the number and you'll jump to that layer.)

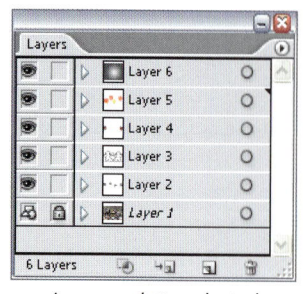

Layers palette selected

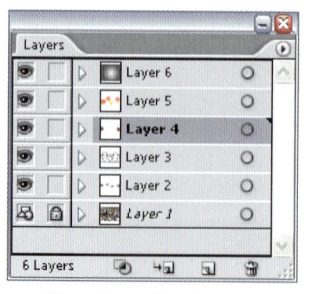

Type 4 to select Layer 4

164 CHAPTER 7 • Layers and Transparency

CUSTOM LAYER ROW SIZE

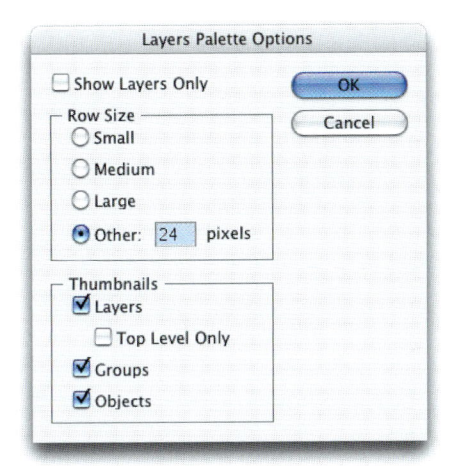

In the Palette Options dialog (found using the Layers palette flyout menu), you can choose between small, medium, and large row sizes. But, in addition to picking between those built-in sizes, you can make your own by choosing Other and entering a specific size. This is another one of these tips that you may not use often, but there are times when it's a perfect solution for those Goldilocks situations (this one is too small, this one is too big, but this one is just right).

EXPAND ALL SUBLAYERS

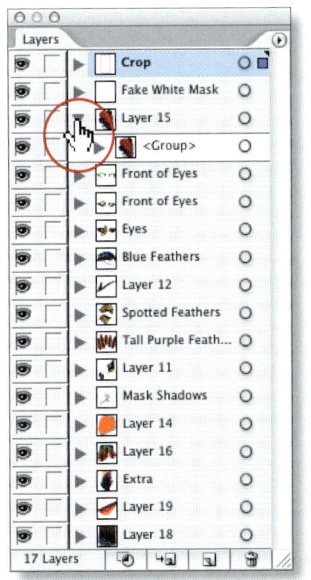

To see all the sublayers in the Layers palette, Option-click (PC: Alt-click) on the expansion triangle beside one of the layers. All the layers will be expanded to display all of their sublayers. (*Note:* This works differently depending on what sublayers you already have expanded.)

Layer expanded without Option-clicking

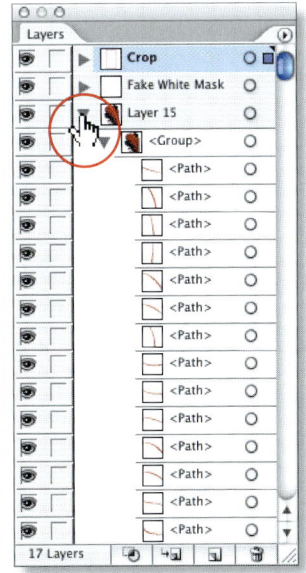

Layer expanded by Option-clicking

CHAPTER 7 • Layers and Transparency   165

NEW LAYER ON TOP

When you click on the Create New Layer icon in the Layers palette, the new layer is created right above the current layer. If you want the new layer to be added at the very top of all the layers, hold down the Command key (PC: Control key) as you click on the Create New Layer icon.

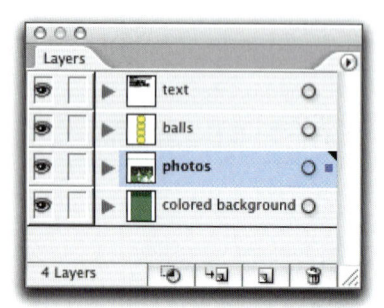

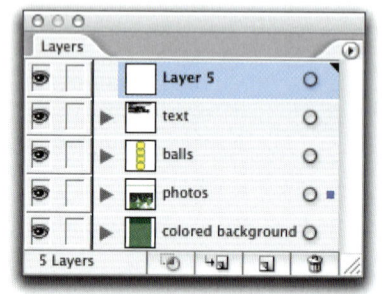

NEW LAYER BELOW

If you want a new layer to be created below the current layer, Command-Option-click (PC: Control-Alt-click) on the Create New Layer icon. The Layer Options dialog will open, but once you click OK, the new layer will be created immediately below the current layer (here we've added a new layer named "additional text" below the layer named "balls").

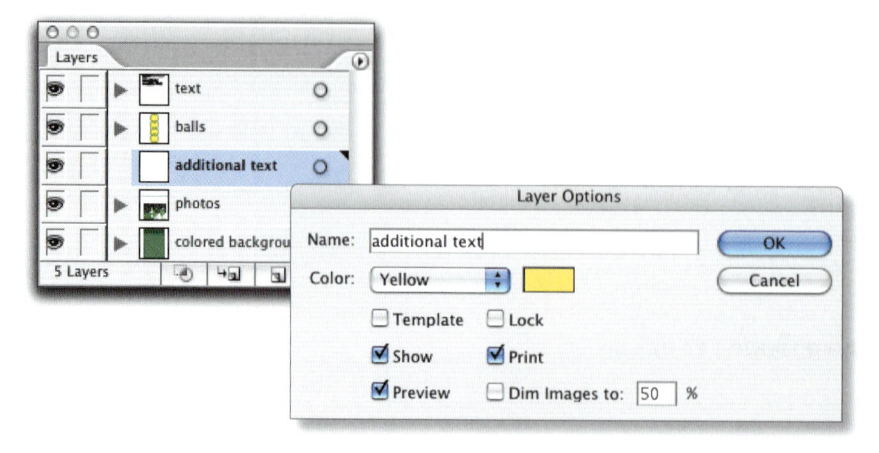

TARGET A LAYER

The empty circle to the right of a layer name serves a very important purpose: When you click on the circle, you are targeting the entire layer. Change the layer's appearance and every object on that layer will have the same appearance. For instance, this applies if you have the layer targeted and then select options in the Appearance and Graphic Styles palettes or use options from the Effect menu, such as Brush Strokes. Once a layer has been targeted and a new appearance applied, the empty circle changes to a shaded circle.

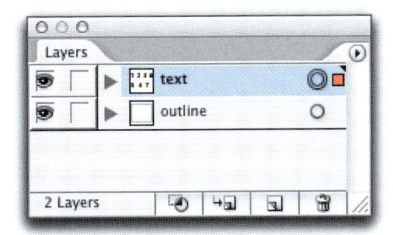

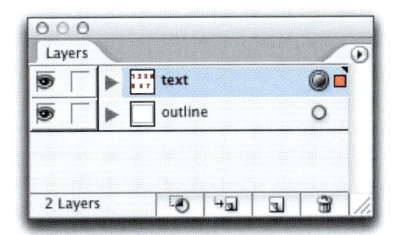

MOVING TARGETS

If you have targeted a layer and have changed its appearance, you can easily change your mind and apply the appearance to a different layer. Just click on the shaded circle and drag it onto an empty circle beside a different layer. The look will be moved from the original layer and applied to the other layer.

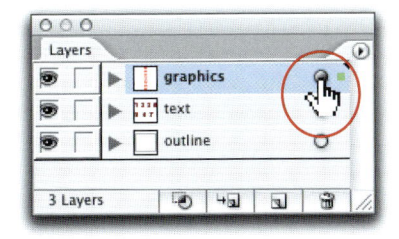

CHAPTER 7 • Layers and Transparency   167

MOVING TARGETS, PART TWO

Here's another possibility: You love the look of one targeted layer so much that you also want to apply that look to another layer. Instead of moving the target, copy it by pressing-and-holding the Option key (PC: Alt key) as you drag the target from the current layer to another layer (note the plus sign beside your pointer).

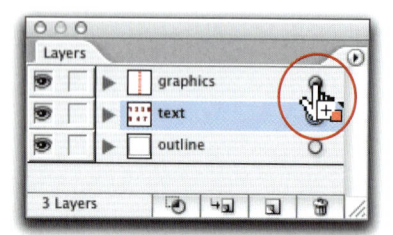

PASTE REMEMBERS LAYERS

This command is very important when copying-and-pasting objects between documents. It is also an important option when copying-and-pasting in the same document. By default this option is turned off, so when you first start working with layers, you may want to go to the Layers palette's flyout menu and select Paste Remembers Layers. Then it will stay on, even when you create new documents.

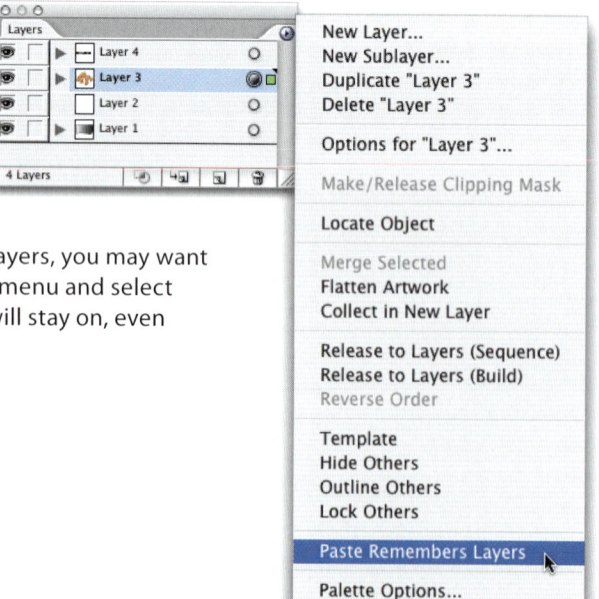

Illustrator CS2
KillerTips

MIRROR REFLECTIONS

Want to create a mirror reflection right inside Illustrator? It's easy. First you'll need to duplicate whatever object you want to create the mirror reflection of so you have two of them. Next, select the object and choose Object>Transform>Reflect. Pick the horizontal option and click OK. Position the duplicate toward the bottom of the original. Next, click the Create New Layer icon at the bottom of the Layers palette to get a blank layer above the layer with your objects. On the new layer, create a rectangle that covers the duplicate object, fill it with a white to black linear gradient, and set the stroke to none. Select both the rectangle and the duplicate object and choose Make Opacity Mask from the Transparency palette's flyout menu. Instant reflection!

©MATT KLOSKOWSKI

CHAPTER 7 • Layers and Transparency   169

LAYER COMPS?

Photoshop CS2 has a great feature called Layer Comps, which helps you save different layer combinations in one document. Although Illustrator CS2 doesn't have the same feature, you can create a similar effect using custom views. Hide one or more layers by clicking on the Eye icons in the Layers palette, and then from the View menu, create a New View, give it a name in the dialog, and click OK. Repeat this to create as many different combinations of layers as you want and then choose your named views from the View menu to look at the different combinations. (*Note:* Custom views work best with top-level layers rather than sublayers.) If you want, you can even add a keyboard shortcut to these "layer comps" using Edit>Keyboard Shortcuts to assign a shortcut to Custom View 1, Custom View 2, etc.

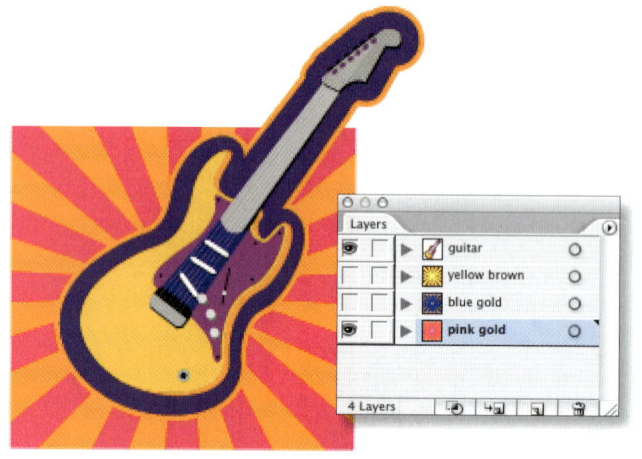

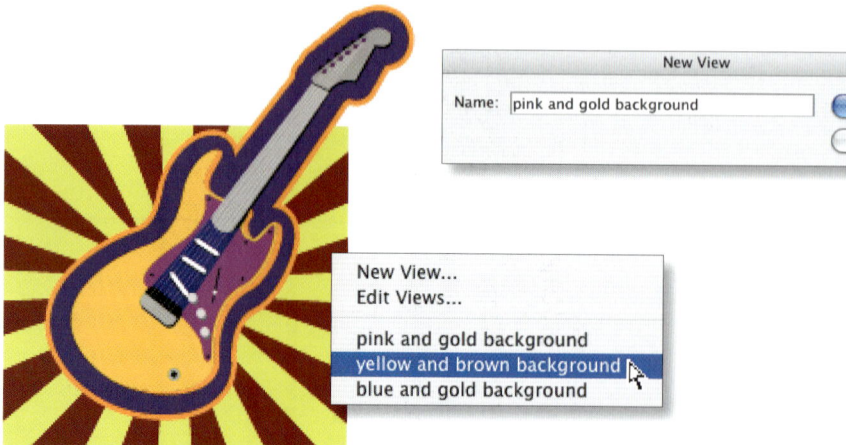

170   CHAPTER 7 • Layers and Transparency

SELECTING MULTIPLE LAYERS

Hold down the Shift key to select more than one layer in the Layers palette (how's that for a staggeringly surprising tip?). Only problem is, you can only select contiguous layers that way (meaning layers that are above or below one another). To select multiple layers anywhere in the list of layers, hold down the Command key (PC: Control key) and click to select non-contiguous layers.

CHAPTER 7 • Layers and Transparency

MOVE OBJECTS TO A DIFFERENT LAYER

As we saw earlier, you move a selected object to a different layer by clicking on the small square and dragging it to a different layer. However, this won't work if you need to move a bunch of objects from various layers to one layer. To do this, you'll have to use the Selection tool (V) and Shift-click to select the objects you need to move and then click on the name of the layer that you want to move them to. Then from the Object menu choose Arrange>Send to Current Layer.

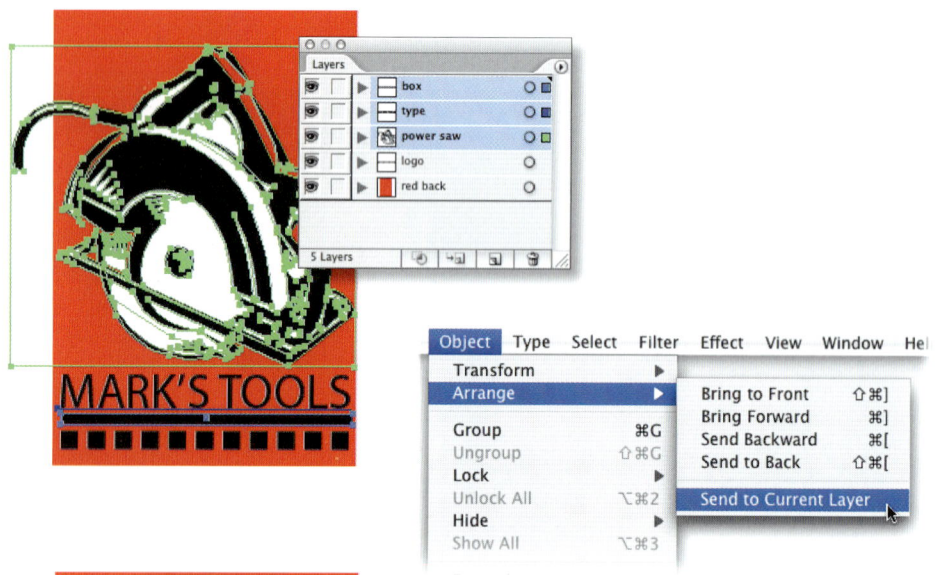

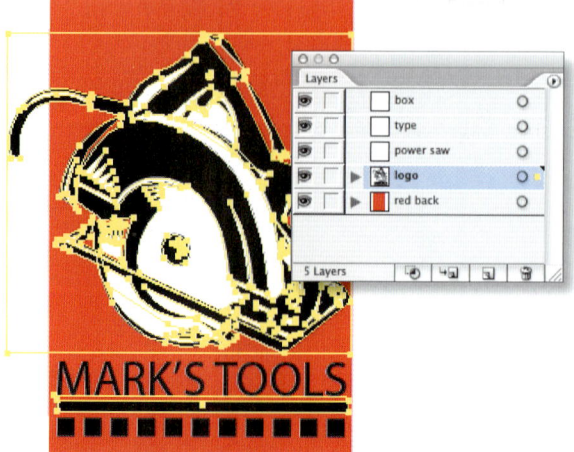

172   CHAPTER 7 • Layers and Transparency

VECTOR TEMPLATES?

Typically, a placed raster image is used as a template to create an illustration. After placing the image (File>Place), choose Template from the Layers palette's flyout menu and if you want, use the Layers Options dialog to further dim the template for easier tracing. Just double-click on your layer name and in the dialog, click the Template checkbox. The Dim Images To field will be editable and you can enter a percentage. But, can you use an Illustrator (vector) object as a template? Well, yes and no. While you can turn a vector layer into a template using the same method just described, you cannot dim an Illustrator object. Another option would be to rasterize the object and then turn it into a template. Choose File>Place to get the vector image, and from the Object menu choose Rasterize. Then use the Layers palette's flyout menu to make the rasterized object into a template. You know the layer is a template when the Template icon appears in the Eye icon box to the left of the layer name. (*Note:* You may want to duplicate the original object before rasterizing just so you have a backup plan.)

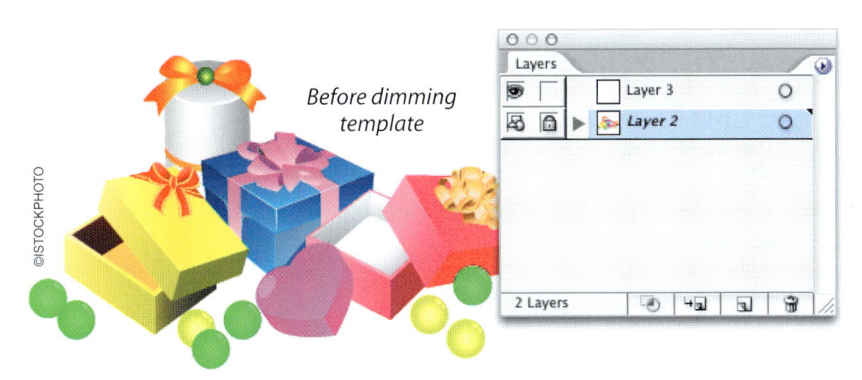

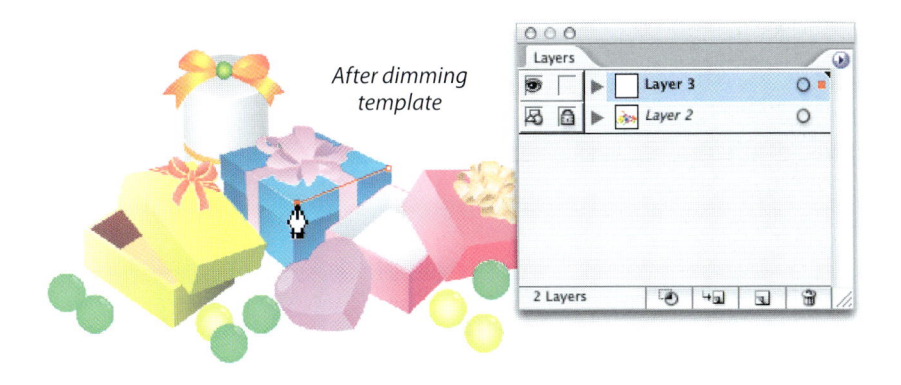

Before dimming template

After dimming template

CHAPTER 7 • Layers and Transparency   173

DON'T PRINT

Here's a simple way to tell at a quick glance if the Print option is turned off in the Layer Options dialog, meaning this layer won't print: Just look at the name of the layer. If the layer name appears in italics, the option to print has been turned off. Double-click on the layer name to open the Layer Options dialog and turn on printing by clicking the Print checkbox (and the display of the layer name will return to standard type).

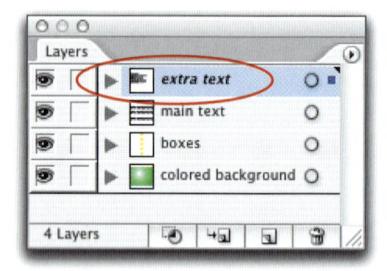

NO SUBLAYERS

To simplify the display of the Layers palette, use the flyout menu to choose Palette Options. In the dialog, check the Show Layers Only box to hide everything except the top-level layers.

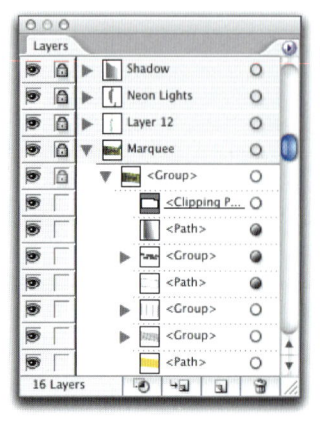

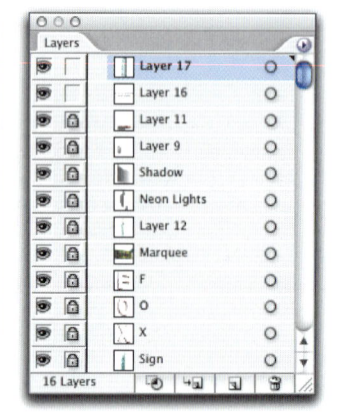

174 CHAPTER 7 • Layers and Transparency

HIDE TEMPLATE

If you've used a template in your document, you can quickly toggle the template on and off (showing and hiding the template) by pressing Command-Shift-W (PC: Control-Shift-W). This command can also be found under the View menu, as shown here.

WHEN SELECT ALL DOESN'T WORK

If you use Command-A (PC: Control-A) to Select All, it may not actually select *all* of your artwork. If you have locked or hidden objects on layers or sublayers, objects on those layers will not be selected. To make sure that Select All will really select everything, use the Unlock All and Show All commands (from the Object menu), then use the Select All command.

CHAPTER 7 • Layers and Transparency   175

MERGE SELECTED

If your Layers palette is getting a little out of hand with way too many layers, there's a simple solution. After selecting the layers you want (see previous tip), use the Layers palette's flyout menu to choose Merge Selected and turn those separate layers into one layer with sublayers. For example, if you select three layers, each with two sublayers, and use Merge Selected, you will get one layer made up of six sublayers. The merged layer will use the name of the last layer you select.

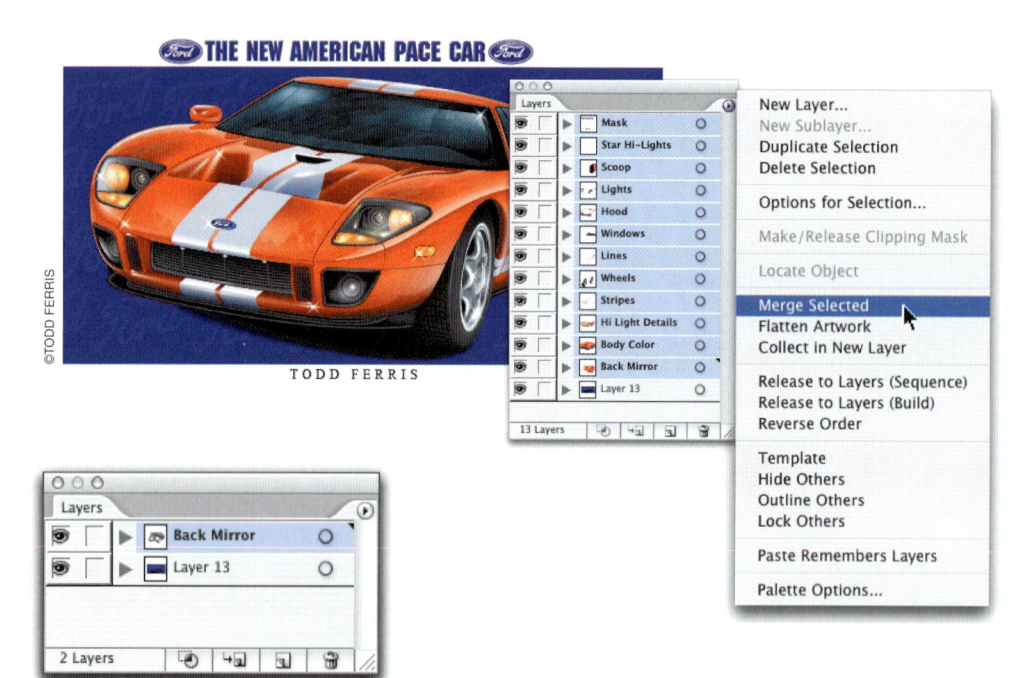

CHAPTER 7 • Layers and Transparency

COLLECT IN A NEW LAYER

As we saw in the previous tip, the Merge Selected command in the Layers palette turns selected layers and sublayers into a new layer with sublayers. If you want to preserve the structure of layers and sublayers, select the layers and from the Layers palette's flyout menu, choose Collect in New Layer. A brand new layer will be created that contains the layers and sublayers from the selected layers. (I just said "layer" 14…no, 15 times, but who's counting?)

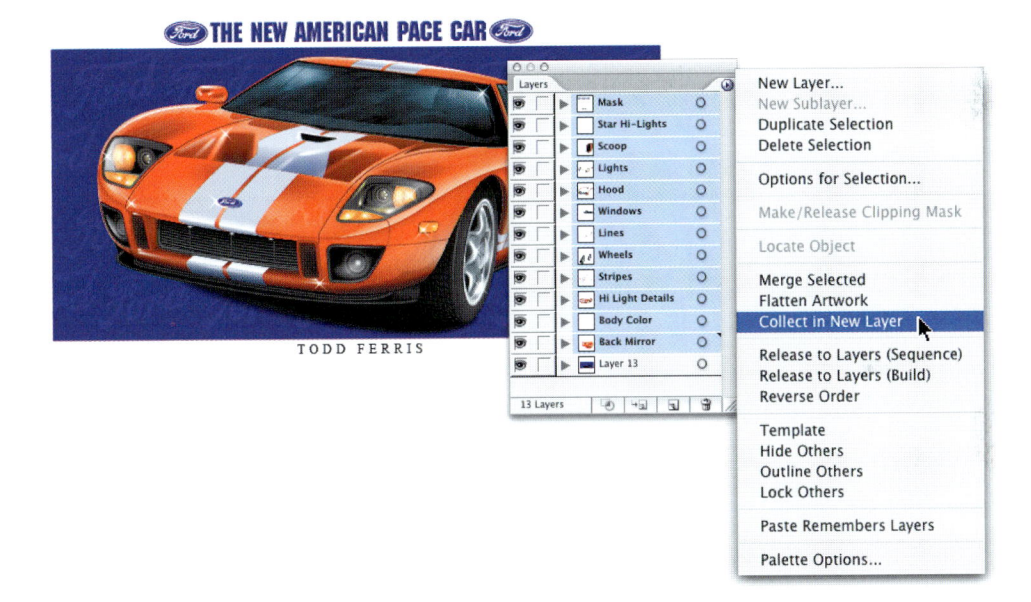

CHAPTER 7 • Layers and Transparency   177

Extreme Makeover

SYMBOLS, BRUSHES, APPEARANCE, FILTERS, AND EFFECTS

Just for fun, we thought we'd present this entire chapter in a Jeopardy *format. You know, answers in the form of questions?*

Extreme Makeover
symbols, brushes, appearance, filters, and effects

Think about it—it would be great: "I'll take the Appearance palette for $500 please, Alex." "It will ensure that all new artwork doesn't take on the appearance of the previously created artwork." "What is the New Art Has Basic Appearance icon?" Ding ding ding ding! Wouldn't that be great? There'd be no other chapter like it! Why do we get the feeling that you're not with us on this one? Okay, okay, how about this: "Name the top reason for creating your own symbol?" Survey says… Wait, don't turn the page, we've got more game show ideas for this chapter…

WHAT IS NEW ART HAS BASIC APPEARANCE?

One important part of the Appearance palette (Window> Appearance) is the New Art Has Basic Appearance icon. It's on by default, which means that every time you create a new object, that object will use the "basic" fill and stroke. What's the basic appearance? The last fill and stroke you've used for that object. However, click on the icon to turn it off if you have created a specific appearance (using styles, effects, etc.) and want to create a whole series of new objects with the same look. In effect, when the icon is on, all new objects will use the basic fill and stroke for that particular object. When the icon is off, all new objects will use the last appearance (including styles, effects, etc.) you created for any object.

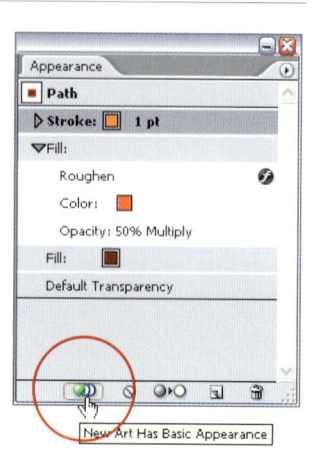

EFFECT GALLERY

Here's a huge speed tip when working with various effects in Illustrator CS2. Choose Effect> Effect Gallery. Your first thought is probably, "What the heck is this?!" Rightfully so, since Adobe really didn't make a big deal out of this one and nobody is talking about it. However, it's a huge time saver because you can preview various effects all within one dialog instead of looking at each effect, canceling out of the dialog, and going through the Effect menu all over again to preview another effect.

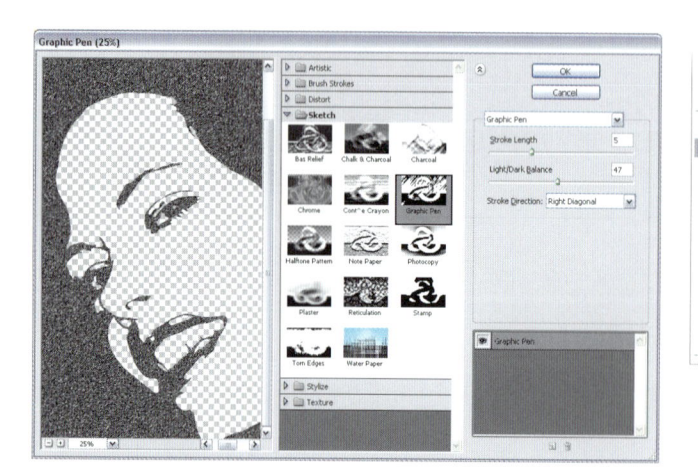

180   CHAPTER 8 • Symbols, Brushes, Appearance, Filters, and Effects

SCRUBBY SLIDERS

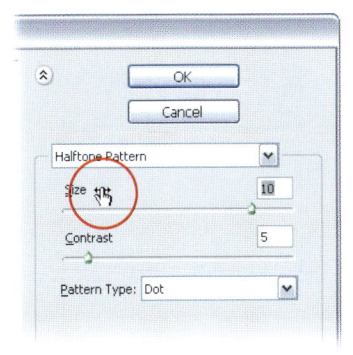

You may first be asking, "What the heck is a scrubby slider?" A scrubby slider is a newer way to adjust settings in dialogs and palettes without using the keyboard. To see what we mean try this: Apply a Halftone Pattern effect to an object in Illustrator (Effect>Sketch>Halftone Pattern). When the dialog opens, position your cursor over the word Size in the settings on the right. Note the little arrows that appear as the cursor. This is a scrubby slider. You can move your mouse to the left or to the right to adjust the setting without ever touching your keyboard. Note that not all settings in Illustrator have been updated with this ability.

CREATING ARROWHEAD DESIGNS

Did you know that you can add an arrowhead to a selected path using Filter>Stylize>Add Arrowheads? No? Well then, that's a bonus tip just for you. Just click on the arrows below the Start and End options to select your arrowheads' style. If you did know that already, then here's your tip: After using the Add Arrowheads filter, use the Direct Selection tool (A) to select the path. Then delete the path (keeping just the arrowhead), and you've got another source for simple shapes that you can use in your artwork.

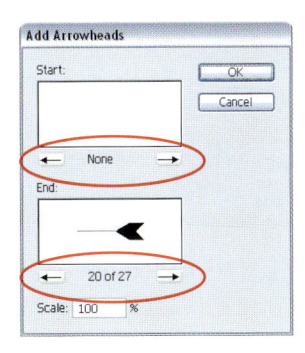

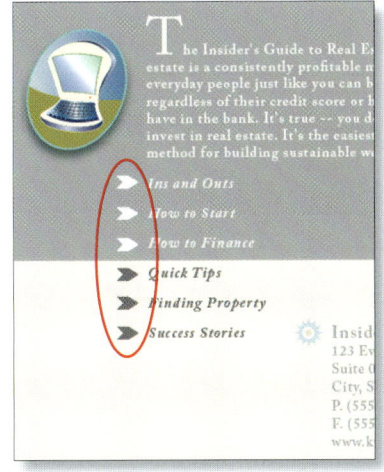

CHAPTER 8 • Symbols, Brushes, Appearance, Filters, and Effects

Illustrator CS2 KillerTips

SYMBOLISM CHOOSER

Here's a cool way (thanks to Mordy Golding, former Adobe Illustrator Product Manager) to switch Symbolism tools on the fly, without using the Toolbox. Just press Control-Option as you click-and-hold (PC: Alt-Right-click-and-hold) with the Symbolism tool you're using, and all the Symbolism tools will appear in a circle. Move toward the tool you want until the cursor changes, release, and start using the new tool.

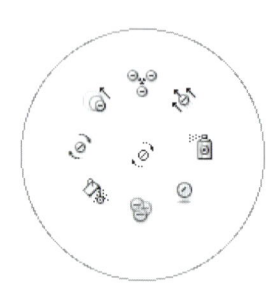

USING THE EYEDROPPER TO SAMPLE APPEARANCE

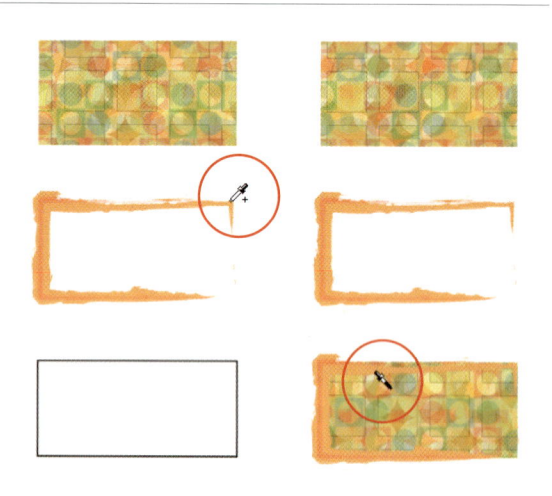

Click on an object with the Eyedropper tool (I) to sample its appearance and then press-and-hold the Option key (PC: Alt key) while using the Eyedropper tool to apply that appearance to another object. Okay, so you probably knew that already. One of the Eyedropper tool's hidden talents is to sample the appearance from multiple objects. (Before you try this, double-click the Eyedropper tool in the Toolbox to make sure that the Appearance options are selected.) With no objects selected in your document, use the Eyedropper tool to select your first color, then press Option-Shift (PC: Alt-Shift) and click on a second object to get your next color. Press-and-hold the Option key (PC: Alt key) and click on an object to apply both (or all) the sampled appearances to that object. If you're not totally satisfied with the result, you can change the order of the various fills and strokes in the Appearance palette.

CHAPTER 8 • Symbols, Brushes, Appearance, Filters, and Effects

DRAG AN APPEARANCE

If you have created an appearance and want to apply the same look to a different object, here's a simple solution. Select the object whose appearance you want to use (in our example, we used an outlined blue and green oval) and click-and-drag its small preview thumbnail from the Appearance palette onto the other object(s) on the artboard (in our example, we dragged it onto the words Speed Clinic). If you don't see the preview, choose Show Thumbnail from the Appearance palette's flyout menu.

MERGE STYLES

If all the built-in graphic styles aren't enough for you, you can create additional styles by merging existing styles together. Find two (or more) styles you like in the Graphic Styles palette (Window>Graphic Styles) and select them. If the styles are adjacent in the Graphic Styles palette, you can press the Shift key and click on them; otherwise, you'll have to Command-click (PC: Control-click) on the styles. Then from the flyout menu, choose Merge Graphic Styles. A dialog will ask you to name the new style that your selected styles will create.

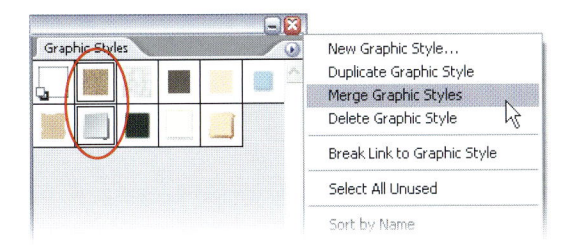

CHAPTER 8 • Symbols, Brushes, Appearance, Filters, and Effects   183

INSTANT LICHTENSTEIN OR POP ART DOT EFFECT

Bet you didn't think you'd get an art history lesson here, did you? Well Roy Lichtenstein (October 27, 1923–September 29, 1997) was a prominent American pop artist whose work borrowed heavily from popular advertising and comic book styles. His illustrations often contained areas of solid color with other areas of dots. You can recreate this style in Illustrator easily. Start out with an illustration and pick a surface that you'd like to add the dot effect to. Duplicate that layer or sublayer by dragging it onto the Create New Layer icon at the bottom of the Layers palette (Window>Layer), so you have two copies (in this example, we've duplicated the layer with the face on it). Next, on the flyout menu in the Swatches palette, select Open Swatch Library>Other Swatch Library. Navigate to the Presets>Patterns>Basic Graphics folder and choose the Basic_Graphics_Dots.ai file. Click on one of the dots patterns to apply it (we used the 10 dpi 40% pattern). Lock all other layers and sublayers except the one that now has the dots on it by Option-clicking (PC: Alt-clicking) in the empty box to the left of the dot layer (to the right of the Eye icon) in the Layers palette. Then go to the Object menu and choose Expand. Deselect everything (Command-Shift-A [PC: Control-Shift-A]). Use the Direct Selection tool (A) to select a single dot, and from the Select menu, choose Same>Fill Color. Choose a color that is slightly darker than your fill color on the surface you duplicated. Deselect everything again and watch your illustration turn into a Lichtenstein!

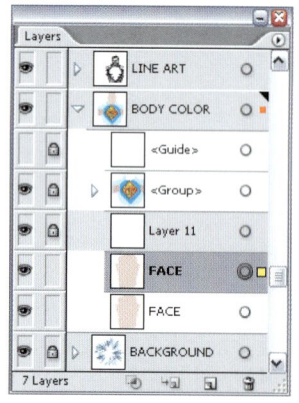

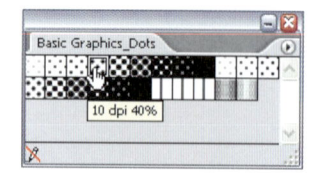

CHAPTER 8 • Symbols, Brushes, Appearance, Filters, and Effects

APPLY THE SAME EFFECT AGAIN

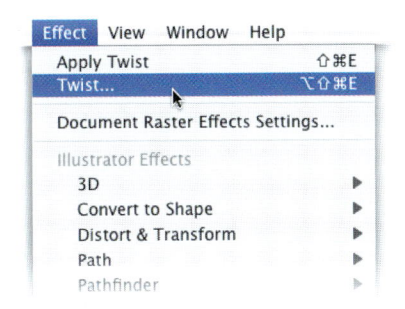

To reapply the last Effect menu command you used with exactly the same settings, press Command-Shift-E (PC: Control-Shift-E). To apply the same effect but change the settings, press Command-Option-Shift-E (PC: Control-Alt-Shift-E) to open a dialog for the effect.

FILTERS VS. EFFECTS? WHAT'S THE DIFFERENCE?

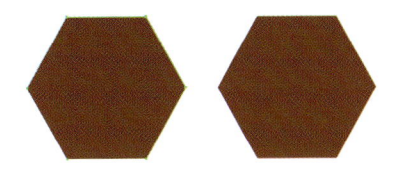

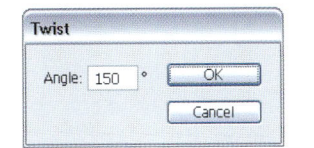

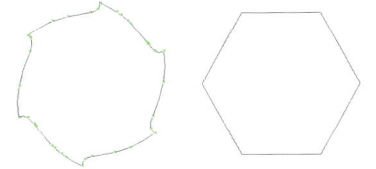

The difference between a filter and an effect is what Illustrator does to the object you apply it to. For example, draw a simple shape on the artboard. Duplicate it so the two are next to each other. Select the first shape and choose Filter>Distort>Twist and change the Angle setting to 150°. Then select the second shape and choose Effect>Distort & Transform>Twist and use the same 150° setting. They should both look identical at this point. But, if you choose View>Outlines, notice how the shape with the Filter applied to it has changed while the other one has not. This is because filters change the underlying structure of any paths they're applied to, while effects only change the appearance. The most important point to glean from this tip is that a filter is permanent and an effect is "live". This means that you can go back and change the settings of the effect (or remove it altogether) at any time.

CHAPTER 8 • Symbols, Brushes, Appearance, Filters, and Effects   185

RESET EFFECT AND FILTER SETTINGS

In many of Illustrator's Effect and Filter menu options, you can "start over" without closing the dialog that appears by pressing the Option key (PC: Alt key). The Cancel button will change to Reset—click Reset to revert all the settings to their default. For instance, we selected an object and chose Effect>Artistic>Dry Brush. After we changed a few of the settings, we decided to revert to the default settings using this tip. To find out which effects or filters dialogs this works in, try it!

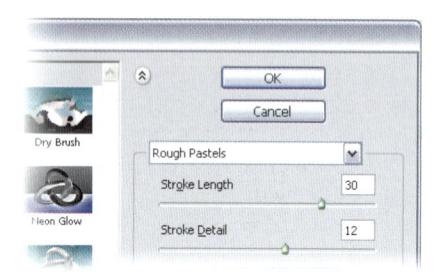

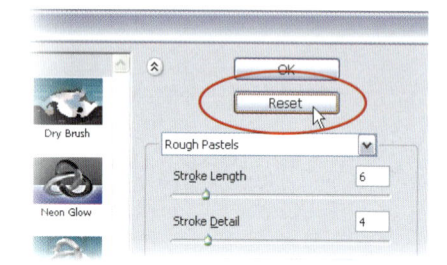

ADD A SECOND STROKE

Unfortunately, you cannot apply a filter or an effect to just the stroke of an object. You could draw the stroke separately, but then you'd have to worry about grouping the two objects. Instead, with the object selected, use the flyout menu in the Appearance palette (Window>Appearance) to choose Add New Stroke. Click on the new stroke to highlight it in the Appearance palette, change its color using either the Color palette or the Swatches palette, and change its Weight by going to Window>Stroke. Then go the Effect menu and pick an effect. That way, if you change the size of the original object, this second stroke will automatically change, too.

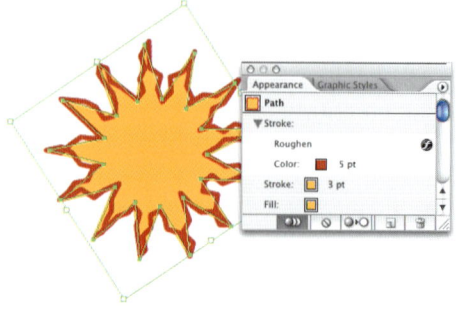

186   CHAPTER 8 • Symbols, Brushes, Appearance, Filters, and Effects

DROP SHADOWS

Here's a great tip for getting a better drop shadow effect in Illustrator. While you can control the offset, opacity, and blur settings of a drop shadow, there's really no way to control the thickness. If you try to do this by changing the offset value too much, it'll just make the drop shadow separate from the overlying object and appear to be raised higher. Instead, try this: Create some type and choose Effect>Stylize>Drop Shadow. Use the following settings:

> Mode: Normal
> Opacity: 100%
> X Offset: 2 pt
> Y Offset: 2 pt
> Blur: 0 pt
> Color: Black

It looks nice, but the effect is too thin. To make it thicker, go to the Appearance palette (Window>Appearance), and just duplicate the Drop Shadow item a few times. Each time you duplicate it the drop shadow effect will get thicker.

CHAPTER 8 • Symbols, Brushes, Appearance, Filters, and Effects   187

CHECK DOCUMENT RASTER EFFECTS SETTINGS

Before you start applying all kinds of raster effects or filters, make sure you have chosen the optimal raster quality settings for your document. From the Effect menu, choose Document Raster Effects Settings. In the dialog, choose the resolution, background (white or transparent), and options for anti-alias and clipping masks. These settings are document-wide, affecting all raster filters and effects. By default, the resolution is set to 72 ppi, so make this decision early on. If you change the resolution after creating objects and applying effects, the new resolution setting will be applied and the effects can change. For example, we had applied the Halftone Pattern effect to a logo, but the effect was changed after we altered the Document Raster Effects Settings.

188 CHAPTER 8 • Symbols, Brushes, Appearance, Filters, and Effects

BREAKING A LINK TO A STYLE

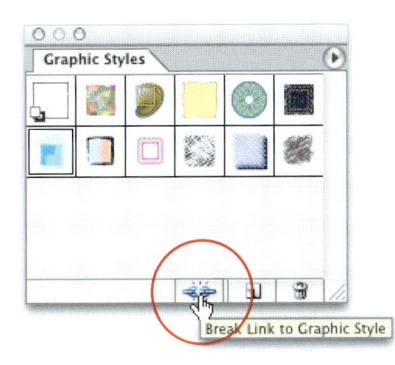

If you have applied a graphic style to a number of objects and later redefine the style in the Appearance palette (Window>Appearance), all the objects will update to the new style (they do not have to be selected). You can also ensure one object does not change from the original style by breaking the link to the style. Select the one object you don't want to change and click on the broken chain icon at the bottom of the Graphic Styles palette (Window> Graphic Styles). Now, if you change the settings for the graphic style in the Appearance palette and choose Redefine Graphic Style from the Appearance palette's flyout menu, the unlinked graphic will not change. There is no re-link icon, so you'll have to reapply the graphic style by selecting the object and clicking on the style in the Graphic Styles palette.

DISAPPEARING EFFECTS WHEN SWITCHING BETWEEN RGB AND CMYK

Some Effect menu options, such as the Artistic set, only work in RGB mode. This means if you change the Document Color Mode to CMYK in the File menu, the effect cannot be preserved (in other words, the effect you applied to an object will disappear, as it did here in our example using Effect>Brush Strokes>Spatter). To avoid this, before changing to CMYK mode, from the Object menu choose Expand Appearance (keeping in mind that your object will be converted to an image that cannot be edited to the same degree as when you started).

Object with Spatter effect

Effect removed in CMYK mode

CHAPTER 8 • Symbols, Brushes, Appearance, Filters, and Effects   **189**

ADD STROKE TO PLACED IMAGE OR PHOTO

If you want to add a stroke to a placed image (File>Place) you can, but it's not as simple as choosing a color for the stroke. You could draw a rectangle the same size, but there's an easier way. With the placed image selected, go to the Appearance palette (Window>Appearance) and choose Add New Stroke from the flyout menu. Then from the Effect menu choose Path>Outline Object. Change the stroke color and weight, and you're all set.

©MATT KLOSKOWSKI

190 CHAPTER 8 • Symbols, Brushes, Appearance, Filters, and Effects

REDEFINE SYMBOLS

If you have created and used a symbol in your document, you can easily change all instances by redefining the symbol. Place an instance of your symbol from the Symbols palette and use the Object>Expand command to edit the original artwork. Make the changes to the artwork and keep it selected. In the Symbols palette, click once on the original symbol, and from the palette's flyout menu, choose Redefine Symbol. All instances will automatically change to the edited symbol.

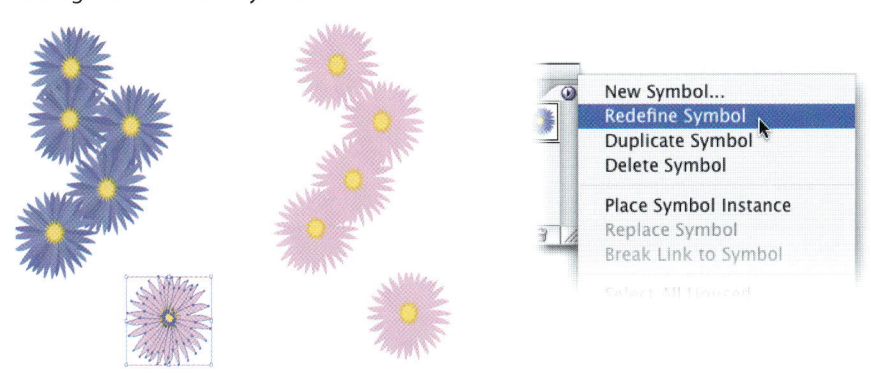

VIEWING THE INTENSITY OF THE SYMBOL TOOLS

To find out the Intensity setting for the Symbolism tools, you could double-click on the active Symbolism tool in the Toolbox (say, for instance, the Symbol Stainer tool). But, for a quick visual clue, check out the brush's outline color. If it's very light gray, the tool has a low Intensity setting; if the brush outline is dark, the Intensity setting is high. Okay, so it's not an incredibly accurate measurement, but it will tell you very quickly if you need to change the setting.

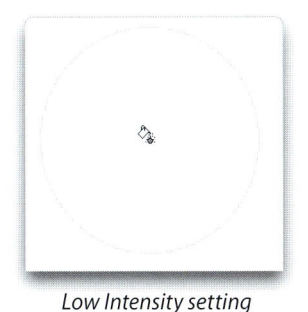

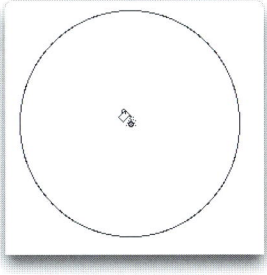

Low Intensity setting   *High Intensity setting*

CHAPTER 8 • Symbols, Brushes, Appearance, Filters, and Effects   **191**

Illustrator CS2
KillerTips

MORE INTENSITY, DIFFERENT SIZE

When you are using any of the Symbolism tools, you can use these keyboard shortcuts: Press Shift-right bracket (]) to increase the brush intensity (the rate of change) or Shift-left bracket ([) to decrease the intensity. Press the bracket keys alone to change the brush size: left bracket to make the brush smaller or right bracket to make the brush bigger.

Lower Intensity setting

Increased Intensity setting

CHANGE MULTIPLE SYMBOLS

By default, the Symbolism tools will affect whatever symbol is selected in the Symbols palette (Window>Symbols). So, if you have multiple symbols on the artboard, only the selected symbol will be affected by the Symbolism tools. The Symbolism tools can influence multiple symbols at the same time: Just Shift-click in the Symbols palette on all the symbols you'd like to work on.

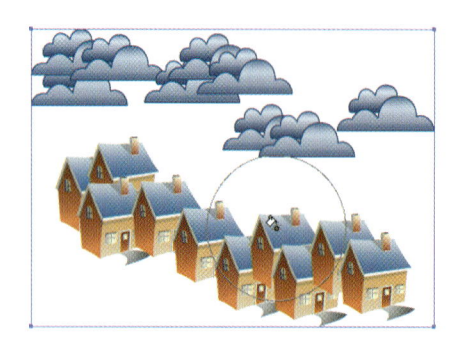

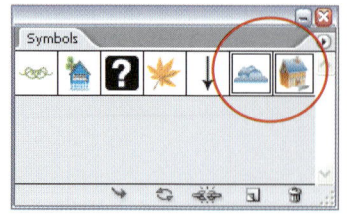

192   CHAPTER 8 • Symbols, Brushes, Appearance, Filters, and Effects

NEW SYMBOL AND INSTANCE

Normally when you drag-and-drop a selected object into the Symbols palette (Window> Symbols), a new symbol is created, but the original artwork has no connection to the symbol—the artwork is not an instance, meaning all its paths are still editable. To create a new symbol *and* turn the original object into an instance of the new symbol, press-and-hold the Shift key as you drag the artwork into the Symbols palette.

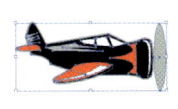

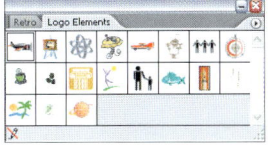

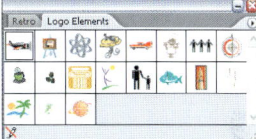

Artwork not a symbol instance

Artwork as a symbol instance

SELECT ALL INSTANCES (AND REPLACE THEM TOO)

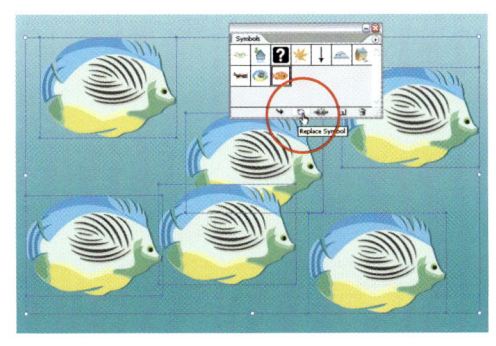

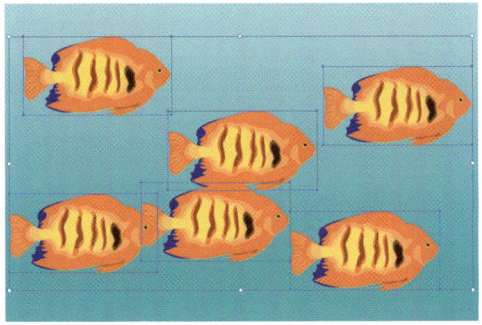

You can create multiple instances of a symbol by placing copies (Edit>Copy; Edit>Paste), or using the Selection tool (V) to select an instance and pressing-and-holding the Option key (PC: Alt key) while dragging to make a copy. But to select all the instances of a symbol in the document, make sure you have nothing selected in your document and click on the symbol in the Symbols palette. Then use the palette's flyout menu to choose Select All Instances. If you want to replace all the selected instances, click on the new symbol in the Symbols palette and press the Replace Symbol icon (the second icon from the left) at the bottom of the palette.

CHAPTER 8 • Symbols, Brushes, Appearance, Filters, and Effects   193

REPLACING SYMBOLS

You know by now (if you read the previous tip) that you can replace all instances of a symbol. What we haven't told you yet is that if you applied effects, changed colors with the Symbol Stainer tool, or resized the instance, all those characteristics will be preserved when you replace the symbol with a new one. For example, in our original symbol instance using the planets, we applied various effects and used the Symbol Stainer tool. When we replaced the symbol (see previous tip), all the instances changed to the cat symbol, while still preserving their individual characteristics.

REVERSE ENGINEERING A GRAPHIC STYLE

One of the best ways to learn all the great things you can do with graphic styles is to apply an existing style and then check out the Appearance palette (Window>Appearance). The entire makeup of the style will be laid out nicely for you—extra fills and strokes, effects, colors, and so on. In addition, if you really like a style and want to make a new one based on an existing style, you can of course, alter the style by selecting it in the Graphic Styles palette and changing style items in the Appearance palette. Then just click the New Graphic Style icon at the bottom of the Graphic Styles palette.

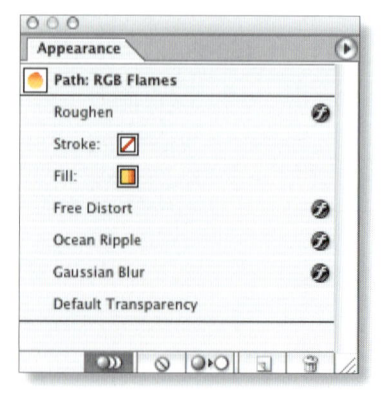

194   CHAPTER 8 • Symbols, Brushes, Appearance, Filters, and Effects

WHY ARE SOME FILTERS AND EFFECTS GRAYED OUT?

If you attempt to access a filter or an effect and it's unavailable (grayed out), there could be several reasons. The bottom half of the Filter menu (from Artistic down) only works on rasterized objects or placed raster images. Moreover, many of the filters only work in RGB mode. Similarly, many Effect menu commands will only work if the document is in RGB mode. As you may know from a previous tip, you cannot switch from CMYK mode to RGB, apply an Effect menu command, and then switch back to CMYK because the effect will be lost.

SEE 3D EFFECTS WHILE YOU'RE APPLYING THEM

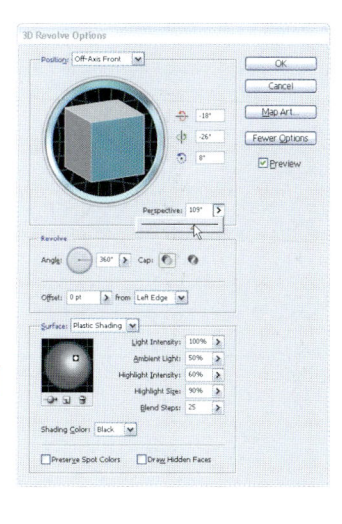

You may not have even noticed this one but when you change settings in the 3D effects dialogs, the settings aren't rendered to the screen until you take your finger off the mouse button. This makes it difficult to see what various settings look like as you're applying them. To get around this, hold down the Shift key as you modify a 3D graphic, and the view on screen will be re-rendered each time you move the setting.

CHAPTER 8 • Symbols, Brushes, Appearance, Filters, and Effects

ROTATE 3D OBJECTS THE RIGHT WAY

If you've tried to use the Rotate tool (R) on a 3D object, you may have noticed that the results can be somewhat unpredictable. Here's a tip: Do all of your rotating within the 3D effect dialog. This rotates the object in true 3D space and it'll leave things looking the way you expected.

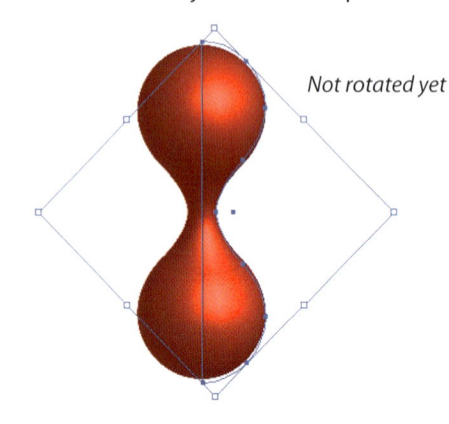

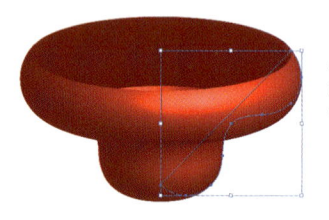

Not rotated yet

Rotated outside of the 3D dialog— very unpredictable

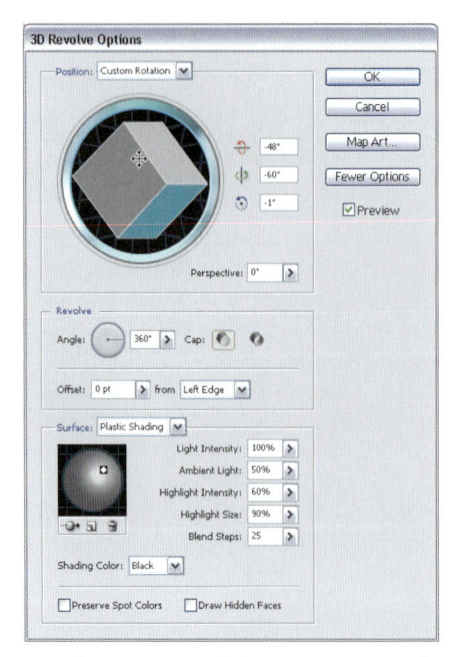

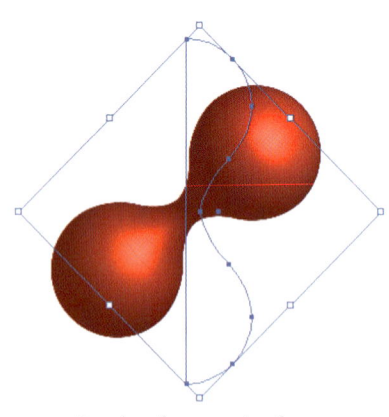

Results after rotating from within the 3D dialog box

Use the 3D Options dialog to rotate instead

196   CHAPTER 8 • Symbols, Brushes, Appearance, Filters, and Effects

CREATING A 3D BANNER

Here's a quick way to create a realistic banner using 3D effects. First, envision what the banner would look like if you were looking straight down at it. Easier said than done, we know. The good news is that you can just draw a path as you see here. Set the Fill for this path to None and change the stroke color to whatever color you'd like the banner to be. Next, choose Effects>3D>Extrude & Bevel. Adjust the Extrude setting in the resulting 3D Options dialog to give some depth to the banner, and move the rotate cube so the banner is facing you. Be sure to check the Preview button so that you can see the changes. That's it. Now you've got a shaded banner without going through all of the hassle of drawing each part manually.

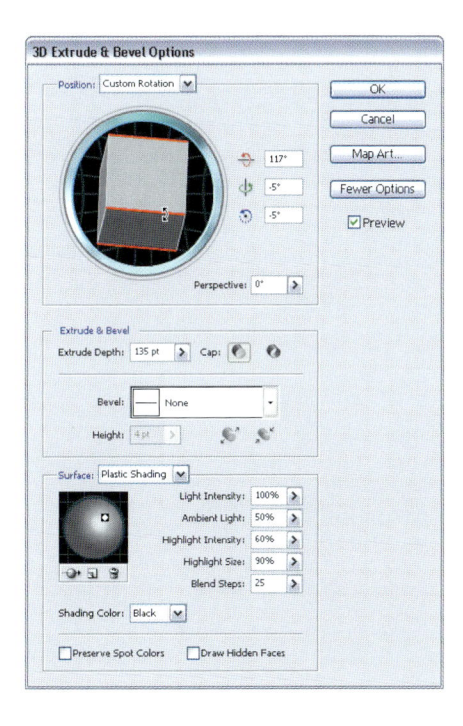

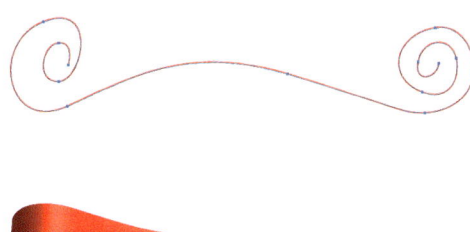

CHAPTER 8 • Symbols, Brushes, Appearance, Filters, and Effects

ADDING TEXT TO THE BANNER

What's a banner in the previous tip without text right? To add text to the banner, simply create the type that you'd like to have flow along the banner. Then drag the text into the Symbols palette (Window>Symbols) to make it a symbol. Now, select the banner and look in the Appearance palette (Window>Appearance). Double-click the 3D Extrude & Bevel item to modify the 3D effect you used to create the banner. Click the Map Art button and cycle through the Surfaces until you find the one of the front of the banner (look at the red highlights on the actual banner to see what surface is currently selected). Then, choose the new text symbol you just created from the Symbols pop-up menu. Position the text as you see fit, and keep in mind that it has a bounding box around it so you can transform it any way you'd like.

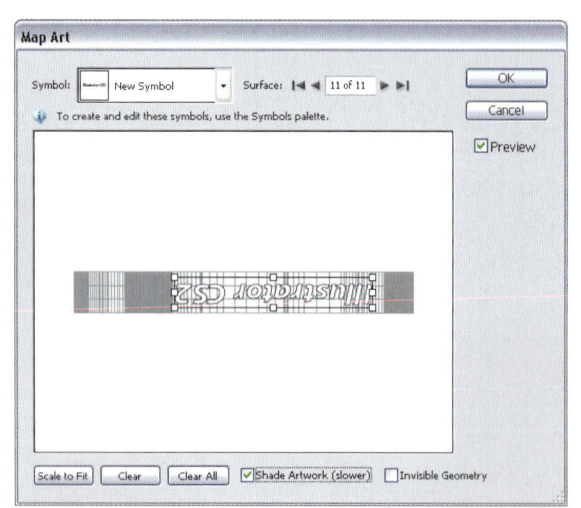

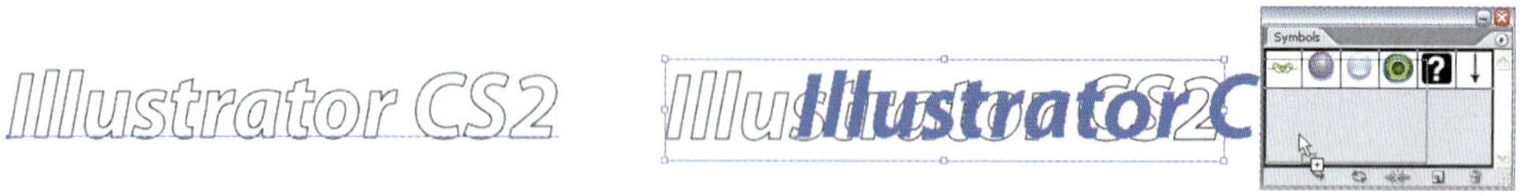

CHAPTER 8 • Symbols, Brushes, Appearance, Filters, and Effects

GET YOUR ARTWORK IN 3D

One of the interesting features of the Effect menu's 3D command is the option to map art onto 3D surfaces. Only symbols can be mapped to the surface, so before heading to the Effect menu, create a symbol that you want to map to the surface of your 3D object, and drag it into the Symbols palette. You can create some very interesting results by using a placed photo as your symbol. Yes, placed raster images can be turned into symbols as long as the images are embedded rather than linked. Try placing (File>Place) an image of a world map (to embed the image, make sure the Link checkbox isn't selected in the Place dialog). Make the image a symbol by dragging-and-dropping it into the Symbols palette (Window>Symbols). Then create a half-circle (by drawing a circle with the Ellipse tool [L] and cutting it in half with the Scissors tool [C]). Next, select your path and choose Effect>3D>Revolve. Click the Map Art button, select your symbol from the Symbol drop-down menu, and size the map to fit the grid by clicking the Scale to Fit button. You can add your symbol to different sides of the shape by using the Surface field. So now, if you ever need to show a different part of the world, double-click on the 3D Revolve effect in the Appearance palette, and use the 3D Revolve Options dialog to change the orientation of your globe.

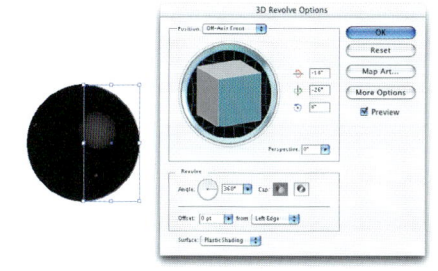

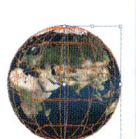

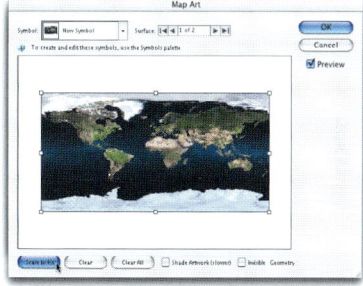

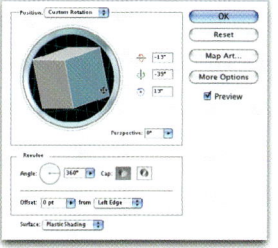

CHAPTER 8 • Symbols, Brushes, Appearance, Filters, and Effects   199

3D AS A STYLE

You can make any of the 3D effects part of a graphic style, but you'll need to do one extra step if you want the color to be part of the style. Apply the 3D effect to your object by selecting it and choosing a command from the Effect>3D menu. Then go to the Appearance palette's flyout menu and choose Add New Fill. Even if your object already has a fill indicated, you'll need to add this second fill for it to register as part of the style. Then go the Graphic Style palette and use the flyout menu to choose New Graphic Style. Give your style a name, click OK, and you're set.

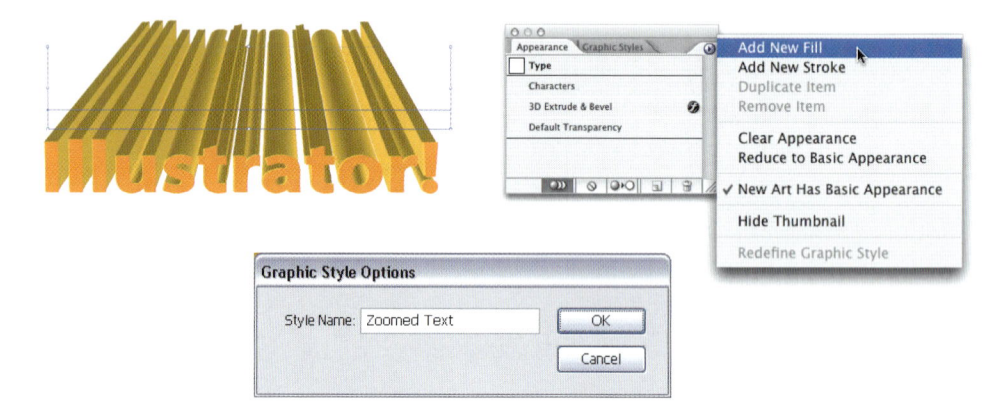

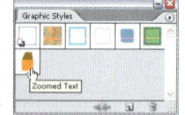

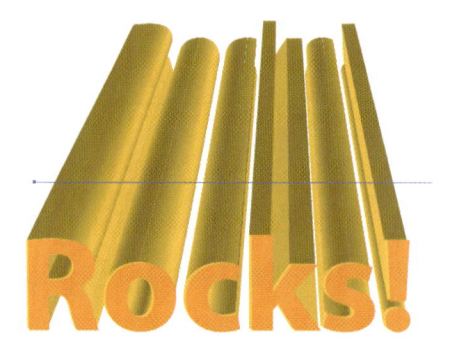

200   **CHAPTER 8** • Symbols, Brushes, Appearance, Filters, and Effects

STAIN REMOVAL

After you've used the Symbol Stainer tool (which is nested under the Symbol Sprayer tool in the Toolbox) to change the color of a symbol, while you still have your symbol instances selected, hold down the Option key (PC: Alt key) to decrease the colorization amount and reveal more of the symbol's original color.

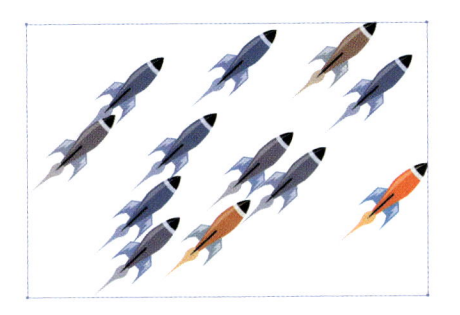

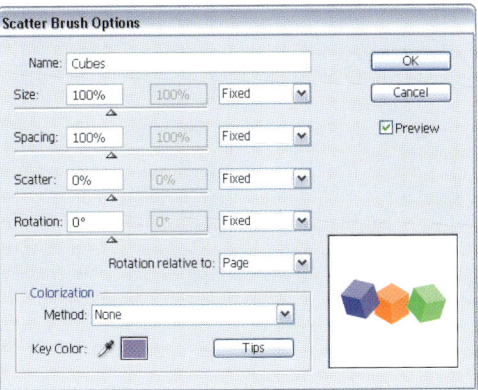

SCATTER BRUSH OPTIONS

There are quite a few factors that determine exactly how a Scatter brush scatters along a path. Rather than trying to figure out the settings you need to create a brush, try this: Select the artwork for your brush and drag-and-drop it into the Brushes palette. When prompted, choose New Scatter Brush. Click OK in the Scatter Brush Options dialog without making any changes. Draw a short, open path with the Line tool and click on the new brush to apply it to the path. With the path still selected, double-click on the new brush in the Brushes palette to open the Scatter Brush Options dialog. Check the Preview box and now you can choose your settings, taking advantage of the preview to see what settings work best.

CHAPTER 8 • Symbols, Brushes, Appearance, Filters, and Effects   **201**

SCATTER ENHANCERS

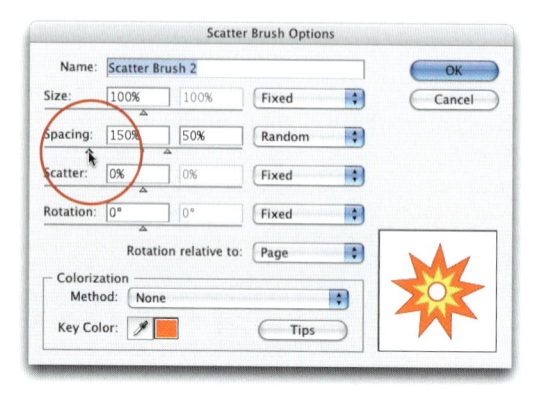

When a Scatter brush's options are set at Random (rather than Fixed), you specify a range of numbers to determine the randomness of the Size, Spacing, Scatter, and Rotation settings. If you're editing these Random settings in the Scatter Brush Options dialog, you can make your life a little easier with these keys. Double-click your Scatter brush to get the dialog, then press-and-hold the Option key (PC: Alt key) to move the minimum and maximum percentage an equal distance apart for one of the settings. For example, if the Spacing slider is set to 100% Fixed and you choose Random in the pop-up menu, hold down Option/Alt and drag the triangle slider to change the minimum to 150% and the maximum to 50% (with nothing held down you'd have to move each slider independently). Once you've set the range you'd like to use, you can move the range higher or lower (while keeping the same distance between the sliders) by holding down the Shift key. (Careful, this last step can be a bit touchy. Try it out and you'll see what we mean.)

SYMBOL STACKING ORDER

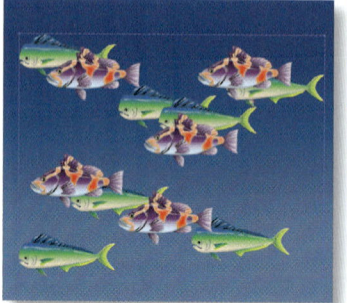

You can change the stacking order of multiple symbols using the Symbol Shifter tool—that is, as long as you have already selected the instances in the Symbols palette (Window>Symbols). To bring symbol instances forward, Shift-click the symbol instance with the Symbol Shifter tool (nested under the Symbol Sprayer in the Toolbox). To send the symbol instances backward, press-and-hold Option-Shift (PC: Alt-Shift) and click the symbol instance.

Symbols brought forward

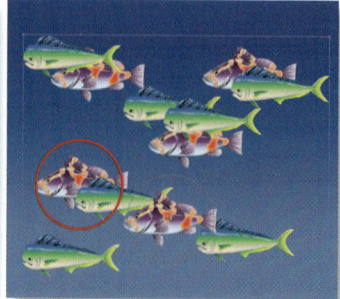

Symbols sent to back

MAKE YOUR OWN BEVELS FOR 3D

If you really want to experiment with the Extrude & Bevel 3D effect, try this: Open the document called Bevels.ai that is located in the Illustrator CS2 application's Plug-ins folder. Draw a short, angled line with the Pen (P) or Line (\) tool and drag the path into the Symbols palette (Window>Symbols) to create a symbol. Save the document, close it, and restart Illustrator. Then, when you choose Effect>3D>Extrude & Bevel, your new bevel will appear in the dialog's Bevel pop-up menu. With a bit of experimentation (each time adding a symbol to Bevels.ai, saving the document, and restarting Illustrator), you can create some pretty interesting results.

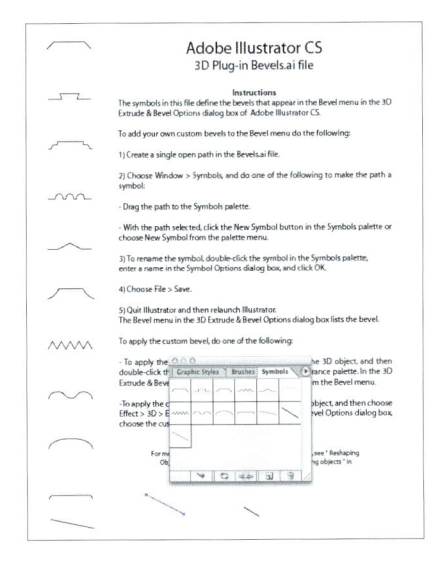

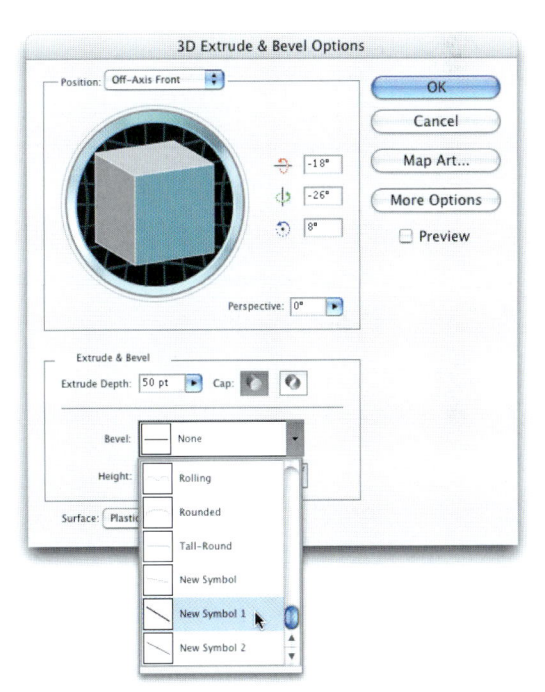

CHAPTER 8 • Symbols, Brushes, Appearance, Filters, and Effects   203

Illustrator CS2 KillerTips

STAIN REPELLANT

This is a pretty basic concept, but if you try to use the Symbol Stainer tool (nested under the Symbol Sprayer in the Toolbox) and nothing happens, it's because the Symbol Stainer tool cannot affect an object that is black. With this in mind, you might want to create a version of your symbol in shades of gray and drag-and-drop it into the Symbols palette. Then if you decide to stain the symbol, you'll have a version on which the Symbol Stainer tool will work.

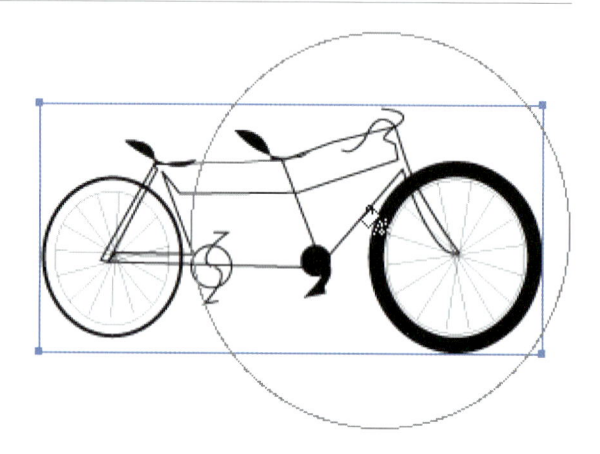

GETTING MORE SYMBOLS IN ILLUSTRATOR

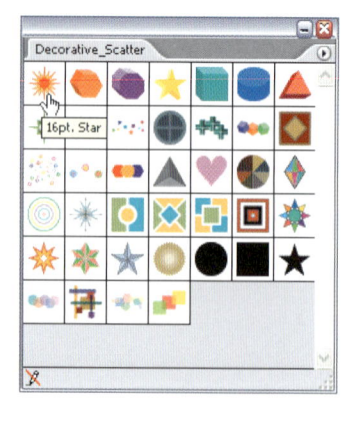

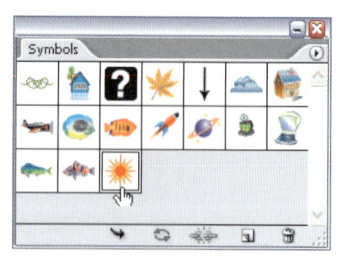

Although Illustrator CS2 comes with a decent selection of symbol libraries, you can easily add many more symbols by using the brush libraries (because there are many more brush libraries included). From the Brushes palette's flyout menu, choose Open Brush Libraries and pick a library (we selected Decorative Scatter). From the library palette that appears, drag a brush onto the artboard and then drag-and-drop it into the Symbols palette. Voilà! New symbol.

204 CHAPTER 8 • Symbols, Brushes, Appearance, Filters, and Effects

FREE! 1,000+ SCIENTIFIC SYMBOLS FOR ILLUSTRATOR

This will possibly be the most read tip in this book. Why? Because it has the word "FREE" in it. Anyway… here's a useful download tip with a ton of free symbols for Illustrator. The Integration and Application Network at the University of Maryland Center for Environmental Science has produced a series of scientific symbol libraries. The libraries contain more than 1,000 custom-made symbols (in 28 categories) designed specifically for enhancing science communication skills for the graphically challenged. Diagrammatic representations of complex processes can be developed easily with minimal graphical skills. The best part about it is the libraries are available cost and royalty free. You can also download a searchable index (PDF) of all the available symbols and an interactive flash tutorial on how to use the symbols with Adobe Illustrator (they require version 10.0 or better). Just go to: http://ian.umces.edu/index.html?http&&&ian.umces.edu/conceptualdiagrams.php and check it out.

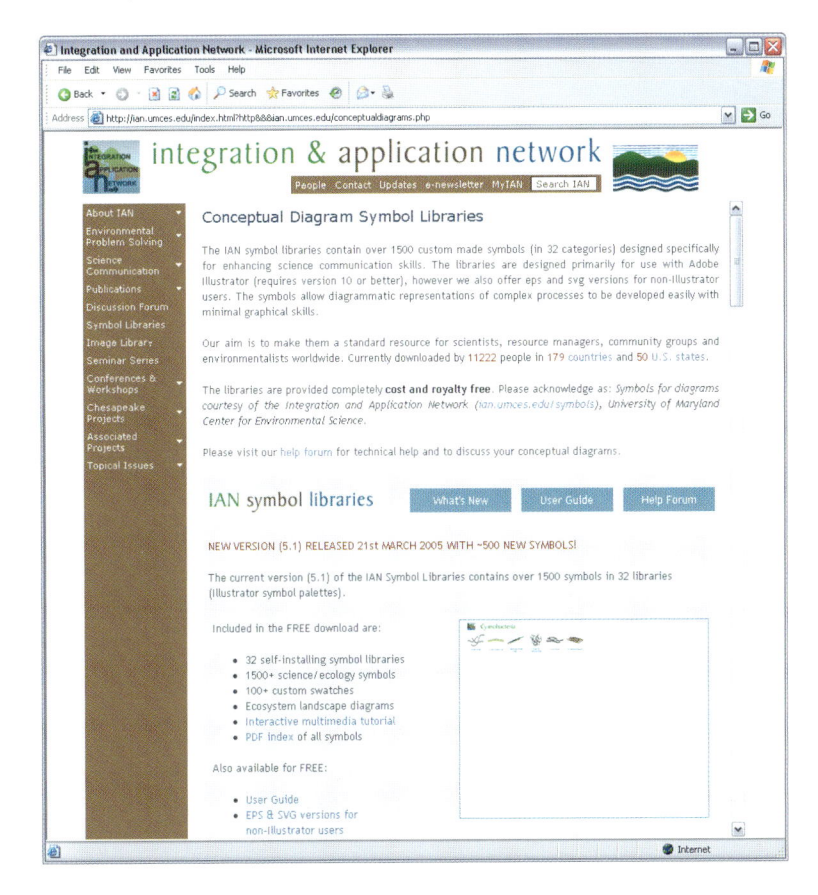

BRUSH OPTIONS VS. OPTIONS OF SELECTED OBJECT

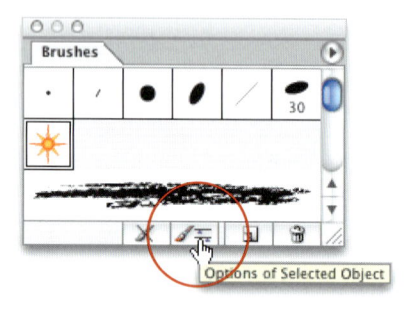

When you want to apply an Art brush to the stroke of an object, there are a couple of different options dialogs that can help you. Double-click on an Art brush in the Brushes palette (Window>Brushes) to set the overall options for the brush—every time you use the brush it will use these settings. Or, to affect only the selected object, select the object, click on the Art brush in the palette to apply the stroke, and click the Options of Selected Object icon at the bottom of the Brushes palette. Change the setting to affect how the brush stroke is applied to only that object. (The same principle applies to Scatter brushes and Calligraphic brushes.)

BIRTHDAY BRUSH

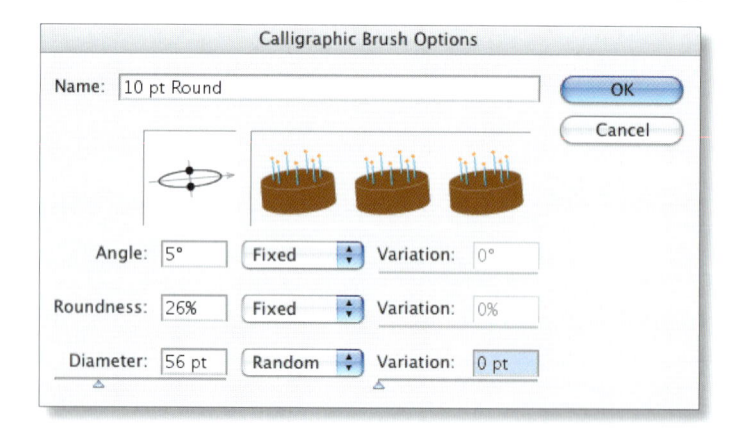

There's an Easter Egg hidden in the Calligraphic Brush Options dialog that was revealed by Deke McClelland in his *Real World Adobe Illustrator* book. Why is it called an Easter Egg? Because it's a little hidden treat that serves no practical purpose whatsoever. Double-click on any Calligraphic brush to open the options dialog and enter these settings: Angle 5°, Roundness 26%, and Diameter 56 points. Click anywhere in the dialog, and you'll get a birthday surprise. Does the brush actually paint with this special design? No, thus the Easter Egg designation—cool but no practical application.

206   CHAPTER 8 • Symbols, Brushes, Appearance, Filters, and Effects

CHAPTER 8 • Symbols, Brushes, Appearance, Filters, and Effects

Trading Spaces

TEXT, TEXT, TEXT →

If a picture's worth a thousand words, how much of a picture can 37 words create? If sticks and stones can break my bones, but words

Trading Spaces
text, text, text

can never hurt me, what in fact is the value of words? It's easy to underestimate the power of text, especially when we're discussing a graphics program like Illustrator. Strange as it may seem, Illustrator's powerful text capabilities can actually create an image—in words—that's worth as much as any picture. So with all that in mind, we decided to present this entire chapter only in pictures, without words. Okay, so that lasted for the first two tips and then we quickly returned to the more traditional words, accompanied by a picture method. It was an interesting thought though, wasn't it?

SELECTING TEXT

For the most part, selecting text in Illustrator CS2 is similar to most applications: Double-click on a word with the Type tool (T) to select it; triple-click to select the entire paragraph (as we did in our example). To select a portion of a paragraph (without clicking-and-dragging), there are a couple of options. Hold down the Shift key and press the Right Arrow key, or click once at the beginning of the text, hold down Shift and click at the end of the text you want to select.

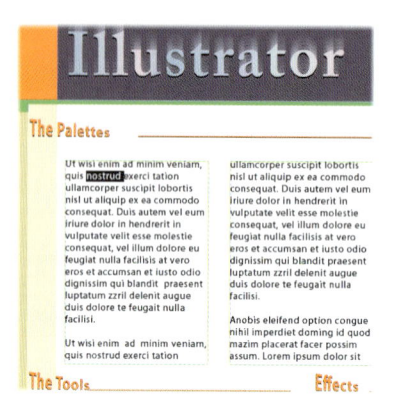

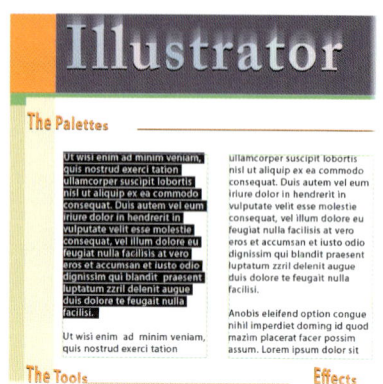

PICKING THE NEXT WORD

To move the insertion point to the start of the previous word, press Command (PC: Control) and the Left Arrow key. We know you'd never guess this, but believe it or not, press Command (PC: Control) and the Right Arrow key to move the text insertion point to the start of the next word (as we did in our example here).

CHAPTER 9 • Text, Text, Text

SELECT BY PARAGRAPHS

To select a paragraph, try this. Press Shift-Command-Down Arrow key (PC: Shift-Control-Down Arrow key) to select from the current text insertion to the end of the current paragraph. Press Shift-Command-Up Arrow key (PC: Shift-Control-Up Arrow key) to select from the current text insertion to the beginning of the current paragraph. To select the paragraph above or below your current selection, use the shortcut and continue to press the Up or Down Arrow keys, with the Down Arrow key selecting the next paragraph and the Up Arrow key selecting the previous paragraph.

CHANGE THE DEFAULT FONT IN ILLUSTRATOR

In case you haven't realized yet, the default font in Illustrator is Myriad. This font is selected in the Font menu, Character palette, and as the Normal Character Style in the Character Styles palette. It is selected even if the document you open doesn't contain that font or if you last used another font before quitting Illustrator. Are you seeing a pattern here? For some reason, Adobe wants us to use Myriad. Heck, it's a nice font, so they may be right. But if this bugs you, then you can always change the default font by editing the startup files. It's a little tricky, but hey… if it really bugs you, then it may be worth it. To change the default font:

1. Quit Illustrator.
2. In the Adobe Illustrator CS2\Plug-ins folder, duplicate the current default startup file—Adobe Illustrator Startup_CMYK or Adobe Illustrator Startup_RGB—and give it a different name. (This creates a copy of the original startup file in case you need it again.)
3. Open one of the default startup files (Adobe Illustrator Startup_CMYK or Adobe Illustrator Startup_RGB, depending on which type of document you intend to use).
4. Choose Window>Type>Character Styles.
5. Select the Normal Character Style and choose Character Style Options from the palette's flyout menu.
6. Select Basic Character Formats on the left side of the dialog, and choose the desired font from the Font Family menu.
7. Click OK, and save the new file as Adobe Illustrator Startup_CMYK or Adobe Illustrator Startup_RGB in the Plug-ins folder.
8. Restart Illustrator.

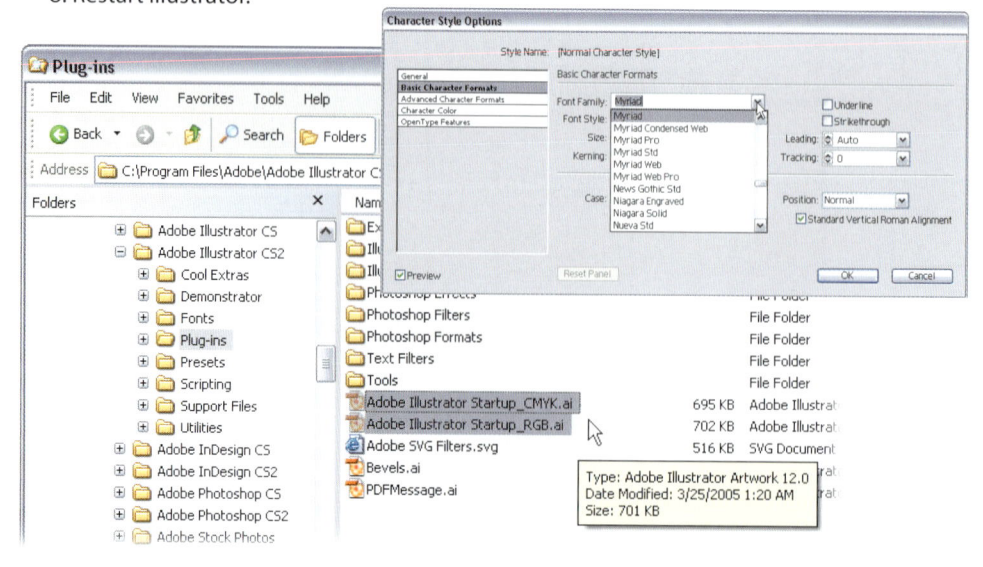

PICK A FONT BY NAME

If you have a big long list of fonts, it can take a while to scroll through the list to find the one you want. Instead, get the Character palette from the Window menu and click just to the left of the font name that appears in the palette. Type the first letter or two of the font name you want (as we did here with Trajan Pro). You'll jump to the first font that matches the letters you type.

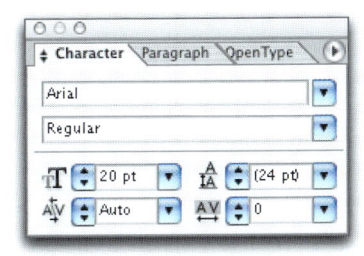

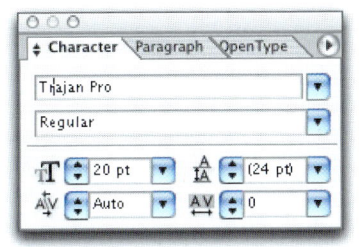

MOVE ALL TABS AT ONCE

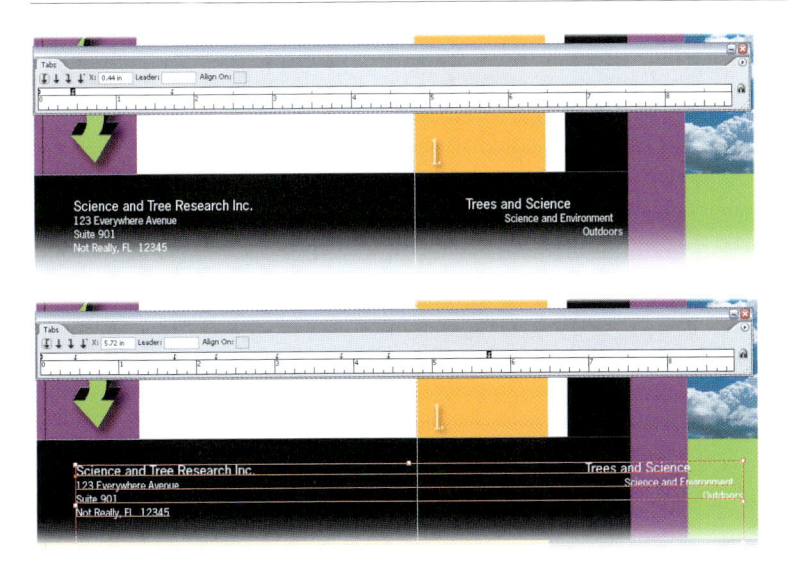

When you're creating a table using the Tabs palette, you may need to move a tab stop, but you still want to keep the rest of your tabs evenly spaced. To do this, first make sure you have the palette open by choosing Type>Tabs from the Window menu (Command-Shift-T [PC: Control-Shift-T]), then select your table with the Selection tool (V), and while pressing the Command key (PC: Control key), drag the tab stop you need to move. In the Tabs palette, all the tab stops to the right of the one you're dragging will also move, preserving the space between them.

CHAPTER 9 • Text, Text, Text   213

CHANGE TAB STYLE

Illustrator lets you add tab stops for left-, center-, right-, and decimal-justified text. Once you have added a tab stop above the Tab Ruler in the Tabs palette (Window>Type>Tabs), you can quickly change between the different tab styles by Option-clicking (PC: Alt-clicking) on the existing tab stop. Each time you click, the tab stop will change to the next style (left-justified, center-justified, etc.).

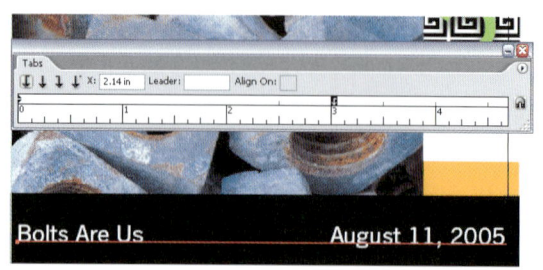

Left-justified text

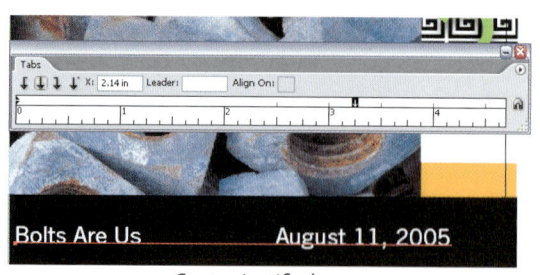

Center-justified text

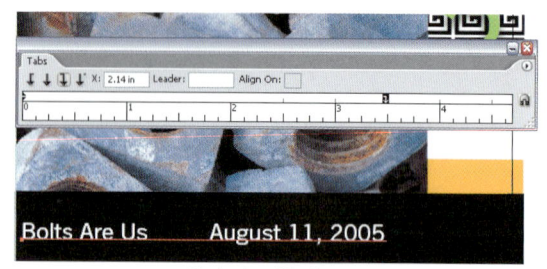

Right-justified text

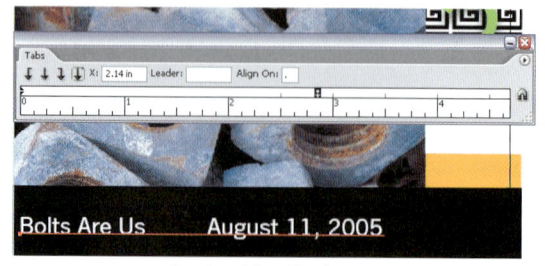

Decimal-justified text

DELETE ALL TABS

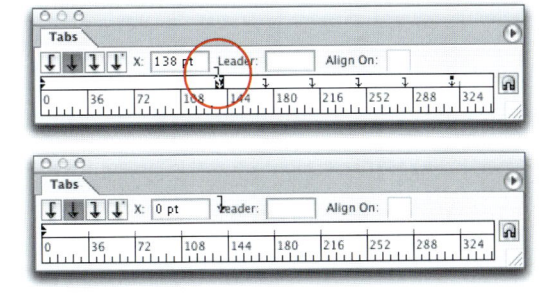

To delete a tab stop in the Tabs palette (Command-Shift-T [PC: Control-Shift-T]), you click-and-drag it off the Tab Ruler. Rather than manually dragging every tab stop to delete them all, hold down the Command key (PC: Control key) and click-and-drag the left-most tab stop off the Tab Ruler. All tab stops will be deleted. Use the same theory anytime you need to delete all the tab stops to the right of a tab stop: Press-and-hold the Command key (PC: Control key) and click-and-drag the first tab stop you want to delete off the palette and all the tab stops to the right of that tab stop will be deleted.

EVENLY SPACED TABS

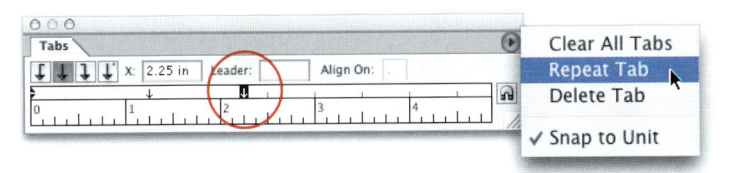

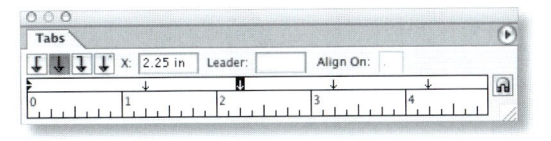

If you need a bunch of tab stops evenly spaced apart, there's an easier way than "doing the math" and figuring out where to position each new tab stop. Select a Tab Alignment icon from the row of four icons near the top left of the Tabs palette, click above the ruler to add the first and then the second tab stop, using the space you want between the two. Then, with your last tab stop still selected, choose Repeat Tab from the Tabs palette's flyout menu to create a whole series of evenly spaced tab stops. (The new, nicely spaced tab stops will appear as wide as you make the Tab Ruler in the Tabs palette. To extend the Tabs Ruler, just click on the bottom-right corner of the palette and drag to the right.)

CHAPTER 9 • Text, Text, Text   215

TAB LEADERS

A nice feature in Illustrator CS2 is tab leaders, which provide the ability to fill the space between the type and the tab with a text character. Click on a tab stop in the Tabs palette, enter a character in the Leader field (such as a period), and then press Return (PC: Enter) or Tab to see the results. You can actually enter up to eight characters in the Leader field, so the possibilities are pretty interesting.

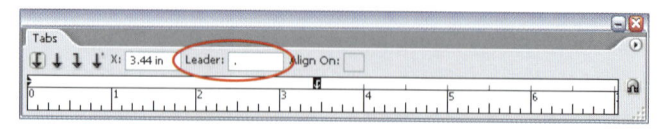

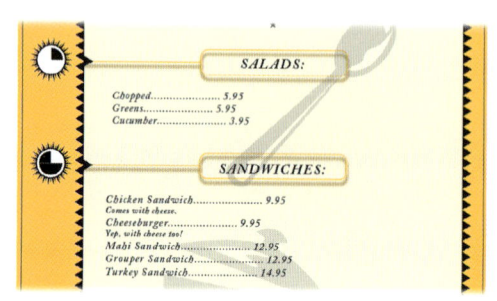

LINE UP THE TAB RULER

When you have a series of text blocks throughout your document and many or all of them use tabs, you'll need to move the Tabs palette (Command-Shift-T [PC: Control-Shift-T]) from one text block to the next to see the Tab Ruler, and edit the tab stops. Rather than dragging the Tabs palette above each text block, just select the text block with either the Type tool (T) or Selection tool (V), and in the Tabs palette, click on the magnet icon along the palette's right side (aka: the Position Palette Above Text icon, but who wants to say that?). The Tabs palette will automatically line up perfectly above the selected text block.

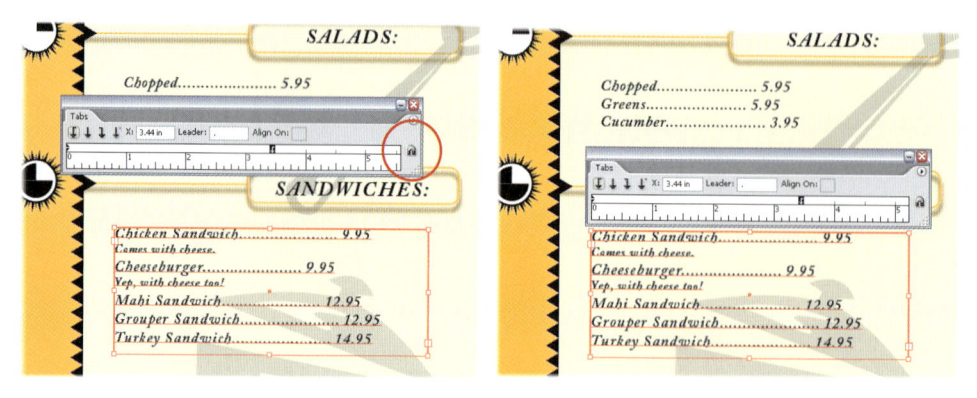

CHAPTER 9 • Text, Text, Text

ALIGN ON

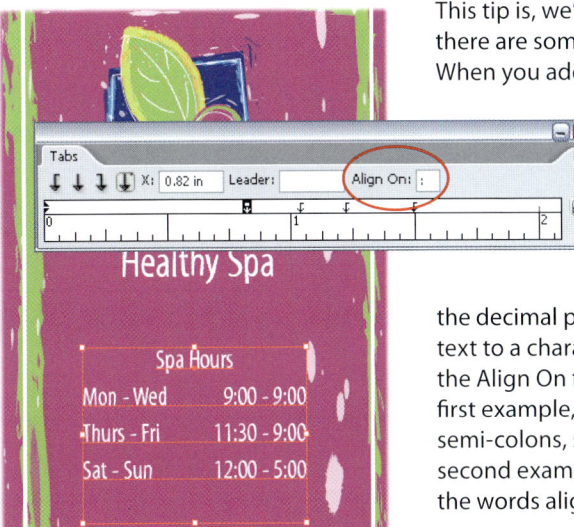

This tip is, we'll admit, a little out there, but there are some interesting uses for this concept. When you add a decimal-aligned tab stop to the Tab Ruler in the Tabs palette (Window>Type>Tabs), by default Illustrator assumes that you want the text to align using the decimal point (a fair assumption). You don't have to be satisfied with aligning to the decimal point, but instead you can align your text to a character by entering any character in the Align On field at the top of the palette. In our first example, all the tabbed text is aligning to the semi-colons, so the workout times all line up. The second example is a little more unusual, with all the words aligning on the letter "a" in each word.

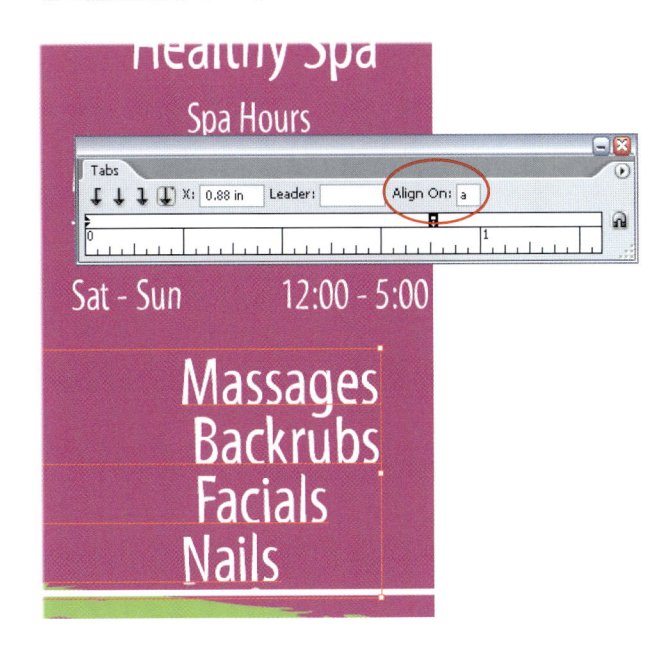

CHAPTER 9 • Text, Text, Text   217

ANGLED TABS

With a bit of effort, you can create what amounts to graphical tabs. Create a text frame with the Type tool (T) and fill it with text information, separating the text with tab stops by using the Tabs palette (or by simply pressing the Tab key as you type information). Then get the Pen (P) or Line (\) tool from the Toolbox and draw paths that will replace the tab stops. You can give your paths a stroke color, such as black, but you should avoid a fill color so you can see the effect you're about to create. Select the paths and the text frame with the Selection tool (V), and from the Object menu choose Text Wrap>Make. Click OK if you get a warning dialog; this is just letting you know that text will be altered. The tabbed text will line up with the paths. To change the text offset or invert the wrap, go to Object>Text Wrap and choose Text Wrap Options. You also may need to use the Direct Selection tool (A) and perform some tweaking to get the ideal result, as we did in our example here.

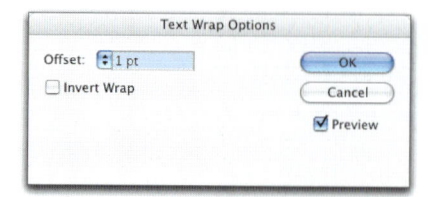

218   CHAPTER 9 • Text, Text, Text

SCROLL THE VIEW WITH TEXT

With most tools, pressing the Spacebar temporarily gives you the Hand tool so you can navigate in the document. Try that while you're typing and, of course, you get spaces. So how do you do that temporary Hand tool thing when you're typing? Press Command-Spacebar (PC: Alt-Spacebar), the shortcut for the Zoom tool. Once the cursor has changed to the Zoom tool, let go of the Command key (PC: Control key), and you'll have the Hand tool, ready to navigate. Let go and you're right back to typing again.

QUICK EDIT

Here's a quick way to switch between the Selection tool and the Type tool, allowing you to start editing some text. Using the Selection tool (V) or the Direct Selection tool (A), double-click on some type. The Type tool will be activated and the text insertion point will appear in the location where you clicked.

CHAPTER 9 • Text, Text, Text   219

HANGING INDENTS

To create hanging indents easily, select your text with the Type tool (T), go to the Window menu, select Paragraph, and use this formula in the Paragraph palette: Enter a positive value in the Left Indent field, and in the First-Line Left Indent field (right below the Left Indent field), enter the same value with a minus sign in front to make it a negative value. Once you get it to work just right, create a paragraph style by choosing Type>Paragraph Style from the Window menu. In the palette that appears, choose New Paragraph Style from the flyout menu. Now you can select your style in the Paragraph Styles palette, and you don't have to go through all that formatting again.

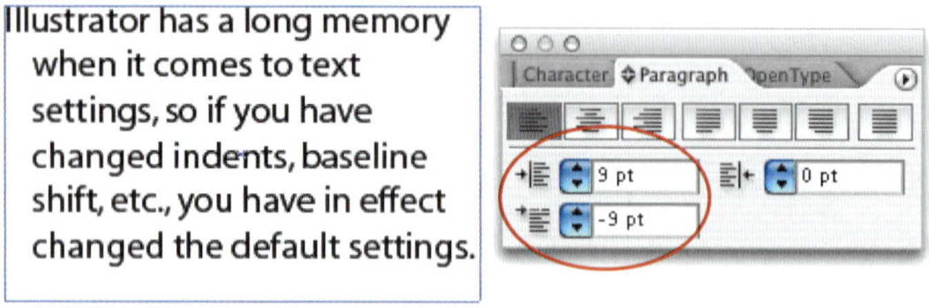

> Illustrator has a long memory when it comes to text settings, so if you have changed indents, baseline shift, etc., you have in effect changed the default settings.

RESET ALL SETTINGS

Illustrator has a long memory when it comes to text settings, so if you have changed indents, baseline shift, etc., you have in effect, changed the default settings. To make sure you don't get unexpected results, you probably want to deselect the text and then either manually change the settings back to "normal," or use the type palette's flyout menu and choose Reset Palette. You'll need to do this for both the Character and Paragraph palettes.

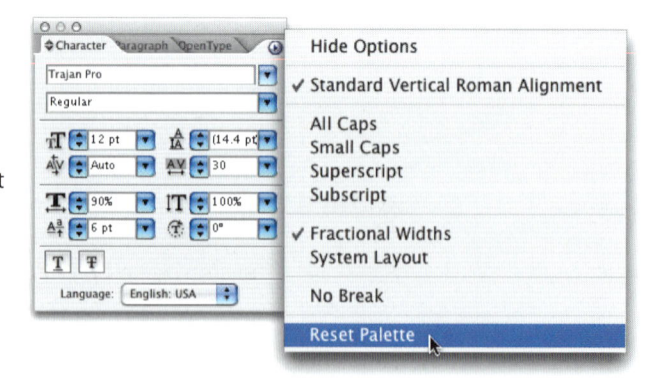

220   **CHAPTER 9** • Text, Text, Text

COLORED TEXT, COLORED BOX

Selected text filled with white   *Text object filled with black*

When you create area type, there are two different objects that can be colored: the type itself and the box that contains the type. To change the fill color of the type, go to the Toolbox, click on the Fill color swatch, and get the Selection tool (V). Then click on the text object and choose a fill color from either the Color or Swatches palette. Use the Direct Selection tool (A) to change a text object's color without affecting the text. First, click away from the object to deselect it, then click directly on the path of the object (typically the text frame). Now when you choose a fill color from the Color or Swatches palette, you will fill the text object, not the text.

HORIZONTAL TO VERTICAL TYPE

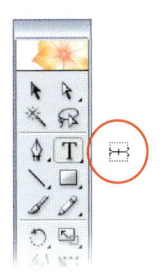

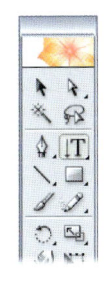

Before using the Type tool (T), you can change from the regular horizontal Type tool to the Vertical Type tool by holding down the Shift key before clicking on the artboard (notice your cursor changes direction). As you may have guessed, the Shift key also works the opposite way if you've selected the Vertical Type tool from the Toolbox. The Vertical Type tool will change into the regular Type tool when you Shift-click.

KERN FROM THE KEYBOARD

Adjusting the space between a pair of letters is known as kerning (yes, you probably knew that, but we needed to be sure). To adjust the kerning between two letters, click between the two letters with the Type tool (T), press-and-hold the Option key (PC: Alt key), and use the Right Arrow key to increase the kerning or the Left Arrow key to decrease the kerning. To change the kerning using larger increments, add in the Command key (PC: Control key), making the shortcut Command-Option-Right (or Left) Arrow key (PC: Control-Alt-Right [or Left] Arrow key), depending on whether you're increasing or decreasing the kerning.

Increasing the kerning between the R and E

TRACKING WITH THE KEYBOARD

Tracking loosens or tightens the amount of space between selected text or a full block of text (again, sorry if that's old news to you). The shortcuts to adjust the tracking with the keyboard are the same as with kerning, except to select a range of text. Highlight all the text you want to adjust using the Type tool (T), press-and-hold the Option key (PC: Alt key), and use the Right Arrow key to increase tracking or the Left Arrow key to decrease tracking. To change the tracking using larger increments, press Command-Option-Right (or Left) Arrow key (PC: Control-Alt-Right [or Left] Arrow key) while you have your text block selected.

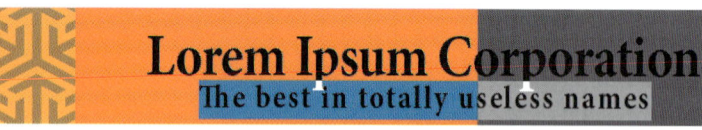

Tracking decreased

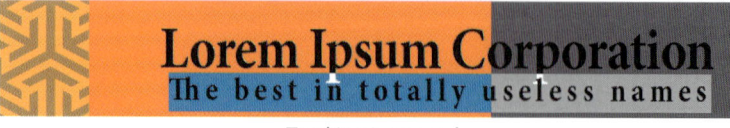

Tracking increased

CONTROL NUMBER OF RECENT FONTS

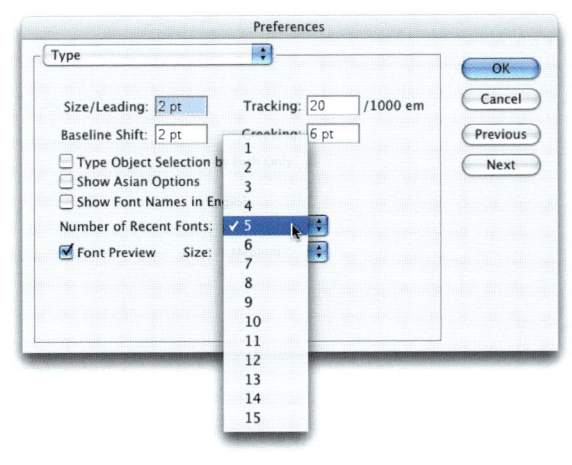

One of the newer options in Illustrator CS2 is to view the most recent fonts you've used in Illustrator. That is, you're not just seeing the fonts you used in the current document, but the fonts you've used since you last launched Illustrator. If you open a new document, your most recent fonts show up in the list under Type>Recent Fonts. You can control how many fonts display in the list through Illustrator's Preferences. Press Command-K (PC: Control-K) to open the Preferences dialog, and from the pop-up menu in the top-left corner, choose Type. Pick a number from 1–15 in the Number of Recent Fonts pop-up menu.

FONT PREVIEW—OR NOT

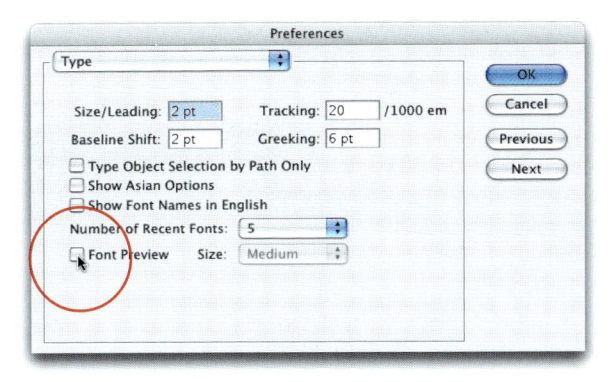

The ability to see the typefaces in the font list is a personal choice: Some people like the option to see what all their fonts look like in the Character palette (Window>Type>Character), others don't like the slight slow down in the font list. To turn off this preview in the font list, go to Illustrator's Preferences (Command-K [PC: Control-K]) and choose Type from the pop-up menu in the top-left corner of the dialog. The checkbox to the left of the Font Preview Size pop-up menu turns the preview on and off.

CHAPTER 9 • Text, Text, Text   223

RESET KERNING AND TRACKING

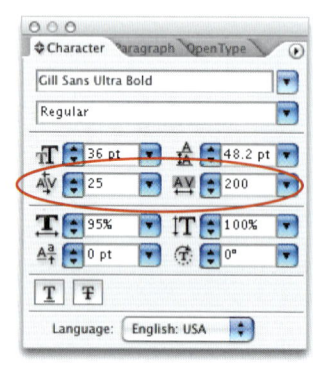

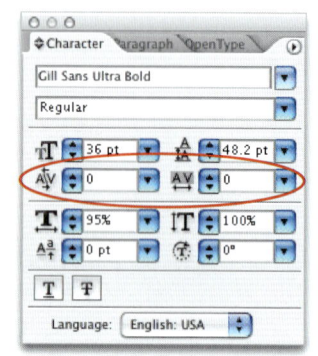

We showed you in an earlier tip how to reset all the settings in the Character and Paragraph palettes (choosing Reset Palette from the respective palette's flyout menu). If you want to keep everything else as-is but reset just the kerning and tracking to zero, here's how: To reset the tracking, highlight your text with the Type tool (T) and press Command-Option-Q (PC: Control-Alt-Q). To reset the kerning, click the Type tool where you've adjusted the kerning and use the same shortcut. Needless to say, make sure you've got the Option (PC: Alt) key held down, or you'll get a very different result!

OPEN AND START EDITING

Here's a cool way to jump right into formatting your text if the Character palette isn't visible—or even open. Press Command-Option-Shift-M (PC: Control-Alt-Shift-M) to highlight the font field in the Character palette, which will also open the palette if necessary (whether you're using the Type tool or not).

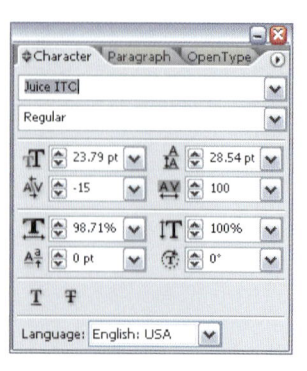

EDIT IMPORTED TEXT

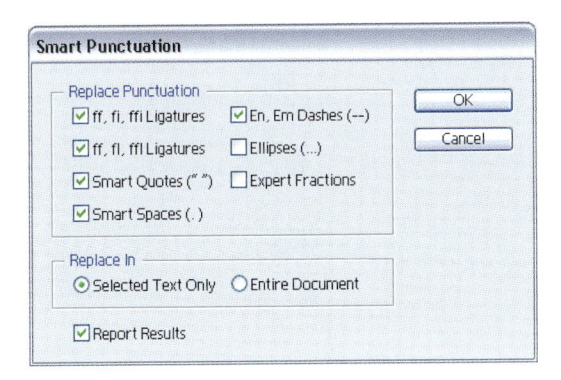

Chances are the text that someone typed for you may not be ideal—perhaps they used two spaces after a period, or typed in inches symbols rather than quotation marks. After placing the text file (File>Place), get Illustrator to automatically strip out all errors using Smart Punctuation. Select the text with either the Selection (V) or Type (T) tool, choose Smart Punctuation from the Type menu, then check the items you want to replace in the resulting dialog.

RESET HORIZONTAL SCALING

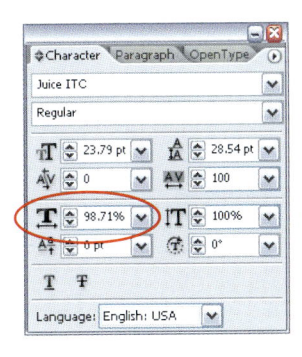

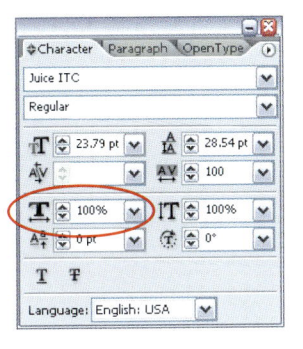

To reset just the Horizontal Scale field to its default setting of 100%, without affecting all the other text settings in the Character palette (Window>Type>Character), press Command-Shift-X (PC: Control-Shift-X). You can use this tip to reset the horizontal scaling of an entire selected text block or to simply change the setting in the Character palette before you create another text object.

CHAPTER 9 • Text, Text, Text   225

SET LEADING TO THE FONT SIZE

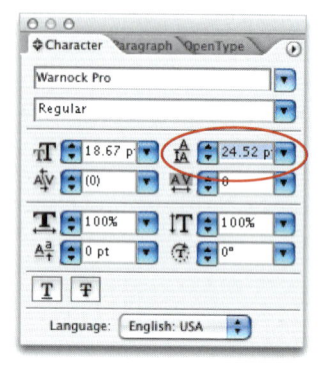

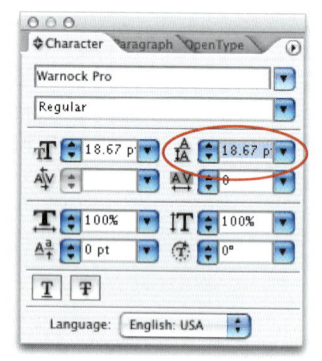

Here's a quick way to set the leading (the space between lines of type) to the same size as the current font size: Highlight your text with the Type tool (T), double-click on the Leading icon in the Character palette (just to the left of the Leading field). Just in case you're interested, equal font and leading sizes is known as solid leading, and it works best when your text is in all caps, so there are no descenders to bump into the type below.

INCREASE OR DECREASE LEADING

To quickly increase or decrease the leading, select text with either the Selection (V) or Type (T) tool and press Option-Up or Down Arrow (PC: Alt-Up or Down Arrow). At first it might seem a little counter-intuitive because the Down Arrow key increases leading (in most palette fields, the Down Arrow makes values smaller). But when you think about it, it makes perfect sense—increased leading makes the second line of type move down, therefore we use the Down Arrow key to increase leading. Here's where it gets a little weird: If you click in the Leading field in the Character palette, the Up and Down Arrow keys work like all the other fields, so you would press the Up Arrow key to increase leading! It's all very logical—really it is!

Decreased leading 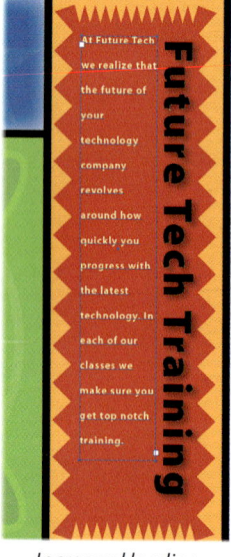   *Increased leading*

226   CHAPTER 9 • Text, Text, Text

CONVERT PARAGRAPH TEXT

Unfortunately, there is no command to convert paragraph text (that is, text you've created using a text box) into regular point type (meaning type that is not confined to a text box). You'll have to do this conversion yourself by highlighting all the text in the text frame with the Type tool (T) and cutting it using the Command-X (PC: Control-X) keyboard shortcut. Then, deselecting the text box (Command-Shift-A [PC: Control-Shift-A]) and clicking with the Type tool on the artboard. This creates a new, single text insertion point and you can press Command-V (PC: Control-V) to paste the text. (You can tell the difference by clicking on the text with the Direct Selection tool (A), which will show a text bounding-box or a path, as seen here.)

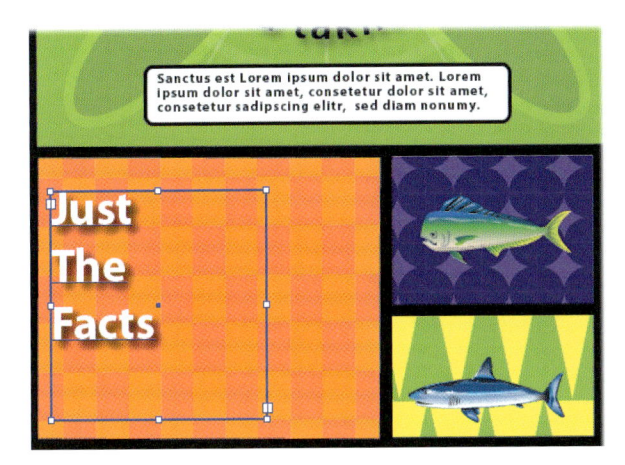

CHAPTER 9 • Text, Text, Text   227

Illustrator CS2 KillerTips

CLEANING UP YOUR TEXT

Each time you click with the Type tool (T) and then decide not to add type after all, you may be adding small text insertion points that could end up causing you grief. You won't see these points in Preview mode, but if you switch to Outline mode from the View menu, you'll see a little X for each insertion point. To automatically remove all of the extra points, go to the Object menu and choose Path>Clean Up. In the dialog, make sure that Empty Text Paths is checked and then click OK. All those unnecessary—potentially troublesome—empty text points will go away.

Image in Preview mode

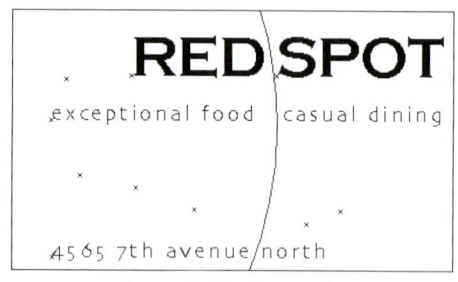

Image in Outline mode

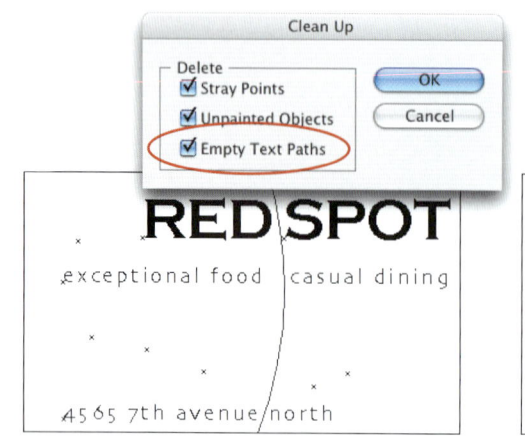

228 CHAPTER 9 • Text, Text, Text

MAKE YOUR OWN TYPEFACE

Okay, it's not exactly making a typeface, but it's a pretty cool way to change the look of type in a way that's very flexible. Enter some text with the Type tool (T), select it with the Selection tool (V), and from the Effect menu choose Stylize>Round Corners. Check the Preview checkbox and then experiment with the Radius field using the Up and Down Arrow keys to get the result you want. Of course, the effect can always be edited by double-clicking the words Rounded Corners in the Appearance palette.

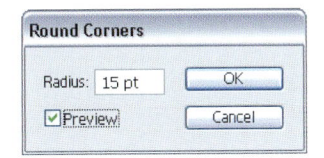

CHAPTER 9 • Text, Text, Text

Whose Line Is It Anyway?

...And More Text

When we were planning the structure of this book, everyone was telling us that it really should have at least ten chapters. Why?

Whose Line Is It Anyway?
...and more text

Apparently, ten is some mystical number that instills confidence in book-buyers, giving them a heightened sense of comfort in their purchase. Problem was, we had pretty much determined the chapters we wanted, giving the book the logical divisions that we felt it needed. "Sorry," we told them, "Nine chapters is all you're going to get, but they will be nine memorable chapters, you can be sure of that!" Well, our stance of "nine is enough" was met with looks of amusement as we were introduced to a new member of the book-editing team. Saying his name aloud brings back too many painful memories, so let us instead introduce Chapter 10, the other half of what we originally had planned as Chapter 9 (and we have to admit it, it was a good call).

CHAPTER 10 • ...And More Text **231**

TRANSFORMING TYPE

Ever notice that you can't use all of the features of the Free Transform tool (E) when you're working with type? You won't be able to use the Command key (PC: Control key) to skew or warp it in certain ways. If you want to do this with the Free Transform tool, you'll first have to convert the type to outlines by selecting it and choosing Type>Create Outlines. Now you're free to transform away.

DRAG-AND-DROP TEXT FROM DESKTOP

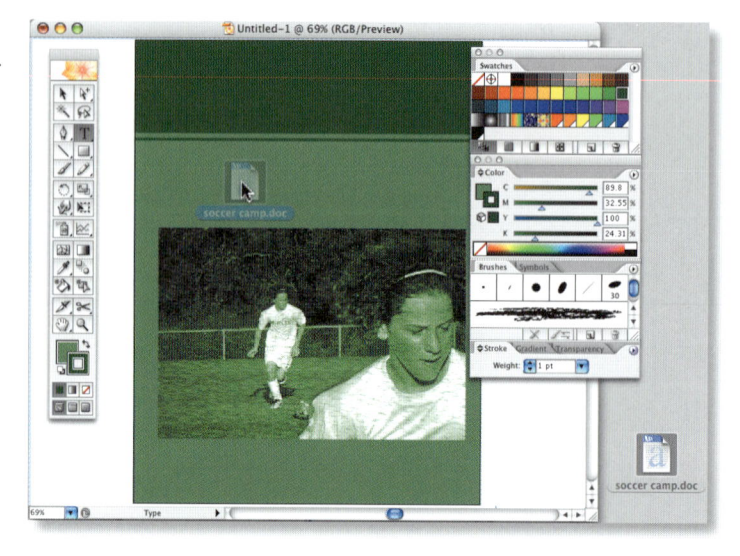

One simple way to add text to an Illustrator document is to drag-and-drop a text document from the desktop into the artwork—just make sure you hold down the Shift key as you drag in the text file. A text block will be created that contains all the text.

232   CHAPTER 10 • …And More Text

BEFORE AND AFTER LEGACY TEXT

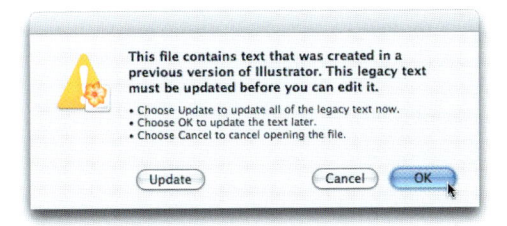

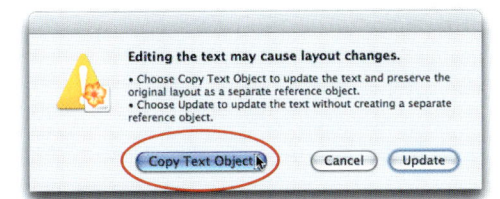

When you open documents from previous versions of Illustrator that contain type, you'll get a warning about updating the legacy text. Although you could choose to update all the text at once, you will not be able to see the difference between the legacy text and the updated text in CS2. Instead, click OK and then update individual pieces of text by using the Type tool (T) to click on the text you want to edit. In the dialog that appears, click the Copy Text Object button and a dimmed copy of the original (legacy) text will appear below the updated text. Use the original text for comparison as you manually adjust the updated type to match the original. Once you're done, go to the Type menu, choose Legacy Text, and from the submenu, choose to hide or delete the copy that was created for you.

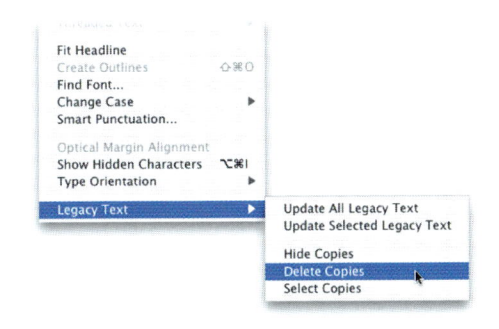

CHAPTER 10 • …And More Text   233

TYPE SIZE BY MATH

For those times where you just don't want to "do the math" yourself, let Illustrator do it for you. In the Font Size field of the Character palette (Window>Character), type * (for multiply) and the number (we used 1.5 in our example). Press Return (PC: Enter) and Illustrator will do the math for you. In our case, change 9-point type to 13.5 points. Use * for Multiply and / for Divide—just remember to click after the unit of measurement.

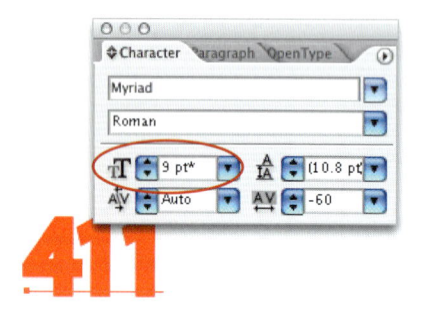

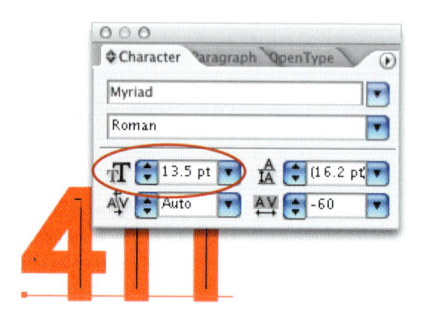

GRADIENT-FILLED TEXT

In order to fill text with a gradient, you cannot simply click on a gradient swatch. Too bad…but there is an easy solution that you can use over and over again. Create an object and fill it with your chosen gradient by clicking on a gradient swatch in the Swatches palette (Window>Swatches). Then with the Selection tool (V), drag the object into the Graphic Styles palette (Windows>Graphic Styles) or choose New Graphic Style from the palette's flyout menu. Now, anytime you need to fill some text with the gradient, just select your text with the Selection tool, and click the gradient in the Graphic Styles palette, applying it to your text. You can still edit the type with the Type tool (T) and change the direction of the gradient using the Gradient tool (G) from the Toolbox. This is simple but effective; especially since you can reuse the graphic style anytime you need it.

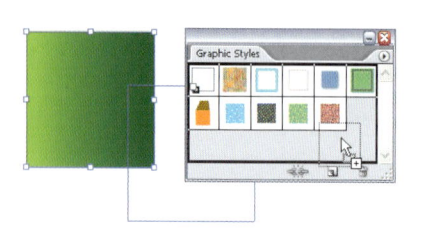

234   CHAPTER 10 • …And More Text

HIDE THE HIGHLIGHT

When you highlight a word using the Type tool (T) and attempt to change its color, the highlight ends up giving you an inversed color effect for the type. So, to keep the text highlighted and see the real color, press Command-H (PC: Control-H) to hide the highlight. Keep in mind that the text is still highlighted, but you just can't see the highlight (as in our example here, where our black type was inverted to white, but by using this tip, we hid the highlight so we could see the black type). Repeat the shortcut to show the highlight again.

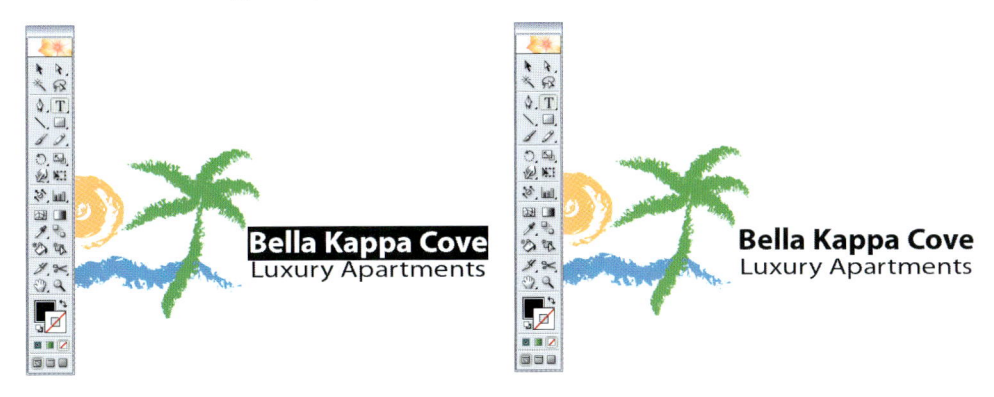

CLEAR THE OVERRIDE

An override is any text attribute in the Character Styles palette (found under the Window menu under Type) that is not part of the style (such as changing the font size). When a style override is made, it is indicated in the Character Styles palette by a small plus sign (+) beside the character style name. To clear the override, select your text with the Selection (V) or Type (T) tool, hold down the Option key (PC: Alt key), and click on the style name in the palette. The selected text will be reformatted to the original character style attributes.

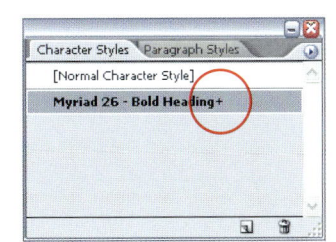

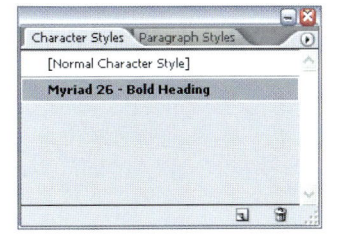

CHAPTER 10 • …And More Text

OVERRIDE THE OVERRIDE

When you apply a new style to some text (by selecting it and choosing a different character style from the Character Styles palette), any overrides will remain from the original style—even though you're changing the type's style. To clear overrides when applying a new style to selected type, press the Option key (PC: Alt key) as you click on the new style name in the Character Styles palette.

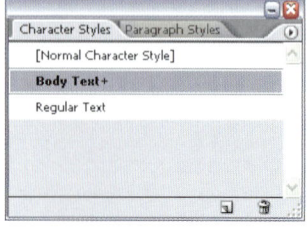

Original style 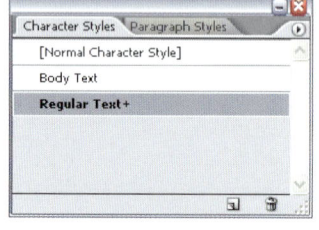 *New style applied* 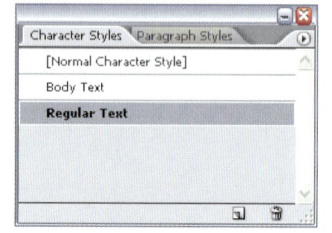 *Overriding style*

LOAD STYLES FROM OTHER DOCUMENTS

Don't re-create character or paragraph styles when you can load them from another document. For example, go to the Character Styles palette's flyout menu (found under the Window menu under Type) and choose Load Character Styles. Then navigate to the document that contains the styles you need. You can choose to load just the character styles (or only the paragraph styles, if you're in the Paragraph Styles palette) or choose Load All Styles to load the document's character and paragraph styles while you're using either palette.

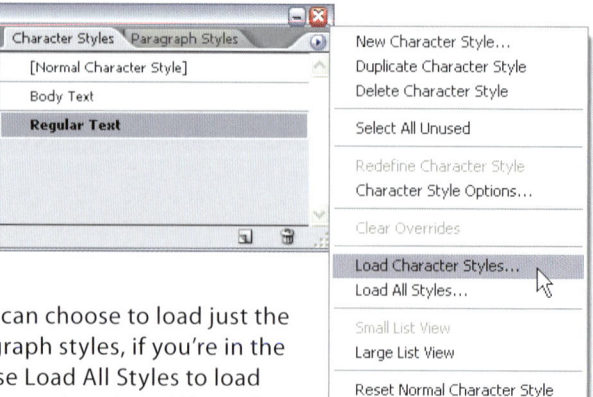

Illustrator CS2 KillerTips

ANGLED MARGINS

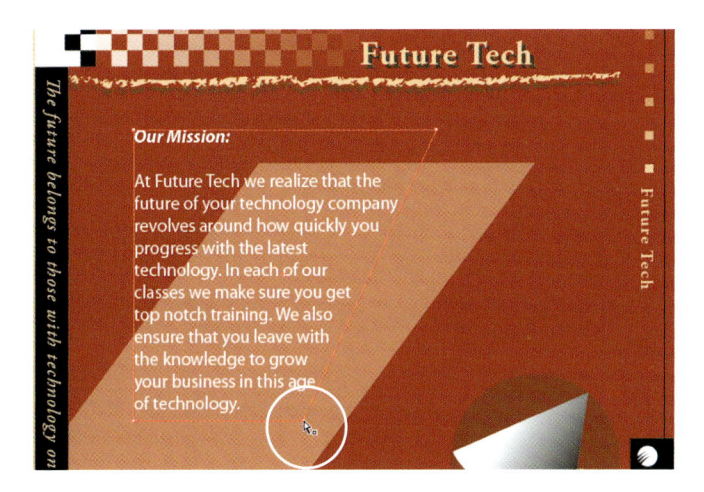

Need to create angled margins for a text box? It's pretty easy with the Direct Selection tool (A): Make sure *only* the text frame is selected with the Direct Selection tool and click on the corner anchor point where you would like to create the angle. Then drag the anchor point to the left or right to create an angle on that side of the text box.

CHARACTER ROTATION

The real tip here is to make sure you don't miss this feature because it's not in the standard view of the Character palette. It's called the Character Rotation field, and it lets you rotate characters (duh) relative to the baseline of the text. To access the control, make sure the Character palette is in its full view by choosing it from the Window menu under Type. When the palette appears, choose Show Options from the flyout menu. You can either highlight individual characters with the Type tool (T) or select an entire block of text with the Selection tool (V), and then pick an angle of rotation from the field's pop-up menu or enter the value you want in the field.

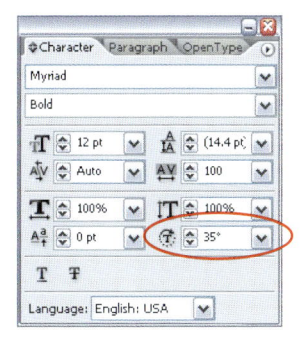

CHAPTER 10 • …And More Text   237

CONVERT WARPED TEXT TO OUTLINES

If you have warped some text—meaning you've selected it the with Selection tool (V), chosen Object>Envelope Distort>Make With Warp, and chosen a style, such as Arc—and now you want to convert the text to outlines (to send to someone who doesn't have that font, for example), you can't use the Type>Create Outlines command. Instead, when you have the warped text selected with the Selection tool, you'll have to use the Object>Expand command to create outlines of your type.

EDIT WARPED TEXT

If you have applied an envelope warp to a text object (Object>Envelope Distort>Make With Warp) and now you want to edit the text, press Command-Shift-V (PC: Control-Shift-V), or go to Object>Envelope Distort>Edit Contents. Once you've finished editing the text with the Type tool (T) and want to re-apply the warp, switch to the Selection tool, and press the same shortcut again.

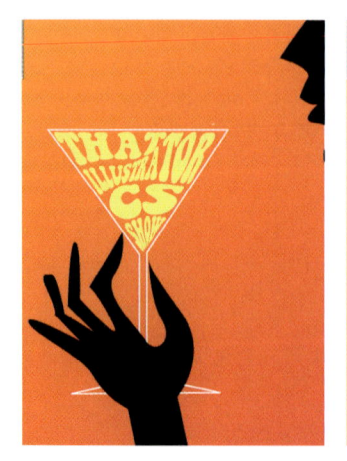

238   CHAPTER 10 • …And More Text

TYPE ON A CIRCLE

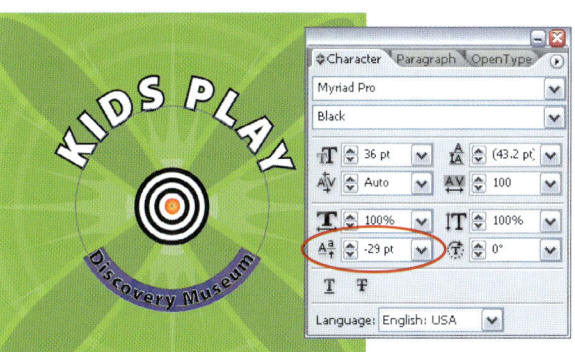

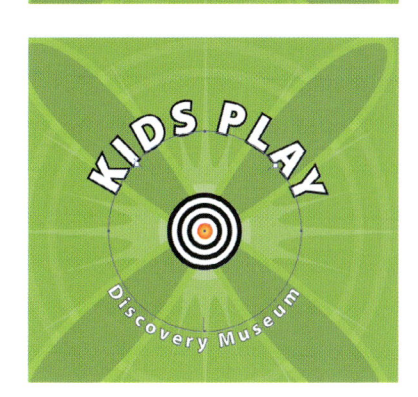

In earlier versions of Illustrator, you could easily create type on both the top and bottom of a circle. You simply had to create the text on the top of the circle, hold down the Option key (PC: Alt key), and drag a copy to the bottom with the Selection tool (V). This shortcut doesn't work in Illustrator CS2. To work around this missing shortcut, do this: Draw a circle with the Ellipse tool (L) while holding the Shift key. Get the Type on a Path tool (which is nested under the Type tool in the Toolbox), click the Align Center icon in the Paragraph palette (found under the Window menu under Type), click on the bottom center of your circle, and enter your text. Your type will be centered at the top of the circle. With the Selection tool (V), select the circle. Then press Command-C (PC: Control-C) to copy and Command-F (PC: Control-F) for the Paste in Front command. Then, drag the copied text to the bottom of the circle by clicking-and-dragging the little line that is sticking up just above the center of your text (avoiding the bounding box). To flip the text so it's reading the correct way, just drag that same line across the path towards the center of the circle. Select the bottom text with the Type tool (T) to edit it, and with your text highlighted, use the Set the Baseline Shift field in the Character palette to position the text below the edge of the circle. (*Note:* Unlike earlier Illustrator versions, you'll have to manually switch to the Selection tool to drag and flip your text. If you switch to the Selection tool using the Command key [PC: Control key] shortcut, it will stop the text from flipping as you drag it.) It sounds like a lot of steps, but do it once…twice… eight times and you'll see how simple it can be.

CHAPTER 10 • …And More Text 239

STOP FLIPPING

Okay, so this is the world's saddest excuse for a separate tip because it was just mentioned in the previous tip. But, just in case you didn't read the previous tip and jumped directly to this one, here we go: To stop text on a path from flipping over as you drag it with either the Selection tool (V) or Direct Selection tool (A), hold down the Command key (PC: Control key).

BASELINE SHIFT AMOUNT

Here's a pretty good guideline when you're applying a baseline shift to text on the bottom of a circle. With most fonts, simply enter a value in the Character palette's Set the Baseline Shift field that's approximately two-thirds of the font size. Highlight your text with the Type tool (T), highlight the Set the Baseline Shift field in the Character palette, enter minus (–) to move the text down, and enter the value that is two-thirds of the font size. (Remember to deselect the type and reset the Character palette's Set the Baseline Shift field back to zero when you're done, or else when you create new type, it will apply your last-used baseline shift setting.)

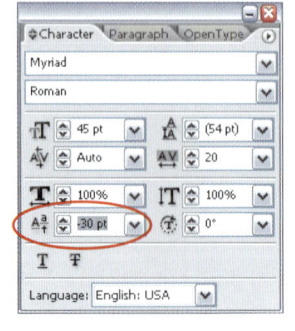

240   CHAPTER 10 • …And More Text

TYPE NOT ON A PATH

If you have created text on a path with the Type on a Path tool (nested under the Type tool in the Toolbox), and then later on decide you don't want it on the path, there is no command called "Remove text from the path." You'll have to do this by selecting just the text with the Type tool (T) and pressing Command-X (PC: Control-X) to cut it. Switch to the Selection tool, delete the path, and then click-and-drag with the Type tool to create a text box, and press Command-V (PC: Control-V) to paste.

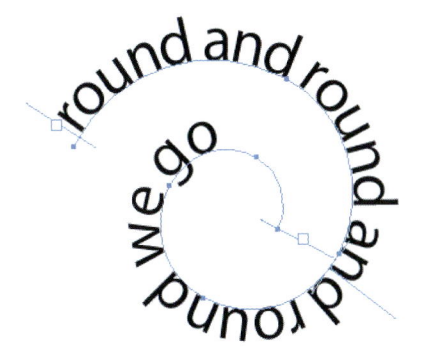

COPY FROM TEXT

You can use the Eyedropper tool (I) from the Toolbox to copy the attributes of existing text onto selected text. By default, the Eyedropper tool will copy fill, stroke, and other text attributes. (To see what your Eyedropper tool's options are, double-click the tool in the Toolbox.) Select the text you want to change with either the Selection (V) or Type (T) tool, and then use the Eyedropper tool to click on the text whose attributes you want to borrow. If you want to copy only the fill color, hold down the Shift key as you click with the Eyedropper tool on the text you're borrowing from.

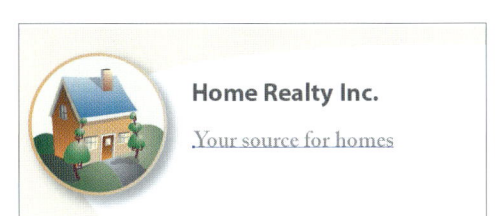

CHAPTER 10 • …And More Text   241

THREAD TEXT INTO A NEW BOX

If you want to create threaded text (meaning you want to create linked text boxes that contain overflow text) and you want to ensure that the next text box is the same size as the first one, it's pretty simple. Select the text frame with the Selection tool (V), and click on the text frame's Out Port icon (located near the bottom-right corner) to load the overflow text—the cursor will change to the Loaded Text icon, which looks like a tiny newspaper page. Then click where you want the second text box to appear. The text is threaded into a new text box, and that box will be exactly the same size as the first text box in the thread. If you want the new text box to be a different size, click-and-drag to draw a box in the size you want while you have the Loaded Text icon showing as your cursor. When you release the mouse button, your text will flow into the box you created.

HIDE TEXT THREADS

Text threads are Illustrator's way to show which text boxes are linked, allowing text to flow from one text box to the next. When you create text threads by using the Selection tool (V) and clicking on a text frame's Out Port icon (the tiny box near the bottom right of the text block), and then clicking on the In Port icon (the tiny box near the top left) of another text frame, Illustrator helps by showing a line that starts at the Out Port icon and ends at the In Port icon of the next text block. While this can be helpful to see where the text is flowing to, it can also be distracting; so to temporarily hide the thread lines for your selected text boxes, press Command-Shift-Y (PC: Control-Shift-Y). To show the thread lines, press the same keys again.

CHAPTER 10 • …And More Text   243

THREADED TEXT BLOCKS OF ANY SHAPE

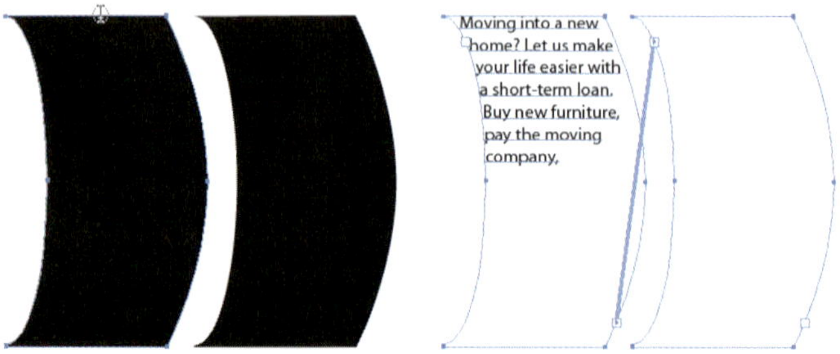

Text can be threaded between objects of any shape, not just rectangles. Draw a shape using any of the Shape tools (or even the Pen tool [P]) from the Toolbox, then click directly on the path of the shape with the Area Type tool (which is nested under the Type tool in the Toolbox) to add some text inside the shape. (*Note:* If your shape had any stroke or fill, those will disappear when you click with the Area Type tool, which converts shapes automatically into text frames.) Create a second shape, select both shapes with the Selection tool (V), and choose Threaded Text>Create from the Type menu. It's magic!

STOP THE THREADING

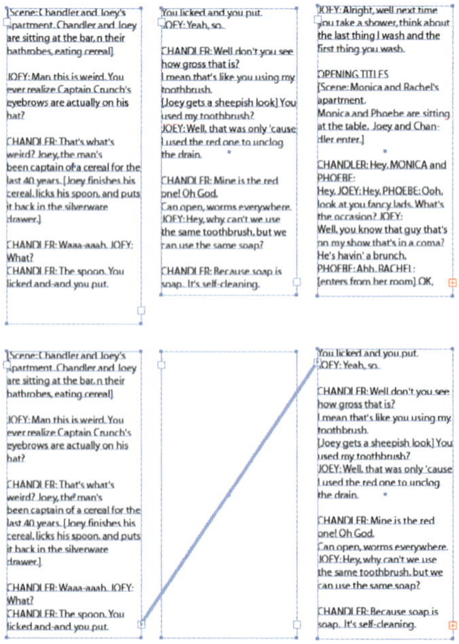

If you created threaded text but then changed your mind, you have a couple of options in the Type>Threaded Text submenu. With your text boxes selected, choose Remove Threading to break the flow of the text—meaning no more text will overflow into the selected text boxes—but you otherwise keep the appearance of the text. For example, if you have threaded three text boxes, the Remove Threading option would unlink the three boxes, but all the text would remain as-is. The other menu option is Release Selection. This command removes a selected text object from the thread. For example, if you had three boxes and selected the middle one with the Selection tool (V), then you chose Type>Threaded Text>Release Selection, the text would flow from the first text box to the third text box, skipping the middle box.

244   CHAPTER 10 • …And More Text

THREAD TEXT ON TWO PATHS

Hey, there's no rule that says you have to use closed shapes as text frames when you're threading text (mind you, in Illustrator 10 there was). You can also thread text on a path to another path, from a closed object to a path, or from a path to a closed object. Use the regular method of clicking on the first text object's Out Port icon (the tiny red box on the path with an plus sign [+] indicating text overflow), and then clicking on the next text object to create the thread.

TEXT WRAP AROUND A PHOTO

Any object in Illustrator can have text wrapped around it—any object created in Illustrator that is. Just position the object on top of a block of text using the Selection tool (V), and with the object still selected, go to the Object menu and choose Text Wrap>Make. If you want to have text wrap around an odd-shaped, placed raster image (File>Place), you'll have to create a path around the object. (In our example, we created and exported the path from Photoshop. See Chapter 11 for more details on exporting a path.) Then place your text box on top of the image and path, select just the path, and choose Object>Arrange>Bring to Front so the graphic is below the text and the path is above it. Then choose Object>Text Wrap>Make. In the Text Wrap Options dialog (Object>Text Wrap>Text Wrap Options), enter an Offset amount, and click OK. (*Note:* This won't work if your text and image are on different layers.)

CHAPTER 10 • …And More Text

MAKE A FRACTION

Another nice feature in Illustrator CS2 is support for OpenType fonts and their built-in special characters, including fractions. Choose an OpenType font by highlighting your text with the Type tool (T) and looking for the *O* symbol to the left of the font name in the Character palette's Font pop-up menu (in Windows, the symbol shows only in the Type>Font contextual menu). The symbol will only be visible if the Font Preview checkbox is turned on in Illustrator's Preferences dialog under Type.) Type the fraction you want as "x/x" (for example, 2/3 or 3/4), select the text, choose Type>OpenType from the Window menu and in the palette, click on the Fractions icon.

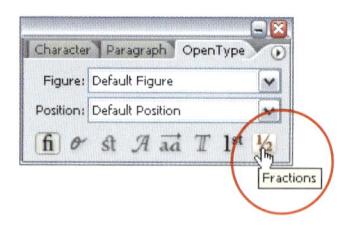

DON'T HAVE AN OPEN TYPE FONT?

But what if you need to make a fraction in a typeface that's not an OpenType font? If you type "1/2" and go to the OpenType palette, the fraction button is grayed-out. Instead, click with the Type tool (T) where you want your fraction to appear but don't type anything, and then open the Glyphs palette (Window>Type>Glyphs). Scroll through the palette to find the figure you need (in this example, a fraction) and double-click on it to add that character. Many fonts will offer the most-used fractions, such as 1/4, 1/2, and 3/4. (Seems obvious once you read it, doesn't it?) Needless to say, you can use this tip for any text symbols whose keyboard shortcut you can't remember, such as trademark, copyrights, accents, etc.

246   CHAPTER 10 • …And More Text

AUTOMATIC ORDINALS

What's an ordinal, you may ask? That's the official name for small, superscript text used after a numeral to denote a rank (e.g., 1st, 2nd, etc.). Rather than go to any trouble to create ordinals manually, some OpenType fonts have this function built right in. (OpenType fonts will have an *O* symbol next to the name in the Character palette's Font pop-up menu or the Type>Font contextual menu.) Just create some type using an OpenType font from the Character palette (found under Window>Type), select the text object with the Selection tool and in the OpenType palette (found under Window>Type), click on the Ordinals icon. The appropriate text will be converted into ordinals. Interestingly, any additional text you add to the existing type will also be converted into ordinals automatically. In our example, if we were to press the Return key (PC: Enter key) and type "5th" it would automatically change the "th" into an ordinal.

CHAPTER 10 • ...And More Text   247

GLOBAL CHANGE CASE

The Change Case command (found under the Type menu) will change the case of highlighted type based on your choice in the Change Case submenu. (First, we chose UPPERCASE and then Sentence Case, in our examples.) You can also perform what you might call a "global" Change Case command by selecting multiple text objects with the Selection tool (V). Then when you use the Type>Change Case option, all text objects will change at once.

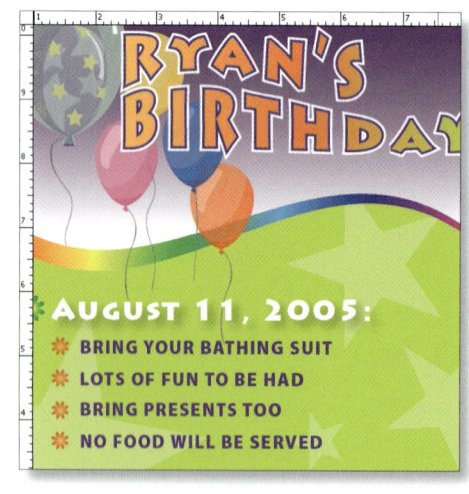

UPPERCASE

Sentence Case

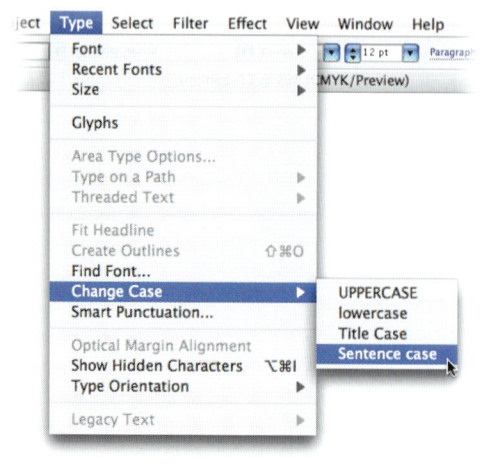

248   CHAPTER 10 • …And More Text

BLEND TWO TEXT OBJECTS

You can create some interesting effects by blending two text objects together, keeping the start and end text editable. Create two text objects that are not in text blocks by clicking once on the artboard with the Type tool (T), entering your text, and then clicking again in another location on the artboard, and creating a second text object. Select them both with the Selection tool and from the Object menu, choose Blend>Make, or press Command-Option-B (PC: Control-Alt-B). If you need to adjust the blend (such as change the number of steps), go back to the Object menu, and choose Blend>Blend Options.

YOUR STYLES IN EVERY DOCUMENT

Once you've created a series of character and paragraph styles, wouldn't it be nice to make them available in every new document you create? Well, if you read a couple of the other chapters, you can probably see where this is going. Save the document that contains your styles and then open the Adobe Illustrator Startup file (Illustrator CS2>Plug-ins folder). Go to the Window menu and choose Type>Character Styles. When the Character Styles palette opens, choose Load All Styles from the flyout menu. Navigate to the document you saved before, click Open, and all your styles should appear on the palette. Save the Startup file, restart Illustrator, and from then on your styles will be in every new document. (You'll have to do this in both the RGB and CMYK Startup files.)

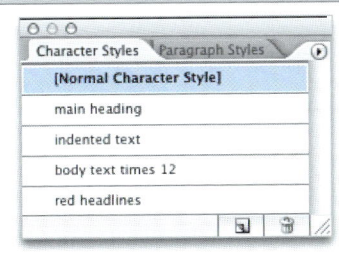

CHAPTER 10 • …And More Text   249

COLUMNS AND ROWS GALORE

Here's a simple way to create multiple columns (or rows) of text: Click-and-drag with the Type tool (T) to create a text block. Then, from the Type menu choose Area Type Options. Enter the number of columns (or rows) you want, the gutter width (space between columns), inset spacing you want, and click OK. Click in the text box, start typing, and the text will flow from one column (or row) to another within the text block.

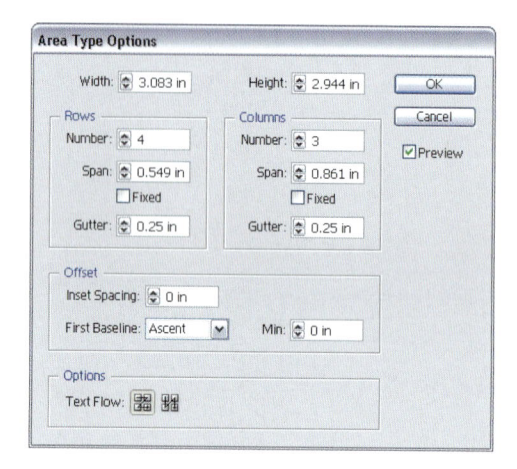

COLUMNS AND ROWS IN ANY SHAPE

We'll admit it, once again this probably could have been part of the previous tip, but we thought we'd separate it, just in case you already knew the previous tip. This is the option to add rows and columns to more than just rectangles. Create any shape you want and then click near the shape's path with the Area Type tool (which is nested under the Type tool in the Toolbox). Then, while still using the Area Type tool, you can go to the Type menu and choose Area Type Options (as in the previous tip) to change the options for columns and rows.

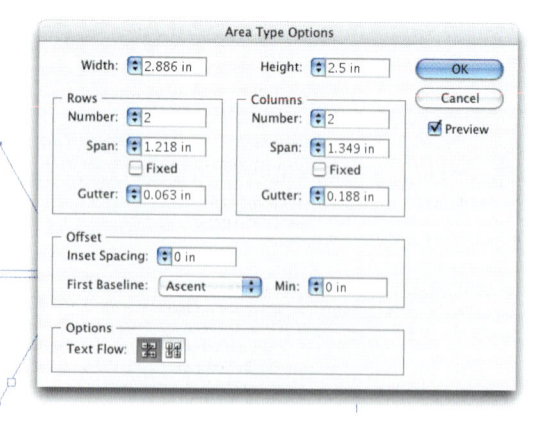

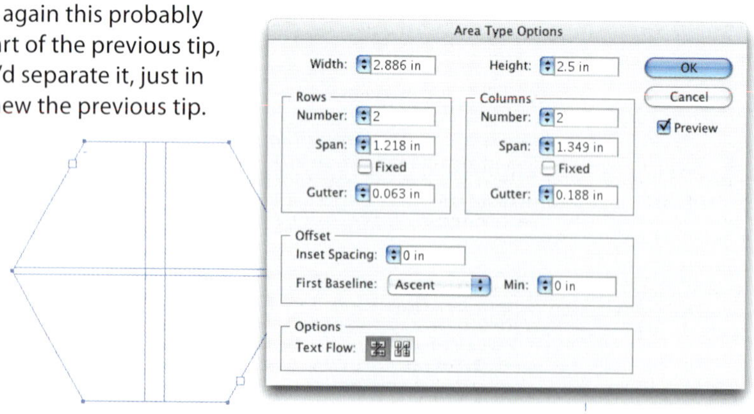

250   CHAPTER 10 • …And More Text

TURN OFF TYPOGRAPHER'S QUOTES

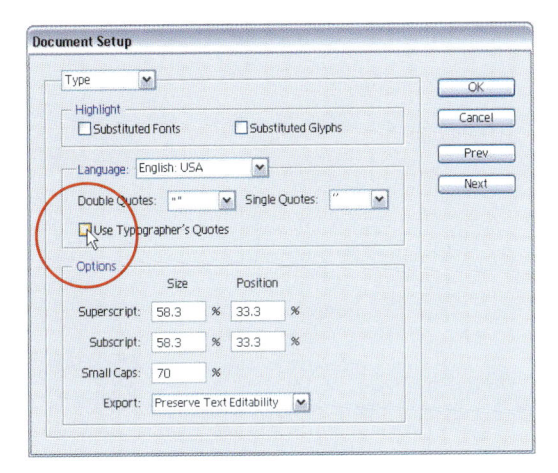

We almost hesitate to mention this one, because hopefully there aren't too many times where you'd want this option turned off. But, in case you don't want the quotation key to automatically turn into typographer's quotes (meaning you want straight quotes), you can turn off this option. From the File menu, choose Document Setup, select Type from the top pop-up menu, and uncheck Use Typographer's Quotes. Of course, if you change your mind, you can always convert "dumb" quotes back into "smart" quotes by selecting your text and choosing Type>Smart Punctuation. Make sure the Smart Quotes checkbox is turned on, and click OK.

PULL IT TOGETHER

Sometimes when you open a PDF file in Illustrator, the text is editable but it comes in as a series of separate text blocks (or lines), instead of one big text block. Luckily, there's an easy fix. Use the Selection tool (V), with the Shift key held down, to select all the text blocks, then cut the text using the Command-X (PC: Control-X) keyboard shortcut. Drag out a text block with the Type tool (T) and press Command-V (PC: Control-V) to paste. Now the text will flow within one text block.

CHAPTER 10 • ...And More Text   251

Friends

ILLUSTRATOR WITH OTHER CS2 APPLICATIONS

By now you are probably either anticipating humorous chapter introductions, or skipping past them completely because you

Friends
illustrator with other CS2 applications

have realized they are pretty meaningless. Well, this one is different, and you should definitely read it. Why, you ask, is this intro more important than the others? Because it actually contains some pertinent information (surprise, surprise). Looking at other Illustrator CS2 books, we were surprised how little information there was about moving files between Illustrator and other applications. So, we have included a few tips that may seem like basic information (and frankly, they are). But we wanted to make sure you were not missing out just because everyone assumed that you knew this stuff already. So please bear with the basic tips that are mixed in with the more killer-esque tips. We now return to our regular chapter intro: "Two vector objects walk into a bar…"

EXPORT IN PHOTOSHOP FORMAT

To convert an Illustrator document into a Photoshop document complete with editable type layers, use the Export command from the File menu. Choose Photoshop (PSD file extension) from the Format pop-up menu at the bottom of the dialog and click Export (PC: Save). In the Photoshop Export Options dialog, choose the color model and resolution you need, but also make sure that the Write Layers radio button is selected, with Preserve Text Editability and Maximum Editability checked. (By the way, you may have read in some Illustrator CS2 books that you cannot export area type to Photoshop and preserve editability, but that's not true—you can.)

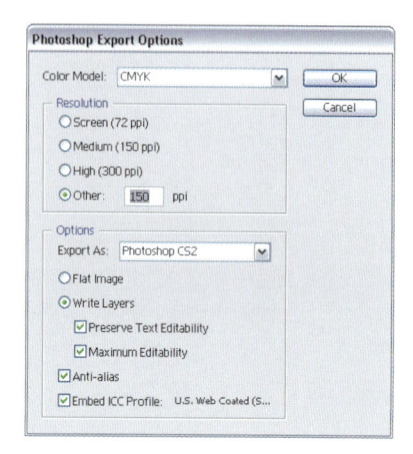

OPEN AN ILLUSTRATOR FILE IN PHOTOSHOP

To convert an Illustrator (.ai file extension) document into raster format, open it in Photoshop. In the dialog, enter the width, height, resolution, and mode for the raster version. Think carefully, because it is not easy to change your mind later without losing quality. If you're unsure, guess on the large side; you can always decrease the size or resolution later.

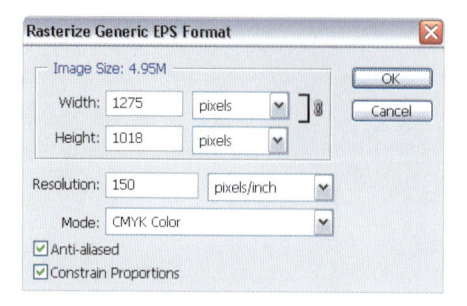

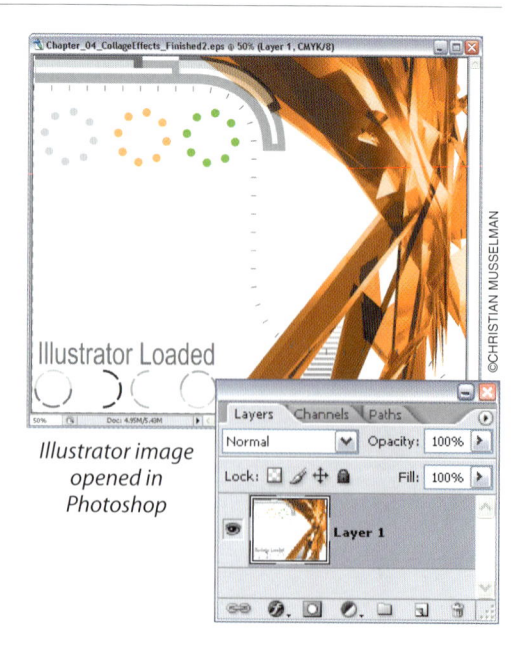

Illustrator image opened in Photoshop

254   CHAPTER 11 • Illustrator with Other CS2 Applications

PLACE AN .AI FILE INTO PHOTOSHOP

Add an Illustrator file into an open Photoshop document by choosing File>Place while in Photoshop. You won't get any options for mode or resolution, as those are set by the existing document. The only factor you can control is the physical size of the placed Illustrator file. After placing—and before the image is rasterized—the image has handles that let you resize it. Press-and-hold the Shift key to keep your image proportionate as you make the image larger or smaller. When you're finished resizing, press Return (PC: Enter) and the object will be rasterized at that size.

DRAG-AND-DROP INTO PHOTOSHOP

Select an object in Illustrator with the Selection tool (V) and drag it into an open Photoshop document. Just as with placing an image, dragging-and-dropping an image results in handles for resizing the image. Is this method better than placing, or vice versa? It's really a matter of personal preference. Some people like to set up Illustrator and Photoshop side by side, and drag from one to the other, while others will prefer placing previously saved files. They both work well—it's really your choice.

CHAPTER 11 • Illustrator with Other CS2 Applications   255

DRAG-AND-DROP FROM DESKTOP

If you can see the photo you want to import into a document, rather than going to the File> Place command, why not just drag it from the Desktop into the document? (Okay, so that was the tip—drag-and-drop from the desktop to place a file into your existing document). The only caveat is you will not get a dialog box with any options—the file will be linked. To embed the file rather than link it, hold down the Shift key as you drag-and-drop the file.

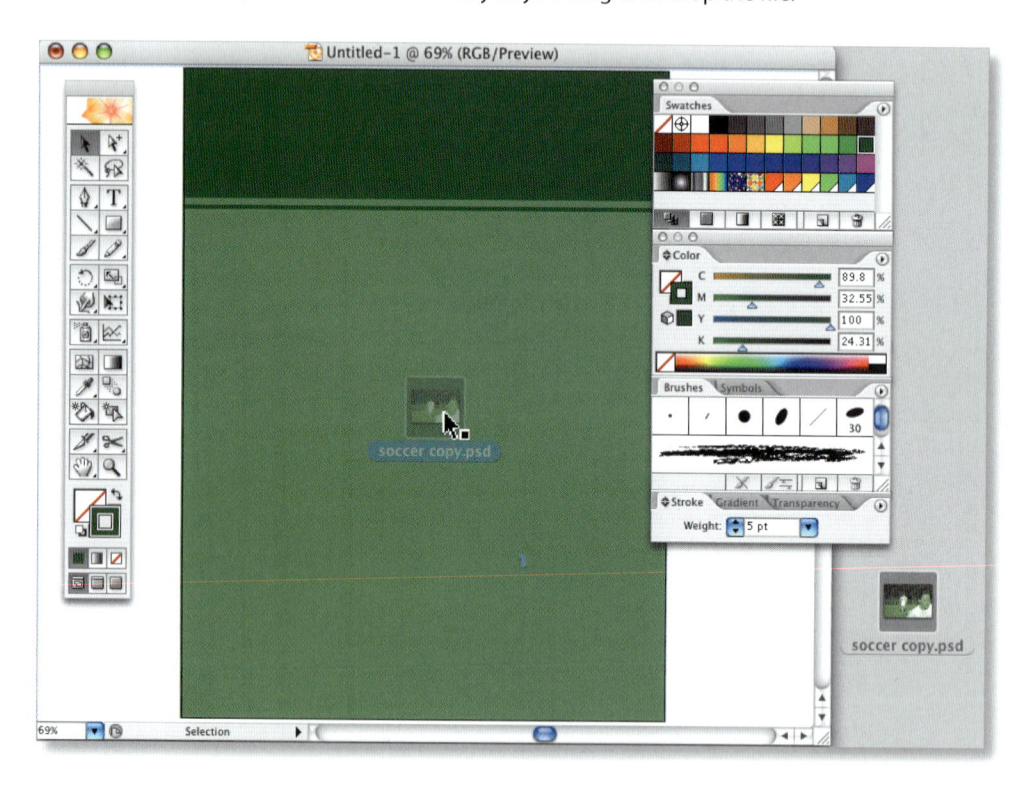

Illustrator CS2
KillerTips

OPEN A PSD FILE IN ILLUSTRATOR

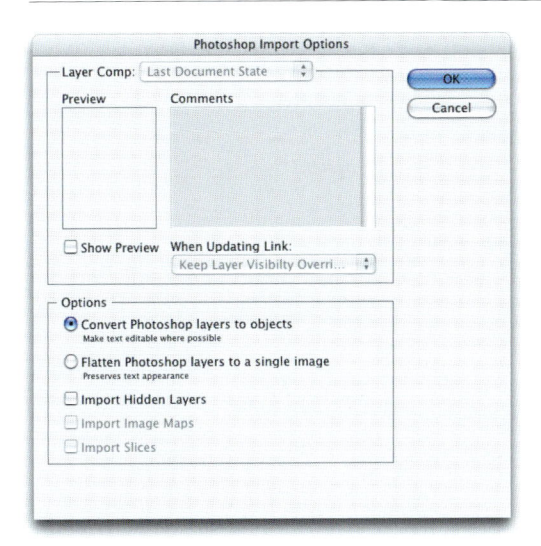

When you open a Photoshop (PSD) document in Illustrator, a dialog will offer two options: "Convert Photoshop layers to objects: Make text editable where possible," or "Flatten Photoshop layers to a single image: Preserves text appearance." Your choice depends on the level of editing you'd like to have. So, if you need to alter any layers in the Photoshop file, choose convert; if you don't need to alter the layered file, choose flatten.

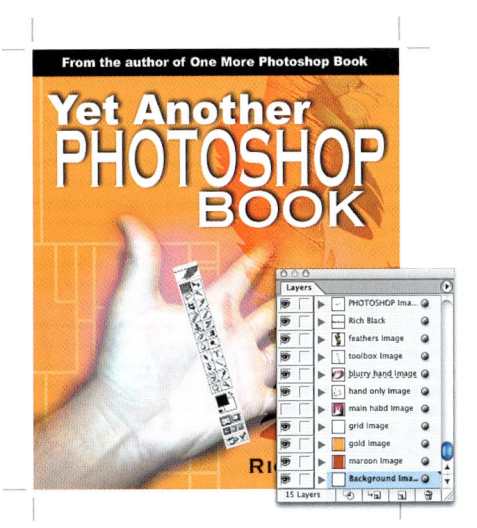

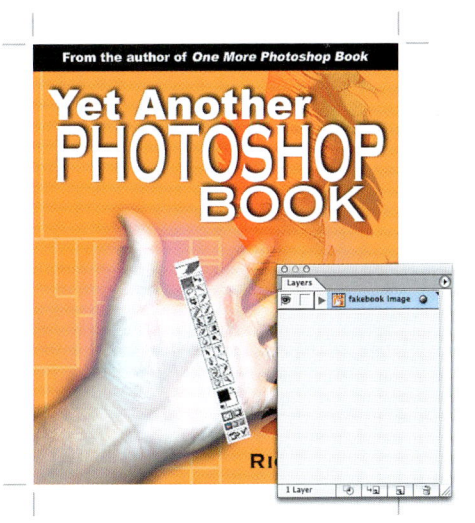

Converted PSD file

Flattened PSD file

CHAPTER 11 • Illustrator with Other CS2 Applications   257

PLACE A PSD FILE INTO ILLUSTRATOR

Use the File>Place command to add a Photoshop document into an existing Illustrator document. In the Place dialog, you can choose to link the file or embed the image. To link the file, just choose the document you want to place and click on the Link checkbox at the bottom left of the dialog before you click the Place button. There actually isn't an option called "Embed," just don't select the Link checkbox in the Place dialog. A linked graphic is easier to edit in Photoshop, while an embedded PSD file makes your image more compatible with other applications.

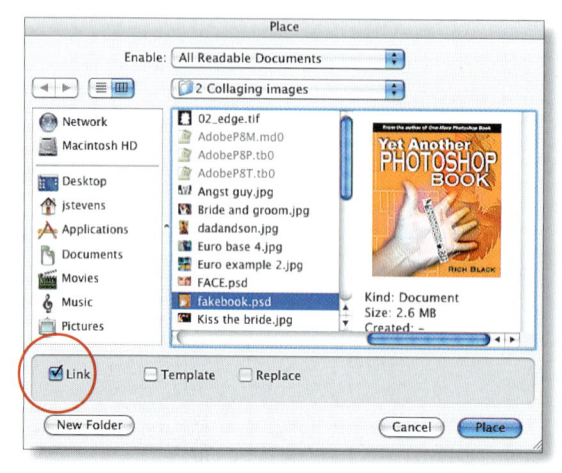

To check if a file is linked or embedded, open the Links palette under the Window menu. An embedded graphic will have a small icon (aka: the Embedded Artwork icon) to the right of the image's name in the Links palette, while linked graphics do not have that icon. Want an even easier way? You can also click on the placed graphic with the Selection tool (V): A linked object has an X through it, while an embedded object does not.

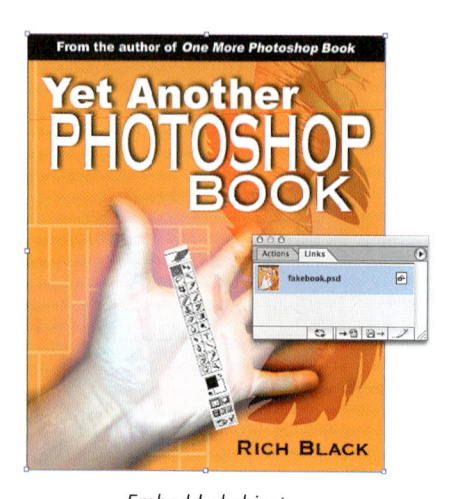

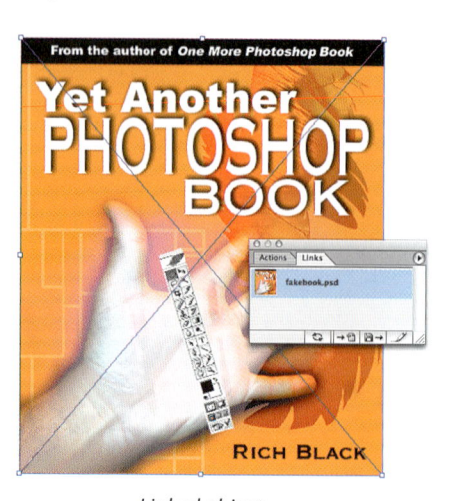

Embedded object

Linked object

258 CHAPTER 11 • Illustrator with Other CS2 Applications

PLACE IN ILLUSTRATOR FROM ADOBE BRIDGE

Check this out! You probably knew that you can open files directly from Adobe Bridge by double-clicking on them. If you have a PSD file, then double-clicking will launch the file in Photoshop. If you have an .ai or EPS file, then double-clicking it will launch that file in Illustrator. However, what if you want to open a Photoshop file in Illustrator or vice versa? You can place an image into Illustrator CS2 (or Photoshop, InDesign, or GoLive for that matter) right from within Bridge. Just choose File>Place and choose which application you'd like to place the file into.

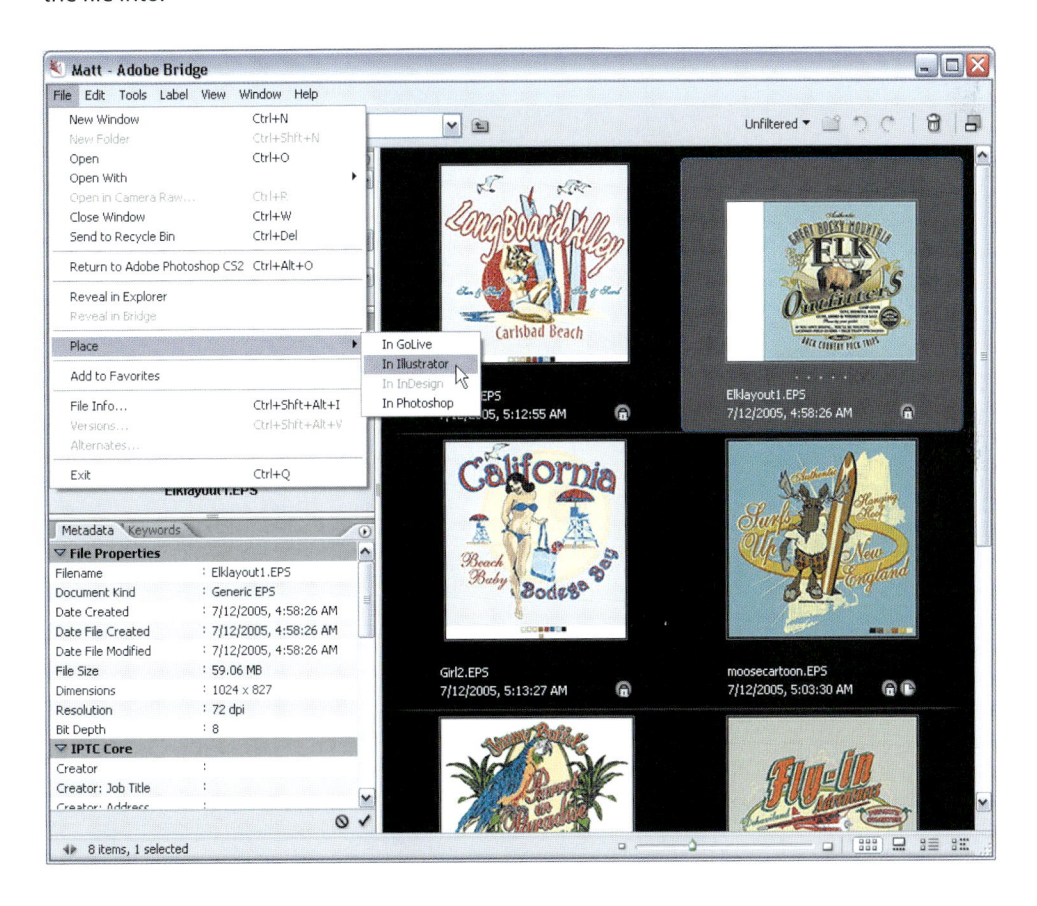

CHAPTER 11 • Illustrator with Other CS2 Applications

CHANGE BETWEEN EMBEDDED AND LINKED GRAPHICS

It's easy to change a linked graphic to an embedded image. Open the Links palette under the Window menu, click on the linked graphic in the palette, and then from the palette's flyout menu, choose Embed Image. If the graphic has layers, you'll have to choose to either flatten it or convert it. It takes an extra step to change an embedded image into a linked image. After selecting the embedded graphic in the Links palette, choose Relink from the palette's flyout menu to open the Place dialog. Find your same graphic, turn on the Link checkbox, and click Place.

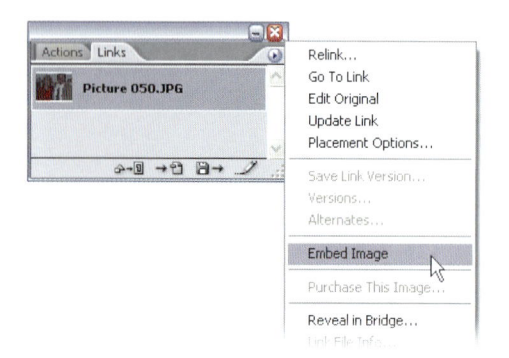

EDITING LINKED IMAGES

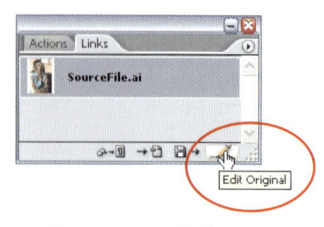

When you place an image into Illustrator, you have two options: embedding or linking. One of the advantages of linking an image is that you can edit it "on the fly" in the original software. Open the Links palette under the Window menu, and click on the Edit Original icon in the bottom-right corner of the palette. Or, to quickly edit the original without having to track down the Links palette, just hold down Command-Option (PC: Control-Alt) and double-click on the placed artwork. The appropriate software will automatically be launched and the image will be opened. Make your changes, save it, and the image will update in your Illustrator document. (You may get a warning dialog asking if you want to update linked files, depending on your preferences—see the tip on page 262.)

260   CHAPTER 11 • Illustrator with Other CS2 Applications

VECTOR SHAPES IN PHOTOSHOP

When you export a document in PSD format, any vector shape is rasterized when it's opened in Photoshop. In order for an Illustrator vector shape to remain an editable vector—meaning you want to create a custom shape layer in Photoshop so you can edit the image—you must do one extra step in Illustrator before exporting. Select the object, choose Window>Pathfinder, and from the Pathfinder palette's flyout menu, choose Make Compound Shape. (*Note:* If your image has objects within it, just select its outermost bounding box. You don't need to flatten the image.) Then choose File>Export, and in the Format pop-up menu choose Photoshop (PSD). When you open the PSD file in Photoshop, the object will appear as a shape layer, preserving its vector editability.

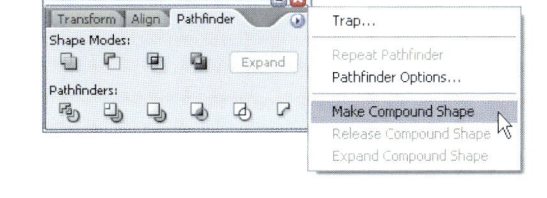

Bull Dog Entertainment
Original vector image

Vector image in Photoshop

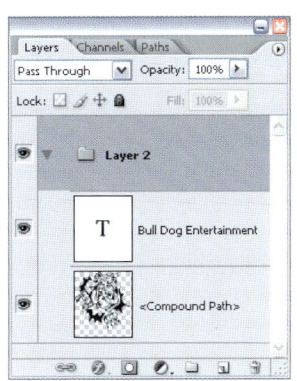

Rasterized vector image in Photoshop

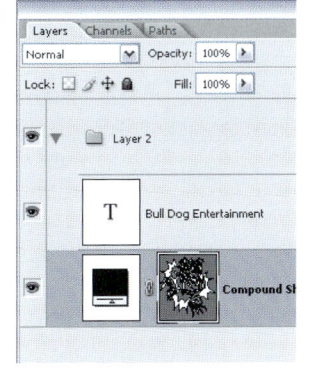

Editable vector image in Photoshop

CHAPTER 11 • Illustrator with Other CS2 Applications   261

WITHOUT WARNING

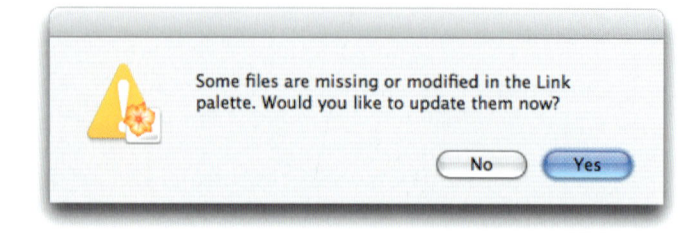

By default, every time you change and save a linked image in another application, you'll get a warning dialog asking you if you want to update the file in Illustrator. To avoid this warning every time you alter a linked image, press Command-K (PC: Control-K) to open the Preferences dialog and choose File Handling & Clipboard from the top-left pop-up menu. In the Update Links pop-up menu, choose Automatically. From then on, linked files will automatically update when you edit them in the original software, without any warning.

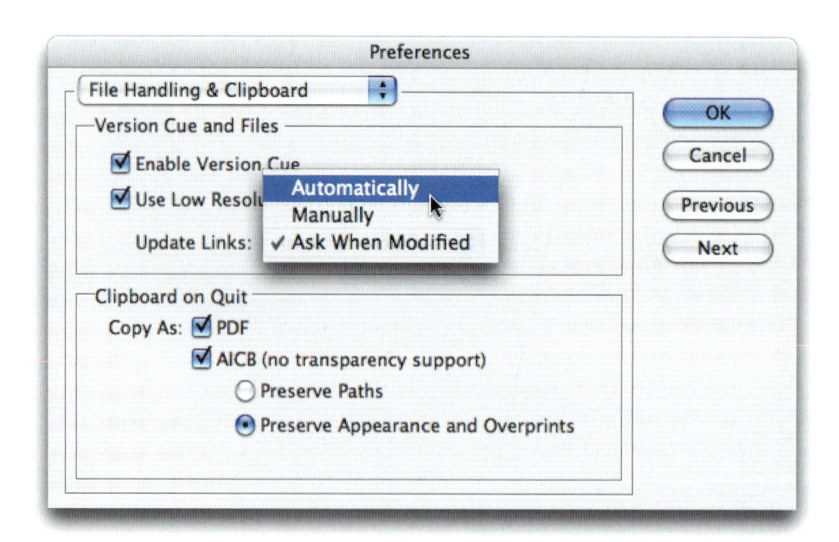

NO VISIBLE IMAGE

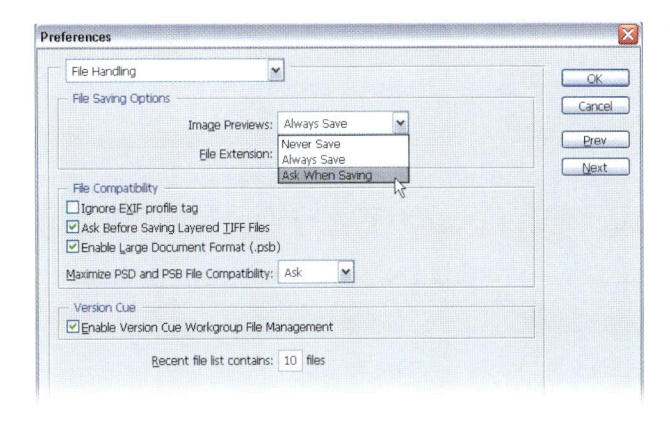

If you place a graphic (File>Place) and nothing shows up except an empty box, it probably means that the preview was turned off in the original program. You'll have to fix this problem by opening your image in its original editing software. In Photoshop, for example, there's an option that's set in the Preferences (Command-K [PC: Control-K]) under the File Handling category in the top-left pop-up menu in the dialog. In the Image Previews pop-up menu, choose Ask When Saving or Always Save. Then resave the image in Photoshop, and relink your selected image in Illustrator by choosing Relink in the Links palette's flyout menu.

COPYING-AND-PASTING BETWEEN ILLUSTRATOR AND PHOTOSHOP

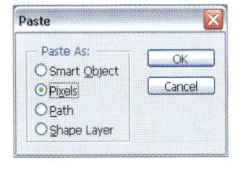

When you choose Copy from the Edit menu to copy a graphic in Illustrator and paste it into a Photoshop document (Edit>Paste), you get four choices: to paste as a Smart Object, as Pixels, as a Path, or as a Shape Layer. If you don't get this dialog offering these choices, you'll have to change a setting in Illustrator. Press Command-K (PC: Control-K) to go to Preferences, choose File Handling & Clipboard from the top-left pop-up menu in the dialog, and make sure that AICB (no transparency support) is checked. Copy the object again (Command-C [PC: Control-C]), and then switch to Photoshop and Paste (Command-V [PC: Control-V]). Now the Paste dialog will appear.

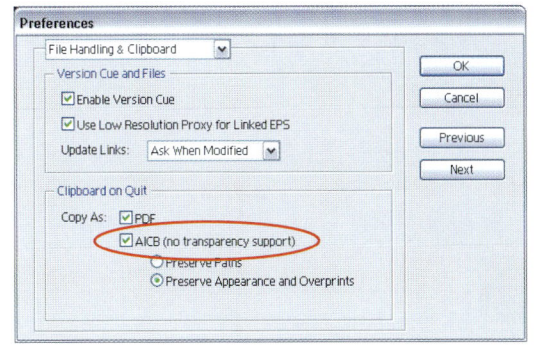

CHAPTER 11 • Illustrator with Other CS2 Applications   263

DRAG FROM ILLUSTRATOR TO MAKE A PATH IN PHOTOSHOP

If you know that you need a path in Photoshop, you can avoid the Paste dialog (see previous tip) by dragging-and-dropping an object from Illustrator into a Photoshop document. Just select your object with the Selection tool (V), hold down the Command key (PC: Control key) to override the Paste dialog, and drag-and-drop the object into your Photoshop document to automatically create a path. To ensure that your object was converted to a path in Photoshop, choose Paths from the Window menu. You should see a Work Path created in the palette for you. (In our example, the copied path was stroked with a brush in Photoshop after we selected Stroke Path from the Paths palette's flyout menu.)

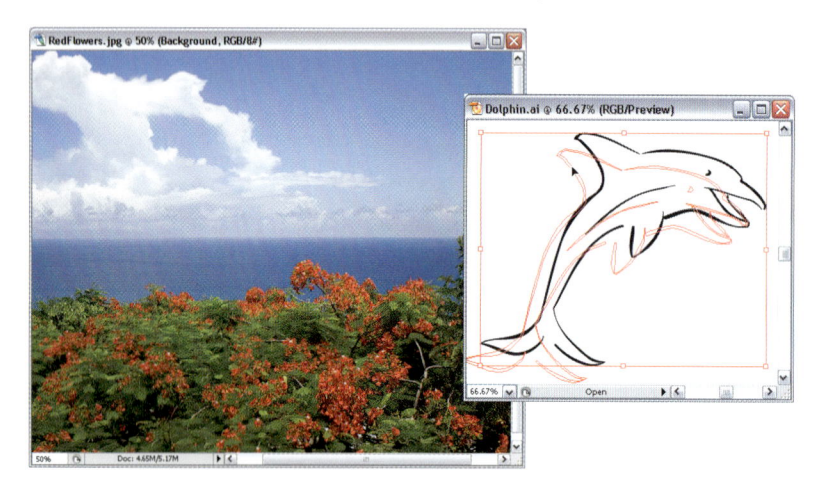

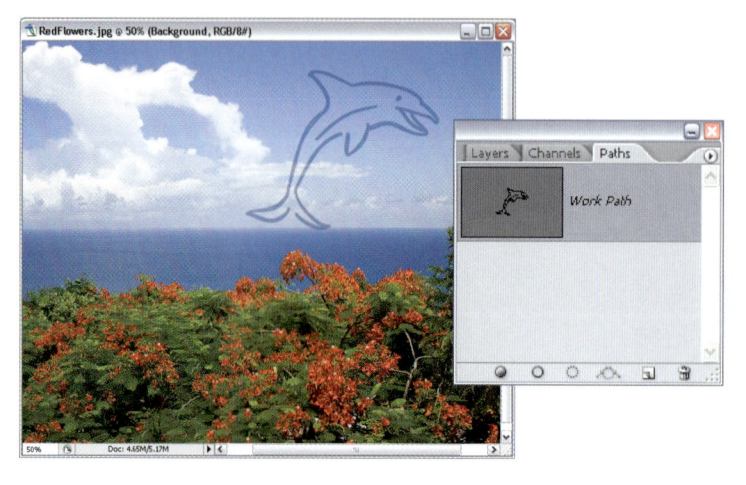

264   CHAPTER 11 • Illustrator with Other CS2 Applications

YOUR ILLUSTRATOR LOGO BUILT INTO PHOTOSHOP

If you would like your one-color logo to be a built-in part of Photoshop, accessible to every document, it's pretty simple to do. Keep in mind that this works best with basic compound shapes; so if you want to add effects, alter opacity, etc., you can simply do that in Photoshop. In Illustrator, select the logo with the Selection tool (V) (if the logo contains text, convert it to outlines by selecting the text with the Selection tool and choosing Type>Create Outlines) and then go to Edit>Copy (Command-C [PC: Control-C]). Switch to Photoshop, and from the Edit menu choose Paste (Command-V [PC: Control-V]). When the Paste dialog appears, choose Shape Layer (to access the Paste dialog, see the tip on page 263). When your logo appears in Photoshop, it will change to whatever fill or stroke color is active in Photoshop's Toolbox, but you can always change this later. So, with the logo still selected, go to the Edit menu and choose Define Custom Shape. Name it, click OK, and from then on your logo will appear in the Shape Picker when you have the Custom Shape tool (U) selected. Just choose a color in Photoshop's Toolbox, get the Custom Shape tool, choose your logo from the Shape Picker in the Options Bar, and click-and-drag with the Shift key held down to add your logo proportionately in any size you want!

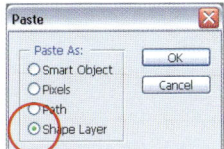

Logo pasted into Photoshop

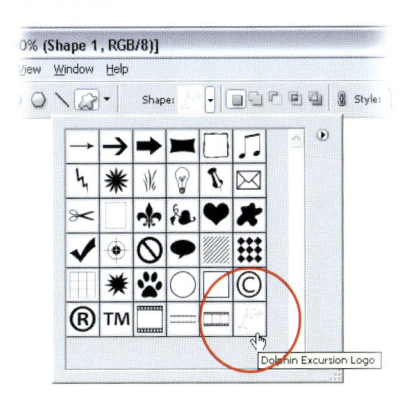

The dolphin logo in a Photoshop document

CHAPTER 11 • Illustrator with Other CS2 Applications   265

EXPORT PATHS FROM PHOTOSHOP

One very effective way to use Photoshop and Illustrator is to create a path in Photoshop (from a selection, for example), and use that path in Illustrator. To do this, go into Photoshop, open your document with your created path, and choose File>Export>Paths to Illustrator. In the resulting dialog, choose the appropriate path (which you saved when you created the path in Photoshop), in the Write pop-up menu, click OK, and open the resulting file in Illustrator. At first, you won't see anything except crop marks, which represent the boundaries of the Photoshop document. Switch to Outline mode from the View menu (Command-Y [PC: Control-Y]) to see, select, and start working with the path. (If you're unable to select or work with the path, you may need to use the Object>Expand command.)

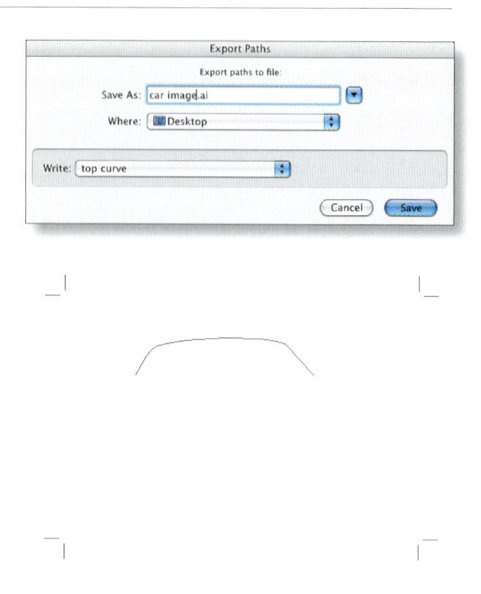

BORROW SHAPES FROM PHOTOSHOP TO USE IN ILLUSTRATOR

Using this theory of exporting paths to Illustrator (see previous tip), why not take advantage of the many custom shapes that are built-in or can be loaded into Photoshop? Get the Custom Shape tool (U) and click the Paths icon in the Options Bar (it's the middle icon in the group of three icons on the left). Select an object from the Shape Picker in the Options Bar, then click-and-drag to create your object with the Custom Shape tool. This will create a Photoshop path. With the object still selected, choose File>Export>Paths to Illustrator to save the path. Now switch to Illustrator and go to File>Open to "transfer" the custom shape.

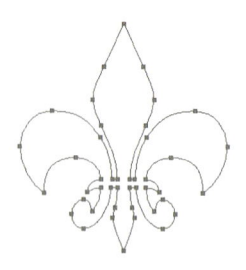

266 CHAPTER 11 • Illustrator with Other CS2 Applications

COMMON COLOR SETTINGS

When placing images created in Illustrator into Photoshop (or vice versa), the colors may appear different. To fix this, ensure that the color management settings for both applications are the same. From Illustrator's Edit>Color Settings dialog, save your color management settings to a color settings file (CSF). From Photoshop's Edit>Color Settings dialog box, click the Load button, and load the CSF you just saved.

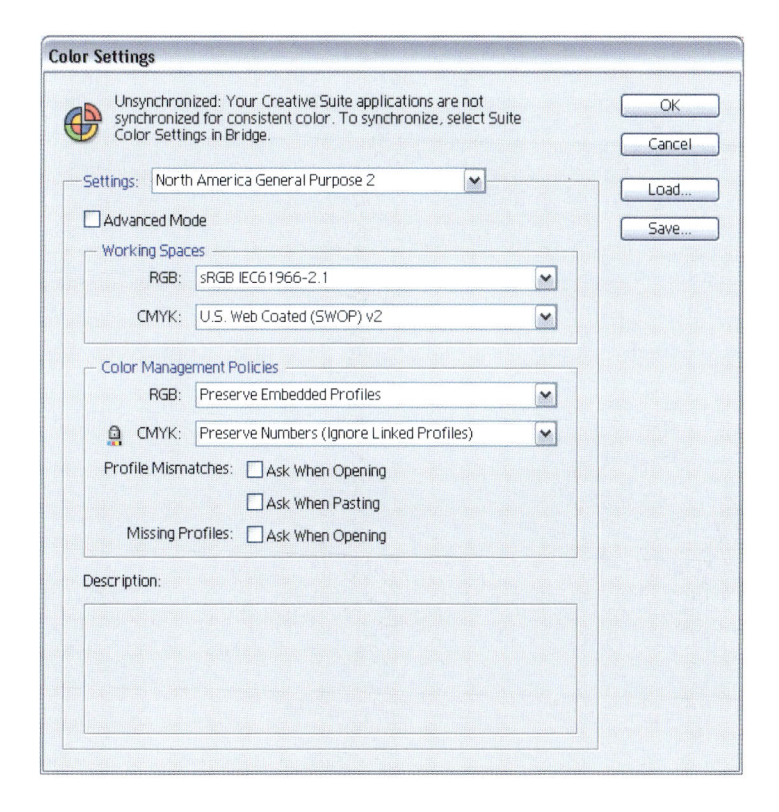

CHAPTER 11 • Illustrator with Other CS2 Applications   267

TAKE YOUR SWATCHES ANYWHERE

Got a swatch set that you're using in Illustrator and want to use it in Photoshop or InDesign? Don't recreate all of the swatches all over again. Try using the new Save Swatches for Exchange function in the Swatches palette flyout menu (Window>Swatches). This will generate an ASE file that can be loaded into Photoshop CS2 and/or InDesign CS2, so you can take your swatches anywhere.

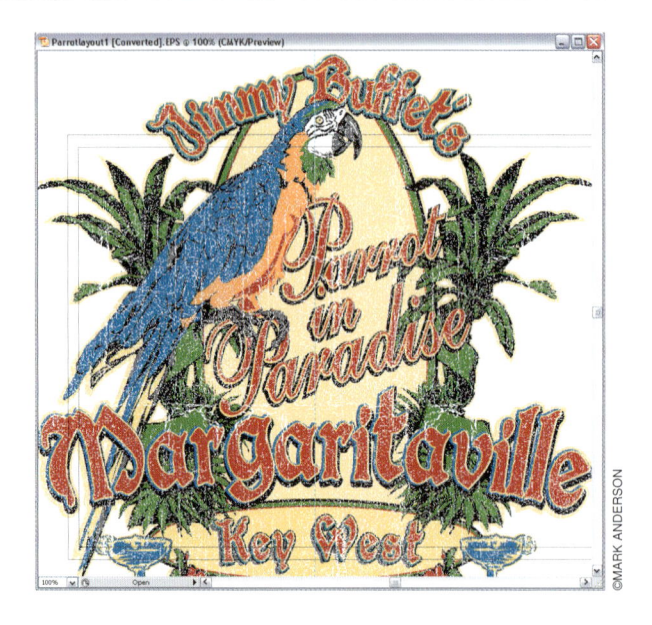

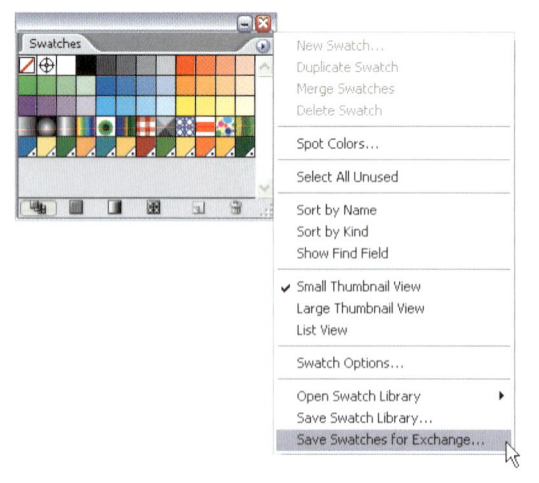

CHAPTER 11 • Illustrator with Other CS2 Applications

INFO FOR PHOTOSHOP

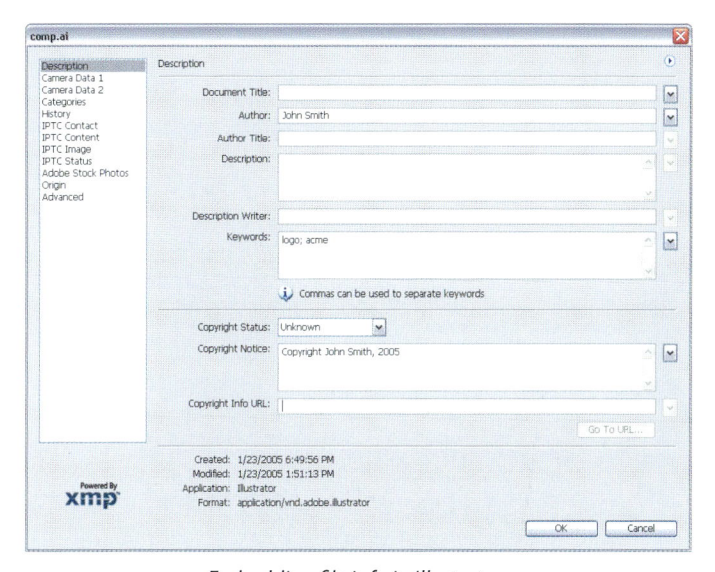

Embedding file info in Illustrator

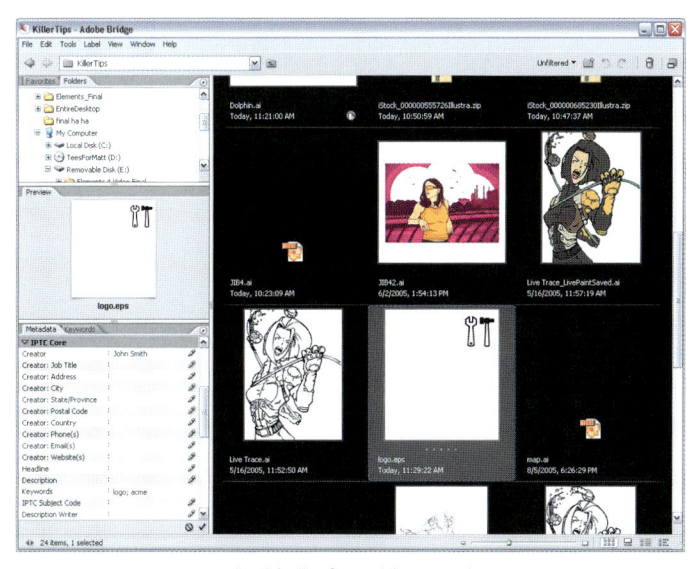

Embedded info visible in Bridge

The File Info command under the File menu is a very useful way to embed details about your document, including the author, keywords, and copyright information. As useful as it can be in Illustrator, the same information can be just as practical in Photoshop because that information becomes searchable metadata in Bridge. For instance, click on the Go to Bridge icon in the far right of Photoshop's Options Bar, navigate to find your Illustrator file, and click on the Metadata palette tab. Here you'll find all the file info that you embedded in your Illustrator document.

CHAPTER 11 • Illustrator with Other CS2 Applications

METADATA TEMPLATES TO SAVE YOU TIME

If there is information that you need to include in multiple documents, you can make your life simpler by creating a metadata template. Use the File Info command under the File menu and enter the information you'd like to embed in your documents. Once you're done, use the flyout menu to choose Save Metadata Template. Anytime you need to embed the same information, go to File>File Info and use the flyout menu to choose from your saved templates. As an interesting aside, the same templates are available in Photoshop (and metadata templates created in Photoshop can be applied in Illustrator).

SHOW IMAGES OR PHOTOS IN OUTLINE MODE

By default, placed images are not visible in Outline mode (Command-Y [PC: Control-Y]). If you'd like to be able to see placed images while you're in Outline mode, go to Document Setup in the File menu. In the dialog that appears, check Show Images In Outline Mode. Any placed image will be visible, albeit in a poor-quality, black-and-white bitmapped version. Still, it can be helpful to see even this mediocre view if you're trying to edit objects in Outline mode.

CHAPTER 11 • Illustrator with Other CS2 Applications

Illustrator CS2
KillerTips

DASHED LINES IN PHOTOSHOP (THANKS TO ILLUSTRATOR)

The only way to create a dotted (or dashed) line in Photoshop is by playing with the Spacing slider in the Brushes palette found under the Window menu. It's a little clumsy, so why not take advantage of Illustrator's ability to create dashed lines? Draw a path with the Line tool (\). With the line selected, open the Stroke palette from the Window menu, choose Show Options from the palette's flyout menu, and turn on the Dashed Line checkbox to create a dashed line. Copy (Command-C [PC: Control-C]) the object in Illustrator, switch to your Photoshop document, and choose Paste (Command-V [PC: Control-V]). Voilà—a quick, dashed stroke! (In this example, we created a path in Photoshop, exported it to Illustrator choosing File>Export>Paths to Illustrator, added a dashed stroke, and pasted it back into Photoshop by choosing Paste in the Edit menu.)

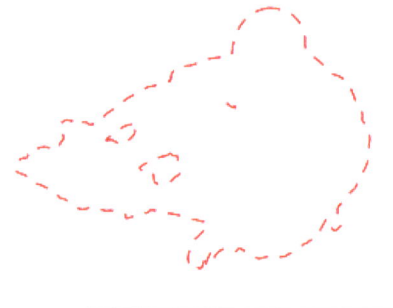

272   CHAPTER 11 • Illustrator with Other CS2 Applications

STOP CLIPPING WHEN SAVING AS AN EPS

Sometimes when you save a document as an EPS file in Illustrator and place it into a page layout program, the EPS file appears to be "clipped"—missing some information at the edges. To make sure that doesn't happen, create a rectangle slightly larger than the artwork, with no fill or stroke. Then choose File>Save As, and in the dialog choose Illustrator EPS (EPS) in the Format (PC: Save as Type) pop-up menu. Clipping should no longer occur.

CHAPTER 11 • Illustrator with Other CS2 Applications

ILLUSTRATOR LAYERS IN ACROBAT

One of the cool features in CS2 is the ability to take an Illustrator (.ai) file with multiple layers and save it as a PDF file, with those layers appearing in Acrobat. Yes, Acrobat 7.0 Professional (as well as Adobe Reader 7.0) has a Layers tab that works like a palette with the option to show and hide your Illustrator layers. Just choose File>Save As and in the dialog that appears, choose Adobe PDF (PDF) in the Format (PC: Save as Type) pop-up menu, then click Save. An Adobe PDF Options dialog will then appear, in which you change the Adobe PDF Preset pop-up menu to Custom, change the Compatibility pop-up menu to Acrobat 7 (PDF 1.6), and click the Create Acrobat Layers From Top-Level Layers checkbox. After you click Save PDF, open your document in Acrobat 7.0, and click the Layers tab on the left side of your document. Imagine having the ability to use Acrobat to show several versions of your document…

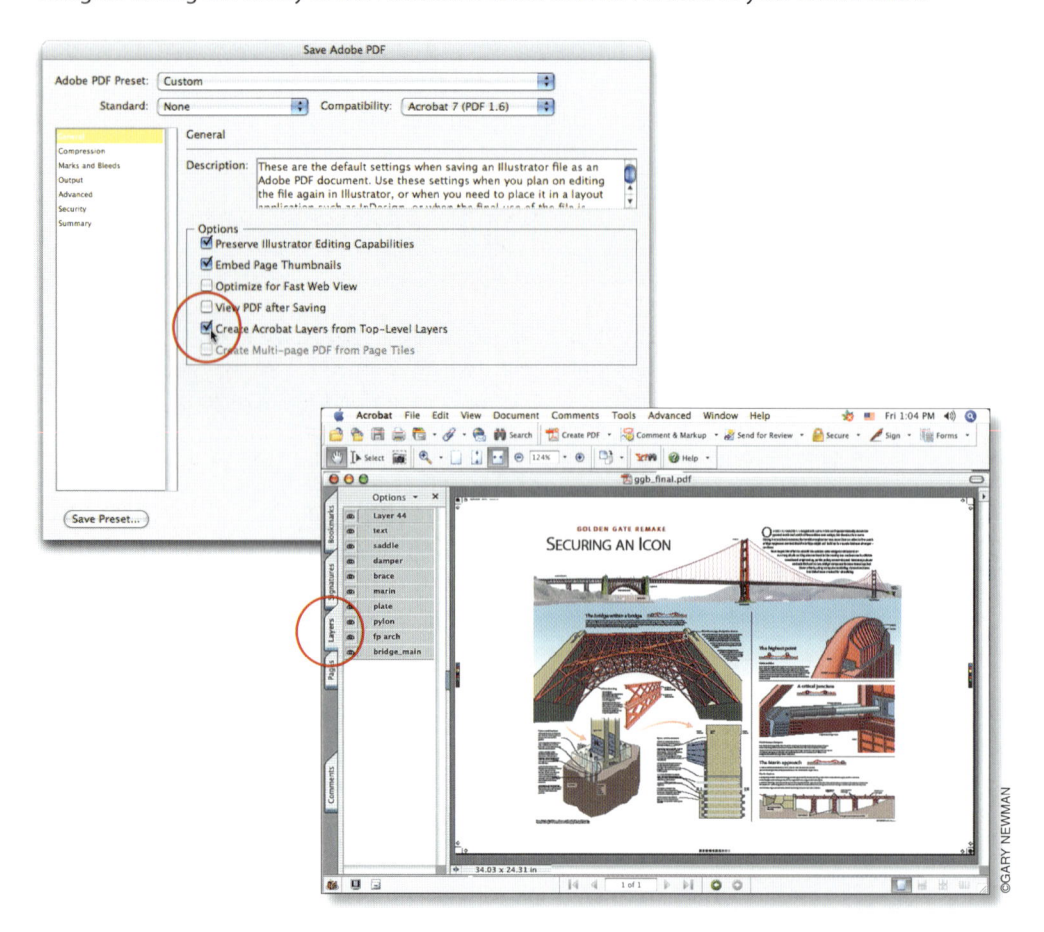

274   CHAPTER 11 • Illustrator with Other CS2 Applications

Illustrator CS2 KillerTips

OPEN A PDF IN ILLUSTRATOR

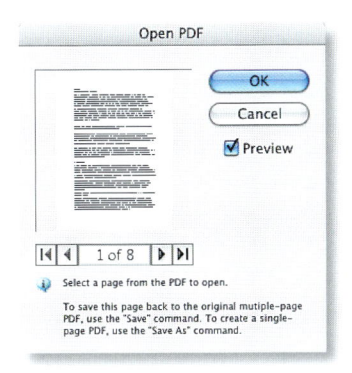

Besides Acrobat, Illustrator is one of the few software programs that can open and edit PDF files. Go to File>Open and target the PDF file. If it is a multipage document, a dialog will appear that allows you to navigate to the single page you'd like to open. (Unfortunately, you'll have to base that decision on a pretty small preview window.) If you open a page, edit it, and choose Save in the File menu, it will be saved back as part of the multipage document. To separate the image from the multipage document—converting it into a one-page PDF file—choose Save As from the File menu, rename the file, and click Save.

PLACE A PDF WITH SPOT COLOR

If you create a spot-color document in Photoshop (that is, with one or more spot color channels) and place it into Illustrator (File>Place), you probably want the spot color to preview. Unfortunately, if you save the file as an EPS file in Photoshop (File>Save As and choose Photoshop EPS in the Format [PC: Save as Type] pop-up menu), and place it into Illustrator, the spot color will import with the EPS file, but it will not show in the placed file. Instead, in Photoshop choose Save As from the File menu and select Photoshop PDF in the Format (PC: Save as Type) pop-up menu (making sure you have the Spot Colors checkbox selected). Switch to your Illustrator document and choose File>Place. When your image appears, go to the View menu and choose Overprint Preview (Command-Option-Shift-Y [PC: Control-Alt-Shift-Y]).

Document placed as Photoshop EPS

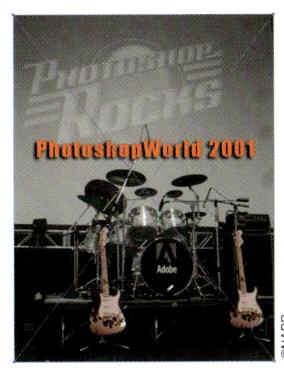

Document placed as Photoshop PDF

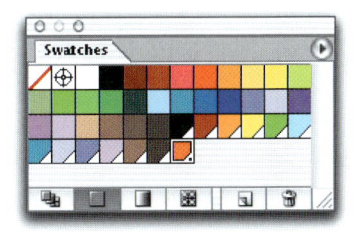

CHAPTER 11 • Illustrator with Other CS2 Applications   275

Illustrator CS2 KillerTips

SENDING A FILE TO A SERVICE BUREAU

Before you create a document that will be printed at an outside service provider (such as a large format printer), see if you can get a copy of the bureau's printer driver. Load it on your system and choose it in the Print dialog (File>Print). That way, you can make sure all the settings are correct and that your document is set up correctly before sending it off to print.

REDUCE FILE SIZE

Before saving a file, you can cut down the file size by removing all unnecessary stuff in the file (in this instance, stuff meaning swatches, symbols, patterns, etc.). Thanks to Adobe, it's pretty easy. In the Actions palette (Window>Actions), look in the Default Actions folder for Delete Unused Palette Items. Click on the action name, and press the Play Current Selection button at the bottom of the palette to run the action. All the unused stuff will be removed, so that when you save the document, it will be a little smaller (not all that much in some cases, but every little bit helps, right?).

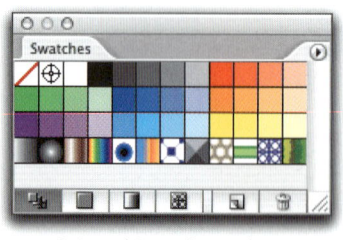

Original Swatches palette

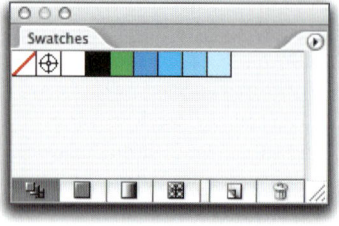

After running action

276 CHAPTER 11 • Illustrator with Other CS2 Applications

CLEANING UP YOUR ILLUSTRATIONS

Before printing a file, you can do yourself a favor by "cleaning it up." First, from the Object menu choose Path>Clean Up. In the dialog, make sure you select the Stray Points and Empty Text Paths checkboxes. Click OK to delete all these unneeded points. If you're sending the document to an outside printing service, you may also want to go to the Swatches palette and use the pop-up menu to choose Select All Unused. Then click on the Trash icon at the bottom of the palette to delete the swatches. Save the document (File>Save), and you're ready to go.

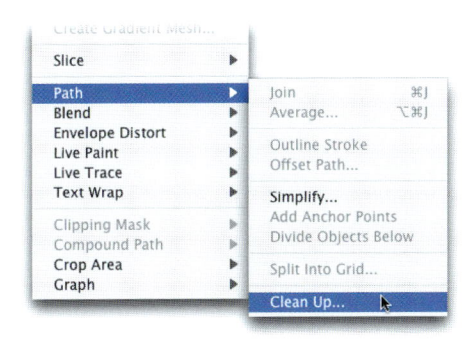

SAVE FOR OLDER VERSIONS OF ILLUSTRATOR

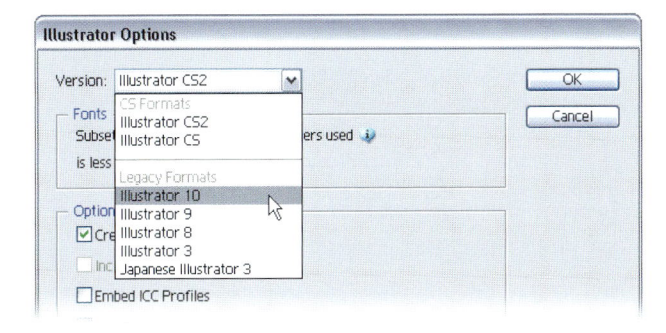

Illustrator is not backwards compatible, which means that you cannot save an Illustrator CS2 file into an older version such as 10, 9, or earlier. The best way to create a document that can be read by an older version of Illustrator is to choose the Save As command in the File menu (Command-Shift-S [PC: Control-Shift-S]). Click Save and from the Illustrator Options dialog, you can choose from older versions of the program in the Version pop-up menu. Be aware that several functions—notably type—will not transfer well from CS2 into earlier versions. (*Note:* If you attempt to open an Illustrator CS2 file in Illustrator 10, you'll get a dialog saying that the file was created in a newer version of Illustrator, but it does give you the option to import the file. Opening a file in this manner does not maintain the CS2 formatting as well as using the Export option.)

CHAPTER 11 • Illustrator with Other CS2 Applications   277

TRIAL SEPARATION

Before sending your file off to the service bureau for color separations, you can (and probably should) print a test separation on your own printer. Use the Print command from the File menu (Command-P [PC: Control-P]) and click on the Output category on the left-hand side of the dialog. Under the Output option, change the Mode pop-up menu from Composite to Separations (Host-Based). That way you can make sure that only the appropriate number of colors print.

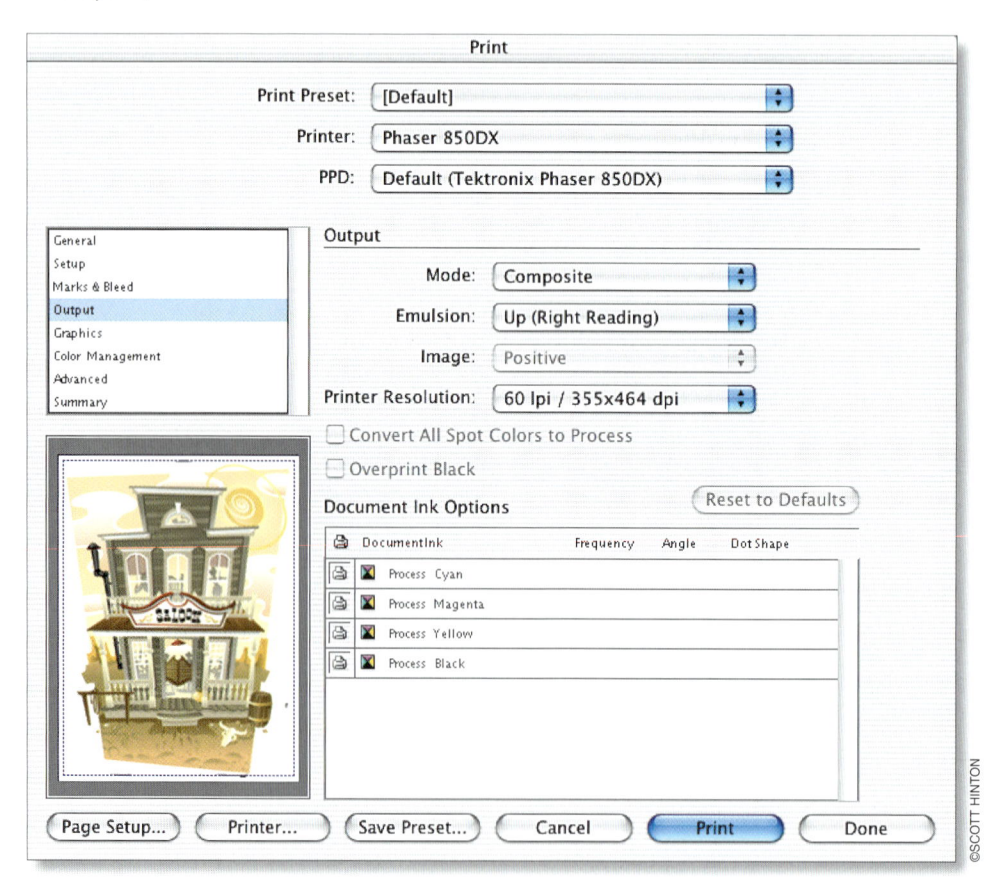

CHAPTER 11 • Illustrator with Other CS2 Applications

PRINTING EVEN LARGER THAN ILLUSTRATOR WILL LET YOU

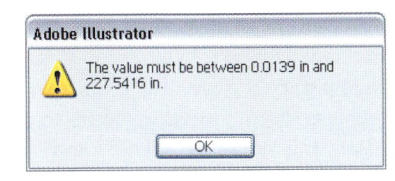

If you haven't figured this out yet, the largest document Illustrator will let you create is 227.54 inches in width or height. How do I know this? Try creating a new document that is 250 inches in size and Illustrator will give you a little reminder of the maximum settings. Well, what if you need to print something out that is larger than this? There's a way to cheat a little and it's in the Print dialog box (Command-P [PC: Control-P]). Under Options, near the bottom of the dialog, just click Custom Scale and enter in a percentage scale value that will get you to the print size you need. For example, if you need to print something that is 260 inches in width and height, then create a document that is 200 inches instead. Then enter 130% in the Width and Height settings under Custom Scale. This will print out at 260 inches (200 * 1.30 = 260).

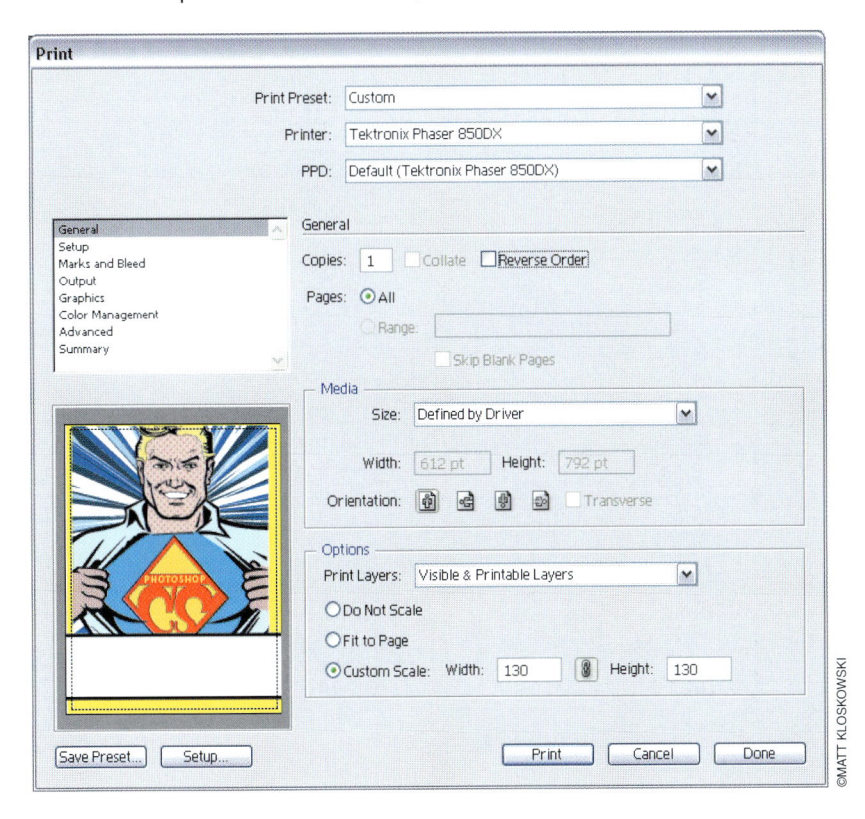

CHAPTER 11 • Illustrator with Other CS2 Applications   279

SAVE PRESET FOR PRINTING

If you have more than one printer in your location, or you send out files to various print shops, you can easily create printer presets for these different locations. Just set up the options in the Print dialog (File>Print) as if you were going to print to one of your printers (or as if you were setting up the file to send to the print shop). Rather than printing, though, click the Save Preset button, name the preset, and then click Done (instead of the Print button). Now, anytime you use the Print command from the File menu, you can choose from a list of presets in the Print Preset pop-up menu in the Print dialog. This can be a great timesaver, avoiding the need to change settings every time you change printers.

280   CHAPTER 11 • Illustrator with Other CS2 Applications

SAVING PRINT SETTINGS

In addition to saving presets (as mentioned in the previous tip), if you need to change the page setup and other settings for a document—without printing—you can do this in the Print dialog. Go to File>Print and just change the settings, such as page setup options, printer marks, etc., and then click the Done button rather than Print. Your settings will reappear when you reopen the Print dialog.

SAVE FOR WEB RIGHT WITHIN ILLUSTRATOR

Many people don't realize that in the File menu, Illustrator has a similar Save for Web interface as Photoshop. This is especially useful if you're saving Web graphic icons, as the PNG format is popular for this type of work. Illustrator's Save for Web dialog even includes a 2- and 4-up view, which really helps get a preview of how your vector artwork will look when compressed using various Web image compression formats.

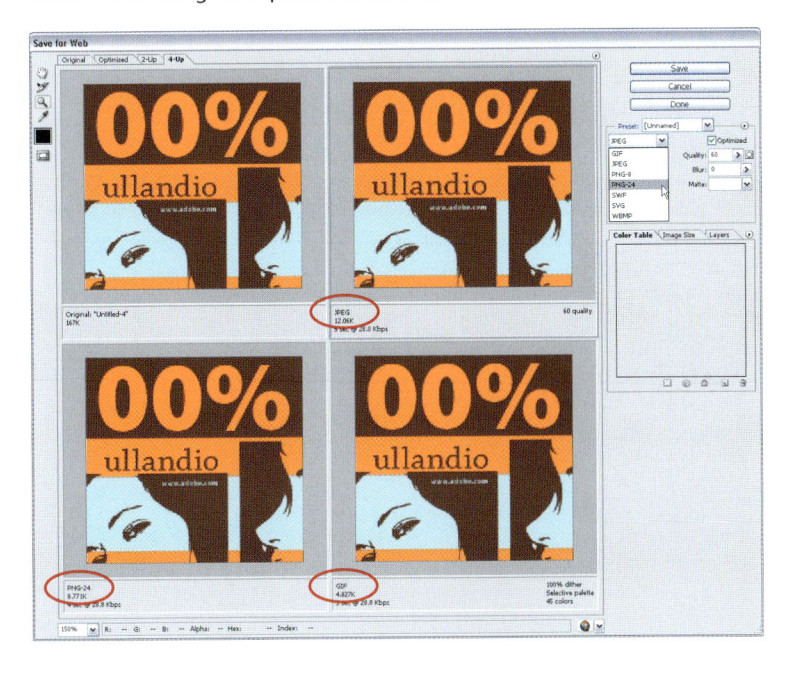

CHAPTER 11 • Illustrator with Other CS2 Applications   281

START OVER IN SAVE FOR WEB

Often, when you're using the Save for Web command in the File menu, you'll find yourself experimenting with various settings. Should you ever want to start again from square one, you can reset all settings in the dialog by holding down the Option key (PC: Alt key). When you do this, the Cancel button changes to Reset. Click Reset to put all settings back to their defaults.

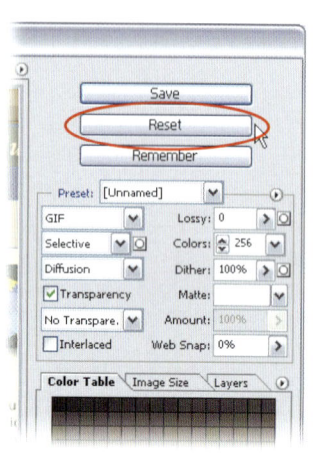

REMEMBER YOUR SAVE FOR WEB SETTINGS

Here's a cool way to remember a setting and then experiment further, knowing you can revert to these settings. To do this, go to the File menu, choose Save for Web, and then choose your settings. When you're finished, hold down the Option key (PC: Alt key) to change the Done button to Remember. Now you can feel free to experiment, knowing that you can go back to this remembered setting by clicking the Reset button. (As mentioned in the previous tip, hold down the Option key [PC: Alt key] to change the Cancel button to Reset.)

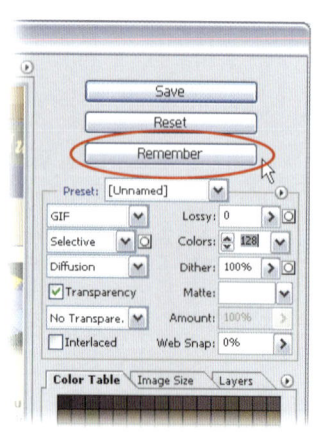

OPTIMIZE BY FILE SIZE

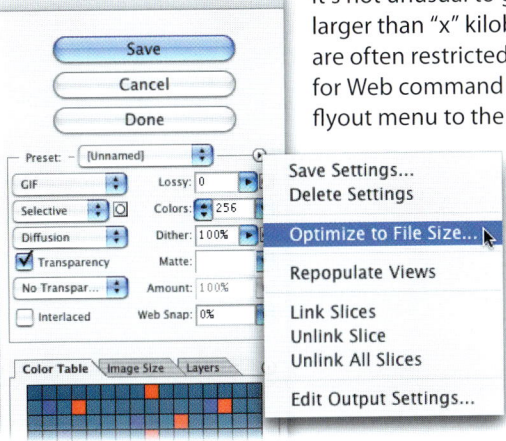

It's not unusual to get a request for a Web graphic to be no larger than "x" kilobytes. Advertising banners, for example, are often restricted to a maximum file size. Luckily, the Save for Web command in the File menu can help with that; in the flyout menu to the right of the preset options in the Save for Web dialog, choose Optimize to File Size. Enter the size for your graphic, click OK, and Save for Web will do the rest.

FLATTENER PREVIEW

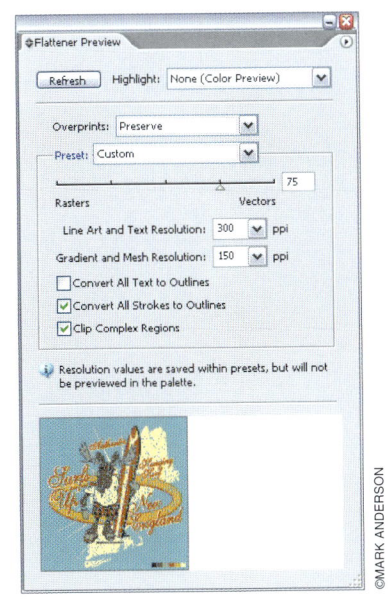

Before sending files off to print, you may need to use the Flatten Transparency command in the Object menu. Unfortunately, the preview function in this dialog can take a while, so here's an alternative: From the Window menu, choose the Flattener Preview palette, then in the palette's flyout menu choose Show Options. There you can get a much quicker preview of the areas that would be affected by flattening, when you select Quick Preview from the palette's flyout menu. To see the preview, be sure to click the Refresh button at the top of the palette. (*Note:* Resolution values cannot be previewed in the palette.)

CHAPTER 11 • Illustrator with Other CS2 Applications   283

GET YOUR GRADIENTS TO PRINT

If you're having trouble getting gradients and gradient meshes to print properly, there is one setting you can change. But be warned, only change this if you're unable to get gradients to print properly, because if you leave this option on, printing can become extremely slow. Open the Print dialog from the File menu, click on the Graphics category in the left-hand side of the dialog, then turn on the checkbox beside Compatible Gradient and Gradient Mesh Printing. (*Note:* You'll likely get a warning dialog informing you that this option should be selected *only* if you're having problems printing.) The current raster resolution will be shown just below the checkbox, and if it's set too low, you'll have to click the Cancel button and use the Document Raster Effects Settings under the Effect menu to change the resolution. If you read the previous chapters, you know that changing raster effects settings after you've applied filters and effects can alter these effects, so remember—only use this if you're unable to print gradients on your printer (this is common in older printers).

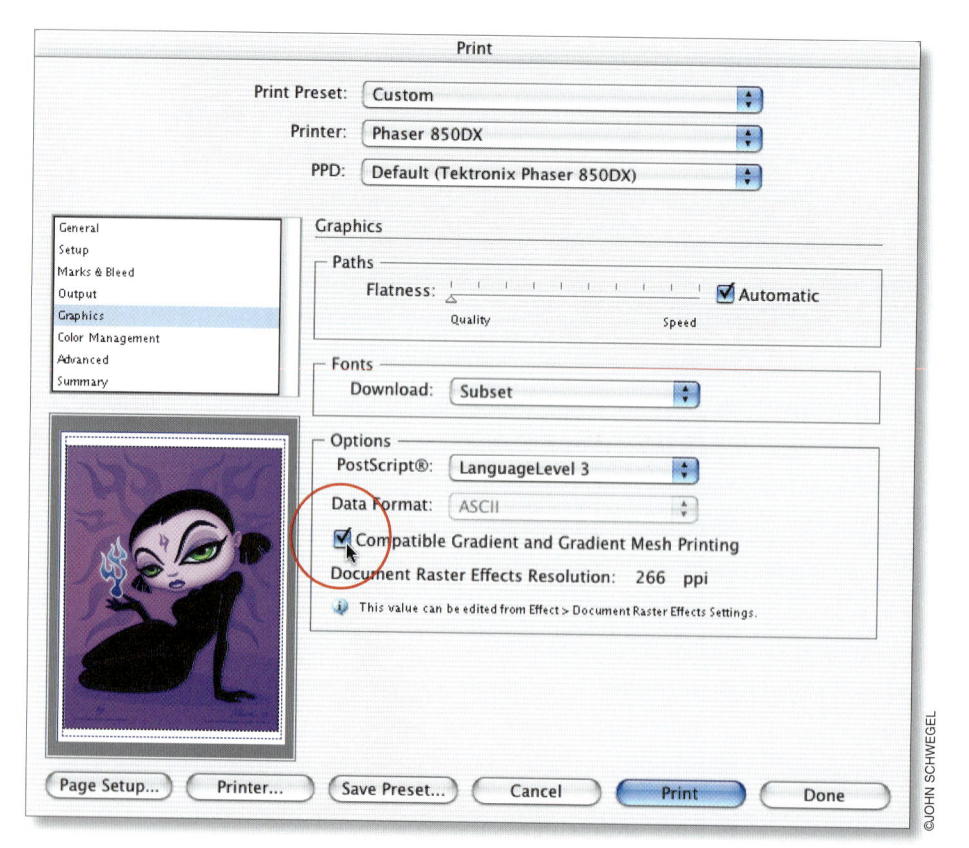

284   CHAPTER 11 • Illustrator with Other CS2 Applications

MISS THE OLD GAL?

Okay, so this really has nothing to do with this chapter, but I thought I'd sneak it in here… just because. For all of its life, Illustrator has always used Botticelli's Venus as its symbol. Then in the CS and CS2 versions, she went away, replaced by flowers. If you miss the old look, you can get a glimpse of the past by holding down the Option key (PC: Alt key) and choosing About Illustrator. In OS X on the Mac, it's under the Illustrator menu; in Windows XP, it's under the Help menu.

CHAPTER 11 • Illustrator with Other CS2 Applications

Index

~ (tilde) key, 69
3D command (Effect menu), 80
3D objects, 80
   artwork, 199
   banner creation, 197
   bevels, 203
   rotating, 196
   style, 200
   view effect while applying, 195
3D Options dialog, 196
3D Revolve Options dialog, 199

A

About Illustrator command (Help menu), 2
Acrobat, Illustrator layers, 274
Acrobat Distiller, multiple pages, 56
actions
   aligning objects, 112
   unrecordable, 52
   within actions, 45
Actions command (Window menu), 24, 31
Actions palette, 24, 31, 52
Actual Size view, 28
Add Anchor Point tool, 81, 94
Add Arrowheads command (Filter menu), 181
Additional Content.pdf, 4
Adjustments command (Image menu), 75
Adobe Bridge, placing file in Illustrator, 259
Adobe Studio Exchange website, 53
Align Center icon, 113
Align command (Window menu), 15, 33, 51
Align palette, 15, 33, 51, 113
aligning
   guides, 33
   objects, 15
   recording action shortcut, 112
   specific objects, 113
   tabs, 217
All command (Select menu), 162
anchor points
   creating shapes, 81
   cutting, 94
   deleting on existing path, 82
   joining, 94–95

   transformations, 111
Anderson, Mark, 152
angled tabs, 218
Appearance command (Windows menu), 21
Appearance palette, 18, 21, 69, 127, 180
appearances. *See also* **effects; styles**
   adding new strokes, 190
   basic, 180
   creating arrowheads, 181
   dragging, 183
   drop shadows, 187
   Eyedropper tool, 182
   style links, 189
Arc tool, 84
arcs, open and closed change, 84
Arrange command (Object menu), 245
arrowheads, creating, 181
Art Brush Options dialog, 41
artist collections, 141–154
Artistic command (Effect menu), 186
Attributes command (Window menu), 43
Attributes palette, 43, 95
Average command (Object menu), 94
axis, graphs, 65

B

banners
   3D, 197
   adding text, 199
Blend command (Object menu), 72
Blend Options command (Object menu), 73
Blend Options dialog, 70, 73
Blend tool, 70–72, 160
blends
   adding to, 71
   bending, 72
   between two objects, 70
   changing, 73
   layers, 71, 160
   shape around circle, 72
   text, 249
Botticelli's Venus, 285
bounding boxes, hiding, 10
Brandsoftheworld.com website, 61

Bring to Front command (Object menu), 111, 245
Brush Strokes command (Effect menu), 189
brushes
   custom, 3–4
   gradients, 77
   options, 85, 206
   sizes, 98
Brushes command (Window menu), 85
Brushes palette, logos, 41
Button mode, viewing actions, 24

C

calculations, 101
Calligraphic Brush Options dialog, 5, 206
centering
   guides, 33
   locating true center, 95
   objects, 51
   points, showing or hiding, 43
Change Case command (Type menu), 248
Character command (Type menu), 223
Character Rotation field (Character palette), 237
Character Styles command (Window menu), 212
Circle N Line Studios website, 145
circles
   blending shapes, 72
   targets, 87
   typing text on, 239
Clean Up command (Object menu), 228
clipping, saving EPS file, 273
Clipping Mask command (Object menu), 60, 82
cloning, scaling object, 97
CMYK mode, switching to RGB mode, 189
collapsed palettes, 7
Collect in New Layer command, 177
collections, artists, 141–154
Color palette, 17, 77, 118, 221
Color Picker, 17

Color Settings command (Edit menu), 267
Color Settings dialog, 267
colors
    apply sampled, 128
    boxes, 221
    changing opposite of active, 120
    complementary, 132
    customizing, 118
    defaults, fill and stroke, 17
    dragging from computer, 123
    fading, 137
    fills, 130
    global, 121
    grabbing, 119, 122
    gradients, 3–4
        brushes, 77
        expanding, 136
        global color, 121
        one-color, 124
        stops, 124–126
    grayscale, 133–134
    inverse, 132
    Live Paint Bucket tool, 129
    loading settings in Photoshop, 267
    mode changes in Color palette, 127
    none, 130
    pantone, 134
    paper simulation, 42
    Preview Bounds, 138
    printer test page, 136
    same again, 129
    selecting from swatches, 99
    slider adjustment, 118
    spots, 131
    strokes, 130
        changes, 126
        multiple, 127
    swapping fills and strokes, 131
    swatches
        replacement, 133
        saving libraries, 135
    text, 221
    View Box, 52
Colors command (Filter menu), 134
Column command (Object menu), 66
commands
    Edit menu
        Color Settings, 267
        Copy, 95
        Keyboard Shortcuts, 25
        Paste, 95
    Effect menu
        3D, 80
        Artistic, 186
        Brush Strokes, 189
        Convert to Shape, 69
        Distort & Transform, 18, 102
        Effect Gallery, 180
        Stylize, 229
        Transform, 102
    File menu
        Export, 24, 254
        File Info, 269
        New From Template, 22
        Place, 19, 60, 156
        Print, 56
        Save As Template, 23
        Save for Web, 282
    Filter menu
        Colors, 134
        Distort, 18
        Stylize, 181
    Help menu, About Illustrator, 2
    Illustrator menu, Preferences, 39
    Image menu, Adjustments, 75
    Object menu
        Arrange, 245
        Blend, 72
        Clipping Mask, 60, 82
        Crop Area, 22
        Envelope Distort, 114, 238
        Expand, 19, 77, 136
        Flatten Transparency, 283
        Graph, 64
        Live Trace, 74
        Path, 73, 78, 86, 94
        Rasterize, 74
        Text Wrap, 218, 245
    Select menu
        All, 162
        Deselect, 13
        Next Object Above, 105
        Next Object Below, 11
        Same, 99
        Save Selection, 92
    Show menu, Number of Undos, 28
    Type menu
        Change Case, 248
        Create Outlines, 41, 60
        Font, 246
        Paragraph Style, 220
        Recent Fonts, 223
        Smart Punctuation, 225
        Tabs, 213
        Threaded Text, 244
    View menu
        Guides, 33, 34
        Hide Artboard, 48
        Hide Page Tiling, 48
        New View, 45
        Show Grid, 43
        Show Page Tiling, 56
        Show Rulers, 37
        Show Transparency Grid, 42
        Simulate Colored Paper, 42
        Snap to Point, 107
    Window menu
        Actions, 24, 31
        Align, 15, 33, 51
        Appearance, 21
        Attributes, 43
        Brushes, 85
        Document Info, 44
        Gradient, 125
        Graphic Styles, 183
        Layers, 53, 156
        Navigator, 46
        Stroke, 73, 186
        Swatch Libraries, 135
        Swatches, 16, 19
        Symbols, 19, 192
        Transform, 15
        Transparency, 157
        Type, 20, 60
        Workspace, 30–31
complementary colors, 132
content, 3–4
Control palette, 32
Convert to Grayscale command (Filter menu), 134
Convert to Shape command (Effect menu), 69
converted PSD files, 257
Copy command (Edit menu), 95
corners, round joins, 128
Creamer, David, 114
Create New Action icon, 33, 52
Create New Layer icon, 53, 156
Create Outlines command (Type menu), 41, 60
Credits, 2
Crop Area command (Object menu), 22
crop marks, creating, 22
Current Tool, 6
cursors, tools, 51
curves, drawing, 12
custom brushes, 3–4

D

dashed lines, converting to outline, 114
Data command (Object menu), 64
data graphs, 64
defaults
   colors, fill and stroke, 17
   fonts, 212
   measurement override, 39
   workspaces, 30
Deselect command (Select menu), 13
Design command (Object menu), 66
designs, graphs, 66
Desktop, drag-and-drop from, 256
dialogs
   3D Options, 196
   3D Revolve Options, 199
   Art Brush Options, 41
   Blend Options, 70, 73
   Calligraphic Brush Options, 5, 206
   Color Settings, 267
   Expand, 77
   Flatten Transparency, 114
   Graph Design, 66
   Graph Type, 65
   Insert Menu Item, 52
   Keyboard Shortcuts, 25
   Layers Options, 156
   Levels, 75
   Move, quick access, 10
   Palette Options, 52, 165
   Photoshop Export Options, 254
   PNG Options, 24
   Preferences, 43
   Save for Web, 283
   Scale, 106
   Scatter Brush Options, 201
   scrubby sliders, 181
   Text Import Options, 19
   Transform Effect, 102
DIM images, layers, 156
Direct Selection tool, 8, 9, 60, 67
Distort & Transform command (Effect menu), 18, 102
Distort command (Filter menu), 18
Divide Objects Below command (Object menu), 78
Document Info command (Window menu), 44
Document Info palette, 44
documents
   automatically adding rulers, 37
   creating multiple pages, 56–57
   duplicating settings, 54
   information, 44
   raster settings, 188
Don't Show Center icon, 43
downloads
   Adobe Studio Exchange website, 53
   free symbols, 205
   presets, 4
drag-and-drop objects, 115
drag-and-drop text, 232
drop shadows, 187
Dry Brush command (Effect menu), 186

E

Edit menu commands
   Color Settings, 267
   Copy, 95
   Keyboard Shortcuts, 25
   Paste, 95
Effect Gallery command (Effect menu), 180
Effect menu commands
   3D, 80
   Artistic, 186
   Brush Strokes, 189
   Convert to Shape, 69
   Distort & Transform, 18, 102
   Effect Gallery, 180
   Stylize, 229
   Transform, 102
effects. *See also* appearances; styles
   3D objects, 80
      artwork, 199
      banner creation, 197
      rotating, 196
   apply same again, 185
   drop shadows, 187
   gallery, 180
   grayed out, 195
   permanent, 63
   pop art dot, 184
   raster settings, 188
   reset settings, 186
   scaling, 106
   switching between RGB and CMYK, 189
   Symbol Stainer tool, 201–202
   three dimensional, view while applying, 195
   versus filters, 18, 185
   vintage texture, 89
embedded objects, 258, 260
Envelope Distort command (Object menu), 114, 238
EPS file, clipping, 273
Expand command (Object menu), 19, 77, 136
Expand dialog, 77
expanded palettes, 7
Export command (File menu), 24, 254
exporting
   Photoshop format, 254
   preview image turned on, 263
Extrude & Bevel command (Effects menu), 80, 197
Eyedropper tool, 119, 123, 128, 182

F

fading colors, 137
feedback, 6
Ferris, Todd, 146
fields, palettes, 54
File Handling & Clipboard command, 262
File Info command (File menu), 269
File menu commands
   Export, 24, 254
   File Info, 269
   New From Template, 22
   Place, 19, 60, 156
   Print, 56
   Save As Template, 23
   Save for Web, 282
files
   clean up, 277
   reducing size, 276
   saving for older Illustrator versions, 277
Fill Color command (Select menu), 99
Fill icon, 17
fills
   colors, 130
   default colors, 17
   effecting, 21
   none, 130
   swapping to opposite, 131
Filter menu commands
   Colors, 134
   Distort, 18
   Stylize, 181
filters
   grayed out, 195
   reset settings, 186
   versus effects, 18, 185

Fit in Window view, 28–29
Flare tool, 63
Flatten Transparency command (Object menu), 283
Flatten Transparency dialog, 114
flattened PSD files, 257
Flattener Preview palette, 283
Flip Horizontal tool, versus Reflect Horizontal tool, 15
flipping objects, 98
Font command (Type menu), 246
fonts, 3–4
    built in, 60
    default change, 212
    locating by name, 213
    OpenType, 246–247
    text, 223
frames, text scaling, 20
Free Transform tool, 104
Full Screen mode, 48

G

Get the Type on a Path tool, 239
global colors, 121
glyphs, multiple choices, 20
Glyphs command (Window menu), 20, 60
Glyphs palette, 20, 60
Golding, Mordy, 182
Gradient command (Window menu), 125
Gradient palette, 77, 123
Gradient Slider, 124, 126
Gradient tool, 123
gradients, 3–4
    brushes, 77
    expanding, 136
    fading colors, 137
    global color, 121
    one-color, 124
    printer, 284
    stops, 124–126
    text, 234
Graph command (Object menu), 64
Graph Data palette, 64
Graph Design dialog, 66
Graph Type dialog, 65
graphic styles. *See* **styles**
Graphic Styles command (Window menu), 183
Graphic Styles palette, 183, 189
graphics. *See* **objects**
graphs
    data, 64
    editing designs, 66
    sliding column design, 67
    value axis, 65
grayscale, 133–134
grids
    angling, 43
    changing, 78
    splitting, 86
groups, selecting, 100
guides
    aligning, 33
    centering automatically, 33
    creating from objects, 34
    direction changes, 34
    layers, 53
    locked changed to path, 35
    locking, 8
    locking to object, 35
    perspective grid, 36
    unlocking, 8
Guides command (View menu), 33, 34

H

Hand tool, 219
    shortcuts, 50
Haya, Erwin, 151
heights, rectangles, 83
Help menu commands, About Illustrator, 2
hidden objects, selecting, 14
hidden tools, menu tear off, 40
Hide Artboard command (View menu), 48
Hide Page Tiling command (View menu), 48
Hinton, Scott, 142
Horizontal Align Center icon, 33
Horizontal icon, 15
Hunt, Jib, 149

I

Illustrator, resetting preferences, 54
Illustrator menu commands, Preferences, 39
Image menu commands, Adjustments, 75
images. *See* **objects**
Insert Menu Item dialog, 52
instances, 193
interlocking objects, live, 79
inverse colors, 132

J–K

Join command (Object menu), 94
joining points, 94–95, 128

kerning text, 222, 224
keyboard shortcuts
    Hand tool, 50
    hidden, 25
    palettes, 49
    Zoom tool, 49
Keyboard Shortcuts command (Edit menu), 25
Keyboard Shortcuts dialog, 25
Knife tool, 108

L

Layer Comps, 170
layers
    Acrobat, 274
    blends, 71
    collecting in new, 177
    copy object to, 160
    creating below others, 166
    custom row size, 165
    DIM images, 156
    duplicating, 161
    expanding sublayers, 165
    guides, 53
    hiding, 158
    jumping to, 164
    Layer Comps, 170
    locating, 164
    locking, 163
    mirror reflections, 169
    moving objects to other, 172
    multiple
        selection, 162
        showing or hiding, 18
    naming, 156
    new on top, 166
    Outline view, 158–159
    paste remembers, 168
    print options, 174
    releasing blends, 160
    selecting
        all, 162
        merging, 176
        multiple, 171
        unlocking all before, 175
    sublayers, not showing, 174
    targets, 167–168
    templates, 173, 175
    unlocking individual objects, 163

layers *(continued)*
    white reflecting transparency settings, 157
Layers command (Window menu), 53, 156
Layers Options dialog, 156
Layers palette, 53, 71, 156
leading, text, 226
legacy text, updating, 233
Levels command (Image menu), 75
Levels dialog, 75
Lichtenstein, Roy, 184
Life In Vector website, 150
linked objects, 258
    automatic update, 262
    changing to embedded, 260
    editing, 260
liquify tools, brush size, 98
Live Paint Bucket tool, 79, 129
Live Trace command (Object menu), 74
locking
    guides, 8
    layers, 163
logos
    online, 61
    Photoshop, 265
    placing in Brushes palette, 41

M

Mac Design Magazine, 114
Magic Wand tool, 110
Make command (Object menu), 22, 60, 82
Make Guides command (View menu), 34
Make With Warp command (Object menu), 238
maps, generating interactively, 61
margins, text, 237
masks
    multiple objects, 82
    opacity, 88
McClelland, Deke, 206
Measure tool, 108
measurements
    entering widths and heights, 83
    moving object, 108
    overriding default, 39
    proportionate, 97
    ruler unit change, 39
    text points, 234
Merge Graphic Styles command (Window menu), 183

Merge Selected command, 176
merging
    selected layers, 176
    styles, 183
mesh points
    make with text, 114
    multiple selection, 101
    selecting, 100
Mesh tool, 76, 100, 114
metadata
    sharing with other applications, 269
    templates, 270
Metadata palette, 269
Microsoft Office, saving for, 24
mirror reflections, layers, 169
Miter Limit field, 128
modifier keys, 6
Move command (Object menu), 108
Move dialog, quick access, 10
move tools, Selection tool, 8
multiple layers, showing or hiding, 18
multiple pages, document creation, 56–57
multiple tools, menu tear off, 40
multiple transformations, 105
Musselman, Christian, 153

N

naming swatches, 16
Navigator command (Window menu), 46
Navigator palettes, 46
Neal, Philip J., 144
New Art Has Basic Appearance icon, 180
New Brush command (Window menu), 85
New From Template command (File menu), 22
New Swatch icon, 16
New View command (View menu), 45
Next Object Above command (Select menu), 105
Next Object Below command (Select menu), 11
Number of Undos command (Show menu), 28
numeric transformations, 104
Nuñez, Brooke, 150

O

Object menu commands
    Arrange, 245
    Blend, 72
    Clipping Mask, 60, 82
    Crop Area, 22
    Envelope Distort, 114, 238
    Expand, 19, 77, 136
    Flatten Transparency, 283
    Graph, 64
    Live Trace, 74
    Path, 73, 78, 86, 94
    Rasterize, 74
    Text Wrap, 218, 245
objects
    3D, 80, 196
    aligning, 15, 113
    blends
        adding to, 71
        bending, 72
        between two objects, 70
        changing, 73
        layers, 71
        shape around circle, 72
    brush options, 206
    center points, showing or hiding, 43
    centering, 51
    copying, 68
    creating, by measurements, 11
    dividing below, 78
    drag-and-drop, 115
    flipping, 98
    guides
        creating, 34
        locking to, 35
    hiding unselected, 50
    information, 44
    live interlocking, 79
    moving to specific area, 107
    multiple as mask, 82
    next object below selection, 11
    opacity masks, 88
    rotating, 102–103
    saving selections, 92
    scaling, 96–97
    selecting
        all but one, 14
        behind, 105
        hidden, 14
        none, 13
    showing in Outline mode, 271
    three dimensional, 80
    wireframe, 80

One Sick Individual website, 151
opacity masks, 88
Open Swatch Library command
(Window menu), 122
OpenType fonts, 246–247
Options of Selected Object
icon, 206
ordinals, text, 247
Outline Stroke command (Object
menu), 73
Outline view
layers, 158–159
showing images in, 271
outlines
dashed line conversion to, 114
text, converting from warped, 238

P

Page tool, tiling, 55
pages, creating multiple, 56–57
Paintbrush tool, 84, 93
Palette Options dialog, 52, 165
palettes. *See also specific palettes*
fields in, 54
quick delete, 7
scrubby sliders, 181
shortcuts, 49
showing and hiding, 47
Pantone palette, 134
paper, simulating color, 42
Paragraph Style command (Type
menu), 220
paragraphs, text selection, 211
Paste command (Edit menu), 95
Path command (Object menu), 73,
78, 86, 94
Pathfinder palette, 63, 103
paths
anchor points
cutting, 94
deleting, 82
closing automatically, 84
editing type, 93
joining, 94
locked guides changed to, 35
reshape
by drawing, 92
by painting, 93
simplifying, 13, 109
smoothing, 109
threading text, 244–245
patterns
edit existing, 19
making own, 119

transformation, 120
PDF files, 275. *See also* **Photoshop**
Pen tool, 12, 67, 81, 86
Pencil tool, 84, 92
Photoshop
borrowing shapes, 266
copying and pasting, 263
dashed lines, 272
drag-and-drop into, 255, 264
exchange swatches, 268
exporting to, 254
loading color settings from
Illustrator, 267
logos, 265
opening file in Illustrator, 257
opening Illustrator file, 254
path export from, 266
placing file
from Illustrator, 255
in Illustrator, 258
sharing file information, 269
vector shapes, 261
Photoshop Export Options
dialog, 254
Place command (File menu), 19,
60, 156
Planiglobe.com website, 61
PNG Options dialog, 24
points
anchor points. *See* anchor points
mesh, selecting, 100–101
Polar Grid tool, 87
Polygon tool, 68
pop art dot effect, 184
Portrait Up icon, 56
Position Palette Above Text
icon, 216
positions, shape changing, 12
Pounds, David, 143
preferences
resetting, 54
tools, 16
Preferences command (Illustrator
menu), 39
Preferences dialog, 43
presets, downloads, 4
Presets folder, 3
Preview Bounds, 138
Print command (File menu), 56
printers
color test page, 136
flattener preview, 283
gradients, 284
large scale values, 279

preset save, 280
sending file to service bureau, 276
settings, 281
trial separation, 278
proportionate measurements, 97

Q–R

raster settings, 188
Rasterize command (Object
menu), 74
Real World Adobe Illustrator, 206
Recent Fonts command (Type
menu), 223
Rectangle command (Effect
menu), 69
rectangles
corner radius, 83
entering widths and heights, 83
split into grid, 86
Rectangular Grid tool, 78
references photos, view using Mesh
tool, 76
Reflect Horizontal tool versus Flip
Horizontal tool, 15
Release command (Object menu),
22, 60
Release Guides command (View
menu), 34
Release Selection command (Type
menu), 244
repeating pathfinders, 103
Replace Spine command (Object
menu), 72
reshaping tools, Direct Selection
tool, 8
Revolve command (Effect menu), 80
RGB mode, switching to CMYK
mode, 189
Rotate tool, 102–103
Roughen commands, 18
Roughen effect, 18
Round Corners command (Effect
menu), 229
round joins, 128
Rounded Rectangle tool, 83
rulers
automatically adding, 37
origin change, 38
resetting, 38
unit of measurement change, 39

S

Same command (Select menu), 99
Save As Template command (File menu), 23
Save for Microsoft Office command (File menu), 24
Save for Web command (File menu), 282
Save for Web dialog, 283
Save Selection command (Select menu), 92
Save Workspace command (Window menu), 31
Scale dialog, 106
Scale tool, 97, 106, 111
scaling
   effects, 106
   objects, 96–97
   strokes, 106
   text frames, 20
Scatter brush
   enhancers, 202
   options, 201
Scatter Brush Options dialog, 201
Scatter brushes, 85
Schwegel, John, 148
Scissors tool, 72, 94
scrubby sliders, 181
Select menu commands
   All, 162
   Deselect, 13
   Next Object Above, 105
   Next Object Below, 11
   Same, 99
   Save Selection, 92
Selection tool, 8, 60
   Move dialog quick access, 10
   next object below selection, 11
   quick selection, 9
selections
   groups, 100
   layers, 162
      all, 162
      merging, 176
      multiple, 171
      unlocking all before, 175
   mesh points, 100–101
   objects behind object, 105
   same again, 99
   saving, 92
   text, 210–211
   tools, 8
Sellers, Mike, 145
Send to Back command (Object menu), 111

Send to Current Layer command (Object menu), 172
shadows, 187
shapes
   anchor points, 81
   blends
      adding to, 71
      bending, 72
      between two objects, 70
      changing, 73
      layers, 71
      shape around circle, 72
   borrowing from Photoshop, 266
   outline strokes, 73
   position change, 12
   text objects, 69
shortcuts
   Hand tool, 50
   hidden, 25
   palettes, 49
   Zoom tool, 49
Show Center icon, 43
Show Grid command (View menu), 43
Show menu commands, Number of Undos, 28
Show Page Tiling command (View menu), 56
Show Rulers command (View menu), 37
Show Transparency Grid command (View menu), 42
Simplify command (Object menu), 109
Simulate Colored Paper command (View menu), 42
slide shows, one slide, 48
sliders, scrubby, 181
Smart Guides, 36
Smart Punctuation command (Type menu), 225
Smooth tool, 109
Snap to Point command (View menu), 107
Spatter command (Effect menu), 189
spirographs, 69
Split Into Grid command (Object menu), 86
spot colors, 131
Sprayer tool, 64
Star tool, 62, 87
stars
   creating perfect, 87
   shape change, 62

startup files
   customizing colors, 118
   modifying, 37
Status Bar, 6
Stroke command (Window menu), 73, 186
Stroke icon, 17
Stroke palette, 106, 128
strokes
   adding new, 190
   adding second, 186
   colors, 126, 130
   convert dashed to outline, 114
   default colors, 17
   effecting, 21
   multiple, 127
   none, 130
   options, 106
   outline, 73
   scaling, 106
   swapping to opposite, 131
styles, 3–4. *See also* **appearances; effects**
   3D, 200
   breaking object links, 189
   merging, 183
   reverse creation, 194
   tabs, 214
Stylize command
   Effect menu, 229
   Filter menu, 181
sublayers
   expanding, 165
   not showing, 174
Swatch Libraries command (Window menu), 135
swatches, 3–4
   exchange with other applications, 268
   gradient stops, 126
   naming, 16
   persistent, 122
   replacement with another, 133
   saving libraries, 135
   selecting color from, 99
Swatches command (Window menu), 16, 19
Swatches palette, 16, 19, 118–119
Symbol Shifter tool, 202
Symbol Stainer tool, 194, 201, 204
Symbolism tools, 182
   brush sizes, 192
   multiple change, 192
   original object as instance, 193
   viewing intensity, 191

symbols, 3–4
   adding, 64
   edit existing, 19
   free downloads, 205
   getting more from brush libraries, 204
   redefining, 191
   replacing, 194
   stacking order, 202
Symbols command (Window menu), 19, 192
Symbols palette, 19, 64, 191–192

T

tabs
   aligning, 217
   angled, 218
   delete all, 215
   evenly spaced, 215
   leaders, 216
   moving together, 213
   ruler line up, 216
   style change, 214
Tabs command (Type menu), 213
Tabs palette, 213
targets, circles, 87
templates
   creating, 23
   layers, 173, 175
   metadata, 270
   opening, 22
test pages, printer colors, 136
text, 209
   adding to banners, 199
   angled margins, 237
   attribute copying, 241
   automatic ordinals, 247
   baseline shift amounts, 240
   blending, 249
   box fill color, 221
   character rotation, 237
   clean up, 228
   colors, 221
   converting to shape, 69
   converting warped to outline, 238
   drag-and-drop from desktop, 232
   editing, 219
      imported, 225
      path, 93
      warped, 238
   flowing multiple blocks into one, 251
   fonts
      controlling recent, 223
      default change, 212
      locating by name, 213
      previewing, 223
   fractions, 246
   frames, scaling, 20
   global case change, 248
   gradient filled, 234
   hiding highlight, 235
   importing, 19
   indents, 220
   insertion point, 210
   kerning, 222, 224
   leading, 226
   legacy update, 233
   loading from other documents, 236
   loading styles in all documents, 249
   make mesh, 114
   multiple columns and rows, 250
   override clear, 235–236
   paragraphs
      converting to regular text, 227
      selecting, 211
   photo inside type, 60
   point calculations, 234
   quick formatting, 224
   removing from path, 241
   reset horizontal scaling, 225
   scroll view, 219
   selecting, 210
   setting reset, 220
   stop flipping, 240
   styling, 229
   tabs
      aligning, 217
      angled, 218
      delete all, 215
      evenly spaced, 215
      leaders, 216
      moving together, 213
      ruler line up, 216
      style change, 214
   threading
      between objects, 244
      hidden, 243
      into new box, 242
      stopping, 244
      two paths, 245
   tracking, 222, 224
   transforming, 232
   typing on circle, 239
   typographer quotes, 251
   vertical, 221
   wrapping around photo, 245
Text Import Options dialog, 19
Text Wrap command (Object menu), 218, 245
Threaded Text command (Type menu), 244
threading text
   between objects, 244
   hidden threads, 243
   into new box, 242
   stopping, 244
   two paths, 245
three dimensional effects, view while applying, 195
three dimensional objects, 80
   artwork, 199
   banner creation, 197
   bevels, 203
   rotating, 196
   styles, 200
thumbnail views, Navigator palette, 46
tilde (~) key, 69
tiling pages, 55
timing, modifier keys, 6
tools, 59
   cursors, 51
   menu tear off, 40
   preferences, 16
   setting changes, 68
   switching quickly between, 55
tracing images, 74–75
tracking text, 222, 224
Transform Again command (Object menu), 21, 111
Transform command
   Effect menu, 102
   Window menu, 15
Transform Each command (Object menu), 105
Transform Effect dialog, 102
Transform palette, 15, 97–98, 107
transformations, 21
   anchor points, 111
   copying, 110
   editable, 102
   multiple, 105
   numeric, 104
   patterns, 120
   scaling objects, 96
   send to back, 111
   text, 232
transparency, opacity masks, 88
Transparency command (Window menu), 157
Transparency palette, 88, 157

true center, locating, 95
Twist command (Effect menu), 115
Twist tool, 115
type. *See* text
Type command
    Object menu, 64
    Window menu, 20, 60
Type menu commands
    Change Case, 248
    Create Outlines, 41, 60
    Font, 246
    Paragraph Style, 220
    Recent Fonts, 223
    Smart Punctuation, 225
    Tabs, 213
    Threaded Text, 244
Type on a Path tool, 241
Type tool, 60, 219
typographer quotes, 251

U

undos, number available, 28
Units & Display Performance Preferences command (Illustrator menu), 39
unlocking guides, 8
unlocking objects, 36
unrecordable actions, 52
updates, linked objects, 262

V

Vertical Align Center icon, 33
Vertical Distribute icon, 15
vertical text, 221
Vertical Type tool, 221
View Box, colors, 52

View menu commands
    Guides, 33–34
    Hide Artboard, 48
    Hide Page Tiling, 48
    New View, 45
    Show Grid, 43
    Show Page Tiling, 56
    Show Rulers, 37
    Show Transparency Grid, 42
    Simulate Colored Paper, 42
    Snap to Point, 107
views. *See also specific views*
    saving, 45
    two of one document, 46
vintage texture effects, 89

W

Wacom pen tablets, 5
warped text, 238
Web, saving for, 281–283
websites
    Adobe Studio Exchange, 53
    Anderson, Mark, 152
    Brandsoftheworld.com, 61
    Circle N Line Studios, 145
    Ferris, Todd, 146
    Haya, Erwin, 151
    Hinton, Scott, 142
    Hunt, Jib, 149
    Life In Vector, 150
    Musselman, Christian, 153
    Neal, Philip J., 144
    Nuñez, Brooke, 150
    One Sick Individual, 151
    Planiglobe.com, 61
    Pounds, David, 143
    Schwegel, John, 148
    Sellers, Mike, 145
    Weichert, Scott, 147
Weichert, Scott, 147
widths, rectangles, 83
Window menu commands
    Actions, 24, 31
    Align, 15, 33, 51
    Appearance, 21
    Attributes, 43
    Brushes, 85
    Document Info, 44
    Gradient, 125
    Graphic Styles, 183
    Layers, 53, 156
    Navigator, 46
    Stroke, 73, 186
    Swatch Libraries, 135
    Swatches, 16, 19
    Symbols, 19, 192
    Transform, 15
    Transparency, 157
    Type, 20, 60
    Workspace, 30–31
windows, switching between multiple, 29
wireframe objects, 80
Workspace command (Window menu), 30–31
workspaces, 30–31
wrapping text, around photo, 245

X–Y–Z

Zoom tool, 28, 219
    shortcuts, 49
    wrong mouse position, 48

COLOPHON

The book was produced by the authors and design team using all Macintosh computers, including a Power Mac G5 1.8-GHz, a Power Mac G5 Dual Processor 1.8-GHz, a Power Mac G5 Dual Processor 2-GHz, a Power Mac G4 Dual Processor 1.25-MHz. We use LaCie, Sony, and Apple Studio Display monitors.

Page layout was done using Adobe InDesign CS. We use a Mac OS X server, and burn our CDs to our CPU's internal Sony DVD RW DW-U10A.

The headers for each technique are set in Adobe Myriad Pro Semibold at 11 points on 12.5 leading, with the Horizontal Scaling set to 100%. Body copy is set using Adobe Myriad Pro Regular at 9.5 points on 11.5 leading, with the Horizontal Scaling set to 100%.

Screen captures were made with Snapz Pro X and were placed and sized within Adobe InDesign CS. The book was output at 150 line screen, and all in-house printing was done using a Tektronix Phaser 7700 by Xerox.

ADDITIONAL RESOURCES

Layers Magazine
Layers—The How-To Magazine for Everything Adobe—is the foremost authority on Adobe's design, digital video, digital photography, and education applications. Each issue features timely product news, plus the quick tips, hidden shortcuts, and step-by-step tutorials for working in today's digital market.

http://www.layersmagazine.com

KW Computer Training Videos
Dave Cross and Matt Kloskowski are featured in a series of Photoshop and Photoshop Elements training DVDs, available from KW Computer Training. Visit the website or call 813-433-5000 for orders or more information.

http://www.photoshopvideos.com

National Association of Photoshop Professionals (NAPP)
The industry trade association for Adobe® Photoshop® users and the world's leading resource for Photoshop training, education, and news.

http://www.photoshopuser.com

Adobe Photoshop Seminar Tour
See Dave Cross live at the Adobe Photoshop Seminar Tour, the nation's most popular Photoshop seminars. For upcoming tour dates and class schedules, visit the tour website.

http://www.photoshopseminars.com

Photoshop World Conference & Expo
The convention for Adobe Photoshop users has now become the largest Photoshop-only event in the world.

http://www.photoshopworld.com

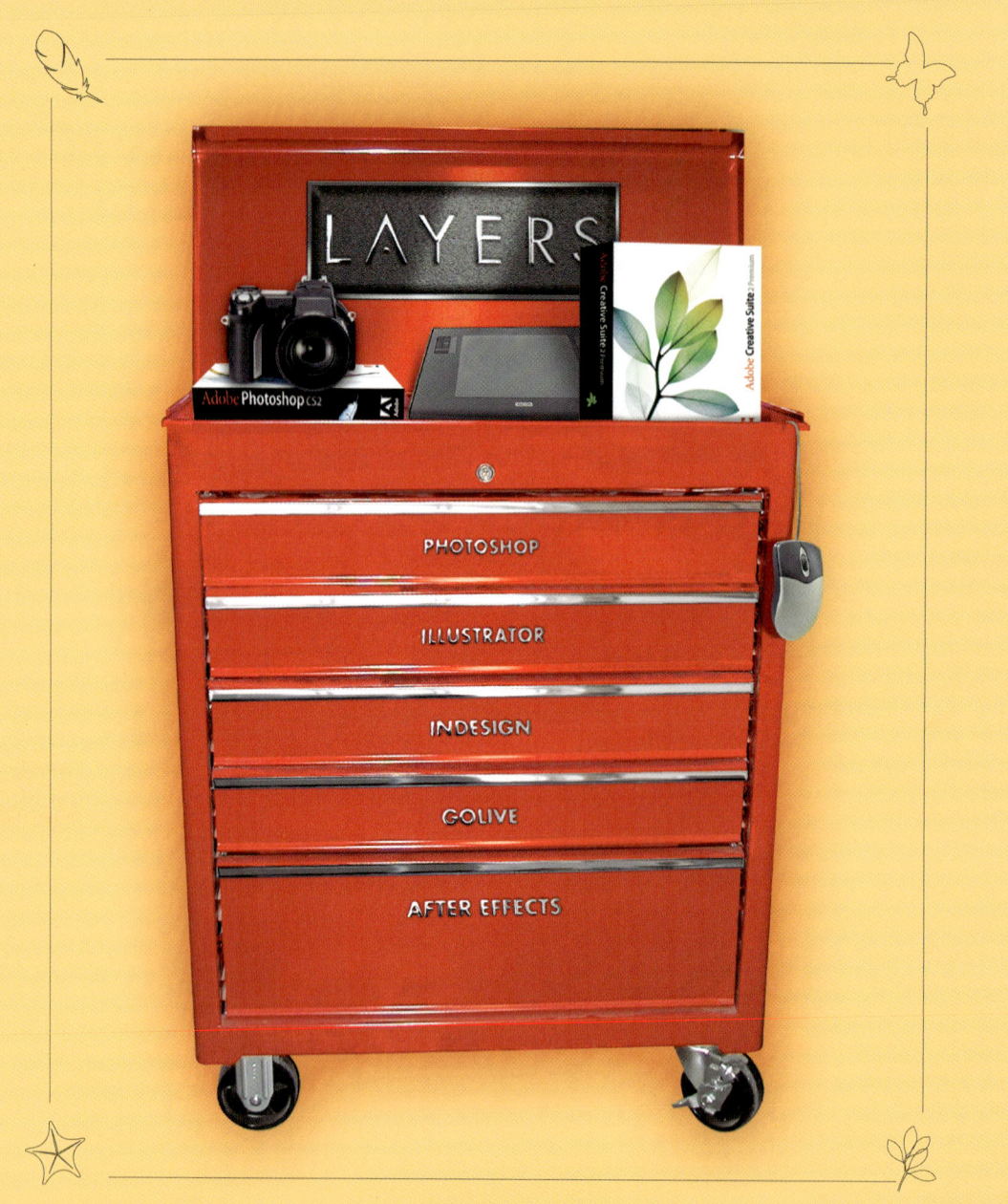

EVERY TOOL... ALL IN ONE PLACE

Layers® magazine equips designers, photographers and multimedia professionals with the crucial tools needed to tackle any task in Adobe Creative Suite. Drill through *Layers'* groundbreaking step-by-step tutorials, get uncompromising product reviews, and read timesaving tips that get the job done fast!

Gear up with your own subscription to *Layers*. One year (six issues) is only $19.95 and two years (12 issues) is just $34.95. That's more than 60% off the cover price!

ORDER TOLL FREE **877-622-8632** OR ONLINE AT **www.layersmagazine.com**

iStockphoto™

Stock illustrations and images for $3 or less

Over 420,000 high-quality files
6,000 new images per week
No subscription fees – ever
Absolutely free to join

istockphoto.com

You've got the people. You've got the projects. You've got the ideas.

(Do you have the technology to bring them together?)

When creativity is your business, you need technology that doesn't get in the way of your ideas. That's why CDW carries all of the technology products a creative professional needs from the brands you trust like Adobe, Epson, Canon, Extensis, Pantone and more. Our account managers will also get you quick answers to your questions. And with fast shipping and access to the industry's largest inventories, you'll get the products you need, when you need them. So give us a call and find out how we make it happen. Every order, every call, every time.

Adobe

CDW

CDW. The Right Technology. Right Away.™
800.PRO.4CDW
CDW.com/CREATIVEPRO

© 2005 CDW Corporation